CONFERENCE PROCE

CHI 2012

it's the experience!

The 30th ACM Conference on Human Factors In Computing Systems (CHI)

AUSTIN • TEXAS • USA

MAY 5-10, 2012

acm Association for Computing Machinery

chi2012.acm.org

SIGCHI

Association for
Computing Machinery

Advancing Computing as a Science & Profession

The Association for Computing Machinery
2 Penn Plaza, Suite 701
New York, New York 10121-0701

ISBN: 978-1-4503-1015-4 (Digital)

ISBN: 978-1-4503-1941-6 (Print Vol 4)

Additional copies may be ordered prepaid from:

ACM Order Department
PO Box 30777
New York, NY 10087-0777, USA

Phone: 1-800-342-6626 (USA and Canada)
+1-212-626-0500 (Global)
Fax: +1-212-944-1318
E-mail: acmhelp@acm.org
Hours of Operation: 8:30 am – 4:30 pm ET

ACM Order Number: 609121

Printed in the USA

Welcome to CHI 2012!

After nearly two years of preparation, we are thrilled to welcome you to CHI 2012 in Austin, Texas. Austin is justifiably proud of being the Live Music Capital of the World (R), and it is home to a world-class university, innovative technology and design firms, superb restaurants, exciting culture and nightlife, and genuinely friendly people--what a perfect fit for our CHI conference. We encourage you to get out and explore the city.

But we also are working hard to lure you back indoors with a phenomenal technical program. At the core of the program are over a hundred technical sessions with research papers and notes, case studies, and other exciting presentations that bring you the best new work on human-computer interaction.

We give thanks to our hundreds of review committee members and our more than one thousand reviewers--they invested thousands of hours to help make sure that we've picked the best content. All of the technical content can be found in the ACM Digital Library.

At the same time, we hope to lure you into our useful courses, engaging panels, and thoughtful invited talks. We're very excited to have Margaret Gould Stewart and Hugh Herr as our keynote speakers. In spanning from Margaret's talk on connecting the world through video to Hugh's talk on designing intelligent orthotics and prosthetics we span the scope of this conference--from social interaction with each other through computing to the very personal and intimate interaction of a human with computerized limbs or other assistive devices. We're also excited to have two special invited talks: Stu Card, SIGCHI's 2000 Lifetime Achievement Award winner, will talk about what interaction science means in today's environment; and Richard Shusterman will bridge HCI and the humanities as he introduces us to Somaesthetics and how it can improve our understanding and experience. We are also honored to have Dan Olsen, Joy Mountford, and Batya Friedman--SIGCHI's Lifetime Research, Lifetime Practice, and Social Impact awardees--each giving talks at CHI 2012. Each of the three of them has made an indelible impact on our field.

The theme of this year's CHI conference is "It's the Experience!" and from the beginning it has been our goal to ensure that CHI 2012 attendees don't only hear about HCI, but experience it with all of their senses. We are therefore delighted to have more than 60 interactivity demonstrations and installations--opportunities for you to see, feel, hear, and interact with exciting new technologies and also to reflect on technologies of the past, thanks to Roger Ibars' HWD collection--a hands-on installation of historic hard-wired input devices. We'll be featuring the full set of interactivity on Tuesday afternoon and Wednesday lunchtime; selected installations will be available at other times--check the Interactivity tab for more details. Our video program will provide another way to experience innovative forms of HCI.

CHI 2012 has new depth in Computer Games (including a new student games competition), digital arts, and the humanities. We have an unusually rich collection of Digital Arts installations--we invite you to take some time to interact with the artists and learn about how art--like science, engineering, and design--has its own ways of posing and exploring challenging questions.

And there's so much more. We will also have over 250 posters representing exciting works-in-progress and much more. Student venues at CHI 2012 include our doctoral consortium--an intimate opportunity for extensive mentoring and peer support; student research and design competitions, and the games competition. Come see the competition finalists! And let's not forget CHI Madness--a frenetic but highly efficient whirlwind tour through each days technical papers.

Even before we "formally" open the conference Monday morning, we will have had an intensive weekend of workshops where CHI attendees gather to address emerging fields, tackle challenging questions, and simply support each other in areas of common interest. The mutual support continues both in formal SIG gatherings and in informal gatherings in the convention center halls and at tables in our exhibit hall. We particularly invite you to gather together in affinity groups built around our nine communities--these communities not only shape our program, they also can help enrich your experience as an attendee.

In the end, though, it is been quite an Experience! for us. We are grateful to all the dedicated volunteers and staff that have made this conference possible. We appreciate the support of our sponsors and participation of our exhibitors. And most of all, we thank you for joining us here at the conference. We hope you find things some things that are useful, some things that are inspiring, and some things that are just plain fun. We hope you have an incredible CHI 2012 Experience!

Joseph A. Konstan
University of Minnesota
CHI 2012
General Conference Chair

Ed H. Chi
Google
CHI 2012
Technical Program Chairs

Kristina Höök
Mobile Life at KTH
CHI 2012
Technical Program Chairs

From ACM SIGCHI's President and Vice President for Conferences

SIGCHI is proud to sponsor the premier annual conference in the field of human-computer interaction. We are extremely grateful to the CHI 2012 Conference Chair Joseph Konstan, to Technical Program Chairs Ed Chi and Kristina Höök, and to their wonderful crew, who succeeded to build an impressive program and experience.

CHI 2012 marks the 30th anniversary of our society. The first conference, on Human Factors in Computer Systems, took place in Gaithersburg, MD, on March 15-17, 1982.

The second and third conferences were a year and a half apart, and from then on CHI, as the conference has been called since 1983, has been an annual event with the official name: "ACM Conference on Human Factors in Computing Systems".

The first conference drew over 900 attendees, and since then CHI has continued to grow and broaden its range of topics and contributing disciplines: the founding psychologists and software engineers began to meet new visions from ethnography, sociology, communication sciences and arts, among others. Relevant industries, as well as research institutes and academia, showed an increasing-and often long-lasting-interest and involvement (through volunteers and through sponsorship for conference expenses).

CHI is an ideal forum for people to meet formally as well as informally, to exchange knowledge and views, to share experiences, and to learn. The CHI conference brings together professionals from research and practice; people from industry, academia, and from government; long-term veterans of HCI, young professionals and students; all in an environment designed to encourage interaction. We invite you to actively participate in that interaction: introduce yourself to people, interact with presenters and speakers, renew old friendships and make new ones.

CHI is organized on behalf of ACM's Special Interest Group on Computer-Human Interaction (SIGCHI), an international community of professionals who share an interest in the many diverse facets of HCI. SIGCHI is committed both to advancing the field of HCI, to facilitate exchange of information within the SIGCHI community, and to support students to enter the domain.

The CHI conference is arguably the single most visible activity of SIGCHI, but we also sponsor and support a wide range of specialized conferences in areas ranging from interactive systems design to user interface technology to computer-supported cooperative work to "intelligent" user interfaces. Visit the SIGCHI website at http://www.sigchi.org to find our conference schedule, listing upcoming as well as past conferences.

SIGCHI and ACM produce some of the most respected publications in the field. All members receive interactions, a highly-acclaimed magazine covering the broad field of HCI and user interface design. ACM Transactions on Computer-Human Interactions (ToCHI), now in its 18th year, is our flagship journal - a quarterly publication with the top-quality archival research aimed at researchers and those translating research into practice.

SIGCHI is truly an international organization, with over 30 local chapters and 3 student chapters in 19 countries on 5 continents. We encourage all SIGCHI members to join their local chapter - or if there isn't one in your area, we would love to help you create one. And don't forget virtual communities! SIGCHI hosts dozens of electronic mailing lists on topics ranging from HCI and the Web, to HCI educations, to public policy and beyond. Those lists range from dozens of subscribers to thousands, and are an excellent way to keep up with the field and with friends and colleagues.

Finally, on behalf of ACM SGICHI, we again want to thank the conference committee and all of the hundreds of volunteers who make this conference possible. Their work makes this a rewarding experience for all of us.

Gerrit C. van der Veer
SIGCHI President

John "Scooter" Morris
SIGCHI Vice-President for Conferences

ABOUT SIGCHI

CHI 2012 is sponsored by ACM's Special Interest Group on Computer-Human Interaction (ACM SIGCHI). ACM, the Association for Computing Machinery, is an educational and scientific society uniting the world's computing educators, researchers, and professionals to inspire dialogue, share resources, and address the field's challenges. ACM strengthens the profession's collective voice through strong leadership, promotion of the highest standards, and recognition of technical excellence. ACM supports the professional growth of its members by providing opportunities for life-long learning, career development, and professional networking. ACM offers its more than 100,000 worldwide members cutting edge technical information through world class journals and magazines, dynamic special interest groups, and globally recognized conferences.

Visit www.acm.org for more information about the ACM.

SIGCHI is the premier international society for professionals, academics, and students who are interested in human-computer interaction (HCI). We provide a forum for the discussion of all aspects of HCI through our conferences, including our flagship CHI conference, publications, web sites, email discussion groups, and other services. We advance education in HCI through courses, workshops, and outreach, and we promote informal access to a wide range of individuals and organizations involved in HCI. Members can be involved in HCI-related activities with others in their region through local SIGCHI chapters. Come to the SIGCHI Town Hall meeting on Wednesday at 12:50 in Meeting Room 16AB, 4th Floor or visit www.sigchi.org to learn more about SIGCHI.

ACM, the Association for Computing Machinery http://www.acm.org/, is an educational and scientific society uniting the world's computing educators, researchers and professionals to inspire dialogue, share resources and address the field's challenges. ACM strengthens the profession's collective voice through strong leadership, promotion of the highest standards, and recognition of technical excellence.ACM supports the professional growth of its members by providing opportunities for life-long learning, career development, and professional networking. ACM offers its 87,000 global members cutting-edge technical information through world class journals and magazines, dynamic specia linterest groups and globally recognized conferences.

Table of Contents

Getting Around: Menus, Scrolling, & Advanced Navigation

Session Chair: Emmanuel Pietriga *(INRIA)*

Spectators

Session Chair: Barry Brown *(University of California, San Diego)*

Immateriality as a Design Feature

Session Chair: Joonhwan Lee *(Seoul National University)*

Privacy + Self Disclosure

Session Chair: Manfred Tscheligi *(University of Salzburg)*

Intimacy & Connection

HCI4D: Business

Pen + Touch

Affective Presence

Games: Community + Communication

Session Chair: Steve Feiner *(Columbia University)*

Critical Perspectives on Design

Session Chair: Peter Wright *(Newcastle University)*

I Am How I Touch: Authenticating Users

Session Chair: Xiang Cao *(Microsoft Research Asia)*

Visionary Models + Tools

Session Chair: Duncan Brumby *(University College London)*

It's a Big Web!

Session Chair: Wayne Lutters *(University of Maryland, Baltimore County)*

Tools & Stats in Evaluation Studies

Session Chair: Jeff Heer *(Stanford University)*

Values in Research Practice

Session Chair: Giulio Jacucci *(Helsinki Institute for Information Technology)*

Space: The Interaction Frontier

Session Chair: Chris Harrison *(Carnegie Mellon University)*

The Tools of the Trade

Session Chair: Jennifer Thom-Santelli *(IBM Research)*

Publics & Civic Virtues

Session Chair: Ann Light *(Northumbria University)*

Promoting Educational Opportunity

Session Chair: Anthony Hornof *(University of Oregon)*

Interfaces for Health & Well Being

Session Chair: Ian Li *(Carnegie Mellon University)*

Needle in the Haystack

Session Chair: Mark Dunlop *(University of Strathclyde)*

Understanding Online Communication

Session Chair: Sharoda Paul *(GE Global Research)*

Performative Emergency Simulation

Session Chair: Olav W. Bertelsen *(Aarhus University)*

Crowdsourcing & Peer Production I

Session Chair: Mira Dontcheva *(Adobe Advanced Technology Labs)*

Pasts + Futures

Session Chair: Siân Lindley *(Microsoft Research Cambridge)*

Mobile Computing & Interaction

Session Chair: Daniel Fallman *(Umea University)*

Future Design

Session Chair: Orit Shaer *(Wellesley College)*

Visualization + Visual Analysis

Session Chair: Luciano Gamberini *(University of Padova)*

Search Interfaces

Session Chair: Remco Chang *(Tufts University)*

Music

Session Chair: Karyn Moffatt *(McGill University)*

ICT4D

Session Chair: Brygg Ullmer *(Louisiana State University)*

Movement-Based Gameplay

Session Chair: Shaun Kane *(University of Maryland, Baltimore County)*

Beyond Paper

Session Chair: Mikael B. Skov *(Aalborg University)*

Sensory Interaction Modalities

Session Chair: Daniel M. Russell *(Google)*

Old Mouse, New Tricks: Desktop Interfaces

Session Chair: Krzysztof Gajos *(Harvard University)*

Social Support & Collaboration

Session Chair: Meredith Ringel Morris *(Microsoft Research)*

Culture, Playfulness, & Creativity

I Did That! Being in Control

Teaching with Games

Health + Design

Check This Out: Recommender Systems

Session Chair: James Fogarty *(University of Washington)*

See Hear Speak: Redesigning I/O for Effectiveness

Session Chair: Eytan Adar *(University of Michigan)*

Triple T: Touch, Tables, Tablets

Session Chair: Bjoern Hartmann *(University of California, Berkeley)*

Defying Environmental Behavior Changes

Session Chair: Alan Borning *(University of Washington)*

Health & Children

Session Chair: Julie Kientz *(University of Washington)*

Comfortable Aging

Session Chair: Volker Wulf *(University of Siegen)*

Touch Text Entry

Session Chair: Brian Bailey *(University of Illinois at Urbana-Champaign)*

Programming & Debugging

Session Chair: Niklas Elmqvist *(Purdue University)*

Organizing the Recovery

Session Chair: Ron Wakkary *(Simon Fraser University)*

Tweet, Tweet, Tweet!

Session Chair: Sadat Shami *(IBM Research)*

Me & My Mobile

Session Chair: Lynne Baillie *(Glasgow Caledonian University)*

Crowdsourcing & Peer Production II

Session Chair: Erika Poole *(Penn State)*

Usability & User Research

Session Chair: Anna Cox *(University College London)*

Do You See What Eye See

Session Chair: Andrew Duchowski *(Clemson University)*

Home & Family

Session Chair: Andrea Grimes Parker *(Georgia Institute of Technology)*

Designing for Learners' Complex Needs

Session Chair: Hilary Hutchinson *(Google)*

Groups @ Work

Session Chair: Eric Gilbert *(Georgia Institute of Technology)*

Use the Force

Session Chair: Mike Horn *(Northwestern University)*

CHI 2012 ORGANIZING COMMITTEE

Conference Chair
Joseph A. Konstan, *University of Minnesota*

TECHNICAL PROGRAM

Chairs
Ed H. Chi, *Google Research*
Kristina Höök, *Mobile Life @ KTH*

Papers
Susanne Bødker, *Aarhus University*
Dan R. Olsen Jr., *Brigham Young University*

alt.chi
Amanda Williams, *Wyld Collective Ltd.*
Erica Robles, *New York University*

Case Studies
Daniela Busse, *Samsung Research*
Elizabeth Buie, *Luminanze Consulting LLC*

Courses
Nancy Frishberg, *MSB Associates*
Gregorio Convertino, *Palo Alto Research Center (PARC)*

Doctoral Consortium
Steve Brewster, *University of Glasgow*
Erik Stolterman, *Indiana University Bloomington*

Interactivity
Patrick Baudisch, *Hasso Plattner Institut*
Florian 'Floyd' Mueller, *Exertion Games Lab*
Eva Hornecker, *University of Strathclyde*
Danielle Wilde, *daniellewilde.com*

Panels
Allison Druin, *University of Maryland*
Joseph 'Jofish' Kaye, *Nokia Research Center*

Special Interest Groups (SIGS)
Daphne Raban, *University of Haifa*
Kaisa Väänänen-Vainio-Mattila, *Tampere University of Technology*

Student Design Competition
Gilbert Cockton, *Northumbria University*
Thecla Schiphorst, *Simon Fraser University*

Student Research Competition
Anne Aula, *Google*
Shaowen Bardzell, *Indiana University Bloomington*

Student Game Competition
Seth Cooper, *University of Washington*
Winslow Burleson, *Arizona State University*

Video
Michael Bernstein, *MIT CSAIL*
Jeffrey Bardzell, *Indiana University, Bloomington*

Work-in-Progress (WIPs)
Lichan Hong, *Google*
Henriette Cramer, *Mobile Life @ SICS*

Workshops
Helena Mentis, *Microsoft Research Cambridge*
Ido Guy, *IBM Research Haifa*

CHI 2012 COMMUNITIES

Chairs
Arnie Lund, *Microsoft*
Bo Begole, *Samsung's User Experience Center*

Core Communities

Design
Ellen Yi-Luen Do, *Georgia Tech*
Patrick Olivier, *Newcastle University*

User Experience
Jhilmil Jain, *Microsoft*
Kath Straub, *Usability.org*

Engineering
Ruven Brooks, *Independent Consultant*
Fabio Paternò, *CNR-ISTI*

Management
Janice Rohn, *Experian*
Dennis Wixon, *Microsoft*

Featured Communities

Child Computer Interaction
Janet C Read, *University of Central Lancashire*
Panos Markopoulos, *Eindhoven University of Technology*
Allison Druin, *University of Maryland*

Digital Arts
David England, *Liverpool John Moores University*
Jill Fantauzzacoffin, *Georgia Tech*

Games and Entertainment
Regina Bernhaupt, *IRIT*
Katherine Isbister, *NYU-Poly*

Health
Karen Cheng, *University of California, Irvine*
Julie Kientz, *University of Washington*

Sustainability
Eli Blevis, *Indiana University at Bloomington*
Samuel Mann, *Otago Polytechnic*

PARTICIPATION AND VOLUNTEERING

Student Volunteer Coordinators
Vicky McArthur, *York University*
Bobby Beaton, *Virginia Tech*

Madness
Paul André, *University of Southampton*
Petra Sundström, *Salzburg University*

Social Media
Cliff Lampe, *Michigan State University*
Sean McNee, *FTI Consulting*

Publicity
Rosemary Stevens, *Ace Public Relations*
Eelco Herder, *L3S Research Center*

Local Experience
Annette Priest, *Revel Insight*

MAKING THINGS HAPPEN

Design Directors
Apala Lahiri Chavan, *Human Factors International*
Srikanth Vellore, *Human Factors International*

Webmaster
William Hudson, *Syntagm Ltd. and Hult International Business School*

Posters
Oleg Komogortsev, *Texas State University-San Marcos*

Proceedings
Max Van Kleek, *University of Southampton*
Nirmal Patel, *Georgia Tech*
Alireza Sahami Shirazi, *University of Stuttgart*
Michael Ekstrand, *University of Minnesota*

Mobile Apps
Stephen Oney, *Carnegie Mellon University*
Jason Wiese, *Carnegie Mellon University*
Eiji Hayashi, *Carnegie Mellon University*

Communications Director
Garett Dworman, Tec-Ed Inc

Program Production
Joan Johnson, *Joan Johnson Design*
Max Van Kleek, *University of Southampton*

Mailing Lists
Adam Sporka, *Czech Technical University*

ACM Staff Liaison
Ashley Cozzi, *ACM*

Sponsors and Exhibits
Carol Klyver, *Foundations of Excellence*

Conference Logistics
Janeé Pelletier, *CLC*
Allison Perrelli, *CLC*

Technology Liaison
Scooter Morris, *University of California, San Francisco*
Sara Drenner, *BI Worldwide*

CMC Liaison
Scooter Morris, *University of California, San Francisco*

Registration
Yvonne Lopez, *Executive Events*

Special thanks for the financial support provided by the following sponsors:

CHI Champion Sponsors

Autodesk®

Bloomberg

Google

ebay® | PayPal™

Microsoft®

NSF

SAP®

CHI Contributing Sponsors

facebook

NOKIA

Friends of CHI

Adobe Systems, Inc. **Disney Research** **University of Michigan School of Information**

Printed on Rolland Enviro 100
100% post-consumer fiber
Certified EcoLogo
Processed chlorine free
Manufactured using biogas energy
Printed using soy-based inks

Beyond Stereo: An Exploration of Unconventional Binocular Presentation for Novel Visual Experience

Haimo Zhang[1,2], **Xiang Cao**[1], **Shengdong Zhao**[2]
[1]Microsoft Research Asia
5 Danling Street, Beijing, China
xiangc@microsoft.com
[2]National University of Singapore
13 Computing Drive, Singapore
{z-haimo, zhaosd}@comp.nus.edu.sg

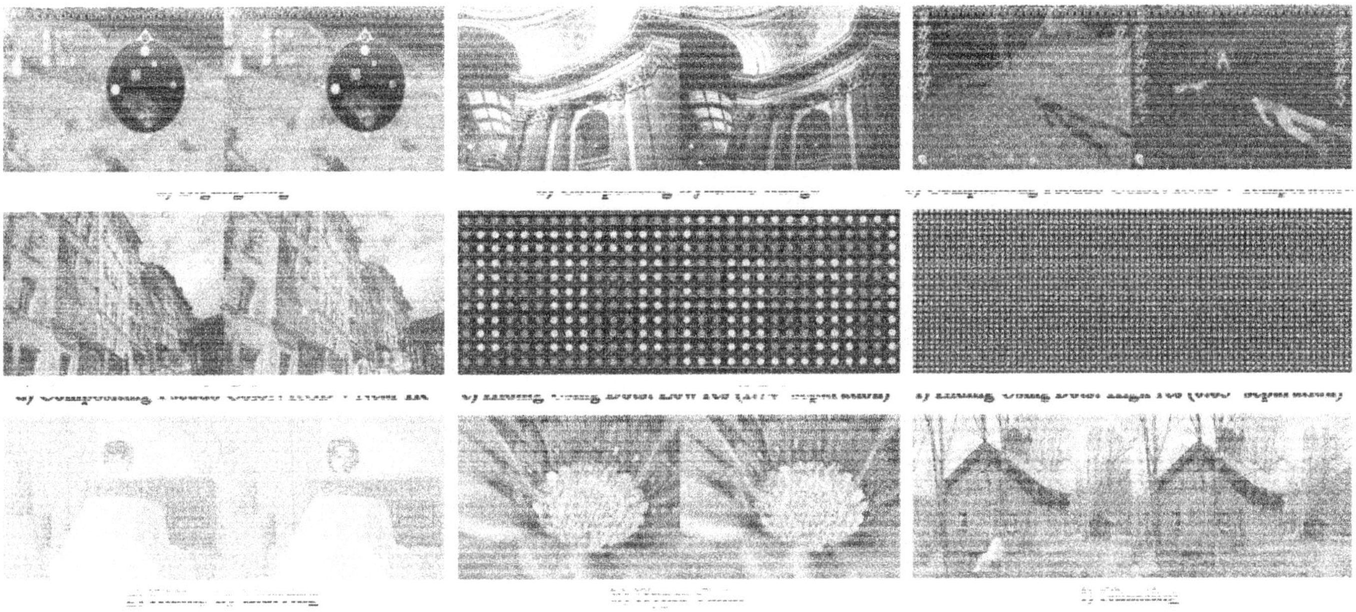

Figure 1. Effects Explored in the Study

ABSTRACT
Human stereo vision processes the two different images seen by the two eyes to generate depth sensation. While current stereoscopic display technologies look at how to faithfully simulate the stereo viewing experience, we took a look out of this scope, to explore how we may present binocular image pairs that differ in other ways to create novel visual experience. This paper presents several interesting techniques we explored, and discusses their potential applications according to an informal user study.

Author Keywords
Binocular vision; special effect; stereo.

ACM Classification Keywords
H.5.2. [Information interfaces and presentation (e.g., HCI)]: User Interfaces – Screen design (e.g., text, graphics, color);

INTRODUCTION
The binocular vision system of two human eyes allows us to see the world in two slightly different perspectives with optical parallax, and our brains process such stereo images to allow us to perceive depth. Numerous stereoscopic display technologies have been created to present prerecorded or synthesized stereo images to our two eyes to simulate 3D sensations, and they are increasingly accessible to the general public. However, these technologies are not necessarily limited to presenting stereo images, but are technically capable of independently displaying an arbitrary pair of images to two eyes. This opens up the question, can we present pairs of images that differ from each other in ways other than stereoscopic, and what does it buy us if we were to deliberately exploit such unconventional binocular vision?

Some cognitive scientists have studied such non-stereo binocular vision in order to understand human perception, especially in terms of binocular rivalry [2, 3, 5, 8], where two dissimilar images are presented to study which features are more dominant in visual perception. Differing from these scientific works, we sought to answer this question from an engineering perspective, i.e. how we can constructively exploit human's binocular vision system in unconventional ways to present novel visual experience for practical applications.

To explore this, we proposed a set of non-stereo binocular presentation techniques inspired by cognitive science literature, and conducted an informal study to validate the viability of these techniques as well as collecting subjective accounts of the actual visual experience. We first describe our study procedure, and then detail the design and findings of each technique.

STUDY PROCEDURE

We used a Vuzix VR920 binocular head-mounted display (HMD). It produces an image of 32° diagonal visual angle at 4:3 aspect ratio, focused at 9 feet, for each eye. The overlap between the two eyes' views was set to 100%. Each participant adjusted the tiltable section of the device to clearly see the entire display. Participants looked with both eyes unless otherwise instructed.

For each presentation technique we tested (see Figure 1 for some examples), six static image pairs were used[1]. As we expect our techniques to be integrated with stereo images in practice, where applicable our stimuli also included regular stereo cues. The stimuli were presented to the two eyes at 30Hz refresh rate each. Each image pair was presented twice with the left/right views swapped; and as a baseline comparison, for each pair of images, we also used the same device to present to both eyes an average image that is equally alpha-blended between the image pair. The stereo cues were kept intact in all three conditions however. Upon participants' request, all stimuli may be freely revisited.

Upon presentation of stimuli, participants were asked to describe in their own words what they were seeing in as much detail as possible. Only when they could not discover the special visual effects by themselves did we provide hints for regions of interest, however without suggesting the actual effect expected. The study was audio recorded for further analysis. Six people (2 females) aged between 24 and 35 participated. All had normal or corrected-to-normal vision, normal stereo vision, and normal color vision. The participants were tested for eye dominance using the Miles test [6] with several repetitions: 3 participants (male) were generally right-eye dominant, while the rest were generally left-eye dominant.

TAXONOMY

Inspired by cognitive science research, we considered three general dimensions along which we can produce non-stereo difference between the pair of images: Color, Sharpness, and Semantic Content. As we are interested in practical applications, we also consider the following four general categories of visual effects: Highlighting, Compositing, Hiding, and Wowing. Table 1 illustrates this design space, and summarizes the techniques we explored and their attributes by these two criteria, to be detailed in the following sections. Due to limited space, for each technique we only reprint one example image pair in the paper, while the full set of image pairs we tested can be found in the supplementary material of this paper.

[1] Some test images based on:
http://pages.cs.wisc.edu/~csverma/CS766_09/HDRI/hdr.html
http://ivrg.epfl.ch/supplementary_material/cvpr11/
http://vision.middlebury.edu/stereo/data/scenes2006/
and Vuzix JPS Viewer:
http://www.vuzix.com/support/downloads_drivers.html

		Color	Sharpness	Semantics
Highlighting	Color Highlighting	√		
Compositing	Dynamic Range	√		
	Pseudo Color	√		
Hiding	Color dot pattern	√		
	Hiding by Blurring		√	√
Wowing	Hyper color	√		
	Ghosting			√

Table 1. Application domains and production procedures.

HIGHLIGHTING

The highlighting effect aims at making certain regions of interest more noticeable to the viewer, and currently includes one technique: color highlighting. This is produced by painting the region with two different colors (90-180 hue difference, 0-13% saturation difference, and 0-66% brightness difference). For example, in Figure 1a, the square icon in the circular game map differs between violet in one image, and green in the other.

Study revealed that regions of highly saturated color pairs that differ in hue were particularly prominent, as long as the size of the region is above a certain threshold (≈0.44° in view angle). Participants described the effect either positively (4/6, i.e. 4 of 6 participants) as "highlighted", "blinking", or negatively (2/6) as "distracting", "annoying". More interesting descriptions include "fluorescent", "bright and colorful emissive light", and "floating". 2 participants were reminded of special optical material they have seen, such as lenticular or refractive films, as these materials may also display view-dependent colors. Eye dominance had a noticeable effect, where different sensations were reported when shown inverted pairs. On the other hand, these sensations were unstabilized, as typical in binocular rivalry [2]. Unsurprisingly, in the baseline image where the two views were averaged, the regions of interest became even less prominent because averaging two contrasting colors results in desaturation.

The power of color highlighting has thus been confirmed. One thing worth noting is that neither single color in the contrasting pair needs to be prominent from the surroundings on its own, so highlighting can be achieved without compromising the image composition.

The highlighting effect could be theoretically suggested by the perceived shininess of a surface [7]: in real world, some "shiny" materials with specular reflection or refraction properties display drastically different hues and brightness from different view angles. Our proposed highlighting technique produces a similar color rivalry [5] effect that resonates with this principle of perceived shininess, thus highlighting the rivaling regions as "shiny" areas.

COMPOSITING

The compositing effect aims at presenting two images of the same scene, however are complementary in terms of information spectrum along a certain dimension. We expect that the human perception system may be able to composite such information to receive a higher bandwidth than is possible with a single view. We explored such compositing effects along two different dimensions:

Compositing Dynamic Range

Compositing dynamic range concerns a pair of photographs taken at different exposures, each missing part of the illumination range of the scene. Figure 1b illustrates.

When shown image pairs with different exposures, participants were able to describe details that are only available in one of the two images, where the corresponding region in the counterpart image is subject to overexposure or underexposure due to limited dynamic range of the camera. This may be explained by contour dominance [8], where the rich contours in one image effectively suppressed the more uniform over/under exposed regions in the other image.

Comparatively, although the baseline average image also incorporates these features, they were less prominent, as averaging reduced the overall image contrast. Interestingly, swapping the left and right eye images also resulted in a perceived change of global brightness; and two participants further perceived change in light source, although they could not determine the nature of that change. The global brightness was biased towards the dominant eye.

Compositing Pseudo Colors

In pseudo color images, pixel values do not represent true visible light intensities, but some other physical channels such as temperature or near infrared (NIR) response. By letting the viewer composite ordinary RGB images with such pseudo color images, we expect that they would be able to make sense of the complementary nature of different channels. Examples are given in Figure 1c and 1d.

For RGB-temperature image pairs, all participants reported seeing bright human figures. It is hard for them to see the human figures' actual color, but they could identify the green color of the background land. One participant described the effect as the contour "shaking". When shown the naïve average between the two images, participants responded that more colors could be observed on the human figure, but that the background color is less obvious. For RGB-NIR image pairs, all participants reported that the boundaries of plants, brightly colored blankets, and sign boards are "bright", "confusing", and sometimes (2/6) "floating", which "does not fit well" into the scene. When shown the averaged baseline, participants reported that the color is not as vivid as in the previous case, but the feeling of "unfitness" also disappeared. The effect of eye dominance is mainly on the overall perceived saturation: when the gray scale NIR image is shown to the dominant eye, participants reported reduced saturation as compared to viewing the other way round.

The response from the participants meets our expectation: in the RGB-temperature image pair, textured background of RGB image suppressed the almost uniform background of temperature map; the strong edges of the human figure in the temperature map suppressed the perception of its normal color; and in RGB-NIR image pairs, large luminance difference of plants and painted sign boards between RGB and NIR images creates strong response that the participants could not overlook. This effect could also be exploited in real-time vegetation inspection applications, by feeding RGB video and NIR video to each eye, while letting the human brain to work out the distracting areas as the possible contours of vegetation.

Besides the contour dominance factor, the aforementioned highlighting effect may also play a role here: regions with rivaling colors would appear bright and catches more attention. The result shows that humans are able to effectively incorporate multi-spectrum visual information through binocular vision and make sense of them. Essentially, by leveraging the "computation power" of the human visual perception system, we may alleviate or eliminate the need for computers to algorithmically fuse such information [4], which is not always possible or straightforward to do.

HIDING

The hiding effect aims at a seemingly counterintuitive goal: to turn visible information in monocular images invisible in the binocular view. In other words, we attempt to hide some information from the viewer when both eyes are open, while revealing it once s/he closes one of the eyes. This may provide a lightweight mechanism for switching between information layers. For example, in video games, users keep both eyes open to see the regular game view, but may occasionally close one eye to access additional information such as player statistics. This is achieved without active sensing the user's eye movement.

Hiding Using Color Dot Patterns

Research in binocular color fusion [5] has discovered several possible outcomes when human brain attempts to fuse two different colors presented to two eyes, ranging from stable uniform fused color, to color sensation that vary both in space and in time. Regardless of the outcome of the color fusion, it is usually difficult for human to determine which eye is seeing which. This suggests that if we present a pair of different colors to both eyes, it may become indistinguishable from the sensation of the same pair presented with left and right eye color swapped. Therefore, by rendering a shape in one eye using a foreground and a background color, and rendering the same in the other eye but with the foreground and background color swapped, it becomes possible that in binocular views at any point the user see the result of color fusion, which are more or less consistent regardless of which color comes from each eye. Thus the information would become invisible to the viewer.

However, such a technique could not work if there exists a visual contour between the colors in either view. As explained previously in [8], such contours are sensed individually by each eye, thus cannot be eliminated by binocular vision. In order to eliminate this, we convert the shape into a dot grid pattern (Figure 1e and 1f), so that it is only encoded by the color contrast but not contours. We generated four test image pairs with two levels of grid resolution (low/high) and two color schemes (complementary/similar colors).

Participants reported that they see dots constantly changing color. Although not seeing clearly to be certain, they were able, after intentionally viewing for some time, to describe the correct pattern in the higher resolution image pairs. They were more confused and uncertain when seeing the low resolution patterns. The minimum time from the onset of the pattern till the participants voluntarily guessed the correct or similar pattern is 10 seconds in the low resolution and 1 second in the high resolution. This period might be the sweet spot to hide information temporarily.

Hiding by Blurring

According to Fahle [3], higher spatial frequency (sharp features) is more dominant than low spatial frequency (blur features) when they are presented to the two eyes respectively. To hide information by this principle, we can create image pairs that show different semantic information in corresponding regions but in different level of sharpness. Contour dominance results in the sharp information masking the blurred information when both eyes are open, while the blurred information becomes visible only when the other eye is closed. We can apply this principle to multiple regions of the image pair, so that each image contains regions that can be either masking the other image or masked by the other, naturally supporting not one, but two individual views that can be revealed by closing either one of the eyes. Figure 1g illustrates one of the image pairs we tested, which shows this technique for both textual and graphical information and in alternate directions between the two eyes.

In general, most participants (5/6) reported seeing the sharper of the text rivalries. With the faces there was more variance between the participants, as 3 of them seeing the sharp face, and others seeing the alternate or mixed information. We suspect this was because the higher-level perception mechanism involved in recognizing faces interacted with our technique. The averaged baseline image appeared confusing and unrecognizable to all participants. When asked to use their single eyes to view the images, the participants were able to recognize all information except for the "NOV" / "DEC" texts, which might be due to the small size of the stimuli. After revelation of the effect, all participants found this effect interesting and fun.

Since no excessive attention is paid to the regions with hidden information, this effect might also be used to hide text or simple graphics to uninformed viewers, and only recognizable by informed users.

WOWING

Wowing effects aim at creating surprising sensations that are not necessarily useful for productivity applications but can facilitate compelling experience in applications such as cinema or gaming. The two effects we explored are as follows:

Hyper Color

We specifically tried to create the effect of "impossible colors" [1] by showing different colors in each eye, as shown in figure 1h. However, participants' responses were not colors that are yellowish blue or greenish red. Instead, 3 participants saw inhomogeneous color patches that change smoothly over time. Other responses include "fluorescent light", "jittering color patches", "bright outline" and "shiny and unstable positions". Based on the same principle as color highlighting, here we are addressing a different application context: we name it "hyper color" and see potential enlargement of color vocabulary in binocular visualizations.

Ghosting Effect

We showed two image pairs where an object is presented only in one eye's image but not the other, thus giving it a ghostly appearance, as illustrated in figure 1i. All participants reported the effect to be similar to transparency. Two participants described temporal change in transparency while the same image pair is presented. One participant explicitly used the word "ghost" in the description without prompting. All participants reported difference in transparency between the ghost effect, its left-right swapped version, and the baseline. Further, this effect demonstrates the temporal fluctuation of perceived transparency, which could not be experienced with transparency rendered in monocular static images.

The ghosting effect partially lies in the unstable perception found in binocular rivalry [2], in which the dominant perception alternates between the two eyes' views, which explains the fluctuation of transparency of the "ghostly" object in the image pair.

CONCLUSION

We have explored several unconventional binocular presentation techniques to create new visual experience. In the future, we would like to further explore how these and other potential interesting effects could be applied in various aspects of human-computer interaction, as well as quantifying the parameters of the techniques and providing a more systematic presentation vocabulary.

REFERENCES

1. Billock, V.A. and Tsou, B.H. Seeing Forbidden Colors. *Scientific American 302*, (2010), 72-77.
2. Blake, R. A Primer on binocular rivalry, including current controversies. *Brain and Mind 2*, 1 (2001), 5-38.
3. Fahle, M. Binocular rivalry: suppression depends on orientation and spatial frequency. *Vision Research 22*, 7 (1982), 787-800.
4. Goshtasby, A.A. and Nikolov, S. Image fusion: Advances in the state of the art. *Information Fusion* 8, 2 (2007), 114-118.
5. Jung, Y.J., Sohn, H, Lee, S., Ro, Y.M. and Park, H.W. Quantitative measurement of binocular color fusion limit for non-spectral colors. *Optics Express* 19, 8 (2011), 7325-7338.
6. Roth, H.L., Lora, A.N. and Heilman, K.M. Effects of monocular viewing and eye dominance on spatial attention. *Brain 125*, Pt 9 (2002), 2023-35.
7. Tyler, C.W. Sensory processing of binocular disparity. *Vergence eye movements: Basic and clinical aspects*. Butterworths, London, UK, 1983.
8. Xu, J.P., He, Z.J. and Ooi, T.L. Surface boundary contour strengthens image dominance in binocular competition. *Vision Research 50, 2 (2010), 155-170.*

1€ Filter: A Simple Speed-based Low-pass Filter for Noisy Input in Interactive Systems

Géry Casiez[1,2,3], Nicolas Roussel[3] & Daniel Vogel[4]
[1]LIFL, [2]University of Lille & [3]Inria Lille, France
[4]Cheriton School of Computer Science, University of Waterloo, Canada
gery.casiez@lifl.fr, nicolas.roussel@inria.fr, dvogel@uwaterloo.ca

ABSTRACT
The 1€ filter ("one Euro filter") is a simple algorithm to filter noisy signals for high precision and responsiveness. It uses a first order low-pass filter with an adaptive cutoff frequency: at low speeds, a low cutoff stabilizes the signal by reducing jitter, but as speed increases, the cutoff is increased to reduce lag. The algorithm is easy to implement, uses very few resources, and with two easily understood parameters, it is easy to tune. In a comparison with other filters, the 1€ filter has less lag using a reference amount of jitter reduction.

ACM Classification Keywords
H.5.2 [Information interfaces and presentation]: User interfaces - Input devices and strategies.

General Terms
Algorithms, Performance, Human Factors

Author Keywords
Signal; noise; jitter; precision; lag; responsiveness; filtering

INTRODUCTION
Noisy signals occur when an original time varying value undergoes undesirable and unpredictable perturbations. These may be caused by things like heat and magnetic fields affecting hardware circuitry, the limits of sensor resolution, or even unstable numerical computation. Noisy signals are a common problem when tracking human motion, particularly with custom sensing hardware and inexpensive input devices like the Kinect or Wiimote. In addition, even signals from established high-end sensing systems can become noisy when interaction techniques use large scaling effects. A common example is using a Vicon tracking system to implement ray casting with a wall display [6]: calibration problems and hand tremor add further perturbations to the ones amplified by the pointing technique.

Noise affects the quality of a signal in two primary ways [9]. It can reduce *accuracy*, by adding an *offset* between the observed values and the true ones. More often, it reduces *precision*, where repeated observations of values exhibit *jitter* – many different values are observed for a single true one. Jitter has a large effect on the way people perceive and act. For example noisy values are harder to read and unstable cursors hinder target acquisition [3, 7, 5]. One usually wants to filter noisy signals to reduce, and possibly remove, the unwanted parts of the signal. However, filtering inherently introduces time latency – commonly called *lag* – which reduces system *responsiveness*. Lag may not be an issue in domains like artificial perception and decision making, but with interactive feedback, it is very important. In fact, it is the combination of precision and responsiveness that are crucial: people can point accurately in spite of an offset, but only with minimal lag and jitter. The difficulty is that implementing and tuning a filter to minimize both jitter and lag is challenging, especially with little or no background in signal processing.

In this paper we describe the 1€ filter ("one Euro filter"), a tool to improve noisy signal quality with a tunable jitter and lag balance. It uses a low-pass filter, but the cutoff frequency changes according to speed: at low speeds, a low cutoff reduces jitter at the expense of lag, but at high speeds, the cutoff is increased to reduce lag rather than jitter. The intuition is that people are very sensitive to jitter and not latency when moving slowly, but as movement speed increases, people become very sensitive to latency and not jitter. We compare the 1€ filter to alternative techniques and show how it can reduce that same amount of jitter with less lag. It is also efficient and easy to understand, implement, and tune: the algorithm can be expressed in a few lines; it uses only basic arithmetic; and it has only two independent parameters that relate directly to jitter and lag. Other researchers and ourselves have already used variations of it in many projects. In fact, the "dynamic recursive low-pass filter" used by the third author in [6] established the basic principle, but it required four parameters and a fixed sample rate. The '1€' name is an homage to the $1 recognizer [10]: we believe that the 1€ filter can make filtering input signals simpler and better, much like the $1 recognizer did for gestures.

After a review of the jitter, lag, and alternative filtering techniques, we describe the 1€ filter in detail with an implementation, discuss tuning with different applications, and conclude with an illustrative comparison.

JITTER, LAG, AND FILTERING
Several studies show jitter and lag have a negative impact on performance. MacKenzie et al. found mouse movement times increased 16% with 75 ms lag, and up to 64% with 225

ms lag [3]. With 3D hand tracking, Ware and Balakrishnan found that only 50 ms lag reduced performance by more than 8% [7]. Pavlovych and Stuerzlinger found no performance degradation below 58 ms lag using a mouse or Wiimote, but increasing jitter from 4 to 8 pixels doubled error rates for small targets [5]. Assuming a 100 PPI screen, 4 pixels corresponds to 1mm of jitter mean-to-peak: close to the 0.4 mm of jitter they found with the established Optitrack system.

Although the precision of an input device may be very good, it does not take into account scaling effects introduced by interaction techniques. Device input is often scaled up, so people can cover more display distance with less device movement. For example, default operating system mouse transfer functions can be scaled up 12× [1] and factors as high as 90× have been used when ray casting on wall sized displays [6]. Regardless of native device precision, scaling amplifies even small sensing perturbations, increasing jitter.

These results highlight the importance of balancing jitter and lag. Jitter should be less than 1mm mean-to-peak, but lag should be below 60 ms. As we shall see, any filter introduces some lag and considering 40-50 ms of inherent system lag [5], that leaves less than 10-20 ms for the filter.

Moving average

By the Central Limit Theorem and reasonable assumptions, averaging enough successive values of a noisy signal should produce a better estimate of the true one [9]. As a result, a *moving average* of the last n data values is commonly used by computer scientists as a kind of filter. For example, Myers et al. [4] used one for laser pointers and reduced hand tremor jitter from ± 8 pixels to between ± 2 and ± 4 pixels using a 0.5s window ($n = 10$). Since all n values are weighted equally, this creates a lag up to n times the sampling period.

Low-pass filters and exponential smoothing

With human movements, noise typically forms high frequencies in the signal while actual limb movements have lower frequencies. A low-pass filter is designed to let these desired low frequency portions pass through, while attenuating high frequency signals above a fixed cutoff frequency. The *order* of a low-pass filter relates to how aggressively it attenuates each frequency: first order filters reduce the signal amplitude by half every time the frequency doubles, while higher order variants reduce the signal amplitude at a greater rate. A discrete time realization of a first order low-pass filter is given by Equation 1 where X_i and $\hat{X}_i$ denote the raw and filtered data at time i and α is a smoothing factor in $]0, 1]$:

$$\hat{X}_i = \alpha X_i + (1 - \alpha) \hat{X}_{i-1} \quad (1)$$

The first term of the equation is the contribution of new input data value, and the second term adds inertia from previous values. As α decreases, jitter is reduced, but lag increases since the output responds more slowly to changes in input. Since the contribution of older values exponentially decreases, a low-pass filter will have less lag than a high n moving average filter.

Smoothing techniques used in business and economic forecasts are similar in approach to a low-pass filter. The equation for *single exponential smoothing* is very similar to Equation 1. As the name suggests, *double exponential smoothing* uses two of these equations to handle trends in the signal. Although not formally documented, the Microsoft Kinect skeleton filters appear to be a variant of this type of smoothing[1]. LaViola extended double exponential smoothing for predictive tracking [2], building on Equations 1 and 2 to predict positions τ time steps in the future (Equation 3):

$$\hat{X}_i^{[2]} = \alpha \hat{X}_i + (1 - \alpha) \hat{X}_{i-1}^{[2]} \quad (2)$$

$$P_{t+\tau} = \left(2 + \frac{\alpha \tau}{1 - \alpha}\right) \hat{X}_i - \left(1 + \frac{\alpha \tau}{1 - \alpha}\right) \hat{X}_i^{[2]} \quad (3)$$

Kalman filters

Unlike the techniques above, Kalman filters make assumptions about the system generating the signal. Typically used for navigation and tracking, they work well when combining data from different sensors (e.g. a GPS and a speedometer) or when the system can be modeled by equations (e.g. determining vehicle acceleration from accelerator pedal position). Kalman filters rely on a *process model* and a *measurement model*. The standard Kalman filter uses a discrete-time linear stochastic difference equation for the process model and assumes that process and measurement noise are independent of each other, white, and are normally distributed [8]. When estimating the true position of a moving object, the process model is typically a linear function of the speed and the previous estimated position. With additional complexity, Extended and Unscented variants of Kalman filters can also model non-linear processes and observations [8].

In the frequent case where the process and measurement noise covariances are not known, one must determine them empirically. This task can be challenging, and an improperly tuned filter can increase and even degrade the signal [9], by creating artificial "overshooting" movements for example. Moreover, understanding Kalman filters requires mathematical knowledge beyond basic linear algebra such as statistics, random signals, and stochastic methods. Implementing them requires a language or library with matrix operations. And, as demonstrated by LaViola for predictive tracking, they can be considerably slower to compute than double exponential smoothing predictors (approximately 135×) with similar jitter and lag performance [2].

THE 1€ FILTER

The 1€ filter is an adaptive first-order low-pass filter: it adapts the cutoff frequency of a low-pass filter for each new sample according to an estimate of the signal's speed, or more generally, its derivative value. Even though noisy signals are often sampled at a fixed frequency, filtering can not always follow the same pace, especially in event-driven systems. To accommodate possible fluctuations, we rewrite equation 1 to take into account the actual time interval between samples. Using a direct analogy with an electrical circuit, where a resistor in series with a capacitor defines a first order low-pass filter, α can be computed as a function of the sampling period T_e and a time constant τ, both expressed

[1] `http://cm-bloggers.blogspot.com/2011/07/kinect-sdk-smoothing-skeleton-data.html`

in seconds (Equation 4). The resistor and capacitor values define the time constant ($\tau = RC$) and the corresponding cutoff frequency f_c, in Hertz, of the circuit (Equation 5).

$$\alpha = \frac{1}{1+\frac{\tau}{T_e}} \quad (4)$$

$$\tau = \frac{1}{2\pi f_c} \quad (5)$$

$$\hat{X}_i = \left(X_i + \frac{\tau}{T_e}\hat{X}_{i-1}\right)\frac{1}{1+\frac{\tau}{T_e}} \quad (6)$$

$$f_c = f_{c_{min}} + \beta\,|\dot{\hat{X}}_i| \quad (7)$$

The sampling period T_e (or its inverse, the sampling rate) can be automatically computed from timestamps, so the cutoff frequency f_c is the only configurable parameter in equation 6. As with any low-pass filter, decreasing f_c reduces jitter, but increases lag. Finding a good trade-off between the two is difficult since people are more sensitive to jitter at low speeds, and more sensitive to lag at high speeds. This is why an adaptive cutoff frequency works well. To reduce jitter, a low f_c is used at low signal speeds, and to reduce lag, f_c is increased as speed increases. We found that a straightforward linear relationship between cutoff frequency f_c and the absolute speed works well (Equation 7). The speed (i.e the derivative $\dot{\hat{X}}_i$) is computed from raw signal values using the sampling rate and then low-pass filtered with a cutoff frequency chosen to avoid high derivative bursts caused by jitter. Our implementation uses a fixed value of 1 Hz, leaving only two configurable parameters: the intercept $f_{c_{min}}$ and the slope β shown in Equation 7. Details of the algorithm are provided in the Appendix.

Tuning and Applications

To minimize jitter and lag when tracking human motion, the two parameters can be set using a simple two-step procedure. First β is set to 0 and $f_{c_{min}}$ to a reasonable middle-ground value such as 1 Hz. Then the body part is held steady or moved at a very low speed while $f_{c_{min}}$ is adjusted to remove jitter and preserve an acceptable lag during these slow movements. Next, the body part is moved quickly in different directions while β is increased with a focus on minimizing lag. Note that parameters $f_{c_{min}}$ and β have clear conceptual relationships: if high speed lag is a problem, increase β; if slow speed jitter is a problem, decrease $f_{c_{min}}$. Rotational input uses a similar tuning process, but rotation axis and angle are filtered separately.

Another application of the 1€ filter is displaying noisy numerical values, such as an unsteady frame rate used to monitor graphical application performance. The goal is to reduce jitter to make the numerical output legible while minimizing lag so the value remains timely. Tuning is similar to above: adjust $f_{c_{min}}$ until the text becomes stable, then increase β until just before the text become unstable.

COMPARISON WITH OTHER FILTERS

To compare the 1€ filter with other techniques, we created a Python application that periodically samples the XY position of the system cursor, adds noise, and displays filtered cursor positions. Each filter can be tuned interactively and all filters can be shown simultaneously making it possible to visually compare jitter reduction and lag across parameter settings and filters. Once tuned, timestamped positions can be logged for the system cursor (with and without noise) and filtered positions of all filters. We used a MacBook Pro with a 1440 × 900 pixel display (109 PPI).

In our comparison, we used independent Gaussian white noises for X and Y with a 50 dB SNR[2], a public implementation of the Kalman filter[3], and custom implementations of a moving average, single exponential, and LaViola's double exponential smoothing. We tuned moving average first and used its performance as a baseline. We found that averaging more than 14 data values did not reduce jitter further and only increased lag, so we used n=14. Then we interactively tuned the other filters to primarily match the jitter reduction of moving average, and secondarily attempting to reduce lag.

Tuning single exponential smoothing to match the reference jitter requires a low alpha value (α=0.11) which introduces lag. This highlights the difficulty of tuning with only a single parameter. For LaViola's double exponential smoothing filter, the reference jitter is obtained with a lower alpha value (α=0.06) and with lower lag. However, this causes overshooting when the pointer abruptly decelerates. For the Kalman filter, we set the measurement noise covariance to the variance of the introduced noise (18.06) as in [2], and adjusted the process noise covariance until we obtained the reference jitter reduction (at a value of 0.3). The amount of lag for this setting was comparable to the moving average and single-exponential. For the 1€ filter, we matched the reference jitter and optimized lag using the tuning procedure described above. In the first tuning step, setting $f_{c_{min}}$ = 1 Hz and β = 0 matched the reference jitter and lag was similar to single exponential smoothing. In the second tuning step, increasing β to 0.007 made the lag almost imperceivable yet maintained the reference jitter when stationary or moving slowly. A supplementary video demonstrates this tuning process and visualizes filter performance.

For a quantitative comparison, we logged the system cursor at 60 Hz for about 1 hour during regular desktop use, then added white noise and applied the filters using the settings above. Figure 1 shows the distance from each filtered cursor position to the true one, binned into four speed intervals. Note that since we tuned the filters to match a reference jitter when not moving, the error between filtered position and noiseless position is primarily due to lag when moving. With higher speeds, the filtered position lags farther and farther behind, increasing this distance (the small distances in the 0 mm/s interval are likely due to offset or overshooting). All filters introduce a similar amount of lag except for the 1€ filter which has less lag across all speed intervals.

As an overall comparison, we computed the Standard Error of the Mean (SEM) in mm for each filter for this data

[2]This signal-to-noise ratio was estimated from Gametrak data using a zero phase shift filter and is consistent with numbers in [2]

[3]`http://greg.czerniak.info/node/5`

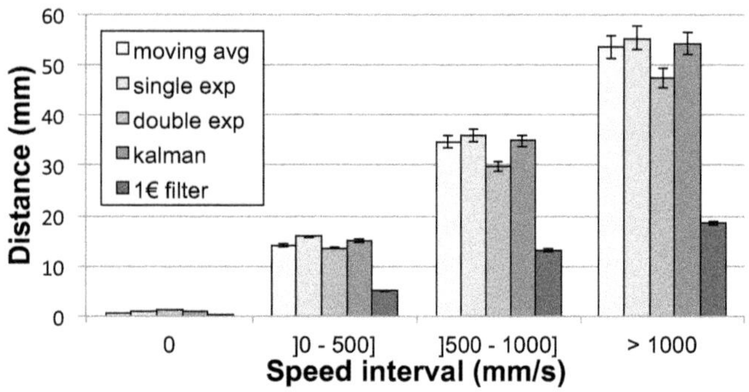

Figure 1. Mean distance between filtered and true cursor position for each speed interval and filter. Error bars represent 95% CI.

set. The 1€ filter has the smallest SEM (0.004) followed by LaViola's double exponential smoothing (0.013), the moving average and the Kalman filter (0.015), and single exponential smoothing (0.016). Our intention for this evaluation is to illustrate the performance of the 1€ filter in an intuitive way under realistic conditions. We are exploring alternative comparisons with user experiments, synthetic reference movements, different noise configurations, and examples of "noisy" hardware.

CONCLUSION

Human-Computer Interaction researchers and practitioners should stop filtering noisy input with a moving average. In most cases, they do not need to wrestle with low-level signal processing issues or with more complex techniques like Kalman filtering – which can be difficult to understand, tune, and implement. The 1€ filter is an intuitive and practical alternative since it is easy to understand, implement, and tune for low jitter and lag. Best of all, it produces better results.

REFERENCES

1. Casiez, G., and Roussel, N. No more bricolage! Methods and tools to characterize, replicate and compare pointing transfer functions. In *Proc. of UIST'11*, ACM (2011), 603–614.
2. LaViola, J. J. Double exponential smoothing: an alternative to kalman filter-based predictive tracking. In *Proc. of EGVE '03*, ACM (2003), 199–206.
3. MacKenzie, I. S., and Ware, C. Lag as a determinant of human performance in interactive systems. In *Proc. of CHI '93*, CHI '93, ACM (1993), 488–493.
4. Myers, B. A., Bhatnagar, R., Nichols, J., Peck, C. H., Kong, D., Miller, R., and Long, A. C. Interacting at a distance: measuring the performance of laser pointers and other devices. In *Proc. of CHI '02*, 33–40.
5. Pavlovych, A., and Stuerzlinger, W. The tradeoff between spatial jitter and latency in pointing tasks. In *Proc. of EICS '09*, ACM (2009), 187–196.
6. Vogel, D., and Balakrishnan, R. Distant freehand pointing and clicking on very large, high resolution displays. In *Proc. of UIST '05*, ACM (2005), 33–42.
7. Ware, C., and Balakrishnan, R. Reaching for objects in vr displays: lag and frame rate. *ACM ToCHI 1*, 4 (Dec. 1994), 331–356.
8. Welch, G., and Bishop, G. An introduction to the Kalman filter. SIGGRAPH course, ACM, Aug. 2001.
9. Wilson, A. D. Sensor- and recognition-based input for interaction. In *The Human Computer Interaction handbook*. CRC Press, 2007, 177–199.
10. Wobbrock, J. O., Wilson, A. D., and Li, Y. Gestures without libraries, toolkits or training: a $1 recognizer for user interface prototypes. In *Proc. of UIST '07*, ACM (2007), 159–168.

APPENDIX A - 1€ FILTER

Algorithm 1: 1€ filter

EXT: First time flag: *firstTime* set to *true*
Data update rate: *rate*
Minimum cutoff frequency: *mincutoff*
Cutoff slope: *beta*
Low-pass filter: *xfilt*
Cutoff frequency for derivate: *dcutoff*
Low-pass filter for derivate: *dxfilt*
IN : Noisy sample value: *x*
OUT: Filtered sample value

```
if firstTime then
|  firstTime ← false
|  dx ← 0
else
|  dx ← (x - xfilt.hatxprev()) * rate
end
edx ← dxfilt.filter(dx, alpha(rate, dcutoff))
cutoff ← mincutoff + beta * |edx|
return xfilt.filter(x, alpha(rate, cutoff))
```

Algorithm 2: *Filter* method of Low-pass filter

EXT: First time flag: *firstTime* set to *true*
IN : Noisy sample value : *x*
Alpha value : *alpha*
OUT: Filtered value

```
if firstTime then
|  firstTime ← false
|  hatxprev ← x
end
hatx ← alpha * x + (1 - alpha) * hatxprev
hatxprev ← hatx
return hatx
```

Algorithm 3: Alpha computation

IN : Data update rate in Hz: *rate*
Cutoff frequency in Hz: *cutoff*
OUT: Alpha value for low-pass filter

```
tau ← 1.0 / (2*π*cutoff)
te ← 1.0 / rate
return 1.0 / (1.0 + tau/te)
```

TeleHuman: Effects of 3D Perspective on Gaze and Pose Estimation with a Life-size Cylindrical Telepresence Pod

Kibum Kim[1], John Bolton[1], Audrey Girouard[1,2], Jeremy Cooperstock[3] and Roel Vertegaal[1]

[1] Human Media Lab
Queen's University
Kingston, ON, K7L 3N6
Canada
{kibum, bolton, roel}@cs.queensu.ca

[2] School of Information Technology
Carleton University
Ottawa, ON, K1S 5B6
Canada
audrey_girouard@carleton.ca

[3] Centre for Intelligent Machines
McGill University
Montreal, QC, H3A 2A7
Canada
jer@cim.mcgill.ca

ABSTRACT

In this paper, we present TeleHuman, a cylindrical 3D display portal for life-size human telepresence. The TeleHuman 3D videoconferencing system supports 360° motion parallax as the viewer moves around the cylinder and optionally, stereoscopic 3D display of the remote person. We evaluated the effect of perspective cues on the conveyance of nonverbal cues in two experiments using a one-way telecommunication version of the system. The first experiment focused on how well the system preserves gaze and hand pointing cues. The second experiment evaluated how well the system conveys 3D body postural information. We compared 3 perspective conditions: a conventional 2D view, a 2D view with 360° motion parallax, and a stereoscopic view with 360° motion parallax. Results suggest the combined presence of motion parallax and stereoscopic cues significantly improved the accuracy with which participants were able to assess gaze and hand pointing cues, and to instruct others on 3D body poses. The inclusion of motion parallax and stereoscopic cues also led to significant increases in the sense of social presence and telepresence reported by participants.

ACM Classification: H.5.2 [Information interfaces and presentation]: User Interfaces - Graphical user interfaces.

General terms: Design, Human Factors, Teleconference.

Keywords: Telepresence; cylindrical display; organic user interfaces; 3D video; videoconference; motion parallax.

INTRODUCTION

Current videoconferencing systems range from the popular, low-end, small displays of Skype and FaceTime to expensive, large-screen business systems such as Cisco TelePresence and Polycom RealPresence, the latter of which can support life-size display. However, all of these systems suffer limitations in their ability to support important nonverbal communication cues such as eye contact, 3D spatial reasoning, and movement of interlocutors. The effect of these cues on remote communication may be difficult to measure, and may not affect typical parameters, such as task performance [33]. However, we believe that differences in user experience of telecommunication versus face-to-face communication may be attributed to subtle violations of such nonverbal communication [31].

Since the Talking Heads system [20], researchers have worked on preserving cues in telecommunication to enhance human telepresence [3]. However, very few systems approach the richness of direct face-to-face communication. Most only preserve a partial set of visual cues or suffer from costly and complex implementations [9]. One approach has been the use of animated 3D avatars of users [8] and head-mounted 3D virtual reality systems [34]. In such systems, a 3D model of the user is produced once, then animated in real time by *measuring* the user's behavior. Since only animation parameters are transmitted in real time, these systems typically require little bandwidth. However, they do so at a cost in realism that results in an Uncanny Valley effect [19].

While recent advances in 3D avatar systems offer highly realistic renditions [1], we believe there are significant advantages to using 3D video instead. Video-based systems differ from avatar systems in that they capture a realistic 3D video model of the user every frame, which is then broadcast and rendered in real time across the network [9]. This results in a highly realistic replication of behavioral cues, but at a cost of network bandwidth. The capturing and transmission of 3D video has, to date, required many special considerations in terms of camera placement and projection environment [9]. The associated requirements of such environments are prohibitive for the typical workplace.

TeleHuman

These observations motivated our development of TeleHuman, a 3D video-based conferencing system that provides the capabilities of 3D capture, transmission, and display in a lightweight, low-cost, low-bandwidth configuration. The system relies on 10 low-cost Microsoft

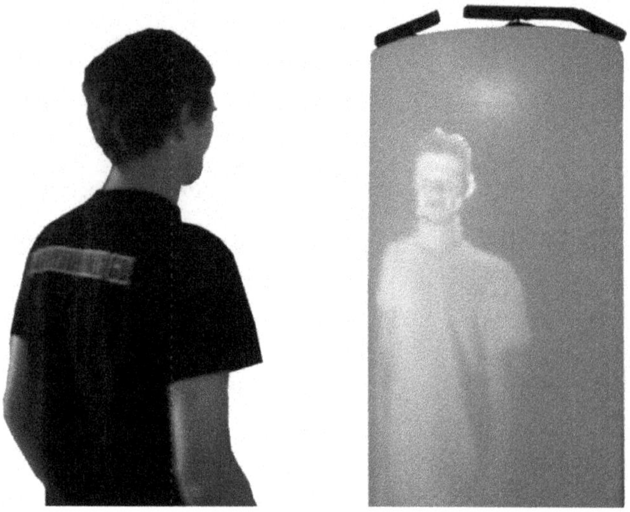

Figure 1. The TeleHuman system: local user (left) interacting with remote interlocutor (right) in 3D.

Kinects for capturing 360° 3D video models of the users. 3D models are efficiently broadcast over the network by adding a grayscale depth map frame to each frame of video. 3D video images are then synthesized locally through texture mapping, in response to actual viewer perspective. The 3D video models are rendered with perspective correction and stereoscopy on a life-sized cylindrical display, using an off-the-shelf 3D projector (see Figure 1).

Contribution

The chief contribution of TeleHuman is that it provides 360° motion parallax with stereoscopic life-sized 3D images of users, using a lightweight approach. Motion parallax is provided via perspective correction that adjusts views as users move around the display. Stereoscopy is provided through shutter glasses worn by the user. There is evidence to suggest that motion parallax and stereoscopy play an important role in the experience of telepresence [25]. To evaluate how these factors might aid in the preservation of basic body orientation cues used in deixis [36] and in pose estimation tasks, we conducted two experiments. The first focused on how well the system preserves gaze directional and hand pointing cues. The second experiment evaluated how well the system conveys 3D body postural cues. For both tasks, the TeleHuman was tested in three different viewing conditions: conventional 2D, 2D + motion parallax, and motion parallax + stereoscopy. Results show the presence of both motion parallax and stereoscopic cues significantly improved the accuracy with which participants were able to assess gaze and hand pointing cues, and instruct others on 3D body posture. These cues also led to significant increases in the sense of telepresence reported by participants.

BACKGROUND

We will first review work from early studies in virtual telepresence systems, after which we review work on gaze awareness in video conference systems. Finally, we will discuss the use of 3D in telepresence systems, and review work on motion parallax.

Telepresence Systems

Research initiatives in electronic transmission of human telepresence trace back to as early as the late 1940s with Rosenthal's work on half-silvered mirrors to transmit eye contact during video broadcasts [30]. In the 1970s, Negroponte developed the Talking Heads project [23]. Driven by the US government's emergency procedures prohibiting the co-location of its highest-ranking five members, Talking Heads proposed a five-site system where each site was composed of one real person and four plastic heads mounted on gimbals that replicated user head orientation. Properly registered video was projected inside a life-size translucent mask in the exact shape of the face, making the physical mask appear animated with live images. However, the system was a mockup that, in practice, would have required head mounted cameras for appropriate registration of faces.

The BiReality system [12] consisted of a display cube at a user's location and a surrogate in a remote location. Both the remote participant and the user appeared life size to each other. The display cube provided a complete 360° surround view of the remote location and the surrogate's head displayed a live video of the user's head from four sides. By providing a 360° surround environment for both locations, the user could perform all rotations locally by rotating his or her body. This preserved gaze and eye contact at the remote location. Although this system presented a life size tele-operated robotic surrogate, only the remote user's head image was rendered realistically. As implemented, the BiReality display was not responsive to viewer position, and thus, did not support motion parallax.

Gaze Direction

A lightweight approach to preserving gaze directional cues was provided by Hydra [31]. Hydra used multiple cameras, monitors, and speakers to support multiparty videoconferencing. It simulated a four-way round-table meeting by placing a camera, monitor, and speaker at the position of each remote participant, preserving both head orientation and eye contact cues. Although initial prototypes suffered from vertical parallax due to the spatial separation of the camera below the monitor, subsequent designs reduced this considerably by placing the camera directly above the display. Another limitation of Hydra was the use of small screens, which limited the size of remote participants. The size of the rendered interlocutor may indeed affect the sense of the social presence [4]. The MAJIC [26] and Videowhiteboard systems [32] projected life size images on semi-transparent surfaces by placing cameras behind the screen. However, these systems did not support 3D stereoscopic cues or motion parallax. The GAZE [33,36] groupware system provided integral support for conveying eye gaze cues using still images. Instead of using multiple video streams, GAZE measured where each participant looked by means of a desk-mounted eye-tracking system. This technique presented a user with the unique view of each remote participant, emanating from a distinct location in space. Each persona rotated around its x and y axes in 3D space, thus simulating head movements. Later, motion video was added via the use of half-silvered mirrors in GAZE-2 [35].

3D Motion Parallax and Stereoscopy

A variety of technical solutions have been devised to explore the preservation of 3D depth cues and motion parallax. Harrison and Hudson presented a method for producing a simple pseudo-3D experience by providing motion parallax cues via head position tracking [10]. Their system required only a single traditional webcam at each end for both scene capture and the creation of head-coupled pseudo-3D views. This system utilized a 2D display that did not provide stereoscopic vision [39]. Some CAVE-like environments provide an immersive VR experience, providing motion parallax for a single user. They typically also require the use of shutter glasses, thus precluding the possibility of eye contact transmission. For example, Blue-C, an immersive projection and communication system [9,22], combines real-time 3D video capture and rendering from multiple cameras. Developing a novel combination of projection and acquisition hardware, it created photorealistic 3D video inlays of the user in real time [22]. The use of auto-stereoscopic display technologies [15,17,24] provides similar capabilities, but without the need for special eyewear and often, adding the ability to support multiple users simultaneously, each with their own perspective-correct view. However, these are restricted to specific optimal viewing zones, may result in significantly reduced resolution, and rely on a flat form factor.

We should note that the above examples all rely on planar screens, limiting the ability of users to walk around the display of a remote interlocutor as is, e.g., possible with LiteFast displays [16]. Another technology, swept-surface volumetric display [11], supports 3D display with motion parallax in a form factor often more suitable for this purpose, but recent examples have been too small to render a full human body at life size.

Empirical Work

Although the benefits of including motion parallax and stereoscopy in the presentation of graphic interfaces have been demonstrated [37], systematic evaluation of the impact of these factors in the context of task performance during video communication, specifically, in assessing pointing or poses of a remote interlocutor, is sparse. Böcker, Rundel and Mühlbach [6] compared videoconferencing systems that provide motion parallax and stereoscopic displays. While their results suggested some evidence for increased spatial presence and greater exploration of the scene, the studies did not evaluate effects on task performance. Subsequently, the provision of motion parallax was shown to generate larger head movements in users of video conferencing systems, suggesting that users do utilize such cues [5].

DESIGN RATIONALE

Our main consideration in the design of our capture and display system was to support 3D cues. These aid in the preservation of information related to head orientation pose, gaze, and overall body posture of a human interlocutor. In this context, we identified a number of relevant design attributes:

3D Cues – TeleHuman supports 3D both through optional use of stereoscopic shutter glasses and motion parallax. The latter results in a change of view and relative shifts of objects in the visual field due to changes in the observer's tracked position, allowing users to walk around and observe a virtually projected interlocutor from any angle.

Form Factor – Providing full 360° motion parallax required the use of a cylindrical form factor display [16] proportionate to the human body. Since this offers an unobstructed 360° field of view, it enables a user to explore different perspectives by natural physical movement.

Directional Cues – Being able to determine where users are looking or pointing has been shown to be an important cue in videoconferencing [34]. These cues can help regulate conversation flow, provide feedback for understanding, and improve deixis [13,20]. The use of 3D video models, as opposed to the direct display of a single 2D video camera output, facilitates preservation of eye contact. However, stereoscopy through shutter glasses inhibits estimation of eye orientation in bi-directional scenarios. We believed that motion parallax alone may suffice for estimation of gaze or pointing direction, as users are free to move to the location in which gaze and arm orientations align to point at the user [5].

Size – Prior work, such as Ultra-Videoconferencing [7] and that of Böcker et al. [4], suggests that to avoid misperceptions of social distance [2] and to aid in a sense of realism, preservation of body size is important [25]. This motivated the conveyance of life-size images in our design.

TELEHUMAN IMPLEMENTATION

Our implementation of TeleHuman revolved around the design of a cylindrical display coupled with 3D tracking and imaging. We first discuss the imaging hardware, after which we discuss software algorithms for capturing, relaying, and displaying live 3D video images.

TeleHuman Cylindrical 3D Display

Figure 2 shows the cylindrical display deployed in TeleHuman. The display consists of a 170 cm tall hollow cylinder with a diameter of 75 cm made of 6.3 mm thick acrylic. The cylinder was sandblasted inside and out to create a diffuse projection surface. The cylinder is mounted on top of a wooden base that holds the projector, giving the entire system a height of approximately 200 cm. These dimensions were chosen to allow for a range in size of remote participants. A DepthQ stereoscopic projector [14] is mounted at the bottom of each display, pointed upwards to reflect off a 46 cm hemispherical convex acrylic mirror.

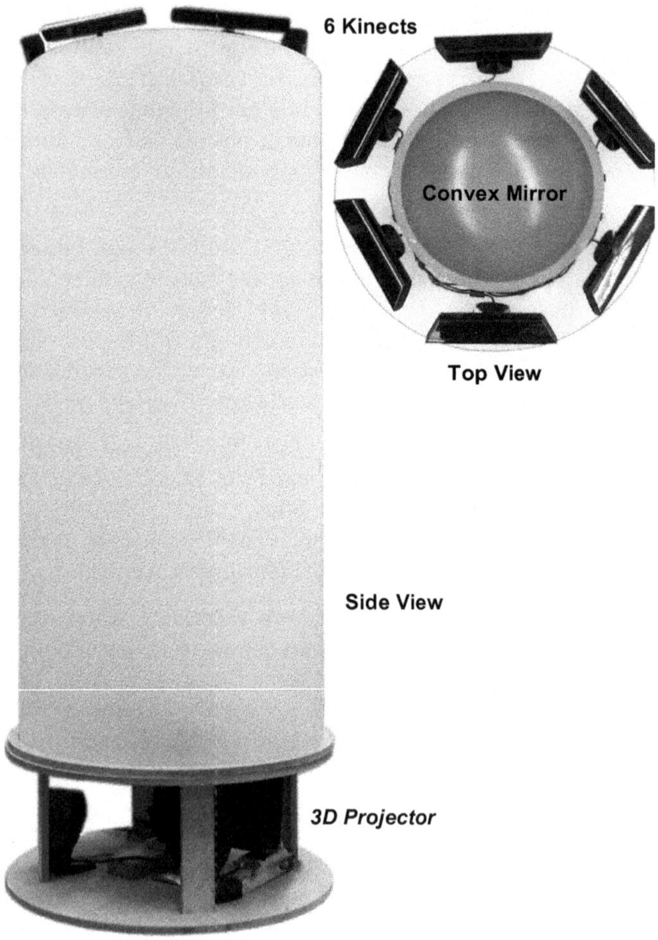

Figure 2. TeleHuman hardware: a cylindrical display surface with 6 Kinects and a 3D projector inside its base.

This allows projections of images across the entire surface of the cylinder. The DepthQ projector has a resolution of 1280 *x* 720 pixels. However, since only a circular portion of this image can be displayed on the surface of the cylinder, the effective resolution is described by a 720 pixel diameter circle, or 407,150 pixels.

An Nvidia 3D Vision Kit [21] is used with the projector to create an active stereoscopic display. This kit provides an IR emitter that connects to a 3-pin sync port on our system's graphics card. Compatible shutter glasses are synced with the IR emitter and projected image, refreshing at 120 Hz. As a result, when viewing the display, a distinct image is shown to each eye, and disparity between these two images creates stereoscopy. By combining depth cues with perspective corrected motion parallax [37] the remote participant appears to be standing inside the cylinder.

User Tracking

We used Microsoft Kinect depth-sensitive cameras [18] to determine the location of users around the cylinder. Six Kinects are mounted on the top of the cylinder, pointed downwards (see Figure 2). These track the location of the user around the cylinder, and obtain frontal images. Four Kinects are located in a square around the cylinder, centered at approximately 2.5 m from its center. These obtain images from the side and back of the user. Images from the Kinects are accessed using OpenNI [29] drivers. Each camera provides a 640 *x* 480 pixel stream at 30 fps with both RGB and depth images. When a user approaches to within 2 m of the TeleHuman, the system starts tracking and broadcasting. The system tracks the location of users around the display until they step out of range. Each Kinect is connected to a PC, which sends the user's position via Open Sound Control [38], along with the user's RGB image and depth map to a Microsoft XNA application that controls the projection. The XNA application calculates the angle between the user and the cylinder and updates the displayed model accordingly. To maintain an appropriate frame rate, we use 1 PC per 2 Kinects, using a total of 5 PCs for preprocessing image data.

Live 3D Model Generation

In order to create a 3D representation of a user, depth values are used to position vertices in a 3D XNA application. Using the depth and RGB streams, the system calculates a four-channel image via OpenCV [28]. This image contains RGB information in the first three channels and depth information in the fourth channel. Images are then sent via a TCP connection with the XNA projection application running on a separate machine. Currently, our system sends images over a gigabit LAN connection, relying on the associated high network speeds to provide multiple live streams with low latency. Note that future versions will use more efficient UDP protocols.

Using the depth map, the XNA display application creates vertices corresponding to each pixel of the user. The depth value is used to determine the vertex locations along the *z* axis. Depth values are also used to remove the scene behind the user, via a basic depth threshold. Vertices are placed in a vertex buffer. The content of this buffer is read and rendered by the XNA application. Based on the distance of the viewer from the cylindrical display, the model is rendered such that the center of mass of the TeleHuman appears to be in the middle of the cylinder, which we treat as the origin. The RGB values from the input image are used to texturemap the resulting mesh model.

Motion Parallax and Projection Distortion

The view of a user on the cylinder is rendered from the perspective of a virtual camera targeted at his or her 3D model. The angular position of the user controls the angle with which this virtual camera looks at the 3D model of the interlocutor. As a user's position changes, the position of the camera changes accordingly, allowing him or her to view a motion parallax corrected perspective of the 3D video model of the other user. This camera view is rendered and stored as a texture. 3D information is preserved during this process allowing the texture to be viewed with stereoscopy. The projected image is rendered using Microsoft's XNA 4.0 framework. A custom distortion class was developed, creating a two-dimensional semi-circular object. The texture coordinates of this object

Figure 3. Textured 3D model with hemispherical distortion. When reflected off the convex mirror onto the cylinder, this produces a 3D model with proper proportions.

are modified to account for the distortions introduced by the hemispherical mirror and the cylindrical display surface. The distortion model is textured using the previously rendered camera view (Figure 3). When reflected off the hemispherical convex mirror, this creates an undistorted projection of the remote participant on the surface of the cylinder. When the user moves around the display, the distortion model ensures that the remote participant remains at the center of the user's field of view. As this projection changes based on user position, it creates a cylindrical Fish Tank VR view that preserves motion parallax [37]. Note that our approach does have the side effects of causing both resolution and brightness to drop off at lower elevations of the cylinder.

EMPIRICAL EVALUATION

We designed two experiments to evaluate effects of stereoscopy and 360° motion parallax on the preservation of nonverbal cues in our TeleHuman system. Our first experiment focused on how stereoscopy and motion parallax might aid in the preservation of basic body orientational cues. The second experiment focused on how stereoscopy and 360° motion parallax around the display might aid in conveying body postural cues.

EXPERIMENT 1: EFFECTS OF 3D PERSPECTIVE ON GAZE AND POINTING DIRECTION ESTIMATES

The first experiment was designed to gauge the effects of motion parallax and stereoscopy on judgment of eye gaze and hand pointing by a TeleHuman 3D video model.

Task

Participants were asked to indicate where a TeleHuman model was looking or pointing. To ensure equal conditions for all participants, we used a static prerecorded TeleHuman 3D video model in all conditions. We used a simplified, asymmetrical setup in which only one TeleHuman pod was used. At each position, participants were first asked if the TeleHuman was pointing or looking directly at them. If they answered negatively, they were asked to indicate where the TeleHuman was pointing or looking, with reference to a tape measure mounted on a

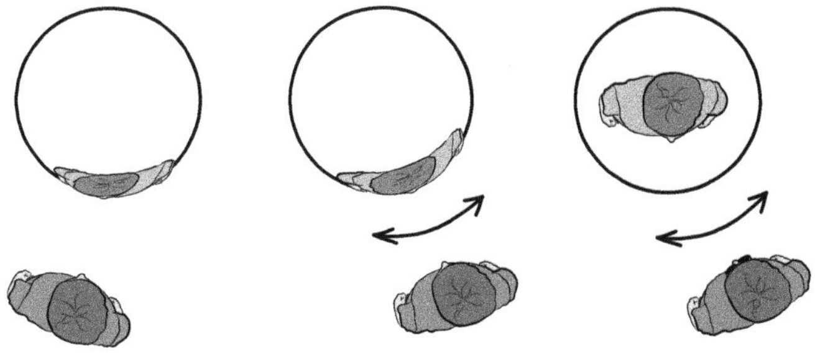

Figure 4. Top-view drawing of perspective conditions: conventional 2D (left), motion parallax (middle), motion parallax + stereoscopy (with glasses, right). In the case of motion parallax, the display would show the remote individual from a slightly side perspective. The black circle represents the cylinder, the person with a green shirt is the perception of the remote participant. The local user is wearing a blue shirt.

wall behind them. Next, participants were asked to move parallel to the wall until they were satisfied that the remote participant was looking or pointing straight at them, at which point we recorded their position.

Experiment Design

We used a within-subjects design in which we evaluated the effect of two fully factorial independent variables: *perspective* and *pointing cue.* To allow for a more realistic scenario, and a richer set of cues, we also varied the participant's location in front of the display: left, center, and right, and the TeleHuman's pointing angle: left, center and right, between conditions.

Perspective

The perspective factor consisted of three levels: *conventional 2D, motion parallax, motion parallax + stereoscopy* (see Figure 4). For the conventional condition, the TeleHuman was shown from the perspective of a front-facing camera, centered on the human. In the *motion parallax* condition, the TeleHuman was displayed with continuous perspective correction based on the location of the participant relative to the display. In the *motion parallax + stereoscopy* condition, participants additionally wore shutter glasses that provided them with a fully stereoscopic image of the TeleHuman, giving the impression that the human was *inside* the cylinder.

Pointing Cue

The pointing cue factor had three levels: *gaze, hand,* and *gaze + hand.* In the *gaze* condition, the TeleHuman indicated the pointing direction by both eye gaze and head orientation directed towards the same location on the wall. In the *hand* condition, the TeleHuman pointed at the target with their arm, hand and index finger. In this condition, the gaze of the TeleHuman was fixated directly to the center, unless the actual target was the center, in which case, gaze was oriented randomly to the left or right of the target. In the *gaze + hand* condition, the TeleHuman's arm, hand and index finger all pointed in the same direction as the eyes and head.

Setup and Procedure

Figure 4 shows a participant standing in front of the TeleHuman. The display was placed 2 m from a wall behind the participant. This wall showed a tape measure with markings at 5 cm intervals from left to right. To ensure presentation of consistent stimuli to all participants, we used a recorded still 3D image to constitute the pointing cues factor. These were rendered according to the perspective factor, as shown in Figure 4. For each condition, participants were asked to stand in between the display and a wall behind them, approximately 190 cm from the display and 10 cm from the wall. Participants experienced the perspective and pointing cue conditions from three locations, distributed between-conditions: directly in front of the cylindrical display, 45 cm to its left, and 45 cm to its right. In addition, in each condition, the TeleHuman pointed in a different angle, selected from left, center, or right. Note that while pointing targets were not visible within our display setup, targets could be projected in the environment in a real videoconferencing scenario.

Trials

Each participant carried out a total of 9 trials, by factorial combination of 3 perspectives (*2D*, *motion parallax*, *motion parallax + stereoscopy*) with 3 pointing cues (*gaze*, *hand*, *gaze+hand*). To allow for a richer set of cues, we also varied the locations of the participant (3 locations) and the directions of pointing between conditions (3 directions). We did not perform a fully factorial presentation as it would have led to 81 trials per participant. The order of presentation of conditions was counterbalanced using a Latin square. All participants were presented with the same set of stimuli, in different orders. The experimental session lasted one hour.

Participants

We recruited 14 participants (mean of 21 years old, 7 male), who were paid $15 for their participation. Three of the participants wore corrective glasses.

Measures

We determined the mean accuracy of pointing location through two measures: 1) *visual assessment*, where participants judged where the TeleHuman was pointing without moving from their initial location; and 2) *visual alignment*, where participants moved to the location at which the TeleHuman appeared to be pointing right at them. Visual assessment allowed us to determine any effects of a more stationary perspective on the accuracy of pointing direction estimates. We expected visual alignment to provide the most accurate method for determining where the TeleHuman pointed or looked, as it allowed users to align themselves such that the TeleHuman appeared to be looking or pointing directly at them. Each measure was calculated as the angular difference between reported viewing direction and the actual TeleHuman pointing direction.

Perspective	2D	Motion Parallax	Motion Parallax + Stereoscopy
Visual Assessment	15.3° (1.6)*	11.5° (1.5)	8.4° (1.2)*
Visual Alignment	21.6° (1.9)†, ‡	5.2° (.89)†	3.9° (.43)‡

Table 1. Angular mean difference between actual and reported target locations and standard error (s.e.) in degrees. There were significant differences, *p = 0.009, †p < 0.001 and ‡p < 0.001.

Questionnaire

To evaluate the degree of telepresence and social presence experienced, participants completed a seven-point Likert scale questionnaire after each *perspective* condition [25]. Telepresence was defined as the feeling of "being there", while social presence was defined as the perceived ability to connect with people through the medium. In the questionnaire, a 1 corresponded to *strongly agree* and 7 to *strongly disagree*.

Results

All results were analyzed using a within-subjects analysis of variance (ANOVA), evaluated at an alpha level of .05.

Pointing Location Estimation

Table 1 shows the accuracy of *pointing location* estimates for our two measures: visual assessment and visual alignment.

Visual Assessment

Results for visual assessment of pointing direction show a significant main effect of *perspective* on accuracy ($F(2,26)=6.35$, $p=0.006$), but no significant effect for *pointing cues* ($F(2,26)=1.92$, $p=0.17$). Bonferroni post-hoc tests showed that mean accuracy of visual assessment was 1.8 times higher in the *motion parallax + stereoscopy* condition than in the *conventional 2D* condition ($p=0.009$). However, there were no significant differences between other conditions.

Visual Alignment

Results for visual alignment show a significant main effect for *perspective* ($F(2,26)=66.51$, $p<0.001$), but not for *pointing cues* ($F(2,26)=0.88$, $p=0.425$). Post-hoc pairwise Bonferroni corrected comparisons of the *perspective* conditions show that mean accuracy was significantly greater in the *motion parallax* condition ($p<0.001$) and in the *motion parallax + stereoscopy* condition ($p<0.001$), compared to the *conventional 2D* condition. There was no significant difference between the *motion parallax* and *motion parallax + stereoscopy* conditions ($p=0.71$).

Questionnaire

Table 2 summarizes the answers to each question for each of the three perspective conditions presented. A Friedman test indicated that there were significant differences between perspective conditions in S1 "*It was as if I was facing the partner in the same room*" ($\chi^2(2)=6.69$,

Statements	2D	Motion Parallax	Motion Parallax + Stereoscopy
*It was as if I was facing the partner in the same room. (S1)**	4.21 (2.0)	3.21 (1.8)	3.14 (2.0)
My partner seemed a real person. (S2)†	4.43 (2.3)	3.86 (2.0)	3.36 (2.2)
I felt immersed in the environment. (T1)‡	4.07 (1.9)	3.14 (2.1)	2.64 (1.8)
I felt surrounded by the environment. (T2)+	4.00 (2.1)	3.21 (1.9)	2.50 (1.4)

Table 2. Means and standard errors (s.e.) for social presence (S) and telepresence (T) scores. Lower scores indicate stronger agreement. There were significant differences between perspective conditions, *p = 0.035, †p = 0.011, ‡p < 0.001 and +p < 0.001.

p=0.035), S2 "*My partner seemed a real person*" (χ^2(2)=9.05, *p=0.011*), T1 "*I felt immersed in the environment*" (χ^2(2)=15.37, *p<0.001*) and T2 "*I felt surrounded by the environment*" (χ^2(2)=16.06, *p<0.001*).

Wilcoxon Signed-Rank post-hoc analysis for social presence showed significant differences in rankings between the *motion parallax* and *conventional 2D* perspectives (Z=-2.22, *p=0.026* for S1, Z=-1.99, *p=0.046* for S2) and between the *motion parallax + stereoscopy* and *conventional 2D* perspectives (Z=-2.70, *p=0.007* for S1, Z=-2.41, *p=0.016* for S2). However, we found no significant differences between the *motion parallax* and the *motion parallax + stereoscopy* conditions.

For the degree of *telepresence*, there was a significant difference between the *motion parallax* and *conventional 2D* perspectives (Z=-2.32, *p=0.020* for T1, Z=-2.37, *p=0.018* for T2), and between the *motion parallax + stereoscopy* condition (Z=-2.65, *p=0.008* for T1, Z=-2.99, *p=0.003* for T2) and the *conventional 2D* condition. However, there were no significant differences between *motion parallax* and *motion parallax + stereoscopy* conditions.

EXPERIMENT 2: EFFECTS OF PERSPECTIVE CUES ON COMMUNICATION OF 3D BODY POSTURAL CUES

In the second experiment, we examined whether support for a 360° life-size stereoscopic view with motion parallax improved the ability to convey the body pose of a remote person on the TeleHuman.

Task

A remote instructor, displayed on the TeleHuman, first positioned herself in one of the predetermined yoga poses (see Figure 5), one per condition. The remote instructor was blind to the conditions. At that point, the main participant ("coach") instructed a co-located partner ("poser") to reproduce the pose as accurately as possible, within a 3 minute time limit. The reason for using a poser, rather than having the coach assume the pose him or herself

Figure 5. Sample Yoga stances used in Experiment 2.

is that this allowed the coach to walk freely around the display, as well as around the poser. Participants were asked to walk around the TeleHuman to examine the pose, and around the poser to examine the result, in all conditions. Note that while participants were allowed to ask the instructor to rotate to show her back conventional 2D conditions, none did, as this would have interfered with her ability to perform the pose.

Experiment Design

We used a within-subjects experiment design to evaluate the effects of the *perspective* factor only, as per the first experiment (see Figure 4).

Setup and Procedure

The coach and the poser were co-located in the same room as the TeleHuman system; but only the coach could see the TeleHuman system. The instructor was in a separate room, and displayed using a live 3D 360° video model on the TeleHuman system. We used an asymmetrical version of the system that allowed for full 360° motion parallax, in which the coach could see and hear the instructor as represented by the TeleHuman, but the instructor could not see the coach. The instructor was not allowed to interfere with the directions of the coach to the poser. Once the coach was satisfied with the poser's posture, the instructor would go to the poser's room to evaluate the poser's stance, while the coach filled out a questionnaire.

We used pairs of participants, unfamiliar with yoga, alternating as coach and poser. To alleviate learning effects, a different yoga pose was used for every condition between pairs of participants, for a total of six yoga poses. All yoga poses, preselected by the yoga instructor, were of the same intermediate level of difficulty as judged by the instructor, and focused on upper body positioning (Figure 5). All poses had limb elements positioned on the back, front and sides of the instructor. The choice of yoga pose was randomly assigned to each coach and condition, and no feedback was provided by the instructor to the poser about the quality of any poses. The three visual perspective conditions were counter-balanced for each coach. The poser was never instructed on the perspective level at hand.

Participants

Eleven of the fourteen participants from the first experiment took part in the second experiment (mean of 22

Perspective	2D	Motion Parallax	Motion Parallax + Stereoscopy
Similarity Score	4.5 (0.71)†	5.5 (0.79)	7.1 (0.55)†

Table 3. Mean pose similarity score and standard error (s.e.) on a scale from 0 to 10 by yoga instructor, per condition. There was a significant difference, †p = 0.04.

years old, 7 male). They were paid a further $15 for their participation.

Measures

The instructor evaluated the similarity between her pose and that of the poser on a scale from 0 to 10 (10 meaning perfectly identical). In this process, she took into account limb angles and orientations, as well as overall posture. After each condition, coaches completed the same questionnaire administered in the first experiment, which evaluated the degree of telepresence and social presence experienced.

Results

We used a within-subjects ANOVA to evaluate differences between conditions, at an alpha level of .05.

Posture Similarity Scores

Table 3 shows the mean pose similarity score and standard error for each perspective condition. Results show that posture similarity scores were significantly different between perspective conditions ($F(2,20)=4.224$, $p=0.03$). Post-hoc tests using Bonferroni correction show that scores in the *motion parallax + stereoscopy* condition were significantly different from scores in the *conventional 2D* condition ($p=0.04$).

Questionnaire

Table 4 summarizes the mean scores for each question, per perspective condition. A Friedman test indicated that there were significant differences between perspective conditions for all social presence ratings (S1, same room $\chi^2(2)=16.06$, $p=0.001$), (S2, real person $\chi^2(2)=12.87$, $p=0.002$), and (S3 acquaintance $\chi^2(2)=11.29$, $p=0.004$). Differences between perspective conditions were also significant for all telepresence ratings (T1, immersion $\chi^2(2)=8.63$, $p=0.013$), (T2 surrounding $\chi^2(2)=12.65$, $p=0.002$), and (T3, involvement $\chi^2(2)=14.4$, $p=0.001$).

Wilcoxon Signed-Rank post-hoc analysis for social presence and telepresence ratings showed significant differences in rankings between the *motion parallax* and *conventional 2D* conditions (Z=-2.83, $p=0.005$ for S1, Z=-2.54, $p=0.011$ for S2, Z=-2.55, $p=0.011$ for S3, Z=-2.85, $p=0.004$ for T1, Z=-2.54, $p=0.011$ for T2, Z=-2.55, $p=0.011$ for T3) and between the *motion parallax + stereoscopy* and *conventional 2D* conditions (Z=-2.69, $p=0.007$ for S1, Z=-2.55, $p=0.011$ for S2, Z=-2.36, $p=0.018$ for S3, Z=-2.54, $p=0.011$ for T1, Z=-2.06, $p=0.040$ for T2, Z=-2.56, $p=0.011$ for T3). However, there were no significant differences between *motion parallax* and the *motion parallax + stereoscopy* conditions.

Statements	2D	Motion Parallax	Motion Parallax + Stereoscopy
It was as if I was facing the partner in the same room. (S1)*	4.82 (1.1)	2.91 (1.1)	3.00 (1.3)
My partner seemed a real person. (S2)†	4.36 (1.5)	2.82 (0.9)	2.82 (1.0)
I could get to know someone that I only met through this system. (S3)‡	4.55 (1.4)	3.18 (1.2)	3.45 (1.0)
I felt immersed in the environment. (T1)$^{+}$	4.45 (1.8)	2.82 (1.6)	3.09 (1.4)
I felt surrounded by the environment. (T2)†	5.18 (1.5)	3.55 (1.6)	3.45 (1.4)
The experience was involving. (T3)*	3.64 (1.4)	2.00 (0.6)	2.27 (0.8)

Table 4. Mean agreement and standard errors (s.e.) with social presence and telepresence statements. Lower scores indicate stronger agreement. There were significant differences between perspective conditions, *p = 0.001, †p = 0.002, ‡p = 0.004, and $^{+}$p = 0.013.

DISCUSSION

We now present a discussion of results from our two experiments.

Effects of 3D Perspective on Pointing Cue Assessment

Results from our first experiment confirmed a strong effect of perspective on the accuracy of assessment of remote pointing cues. Motion parallax + stereoscopy increased the accuracy of angular judgment by a factor of 1.8 over traditional 2D conditions in cases where participants were stationary. As expected, motion parallax alone, in this situation, was limited, and thus, the addition of stereoscopy was important. When participants were allowed to move, motion parallax was shown to provide the dominant effect, with participants achieving four times higher accuracy on average in angular judgment of remote pointing cues as compared to 2D conditions. In this case, stereoscopy appeared to provide little additional benefit. Note that the type of pointing cue: *gaze, hand only,* or *gaze + hand*, had no significant effect on accuracy measures.

Qualitative measures support the above analysis. Social presence rankings were significantly higher in conditions where motion parallax cues were supported, with no significant additional effect for motion parallax augmented by stereoscopy. As for the degree of telepresence or immersion, the combined effect of motion parallax and stereoscopy was critical for obtaining significant differences from 2D conditions.

Stereoscopy therefore appears to be beneficial for judgment of pointing angle when motion parallax cannot be exploited. However, this comes at the cost of preventing reciprocal gaze awareness if shutter glasses are deployed. Motion parallax, even in the absence of a stereoscopic display, may, however, suffice for preservation of social presence or pointing cues.

Effects of 3D Perspective on Body Pose Assessment

Results for our second experiment, in which we evaluated the effects of perspective cues on preservation of postural cues, were in line with those from Experiment 1. The presence of *motion parallax + stereoscopy* cues increased the accuracy of pose scores by a factor of 1.6 over conventional 2D conditions. These results suggest that both motion parallax and stereoscopy needed to be present in order to judge and convey poses accurately. Surprisingly, the presence of motion parallax cues alone only marginally improved scores. This was likely due to the fact that while motion parallax allowed users to see the sides and back of poses, stereoscopy helped improve their judgment of the relative angles of the limbs.

Qualitative measures indicate little additional effect of the presence of stereoscopic cues. Social presence rankings were significantly higher in conditions where *motion parallax* or *motion parallax + stereoscopy* were supported. As for the degree of telepresence, rankings were significantly higher in cases where *motion parallax* or *motion parallax + stereoscopy* were supported. However, there appeared to be little additional effect of the presence of stereoscopic cues over *motion parallax* only. While the presence of stereoscopy did not significantly affect qualitative measures, we can conclude that in this task both motion parallax and stereoscopy were required.

LIMITATIONS, APPLICATIONS & FUTURE DIRECTIONS

Our first study was limited by the fact that the TeleHuman was a static 3D image, and communication was not reciprocal. Although this permitted us to evaluate the effect of stereoscopy on pointing cue assessment, it necessitated an artificial communication condition in which the shutter glasses had no detrimental effect on perception of eye contact. There is an obvious tradeoff between supporting eye contact between interlocutors and presentation of a stereoscopic display requiring the use of shutter glasses. However, other display technologies, such as autostereoscopic and volumetric displays do support glasses-free stereo viewing. We hope to conduct future experiments to evaluate the added benefit that such technologies might offer in terms of eye contact perception with TeleHuman. Note that participants in our study did not ask the instructor to rotate in the 2D condition. There may be cases in which such rotation would provide adequate information to complete a 3D pose task. To avoid introducing confounding factors, we did not specifically compare results with traditional 2D flat display conditions. However, we believe that the results of our 2D conditions would generalize to such conditions.

Future Application Scenarios

The TeleHuman system has potential applications in a number of areas where 2D displays may limit the users' viewpoints. One example is in remote sports instruction. As Experiment 2 demonstrates, examination of the mechanics of limb movement may benefit from the ability to review movement and posture from any angle. For example, this may be helpful in teaching golfers to improve their swing. Applications also exist in telemedicine and remote medical instruction, for which the benefits of arbitrary view control were demonstrated previously in the context of surgical training [27]. TeleHuman could similarly offer doctors the ability to examine remote patients from any angle, but at full scale. This may be particularly beneficial for orthopedic or postural conditions, where the patient cannot reorient herself for a side view. Finally, applications exist in gaming, as the ability to render a 3D gaming character or another online gamer in a 360° view allows for a more immersive gaming experience in first-person shooter scenarios.

Support for Multiparty Videoconferencing

In the near future, we hope to leverage TeleHuman for *multiparty* teleconferencing scenarios. To support such experimentation, we will be replacing the current TCP communication layer with a UDP-based alternative, suitable for low-latency interaction over larger distances. Support of a teleconference with n users requires n^2-n setups and, barring multicast support, a similar number of data streams. This entails significant bandwidth requirements for transmission of 3D video models. However, our design allows for such scaling without modifications to the TeleHuman hardware.

CONCLUSIONS

In this paper, we presented the TeleHuman system, a cylindrical display portal for life-size 3D human telepresence. The system transmits telepresence by conveying 3D video images of remote interlocutors in a way that preserves 360° motion parallax around the display, as well as stereoscopy. We empirically evaluated the effect of perspective on the user's accuracy in judging gaze, pointing direction, and body pose of a remote partner using an asymmetrical version of the system. Results for pointing directional cues suggest that the presence of stereoscopy is important in cases where the user remains relatively stationary. However, when users move their perspective significantly, motion parallax provides a dominant effect in improving the accuracy with which users were able to estimate the angle of pointing cues. As for pose estimation, the presence of both 360° motion parallax cues and stereoscopic cues appeared necessary to significantly increase accuracy. Both motion parallax and stereoscopy appear important in providing users with a sense of social presence and telepresence. We conclude that we recommend inclusion of both motion parallax and stereoscopic cues in video conferencing systems that support the kind of tasks used in our evaluation, with the caveat that tools such as shutter glasses, which obstruct views of the remote participants eyes, are most likely not recommendable for bi-directional communication systems.

ACKNOWLEDGEMENTS

This work was supported by grants by the Natural Sciences and Engineering Council of Canada (NSERC) and the Ontario Research Fund. We also thank Autodesk Research.

REFERENCES

1. Alexander, O., Lambeth, W., and Debevec, P. Creating a Photoreal Digital Actor : The Digital Emily Project Previous Efforts at Photoreal Digital Humans. *Proc. SIGGRAPH*, (2009), 1-15.
2. Argyle, M. and Ingham, R. Gaze, Mutual Gaze and proximity. *Semiotica 6*, 1 (1972), 32-49.
3. Buxton, B. Telepresence: Integrating Shared Task and Person Spaces. *Proc. GI*, (1992), 123-129.
4. Böcker, M. and Mühlbach, L. Communicative Presence in Videocommunications. *Proc. Human Factors and Ergonomics Society*, (1993), 249-253.
5. Böcker, M., Blohm, W., and Mühlbach, L. Anthropometric Data on Horizontal Head Movements in Videocommunications. *Proc. CHI*, (1996), 95-96.
6. Böcker, M., Rundel, D., and Mühlbach, L. On the Reproduction of Motion Parallax in Videocommunications. *Proc. HFES*, (1995), 198-20.
7. Cooperstock, J.R. Multimodal Telepresence Systems: Supporting Demanding Collaborative Human Activities. *IEEE Signal Processing Magazine, Special Issue on Immersive Communications 28*, 1 (2011), 77-86.
8. Garau, M., Slater, M., Vinayagamoorthy, V., Brogni, A., Steed, A., and Sasse, M.A. The Impact of Avatar Realism and Eye Gaze Control on Perceived Quality of Communication in a Shared Immersive Virtual Environment. *Proc. CHI*, 5 (2003), 529.
9. Gross, M., Würmlin, S., Naef, M., et al. Blue-c: A Spatially Immersive Display and 3D Video Portal for Telepresence. *ACM Transactions on Graphics 22*, 3 (2003), 819-827.
10. Harrison, C. and Hudson, S. Pseudo-3D Video Conferencing with a Generic Webcam. *Proc. IEEE International Symposium on Multimedia*, (2008), 236-241.
11. Jones, A., Lang, M., Fyffe, G., et al. Achieving Eye contact in a One-to-many 3D Video Teleconferencing System. *ACM Transactions on Graphics 28*, 3 (2009), 64:3-64:8.
12. Jouppi, N.P., Iyer, S., Thomas, S., and Slayden, A. BiReality: Mutually-immersive Telepresence. *Proc. MM*, (2004), 860-867.
13. Kendon, A. Some Functions of Gaze Direction in Social Interaction. *Acta Psychologica 26*, 44 (1967), 22-63.
14. Lightspeed Design. DepthQ Stereoscopic Projector. http://www.depthq.com.
15. Lincoln, P., Nashel, A., Ilie, A., Towles, H., Welch, G., and Fuchs, H. Multi-view Lenticular Display for Group Teleconferencing. *Proc IMMERSCOM*, (2009).
16. Litefast. http://www.litefast-display.com/
17. Matusik, W. and Pfister, H. 3D TV: A Scalable system for Real-time Acquisition, Transmission, and Autostereoscopic Display of Dynamic Scenes. *ACM Transactions on Graphics*, (2004), 814–824.
18. Microsoft. Kinect. http://www.xbox.com/kinect
19. Mori, M. The Uncanny Valley. *Energy 7*, 4 (1970), 33-35.
20. Morikawa, O. and Maesako, T. HyperMirror: Toward Pleasant-to-use Video Mediated Communication System. *Proc. CSCW*, (1998), 149-158.
21. NVidia. nVidia 3D Vision Kit. http://www.nvidia.com/object/3d-vision-main.html
22. Naef, M., Lamboray, E., Staadt, O., and Gross, M. The Blue-c Distributed Scene Graph. *Proc. IPT/EGVE Workshop*, (2003), 125-133.
23. Negroponte, N. *Being Digital*. Vintage Books, New York, NY, USA, 1995.
24. Nguyen, D. and Canny, J. MultiView: Spatially Faithful Group Video Conferencing. *Proc. CHI*, (2005), 799–808.
25. Nowak, K.L. and Biocca, F. The Effect of the Agency and Anthropomorphism on Users' Sense of Telepresence, Copresence, and Social Presence in Virtual Environments. *Presence Teleoperators and Virtual Environments 12*, 5 (2003), 481-494.
26. Okada, K.-I., Maeda, F., Ichikawaa, Y., and Matsushita, Y. Multiparty Videoconferencing at Virtual Social Distance: MAJIC Design. *Proc. CSCW*, (1994), 385-393.
27. Olmos, A., Lachapelle, K., and Cooperstock, J.R. Multiple Angle Viewer for Remote Medical Training. *Proc. International Workshop on Multimedia Technologies for Distance Leaning*, (2010), 19–24.
28. OpenCV. http://opencv.willowgarage.com/
29. OpenNI. http://openni.org/
30. Rosenthal, A. Two-way Television Communication Unit. (1947).
31. Sellen, A., Buxton, B., and Arnott, J. Using Spatial Cues to Improve Videoconferencing. *Proc. CHI*, (1992), 651-652.
32. Tang, J.C. and Minneman, S. VideoWhiteboard: Video Shadows to Support Remote Collaboration. *Proc. CHI*, (1991), 315-322.
33. Vertegaal, R. and Ding, Y. Explaining Effects of Eye Gaze on Mediated Group Conversations : Amount or Synchronization ? *Proc. CSCW*, (2002), 278-285.
34. Vertegaal, R., Slagter, R., Van der Veer, G., and Nijholt, A. Eye Gaze Patterns in Conversations: There is More to Conversational Agents than Meets the Eyes. *Proc. CHI*, (2001), 301-308.
35. Vertegaal, R., Weevers, I., Sohn, C., and Cheung, C. GAZE-2: Conveying Eye Contact in Group Video Conferencing Using Eye-controlled Camera Direction. *Proc. CHI*, (2003), 521–528.
36. Vertegaal, R. The GAZE Groupware System: Mediating Joint Attention in Multiparty Communication and Collaboration. *Proc. CHI*, (1999), 294-301.
37. Ware, C., Arthur, K., and Booth, K.S. Fish Tank Virtual Reality. *Proc. CHI*, (1993), 37-42.
38. Wright, M. and Freed, A. Open Sound Control: A New Protocol for Communicating with Sound Synthesizers. *Proc. International Computer Music Conference*, (1997), 101-104.
39. Zhang, C., Yin, Z., and Florencio, D. Improving Depth Perception with Motion Parallax and its Application in Teleconferencing. *Proc. IEEE International Workshop on Multimedia Signal Processing*, (2009), 1-6.

MUSTARD: A Multi User See Through AR Display

Abhijit Karnik, Walterio Mayol-Cuevas, Sriram Subramanian
Department of Computer Science,
University of Bristol, UK
karnik, wmayol, sriram @cs.bris.ac.uk

ABSTRACT
We present MUSTARD, a multi-user dynamic random hole see-through display, capable of delivering viewer dependent information for objects behind a glass cabinet. Multiple viewers are allowed to observe both the physical object(s) being augmented and their location dependent annotations at the same time. The system consists of two liquid-crystal (LC) panels within which physical objects can be placed. The back LC panel serves as a dynamic mask while the front panel serves as the data. We first describe the principle of MUSTARD and then examine various functions that can be used to minimize crosstalk between multiple viewer positions. We compare different conflict management strategies using PSNR and the quality mean opinion score of HDR-VDP2. Finally, through a user-study we show that users can clearly identify images and objects even when the images are shown with strong conflicting regions; demonstrating that our system works even in the most extreme of circumstances.

Author Keywords
Display; Random hole display; see-through; multi-view; multi-user; Augmented Reality.

ACM Classification Keywords
H5.2 [Information interfaces and presentation]: User Interfaces - Graphical user interfaces;

General Terms
Design, Human Factors

INTRODUCTION
There are many settings in which users are expected to experience physical objects through a glass cabinet. Such settings exist in museums, shops and vending machines. In a museum it is common for users to view delicate real objects placed behind a protective glass without direct access to handle them. In the case of shopping windows or vending machines where some transaction may be required to gain access to the physical object they also offer a means of finding out more about the item prior to purchase. Retailers have already trialed simple systems aiming at combining real objects and interactive information. For e.g., Polo Ralph Lauren unveiled an interactive shopping window (engadget, Aug. 10, 2006), in which shoppers could view clothing and make purchases via an interactive touch screen.

However these and similar systems are limited to being tailored to work for one user at a time and information is not spatially situated. Thus the experience is closer to navigating a web catalog than properly augmenting the object behind the glass. The most beneficial aspect of an augmented reality see-through glass in a museum or retail setting would be its ability to support multiple users with distinct views. Shop windows are often explicitly designed to encourage multiple users to engage with their content.

The two opposing challenges are: a) delivering unimpeded visibility of the physical object behind a semi-transparent layer and b) simultaneously providing viewer-dependent information for multiple viewers.

Although Parallax barriers and lenticular arrays may be used to provide viewer-dependent information to multiple viewers they have not been shown to support the see-through feature described above. Especially, lenticular arrays distort views of the objects placed behind them limiting their use as a multi-view see-through display.

Figure 1. MUSTARD Prototype (center) with one of the augmented views (left) and the physical objects (right).

To make inroads into these challenges we present MUSTARD: a multi-user see-through augmented reality display as shown in Figure 1. MUSTARD allows users to inspect objects behind a glass panel while delivering view dependent information through the glass. The system consists of two liquid crystals (LC), as shown in Figure 3 (b), which are separated by a short distance within which physical objects can be placed. We use the front LC as the data-panel where the augmenting information is displayed whereas the back LC serves as a dynamic mask-panel that deals with enabling the multiple viewers' capability. We also identify several ways in which view conflicts, resulting from two or more views being displayed at the same location on the data-panel, can be managed. To identify best design strategies we built a prototype system and tested various cross-talk functions. We finally report on a user study that examines the usability and effectiveness of the system from a users' perspective.

The main contributions of this paper are:

1. Design and implementation of a multi-user see-through display which is *not* based on head-worn displays.
2. Using a sandwich of liquid-crystals to create a dynamic random hole display (RHD) which provides better image quality through improved coverage of the entire data-panel.
3. Implementation of a range of crosstalk algorithms for the determination of the color value of conflict pixels.
4. A systematic evaluation of the crosstalk functions using image-quality metrics such as HDR-VDP2 and PSNR followed by a user-study showing that users are able to see and recognize images; demonstrating the system works.

RELATED WORK

The most common see-through display nowadays has to be worn. Such embodiments have been around since the 1960's in the form of optical (and video) see-through head-mounted displays (HMD) to support mixed-reality applications such as medical visualization, maintenance and repair, and robot path planning. An alternative compromise recently available is to force real object's appearance through small displays and cameras as present in hand held tablets or mobiles.

Both the above are suitable from an egocentric model driven augmentation of physical objects. However, there are many situations where users expect to be able to walk-up and engage with the physical environment without having to adorn themselves with extra devices. We are interested in supporting such walk-up and use scenarios.

DigiScope [3] is an early implementation of a system that uses a transparent see-through display to allow users to see information and physical objects through a transparent screen. A typical approach to this form of projection-based systems is to use a translucent projection film. The film reflects or transmits perpendicular to the plane of the glass any incident light coming for a specific acute angle. This allows users to observe both the projected digital data and the physical object behind the glass-pane to which the projection film is attached. A direct extension to this to support stereoscopic see-through displays has been demonstrated with ASTOR [14] that uses HOEs (Holographic Optical Elements) on the glass pane to direct different light sources to each eye.

See-through displays are not limited to displaying information only. Wilson [20], Hirakawa et al. [4] and Hirsch et al. [5] propose different interaction techniques to allow pointing at the screen or the physical object. WaveWindow [16] is another system that supports gesture based interactions with see-through displays. However, the different solutions proposed so far allow a single user to view and use the system at a time. There is need to explore how see-through displays can be extended to allow multiple users to use the same display space at the same time.

Without the see-through capability, multi-view display systems have been demonstrated to work using different principles. One method is to use parallax strip barriers to occlude certain parts of the screen from one eye while allowing another eye to see them. Systems like Perlin et al.'s autostereoscopic display [15], Varrier [19], and Dynallax [17] demonstrate this concept. Lenticular barriers unlike parallax barriers are not limited to two views. Kooima et al.'s work [8], the MERL display [11], RCL3D [12] all of which are based on lenticular barriers allow more than two unique views. Another approach based on directional diffusion films is demonstrated with Lumisight [10]. Sakurai et al.'s work [18] using polarized lighting is another technique used to present multiple views to users.

Extending such displays for see-through is fraught with difficulties; use of lenticular barriers or diffusion films results in distortions in views of any object placed behind.

Of particular interest to us is the Illusion Hole [7] which moves away from traditional linear parallax barriers and uses a single circular viewport per viewer. Naschel et al.'s RHD prototype [13] extends their approach by using a large number of micro viewports and demonstrates its advantages over parallax barrier displays. Gu et al. [21] demonstrates a full multi-user multi-view system using this concept with their Tabletop Autostereoscopic Display (TAD). All these approaches to multi-view displays are based on viewing the data through a hole-mask that is placed at a certain distance from the data to serve as a barrier that mediates the view for different users.

While these approaches also break when we place an object between the data and the hole, it is possible to adapt them to create a multi-user see-through display. We present MUSTARD which overcomes the challenges of simultaneous multiple-user and multi-view augmentation for objects in a cabinet.

MUSTARD: PRINCIPLE AND DESIGN

MUSTARD allows users to inspect objects behind a glass panel while projecting view dependent information through the glass. The system consists of two liquid-crystal elements: a) a dynamic *hole-mask* that restricts the amount of data visible to each user; b) a *data-panel* where data for multiple views is displayed simultaneously. Data shown on the data-panel can be seen from a specific view only when light passes through the hole-mask. This procedure generates location specific views, as only parts of the data panel are visible through the mask for each user.

This principle of MUSTARD is derived from the IllusionHole [7] and TAD [21]. However there are four key distinctions:

- Mask Type: Previous approaches use a static hole-mask. A static hole-mask like in IllusionHole [7] and TAD [21] blocks parts of the data plane from being viewed by a user. In MUSTARD we used a dynamic random hole-mask allowing coverage of the entire screen by constantly changing the hole-mask from frame to frame.
- See-through: MUSTARD allows uninterrupted viewing of a physical object placed between the data-panel and the hole-mask. This object can be separately lit by non-polarized light with the only restriction of not saturating the light used for showing the data on the data-panel.
- Ordering: While previous approaches place the mask between the user and the data, we place the data-panel between the user and the mask allowing us greater flexibility in managing the views generated.
- View Conflict Management: View conflict results from two or more views being displayed at the same display location (pixels) on the data-panel. Through a careful and systematic analysis of various conflict management strategies we identify approaches to manage conflicts.

We now explain the design choices we made for arriving at our implementation of MUSTARD.

Hole-mask with see-through capability

When designing a hole-mask one needs to consider the *mask type* and *the ordering* of the data-panel and hole-mask with respect to the viewers. The mask type influences visibility of the object and the type along with ordering can affect see-through capabilities.

Static v/s Dynamic Mask

As mentioned before, IllusionHole [7] and TAD [21] rely on the ability of the system to block visibility of certain parts of the data panel to present view-specific information. Placing a large panel - the hole-mask, at a certain distance from the data-panel, does the blocking action.

A side-effect of a static hole-mask is that only a small part of the screen is visible to any user at any time resulting in reduced display coverage. An alternative approach to a static hole-mask is a controllable and dynamic hole-mask. Such dynamic hole-mask would allow its pattern to change over time in order to show the entire display screen to any user over a short period of time.

Conflict Management: The other advantage of a dynamic mask is related to the management of conflict pixels. Conflict pixels are regions of the data-panel that are simultaneously visible to more than one viewer. The data shown in these regions is visible to more than one viewer and leads to crosstalk for one or more users.

For a static mask (and with stationary users) the regions of conflict are fixed and the effect of crosstalk is more pronounced. While it is possible to minimize the effect of crosstalk in conflict pixels for a fixed mask [21], increasing the number of users increases the collision pixel count and gradually degrades the image quality. For a dynamic mask, due to change in the position of the hole-mask the position of the conflict pixels changes over time. This change reduces the crosstalk at a single location and spreads it over the entire display screen.

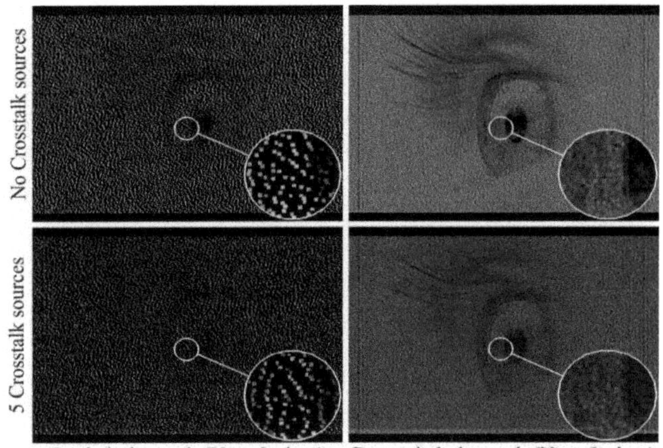

Figure 2. Effect of coverage & crosstalk on image quality with static & dynamic masks. Reddened pixels show crosstalk locations. Bright red indicates more crosstalk sources. Dynamic mask views are averaged over $^1/_2$ s or 30 frames.

Comparison of Mask Types: A comparison between a static mask and dynamic mask is shown in Figure 2. The static mask (Figure 2-Left) demonstrates a lower coverage. The black areas are regions where the view is blocked by the hole-mask. In case of the dynamic mask (Figure 2-Right), the view coverage is larger. The lower half of Figure 2 shows the effect of crosstalk sources. The red dots represent the location of the conflict pixels. A higher number of crosstalk sources leads to a more pronounced red dot. With the static mask, the locations of conflict pixels are constant. In case of the dynamic mask, the conflict pixels are distributed over the whole display. This minimizes the crosstalk effect at any single location.

Implementation Issues: A static hole-mask can be implemented as a printed mask on a transparent media. Dynamic hole-mask requires an active element. LC panels inside commonly available LCD screens can act as the active element. The linear polarizer inside an LCD screen is designed to attenuate light not polarized in the same direction as the polarizer. An LC panel is sandwiched between two crossed polarizers with polarization directions at 90° to each other as shown in Figure 3 below. The LC generates a twisting action on polarized light thereby controlling its passage through the front polarizer. This capability of LC panels can be used to generate a dynamic hole-mask by displaying a black and white dot pattern.

See-through and Panel Ordering

A simple implementation using two LC panels can work as a multi-user display. The hole-mask LC panel consists of an unmodified LCD screen with its backlight removed. This is placed in front of another LCD screen which serves as the data-panel. If the polarization directions of the front polarizer of the data-panel LC to the rear polarizer of the hole-mask LC panel are aligned, then the system works as a multi-user display. When a white spot is displayed on the hole-mask LC, that region of the LC allows all the light from the data-panel to pass through to a viewer.

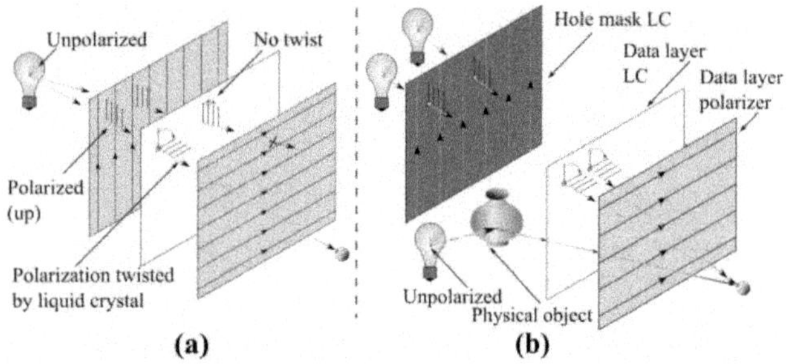

Figure 3. Operating principle for MUSTARD (a) Normal LC operation (b) Two LC setup with polarized light for data and unpolarized light for see-through aspect of the display.

The hole-mask LC will polarize all incident light passing through its rear polarizer. Hence such a naïve implementation cannot serve as a see-through display. To be see-through, the device needs to distinguish between light related to the displayed information and reflected light from the physical object. The hole-mask either allows the light related to the displayed information to pass through (a hole) or blocks it (mask). At the same time, the hole-mask allows all light from the physical object to pass through.

It is possible to achieve see-through capability by modifying an LCD screen. By design, if the rear polarizer is absent the remaining LC and front polarizer will allow unpolarized light to pass through it (except for a tiny fraction that is polarized 90°). It will also actively block any incident light that is polarized 90° to the front polarizer.

Anything displayed on this modified panel is not visible unless illuminated by correctly polarized light. Now if we were to display the information on such a panel and then illuminate it from behind with a polarized light source, a viewer should be able to see the information. At the same time, an object placed behind such a modified panel and illuminated by an unpolarized light source will be visible through the panel all the time.

This arrangement (see Figure 3(b)) is used to achieve see-through capability. The key difference of the order of the hole-mask and the data-panel now becomes apparent. The data-panel is in front of the hole-mask and the physical object is placed in between them. This arrangement converts the hole-mask into a grid of randomly distributed point-light sources. These holes emit polarized light necessary to view information on the data-panel. Also, each one of these holes illuminates any point on the data layer lying directly in line of sight to a viewer. As shown in Figure 3 above, two holes on the mask allow two points on the data layer to become visible to the viewer.

Conflict Management: With this arrangement, a single hole lies in direct line of sight of all users. But based on the user positions, the corresponding points on the data-panel are different. However, with a grid of holes, a single point on the display-panel may be illuminated by different holes for different users. So, the existence of conflict pixels is not eliminated and still needs to be managed. The process of generation of the hole-mask pattern and the final data-layer view are described next along with methods for conflict resolution for conflict pixels.

Mask and View Rendering

MUSTARD is designed to deliver different views to different users by using the same data-panel for display purpose. The rendering process is shown in Figure 4 below. The hole-mask illuminates only a part of the data-panel as seen from any one user's perspective. Thus only that part of the data-panel is visible to the user. This is referred to as the per-user data view. The data-panel displays a composite image which is generated from the combination of all the per-user data views. Per-user data views are generated using the user's eye-positions and the hole-mask pattern.

Mask Rendering: The hole-mask is an image with a collection of black-and-white dots. The white dots act as holes while the black dots act as masks. The locations of the white dots need to change over time so that over *10-frames* the white dots cover the entire display area. The ideal algorithm to compute this pattern is the Fast Poisson Disc Noise algorithm proposed by Bridson [1]. It has been used for static hole-masks by previous implementations [13,21]. This algorithm outputs a pattern of points at random locations but with uniform density. Since in our case the hole-mask is dynamic, a new pattern needs to be computed for every frame. Details of how this is done are given in the Algorithm Implementation section.

Generating Composite View Image: To generate data-panel's composite image the perspective-corrected view for each viewer has to be constructed using the eye-positions of each viewer. This step assumes that the entire view will be seen by the viewer. Then the per-viewer data view is processed against the hole-mask pattern to determine the visible parts of the view. This involves finding the point on the mask which is collinear to an eye position and a point on the data layer. If the point on the hole-mask pattern is a hole then the color data from per-viewer data view is retained for further processing. This process is carried out for all active users.

Conflict Management: The next step is to determine if there is a conflict at any point on the composite view by checking if more than one per-viewer data view has color data at the same position. In the absence of conflict, a single per-viewer data view contributes its value to the composite view. In case no data view contributes color, the output is black. Due to lack of a hole directly in line of sight from that point to any active viewer, the point is not of any interest for display purposes.

The final step is to resolve the conflicted pixels by using one of the functions (described next) to determine the color of the conflict pixel. Once the conflict is resolved, the output color is inserted at the conflict pixel location in the data layer. Finally both the hole-mask pattern and the data-panel views are displayed on the respective screens.

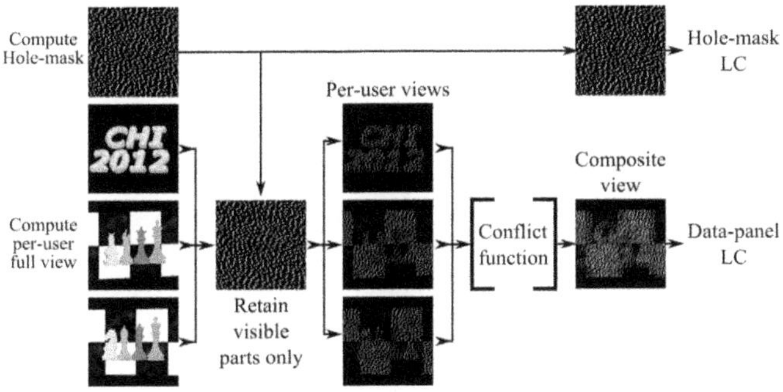

Figure 4. Steps involved in mask and view rendering.

Conflict Resolution Functions

MUSTARD's dynamic mask ensures that the conflict pixel locations are not constant from frame to frame. However resolving the color output for the conflict pixels is a critical part of the data display process. While TAD uses an error diffusion technique that spreads the error over neighboring pixels, we chose to apply the conflict resolution on the conflict pixel itself. The error for any single view is a function of the distance between the output color value and view's color value. The objective of the conflict resolution function is to choose the value that minimizes the sum of the absolute errors for all the contributing views.

At the pixel location where there is a conflict we convert the color values of each contributing view using a conflict resolution function (described below) and selecting the median of those contributing values.

The geometric median for a set of n points in the Euclidean space represents the point whose sum of distances from the n points is the least. This point also described as the 1-median provides the central tendency for the n points representing the user view colors. Computing the geometric median in two or more dimensions is a costly iterative process [2]. We use a simpler approach by processing color values over separate 1-dimensional channels. Our median function generates the median value from an nx1 kernel where each of the n values is contributed by a user view.

The input to the median function is perhaps the principal conflict resolution function that can be varied and there are many possible ways in which this function can be implemented. Following we describe six such options.

Full Range Method (FR): This is the simplest approach for determining the color of the conflict pixel. The color values contributing to the conflict pixel are directly passed to the median function for processing as shown in Figure 5 below.

Non-intersecting 1/n ranges method (NI1NR): This method relies on splitting the overall dynamic range output into equal ranges of size $1/n$ for each user view.

Intersecting half ranges method (IHR): For this method the output range is also divided into n ranges however these ranges overlap with an offset of $1/(2(n-1))$ units as illustrated in Figure 5 (C). Note that for a 2-user view setting, the output of NI1NR and IHR methods is same.

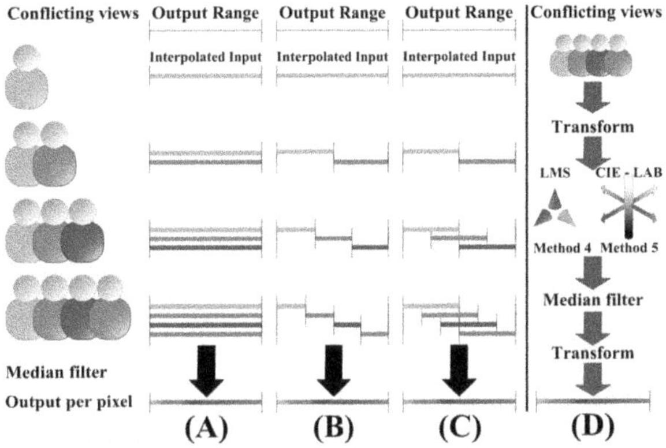

Figure 5. (A-D) Five of the six conflict resolution functions: (A) Full Range method, (B) Non-intersecting 1/n ranges method, (C) Intersecting half-ranges method, (D) LMS and CIE-LAB conversions. Each method is the input to the median filter that outputs the final value.

CIE-LAB and LMS Methods: The previous three methods operate on the RGB values and the median values are computed per channel. These methods are device-oriented. CIE-LAB and LMS methods operate in color spaces that are more suited for perceptual intent. The operation is similar to the FR method. The only difference is that the operations happen in CIE-LAB and LMS color spaces respectively. To achieve the conversions, the color values are converted to CIE-XYZ values and then to CIE-LAB and LMS. After applying the median function to the results, the output is obtained by re-conversion back to RGB values.

Alpha-Kern Method (AK): The Alpha-Kern, shown in Figure 6 below uses a scaled down version of the user view while retaining its original size. The downscaling process without resizing generates regions of no data which are filled with pixels from the original image at higher transparency. This generates an additional level for conflict source prioritization. The pixels belonging to the downscaled part of the view are given higher priority than the original pixels with higher transparency.

Thus if there are one or more user views which contribute color from their downscaled regions, the other sources with higher transparency are rejected from further processing. If there are no user views contributing color from their downscaled regions, all the higher transparency sources are considered for processing (while ignoring their transparency). The downscaling is achieved by a weighted average 3x3 kernel that colors the central pixel with the result of the weighted average.

MUSTARD IMPLEMENTATION

To evaluate the different conflict resolution functions we built a real prototype which is described next.

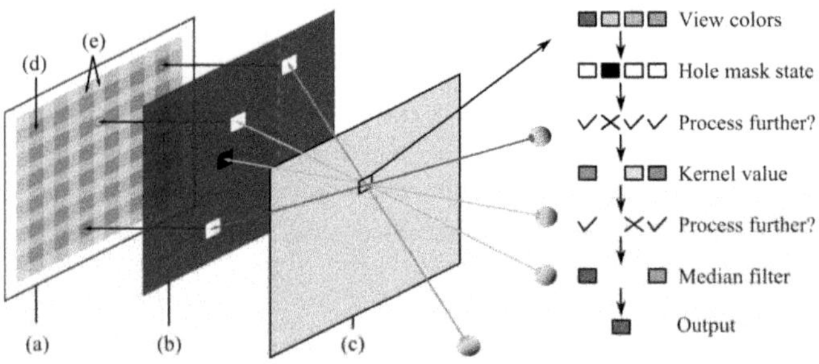

Figure 6. Alpha-Kern method. (a) Alpha mask, (b) Hole-mask pattern, (c) Data-panel. Output is the median of viewpoints indicated by blue and orange eye positions. Cyan eye view is rejected due to absence of hole. Green is rejected due to partial alpha contribution (e) in presence of (d) full alpha (blue and orange).

Physical Implementation

Our implementation consists of two 17" (1280x1024px) Matsushita LC panels extracted from existing PC monitors to simplify interfacing with a computer. We removed the rear polarizer from the front LC. The backlight setup consists of ten (30W, 6400K, 1535 lumens) compact fluorescent lamps behind a lenticular lens array (A4, 40 lpi). This provides a uniform diffused backlight.

The rear hole-mask LC and the front data-panel LC are 70 mm apart so as to accommodate a physical object within a 420 cm^3 space while maintaining an object-to-display area ratio of 0.062:1. Any variation in this distance requires a one-time calibration necessary to convert the physical distance into coordinates used by the algorithm described next. We did not track the user's eyes as it can be achieved with existing technology and was not necessary to demonstrate the prowess our system.

Algorithm Implementation:

Coordinate Space Conversion

An Intel Core 2 Duo CPU and NVIDIA GeForce 9500 GT GPU were used. We selected the display area dimensions such that the texture coordinates of textures could be mapped 1:1 to the pixels of the displays. Using a one-time calibration the physical distance between the hole-mask LC and the data-panel LC is converted to coordinates in the texture-space coordinate system. Similarly, the user eye coordinates are mapped to texture-space coordinates. For the repeatability of the experiment across different conflict functions, the eye coordinates were held fixed. This was done by marking the physical locations of the viewer and not changing them for the duration of the experiment.

Cg Fragment Shaders

The steps for conflict pixel resolution are carried out at the GPU level per frame. The data-panel information is processed as a texture and all operations are carried out on every texture coordinate. The perspective corrected views for each eye are drawn into FBO textures. The textures are processed as per the hole-mask pattern (another texture). The resulting output is passed through the conflict resolution function and the output is the final texture which is drawn to the data-panel LC. A single Cg-based fragment shader program performs all these actions.

Poisson Disc Noise for Hole-mask

In our implementation the hole-mask pattern consists of a black-and-white checkered pattern with a block size of 3x3 pixels. The location of the blocks in the pattern is computed first using the Poisson Disc Noise function. GPU based computation of the Poisson Disc Noise function is not optimal. Also, the dynamic pattern requirement doesn't preclude the reuse of a previous pattern as long as it is not reused in the very next frame. Thus, by pre-computing a set of m patterns the CPU can provide a list of patterns for the GPU to use. This frees the CPU to refresh the m patterns one at a time. Our implementation of Bridson's algorithm [1] (r=5 and k=32) gives us a hole coverage between 13 to 14% of the hole-mask per frame. The calculation time per hole-mask pattern is 10*ms*. We start with a pre-computed set of 4 masks and refresh one every 12 frames. Thus, the users see 8 different hole-masks every second at 60 fps.

Conflict Function Implementation

Processing conflict functions in the CIE-LAB and LMS color spaces requires conversion. To achieve this, the existing RGB values are converted to CIE-XYZ and then to the respective color spaces. All conversions use the formulae specified for Observer = 2° and Illuminant = D65.

Since the user views are dynamic and only a small part of each view is seen at a time, it is not practical to perform down-sampling on the entire view in the Alpha-Kern method. Instead, a fixed pre-computed alpha mask is used. The alpha mask consists of 3x3 pixels with weighted values of 16/256 for corners, 32/256 for edges and 64/256 for center. Once the position on the hole-mask pattern is identified to be a hole, the corresponding alpha value (at the same position) is retrieved from the alpha mask. If the value is greater than 32/256, the position is the central position in the 3x3 grid. The weighted average of the user view is calculated at the corresponding point on the data layer and its value is returned for further processing. If the position is not central, the returned color value is the original color value multiplied by the alpha value of the point. Prioritization based on the alpha values is performed and the final output is the median value of the prioritized inputs.

STUDY 1: EVALUATION OF CONFLICT FUNCTIONS

To examine the quality of output from a conflict function we compare the output in presence of crosstalk (test-source) with the expected output in the absence of crosstalk (reference-source). The reference-sources were derived from three different usage scenarios.

High-conflict Scenario: This scenario assumes that one user is presented with extreme conflict. This happens when all the other users are viewing nearly similar information but very different to the view of the first user. The user views are shown in Figure 7. The first user view (Figure 7-left) has large areas of black space and the text has very large regions of white. This is contrasted against the chess piece set which is the scene for all the crosstalk source views (see Figure 7-center). Since all crosstalk sources have near similar contents, the crosstalk effect should be additively adverse to the first user view. This is apparent in the regions which are not black in Figure 7-right.

Figure 7. High-conflict scenario for conflict function evaluation. *Left*: First user view showing 'CHI 2012', also the view of interest. *Center*: One of the crosstalk sources for generating conflict pixels. *Right*: XOR of the two images showing conflict regions and color. Black indicates no conflict.

Perspective Visualization Scenario: In this scenario all users see a different view albeit from the same 3D scene. Such a scenario would exist when all users are shown a virtual 3D object that looks slightly different depending on the user's location as seen in Figure 8-left.

Figure 8. Other scenarios for evaluation of conflict functions. *Left:* 6 closely related views of the same 3D scene from different positions. *Right:* 6 views showing an example of possible personalized content.

Personalized Views Scenario: In this scenario all the users are viewing different content. For example, in a museum cabinet displaying a crown, and depending on their location, all the viewers can be shown a king's portrait each, from a chronologically ordered series of regents who have worn the crown. Figure 8-right shows this scenario.

Evaluation Technique

Using a camera to capture the view introduces an external factor to the visualization of the results. Hence we compared the conflict functions using screen-grabs of the outputs. Our first metric is the Peak Signal to Noise Ratio (PSNR) which is relevant due to the temporal nature of the views [6]. The second metric is Mantuik's HDR-VDP-2 [9] which is a visual differences predictor that measures how much difference will be visible between our test source and reference source images. Specifically the quality mean opinion score (Q_{MOS}) allows us to compare the outputs by using the score for ranking.

One data-panel frame contains only 13-14% of a single per-user view. Also the dynamic mask is integral to uniform distribution of crosstalk which itself is a small part of the per-user view. Hence an image averaged over 10 frames is used for evaluation. Both metrics would output better scores for a single frame. The 10-frame average allows us to avoid this positive bias.

Figure 9. Sample of test source images. Top row: Views with two crosstalk sources. Bottom row: Views with four crosstalk sources. Methods shown (left to right): FR, CIE-LAB, AK.

Procedure

We used the algorithm implemented on our MUSTARD prototype for generating the data to be evaluated. To standardize the conditions, the user eye positions were considered fixed for the duration of the evaluation. The algorithm generated images meant for the first user view with (test source) and without crosstalk (reference source).

Screen grabs were then averaged over 10 frames for both sources. A sample set of images for the high-conflict scenario is show in Figure 9. For PSNR we used the implementation available on Max-Plank Institute's website (http://driiqm.mpi-inf.mpg.de/generator.php). The Q_{MOS} metric was generated using the original reference implementation.

Results

PSNR Analysis

With PSNR a higher value is an indicator of better quality. The left column of Figure 10 shows the PSNR values for each of the test scenarios.

The average PSNR value is the lowest for the high-conflict scenario (125.59 dB), followed by perspective visualization scenario (133.23 dB) and personalized views scenario (138.16 dB). The high-conflict scenario was designed to demonstrate the ability of the system to generate viewable images even in the most adverse conditions. From Figure 9 we can see that the images are recognizable even when there are up to 4 strong crosstalk sources conflicting with the current view. As expected the PSNR value for each image drops as the number of crosstalk sources increases.

Our results also show that AK method has the highest PSNR values of all conflict management functions for each of the three scenarios. The AK method results in PSNR values of 128.36 dB, 140.38 dB and 143.88 dB for the three scenarios which is higher than the PSNR values of all other techniques. It is also visible in Figure 9 that the images on the right column (corresponding to AK method) have better quality than the other images. The PSNR value for each of the scenario also suggests that CIE-LABS and CIE-LMS are almost identical in performance. It is also worth nothing that NI1NR method performs the worst in terms of PSNR.

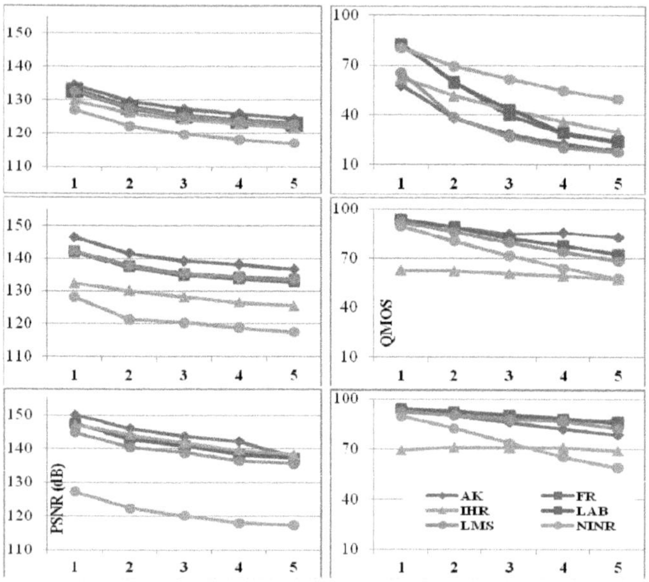

Figure 10. PSNR and Q_{MOS} results. Top: High-conflict scenario, middle: Perspective visualization scenario, bottom: Personalized views scenario. X-axis: Crosstalk source count.

Q_{MOS}

The Quality mean opinion score (Q_{MOS}) is a score between 0 and 100 with 0 implying worst quality and 100 implying best quality. Like the PSNR results, average Q_{MOS} scores are much lower for the high-conflict scenario when compared with the other two scenarios.

From Figure 10 we can see that for Q_{MOS} there is no clear winner in terms of Conflict functions. In the high-conflict scenario NI1NR turns out to be better than the rest with AK and LMS seeming to be the worst techniques. However when looking at the two scenarios that are closer to what one might encounter in a real-world application it seems like NI1NR starts to degrade quickly as the number of conflict sources increases. Whereas the AK technique performs well even when there are 4 or 5 cross-talk sources.

Discussion

The results of this study show that there are no clear winners in terms of best suited conflict function. However our AK method frequently performs better than the other methods and seems more resilient to quality degradation due to more cross talk sources.

We also find that NI1NR and IHR generally performed worse than most other techniques. Although NI1NR performed better than the other techniques when looking at Q_{MOS} scores for the high-conflict scenario we feel that this is more an artifact than a reflection of the quality of the technique (in the remaining 5 cases it was at the bottom). Based on the results of this study and on Figure 9 it seems that visual quality in these cases might be better aligned with PSNR values than with Q_{MOS}.

USER STUDY

In order to further understand whether users are able to look at both the physical object and the image on the data-panel we carried out a user study where participants had to look at both the object and the data-panel to complete the trial.

We carried out a 3x3x3 factor within-subjects experimental design with the number of crosstalk sources, the conflict functions and the viewport as the factors. We used FR, AK and CIE-LAB as the conflict functions with 2, 4 and 5 crosstalk sources.

The conflict functions were chosen based on the results of our previous study. NI1NR and IHR were discarded based on their performance while CIE-LMS was not included as it was similar in performance to CIE-LAB. Each participant had to perform the task from three distinct viewports (Left, Center and Right). The position of the viewports was fixed.

Task

The task was a symbol matching task. For each trial, the participant had to look at the see-through display through a viewport. One of six pre-determined symbols appeared at the top of the data-panel. The same six symbols appeared as annotations, one above each of six physical objects behind the data-panel. The physical objects were 25mm square cardboard cutouts (see Figure 11-right) with the numbers 1 to 6 printed on them. The participant was asked to identify the physical object above which the matching symbol appeared and then call out the number printed on the matched object. The experimenter entered the number in the system through a keyboard. The system then moved to the next trial. Depending on the experimental condition there were 2 or more crosstalk sources.

After each trial, the mapping of the symbols to the physical objects was changed for both the participant's view as well as the crosstalk source views. No two views had the same symbol order during a trial.

Participants and Setup

10 volunteers (4 female) aged 20-40 yrs participated in this study. None of them had any experience with a multi-view system or a see-through display. The participants were given time to acclimatize themselves to MUSTARD. The trials commenced after suitable explanation of the device and task. Each participant completed 5 repetitions for each combination of factors resulting in a total of 135 trials per participant (3x3x3x5 = 135). Participants were free to rest at any point when not performing a task.

The system was pre-calibrated to work with each of the viewports so there was no need for the system to include an eye-tracker (which would also have introduced an additional level of complexity in the data-analysis). The viewports were within 800-1000 mm of the system. None of these offered any advantage by way of placement.

Procedure

The order of presentation of the crosstalk sources was first balanced using Latin Squares then the order of presentation of the conflict functions was balanced to remove any order effects. The participants completed all trials at any one specific viewport before moving to the next viewport.

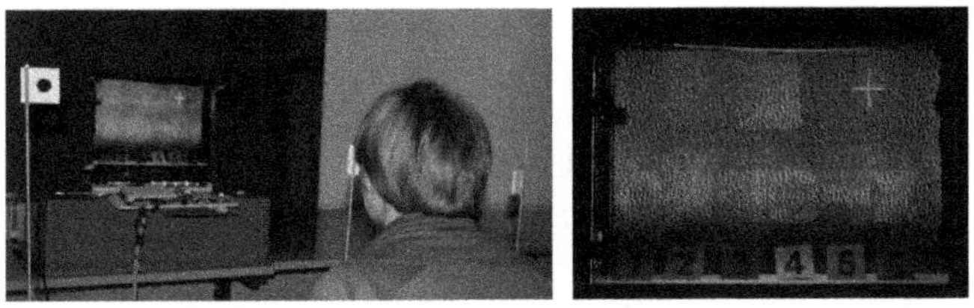

Figure 11. Left: Experimental setup. White squares with holes are the viewports. Right: View as seen by the user on the left. View has 2 crosstalk sources and CIE-LAB is the conflict resolution function in use. The view-dependent virtual annotations are shown above the real numbered objects.

Measures

The experimental program recorded whether the user identified the right object or not. If the user called out the wrong number then the system registered an error and the experiment progressed to the next trial. We also asked the users to tell us how confident they were of their answers on a scale of 0 to 2. '0' meant it's a pure guess and '2' meant they are extremely confident of their answer.

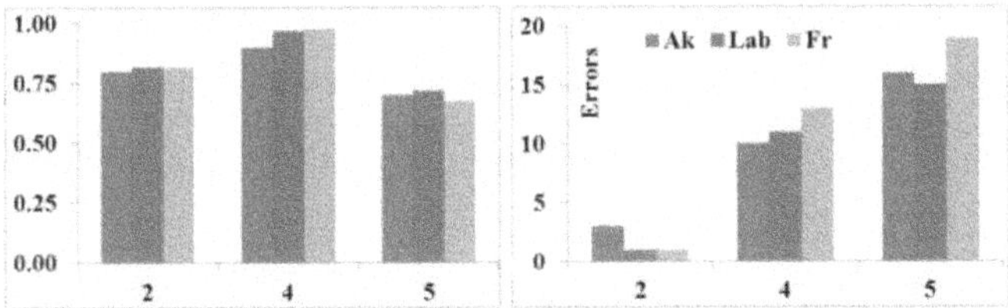

Figure 12. Left: Total Number of error across for each conflict function and crosstalk source. Right: Average weighted accuracy for each conflict function and crosstalk source.

Results

From the 10 participants we recorded a total of 1350 trials, of which only 89 trials resulted in an error giving an overall accuracy of 93%. As seen in Figure 12(Left) with the increase in the number of crosstalk sources the error rates increased significantly ($F_{2,18} = 57.4$, $p<0.05$ – Univariate ANOVA with users as random factors). However we found no statistical difference in error rates between the different conflict resolution techniques. We created a weighted accuracy as (Accuracy x Confidence score)/2. This score reduces the weighting for trials where the users were not confident. The score was 0 if the answer was wrong or if the user had no confidence in their answer. Figure 12 (right) shows the average score of the weighted accuracy.

The results of this user study demonstrate that the users are able to successfully identify objects even in the high-conflict scenario with up to 5 crosstalk sources. Users were able to successfully complete the task with the conflict functions tested further reiterating our claim that these functions are effective in reducing effect of crosstalk.

DISCUSSION

Hole-Mask

With MUSTARD, we demonstrated the concept of using two LCs to create a dynamic RHD which allows use of polarized and unpolarized light for achieving a multi-view see-through display. We also demonstrate that a dynamic mask based system provides better coverage over static mask. Below we discuss some of our observations.

Hole-mask Pattern

The size of the hole is governed by two extreme cases. The smallest size of the hole depends on the smallest pixel pitch of the hole-mask LC. The largest possible size of the hole is the one that doesn't allow any one data-panel pixel to be visible to two eyes at the same time. This size is given by the formula: $h_w = IPD * d_{LC} / d_{EYE}$. Here h_w is the hole width, *IPD* is the interpupillary distance (essentially the closest any two user eyes are assumed to be), d_{LC} is the gap between the data panel LC and the hole-mask LC and d_{EYE} is the distance of the user from the data panel LC.

Conflict Functions

We presented a set of conflict functions that can be used for MUSTARD. Our analysis of the methods based on image quality metrics showed that AK method performs better than others in certain conditions. However we found no difference between AK, CIE-LAB and FR in our user-study. These findings suggest that all these functions might be suitable as conflict function.

MUSTARD could be setup to select a conflict functions on the fly. The content to be delivered can determine the choice of function. Since our methods operate on a pixel level, individual pixels or regions can use entirely different functions. Thus the system could deliver a uniform user experience across the user group. Alternately, at the cost of quality of view for the group, a single user with higher priority could have access to the best view possible.

LC Selection

Hole-mask LC: The rear LC panel only serves as a white light source. A specialized LC panel with larger monochromatic pixels can be used so as to reduce the ringing effect caused by the fixed color filter coating on the LC. At the same time, it is necessary to resize the rear LC such that optimal coverage of all view positions is achieved.

Limitations: The LC gap and hole-size are limiting factors for MUSTARD as they affect the view distance. While the current implementation focuses on the effectiveness of conflict functions, we feel that the individual investigation of these factors could be undertaken as future work.

Physical Objects and User Experience

Objects Sandwiched Between Two LC Panels

With our prototype, the physical object is placed between the two LC panels. This arrangement is not a conceptual limitation. A wedge waveguide placed immediately behind the data layer could be an alternate implementation. The angle of input of the light fed to the bottom of the wedge determines the position of exit. The input to the wedge would be MUSTARD's hole-mask pattern (compensated for polarization shift due to reflection) and the conflict resolution methods described previously will still be valid for such an implementation.

User Experience:

The physical object is visible to any user and is not occluded by the displayed content. While there may be arguments in favor of overlaid object annotations, MUSTARD's multi-view approach prefers annotations around the object. This can be particularly important in the intended usage scenarios wherein a user in a group is interested in the physical object only. In this case MUSTARD is delivers an unobstructed view to that particular user while presenting data to the other users.

CONCLUSION

We have demonstrated the concept of MUSTARD for achieving multi-user see-through effects suitable for walk-up and use scenarios. Through a two LC based prototype system we show the feasibility of a random hole display that includes a dynamic mask to improve image quality. We examine various functions to mange conflicts in pixel color due to multiple user views. We show that the alpha kernel conflict management functions provides good image quality scores as well as performing well in a user study.

ACKNOWLEDGEMENTS

We thank Dr. Tania Pouli for the help with the HDR-VDP and Benjamin Long for advice on Cg. This work is partially supported by Microsoft Research through the PhD Scholarship Programme & by a UoB Pump Priming grant.

REFERENCES

1. Bridson, R. Fast Poisson disk sampling in arbitrary dimensions. In SIGGRAPH 2007 Sketches.
2. Chandrasekaran, R. and Tamir, A. Open questions concerning Weiszfeld's algorithm for the Fermat-Weber location problem. Mathematical Programming (1989).
3. Ferscha, A. and Keller, M. DigiScope: An Invisible Worlds Window. In Ubicomp 2003 (2003), 261-264.
4. Hirakawa, M., Kojima, Y. and Yoshitaka, A. Transparent interface: a seamless media space integrating the real and virtual worlds. In Proc. Human Centric Computing Languages and Environments (2003). 120-122.
5. Hirsch, M., Lanman, D., Holtzman, H. and Raskar, R. BiDi screen: a thin, depth-sensing LCD for 3D interaction using light fields. In SIGGRAPH Asia 2009.
6. Huynh-Thu, Q. and Ghanbari, M. Scope of validity of PSNR in image/video quality assessment. Electronics Letters 44 (2008), 800-801.
7. Kitamura, Y., Konishi, T., Yamamoto, S. and Kishino, F. Interactive stereoscopic display for three or more users. In SIGGRAPH 2001, ACM (2001), 231-240.
8. Kooima, R., Prudhomme, A., Schulze, J., Sandin, D. and DeFanti, T. A multi-viewer tiled autostereoscopic virtual reality display. In Proc. VRST 2010, (2010).
9. Mantiuk, R., Kim, K. J., Rempel, A. G. and Heidrich, W. HDR-VDP-2: a calibrated visual metric for visibility and quality predictions in all luminance conditions. In SIGGRAPH 2011, ACM (2011), 1-14.
10. Matsushita, M., Iida, M., Ohguro, T., Shirai, Y., Kakehi, Y. and Naemura, T. Lumisight table: a face-to-face collaboration support system that optimizes direction of projected information to each stakeholder. In CSCW '04.
11. Matusik, W. and Pfister, H. 3D TV: a scalable system for real-time acquisition, transmission, and autostereoscopic display of dynamic scenes. In SIGGRAPH 2004, (2004).
12. Morishima, H., Nose, H., Taniguchi, N., Inoguchi, K. and Matsumura, S. Rear-cross-lenticular 3D display without eyeglasses. In Stereoscopic Displays and Virtual Reality Systems V, (1998).
13. Nashel, A. and Fuchs, H. Random Hole Display: A non-uniform barrier autostereoscopic display. In 3DTV Conference: The True Vision - Capture, Transmission and Display of 3D Video, (2009), 1-4.
14. Olwal, A., Lindfors, C., Gustafsson, J., Kjellberg, T. and Mattsson, L. ASTOR: An Autostereoscopic Optical See-through Augmented Reality System. In ISMAR '05.
15. Perlin, K., Paxia, S. and Kollin, J. S. An autostereoscopic display. In SIGGRAPH '00, (2000).
16. Perry, M., Beckett, S., O'Hara, K. and Subramanian, S. WaveWindow: public, performative gestural interaction. In ITS '10, ACM (2010), 109-112.
17. Peterka, T., Kooima, R. L., Sandin, D. J., Johnson, A., Leigh, J. and DeFanti, T. A. Advances in the Dynallax Solid-State Dynamic Parallax Barrier Autostereoscopic Visualization Display System. IEEE Transactions on Visualization and Computer Graphics 14, (2008).
18. Sakurai, S., Kitamura, Y., Subramanian, S. and Kishino, F. A visibility control system for collaborative digital table. Personal Ubiquitous Comput. 13, (2009).
19. Sandin, D. J., Margolis, T., Ge, J., Girado, J., Peterka, T. and DeFanti, T. A. The Varrier autostereoscopic virtual reality display. ACM Trans. Graph. 24, (2005), 894-903.
20. Wilson, A. D. TouchLight: an imaging touch screen and display for gesture-based interaction. In ICMI, (2004).
21. Ye, G., State, A. and Fuchs, H. A practical multi-viewer tabletop autostereoscopic display. In ISMAR '10 (2010).

SphereAvatar: A Situated Display to Represent a Remote Collaborator

Oyewole Oyekoya, William Steptoe, Anthony Steed
Virtual Environments and Computer Graphics
Department of Computer Science, University College London, UK
w.oyekoya, w.steptoe, a.steed@cs.ucl.ac.uk

ABSTRACT
An emerging form of telecollaboration utilizes situated or mobile displays at a physical destination to virtually represent remote visitors. An example is a personal telepresence robot, which acts as a physical proxy for a remote visitor, and uses cameras and microphones to capture its surroundings, which are transmitted back to the visitor. We propose the use of spherical displays to represent telepresent visitors at a destination. We suggest that the use of such 360° displays in a telepresence system has two key advantages: it is possible to understand the identity of the visitor from any viewpoint; and with suitable graphical representation, it is possible to tell where the visitor is looking from any viewpoint. In this paper, we investigate how to optimally represent a visitor as an avatar on a spherical display by evaluating how varying representations are able to accurately convey head gaze.

Author Keywords
Spherical displays; remote collaboration; telepresence; telerobotics; avatars; mixed reality

ACM Classification Keywords
H.4.3 Communications Applications: Computer conferencing, teleconferencing, and videoconferencing; H.5.1 Information Interfaces and Presentation: Multimedia Information Systems—*Artificial, augmented, and virtual realities*

General Terms
Design, Experimentation, Human Factors.

INTRODUCTION
Technologically asymmetric telecollaboration systems are an emerging form of telecommunication. In these systems, one or more remote participants use computer supported means to collaborate with others who are physically located at a specific destination space. These systems are based on the paradigm that the actions and behaviors of remote participants (*visitors*) are acquired at their physical location, and transmitted and represented at the *destination* site. Acquisition technology at the visitor sites include cameras, motion capture systems, and microphones, which capture digital representations of the visitor ready for real-time transmission to the destination site. Display technology at the destination site aims to represent visitors with physical presence, and may include humanoid robots or situated displays.

Technologically asymmetric telecollaboration can be contrasted with conventional video conferencing or collaborative virtual worlds, in which each participant's experience is mediated by approximately identical technology, and thus presents similar social affordances. Video conferencing is able to faithfully represent participants' appearance across a distance, but typically employs flat displays, which compress the representation of each participant's local 3D space. Participants have access to a range of verbal and non-verbal communicational cues that are well-supported by the medium: movement of the eyes and head, turn-taking and facial expressions [12]. However, the 2D nature of standard video and the typically narrow camera field-of-view limits the spatial nature of non-verbal communication [11]. In collaborative virtual worlds, visitors are represented by avatars. Avatars represent the presence and activities of a participant and can be visualized using standard displays or projection surfaces at a destination. Avatars are capable of eliciting appropriate responses from observers. For instance, it has been shown that the attractiveness of a participant's avatar influenced how intimate participants were willing to be with a stranger [38]. The ability of a visitor to choose different avatar representations may also be helpful in distributed meetings that include a social component [29].

This paper presents a novel method of visualizing a visitor using a spherical display as part of a technologically asymmetric telecommunication platform. The sphere we have used is 16" diameter which is conveniently somewhat bigger than the human head and thus we will depict the visitor's head on all or some of the display. A key observation is that flat displays are only visible from the front, and lack the 360° view offered by spherical displays. Exploiting the unique characteristics of such displays may bestow a participant represented on the sphere with a greater degree of social presence, as observed by those at the destination. We believe that this is for two reasons. First the display is visible from all sides so the identity of the person depicted on the display can be determined by any viewer. Second, from no position is the display seen obliquely, so it should be possible to support the display of head gaze direction more accurately.

We have chosen to focus on the display of a head because when we interact with others we pay the most attention to the face. Faces are interesting because they convey eye gaze, expressions and gestures and are used as a central channel of communication. Detecting the gaze direction of a person is important for human-computer interaction applications, such as meeting or shared collaborative workspaces. Head gaze, or the orientation of the head during communication of attention, is crucial in interaction. Humans are very good at estimating focus of attention in meeting scenarios [32]. It has been shown that the perceived direction of eye gaze can be influenced by the angle of rotation of the head [37], affirming the importance of the head as a cue to attention direction. Consequently, any new display method needs to evaluate the ability of users to discern the focus of attention based on head gaze direction.

Therefore, in this paper, we present an implementation of a novel display of a visitor's head called *SphereAvatar*. We demonstrate three different modes of presenting the visitor which use different modes of rendering and configuration: *inflated*, *normal* and *surface* (see Figure 1). SphereAvatar is part of a larger experimental distributed collaboration system discussed in [30], which provides a heterogeneous and multimodal platform for telecollaboration. In the current paper, we investigate the use of a novel spherical display technology to embody a remote visitor. We perform an experiment to measure how accurately observers are able to determine the SphereAvatar's direction of head gaze across three varying modes of representation.

In the following sections, we review related work and present the software and hardware components needed to implement SphereAvatar. This is followed by an experimental evaluation of SphereAvatar and results. Finally, we present discussions of the results, implications for future designs, conclusions and future work.

RELATED WORK

Spherical Displays

Spherical displays have been used as a multi-touch sensitive interactive surface. Benko et al. designed a multi-user, multi-touch sensitive spherical display that facilitates collaborative interactions around the sphere [4]. An infrared camera is used for touch sensing and shares the same optical path with the projector used for the display. They placed their spherical installation in three high traffic locations and observed collaborative activities from several people interacting with the sphere. They reported that the sphere's unusual shape, large size and visibility from all directions attracted large crowds (also noted in [2]). Most described the experience as "like interacting with a crystal ball". The authors [4, 5] highlight two unique characteristics of the display: borderless but finite display and visible content changes with position and height.

Spherical displays have also been explored by Kettner et al. [17] for interacting with data projected on a spherical surface. Using external projectors, they were able to physically rotate the ball in place (like a large trackball). Grossman et al. [10] used a spherical volumetric display to allow gestural interaction and visualization with the 3D data within the display, using the 360° viewing volume. The focus of these systems have been more on how to use the spherical form factor to improve interaction. The exception is Jones et al. [16], which uses an autostereoscopic light field display to present interactive 3D graphics to multiple simultaneous viewers around the display. The spinning display surface was optimized in [15] for the display of a life-sized human face for real time teleconferencing, but the setup omits views of the back of the head. The borderless display and 360° visibility of spherical displays makes for an interesting display mode for an avatar head, as observers are potentially able to understand head direction from any perspective.

Collaborative Mixed Realities

The virtuality continuum [22] describes virtual reality (VR) related display technologies in terms of their relative extents of presenting real and virtual stimuli. The spectrum ranges from the display of a real environment (for instance video) at one end to a purely synthetic virtual environment (VE) at the other. Mixed reality (MR) occupies the range of the continuum between these extrema, merging both real and virtual objects together. MR was originally considered on a per *display* basis, and later, broadened to consider the joining together of distributed physical locations to form MR *environments* [3]. When discussing MR displays it is sufficient to do so with regard to Milgram and Kishino's evolving taxonomy [22] that ranges from hand-held devices through to immersive projection technologies. However, MR environments as outlined by Benford et al. [3] bring together a range of technologies, including situated and mobile displays and capture devices, with the aim of supporting high-quality spatial telecommunication.

Several means of representing people virtually in such MR environments have been investigated. This includes the use of situated displays [36], mobile personal telepresence robots [35], and optical or video see-through Augmented Reality (AR) displays [27]. Regarding AR displays, in order to obtain an enhanced view of the real environment, an AR display would have to be worn by each user at the destination. Live capture of 3D content and simultaneous presentation, using fiducial markers and video-see-through AR, has been demonstrated by Prince et al. [25]. Video see-through displays capture the real world with video cameras mounted on the head gear, and virtual world views are electronically combined with the video stream from the camera. Disadvantages of these displays includes narrow field-of-view and low contrast. Optical see-through displays fare much better, as the physical world is seen through semi transparent mirrors placed in front of the user's eyes. These mirrors reflect the virtual world views into the user's eyes thus optically combining of real and virtual world views. There is no limitation to the wearer's field-of-view. However the obstruction of the face, although somewhat limited with the optical display, may still hamper the ability of the visitor at the remote site to maintain good face-to-face communication with users at the destination.

Telepresence Robots

In robotics, a range of systems exist to support remote telepresence. Two complementary approaches can be found: mobile robots that represent the movement of users and situated humanoids that mimic the appearance of the head or body of users. For example, telepresence robots [7, 20] can offer video conferencing with mobile capabilities. These devices tend to have a built-in flat screen to display the video stream. Lee et al. [20] conducted a field study over 2–18 months in the use of this mobile remote presence system and commented that most people could not identify the remote pilot without walking around to check the front of the side of the screen. Robots such as Robovie [13] focus more on the interactional capabilities and do not show a video representation of the controlling user.

In the field of humanoid robotics, examples such as Geminoid [28] are very human-like in both appearance and movement. They can potentially be used to represent specific visitors at a destination but they are limited in terms of their flexibility in representing other teleoperators. Research on the dynamic characteristics of humanoid robots has been limited. Research on TeleHead [33], an acoustical telepresence robot, showed that dynamic cues from head movement play important roles in auditory localization. Head movement is an important factor in telepresence, from turn-taking during conversations to both showing and observing attention.

Earlier work by Naimark demonstrated a talking head: a technique where an image is projected onto a screen whose shape physically matches the image itself [24], to enhance telepresence. Animatronic Shader Lamps Avatars (SLA) [21] takes this technique further by using cameras and projectors to capture and map both the dynamic motion and the appearance of the embodied user onto a humanoid animatronic model. The SLA's use of front projection to texture the 3D facial geometry makes it less practical than one with internal (rear) projection, as commented by the authors. The feature-points expression face robot WD-1(Waseda-Docomo face robot No.1)[14] uses rear projection to texture a real user's face onto the robot's surface but will need further miniaturization for wider use. REFLCT [19] personalizes the experience by using head-worn projective displays to overlay multiple user-specific, customized views of an avatar on a common abstract mannequin head in a shared environment, enabling projection of animated facial expressions, similar to SLA.

The most obvious question that one can ask about a humanoid robot is whether it is actually treated as if it were a real-person. A remote-controlled android system called Geminoid HI-1 [28] was judged to be more human-like and natural than a video conferencing system but it was described by users as very *uncanny*. Uncanny is a term often used to described robots and computer generated avatars; the term was used in Mori's description of the uncanny valley [23] where it was advocated that the degree of intimacy increases with a robot's humanlike appearance and behavior but that at a certain level of humanlike appearance and behavior, however, the degree of intimacy drops sharply. A spherical display could easily be integrated into a robotic platform. Compared to current telepresence robots, the visibility of the display would be a distinct advantage. The sphere display offers flexibility compared to humanoid robotics as it isn't constrained to a single head size or shape.

Perception of Head and Eye Gaze Direction

Whilst the 360° and multi-view capabilities of a spherical projection are novel, it is not clear whether observers can interpret gaze direction on closely-spaced target objects. The direction of a person's gaze is one feature that is relevant in judging objects of interest in an environment. Early work indicates that gaze direction may be perceived by both the direction in which the head is oriented and the eye's position relative to the head [8]. Previous research has focused on studies in which the eyes and the head were counter-rotated to varying degrees while maintaining fixation on the subject [8, 1]. These studies consistently showed an interaction between eye and head position in the perception of gaze direction. Gibson et al. [8] examined three head gaze conditions: head to front, left and right. In each condition, an observer at a distance of 2m gazed at seven positions in a prearranged random order, each 0.1m apart on a wall behind participants. Participants made yes or no judgment of whether or not they felt they were being looked at. The frequency distributions of 'yes' judgments showed a *head-turn* effect such that when the target's head was rotated in one direction, participants' judgments tended to perceive gaze to be rotated in the opposite direction. In addition to the three head gaze conditions, Anstis et al. [1] investigated three orientations of a TV screen. They found: the same *head-turn* effect; *TV-screen-turn* effect, apparent displacement of the perceived direction in the same direction as the turn of the screen; and an overestimation of the deviation of looker's gaze from the straight ahead. They suggested that the convex curvature of the screen probably caused the *TV-screen-turn* effect. Overestimation was found to increase with the complexity of the viewing condition. Overall, these studies suggest that observers may be constructing a mental line based on the head orientation before judging the eye direction relative to the head.

Despite the importance of the head as an attentional cue, there has been relatively little research on the perception of its orientation. Troje and Siebeck [34] quantified accuracy of head orientation discrimination under varying illumination conditions with the eyes pointing directly forwards. Discrimination was shown to be most accurate within the $\pm 15°$ range of forward gaze directions but was markedly poorer at 30° head rotation. This was also observed by Wilson et al., who also found that changes in head orientation could be perceived even when the internal features of the head or the outline head contour is removed, suggesting that the deviation of nose angle may be a likely cue [37].

Troje and Siebeck [34] also concluded in their third experiment that subjects were not influenced by potential changes in eye gaze direction but in fact judged the head orientations as instructed. Perception of an avatar's gaze direction has also been studied in virtual environments [26, 31]. In an object-focused multiparty immersive collaborative virtual environment scenario, tracked eye gaze has been shown not to provide statistically significant advantage over just tracked head gaze

[31]. With both tracked eye and head gaze, avatars' eyes and heads were controlled by head-mounted mobile eye trackers and head tracking worn by participants, while head tracked avatars featured static centered eyes with no gaze control, so visual attention must be inferred from head orientation only. Therefore, in this initial study into the use of spherical displays for representing remote participants, we employ the static gaze condition in evaluating SphereAvatar, although the underlying system supports full eye gaze as well as facial expressions.

SYSTEM DESIGN

The SphereAvatar system is a part of a larger distributed system [30] supporting both avatar- and video-mediated communication. The aim of the overall system is to allow a visitor to have multiple presences in a real environment through fixed and mobile display units. The visitor is tracked using motion capture and video systems. In this study, we focus specifically on one aspect of the system: the forms of representation of the visitor that are possible on a spherical display. The spherical display is chosen because it is small enough to situate almost anywhere in a room, but it is visible from all directions. For example, it could be positioned in a seat around a table and all others at the table would see a wide aspect of the display unlike they would with a flat panel display where even if the display could rotate, some participants would see face-on views whereas others would see oblique views.

The SphereAvatar system has the ability to show video captured content and computer generated content. However for the purposes of the experiment described in this paper, we have chosen to focus on a photorealistic computer generated head so as to provide reproducibility of cues between the conditions. In the discussion section, we describe how we can support novel real-time video-based rendering using multi-view video or could support 3D reconstruction: however these are both research topics and the visual quality achievable is not fairly comparable. Using a rendered avatar allows us to consider the ideal representations for a human head on such a spherical display without potential confounds because the detail of the representations is significantly different. The computer generated head is also precisely controllable whereas video content would have to be captured from a person performing the actions.

Hardware

SphereAvatar uses the commercially available Magic Planet display by Global Imagination®. The Magic Planet is a projection display device with a 16" sphere-shaped surface. The spherical surface is an empty plastic ball coated with a diffuse material that serves as a passive curved projector screen. It features a standard 1024×768 projector at 60Hz, coupled with a fisheye lens to project imagery. The projected light travels through the bottom of the sphere. Hence the sphere is completely illuminated except for the area immediately around the lens itself. The unique aspect of such displays are their 360° horizontal visibility, allowing the displayed avatar head to face any direction in the destination.

Software

In order to project an avatar's head onto the sphere there are two main stages: first the scene is rendered in to an environment map, and then a 3D sphere is drawn using the environment map as its sole texture. The second stage of the process is the same for each display mode. The first stage is different and the various methods are explained in the following sections.

An environment map is an image that represents the complete scene around a point. Greene proposed the idea of storing environment maps as cube maps [9] where six subimages representing the six different faces of a cube. Figure 2(a) depicts a cube map where every cube map face is a different solid color. This corresponds to scene which comprises a cube where each wall was a different color, left yellow, top blue, etc. The output of the second stage is to create an image from this environment map that can be projected through the fisheye lens. With the given environment the image to project should be as shown in Figure 2(b). The most common way of performing the relevant distortion is to use environment mapping, and to render a sphere with the environment map as its texture. Environment mapping was first proposed by Blinn and Newell [6]. It simulates the reflectance of a surface, by using the reflected eye vector as a lookup in to the texture rather than a simple texture coordinate. OpenGL and Direct3D have both supported environment mapping for many years, and it is built in to most recent graphics processing units on graphics cards. We have implemented this process in OpenGL and GLUT. We render the scene in to an environment map using six cameras, but see the following sections for how these cameras and the objects are configured. The environment map is rendered in to a frame buffer object (FBO) which means the rendering process can be real-time. This two-stage rendering approach is a standard process and, for example, a similar implementation can be found in the open source OpenSceneGraph software. Figures 2(c) and 2(d) show example of the results of renderings of the environment mapping stage. Once projected on through the fisheye lens and onto the spherical surface these would appear similar to the images in Figure 1.

Display Modes

We implement three methods for displaying the animation of an avatar's head. As described above, in this first stage a cube map must be generated by rendering six views of the avatar head. The key difference between the three display modes is the positioning and orientation of the camera to capture the views of the six cube faces.

Inflated

With this display mode, the camera center is positioned inside the avatar's head at the center and six views are rendered facing out to each cube face. However, in this state, the camera would render the inside of the head. In order to get the correct rendering, we reverse the OpenGL depth ordering and polygon direction, so the head is rendered from the inside, but also inside out. This creates a cube map, which when environment mapped in the second stage always covers the whole sphere, see Figure 2(c). Due to the inherent differences between the shape of the human head and the sphere, this mode is

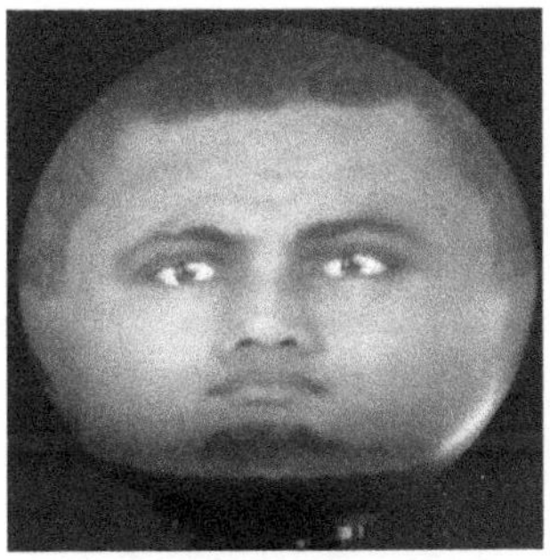

(a) Inflated Mode 1

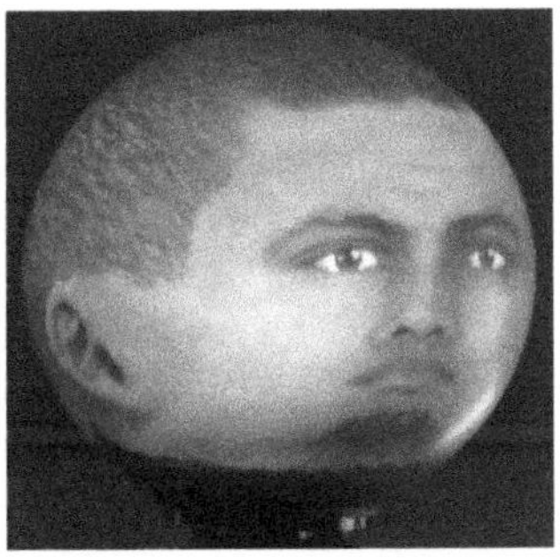

(b) Inflated Mode 2

(c) Normal Mode 1

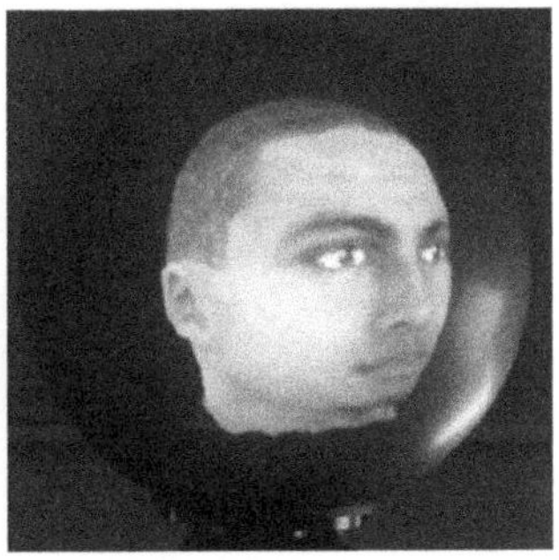

(d) Normal Mode 2

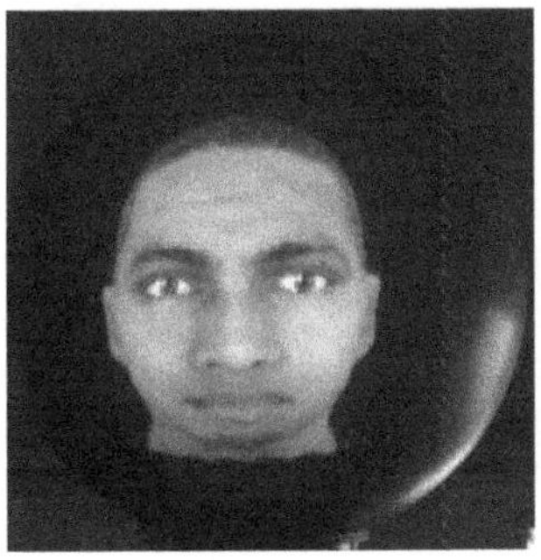

(e) Surface Mode 1

(f) Surface Mode 2

Figure 1. Examples of inflated, normal and surface display modes. In the left column the avatar head is looking at the same angle approximately 10° **to the right of the viewer. In the right column the avatar head is at the same angle approximately** 45° **to the left of the viewer.**

somewhat distorted on the spherical display (see Figures 1(a) and 1(b)) and the head looks like it has been blown up to a sphere. Hence the name of the display mode. Despite the distortion, all the features are locally consistent and the shape of the features in the center of the face are nearly correct. It is obviously a head and it is easy to determine the direction in which it is looking.

Normal

With this display mode (Figures 1(c) and 1(d)), the camera is positioned outside the cube at the position of the observer's head. A cube map is rendered using the now non-symmetric view volumes. The resulting cube map looks as if the head is outside looking in, but once reflected in the environment mapping, it gives the illusion that the head is situated within the spherical display.

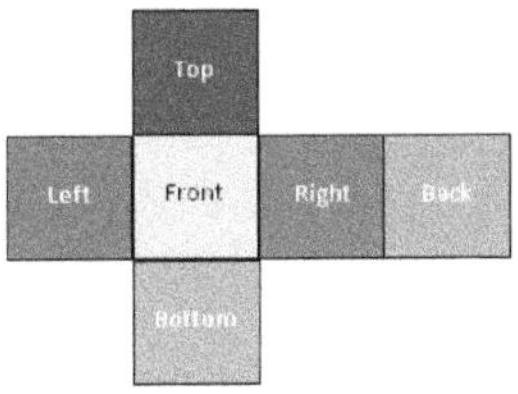

(a) Cube map

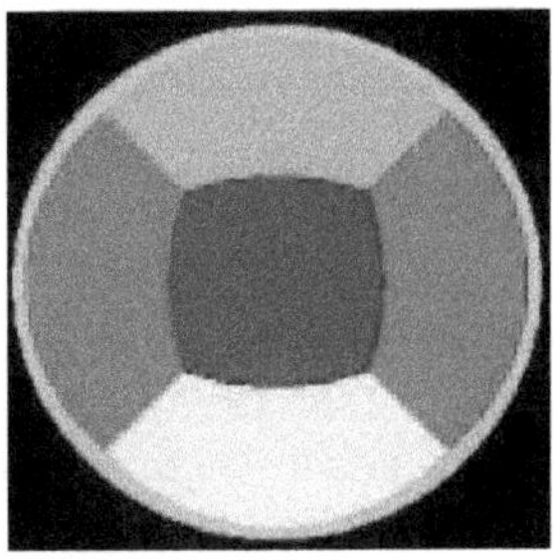

(b) Distorted cube map for projection

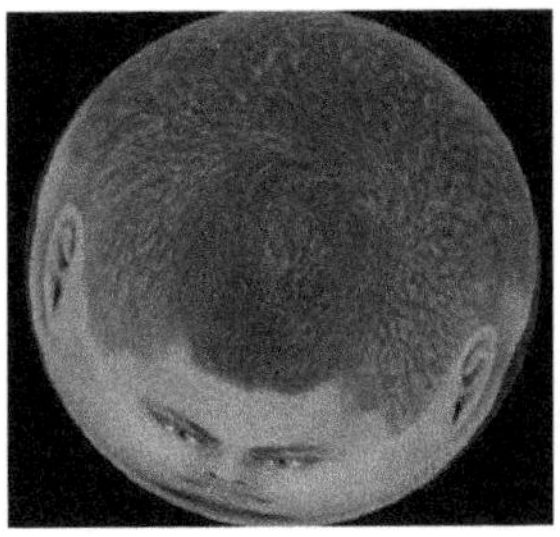

(c) Inflated display mode as generated for projection

(d) Normal display mode as generated for projection

Figure 2. Illustrating stages of the rendering pipeline.

If the head were situated inside the spherical display, as an observer moved around the view of the head would change. In our implementation we can take this into account by tracking the position of the user's head using Microsoft Kinect. This mode can thus only support a single viewer as the image on the sphere can only be adjusted based on one person's position. It does however mean that the head appears solid: if the user walks around to the back of the sphere, the image will be adjusted accordingly (i.e. the back of avatar's head would be displayed at the back of the sphere). To ensure accuracy and stability, in the experiment described in the next section, head tracking was disabled and the participant sat in fixed positions. An operator keyed in the correct position.

Surface

With this display mode (Figures 1(e) and 1(f)), the avatar's head is rendered always looking straight ahead on the spherical display but rotation of the head is depicted by moving the head around the sphere. This is done by setting the cameras inside the cube as for the inflated mode, but then positioning the head outside the cube looking directly toward the center of the cube. This rendering type lends itself to rendering of face images and video as well as 3D models: the image or video could be placed on a planar billboard facing the cube center.

EXPERIMENT

In this experiment, we explore the accuracy with which participants can discriminate the SphereAvatar's head orientation for all three display modes. Specifically we measure the ability of participants to identify which of a set of targets the avatar head appears to be gazing toward. Given the three display modes, we expect that participants viewing the normal mode will be able to identify more correct targets compared to those viewing the surface mode. We expect the inflated mode to lie between these two in performance.

Method

Apparatus and Materials

We captured a visitor's head motion in a CAVE-like system with Intersense IS-900 head tracking when looking at virtual balls in a prearranged random order (Table 1). The balls (stimuli) were placed in a 7 × 7 grid, excluding the central position, hence producing 48 target positions. The balls were 5.5cm in diameter, and were spaced 0.3m (9.46°) apart both horizontally and vertically. The most extreme head orientation to the outer-most ball horizontally or vertically was 26.56°, while the diagonal extreme was 35.26°. As the visitor moved his head during the recording process, he would call out a target number currently being looked at (i.e. "Target 1", "Target 2", ... , "Target 48").

Table 1. Target Order

23	38	3	9	44	5	20
11	17	24	32	27	47	28
29	42	31	40	14	25	4
35	2	37	-	34	46	12
18	48	33	6	19	16	41
7	15	26	43	30	1	22
39	45	10	21	8	36	13

A real environment was set up to accurately match the virtual environment (Figures 3 and 4). Alignment between the two frames of reference as seen at the visitor site and the destination site ensures consistency between the visitor's head movements as he perceives the virtual destination and the where the embodied avatar head at the physical destination is objectively facing. At the physical destination site, the spherical display is used to visualize the avatar head. 48 real balls (with the same radius as their virtual counterparts) were hung from the ceiling with thin thread in the same locations as the match the virtual balls. To improve discriminability, the balls were color-coded by horizontal rows in the following order: green, blue, red, yellow, red, blue, green. The target balls were situated centrally between the spherical display and the participants' seated position at a distance of 1.8m to each. There were three seating positions for the participants with a horizontal spacing of 0.9m, enabling the investigation of viewing effects from different angles. The viewing distance from participant to avatar for the center position was 3.6m. We ensured that participants' eye level were roughly the same as the avatar's eye position by seating them on a chair.

Design

Each participant judged only one of three display modes (between subjects design), but a within-subjects design was employed regarding the two factors of seating position (left, center or right) and the 48 target positions. The target positions were split into three groups: 1–16, 17–32, 33–48. Using a counterbalanced measures design, we mixed the three seating positions in order to reduce any confounding influence of the orderings such as learning effects or fatigue.

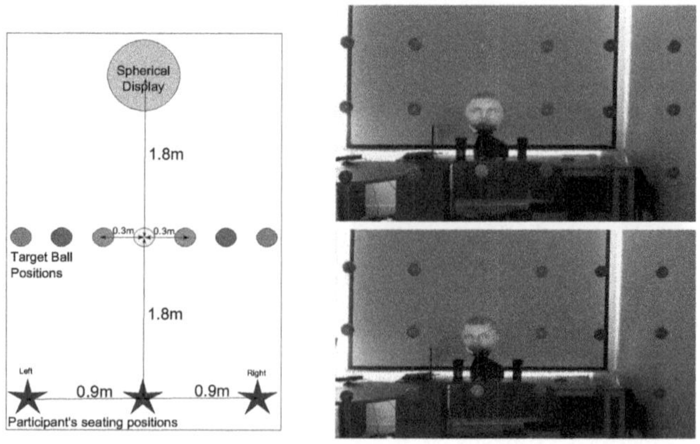

Figure 3. Experiment Setup: (a) Schematic Layout, (b) Inflated Views.

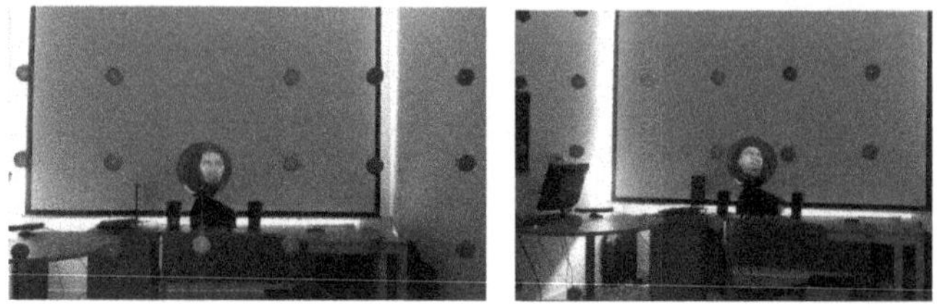

(a) Rotated Surface Display Mode (b) Rotated Normal Display Mode (Right seating position)

Figure 4. Picture of experiment room taken from different perspective of the participant

Procedure

Thirty-six unpaid participants made up of students and staff were recruited to take part in the study. Each participant only judged one of three display modes. Participants were initially seated in one of the three positions depending on the ordering that applied. Participants were given a sheet of paper with an empty 7 × 7 grid. Each time the avatar's head reoriented to face a new target and uttered a target number, the participant was instructed to judge which target was being gazed at, and write the uttered target number in the corresponding position in their grid sheet. They were advised that they could write multiple targets in the same grid location if that is where they perceived the avatar to be facing. Following each target gaze iteration, the avatar head returns to the central gaze position and pauses for around 10 seconds before proceeding to gaze at the next target. This provided time for participants write their judgment in the grid. At each 16th iteration, the session was paused to allow the participants to change to the according seating position. Additionally for the normal mode, the viewing frustum was manually adjusted by $\pm 14°$ depending on the left or right seating position in order to correct the rendering perspective as discussed earlier.

Results

Accuracy

The accuracy of participants' judgments was tabulated. The dependent variable data (accuracy) were entered into a mixed design Analysis of Variance (ANOVA) with the three factors of display mode, seating position, and target position. There was a significant main effect of display mode, ($F_{(2,9)} = 9.692, p < 0.01$) with higher accuracies for the inflated (*Mean, M = 0.464*) and normal modes (*M = 0.465*) than the surface mode (*M = 0.248*). Post-hoc Tukey tests revealed significant mean differences between surface and inflated modes ($p = 0.011$)) and between surface and normal modes ($p = 0.010$)). There was no difference between normal and inflated modes ($p = 1.000$)). Both normal and inflated outperformed the surface mode. We employed Mauchly's test of sphericity to validate our repeated measures factor ANOVAs, thus ensuring that variances for each set of difference scores are equal. Mauchly's test indicated that the assumption of sphericity had not been violated ($\chi^2 = 2.652, p > 0.05$). The main effect of seating position was not significant ($F_{(2,8)} = 1.541, p => 0.05$), with similar levels of accuracy for left (*M = 0.405*), center (*M = 0.410*) and right (*M = 0.363*) positions. The main effect of target position was significant ($F_{(47,423)} = 2.575, p < 0.0001$). While this absolute accuracy is a good basic measure, it reduces measurements to the binary rating scale of correct or incorrect. In order to get a more detailed view of accuracy, horizontal and vertical errors must be taken into account.

Horizontal Errors

Horizontal error was determined by the difference between the correct target and the misjudged target position. The dependent variable data (horizontal error) were entered into a mixed design ANOVA with the three factors of display mode, seating position, and target position. There was a significant main effect of display mode, ($F_{(2,9)} = 6.945, p < 0.05$) with lower horizontal errors for the inflated (*M = 0.299*) and normal modes (*M = 0.344*) than the surface mode (*M = 0.785*). Post-hoc Tukey tests revealed significant mean differences between surface and inflated modes ($p = 0.020$)) and between surface and normal modes ($p = 0.033$)). There was no difference between normal and inflated modes ($p = 0.948$)). Both normal and inflated had significantly lower horizontal errors than the surface mode. Mauchly's test indicated that the assumption of sphericity had not been violated ($\chi^2 = 1.025, p > 0.05$). The main effect of seating position was not significant ($F_{(2,8)} = 2.217, p => 0.05$) with similar horizontal errors for left (*M = 0.434*), center (*M = 0.446*) and right (*M = 0.547*) positions. As expected, there was a significant main effect of target positions ($F_{(47,423)} = 2.839, p < 0.0001$).

Vertical Errors

Vertical error was determined by how many balls away from the the correct target ball to the misjudged target ball position vertically. The dependent variable data (vertical error) were also entered into a mixed design ANOVA with three factors of display mode, seating position, and target position. There was a significant main effect of display mode, ($F_{(2,9)} = 11.365, p < 0.05$) with lower vertical errors for the inflated (*M = 0.431*) and normal modes (*M = 0.378*) than the surface mode (*M = 0.856*). Post-hoc Tukey tests revealed significant mean differences between surface and inflated modes ($p = 0.010$)) and between surface and normal modes ($p = 0.005$)). There was no difference between normal and inflated modes ($p = 0.885$)). Both normal and inflated had significantly lower vertical errors than the surface mode. Mauchly's test indicated that the assumption of sphericity had not been violated ($\chi^2 = 0.687, p > 0.05$). The main effect of the seating positions was not significant ($F_{(2,8)} = 3.393, p > 0.05$) with similar vertical errors for left (*M = 0.519*), center (*M = 0.550*) and right (*M = 0.595*). Regardless of seating positions, the level of vertical errors did not significantly differ. There was a significant main effect of target positions ($F_{(47,423)} = 6.042, p < 0.0001$).

DISCUSSION

The main findings of the study are:

- Participants' could interpret the direction of the normal and inflated modes more accurately than the surface mode. This was also backed up by results from the vertical and horizontal errors.
- The differences in accuracy and errors between the normal and inflated modes were not statistically significant.
- The differences in accuracy and errors between the left, center and right seating positions were not statistically significant.

In the experiment, participants judged the direction of three different display modes of an animated avatar's head rendered a spherical display, which fixated on 48 target points arranged 9.46° apart with a maximum horizontal or vertical range of 26.56° and maximum diagonal range of 35.26°. This allowed us to explore how subjects perceived a range of horizontal and vertical head orientations. We also computed an estimate of the mean angular error from the vertical and horizontal errors of each display mode. The mean angular error for the inflated mode was 5.00°, normal mode was 4.87°, and surface mode was 10.96°. The average deviation of participants' inaccurate judgments of the surface mode was twice as large as the other two modes.

An analysis of the heat maps in Figure 5 shows that subjects' accuracy when viewing the inflated mode was more evenly distributed (Figure 5(a)) than when viewing the normal mode, which resulted in higher accuracy when viewing the edges of the grid than the more central locations (Figure 5(b)). The surface mode was biased subjects' judgments toward the central targets (Figure 5(c)).

Our results should be discussed in relation to the finding by Wilson et al. that internal features or outline head contour can be used to perceive changes in head orientation [37]. The third experiment reported by Wilson et al. investigated what cues subjects use to discriminate head orientation. The example stimuli presented in the paper shows a face with the head contour alone and another with the isolated internal features (eyebrows, eyes, nose and lips). The authors found no statistically significant difference between the full face, head and features conditions. They concluded that both the head contour and internal features provide cues of equivalent strength. Likewise in our findings, the inflated mode does not have a defined outline head contour, as the display hardware is always spherical regardless of the rendered head orientation. However, the avatar does have well-defined internal features that participants successfully used to make good judgments. The normal mode has defined internal features and outline head contour

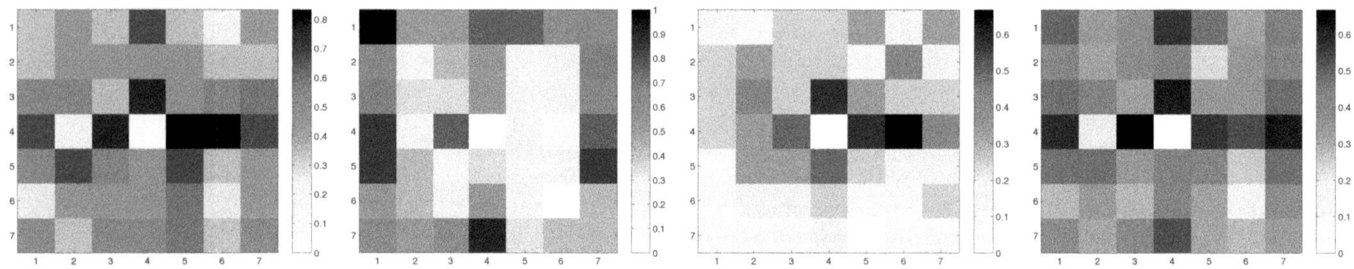

(a) Accuracy - Inflated (b) Accuracy - Normal (c) Accuracy - Surface (d) Accuracy - Combined

Figure 5. Heat maps showing the level of accuracy for each display mode and target position.

that changes with head orientations which helped participants when making judgments. The lack of statistical significance in difference we found between these two display modes is similar to Wilson et al.'s findings. We conclude that the internal features of the face may provide sufficient information for discerning direction of head gaze. Unlike the normal display mode, the internal features and the outline head contour of the surface mode always remains the same regardless of orientation, which is likely to have reduced its effectiveness in discerning targets.

System Design Implications

Head Representation

Perhaps the most surprising aspect of our study is that the inflated avatar head is as accurate as the normal head display mode. We expected the normal mode to be the most accurate because, to the observer, it has the same dimensions as an average human head and has a similar appearance. The inflated mode was originally added as an interim test of the rendering pipeline, and although casual visitors to the lab who have seen this display have described it as being a bit unusual, they have not been averse to interacting with it. One potential advantage of the inflated mode is that it is larger than life and thus features on the display are perhaps easier to see than the normal or surface modes, thus it might be better for use in a larger space.

The poor performance of the surface mode was expected because the head is always rendered exactly face-on, and as it moves to the side of the display (i.e. the head turns) the number of visible pixels from the experimental seating positions reduces. Although greater angles such as 90° were not considered, in such a case, the head would only be partially visible from the front, as it would be positioned on the side of the display.

A related issue is the performance with multiple viewers. The inflated display mode has the distinct advantage that the head is always visible from all angles. Thus any number of observers can watch the sphere and can determine the direction the head is looking. This immediately solves a problem identified by Lee et al. [20] in their study of a mobile remote telepresence system where users could not identify the remote visitor without seeing the front of the telepresence robot. In contrast, the normal mode can only be correct for one viewer. This is because the position of the observer is needed in order to render the head correctly for that perspective. The surface display mode also has visibility problems with multiple viewers, though they are slightly different from those encountered with the normal display mode. Specifically, as the surface mode turns through a complete horizontal revolution, it is sometimes visible and invisible to any viewer, whereas as the normal mode turns, it is always visible to the one selected viewer and it may or may not be visible to the other viewers.

View Generation

With our current demonstration we are using computer generated renderings of avatar heads. Although the animation we have used in the experiment is simple, the software system provides a fully animated head with mouth movement, eye movement and facial expression. It can also render an avatar body, but since this would not be visible on the inflated display, we did not consider this in the current study. All three display modes are easily generated from 3D models.

An interesting question is the potential support for live video streaming. Telepresence robots have, so far, generally used flat screens, with a webcam view of the remote participant. This webcam view could be rendered on to a spherical display and oriented, independent of the robot base, to face in any direction. This would support more rapid head movement than turning the base itself. This could help in social situations where attention needs to be directed quickly. The direction of this surface video view could be driven in multiple ways, including following the eye or head direction of the visitor.

Given that determining gaze direction from the surface display mode is difficult, this suggests that image-based rendering or computer vision reconstruction techniques might be appropriate in order to construct normal or inflated video-based views. An equivalent normal display mode could be supported using multiple video cameras that surround the visitor. The correct video could then be selected to be shown on the sphere, by choosing the camera whose viewing angle was closest to the user viewing the SphereAvatar. The construction of a video equivalent to the inflated mode is not so simple and would require reconstruction of some proxy geometry for the head (perhaps a spheroid) that could then be re-rendered. This seems eminently tractable given the current state of the art in computer vision for reconstruction of objects from video (e.g. [18] focuses on full body avatars, but similar approaches would work for the head or head and shoulders).

CONCLUSIONS AND FUTURE WORK

We have presented a novel display system for technologically asymmetric telecollaboration called the SphereAvatar. It comprises a spherical display on to which we project an avatar representation of a remote visitor. The SphereAvatar can represent the identity and presence of the remote visitor and we have also shown that it can successfully convey that person's direction of attention. We demonstrated three potential ways of rendering the remote visitor's head, and have discussed how these afford support for different numbers of people viewing the display. We have also discussed how these modes might be created directly from video. The key advantage of using a sphere is that it can be seen from all directions, and for no observer is the display at an oblique angle. Perhaps the most surprising finding was that the inflated display mode was very successful at conveying direction of head gaze. This is despite the inflated mode showing a head that was overly large and distorted to fit a sphere. It is thus a promising line of development. We suspect that the normal display mode which we demonstrate might still be preferable for a single user viewing the display, but it can't support multiple viewers.

The repetitive nature of the experimental task, combined with the minimal avatar animation, which did not feature eye movement or facial expression, were critical to the core aims of the experiment, which sought to determine how accurately people could identify direction of head gaze. This scenario is clearly an unusual one to perform over a telepresence system built to support normal remote interaction, and hence, we decided not to collect subjective opinions of the SphereAvatar from experimental subjects. Future studies will be designed to enable collection of such subjective data. We will also concentrate on analyzing the head-eye coordination of this display medium. Another limitation of this study is the lack of investigation along the depth dimension, as targets were arranged in a 2D plane.

SphereAvatar is technically quite simple to build and can be constructed very cheaply in comparison to volumetric displays, robotics and animatronic shader lamp avatars. An alternative approach would have been to project onto an ellipsoid that is more "head-shaped" than a sphere, however this would have worked for head rotations around the vertical axis (heading/yaw) while the projection would be severely distorted for rotations around other axes.

SphereAvatar can be statically situated or it could be mounted on a robot. In future work we want to investigate the use of a mobile SphereAvatar and how this might alleviate the need to have the robot continually turn to face the target of interest in order to properly convey the remote visitor's interest. We will also work on integration of video-based representations. There is also more work to be done on altering the rendering modes or systematically changing cameras so that the poor performance of the surface display mode is raised. Subtle shading or exaggerating the angle of the head might better represent head gaze in the surface display mode, but this might restrict it to being a single-view only display. Finally, in the larger context of heterogeneous multimodal mixed reality telecommunication [30], we will study how we might have a static or mobile SphereAvatar represent the dynamic free movements of a remote person. Thus upcoming experiments will focus on case studies of more complex telecollaboration scenarios.

REFERENCES

1. Anstis, S., Mayhew, J., and Morley, T. The perception of where a face or television'portrait'is looking. *The American Journal of Psychology 82*, 4 (1969), 474–489.

2. Barthel, C., and Rowe, S. Visitor interactions with 3-d visualizations on a spherical display at a science museum. In *OCEANS 2008* (sept. 2008), 1.

3. Benford, S., Greenhalgh, C., Reynard, G., Brown, C., and Koleva, B. Understanding and constructing shared spaces with mixed-reality boundaries. *ACM Transactions on computer-human interaction (TOCHI) 5*, 3 (1998), 185–223.

4. Benko, H., Wilson, A., and Balakrishnan, R. Sphere: multi-touch interactions on a spherical display. In *Proceedings of the 21st annual ACM symposium on User interface software and technology*, ACM (2008), 77–86.

5. Benko, H., and Wilson, A. D. *Design Challenges of Interactive Spherical User Interfaces*. 2009, 1–4.

6. Blinn, J., and Newell, M. Texture and reflection in computer generated images. *Communications of the ACM 19*, 10 (1976), 542–547.

7. Desai, M., Tsui, K., Yanco, H., and Uhlik, C. Essential features of telepresence robots. In *Technologies for Practical Robot Applications (TePRA), 2011 IEEE Conference on*, IEEE (2011), 15–20.

8. Gibson, J., and Pick, A. Perception of another person's looking behavior. *The American Journal of Psychology 76*, 3 (1963), 386–394.

9. Greene, N. Environment mapping and other applications of world projections. *Computer Graphics and Applications, IEEE 6*, 11 (nov. 1986), 21 –29.

10. Grossman, T., Wigdor, D., and Balakrishnan, R. Multi-finger gestural interaction with 3d volumetric displays. In *Proceedings of the 17th annual ACM symposium on User interface software and technology*, ACM (2004), 61–70.

11. Hauber, J., Regenbrecht, H., Billinghurst, M., and Cockburn, A. Spatiality in videoconferencing: trade-offs between efficiency and social presence. In *Proceedings of the 2006 20th anniversary conference on Computer supported cooperative work*, ACM (2006), 413–422.

12. Isaacs, E., and Tang, J. What video can and cannot do for collaboration: a case study. *Multimedia Systems 2*, 2 (1994), 63–73.

13. Ishiguro, H., Ono, T., Imai, M., Maeda, T., Kanda, T., and Nakatsu, R. Robovie: an interactive humanoid robot. *Industrial robot: An international journal 28*, 6 (2001), 498–504.

14. Itoh, K., Miwa, H., Onishi, Y., Imanishi, K., Hayashi, K., and Takanishi, A. Development of face robot to express the individual face by optimizing the facial features. In *Humanoid Robots, 2005 5th IEEE-RAS International Conference on*, IEEE (2005), 412–417.

15. Jones, A., Lang, M., Fyffe, G., Yu, X., Busch, J., McDowall, I., Bolas, M., and Debevec, P. Achieving eye contact in a one-to-many 3d video teleconferencing system. In *ACM Transactions on Graphics (TOG)*, vol. 28, ACM (2009), 64.

16. Jones, A., McDowall, I., Yamada, H., Bolas, M., and Debevec, P. Rendering for an interactive 360 light field display. *ACM Transactions on Graphics (TOG) 26*, 3 (2007), 40.

17. Kettner, S., Madden, C., and Ziegler, R. Direct rotational interaction with a spherical projection. In *In Interaction: Systems, Practice and Theory Proceedings* (2004).

18. Knoblauch, D., Font, P. M., and Kuester, F. Virtualizeme: Real-time avatar creation for tele-immersion environments. In *IEEE Virtual Reality 2010 Proceedings*, IEEE (2010), 279–280.

19. Krum, D., Suma, E., and Bolas, M. Augmented reality using personal projection and retroreflection. *Personal and Ubiquitous Computing*, 1–10. 10.1007/s00779-011-0374-4.

20. Lee, M. K., and Takayama, L. "now, i have a body": uses and social norms for mobile remote presence in the workplace. In *Proceedings of the 2011 annual conference on Human factors in computing systems*, CHI '11, ACM (New York, NY, USA, 2011), 33–42.

21. Lincoln, P., Welch, G., Nashel, A., State, A., Ilie, A., and Fuchs, H. Animatronic shader lamps avatars. *Virtual Reality* (2009), 1–14.

22. Milgram, P., and Kishino, F. A taxonomy of mixed reality visual displays. *IEICE Transactions on Information and Systems E series D 77* (1994), 1321–1321.

23. Mori, M. The uncanny valley. *Energy 7*, 4 (1970), 33–35.

24. Naimark, M. Elements of realspace imaging: A proposed taxonomy. In *Proc. SPIE*, vol. 1457 (1991).

25. Prince, S., Cheok, A., Farbiz, F., Williamson, T., Johnson, N., Billinghurst, M., and Kato, H. 3d live: Real time captured content for mixed reality. In *Mixed and Augmented Reality, 2002. ISMAR 2002. Proceedings. International Symposium on*, IEEE (2002), 7–317.

26. Roberts, D., Wolff, R., Rae, J., Steed, A., Aspin, R., McIntyre, M., Pena, A., Oyekoya, O., and Steptoe, W. Communicating eye-gaze across a distance: Comparing an eye-gaze enabled immersive collaborative virtual environment, aligned video conferencing, and being together. In *Virtual Reality Conference, 2009. VR 2009. IEEE*, IEEE (2009), 135–142.

27. Rolland, J., and Fuchs, H. Optical versus video see-through head-mounted displays in medical visualization. *Presence: Teleoperators & Virtual Environments 9*, 3 (2000), 287–309.

28. Sakamoto, D., Kanda, T., Ono, T., Ishiguro, H., and Hagita, N. Android as a telecommunication medium with a human-like presence. In *Proceedings of the ACM/IEEE international conference on Human-robot interaction*, ACM (2007), 193–200.

29. Shami, N., Cheng, L., Rohall, S., Sempere, A., and Patterson, J. Avatars meet meetings: Design issues in integrating avatars in distributed corporate meetings. In *Proceedings of the 16th ACM international conference on Supporting group work*, ACM (2010), 35–44.

30. Steptoe, W., Normand, J. Oyekoya, O., Pece, F., Giannopoulos, E., Tecchia, F., Steed, A., and Slater, M. Acting in collaborative multimodal mixed reality environments. *Presence: Teleoperators & Virtual Environments* (In Press).

31. Steptoe, W., Oyekoya, O., Murgia, A., Wolff, R., Rae, J., Guimaraes, E., Roberts, D., and Steed, A. Eye tracking for avatar eye gaze control during object-focused multiparty interaction in immersive collaborative virtual environments. In *Virtual Reality Conference, 2009. VR 2009. IEEE*, IEEE (2009), 83–90.

32. Stiefelhagen, R., and Zhu, J. Head orientation and gaze direction in meetings. In *CHI'02 extended abstracts on Human factors in computing systems*, ACM (2002), 858–859.

33. Toshima, I., and Aoki, S. The effect of head movement on sound localization in an acoustical telepresence robot: Telehead. In *Intelligent Robots and Systems, 2006 IEEE/RSJ International Conference on*, IEEE (2006), 872–877.

34. Troje, N., and Siebeck, U. Illumination-induced apparent shift in orientation of human heads. *PERCEPTION-LONDON- 27* (1998), 671–680.

35. Tsui, K., Desai, M., Yanco, H., and Uhlik, C. Exploring use cases for telepresence robots. In *Proceedings of the 6th international conference on Human-robot interaction*, ACM (2011), 11–18.

36. Venolia, G., Tang, J., Cervantes, R., Bly, S., Robertson, G., Lee, B., and Inkpen, K. Embodied social proxy: mediating interpersonal connection in hub-and-satellite teams. In *Proceedings of the 28th international conference on Human factors in computing systems*, ACM (2010), 1049–1058.

37. Wilson, H., Wilkinson, F., Lin, L., and Castillo, M. Perception of head orientation. *Vision research 40*, 5 (2000), 459–472.

38. Yee, N., and Bailenson, J. The proteus effect: The effect of transformed self-representation on behavior. *Human communication research 33*, 3 (2007), 271–290.

Trajectory-Aware Mobile Search

Shahriyar Amini[1,2], A.J. Bernheim Brush[1], John Krumm[1], Jaime Teevan[1], and Amy Karlson[1]

[1]Microsoft Research
One Microsoft Way, Redmond, WA
{ajbrush,jckrumm,teevan,karlson}@microsoft.com

[2]Carnegie Mellon University
5000 Forbes Avenue, Pittsburgh, PA
shahriyar@cmu.edu

ABSTRACT
Most location-aware mobile applications only make use of the user's current location, but there is an opportunity for them to infer the user's future locations. We present Trajectory-Aware Search (TAS), a mobile local search application that predicts the user's destination in real-time based on location data from the current trip and shows search results near the predicted location. TAS demonstrates the feasibility of destination prediction in an interactive mobile application. Our user study of TAS shows using predicted destinations to help select search results positively augments the local search experience.

Author Keywords
Mobile local search; mobile systems; location prediction;

ACM Classification Keywords
H.5.m [Information Interfaces and Presentation]: Misc.;

INTRODUCTION
Mobile applications often take advantage of user location to provide a localized experience. However, most only use a single snapshot of the user's current location. When users are moving (e.g., in a car), their current location can quickly end up behind them. Some tools, like GPS travel systems, are designed to support mobility, but require an explicit destination, which their users specify for only about 1% of their trips [6]. In this paper, we use location trajectory and destination prediction to implicitly incorporate information about where users are going, and not just where they are.

The application we explore is mobile local search. *Local searches* are searches for places with a geographic location; common examples include restaurants, gas stations, stores, or area attractions. A recent survey of 929 mobile searchers found that respondents often search while in motion (e.g., in a vehicle or walking), and that more than half of the time searchers wanted their results to be near their route or destination rather than their current location [9]. This suggests using the searcher's location trajectory could help find more relevant results than using current location alone.

Although destination prediction algorithms have been proposed and validated [e.g., 5], we are unaware of any user-focused applications that incorporate them. Amin et al. [1] show users conduct searches most often along regularly used routes and near regularly visited places where users would not be likely to specify a destination. A few prior projects have proposed or looked at using the user's speed and direction. Gui et al. [3] mention that a user's speed could be used as a ranking feature for a context-aware proxy for mobile search, but do not describe exactly how this might be done. COMPASS, a mobile tourist guide prototype, uses user speed to present relevant points of interest [8], and Console et al. [2] consider speed and direction of travel to offer points of interest with respect to what can be reached and what is in the direction of the trip. These works focus on the use of location context for tour guide applications. Our work is unique in that we build and study an interactive trajectory-aware search prototype, and we use destination prediction within the search domain.

To demonstrate the value of incorporating destination prediction into mobile search applications, we implemented and studied the Trajectory Aware Search (TAS) prototype. TAS takes multiple samples of a user's GPS location to establish the user's trajectory and predicts a likely destination that is used to identify appropriately located search results. Our trajectory prediction method is based on an algorithm that is both user and history agnostic [5], meaning it is immediately useful to first-time users and in unfamiliar locations. It also mitigates privacy concerns by only using location data from the current trip.

We studied the use of TAS with a restaurant search task. Our studies in the lab (N=18) and car (N=6) found that restaurants suggested using destination prediction were well-located and relevant, in particular during the first few queries of a search session. We conclude with a discussion of how trajectory data could be used to further improve mobile search and other mobile applications and services.

TRAJECTORY-AWARE SEARCH PROTOTYPE
Given the popularity of restaurant searches (representing 45% of all local mobile searches [9]) we designed the TAS prototype to support local restaurant searches. Figure 1 shows screenshots of the TAS Mobile Client, implemented for Windows Phone 7. TAS has a textbox to input search queries (e.g., *pizza*), and an interactive map displaying results as flags. Results are fetched from the server once the user sends a query. Clicking on a particular flag provides more information about the associated restaurant at the bottom of the screen. Tapping on the description takes the user to another screen with restaurant reviews.

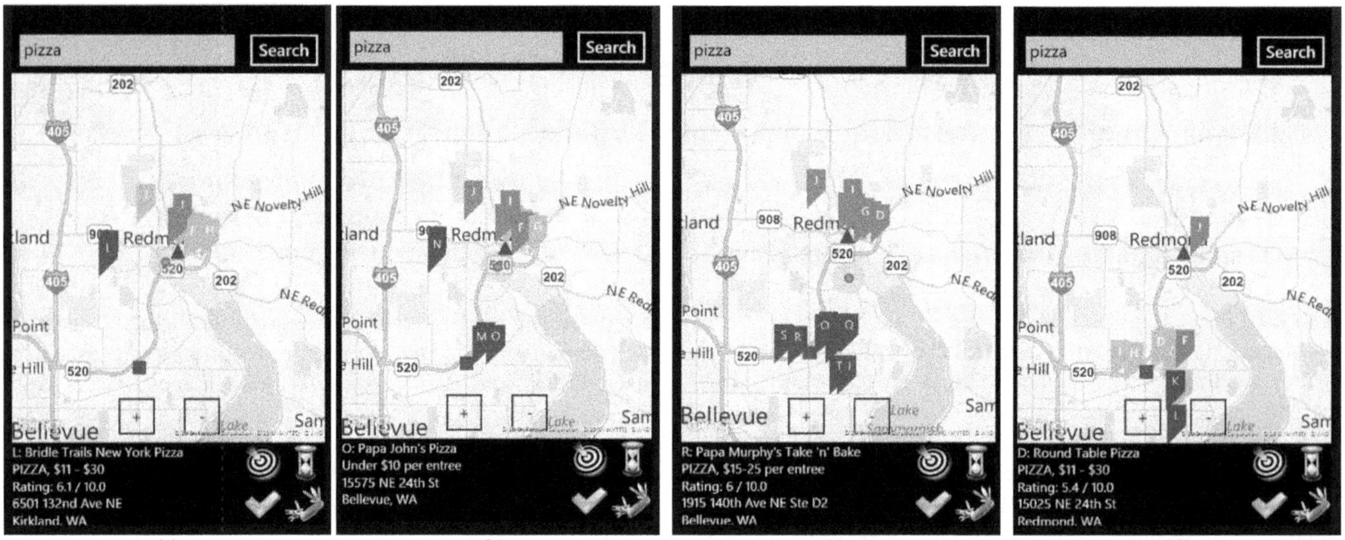

(a) (b) (c) (d)

Figure 1. Trajectory-Aware Search Interface. User is traveling from the purple triangle to the red square with their current location shown by a blue dot. Trajectory results are shown in blue, conventional results are gray, and results returned by both are orange.

TAS discretizes space into square cells. The TAS application samples the GPS sensor every 5 seconds and determines the cell that the user is located in (see Figure 2). When the user issues a query, the mobile client sends both the query and the sequence of cells that the user has traversed to the TAS server, which performs destination prediction and retrieves two sets of search results from Bing™ Local: 1) *Conventional* results, based on the user's current location, and 2) *Trajectory* results, based on the user's predicted destination. By building on top of an existing search engine, we prevent the need to directly modify the search algorithm and provide a solution for how legacy location-aware services may be enhanced through destination prediction.

TAS presents the Trajectory and Conventional results using blue and gray flags. Occasionally the two result sets overlap, shown as orange flags. Figure 1 shows the series of results that occur as a user moves from an initial location (the purple triangle) towards the destination (the red square), with the blue circle indicating the user's current location. Figure 1a represents the start of the trip, so the predicted destination is very similar to the current location and most of the results are in both sets (orange). As the user moves, the separation between the Conventional (gray) and Trajectory (blue) results becomes evident. Almost half-way through the trip (Figure 1c), the Trajectory results converge around the user's true destination. The Conventional results, however, remain at the user's starting location. This is because there are no restaurants near the halfway point of the trip, so the Conventional results continue to show restaurants from the starting location. Once the user is almost at the destination (Figure 1d), the Conventional search results again converge on the user's destination.

Destination Prediction

Destination prediction is based on prior work by Krumm [5]. The approach assumes drivers choose efficient routes to reach their destination. A discrete grid of cells is placed over a region of interest, such as the metropolitan area shown in Figure 2. For each trip, the user's path up to the current time is recorded as a sequence of cells. Based on how efficiently the user has approached any particular cell in the grid, the algorithm computes the probability of that cell being the user's destination. Cells to which the driver is taking an efficient route are considered more likely destinations than cells the driver has apparently decided to pass up. We limit prediction to locations reachable within 30 minutes from the trip's start, since a majority of driving trips take less than 30 minutes [4]. Figure 2 shows a partial trajectory going south through four cells. The higher probability cells, shown with darker outlines, are those to which the partial trajectory is an efficient route.

TAS contributes a novel application of Krumm's algorithm to generate a trajectory-aware local search experience in real-time. To conform to existing local search APIs, which expect a single GPS location and radius, the prediction

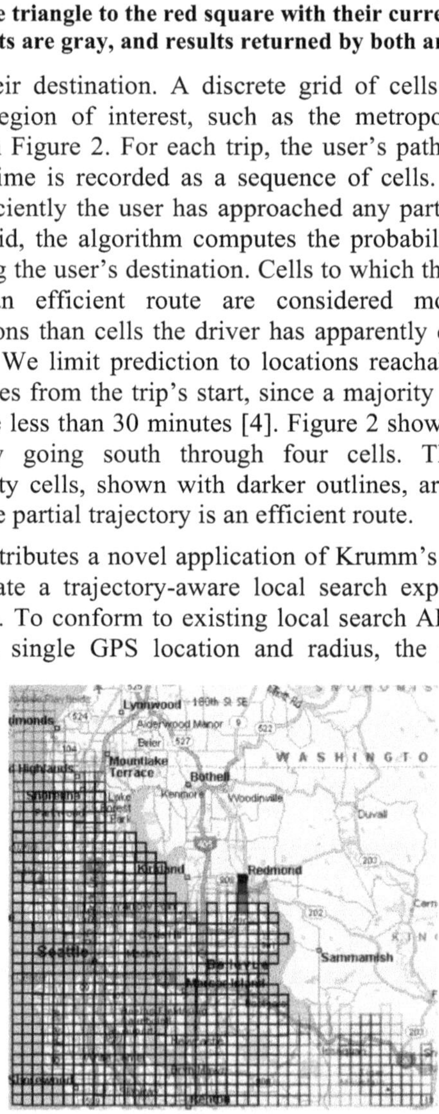

Figure 2. An example of the prediction grid after a driver has traversed south through the four filled cells. Cells with higher probabilities given that route have a darker outline.

algorithm computes the spatial centroid and standard deviation of the cell probabilities, essentially fitting a 2-D circularly symmetric Gaussian to the computed probability distribution. We use a circle with a radius of one standard deviation centered at the centroid of the Gaussian as the search region for the predicted destination.

USER STUDY METHODOLOGY

We evaluated TAS by asking participants to select a restaurant for lunch while en route to a destination. We provided participants Samsung Focus Windows Phones running the TAS Mobile client. Each participant received an introduction to the mobile client interface, and was told that we were comparing different local mobile search algorithms, the results of which were represented by different colored flags. We varied the mapping between flag color and search result type across participants to avoid a potential selection bias based on flag color. To motivate participants to choose a restaurant they actually wanted to eat at, they were told they would receive a gift certificate to one of the four restaurants they selected.

We tested TAS in a controlled laboratory environment with 18 participants (9 M, 9 F). We simulated four trips to nearby suburban centers using pre-recorded GPS data. During pilots we found the GPS playback felt slow, so we played it back at double speed. In addition to these lab studies where we could ensure each participant experienced the same "trip," we also drove 6 participants (3 M, 3 F) to the same four suburban centers following the path of the pre-recorded GPS to evaluate the use of TAS in-situ. The trips studied were approximately 15 minutes long driving. In our analysis, C denotes an in-car participant, while L denotes lab. All participants worked at Microsoft and had previously used mobile search. We compensated participants with either a $10 (lab) or $25 (car) gift card.

We collected qualitative data about the participants' experiences and logged interactions with TAS. Following each task, participants filled out a brief questionnaire asking them about the restaurant they chose (e.g., had they heard of or been to it before?), the location of the search (e.g., was it familiar and were the results nearby?), and their search experience (e.g., was the experience satisfying or frustrating and did they have enough choice?). All participants chose 4 restaurants in 4 locations, for a total of 96 restaurants across 24 participants. Logging failed for two participants (1 car male, 1 lab female). The logged participants issued a total of 464 queries.

USER STUDY RESULTS

Overall, we found that participants found a restaurant that they would like to eat at faster with Trajectory search than they did with Conventional search, and that they were more satisfied with the Trajectory search results. The results identified via destination prediction appeared particularly useful early in the search process, when the destination was some distance away, and for participants who employed exploratory search strategies by entering short, vague queries, versus long, targeted queries.

Target Restaurant Found Sooner with Trajectory Search

The process of selecting a specific restaurant to eat at (referred to as the *Selected restaurant*) took most participants about five minutes, and, on average, 5.3 queries. When we look at the first query within the search session to return the Selected restaurant somewhere in its result list, we observe that 56% of the time the restaurant appeared in both the Trajectory and Conventional results sets. However, when the Selected restaurant was initially found by only one approach, the restaurant was more likely to be found in the Trajectory results (32%) than the Conventional results (13%). Participants were equally familiar with the areas where the Selected restaurant was first found in Conventional or Trajectory results (Median response "Familiar"). However, they were more familiar when the restaurant was returned in both sets (Median response "Very Familiar"). This was particularly true for the in-car studies. Of the 20 search tasks logged in the car studies, 50% of the time the Selected restaurant was first returned only in the Trajectory results. The rest of the time the Selected restaurant was returned by both the algorithms. We conjecture the two search result sets being distinct longer in slower-paced car studies account for this fact.

Participants More Satisfied with Trajectory Search

Trajectory search also led to a more satisfying experience. When a participant's Selected result was first found in the Trajectory results, they reported having a more satisfying search experience (median 3 out of 5, 1 = least satisfying) than when the Selected restaurant was first returned in the Conventional results (median 2). Participants' comments supported the relative lack of value they found in Conventional results. For example, C2 said she "never saw the [conventional] results," and C4 said "I never picked [conventional], I did not see many." In contrast, C5 commented after finding a restaurant returned in Trajectory results: "It gives plenty of options at [my] destination vs. where we are presently."

Trajectory Search Useful Early in the Search Process

During the study we observed that Trajectory search was particularly useful to our participants early in the search process, while they were still far enough from their destination that Conventional search could not retrieve results near where they were heading. Our search logs corroborate this observation, revealing that the Conventional and Trajectory results were most distinct during the first query and became more similar as participants' tasks progressed. C5, who selected restaurants returned first in Trajectory results for all four suburbs, reflected, "I chose while we were not that close to destination," indicating his use of Trajectory results to select restaurants ahead of him.

Trajectory Search Supports Exploration

We also found that the participants who successfully used the Trajectory approach often adopted an exploratory approach, issuing short, general queries. The average query length when the Selected restaurant was first found in the

Trajectory results was much shorter than those issued when results were first found with only the Conventional algorithm (1.2 words vs. 2.5). L2's comment, "I began to trust that I didn't have to specify location because I was 'close enough' even if we were going between towns," suggests users also noticed that the correct prediction of trajectory allowed them to type shorter queries.

In order to examine how exploratory the queries participants used were in different conditions, we manually coded the 147 queries that returned the Selected restaurant in the results by whether the query contained:

- location information (e.g., *[city name] pizza*),
- the name of a specific restaurant (e.g., *pizza hut*),
- a restaurant genre (e.g., *italian*), or
- generic (e.g. *restaurant* or *food*).

Given the TAS focus on location, if the query referenced a location it was categorized as such, regardless of other content. One author coded all of the queries and another coded 40%, with 100% agreement. We observed that 87% of the time when the Selected restaurant was returned only in the Trajectory result set, the participant used a generic or restaurant genre query to find it, compared with only 40% of the time when it was returned in the Conventional result set. In contrast, the queries used to find the Selected restaurant in Conventional results were much more likely to include a location or the name of a specific restaurant (doing so 60% of the time) than those used to find it in the Trajectory results (doing so only 12% of the time).

Overall, the search patterns we observed by participants whose Selected restaurant was first found in the Trajectory results exemplify the scenarios for which destination prediction may have highest value: when the issuer does not have a particular restaurant in mind, and when the destination is not specified (because the user does not want to bother, cannot name the destination, or would accept several destinations along the route). In Teevan et al.'s survey, 31% of mobile-issued local searches had the characteristics that the searcher is both moving and searching for a non-specific result [9]. We expect trajectory-augmented search results to have the highest potential value for these searches.

CONCLUDING REMARKS

By building and studying TAS, we demonstrated destination predication can usefully augment mobile local search. Identifying results near a mobile user's predicted destination appears to be a simple means of augmenting and personalizing conventional local search. Our experience also suggested to us other ways destination predication could enhance the mobile search experience. For example, trajectory information could be used to inform auto-complete query suggestions, thus reducing the amount of user input. Destination prediction could also help determine the most appropriate focus and zoom level of the map to display results (e.g., perhaps centering the map so that the predicted destination is visible).

We believe using trajectory prediction to enhance mobile search works well because the destination prediction does not have to be perfect to usefully restrict the search region. A range of other mobile applications could likewise benefit from prediction; for example, location based reminders could be presented in advance of reaching a location [7] and traffic warnings could enable drivers to an alternate routes.

More generally, our design and implementation of TAS demonstrate a feasible approach for evolving a legacy location-based service to become trajectory-aware. Specifically, we did not make any changes to the underlying search engine to produce a trajectory-aware search engine. With respect to the vast number of location-based services available, we envisage other services that could easily provide trajectory-awareness without modifications to the underlying service (e.g., a friend finding application might show friends near a predicted destination rather than a current location). Based on our experiences with TAS, we see tremendous potential in using richer location information in mobile applications.

REFERENCES

1. Amin, A., Townsend, S., Ossenbruggen, J. and Hardman, L. Fancy a Drink in Canary Wharf?: A User Study on Location-Based Mobile Search. In *Proc. INTERACT 2009*, 736-749.
2. Console, L., Gioria, S., Lombardi, I., Surano, V. and Torre, I. Adaptation and personalization on board cars: A framework and its application to tourist services. In *Proc. Adaptive Hypermedia and Adaptive Web-Based Systems 2002*, 112-121.
3. Gui, F., Adjouadi, M. and Rishe, N. A contextualized and personalized approach for mobile search. *Advanced Information Networking and Applications Workshops*, 2009, 966–971.
4. Hu, P.S. and Reuscher, T.R. Summary of travel trends: 2001 national household transportation survey. *Oak Ridge National Laboratory Technical Report* ORNL/TM-2004/297, 2004.
5. Krumm, J. Real time destination prediction based on efficient routes. Paper 2006-01-0811. *SAE International*, 2006.
6. Krumm, J. Where will they turn: Predicting turn proportions at intersections. *Personal and Ubiquitous Computing*, 2009.
7. Ludford, P., Frankowski, D., Reily, K., Wilms, K., and Terveen, L. Because I carry My Cell Phone Anyway: Functional Location-Based Reminder Applications. In *Proc. CHI 2006*.
8. Setten, M.V., Pokraev, S. and Koolwaaij, J. Context-aware recommendations in the mobile tourist application COMPASS. In *Proc. Adaptive Hypermedia and Adaptive Web-Based Systems*, 2004, 235-244.
9. Teevan, J., Karlson, A., Amini, S., Brush, A.J. and Krumm, J. Understanding the importance of location, time, and people in mobile local search behavior. In *Proc. MobileHCI 2011*.

360° Panoramic Overviews for Location-Based Services

Alessandro Mulloni[1], Hartmut Seichter[1], Andreas Dünser[2], Patrick Baudisch[3], Dieter Schmalstieg[1]
[1] Graz University of Technology, Graz, Austria
[2] HITLab NZ, Univ. of Canterbury, Christchurch, New Zealand
[3] Hasso Plattner Institute, Potsdam, Germany
[lastname]@icg.tugraz.at, andreas.duenser@hitlabnz.org, patrick.baudisch@hpi.uni-potsdam.de

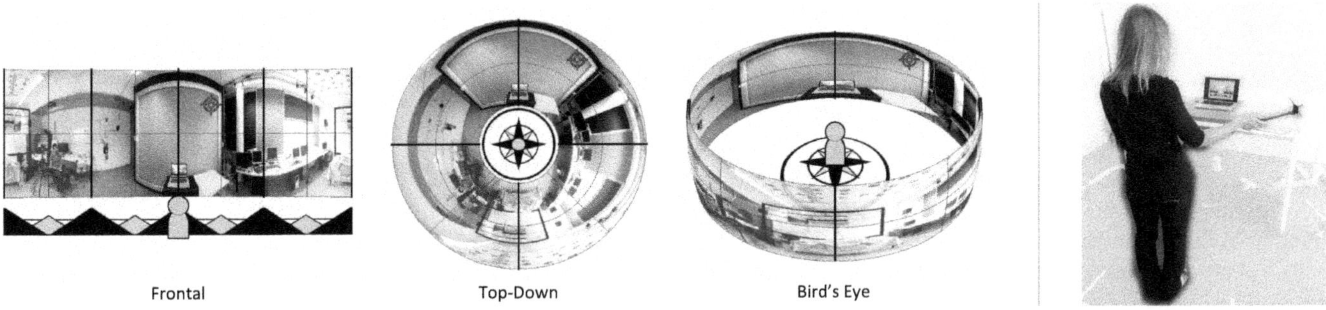

Figure 1. Left: 360° panoramic overviews of a laboratory room. We consider three different shapes for visualizing the panorama. Right: the setup for our user studies consisted of a static display and a tracked wand (used for pointing in the environment).

ABSTRACT
We investigate 360° panoramas as overviews to support users in the task of locating objects in the surrounding environment. Panoramas are typically visualized as rectangular photographs, but this does not provide clear cues for physical directions in the environment. In this paper, we conduct a series of studies with three different shapes: *Frontal*, *Top-Down* and *Bird's Eye*; the last two shapes are chosen because they provide a clearer representation of the spatial mapping between panorama and environment. Our results show that good readability of the panorama is most important and that a clear representation of the spatial mapping plays a secondary role. This paper is the first to provide understanding on how users exploit 360° panoramic overviews to locate objects in the surrounding environment and how different design factors can affect user performance.

Author Keywords
Panorama; visualization; location-based service; magic lens

ACM Classification Keywords
H.5.2 Information Interfaces and Presentation: User Interfaces – Graphical User Interfaces (GUI)

INTRODUCTION
In this paper, we target users of location-based services (e.g., a navigation system) who are looking for objects within their visibility range. A typical scenario might require highlighting a building entrance. In such scenario, a panorama provides omnidirectional overview of the environment. Further, since it is a first-person overview, users do not need to switch to other representations such as maps.

Panoramas can be rendered in any geometrical shape, but rectangles are typically used, similar to any other photograph. If we use the term *readability* qualitatively, as the ease of reading panorama elements, rectangles offer good readability of the panorama but do not clearly represent the fact that the environment surrounds the user: i.e., leftmost and rightmost points in the rectangle depict a part of the environment that is located behind the user. This paper is the first to investigate 360° panoramic overviews for users co-located with the panorama, rather than remote. In our scenario, users try to understand where points on the panorama are physically located in the environment. The spatial mapping between panorama and environment must be therefore clear.

In this paper we consider – in addition to *Frontal* – two shapes that provide a clearer representation of the spatial mapping: *Top-Down* and *Bird's Eye* (Figure 1, left). We conduct a sequence of user studies, asking participants to use panoramic overviews for locating points in the environment. Our results highlight that good readability of the panorama is the most important factor when a panorama is available, while a clear representation of the spatial mapping is advantageous when no panorama is available. We contribute to understanding how 360° panoramic overviews support users locating objects in their surroundings and how different design factors affect user performance.

RELATED WORK
Panoramas are widely used to explore remote locations, e.g. on 360 cities[1] or Google Street View[2]. Multi-perspective visualizations are also popular to gain overview on remote

[1] 360 Cities: http://www.360cities.net/
[2] Google Street View: http://www.google.com/streetview

paths. Zheng [3] presents route panoramas, a technique to join a sequence of images of a path into a single panoramic image. Similarly, Kopf et al. propose StreetSlide [4] where street-level images of a street's façades can be browsed as a single image strip. These works focus on the exploration of remote environments and do not aim at communicating the spatial mapping between visualization and environment.

First-person imagery can be advantageous in location-based services. Chittaro and Burigat [2] show that photos allow faster navigational decisions at road intersections, as compared to a map. Similarly, Google Maps for mobile[3] supports navigation with Street View images. Wither et al. [6] let users browse co-located panoramas through a *magic lens* – users physically turn the device in the environment to see corresponding portions of the panorama. Users successfully identify buildings in the environment from the panoramas, even if there is an offset between the users' location and the position in which the panorama was captured. In these works the panorama only provides a limited field of view, while our goal is to provide omnidirectional overview.

Baudisch et al. [1] target the necessity of overview for magic lenses in the context of online panorama capturing. They dynamically enlarge the field of view to fit the whole panorama, to help users capturing a gapless panorama. In a previous paper [5], we present a similar approach for augmented reality. We propose zooming between live video and an online-captured 360° panorama, showing that the overview is beneficial for complex tasks of spatial search in augmented reality. Similarly to this paper, both works provide omnidirectional overview for magic lenses. However, they visualize the panorama as a rectangle and give no clear indication of whether users understand the spatial mapping between panorama and environment from the rectangle.

DESIGN SPACE: CHOOSING ALTERNATIVE SHAPES

The choice of a shape for a panoramic overview is guided by two design factors: good *readability* of the panorama, and clear *representation of the spatial mapping* between panorama and environment. For our experiments, we considered three shapes (Figure 1). We also add further cues to each shape, visualizing an avatar, a wind rose and a grid.

Frontal. A rectangular shape provides good readability of the panorama, but no clear mapping to the environment.

Bird's Eye. A cylindrical shape maps panorama and environment in a direct way, but sacrifices readability. Due to the 3D view, the panorama is warped and occluded on the sides (we use 15% transparency to resolve occlusions).

Top-Down. A circular shape provides good readability of the panorama and direct mapping of the yaw. However, since the pitch is mapped to the distance from the center of the circle, the panorama is distorted for high pitch, and upside-down in the area of the panorama, which is behind the user.

[3] Google Maps for mobile: http://www.google.com/mobile/maps/

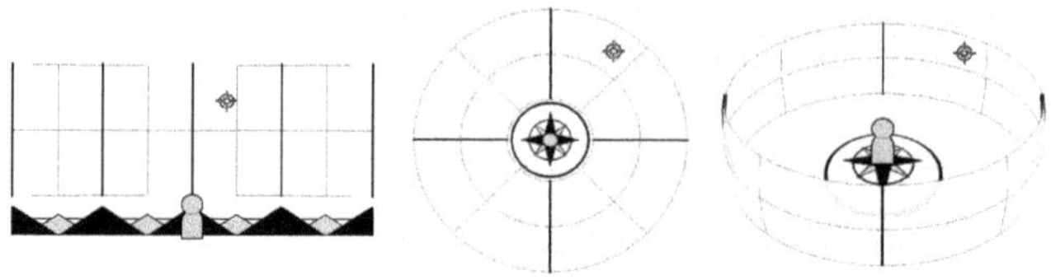

Figure 2. The three shapes in the condition with no panorama.

PILOT STUDY: USER STRATEGIES

We conducted a pilot study to gain first understanding on how users exploit panoramic overviews to locate points in the environment. We tested four conditions, defined by the variables Shape (*Bird's Eye* or *Frontal*) and Image (*without a panorama*, as in Figure 2, and *with a panorama* of the room, generated using a Ladybug camera[4], as in Figure 1).

We recruited 4 participants from our university. We showed them a sequence of panoramas, marked one point with a green crosshair, and asked them to point to the corresponding location in the environment. All participants used all conditions. We counterbalanced the order of conditions with a balanced Latin square and randomized the crosshair position.

To isolate and accurately measure comparative performance with the visualizations, we chose a controlled lab setup. We showed panoramas on a 13.3" screen, in a window of 1024 × 768 pixels. Participants pointed with a wand and then clicked a button on the wand (clicks were recorded by a laptop via a wireless receiver). We used a wand to acquire accurate motion and timing data via an infrared tracker[5].

Afterwards, we interviewed participants and asked them to describe the strategy they used, for each shape. From the interviews, we isolated two types of strategy: using grid and wind rose to determine *body-aligned directions* (left, right, front, back), and *visual matching* of objects in the panorama with corresponding objects in the environment.

We decided to conduct three experiments to isolate the effects of the two strategies: the first study with no panorama (no visual matching), the following two studies with a panorama (to support visual matching). During the three experiments, we collected questionnaire data on expertise with panoramas (browsing, capturing), maps and games (radars, 3D graphics). Expertise was balanced within the participants.

USER STUDY 1: ONLY THE SHAPE

In the first study, we evaluate how different shapes impact on the performance of the pointing task, assuming that no panorama is available (see Figure 2).

Independent variable. Shape: *Frontal*, *Top-Down*, *Bird's Eye*.

Hypothesis. We expected a difference in time: Top-Down < Frontal and Bird's Eye < Frontal, because Top-Down and Bird's Eye, in contrast to Frontal, provide a direct representation of the mapping between panorama and environment.

[4] Ladybug is a product of Point Grey: http://www.ptgrey.com/

[5] ARTTracker1 is a product of A.R.T.: http://www.ar-tracking.de/

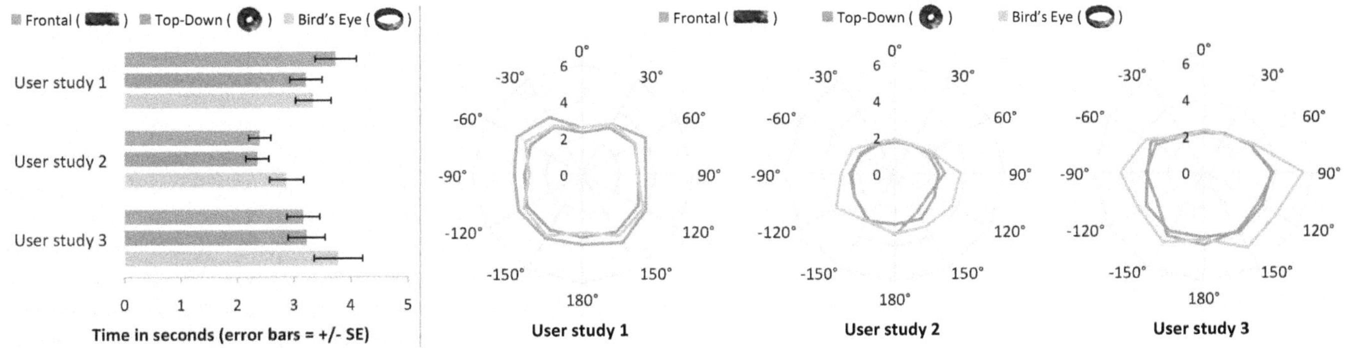

Figure 3. Left: mean time for each shape. Right: mean time for each shape and annotation angle (distance from center = seconds).

Experimental design. We selected 12 distinct intervals of size 30°, starting from [-15°, 15°]. The crosshair was assigned a random yaw angle within one of the intervals, and a constant pitch angle of 0°. Participants performed 5 repetitions of 3 (shape) × 12 (angle) trials, for a total of 180 measurements. We used balanced Latin squares to counterbalance the order of shape and angle intervals.

First, we introduced participants to the three experimental conditions. We clearly indicated to all participants the front, left, right and back lines in the visualization. Participants were allowed 6 practice trials for each shape. We instructed all participants to be as fast and accurate as possible but to give higher importance to accuracy. Finally, we conducted a short interview asking participants to describe the strategy they used to complete the task with each shape.

Apparatus. We used the same setup as in the pilot study.

Participants. We recruited twelve university students and staff (6m/6f), aged between 16 and 44 years (*mean* = 29.5, *sd* = 7.4). All participants used their dominant hand.

Results. For each of the 180 repetitions, we recorded task completion time (seconds) and unsigned error in yaw (degrees) between the target and the selection. For each shape × angle condition and participant, we calculated median time and error of the 5 repetitions.

Mean error values were 13.9° (*sd* = 4.0) for Frontal, 13.4° (*sd* = 2.6) for Top-Down and 14.1° (*sd* = 1.4) for Bird's Eye. A Friedman test did not show any effect of shape on error. In the following, we analyze time measurements under the assumption of comparable accuracy.

Mean task completion time (Figure 3, left) was 3.7s (*sd* = 1.3) for Frontal, 3.2s (*sd* = 1.0) for Top-Down, and 3.3s (*sd* = 1.1) for Bird's Eye. Since the data violates normality and sphericity (ANOVA requirements), we conducted a non-parametric Friedman test, which revealed a significant effect of shape on time ($\chi^2(2) = 16.67$, $p < .001$). Post-hoc Wilcoxon Signed Ranks tests with Bonferroni correction showed that all pair-wise differences are significant: Top-Down was significantly faster than Bird's Eye ($p = .005$) and Frontal ($p = .003$), and Bird's Eye was significantly faster than Frontal ($p = .015$). Bird's Eye was on average 3.5% slower than Top-Down; Frontal was on average 16.3% slower than Top-Down and 12.3% slower than Bird's Eye. In Figure 3 (right), we can see that Frontal was generally slower than Top-Down and Bird's Eye, besides for target locations around 0°. A Friedman test shows no effect of repetition on time, highlighting no significant learning effect.

In the interviews, participants reported orientating to body-aligned directions (left, right, front, back) using grid and wind rose, and then refining the pointing direction. Participants reported imagining themselves "in the middle of the visualization" for Top-Down and Bird's Eye. For Frontal, more "thinking" with respect to body-alignment was required.

Discussion. Our results support our initial hypothesis, and highlight a further significant difference between Top-Down and Bird's Eye. In general, we see that, if no panorama is available, users rely on body-aligned reference lines to orient themselves and refine the orientation of annotations between these lines. Shapes which correctly represent the spatial mapping of the panorama to the environment result in significantly shorter task completion times.

USER STUDY 2: ADDING A PANORAMIC IMAGE

In the second study we evaluate how user strategies and performance change when a panorama is available.

Experimental design. We used the same setup and design as in study 1. However, in this study we used a panorama of the room in which the study took place (a quiet laboratory room, see Figure 1, left). The panorama was up-to-date with the room's appearance during the study. The panorama covers 360° in yaw, and [-45°, 45°] in pitch (in most real-world cases little information is present outside such range).

Hypothesis. We expected a difference in time: Top-Down < Bird's Eye and Frontal < Bird's Eye, because we expected good readability to be advantageous for completing the task and more advantageous than the strategy used in study 1.

Participants. 12 university students and staff (6m/6f), aged between 17 and 34 years (*mean* = 24.4, *sd* = 6.5). None of the participants had taken part in the previous study.

Results. In this experiment, we calculated error as the great-circle distance (to include error in pitch) in degrees between the target and the selection. Mean error was 16.5° (*sd* = 8.4) for Frontal, 15.7° (*sd* = 7.6) for Top-Down, and 17.1°

(*sd* = 8.0) for Bird's Eye. A Friedman test showed no significant effect of shape on error.

Mean task completion time (Figure 3, left) was 2.4s (*sd* = 0.7) for Frontal, 2.4s (*sd* = 0.7) for Top-Down, and 2.9s (*sd* = 1.0) for Bird's Eye. A Friedman test revealed a significant effect of shape on time ($\chi^2(2) = 20.67$, $p < .001$). Post-hoc Wilcoxon Signed Ranks tests with Bonferroni correction showed that Bird's Eye was significantly slower than Top-Down ($p = .002$) and Frontal ($p = .002$). Bird's Eye was on average 21.9% slower than Top-Down, and 19.8% slower than Frontal. Friedman tests showed an effect of repetition on time, for all shapes ($p < .001$). However, Wilcoxon Signed Ranks tests only highlighted a significant learning effect between the first repetition and the others. This is not a problem for our analysis, since we perform it using the median values of the five repetitions.

In the interviews, participants reported looking for objects in the panorama and corresponding objects in the room (*e.g.*, a whiteboard, a fire extinguisher). For this strategy, most participants reported that Bird's Eye is inconvenient, as the sides are either not visible or warped and hard to see. One participant also reported issues with the backside of Bird's Eye, where the panorama appears mirrored. Figure 3 (right) illustrates this: we can see that Bird's Eye was slower than Top-Down and Frontal mostly around +/- 90°, in the warped or occluded regions.

Discussion. The results show that users adopt a strategy predominantly based on visual matching when a panorama is available, *independently* of the shape. As hypothesized, Top-Down and Frontal were significantly faster than Bird's Eye.

USER STUDY 3: VARYING PITCH ANGLE

In the third study, we aimed at corroborating the results from study 2 in the case of varying pitch angle.

Experimental design. Same as in study 2. In this study, the crosshair was assigned random pitch within [-45°, 45°].

Hypothesis. Same as in study 2: we expected a significant difference in task completion time: Top-Down < Bird's Eye and Frontal < Bird's Eye. This is because we expected visual matching to work also for non-zero pitch angles.

Participants. 12 university students and staff (6m/6f), aged between 23 and 50 years (*mean* = 30.1, *sd* = 7.8). None of the participants had taken part in the previous studies.

Results. Mean error was 15.0° (*sd* = 5.2) for Frontal, 16.6° (*sd* = 4.7) for Top-Down and 18.5° (*sd* = 4.3) for Bird's Eye. A Friedman test showed a significant main effect of shape on error ($\chi^2(2) = 12.17$, $p = .002$). Post-hoc tests showed a significant difference between Frontal and Bird's Eye.

Mean task completion time (Figure 3, left) was 3.8s (*sd* = 1.5) for Bird's Eye, 3.2s (*sd* = 1.1) for Top-Down, and 3.2s (*sd* = 1.0) for Frontal. A Friedman test revealed a significant effect of shape on time ($\chi^2(2) = 15.17$, $p = .001$). Post-hoc tests showed that Bird's Eye was significantly slower than Top-Down ($p = .002$) and Frontal ($p = .003$). Bird's Eye was on average 16.1% slower than Top-Down, and 17.1% slower than Frontal. A Friedman test showed no effect of repetition on time.

In the interviews, reported strategies and issues with Bird's Eye were in line with study 2. Figure 3 (right) illustrates that Bird's Eye was again slower than Top-Down and Frontal mostly in the warped areas. Participants reported that Frontal was the easiest to find the pitch of points, whereas finding the yaw was considered harder. With Top-Down, participants had issues with the outermost third of the visualization (high pitch in the panorama), due to the strong distortion effect.

Discussion. The results of this study replicate the results of the previous study for the case of varying pitch angle.

DISCUSSION AND CONCLUSION

Our results show that, in the presence of a panorama, users mainly perform visual matching of objects in the panorama with correspondences in the environment. Consequently, good readability of the panorama has primary importance in the design of a panoramic overview. As a secondary strategy – and the main one when no panorama is available – users look for body-aligned directions within the visualization. A panoramic overview designed to represent the mapping between panorama and environment provides therefore a fallback, whenever a panorama is not available.

We are looking forward to apply this work to location-based services in outdoor scenarios. Here the environment is mutable and visual matching is not always feasible. Challenging scenarios are, for example, incomplete panoramas (as in our previous work [5]), outdated panoramas, or panoramas recorded from a slightly different location (as in Wither et al. [6]). In those scenarios, we will investigate how user strategies intertwine. Our results inform us on how design choices will affect support for visual matching and communicating body-aligned directions.

Acknowledgments. Thanks to B. Kainz for the tracking setup, to S. Gustafson and all the HCI Lab at HPI for the positive discussions. This work was supported through the CDL for Handheld AR.

REFERENCES

1. Baudisch, P., Tan, D., Steedly, D., et al. Panoramic viewfinder: providing a real-time preview to help users avoid flaws in panoramic pictures. *Proceedings of OZCHI 2005*, (2005), 1–10.
2. Chittaro, L. and Burigat, S. Augmenting audio messages with visual directions in mobile guides. *Proceedings of MobileHCI 2005*, (2005), 107–114.
3. Jiang Yu Zheng. Digital route panoramas. *IEEE Multimedia 10*, (2003), 57–67.
4. Kopf, J., Chen, B., Szeliski, R., and Cohen, M. Street slide: browsing street level imagery. *ACM Transactions on Graphics (TOG) 29*, (2010), 96:1–96:8.
5. Mulloni, A., Dünser, A., and Schmalstieg, D. Zooming interfaces for augmented reality browsers. *Proceedings of Mobile-HCI 2010*, (2010), 161–170.
6. Wither, J., Tsai, Y.-T., and Azuma, R. Indirect augmented reality. *Computers & Graphics 35*, 4 (2011), 810–822.

On the Use of Virtual Environments for the Evaluation of Location-Based Applications

Arief Ernst Hühn[1], Vassilis-Javed Khan[1], Andrés Lucero[2], Paul Ketelaar[3]
[1]NHTV Breda, University for Applied Sciences, P.O. Box 391, 4800 DX Breda, The Netherlands
[2]Nokia Research Center, P.O. Box 1000, FI-33721 Tampere, Finland
[3]Radboud Universiteit, P.O. Box 9104, 6500 HE Nijmegen, The Netherlands
{huhn.a, khan.j}@ nhtv.nl; andres.lucero@nokia.com; p.ketelaar@ru.nl

ABSTRACT
User experience (UX) research on pervasive technologies faces considerable challenges regarding today's mobile context-sensitive applications: evaluative field studies lack control, whereas lab studies miss the interaction with a dynamic context. This dilemma has inspired researchers to use virtual environments (VEs) to acquire control while offering the user a rich contextual experience. Although promising, these studies are mainly concerned with usability and the technical realization of their setup. Furthermore, previous setups leave room for improvement regarding the user's immersive experience. This paper contributes to this line of research by presenting a UX case study on mobile advertising with a novel CAVE-smartphone interface. We conducted two experiments in which we evaluated the intrusiveness of a mobile location-based advertising app in a virtual supermarket. The results confirm our hypothesis that context-congruent ads lessen the experienced intrusiveness thereby demonstrating that our setup is capable of generating preliminary meaningful results with regards to UX. Furthermore, we share insights in conducting these studies.

Author Keywords
User experience evaluation; mixed reality; location-based services; pervasive computing.

ACM Classification Keywords
H.5.m [Information interfaces and presentation (e.g., HCI)]: Miscellaneous.

INTRODUCTION
The advent of new mobile devices like smartphones and tablets has contributed substantially to the momentum of the adoption of pervasive computing. Although these devices share many characteristics with their static counterpart, the desktop computer, their mobile nature enables applications to bring their functionalities into the user's dynamic context. Apart from location independence, applications also gain the ability to interact directly with the specific context of the user, due to context-sensitive technologies (e.g. camera, GPS, compass, accelerometer, etc.). Augmented reality and location-based services (or a combination of these) on a mobile device are popular examples that tie in closely with the ever-changing environment of the user and have attracted much attention from advertisers and marketing scholars [10]. However, advertising research is limited when it comes to the evaluation of context-sensitive applications because of the lack of means to deal with the context-prone and dynamic research setting pervasive technology poses. Because of the lack of better alternatives advertising researchers mostly focused on simple forms of advertising (simple push SMS/MMS-advertising) and their methods generally relied on surveys with scenario descriptions [4,6,40,42,43], thereby generating questionable results.

In contrast, to the field of human-computer interaction (HCI), mobility and context-sensitivity are already familiar challenges when it comes to the evaluation of pervasive applications. Until relatively recently mainly two types of studies were engaged to evaluate mobile applications: laboratory and field-test studies [19]. Researchers have been divided about which method is more effective and efficient [30]. Main objections to field studies are concerned with the lack of control and the expensive and time-consuming endeavours associated with this type of research [21, 35]. In contrast, lab studies do not offer an immersive and interactive context for the user, thereby overlooking possible important influences that determine the everyday practice of these pervasive applications [21]. Furthermore, some mobile applications are currently difficult to deploy because the supporting technology (e.g. indoor positioning, RFID, etc.) is not yet in place [5].

These shortcomings have given rise to a new line of research where lab studies have been extended with the utilization of virtual environments (VEs). This offers participants a dynamic and interactive context during their experience while researchers gain a controllable and malleable research setting [24]. Although very promising, the aforementioned studies are mostly limited to usability studies. Moreover, the setups from these studies leave room for improvement in terms of display methods, navigation, and interactivity between the VE and the mobile app.

This paper builds on this line of work by introducing a working concept with a distinct combination of features: a mixed reality setup consisting of an interactive 360° CAVE (Cave Automated Virtual Environment) installation interacting with a location-based advertising application running on a smartphone [18]. To show the potential relevance of this approach we present a case study in which we conduct two experiments with this setup. These studies evaluate the UX of a location-based advertising application within the context of a virtual supermarket. Based on literature and empirical data, it is our aim to tentatively answer the following explorative research question: *Can we generate meaningful research conclusions about the UX of pervasive advertising apps in our mixed reality setup?* The answers and provided insights should help advertising and HCI researchers to conduct virtual reality aided evaluation studies of their own, thereby benefitting the design process of location based advertising applications and pervasive applications in general.

Before we discuss the specifics of our case study, we present the limitations in advertising research and review the different mobile evaluation methods in HCI.

BACKGROUND

Mobile Advertising Research

Since the advent of pervasive computing the advertising business has increasingly concerned itself with mobile technology as means to disseminate ads. As a consequence, mobile advertising has attracted the attention of advertising scholars to scrutinize its effectiveness. These studies investigated several mobile ad properties like for example text versus graphic [43], push versus pull [40], permission based versus non-permission based [8] situational context [42], location congruent versus location incongruent [4] and their influence on subjective experience either based in cognition or attitude (e.g. ad irritation, ad intrusiveness and attitude towards the mobile ad, perceived usefulness). Subsequently Theory of Reasoned Action [14], Theory of Planned Behavior [3] and Technology Acceptance Model [9] offer a theoretical framework which links cognition and attitude to the behavioral intentions and behaviors that are of relevance to advertisers (e.g. intention to use a technology, intention to buy).

Results are usually obtained through surveys using scenario descriptions of use-context. Marketing studies using real encounters with mobile applications (e.g. [23]) are on the other hand scarce. Although these scenario-based studies still yield interesting results regarding expectations people have, they are questionable since the participants have not interacted with the application itself, let alone within the use context [42, 43].

This lack of data based on real contextual interaction signals the need for new approaches to study these phenomena. In this respect HCI methodology could be valuable to the field of mobile ad research since it is already familiar with the challenges of evaluating mobile applications. Mobile advertising on the other hand serves as an appropriate vehicle to illustrate the potential of these evaluation methods within the field of HCI.

Mobile Application Evaluation: Field Versus Lab

Field studies are praised for taking the real life context into account. When it comes to studying the UX of mobile context-sensitive apps, where a dynamic context is salient, field studies seem to be even more appropriate. However, methods examining phenomena in a real life context are not widely used [19]. A possible reason is that these methods are time consuming, costly [35] and sometimes rely on third parties to acquire the necessary infrastructure [42]. Moreover, some future concepts are hard to deploy in the real world, due to current technical constraints [5].

In addition to these practical issues, there are also some methodological challenges that keep researchers from using field studies on a frequent basis when evaluating mobile apps. Kjeldskov and Stage [20] argue that the mobile nature results in an unstable context with detrimental consequences. They report difficulties in terms of observation, manipulation and control of the use-context. In line with this conclusion Roto et al. [35] report that investigating mobile phone use in the wild with a quasi-experiment *"is a laborious method and requires careful planning and vast technological resources."*

Instead, a great amount of user studies is conducted within laboratory settings. Kjeldskov & Graham [19] conclude that 71% of the mobile evaluation studies they reviewed take place in laboratories. The main advantage is the control researchers have on the use context thereby excluding confounding variables and securing reproducibility. Certain evaluations are reasonably executable in lab settings when they only take the necessary environmental aspects into account. Lumsden [27] for example evaluated the quality of three mobile speech recognition systems where the environmental noise was artificially recreated with a 7.1 surround system.

Nonetheless there are drawbacks to laboratory studies, such as the lack of a realistic and immersive context [19]. Although real life environments can be recreated physically within lab studies to a certain extent, most mobile use contexts ask for an extensive and dynamic environment instead of a small sized living room or shop, as is the case with most lab studies (e.g. [23]). In the case of evaluation of context-aware mobile systems the limitations of lab studies are even more prevalent since context not only serves as a backdrop, but also plays an active role in the use of the application [1,36]. Contrary to the findings of Kaikonen et al. [16] and Kjeldskov et al. [21], Nielsen et al. [30] and

Duh et al. [12] found more usability problems in the field than in the lab attributed to a different interaction style, cognitive load and a richer environment in the field.

These shortcomings on both field and lab studies, point out the need of an approach that provides on the one hand a controllable setting and on the other hand a rich context users can relate to and interact with while keeping costs, time and organizational effort as low as possible [20,24,36].

Evaluation with Virtual Environments (VEs)

Inspired by the shortcomings of these traditional methods recent studies have tried to address these issues by using virtual environments (VEs). Ubiwise [5] is one of the first research efforts to evaluate pervasive applications with the assistance of a VE. Since that first attempt there have been several other prototypes presented with the same approach [5,24,32,34,36,38,39].

Not only do VEs improve control [24,39], but they also give the researcher the possibility to test mobile concepts that are hard to deploy in the real world [5]. Furthermore, the opportunities regarding measurement will improve when conducting studies with the use of VEs. Advanced methods like psychophysiological measurements, video recording and behavioral tracking are easier to implement because the researcher is given a stable research setting which simplifies the placement of measuring equipment. In the study by Schellenbach et al. [36], VEs enabled them to use a motion capture system to measure the effect of specific interactions with a mobile navigation system on the gait of participants. To set up such a motion capture system in the field or recreate the use-context (in their case study a museum) would be a daunting task.

When comparing the different setups reported in literature, we noted important similarities and differences. Most of these setups have in common that they use hybrid simulations, i.e. "*setups that rely on the integration and combination of the real and virtual world.*" This enables participants to directly interact with a physical mobile device [24], whereas full virtual simulations would have represented the device virtually, forcing its interaction to take place indirectly (e.g via keyboard and mouse), which could disrupt the usage [24]. In terms of differences we noted that some evaluation studies used desktop setups (e.g. [5,24]) while others have moved to large-scale panoramic screens [39,38,22], which increases the feeling of presence and immersiveness [26,39]. Although not necessarily detrimental for their research goal, these screens displayed only environments using prerecorded photos or video lacking the possibility to navigate through the represented environment. In contrast, evaluations that relied on a navigable environment used 3D computer rendered environments [5,24,32,36]. Navigation style within these studies ranged from traditional input methods to more natural forms like treadmill based movement. The latter seems preferable since controls involving the mapping of body movement not only evoke higher presence [37] but also seem to result in a better representation of the cognitive state during the use of applications in the real world [39]. In addition, audio, haptic and olfactory stimuli in a VE could also increase the sense of presence even further [11]. Nonetheless the development of these test beds cannot only rely on theory but should also be validated in the field to strengthen its external validity. Concordantly, several studies have already planned to replicate their evaluation study in the field [22,36,39].

Based on these comparisons we can reason that our CAVE-smartphone interface apparently extends earlier approaches by having a distinct combination of features: a 360° view CAVE, surround sound, navigation through full-body movement and the direct interaction between virtual location and the mobile application.

Furthermore, we have not yet encountered a study within VE aided evaluation focusing on the UX of pervasive applications. Instead most studies have focused on usability evaluation and the technical realization of these test beds. Our case study gives some preliminary insights into how VEs can contribute to the UX evaluation of mobile apps.

UX and Ad Intrusiveness

UX in HCI is a very broad concept and still undergoes semantic negotiations. Generally there are two approaches to UX: reductionist and holistic [17]. The reductionist approach chooses to identify distinct psychological constructs, while the holistic approach looks at experience as unique, highly depending on the specific situation and people. Since our case study is grounded in the motivation of advertisers, we are specifically interested in the way location-based applications can improve the user's experience of advertising. This involves a construct that takes into account the subjective experience of the user in relation to: 1) the medium (application), 2) the content of the medium (in our case advertising), and 3) the context. Moreover, the construct needs to be a good predictor for behavioral intention/behavior to be of use to advertisers. These requirements obviously place us within the reductionist approach.

The concept of perceived intrusiveness, originally used within persuasive communication, concerns itself with the experience people have when their cognitive processes are interrupted by an advertisement, which have proven to be good indicators for behavioral intentions (e.g. ad avoidance, [25,28]. Intrusiveness regarding context is originally defined by Ha [15] as 'the degree to which ads in a media vehicle interrupt the flow of an editorial unit'. Li et al. [25] expands the concept by redefining "editorial unit" as "all new environments in which ads appear", thereby including advertising formats that not only interrupt media content but also other contexts, as is the case with mobile advertising. Since mobile devices are ubiquitous due to their mobile nature, mobile ads can potentially interrupt the user anytime and anywhere [6]. Location-based applications offer the opportunity to adjust the ad to the physical environment of the user. Edwards et al. [13] state that context-congruent ads can lower the intrusiveness by reducing the divergent knowledge structures that would normally be activated by context-independent ads. Based on the existing theory, our hypothesis for our case study is:

H1: Location-based ads will be perceived as less intrusive compared to location-independent ads.

METHOD

Before presenting the two experiments, we describe the general setup and procedure that both experiments shared.

General Setup

The experiments took place within a virtual supermarket simulated by a CAVE. A supermarket seemed to be the most suitable setting since mobile ads are more effective if they are aimed at low-priced and frequently bought products [8]. The VE (modelled in Maya and rendered in OGRE) is projected onto four rear- projection screens (each 3.6 meters wide by 2.6 meters high). The screens form a closed space, thereby offering the participant a 360° view of the environment. Participants can move in the virtual setting with the help of a head-tracking system based on four Wii-mote IR cameras. In contrast with head-mounted displays, the CAVE does not block out the physical world, which offers the opportunity to use physical objects and the representation of the participant's own physical body. In this particular case, it gave us the possibility to use an actual smartphone, with which participants were able to receive location-based ads. The tracking device (Figure 1, left) determines the participant's head position in the physical room, which is then used to control motion in the virtual supermarket. In essence, the participant acts as a "human joystick": when the participant stands in the centre of the CAVE the virtual camera stands still, whereas when the participant takes one step in a certain direction, the virtual camera moves accordingly, thus giving the illusion of movement within the virtual space. The participant is able to turn and step in every direction relative to the CAVE's centre. The simulation is also sensitive to the magnitude of the participant's distance from the centre of the physical room. This distance, determines the speed with which a participant walks within the environment. The simulation also corrects the first person view for the vertical axis. Thus, in the case in which one, for example, jumped or ducked the simulation corrected the perspective according to the vertical position of the participant's head. When it comes to shopping within the supermarket our simulation does not yet support interaction with virtual products. To simulate the act of selecting a product, participants were asked to make a grabbing gesture, without actually attempting to interact with the virtual product (Figure 1, left). When the participant made this grabbing gesture, they received auditory feedback.

Figure 1. Left: Participant (wearing a headtracker and holding smartphone) makes a 'grabbing' gesture in the virtual supermarket Right:. The chewing gum ad (study 1) after entering trigger area. With 'know more' & 'no, thanks' buttons the participant can pull more info.

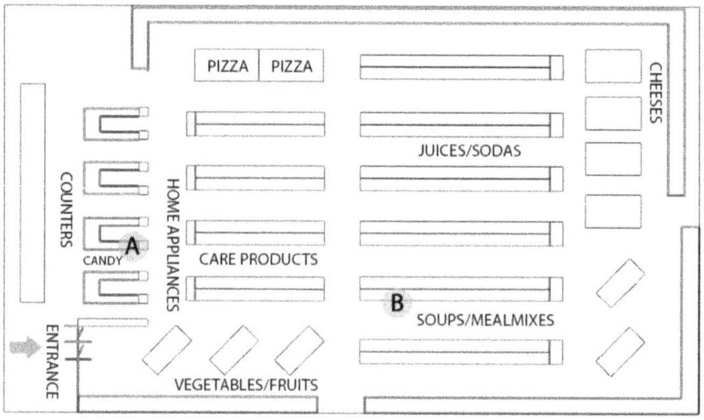

Figure 2. Floor plan of the virtual supermarket; location-congruent trigger area study 1 (A). Location incongruent area study 1 (B). Location (in)congruent area study 2 (B)

The interior of the supermarket (Figure 2), with regards to corporate style and spatial arrangement, was based on common denominators found in stores of popular Dutch supermarkets. The entire supermarket inventory was apparent and about one sixth of the shelves were filled with products at the time of the experiments. In the future it will be filled with a representative product set.

An Android application was developed, which connected the phone with the CAVE through Bluetooth. The application would play an audio message, vibrate and present the ad to participants. The application offered the option of receiving or rejecting more information about the product offer by using yes/no buttons. This ad was presented when the user was within a specific trigger area of the virtual supermarket.

General Procedure

During the briefing of both experiments we covered different topics: interacting with the smartphone and the CAVE, shopping instructions, notice for the slight risk of physical inconveniences (dizziness and nausea) due to disorientation in the CAVE, the length of the experiment (~30 minutes) and the confidentiality clause regarding the collected data. In addition, participants received tasks they had to complete during their virtual supermarket experience. These tasks involved doing shopping and varied slightly for each study to serve the specific research goal. After the briefing, participants were led to the CAVE where the head tracker was mounted and calibrated according to the specific height of the participant. Depending on the group the participant belonged to, the researcher had to start the corresponding supermarket version (congruent or incongruent). After the experiment the participant was asked to fill out a questionnaire.

STUDY 1: PILOT

Our aim with our pilot study was to investigate the user's experienced intrusiveness when receiving a location-based ad. For clarity reasons we repeat our hypothesis:

H1: Location-based ads will be perceived as less intrusive compared to location-independent ads.

Experimental Design

A between-subjects design was used to test the hypothesis. Participants were randomly assigned to two conditions. Location-congruent: The ad with product X was presented when the user was on location A, in proximity of product X. Location-incongruent: The ad with product X was presented when the user was on location B, not in proximity of product X. Proximity was set to 0.5 meter distance to the product. Product X was chewing gum; location A was at the counter close to the chewing gum; location B was at the soup shelf instead (Figure 2). The ad advertised chewing gum (Figure 1, right).

Participants

While having 27 participants, for the results described in this paper we decided to include the 12 participants whose experiment proceeded according to protocol; i.e. they noticed the ad on the mobile phone. These 12 consisted of 8 who witnessed the location-incongruent setup (4 male and 4 female; average age: 23) and 4 who witnessed the location-congruent (2 male and 2 female; average age: 21). All of them were international university students. Moreover, they all owned a mobile phone and were familiar with smartphones equipped with a touch screen interface. For their effort participants received a 5€ gift coupon.

Tasks

The initial task was to navigate through the supermarket for a few minutes to get familiar with the controls and the interaction. Next, participants were asked to go to the main entrance of the supermarket to receive the second task: buying a pizza. While executing the second task participants were given a pre-scripted phone call before reaching the pizza refrigerators. During this call the extra task of getting a soft drink and a soup package was given. After completing the task participants had to go to counter number 3. The shelves above the conveyor belt at that counter were filled with products including the advertised chewing gum. Depending on the condition a participant was assigned to, the chewing gum ad was triggered at one of two locations. The location-congruent condition triggered the ad within 0.5 meters of the chewing gum shelf (Figure 3, left) while the location-incongruent condition triggered the same ad within 0.5 meters of the soup shelf (Figure 3, right). The half-meter radius was determined by the researchers based on the observation that people usually enter this area when they want to look at products, whereas people that just walk by in the aisle do not trigger the ad.

Figure 3. Left: Participant from the context-congruent group receives a chewing gum mobile ad in front of the chewing gum shelf. Right: Participant from the context-incongruent group receives a chewing gum mobile ad in front of the soup shelf.

These tasks ensured that both groups visited their trigger area without giving away our research goal. In the case of the location-congruent group we did not need to ask participants to seek the chewing gum shelf, since they would visit it while checking out at counter 3. For the location-incongruent group the task to pick up soup ensured all participants within the incongruent group experienced similar conditions while receiving the mobile ad.

Measurement

Immediately after the virtual shopping experience, participants filled out a questionnaire that assessed their perceived ad intrusiveness of the received mobile ad. In order to take into account the complexity of an everyday commercial setting we also measured several control variables that have proven to affect the evaluation of advertising and location-based advertising. Based on our literature study we included the following scales: product involvement [41], privacy concerns [7] and the attitude towards advertising in general [29].

Results

The 12 respondents rated homogeneous with regards to the control variables, thereby excluding the possibility of these variables explaining the measured effect. The median scores on the ad intrusiveness scale for the congruent and incongruent group were respectively 3 and 5 (7 point scale). Based on the Mann Withney U test we conducted we can conclude that the median scores on the intrusiveness scale differed significantly ($z=-2.722$ $p=0.003$). It can be further tentatively concluded that mobile context-congruent ads lead to less ad intrusiveness than mobile ads which are not context-congruent.

Figure 4. 'Incongruent Group' shelf setup (left): all six shelves offer only meal mixes. 'Congruent Group' shelf setup (right): top three shelves offer soup, including the advertised soups (highlighted); bottom three shelves offer meal mixes

STUDY 2: LARGE SCALE

Our second study approaches the same research hypotheses as our pilot. For clarity reasons, we state once again:

H1: Location-based ads will be perceived as less intrusive compared to location-independent ads.

For this study we also extended our theoretical scope to the consequences of intrusiveness for behavioural intentions. Theory of Reasoned Action [14], Theory of Planned Behavior [3] and Technology Acceptance Model [9] predicts that positive perceptions lead to a favourable attitude, which in turn has a positive influence on behavioural intentions. This theoretical framework has already been successfully applied to intrusiveness in the context of web ads [28]. Thus, we hypothesize:

H2: Lower level of perceived ad intrusiveness results in more favourable attitude toward the mobile advertising application

H3: Attitude towards the mobile advertising application is positively related to the intention to use the mobile advertising application

In the following section we present the motivations for the changes we introduced compared to our pilot (Study 1).

Experimental Design

For this study we again used a between-subjects design to test our hypotheses. Participants were randomly assigned to two conditions: 1) Location-congruent: the mobile ad with product x was presented when the user entered location B where product x, product group X and product group Y were available, 2) Location-incongruent: the mobile ad with product x was presented when the user entered location B where only product group Y was available (Figure 4). Contrary to study 1, we kept location constant and manipulated the products on the shelf to keep as many circumstantial factors constant as possible. Location B could be found approximately in the centre of the supermarket and covered the space with again a radius of 0.5 meter from the manipulated shelf (Figure 2). For product x, a well-known Dutch soup product was used. Accordingly, the ad showed an offer with this specific soup product (Figure 5). Further, product group X consisted of soups and product group Y consisted of meal mixes.

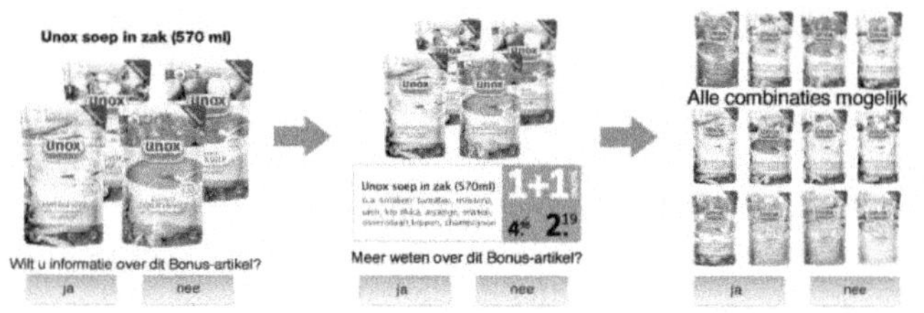

Figure 5. The soup ad for study 2 (left) the participants received when they reached the trigger location. Subsequently, participants could pull more information about the offer by using 'yes' and 'no' buttons (middle, right).

Setup

Compared to the pilot study, we improved the realism of our scenario by creating a simple UI of the application using the supermarket's corporate style. Furthermore, participants had to start the application themselves in contrast to the pilot where the application was already started and was running in the background. In this way we wanted to convey the idea to the participant that this is an opt-in service within the environment of an application instead of a simple push message.

Participants

We recruited 70 participants through a marketing research company. From the 70 participants 15 participants received the ad outside the perimeter as a consequence of an unstable Bluetooth connection and 2 participants did not notice the ad. The remaining 53 participants (31 male, 22 female; age range 17-64 years, M= 28.57 years, SD=11.60) consisted of 26 who witnessed the location-incongruent setup (15 males and 11 females; M=28.96 years, SD=14.22) and 27 who witnessed the location-congruent (16 male and 11 female; M=28.19 years, SD=11.22). Moreover, they all owned a mobile phone and were familiar with smartphones equipped with a touch screen interface. For their effort participants received a 5€ coupon.

Tasks

Participants were given two tasks during the briefing: first, they freely navigated in the supermarket for a few minutes to get familiar with the controls and the interaction. Second, they had to pick five different food products and then to go to the counter. The central location of our trigger area, the task of shopping five products and the limited product set of the virtual supermarket ensured that both groups visited the trigger area. In this way we did not have any specific instructions for participants to visit the manipulated shelf, thereby keeping our research goal concealed.

Measurement

After the virtual shopping experience, a questionnaire assessed the perceived intrusiveness (C's alpha=.841), based on the scale of Li et al. [25], attitude toward the mobile application (single item) based on a scale of Bergkvist and Rossiter and measured their intention to use the application (C's alpha=.921) based on a scale of

Kowatsch and Maas [23]. As was the case with our pilot study we also took into account relevant control variables: product involvement (C's alpha=.842) [41], the attitude towards advertising in general (C's alpha=.841) [29] and personal innovativeness (C's alpha=.845) [2].

Results

The variable *intrusiveness* shows a statistically significant higher value with the incongruent-group (M=3.15, SD=0.90) than with the congruent-group (M=2.45, SD=1.07); (t(51, N=53)=-2.546, p<.05), thereby pointing in the direction expected by H1. The ANCOVA (see Table 1) confirms the significant effect of the congruent/incongruent condition when controlled for *product involvement* and *attitude toward advertising in general*. It also shows that the congruent/incongruent condition has the greatest effect (η^2=0,094). H1 is thereby supported by the data. Furthermore, we tested the remaining hypotheses by conducting a regression analysis. We once again took the congruent/incongruent condition (incongruent=0, congruent=1) into account and found a significant effect in the expected direction (β=-0.286, p<.05). The congruent/incongruent condition explains together with the control variables 23.2% of the variance of *intrusiveness*. *Intrusiveness* in turn has a significant effect on the *attitude toward the app* (β=-0.173, p<.05) and is responsible for 14.1% of the variance, thereby supporting H2. *Attitude toward the app* has a positive influence on 'intention to use the application' (β=0.393, p<.001) when controlled for *innovativeness* (H3 supported). Together they explain 48.1% of the variance of *intention to use the application*.

Variable	*df*	*MS*	*F*	partial η^2
Product involvement	1	1.621	1.826	.036
Attitude ad in general	1	4.369	4.921	.091*
Context congruency	1	4.514	5.085	.094*
Error	49	.888		
Total	53			
Corrected Total	52			

Table 1. ANCOVA for 'intrusiveness'

GENERAL RESULTS AND LESSONS LEARNED

The results from both studies show us that location congruency is a significant factor when it comes to lowering the intrusiveness people experience when using a mobile (advertising) application. Furthermore, users of a context-congruent application tend to form more positive attitudes toward the application and as a consequence are more likely to use it in the future.

In addition to the gathered quantitative data, these studies also provide insight into the specifics of conducting pervasive application evaluations using VEs. With regards to the setup, scenario and experimental design we had to be creative to deal with the challenges that this kind of research poses. Firstly, given the fact that the setup did not support any interaction with the virtual products, the participants were asked to make a 'grabbing' gesture towards the product of their choice. To give participants feedback on whether they were successful in their attempt, a 'wizard of Oz' procedure was implemented: as soon as the participant made the grabbing gesture the researcher manually played a confirmation sound. Since the CAVE installation formed a closed space, separating participants from the researcher, the use of video cameras was essential in observing the participant's actions within the CAVE.

When it comes to the experimental design, the concept of 'context-congruency' can be operationalized by manipulating one of the following factors: 1) by altering the product in the advertising application, 2) by altering the location where the ad is triggered (thereby obviously altering the context in which the ad is received) or 3) by replacing the advertised product in the shelf with a different product. In our pilot study (Study 1) we altered the trigger location thus manipulating the aforementioned factor 2. This resulted in the 'context-congruent' group receiving a chewing gum ad at the counter where chewing gum was displayed while the 'context incongruent' group received the chewing gum ad at the soup shelf. Although altering the location seemed a rational choice, we realized that it compromises the requirement for experiments to keep circumstantial factors constant. Receiving an ad at the supermarket counter compared to receiving an ad at a supermarket aisle not only manipulates context-congruency but also possibly includes other situational factors that could unintentionally affect our dependent variable. Therefore, in our second study we decided to keep the location of the trigger area for both groups the same and to change the products that are within the vicinity of the trigger location instead. Because of the plasticity of our VE it was fairly easy to replace the congruent products (soup) with incongruent products (meal mixes). The third aforementioned factor we could manipulate, i.e. changing the product within the ad, was discarded as an alternative since it could affect the participant's product involvement towards the advertised product, which in turn influences their experienced intrusiveness [42].

When scrutinizing the effect of context-congruency, it is important for the research goal that participants reach the trigger area and notice the products. The importance lies in controlling any biases participants might experience in case their task description includes products in the ad's location-triggering area. Since the empty shelves were already common in the virtual supermarket, we were able to empty the opposing shelf to ensure that the participants would only notice the (in)congruent products while receiving the ad with their application. In addition, we placed the trigger area in a central location of the supermarket to increase its accessibility. This once again illustrates the benefits of the dynamic configuration of the VE in helping the researcher to adjust the setting to the needs of the study. Furthermore, participants can also be 'guided' towards the trigger area through the task scenario. In our first study we used the shopping list and counter to draw people towards their respective trigger areas. The second study had a different approach. During our pilot we experienced that the limited product set of the supermarket already 'forced' the participants to visit all the filled shelves, since there were not many other places of interest. Just by giving a generic task where participants had to shop for five products sufficiently increased the chance they reached the trigger area. This caused all participants to visit the trigger area.

CONCLUSION

This case study presented a setup with a CAVE-smartphone interface that was used to evaluate the UX of a location-based advertising application. We conducted two experiments that evaluated the perceived intrusiveness of location congruent versus location incongruent mobile ads. The results from both studies show a statistical significant difference between the two groups; participants receiving a location-congruent mobile ad perceived it as less intrusive compared to participants receiving a location-incongruent mobile ad, thus confirming our central hypothesis. Furthermore, our second study confirmed our other hypotheses: users of a context-congruent application tend to form more positive attitudes toward the application and as a consequence are more likely to use it in the future and to buy the advertised product. Thereby the results seem to support the underlying theory [3,9,14,25] and contribute to the knowledge of persuasive communication by applying the construct of intrusiveness to pervasive advertising.

A more abstract, yet tentative methodological conclusion (see Limitations and Future Work section) is that such a setup enables mobile and pervasive computing researchers as well as advertisers/advertising scholars to conduct experimental studies to yield meaningful results regarding the UX of mobile applications. Our literature study showed that such a setup has substantial advantages when compared to field and lab studies. When compared to field studies, such a setup can help researchers control and manipulate context parameters, enable the replication of studies and apply extensive measurement. When compared to lab studies, this setup can introduce malleable, immersive and interactive experiences with the envisioned context of use [39]. As described earlier, we were able to manipulate location (study 1) and context (study 2) fairly easily when compared to the effort one would need in the field. In contrast, Nurmi et al. [31] conducted a field study in a real supermarket and reported difficulties in modifying the environment due to restrictions from the supermarket. Compared to the existing literature our setup is a useful expansion as it offers a distinct combination of features like an interactive virtual environment (VE), 360° view, navigation controls with body movement and a virtual localizing system interacting with a physical smartphone. Nonetheless, its value needs to be verified by comparing this setup with other approaches.

Furthermore, based in our experience we provided guidelines for researchers planning to use such setups for evaluating context-aware pervasive computing applications.

Naturally, developing such an installation would initially require a considerable investment, but in the long run it would save time and money when it comes to performing user evaluations [24]. Furthermore, since the setting as well as the pervasive technology infrastructure takes place within the simulated environment, it does not rely on third parties for the operationalization.

LIMITATIONS AND FUTURE WORK

Although our results resonate with theory and expectations, they remain tentative due to certain limitations. Since we have not yet conducted a validation study, there is still uncertainty with regards to the external validity. We see two important factors that could have decreased the generalization of our results. In the first place we observe a potential tradeoff between the ecological validity and the internal validity. To strengthen the internal validity of our study we had to investigate the relationship between the UX and context-congruency within a vacuum of some sort. Conducting the experiments within a VE helped us achieve that goal, due to high control and manipulability; we were able to customize the shelves and filter out confounding variables. However, these adjustments could have affected the outcome in such a way that the results cannot speak for the use context we wanted to investigate in the first place (i.e. real world supermarkets). This obviously has little to do with the use of VEs but more with the inherent properties of an experimental setup that investigates a specific causal relationship.

Secondly, we can speculate about the possibility that the limitations of our setup and simulation affected the ecological validity. The interaction with the VE, like the navigation style and manipulation of objects differed from physical reality. The absence of a complete product set is also a noteworthy difference. Furthermore, the presence of supporting equipment (head tracking system, beamers etc.) could have impaired the level of immersiveness. Validation studies that compare the results of a CAVE with a real life supermarket, could give some insight in to what extent the results are affected by these limitations. However, we must note that these shortcomings are not necessarily inherent to the principle of a virtual reconstruction of UX, but are caused by our specific operationalization and by the limitations of current technology. As technology progresses certain aspects of the setup could be improved. In our case we are already in the process of extending our product set, improving the graphics and have already replaced the Wii-mote based head-tracking with the help of a Microsoft Kinect, thereby making the facilitating technology transparent to the user. Finally this issue raises the philosophical question whether such setups can become truly invisible and match field studies in realism. A pragmatic approach would be that the facilitating technology should be as unobtrusive as possible so that the participant can focus better on the reconstructed UX. Results from validation studies should guide us in this process of improvement.

In addition, the setup could also affect the outcome as a consequence of Hawthorne effects. Even though participants got the chance to get used to the setup, there is the risk that they behaved differently because the setup still reminded them they were taking part in an experiment.

Apart from the external validity we also see some room for improvement in terms of measurement. In our case we relied on questionnaires to gather our data. Even though the construct of intrusiveness is usually measured with self-report Likert scales, the delay between the stimulus and measurement could have affected the outcome. Since the use of the CAVE setup allows for elaborate measurements, direct measures like observations or psychophysiological measurements should be considered in the future.

ACKNOWLEDGMENTS

We would like to extend our gratitude to our financial sponsors: the Dutch Ministry of Education, Culture and Science (OCW), RAAK scheme (RAAK Pro) and Popai Benelux. Moreover, we would like to thank Hans Bouwknegt, Koos Nuijten and Marnix van Gisbergen for their essential contribution to this project. A special thanks goes out to our colleague Nils Deslé for his exceptional work on developing the virtual supermarket.

REFERENCES

1. Abowd, G. and Mynatt, E. Charting past, present and future research in ubiquitous computing. *ACM Trans. Comput.-Hum. Interact. 7*, 1 (March 2000), 29-58
2. Agarwal, R. and Prasad, J. The role of innovation characteristics and perceived voluntariness in the acceptance of information technologies. *Decision Sciences 28,* 3 (1997), 557–582.
3. Ajzen, I. The Theory of Planned Behavior. *Organizational Behavior and Human Decision Processes 50,* 2 (1991), 179-211.
4. Banerjee, S. and Dholakia, R.R. Mobile advertising: does location-based advertising work? *International Journal of Mobile Marketing 3,* 2 (2008), 68-74.
5. Barton J.J. and Vijayaraghavan, V. Ubiwise: A ubiquitous wireless infrastructure simulation environment. Tech. report HP Labs, 2002.
6. Bauer, H.H., Reichardt, T., Barnes, S.J. and Neumann M.M. Driving Consumer Acceptance of Mobile Marketing: A Theoretical Framework and Empirical Study. *Journal of Electronic Commerce Research 6*, 3 (2005), 181-192.
7. Barkhuus, L. and Dey, A. Location-based services for mobile telephony: A study of users' privacy concerns. *Proc. INTERACT '03,* IOS Press (2003).
8. Barwise, P. and Strong, C. Permission-Based Mobile Advertising. *Journal of Interactive Marketing 16*, 1 (2002), 14-24.
9. Davis, F.D. Perceived usefulness, perceived ease of use, and user acceptance of information technology. *MIS Quarterly 13* (1989), 319-340.
10. Dhar, S. and Varshney, U. Challenges and business models for Mobile Location Based Services and Advertising. *Commun. ACM 54, 5 (May 2011)*, 121-129.
11. Dinh, H.Q., Walker, N., Song, C., Kobayashi, A., and Hodges, L.F. Evaluating the Importance of Multi-sensory Input on Memory and the Sense of Presence in Virtual Environments. *Proc. VR'99,* IEEE (1999), 222.
12. Duh, H.B.-L., Tan, G.C.B. and Chen, V.H.-h. Usability Evaluation for Mobile Device: A Comparison of Laboratory and Field Tests. *Proc. Mobile HCI '06,* ACM Press (2006), 181-186.
13. Edwards, M., Li, H. and Lee, J-H. Forced exposure and psychological reactance: Antecedents and consequences of the perceived intrusiveness of pop-up ads. *Journal of Advertising 31* (2002), 83-95.
14. Fishbein, M. and Ajzen, I. *Belief, Attitude, intention and behavior: An introduction to theory and research.* Addison-Wesley, 1975.
15. Ha, L. Observations: advertising clutter in consumer magazines: dimensions and effects. *Journal of Advertising Research 36*, (1996), 76-83.
16. Kaikkonen, A., Kallio, T., Kekäläinen, A., Kankainen, A. and Cankar, M. Usability testing of mobile applic*ations: A comp*arison between laboratory and field testing. *Journal of Usability Studies 1*, 1 (2005), 4-16.
17. Karapanos, E. *Quantifying Diversity in User Experience.* PhD Thesis, Eindhoven University of Technology, 2010.
18. Khan, V.J., Nuijten, K. and Deslé, N. Pervasive Evaluation Application within Virtual Environments. *Proc. PECCS '11*, 261-264.
19. Kjeldskov J. and Graham C. A Review of MobileHCI Research Methods. *Proc. MobileHCI '03,* LNCS Springer-Verlag (2003), 317-335.

20. Kjeldskov, J. and Stage, J. New techniques for usability evaluation of mobile systems. *International Journal of Human-Computer Studies 60*, 5-6 (2004), 599-620.

21. Kjeldskov J., Skov M.B., Als B.S. and Høegh R.T. Is it Worth the Hassle? Exploring the Added Value of Evaluating the Usability of Context-Aware Mobile Systems in the Field. *Proc. MobileHCI '04,* Springer-Verlag (2004), 61-73.

22. Klompmaker, F., Stern, C., Reimann, C. and Santelmann, H. A Mock-up System for the Early Testing of Location Based Services. *In: Mobile Interaction with the Real World 2007/5th Workshop on HCI in Mobile Guides. Singapore: ACM*

23. Kowatsch, T. and Maass, W. In-store consumer behavior: How mobile recommendation agents influence usage intentions, product purchases, and store preferences. *Computers in Human Behavior 26*, (2010) 697-704.

24. Leichtenstern, K., André, E. and Rehm, M. Using the Hybrid Simulation for Early User Evaluations of Pervasive Interactions. *Proc. of NordiCHI '10*, ACM Press (2010), 315-324.

25. Li, H., Edwards, S.M. and Lee, J. Measuring the Intrusiveness of Advertisements: Scale Development and Validation. *Journal of Advertising 31* (2002), 37-47.

26. Lin, J.J.W., Duh, H.B.L., Abi-Rached, H., Parker, D.E., and Furness, T.A. Effects of Field of View on Presence, Enjoyment, Memory, and Simulator Sickness in a Virtual Environment. *Proc. VR '02,* IEEE (2002), 164-171.

27. Lumsden, J., Kondratova, I. and Durling, S. Investigating Microphone Efficacy for Facilitation of Mobile Speech-Based Data Entry. *Proc.BCS-HCI '07,* BCS Swinton (2007), 89-97.

28. McCoy, S., Everard, A., Polak, P. and Galletta, D.F. An experimental study of Antecedants and consequences of online ad-intrusiveness. *Journal of Human-Computer Interaction 24*, 7 (2008), 672-699.

29. Muehling, D.D., Stoltman, J.J. and Grossbart, S. The impact of comparative advertising on levels of message involvement. *Journal of Advertising 19*, 4, 41-50.

30. Nielsen, C.M., Overgaard, M., Pedersen, M.B., Stage, J. and Stenild, S. It's worth the hassle!: the added value of evaluating the usability of mobile systems in the field. *Proc. NordiCHI '06*, ACM Press (2006), 272-280.

31. Nurmi, P., Salovaara, A., Bhattacharya, S., Pulkkinen, T. and Kahl, G. Influence of Landmark-Based Navigation Instructions on User Attention in Indoor Smart Spaces. *Proc. IUI'11,* ACM Press (2011), 33-42.

32. O'Neill, E., Klepal, M., Lewis, D., O'Donnell, T., O'Sullivan, D. and Pesch, D. A testbed for evaluating human interaction with ubiquitous computing environments. *Proc. Tridentcom '05*, IEEE (2005), 60-69.

33. Pramanik, A. The use of a virtual environment as a method of wayfinding research in architecture. Master's Thesis, Texas Tech University, 2006.

34. Reynolds, V., Cahill, V. and Senart, A. Requirements for an ubiquitous computing simulation and emulation environment. *Proc. InterSense '06,* ACM Press (2006).

35. Roto, V. Oulasvirta, A. Haikarainen, T. Lehmuskallio, H. and Nyyssönen, T. Examining mobile phone use in the wild with quasi-experimentation. *HIIT Technical Report 2004-1*, August 13 2004.

36. Schellenbach, M., Krüger, A., Lövdén, M. and Lindenberger, U. A laboratory evaluation framework for pedestrian navigation devices. *Proc. Mobility '07,* ACM Press (2007), 495-502.

37. Slater,M, Steed,A., McCarthy, J. and Marinelli, F. The Influence of Body Movement on Presence in Virtual Environments. *The Journal of the Human Factors and Ergonomics Society 40,* 3 (1998), 469-477.

38. Singh, P., Ha, H.N., Kuang, Z., Olivier, P., Kray, C., Blythe, P. and James, P. Immersive video as a rapid prototyping and evaluation tool for mobile and ambient applications. *Proc. MobileHCI '06,* ACM Press (2006), 264-264.

39. Snowdon, C. and Kray, C. Exploring the use of landmarks for mobile navigation support in natural environments. *Proc. MobileHCI '09*, ACM Press (2009), Article 13, 10 pages.

40. Unni, R. and Harmon, R. Perceived effectiveness of push vs. pull mobile location-based advertising. *Journal of Interactive Advertising 7*, 2 (2007), 28-40.

41. Verbeke, W. and Vackier, I. Profile and effects of consumer involvement in fresh meat. *Meat Science, 67,* 1 (2004), 159-168.

42. Wehmeyer, K. Mobile Ad Intrusiveness – The Effects of Message Type and Situation. *eMergence: Merging and Emerging Technologies, Processes, and Institutions 6* (2007), 1-18.

43. Xu, H., Oh, L-B. And Teo, H-H. Perceived effectiveness of text vs. multimedia Location-Based Advertising messaging. *International Journal of Mobile Communications 17*, 2 (2009), 154-177.

The Impact of Three Interfaces for 360-Degree Video on Spatial Cognition

Wutthigrai Boonsuk
Iowa State University
Ames, Iowa, USA
wutthigraib@gmail.com

Stephen B. Gilbert
Iowa State University
Ames, Iowa, USA
gilbert@iastate.edu

Jonathan W. Kelly
Iowa State University
Ames, Iowa, USA
jonkelly@iastate.edu

ABSTRACT
In this paper, we describe an experiment designed to evaluate the effectiveness of three interfaces for surveillance or remote control using live 360-degree video feeds from a person or vehicle in the field. Video feeds are simulated using a game engine. While locating targets within a 3D terrain using a 2D 360-degree interface, participants indicated perceived egocentric directions to targets and later placed targets on an overhead view of the terrain. Interfaces were compared based on target finding and map placement performance. Results suggest 1) non-seamless interfaces with visual boundaries facilitate spatial understanding, 2) correct perception of self-to-object relationships is not correlated with understanding object-to-object relationships within the environment, and 3) increased video game experience corresponds with better spatial understanding of an environment observed in 360-degrees. This work can assist researchers of panoramic video systems in evaluating the optimal interface for observation and teleoperation of remote systems.

Author Keywords
360-degree view; panorama; virtual navigation; spatial cognition.

ACM Classification Keywords
H.5.2 User Interfaces - Evaluation/methodology, Graphical user interfaces (GUI), User-centered design;

General Terms
Evaluation, Interface Design, Navigation, Spatial cognition

INTRODUCTION
A surveillance system typically involves monitoring multiple video feeds of cameras in an extensive area. We can divide this system into two categories: stationary systems and mobile systems. In this paper, we focus on the mobile system in which cameras are attached to dynamic objects such as persons, vehicles, or aircrafts to provide a remote 360-degree view. The video feeds from the mobile system are usually monitored in real-time and require significant vigilance to examine their contents. The design of the view interface can be essential in providing the effectiveness of observation. Traditional interfaces for remote camera systems (e.g., Google Street View [25] or HMDs connected to 360-degree environments [7] or immersive systems with displays surrounding the user [5, 12, 19, 24] require multiple views or active remote panning of the view to observe occluded regions. An interface that provides observers with a complete view at a single glance without leading to perceptual distortion of spatial information would represent an improvement.

Human eyes have a horizontal field of view (FOV) of approximately 200 degrees, and so displaying a 360-degree panorama to a human observer requires compressing the display horizontally. The resulting horizontal distortion could disrupt the viewer's ability to accurately perceive spatial relationships between multiple objects in the camera's view. Egocentric (self-to-object) directions of objects in the display will not necessarily correspond to the egocentric directions of the objects relative to the person wearing the camera. Human spatial orientation is thought to be largely based on the egocentric directions and distances to known landmarks [8, 26]. Misperception of those egocentric directions could result in large errors in determining one's position within a remembered space. In light of the potential disruption of normal spatial cognitive processes, the interface should augment the view to leverage our natural sense of presence and spatial awareness. In this paper, we describe an experiment investigating the effectiveness of three designs for a 360-degree view interface, part of an ongoing project to build a wireless 360-degree life-sharing system.

Acquiring 360-Degree Video
The two approaches to producing 360-degree video are combining images from multiple cameras, each with limited field of view (FOV), and using a single panoramic camera. The first approach requires use of software techniques such as image blending [4], piecewise image stitching [9, 22], or 2D projective transformation [17, 20, 23]. The single camera approach may use a fish-eye lens [28], omni-directional camera [14], or a conic mirror camera [3]. The current study simulates video feeds within a virtual game

Figure 1. Three 360-degree interfaces from the same viewpoint: (a) 90-degree x 4, with left, front, right, rear; (b) 180-degree x 2, with front and rear and (c) 360-degree x 1, panorama. Original 3D model created by HORSE-A-F; used with permission.

engine environment by utilizing multiple cameras situated around the head of a virtual character. This approach is similar to piecewise image stitching, and the choice of multiple cameras enabled tight control of distortion, which is reduced by using multiple cameras with small FOV (25-30 degrees). The interfaces were designed to maintain the same size of objects in the 3D scene across all three interfaces.

Previous 2D Displays of 360-Degrees

The primary reason to transform a 360-degree view to a 2D flat interface is to offer observers the ability to use standard computer displays and to enable monitoring of multiple video feeds simultaneously (e.g., from multiple people or vehicles using 360-degree camera rigs). The 360-degree interface should help observers attend to both center and peripheral information and maintain spatial orientation within the displayed environments.

Past research has used a variety of interfaces to display a 360-degree video feed on a single monitor. Three examples highlight the diversity of interface designs. Kadous et al [13], for a robot search and rescue system, displayed a main front view with smaller additional views (left, right, and rear) arranged around the border of the main view. Meguro et al [15], for a mobile surveillance system for an autonomous vehicle, presented two views, each with 180-degree FOV (front and rear). Greenhill and Venkatesh [11], for a mobile surveillance system for city buses, presented a single uncut 360-degree view. While a variety of interface arrangements exist, the authors are not aware of a thorough investigation of the characteristics of an effective 360-degree display.

Potential Impact on Spatial Cognitive Tasks

A remote 360-degree surveillance system allows the surveillance operator to detect objects of interest in any direction, thereby exceeding the abilities of the camera-wearer. For example, a surveillance operator could detect a navigational goal or target behind the wearer and direct him/her to approach the goal. Alternatively, the operator could remember the goal location for later use. In both of these tasks, performance might be impaired by displaying 360-degree video on a 2D monitor because of disruptions in judging egocentric directions.

Accurate perception of the egocentric direction of a goal relative to the camera-wearer requires mapping the 360-degree image onto a representation of the wearer's body. When displaying a 360-degree view in a single, uninterrupted image on a monitor, an object appearing on the far left or right of the image is actually directly behind the camera-wearer. This mapping between display and body coordinates is unnatural and will likely cause errors in estimating egocentric object locations. Adding visual borders to the image might improve judgments of egocentric direction by providing multiple points of reference between the image and the wearer's body. For example, segmenting the display into four 90-degree sections separated by borders indicating front-left, front-right, back-left and back-right in body coordinates would facilitate mapping between image and body coordinates. This hypothesis is tested in the current experiment.

Direction Performance Tied to Mapping Performance?

Errors in judging egocentric directions to objects may or may not lead to errors in generating a cognitive map of the environment, and different spatial cognitive theories make different predictions regarding this relationship. For the purposes of this study, a cognitive map is considered to be a mental representation of object-to-object, or exocentric, locations in the environment. A cognitive map is required when retrieving remembered locations, such as when drawing a map of the environment or navigating to a remote goal. If accurate perception of egocentric direction is necessary in order to construct an accurate cognitive map, then there should be a direct relationship between egocentric and exocentric errors. That is, misperception of a target's egocentric direction should lead to errors in placing that object within a cognitive map [8, 26]. This would result in a positive correlation between egocentric pointing errors made within the environment and map placement errors made when reconstructing the layout from memory.

However, if exocentric relationships are stored independently of egocentric directions, then errors in egocentric and exocentric judgments should be unrelated. If cognitive maps are constructed on the basis of object-to-object relationship (e.g., the barrel is on the north side of the shed), then an accurate cognitive map could be formed even if egocentric directions to individual objects are misperceived. This would result in no correlation between egocentric pointing errors made within the environment and map placement errors made when reconstructing the layout from memory. These alternative hypotheses are also tested in the current experiment.

RESEARCH APPROACH

The goal of this project is to identity which of three design interfaces offers the best spatial task performance in an observed remote environment. For this study, active navigation is used instead of passive observation since active navigation benefits peripheral perception in a large FOV display [18]. Participants performed several spatial tasks using each interface, and their performance was recorded and used to determine the effectiveness of the interfaces. The best interface should provide appropriate utilization of the edges of the display, including the corners, as is commonly used in first-person shooter games to display status information, and should promote accurate judgment of egocentric object directions as well as accurate creation of a cognitive map of the virtual environment.

Interfaces

The three interface configurations chosen for comparison were based on the previous work described above and on an informal pilot study of these and additional interfaces. The interfaces are shown in Figure 1 and the accompanying video figure.

The first interface, "90-degree x 4," is a combination of four views: front, left, right, and rear. As illustrated in Figure 1a, each view has 90 degree FOV and is placed 10 pixels apart from the other. The rear view is placed underneath the front, left, and right views. This first interface is designed based on the common size of FOV for a video game with additional views to cover 360 degrees. The borders of the four views provide visual landmarks indicating the camera boundaries at the front-left, front-right, back-left, and back-right relative to the user's heading within the virtual environment.

The second interface, "180-degree x 2," comprises two views with 180 degree FOV (Figure 1b). We designed this interface based approximately on the natural horizontal FOV of human eyes. The left and right borders of the images provide visual landmarks indicating the camera boundaries directly left and right relative to the user's heading within the virtual environment.

The last interface, "360-degree x 1," is a single 360-degree panoramic view as illustrated in figure 1c. We believe this interface may reduce visuospatial working memory load since the views are grouped into a single element. While this interface has been perceived by some to be the obvious "winner" because of its familiarity, the results below suggest that a careful analysis is merited. The left and right borders of the image both provide visual landmarks indicating the camera boundary directly behind the user's heading within the virtual environment

Each interface was displayed on a 22-inch monitor with the participant sitting approximately one foot away, yielding a visual angle on the eye of ~30-40 degrees horizontally and ~10 degrees vertically.

METHODS

The virtual environment used in this study was created using the graphics game engine Irrlicht [1] with C++ and OpenGL. Our experiment utilized a 22-inch 3M multi-touch display to present the views from virtual cameras of the game engine and receive participants' responses in given tasks. Participants used the keyboard arrow keys to navigate through the virtual environment.

Tasks

For each interface, the experiment was broken up into three phases, a familiarization phase, a target search phase, and a map reproduction phase. Interface order was counterbalanced to prevent order effects from contaminating the analyses. The familiarization phase occurred at the beginning of each interface session. During familiarization, participants were given 5 minutes to familiarize themselves with the navigation controls and the interface. Familiarization took place within a 3D model of an urban environment; the subsequent target search phase

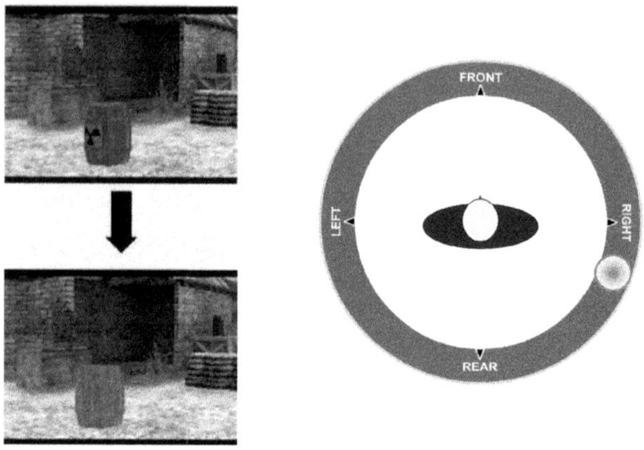

Figure 2, left: Participants tapped 10 red barrels in the environment to "clear" them to green. At right: Compass rose, showing front, right, left, and rear, where a participant has tapped to indicate that a target barrel sits about 100° to the right of her. Original 3D model at left created by HORSE-A-F; used with permission.

took place within a different 3D model of a small hilly village (measuring 360 x 360 feet). During the target search phase, participants had 10 minutes to locate 10 targets (red wooden barrels). Participants were instructed to select the target as soon as it appeared anywhere on the display. To select a target, the participant tapped it with a finger, and the target color changed from red to green (Figure 2, left). To accommodate colorblindness, red barrels also lost their radioactivity logo when touched. Immediately after selecting the barrel target, participants were asked to identify the target direction relative to their current heading in the virtual environment by tapping a compass rose (Figure 2, right), herein referred to as the pointing response.

The map phase began after participants had located all 10 targets or after 10 minutes had elapsed. Participants were asked to place 10 targets on an overhead map (Figure 3), herein referred to as the map response. Barrels were not uniquely identifiable except by their spatial location. After placing all 10 targets on the map, participants were introduced to the next interface and the entire process was repeated.

Three different target layouts were created and randomly paired with the three interfaces so that each participant experienced all three layouts. The primary dependent measures were errors committed on pointing and the map responses. We also recorded the total number of targets found during the target search phase, the total time required to find all targets during the target search phase, and the egocentric directions and distances of selected targets during the target search phase.

Questionnaire

At the end of the three interface sessions, a questionnaire was administered to assess participants' satisfaction with each interface, and also to identify whether participants reported using the display periphery on each interface.

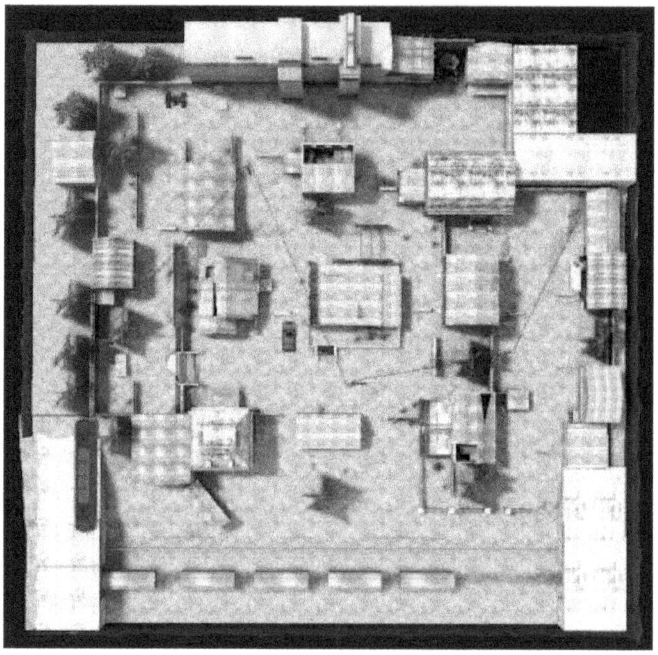

Figure 3: Overhead map of terrain, on which participants located the target barrels that they had selected in first-person view. Original 3D model created by HORSE-A-F; used with permission.

Participants

A total of 20 participants (4 females and 16 males), ages 18 - 35, were recruited. To gauge their ability to understand a video-game-like virtual environment and navigate using the keyboard control, participants were asked for number of hours of video game playing per week. The median number of hours was one; most participants did not routinely play video games.

RESULTS

Data from two of the 20 participants were excluded from all analyses because their pointing errors were extremely high (more than 6σ) and inconsistent with errors made by the remaining participants.

Across all three interface sessions, 13 of the 18 participants found all 10 targets. The remaining 5 participants sometimes found only 8 or 9 targets. Participants who found all 10 targets spent 5 minutes on average. In particular, average time for 90-degree x 4 was 4.8 minutes, 180-degree x 2 was 5.0 minutes, and 360-degree x1 was 5.3 minutes. However, times could range from 2 to almost 10 minutes.

Target Location

The degree to which participants made use of the entire 360-degree display can be determined by analyzing the actual angles of target barrels at the time they were selected during the target search phase.

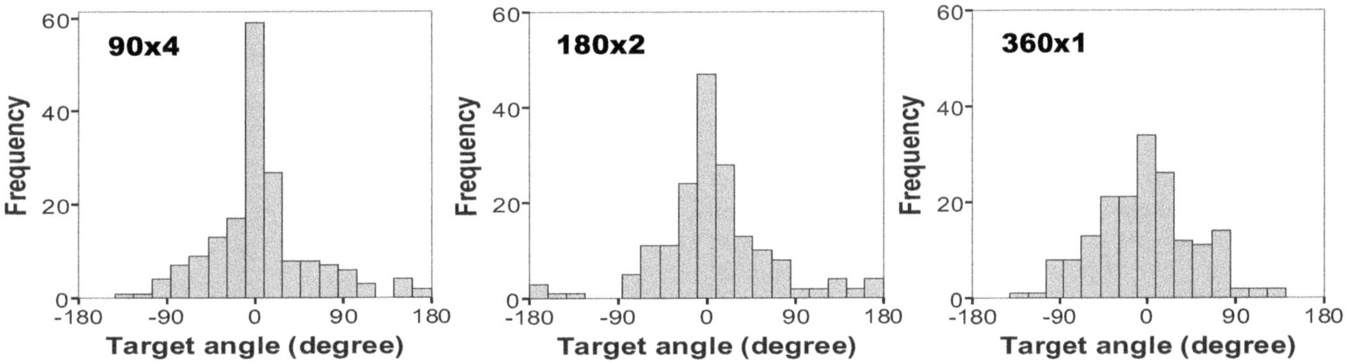

Figure 4: Histograms of actual barrel target angle at the time of participant selection. More barrels were chosen in the periphery in the 360-degree x 1 interface.

The frequency distribution of actual target directions at the time they were selected is shown in Figure 4. Directions displaced rightward from the participant's heading at the time of selection were arbitrarily labeled as positive angles, and leftward directions were labeled as negative angles, where 0 degrees is straight ahead and 180 degrees is directly behind. In all three interfaces, the peak frequency occurs at 0 degrees and decreases with increasing distance from 0 degrees. This indicates that participants tended to select targets when they were near the center of the display. Furthermore, the distributions of target directions vary across interface. When using the 90-degree x 4 interface, 52% of targets were selected when they fell in the center 45 degrees of the display. This value drops to 50% in the 180-degree x 2 interface and 41% in the 360-degree x 1 interface. Considering an even smaller window defined by the center 15 degrees of each interface accounts for 31% of targets in the 90-degree x 4 interface, 23% of targets in the 180-degree x 2 interface, and 15% of targets in the 360-degree x 1 interface. These differences in target direction distributions indicate that the interface influenced participants' focus of attention, such that attentional distribution across the display was broadest in the 360-degree x 1 interface and most narrow in the 90 x 4 interface (and intermediate in the 180 x 2 interface).

Target distance (the distance from the participant's point of view to the barrel at the time it was selected) affected the size of the target in pixels within the interface. The size of the target was expected to have little impact on pointing performance (angular pointing error or the time to choose the pointing angle on the compass rose), since the pointing action is based on the horizontal position of any green barrel pixels on the display. As predicted, target distance was not significantly correlated with pointing error, $r(18) = .135$. However, target distance was positively correlated with the time required to indicate the target's direction on the compass rose, $r(18)=.570$. This suggests that participants processed the scene three-dimensionally during the pointing task, noting a target's distance from themselves, or possibly associating the distant barrels with distant landmarks. This spatial processing implies that, as desired, participants are engaged with a 3D environment rather than a 2D projected image.

Reaction time

Reaction time was evaluated using a log of participants' actions in the virtual environment. This log was an output text file that contained participants' directions and positions that were recorded every second during the experiment. The reaction time was analyzed by replaying this data and then measured the time delay between target appearance and target selection.

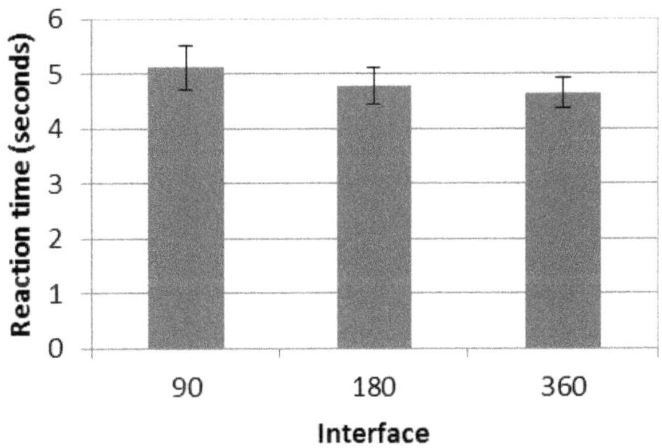

Figure 5: Time delay between target appearance and target selection

The differences of average reaction times were small across three interfaces (less than 1 second) as shown in Figure 5. Reaction time was analyzed in a one-way repeated-measures ANOVA to determine the effect of interface on reaction time. The main effect of interface was not significant indicating that reaction times did not differ across the interfaces, $F(2,34)=0.871$, $p = 0.428$.

Pointing error

Absolute pointing errors were evaluated in order to assess the accuracy with which participants could map the 360 degree images onto egocentric target directions relative to the participant's heading in the virtual environment. Pointing errors were computed by finding the minimum absolute difference between the actual angle of the target and the angle indicated by the participant. Pointing errors (shown in Figure 6) otherwise were generally low with approximately 75% of pointing responses being within 20 degrees of the actual target direction. Absolute pointing error was analyzed in a one-way repeated-measures ANOVA to determine the effect of interface on pointing error. The main effect of interface was significant, $F(2, 34)=5.54$, $p = 0.008$. Post-hoc analyses indicated that pointing errors in the 90-degree x 4 and 180-degree x 2 interfaces did not differ from one another (p=.809), but pointing error when using the 360-degree x 1 interface was significantly greater than when using the 90-degree x 4 (p=.032) and the 180-degree x 2 interface (p=.003).

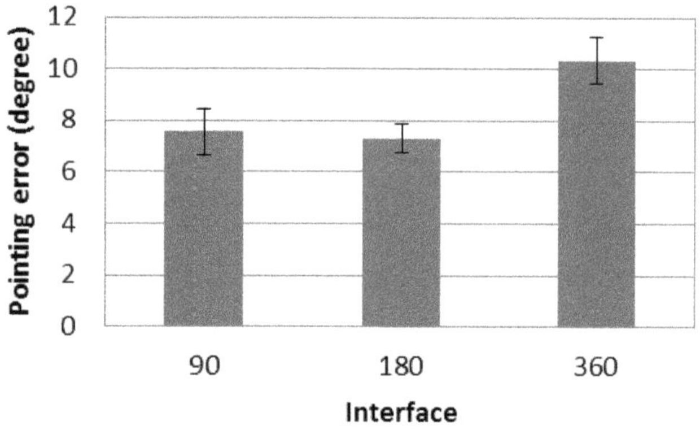

Figure 6: Pointing errors by interface

Map error

Map error was calculated as the mean Euclidean distance between the participant's selected locations on the map task and the actual target locations. In many cases there was a clear correspondence between the barrel placed by the participant and the actual location of a barrel in the environment (Figure 7, top). In other cases, participants placed barrels in locations midway between two actual barrel locations (Figure 7, bottom). Because the barrels were non-unique, it was impossible to determine which barrel response corresponded to which actual barrel location. As such, we calculated the sum of squared distance errors for all possible pairings of barrel responses with actual barrel locations for each participant on each map. The barrel pairings which minimized the sum of squared errors (SSE) were used to calculate average barrel placement error (see Figure 7 for an example of barrel pairings).

The map task was challenging for some participants, and map error varied considerably across individuals. The virtual environment was 360 feet x 360 feet in dimension.

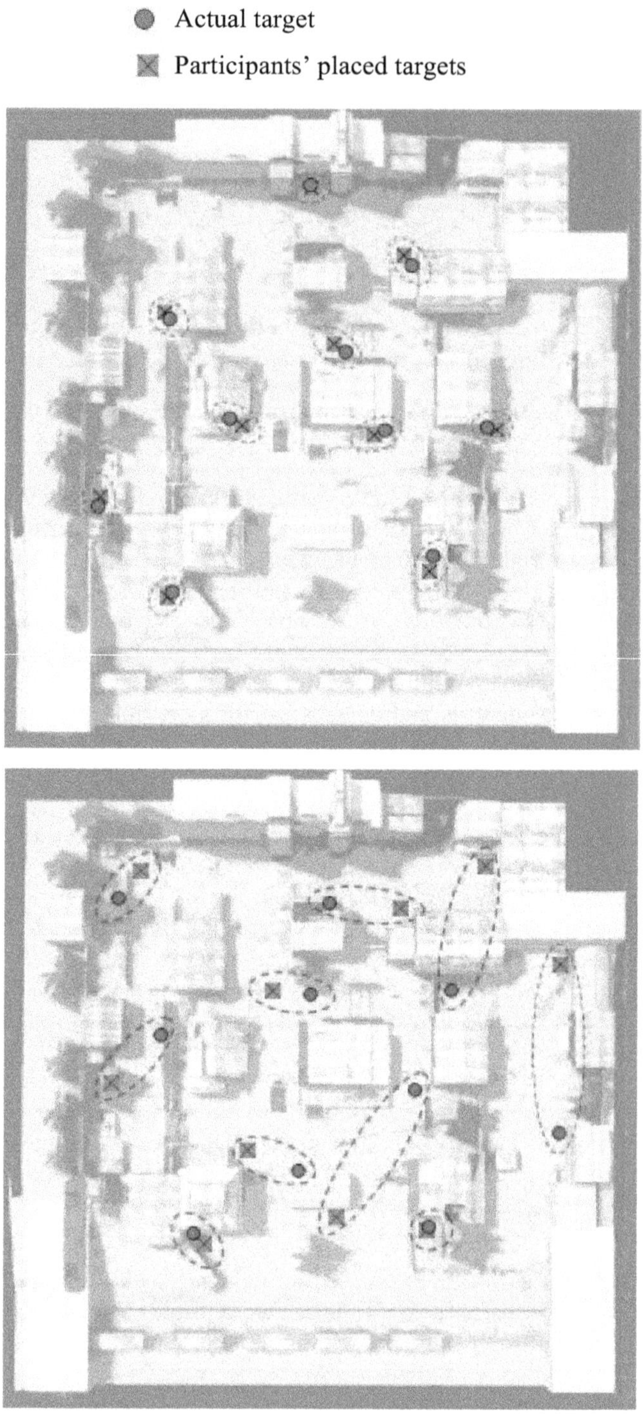

Figure 7: Two maps showing large differences in map error. The top map shows targets placed highly accurately, while the bottom map shows a more typical placement. Pairings show the map error scoring method, minimizing the sum of squared errors across all possible pairings. Original 3D model created by HORSE-A-F; used with permission.

Average map error for all participants (n=18) was 26.7 feet, but average map error for individuals (averaged across their 10 barrel placements) ranged from 6 – 48 feet. However, a simulation of repeated random barrel placements yielded a

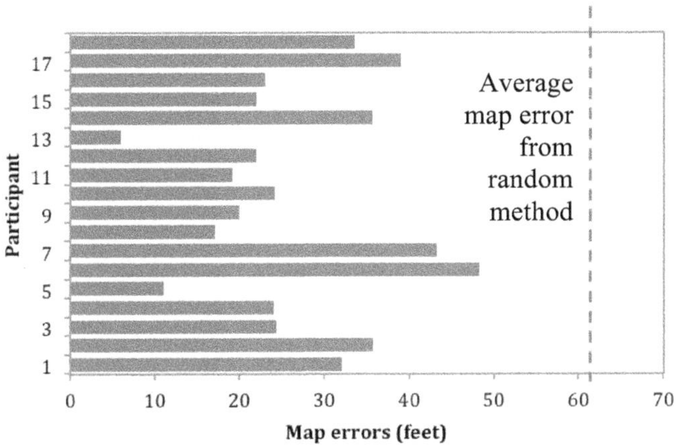

Figure 8: Participants' map errors vs. random map error

map error of greater than 60 feet (Figure 8). Thus, individuals varied but were always better than chance performance. Also, because participants varied in how far they travelled through the environment during the target search phase (even though the experience was capped at 10 minutes) it could be posited that a longer travel path would lead to more exposure to relevant landmarks and object-to-object relationships, which in term may lead to more familiarity with the map and lower map error. However, map error and travel distance were not significantly correlated, $r(18) = -.172$ Map error was analyzed in a one-way repeated-measures ANOVA to determine the effect of interface on map error (Figure 8). The main effect of interface was not significant, indicating that map errors did not differ across interfaces ($F(2,34)=1.589$, $p = .219$).

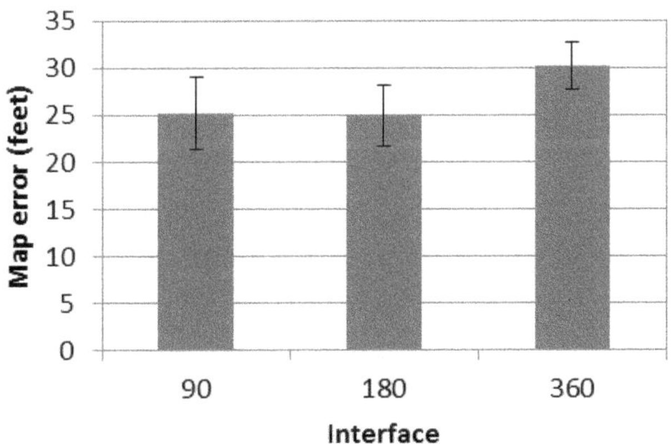

Figure 9: Map errors by interface

Correlation between pointing error and map error

If accurate perception of egocentric direction is necessary in order to construct an accurate cognitive map, then there should be a positive correlation between egocentric pointing errors and map errors. Spearman's rank correlations were calculated between absolute pointing errors and map errors. The between-participant correlation was not significantly different from zero, $r(18)=.164$.

Survey Results

Survey results (Figure 10) serve as additional data for triangulation of participants' experiences using the interfaces. Answers to Question 1 (Which interface for 360-degree viewing did you prefer?) and Question 2 (Which interface for 360-degree viewing provided the most natural feel for navigating through the environment?) both indicate a minority of preference for the 360 degree x 1 interface (preferred by 22% and 11% of participants in Questions 1 and 2, respectively). The remaining responses are evenly split between the 90 degree x 4 interface and the 180 degree x 2 interface. Question 3 (Which interface for 360-degree viewing allowed you to determine the direction of objects in the scene accurately?) shows that a strong majority preferred the 90-degree x 4 interface (72%), and only a single participant (6%) preferred the 360-degree x 1 interface for target angle identification (pointing). Question 4 (Which interface for 360-degree viewing allowed you to place the barrels on the top-down map most accurately?) shows a somewhat even distribution with no clear preference of the best interface to help build a cognitive map.

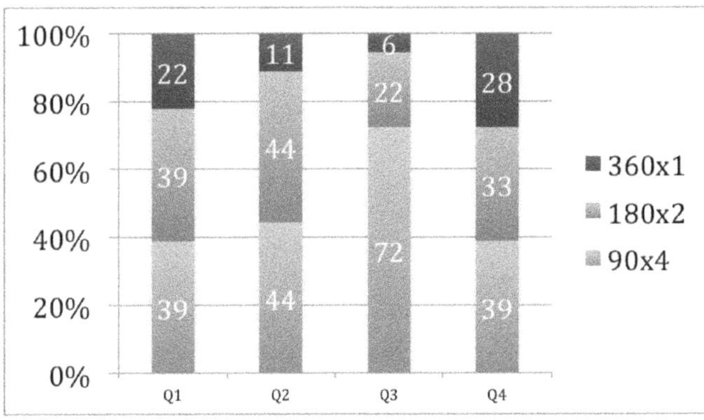

Figure 10: Survey results. Q1: Preferred interface. Q2: Most natural feel for navigation. Q3: Most accurate interface for pointing task. Q4: Most accurate interface for map task.

When comparing these preferences with performance on the pointing and map tasks, Q1, Q2, and Q3 results match the pointing error performance data, in that participants performed significantly worse when using the 360-degree x 1 interface compared to the other two interfaces. Q3 highlights a slight difference between self-reported preferences and pointing errors: a majority of participants preferred 90-degree x 4 over 180-degree x 2 for accurate pointing, even though their pointing error performance did not significantly differ in the two interfaces. This result suggests that the 90-degree x 4 may be preferred for reasons other than the tasks themselves, such as familiarity of the 90-degree FOV from first-person shooter video games. Q4 results also match the map error data in that map errors did not differ by interface, and neither did preferences.

Individual Differences

Previous work has shown that video game experience improves general spatial skills such as spatial allocation of attention and mental rotation [6]. We investigated whether individual differences such as video game experience influenced performance on the pointing and map tasks. Participants with greater or equal to 3 hours per week of video game experience were considered gamers, and those with fewer than 3 hours per week of video game experience were considered non-gamers. Video game players exhibited overall lower errors on the map task ($F(1, 16) = 6.174$, $p = .024$), but the pattern of map errors across the three interfaces was no different for gamers and non-gamers (i.e., the interaction between video game play and interface was non-significant, $F(2, 32) = 1.4$, $p = .261$. Video game play did not affect pointing performance ($r(18) = .026$).

Although the primary analysis of map performance data revealed no differences between the three interfaces (see Map Error section, above), we also considered the possibility that there may be individual differences in the effect of the three interfaces on map error. To evaluate this, we divided participants into two groups based on their average map error. A cutoff of 25 feet was used to distinguish participants who committed high and low map errors. This cutoff was chosen because it was near the median error score, and because there was a large gap between the next largest and next smallest error scores. Map errors were analyzed in a mixed-model repeated-measures ANOVA with terms for map score (high or low) and interface. The interaction between the two variables was not significant, $F(2,20)=2.143$, $p=.143$, nor was the main effect of interface (reported previously in the Map Error section), indicating that participants who scored high or low on the map task were not differentially affected by the three interfaces. These results show that the lack of significant difference in map error across interfaces is not likely due to individual differences.

DISCUSSION

During the target search phase, participants attempted to find 10 target barrels distributed throughout the environment. Upon finding each barrel, participants judged its egocentric direction relative to their heading in the virtual environment.

The actual egocentric directions of selected targets varied as a function of the interface used to display the 360-degree view of the environment. Participants tended to select targets close to their heading at the time of selection, and this tendency was most pronounced in the 90 degree x 4 interface, somewhat reduced in the 180 degree x 2 interface, and further reduced in the 360 degree x 1 interface. One possible explanation for this finding is that image segmentation affects spatial allocation of attention. In all three interfaces, participants preferred to allocate their attention in the direction they were moving. In the 360 degree x 1 interface, participants were able to spread their attention horizontally over a relatively wide area of the display, centered on their heading. In the 180 degree x 2 interface, participants needed to attend to the upper 180 degree view in order to center their attentional focus around their heading, which reduced their ability to detect targets in the far periphery (e.g., targets appearing on the lower view). In the 90-degree x 4 interface, participants focused their attention on the central (forward) view, and the visual borders around the central view restricted their attention to that view. Furthermore, since the reaction times between target appearance and target selection were not influenced by different interfaces, it suggests that participants were able to focus their attention to detect targets in the periphery of the wider view. We interpret these findings as evidence in favor of the 360 x 1 interface, which allowed participants to make better use of the 360-degree view of the environment.

Pointing errors when judging the egocentric directions of targets also depended on the interface. Errors were lowest in the 90 x 4 and 180 x 2 interface, compared to the 360 x 1 interface. This difference might be due to a benefit conferred by the visible image borders, which could serve as landmarks to identify key orientations relative to the participant's heading. However, the additional borders in the 90 degree x 4 interface did not lead to superior pointing performance compared to the 180 x 2 interface. One possible explanation for this is that the borders in the 180 x 2 interface were more helpful than those in the 90 x 4 interface because they distinguished between the front and back hemi-fields. The front-back distinction in body coordinates is more salient than the left-right distinction [10].

Unlike the pointing errors, which favored the 90 x 4 and 180 x 2 interfaces, map errors did not differ as a function of interface. This suggests that participants were able to create a cognitive map of the environment equally well in all three interfaces. The distinct error patterns in the pointing and map tasks suggest that the processes might be dissociable. Specifically, the data indicate that cognitive maps may have been formed on the basis of exocentric (object-to-object or object-to-environment) directions rather than egocentric directions. This conclusion is contrary to the notion that cognitive maps are formed by integrating egocentric directions with perceived self-position and orientation [8, 26]. The lack of correlation between egocentric pointing errors and map errors provides further evidence for the dissociation between perception of egocentric object directions and creation of a cognitive map.

SUMMARY AND FUTURE WORK

The goal of this study was to investigate the effectiveness of three designs of a 360-degree view interface for a mobile surveillance system. Interfaces were evaluated based on participants' performance of two spatial tasks and their surveyed preferences.

We plan to extend our findings on the usage of peripheral views to evaluate the mechanism underlying the observed differences across the three interfaces. By experimentally placing targets in the periphery and measuring eye and head movements, we will be able to evaluate whether selected target direction is dependent on eye gaze direction. Adding visual boundaries (e.g., dash lines) on a wider view interface such as 360-degree x 1 may significantly improve the ability to determine target directions. However, it may also interrupt the distribution of attention across the display. This enhancing technique will need to be carefully investigated to the extent of designing an effective interface. We also plan to expand our work to a passive viewing situation rather than active navigation, since passive viewing corresponds more closely with a real-world surveillance task (e.g., "Watch this 360-degree video from a panoramic-camera wearer in the field and report anything suspicious."). Additional field agents can be added for observation to explore the maximum number of agents that can be observed reliably and the ability of an observer to build a cognitive map successfully by integrating 360-degree views from multiple field agents. Results of such a passive study may differ significantly from the current study given Noë's suggestion that the ability to act on an environment is critical to perception of it [16].

An important extension of this work will be to evaluate how experience and training with each interface affects task performance. Participants in the current study experienced each interface for a total of 15 minutes (5 minutes during the familiarization phase and 10 minutes during the target search phase), but professional operators might acquire hundreds of hours of experience with a given interface. Therefore, more extensive training studies are needed before the design implications can be fully realized. The results of the current study that favor those with more video game experience suggest that additional time with a novel interface may lead to higher performance and an increased sense of naturalness. This idea is consonant with early prism glasses research that showed that over time participants could adapt and perform normally even if their right-left and up-down were reversed or distorted [21, 27].

A practical contribution of this work is the identification of a previously unreported tradeoff that designers face when choosing the optimal interface for observation and teleoperation of remote systems capable of capturing live 360-degree video. If accurate judgment of egocentric directions is of critical importance to the task, then the 90-degree x 4, the 180-degree x 2, or another interface with visual angle markers or boundaries will be most appropriate. This applies to situations in which an observer watches the video feed and relays information to the person carrying the video cameras about the egocentric location of an important navigational goal (e.g., "The building entrance is to your right at 4 o'clock."). However, if surveillance of the entire display is the primary task, then the 360-degree x 1 interface, or perhaps another seamless interface, would be more appropriate, since it would allow for the broadest distribution of attention. This applies to situations in which an observer provides a simple but fast alert about the presence of a person or object near the person carrying the cameras, but egocentric location is of secondary importance (e.g., when identifying the presence of an enemy combatant and that personnel should immediately seek cover).

This project represents a first attempt to determine the necessary display characteristics that allow viewers to correctly interpret 360-degree video images displayed on a 2D screen. By examining performance on two spatial tasks and user preferences using three interfaces, we have established that the best design of the interface is not obvious and have offered practical guidance for practitioners creating such displays. Also, we have revealed evidence that egocentric and exocentric spatial tasks may be dissociable, which has broader implications for the design of any navigation system or virtual environment.

ACKNOWLEDGMENTS

We thank the U.S. AFOSR and U.S. Army Research Lab for support for this research. The 3D village model is based on *ut4_blitzkrieg* created by HORSE-A-F and is used with permission.

REFERENCES

1. Irrlicht Engine - A free open source 3d engine.
2. Agarwala, A., Zheng, K.C., Pal, C., Agrawala, M., Cohen, M., Curless, B., Salesin, D. and Szeliski, R. Panoramic video textures. *ACM Trans. Graph.*, *24*, 3 (2005), 821-827.
3. Baldwin, J., Basu, A. and Zhang, H., Panoramic video with predictive windows for telepresence applications. in *IEEE International Conference on Robotics and Automation*, (1999), 2884-2889.
4. Burt, P. and Adelson, E. A multiresolution spline with application to image mosaics. *ACM Transactions on Graphics*, *2*, 4 (1983), 217-236.
5. Cruz-Neira, C., Sandin, D.J., DeFanti, T.A., Kenyon, R.V. and Hart, J.C. The CAVE: audio visual experience automatic virtual environment. *Commun. ACM*, *35*, 6 (1992), 64-72.
6. Feng, J., Spence, I. and Pratt, J. Playing an Action Video Game Reduces Gender Difference in Spatial Cognition. *Psychological Science*, *18*, 10 (2007), 850-855.
7. Fiala, M., Pano-presence for teleoperation. in *Intelligent Robots and Systems, 2005. (IROS 2005). 2005 IEEE/RSJ International Conference on*, (2005), 3798-3802.
8. Foo, P., Warren, W.H., Duchon, A. and Tarr, M.J. Do humans integrate routes into a cognitive map? Map-

versus landmark-based navigation of novel shortcuts. *Journal of Experimental Psychology: Learning, Memory, and Cognition*, *31*, 2 (2005), 195-215.

9. Foote, J. and Kimber, D., FlyCam: Practical panoramic video and automatic camera control. in *IEEE International Conference on Multimedia and Expo*, (2000), 1419-1422.
10. Franklin, N. and Tversky, B. Searching imagined environments. *Journal of Experimental Psychology: General*, *119*, 1 (1990), 63-76.
11. Greenhill, S. and Venkatesh, S. Virtual observers in a mobile surveillance system *Proceedings of the 14th annual ACM international conference on Multimedia*, ACM, Santa Barbara, CA, USA, 2006, 579-588.
12. Hirose, M., Ogi, T. and Yamada, T. Integrating live video for immersive environments. *Multimedia, IEEE*, *6*, 3 (1999), 14-22.
13. Kadous, M.W., Sheh, R.M. and Sammut, C., Effective user interface design for rescue robotics. in *1st ACM Conference on Human-Robot Interaction*, (2006), 250-257.
14. Liu, H., Javed, O., Taylor, G., Cao, X. and Haering, N. Omni-directional surveilance for unmanned water vehicles *8th International Workshop on Visual Surveillance*, 2008.
15. Meguro, J., Hashizume, T., Takiguchi, J. and Kurosaki, R., Development of an autonomous mobile surveillance system using a network-based RTK-GPS. in *2005 IEEE International Conference on Robotics and Automation*, (2005), 3096-3101.
16. Noë, A. *Action in perception*. MIT Press, Boston, MA, 2004.
17. Park, J. and Myungseok, A. A novel application of panoramic surveillance system *IEEE International Syposium on Industrial Electronics*, Seoul, Korea, 2009, 205-210.
18. Richman, J.B. and Dyre, B.P., Peripheral Visual Stimulation Benefits Heading Perception during Active Control in *Human Factors and Ergonomics Society Annual Meeting*, (1999), 1411.
19. Schmidt, M., Rudolph, M., Werther, B. and Furstenau, N., Remote airport tower operation with augmented vision video panorama HMI. in *2nd International Conference Research in Air Transportation*, (2006), 221-230.
20. Shum, H.Y. and Szeliski, R. Panormic image mosaics *Microsoft Research Technical Report*, 1997.
21. Stratton, G.M. Some preliminary experiments on vision without inversion of the retinal image. *Psychology Review*, *3*, 6 (1896), 611-617.
22. Sun, X., Foote, J., Kimber, D. and Manjunath, B.S. Panoramic video capturing and compressed domain virtual camera control *Proceedings of the ninth ACM international conference on Multimedia*, ACM, Ottawa, Canada, 2001, 329-347.
23. Szeliski, R. Image mosaicing for tele-reality applications *DEC and Cambridge Research Lab Technical Report*, 1994.
24. Tang, W.-K., Wong, T.-T. and Heng, P.A. A system for real-time panorama generation and display in tele-immersive applications. *Multimedia, IEEE Transactions on*, *7*, 2 (2005), 280-292.
25. Vincent, L. Taking Online Maps Down to Street Level. *Computer*, *40*, 12 (2007), 118-120.
26. Waller, D., Loomis, J.M., Golledge, R.G. and Beall, A.C. Place learning in humans: The role of distance and direction information. *Spatial Cognition and Computation*, *2*, 4 (2000), 333-354.
27. Welch, R.B. Discriminative conditioning of prism adaptation. *Perception and Psychophysics*, *10*, (1971), 90-92.
28. Xiong, Y. and Turkowski, K., Creating image-based VR using a self-calibrating fisheye lens. in *IEEE Computer Society on Computer Vision and Pattern Recognition*, (1997), 237-243.

MOSOCO: A Mobile Assistive Tool to Support Children with Autism Practicing Social Skills in Real-Life Situations

Lizbeth Escobedo[1], David H. Nguyen[2], LouAnne Boyd[3], Sen H. Hirano[4], Alejandro Rangel[1], Daniel García-Rosas[1], Monica Tentori[1], Gillian R. Hayes[4]

[1]Computer Science School, UABC {lescobedo, arangel, jose.daniel.garcia.rosas, mtentori} @uabc.edu.mx

[2]Nokia Research Center david.h.nguyen @nokia.com

[3]Division of Special Education, NOC SELPA lboyd@ocde.us

[2]Department of Informatics, University of California, Irvine {gillianrh, shirano} @ics.uci.edu

ABSTRACT
MOSOCO is a mobile assistive application that uses augmented reality and the visual supports of a validated curriculum, the Social Compass, to help children with autism practice social skills in real-life situations. In this paper, we present the results of a seven-week deployment study of MOSOCO in a public school in Southern California with both students with autism and neurotypical students. The results of our study demonstrate that MOSOCO facilitates practicing and learning social skills, increases both quantity and quality of social interactions, reduces social and behavioral missteps, and enables the integration of children with autism in social groups of neurotypical children. The findings from this study reveal emergent practices of the uses of mobile assistive technologies in real-life situations.

Author Keywords
Assistive technology; autism; child-computer interaction; social skills; augmented reality; mobile applications

ACM Classification Keywords
K.3.1 [Computers and Education]: Computer Uses in Education; K.4.2 [Computers and Society]: Social Issues-Assistive technologies for persons with disabilities

INTRODUCTION AND MOTIVATION
Autism is characterized by social skills impairments [1]. Children with autism exhibit problems when initiating and terminating interactions, learning the interests of others, and joining social groups [12]. Direct instructions for skill acquisition are an effective way to teach them social skills, helping to cope with these social challenges [35].

Most of the available social skills tools use visual supports (*i.e.,* "those things we see that enhance the communication process" [19]. See Figure 1) and social stories (*i.e.,* "picture or written description of social situations" [13, 32]). Taken together, these tools go beyond the teaching of basic social skills and tackle such broad social issues as how situational contexts evolve in ongoing social interactions [13].

The Social Compass curriculum is a behavioral and educational curriculum identified as the best social curriculum for social skills training. It uses social stories and paper-based visual supports for teaching children with autism social skills [6]. The minimal social skills required for a "basic and complete social interaction" are addressed by six core lessons from the Social Compass curriculum: eye contact, space and proximity, start interaction, asking questions, sharing interests, and finishing interaction [33].

Each Social Compass lesson is composed of eight steps and is conducted in groups of both students with autism and neurotypical (NT) students. First, (1) the teacher introduces the social skill to be learned and (2) its related visual support. Then, (3) the teacher reads a social story that helps students connect the visual support, the social skill and the social situation. Later, (4) the teacher demonstrates how the skill is used in social contexts, and (5) students rehearse the skill in pairs. Next, (6) students role-play to practice the skill in four scenarios and (7) self-rate their performances. Finally, (8) students are encouraged to practice the newly learned social skill in different real-life social situations. A central aspect of the Social Compass training—as with

Figure 1. The visual supports of the Social Compass' basic social skills lessons. From left to right: eye contact, space and proximity, start an interaction, asking questions, sharing interests, and finish an interaction.

other social skills training [12, 23, 32, 35]—is enabling students to use newly learned skills in daily social contexts, supporting maintenance and generalization in real life.

Although the Social Compass curriculum has been successfully used during social skills activities in classrooms [6], there are still open questions as to how students might generalize their newly learned social skills to situations outside the classroom. However, there is currently limited support for this kind of mobile, dynamic instruction. To offset this challenge, we explored the use of mobile and augmented reality technologies to provide "anytime and anywhere" support for students practicing social skills in their daily lives.

In this paper, we first describe the design and implementation of the **Mobile Social Compass** (MOSOCO), a mobile assistive application that extends the Social Compass training and supports real-life social situations [33]. Then, we present the results from a deployment of MOSOCO. Finally, we close discussing with directions for future work.

RELATED WORK

Interactive technologies have the potential to provide a wide variety of support to children with autism. For example, interactive visual supports [15] help children with autism manage their schedules [17], remediate their speech and language disabilities (*e.g.,* [5, 27]) and provide feedback on their pronunciation (*e.g.,* [10, 14]).

Other projects have focused more directly on the development and practicing of social skills. Both games (*e.g.,* SIDES [29]) and multitouch displays (*e.g.,* Tablets [21]) have been developed to engage children with autism in social activities and enable novel forms of social expression. These entertainment-based assistive technologies also help children with autism learn how to work with others, be patient and understand emotions [29]. These research projects have made the compelling argument that children with autism are more willing to initiate play and to interact appropriately when using entertainment-based assistive technologies. However, there is limited evidence of a sustained improvement in their social skills following the use of these tools.

To cope with this challenge of sustainability of skill development, the StoryTable project focused on the use of storytelling to encourage socialization and enable practicing of appropriate social skills [11]. This research has shown that support during social engagements increased appropriate expression of emotions and responses to peer questions by children with autism [11]. However, most of these assistive technologies are often available only for use inside classrooms or during group therapies. Children with autism still struggle when generalizing what they learned to real-life situations outside the classroom [3].

Supporting real-life social situations poses new research questions and strains the design and use of currently

Figure 2. The MOSOCO system

available assistive technologies. One of the main challenges in this context is mobility. Although mobile systems have been theorized as an effective educational method enabling "anytime and anywhere" social skills practicing and learning [8, 28], mobile assistive technologies that support socialization and social skills practice for children with autism in this context are scarce. Some mobile applications for encouraging and supporting socialization of NT children have been proposed (*e.g.,* Camelot [34], Mobile Stories [8]), others have explored other domains, (*e.g.,* Personal Travel Assistant [7]), but none of these solutions have been used to support the socialization of children with autism.

These related efforts open new research questions around how mobile assistive technologies for encouraging socialization and learning and practicing of social skills improve the quality of interactions of students with autism and their NT peers. Additionally, the lack of exploration of tools for both children with and without autism opens questions around whether these tools might foster integrated social groups.

In light of the related literature, this work has three contributions. First, although many other researchers have explored the use of assistive technologies for social skills practice in classrooms (*e.g.,* [9, 16, 20]), we examine the usability and usefulness of socially assistive technologies in real life situations outside classrooms. Second, we present a mobile assistive tool that could be useful to other researchers in designing and evaluating mobile assistive technologies for use in real-life situations. Third, the results of our deployment study reveal how new social practices mediated by MOSOCO can improve the quality of interactions and social skills in generalized settings.

THE MOSOCO SYSTEM

MOSOCO is a mobile augmented reality application inspired by previous research on the Social Compass curriculum [33] (see Figure 2). In our previous work, we focused to analyze interactions among students, which led to design insights. Those insights, along with the Social Compass curriculum, inspired the design and development of MOSOCO. MOSOCO facilitates practicing social skills in real-life situations, guiding students through the six fundamental social skills of the Social Compass curriculum. MOSOCO provides children with autism with interactive

Figure 3: Students using MOSOCO during recess (left) two students making eye contact (right) Learning and tagging PIP's interests

features to encourage them to make eye contact, maintain appropriate spatial boundaries, reply to conversation initiators, share interests with partners, disengage appropriately at the end of an interaction, and identify potential communication partners. MOSOCO runs on an Android smartphone wirelessly connected to a server. MOSOCO uses the smartphone's camera to augment a real-life social situation with visual support—mimicking the Social Compass curriculum that augments social stories with paper-based visual supports.

MOSOCO was designed with both individual and group features in mind, augmenting each individual student's social skills, needs, and capabilities, and enabling synchronized group interactions and shared experiences. Individual features include: a unique identifier for each student using the system (typically a name), visualization of student progress in the form of stars that can be earned, an interaction self-report form, and social cues, *i.e.,* what a user should do (*"DOs"*) and should not do (*"DONTs"*) when interacting with others. Collaborative and group features include: the **Interaction Visual Schedule** (IVS) (*i.e.,* a six-step visual schedule that provides step-by-step guidance through the six basic social skills learned during the Social Compass training), a **Potential Interaction Partner** (PIP) suggestion (*i.e.,* a student who might like to interact with the student using the device), and a roster of connected students (*i.e.,* a listing of student profiles including photographs and personal interests).

When they first start MOSOCO, students are instructed to find a suggested PIP. MOSOCO suggests the PIP by showing the partner's name and photograph (see Figure 4). When the system detects that the user is in close proximity to the suggested PIP, both students are automatically "paired up," indicating that they have started an interaction. At this point, their Interaction Visual Schedules (IVS) are synchronized. Students may also manually pair themselves with another student.

Once MOSOCO's IVS is activated, the first visual support, eye contact, is colored. MOSOCO suggests skill-appropriate do's (*e.g., "smile if somebody looks at you"*) and don'ts (*e.g., "don't stare"*). These suggestions mimic verbal support available from teachers during the Social Compass classroom activities and can be used to practice the skills (Figure 3). MOSOCO monitors skill completion to mimic teacher support further. For example, the system detects eye contact through a vision-based algorithm for eye detection. If MOSOCO infers that eye contact was not properly achieved, it shows a warning notifying that a social misstep has occurred alongside a picture and text-based advice suggesting how to recover from it (*e.g.,* "*look at your partner*'s *eyes*"). Some common social missteps observed in our data include students using an inappropriate tone of voice (*e.g.,* shouting), avoiding eye contact or staring, invading personal space, and interrupting or breaking an interaction (*e.g.,* students with autism usually break an interaction without an explicit farewell). Once MOSOCO detects that both students have made eye contact, it emits a sound and highlights the next step. Students repeat this process to follow each of the rest of the IVS steps until it is time to "end a conversation" (step 6). During a successful sustained interaction, students perform "verbal or physical social activities" (Figure 3). Verbal interactions include activities like asking questions and learning and marking interests from the Social Compass curriculum. Physical interactions include traditional activities performed during recess, such as playing sports or board games.

After each interaction, students complete self-report forms to grade themselves on the six practiced social skills. They select "thumbs up" or "thumb down" on the interface, matching the simple self-grading students do during classroom social skills activities. If no social missteps were detected directly by the system, students earn stars based on the number of times *both* partners grade the interaction with a "thumbs up," encouraging students to help each other master the different skills. Finally, after the interaction and self-evaluation, MOSOCO calculates a new PIP suggestion for both students giving them the opportunity to interact with other students.

By receiving this information through a personal device, each student gets direct assistance and reinforcement for practicing their social skills, similar to the kind of human prompting and reinforcement they might receive during classrooms activities. Meanwhile, every activity is logged in the background, enabling automatic report generation for teachers to measure student progress.

METHODS

MOSOCO was deployed in a public school in Southern California during regularly scheduled lunch and recess breaks. All students enrolled in the Social Compass training were between the ages of 8 and 11 (m=10.08, sd=0.90). From this group, we selected three students with autism who demonstrated minimal social skills but otherwise demonstrated age-appropriate functioning; for each of them, we invited three NT students to serve as their PIPs (n = 12 total). This ratio of NT students mimics the school population. The evaluation included three stages: *pre-deployment* (3 weeks), *deployment* (3 weeks) *and post-deployment* (1 week).

During pre-deployment, students participated in the standard Social Compass curriculum in the classroom, which included direct instruction from trained specialists and paper-based tools. Researchers then installed MOSOCO and gave a training session on the system to the students and teachers. During the deployment phase, the students used MOSOCO during the Social Compass class and during their breaks. Finally, during post-deployment, the students participated in no lessons, and the system was not available to them.

To meet the regulations of the school and the university research ethics board, students enrolled in the study were confined to a private playground area during recess and lunch breaks (approximately 25 minutes per day). This area (150x50 ft) was separated from the rest of the playground by cones but incorporated common landscape elements (*e.g.*, a tree, a wall, and benches) and traditional school playground items (*e.g.*, balls, ropes, board games).

Data Collection

At the beginning of each session, researchers set up video cameras and sectioned off the playground for the study using bright orange cones. The sectioned-off playground

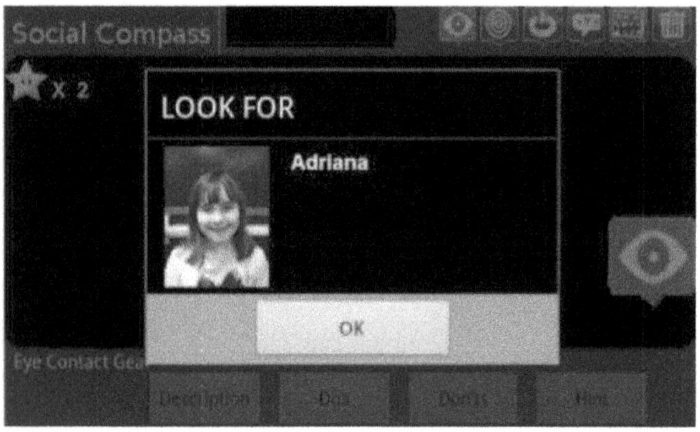

Figure 4: MOSOCO suggesting a PIP

area was surrounded with six HD video cameras, thus recording the children's interactions from six different angles. Researchers observed the students during both the Social Compass training and breaks, including lunch and recess for a total time of observation of just under 11 hours, (pre-deployment: 4 hr. 3 min., deployment: 4 hr. 37 min., post-deployment: 2 hr. 12 min.).

Weekly interviews were recorded and conducted with the participants across each study phase. Interviews were face-to-face and semi-structured, and students were divided in three groups (*i.e.*, g1 = 5 NT students, g2 = 4 NT students, g3 = 3 students with autism). Interviews generally lasted between 15 minutes to half an hour, in keeping with the short blocks of time available to talk with school students.

During pre-deployment, students were asked about daily routines and general communication practices. During deployment, students were asked to discuss how the use of the system went during that particular week, comment on how MOSOCO impacted their interactions and social groups, and encouraged to tell stories and discuss what they found interesting, surprising, or different that week. At the end of the study, the teaching staff and students completed surveys about their experiences with MOSOCO and took part in a 60-minute group interview. Unlike in the previous interviews in which the students were broken into small groups, in this final interview, all students met together. Recorded interviews and videos were transcribed.

Analysis

All field notes, interview and videos transcripts were inspected together using a mixed-methods approach. Researchers first analyzed the data for evidence of whether MOSOCO supported the needs of students. Researchers used open coding [31] and multi-phased affinity analysis [24] to uncover emergent themes from the interview data, in particular in relation to uses of the system. We then developed a coding scheme focused on student social experiences. This coding scheme was cross-analyzed during discussions among the research team to validate and refine its categories and properties.

A quantitative analysis was conducted to estimate the time students spent in different interactions and social groups as well as the number of social missteps committed. Using our coding scheme, the research team coded the recorded videos for interactions, behaviours, and social missteps. Inter-observer reliability[1] was acceptable (r=.912). For each participant under each condition, we calculated:

- *total and descriptive statistics* (*i.e.*, average and standard deviation) of interactions, social missteps, and topic of conversations
- *average time in a sustained* interaction, social misstep and topic conversation

[1]Refers to the degree of agreement between two data sets, scored independently by two different observers.

Finally, a single t-test was used to compare students with autism social missteps and behaviours, and an independent sample t-test was conducted to compare the number of physical, verbal and total of interactions using and not using MOSOCO, of both students with autism and NT students. The data presented a normal distribution.

RESULTS

New social practices mediated by MOSOCO emerged during our deployment. In particular, MOSOCO had an impact on the practicing and learning of social skills and changed the makeup and character of student peer groups.

General Use and Adoption

Overall, students positively received MOSOCO, finding it useful, fun, and helpful. Students showed excitement while using the system, and learned how to use it with minimal training in less than an hour. At the beginning of each session, they typically ran to the area where the phones were stored to start using them.

> *"It's really cool... I was very comfortable... I'm always waiting for this part of the school day." (s10, student with autism)*

> *"It was good, really good, and really awesome." (s11, student with autism)*

Students were more interested in using MOSOCO and other smartphone applications than the typical playground items available, calling out features they liked.

> *"I liked that you can earn stars. [That] was fun." (s1, NT student)*

> *"...I'm more interested in the phone and [MOSOCO], because I can learn a lot of different things." (s2, NT student)*

The primary motivation for using MOSOCO was to learn and to practice social skills, with all students reporting that they learned the Social Compass lessons. When discussing what they learned specifically, students referenced the six fundamental social skills (*e.g.*, "space and proximity," "ending a conversation," and "eye contact").

> *"I got to learn, because I didn't know about how far [away from another person] you are supposed to be." (s4, NT student)*

> *"... I've learn how to end [a conversation properly]." (s12, student with autism)*

> *"[MOSOCO] helped me how to make eye contact and ask questions." (s10, student with autism)*

Both sets of students expressed that they would like to use MOSOCO for longer integrated in their everyday lives, rather than only in the restricted areas of the study.

> *"I'll want to do it again. Yeah I think it would be helpful for kids that are still learning [the Social Compass curriculum]." (s4, NT student)*

During the three weeks of intervention, all of the students mastered the features of MOSOCO and the smartphone itself. This allowed them to explore uses for both the smartphone and MOSOCO, sometimes circumventing the prescribed lessons. For example, at the end of the third week, students started to "skip" practicing of some of the more basic skills in MOSOCO, shortening interactions to earn more stars while competing with other students.

> *"....I pressed ok ok ok and then I got so much stars, and I was like wow!" (s5, NT student)*

The students provided suggestions for encouraging greater adherence to the lessons during interviews:

> *"To really go with the person suggested by [MOSOCO], it would be interesting to have in [MOSOCO] more sophisticated functions, like face detection gear." (s4, NT student)*

> *"Find games that are like appropriate—that are mixed with the social compass—you have to do eye contact. Oh, and then you get a point or something like that? Make it more game like." (s7, NT student)*

Another, particularly remarkable interaction that exemplifies how students mastered the smartphone occurred during the third week of use. Even though all of the phone's buttons were deactivated, Student 5 (NT) closed MOSOCO's application and launched other applications. He then taught this skill to other students who began occasionally to listen to music, select different ringtones, take pictures, and play games with the GPS.

> *"Well I found this app thing that said; GPS Test. So I hit it so I could test it. It's cool; it also tells you your speed." (s6, NT student)*

> *"I just spent time with myself listening to ringtones sitting down." (s3, NT student)*

These results demonstrate that assistive technologies are important and useful outside classrooms but that classroom management strategies will continue to be needed to support students in staying focused on their tasks rather than playing with the technologies in other ways.

Impact on Student Behavior and Performance

During the deployment phase, the smartphone and MOSOCO evolved from a novel artifact and a "toyish" application to a true assistive support and means for social skills learning and practicing outside the classroom. Overall, the use of MOSOCO positively impacted student interactions with each other. Students learned the basic steps of a "proper" interaction, how to avoid and identify missteps, and how to help others interact.

Social Skills Practice and Learning

Generalizing skills beyond classroom learning is a challenge for any student, but particularly so for students with autism. Thus, the ability to practice social skills outside the classroom was a key feature of the MOSOCO system.

"It really does help me practice the Social Compass lessons." (s11, student with autism)

"[It helps me] to do the social things, eye contact, proximity, and all those things, so I can practice them." (s6, NT student)

In addition, students noted that the system provides them confidence when interacting with others, reassuring them of what they should or should not be doing.

"I forgot something; I'll look into [MOSOCO's social cues]." (s12, student with autism)

"It usually gives me hints." (s5, NT student)

"The eye contact and all the other tools and the do's and don'ts—I found those useful for any of the conversations I start." (s8, NT student)

MOSOCO can help students learn by repetition, in keeping with many other therapies for children with autism (*e.g.*, discrete trial training [30] and rote learning [22]).

"It helps me practice and practice." (s10, student with autism)

"To reenact" (s11, student with autism)

After so many repetitions, students were able to quickly recall the goal of the lesson and how to use the social skill in a given particular situation.

"[MOSOCO] helps you, because if you forgot to put that into your brain, it then remembers you [sic]." (s10, student with autism)

Students with autism and NT students differed somewhat, however, in their motivation for continued use of the system once the novelty wore off. While students with autism continued describing wanting to practice newly learned social skills, NT students adopted "mentoring" behavior. They described feeling responsible for assisting the practicing of social skills with the students with autism and helping them to improve their interactions.

"I like to help those shy children [the students with autism] to have a fun time. It's awesome." (s4, NT student)

"Yeah! I practice with [a student with autism] eye contact and all those things." (s5, NT student)

Most of the interactions we observed with NT students involved hints and explanations about a particular social skill. When children with autism would get "stuck" in a step, NT students would help them to "stay on task." This mimics the physical prompting given by teachers during classroom lessons.

Improving the quality of interactions

Both NT students and those with autism repeatedly expressed that MOSOCO helped them to improve the quality of their interactions.

"Talking certainly to a person in the way that they taught us: how to talk 'formally.' " (s7, NT student)

"It helps me like to socialize better." (s10, student with autism)

The time students with autism were involved in social missteps was 56% lower on average using MOSOCO (no-support: 2 hours 2 min 13 sec; using-MOSOCO: 54 min 38 sec; $t=3.42$, $p=.003$). This reduction can be attributed to greater student awareness and improved ability to identify social missteps using the prompts provided by MOSOCO. Additionally, the system augmented understanding of the usage of specific social skills given particular situations.

"Like sometimes before Social Compass, when I was doing eye contact, I looked away, but after the lessons I know eyes should go on." (s5, NT student)

"[MOSOCO] helped reduce the social missteps." (s10, student with autism)

Having social skill awareness with MOSOCO, the total time a student continually remained engaged in a social misstep reduced 76.52% (no-support: 3 min 33 sec; using-MOSOCO: 50 sec; $t=3.75$, $p=.002$). In addition to reducing missteps for students with autism, MOSOCO supported NT students in learning how to be more understanding and permissive if such missteps were presented. NT students developed new strategies for handling the social missteps instead of mocking or teasing the students with autism as they had done before.

Of course, for young children, encountering this kind of difference can still be challenging, as exemplified by the student below who describes being understanding most of the time but resorting to antisocial behaviors at other times to handle social missteps.

"I ask [a student with autism] what he wants to tell me and then we just get along, but sometimes I just ignore him because he does that [referring to social missteps] way too many times" (s5, NT student)

As with social missteps, we observed that other behavioral issues (*e.g.*, rocking, jumping or making noises), traditionally demonstrated by students with autism when interacting with others were substantially reduced during the deployment of MOSOCO (no-support: 50; using-MOSOCO: 1). This large difference warrants further investigation with a larger sample. These behaviors may have been limited by the interest in and engagement with the smartphone and MOSOCO.

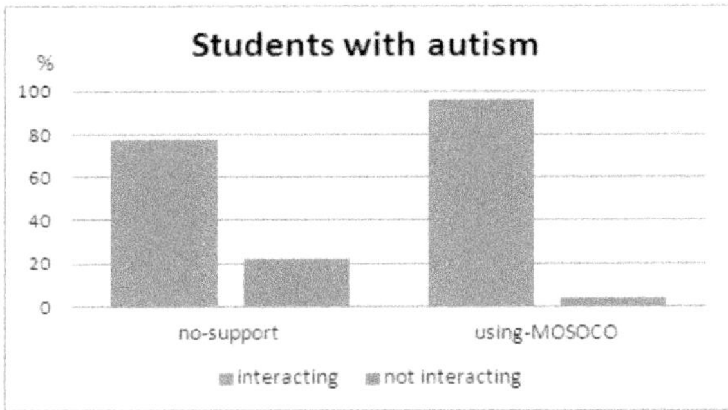

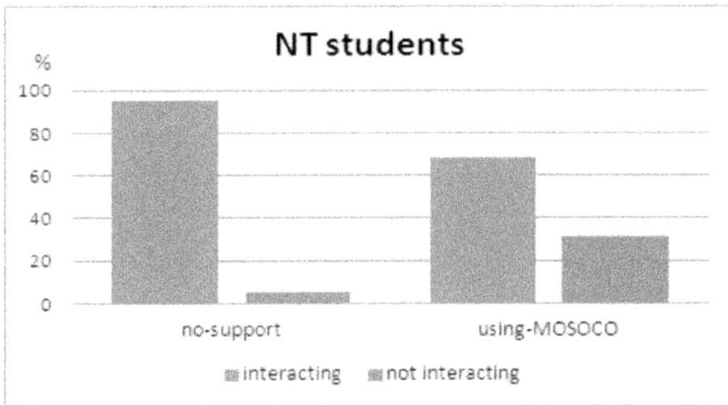

Figure 5. Percentage of students' number of interactions: Children with autism (left) and NT children (right)

Students with autism struggle to make eye contact when interacting with others [26], a problem one might imagine could be exacerbated by concentration on a mobile device. However, all students agreed that with MOSOCO they never had problems making eye contact during an interaction.

> *"It tells me to find somebody, and then I found a person and then I hear the buzz sound and it tells me to do eye sight, I mean eye communicate. Yes you have to communicate with somebody's eyes I guess." (s4, NT student)*

Similarly, "how to end a conversation" was another basic social skill that students agreed MOSOCO helped them to improve. Before the use of MOSOCO, students said that is very common to end up being alone because their partner walked away without saying anything.

> *"I've been improving on how to like end conversations, usually I'm like 'bye' then walk away." (s5, NT student)*

> *"First you would say 'hi' and then walk away without ending the conversation. Now you know how to end the conversation..." (s10, student with autism)*

Students made references to their interactions before using MOSOCO, highlighting that this application serve as a milestone for improving their social behavior.

> *"I've been like starting and ending conversations differently. We had less way less blanks [using MOSOCO]." (s1, NT student)*

Eleven of the twelve students expressed that MOSOCO helped them to understand that an interaction has an "interactive behavior," involving at least three of the basic social skills.

> *"In the beginning, you have to make eye contact, and the next step is proximity I think, and then asking questions and then asking interests, and then is cleaning up the conversation—like how to end it, like say "bye" or something." (s2, NT student)*

> *"...you have to make good eye contact, study your things to make sure you made the right move, ending the conversation instead of just walking away." (s10, student with autism)*

MOSOCO also helped students improve awareness of space and proximity when interacting with others. Beyond just understanding the anatomy of a "proper" interaction, students learned about the implications of not maintaining socially acceptable distances.

Students also learned that one of the main goals of social interactions is to know the personality of your interaction partners (*i.e.*, interests, likes, and dislikes). They began to recognize the need for multiple conversation topics and to develop new relationships through these conversations.

> *"[MOSOCO] guided us through a 'proper' conversation and taught us how to input emotions and feelings." (s1, NT student)*

These findings indicate that MOSOCO helped both students with autism and their NT peers to enhance the quality of interactions by encouraging them to follow basic steps. The reminders then solidified these directions during interactions.

Student interactions and social groups

In this work, we were interested in two types of interactions. First, given that MOSOCO is largely about helping students with autism communicate with peers, we were interested in investigating how their one-on-one interactions can be assisted or improved by mobile assistive technologies. Second, we were interested in how communication patterns amongst students influence social groups through interactions mediated by MOSOCO.

Student-Student

Overall, the number of interactions between students increased 56.73% when using MOSOCO (no-support: 386 interactions; using-MOSOCO: 605 interactions) (Figure 5). Surprisingly, we observed less time spent not interacting with others for students with autism during use of MOSOCO (no-support: 27; using-MOSOCO: 7), NT students spent more time alone (no-support: 14; using-MOSOCO: 136) (Figure 5). We hypothesize that this result could be related to the interest of NT students in interacting with the smartphone, like other youth their age [2]. The large differences in these initial comparisons warrant further detailed exploration. In contrast, students with autism, who are typically considered at a greater risk for fixating on a tool, appeared to embrace the application as a support that seamlessly mediated their interactions.

Although in our observations, NT students interacted physically with other students less while using MOSOCO (no-support: 145; MOSOCO: 13), students with autism interacted physically more with MOSOCO (no-support: 50; MOSOCO: 60). Likewise, students using MOSOCO displayed substantially, but not significantly, more verbal interactions than without (no-support: 160; using-MOSOCO: 389). These preliminary results warrant further detailed exploration with a larger sample to understand the potential trends we see in these non-significant comparisons. However, these initial results imply that MOSOCO may be better at supporting conversations than physical games, which is in keeping with the goals of social skills training in schools. Students' highlighted that after the use of MOSOCO they got to know their partners better, knowing their interests and dislikes. Additionally, we observed conversations that were qualitatively more intimate during the deployment than in the pre-deployment condition, an effect that could be in part due to the greater familiarity the students had with one another having been in class together for weeks.

With MOSOCO we observed that students with autism learn new and traditional strategies for starting an interaction, even though it has been reported that children with autism find it difficult to properly start a conversation [18], read others body language [4] or join a group of children playing [25]. Students expressed that MOSOCO helped them to understand body language and recognize invitations for starting an interaction.

> *"[MOSOCO] helped me play with others." (s12, student with autism)*

In our observations, students with autism spent more time continuously engaged when using MOSOCO (no-support: 6 min 8 sec; using-MOSOCO: 8 min 49 sec). This result warrants further investigation with a larger sample size as well as a more detailed observation of the types of engagement and the potential ramifications of use of MOSOCO on those activities.

Group Interactions

Social skills used during one-on-one interactions also bled over into groups. In particular, students exhibited new strategies for joining a group of children already playing. Before the deployment of MOSOCO, the strategies were fairly *ad hoc* and tended to encourage socialization with known classmates:

> *"I just look around for one of my friends." (s1, NT student)*

While using MOSOCO, however, the students appeared more motivated to interact with everyone. This motivation enabled students to flow more easily between groups or to enter large groups without explicitly requesting to do so. What could be happening here is that MOSOCO is providing students a "ticket to talk". MOSOCO provides the "ticket" for them so that it is easier to start conversations and talk with each other.

> *"We see each other in the face and we just play." (s4, NT student)*

After the removal of MOSOCO during post deployment, NT children integrated children with autism into their playgroups, and the students with autism joined without resistance. This kind of social integration was not seen during our baseline data collection nor reported by any staff members prior to that. Moreover, this change did not go unnoticed by the students with autism who told us during interviews that now they can join groups more easily.

> *"All you do is just go and have eye contact and they know you're playing with them and they know they're playing with you." (s10, student with autism)*

MOSOCO provided new strategies for the creation and transformation of social groups. Students universally reported that before using MOSOCO they had clearly defined social groups of friends with a sort of social protocol dictated by the social group's leader for admitting new members. These social protocols, typical of school circles, tend to demand from an individual an attempt to be integrated into the group.

> *"She has to agree and I have to agree and she has to agree too." (s9, NT student)*

The complexity of these interactions combined with limited social skills means that most children with autism tend not to be part of a social group and instead spend recess by themselves. However, after using MOSOCO, we observed that students with autism learned new strategies for creating and entering a predefined social group.

> *"Just walk up and stand in line. Then they play." (s10, student with autism)*

This kind of breaking down of the barriers of strict social groups provides some indication that even in schools with no students with autism, such tools might be useful. Additionally, making group integration a more straightforward process allowed students with autism to enjoy topics of conversation and the company of classmates rather than just the execution of an activity (*e.g.*, a game).

> *"I just face them and then I say hello and then they start talking to me and then I talk so we start a big conversation." (s7, NT student)*

CONCLUSION AND FUTURE WORK

Appropriately designed assistive technologies can play a crucial role in improving social learning and social skill practice in real-life social situations for students with autism and their NT peers. A key contribution of this work are the results of the deployment of MOSOCO in order to understand the design space and the user experience of this mobile assistive tool in real-life social situations. The exploration of 12 students' use and experience with MOSOCO throughout its deployment provides a set of emergent practices of the use of assistive technologies in real situations complementing classroom activities.

Our results demonstrate that MOSOCO is easy to use and helps students practice their social skills. In our evaluation, use of this tool reduced students with autism social missteps 56% and behavioral issues 98%, increases the number of interactions and their quality 52% of both students with autism and NT students. We found out that instead of the smartphones pulling children out of interactions, students were motivated towards social interactions and used the system without additional prompting by teachers. This behavior occurred because both students with autism and NT students were interested in sharing what they discovered, practicing the newly learned social skills and earning the rewards designed into MOSOCO. By freeing students from teachers' prompts, MOSOCO also allowed students to discover other functionalities of the smartphone that played a positive role in improving student's interactions. A deeper and bigger study is needed to explore this sort of assisted independence and its relevance to long-term MOSOCO use. Additionally, our results indicate that using mobile assistive technologies in real-life social situations have an impact on children's social groups. But open questions remain as to how social group dynamics are currently changing due the use of an assistive technology that mediates topics of conversation, with which potential users more likely choose to interact, and the creation and transformation of their existing social groups—an analysis in this direction is currently in progress.

Future work should also focus on use of tools such as these outside of schools with interaction partners who have limited knowledge of the tools and lessons. Additionally, the experience of teachers, other school staff, and parents in setting up and using such tools for students should be explored with new tools built to support these activities if necessary.

The deployment and evaluation of MOSOCO exposed tensions around its use outside classrooms and contributes important implications for the design of assistive technologies in the future, especially those destined for use in real-life situations and in mobile contexts. Our results indicate that students were highly interested in earning stars so assistive technologies should incorporate the potential for game-like interactions to earn points and rewards. Also, we noted that social cues play an important role for helping students "stay on topic" when interacting with peers. However, social cues were sometimes triggered at inappropriate times, as the application was highly unaware of the topic of conversation. Context-aware tools with voice recognition capabilities will enable the application to recognize the conversation context and react accordingly.

There are some limitations to this work. First, the design of MOSOCO is based on the application of one particular classroom-based social skills training. Use of this tool in schools in which the Social Compass *curriculum* is not currently the norm would broaden our understanding of its general applicability. Likewise, open questions remain in exploring other assistive technologies based on a different social skills training techniques in this context. Finally, as in any deployment study, perfectly controlled conditions are not possible, and some effects may be related to the sustained engagement of the students in the Social Compass *curriculum* over the course of the study rather than to tool use alone. Also our study is limited by the small number of participants. With the current sample, it's not possible to derive findings that can extend across larger populations. We want to clarify that our effort centered on acquiring a vast and detailed understanding of the practices of a few individuals across the multitude of experiences of a shared playground. Therefore, the significance of our results lies on the qualitative nature of the inquiry and analysis. We leave open for future work the study of the impact of MOSOCO with a bigger sample or in another context.

ACKNOWLEDGMENTS

This work was supported by grants from NSF CAREER #0846063, UC Mexus, PROMEP #9044, and CONACYT #10256. We thank the STAR group at UCI for reviewing early drafts of this paper. And importantly, we thank the participants and their school for helping with this study.

REFERENCES

1. American Psychiatric Association (1994). *Diagnostic and statistical manual of mental disorders (4th ed.)*
2. Berg, S., Taylor, A. and Harper, R. Mobile phones for the next generation: Device designs for teenagers. In *Proc. CHI 2003,* ACM Press (2003), 433-440.
3. Betz, A., Higbee, T. and Pollarda, J. Promoting generalization of mands for information used by young children with autism. *Research in autism spectrum disorders*, (2009), 4(3).
4. Blake, R., Turner, L., Smoski, M., Pozdol, S. and Stone, W. Visual recognition of biological motion is impaired in children with autism. *Psychological science, 2003*, 14(2).
5. Bowker, S. A,. Autism, AAC, and Proloquo2go. In *perspectives on augmentative and alternative communication*, (2009), 137-145.
6. Boyd, L., Mcreynolds, C. and Chanin, K. The social compass curriculum: a story-based intervention package for social skills. *NOC SELPA, editor 2010*, Fullerton, CA, USA, 190.
7. Carmien, S., Dawe, M., Fischer, G., Gorman, A., Kintsch, A. and Sullivan, J. F. Socio-Technical Environments Supporting People with Cognitive Disabilities Using Public transportation. In *ToCHI 2005*, 12(2), 233-262.
8. Fails, J., Druin, A. and Guha, M. Mobile collaboration: collaboratively reading and creating children's stories on mobile devices. In *IDC 2010*, 20-29.

9. Farr, W., Yuill, N. and Raffle, H. Collaborative benefits of a tangible interface for autistic children. In *Proc. CHI 2009.*

10. Fell, H., Cress, C., MacAuslan, J., and Ferrier, L. visiBabble for reinforcement of early vocalization. In *Proc. of the 6th international ACM SIGACCESS on Computers and accessibility*, ACM Press, 2003, 161-168.

11. Gal, E., Bauminger, W., Pianesi, F., Stock, O., Zancanaro, M., and Weiss, P. Enhancing social communication of children with high-functioning autism through a co-located interface. *AI Soc.* 24, 1 (2009), 75-84.

12. Gonzalez-Lopez, A. and Kamps, D. M. Social skills training to increase social interactions between children with autism and their typical peers. *Focus on autism and other developmental disabilities, 1997*, 12, 2-14.

13. Gray, C., Social stories and comic strip conversation with childs with asperger syndrome and high functioning autism. In *Asperger syndrome or highg-functioning autism.* Schopler et. Al. (eds.) Plenum press, NY, 1998, 167-198.

14. Hailpern, J., Karahalios, K., Dethorne, L., and Halle, J. Vocsyl: Visualizing syllable production for children with ASD and speech delays. In *Proc. of the 12th international ACM SIGACCESS conference on Computers and accessibility* 2010, ACM Press, 297-298.

15. Hayes, G.R., Hirano, S., Marcu, G., Monibim M., Nguyen, D.H., and Yeganyan, M. Interactive visual supports for children with autism. *Personal and ubiquitous computing,* 2010, 14(7).

16. Hendrix , K., L., van Herk, R., Verhaegh, J., and Markopoulos, P. Increasing children's social competence through games, an exploratory study. In *IDC 2009.*

17. Hirano, S.H., Yeganyan, M. T., Marcu, G., Nguyen, D. H., Boyd, L., and Hayes, G. R. Vsked: evaluation of a system to support classroom activities for children with autism. In *Proc. CHI* 2010, ACM Press, 1633-1642.

18. Hobson, R.P. and Lee, A. Hello and goodbye: a study of social engagement in autism. *Journal of autism and developmental disorders,* 1998, 2(1): 117-127.

19. Hodgdon, L.A. Visual strategies for improving visual communication. *Practical support for school and home.* Quirk roberts publishing, 1999.

20. Hourcade, J.P., Bullock-Rest, N.E. and Hansen, T.E. Improving the quality of communication and social interactions for children with autism spectrum disorders through multi-touch tablet applications. In *clinical aac research conference 2010.*

21. Hourcade, J.P., Bullock-Rest, N.E. and Hansen, T.E. Multitouch tablet applications and activities to enhance the social skills of children with autism spectrum disorders. *Personal and ubiquitous computing,* 2011, 1-12.

22. Koegel, R.L. and Kern, L. Pivotal response treatments for autism: communication, social, and academic development. (2006) *Brookes publishing company.*

23. Krantz, P.J. and Mcclannahan, L.E. Social interaction skills for children with autism: a scriptading procedure for beginning readers. *Journal of applied behavior analysis,* 1998, 31,191–202.

24. Kuniavsky, M. Observing the user experience: a practitioner's guide to user research. (2003) M*organ kaufmann.*

25. Libby, S., Powell, S., Messer, D. and Jordan, R. Spontaneous play in children with autism: a reappraisal. *Journal of autism and developmental disorders*, 1998, 28(2), 487-497.

26. Mcarthur, D. and Adamson, L.B. Joint attention in preverbal children: autism and developmental language disorder. *Journal of autism and developmental disorders*, 1996, 26(3), 481-496.

27. Monibi, M. and Hayes, G. R. Mocotos: Mobile communications tools for children with special needs. In *IDC* 2008, ACM Press, 121-124.

28. Patten, B., Sánchez, I.A. and Tangney, B. Designing collaborative, constructionist and contextual applications for handheld devices. *Computers & education,* 2006, 6(3).

29. Piper, A.M., O'Brien, E., Morris, M. and Winograd, T. Sides: a cooperative tabletop computer game for social skills development. In *Anniversary conference on CSCW* 2006, ACM Press, 1-10.

30. Smith, T. Discrete trial training in the treatment of autism. *Focus on autism and other developmental disabilities,* 2001, 15(2), 86-92.

31. Strauss, A. and Corbin, J. Basics of qualitative research: techniques and procedures for developing grounded theory. Ed. Sage. 1998, thousand Oaks, CA.

32. Swaggart, B.L., Gagnon, E., Jones-Bock, S., Earles, T.L., Quinn, C., Smith-Myles, B. and Simpson, R.L. Using social stories to teach social and behavioral skills to children with autism. *Focus on autism and other developmental disabilities*, 1995, 10, 1-6.

33. Tentori, M. and Hayes, G.R. Designing for interaction immediacy to enhance social skills of children with autism. In *ubicomp* 2010, ACM Press, 51-60.

34. Verhaegh, J. Soute,I., Kessels, A. and Markopoulos, P. On the design of camelot, an outdoor game for children. In *IDC* 2006, ACM Press, 9-16.

35. Wise, M.J. and Harris, S.L. Teaching social skills to people with autism. *Behavior modification*, 2001, 25(5), 785-802.

Developing IDEAS: Supporting Children with Autism within a Participatory Design Team

Laura Benton[1], Hilary Johnson[1], Emma Ashwin[2], Mark Brosnan[2] and Beate Grawemeyer[1]

[1]Department of Computer Science
University of Bath, UK, BA2 7AY
{L.J.Benton, H.Johnson, bg230}@bath.ac.uk

[2]Department of Psychology
University of Bath, UK, BA2 7AY
{E.L.Ashwin, M.J.Brosnan}@bath.ac.uk

ABSTRACT

IDEAS (Interface Design Experience for the Autistic Spectrum) is a method for involving children with Autism Spectrum Disorders (ASD) in the technology design process. This paper extends the IDEAS method to enable use with a design team, providing specific added support for communication and collaboration difficulties that may arise. A study to trial this extended method was conducted with two design teams, each involving three children with ASD, in a series of six, weekly design sessions focused on designing a math game. The findings from this study reveal that the children were able to successfully participate in the sessions and collaborate with other children. The findings also highlight the *positive experience* that involvement in such a process can offer this population.

Author Keywords

Participatory design; autism; children; educational games

ACM Classification Keywords

H.5.2 [Information Interfaces and Presentation]: User Interfaces - User-centered design;

General Terms

Design, Human Factors

INTRODUCTION

Technology is increasingly being seen as a beneficial addition to the strategies for supporting children with Autism Spectrum Disorders (ASD) [8]. Children with ASD typically exhibit an affinity for computers [3,20], which provide a safe environment to learn and practice skills that they may find difficult in everyday life. Computers have a number of features particularly appealing for children with ASD, such as the ability to repeat tasks and easily correct errors [20]. However, technology aimed at this population is often designed without the involvement of the children themselves. This may be due to the impairments typically associated with ASD [1,25], and the challenge of managing these impairments to allow the children to participate successfully in the technology design process.

A triad of impairments typically characterizes ASD including social impairments, communication difficulties (incorporating a lack of imagination) and rigid and repetitive behaviors [1,25]. Each of these impairments present a unique challenge for designers intending to work with this population. The process of designing technology often involves working with others as well as generating, communicating and progressing creative ideas which, given the triad of impairments, could be particularly difficult for children with ASD. However, involvement in the technology design process does offer an opportunity to practice social interaction and creative thinking in a more structured environment, which may be more suited to this population.

Participatory design (PD), a means of involving end users in the design process, is one method that has successfully involved children in the design of technology. Involving children as equal stakeholders or 'design partners' through PD offers a number of potential benefits. These include giving the children a sense of empowerment and challenge, providing them with an opportunity to develop new skills, and building their confidence both academically and socially [6,10]. This approach can also potentially result in more innovative technologies [6] and can give the children a feeling of ownership over the final product [11,24]. However, it is not known if these benefits would generalize to children with ASD or if children who have not participated would feel the same about the final product.

Benton et al. [4] began an investigation of the potential use of PD with children with ASD. The authors adopted a phased, analytical approach to overcome the different obstacles of involving children with ASD in PD sessions. The first phase, described in [4], involved a pilot study using a tailored design method, IDEAS, to investigate if this population were able to ***individually*** undertake activities typically involved in PD sessions. It was found that children with ASD do have the potential to be involved in these design activities, but often require additional appropriate support. Although there have been a few examples of similar work in this area [7,19], the benefits of the IDEAS method are that it is firmly grounded in the autism literature [1,25] and is based on the TEACCH culture of autism [18]. TEACCH is a program that is "an internationally recognized treatment and support modality for individuals of all ages with autism spectrum disorders" [18]. This ensures the IDEAS method takes into account and mitigates the full range of potential difficulties that might arise when working with this population.

The three main research aims of this paper are:

1. Can children with ASD work within a collaborative design environment, how does the existing IDEAS method need to be modified to support this and what implications does this have for them becoming full 'design partners'?
2. What are the potential benefits of involvement in a PD process for children with ASD?
3. Can using a PD process also provide benefits for children with ASD not involved in the product design?

This paper extends the IDEAS method by incorporating ***collaboration*** support, enabling it to be used with a design team including children with ASD. The extended IDEAS method, described in this paper, has been trialled with two groups of children with ASD over six design sessions focused on developing a math game. A detailed description of the method used is given with the intention of enabling other researchers to replicate the method in different scenarios to build on the results presented here. Due to the even greater social interaction and communication difficulties faced by children at the lower end of the autism spectrum this research is *initially* focused on those individuals diagnosed with high-functioning autism or Asperger Syndrome (AS). The research reported in this paper is closely related to, and will feed results into, a larger scale funded project. This project is focused on developing math-based tutoring software tailored to the needs of children with ASD, and so forms part of a coherent, integrated research agenda.

RELATED WORK

Participatory design has been used successfully with typically developing children for over a decade. Druin [5] has developed one of the most frequently used methods, Cooperative Inquiry (CI), and has also defined different roles that children can undertake within the design process [6]. These roles include user, tester, informant and design partner. The role of design partner provides children with the greatest opportunity to contribute to the design process, allowing them to become an equal stakeholder in the process. This involvement can help children to feel empowered, which can be a rare experience in childhood; particularly for children with special needs. However, as Frauenberger et al. [7] point out "the balance between empowering children and overburdening them with responsibility is a difficult one to manage" and therefore an important consideration in the development of any PD method for children. Additionally, much of the previous research in this area has focused on the benefits to the technology design rather than any potential benefits to the children themselves [10]. There has been some anecdotal evidence of typically developing children benefitting from participating in the design process, but this is often a secondary focus [15,17]. The difference in feelings of ownership and empowerment between children involved in the design process and non-participants within the same target population, has also rarely been considered.

There has been a limited amount of work undertaken to involve children with particular special needs in the design process. Guha et al. [9] have developed a framework for involving this population, based on the CI method. They highlight important aspects to be considered such as the nature/severity of the child's disability and the availability/intensity of support. Frauenberger et al. [7] state that using PD to give children with special needs control over creative processes "can be very liberating for them." In conducting a literature survey into different PD approaches they found 11 projects in which children with special needs, such as cerebral palsy, vision/hearing impairments and learning difficulties, were involved to some extent. Five of these projects included children with ASD, typically within a testing role, with some also incorporating parents or teachers as proxies for the children (e.g. [12,24]). In addition to these projects Kientz et al. [13] have also used parents and caregivers of children with ASD as proxies in the design of pervasive technology, and children with ASD were involved as testers and informants in designing facial expression recognition software [16] and a social skills development game [22].

Researchers have recently begun to involve children with ASD more fully within the design process, allowing them to undertake roles more akin to a design partner. Frauenberger et al. [7] involved a group of children, two boys with ASD and one girl with other special needs, in the design of ECHOES, a learning environment for social skills development. A separate group of typically developing children were also involved in the project. Both groups undertook a series of design activities specifically developed for the ECHOES project, as well as evaluating the prototype system. Although some of the activities were slightly adapted for the ASD group and allowed children to contribute some valuable ideas to the design process, they did not participate in every activity due to "logistical difficulties". Millen et al. [19] have taken the work in this area a step further and developed a method that could be adapted for use in other projects. Their PD method has been developed for involving children with ASD in the design of collaborative virtual environments and incorporates a series of structured activities. It has been trialled successfully with three boys (aged 13-14) with ASD, but does not appear to offer explicit support for collaboration within the group.

THE IDEAS METHOD

The IDEAS method was first presented in Benton et al. [4]. The development of IDEAS was guided by both the literature on the triad of impairments [1,25] and the TEACCH characteristics of the culture of autism [18]. The TEACCH characteristics cover the fundamental features of autism, with each characteristic being a result of impairments in one or more areas of the triad. These characteristics (with some resulting behaviors highlighted in brackets) include: difficulties with the concept of meaning; focus on details and lack of ability to prioritize their relevance; distractibility; concrete vs. abstract thinking (inc. limited social skills/emotion empathy); combining or integrating ideas; organizing and sequencing; generalization; visual vs. auditory learning; prompt dependence (inc. difficulty with initiation); strong impulses and, excessive anxiety (inc. attachment to routines). The IDEAS method was designed to support each one of these characteristics, to prevent any one of them becoming a barrier to successful involvement in the design process.

The original IDEAS method provided support to help children with ASD *participate* in typical PD activities. It was designed for use with *individual* children in a one-off design session involving (1) an introduction to the design topic, (2) discussion of previous experience/demonstration of similar software, (3) generation of own design ideas, (4) drawing out interface design of their best idea [4]. The method also included a visual schedule that displayed the sequence of these activities and acted as a checklist to document the child's progress. The IDEAS method was trialled with 10 children with ASD. The amount of support provided in each session (incorporating example ideas and template interface designs) was varied according to the needs of each child. It was found that children with ASD had the potential to take part in these creative activities, but some needed the additional support to participate fully.

In this paper the IDEAS method has been extended to further support children with ASD to *collaborate* within a design team. The extended method includes similar activities, but these activities are undertaken in more detail over six sessions with the ideas developed into a working prototype. It also uses a visual schedule in the form of a whiteboard to again allow the children to check off the tasks, as well as displaying other information about the session (Fig. 1). The design team incorporates children with ASD, specialist teaching staff and university researchers (including a researcher with the technical skills to build a computer-based prototype and another researcher with specialist autism knowledge). It is important that there are enough adults within the team to provide one-to-one support for each child if necessary. Adult team members help mediate social interaction where needed, enforcing social rules like turn taking and listening to others. Children are also praised for good examples of social interaction to highlight correct behaviour. This support can be decreased in later sessions, but is still available if required.

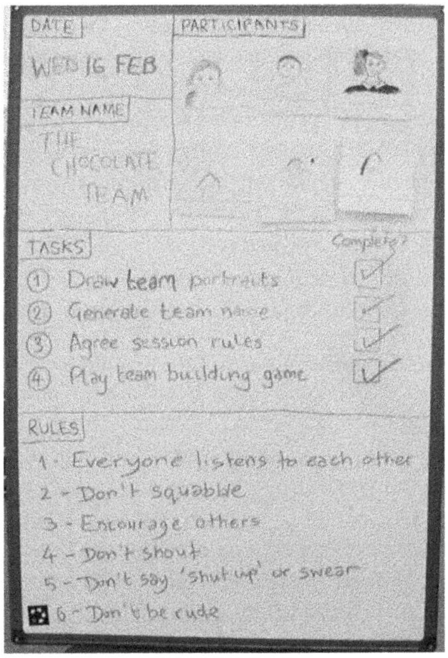

Figure 1: Visual Session Schedule

METHODOLOGY

Participants

The IDEAS method has been trialled with two groups of children with high-functioning ASD and two groups of typically developing children. However, this paper focuses solely on the results of the ASD groups. Each design team comprised three children with ASD (who knew each other), one teaching staff member from the children's school with whom they were familiar, and two university researchers with appropriate skills/knowledge. The children were aged 12-13 years, diagnosed with high-functioning autism by clinicians following DSM-IV criteria, and attended two different urban, non-faith specialist ASD schools. Group 1 contained two boys and one girl, and Group 2 contained three boys. The sessions took place on a weekly basis at the children's school and were run in a separate classroom. Following appropriate consents and ethical considerations all sessions were video-recorded, to ensure all ideas/discussions were captured. As a reward for taking part, the children were allowed five minutes at the end of each session to play a game of their choice on an iPad.

Session Content

The sessions were centered around designing a math game, chosen partly because children enjoy playing computer games, so this would add a fun element to the sessions. Also, as well as being a core curriculum subject, math is a subject high-functioning individuals with ASD often have an affinity for [14]. To help provide structure to the idea generation process the children were shown an existing math game, which involves answering basic math questions by shooting planes with the right answer on. They were then asked to focus their ideas on how to improve the way the game could give them positive or negative feedback and how they could be rewarded for winning the game, with the potential of feeding these results into the reward scheme of the math tutor. The reason for not giving the children a 'clean-slate' design problem was that in the previous IDEAS paper [4] it was clear some children with ASD were unable to generate ideas from scratch and it was important that this did not become a barrier to collaboration, the focus of this study. Below is a description of each of the six design sessions (with the TEACCH characteristics specifically supported during that session in brackets):

Session 1 Team Building *(concrete vs. abstract thinking - limited social skills/emotional empathy):* this involved structured activities such as agreeing to a team name, drawing each other's 'team portrait,' thinking of team rules (see Fig. 1) and building/playing a LEGO® team game (based on LEGO® Therapy [21] where each child was given a role i.e. designer, supplier and builder). These activities help initiate and structure the initial interaction between team members to support potential social difficulties.

Session 2 Context Setting *(concept of meaning; generalization):* this involved discussing the children's prior experiences of receiving feedback and being rewarded in school. The children then observed and interacted with four existing online and iPad-based math games, and discussed the positives/negatives/potential improvements of these. The discussion task helps the children to generalize past experiences within this new context and then the concrete examples of the design topic support potential difficulties grasping the topic context, i.e. a math game.

Session 3 Idea Generation *(combining and integrating ideas; prompt dependence):* this involved demonstrating an existing math game that was poor at giving feedback and rewarding the player. Each team member then drew out their own ideas, based on this game, onto three separate paper template interfaces (e.g. Fig. 3) for what happens if they get a math question correct (correct feedback), what happens if they get a question wrong (incorrect feedback) and how the game should reward them for winning. These ideas were then presented to the rest of the team. Templates were used to prevent the children being overwhelmed by a totally blank piece of paper, but at the same time to give plenty of scope to use their creativity and imagination. The individual ideas were then combined into three team ideas (correct, incorrect, reward), with each child responsible for making decisions as to which ideas to include for one team idea (supported by an adult), but no idea explicitly rejected. Any difficulties with combining ideas were supported through this gradual integration process and the one-to-one adult support. The idea generation process begins with paper prototyping, as using basic art supplies is an activity children are typically familiar with [6] and negates the need to teach the technical skills required to use specific computer software. Between sessions 3 and 4 the combined team ideas were transferred into Adobe® Photoshop® by a researcher with appropriate technical skills.

Session 4 Design Development *(concrete vs. abstract thinking)*: this involved showing team members the combined group ideas for the math game, now on the computer to help make the ideas more concrete. The team members then collectively discussed and agreed how to animate the prototype game, annotating ideas on a paper version of the interface (e.g. Fig. 4). Between sessions 4 and 5 an animated computer-based prototype was built, based on the annotated templates, by a researcher using Adobe® Flash®.

Session 5 Design Refinement *(concrete vs. abstract thinking)*: this involved refining the team's ideas into 'a polished product'. Team members were shown the initial computer animated (non-interactive) math game prototype and then collectively adapted printed storyboards of the prototype to improve upon the animation, sounds, look, etc. (e.g. Fig 5). Between sessions 5 and 6 a researcher refined the computer-based prototype to include these further ideas.

Session 6 Evaluation and Reflection: this involved evaluating the final prototype and reflecting on the PD experience. The children were shown the final math game prototype and completed surveys about their opinions of the prototype and of being involved in the PD sessions. They then produced a display of work from the previous five sessions, which involved writing down a list of activities and their likes/dislikes for each session. They presented this work to their Head Teacher. This overview of the sessions helps the children link what they have done and grasp the 'big picture' as well as a chance to show off their work.

The remaining TEACCH characteristics were supported through the overall session structure. To support difficulties with *organizing and sequencing,* each session began with an introduction and explanation of the tasks, a reminder of the team rules from the first session and a visual recap of the previous sessions. To support the preference for *visual learning* each task incorporated a visual component and a whiteboard was used to visually display session information including tasks and rules (Fig. 1). These explicit rules may also help to govern the social environment making children with ASD happier to participate within it. A different child in each session was assigned the role of ticking the completed tasks off to track progress. The whiteboard was also designed to help children focus on the 'big picture' rather than *irrelevant details,* by highlighting the key tasks. To help *reduce distractions* the sessions were conducted in a quiet environment and were designed to be engaging and fun with a relaxed atmosphere. Additionally to mitigate *strong impulses* related to special interests and *excessive anxiety* about the unfamiliar nature of the sessions, the sessions were run in school and incorporated a member of teaching staff familiar with the children's hobbies and interests. Finally to *reduce anxieties* about the change from their normal routine the session structure was kept consistent throughout and undertaken at the same time and place each week.

Surveys

During the final *evaluation and reflection* session the children were asked to fill in a survey to determine their opinion of the final math game prototype. The teachers were then asked to administer another survey to find out the children's opinions about the overall experience of participating in the sessions. The display of work produced in session 6 served as a memory aid for this to help the children remember the previous sessions. The teachers also filled in a separate survey to gather their personal feedback on the sessions and whether they thought it was a positive or negative experience for the children. The surveys given to the children used simple language, included 11-12 questions and incorporated a Smileyometer Likert rating scale [23] (Fig. 2) to determine the children's opinion of different elements of the game as well as the different PD activities they took part in. The Smileyometer is an established instrument, co-designed by children, who altered the neutral state as it was deemed to look angry [see 23]. This rating scale was explained before the children began the first survey and there were no difficulties understanding it. Although children with ASD can have emotional-processing difficulties, this does not extend to such stereotypical images of faces [2]. The remaining questions were multiple choice and the options for each question were typically Yes/No/Not Sure (or Maybe).

Figure 2: Smileyometer rating scale used in surveys

After each of the final sessions the researchers returned to the respective schools to show the prototype math game to a further 5-6 children with ASD who were *not involved* in the sessions. The children were not told who was involved in the design of the game. After seeing the prototype game the non-participants were asked to complete a very similar survey about their opinions of the game. This was done to compare their sense of ownership and motivation for using the game against the children that had been involved in actually designing the game.

RESULTS

The video data from each session was transcribed and coded using the triad of impairments and the individual TEACCH characteristics to highlight occurrences of successful participation as well as any specific difficulties related to typical ASD characteristics. The ideas and final prototype designs were also analyzed to look for common or distinctive themes and the processes the idea development had followed to achieve the final prototype design. The results of this analysis are discussed below.

(1) Working within a collaborative design environment

The children in both teams were able to undertake all of the tasks set during the sessions. All the children contributed ideas, gave their opinions on other ideas, and were able to collectively agree on a final idea (Figures 3 – 5 show how Group 2 progressed one of their prototype designs.).

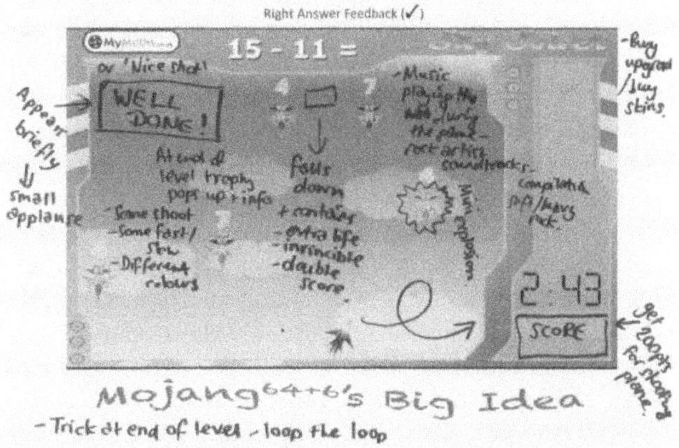

Figure 3: Group 2 combine their individual correct feedback ideas during Idea Generation session

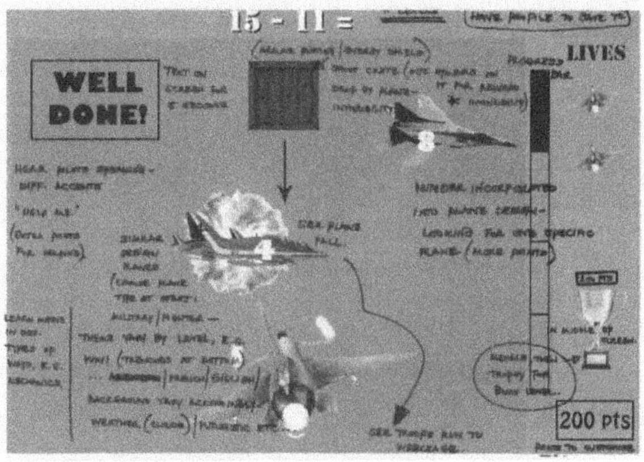

Figure 4: Group 2 add sound/animation to correct feedback ideas during Design Development session

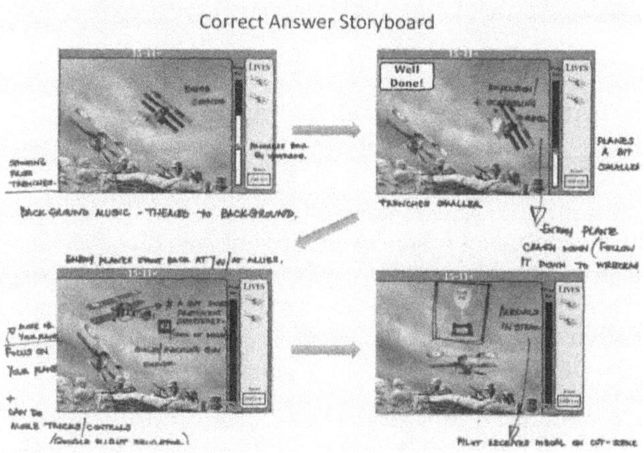

Figure 5: Group 2 refine the correct feedback prototype game storyboard during Design Refinement session

(Larger images can be viewed at: http://goo.gl/oc96f)

During the *idea generation* session all of the children were able to generate their own individual ideas (sometimes with extra support from an adult, who would ask questions/make suggestions as a prompt) and contribute to the group idea during later sessions. Some children contributed more ideas than others, but this is often the same with typically developing children. Idea initiation varied quite significantly between groups. Group 2 rarely needed prompting and began generating ideas from the start of the session, sometimes without prompting. In contrast, Group 1 were not initially forthcoming with any ideas and the adults adopted a method of prompting the children to think of ideas for a specific element of the game. It was observed that as sessions progressed the children gained more confidence in initiating ideas without direct prompting and in later sessions were able to generate many ideas without any adult support. The children in both groups generally preferred to express their ideas verbally with an adult annotating these ideas on a paper template of the interface. They occasionally drew specific interface elements, but most disliked writing and in both groups there was one child that had very limited reading/writing skills.

The social interaction across the two groups varied dramatically and this influenced the level of collaboration between the children. In the early sessions any form of interaction between the children in Group 1 was extremely limited, with the adults mediating the interaction that did happen. However, by the fourth session the children began to acknowledge each other's ideas, suggested further ideas based on another child's idea and even occasionally had social conversations without an adult involved. This progress in social interaction continued throughout the remaining sessions. The vignette below shows two children in Group 1 compromising on an idea for giving feedback:

[C wants the plane to turn into confetti if you shoot the right answer and M wants it to burst into flames]

C: Maybe if you get the wrong one it burns into flames

M: Yeah ok that's alright

Teacher: Yeah..well done that's a good one

C: Compromise [plane can burst into flames if you shoot the wrong plane and turn into confetti for the right one]

There were many more occurrences of social conversation in Group 2, particularly as two of the boys had a shared interest in gaming. This appeared to help collaboration between these boys as they were happy to expand on each other's ideas from the start, for example:

[L and G discuss mini game ideas for the reward scheme]

L: Yeah I think that shooting the right crate would be a good one

G: Yeah you could have 3 modes

L: Yeah 3 I think

G: So you could have like a survival mode, a sort of shooting crates one and endless just sort of mode

This greater collaboration helped increase the creativity of the ideas generated by this group involving imaginative concepts such as incorporating feedback through newspaper stories and an incremental storyline as an intrinsic reward. However, it is not known whether this is due to different manifestations of ASD or simply individual differences between the children. This would be a focus of future work.

The third boy in Group 2 often struggled to get his ideas heard and an adult had to step in and share his ideas so the others would listen. During the later sessions the other boys listened to him more and considered his ideas. By the end of the six sessions both groups demonstrated the ability to build on each other's ideas, suggest compromises where there were disagreements and compliment other's ideas:

[L is describing his idea for the progress bar]

G: Yeah that's actually not bad

L: And also the plane should be moving upwards on the bar

G: That works yeah…that's quite good

In both groups one of the children emerged as the dominant group member dictating the discussion and initiating significantly more ideas than the other children. In Group 2 this was evident right from the first session as one boy regarded himself as a 'gaming expert' and saw himself as having more knowledge than the other two boys. In Group 1 this happened in later sessions as one boy grew in confidence and often 'jumped in' with ideas if other group members were taking time to think. When the dominant group members took over the idea discussions the adults often had to ask the other group members for their thoughts to get them involved in the discussion again.

(2) Potential benefits of PD for children with ASD

Involvement in the PD sessions was a significant deviation from the children's normal routine. However, no child appeared distressed due to participating in the sessions, nor was any unable to participate because of anxiety related to the routine change. The children frequently checked the whiteboard displaying the visual schedule as they came into the classroom to see what they would be doing. The action of ticking off the tasks on the board helped increase the children's engagement in the sessions and they often volunteered to undertake the role for that session. Very few deviations from task were noted in either group and the children generally appeared to be engaged in the tasks. The task of designing a game proved to be a very successful topic in capturing the children's interest. It also tapped into a vast area of knowledge all of the children appeared to have, which in turn gave them confidence to participate by sharing their own ideas and opinions.

Some minor incidents of repetitive behaviour were noted in both groups. In Group 1, one boy would repeatedly share his opinion of a particular game element he did not like, finding it difficult to move on and accept this could be changed for the next session. This was overcome by repeated reassurance it could be changed, and prompting him to re-engage in the current discussion by asking for his opinion on suggested ideas. In Group 2 another boy frequently brought up the same idea and was fixated on everything being as realistic as possible. It was difficult to mitigate this particular issue during the sessions, due to the difficulty of finding the balance between progressing ideas and not discouraging the children from sharing their ideas.

The survey results were analysed to determine the success of the overall PD experience as well as the final prototype. For the PD experience the level of success was measured by the children's enjoyment of the tasks and working in a team as well as if they would choose to take part again and recommend a friend to take part. In this survey all the children were positive in their feedback stating that the activity of designing a math game as well as the experience of working in a team was either 'Good' or 'Really Good'. All the children except for one would definitely take part again (the other child said 'Maybe') and they would all rather work with the team than on their own to design the game.

(3) Potential benefits for non-participants

For the final prototype the level of success was measured in terms of whether the feedback elements would enforce the desired behaviour in the game (i.e. getting the answer right), if the reward scheme would encourage the child to continue playing the game, if the child liked the different elements of the game as well as whether they would choose to play it and recommend it to a friend. Both the children in the design teams and the children that were *not involved* were happy with the way the game gave feedback, but were less sure about the reward scheme with just under half the children from both groups saying the reward would encourage them to play the game for a long time. In terms of the look, sounds and animations in the game both groups of children rated them on average 'Good' to 'Really Good'. However the children *not involved* wanted to change a lot more game elements, frequently not because they disliked it but because they had their own idea that they thought would be better. Five out of six design team members, if given the choice, would choose to play the game, whereas just over half the children who were *not involved* would do the same.

DISCUSSION

The trial of the extended IDEAS method has so far produced some promising results regarding the involvement of children with ASD in PD sessions. The discussion has been framed around the TEACCH characteristics [4], which underpin the IDEAS method, to determine the successful elements of the method and where further work is needed.

The Concept of Meaning: introducing the design task within the context of existing games the children were familiar with helped engagement. Building up the low-tech prototype game excited them and helped them to imagine what the final game would be like.

Focus on Details: with respect to the session the visual timeline helped the children progress and know what they had to achieve before the end of each session. Having one-to-one adult support available helped children who got stuck on one idea to move on and re-engage, without affecting the rest of the group's progress.

Distractibility: the game design topic helped spark the children's interest in the sessions decreasing the likelihood of distraction from task. One-to-one adult support helped children concentrate on individual tasks and also helped bring disengaged children back into the group discussion.

Concrete vs. Abstract Thinking: the incorporation of concrete computer-based versions of the ideas at each stage helped the children imagine the possibilities and generate more creative ideas, for example the idea that integrated a storyline within the game and doubled up as a reward at the end of the game. The use of weather to show feedback as well as showing popularity through newspaper articles showed capability within both groups to generate more abstract ideas. Adults facilitating the interaction between the children was important, asking questions such as '*M what do you think of C's idea?*' to encourage the children to acknowledge each other and not just talk to the adults. This facilitation was required throughout but the children gradually initiated more interaction with each other during later sessions, demonstrating the ability to build on others ideas, compliment each other and start social conversations.

Combining or Integrating Ideas: the staged collaboration process ensured the children became comfortable with idea generation before working as a group. The consistent structure of the idea generation tasks also gave the children plenty of opportunities to practice their idea generation and collaboration skills. This was evident in the later sessions where children were increasingly building on each other's ideas. This process ensured no child became upset when, for example, their idea was not included. The adults helped support the children to come up with solutions to combine their ideas where they wanted different things.

Organising and Sequencing: beginning the session with a recap, going over the session tasks and ending with a description of what would happen next helped children understand where they were in the process. The act of ticking off each task also helped the children keep track of the current task and what was still to come. The idea generation tasks were kept to the same format across each session starting with ideas for i) correct feedback, then ii) incorrect feedback and lastly iii) the reward scheme, so the children became very familiar with the session structure.

Generalisation: the children demonstrated the ability to apply their knowledge of other games appropriately within the context of the group's idea. For example, the incorporation of a player viewpoint similar to Google flight simulator and using only non-lyrical music based on the failure of other games to include lyrical music successfully.

Visual vs. Auditory Learning: the children were given a visual representation for each iteration of the idea, which appeared to be enough to support discussions. They were happy to verbally discuss ideas by pointing at the design. The visual nature of the sessions was particularly important for involving the children who were unable to read and adult support was required for any writing, again highlighting the need for one-to-one adult support. One teacher also commented "*I think the way the sessions were structured, visual and recapped was brilliant! There were visual examples for them to get ideas from but not copy which made them use their imagination.*"

Strong Impulses: the children were given time to discuss any special interests and the adults tried to suggest ways of incorporating these into design where appropriate, if the children were unable to. The teachers were very good at trying to incorporate their interests into the design tasks, e.g. for a child that liked The Simpsons reframing the question as '*What would Homer say?*' This highlighted the importance of involving teachers as well as incorporating the children's hobbies and interests.

Excessive Anxiety: the children were told during the first session that they were free to leave any time they needed a break, but the familiar environment, the involvement of a familiar teacher and the one-to-one adult support helped ensure that no children had to leave the sessions for any reason. The children's preference for routines was used positively in the consistent session structure and the same regular weekly time slot. Adult support was needed for discouraging some negative behaviour such as a child answering every question with the same answer '*alright*', even when this was an inappropriate answer. The child was encouraged to give another answer and praised for doing so.

Prompt Dependence: this was one of the main challenges with Group 1. The teacher adopted a method for dealing with the children not initiating ideas, using lots of prompts. These prompts began as direct questions about specific parts of the design and then gradually moved on to more open-ended questions as the children's confidence in sharing their ideas with the group increased. This indicates that the adults may need to start off in a directing role and move to a supporting role in later sessions, to give extra help at the idea initiation stage and then allow the children more freedom to develop their ideas. This prompting technique should be formalized, in future work, within the IDEAS method so any adult can use it. However, the teacher's role should also include reinforcing social behaviour as it is taught in class.

CONCLUSION AND FUTURE WORK

This paper described the further development of the IDEAS method for involving children with ASD in PD. This work started with three main research aims and the extent to which these have been achieved are discussed below.

(1) Can children with ASD work within a collaborative design environment and potentially be design partners?

The outcomes of the study indicate that children with ASD can take part in PD sessions and potentially offer value as design partners with the support provided by the IDEAS method. The children were able to generate appropriate creative ideas, collaborate with both adult and child team members and compromise to collectively agree on a final group idea that fulfilled the initial brief. To support this collaboration the IDEAS method was extended to include one-to-one adult support for each child within the design team, providing additional prompts where the children struggled to generate ideas or communicate with other team members effectively. The method also included rules to help govern the social environment and began with 'team-building' activities to provide further structure to the initial social interaction. Finally the idea generation process was staged to gradually introduce the children to combining their ideas with others and making compromises where there were differences of opinion. Collaborating with others certainly did not come naturally to the children in this study, but what has been shown is their ability to learn to improve this skill over a series of sessions involving a consistent structure and adult support.

The outcome of this study indicates the potential this population has in becoming design partners. It is also important to recognize not every ASD characteristic is a possible barrier to participation in PD; this population has a number of strengths that could be of benefit to this process. For instance repetitive behaviors in activities related to their special interest and a predisposition to technology [3,20] can help increase engagement in sessions. However, during the PD process more time does need to be dedicated to building up the children's collaboration skills, with adults providing extra support for this initially and then gradually fading it out as the children demonstrate the ability to discuss ideas, listen to others and compromise unprompted.

(2) What are the benefits of PD for children with ASD?

The teachers in both design teams cited a number of benefits resulting from the children's involvement including: learning better team work skills, turn taking, compromising ideas and gaining confidence to voice opinions. These positive effects were reflected in the children's desire to take part again and continue working within the team environment. The children rated being able to generate their own ideas as either 'Good', 'Really Good' or 'Brilliant'. Furthermore, the teachers involved in the sessions, and the Head Teachers that the children presented their work to, were very positive about the overall experience, particularly about the team-working skills the children gained, and one teacher commented:

"All the sessions were positive, but I think it [the most positive aspect] *was watching their confidence grow and the relationship between the children and different adults grow, which was done by each session seeing their ideas come to life and the adults listened and took on board what they said."*

The teachers' comments also highlighted the sense of empowerment the children experienced with one teacher remarking: *"They got to do something fun and be part of the process"* and another *"...it was also a big confidence boost for all 3 to be part of something and see their own idea develop"*.

(3) Do any benefits extend to non-participants?

There was a difference in the ownership and motivation to use the final prototype between the participants and non-participants. It was clear that involvement in the design process increased the children's sense of ownership and motivation, with less suggested changes and an increase in likelihood to play the game and recommend to a friend. This was also highlighted in the importance for the children in Group 2 to be acknowledged in the credits of the game, with one child stating *"I'd play the whole game just to see credits with my name in."*

Limitations of this study

Due to the time consuming nature of running PD sessions it has not been feasible to trial the IDEAS method with more groups. Therefore despite the positive outcome of this study it is difficult to generalize the results and conclude that all high-functioning children with ASD would be able to participate in PD using the IDEAS method. These results also do not currently apply to individuals with low-functioning autism. It is acknowledged that the task of 'designing a game' was chosen to specifically appeal to this population and the choice of a different design topic may have been less successful. However, it was important that the appeal of the task was not initially a barrier to collaboration and it is hoped that the lessons learned in this study could be applied in a research scenario with a less appealing design topic. It is possible that missing lessons could have contributed to the children's positive view of the sessions, however pleasant reward times are incorporated into most lessons, the children are often brutally honest and can find disruption to their familiar routine stressful, which would make a 'halo' effect unlikely.

A number of other external factors could also influence the success of the method such as the children's individual interests and motivation to take part, having a teacher willing to support the process, as well as choosing the right mix of children who are willing to work with one another. It is also important to point out that the IDEAS method is being developed incrementally with the end goal being the full inclusion of children with ASD as design partners within the PD process. Although this work has shown there is the potential to achieve this, a full PD study would need to be undertaken over a longer period of time and result in the full design/build of a product to verify these results. What has been shown though, in two different schools, is that children with ASD do have the potential to participate. Furthermore by undertaking careful planning before the sessions and using a method like IDEAS to support the process, then there is a good chance of success as well as to give the children a positive experience.

PD Session Guidelines

From the experiences in this study we offer the following preliminary set of guidelines, framed by the relevant TEACCH guidelines, to heighten the pleasure and well-being effects of participants with ASD in PD sessions:

1. *Concept of Meaning:* Ensure the children are familiar or can identify with the design topic in some way.
2. *Distractibility:* Identify the hobbies and special interests of each child and incorporate these within examples and discussions, particularly as a way of engaging a distracted child.
3. *Concrete vs. Abstract Thinking:* Be prepared for very direct criticism. If the children do not like something, expect them to say so. Do not take offense and give clear explanations/solutions to issues.
4. *Organising and Sequencing/Visual vs. Auditory Learning:* Ensure the children know what activities to expect during each session and represent these in a visual way wherever possible.
5. *Excessive Anxiety/Prompt Dependence:* Involve an enthusiastic member of teaching staff, who 'gets' the project, knows the children well and is able to reinforce the support structure and improvise where necessary.
6. *Strong Impulses:* Use the personal strengths of each child to build up their confidence in the sessions.
7. Finally, involve researchers from a range of backgrounds, as it is important to have adult team members with technical skills as well as the psychological knowledge to best engage the children.

As both groups were able to generate ideas given a basic game framework as a starting point, future work could determine whether the children can cope with less support for the initial idea allowing them even greater scope for creativity. The method could also be trialled with lower functioning children to see if they are able to participate with the same level of support, need an increased level, or whether the type of contribution they could make to the design process would need to be reconsidered.

The positive results reported in this paper demonstrate that the potential benefits of incorporating typically developing children in PD are also applicable to children with ASD. Therefore excluding this population from involvement in the design process is not only a possible detriment to the end product, but is also depriving this population of a potentially rewarding and pleasurable experience. It is hoped though, that as a result of this work, designers will recognise the valuable contribution children with ASD can make to the design process and seek to involve them by using a supported design method such as IDEAS.

ACKNOWLEDGMENTS

We would like to thank the schools for agreeing to take part in this study, the teachers for giving up their time to be involved and the children for sharing their ideas with us.

REFERENCES

1. APA. *DSM-IV Diagnostic and Statistical Manual of Mental Disorders* (4th edition). American Psychiatric Association, Washington DC, 1994.
2. Ashwin, E., Brosnan, M., Johnson, H., Grawemeyer, B. and Benton, L. Social functioning, systemizing ability and emotion recognition in autism spectrum conditions. *Autism Neuroscience Conference 2010,* Cambridge, UK.
3. Barry, M. and Pitt, I. Interaction design: a multidimensional approach for learners with autism. *Proc. IDC 2006,* ACM Press, 33-36.
4. Benton, L., Johnson, H., Brosnan, M., Ashwin, E. and Grawemeyer, B. IDEAS: an interface design experience for the autistic spectrum. *Ext. Abstracts CHI 2011*, ACM Press, 1759-1764.
5. Druin, A. Cooperative inquiry: developing new technologies for children with children. *Proc. CHI 1999*, ACM Press, 595-599.
6. Druin, A. The role of children in the design of new technology. *Behaviour and IT 21*, 1 (2002), 1-25.
7. Frauenberger, C., Good, J. and Keay-Bright, W. Designing technology for children with special needs – bridging perspectives through participatory design. *CoDesign 7*, 1 (2011), 1-28.
8. Goldsmith, T.R. and LeBlanc, L.A. Use of technology in interventions for children with autism. *Journal of Early and Intensive Behavior Int. 1,* 2 (2004), 166-178.
9. Guha, M.L., Druin, A. and Fails, J. Design with and for children with special needs: An inclusionary model. *Proc. IDC 2008*, ACM Press, 61-64.
10. Guha, M.L., Druin, A. and Fails, J. Investigating the impact of design processes on children. *Proc. IDC 2010*, ACM Press, 198-201.
11. Kam, M., Ramachandran, D., Raghavan, A., Chiu, J., Sahni, U. and Canny, J. Practical considerations for PD with rural school children in underdeveloped regions: early reflections from the field. *Proc. IDC 2006,* ACM Press, 25-32.
12. Keay-Bright, W. The reactive colours project: demonstrating participatory and collaborative design methods for the creation of software for autistic children. *Design Principles and Practices: An International Journal 1*, 2 (2007), 133-151.
13. Kientz, J.A., Hayes, G.R., Westeyn, T.L., Starner, T. and G.D. Pervasive computing and autism: assisting caregivers of children with special needs. *IEEE Pervasive Comp. Magazine 6*, 1 (2007), 28-35.
14. James, I. Autism and Mathematical Talent. *The Mathematical Intelligencer 32,* 1 (2010), 56-58.
15. Large, A., Nesset, V., Tabatabaei, N. and Beheshti, J. Bonded design re-visited: involving children in information visualization design. *Canadian Journal of Inform. and Library Science* 32, 3/4, (2008), 107-139.
16. Madsen, M., el Kaliouby, R., Eckhardt, M., Hoque, M.E., Goodwin, M.S. and Picard, R. Lessons from participatory design with adolescents on the autism spectrum. *Proc. CHI 2009*, ACM Press, 3835-3840.
17. Mazzone, E., Read, J. and Beale, R. Design for and with disaffected teenagers. *Proc. NordiCHI 2008,* 290-297.
18. Mesibov, G.B., Shea, V. and Schopler, E. *The TEACCH approach to autism spectrum disorders*. Springer, New York, 2004.
19. Millen, L., Cobb, S. and Patel, H. A method for involving children with autism in design. *Proc. IDC 2011,* ACM Press, 185-188.
20. National Autistic Society. Computers: applications for people with autism. http://www.autism.org.uk.
21. Owens, G., Granader, Y., Humprey A. and Baron-Cohen, S. LEGO©Therapy and the social use of language programme: an evaluation of two social-skills interventions for children with high functioning autism and asperger syndrome. *J Autism Dev Disord 38*, (2008) 1944-1957.
22. Piper, A.M., O'Brien, E., Morris, M.R. and Winograd, T. SIDES: a cooperative tabletop computer game for social skills development. *Proc. CSCW 2006*, ACM Press, 1-10.
23. Read, J.C. and MacFarlane, S. Using the fun toolkit and other survey methods to gather opinions in child computer interaction. *Proc. IDC 06*, ACM Press, 81-88.
24. van Rijn, H. and Stappers, P.J. Expressions of ownership: motivating users in a co-design process. *Proc. PDC 2008,* 36-39.
25. Wing, L. and Gould, J. Severe impairments of social interaction and associated abnormalities in children: epidemiology and classification. *J Autism Dev Disord 9,* (1979) 11-29.

Supporting Face-To-Face Communication Between Clinicians and Children with Chronic Headaches Through a Zoomable Multi-Touch App

Juan Pablo Hourcade, Martha Driessnack, and Kelsey E. Huebner
University of Iowa
Iowa City, IA 52242 USA
{juanpablo-hourcade, martha-driessnack, kelsey-huebner}@uiowa.edu

ABSTRACT

Chronic headaches are one of the top five health problems for young children in the United States, negatively affecting their quality of life and learning opportunities. A clear understanding of children's headache characteristics is crucial for delivering appropriate treatment. However, current data collection methods were designed for adults often resulting in insufficient information. In this paper we present a novel method to help children communicate with health care providers and researchers about their headaches. It augments an existing child-centric method called Draw-and-Tell Conversation, which has already been shown to provide more actionable information from children than standard data collection methods. It does so by enabling children to draw their symptoms on a zoomable drawing application, giving them the ability to provide more details and context than on paper. We present a study conducted with nineteen children aged 7 to 12 suggesting that children provided more information about their headaches when using the zoomable drawing application than when drawing on paper. This study provides a rare example of a mobile device used to enhance face-to-face interactions and contributes evidence of a specific benefit of zoomable user interfaces.

Author Keywords

Children; pain; communication; headaches; draw; zoomable user interfaces; mobile devices; tablets.

ACM Classification Keywords

H.5 [Information interfaces and presentation (e.g., HCI)]: Miscellaneous; J.3 [Life and medical sciences]: Health;

INTRODUCTION

Mobile devices are making it increasingly easy to connect remotely with others, as well as access information anytime, anywhere. At the same time, they may often be getting in the way, or at the very least discouraging face-to-face interactions. For example, a decade ago, it would not have been unusual to see strangers strike a conversation when sitting next to each other in public transportation, or in a commercial flight. Nowadays, it is more likely that many passengers will be wearing their headphones while playing games or listening to music on their mobile devices, broadcasting to those near them that they are not interested in face-to-face interactions. Likewise, when traveling to another city, there is less of a need to interact with locals since it is easy to find a good restaurant or the closest automatic teller machine by going online. The time spent interacting with devices instead of people could end up affecting our ability to engage in face-to-face interactions as suggested by a recent study of high school students in the United States that found a positive relationship between social anxiety in face-to-face situations and communicating with others online or via text messaging [35].

While one could argue about the relative merits of remote versus face-to-face interactions, there are situations when face-to-face interactions are not only necessary, but may not be sufficiently rich if limited to unassisted communication. The specific situation we address in this paper is communication between children with chronic headaches and health care providers. A clear understanding of headaches is crucial to make a proper diagnosis and provide appropriate treatment to the child. Regretfully, current practice emphasizes the use of data collection techniques developed for adults, which often results in insufficient information. The need for better communication between children and health care providers and researchers is such that the United States National Institutes of Health recently launched an initiative titled *No More Hand-Me-Down Research*, calling in part for novel data collection methods when interacting with children.

To address the shortcomings of current approaches to communicating with children, Driessnack developed the Draw-and-Tell Conversation (DTC) method. DTC is a child-centric approach in that it begins by offering children the opportunity to collect their thoughts before they respond through drawing. For example, children can be asked to draw their pain before they are asked to describe it verbally. In earlier studies, providing children the opportunity to draw, such as proposed in DTC, results in more information being shared [17]. Further, the increased information provided by the children not only provided new data, but it also provided clinicians and researchers with accurate, relevant, and actionable insights [18].

In this paper we augment DTC through the use of a zoomable drawing application on a multitouch tablet, thus providing a rare example of a zoomable user interface and a mobile application to improve and augment face-to-face communication. An exploratory evaluation comparing paper-based DTC to zoomable DTC suggests that when using zoomable DTC children with chronic headaches provide more information about their headaches. The main contribution of the paper is empirical evidence of the advantages of a mobile, zoomable drawing tool to facilitate face-to-face communication for a vulnerable population. In fact, this is the first empirical evidence of the benefits of zoomable user interfaces to facilitate face-to-face communication. It is also the first research study in our field focused on children with chronic headaches.

RELATED WORK

Chronic headaches

Chronic headaches are one of the top five health problems for young children in the United States and there are indications that existing rates are on the rise [30]. Chronic headaches are intrusive, they interfere with learning, and they negatively impact the quality of children's lives. Headaches currently account for over a million lost school days each year in the United States [40]. Further, more than 70 percent of children with chronic headache complaints continue to experience headaches into adulthood, leaving to question whether or not existing measures and intervention efforts are adequate [1] [10] [14]. Recent advances in both the developmental and biological sciences build an increasingly persuasive case for a need to redirect health-related research efforts to children and childhood [38]. Refocusing efforts to childhood health and illness experiences, especially those such as headaches that appear to follow children into adulthood, may lay the groundwork for enhancing self-management skills and play an important role in primary prevention. Ultimately, these upstream efforts with children may also prove to be a powerful strategy for reducing the population-level burden of chronic morbidity, as more effective interventions early in life have the potential to produce measureable benefits later in educational achievement, economical productivity, and responsible citizenship [38].

While childhood headaches are a serious challenge, it is also significant that data collection tools being used today in the assessment, classification, and evaluation of childhood headaches were developed with and for adults with headaches, not children. These tools focus primarily on headache frequency, duration, and intensity as the sole outcome criteria reported using numeric rating scales and/or picture charts of facial expressions in retrospective diaries. The tools were handed down in spite of continued evidence that pediatric headaches manifest themselves differently than adult headaches and existing tools do not seem to capture the acute or chronic impact of headaches in children's life experiences [14] [24] [39]. It has been suggested that adding a developmental perspective to assessment and evaluation of childhood headaches could enhance treatment approaches and effects [1] [10] [28] [41]. New efforts are being made to computerize existing rating scales and picture charts. However, adding a 'technological face lift' does not address the underlying concern, which is the validity of data obtained from children using adult-centered tools. Instead, we need to expand the armamentarium of self-report tools to include new tools that match children's information processing capabilities. This back-to-the-future approach to tool development may open the door to the collection of more accurate, complex, relevant, and actionable information collected from children. Improving the quality of self report in one focused sample of children may also provide insights into how to access health-related experiences from children with other challenging conditions, opening the doors for improving child health care and outcomes across the health care continuum.

Draw-and-Tell Conversation

DTC begins with an *a priori* art directive that includes either an original drawing or a drawing-completion task. The art directive is specifically developed to reflect the study purpose and, along with the interview guide, is used by the researcher or clinician to facilitate the conversation that follows. For this study, the art directive focused on headache pain. In DTC, the opportunity to draw provides children with a transitional space where their thoughts can be externalized and organized before they are asked to share them with the researcher [31]. DTC has been shown to be more effective in bringing out the complexities of children's experiences than the more typical adult-centered approaches to data collection e.g., directed interviews, surveys, and questionnaires [13] [16] [17] [18] [19].

Computing Technologies for Children in Medical Settings

Children also need help when in stressful and uncomfortable situations while they are hospitalized. There have been a few efforts in the HCI community to address this challenge. For example, Weiss et al. [43] helped children stay connected with their classrooms through video-conferencing. Bers et al. [9] assisted pediatric patients in a dialysis unit by providing them with a virtual community. This enabled the children to receive support while they were in a situation where they could not physically interact with others as they received treatment. By providing a way to communicate with others, the tool helped children think of other things while having dialysis, which helped reduce stress and anxiety.

The same research group had previous experience in hospital settings through the use of text-based storytelling technologies with children in a hospital's cardiology unit [8]. More recently, Chin and Tsuei [12] also developed a storytelling system for hospitalized children with chronic illness to share and co-narrate stories. None of these efforts were meant to facilitate communication between patients and health professionals.

There has also been evidence of computing technologies used to distract children in order to lessen the impact of pain while reducing stress and anxiety. For example, Dahlquist et al. [15] found playing video games improved pain tolerance in children experiencing cold pressor pain. Similarly, van Twillert et al. [42] used immersive virtual reality to reduce pain in pediatric and adult burn patients during wound dressing changes. These efforts were limited at helping children as pain occurs, as opposed to helping health professionals better understand pain in order to better treat it.

Augmentative and Alternative Communication Devices

Augmentative and Alternative Communication (AAC) devices enable people, including children, with communication impairments to verbally interact with others [22]. They typically do so by providing visual menus of items that can be put together into phrases, which are then spoken by the computer through a speech synthesizer. Populations who use these devices include autistic people and people with aphasia. AAC is currently delivered in most cases through dedicated tablets (e.g., the Dynavox [21]), or through applications available for multi-purpose tablets such as iPads (e.g., Proloquo [37]). They represent a rare example of the use of mobile devices to enable face-to-face communication. While these devices are very helpful, they do limit communication choices to those available in the device at the time of use.

Zoomable User Interfaces

Since being introduced in the early 90s [34] zoomable user interfaces (ZUIs) have moved from being used largely in research projects to increasingly wide use [7]. ZUIs have proved particularly powerful in handheld devices where smaller displays limit the amount of data that can be presented.

The most popular ZUIs have been geared at helping users explore data. Examples include browsing personal photo collections [6][3], browsing and navigating through notes [32], launching and closing applications [2], and navigating web pages [4]. ZUIs have also been used to support authoring of zoomable media. The most popular example is the authoring of slide presentations [23][33][36].

Closer to our research are ZUIs designed for children to author content. KidPad [25] is a collaborative storytelling tool that enables children to create content on a large zoomable canvas, mostly by drawing. KidPad was designed and developed before multitouch displays and tablets were available, so it supported collaboration through multiple mice and the use of "local tools" in the user interface (a user's mode was represented in the user's cursor).

In spite of the above-mentioned examples and plenty of anecdotes, there is little empirical evidence of the advantages of ZUIs for authoring media. In particular, while there is anecdotal evidence from KidPad, for example, that children may put together richer stories in these environments [25], no research studies have been conducted to back up this claim. As a matter of fact, in a recent review of ZUIs, Bederson lists "definitive understanding of the benefit" as the first to-do item for further research on ZUIs [7]. In this paper, we provide empirical evidence of the advantages of ZUIs for communication, in particular as they enable children to provide a richer description of their headaches when compared to using paper and pencil.

RESEARCH OBJECTIVE

Our goal was to explore the use of multitouch tablets to augment the benefits of DTC. In particular, we wanted to compare the feasibility and possible benefits of two tablet-based approaches to paper-based DTC. One was based on showing the children a picture of their face that they could squeeze and stretch with their fingers and draw on with a digital pen. We call the application Photogoo. The rationale for using Photogoo was that seeing their own faces the children could better contextualize their symptoms and express symptoms such as the head feeling like it is being squeezed.

The other was a simple drawing application that enabled children to draw on a large zoomable canvas and change colors. The rationale for using this application was that it could enable children to provide more information about headaches by enabling them to zoom into a region that caused pain while also moving from drawing symptoms on the head and the rest of the body. We provide more details on the applications in the materials section below.

STUDY SETUP

Participants

The participants were nineteen 7 to 12 year old children. While the median age was 10.5 years, the primary focus of recruitment efforts was to achieve maximum variation across this age span to ensure inclusion of children from each year of age. Ten were female and nine were male. To ensure representation from various socio-economic levels, parents were asked if their child was eligible for/participated in the state free/reduced lunch program (10 were eligible; 9 were not). Recruitment was coordinated through two pediatric neurology clinics. All children had a primary headache diagnosis (e.g., migraine or tension-type headaches). Children with secondary headache diagnoses (e.g., brain tumor) were excluded. We do not take into account data collected from a 20th child diagnosed with autism due to the child's significant challenges in communication. Given the high variability between children with autism though, we want to emphasize that this does not mean that our approach will not work for all children with autism.

Materials

For paper-based DTC, we provided children with two sheets of paper, one with the outline of a human head, the other with the outline of a human body (see Figure 1). We also gave them an assortment of colored pencils and markers.

For the tablet applications, we used a Dell XT2 tablet with a 12 inch multitouch display and a digital pen. It runs Windows 7, and when the children used it, we folded the screen over the keyboard so it would be in tablet mode.

We used two open source applications we developed for a separate research project to enable children to conduct DTC on the tablet. We selected them because they are very simple, with a minimal user interface. A zoomable drawing application (see Figure 2), enabled children to draw with the digital pen on a large zoomable canvas. In the application they could pan by dragging one finger on the display, zoom and rotate by using the "pinch" gesture with their fingers [29], change colors by touching the color palette, or draw by using the digital pen.

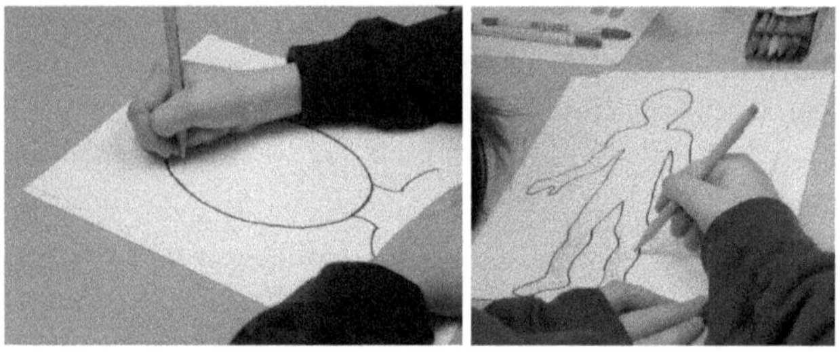

Figure 1. Children drawing on paper with and outline of a human head on the left, and a human body on the right during paper-based DTC.

Figure 2. Child drawing on zoomable drawing application on a Dell XT2.

The other application is called Photogoo. It enables users to modify a picture shown on the screen using their fingers to squeeze or stretch it. Users can also draw on top of the picture.

Procedure

We conducted study sessions in quiet rooms at two large hospitals in two metropolitan areas in the United States Midwest. We began sessions with introductions and then obtained assent and consent from the participants and their parents. A pediatric nurse experienced in using DTC with children facilitated the sessions (the same nurse facilitated all the sessions).

When conducting paper-based DTC, the pediatric nurse gave children first the outline of a head on which they could draw while having a conversation with her (as in Figure 1). She then gave them the outline of the body (also in Figure 1) asking them if there were any symptoms elsewhere in the body.

When conducting zoomable DTC, we started the zoomable drawing application and quickly drew a couple of lines and demonstrated how to pan and perform the "pinch" gesture. We then drew head and body outlines for the participants unless they asked to do it themselves before they began using the software.

When children used Photogoo, we first demonstrated the application using someone else's picture and showed them how to distort it and draw on it. Then, we uploaded a picture of their head (shot from the front) onto the display. Children could then distort their picture using their fingers, or draw on it with the digital pen.

Design

This was an exploratory within-subjects study. All participants used all three methods. We began the study by having participants use paper-based DTC, followed by the two tablet applications, with Photogoo always first and zoomable drawing second. Toward the end of the study we switched order so that six of the participants experienced DTC with the tablet first (Photogoo first, then zoomable drawing), followed by paper-based DTC.

Therefore, the independent variable was the media used to conduct DTC. The dependent variables include the time to conduct each DTC, the headache descriptors provided through each DTC, and the drawings themselves.

RESULTS

As we completed the sessions it quickly became clear that Photogoo was not appropriate. The children either did not like having to manipulate their own faces to show how headaches feel and perhaps more important, they also told us they did not know what they looked like when they have headaches. We therefore focus our presentation of results on paper-based DTC and zoomable DTC.

Coding of Headache Descriptors

Each data collection session was videotaped, transcribed verbatim, and then analyzed using qualitative content analysis [27]. Each transcript was reviewed and coded individually and then compared across all the children for overlap and convergence of content and/or themes [5]. An organizational matrix was then developed.

The initial sort of the data created three (3) categories of descriptors: 1) location, 2) symptoms, and 3) actions. The first category included descriptors about the location(s) of the children's headaches. The second category included specific descriptions and characteristics of the children's headaches. Descriptive units within this second category were further subdivided by site: head, eyes, stomach, and other body areas (see Table 1 for examples). The third category reflected children's actions or behaviors that accompanied their headaches (see Table 2 for examples).

Table 1. Examples of descriptors of children's symptoms.

HEAD
Feels like someone hit me in the head really hard
Crack/Like an earthquake/plates move apart
Pushing/Squeezing/Squished
Pressure all at once/Three places coming into it
Loud (inside my head)
Swollen (my head feels swollen)
Stings/stinging
Like nail(s)
Pounding/Throbbing
Being hit over and over
Like a heartbeat in your head/Blood pumping
Hammer hitting you/Sledge hammer
One Pound all at one time
EYES
Sometimes it goes into your eyes
See bright lights
Blurry/Tearing/Droopy
STOMACH
Pain/Cramps
Stomach Pressure/Squeezing/Tight like a knot//No room
Nausea/Swishing around/Like waves in your stomach
Vomiting
OTHER PARTS OF THE BODY
Look pale
Feel warm/Hands sweaty
Dizzy/ Things go round and round
Arm/Leg pain

Table 2. Examples of descriptors of children's actions/behaviors.

Close eyes
Take glasses off
Can't concentrate
Lie down/lay still/sleep
Ice pack/cold rag

The number of individual descriptive units within each category was calculated within and then totaled across categories for comparison.

Analysis of Descriptors

Since all participants used all DTC methods, we compared paper-based DTC to zoomable DTC by recording how many additional descriptors were provided by the second method used by participants (not mentioned when using the first method). We found that when participants used paper-based DTC after zoomable DTC no new descriptors were added. On the other hand, when participants used paper-based DTC first and zoomable DTC second, participants mentioned a median of four additional descriptors (mean=3.54) when using zoomable DTC. The difference between additional descriptors was statistically significant based on a t-test ($p<.005$).

We also compared the number of descriptors participants mentioned during their first method. The difference was statistically significant based on a t-test ($p<.05$), with participants mentioning more descriptors when using zoomable DTC. See Figure 3 for box plots.

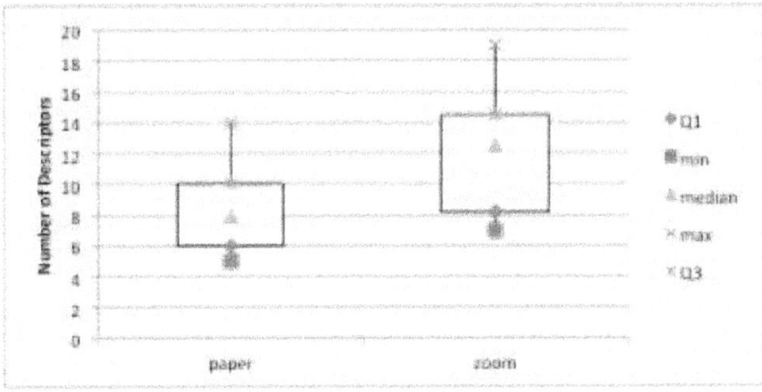

Figure 3. Box plots of number of descriptors based on first method used.

Session Time

We completed DTC sessions, either paper or zoomable in a short amount of time, with only one child taking more than 10 minutes during a paper-based DTC session. This suggests that both forms of DTC can be reasonably incorporated into clinic visits. Figure 4 shows that most participants who used paper-based DTC first spent a bit more time on zoomable DTC, while Figure 5 shows that when zoomable DTC was used first participants spent more time on it than on paper-based DTC. Actually, participants seemed to spend a similar amount of time on zoomable DTC no matter in what order it was experienced, while they spent more time on paper-based DTC when it was experienced before zoomable DTC than when it was experienced after it. This agrees with our general assessment that participants had more to add when using zoomable DTC after paper-based DTC than when experiencing DTC types in the opposite order.

Drawing Characteristics and Quotes

While coding for descriptors gives us a sense of the amount of data collected through each method, the drawings themselves together with quotes from the participants provide a better sense for how the methods differed, and for the reasons why zoomable DTC provided advantages. They also enable us to understand the great needs of this population and how clearly and acutely the children managed to describe their pain, illustrating it in heart-wrenching ways that nonetheless could help them obtain more appropriate treatment. Below are the children's voices and their drawings.

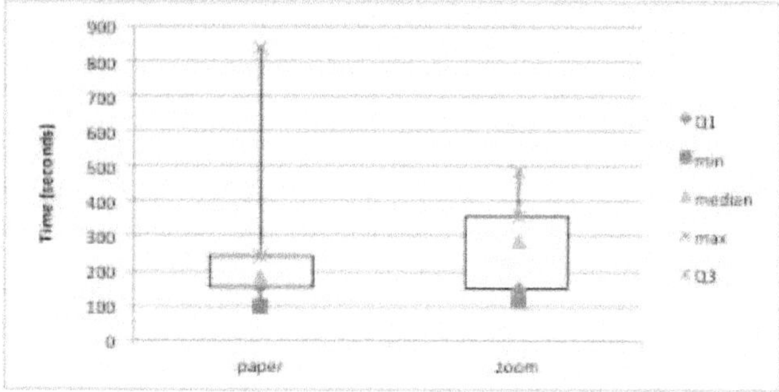

Figure 4. Box plots of session time in seconds when paper-based DTC was conducted first by DTC type.

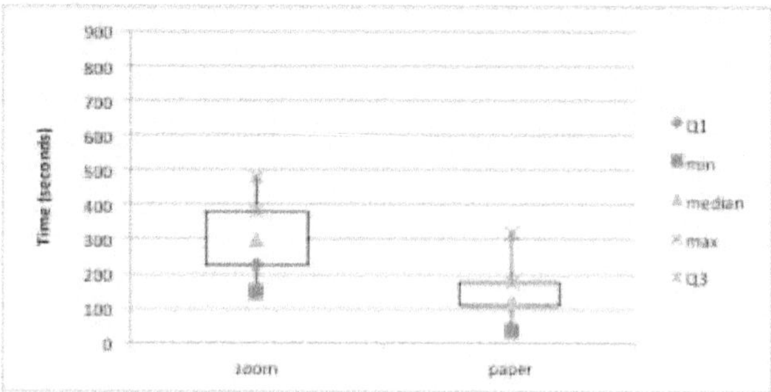

Figure 5. Box plots of session time in seconds when zoomable DTC was conducted first by DTC type.

Zooming to Provide More Details

One of the main advantages of zoomable DTC is that it enabled many of the children to provide more details on their symptoms by zooming into areas of pain. Below are several examples of children making use of this possibility. In many cases we also contrast the zoomable drawings with the drawings on paper.

For example, participant 3 only drew arms holding the area of the head that hurt when using paper-based DTC. When moving on to zoomable DTC, the participant drew two heads for two types of headaches experienced, and zoomed in to reveal a throbbing headache while saying "It would like be bum bum.. bum bum... bum bum.. like that. It usually starts out really big then gets littler and littler then the littlest." The child also drew what one of the circles in the head looks like inside and described it as "kind of like termites eating at wood." See Figure 6.

Another example comes from participant 9 who had drawn crosses on the head during paper-based DTC to note the location of the pain. Under zoomable DTC, the child was able to zoom into them and provide extra details. The child drew green lines around the cross-like drawings representing pain and added "It's all the pain coming into it and putting more pressure." See Figure 7.

Participant 6 had drawn circles above the eyes to show the location of the pain using paper-based DTC. The child did the same when using zoomable DTC, but in addition zoomed into one of the pain areas and added extra spots inside of it saying "like on the outside it doesn't hurt, but right there it stings." See Figure 8.

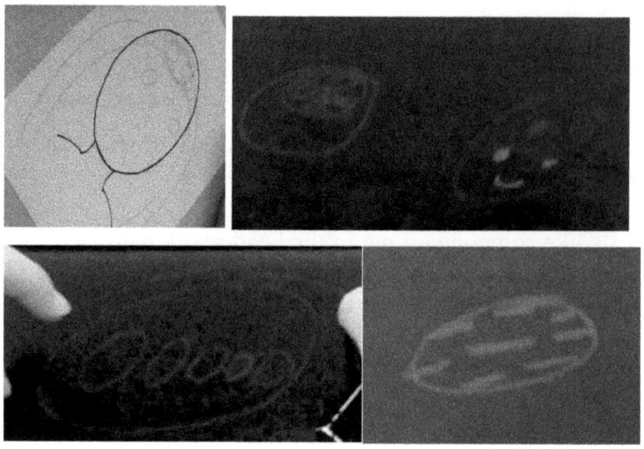

Figure 6. Participant 3's paper-based DTC drawing (top left), and various zoom levels for his zoomable DTC.

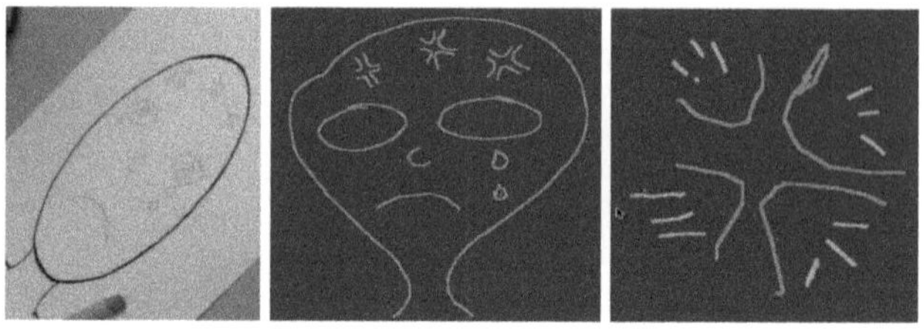

Figure 7. Participant 9's head drawings, zooming in to provide extra detail on the headaches.

Participant 10 referred to the headache feeling like cracks in the head when using paper-based DTC. "It's like there's a crack," the child said. When using zoomable DTC, the child added extra lines to the crack on the head and added it was "kind of an area like an earthquake when the plates move; like just one area feels irritated." See Figure 9.

Participant 13 explained the headache as having a nail and a knife being driven into the head. When asked about how it feels at those spots the child said the pain "spreads out" and drew accordingly. The child then zoomed into the knife spot and explained that it felt like it was "going in and out." This is something the child was not able to do with paper-based DTC. After zooming out, this participant provided more context saying "sometimes my neck hurts," drawing lines around the neck and saying it was "sore...kind of bumpy feeling." See Figure 10.

Participant 18 began by locating the headache on both sides of the head, drawing and telling us "it hurts really bad on the sides." We asked the child to zoom into one of the areas of pain to see what it felt like inside. The child drew hammers coming into a particular point while adding "it feels like it's being hit like pounded I guess."

The child also told us about feelings of nausea and stomach pain, proceeding to draw the location of the pain saying it hurts in one spot. Participant 18 was not able to provide the same level of detail when using paper-based DTC. See Figure 11.

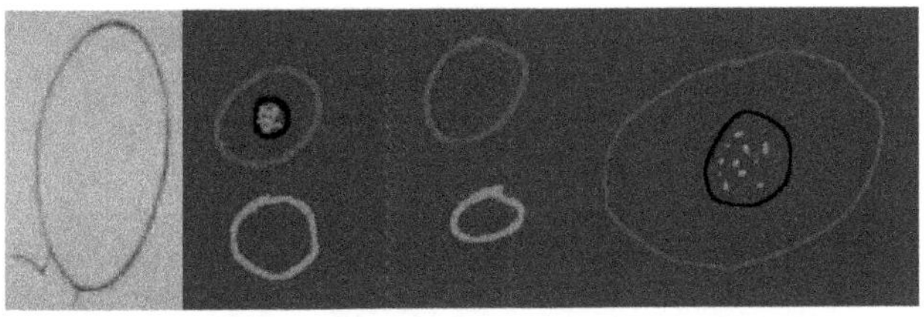

Figure 8. Participant 6's drawings. The zoomable DTC drawings show detail of pain areas above the eyes.

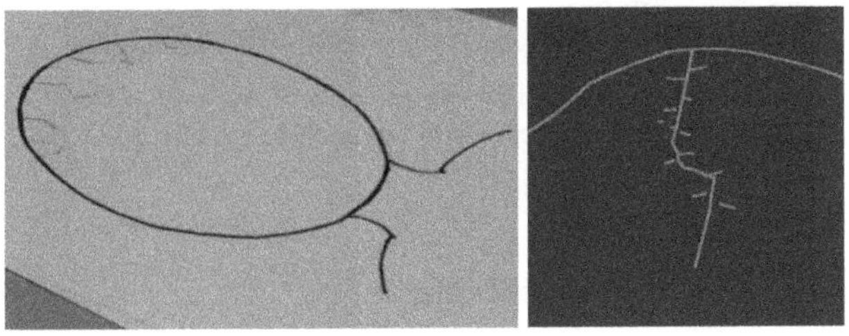

Figure 9. Participant 10's drawings showing the "cracks" in the child's head.

Zooming to Provide Context

Zooming out could also be useful in providing a better context for the symptoms involved in a headache. For example, participant 2 only drew a somewhat sad face on paper, but provided a bit more information about location in zoomable DTC, and added a connection between the headache and discomfort in the stomach while saying "the stomach is down here and it doesn't feel good." See Figure 12.

Participant 11 experienced zoomable DTC first and is a great example for all the levels of detail that can be provided, from locating pain in different parts of the body, to providing detail on the head, and then additional information about each spot where it hurts. This participant also had a throbbing headache and provided a somewhat similar visual description to participant 3. See Figure 13.

Participant 15 also used zooming to provide context, starting out by drawing an outline of the upper half of the body, then zooming into the head to show a headache the child described as "loud." Then, the child zoomed out, added information about the face (eyes, mouth), and proceeded to show what happens in the stomach at the same time drawing cramps described as "all tight...like a knot." See Figure 14.

Participant 15 had headaches similar to participant 10's. This child started by drawing the headache with a ray-like item running through the head, saying "my brain is cracking". The child then drew the eyes, providing better context for the location of the pain and saying that "they are splitting." Participant 15 then zoomed out and zoomed into the stomach area to describe the pain there. "It's like boiling water," the child said. See Figure 15.

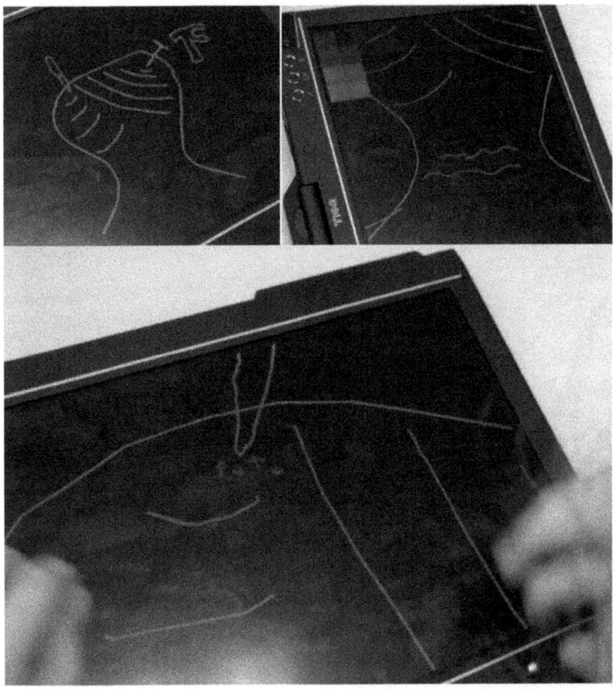

Figure 10. Participant 13's drawings on zoomable DTC showing details of the in and out feeling of the knife-like pain at the bottom (with small arrows), and a sore neck on the right.

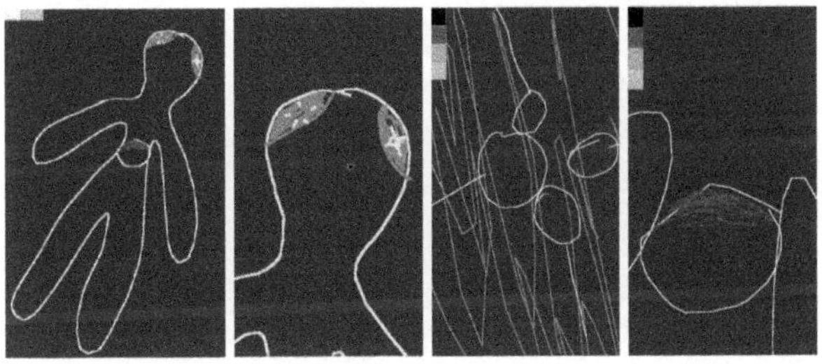

Figure 11. Drawings with zoomable DTC by Participant 18, providing more detail by zooming into the head to show a pounding headache and into the stomach showing pain and nausea.

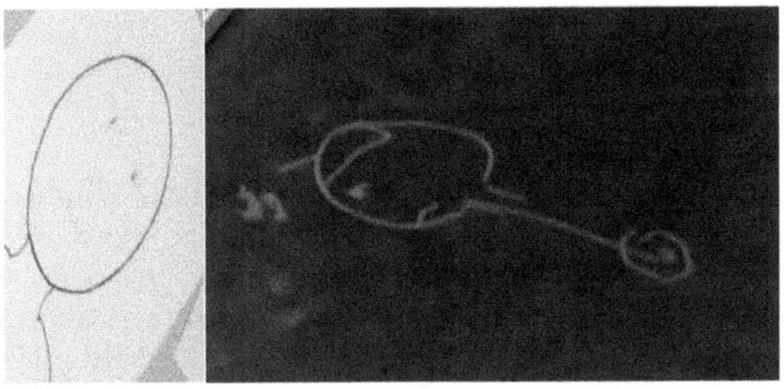

Figure 12. Participant 2's drawings.

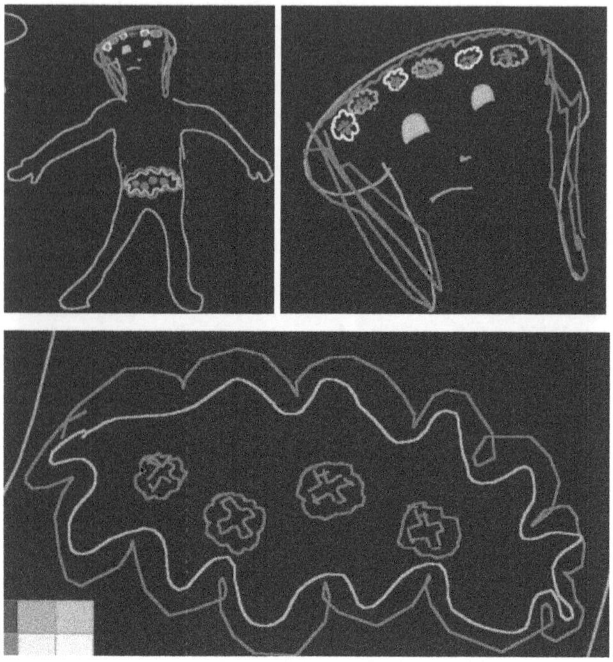

Figure 13. Part of participant 11's zoomable DTC drawings showing several levels of detail through zooming.

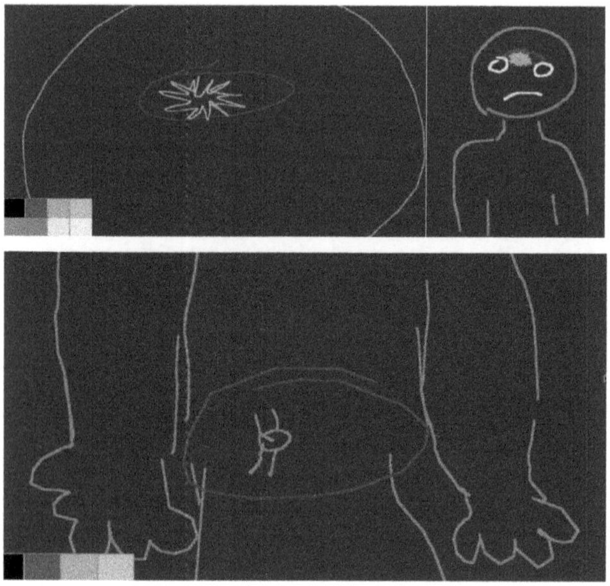

Figure 14. Participant 15's drawings with zoomable DTC going from a "loud" headache to providing context in the head, to drawing a "knot" in the stomach.

Other Observations

Something else we noticed is that none of the children who experienced paper-based DTC first used more than one color, while all the children who experienced zoomable DTC used multiple colors, and all the children who experienced paper-based DTC after zoomable DTC also used multiple colors. This was unusual in terms of earlier DTC research and may be unique to headache pain experiences. It may also be due to the color palette being very visible in the software, although children had colored pencils and markers right in front of them while drawing on paper.

An advantage we did not expect from zoomable DTC is that it was more flexible in providing children the ability to draw in ways we did not expect. For example, being able to draw the head sideways enabled two of the children to better communicate the location of their headaches.

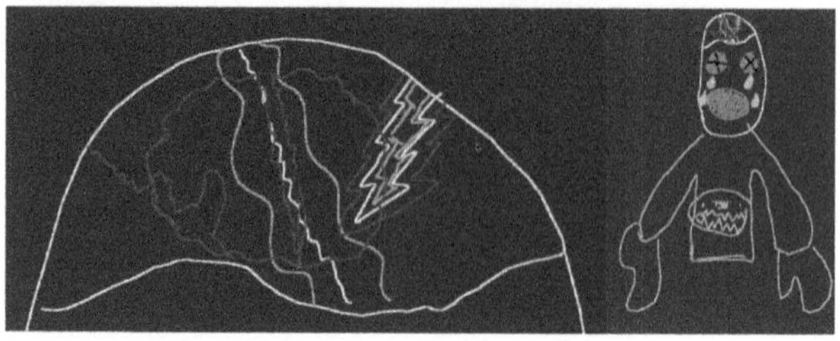

Figure 15. Participant 15's drawings showing a "cracking" headache, "splitting" eyes and stomach pain "like boiling water."

DISCUSSION

A Rare Role for Mobile Devices

Mobile devices excel at helping us communicate remotely, but they rarely help us communicate with those next to us. In this paper we presented an example of a way of using mobile devices to enhance communication in a much-needed context for a population that has rarely been the focus of HCI research. We hope that this research encourages further research on similar use of mobile devices.

A Validation of Zoomable User Interfaces

This study also provides a rare example of a ZUI providing benefits in a task involving authoring media and communicating face-to-face. This is significant given the small number of studies supporting specific benefits of ZUIs. Thus, it helps fulfill Bederson's request [7] for a better understanding of the benefits of ZUIs.

Applicability to a Clinical Setting

Working at a university with a research hospital, it is not unusual to hear medical doctors and nurses complain about computers getting in the way of interactions with patients, especially when having to enter information in Electronic Medical Records (EMR) software. A recent study provides empirical evidence of this phenomenon, finding that health professionals spend more time with patients when using EMRs, yet during this time there may be as little as half the amount of verbal and visual interaction that is found if an EMR is not used [20].

With zoomable DTC we see the exact opposite, with computing technology in the role of improving communication and providing health professionals with the information they need to make a correct diagnosis. The time it took to complete a session was certainly not an issue as it would fit into a regular visit. In addition, as the cost of data storage continues to decrease, it is certainly possible to record a patient's drawings as well as their voice (we used Camtasia [11] in our study) and store the session in the patient's medical record.

Limitations

The main limitation of this study relates to its exploratory nature. This involves both a small sample of participants and a design that was not fully balanced between conditions.

Participants were difficult to recruit. It took over six months to recruit the participants for this study and larger studies would require working with even more hospitals. However this is likely necessary to reach more solid conclusions given the variability in the population. For this same reason (small sample and high variability), we believe the results from inferential statistical tests presented in this paper should be received with caution.

In spite of these limitations, we believe the combination of quantitative and qualitative data in this study provides enough evidence of the likely benefits of the use of zoomable drawing to support communication between children with chronic headaches and clinicians.

An additional limitation is that we did not isolate zooming in our design by having an additional condition where children could draw on the computer without zooming (Photogoo enabled this, but with a photo of the child). However, based on a review of the sessions, and as illustrated through the examples above, the gains that resulted from zoomable DTC largely had to do with zooming with the exception of the use of color.

Finally, given its visual nature and the need to use a digital pen, our approach would not work for children with severe visual or motor impairments. On the other hand, there has been research on enabling people with motor impairments to draw [26], making it possible for the concept of zoomable DTC to still work.

Future Work

A next step for this research is a larger multi-site, between-subjects trial. We are excited about this possibility as we expect zoomable DTC will enable children to better describe their headaches, leading to better diagnoses and more effective treatment. Another extension would be the inclusion of children with other types of chronic pain (e.g., juvenile rheumatoid arthritis).

We also believe this type of zoomable drawing applications could be used in other situations when children need to communicate something that is difficult to communicate verbally. For example, we think clinical psychologists working with children could find these useful during therapy sessions to augment current practices that already use drawing.

Adults may also benefit, as there may be some situations where it is easier to illustrate a medical issue visually rather than verbally. This could be particularly useful for people with limited verbal ability, or in situations where the clinician and patient do not speak the same language.

CONCLUSION

We have presented empirical evidence supporting the use of zoomable Draw-and-Tell Conversations as a method to obtain symptom information from children with chronic headaches during medical appointments. In doing so we provide a rare and novel example of the use of a mobile device to support face-to-face communication, contribute evidence of a specific benefit of zoomable user interfaces, and serve a special needs community. We believe our approach can have a broad and direct impact in clinical settings, helping children with chronic pain better communicate their symptoms and medical professionals identify appropriate treatments.

ACKNOWLEDGEMENTS

We would like to thank all research participants and their parents. This research was funded in part by a University of Iowa SSFP grant.

REFERENCES

1. Andrasik, F. & Schwartz, M.S. (2006). Behavioral assessment and treatment of pediatric headache. *Behavioral Modification, 30* (1), 93-113.
2. Apple iPhone. (2011). http://www.apple.com/iphone/
3. Apple iPhoto. (2011). http://www.apple.com/iphoto/
4. Apple Safari. (2011). http://www.apple.com/safari/
5. Ayres, L., Kavanaugh, K., & Knafl, K. A. (2003). Within-case and across-case approaches to qualitative data analysis. *Qualitative Health Research, 13*(6), 871-883.
6. Bederson, B. B. (2001). PhotoMesa: a zoomable image browser using quantum treemaps and bubblemaps. *Proc. of UIST 2001*. ACM, 71-80.
7. Bederson, B.B. (2009). *The promise of zoomable user interfaces*. U. of Maryland, HCIL, TR 2009-21.
8. Bers, M.U et al. (1998). Interactive storytelling environments: coping with cardiac illness at Boston's Children's Hospital. *Proc. of CHI 98*. ACM, 603-610.
9. Bers, M.U., Gonzalez-Heydrich, J. & DeMaso, D.R. (2001). Identity construction environments: supporting a virtual therapeutic community of pediatric patients undergoing dialysis. *Proc. of CHI 01*. ACM, 380-387.
10. Brna, P.M. & Dooley, J.M. (2006). Headaches in the pediatric population. *Seminars in Pediatric Neurology, 13*, 222-230.
11. Camtasia. http://www.techsmith.com/camtasia/
12. Chin, J. & Tsuei, M. (2009). Multi-user Narrative Sharing System for Children with Chronic Illness. *Advanced Learning Technologies 2009,* 479-481.
13. Coad, J. (2007). Using art-based techniques in engaging children and young people in health care

consultation and/or research. *Journal of Research in Nursing, 12*(5), 487-497.

14. Cvengros, J.A., Harper, D. & Shevell, M. (2007). Pediatric headache: An examination of process variables in treatment. *Journal of Child Neurology, 22* (10), 1172-1181.

15. Dahlquist, L.M et al. (2009). Effects of Videogame Distraction using a Virtual Reality Type Head-Mounted Display Helmet on Cold Pressor Pain in Children. *J. Pediatr. Psychol., 34*(5), 574-584.

16. Driessnack, M. (2005). Children's drawings as facilitators of communication: A meta-analysis. *Journal of Pediatric Nursing, 20*(6), 414-423.

17. Driessnack, M. (2006).Draw and Tell Conversations with children about fear. *Qualitative Health Research, 16*(10), 1414-1435.

18. Driessnack, M. (2009). Using the Colored Eco-Genetic Relationship Map with children. *Nursing Research, 58*(5), 304-311.

19. Driessnack, M. & Furukawa, R. (*in press*). The use of participatory arts-based inquiry in child. *Journal for Specialists in Pediatric Nursing.*

20. Duffy, W.J., Karasch, M.S. & Du, H. (2010). Point of Care Documentation Impact on the Nurse-Patient Interaction. *Nursing Administration Quarterly, 34*(1), 1-10.

21. Dynavox (2011). Avaiable at http://www.dynavoxtech.com/

22. Glennen, S.L. & DeCoste, D.C. (1997). *The handbook of augmentative and alternative communication.* San Diego, CA: Singular Publishing Group.

23. Good, L. & Bederson, B. B. (2002). Zoomable user interfaces as a medium for slide show presentations. *Information Visualization 1*(1), 35-49.

24. Heinrich M., Morris L., & Kroner-Herwig B. (2009). Self-report of headaches in children and adolescents in Germany: Possibilities and confines of questionnaire data for headaches classification. *Cephalgia, 29*, 864-872.

25. Hourcade, J.P., Bederson, B.B. & Druin, A. (2004). Building KidPad: An Application for Children's Collaborative Storytelling. *Software Practice and Experience, 34*, 895-914.

26. Hornof, A.J. & Cavender, A. (2005). EyeDraw: enabling children with severe motor impairments to draw with their eyes. *Proc. of CHI '05.* ACM, 161-170.

27. Hsieh, H.F. & Shannon, S.E. (2005). Three approaches to qualitative content analysis. *Qualitative Health Research, 15*, 1277-1288.

28. Johnson, R. & Spence, S. (1994). Pain, affect and cognition in children: Recall bias associated with pain. *Progress in Pain Research and Management, 2*, 877-884.

29. Krueger, M.W. (1983). *Artificial Reality.* Reading, MA:Addison-Wesley.

30. Lewis D.W. (2007). Headaches in children and adolescents. *Current Problems in Pediatric and Adolescent Health Care, 37*, 207-246.

31. Malchiodi, C.A. (1998). *Understanding children's drawings.* New York: The Guilford Press.

32. Microsoft Canvas For OneNote. http://www.officelabs.com/projects/canvasforonenote/Pages/default.aspx

33. Microsoft pptPlex. (2011). http://www.officelabs.com/projects/pptPlex/Pages/default.aspx

34. Perlin, K. & Fox, D. (1993). Pad: an alternative approach to the computer interface. *Proc. of* SIGGRAPH 1993. ACM, 57-64.

35. Pierce, T. (2009). Social anxiety and technology: Face-to-face communication versus technological communication among teens. *Computers in Human Behavior, 25*(6), 1367-1372.

36. Prezi. (2011). http://prezi.com/

37. Proloquo (2011). Available at http://www.assistiveware.com/proloquo.php

38. Shonkoff, J.P., Boyce, T.W. & McEwen, B.S. (2009). Neuroscience, molecular biology, and the roots of health disparities: Building a new framework for health promotion and disease prevention. *JAMA, 301*(21), 2252-2259.

39. Stafstrom C.E., Rostasy K. & Minster A. (2002). The usefulness of children's drawings in the diagnosis of headaches. *Pediatrics, 109* (3), 460-472.

40. Trautmann, E., Lackschewitz, H. & Kroner-Herwig, B. (2006). Psychological treatment of recurrent headache in children and adolescents: A meta-analysis. *Cephalgia, 26*, 1411-1426.

41. van den Brink, M., Bandell-Hoekstra, E.N.G. & Abu-Saad, H.H. (2001). The occurrence of recall bias in pediatric headache: A comparison of questionnaire and diary data. *The Journal of Head and Face Pain, 41*(1), 11-20.

42. van Twillert, B., Bremer, M. & Faber, A.W. (2007). Computer-Generated Virtual Reality to Control Pain and Anxiety in Pediatric and Adult Burn Patients During Would Dressing Changes. *Journal of Burn Care & Research, 28*(5), 694-702.

43. Weiss, P.L et al. (2001). Pebbles: A personal technology for meeting educational, social and emotional needs of hospitalized children. *Personal and Ubiquitous Computing, 5*, 157-168.

Design of an Exergaming Station for Children with Cerebral Palsy

Hamilton A. Hernandez[2], T.C. Nicholas Graham[2], Darcy Fehlings[1,3], Lauren Switzer[1], Zi Ye[2], Quentin Bellay[2], Md Ameer Hamza[2], Cheryl Savery[2], Tadeusz Stach[2]

[1]Bloorview Research Institute
Holland Bloorview Kids Rehabilitation Hospital
Toronto, ON, Canada

[2]School of Computing
Queen's University
Kingston, ON, Canada

[3]Department of Paediatrics
University of Toronto
Toronto, ON, Canada

(hamilton, graham, zi, bellay, ameer, savery, tstach)@cs.queensu.ca,
(dfehlings, lswitzer)@hollandbloorview.ca

ABSTRACT
We report on the design of a novel station supporting the play of exercise video games (exergames) by children with cerebral palsy (CP). The station combines a physical platform allowing children with CP to provide pedaling input into a game, a standard Xbox 360 controller, and algorithms for interpreting the cycling input to improve smoothness and accuracy of gameplay. The station was designed through an iterative and incremental participatory design process involving medical professionals, game designers, computer scientists, kinesiologists, physical therapists, and eight children with CP. It has been tested through observation of its use, through gathering opinions from the children, and through small experimental studies. With our initial design, only three of eight children were capable of playing a cycling-based game; with the final design, seven of eight could cycle effectively, and six reached energy expenditure levels recommended by the American College of Sports Medicine while pedaling unassisted.

Author Keywords
Exergame; exertion interface; video game design; exergaming station; accessibility.

ACM Classification Keywords
H.5.2 [Information Interfaces And Presentation]: User Interfaces – Input devices and strategies;

General Terms
Human Factors, Design.

INTRODUCTION
Cerebral palsy (CP) is a group of disorders affecting the development of movement and posture, causing activity limitations attributed to disturbances in the development of the fetal or infant brain [21]. As children with cerebral palsy become teenagers, they can experience a cycle of deconditioning resulting in deteriorating physical function. Children who walk with the use of a mobility aid (those classified as Gross Motor Function Classification System (GMFCS) level III [11]) show a significant functional decline through adolescence and during the transition to adulthood. This loss of gross motor function in adolescents with CP is multifactorial, but proximal muscle weakness secondary to disuse, poor physical fitness, changes in body composition, limitations in range of motion, spinal misalignment, and pain are significant contributors [3,11].

Exergames, video games whose play requires physical activity, represent a promising way of enabling children with cerebral palsy to perform exercise while having fun. Exergames can be designed to match the children's abilities. They can be played from home, removing the significant logistical difficulties of travelling to a specialized rehabilitation centre. They can be played with others over a network, providing social contact with peers. Experience with a cycling-based exergame for people without motor impairments has found them to be more motivational than traditional exercise, to encourage more vigorous exercise, and to lead to health benefits over a six-week period [24].

The use of Wii Sports and Wii Fit has been reported in an increasing number of studies involving people with motor deficits resulting from CP. Almost uniformly, these have focused on extending range of motion [6] and improving balance [1,7,8]. The Wii system has also been applied to rehabilitation of people with motor impairments resulting from other causes such as stroke [5,23]. However, these studies have focused on rehabilitation therapy, as opposed to physical fitness.

In this paper, we present the results of a design study of an exergaming station suitable for children with Cerebral Palsy. In this study, we addressed the question of how to design a station allowing children with CP to play exergames involving vigorous activity in a safe, convenient and enjoyable manner. The scope of our work includes the physical design of the station and its software interface to games. In this paper, we do not consider the design of exergames per se, or the long-term effectiveness of an exergaming program. We carried out the study using iterative design over a six month period, using a collaborative design process involving paediatricians and physiotherapists specializing in CP, kinesiologists, computer scientists and eight children with CP. Our central findings were:

- Custom-designed hardware is required, allowing easy entry and exit from a walker or wheelchair, and stable support while gaming.
- Input provided by an exercise ergometer must be transformed before being sent to a game to enhance smooth and accurate control of an in-game avatar.

The resulting design was highly successful. While only three of eight children with CP who were tested were able to play a pedaling-based game with an initial prototype, seven of eight could play unassisted using the final version. Six of these seven exercised vigorously enough to meet the recommendations of the American College of Sports Medicine (ACSM). The eighth child also met ACSM recommendations, pedalling with the assistance of an adult.

The paper is organized as follows. We first review related approaches. We then discuss the goals and challenges in designing an exergaming station for children with CP. We discuss the design of hardware and the software challenges of interfacing this hardware to games. Finally, we report on methods for using this hardware to accurately and smoothly control an avatar on screen.

RELATED WORK

Active games are digital games where gameplay involves physical activity. Commercial examples include Wii Sports, where players swing their arm to control a tennis racquet, and Dance Dance Revolution, where players must carry out increasingly complicated dance steps. Some active games are designed explicitly to help improve the physical health of their players; these are commonly termed *exergames*. Commercial examples of exergames include Wii Fit and EA Sports Active. Examples from the research domain include personalized exergames [10], Jogging over a Distance [16] and Breakout for Two [17].

The physical hardware supporting exergames follows three main branches. Many games are based around motion-capture hardware such as the Microsoft Kinect and the Wii Remote. Studies of such games are divided as to whether they are sufficiently vigorous to lead to health benefits. For example, Graves et al. have shown that Wii Tennis leads to half the energy expenditure of traditional tennis [9]. A second approach is ubiquitous games, where gameplay involves navigation of the real world [14]. The third approach is based on traditional exercise equipment (or ergometers), such as the commercial PCGamerBike Mini (figure 3) or the CateEye Gamebike. Since this approach is based on equipment intended for exercise, high levels of exertion can be obtained. Warburton et al. have shown that exergames on the GameBike can lead to better exercise adherence and improved health measures versus traditional exercise on a stationary bicycle [24].

Health benefits have been shown to accrue from exergaming. Motivation to perform physical activity has been shown to increase among people without motor impairments [10,20,24] and with motor impairments [7,26]. Additionally, exergames have been successfully applied to the rehabilitation of people with motor impairments. Both custom-designed games [6,18,23] and commercial games [7,22] have been used to help improve upper extremity impairment in children with CP, improve oxygen uptake and maximum work capability in adolescents with spinal cord dysfunction [26], and improve balance in patients with stroke [1,5,8].

Apart from the work of Widman et al. [26], there has been little work on games for improving the cardio-vascular health of people with motor deficits, particularly from CP. What work there is tells at best a mixed story. Graves et al. showed that for people without motor impairment, Wii Sports games played in bursts of 15 minutes or more provide less vigorous exercise than required for health benefits [9]. Hurkmans et al. [12] showed that in a population with CP, sufficient energy expenditure was obtained under similar conditions (but this population was at the highest level of function, mainly GMFCS level II or higher). This allows cautious optimism, but clearly calls for more study.

More disappointingly, home-based interventions based on the Wii have shown sharply declining interest over periods of 12 weeks or more [2,19,22]. Some interventions have shown positive results, but only in the presence of extraordinary support [4,15].

Much of the difficulty is that few Wii/Kinect/Move games require vigorous use of the controller (as with Wii Sports Tennis and Boxing). Popular Wii games such as MarioKart or Zelda that use a controller do not require physical exertion. The limited selection of truly active game styles available for these gaming platforms leads to loss of interest over time. Games based on cycling ergometers are promising as they allow pedaling motions to control an avatar in a game, matching a wide range of game styles.

THE DESIGN CHALLENGE

A successful exergaming station for children with CP needs to address three challenges: the design of the physical apparatus supporting exercise; the interpretation of input from such a device; and the design of the station as a whole to enable exercise that is sufficiently vigorous to lead to health benefits. While these challenges must be solved for any exergaming station, they are exacerbated when designing for children with motor impairments, and failure to solve them represents a significant barrier to adoption of such a system.

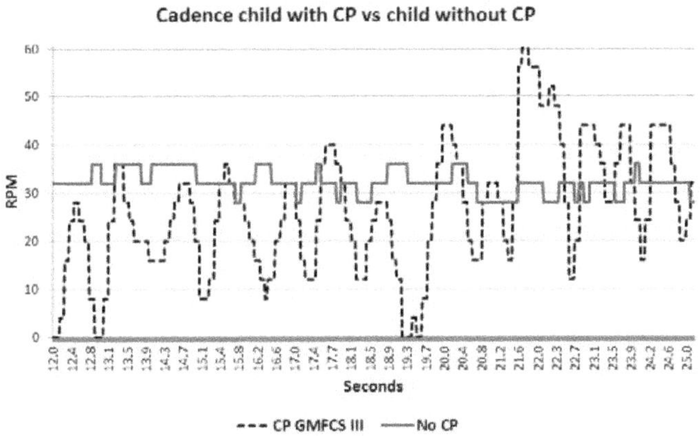

Figure 1. Comparison between typical cadence information of child with CP and child without CP in GMFCS level III pedalling a cycling ergometer

Physical challenge

Children with CP have muscle weakness, reduced range of motion, and poor control over their movements. These aspects of their disability pose difficulties with most existing exergaming infrastructures: many children with CP who use mobility aids have challenges with the finely controlled movement required by Kinect or Wii titles; they cannot balance on a Wii balance board, or sit on a GameBike. As we shall see, these limitations caused us to settle early on a cycling-based device with a custom-designed seat.

The physical station must permit easy transfer from a wheel chair or walker, preferably without the intervention of an adult. This means that children must be able to use their hands to support their weight as they transfer, and there must be no obstacles to impede them as they move. Children with GMFCS level III CP may have poor upper-body strength, and have a hard time supporting their own body while holding a game controller in their hands. Finally, an exergaming station must be sufficiently transportable and compact that it can be installed in a child's bedroom or living room without dominating the space.

Control challenge

Most children with GMFCS level III CP have spasticity and decreased motor control of both their legs. This means that they cannot pedal smoothly. Figure 1 compares the pedalling cadence of a typical child with GMFCS level III CP with that of a typical child without CP. The child with CP has considerably higher variance in cadence. Normally, in pedalling-based exergames, the player powers an avatar with the bicycle. The faster the player pedals, the faster the avatar moves. This literal translation leads to jerky movement of the avatar which is unaesthetic and can hinder typical gameplay tasks such as aiming to stop at a particular location.

The children can use traditional game pads such as an Xbox 360 controller, but their manual ability prevents them from quickly moving between buttons, or from using different controls simultaneously (e.g., pressing a button with one finger while pulling a trigger with another finger on the same hand.) As shown in figure 2, a typical usage involves holding all fingers together and moving them as a unit from button to button.

These issues imply two design constraints. First, pedalling input must be filtered to improve smoothness and accuracy of the movement of an avatar in the game. Second, hand controls must not require rapid hand movements, use of multiple controls at once, or stringently time-sensitive (colloquially "twitch") operation.

Vigour challenge

Finally, the hardware must be designed so that the players are capable of exercising vigorously enough to reach heart rate targets associated with health benefits. For example, the American College of Sports Medicine specifies that 150 minutes per week of moderate activity in 10 minute sessions is sufficient to lead to health benefits [25]. "Moderate activity" is defined as 64%-76% of maximum heart rate.

As we have discussed, exergaming systems for people without motor impairment frequently fail to meet this requirement (although youth with CP GMFCS level III may have lower levels of conditioning, and may therefore require a lower level of activity to raise heart rate). Given the challenges that children with CP face with movement, it is not obvious how to design an exergaming station that supports this level of vigour.

Existing systems do not meet these three design constraints as, being designed for people without motor impairment, they do not solve the physical or control challenges. Worse, they frequently fail to require sufficiently vigorous activity to meet ACSM requirements.

Our research question is therefore whether it is possible to build such a cycling-based exerstation that is safe, usable by people with motor deficits consistent with CP GMFCS level III, and supports exercise at a level of vigor associated with health benefits. To our knowledge, we are the first to address this question.

Figure 2. Child with CP holding Xbox 360 controller

Figure 3. PCGamerBike mini and Xbox 360 controller

DESIGN METHOD

The design constraints identified above led us to favour a custom-designed cycling-based gaming system. For reasons of price and availability of application programming interfaces, we chose the PCGamerBike Mini cycling ergometer and the Xbox 360 game controller (figure 3). From this starting point, we set out to solve: (1) the physical challenge of integrating these controllers into an exercise station suitable for children with CP, (2) the control challenge of interpreting input from the ergometer, and (3) the vigour challenge of ensuring that exercise meets ACSM guidelines.

We followed a participatory, iterative design approach, including eight children with CP, computer scientists, a medical doctor specializing in children with CP, a physiotherapist, and a mechanical engineer. We also received offline advice from a professional game designer, an exercise psychologist, and a kinesiologist.

We held four design and evaluation sessions with the eight children, and an additional experimental session with each child individually. Three children were females and five were males. The mean age was 15.6, with a minimum of 12 and maximum of 18. Five children had spastic diplegia and three had spastic triplegia. Seven of the children were at GMFCS level III and 1 at GMFCS level IV.

HARDWARE

We experimented with four chair designs. In this section, we summarize the design constraints that emerged through our testing process. This process emphasizes the importance of iterative testing with members of the user group, and the difficulty of anticipating design problems.

We met with eight children with CP through four design sessions, and allowed them to try different alternative designs. We assessed the efficacy of each chair design through observation by a paediatrician and a physiotherapist specializing in CP, and from discussions with the children. We first summarize the four design types, and then summarize our findings. The four chair types are shown in figure 4.

MSS Tilt and Recline Chair: this is a commercial chair designed specifically for children with CP. On paper, it is a perfect match with our requirements: it allows children to sit in a semi-reclined position suitable for recumbent cycling; it provides a stable back and arm rests, and it provides optional straps for holding the child in the chair. Our initial plan was simply to adapt this chair by removing its foot rest and bolting it to a platform where the PCGamerBike mini cycling ergometer was also attached.

However, initial feedback ruled out this design, as the device was perceived as being too specific to people with disabilities. This detracted from the "cool" factor of exercising while playing video games. Moreover, the device was over-engineered for some of the candidate children, some of whom were capable of sitting in standard chairs, and who did not like to be provided with equipment that over-stated the degree of their disability.

Bean bag chair: this chair could be placed against a wall, providing stability while seated. The chair naturally conforms to the body, providing comfort and stability while sitting in a wide range of positions, including the reclined position best suited to recumbent cycling. Furthermore, it is easily portable, and fits well with existing furniture in the home. In initial tests with people without motor impairment, we were excited by the potential of this chair.

In practice, however, it was resoundingly rejected by the youth with CP. They found it uncomfortable being low to the ground, doubted the stability that the chair would provide, and felt a lack of control around chair exit/entry. On the chair's height, children said: "You're more sunk into it… and if you move you get sunk even more", and "Your feet are up… but it makes it feel like your feet are more off the ground. It's more unstable." On entry/exit, one child said "I think the higher it is, the easier it is to sit [down] on it." On stability in general, one stated "I like having an actual chair so I can lean my back against it."

This example emphasizes how misleading experience with people without motor impairment can be in predicting the experience of those with motor impairment.

Customized office chair: Our third chair was a traditional office chair, modified to our specifications by the chair's manufacturer. The original chair was designed for use by police officers. Its arms could easily drop, allowing entry by people wearing firearms. We hypothesized that this would allow the children to more easily enter and exit, as the arms could be dropped on entry, then returned to upright position once the child was seated. The chair was modified to replace its castors with a fixed base and to remove the ability of the chair to swivel.

The chair's drop-arms were successful as predicted, but the chair had too much rotational flex; as one child said, "I found it moved too much". We observed that the chair's soft back impeded pedalling, as some children pushed against the chair back to help them deliver force to the pedals. Interestingly, the children themselves did not report this difficulty, saying for example "I think it has a good back support and it's long enough to support our whole back" and "The fact that it's soft, it doesn't matter for me personally."

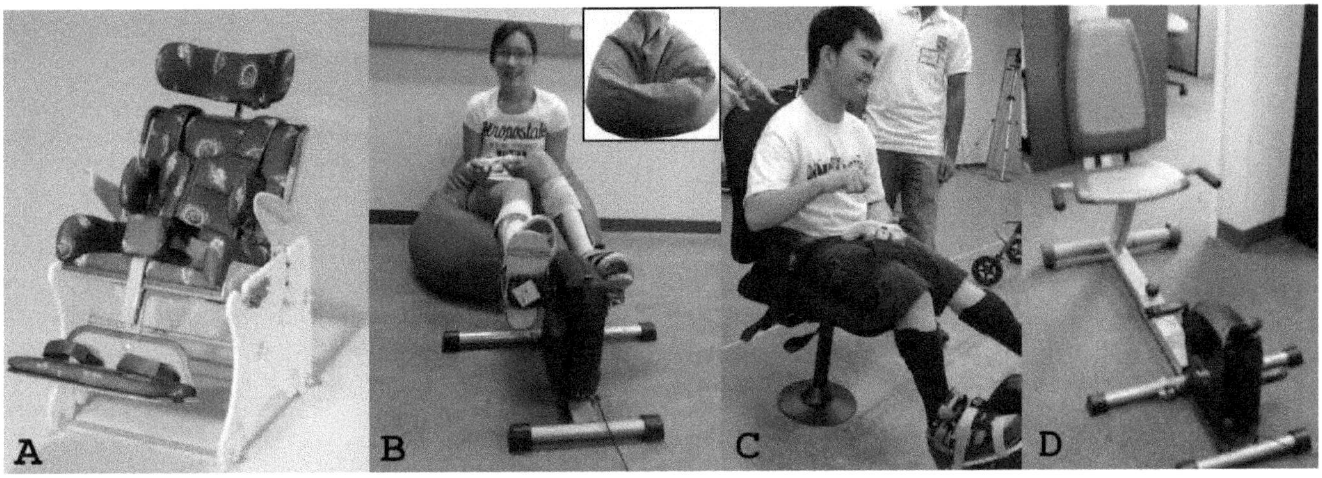

Figure 4. Four chair designs: (A) commercial MSS tilt and recline chair, (B) bean bag chair, (C) modified office chair, and (D) custom designed "racer" chair

The children were split on the presence of the arm rests. Some children found the position of the arm rests was incorrect for their physiology, and forced them into an uncomfortable position (e.g., "I prefer when they [the arms] are down.") Others preferred being able to lean on the arm rests, saying "I liked the arm rests so I can lean my elbows", and "It's easier to pedal if there's arm rests on the chair. If I'm supported by the arm rests I think I can go faster."

Racer chair: Our final design iteration was a custom-built platform. The arm rests are flush with the seat, allowing easy entry/exit. The cycling ergometer is attached to the platform, and adjustable for leg length. The seat back is full-height and rigid for stability. The wide attachment for the cycling ergometer does not interfere with the large pedalling attachments.

We found that seven of the eight children were able to pedal without assistance using this device. One initial concern was that the absence of arm rests would be difficult for the children. In practice, some children reported having to work harder to stabilize themselves than with the earlier customized office chair design. We view this as positive, as this self-stabilization provides an additional form of beneficial exercise.

Lessons on Hardware Design

We learned several lessons from this hardware design exercise, which we believe are broadly applicable when designing for people with motor impairment.

We faced considerable logistical difficulties in testing our designs. Even within our small group of eight children, we observed large individual differences. For example, the children were split on their preference of arm rests versus no arm rests on the chair. It is positive that even a small group can provide such a wide range of experience, which highlights the importance of consulting a group at least as large as we did, despite the logistical challenges.

We were surprised by the degree to which we were unable to predict what technologies would work well for children with CP. For example, we believed that the bean bag chair would be successful, but it was met with uniform dislike. This highlights the importance of iterative design grounded by significant testing with the target users.

Another challenge was the difficulty of isolating features of the platform while testing. For example, early problems with the pedals (early versions were loose) had cascading effects on other aspects of the platform.

We saw a significant difference between observed and reported behaviour. For example, all children had difficulty with the padded seat on the custom office chair, but none reported this as a difficulty. Even children who reported problems with the lack of an armrest in the racer chair were in fact able to pedal successfully while using the game controller. This emphasizes the importance of observation, by domain experts such as our medical professionals, in addition to questionnaires and interviews.

CONTROL

The station supports two forms of control: pedaling a cycling-based ergometer propels an avatar in the world, and manipulating buttons and joystick on a controller aims, specifies direction and performs game actions (e.g., jumping or firing a weapon.)

Pedaling Control

Games based on cycling ergometers typically use pedaling to control an avatar. Pedaling faster speeds up the avatar; pedaling slower reduces its speed. Children with CP have difficulty maintaining a smooth pedalling cadence, resulting in problems of *smoothness* and *accuracy* when controlling the avatar. Smoothness is an important aesthetic issue – the avatar should not move in a jerky fashion. Accuracy is important in game tasks where precise positioning of the avatar is important, for example stopping at the foot of a ladder to climb up, or navigating around obstacles. Figure 1 graphs the cadence of a typical child with CP.

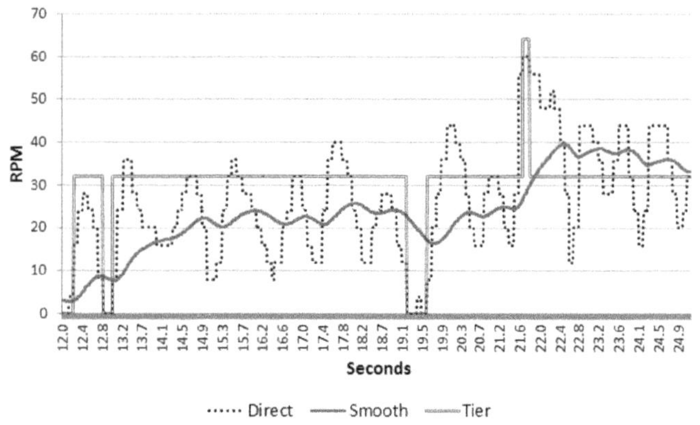

Figure 5. Typical pedaling cadence of a child with CP interpreted via the direct, smooth and tier algorithms.

Smoothing algorithms are broadly employed in video games using handheld controllers [13]. The high variance in cadence of children with CP requires more aggressive smoothing than is typically used. We therefore require a software layer that filters raw cadence information provided by the ergometer into a smoother signal that can be used to modify the avatar's position in a game. We carried out a study to investigate three such algorithms (compared to a fourth control condition). These algorithms are:

1. *Direct Drive* is the control condition where cadence information is transmitted directly to the game.
2. *Smooth:* cadence information is smoothed using a weighted average over a 3 seconds window. This algorithm removes jitter, at the cost of latency.
3. *Tier:* only three game speeds are possible – "stopped", "walking", and "running". This allows considerable variance in cadence while reducing changes in visible speed. The tiers overlap in order to avoid oscillation.
4. *Inchworm:* under this algorithm, the world is divided into a grid of size 1m x 1m blocks (in world units). The avatar remains stationary until the distance to the next block has been pedaled, at which point it jumps to the next block. The avatar is animated to show progress towards the next jump. This algorithm aims to provide excellent accuracy, at the cost of resolution of smoothness in movement.

Figures 5 shows how pedalling input of figure 1 (input from a typical child with GMFCS level 3 CP) is interpreted under the direct, smooth and tier algorithms.

Method

Participants carried out two game-like tasks, one measuring smoothness (variance of in-game speed when the player attempts to move at constant speed) and the other measuring accuracy (players' ability to stop close to the centre of a target). For both tasks, the players used the "racer" bike (described above) and an Xbox 360 controller. Players practiced the task for two minutes. They then performed the task using each of the four algorithms. To balance for order effect, the algorithms were rotated twice according to a balanced Latin square of size = 4, adequate for four conditions and eight participants.

The smoothness task involved pedaling an avatar riding a unicycle while carrying a tray full of eggs in each hand (Figure 6). Players were instructed to pedal as smoothly as they could, so that the avatar could deliver his eggs without dropping any. As the players pedaled, the unicycle wobbled in response to changes in cadence. Players were provided with visual feedback: at every 100 pixels travelled in the game, the variance in cadence over the last two seconds was computed; if it exceeded 10 RPM, an animation showed an egg dropping and a crashing sound was reproduced. The course was 6,000 pixels in length. Variance in pedal cadence was recorded over the course.

The accuracy task was to play the "pipes" game (Figure 7). Players were instructed to pedal their avatar as close to the centre of the pipe door as they could manage, and then push the "A" button on their Xbox 360 controller. For each algorithm, accuracy and time were recorded. Accuracy was measured in pixels from the centre of the pipe, and time was measured in elapsed milliseconds from start of the condition until the player pressed the "A" button.

Results: Smoothness

For the Unicycle game, a within subjects RM-ANOVA was used to determine the effect of each algorithm on player's ability to move the character smoothly through the course.

Figure 6. The unicycle game used to measure smoothness. The avatar drops an egg in response to uneven pedaling.

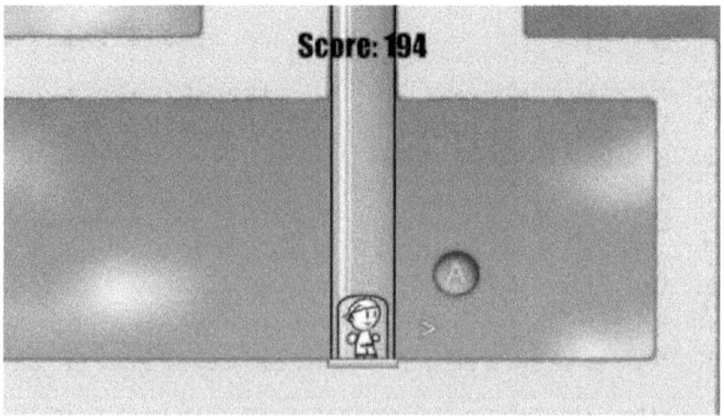

Figure 7. The pipes game used to measure accuracy. Here the avatar is at the center of the pipe door.

We applied Bonferroni correction, giving a significant $p < 0.009$. We found a significant effect of the algorithm on the score ($F(3,21)=45.323$, $p<0.001$, partial $\eta^2=0.866$).

Follow-up pairwise comparisons showed that players' score was higher using the smooth algorithm (M=99.9, SD=0.4) than direct drive (M=65.5, SD=12.5, p<.001), tier (M=82.5, SD=13.8, p=.009) and inchworm (M=52, SD=0.0, p<.001). Additionally, inchworm led to lower scores than tier (p<.001). Direct drive led to higher scores than inchworm (p=.018), and tier led to higher scores than direct drive (p=.015), but both cases are not significant at the level required by Bonferroni correction.

Player comments showed that they found direct drive more difficult than other conditions; one remarked "Are you altering the game? Cause this time it was like... more challenging". One participant noted that the tier algorithm was not responsive to changes in cadence: "I noticed that even though I was pedaling harder, it was always going at the same speed". Two participants commented on the difficulty of playing with inchworm: "I do have a smooth pace but he keeps on dropping eggs", and "It was difficult because he was jerking around".

Results: Accuracy

A within subjects RM-ANOVA was conducted to compare the effect of each of the four tested algorithms on players' ability to accurately navigate to the centre of each pipe. There was a significant effect of the chosen algorithm at the p<.009 level for the three conditions [$F(3,21) = 12.257$, $p < 0.001$, partial $\eta^2=0.636$].

Follow-up pairwise comparisons showed that the inchworm algorithm led to significantly higher accuracy (M=0.0 pixels, SD<0.001) than direct drive (M=9.9 pixels, SD=6.6, p=.004), smooth (M=16.4, SD=11.1, p=.004) and tier (M=13.6, SD=8.6, p=.003). There was no significant difference between the other algorithms.

A RM-ANOVA was also conducted to compare the effect of each of the four algorithms on the time that players spent on the pipes task. Here we found a significant effect of the choice of algorithm on the time (*$F(3,21)=11.583$, $p<0.001$, partial $\eta^2=0.623$*).

With the smooth algorithm (M=34.3 seconds, SD=12.7), players were significantly slower than with direct drive (M=22.8 seconds, SD=15.0, p=.005), tier (M=21.4, SD=11.5, p=.003) and inchworm (M=15.6, SD=7.1, p=.001).

A linear regression was conducted to determine the correlation between time and score for each algorithm. The inchworm algorithm was excluded because all players received the maximum score. The other algorithms showed a negative correlation (as time increases the distance to the center of the pipe decreases), but none were statistically significant (direct drive: r=0.351, p=0.395. Smooth: r=0.351, p=0.394. Tier: r=0.317, p=0.445).

Participants noticed the effect of the smooth algorithm on latency; one remarked "it slides more than you want him to". Participants commented that inchworm was significantly easier than the other conditions, stating that "it was extremely easy" and "I didn't have fun because I think what was going on this time was automatic, as long as you pedal he will move the same on the floor."

Discussion: Pedaling Control

The choice of algorithm for pedal control requires designers to trade off accuracy, smoothness and responsiveness to changes in speed. The smooth algorithm provided the smoothest input, as evidenced by the highest scores in the unicycle game. However, it also provided the worst accuracy scores and highest times in the pipe game.

Conversely, the inchworm algorithm performed so well in the accuracy task that players complained that the game was too easy. However, this comes at two costs. First, the avatar moves in a sequence of jumps rather than smoothly (as shown by its poor performance in the unicycle game.) Second, entities in the game world must be positioned on a grid corresponding to the algorithm's step size.

The tier algorithm acted as a middle ground, balancing smoothness and accuracy, but not excelling at either.

We conclude that for games that require high accuracy, designers should consider using inchworm, or should redesign the game so that accuracy is less important. While the smooth algorithm is most effective for reducing variance in cycling cadence, for most game situations, its lagged response to changes in cadence outweigh its advantages.

Button and Joystick Control

All eight children were capable of holding and manipulating game controllers similar to that of figure 2, but with significant limitations. Specifically, they had difficulty with time-sensitive manipulation of controller buttons, and found it challenging to manipulate multiple controls concurrently. Some children had difficulty manipulating the controller with two hands, as they used the other hand to support themselves.

The children used a variety of strategies to manipulate the controller. A typical strategy was to use one hand to hold the controller, and the other to manipulate the buttons, joysticks and triggers. Another was to use all four fingers on one hand to manipulate a single button or joystick. Figure 2 shows a child using his right hand to stabilize the controller while manipulating a button with his right thumb, and using the left hand to use a joystick.

The restrictions of CP lead to difficulties manipulating the controller to play many commercial games. Some games require time-sensitive manipulation of the controller's buttons. For example, platformer games such as Ubisoft's Assassin's Creed require the player to run using one control and initiate a jump using another at exactly the right time in order to climb an obstacle. In our exploratory sessions, several of the children found such time-sensitive actions too difficult, and we conclude that games for children with CP should not require them.

Similarly, commercial games frequently require players to rapidly manipulate multiple controls. For example, in Activision's Call of Duty games, players simultaneously use one joystick to control movement speed and direction, another joystick to aim their weapon, and a trigger to fire. We observed that the children typically do not have the manual dexterity to perform such actions concurrently.

In interviews, one child expressed a preference for Sony's PS3 controller, because it is small and allows them to reach all of the buttons without moving their grip. Two others preferred Nintendo's Wii Remote controller because it can be used one-handed, allowing the other hand to be used to support their body while seated on a couch. However this preference extended only to games using the Wii Remote as a traditional controller with buttons and trigger, not as a motion-control device.

In general, the children prefer to have their arms supported while playing, but only when the arm support is flexible and can be customized for comfort.

Despite these findings, all eight children reported attempting to play action-oriented commercial games such as EA's NHL and Activision's Call of Duty at either their own or friends' houses. This highlights the strong desire of the children to overcome the challenges of using these controllers, and their willingness to improvise with complex control schemes.

We summarize with the following lessons for designers: first, for GMFCS level III youth with CP, it is not necessary to develop custom game controllers; stock gaming controllers can be used. However, the control scheme should be simplified over those found in many commercial games. Designers should assume that only one control at a time can be used, and that controls should not be time-sensitive. Where possible, the control scheme should be designed to permit one-handed use.

VIGOUR

The goal of our exergaming station is to enable improved health through exercise. As described earlier, the American College of Sports Medicine recommends that health benefits can occur from as little 10 minute sessions of moderate exercise, as long as it is 150 minutes in total per week [25]. Exercise is considered moderately vigorous if the participant exceeds a threshold of between 64-76% of their maximum heart rate, where the lower threshold value is applicable to people with lower levels of aerobic fitness, as would be the case for our target population.

To see whether children with GMFCS level III CP could achieve this level of exercise intensity using our exergaming station, we asked our eight participants to play a vigorous game while their heart rate was monitored. This activity was performed following the input control study described in the last section.

Participants played a game in which they controlled a spikey ball rolling across the screen. The goal of the game was to roll over (and burst) as many balloons as they could within a two minute period. The game required no strategy; it simply required players to pedal as hard as they could for two minutes.

Before the session, we captured resting heart rate and the participant's age, and then used the Karvonan formula [25] to estimate the participant's maximum heart rate. Heart rate was logged during the two minutes of play using a Polar heart rate monitor worn using a chest strap. Figure 8 shows that seven of eight participants reached the heart rate threshold for moderate exercise intensity, and all eight reached the "warm up" threshold of 40% of maximum heart rate. Seven participants pedaled without assistance. One participant (the single participant at GMFCS level IV) pedaled with assistance of an adult.

The participants reacted positively to the level of exercise, reporting "this is like therapy – I can feel it", "I like it, is difficult, is something I would do for exercise", and "it would push you to go faster. I think it's productive."

While more study is required with longer exercise sessions, this result indicates that the exergaming station can allow the target population to perform exercise at a sufficiently vigorous level to see health benefits.

DISCUSSION

Our biggest lesson from this study was the multi-faceted nature of the design challenges. Building an exergaming station for children with CP required us to address the physical platform itself, the design of the handheld controller, and algorithms for interpreting pedaling input. From our design sessions, we learned that all three aspects of the problem must be solved well in order for the station to work at all. For example, early problems with the pedal support mounts made it impossible to test the pedaling input algorithms. This required an incremental and iterative design process where slow but steady progress was made on all design fronts simultaneously.

Participant	HR max	40%	64%	70%	Achieved HR
1	203	81.2	130	142	**133**
2	206	82.4	132	144	**149**
3	202	80.8	129	141	**177**
4	206	82.4	132	144	**153**
5	208	83.2	133	146	**141**
6	206	82.4	132	144	126
7	204	81.6	131	143	**157**
8	205	82	131	144	**131**

Figure 8. Heart rates achieved using exergaming station

Working with children with CP introduced challenges not seen in traditional participatory design environments. Parents or guardians needed to bring the children to the sessions at the hospital where they took place, sometimes requiring the booking of special vehicles. Because of the demands this placed on the families we were working with, we were restricted in the number and frequency of the sessions. This imposed limitations on the studies we performed. For example, the study on exercise vigour was performed immediately following the study on pedaling input control in order to avoid the need for a second visit. This limited the length of the vigour study, as the children were already tired from the previous study.

There were enormous individual differences between the children. Some could walk with canes, while others required wheelchairs. Some could use an Xbox 360 controller adeptly, while others were significantly challenged. Initially, some could not pedal at all, while others pedaled comfortably. This highlights the importance of dealing with a group that is large enough to be representative of the broader community, despite the logistical difficulties described above.

One way of reducing logistical overhead is the use of interviews rather than direct observation. We observed, however, a significant gap between our participants' self-reporting and their observed capabilities. For example, several participants reported needing arm rests to be able to cycle and use a controller, yet were in fact capable of using the racer bike. All participants reported that they played action-oriented commercial video games, which led us to believe that they were far more adept with game controllers than direct observation showed them to be. Direct observation was therefore critical to gaining an accurate understanding of the participants' capabilities.

Since design sessions were separated by weeks, ongoing testing was difficult. It was not practical to use participants without motor impairment as proxies for children with CP, as their capabilities were too different to lend any predictive value. We found it useful to record input data from the children, and to instrument our games to run in simulation mode, taking recorded rather than live input.

In general, we found it important to separate the design of the exergaming station from the design of the exergames themselves. This approach reduced the risk of conflating problems with the design of the game with those of design of the station, and helped reduce the scope of what proved to be a challenging design problem. Nevertheless, this study did suggest several lessons for game designers:

Avoid "twitch" gameplay: ensure that the game does not rely on time-sensitive actions such as pushing two buttons in quick succession, or operating multiple controls at once.

Avoid the need for accurate positioning or targeting, since the children experience difficulties with accurate movement.

Avoid the need for frequent starts and stops, as some children with CP find it challenging to start pedaling.

Build in customizability, allowing algorithmic parameters to be set at runtime, e.g., to allow easy tuning of the mapping of cadence to in-game speed.

CONCLUSION

In this paper, we have presented the design of an exergaming station for children with CP. The resulting station showed dramatic improvement over early prototypes, allowing seven of eight children tested to pedal effectively within a game, and allowing seven of eight to reach energy expenditure levels recommended by the ACSM. We have identified a series of challenges and tradeoffs in the design of such stations, and have provided practical advice both to designers of the physical apparatus and the software underlying its operation. Our next steps will involve continued design of games for this station, and their evaluation in longitudinal trials.

ACKNOWLEDGEMENTS

This work was carried out within the NEUROGAME project, supported by the NeuroDevNet and GRAND Networks of Centres of Excellence. The work was further supported by an NSERC Research Tools and Instruments grant.

REFERENCES

1. Anderson, F., Annett, M., F. Bischof, W., and Bischof, W.F. Lean on Wii: physical rehabilitation with virtual reality Wii peripherals. *Studies in Health Technology and Informatics 154*, (2010), 229-234.
2. Baranowski, T., Abdelsamad, D., Baranowski, J., O'Connor, T., Thompson, D., Barnett, A., Cerin, E., and Chen, T.A. Impact of an active video game on healthy children's physical activity. *Pediatrics*, (2012).
3. Bartlett, D.J., Hanna, S.E., Avery, L., Stevenson, R.D., and Galuppi, B. Correlates of decline in gross motor capacity in adolescents with cerebral palsy in Gross Motor Function Classification System levels III to V. *Developmental medicine and child neurology 52*, 7 (2010), e155-e160.
4. Boschman, L. Exergames for adult users: a preliminary pilot study. *Proceedings of Futureplay*, (2010), 235-238.
5. Brown, R., Sugarman, H., and Burstin, A. Use of the Nintendo Wii Fit for the treatment of balance problems in an elderly patient with stroke: a case report. *International Journal of Rehabilitation Research 32*, (2009), 109-110.
6. Chen, Y.P., Kang, L.J., Chuang, T.Y., Doong, J.L., Lee, S.J., Tsai, M.W., Jeng, S.F., and Sung, W.H. Use of virtual reality to improve upper-extremity control in children with cerebral palsy: a single-subject design. *Physical Therapy 87*, 11 (2007), 1441-1457.

7. Deutsch, J.E., Borbely, M., Filler, J., Huhn, K., Guarrera, P., and Guarrera-Bowlby, P. Use of a low-cost, commercially available gaming console (Wii) for rehabilitation of an adolescent with cerebral palsy. *Physical Therapy 88*, 10 (2008), 1196-1207.
8. Geurts, L., Vanden Abeele, V., Husson, J., Windey, F., Van Overveldt, M., Annema, J.H., and Desmet, S. Digital games for physical therapy: fulfilling the need for calibration and adaptation. *Proceedings of the Fifth International Conference on Tangible, Embedded, and Embodied Interaction*, ACM (2011), 117-124.
9. Graves, L., Stratton, G., Ridgers, N.D., and Cable, N.T. Serious games for health: personalized exergames. *BMJ (Clinical research ed.) 335*, 7633 (2007), 1282-4.
10. Göbel, S., Hardy, S., Wendel, V., Mehm, F., and Steinmetz, R. Serious games for health: personalized exergames. *Proceedings of the International Conference on Multimedia*, ACM (2010), 1663-1666.
11. Hanna, S.E., Rosenbaum, P.L., Bartlett, D.J., Palisano, R.J., Walter, S.D., Avery, L., and Russell, D.J. Stability and decline in gross motor function among children and youth with cerebral palsy aged 2 to 21 years. *Developmental Medicine and Child Neurology*, (2009), 295-302.
12. Hurkmans, H.L., van den Berg-Emons, R.J., and Stam, H.J. Energy expenditure in adults with cerebral palsy playing Wii Sports. *Archives of Physical Medicine and Rehabilitation 91*, 10 (2010), 1577-1581.
13. Lürig, C. and Carstengerdes, N. Filtering joystick data for shooter design really matters. *Proceedings of the International Conference on Entertainment Computing*, (2011), 264-269.
14. Magerkurth, C., Cheok, A.D., Mandryk, R.L., and Nilsen, T. Pervasive games: bringing computer entertainment back to the real world. *Computers in Entertainment 3*, 3 (2005), 4.
15. Moyà Alcover, B., Jaume-i-Capó, A., Varona, J., Martinez-Bueso, P., and Mesejo Chiong, A. Use of serious games for motivational balance rehabilitation of cerebral palsy patients. *Proceedings of the 13th International ACM SIGACCESS Conference on Computers and Accessibility*, (2011), 297-298.
16. Mueller, F., Vetere, F., Gibbs, M.R., Agamanolis, S., and Sheridan, J. Jogging over a distance: the influence of design in parallel exertion games. *Proceedings of the 5th ACM SIGGRAPH Symposium on Video Games*, ACM (2010), 63-68.
17. Mueller, F. and Agamanolis, S. Breakout for Two : An example of an exertion interface for sports over a distance. *Ubiquitous Computing*, (2003), 2-3.
18. Odle, B.M., Irving, A., and Foulds, R. Usability of an adaptable video game platform for children with cerebral palsy. *35th IEEE Annual Northeast Bioengineering Conference*, (2009), 1-2.
19. Owens, S.G., Garner, J.C., Loftin, J.M., Van Blerk, N., and Ermin, K. Changes in physical activity and fitness after 3 months of home Wii Fit use. *Strength and Conditioning 25*, 11 (2011), 3191-3197.
20. Rhodes, R.E., Warburton, D.E.R., and Bredin, S.S.D. Predicting the effect of interactive video bikes on exercise adherence: An efficacy trial. *Psychology, Health & Medicine 14*, 6 (2009), 631-640.
21. Rosenbaum, P., Paneth, N., Leviton, A., Goldstein, M., Bax, M., Damiano, D., Dan, B., and Jacobsson, B. A report: the definition and classification of cerebral palsy April 2006. *Developmental Medicine and Child Neurology. Supplement 109*, (2007), 8-14.
22. Sandlund, M., Waterworth, E.L., Häger, C., and Lindh Waterworth, E. Using motion interactive games to promote physical activity and enhance motor performance in children with cerebral palsy. *Developmental Neurorehabilitation 14*, 1 (2010), 15-21.
23. Saposnik, G., Teasell, R., Mamdani, M.M., Hall, J., McIlroy, W., Cheung, D., Thorpe, K.E., Cohen, L.G., and Bayley, M. Effectiveness of virtual reality using Wii gaming technology in stroke rehabilitation: a pilot randomized clinical trial and proof of principle. *Stroke 41*, 7 (2010), 1477-1484.
24. Warburton, D.E.R., Bredin, S.S.D., Horita, L.T.L., Zbogar, D., Scott, J.M., Esch, B.T.A., and Rhodes, R.E. The health benefits of interactive video game exercise. *Applied Physiology, Nutrition, and Metabolism 32*, 4 (2007), 655-663.
25. Whaley, M.H., Brubaker, P.H., Otto, R.M., and Armstrong, L.E. *ACSM's Guidelines for Exercise Testing and Prescription*. American College of Sports Medicine, Indianapolis, 2006.
26. Widman, L., McDonald, C., and Abresch, T. Effectiveness of an upper extremity exercise device integrated with computer gaming for aerobic training in adolescents with spinal cord dysfunction. *The Journal of Spinal Cord Medicine 29*, (2006), 363-370.

Enabling Self, Intimacy and a Sense of Home in Dementia: An Enquiry into Design in a Hospital Setting

Jayne Wallace[1], Anja Thieme[2], Gavin Wood[2], Guy Schofield[2] and Patrick Olivier[2]

[1]School of Design
Northumbria University
Newcastle Upon Tyne, NE1 8ST, UK
jayne.wallace@northumbria.ac.uk

[2]Culture Lab
School of Computing Science
Newcastle University
Newcastle Upon Tyne, NE1 7RU, UK

ABSTRACT

Design and digital technologies to support a sense of self and human relationships for people living with dementia are both urgently needed. We present an enquiry into design for dementia facilitated by a public art commission for an adult mental health unit in a hospital in the UK. The interactive art piece was informed by the notion of personhood in dementia that foregrounds the person's social being and interpersonal relationships as sites where self is maintained and constructed. How clients, clients' family members and staff used the piece is reported and insights related to the notions of home, intimacy, possessions and self are presented. The art piece served as window on both dementia and the institution leading to a number of insights and implications for design.

Author Keywords

Dementia; intimacy; self; home; empathy; dignity; design.

ACM Classification Keywords

H.5.m. [Information interfaces and presentation (e.g., HCI)]: Miscellaneous;

General Terms

Design, Human Factors.

INTRODUCTION

Dementia and the context of life for people living with dementia has become an increasingly important topic in HCI and Design over recent years [cf., 25]. Dementia has a profound effect globally and on each individual living with the condition. Globally, there are estimated to be 35.6 million people with dementia and this is expected to rise to 115.4 million by 2050. In fact, about one-quarter of all hospital patients aged 65 and older are people with Alzheimer's disease and other dementias [2]. Despite this, it is the focus of little research in the field of HCI, with efforts primarily being directed towards supporting ageing in place [cf., 23]. Likewise, research that foregrounds the role of design in dementia is still under-explored [14].

This paper describes an interactive art piece (Tales of I) that was commissioned for a hospital in the UK specialized on the assessment and treatment of older adults with severe dementia. The development of *Tales of I* enabled us to engage with staff in the unit and gain an in depth understanding of the care environment and the routines of hospital life. This revealed certain complexities and a set of particular design challenges. Furthermore the art piece served as a window on dementia and the institution itself. We detail the design of *Tales of I* and the design rationale, which has been informed by the concept of personhood [16] in the philosophy of dementia care. The piece was motivated by the desire to create a valuable resource for clients and staff that centered on a notion of home and offered connections to a number of themes which were suggested by staff through workshops.

Through interviews with staff, we were able to gain insights into nuanced complexities of their practice when engaging with people with dementia and from these propose a number of implications for design. We also unpacked key dynamics occurring around clients' interactions with the piece. These related to intimacy, home, sense of self and possessions. Our account is not intended as an evaluation of an art piece and its design. Rather, we describe how the art piece can serve as a lens onto this care environment and the people within it in the spirit of Gaver et al.'s Prayer Companion [12]. As a tool of enquiry it revealed valuable spaces for design in dementia that have wider implications for interaction design.

This paper centers on understanding users in the extreme context of severe dementia within a hospital setting. We highlight dynamics and challenges in the hospital setting that were revealed through the use of the art piece, which help us to understand severe dementia and staff-client exchanges more holistically. We reveal nuanced and multi-textured aspects of what it means to have severe dementia and the themes of personhood, intimacy, sense of self and home are shown to enable a rich understanding of this context and how this can help us to design in this environment. We highlight spaces for design to make a positive difference and show how understanding users can inform sensitive empathic design. We suggest that a designer should step back from constraints emphasizing the institutional environment or cognitive impairment and instead focus on enabling the full person.

THE PUBLIC ART COMMISSION

The art piece *Tales of I* came into being through a public art commission for a specific care and treatment unit (which we will refer to as Francis Place) in a new annex of a hospital in the UK. Francis Place is a secure unit for up to 16 clients with psychiatric disorders (predominantly severe dementia) and mainly accommodates male clients. The unit specializes in the assessment and treatment of these clients, who are usually transferred from care homes following extreme changes in their presentation or displays of anti-social behavior. A client's stay in the unit ranges typically from 2-4 weeks depending on diagnosis and treatment plan.

Francis Place was a newly constructed facility, predominantly white and unornamented, with a wide corridor that meandered through the whole unit around a series of courtyards. There were a number of spacious dayrooms, individual bedrooms for clients, a dining room, and a few much smaller rooms.

Workshops with Staff

We ran two workshops with staff from the hospital. The informal brief for the art commission indicated that pieces should reflect the care conditions and context of the unit. On our part we wanted to use the opportunity to build on our previous projects with people living with dementia [31] and create an interactive art piece that enhanced the lives of clients and staff within the unit.

The All About Me Books

From the workshops we learnt about staff practice, the kinds of activities that clients' engage in at Francis Place, general context of clients' experiences within the unit and gained insights into clients' behaviors (without any identification of specific clients). Staff members' work with clients included: support of their moods, engagement in acts of reminiscence by using photographs of objects to promote recognition and conversation. They work to de-escalate feelings of distress through the use of gentle hand holding, walking together and calm conversation about things that were meaningful to clients. This last point was enriched by the use of *All About Me* books, which staff members produce for each client. These A4 paper books detail a client's life story, likes and dislikes and include personal photographs. Family members supply much of this content, and photographs are scanned and printed for the book by staff. The simple premise of the *All About Me* books underplays their value in the unit. The books offer family members a way to contribute to the wellbeing and care of their relative both in the supply of information and in the use of the book during visits. Moreover, the books enable staff to get to know a client and see him or her as a multi-faceted person; someone who has had a life's worth of experiences and achievements; an individual.

Exchanging Existing Practice

The workshops and subsequent visits to the unit enabled us to spend time with staff fulfilling different roles including occupational therapists, qualified nurses and auxiliary staff. We were able to show staff previous projects that had involved a sustained and meaningful engagement with people with dementia in the research process [31] and that typified our person-centered design practice [24, 30, 35]. This prior experience allowed us to engage in rich and creative conversations with staff about what the art piece could be. Our commission was the last to be developed for the site; therefore, we were able to see the other pieces of art in situ in the unit. These included wall based sculptures, each with tactile qualities. A variety of material and color has been used and the pieces were made by a number of different artists. In each case the forms were abstract. However, staff explained that these pieces were rarely acknowledged, touched or interacted with by the clients.

THE ART PIECE

Influences & Insights from Previous Projects

As noted the Francis Place art piece was informed by a previous project in which we had engaged with Gillian, a woman living with dementia, and John, her husband, through a co-creative and design-led enquiry [31]. Within this enquiry the notion of *Personhood* had central importance to us. Arising from the philosophy of dementia care, the concept of *Personhood* [15, 16] counteracts many of the damaging effects that traditional accounts of dementia have on common assumptions of self and identity for someone living with dementia. Early accounts present the view that "individuals with dementia experience a steady erosion of selfhood to the point at which no person remains" [17], or in the extreme that dementia causes the "death of self" [9]. In contrast *Personhood* regards self as something not solely constructed internally, but created, nurtured and sustained by an individual's relationships with other people. For Kitwood "personhood is a standing or status that is bestowed upon one human being, by others, in the context of relationship and social being" [15]. As such, *Personhood* provides a valuable extension to the notion of self. Drawing from this perspective we can understand that, in order to support personhood in dementia, we need to see the person as far more than the sum of his or her cognitive ability. We need to support the 'social being' of an individual, which relates to his or her relationships to things, events and experiences which strengthen connections to the many facets of who the person is. We therefore need to nurture and support an individual's relationships with other people as this is where the person's self is most sustained. Hughes et al. [13] suggest that the people closest to an individual with dementia become guardians of their personhood.

Through our engagement with Gillian and John in the Personhood project we were able to gain a rich understanding of what life was like for them, how dementia had changed their lives and enact the notion of personhood

Figure1. From left to right: The wall cabinet containing themed globes, the television cabinet with the *Nature* globe and *Nature* film playing, detail of *Holiday* globe with its specific color (top) and detail of the room locating the art piece (bottom).

within the design process to make pieces that were both social and relational. We were able to see how artifacts and digital technologies could play valuable roles for them. We saw how they used the artifacts we made (including a digital locket holding Gillian's photographs, a digital jewelry box through which they could record memories to different jewelry objects) as tools for self reflection, for reminiscence, for comfort, reassurance and as receptacles of aspects of identity to be passed on to their children. It is key to mention that this engagement deeply informed our approach at Francis Place.

Elements of the Art Piece

Tales of I comprises two pieces of furniture: a wall cabinet and a television cabinet (see Figure 1). The sculpted casing of the wall cabinet has colorful vinyl graphics on its surface and a thick, transparent acrylic door that locks. The interior of the cabinet is made from walnut inlayed with resin in various colors and houses a series of globes. Each globe is made from clear cast resin of optical quality to reduce discoloration over time and each encases objects that relate to a different theme: *Holiday, Football, Nature, Local, Objects* and *Making*. Beneath each globe is a wooden drawer containing tactile materials that relate to the particular theme (for example velvets, feathers and spiky textured objects accompany the *Nature* globe). The base of each has a resin inlay of a specific color that corresponds to the recess in which it sits (see Figure 1). In its aesthetics and materials the television cabinet echoes the wall cabinet and has a colorful vinyl graphic of a doily with a central circular recess that a globe fits into. The screen is fronted with a thick sheet of clear acrylic and the cabinet has a prominent volume control dial to the top right hand of the screen. Hidden behind a sliding door is an on/off button and a USB port.

The television cabinet houses a computer, a screen, an RFID reader and a USB hub. Once a globe is selected from the wall cabinet and placed onto the television cabinet a film begins to play. Radio frequency identification or RFID tags in the base of each globe connect with an RFID reader positioned under the top surface of the television cabinet, which triggers the correct film to play. Each bespoke film is between ten and fifteen minutes long and relates to the theme of that globe. Films were made from a combination of footage that we took ourselves on location, footage shot of domestic and popular culture artifacts from the archives of a local museum dating from the 1930s to present day, footage from a local creative film archive and footage from the archives of the particular football club of the area. Films loop if a globe remains in place on top of the television cabinet and a new film begins once a different globe is placed on the cabinet. Different films have different qualities and tempos. For example, the *Holiday* film has a lively cadence with much color, the *Nature* film has a much calmer, slower feel to it and the *Football* film has a more reportage nature using old television coverage of matches, which have commentary running over the top of them along with audio tracks of crowds from matches running over the top of film footage from the stadium over the years and images of different players from the team.

Finally there are in addition a large number of USB memory sticks that accompany the piece. Each memory stick is associated with a client, onto which staff can place any personally meaningful images and film clips supplied by a client's relatives and friends. Once a client's memory stick is plugged into the television a slideshow of this content plays. The software of the cabinet is set up to play files in alphabetical and alphanumerical order; images stay on screen for ten seconds before moving onto the next image and the full sequence loops once it reaches its end.

Design Rationale

Through the workshops we developed ideas that were grounded in both daily life in the unit and staff practice. We were motivated by several dynamics. Firstly, the *All About Me* books, which were clearly a valuable resource, used for many purposes and supported creative interaction with clients. Secondly, as a newly built unit Francis Place did not offer many vibrant spaces or any stimuli that a client would recognize from the outside world. The unit, although clean and bright, looked and felt like a medical institution. Other than a client's bedroom there were few spaces that felt private or cozy, which motivated us to create a home-like space.

A Home-Like Space

A couple of rooms within the unit had signage describing spaces as *quiet rooms*, but we learned that they were rarely used and had yet to be given a purpose. We developed the art piece for one of these rooms with the aim of both enlivening the space and creating a welcoming but private space – akin to a living room – that family members might sit in with their relative to watch the *Tales of I* films together, and talk about the different stimuli that the films presented. Likewise, staff would be able to use art pieces here for reminiscence activities, to de-escalate someone's anxious behavior and to build on current practice, to enhance an individual's sense of wellbeing, through discussion of things that were meaningful to the client and the use of stimuli that a client found visually and aesthetically pleasing.

The Role of Aesthetics and Beauty

By placing the cabinet just outside the quiet room we hoped that clients would naturally see it during the many hours they spend walking in the corridors, be attracted to it, and want to interact with its contents. To this end a sweetshop window and a cabinet of curiosities inspired the design with a view to engaging interest and fostering a sense that something 'good' was inside. We were aware that clients had little interest in the abstract sculptures that made up other art pieces in the unit. As such our use of color, variety of materials and detailed colorful scenes that were captured in resin globes were all intended to catch the eye and provoke curiosity and fascination. The detail inside each globe was intended to hold someone's attention and interest on closer examination as he or she drew closer to it. We used walnut with an expressive grain and the vinyl graphics and resin inlays were added with precision. It was important to us that the piece was well made, interesting and beautiful as we wanted to convey to clients that they were valued and deserved beautiful things. The value of beauty and aesthetics in attracting people to artifacts is a well-documented phenomenon, but particularly well articulated in Killick and Craig's work [14], in the field of occupational therapy, who emphasize the value of creativity and beautiful artifacts for people with dementia.

The value of Recognition and Familiarity

The television cabinet referenced 1950-60s furniture; something that would be *known* by clients from their youth and that suggested *sitting* and *watching*. The piece was intended to be suggestive of a home environment, and staff helped to provide curtains, a lamp, comfortable chairs and a sofa. In doing these things we were able to start to shape the room into something that offered an intimate space. In this way the art piece became connected to the room, and the room reflected a home-like space. *Tales of I* offered a tailored experience with a variety of film content that spanned very general subject matter, as well as local identity and very personal things.

We hoped that we had provided an informal space where families could behave in more natural ways than the rest of the unit afforded. It was also important to us that we provided the means through the art piece for family members to be able to make connections with their relative through the use of the films and various artifacts of the piece and so aid more positive visits.

Themes

The themes of the globes arose through conversation with staff in the unit, who made specific requests relating to content that would hold relevance for their clients. Each globe encases a scene or a series of small objects. For example *Nature* holds butterflies that are local to the area and *Football* encases images of well-known footballers from the local team over past decades. The globes were made to be light and easily held or cradled in the hand. Tangible interaction with the globes by clients was an important design consideration and we hoped that they would be touched and explored. To add to this drawers beneath each globe held a mixture of tactile materials to allow a multi-sensory experience when watching the films. Through the films we aimed to draw on the local identity of the area, which we hoped would resonate on a personal level for many of the clients as almost all had lived in the area all of their lives. This allowed us to involve close detail of the local character, culture and industry of the region.

Another of our goals was to build on the practice of using *All About Me books* and create a way that personal imagery and video from a client's life could be made into a short film that could be played for them on the television cabinet. Staff had already invested time scanning in photographs brought in by clients' relatives for the books; these images could now also be used as part of a personal film for a client and be supplemented by short film clips provided by relatives. The dynamics of the display of films (timings and cut effects) were discussed with staff in the unit using demos in situ as the piece developed. We hoped that these films would enable a truly personal experience for the client, that they would supplement the varied uses of the *All About Me* books and would give family members a greater opportunity to contribute to the care of their relative and communicate with them during visits. However, at the point in time of our evaluation the 'All about me' memory sticks had not been deployed (due to staff changes on this unit).

FINDINGS & IMPLICATIONS

As part of a service evaluation for the art piece, we conducted semi-structured interviews with members of staff in the unit, including 2 ward managers, 1 occupational therapist, 1 auxiliary and 7 qualified staff nurses. Interviews were conducted on the day of installation, and in months 1 and 3, lasted on average 30 minutes and were audio recorded, transcribed and analyzed in-depth by following Braun and Clarke's thematic analysis approach [6]. We asked staff about their experiences and observations of using the piece with clients and adopted the most ethical approach that we could in this context: one that added no additional burden for clients. Clients in the unit have extremely challenging and complex behaviors and the staff group, who have a very person-centred form of care working one-to-one with clients were perfectly positioned to act as client advocates to give us feedback over the prolonged period of use that formed our evaluation.

General Engagement with the Piece

The log data for 143 days of deployment indicate that globes were placed on the cabinet to trigger a video on 308 occasions. On 57 days no interaction was logged. However, these non-interaction days are evenly distributed over time (see Figure 2).

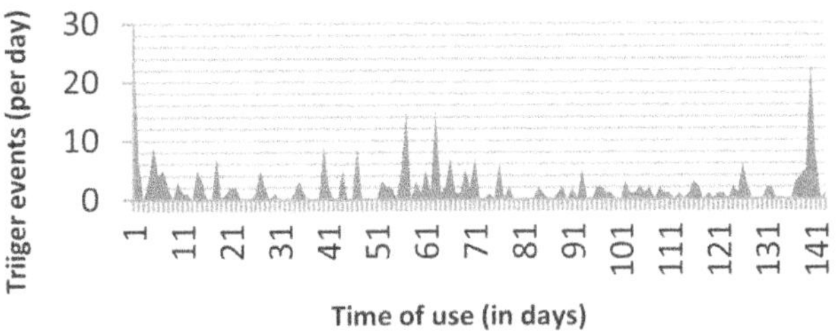

Figure 2. Number of video events triggered per day.

On average, videos were triggered 5 times per day (*modal value*), with a maximum of 27 interactions on one day alone. The *Football* and the *Holiday* globes were used most commonly (73 times each); *Objects* (54 times); *Nature* (35 times); *Local* (28 times); and Sewing (23 times).

Our interviews with members of staff revealed that the piece has been appropriated for different purposes: for individual reminiscence practices; to calm, relax and engage clients who were exhibiting challenging behaviors; to assess a client's memory span and life history; and to assess and improve the communication skills of trainees learning to work with dementia clients. The room became several different spaces within the hospital environment.

Space for Relaxation for both Clients and Staff

The room had been used to calm clients down, when their behavior escalated or when they felt anxious or agitated, and was also found to be relaxing space, where staff could sit with a client quietly. Here, clients could be distracted from experiencing distress and become more settled in their presentation. Interestingly, the room was also used to calm down members of staff. For example after a serious assault by a client. *Nature* was described as being particularly good for relaxing clients and easing conversation. Expanding on this, one ward manager (Amy) explained:

"The other thing we're exploring is, you know the nature one? If we've got somebody that we want to do relaxation with, we want to engage with them, it's to put them on. It's the ambience it creates with the music and the pictures. If you're sitting there and you've got long, silent periods, there is something for them to focus on and it doesn't make them feel uncomfortable."

Beyond providing a calming and relaxing atmosphere, the *Tales of I* provided activities that had different characteristics to the more functional activities of care in a hospital environment (e.g. taking medication, being washed or fed). It allowed clients to take part in a personally meaningful activity, something that they could focus their attention on. Clients were generally very restless and tended to wander around the corridors for long periods of time each day. They also had only a short attention and memory span making it difficult for them to concentrate or to focus their attention. Getting the client to sit down in the room, to engage with the piece and watch one of the films, even if only for a short period of time, was described by staff as remarkable. Amy described an event relating to a client:

"And actually their dad [the client] actually sat for ten minutes which was really good because normally he would walk round and round. He would sit for his meal because his meal was in front of him but then he'd get up and he'd continuously walk. And he used to get into a lot of altercations with people. (...) She [the nurse] put it on for him and he sat there. It was [the] football one again. But he sat there and he sat for ten minutes."

A space for Intimacy

Issues of intimacy arose from people's engagements with the art piece and the room in which it was located. It also brought the client's desire for interactions and conversations with other people to the forefront, and the need to have an appropriate space to be intimate and private with somebody within the formal setting of a hospital.

Inter-Personal Communication

Staff described how interactions with the art piece enabled and stimulated conversations about things that were central to the film, but also about a wider scope of topic as this quote describes:

Clare: "...for a particular patient say it's football they might play football or you can talk about when they were younger playing, if they had children or...So it does bring things out.. And then they would talk about like the old football boots..."

This functioning of the piece was as expected and confirms that it was facilitating the kinds of conversations that it was designed to support. Interestingly the piece also created situations whereby the client was the expert about a particular topic shown in the films.

Amy: "[the piece] is also there for educational purposes. You'd be amazed, some of the staff don't even know what half the objects are. (...) prompting them "Well, what's that?" gives some leverage to the client and to instigate conversation."

Staff described this dynamic as exceedingly unusual in the unit and that an occurrence whereby a member of staff learned something from a client was extremely rare. This dynamic is bolstered further through description of how the art piece functioned when staff, who had not grown up in the area or country used the piece with clients.

Amy: "Our ethnic minority staff. You know the one [globe] for industry? One of the auxiliaries, (...) he was fascinated to find out why ships were painted half red under the water, and one of our clients was able to tell him."

This dynamic was one that the ward manager prized about the piece. She described how as a result she encourages staff to use the piece to ask the client questions about things that they genuinely don't know about, rather than merely asking about the known aspects of the film in an effort to engage the client.

Amy: "That's something else; you've got to get students and staff to say (...) If you don't know where it is, ask. The patient will remember and if they don't you can say 'Well, maybe we can go and find out'... Why can't you go and find out?"

Moreover staff expressed how such interactions with the art pieces had enabled a more balanced communication with clients than is often possible; staff commented that the interactions were *"proper conversations, even if only for a short time"*, *"encourage[d] two-way conversation"* and were *"more equal"*. Engagement with the piece was perceived as *"an activity where no one's in control of it"*. Normally, the professional relationship between staff and clients does not allow for a reciprocal exchange of personal information. Clampitt [8] describes inter-personal communication as a dance, where partners have to coordinate their movements in order to both understand where they are going. Within the dance he suggests that there are rules and skills, but there are also flexibilities whereby dancers can interject their own styles into the movement. If we consider this analogy within Francis Place it seems that there are a number of common 'dances' that typically occur, where staff predominantly take the lead. What staff were describing around the use of the piece suggests that a few more dance styles and tempos have been enabled in the unit, that the client has been able to take the lead or to change the movement and that this has been enjoyable for the client and staff.

Paula: "They [the clients] actually, they're toe tapping and some of them have been dancing. The thing is the staff do it as well you know and it's getting to the point where it's a more natural setting."

As noted earlier we drew heavily on local references and culture for the creation of the films and staff described how these aspects often acted as very strong memory triggers for clients. Staff were encouraged to build an active rather than a passive engagement with the piece. If content in the film was unknown they were motivated to find out about the meanings either from a client or from a different source. The ward manager saw this as a dynamic that had developed because of the piece that created interesting and new opportunities for connection between staff and clients and also between staff and the unit itself.

Staff described how the piece has often stimulated clients who usually didn't talk very much to instigate or be part of a conversation and how this could then lead on to the client continuing this conversation with other clients when he or she left the room and went back into the main unit.

Anna: "Even with patients who normally wouldn't chat you know? It would just be like constant observation and just wondering around in their own world – we got them in here and then we were able to discuss something."

The desire staff had to find *ways in* to a client becomes acute when he or she has limited ability to articulate something. We were told about a client who only used one term to describe whatever she wanted to say. Working with her became about trying to pick up on nuances of her behavior, gestures and intonations to try to understand what she wanted to communicate. This would clearly frustrate her at times, as she would repeatedly say the term in increasing efforts to communicate. Equally, staff would want to understand her and help her and in some situations this would become extremely difficult for them. Staff described how they were able to use *Tales of I* with her to connect with her in new ways, for example through her gestures towards certain aspects of different films or through words that she would say stimulated by the films.

Need for Self-Disclosure, Intimacy & Relationships to Others

This, and other examples outlined earlier, demonstrate clients' need to communicate and self-disclose information to others [19]. In unfolding their inner life by disclosing personal or private information, the client communicates something about her or himself (e.g. personal experiences, meanings attached to events, fact's about their life). The sharing of information with others can increase mutual knowledge and understanding and allows people to better meet each other's needs [28]. As such, self-disclosure supports the development of closeness with others, can increase interpersonal liking and trust, and offers opportunities for sympathetic and supportive responses [19]. Thus, communication in this context should not only be understood as the interpersonal exchange of information on a content level (e.g. a person's memories or feelings), but incorporates what Watzlawik et al. [32] termed the 'relational level' of communication, whereby the relationship between the people is defined through the exchange itself (e.g. as a caring relationship).

The desire to communicate with others and to feel close to them, describes the very fundamental human need of belonging [4, p.497] suggesting that "human beings have a pervasive drive to form and maintain at least a minimum quantity of lasting, positive, and significant interpersonal relationships". Thus, to fully satisfy this need, individuals have to have frequent interactions with other people which should be perceived as providing an interpersonal bond marked by stability, continuation and affective concerns (e.g. that one cares about one another).

In this regard, intimacy is a valuable aspect of interpersonal relationships as it enables the experience of warmth, closeness, commonality and caring [28]. However, establishing a clear and specific definition of the concept is rather difficult. Moss and Schwebel [22] identified five key components describing intimacy as a mutual exchange between people, that is characterized by the receipt and expression of affect (e.g. feelings of compassion, validation of a person's worth, providence of assistance), cognitions (e.g. information about beliefs, values or experiences), physical closeness and commitment. This human need for intimacy, for touch, hugs and kisses and the desire to feel connected to others does not diminish with age. Yet, aspects of closeness, intimacy or even sexuality are often overlooked in discussions about the well-being of clients with dementia in hospital or care settings [11, 18]. People with dementia have the same psychosocial needs as other individuals: "They need stimulation and companionship, they need to feel secure, to feel they are unique and valued individuals, and to feel a sense of self-esteem" [3]. According to Kuhn [18, p.165], enabling them to "maintain their social skills and sense of self in close relationships is essential to enhancing their quality of life".

The Relationship to Staff

Having more natural and equal conversations between members of staff and clients, in which both parties disclose and exchange pieces of information about themselves, facilitates the building of a relationship. Against the backdrop of the fundamental human need to belong to others [4], clients may benefit from the opportunity to develop a relationship with the nurse [33]. They also have the need for closeness in a relationship. Buckland [7, p.33] describes, "the insecurity and loneliness of a dementing illness can make the interpersonal relationship the most important aspect of care". This suggests identifying new ways for members of staff to support residents in their desire for closeness and social engagement with others [18].

In the past, the role of the nurse was characterized by a professional detachment from clients, meaning that the nurse could appreciate the client's situation but was emotionally detached and distant to them. This definition was driven by the idea of a desexualizing of the nurse-client-relationship, where the nurse stays in control over any interaction with the client [cf., 33].

With the redefinition of nursing care as 'The New Nursing' [26], the emphasis of care was extended to include both the caring *for* and caring *about* clients, which includes emotional involvement and commitment to the patient. In this context, closeness or intimacy between nurse and client does not mean having an intimate relationship which is characterized by a deep emotional and personal attachment to the client, which could be an example of over-involvement increasing the vulnerability of the nurse. Instead, intimacy in nursing can simply mean to spend time with clients, to demonstrate appreciation of their experiences, to self-disclose personal information to facilitate mutual understanding and acceptance in order to build a confiding relationship as a base for an empathic engagement with one another [cf., 33].

Relationship to Family and Friends – Creating a Visit

Clients usually perceive the transition from their home to the hospital as a 'reality shock' [1], and also their relatives can experience emotional distress about their loved one being institutionalized [29]. Involving family and friends in the care of the person with dementia, and facilitating a sense of purpose beyond the 'visit', can be of great benefit to both parties [10]. Family engagements in care are generally valued for "empowering the client and protecting against feelings of helplessness, improving compliance and supporting early hospital discharge" [1, pp.150-151]. They can best fulfill the more intimate and affective needs of clients, but they often feel disempowered to contribute in a hospital setting, and at times do not know how to engage with a person living with severe dementia. *Tales of I* had so far only been used a few times by family members, but was found to settle the client and to help them in visiting their relative Amy described:

"We had a relative (...) use it. They were concerned about their mother. They were struggling when they were visiting, so this was more of an aid for them than anything else, and what the staff were doing was taking them through and leaving them with the key [to the globes], going back for them later."

As such, the room and the engagement with the piece may provide family and friends with an avenue into involvement and care for their relative, without invading the workspace and care practices of members of staff [cf.,1,29].

The Room and the Art Piece

As staff talked about the room and the art piece it was clear that they had become one and the same thing within the unit. The room was described repeatedly by different staff as "*cozy*" and the intimate setting of the room and what this enabled were reflected upon by the ward manager in terms of privacy and dignity. She described how important it was to give clients and family members privacy during visits. Intimate gestures such as holding hands and having cuddles are needed by both clients and relatives, and staff did their best to give people the space to be intimate.

"We encourage people to visit in the bed areas, as well as the day areas, but we encourage especially couples to visit in the bed areas, because people like privacy and they like to be intimate in the sense of holding hands, having cuddles, pecks on the cheek"

Tales of I had now provided an additional space in the unit for couples to be alone. One point worth noting here is that because the room is accessible to everyone and is located along the meandering corridor people can walk into it not knowing what kinds of conversations are already happening inside, which may feel intrusive. So whilst the room has successfully enabled people to feel that it is a cozy space where intimacy can be displayed it highlights the challenges to the design of such spaces within this extreme context and shared environment.

Sense of Self

The triggering of memories and past experiences had deep implications for care in terms of the sense of self of someone with dementia. The role of familiarity, possessions and home were all key factors in the re-connecting with self that occurred in interactions with the piece.

Value of the Act of Remembering

As described, clients were reconnected to past memories through their interactions with the piece. A key example of this is worth sharing as it demonstrates how important the act of remembering something can sometimes be to someone and how powerful this can be.

Amy: "This gentleman, (...) he watched the football one, stimulated when he remembered that when he was young his dad had gone to [a famous footballer's] house. His dad had been a friend of [the famous footballer]and he'd sat on his knee. Now, he remembered that, not in the full format of what he remembered at the time. This was before breakfast, about 8 o'clock in the morning. At 3 o'clock in the afternoon he was still talking about sitting on [the famous footballer's] knee. That was fixed, it was there and he was going round engaging with people, telling them."

This was an exceptional occurrence for this particular client who would typically walk around the unit for hours each day, only stopping to eat meals. Staff were able to get him to sit for ten minutes to watch the football film, which in itself was remarkable. And as the quotes describe he connected with a past personal experience powerfully and moreover this memory stayed with him for hours. Staff described how this had given them something to work with for this client. They used football related imagery and conversation as well as the globe and the football film to connect with the client and build on the sense of wellbeing that he experienced from watching the film.

Furthermore the powerful connection that the client had with the film about his football club suggests that aspects of his identity were bound up with being an avid football fan. Belk [5] states that people define themselves through their possessions by which he is referring to more than artifacts. Personal skills, how someone relates to other people, places and groups all factor in this way. Such 'possessions' Belk asserts contribute and reflect a person's identity and as such are an important component of their sense of self.

As such we can posit that in the case of this client the football film offered him a connection to a piece of himself kept within signifiers of his football club. The film itself contained a piece of him and he was a part of it. This sense of rich connection is a form of ownership. Through this example we can see how even for people who will stay in an environment such as Francis Place only fleetingly it is possible to offer connections to things that resonate with self on a deep level. This example was not an isolated occurrence and staff described other similar accounts. Again, as previously noted, a connection to things that are local and from the local community where an individual is from enable relatively general referents to strike a rich chord. As Belk [5, p.152] describes: "we exist not only as individuals, but also as collectivities."

Ways in such as the football club for this client are things that staff used to develop a richer understanding of a client's life history. The value of narratives and telling your life story are things that staff frequently mentioned. We tell our life stories to disclose who we are to others, but also to reflect on a personal sense of self and to understand self more. In Francis Place the enabling of clients to tell their life stories is regarded as good care for this reason. Furthermore as part of the assessment process staff are searching to connect a client's current presentation to events from their pasts in order to gain an understanding of why they are behaving as they are.

Amy: "On the organic side we link it to the life history and what we do is we're trying to find out can we link somewhere in the person's past the presentation we're seeing now."

Amy: "You know is what they're displaying to us anything from there or around there and can we work with it."

Gaining knowledge about an individual's life story was described by the ward manager as a way for staff behavior to be appropriate for a client, which she describes as staff conforming to a client rather than the reverse occurring:

"You know and if you keep people's identity (...) you working with them so even though we have our standard environment (...) we are conforming to them they're not conforming to us."

Transitory Space and Possessions

Francis Place, as already noted, is an assessment and treatment unit. Thus, clients are there for a relatively short period of time. Like most hospitals it is a transitory space. This makes it challenging for staff to get to know clients and to engage them in personal care when the emphasis is often on functional aspects of assessment and daily routine.

Designs that help change a client's perception of the environment from a 'place-less' space to something more recognizably relaxing and homely aids the personal care that staff are able to give. The new build construction of Francis Place meant that, as an environment, there was little or nothing that was old. There were subsequently no other referents of anything 'old' for the clients to relate to or have memories triggered by. Many of the films and objects like the old coins and badges in one of the globes provided a resource for nostalgia. Davis [1979, p.31 as cited in 5] notes the relevance of such longing to the self:

"nostalgia (like long-term memory, like reminiscence, like daydreaming) is deeply implicated in our sense of who we are, what we are about (...). In short, nostalgia is (...) a readily accessible psychological lens (...) for the never ending work of constructing, maintaining, and reconstructing our identities."

You could posit that in the relatively unadorned, new environment of the unit there were few objects that could tell a story and therefore few objects that could fundamentally connect clients to things outside of the unit; to their own lives or to different times from their pasts. Belk [5] and McCracken [21] relate environments in which people are denied their personal objects or objects that connect them more generally to things that are meaningful in their lives to a dehumanizing of the person. Although within the unit it clearly was not staff practice to dehumanize clients the severity of the clients' dementia meant that they would often unintentionally damage or break any personal possessions. As such each client would commonly own only a few personal artifacts. Therefore Belk's perspective that a lack of personal possessions leads to a "traumatic lessening of the individual's sense of self" [5, p.142] is very relevant in the context of any environment where people with severe dementia live without the evidence of many of their life experiences referenced through artifacts around them. To regard this more generally we could argue that environments in which residents are treated as the same and have the same clothing, the same rooms and the same artifacts is a form of standardization that Belk relates to an elimination of uniqueness and again to a lessening of a sense of self. Furthermore such standardization often relates to an institutional identity being the dominant voice in such situations.

The contexts of *home* and *neighborhood* are argued by Belk to counteract such lack of personal sense of self:

"As with more personal possessions, home and neighborhood have been hypothesized to contribute to sense of self to the degree that a person feels control over them" [5, p.143].

This hypothesis resonates with the work of many anthropologists such as Miller [21, p.1] who stated that:

"We live today in a world of ever more stuff (...) We tend to assume that this has two results: that we are more superficial, and that we are more materialistic, our relationships to things coming at the expense of our relationships to people (...) in many ways , the opposite is true; that possessions often remain profound and usually the closer our relationships are with objects, the closer our relationships are with people."

Tales of I offered a different space in the unit; somewhere where objects *do* feature and objects that reference different aspects of the past at that and staff still had plans to decorate the room further:

Sara: "what I would plan to do is put some pictures and things on the wall and put some cushions and things in here."

Jess: "we still need to get the furniture and things, put in here, to make it look a bit more homely. And a few soft furnishings."

Possessions can be instrumental to maintaining a concept of self for individuals [5]. Through possessions we create and preserve our own sense of who we are; acts that in themselves contribute towards a healthy identity. For people who have severe dementia possessions clearly have a powerful potential in this respect. Through possessions an individual can reconnect to past identities, to skills once possessed and to the knowledge that he or she has been loved and has commanded respect.

Along with possessions, the role of home equally cannot be underestimated in a care or hospital context. As we have noted 'home' can engender calm, enable intimacy between individuals and support a sense of self through a connection to things that are known and have a deep meaning. The ward manager also described how the room could act as a form of security and reassurance for clients.

"It's like, some people when you're driving down the street, and you start seeing sign posts that you know, you become more familiar "Well, I'm getting closer to home now, this is now my home." You go down your drive, in your house. Patients on the organic side, they miss them triggers. It could be that they're in a room full of colors or maybe an object, or it even be an individual. Wherever that individual is, they're there with them, that could be their security blanket. They're their signpost."

The environment of the hospital can feel very alien and things that denote a sense of home for someone can act like recognizable and reassuring triggers within these unknown places. For someone with severe dementia who has a very short memory span ways of regularly triggering and retriggering a sense of reassurance and a connection to a personal sense of home has extremely high value.

CONCLUSION

Through *Tales of I* we were able to explore the environment of a hospital unit to draw out implications for design in dementia. The piece became a window on dementia and the institution itself. The ways that the piece was used and experienced by clients, staff and relatives revealed many rich insights.

Home was shown to be an intensely important concept. Home-like spaces can function as a retreat, a space for relaxation and a natural setting to help de-escalate anxiety and challenging behaviors. Home is something familiar, that is recognizable and that a client can relate to. Unlike the hospital environment referents that speak of home reflect the person, aspects of their identity and life history with all its achievements and experiences. By connecting with a client's past staff were able to 'meet them there'.

Possessions, in their widest sense, for instance artifacts, places, groups or local culture can hold parts of a person; they can define and extend a person's sense of self. Therefore preserving parts of the person's self means that possessions play a crucial role in dementia. To design for the support of self we need to value the client's dignity and acknowledge the potential of possessions and of beauty.

When a person reconnects with aspects of self that are triggered by these things staff are able to see them more as a full person. Supporting these re-connections to self enables staff to find *ways in* to a client. Design needs to promote more reciprocal conversations in which clients can contribute their knowledge and share their expertise with staff. Through self-disclosure of personal information a client opens the space for staff to give an empathic response and value the person for who they are. This also fulfills the fundamental human need to connect to others and to be emotionally close to them. Our findings show that there was an urgent need for privacy and intimacy in the hospital setting. This is often neglected in design for these contexts. In short design should empower the person with dementia. To this end a designer should step back from constraints that emphasize the institutional environment or cognitive impairment and instead focus on enabling the person.

ACKNOWLEDGMENTS

This research was conducted within the RCUK Digital Economy Research Hub on Social Inclusion through the Digital Economy (SiDE).

REFERENCES

1. Allan, D. Negotiating the role of expert carers on an adult hospital ward. *Sociology of Health & Illness, 22*(2), 2000, 149-171.
2. Alzheimer's Disease Facts and Figures report 2011, p.36, from www.alz.org/downloads/Facts_Figures_2011.pdf
3. Alzheimer Society of Canada. Guidelines for Care. Toronto: ASC; 1992, p.3.
4. Baumeister, R.F., and Leary, M.R., The need to belong: Desire for interpersonal attachments as a fundamental human motivation. *Psychological Bulletin, 117*(3), 1995, 497–529.
5. Belk, R.W. Possessions and the extended self. *Journal of Consumer Research, 15*(2), 1988, 139–168.
6. Braun, V., and Clarke, V. Using thematic analysis in psychology. *Qualitative Research in Psychology, 3*, 2006, 77-101.
7. Buckland, S. Well-being, personality and residential care. In: Kitwood T, Benson S, eds. *The New Culture of Dementia Care.* Hawker Publications, 1997, 30–34.
8. Clampitt, P.G. *Communicating for managerial effectiveness*. Sage, 1996.
9. Cohen, D. and Eisdorfer, C. *The loss of self: A family resource for the care of Alzheimer's disease and related disorders*. Norton, 1986.
10. Davies, S. 'Making the move': relatives' experience of the transition into a care home. *Health and Social care in the Community, 12*(6), 2004, 517-526.
11. Ehrenfeld, M., Bronner, G., Tabak, N., Alpert, R., and Bergman, R. Sexuality among institutionalizes elderly patients with dementia. *Nursing Ethics, 6*, 1999, 144-149.
12. Gaver, W., Blythe, M., Boucher, A., Jarvis, N., Bowers, J. and Wright, P. The Prayer Companion: Openness and Specificity, Materiality and Spirituality. *In Proc. CHI 2010*, ACM Press (2010), 2055-2064.
13. Hughes, J.C., Louw, S.J., and Sabat, S.R. *Dementia: mind, meaning, and the person*. Oxford Medical Publication, 2006.
14. Killick, J. and Craig, C *Creativity and Communication in Persons with Dementia: A Practical Guide Jessica*, Kingsley Publishers, 2011.
15. Kitwood, T. *Dementia reconsidered: The person comes first*. Open University Press, 1997.
16. Kitwood, T., and Bredin, K. Towards a theory of dementia care: Personhood and well-being. *Ageing and Society, 12*, 1992, 269–287.
17. Kontos, P. C. Embodied selfhood in Alzheimer's disease – Rethinking person-centred care. *Dementia, 4*, 2005, 553-570.
18. Kuhn, D. Intimacy, Sexuality, and Residents with Dementia. *Alzheimer's Care Quarterly, 3*(2), 2002, 165-176.
19. Larson, J.H., Hammond, C.H., and Harper, J.M. Perceived equity and intimacy in marriage. *Journal of Marital and Family Therapy, 24*, 1998, 487–506.
20. McCracken, G. Culture and consumption among the elderly: Three research objectives in an emerging field. *Aging and Society, 7*(2), 1987, 203-224.
21. Miller, D. *The comfort of things*. Polity Press, 2008.
22. Moss, B.F., and Schwebel, A.I. Defining intimacy in romantic relationships. *Family Relations, 42*, 1993, 31–37.
23. Mynatt, E.D., Melenhorst, A.-S., Fisk, A.D., and Rogers, W.A. Aware Technologies for Aging in Place: Understanding User Needs and Attitudes, *IEEE Pervasive Computing, 3*(2), 2004, 36-41.
24. Olivier, P., and Wallace, J. Digital technologies and the emotional family. *International Journal of Human Computer Studies, 67*(2), 2009, 204 – 214.
25. Orpwood, R. et al. Designing technology to support quality of life of people with dementia. *Technology and Disability, 19*, 2007, 103-112.
26. Salvage, J. The theory and practice of the `New Nursing'. *Nursing Times, 86*, 1990, 42-45.
27. Schaefer, M.T., and Olson, D.H. Assessing intimacy: the pair inventory. *Journal of Marital and Family Therapy, 7*(1), 1981, 47–60.
28. Thieme, A., et al. Lover's box: Designing for reflection within romantic relationships. *International Journal of Human Computer Studies, 69*(5), *2011*, 283-297.
29. Tornatore, J.B., and Grant, L.A. Burden among family caregivers of persons with Alzheimer's disease in nursing homes. *The Gerontologist, 42*(4), 2002, 497-506.
30. Wallace, J., Dearden, A., and Fischer, T. The significant other: the value of jewellery in the conception, design and experience of body focused digital devices. *AI & Soc, 22*, 2007, 53-62.
31. Wallace, J., McCarthy, J., Wright, P. and Olivier, P. Beyond reminiscing: Looking back to look forward in dementia. *CHI 2011 Workshop on Bridging Practices to Support Reminiscence.* http://www.cs.cornell.edu/~danco/remchiwork/papers/Wallace_CHI2011_wkshp.pdf
32. Watzlawik, P., Beavin, J.H., and Jackson, D.D., *Menschliche Kommunikation: Formen, Stoerungen, Paradoxien*. Hans Huber, Vol. 10. 2003, 1–170.
33. Williams, A. A literature review on the concept of intimacy in nursing. *Journal of Advanced Nursing, 33*(5), 2001, 660-667.
34. Wimo, A. and Prince, M., *World Alzheimer Report: The Global Economic Impact of Dementia,* Alzheimer's Disease International (ADI), London, 2010.
35. Wright, P., Wallace, J. and McCarthy, J. Aesthetics and experience-centred design. *ACM Trans. Computer-Human Interactions, 15* (4), 2008, 1 – 21.

ICT-Development in Residential Care Settings: Sensitizing Design to the Life Circumstances of the Residents of a Care Home

Claudia Müller, Cornelius Neufeldt, David Randall, Volker Wulf
Information Science and New Media
University of Siegen
Hölderlinstr. 3, 57068 Siegen, Germany
{claudia.mueller, cornelius.neufeldt, volker.wulf}@uni-siegen.de; daverandall2008@gmail.com

ABSTRACT

In this paper we wish to contribute to the recent ICT-design for and reflection of the application field of residential care homes. In doing so, the contribution of the paper is twofold: we wish to highlight some aspects of the every-day life of institutionalized elderly people – trust, sociality, and memory – which not only provoke reflection on design ideas but also on the socio-technical nexus in which design for the elderly has to take place. This domain, we suggest, is one where the 'parachuting in' of technology is unlikely to prove successful, for reasons we examine below. Further, we suggest that design for and with the elderly carries with it some specific problems. We illustrate our methodological reflections by means of an ongoing empirical research project which aims at the development of a large-screen display for a residential care home.

Author Keywords

Elderly people; residential care; design, methodology; action research; large-screen display

ACM Classification Keywords

H.5.2 [Information Interfaces And Presentation]: User Interfaces – Theory and methods;

General Terms

Human Factors; Design.

INTRODUCTION

Ethnographic and related qualitative research in the context of HCI has progressively extended its remit. One such area is that of assistive technology and, more specifically for our purposes, support for elderly people. Such research confronts unique problems insofar as traditional ethnographic methods, reflecting notions of the 'native', the 'stranger' and processes of enculturation, may not be entirely appropriate. This, we suggest, is particularly the case where the elderly population in question is living in a residential nursing home. If so, then a more creative and opportunistic approach to ethnographic work may prove necessary. In this paper we further elaborate on a broadly ethnographic approach which attempts to deal with three interlinked issues.

Firstly, we argue, the idea of a generic concept of the 'elderly' itself needs to be challenged, since there are specific cultural, institutional, professional policy and age- and health- related issues [1,32] that are implicated here (we have no space to go into theoretical debates concerning the best way to understand 'aging' in society but of relevance here would be so-called 'structured dependency theory' and its critics. The former aims to isolate the specific factors which cause varied experiences of aging whilst critics tend to see such arguments as 'disempowering'(See e.g. [13] for a discussion).In detail, therefore, our research focuses on a very elderly population and one, moreover, which has had to contend with a transition from family to care home. This issue of 'transition', we argue, is a major issue when reflecting on ICT usage for the improvement of quality of life.

Secondly, there are issues relating to the appropriate level of 'granularity' associated with the analysis of 'situated practice' [33], and thirdly in this specific case there are issues which have to do with the relationship between ethnographer and 'user' and which implicate some form of action-based or interventionist approach (see [7]). Specifically, we were confronted with the problem of getting a very elderly user population (aged on average between 80 and 90) in a residential home interested in, and motivated about, potential ICT applications. In the residential home in question, known features of the 'digital divide', notably the poor take-up of ICTs by the elderly and by those of low socio-economic status (most of the residents were from relatively poor backgrounds), compounded by experience of very disruptive life processes during and after the war had a significant impact. In much the same way, the care home instantiates known issues of the 'digital divide' [23,37]. It provided nothing in the way of Internet access, few (if any) residents had computers, and only a very small number had any experience at all of using computer technology. We were not, then, able to conduct studies of their routine ongoing, ordinary experience and use of IT in quite the way we might have wanted. On the other hand previous research has consistently shown that there are significant benefits to IT adoption for the elderly and even for the very old living in residential settings [24] and so we had good grounds for pursuing, by whatever means we could find, methods for engaging this potential user population. In detailing our own work here, we draw on certain perspectives on 'action research', notably those which stress the 'process of systematic reflection, enquiry and action carried out by individuals about their own professional practice' [11]. In other words, there was a process of learning for us as well. Here, we draw on approaches to the 'cultural probe' and on the notion of 'co-construction' as adjuncts to the existing methodological tool box in an effort to address this challenging application field [6,9,17,20].

In what follows, we describe the methods we adopted, the analytic results and some reflections on the development of a large screen display in the care home. Some design implications are then introduced stemming from our empirical investigation.

ICT-DESIGN FOR RESIDENTIAL CARE RESIDENTS: DEALING WITH 'CONTEXT'

The topic "ICT development for old people" and especially in the context of residential homes has not been extensively studied. Indeed, it is sometimes argued that the topic is often neglected, trivialized or treated as merely usability challenges [5,21]. Other researchers report on experiences we also have had, namely being confronted with rather cynical questions about whether it is worthwhile engaging in ICT-design for these old people [2,6]. They are, in other words, classic exemplars of the 'digital divide'.

But there are several reasons for going on with research in this domain. Besides the fact that digital – and social – exclusion remains a vibrant research topic, demographic changes mean that it will become more, not less, important. The fact of an increasing number of single households and increased geographical mobility means that residential care will become an alternative for more elderly citizens in the future. If so, then solutions to the social problems the elderly face will become urgently sought. Such solutions will need to address sociality and 'quality of life' issues as much as those of health and security (for examples of the latter, see [38]). Moreover, 'parachuting' ICT into a care home is unlikely to have the desired effects since issues of the institutional framework, professional practice, family rights and responsibilities and so on will all be relevant. [10,31]. On the face of it, then, engagement on the part of both researchers and participants will be critical.

How this is to be achieved, however, is non-trivial. To some extent, our difficulties are similar to those encountered by Crabtree et al. in their study of a halfway house for psychiatric patients [7]. We learned over time that simple observation of the behavior of the 'older old' revealed relatively little. Sadly, and perhaps because of the institutional setting in which they found themselves, there were relatively few examples of spontaneous 'social' behavior on display and fewer examples of 'activity' than we might have wished for. Being institutionally confined can be an isolating and relatively inactive experience. Where activities were available, they tended to be of the organized kind, provided by staff for groups. Equally, the 'older old' do not necessarily make good respondents. In this case, they knew very little about the possibilities inherent in ICTs and we perhaps were naïve in our initial assumptions about the kinds of question we wanted to ask them. This implicates both problems of method and of analysis. User-centered design approaches are without doubt a 'consummation devoutly to be wished' but are not easily managed when users do not wish, or do not know how, to be at the centre of the design process.

We already know that the move to 'non-work' settings has brought with it some controversy about method, perspective and paradigm [8], largely predicated on the irrelevance of an 'efficiency' or 'task' oriented paradigm. This has led to suggestions such as, from the inclusive technologies research arena, the need for "user sensitive inclusive design" [22]. Similarly, it has been argued that more playful and experiential user involvement endeavors in user-centered design projects would better serve the challenge of engaging elder people [2,16,21,34].

Analytically, it is evident, as Räsänen and Nyce [25] stress, that there is more than one way to conceptualise the socio-cultural context in ethnography-based design processes in HCI. A detailed focus on task, sequential organization, naturally occurring talk, and so on – the kinds of things that have proved enormously revealing in other contexts, proved – as it turns out – less helpful here for the reasons we give above. Below, we reflect on these methodological and analytic difficulties, on the factors which led to our evolving choices, and on their relationship to design decisions. We identify three major themes which, we argue, closely relate to the transitional experiences of the very elderly. They provide an analytic framework for understanding the way in which changing life circumstances intersect with the possibilities that new technology can afford for this population. The themes in question are: *Memory*, *sociality* and *trust*.

EMPIRICAL STUDY: DEVELOPMENT OF A LARGE-SCREEN DISPLAY FOR A RESIDENTIAL CARE HOME

Setting and Project Focus

The original impetus for the project came from an inquiry from the manager of a residential care home. His initial idea was to position a large-screen display for mainly promotional purposes in the entrance hall. Elderly people and their relatives often come to visit the home in order to assess its suitability. Besides that, he was looking for workable ways of providing internet access to the residents, and supporting their every-day activities in terms of social activities, games, and multimedia offers by means of the large-screen display. In meetings with him, we learned that he and his team were very open-minded towards new ICT-based solutions and also flexible and open towards an exploratory, ethnography-based research approach which we perceived as a necessary and fruitful prerequisite for the design process that would follow.

The residential care home houses about 90 elderly residents who mostly have physical or mental problems and who are mainly of advanced age (80+). The home is located in the center of a small city, which is representative of this region (which has very few large cities). Most of the residents have lived their whole life or at least for a long time in the city or one of its neighboring villages.

The support staff offers many regular daily and weekly group activities to their residents. In terms of media usage few seniors had used the internet before and neither did the social workers and other support staff for the activities they offered; the main media the residents consumed were, variously, television, radio and newspapers.

Methodological Challenges when Designing for a Residential Care Setting

As our usual set of methods and research designs in the area of user- and practice-based computing had proved to be successful in our other projects in several application fields we initially planned the research as in a fairly standard way: an extensive pre-phase based on semi-standardized interviews and participant observation, followed by a diary-study in order to gather an extensive understanding of the living context and of daily routines, of patterns of communication and interactions, and the media use of the residents. We were interested in their every-day activities, their information needs and wishes, as well as their interests in communal activities, such as games, music listening, and watching TV.

We started with interviews with staff and residents who had been proposed by the manager and who had signaled their willingness to talk to us. The interviews with residents took place in their rooms, which are partly furnished with their private furniture and decorative elements, such as family pictures. We deliberately choose the rooms as interview settings in order to be able to integrate talking about personal artifacts during the interview, especially photographs of loved ones displayed on the walls or on cabinets.

We initially undertook 13 semi-standardized interviews and 30 hours of participant observation. After the "internet days" (see below) (altogether 15 hours), we accomplished another 15 semi-structured interviews to reflect on these activities together with the participants. The interviews were recorded and transcribed, and field notes were taken both during the participant observation and the "internet day" activities. Data analysis broadly followed the precepts of grounded theory methodology. Analysis was conducted in several steps. We started with open coding, describing loose categories which came up in the interview transcripts. Subsequently, the codes were clustered to higher level categories. Some of the results of this process are the themes we describe in this paper. Our interviews allowed us to identify some recurring themes in relation to perceptions by the elderly of their lives. These were *coping with the current situation* and the *positioning of elderly people*. That is, we were provided in the main with fairly general observations concerning what it is like to be elderly and to live in a care home. These turned out to be very useful insofar as they gave us a picture of a level of acceptance, even fatalism, which prompted us towards a more interventionist stance.

Coping with the Current Situation

Coping with the actual situation in terms of accepting one's fate is a core theme we identified in the analysis of the interviews. We noticed this attitude permeated reflections about their actual every-day life in the home and specifically in relation to themes such as their poor health status and their relative lack of autonomy. Thus and for instance, one respondent told us that, although in the summer he likes to take walks through the village and enjoys being mobile and meeting his former neighbors, in winter he does not leave the home because he is too afraid of falling down. Another example involved a woman who possesses a radio but cannot listen to it: *"I have a radio, but with these buttons, it is too complicated. That's why I do not use it. [...] I would like to listen to it if it were simpler."*

A further example demonstrating this attitude involved a woman talking about games she likes: *„I like to play Rommé very much. But most of the time I do not have partners. There are also many other board games available in the house, but only few like to play. But that's ok."*

What is common to all is their acceptance of the current situation and their unwillingness to complain. Even when possible solutions were suggested, our respondents were unlikely in the first instance to respond with any enthusiasm.

Positioning of Elderly People

The same attitude was apparent when the elderly reflect on their own position: *„My grand-children do not visit me very often. It's because the young do not like old peoples' homes. But that's all right, I can understand this."* Although this woman would like to see her relatives more often, she accepts their choices as 'natural' and more or less inevitable features of the interaction between younger and older generations.

Relating to this general attitude, and of specific relevance to our themes, was the relative absence of self-organized activities. As we have said, the home regularly provides organized activities for its residents but it is in the nature of such activities that they are fairly undifferentiated – they are organized for the group, not for the individual. Some residents admit that they regret this low level of activity and would like to have more individual exchanges and encounters with other residents. On the other hand, there seems to be a tension between being seen as a "social petitioner" or as a "lone wolf".

One man told us in this respect: *„One talks to the others. One should not think that I am a lone wolf. In the summer I am always outside. I also have contacts. I often participate at organized activities in the house. I do not exclude myself.“*

Altogether, the interviewees manifested considerable caution in expressing wishes and desires, were unwilling to sound critical and had a more or less fatalistic attitude to the conformities associated with living in a residential home. In a very real sense, they seemed to have given up some part of their individuality. Comments of the following kind were common: *"one must think of the commonality"*, or: *"Of course I adapted myself – that's what you must do here."*

This in no way reflects on the home. Residents commended practices in the home, stressed the quality of activities on offer, the personnel, especially the manager, and the food: *"It must be forcefully stated that they do so much for elderly and disabled persons. They are really very caring!"*

In much the same way, our research in the house is seen very positive by the elderly, with statements like *"it`s nice to see that the young people don`t forget us"* often heard. At the same time, these utterances rather reflect the sense that these elderly people have of something 'abnormal' taking place when potential interventions take place. Being very old, it seems, meant a forcible disengagement from the world. Again, it was not uncommon to hear contrasting stories about past and present. Respondents would, for instance, report on their previously very fulfilling lives and implicitly contrast them with their current situation. One person reported on her prior life in a big family and made the contrast by pointing to how, *"Today, only one sister is left"* and going on to talk about how mobility problems meant that they were seldom able to meet in person. It is all the more surprising, then, that when we reflected together with her on possible options for supporting them by e.g. video chat and other community tools, there was an unenthusiastic response. The 'fact' of her inability to use new communication technology was too big a barrier. The massive reality of their current situation, the lack of expertise amongst both residents and support staff, and a contrastive orientation to the past seemed to mitigate against engagement with technological change. However, indirectly, we learnt an important lesson on identity construction, on self-perception and perception of the other by the elderly residents which have a huge impact on the design, acceptance, appropriation, and use of new media by elderly people who live in residential care homes. We see these themes also belonging to the research on socio-cultural context of the prospective users. This group were, in a sense, and quite understandably, 'unreliable witnesses' to their own lives. As such, they form something of a marginal case in terms of a conventional ethnographic project and, on reflection, we decided that some kind of stimulus was necessary, a stimulus that has much in common with the notion of 'cultural probes' [12]. In the absence of a clear means to identify interests and desires through observation and interview, we needed to find additional strategies for the engagement that was otherwise lacking. We will elaborate on that further on below.

'Internet Days' as Action Research-Based Approach

Confronted with a lack of any clear direction concerning relevant possibilities, we decided to establish 'internet days' for the residents. Part of the reason for this was the recognition that the residents were familiar with and willing participants in, organized activity.

'Internet Days' – The Setting

The events were planned to take place on two Saturday mornings at a time when no other organized activity were planned. They were promoted as special events in the residential care home and in the village where the home is located, by giving flyers to the elderly and by putting up posters in the building. The project group consisted of a student group of 8 persons and of three lecturers. The event was planned to start at 10am, but in fact, when we started to prepare the desks and switch on the computers at 9am, there were already many elderly people arriving to see what was happening here. During the event the elderly were mostly brought to the stations by the people from the social services and the manager of the old people's home. Other elderly people, who had not previously taken notice of the posters, noticed that there was something going on by other signs which caused their curiosity, e.g. more cars in the parking lot and more younger people in the home, so they got interested in the event, too. The net result was a high degree of participation throughout the course of the day.

During the 'internet days' we presented different online services at five stations, four with computers with large monitors (24") and one with a Wii console connected to a large screen television.

To begin with, and in the absence of any strong sense of 'need' from our initial studies, we structured our provision through discussion with our student volunteers, using readily available resources that they (the students) would regularly use. Students, in other words, were showing the services that they habitually used to residents. We were demonstrating well-known, real world applications to them. These included Facebook, media libraries (TV and broadcast), YouTube, and Google Earth (see figure 1 below). The event was recorded on video and audio, photos and notes were taken during the event.

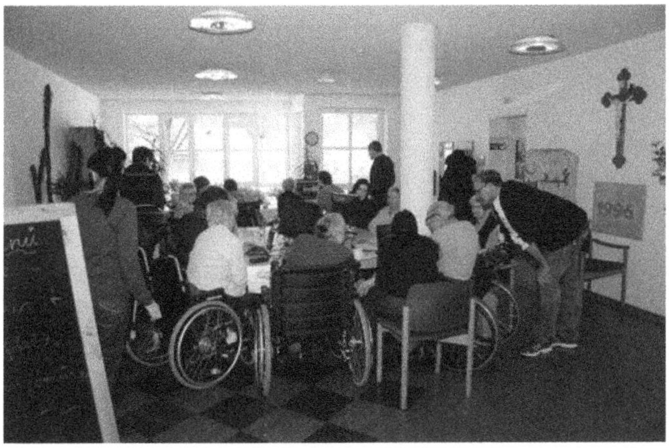

Figure 1: An 'internet day' in the care home

Figure 2: An elderly resident and a student are commonly exploring YouTube

Acceptance of and Interest in the Different Internet Stations

At each station, we saw very different patterns and degrees of engagement. The students consistently tried to involve as many of the elderly sitting at their stations as possible, which was not always easy. In part this was a function of the large numbers, prompted by curiosity about the event itself, the presence of young people interacting with the elderly, the technology we were presenting and the contents shown on the computers. Examples of this varied reaction are as follows:

At the first station we presented the *online media library* of a German television channel. Our intention was to show news and content from the neighborhood of the old people's home as we prior interviews indicated that the elderly were mostly interested in those news stories. We also had evidence from other studies that some content in the library was of special interest for people above 50 years of age. At the internet day we noticed that the content was not as widely accepted as planned. We found two possible explanations for this fact: First was that the group of 50+ is a large group of individuals with different and varied interests. It became apparent that a much more nuanced and differentiated view of the 'elderly' and their interests was necessary. The other fact was that the elderly have quite a bit of time on their hands to consume TV content and consequently have no need for getting content they might have missed. This can be seen at the example of clips from the Olympic Games which were running during the study. The elderly explained to us that they have enough time to keep awake to see the Olympic games coming at night in the TV, so they don`t need the recorded clips from the digital library.

In contrast, *YouTube* was a perfect tool to *collaboratively explore* media content to be of interest for the residents. Together with a student the elderly successively browsed through old films and series they liked to watch in the 60s, to former musicians and pieces of music they liked but had forgotten about and also to actual media content, such as cooking shows (see figure 2).

At the *Facebook* station we could see many interested elderly people searching for relatives – mainly their grandchildren – and writing comments to them. They also had fun looking at the account of the manager of the home and leaving messages on his wall. We presented Facebook as the "yearbook of today" and the seniors had no problems of understanding what it offered. They knew yearbooks very well and were interested in the content. This result was not entirely unexpected, since it is known that social bonds between grandparents and grandchildren can be very strong (see e.g. [19]).

The most intensive use, besides *YouTube*, could be observed at the stations where we switched to use *Google Earth* and webpages from different cities to give the elderly the possibilities to see pictures from their cities of birth again, their favorite former holiday regions or other stations of their individual biographies. The initial start of such a session started usually by a question of a student asking what they would like to see. Some of the elderly directly mentioned some regions, but some did not know what to say. Students explored various websites in response to comments, which prompted further remembrances and reflections. This mutual engagement was what we can call a 'trustful' encounter.

An example of this was a 98-year-old person who was on the internet for the first time in his life on this particular day and expressed delight at being able to see his place of birth and the company where he had worked for almost 50 years. As he was so enthusiastic we offered him an extra space on a laptop on which he browsed for over three hours. At the end of the day the manager printed his favorite pages for him. This gentleman was still showing and explaining them to other people several weeks later (see figure 3).

Again, this linked very closely to biographical memory. Three women in particular, with a biography as displaced persons, expressed great happiness at seeing the places where they were born and had spent their early lives. Another feature of this was that their experiences generated narratives. This was not a passive experience for our group

– they showed a great eagerness to tell stories associated with the text and images they were discovering.

Figure 3: A 98-year old browsing through his past

The action-research based approach in bringing the technology and content to the residents, and trying them out with them helped us in finding anchor points to their interests in media use in a deeper way. All participants – the residents, the students and researchers, and the staff were engaged in a mutual learning process regarding their own attitudes and their perceptions of self and others. For the residents, besides the evident fact that the 'internet days' were fun, the activities also generated a certain trust in their own bodily and cognitive capabilities: One lady told us *"playing the game was so much fun because I noticed that I could do it. I first thought I was not able to do it, but then I was really surprised and happy that I made it."* This utterance of the feeling of success is an indicator of a problem which is experienced by many elderly people with physical handicaps: they often feel uncomfortable exposing their frailty in public and even to an intimate circle of other inhabitants assembled in front of the game. 'Front', in Goffman's sense [14], remains important even to the very old. This game was not only fun for her but also gave her back a little trust in her physical capabilities.

Another elderly lady admitted that she had *"exercised theoretically"* the arm movement for the *Wii* bowling game. She had participated at a *Wii* bowling session which had been organized by the social workers before the 'internet days'. At that time she had felt embarrassed when she could not manage to press the buttons as required. After that session she did not participate in that event again, even when the social workers invited her to. After having exercised the movement she had 'the feeling she could dare' to try it again with us. These physical and confidence issues also produced the phenomenon whereby residents sometimes preferred to instruct the students rather than handle the input devices (*Wii* controller, mouse and keyboard) themselves, despite regular opportunities to try it for themselves. All in all, it was clear that mouse and keyboard are very hard to handle for elderly people who often have fine-motor problems.

Also for the staff the 'internet days' were helpful in adjusting their attitude towards their quite fixed perceptions of the residents. The 'internet days' aroused so much attention that social workers and support staff expressed considerable surprise: *"We see here that we often have too little confidence in capabilities and interests of our inhabitants"*. The social workers also had many insights and ideas themselves towards a possible integration of the media contents into the activities they offer regularly or for setting up new activities. Some of them, mainly women not familiar with new media themselves and as a result rather skeptical about our endeavor, took the chance to learn themselves in the sessions. To different extent, they – due to their own familiarity with new media – considered the use of internet applications as interesting in their work with the residents in the area of "biography work". Biography work is seen as an important task in the house. Especially when new residents enter the house, the personnel tries to get to know the person and aims at documenting as much as possible about the resident's former life in order to be able to offer person-centered care. This is especially important for both building up relationships and a good care atmosphere with persons who have symptoms of dementia. Also in the regular activities offered by the social workers links to historical topics and to remembering the past take up a lot of space. They offer, for example, discussion groups guided by topics such as "how children played 60 years ago" and then they introduce pictures to the group which they found in the literature or somewhere else, such as their own family picture archive or the residents' archives. However, personal chats with the residents in spontaneous face-to-face situations take up most of the time in biography work, e.g. when a social worker and a resident go for a walk and then the resident talks about his life, being happy that someone has time to listen to his personal story. To different extents, the staff started to use the internet to augment the chats with the people after the 'internet days'. Before our activities in the house, they were provided with a laptop, but had no internet access beyond the manager's office. One of them, a young, internet-affine social worker, downloaded pictures from the internet and then took the laptop to bedridden people. As we needed to install WLAN for the 'internet days', we left a new infrastructure in the house, which was later used by this person to be more spontaneous when it comes to searching for pictures and other illustrative material linked to topics that had arisen in chats with residents.

DISCUSSION

The 'Internet Days': Collaborative Exploration and the Setting-up of a Common Space of Thinking

The action-research based approach, which led us from fairly orthodox ethnographic observation to more interventionist strategies has similarities to other design approaches which are based on playful and experiential endeavors, such as Gaver et al.'s "cultural probes" [12], Svenssons and Sokolers "tickets-to-talk", Blythe et al.'s ludic engagements in residential care settings or Harper et al.'s SenseCam [2,16,34]. Blythe et al. coined the term 'interpassivity' to describe some of the features we had also observed. In our view, however, the 'internet days' supported, to a significant degree, more active interactions on the part of the residents and at the same time produced valuable data for informing our further design of the display. The different internet stations, guided by the students, offered a variety of "tickets-to-explore" and "tickets-to-reflect" on further design alternatives but also our general design work in the field of residential care. Similar to the SenseCam research [2,15,33], the 'internet days' drew attention to interests and (past) moments in the residents' lives which otherwise would have been neglected – as the limits of our first interview series have shown. However, what is different to the SenseCam approach is the collaborative moment of the 'internet days'. It seems that, in a context where interview and observational data confronts the problem of the 'unreliable' or 'unwilling' witness, then additional triggers need to be found. Our collaborative engagement was one such. The ongoing exchange between residents, staff and students/ researchers generated mutual knowledge in an ongoing dialogue of offering, asking, exploring and listening – "what can the students and the technology offer for me" and "what could be of interest for her/him" . These evolving methodological and analytic choices led us to three important empirical categories which were helpful to understand the very specific life circumstances of residents in a German care home, residents who have experienced a number of transitions in their lives. These categories are "sociality", "trust", and "memory". The categories have significance for a comprehensive understanding of the very specific social setting and its relation to questions of ICT development and appropriation.

Trust, Sociality and Memory

Trust

It is easy for the young and able-bodied to ignore physical and mental decline. At the same time, and as disability rights campaigners (see e.g. [4]) have constantly reminded us, we should not view 'them' as the problem. The issue of trust here refers not only to the level of faith the very old have in their own capacities but also to the assumptions made by us and by professionals about the appropriateness of what we do. There are some fairly evident design issues relating to physical and mental capacity: Thus, whilst some people were eager to experiment with the controllers, mouse and keyboard themselves, others were not. It was evident to us, for instance, that we needed to experiment with input devices which must be very easy to handle for the elderly, and which connect directly to basic functionalities and information like weather information, news from the city and recent photos from organized activities. On top of that, we learned that the display was quickly recognized and adopted by the social workers and caregivers, as well as the elderly, as a new tool for their activities. Thus, there are two quite distinct user role concepts for the development of the devices and the media accesses – 'the elderly resident user' and 'the social worker user'.

Importantly, our subsequent interviews revealed that trust and confidence were not an issue just for elderly people. Caregiver confidence, as Li and McLaughlin have also pointed out [18] is an important issue which has direct consequences on the residents' self-perception and their practices. As they suggest, caregiver confidence has direct impacts on evaluation by the elderly of their health status and their ability to accomplish activities in daily life. Our observations indicate that this also holds true for the residents' evaluation of new media as a sensible tool for their leisure activities. When caregivers think that new media are not especially useful for the residents, then this is a huge barrier for the residents as the caregivers in the house dominantly affect their possibility of taking part in such events as the 'internet days'. This is especially true for those people who need help due to their restricted mobility so that they need to be accompanied to the place where the activity takes place. During the events, the caregivers came to experience many surprising moments and saw that *"we often have not enough confidence in our residents"*. They, in other words, needed to be 'enlisted'. Whether or not, their prior assumptions can be thought of as "ageism" [29], we have no doubt that our interventions prompted some serious reflections on their part about their own assumptions. Their 'enlistment' in the 'internet days', and afterwards, had a powerful effect on their decisions over which services and treatments are to be offered to elderly people and which are not.

In addition, caregivers' confidence towards media interest and capability of the residents is often affected by their own personal access to new media. Perhaps surprisingly, many of the caregivers themselves had limited access to the new media in their private lives and had limited knowledge of how to integrate new media into their activities with the residents.

With ongoing ICT diffusion into the private arena, there will be a demand for new professional roles. Since relatives and interested elderly persons who come to inspect the care home increasingly ask for internet access and about the role of ICT in activities in the house, new tasks and role requirements for the caregivers working in the house become salient. From this stance, our project can be seen in terms of a coupling of professional, organizational and technological development approaches [28]. This means, that we need to have a more sensitive view of the media learning needs and requirements of all stakeholders, and not only the elderly residents. This requires us to give stakeholders training options, and to co-develop new practices around media usage in their daily work.

Sociality
For the elderly, sociality is something of a problem. Interaction with family, whilst often regular, is no longer under their control. There is, as we have seen, a moral imperative not to be a 'lone wolf' but at the same time there is a certain contempt for those who show an unacceptable 'neediness'– the 'social petitioners'. There is, in other words, something of a tension in place. Elderly people wish to preserve their privacies (and other rights) but at the same time have a clear collective orientation to the activities in the home predicated on the need for a level of organization.

Our respondents, then, whilst reacting with considerable enthusiasm to the displays we put in place and the collectively organized events associated with them would also like, in principle, to engage in some more individual or spontaneous activities. They nevertheless have little idea about how to go about this. Our own view is that this has to do with certain cultural-historical facts – that this generation has tended to come from small and homogeneous communities with strong family and community ties, and hence that relocation has had major consequences in relation to self-marginalization and self-identification. This in turn has consequences for the 'quality of life' agenda associated with, for instance, the gerontological literature and the constraints that institutional settings place on it [27,36]. This problem can be conceptualized in terms of an incommensurability between life-historical narratives on the part of the elderly – their identities are, unsurprisingly, constructed out of their life experiences – and the adjustments that are required in institutional frameworks. The so-called "culture change" movement in the US [30,35], one which we are entirely sympathetic to, aims to promote a more humane institutionalized care as important approaches for an individualized, patient-centered and autonomy-oriented care philosophy. However, in the light of our own findings, it is apparent that balancing the demands of individual 'narrative' and institutional life is non-trivial (see e.g. [30]).

Taking this view, we have learned that relocation into a care home involves a renegotiation of sociality, one which is often troublesome for residents. Individual attitudes and ways of moderating sociality, i.e. personal distance and closeness, which stem from individual and collective biographical experiences which are often hard to express verbally have to be measured against institutional expectation. Appropriation of technology will reflect this. Additionally, design criteria need to reflect the constantly changing nature of the group in question, a group that has developing needs and wishes. As people age and their health status deteriorates. Hence, in our design work, we must think of "the elderly" as a continuum [26] and related needs and wishes as being in a constant state of change. Our reflections on sociality, that is, need to reflect this as well.

Memory
Perhaps the clearest and most unambiguous finding from our work is the importance of acts of remembering. Reminiscence, we find, is important in many different ways – in the use of Google maps to identify previous location in a life history; in 'madeleine' moments prompted by music and other media; in photographic records, and in searches on Facebook. Gerontopychology suggests that older adults actively use reminiscence in social interactions for emotion regulation and promotion of psychological wellbeing. Self-identity and self-continuity, the meaning and coherence of life, promoting acceptance and reconciliation, and especially for institutionalized elderly, dealing with boredom (for an extensive theoretical overview see [3]) all prompt these acts.

Our studies powerfully confirm this. Anecdotes, reminiscences, and other narratives drove many of our interviews with elderly people, often to contrast previous and current existence. Harper [15] has described how photographic elicitation (and other visual representation) can be used as an aid to narrative work and one of the unequivocal results of our 'internet days' was the fact that they provided a strong and clear opportunity for residents to do narrative work of this kind. They provided a fruitful space for the stimulation of remembrance and narrations, framed by social interaction and common activity.

In sum, we learned that internet content and applications which support and stimulate reminiscence activities can contribute to meaningful and joyful activities in the home. Our design work aims precisely at supporting both individual memory activities through the prompts entailed in music and photographs, and through the co-construction with care givers and elderly people of collective content which can be used in group activities on the large screen.

First Prototypes
A reflection of the study results let to the introduction of a first set of prototypes which subsequently were the basis of our ongoing research and development process up to the present.

The first set of prototypes consists of a large-screen display (55'), input devices and a small collection of 'programs'. The display system is a common windows-based PC. We will briefly elaborate on the elements.

Although at first we were skeptical about the designated location of the display in a corner in the entrance hall which initially seemed to us a fairly hectic and uncomfortable space we learned that the hall had some certain meaning for sociality. On one hand, the manager's office, which is located at the end of the hall, serves as a focal point for many residents, who will typically walk over for a quick chat or to hear what is happening in the house and around. In addition, some people like to sit on a sofa next to the entrance and to see what is going on there. The dining hall is also next to the entrance hall, another reason for action around that place three times a day. That is, what we considered to be an unsuitable site was viewed quite differently by the people on-site. This was supported by the manager's plans to restructure the display area, with the introduction of a nicely fitted cafeteria, which he implemented immediately. From a sociality perspective, the place offers two options, to start individual interaction with the system and to use it as the basis for group activities. As discussed above, there is a tension between the desire to socialize and to be informed about things happening, but at the same time to be restrained in one's orientation to 'group' activities. Elderly people (and perhaps like the rest of us) do not want to be thought of as 'bothersome' or 'needy'. The display in its very location somehow provides new options to deal with this tension. People now can stop by the display on their stroll through the house, and use it to just briefly get some information or to take up a more intensive interaction, on their own or with others. Meanwhile, the display area has led to some new forms of interaction among residents distinct from organized group activities which are linked to obligations. In this way, the technology mediates social activity. It "legitimizes" cooperative endeavor, but does not bind people to it. This is true for both social constellations, between residents and also between residents and staff, who can, when they choose, explore mutual likes and interests.

In terms of content we chose four programs: (1) a photo album which is constantly actualized by the manager with photos from activities in the home, such as festivities. We chose the photo album because a culture of picture taking and displaying in the house already existed. (2) a program of "short films" with *YouTube* videos which are selected collaboratively by the research team and the staff on the basis of our experience from the 'internet days', and which reflected biographical interests,(3) a news channel which is frequently watched by many residents at the classic daily 'prime time'. With this application they now are able to stop by and get the actual news from the broadcast's media library, and (4) a "local news" programme. The news, we find, functions as a "ticket-to-talk", i.e. a kind of legitimation for communication with others.

General internet access is also provided via a browser, at the moment mainly to be accessed by the social workers. This is most likely not the final set of programs, but is based on the first empirical findings and in our ongoing evaluation and development cycles we learned that people very much liked to stop by or sit for a longer time to interact with the display. Besides this, it offers a first approach for remembrance work led by the social workers.

Besides keyboard and mouse we looked for a simple input device for the residents. As a first approach, we modified the *PlayStation* buzzer. The buzzer consists of five differently colored buttons which were connected to fixed functionalities on the screen (e.g. "would you like to see the photo album then press the red button"). This is sufficient and works well for access to this small program. However, for the future we need to find another solution as complexity of the program increases. Other prototypes are on the way, such as an easy-to-use music device, an input device which provides access to *google maps* and annotated content, and a device which enables residents to annotate places with personal narrations. With the ongoing prototype design and implementation also additional questions will need to be dealt with, such as how to organize the growing material, searchability, and, most importantly, privacy issues.

CONCLUSION

Our study contributes to research on ICT for the elderly and serves as a window to better understand the life circumstances of institutionalized elderly people and the methodological challenges involved in the set-up of a user-centered design process. By applying a set of methods containing interviews and collaborative and explorative action-based research we could identify some core socio-technical themes – sociality, trust, and memory – which constitute the contours of every-day life in a residential home and impact on interactions between not only the elderly themselves but also the other stakeholders involved in their care. These analytic categories help to understand respective specificities of life in an institutional setting and certain social issues which come to the fore as elderly people experience a major transition in their lives, a transition which has material, spatial and social elements, as we have shown. Participatory design adherents often speak of 'mutual learning'. As we have seen, work with the very elderly is something of a limiting case in respect of participation. Mutual learning, nevertheless, very well describes our experience.

REFERENCES

1. Bengtson, V.L., Silverstein, M., and Putney, N. *Handbook of theories of aging*. Springer, 2009.
2. Blythe, M., Wright, P., Bowers, J., et al. Age and experience: ludic engagement in a residential care setting. *Proc. DIS 2010*, ACM (2010), 161-170.
3. Bohlmeijer, E. *Reminiscence and depression in later life* (Dissertation) 2007. http://dare.ubvu.vu.nl/bitstream/1871/12886/2/proefschrift_reminiscence_and_depression_in_later_life.pdf (15.09.2011)
4. Campbell, F.K. *Contours of ableism: The production of disability and abledness*. Palgrave Macmillan, 2009.
5. Clarkson, J. *Inclusive design: design for the whole population*. Springer, 2003.
6. Coleman, G.W., Gibson, L., Hanson, V.L., Bobrowicz, A., and McKay, A. Engaging the disengaged: how do we design technology for digitally excluded older adults? *Proc. DIS 2010*, ACM (2010), 175-178.
7. Crabtree, A., Hemmings, T., Rodden, T., et al. Designing with care: Adapting cultural probes to inform design in sensitive settings. *Proc. OZCHI 2003*, 4-13.

8. Crabtree, A., Rodden, T., and Benford, S. Moving with the times: IT research and the boundaries of CSCW. *Journal Computer Supported Cooperative Work* 14, 3, (2005), 217-251.
9. Duh, H.B.-L., Do, E.Y.-L., Billinghurst, M., Quek, F., and Chen, V.H.-H. Senior-friendly technologies: interaction design for senior users. *Ext. Abstracts CHI 2010*, ACM (2010), 4513-4516.
10. Eaton, S.C. Eldercare in the United States: Inadequate, Inequitable, but Not a Lost Cause. *Feminist Economics* 11, 2 (2005), 37-51.
11. Frost D. and Durrant J. Teachers as Leaders: exploring the impact of teacher-led development work. *School Leadership and Management* 22, 2 (2002), 143-161.
12. Gaver, B., Dunne, T., and Pacenti, E. Design: Cultural probes. *interactions 6*, (1999), 21-29.
13. Gilleard, C.J. and Higgs, *P. Cultures of ageing: self, citizen, and the body*. Pearson Education, 2000.
14. Goffman, E. *The Presentation of Self in Everyday Life*. Anchor, 1959.
15. Harper, D. Talking about pictures: a case for photo elicitation. *Visual Studies* 17, 1 (2002), 13-26.
16. Harper, R., Randall, D., Smyth, N., Evans, C., Heledd, L., and Moore, R. The past is a different place: they do things differently there. *Proc. DIS 2008*, ACM (2008), 271-280.
17. Ijsselsteijn, W., Nap, H.H., Kort, Y. de, and Poels, K. Digital game design for elderly users. *Proc. Future Play 2007*, ACM (2007), 17-22.
18. Li, L.W. and McLaughlin, S.J. Caregiver Confidence: Does It Predict Changes in Disability Among Elderly Home Care Recipients? *The Gerontologist* (2011).
19. Lindley, S.E., Randall, D., Sharrock, W., Glancy, M., Smyth, N., and Harper, R. Narrative, memory and practice: tensions and choices in the use of a digital artefact. *Proc. British HCI*, (2009), 1-9.
20. Massimi, M., Baecker, R.M., and Wu, M. Using participatory activities with seniors to critique, build, and evaluate mobile phones. *Proc. ACM SIGACCESS* 2007, ACM (2007), 155-162.
21. Newell, A., Arnott, J., Carmichael, A., and Morgan, M. Methodologies for involving older adults in the design process. Proceedings of the 4th international conference on Universal access in human computer interaction:coping with diversity, (2007), 982-989.
22. Newell, A.F. and Gregor, P. User sensitive inclusive design; in search of a new paradigm. *Proc. Universal Usability 2000*, ACM (2000), 39-44.
23. Norris, P. Digital Divide: *Civic Engagement, Information Poverty, and the Internet Worldwide*. Cambridge University Press, 2001.
24. Piper, A.M., Campbell, R., and Hollan, J.D. Exploring the accessibility and appeal of surface computing for older adult health care support. *Proc. CHI 2010*, ACM (2010), 907-916.
25. Räsänen, M. and Nyce, J.M. A new role for anthropology?: rewriting „context" and „analysis" in HCI research. *Proc. NordiCHI 2006*, ACM (2006), 175-184.
26. Roberts, S. *The Fictions, Facts and Future of Older People and Technology*. ILC-UK, 2009.
27. Robichaud, L., Durand, P.J., Bédard, R., and Ouellet, J.-P. Quality of life indicators in long term care: Opinions of elderly residents and their families. *Canadian Journal of Occupational Therapy* 73, 4 (2006), 245-251.
28. Rohde, M. *Integrated organization and technology development (OTD) and the impact of socio-cultural concepts: a CSCW perspective*. http://rudar.ruc.dk /handle/1800/3112 (15.10.2011)
29. Rosowsky, E. Ageism and Professional Training in Aging: Who Will Be There To Help? *Generations* 29, 3 (2005), 55-58.
30. Shura, R., Siders, R.A., and Dannefer, D. Culture Change in Long-term Care: Participatory Action Research and the Role of the Resident. *The Gerontologist* 51, 2 (2011), 212-225.
31. Stark, A. Warm Hands in Cold Age – On the Need of a New World Order of Care. *Feminist Economics* 11, 2 (2005), 7-36.
32. Stolk, R.P., Hutter, I., and Wittek, R.P.M. Population ageing research: a family of disciplines. *European Journal of Epidemiology* 24, 11 (2009), 715-718.
33. Suchman, L.A. *Plans and situated actions: the problem of human-machine communication*. Cambridge University Press, 1987.
34. Svensson, M.S. and Sokoler, T. Ticket-to-talk-television: designing for the circumstantial nature of everyday social interaction. *Proc. NordiCHI 2008*, ACM (2008), 334-343.
35. Thomas, W.H. *Life Worth Living: How Someone You Love Can Still Enjoy Life in a Nursing Home - The Eden Alternative in Action*. Vanderwyk & Burnham, 1996.
36. Timonen, V. and O'Dwyer, C. Living in Institutional Care: Residents' Experiences and Coping Strategies. *Social Work in Health Care* 48, (2009), 597-613.
37. Warschauer, M. *Technology and Social Inclusion: Rethinking the Digital Divide*. MIT Press, 2003.
38. Yeunsook Lee, Z. Zenn Bien, Mounir Mokhtari, et al. ed. Aging Friendly Technology for Health and Independence: *8th International Conference on Smart Homes and Health Telematics, ICOST 2010*, Seoul, Korea. Springer, Berlin, 2010.

Investigating Interruptions in the Context of Computerised Cognitive Testing for Older Adults

Matthew Brehmer[1], Joanna McGrenere[1], Charlotte Tang[1], Claudia Jacova[2]
[1]Deptartment of Computer Science, [2]Deptartment of Medicine
University of British Columbia, Vancouver, Canada
{brehmer, joanna, scctang} @cs.ubc.ca, cjacova@mail.ubc.ca

ABSTRACT

Interruptions in the home pose a threat to the validity of self-administered computerised cognitive testing. We report the findings of a laboratory experiment investigating the effects of increased interruption workload demand on older adults' computerised cognitive test performance. Related work has reported interruptions having a range of inhibitory and facilitatory effects on primary task performance. Cognitive ageing literature suggests that increased interruption workload demand should have greater detrimental effects on older adults' performance, when compared to younger adults. With 36 participants from 3 age groups (20-54, 55-69, 70+), we found divergent effects of increased interruption demand on two primary tasks. Results suggest that older and younger adults experience interruptions differently, but at no age is test performance compromised by demanding interruptions. This finding is reassuring with respect to the success of a self-administered computerised cognitive assessment test, and is likely to be useful for other applications used by older adults.

Author Keywords

Interruptions; experiment; task resumption; computerised cognitive assessment; older adults.

ACM Classification Keywords

H.5.2 [Information Interfaces and Presentation]: User Interfaces - Evaluation/methodology;

General Terms

Experimentation, Human Factors.

INTRODUCTION

Interruptions are common in everyday life, occurring in all contexts, affecting all people, young and old. Interruptions can have detrimental effects on ongoing tasks, incurring costs to productivity [21] and increases in errors [13].

Effects of interruptions have been studied in many naturalistic and experimental settings, resulting in implications for designing applications to support productivity [2], decision-making [25], and vigilance [1].

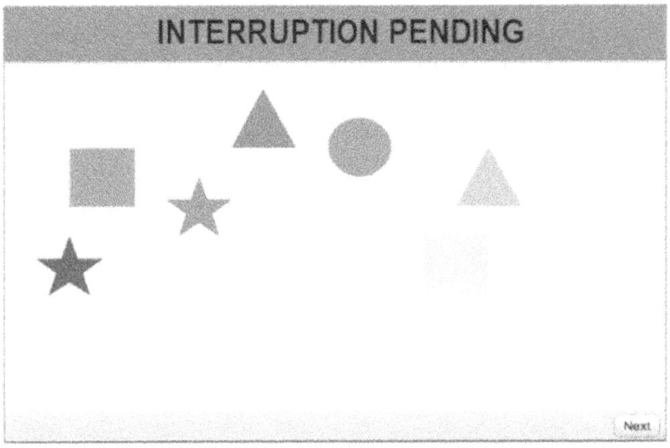

Figure 1. Notification of a pending interruption in a verbal memory task, adapted from a cognitive assessment task.

These implications largely focus on younger adults in workplace contexts. They have only minimally addressed how the ageing mind is affected by interruptions to ongoing primary tasks, which is the focus of our current work.

Our motivation stems from an initiative to develop Cognitve Testing on a Computer (C-TOC), a self-administered web-based computerised cognitive assessment that individuals will be able to take independently from their home [18]. With ongoing advances in modern medicine, people are living longer. This is associated with an increase of older individuals (55+) experiencing cognitive decline and presenting concerns regarding cognitive health. Currently, the screening for pathological cognitive decline as a result of Alzheimer's disease and related dementias are conducted using paper-based tests including the Mini-Mental State Examination [12] and the Montreal Cognitive Assessment [20]. They are administered by professionals in clinical settings during a visit. There is currently no opportunity to identify potential impairments before a visit. At our clinic for Alzheimer's and related dementias, which is representative of those in major urban centres in Canada, wait times for in-depth diagnoses and consultation regarding cognitive concerns ranges between 6 and 24 months. Thus, innovation in cognitive testing is an urgent yet unmet need due to the growing demand for diagnostic services.

The intent of C-TOC is to make preliminary cognitive testing more widely available and to triage individuals that exhibit pathological decline to fuller diagnostic testing as promptly as possible. This novel testing tool brings together existing non-computerised tests and new test paradigms.

Since users will be accessing C-TOC at home, it is imperative to address the issue of interruptions and distractions that are pervasive in home environments. Interruptions may hinder older adults' progress in completing the test, potentially affecting their task performance which will in turn affect the validity of test results. Our research aim is to understand these effects, which will help inform designs for detecting and mitigating interruptions, specifically in C-TOC, and more generally in other applications designed for the ageing population.

The cognitive ageing literature suggests that interruptions will affect older adults to a greater extent than young adults [5,11,14,29]. We conducted an experiment to determine the effects of interruption on older adults' performance on two primary tasks adapted from C-TOC tests. A group of old adults (70+) was compared against two other age groups (19-54, 55-69). We did not include individuals with diagnosed cognitive impairments, as the effects of interruption must be gauged first when cognition is not impaired. We expected to find an increased cost of interruption for older adults, with disproportionally worse performance as interruption workload increases. We also expected a greater cost of interruption on a verbal working memory (WM) task than on a spatial problem solving task, as the former places a greater demand on WM.

Our findings indicate a cost to task resumption time incurred by interruptions, as well as possible compensatory behaviour in older adults' verbal memory task performance following an interruption: older adults were disproportionally slower than young adults to resume the task, but not disproportionally slower to complete the task. In a spatial problem solving task, we found evidence that interruptions were experienced differently by the different age groups. For both tasks, test scores were not compromised by interruptions.

The contributions of this research include the finding of divergent effects of increased interruption demand between different age groups for different primary tasks. These findings led to implications for the design of C-TOC; many of these implications are also promising for the design of other applications used by older adults.

RELATED WORK

We situate our work within a well-established body of research investigating the effects of interruptions on primary task performance. We review empirical costs of interruption and discuss factors for predicting these costs, including the age of the interrupted individual.

Measuring the COI

The cost of interruption (COI) on an ongoing primary task has been examined in naturalistic and experimental settings, and can be defined by several measures. A coarse COI measurement is the frequency of non-resumption of a primary task following an interruption, leaving the primary task uncompleted [21]. When primary task performance following an interruption is considered, the COI could be measured as the difference in task completion time between uninterrupted and interrupted conditions [33]. This measurement may not capture variation in behaviour immediately following an interruption [19]. Task resumption lag, the time elapsed when switching from an interrupting task back to the primary task, can be a precise local COI measurement [1,17,27]. Finally, COI can be measured in terms of the difference in a primary task's error rate between uninterrupted and interrupted conditions [13,22,25,26]. Many studies, including our own, report on several measures of COI.

Predicting the COI

Experimental approaches have attempted to isolate factors of primary and interrupting tasks predictive of the COI, however many divergent findings exist in the literature.

Interrupting task demand. Increased workload demand of the interrupting task has been shown to be predictive of the COI in some cases [13,19], but not in others [22]. However, low-demand interrupting tasks can sometimes improve performance on a primary task [33]. This phenomenon of improved performance on an interrupted primary task, compared to an uninterrupted task, was first reported by Zeigarnik [32] in the 1920s, and is now known as the *`Zeigarnik effect'*. If primary task representations can be encoded in long-term WM, increased interruption demand has no effect on primary task performance, otherwise increased interruption workload demand is disruptive [22].

Primary task demand. Bailey [2] examined the COI for two interrupting tasks on six primary tasks, finding memory demand in the primary task at the point of interruption to be most predictive of COI, rather than any demand incurred by the interrupting task. Similarly, an effect of primary task workload demand was also found by Speier [25], wherein for highly-demanding primary tasks, interruptions can inhibit performance; conversely, they also found that interruptions can actually improve performance on low-demand primary tasks, another *Zeigarnik effect* [32].

Similarity of primary & interrupting tasks. Gillie [13] found that a high degree of similarity between interrupting and primary tasks was predictive of greater COI (i.e., when tasks interfere with one another, engaging the same cognitive processes). However, later work failed to find an effect of similarity between primary and interrupting tasks [2].

Interruption duration. Earlier studies did not find interruption duration to be predictive of the COI [2,13], however this finding has recently come into question. Oulasvirta [22] found that increased interruption duration was found to incur a greater COI when primary task representations cannot be encoded into long-term WM . Monk [19] have also found that increased interruption duration contributes to lower primary task performance, at odds with earlier findings [2,13]. They resolved that activation of primary task goals decays as a function of interruption duration.

Interruption lag. Prior research [1, 27] has examined the role of the interruption lag, the brief period of time in which an individual is alerted of an imminent interruption but is still focused on the primary task. This addresses the observation that switching to an interrupting task is seldom an immediate action (e.g., a ringing telephone preceding a conversation). A short interruption lag, as brief as 1-2s, may be sufficient for encoding primary task cues and prospective goals [1]. Retrospective rehearsal following an interruption can retrieve these goals [27].

Contextual factors. Observational and simulated naturalistic studies of interruptions have addressed the many contextual, temporal, and social factors found to be predictive of COI. These have included task structure [16], primary task visibility during an interruption [17], the frequency of interruption [33] and the source and modality of an interruption [26]. Incorporating these factors was outside the scope of our laboratory experiment, but we plan to assess the impact of interruption frequency and modality on COI in the near future.

The COI for Older Adults

Many cognitive processes change as we age, and each may contribute to the COI for older adults. Normal age-related changes in cognition can be attributed in part to slower processing speed [24]. Changes in cognition may also be attributed to reduced activation of WM [7]. Prospective memory, the ability to remember intentions, is also inhibited in older adults [29], and can be compromised by interruptions [11]. The ability to suppress reactions to distracting or irrelevant information appears to be reduced [15]. Given these changes, it is no surprise to find that older adults have a reduced capacity for multitasking [30] and attention switching [5]. However, age-related cognitive changes are not always marked by losses in functioning; there is evidence for compensatory brain activity in old adults, activating additional areas of the brain such that they perform as well as young adults on WM tasks [4].

Related work discussed in the previous section was largely carried out with younger adults, and did not analyse participant age as a factor for predicting COI. While older adults have been found to be susceptible to distractions [15] and have a reduced capacity for task switching [30], few studies have directly addressed the COI for older adults. Clapp [5] conducted an experiment to compare WM performance between young and old adults in interrupted conditions, where they found that older adults perform disproportionately worse than young adults on a short facial comparison task when distracted or interrupted. In terms of attentional modulation, they asserted that older adults attend to interrupting stimuli more than younger adults. In a naturalistic prospective memory task, older adults' ability to remember intentions was inhibited when it was interrupted with a demanding verbal fluency task [11]. To our knowledge, no previous studies have directly compared the COI in the setting of computer applications involving multiple task types in an older population.

EXPERIMENT

We conducted an experiment to investigate the effects of age, primary task, and interrupting task demand on C-TOC test performance. As in previous work, we measured COI on primary task performance in terms of task resumption lag, completion time, and accuracy. We manipulated primary task type and interruption workload demand as independent variables. We maintained fixed levels of interruption duration, frequency, and lag visibility.

Methodology

Primary Tasks

Two primary tasks were used in this study, adapted from C-TOC test components: a verbal WM sentence comprehension task and a spatial problem solving task, hereby referred to as the VERBAL task and the SPATIAL task. In the VERBAL task, participants arrange geometric figures according to an instruction. In each trial, an single puzzle instruction (Figure 2a) is read before advancing to the execution step (Figure 2b), at which point the instruction is no longer accessible; thus the participant must hold the task instruction in verbal WM. In the SPATIAL task (Figure 2c), the participant is given vertical and horizontal lines, and is instructed to arrange them to create a number of complete squares in a specified number of moves (Figure 2d). Instructions remain visible throughout a trial, but the original layout or number of moves remaining must be held in WM. Comparitively, less information is held in WM this task than in the VERBAL task. Unlike previous studies of interruptions and older adults [5,11], our tasks are open-ended, and allow for partially-correct solutions.

Interruption Conditions

Three interruption conditions were used in this study. The first of which was an UNINTERRUPTED control condition. The other two conditions presented interrupting tasks. These filled the entire screen, occluding the primary task. In both types of interrupting tasks, an automated randomised sequence of a dozen cartoon images was shown at a rate of 1 image every 1.5s. Total interruption time was roughly 20s After this, the participant was prompted to click in order to dismiss the interruption and return to the interrupted primary task trial. The high-demand ACTIVE interruption (Figure 2f) is a variant of the established '*n*-back' working-memory task [23], in which participants must vigilantly monitor the series of images and click whenever an image is presented that is the same as the one presented two images prior in the sequence. Hence we used the '*2*-back' variant of the task (23 of 24 studies surveyed in Owen's meta-analysis [23] studied the *2*-back variant). This task was intentionally chosen to interfere with the WM demands of the primary tasks. In a low-demand PASSIVE interruption (Figure 2e), participants were instructed to watch the

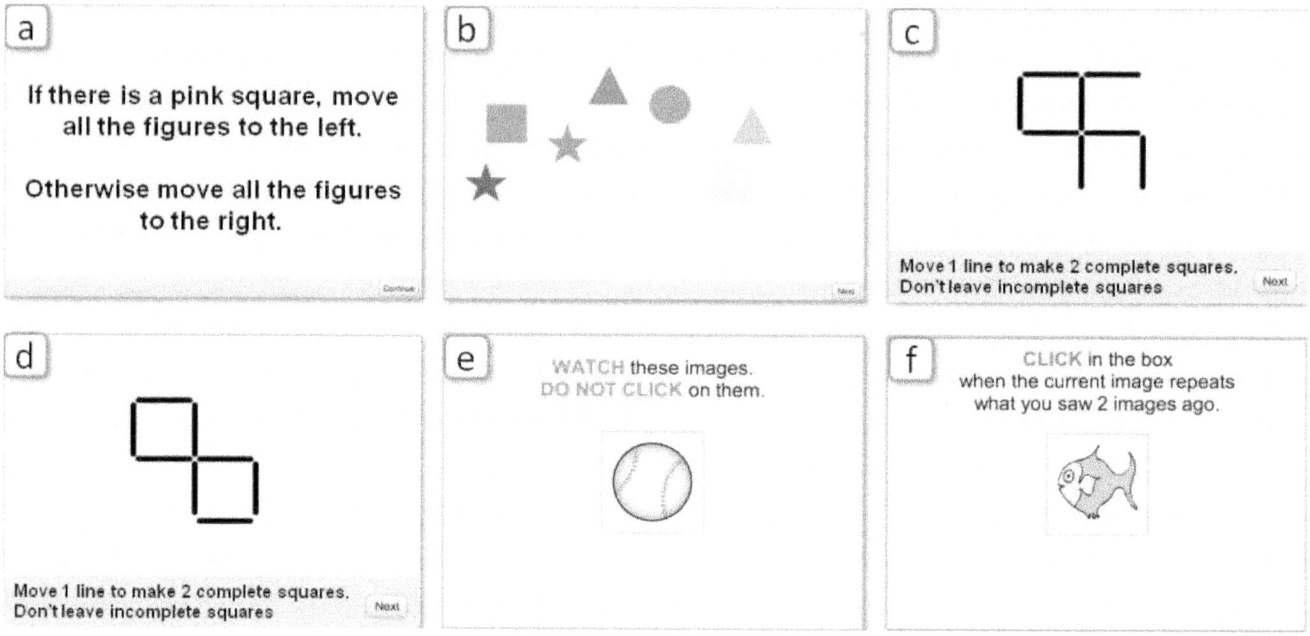

Figure 2. Primary & interrupting tasks used in the study: VERBAL task (a) instruction screen (b) execution screen prior to any user interaction; SPATIAL task (c) initial view (d) same view, completed task; Interruption tasks (e) PASSIVE (f) ACTIVE.

sequence of images passively until prompted to dismiss the interruption. The low-demand PASSIVE condition places no demand on WM. The similarity between interrupting tasks is deliberate; the visual stimulus remains constant, however a response to the stimulus is only required in the high-demand condition. The interrupting tasks are meant to simulate different levels of WM demand posed by interruptions which occur in the home. It is not our intention to map our interrupting tasks to specific household interruptions, but rather to represent a range of possible naturalistic interruptions.

Coordination of Primary and Interrupting Tasks

The two primary tasks each had three blocks of trials, one block for each of the three interruption conditions, counterbalanced across participants. Three isomorphic sets of trials were randomly allocated per participant to each block. Task instructions were unique between and within each set of trials, and corresponding trials between sets were isomorphic in terms of instruction complexity. In the PASSIVE and ACTIVE conditions, a subset of trials contained interruptions. This subset was selected at random for each participant; a subset of 4 out of 10 trials were interrupted in the VERBAL task while a subset of 3 out of 8 trials were interrupted in the SPATIAL task. For example, a participant interrupted on trials 2, 5, and 7 in the PASSIVE condition would also be interrupted on trials 2, 5, and 7 in the ACTIVE condition. This was necessary as corresponding trials between blocks had isomorphic task instructions. A diagram illustrating the coordination of primary and interrupting tasks can be found in the first author's thesis on p.50 [3]. Interruption onsets were fixed for each VERBAL trial, and would occur between 1s and 3s into the execution step, typically during or before a first move action is attempted. Therefore, the interruption onset was the same between PASSIVE and ACTIVE conditions for trial *n*. In SPATIAL trials, interruption onsets would occur 500ms after the first or second completed move action, such that one or two outstanding moves were required after the interruption. Different interruption onsets for the two primary tasks was necessary due to differences in task structure and task completion time observed in pilot studies. Following from the observations of related work [1,27], our interrupting tasks were preceded by an interruption lag lasting 2s. During the interruption lag, the primary task is still visible but interaction is disabled; meanwhile a highly-salient interruption notification appears at the top of the screen (Figure 1). As discussed in related work, two seconds provides a sufficient amount of time to encode task goals and form cues for task resumption. Following the interruption lag, the interrupting tasks occupy the entire screen, the intent being to disrupt the primary task to a greater extent than what a partially-occluding or non-occluding interrupting task could accomplish [17,26]. At the end of the interrupting task, the user is prompted to click to dismiss the interruption, returning to the interrupted primary task at the point where it was interrupted.

Quantitative and Qualitative Measures

Three dependent measures were recorded for both primary tasks: Task resumption lag time, completion time, and accuracy. We considered data from the subset of trials in which interruptions occurred. For completion time and accuracy, we also considered the corresponding subset of trials from the UNINTERRUPTED condition. We measured task resumption lag as the time elapsed between returning to the primary task following an interruption and the completion of the first subsequent action (e.g., dragging a shape or line). Beginning at trial onset, we measured completion time as the total *uninterrupted* time elapsed completing the subset of interrupted trials, which included task resumption time. The total time to complete the corresponding subset of trials was measured in the UNINTERRUPTED condition. We did not include the time spent reading trial instructions in the VERBAL task as part of trial completion time. We measured accuracy, a percentage score, according to a clinical scoring scheme used for C-TOC, based on scoring scheme used in the *Token* test [9]. This scheme accounts for the number of moves and correct relative positioning of shapes or lines, allowing for partially correct responses. Accuracy in the ACTIVE interrupting task was also recorded.

Subjective data concerning task difficulty and demand was collected on a questionnaire following each condition. The questionnaire was adapted from the NASA-TLX [14], a standardised instrument for assessing various dimensions of workload. Six questions were posed regarding mental and physical demand, annoyance, perceived performance, and fatigue. Responses were along a 10-point scale. At the end of the study, we interviewed participants to probe perceptions of task difficulty and task resumption strategies.

Apparatus

A laptop computer running Microsoft Windows XP was used for the experiment. A mouse was also used. The experimental software was written in Adobe Flex 4.0.

Participants

Thirty-six healthy participants were recruited from three age groups (12 each). The justification for these age groups rests on age-related changes in cognition that occur around the ages 55 and 70 [8]. Participants were recruited through advertisements placed throughout the community, and received financial compensation for their participation.

YOUNG *(19-54)*	Range: 19-50, ($M = 31.0$)	8F / 4M
PRE-OLD *(55-69)*	Range: 57-69, ($M = 63.4$)	9F / 3M
OLD *(70+)*	Range: 70-86, ($M = 74.8$)	6F / 6M

Procedure

The experiment was designed to fit into a single 90 minute session, which took place either in an exam room at our clinic or in a private room at a nearby community centre. We first administered the Montreal Cognitive Assessment (MOCA) [20] to help ensure that participants had no existing cognitive impairment. We then administered the North American Adult Reading Test (NAART) [28] to help ensure participants had sufficient English fluency to follow our instructions. Cutoff criteria were used for both tests: participants required a score of 26 or higher (out of 30) on the MOCA and were required to read at least 25% of words used in the NAART correctly. Based on these criteria, we excluded five participants (not included in the 36 above). They were allowed to finish the study, but their data were not included in our analysis. Those who scored less than 26 on the MOCA were later contacted by clinicians to arrange further consultation. For the remaining participants, MOCA and NAART scores were comparable between age groups.

Participants were first given examples of the interrupting tasks and asked to practice the ACTIVE interrupting task until they were familiarised with it. Participants then completed 4 blocks of trials for both primary tasks. The first block in each task was a short 4-trial practice block containing UNINTERRUPTED and interrupted trials. Consistent with the C-TOC battery, the remaining three test blocks in the VERBAL task contained 10 trials, while test blocks in the SPATIAL task contained 8 trials. The number of trials in a test block were representative of the number of trials appearing in the corresponding C-TOC tests. Participants were asked to complete each trial as quickly and as accurately as possible. After each block, participants filled out a copy of the questionnaire. Finally, participants were interviewed.

Design

A 3x3x2 mixed design was used; age (YOUNG, PRE-OLD, and OLD) was a between-subjects factor, and level of interruption demand (UNINTERRUPTED, PASSIVE, or ACTIVE) and primary task type (VERBAL, SPATIAL) were within-subject factors. Order of presentation for the within-subjects factors was fully counterbalanced, such that a participant began with all of either the VERBAL or SPATIAL task blocks.

Hypotheses

H1. Age & Interruption Demand.

1. *Overall,* YOUNG *adults will perform better than older (*PRE-OLD, OLD*) adults on the primary tasks.*
2. *Older (*PRE-OLD, OLD*) adults will incur a disproportionately larger* COI *when interruption demand increases.*

H2. Age, Task & Interruption Demand.

1. *Given that the* VERBAL *task places a greater load on memory, increased interruption demand will incur a disproportionately greater* COI *on the* VERBAL *task than on the* SPATIAL *task.*
2. *This difference in* COI *will be greater for older (*PRE-OLD, OLD*) adults.*

Results

Task resumption lag and task completion time results were log-transformed, correcting for positive skews. We performed a 2x3 (level of interruption demand x age) ANOVA on the task resumption lag data and a 3x3 (level of interruption demand x age) ANOVA on the completion time data. The accuracy data for both tasks was negatively skewed, so we performed nonparametric factorial 3x3 ANOVAs using the aligned rank transform [31], a method that can accommodate repeated measures designs and examine interaction effects. Pairwise comparisons were protected against Type I error using a Bonferroni adjustment. We report on measures that were significant ($p < .05$) or represent a possible trend ($p < .10$). Along with statistical significance, we report partial eta-squared (η^2), a measure of effect size, where 0.01 is a small effect size, 0.06 is medium, and 0.14 is large [6]. We report significant findings on data from 36 participants (Figure 3).

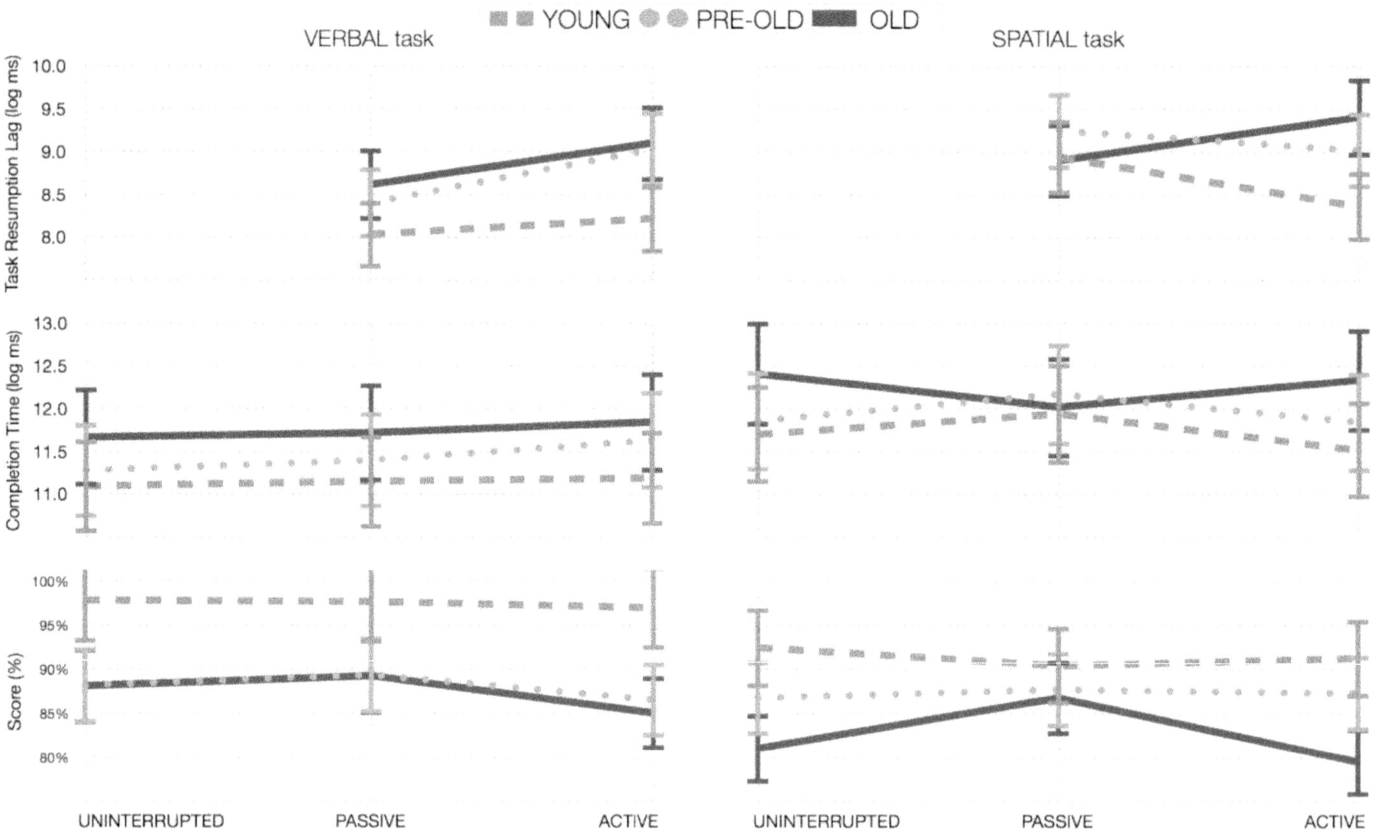

Figure 3 Quantitative results from the Verbal task (left) and the Spatial task (right). Top to bottom: log task resumption lag times, log completion times, and accuracy scores. Error bars show 95% CI (N = 36).

Verbal Task

Task resumption lag increases with age and interruption demand. With ACTIVE interruptions, OLD adults appear to be disproportionally slower than YOUNG adults to resume the task. The main effect of age was significant ($F_{2,33}$ = 11.89, p < .001, η^2 = .420). Pairwise comparisons showed that OLD YOUNG adults (p < .001, p = .002, respectively).

The main effect of interruption demand is also significant ($F_{1,33}$ = 35.99, p < .001, η^2 = .522); participants were slower to resume the task following ACTIVE interruptions than PASSIVE ones (p < .001). A trend suggests, as hypothesised, an interaction between age and interruption demand ($F_{2,33}$ = 3.22, p < .053, η^2 = .163). Pairwise comparison on the interaction effect showed that PRE-OLD and OLD adults were slower to resume the task following ACTIVE interruptions than PASSIVE ones (p < .001, p = .005, respectively).

Completion time increases with age and interruption demand. Closely mirroring the resumption lag results, there was a main effect of age on completion time ($F_{2,33}$ = 12.00, p < .001, η^2 = .422). Pairwise comparisons showed that OLD adults were slower than YOUNG adults (p < .001). There was also a significant main effect of interruption demand ($F_{2,66}$ = 12.47, p < .001, η^2 = .274) . Completion times were longer in the ACTIVE condition than in the PASSIVE and UNINTERRUPTED conditions (p < .001, p = .006, respectively). Unlike the resumption lag results, however, there was no interaction of age and interruption demand.

OLD are less accurate than YOUNG. The main effect of age was significant ($F_{2,33}$ = 10.46, p < .001, η^2 = .388), where OLD were less accurate than YOUNG adults (p = .001). The latter performed at ceiling levels.

Spatial Task

Task resumption lag increases with age, however YOUNG resume the task faster with ACTIVE interruptions, whereas OLD do not. The main effect of age was significant ($F_{2,33}$ = 3.40, p = .046, η^2 = .171). The effect of interruption demand was not significant, however the interaction between age and interruption demand was significant ($F_{2,33}$ = 5.60, p = .008, η^2 = .253). YOUNG adults resumed the task faster after ACTIVE interruptions than after PASSIVE ones (p = .019). A trend suggested that OLD adults were slower to resume the task after an ACTIVE interruption than after a PASSIVE one.

Completion time increases with age, however, no significant difference between OLD and YOUNG with PASSIVE interruptions. There was a main effect of age ($F_{2,33}$ = 4.09, p = .026, η^2 = .199). Pairwise comparisons showed that OLD adults were slower than YOUNG adults (p = .022). There was no significant effect of interruption demand. However, different levels of interruption demand affected the age groups differently (interaction effect: $F_{4,66}$ = 3.28, p = .017,

η^2 = .166). Pairwise comparison on the interaction effect showed that OLD adults are slower than YOUNG adults in the UNINTERRUPTED condition (p = .010). Surprisingly, there were no significant differences between groups in the PASSIVE condition. In the ACTIVE condition, OLD adults are again slower than YOUNG adults (p = .004).

With regards to accuracy, the main age effect was at a trend level (p = .078). Future inquiry is needed here.

Between-Tasks Analysis

Differences in performance between the two primary tasks were expected. Results of omnibus 3 (age) x 3 (interruption demand) x 2 (primary task) ANOVAs were thus not surprising: less time was taken to resume and complete the VERBAL task than the SPATIAL task (both $p < .001$). As expected, interactions between age, task, and interruption demand were also found, as shown in Figure 3. Accuracy did not differ as a factor of task or interruption demand.

Active Interruption Task

Participants attended to the ACTIVE interrupting task. YOUNG adults performed at ceiling, better than OLD adults. Mean scores on the ACTIVE 'n-back' task were 9.5 (YOUNG), 8.8 (PRE-OLD), and 8.2 (OLD) out of 10, indicating that participants attended to the task, as instructed. There was a significant main effect of age on score ($F_{2,33}$ = 12.08, p < .001, η^2 = .437). Pairwise comparisons showed that OLD adults were less accurate than YOUNG adults (p < .001).

Subjective Findings: Questionnaire Responses

Responses to questionnaire questions revealed that OLD adults reported higher levels of mental demand than YOUNG adults (p = .050) and PRE-OLD adults (p = .030). Not surprisingly, the UNINTERRUPTED condition was reported to be less annoying than both the interrupted conditions (PASSIVE: p = .003; ACTIVE: p < .001). Surprisingly, the PASSIVE condition was not seen as less annoying than the ACTIVE condition. Consistent with our quantitative results, OLD adults reported lower performance than YOUNG adults (p = .012). Furthermore, in the SPATIAL task, OLD adults reported highest performance in the PASSIVE condition (p = .061), mirroring what is shown in Figure 3 (right column).

Subjective Findings: Interview Comments

The quantitative results include several divergent and trend levels results. This suggests that interruptions are experienced differently by the three age groups on the two primary tasks. We reviewed participants' interview comments regarding these differences.

When asked about the relative difficulty of the two primary tasks, regardless of interruption condition, the majority of participants (7 YOUNG, 8 PRE-OLD, 8 OLD) said that the SPATIAL task was more difficult. However, a majority (9 YOUNG, 6 PRE-OLD, 12 OLD) said that the VERBAL task was disrupted to a greater extent by interruptions.

When asked about task resumption strategies, there were no clear dominant strategy across age groups. All participants agreed that the ACTIVE interruption was too demanding to allow continued thinking of the primary task. Many participants, particularly those in the OLD group, did not form any task resumption strategy for the SPATIAL task. They claimed that interruptions had little or no effect on their performance, which is at odds with empirical findings.

Altogether, participants' comments do not decisively explain why ACTIVE and PASSIVE interruptions give rise to different performance effects for YOUNG and OLD participants, particularly in the SPATIAL task. However, we noted different reported behaviour among participants who did not rehearse primary task cues during the PASSIVE interruption: some YOUNG participants reported attending to the PASSIVE interruption while others let their mind wander. OLD participants reported ignoring it and feeling impatient.

Summary

Task	Resumption lag	Completion time	Accuracy
VERBAL	OLD disproportionally slower than YOUNG in ACTIVE	all groups slower in ACTIVE	
SPATIAL	YOUNG faster in ACTIVE than PASSIVE	no age differences in PASSIVE *	age effect not sig. *

Table 1. Summary of quantitative findings from the experiment. The effect of age was found everywhere except in those cells with an *.

We summarise our results according to our hypotheses:

H1. Age & Interruption Demand.

1. *Overall,* YOUNG *adults will perform better than older (*PRE-OLD, OLD*) adults on the primary tasks.* Supported. OLD adults took longer to resume and complete a primary task and were less accurate than YOUNG adults. However, there was no difference in accuracy in the SPATIAL task.
2. *Older (*PRE-OLD, OLD*) adults will incur a disproportionately larger* COI *when interruption demand increases.* Partially supported. OLD adults take disproportionally longer than YOUNG adults to resume the VERBAL task in the Active condition, when compared to the PASSIVE condition. This is not supported by completion time or accuracy results, nor by SPATIAL task results.

H2. Age, Task & Interruption Demand.

1. *Given that the* VERBAL *task places a greater load on memory, increased interruption demand will incur a disproportionately greater* COI *on the* VERBAL *task than on the* SPATIAL *task.* Partially supported. The effect of increased interruption demand was significant for the VERBAL task but not for the SPATIAL task, in terms of completion time and resumption lag time, but not accuracy.
2. *This difference in* COI *will be greater for older (*PRE-OLD, OLD*) adults.* Partially supported. OLD adults have disproportionately longer task resumption lags than YOUNG adults following an Active interruption in the VERBAL task, however completion times were not disproportionally longer. In the SPATIAL task, OLD and

Young experience the PASSIVE and ACTIVE interruptions differently. Subjective responses fail to explain this finding. Despite this, there is no significant COI as a factor of interruption demand.

DISCUSSION

In this section, we reflect on the key quantitative findings listed in Table 1. Qualitative findings from questionnaires and interviews are also considered.

Old adults compensate for slower task resumption. We reported a COI on a verbal memory task, where increased interruption demand incurred disproportionally longer task resumption times among OLD adults. This finding is also supported by cognitive ageing literature [30], where task switching response times have been shown to be greater for older adults. Unexpectedly, however, our OLD participants were not disproportionately slower to complete the task. Therefore, after being initially slow to resume the task, OLD adults compensated by increasing their rate of completion, relative to their rate of completion in the UNINTERRUPTED condition. We speculate that this behaviour is the result of an age-specific *Zeigarnik effect* [32] for older adults: a motivated effort to work with heightened efficiency after being interrupted, making up for lost time incurred by the initial COI. Alternatively, longer resumption lags may have allowed for the formulation of more efficient strategies for completing the primary task. However, this was not confirmed by interview responses.

Primary task accuracy was not affected by interruptions, regardless of age. This indicates that task goals, such as instructions in trials of the verbal memory task, were successfully encoded into WM before an interruption took place [22]. Thus, task goals were largely resistant to interference caused by demanding interruptions.

Methodological Implications

Low-demand interruptions affect age groups differently. While there was no COI in the SPATIAL task, we observed that different age groups experienced low- (PASSIVE) and high-demand (ACTIVE) interruptions differently. In particular, YOUNG adults were faster than OLD adults to resume and complete the task in the ACTIVE condition, but the groups did not differ in the PASSIVE condition. In the PASSIVE condition, mind-wandering may have caused young adults' performance to slip, as suggested by some interview comments. This mind-wandering afforded by the low-demand interruption may have actually had a greater negative effect on primary task performance than the high demand interruption. It is also possible that older adults were more conscientious than younger adults, and resisted mind-wandering. Cognitive testing is a sensitive topic for older adults [10], and thus a fear of poor performance may have resulted in increased conscientiousness. We deliberately designed our low-demand interruption task to require no action, while maintaining a high visual similarity to the high-demand interruption task. We expect a low-demand interruption task that requires a simple action (i.e., clicking on every image) would reduce mind-wandering.

Regardless of age, low-demand PASSIVE interruptions give participants a choice: they can allow their mind to wander, or they can use the opportunity to rehearse primary task cues. Interviews with participants revealed no age-specific trends with regards to their cognitive processes occurring during PASSIVE interruptions. An aim of future research will be to identify any age-related differences in strategy.

High-demand interruptions may not have been difficult enough for our YOUNG *adults.* Among our YOUNG participants, there were no significant differences in task performance between the interruption conditions, with the exception that young participants' task resumption lag times in the SPATIAL task were significantly shorter with high-demand ACTIVE interruptions than with low-demand PASSIVE interruptions. By contrast, Monk [19] showed that increased interruption demand incurs a COI in terms of longer task resumption lag times. This suggests that our ACTIVE interruption task may not have been sufficiently demanding for our young participants. We also observed a ceiling effect for young participants in terms of score on the ACTIVE interruption task; our OLD participants performed worse, but were still far from floor levels, and thus could have endured a more challenging task. While the 2-back variant of the *n*-back task is the most studied in the literature [23], future work could increase *n* in the '*n*-back' task, beyond we used, until ceiling effects are avoided.

An alternate explanation is that *the combination* of primary and interrupting tasks was not sufficiently difficult for our young adults. This would not be altogether surprising, as the C-TOC tasks are intended for older adults, and should be considerably easier for young adults.

Design Implications

Our primary tasks were adapted from C-TOC, a self-administered computerised cognitive assessment. As a reminder, C-TOC need not be as accurate as a full clinical assessment; it is only needed to triage patients. In light of our results, we address implications for preventing, detecting, and mitigating interruptions in terms of UI design for the purposes of preserving test validity.

Prevent interruptions with prompts tailored to each test. A prompt to prevent external interruptions and distractions currently appears in the preparation screen displayed once at the beginning of C-TOC (Figure 5). Since we found divergent effects of interrupting tasks on different C-TOC tasks, it may be necessary to repeat this prompt at the outset of tasks that are particularly sensitive to the effects of interruptions, such as the VERBAL task. Performance is currently weighted differently between completion time and accuracy for each test. Weights could be made explicit to test-takers, to increase awareness of how each test is scored and how an interruption may affect their score.

Detect interruptions by requiring user response. Mitigate interruptions with trial replacement and test restarts. Periods of inactivity and unusual variation in test performance cannot always be assumed to be caused by an interruption: an older individual may be challenged by the test and a lack of activity may represent genuine performance. A threshold amount of inactive time should be determined for each C-TOC test. Once this threshold is reached, a highly salient prompt should appear, querying the test-taker to determine if the current inactivity is due to an interruption; mouse movement or a key press would dismiss the prompt, allowing immediate continuation of the primary task trial. If the prompt is not quickly dismissed, C-TOC could resolve that an interruption has occurred. In this case, the interrupted primary task trial should be discarded and replaced with an isomorphic trial upon task resumption. Finally, in cases of prolonged interruptions, a global inactive time threshold should also be determined; once passed, the test-taker would be required to restart the current test, or, if need be, the entire C-TOC battery.

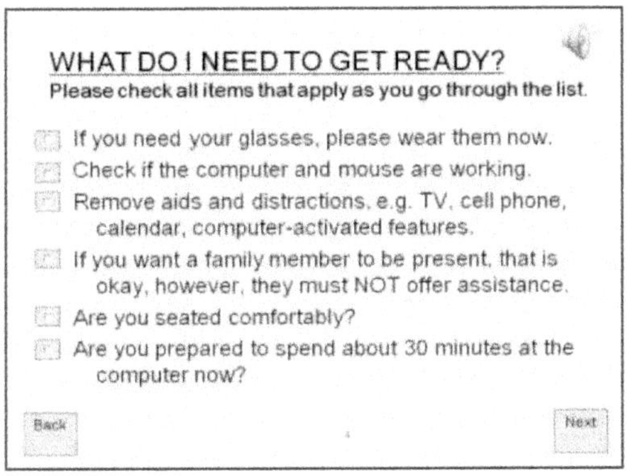

Figure 5. Preparation screen displayed before beginning C-TOC, which includes a prompt to prevent external interruptions and distractions.

Detect interruptions by examining variation in rate of activity. If the task is one in which older adults are known to compensate following task resumption (such as our VERBAL task), the rate of activity, or average time between valid actions in a task (i.e., moving objects), before and after the period of inactivity should always be compared, once the trial is completed. When it appears likely that an interruption occurred, the performance could be classified as invalid and the user could be required to complete an isomorphic replacement trial.

The user was interruped. Is their performance invalid? Effects of interruptions on primary task performance may not always incur a cost to performance, as was observed in the SPATIAL task. In these cases, trial completion time (minus inactive time) can be retained for assessment purposes. In cases such as the VERBAL task, completion time results may no longer be valid, however accuracy results will still be reliable. The decision to retain performance data despite the occurrence of interruptions will vary from test to test and will depend greatly on how the test is scored. Alternative scoring schemes may need to be developed for interrupted tests.

Accuracy ultimately remains the most important performance criteria, in C-TOC and in existing clinical testing. Completion time is a secondary measure of performance. Given our result that accuracy remains unaffected by interruptions, C-TOC test results remain largely valid even if the user was interrupted.

In general, segment tasks and determine inactivity thresholds. Our findings are relevant to the design of all applications used by older adults in contexts where interruptions and distractions might occur and have potentially detrimental effects, such as online banking or booking a travel itinerary. Segmenting longer tasks into smaller sub-tasks and setting inactive time thresholds based on the task structure can limit the effects of interruptions.

CONCLUSION AND FUTURE WORK

Our contributions include the significant finding of divergent effects of increased interruption demand on older adults' primary task performance. Increased interruption demand can incur a cost to performance for older adults; however, these effects are dependent on the cognitive processes required by the primary task. We also contribute design implications for C-TOC, a self-administered computerised cognitive assessment test. Many of these implications are promising for the design of other applications used by older adults.

Increased interruption demand did not affect task accuracy. Highly demanding interruptions caused longer task completion times in a verbal memory task, but this was true of both YOUNG and OLD participants. Overall, the results suggest that healthy older individuals are fairly robust to interruptions, even when they are demanding. This is a reassuring result with respect to the viability of C-TOC in the home. As individuals with memory impairments are expected to struggle following interruptions, lower task accuracy will help identify impaired individuals.

In parallel to the study reported in this paper, we have been investigating the behaviour of older adults as they complete C-TOC in home settings, while documenting the types and effects of naturalistic interruptions and distractions. We are also currently replicating this study's methodology with different clinical groups (i.e., those diagnosed as having Mild Cognitive Impairment) and with different levels of low and high interruption demand. This investigation will also examine interactions of age and interruption demand on other C-TOC tests, engaging cognitive processes other than verbal memory and spatial problem solving. We hope to attain a deeper qualitative understanding of age differences in strategy in response to different primary tasks and levels of interruption demand, as well as the impact of varying levels of computer literacy. Finally, we plan to evaluate methods for preventing, detecting, and mitigating interruptions, as well as the effects of these methods on test validity.

ACKNOWLEDGEMENTS

We thank Carmen Li, NSERC, CIHR, & the GRAND NCE.

REFERENCES

1. Altmann, E. M. & Trafton, J. G. Task interruption: Resumption lag & the role of cues. In *Proc. Cognitive Science Society*, 43-48, 2104.
2. Bailey, B. P., Konstan, J. A., & Carlis, J. V. Measuring the effects of interruptions on task performance in the user interface. In *Systems, Man & Cybernetics*, 757-762, 2000.
3. Brehmer, M. M. *Usability and the effects of interruption in C-TOC: Self-Administered Cognitive Testing on a Computer.* M.Sc thesis. University of British Columbia, 2011.
4. Cabeza, R. Task-independent & Task-specific Age Effects on Brain Activity during Working Memory, Visual Attention and Episodic Retrieval. *Cerebral Cortex, 14*(4):364-375, 2004.
5. Clapp, W. C. & Gazzaley, A.. Distinct mechanisms for the impact of distraction and interruption on working memory in aging. *Neurobiology of Aging*: 1-15, 2010, In Press.
6. Cohen, J. Eta-squared and partial eta-squared in communication science. *Human Communication Research, 28*:473-490, 1973.
7. Craik, F .I. M. & Byrd, M. Aging and cognitive deficits: The role of attentional resources, 19--222. In Craik, F. I. M. & Trehub, S. E. (eds.), *Aging & Cognitive Processes*. Plenum Press, 1982.
8. Craik, F. I. M. & Salthouse, T. A., Eds. *The Handbook of Human Aging & Cognition*. Erlbaum, Hillsdale, NJ, 2nd edition, 1992.
9. De Renzi, E. & Vignolo, L. A. The token test: A sensitive test to detect receptive disturbances in aphasics. *Brain: A Journal of Neurology 85*: 665-678, 1962.
10. Dickinson, A., Arnott, J., & Prior. S. Methods for human-computer interaction research with older people. *Behaviour & Information Technology 26*(4):343-352, 2007.
11. Farrimond, S., Knight, R. G., & Titov, N. The effects of aging on remembering intentions: performance on a simulated shopping task. *Applied Cognitive Psychology, 20*(4):533-555, 2006.
12. Folstein, M. F., Folstein, S. E., & McHugh, P. R. Mini-Mental State: a practical method for grading the cognitive state of patients for the clinician. *Journal of Psychiatric Research*, 12:189-198, 1975.
13. Gillie, T. & Broadbent, D. What makes interruptions disruptive? A study of length, similarity, and complexity. *Psychological Research, 50*(4):243-250, 1989.
14. Hart, S.G. & Staveland, L.E. Development of NASA-TLX (Task Load Index): Results of empirical and theoretical research, 139-183. In Hancock, P. & Meshkati, N. (Eds.). *Advances in Human Psychology: Human Mental Workload.* Elsevier Science, 1988.
15. Hasher, L. & Zacks, R. T. Working memory, comprehension, and aging: A review and a new view. *Psychology of Learning & Motivation, 22*:193-225, 1988.
16. Iqbal, S. T. & Bailey, B. P. Leveraging characteristics of task structure to predict the cost of interruption. In *Proc. CHI*, 741-750, 2006.
17. Iqbal, S. T. & Horvitz, E. Disruption and recovery of computing tasks: Field study, analysis, and directions. In *Proc. CHI*, 677-686, 2007.
18. Jacova, C., Lee H. S., Le Huray, S., McGrenere, J., Beattie, B. L., Feldman, H., and Hsiung G-Y. R. Cognitive Testing on Computer (C-TOC): Designing a computerized test battery for evaluation of cognitive impairment with user and community health professional input. *Alzheimer's & Dementia, 6*(4):S317-S318, 2010.
19. Monk, C. A., Trafton, J. G., & Boehm-Davis, D. A. The effect of interruption duration and demand on resuming suspended goals. *Journal of Experimental Psychology: Applied, 14*(4):299-313, 2008.
20. Nasreddine, Z. S., Phillips, N. A., Bédirian, V., Charbonneau, S., Whitehead, V., Collin, I., Cummings, J. L., & Chertkow, H. The Montreal Cognitive Assessment, MoCA: a brief screening tool for mild cognitive impairment. *Journal of the American Geriatrics Society, 53*(4):695-699, 2005.
21. O'Conaill, B. & Frohlich, D. Timespace in the workplace: Dealing with interruptions. In *Proc. CHI*, 262-263, 1995.
22. Oulasvirta, A. & Saariluoma, P. Surviving task interruptions: Investigating the implications of long-term working memory theory. *International Journal of Human-Computer Studies, 64*(10):941-961, 2006.
23. Owen, A. M., McMillan, K. M., Laird, A. R., & Bullmore, E. N-back working memory paradigm: a meta-analysis of normative functional neuroimaging studies. *Human Brain Mapping, 25*(1):46-59, 2005.
24. Salthouse, T. A. The processing-speed theory of adult age differences in cognition. *Psychological Review, 103*(3):403-428, 1996.
25. Speier, C., Vessey, I., & Valacich, J. S. The effects of interruptions, task complexity, and information presentation on computer-supported decision-making Performance. *Decision Sciences, 34*(4):771-797, 2003.
26. Storch, N. A. *Does the user interface make interruptions disruptive? A study of interface style and form of interruption.* Technical report, Lawrence Livermore National Laboratory, Springfield, 1992.
27. Trafton, J. G., Altmann, E. M., Brock, D. P., & Mintz, F. E. Preparing to resume an interrupted task: effects of prospective goal encoding and retrospective rehearsal. *International Journal of Human-Computer Studies, 58*(5):583-603, 2003.
28. Uttl, B. North American Adult Reading Test: age norms, reliability, and validity. *Clinical & Experimental Neuropsychology, 24*(8):1123-1137, 2002.
29. Uttl, B. Transparent meta-analysis of prospective memory and aging. *PloS ONE, 3*(2):e1568 1--31, 2008.
30. Wasylyshyn, C., Verhaeghen, P., & Sliwinski, M. J. Aging and task switching: a meta-analysis. *Psychology & Aging, 26*(1):15-20, 2011.
31. Wobbrock, J. O., Findlater, L., Gergle, D., & Higgins, J. J. The aligned rank transform for nonparametric factorial analyses using only ANOVA procedures. In *Proc. CHI*, 143-146, 2011.
32. Zeigarnik, B. Das behalten erledigter und unerledigter handlungen. *Psychologische Forschung, 9*:1-85, 1927.
33. Zijlstra, F. R. H., Roe, R. A., Leonora, A. B., & Krediet, I. *Temporal factors in mental* work: Effects of interrupted activities. *Journal of Occupational & Organizational Psychology, 72*(2):163-185,1999.

Observational and Experimental Investigation of Typing Behaviour using Virtual Keyboards on Mobile Devices

Niels Henze
University of Oldenburg
Oldenburg, Germany
niels.henze@uni-oldenburg.de

Enrico Rukzio
University of Duisburg-Essen /
Lancaster University
enrico.rukzio@uni-due.de

Susanne Boll
University of Oldenburg
Oldenburg, Germany
susanne.boll@uni-oldenburg.de

ABSTRACT
With the rise of current smartphones, virtual keyboards for touchscreens became the dominant mobile text entry technique. We developed a typing game that records how users touch on the standard Android keyboard to investigate users' typing behaviour. 47,770,625 keystrokes from 72,945 installations have been collected by publishing the game. By visualizing the touch distribution we identified a systematic skew and derived a function that compensates this skew by shifting touch events. By updating the game we conduct an experiment that investigates the effect of shifting touch events, changing the keys' labels, and visualizing the touched position. Results based on 6,603,659 keystrokes and 13,013 installations show that visualizing the touched positions using a simple dot decreases the error rate of the Android keyboard by 18.3% but also decreases the speed by 5.2% with no positive effect on learnability. The Android keyboard outperforms the control condition but the constructed shift function further improves the performance by 2.2% and decreases the error rate by 9.1%. We argue that the shift function can improve existing keyboards at no costs.

Author Keywords
touchscreen; virtual keyboard; mobile phone; public study.

ACM Classification Keywords
H.5.2 Interfaces and Presentation: User Interfaces - Input devices and strategies.

General Terms
Design, Human Factors, Experimentation.

INTRODUCTION
Since the introduction of the iPhone, mobile phones with touchscreens began to dominate the smartphone market. Today, all major phone makers have touchscreen devices in their portfolio. In contrast to earlier devices, today's smartphones are operated by touching the screen with the fingers and only a few devices have a physical keyboard. Instead, users rely on virtual keyboards that are operated by touching the screen.

While touchscreens and virtual keyboards have been studied for years, understanding users' touch behaviour remains challenging. Previous work usually studies the effect of single aspects, such as key size or keyboard layout, on the users' performance. Due to limited resources corresponding user studies are often conducted with a homogenous sample and a single device. Such studies usually try to seek a balance between internal validity (the extent to which variance is due to the test conditions) and external validity (the extent to which results are generalizable). Experimenters control most variables and conduct studies with a small number of participants in a lab (high internal and low external validity). Many results from related work are therefore based on the performance of male right-handed students from a technical discipline that live in the same region i.e. no equal gender split and mainly participants from the authors' institution.

In contrast to previous work, our aim is to observe and manipulate the touch behaviour of a diverse sample, a large number of devices, and various contexts. To collect the required large amount of keystrokes on a virtual keyboard we developed a mobile typing game. To attract a large number of participants the game has been published to the Android Market. Our approach thus allows studying a large number of users with varying backgrounds in a large number of realistic contexts with their own devices (low internal validity due to a high variance but high external validity). This allowed analysing the typing performance of users whose behaviour would have been significantly altered in a very controlled setting. Because external factors cannot be ruled out and we have little control over the participants the study has a low internal validity as there was no possibility to control any contextual factors. The flip side is that the diversity of the environment provides a higher external validity than common lab studies.

After discussing related work, we describe the game that we developed to collect the data. We provide an overview about the data we collected after publishing the game to the Android Market. Following this, an analysis of the touch distribution is provided that shows how touch contacts are skewed relative to the keyboard's keys' centre. Afterwards, three approaches to influence the users' typing behaviour are proposed. We report how we evaluated these approaches in an experiment by publishing an update of the game to the Android Market. We show that our adapted shift function improves the performance, elevating the position of the keys' labels is not beneficial, and informing the user about the touched position decreases the error rate but also decreases the speed. We close the paper with a conclusion and an outlook on future work.

RELATED WORK

In the last decade and in particular since the emergence of the iPhone we observed a shift from using keypads and stylus-based interaction to finger-based interactions with touch-screens on mobile devices. One important aspect to be considered in the design of virtual keyboards is that the output resolution of such a touchscreen is much higher than the input resolution of a human thumb or finger. This leads to the "fat-finger-problem" due to the difficulty to select small targets with a much larger finger and the aspect that the finger occludes the target as well. Current smartphones address this aspect e.g. through a visual confirmation of what has been touched or trough callouts that show the region currently touched in order to perform fine granular selections.

One strand of research focuses on interaction techniques that allow the selection of small targets with a finger without changing the size of the target while achieving an acceptable error rate. In Shift [20] this has been achieved through callouts showing a copy of the area occluded by the finger in a non-occluded area and the possibility to move a pointer in the callout via finger movement to select the desired target. In TapTap [15] the occluded area is also shown in a callout but here a zoomed in copy of the occluded area is shown and the user has to touch the desired target in the callout with a second touch. In Escape [21] the small targets are visually changed and indicate a direction in which the user has to drag its finger after touching it in order to select it. Those interaction techniques are not well suited for text input as additional interactions are required, which requires more time and a higher mental effort, when compared with a simple touch.

Further research focused on the optimal size of targets while considering the trade-off between finger size and user interfaces design. For almost perfect accuracy targets need to be larger than 20 x 20 mm [10]. This means that current touch-screen phones would be able to display only around 8 targets while showing no other information. According to the iOS Human Interface Guidelines [1] the optimal size of a tapable UI element on the iPhone is 6.74 x 6.74 mm which is a compromise between an acceptable error rate and the available screen size. A significant body of research investigates the influence of target size and context on time needed for selecting a target and the error rate [12, 19]. Considered contextual aspects were e.g. the actual task (e.g. inspired by Fitts' law or text input), device- and display-size and -type, thumb size [2], activity [17], touch feedback [9] or one-handed or two-handed interaction. The outcome is often a suggestion regarding an optimal target size and location under consideration of the given context and an assumption regarding acceptable error rate, task load or user satisfaction.

Relatively little research analysed how the actual location of a target on the screen or a device's orientation affects effectiveness and efficiency. Early research, focusing on fixed touch-screens mounted on a table, showed that users touch slightly below the actual target if the screen is tilted away from the user and that they touch above the target if its tilted towards the user [18]. Other research showed that the location of targets on the screen has an effect on effectiveness, efficiency and user satisfaction. Himberg et al. developed an adaptive numerical on-screen keyboard that observes where the user is touching the display in relationship to the displayed key [5]. This information is used to adapt the shape of the virtual keys to improve the error rate. Similar work by [8] uses geometric pattern matching to reduce the error rate for stylus-based text entry. [3] developed an anchored keyboard adaptation and a simulation suggests that it reduces the errors rate. Holz and Baudisch investigated how crosshairs are targeted and present a model that can reduce the error offset [6].

Karlson showed that regions which are easily to reach with the thumb when considering one-handed interaction achieve the best task performance and lowest perceived difficulty [7]. Karlson concludes that frequently used buttons should be placed in those regions. Perry and Hourcade showed again that targets within easy reach of the thumb can be reached quicker but the accuracy is best when the targets are located on the left, right and top edges of the screen [14]. Park et al. analysed the success rate, error rate and convenience of 25 regions of a touchscreen when using one-handed thumb input [13]. The authors also analysed the offset between indicated target and actual touch events. They observed location-specific offsets and discuss the idea of adjusting the location of the touch recognition area to improve the overall performance. Those findings have been extended by Henze et al. who analysed those offsets using a very large data set and showed that a corresponding compensation function can reduce the error rate significantly [4]. Recent work of Ruchenko et al. tried to improve the performance of virtual keyboards through data collected in a game [16]. They showed the positive effects of providing feedback about where users touched so user could adapt their behaviour. Unfortunately, only 6 persons participated in the laboratory study and the potential advantages of key-target resizing were only shown in a simulation and were not tested.

Our paper is the first that analyse the offset between the displayed keyboard keys and the actual hit locations based on a very large data set collected in a realistic context. This allows us, in contrast to previous research that was performed in laboratory settings or which is based on a small number of touch events, to calculate those offset vectors very precisely. Furthermore are we the first to show that the application of corresponding compensation functions improves performance and reduce error rate significantly for a very large number of users who typed in various contexts using various devices.

DESIGN OF THE GAME

To collect a large number of keystrokes on a virtual keyboard from a number of different devices and diverse participants we decided to collect data using a mobile typing game. During the design of 'Type It!' we had to find a balance between providing players with a game that is worth playing and a test application that collects meaningful data.

Game play

The game play focuses on collecting basic keystrokes that form independent words. Words are presented to the player and the task is to type these words. The game is structured in

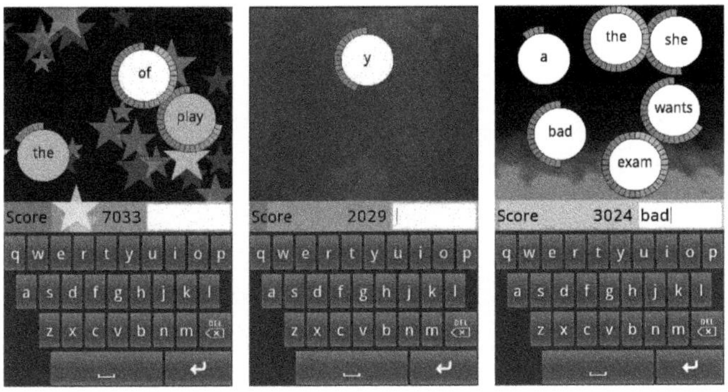

Figure 1. Screenshots of the game's three stages: stars, water, and fire.

three stages called stars, water, and fire. Each stage contains four levels and each level consists of multiple words that must be typed. As shown in Figure 1 the keyboard is displayed in the lower half of the screen and the words are shown in the upper part of the screen. While playing, words are presented in white circles with a fixed size. A circular progress bar around the circles shows the remaining time until the word must have been typed. The bar is coloured from red to green to also highlight the remaining time. While the time to type a word expires, the progress bar gets shorter. The available time to type a word depends on the level and the number of characters. Depending on the level, multiple words are presented simultaneously and can be typed in any order.

A word's characters must be typed to complete it. While typing, the characters appear in a textbox just above the keyboard. The player must confirm the words by either tapping the space bar or the enter key. If a word has been typed correctly the word's background becomes green, the progress bar accelerates, and a rattle sound is played. If the progress bar gets empty the word disappears. To make a game out of the basic task the player must complete a word in a certain timeframe. The timeframe is reduced from word to word while the player proceeds through a level and also depends on the word's number of characters. Players receive a penalty point if a word has not been completed in the given timeframe. The game is lost when the player collected three penalty points in one level. Players receive scores when they complete a word. The faster a word is typed the higher the score.

To increase the study's internal validity, the same keyboard is used for all devices. We used the source code of the standard Android 2.2 ('Froyo') keyboard as basis. The Android keyboard is designed to scale across different devices, screen sizes, and resolutions. We adapted the keyboard by removing keys that are not required to play the game and added code to measure the players typing behaviour. An interesting aspect of the Android keyboard is that the position of touch events is internally shifted upwards by 10 'density-independent pixels' (dp). Dp is an abstract unit based on the physical density of the screen. These units are relative to a 160 dots per inch screen and designed so that 160dp is one inch. According to the Android Developer Guide the ratio of dp-to-pixel changes with the screen density, but not necessarily in direct proportion[1]. In addition, if there is free space to the left (as for the 'a') or to right of a key (as for the 'l') this area is part of the keys interactive region. Touching, for example, on the free space left of the 'a' is still considered as typing on the 'a'.

level	max. characters	source
1	4	MacKenzie et al.
2	5	MacKenzie et al.
3	1	one character
4	7	MacKenzie et al.
5	1	one character
6	2	two characters
7	3	three characters
8	2	two random characters

Table 1. The text sources used for the first eight levels of the game.

We made the game visually appealing to motivate intensive usage. Each stage has a different animated background shown in Figure 1. The total score is shown above the keyboard next to the text box. Furthermore a player receives "badges" when successfully completing a level or achieving other goals. To increase the long term motivation we implemented a global and a local high score lists shown in Figure 2. Players can share their score via twitter if they achieve a high score.

Levels and text sources

To increase the external validity and the players' fun we use words with different length and from different sources throughout the levels. Table 1 provides an overview about the first eight levels and the used words. For most levels we randomly select words from the phrase set provided by [11] with a fixed maximum number of characters. In addition, for some levels we use all words with two or three characters from the Official Tournament and Club Word List for Scrabble[2] and words consisting of one or two random characters. We also vary the available time to complete the words and the number of words. In general, the game gets more challenging from level to level. While the first levels are very easy we assume that the very last level is impossible to finish successfully.

Measures and consent

We collect various data about the used devices and the performance of the players. An identifier for each installation is derived from a device's "Android ID" to anonymize the data. Furthermore, we collect the user's locale (e.g. "en_GB" or "es_ES"), the device's name (e.g. "GT-I9000" for the Samsung Galaxy S), the time zone as well as the width and the height of the virtual keyboard in pixels. During the game we record the presented words and the position where the player taps the virtual keyboard. We record the position where the player's finger initially hit the screen and the position where the finger lifts-off the screen. We do not record intermediate movement as this would have led to very large data sets to be logged and transmitted to our server later on. For the taps we record the position before the Android keyboard shifts the

[1]Android Developer Guide - More Resource Types: http://developer.android.com/guide/topics/resources/more-resources.html

[2]Scrabble tournament and club word list: http://www.isc.ro/en/commands/lists.html

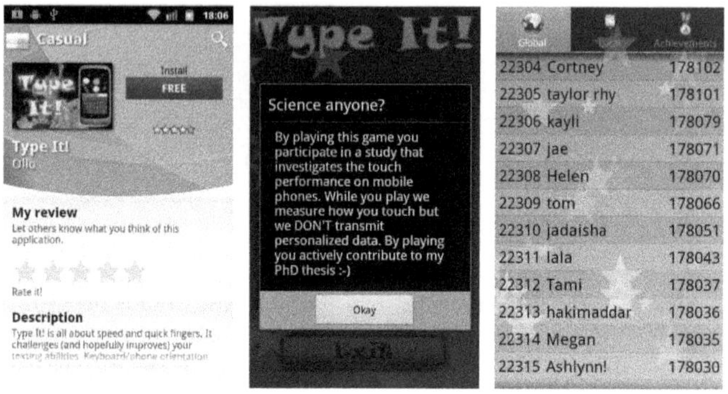

Figure 2. Type It! in the Android market (left), a modal dialog that informs the player about the study (centre), and the high score list (right).

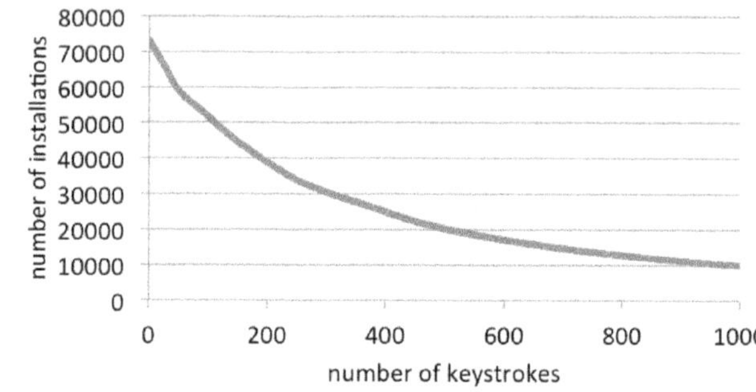

Figure 3. Number of collected keystrokes. The graph must be interpreted as on y installations more than x keystrokes have been recorded. E.g. 40.000 installations contributed more than 200 keystrokes.

touch events by the 10dp mentioned above. For all events we log the time elapsed since the start of the level.

The properties of the used device are transmitted to our server when a game is started and the data collected while playing is transmitted after a level is finished. The data is stored internally on the phone and retransmitted after the next level if the transmission failed. We do not store data that allows identifying individual players or installations. We inform players about the fact that data is collected to act ethically and to conform to corresponding legislation in many countries. The modal dialog shown in Figure 2 tells players that they are about to participate in a study when the game is started for the first time. In addition, the description in the Android Market briefly outlines our intention, what we record, and what we are trying to achieve with the collected data.

PUBLISHING IN THE MARKET

We published Type It![3] in the Android Market on April 29, 2011. Figure 2 shows the appearance of the game in the Android Market. Till July 31, 2011 the game got installed 89,262 times according to Google's Developer Console. In total the game received 880 ratings with an average of 3.98 on the five point scale (the higher the better). On our server we collected data from 80,424 installations but only 72,945 installations provided meaningful data (see below). We provide an overview about the data in the following.

Demographics

We collected data from devices with 581 different names. Most of these names appeared, however, only a few times and are rather exotic such as the "Pulse Mini MG Mod". For 104 names we collected data from more than a hundred installations. As the mobile network operators give different names to the same device type there are in fact much less different devices than the 581 names suggest. The Galaxy Tab, for example, appears with at least six different names. After harmonizing the names for common devices, the 15 most common devices represent 44.13% of all installations.

The collected locales and time zones show that there is a bias towards western countries among the players. The most common locales are English speaking US ("en_US", 65.94%) and English speaking Great Britain ("en_GB", 10.44%). This is followed by Germany ("de_DE", 1.84%), Spanish speaking US ("es_US", 1.68%), and France ("fr_FR", 1.37%). The other 191 locales together result in 18.72% including 64 further English locales representing 4.77% of all installations. The recorded time zones show a similar picture. The only non US American or European time zone among the ten most common ones is Asia/Calcutta.

[3]Type It! in the Android Market: `http://tiny.cc/type_it`

Collected data

While we received data from 80,424 installations, not all of them provided meaningful data. We only use data from 72,945 installations because installations provided inconsistent data or we did not record a single played level. In total 952,487 levels have been played and on average 13.06 levels (SD=58.88) have been played on each installation. On 45.94% of the installations less than 5 levels have been played. There are, however, a few very intensive players and 21 installations, for example, contributed more than 1,000 levels each. The number of keystrokes per installation is analogue. In total 47,770,625 keystrokes have been recorded and on average 654.89 keystrokes (SD=4,149.46) have been produced on each installation. Figure 3 provides an overview about the number of keystrokes per installation.

OBSERVED TOUCH BEHAVIOUR

We computed the distribution of the positions where the players' fingers lift-off the screen for each key using our entire dataset. To compute the distribution, we could either assign a touched position to the key that fits the presented word or to the key that is recognized by the keyboard. As the touches are normally distributed and the error rates are low we assign the position to the key recognized by the keyboard. Figure 4 shows the touch distribution for the two most common devices: the Optimus One, a device with a 3.2 inch screen by LG, and the Ascend, a device with a 3.5 inch screen by Huawei. In the following we analyse the horizontal and the vertical skew in the distribution of taps.

Vertical offset

For each key, we analysed the distribution of touch events by computing the distance between the centre of the touch distribution and the centre of the visual area of the respective key.

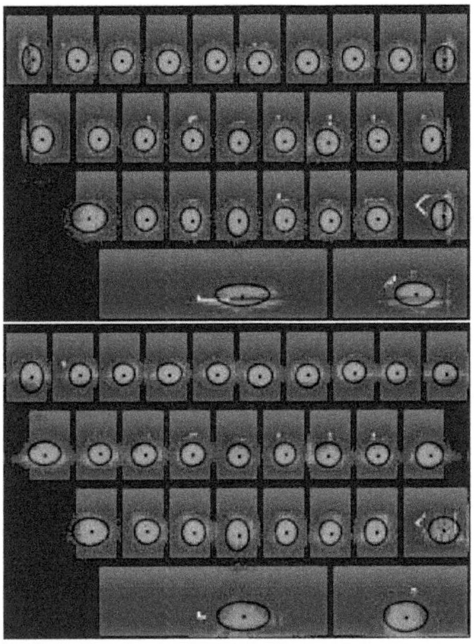

Figure 4. Touch distribution of the Optimus One based on 2,407,164 keystrokes (top) and the Ascend based on 4,589,967 keystrokes (bottom). Green regions cover 50% of all taps. Red and green regions combined cover 80% of the taps. Black dots show the distributions' centre and black ellipses one standard deviation.

On average the centre of the touch distribution is 10.60 pixels (SD=8.79 pixels) below the keys' centre for the Optimus One and 8.02 pixels (SD=8.34 pixels) below the keys' centre for the Ascend. The 95% confidence intervals for the centre of the touch distributions are ±0.01 pixels wide. Taking the screen's physical size into account this means that on the Optimus One players hit on average 2.24 mm below the keys' centre and on the Ascend 1.85 mm below the keys' centre.

The deviation from the centre varies for the different character keys but the difference between the two devices is consistent for all keys. Using the distance between the keys' centres and the centre of the touch distribution for the 26 character keys as the sample, an unpaired t-test shows that the distance is significantly different ($p<.10^{-12}$, d=.91). Even though, we found this difference using post-hoc analysis the high effect size and the low significance level let us assume that we did not observe the difference by chance. Table 2 shows how far, on average for all keys, the players input is shifted below the centre of the respective key. The 95% confidence intervals for the centre of the touch distributions are ±0.02 pixels wide or smaller. There is no correlation between the physical size of the offset and the size of the screen (r=.13) but a correlation between the physical size of the keys' distributions standard deviation and the size of the screen (r=.89). Thus, the data suggest that the vertical offset does not increase with an increasing screen size but the variability does.

Horizontal offset

While the vertical offset is very consistent across all character keys the horizontal offset varies across the keyboard and is much smaller. For the above mentioned Optimus One, the average horizontal offset is negligible 0.03 mm and the Ascend's offset is 0.07 mm. For the 50 most common devices the average horizontal offset is below 0.1 mm. This is mainly caused by the different offsets for individual keys. E.g. for the Optimus One the horizontal offset for 'a' is 5.58 pixels/1.18 mm ($conf_{95\%} \pm 0.05$ pixels) while the offset for the 'l' is -5.13 pixels/1.08 mm ($conf_{95\%} \pm 0.06$ pixels). Thus, the individual keys must be treated separately. Figure 5 shows the average horizontal offset for all devices with a resolution of 480x800 pixels among the 50 most common devices. A negative value means that players typed right of a key's centre and a positive value means that players typed left of the key's centre. One must, however, notice that the top row covers the whole width of the screen while the two lower rows have free space to the left that also activates the key. In addition, the row in the centre has also free space to the right. With this in mind it can be seen that the average touch position is slightly skewed towards the centre of the screen for all but those keys with adjacent free space next to them (i.e. 'a', 'z', and 'l').

device	screen	pixel offset	mm offset	SD
Ally	3.2in	13.23px	1.15mm	1.15mm
Droid Inc.	3.7in	14.72px	1.48mm	1.39mm
Glacier	3.8in	6.93px	0.72mm	1.32mm
Galaxy S	4.0in	12.72px	1.39mm	1.33mm
Captivate	4.0in	13.78px	1.50mm	1.34mm
Vibrant	4.0in	12.80px	1.39mm	1.35mm
Fascinate	4.0in	12.98px	1.41mm	1.37mm
Epic 4G	4.0in	13.55px	1.48mm	1.43mm
Desire HD	4.3in	9.05px	1.06mm	1.49mm
Evo 4G	4.3in	10.88px	1.27mm	1.54mm

Table 2. Average vertical offset for ten devices with a resolution of 480x800 pixels. 95% confidence intervals are ±0.02 pixels or smaller.

Discussion

Analysing the collected data, we found that players' taps are systematically skewed towards the bottom of the screen along the vertical axis. We also found that taps on keys that have no adjacent free space next to them are skewed towards the centre of the screen along the horizontal axis. Furthermore, we could show that the touch-distribution differs for different devices even if they have the same resolution and the same screen size.

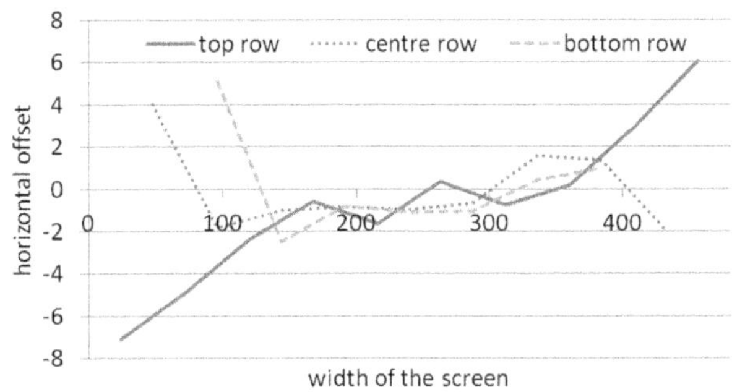

Figure 5. Average horizontal offset (in pixels) for the character keys of the 21 most common devices with a resolution of 480x800 pixels. Negative values mean that players taped right of a key's centre and positives values means that players taped left of the key's centre.

Besides the general limitations of our approach the results are mainly limited by the fact that comparing different devices means conducting a quasi-experiment. Thus, we cannot know if the observed differences are because of the devices itself or because of other factors. E.g. some devices might be preferred by a person group that tends to have smaller hands than the average (e.g. kids), users with different background might hold the device differently, and the devices' form factor might also have an impact. As our knowledge about the players is very limited we cannot factor out those aspects. Furthermore, the analysis is based on data collected using the standard Android keyboard that shifts the users input. Even though players still tap below the keys' centre and the majority is certainly not aware of this shift, we cannot know the influence of this approach.

The analysis of touch behaviour revealed a systematic skew in the distribution of taps. By shifting the users' input by 10dp towards the top of the screen the Android keyboard already tries to compensate this systematic skew. To our knowledge, however, no published work actually showed if this rather simple compensation function improves the users' performance. Another potential approach to influence the users' touch behaviour is to change the design of the keys. Assuming that the users try to hit the keys' labels, shifting the position of the labels towards the upper part of the keys might influence the users to also move their taps upwards. Finally, it seems reasonable to assume that users are not aware that their touch distribution is distorted. Visualizing the position where the device recognized a touch event, users might be able to adjust their behaviour according to the provided feedback.

INFLUENCING TOUCH BEHAVIOUR

To analyse the three approaches to influence the users touch behaviour proposed in the previous section we design according implementations which are discussed in the following.

Shifting touch positions

To analyse how shifting the users' input influences the touch behaviour we use three different ways to shift the users' taps. The first technique, that we call 'no shift', does not shift the touch events and simply uses the touch events' raw position. As the second technique, that we call 'native shift' we use the standard Android keyboard that shifts the touch events by 10 density independent pixels towards the upper part of the screen.

For the third technique, called 'adapted shift', we derived a compensation function from the data described in the previous section. The technique follows the assumption that it is best to shift the users' input in a way that moves the centres of the touch distributions to the centres of the keys. Figure 6, exemplarily visualizes the compensation function computed for the Galaxy S. For each key, we use the centres of the distribution of touch events as support points (highlighted by a white dot in Figure 6). For each key a vector to the key's centre is derived (shown in blue). Using linear interpolation the shift vectors for the corners of all keys are computed based on the support points. To avoid shifting taps off the keyboard the respective component of the vectors located at the keyboard's

Figure 6. Touch distribution and computed compensation function for the Galaxy S based on 3,242 installations that provided 1,831,489 keystrokes. The white dots show the origin of the shift vectors, the yellow dots their destination, and the blue lines show the actual vectors.

border are set to zero. E.g. the y-component of vectors located at the upper boundary of the keyboard is set to zero to avoid shifting taps above the keyboard. Finally, shift vectors for further positions are derived using linear interpolation to produce an array of 21x5 shift vectors. All touch events on the keyboard are shifted according to the surrounding vectors.

The touch distribution differs for different devices. Therefore, a compensation function is computed for each of the 50 most common devices in the dataset. For the remaining devices a function is computed using data from all devices with this particular resolution. However, all resolutions with less than 150,000 keystrokes in the dataset are rejected which leads to 58 different functions. The compensation functions are integrated in the Android keyboard and applied before touch events are processed by the keyboard.

Shifting key labels

This approach is based on the assumption that users are influenced by the locations of the keys' labels and, at least to some degree, try to hit the label. The labels are either shifted to the upper part of the keys ('elevated labels') or not ('default labels'). To maintain the labels' font size and leave room for larger upper case characters the labels are only slightly shifted. The centre of the labels is shifted from the centre of the key to the upper third of the key depending on the device's resolution. E.g. for the Optimus One the labels are shifted by 11 pixels towards the top of the screen, the same amount of pixels that players touches are skewed towards the bottom of the screen. As the labels' shift only depends on the device's resolution, it only roughly approximates the skew we found in the previous section. The horizontal position is not altered. Figure 7 shows the difference between the default and the elevated labels.

Showing touched positions using dots

The third approach tries to inform the user about the touched position in an unobtrusive way. A small red dot appears as soon as the user's finger touches the screen. The dot follows the touch events until the finger lift-off again and remains at

Figure 7. The two different positions of the keys' labels. The green labels show the default Android keyboard and the white labels show the elevated labels.

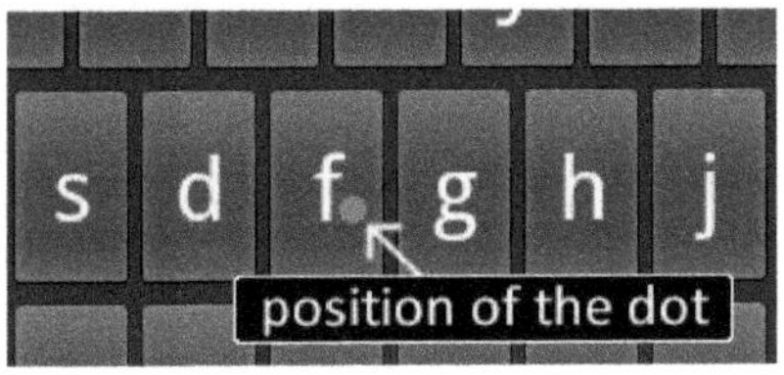

Figure 8. Keyboard that shows a red dot at the position where the user touches the screen after typing an 'f'.

this position. Thereby, the dot always shows the last touched position. We refrain from showing former touch positions or the movement of the finger to keep the visualization as simple as possible to increase the understandability and minimize the obtrusiveness. Figure 8 shows the keyboard after the user just tapped on the 'f'.

EXPERIMENT

We conducted an experiment to analyse the effect of the proposed approaches. The game was published as an update to the Android Market after integrating the three approaches. In the following we describe the design of the experiment, followed by the results, and a discussion of our findings.

Design

The experiment follows an independent measures design to allow players adapting to the respective keyboard. The three approaches described in the previous section are used as the independent variables. Table 3 provides an overview about the independent variables and their degrees of freedom. In total, the design results in 12 conditions. Installations are randomly assigned to one of the conditions when the game is started for the first time or when the updated version is started for the first time. By randomly assigning installations to one condition we assume that players are almost evenly distributed across the 12 conditions.

Three measures are used to assess the players' behaviour. We assess the players' *speed* by counting the number of keystrokes and measuring the time to complete a level to derive the number of keystrokes per second. In addition, we determine the players' *performance* by counting the number of keystrokes that contribute to the given words. E.g.

independet variable	degrees of freedom
touch	no shift native shift adapted shift
label	default labels elevated labels
dot	no dot dot

Table 3. The three independent variables and their degrees of freedom.

keystrokes that produced characters that are deleted afterwards are excluded. This is used to compute the number of correct keystrokes per second. Finally, we assess the *error rate* by dividing the number of keystrokes that lead to incorrect characters or compensate errors by the total number of keystrokes.

Results

We deployed an update of the game to the Android Market on July 31, 2011 and collected data until September 19, 2011. We use the data provided by installations that updated or newly installed the game. In total we received data from 26,586 installations. For the analysis we only consider data provided by devices that can use one of the computed compensation functions. Thereby, we consider only data from the 50 most common devices and from the 8 most common resolutions. Furthermore, we removed the first played level from the data provided by each installation and data from all installations that contributed only a single level or provided inconsistent data, to reduce the noise in the data.

We use data from 13,013 installations that contributed 6,603,659 keystrokes by playing 120,662 levels for the following analysis. On average an installation contributed 9.27 levels (SD=25.54) and 507.47 keystrokes (SD=1,556.69). The average number of installations per condition is 1084.42 (SD=36.24), the average number of played levels per condition is 10,055 (SD=938.46), and the average number of keystrokes per condition is 550,304 (SD=53,537). Because the device types and players' locales are consistent with our first observation we refrain from a detailed description.

In the following we analyse the effect of the independent variables using a three-way independent analysis of variance (ANOVA). The differences between the individual conditions are analysed using Fisher's Least Significant Difference (LSD) post-hoc test. The levels of significance when comparing the conditions are shown in Figure 12. The term 'control condition' is used for the condition with no shift, default labels, and no dot - i.e. the Android keyboard without shifting the touch events by 10dp.

Speed: To assess the effect of the independent variables on the players' speed we compare the number of keystrokes per seconds. The ANOVA show that the three main effects as well as all interaction effects are significant ($p<.001$). Figure 9 shows the average number of keystrokes per second for all conditions. In particular, the 'native shift with default labels and no dot' together with the two 'adapted shift with default labels' conditions result in a significantly higher number of

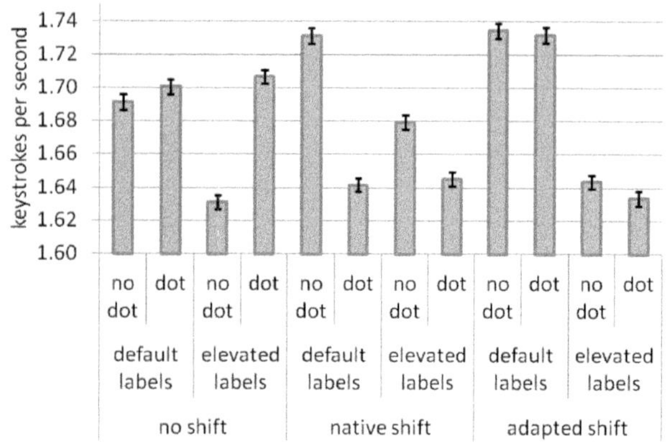

Figure 9. Average speed assessed through the number keystrokes per second (error bars show standard error).

keystrokes per second than all other conditions. The difference between these three conditions is, however, not significant. Players are 2.5% faster with one of the three conditions compared to the control condition and players are 6.4% faster with the fastest condition (adapted shift with default labels and no dot) compared to the slowest condition (no shift with elevated labels and no dot).

Performance: To assess the players' performance we investigate the independent variables' effect on the correct keystrokes per second (i.e. those keystrokes that are not errors and do not compensate an error). The ANOVA show that the two main effects touch and label ($p<.001$) as well as the effect of dot ($p<.05$) are significant. All interaction effects are also significant ($p<.001$). Figure 10 shows the performance for all conditions. For all conditions with native shift or adapted shift, elevating the labels results in a lower performance (between 2.2% and 6.1%). For the same conditions with native shift or adapted shift, the dot also results in a lower performance (between 0.8% and 3.5%). The results for the conditions without shift are mixed. For these conditions, however, the dot increases the performance. Comparing the native shift and the adapted shift with default labels and no dot, shows that that performance increases by 2.3% with the adapted shift. Compared to the control condition, the adapted shift with default labels and no dot (the condition with the highest performance) has a 5.0% higher performance.

Error rate: To determine the error rate we divide the number of keystrokes that are errors or compensate an error by the number of the remaining keystrokes. The ANOVA shows that all main effects as well as all interactions are significant ($p<.001$). Figure 11 shows the error rate for all conditions. Pair wise comparison of conditions with the same shift function and the same labels show that the dot always reduces the error rate (between 3.8% and 18.3%). Compared to the control condition, the native shift with default labels and no dot (the standard Android keyboard) has a 2.2% higher error rate. Adapted shift with default labels and no dot (the Android keyboard with adapted shift) decreases the error rate by 7.1% compared to the control condition. The native shift with default labels and dot (the condition with the lowest error rate) has a 16.4% lower error rate than the control condition.

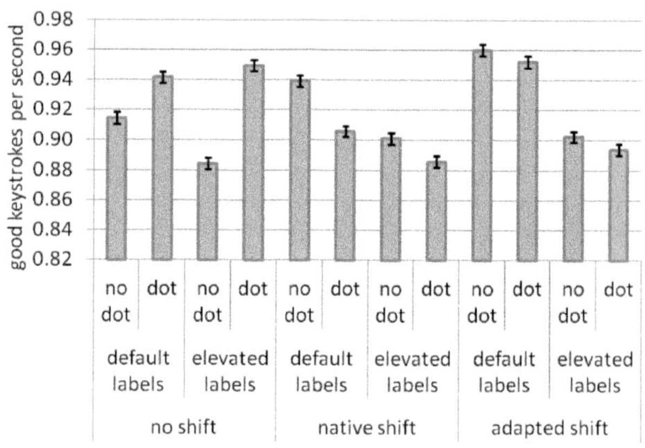

Figure 10. Average performance assessed through the number of correct keystrokes per second (error bars show standard error).

Learnability with dots: The assumption behind showing the touched position to the user was that users can adapt their behaviour using the provided feedback. Therefore, we analyse how the error rate, with and without dots, changes over time. We computed the error rate after playing 2 to 11 levels. To determine the difference between installations in the 'no dot' conditions and those in the 'dot' conditions we normalized the error rate to a percentile scale. Thus, 100% is the average error rate over all conditions after playing a certain number of levels. A larger percentage means an above-average error rate while a lower percentage means a below-average error rate. Figure 13 contrasts the results for installations in the 'dot' conditions with installations in the 'no dot' condition. The correlation between the number of played level and the difference of the error rate is $r=-0.41$. This small inverse correlation suggests that the difference of the error rate slightly decreases when players get more experienced. Thus, players in the 'dot' conditions do not further improve their error rate compared to players in the 'no dot' conditions.

Discussion

Using an experiment we compared three approaches to influence the users' behaviour when typing on a virtual keyboard

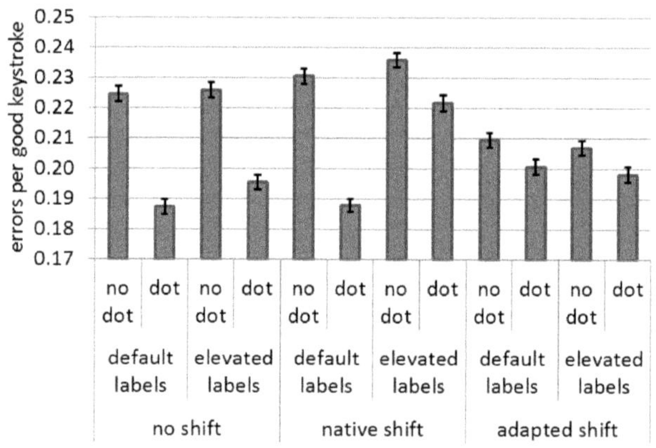

Figure 11. Average error rate assessed by dividing the number of keystrokes that are errors or compensate an error by the total number of keystrokes (error bars show standard error).

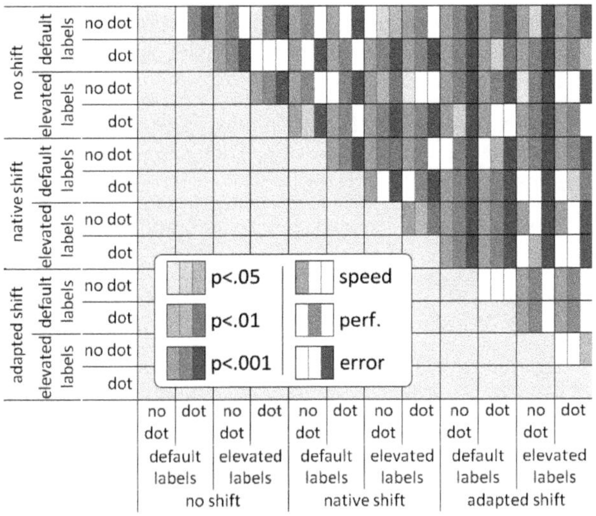

Figure 12. Significance levels for comparison of the individual conditions and the three depended variables using Fisher's LSD.

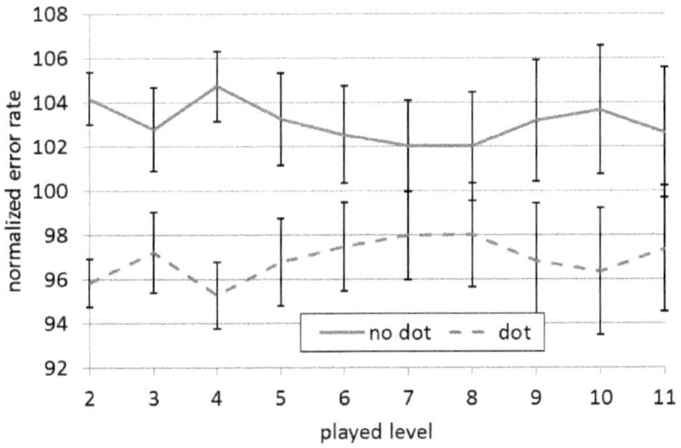

Figure 13. Normalized error rate for installations in the 'dots' and the 'no dots' conditions for the first 11 played levels. Error bars show standard error.

using data provided by 13,013 installations, 120,662 played levels and 6,603,659 touch events.

Shifting touch positions: Using the default labels and no dot the shift function provided by the Android keyboard results in 2.4% higher speed, 2.7% higher performance, and a 2.2% higher error rate compared to the control condition. The advantage for the adapted shift function is even higher. Using the adapted shift results in 2.6% higher speed, 5.0% higher performance, and a 7.7% lower error rate compared to the control condition. The results show that the native shift function improves the users' typing. The adapted shift function can, however, further improve the users' performance by 2.2% and decrease the error rate by 9.1% when compared to the standard Android keyboard.

Shifting key labels: For all conditions with a shift function elevating the labels' position decreases the speed, decreases the performance, and increases the error rate for the Android keyboard. The only condition that improved by elevating the labels is without shift and with dot. Still, the overall results strongly suggest that elevating the labels' position to the upper part of the key does not improve the users' typing.

Showing touched positions using dots: It is found that visualizing where the user's finger lift-off the keyboard using a dot decreases the error rate for all conditions. Adding the dot to the control condition, for example, decreases the error rate by 16.9% and adding the dot to the Android keyboard decreases the error rate by 18.3%. For all conditions with the native or the adapted shift function, however, the dot decreases the speed up to 5.2% and also decreases the performance. To reduce the error rate users must pay attention to the dot. We assume that this attention spend on the dot reduces the speed and as a consequence also the performance.

Limitations: In line with previous work that investigates typing on virtual keyboards one limitation of the study lies in the task that is used to collect the data. While other work asks participants to copy text, often in a highly controlled environment using a single device, our task is part of a typing game. Using a public game, however, has the advantage that the study has a high external validity. It can be assumed that users have more diverse backgrounds and use the game in more diverse contexts than what can be achieved in common lab studies. Furthermore, the study is not limited to one specific device but considers a broad range of devices. This is especially important because our observation of the touch behaviour showed that the device influences how users type.

As we collected data from players that installed the game at their own will we have very limited control over the participants. We cannot control who plays the game and when they stop playing. E.g. the probability that players with a low performance stop playing early might be higher than for players with a high performance. The used approach, however, enables to attract a truly large sample from all over the world. Instead of conducting a study with a small homogeneous sample, as it is often common in other studies, the large sample and the participants diversity increases the study's validity.

CONCLUSION

We investigated the touch behaviour on mobile devices' virtual keyboards. To observe the behaviour of a large number of users we developed a typing game. Using this game we collected 47,770,625 keystrokes that have been produced by 72,945 installations playing 952,487 levels. Analysing the data shows that players touch systematically below the centre of the keys (e.g. 12.72px or 1.39mm for the Galaxy S). Furthermore, we found no strong correlation between the touch skew and the devices' size. It can be concluded that other factors, such as the devices' form factor or the devices' user groups, have a stronger effect on the typing behaviour. We used the collected data to identify three approaches that might influence the typing behaviour positively. We developed a function that compensates the systematic skews found in the touch distribution. Furthermore, we shift the keys' labels to the upper part of the keys and show the position where the user's finger lift-off the screen using a simple dot.

To compare the three approaches we conducted an experiment by publishing an update of the game. For the experiment with three independent variables we collected data from 13,013 installations that contributed 6,603,659 keystrokes by playing 120,662 levels. The results disprove our assumptions that elevating the position of the keys' labels is beneficial. Showing the users where they touch using a dot clearly improves the error rate. The error rate for the standard Android keyboard, for example, is decreased by 18.3%. The dot, however, also decreases the typing speed and has no positive effect on learnability. The usefulness of this feedback therefore depends if the error rate or speed is more important. We showed that the simple shift function provided by the standard Android keyboard improves the users' speed but provides no relevant improvement for the error rate. The adapted shift function that we derived from our observation, however, further improves the performance by 2.2% and decreases the error rate by 9.1% compared to the Android keyboard. Because this shift function can be used as a drop-in replacement for the Android keyboard's shift function we assume that it can improve the typing on current smartphones at no costs.

The conducted studies have a low internal validity but, compared to common lab studies, a very high external validity. Our approach has the advantage that the results are based on a very large number of users, the participants are likely representative for Android users, and the data has been collected in real life contexts from users using their own devices. We assume that the very large number of observed users is by nature representative for smartphone users. There are, however, also disadvantages of the used approach. Studies with a high external validity, such as ours, enable to observe the users real behaviour. In contrast, studies with a high internal validity that investigate isolated aspects might be better suited to find the causes for the observed behaviour.

The collected data provides a rich source of information. We would like to share the data with other to enable further analysis. In particular, analysing the data provided by different devices could provide interesting insights. Furthermore, the data could be used for analysing touch sequences to dynamically adapt the keyboard while typing words. We are interested in using the game to investigate further aspects that influences the users' typing behaviour. E.g. testing further visual keyboard designs and shift functions. We also aim at investigating more radical keyboard designs and if other widgets can be investigated using mobile games.

Acknowledgments: Parts of this work were conducted within the context of the Emmy Noether research group Mobile Interaction with Pervasive User Interfaces funded by the German Research Foundation (DFG).

REFERENCES

1. Apple Inc. iOS Human Interface Guidelines, 2010.
2. Balakrishnan, V., and Yeow, P. A study of the effect of thumb sizes on mobile phone texting satisfaction. *Journal of Usability Studies 3* (2008).
3. Gunawardana, A., Paek, T., and Meek, C. Usability guided key-target resizing for soft keyboards. In *Proc. IUI* (2010).
4. Henze, N., Rukzio, E., and Boll, S. 100,000,000 taps: Analysis and improvement of touch performance in the large. In *Proc. MobileHCI* (2011).
5. Himberg, J., Häkkilä, J., Kangas, P., and Mäntyjärvi, J. On-line personalization of a touch screen based keyboard. In *Proc. IUI* (2003).
6. Holz, C., and Baudisch, P. Understanding touch. In *Proc. CHI* (2011).
7. Karlson, A. Interface Design for Single-Handed Use of Small Devices. In *Proc. UIST* (2008).
8. Kristensson, P.-O., and Zhai, S. Relaxing stylus typing precision by geometric pattern matching. In *Proc. IUI* (2005).
9. Lee, S., and Zhai, S. The performance of touch screen soft buttons. In *Proc. CHI* (2009).
10. Lewis, J. R. Literature review of touch screen research from 1980 to 1992. In *IBM Technical Report 54.694* (1993).
11. MacKenzie, I., and Soukoreff, R. Phrase sets for evaluating text entry techniques. In *Adjunct Proc. CHI* (2003).
12. Parhi, P., Karlson, A., and Bederson, B. Target size study for one-handed thumb use on small touchscreen devices. In *Proc. MobileHCI* (2006).
13. Park, Y., Han, S., Park, J., and Cho, Y. Touch key design for target selection on a mobile phone. In *Proc. MobileHCI* (2008).
14. Perry, K., and Hourcade, J. Evaluating one handed thumb tapping on mobile touchscreen devices. In *Proc. GI* (2008).
15. Roudaut, A., Huot, S., and Lecolinet, E. TapTap and MagStick: improving one-handed target acquisition on small touch-screens. In *Proc. AVI* (2008).
16. Rudchenko, D., Paek, T., and Badger, E. Text text revolution: A game that improves text entry on mobile touchscreen keyboards. In *Proc. Pervasive* (2011).
17. Schildbach, B., and Rukzio, E. Investigating selection and reading performance on a mobile phone while walking. In *Proc. MobileHCI* (2010).
18. Sears, A. Improving touchscreen keyboards: Design issues and a comparison with other devices. *Interacting with computers 3* (1991).
19. Sears, A., and Zha, Y. Data entry for mobile devices using soft keyboards: Understanding the effects of keyboard size and user tasks. *International Journal of Human-Computer Interaction 16* (2003).
20. Vogel, D., and Baudisch, P. Shift: a technique for operating pen-based interfaces using touch. In *Proc. CHI* (2007).
21. Yatani, K., Partridge, K., Bern, M., and Newman, M. Escape: a target selection technique using visually-cued gestures. In *Proc. CHI* (2008).

Multidimensional Pareto Optimization of Touchscreen Keyboards for Speed, Familiarity and Improved Spell Checking

Mark D Dunlop and John Levine
Computer and Information Sciences, University of Strathclyde
Richmond Street, Glasgow, G1 1XH, Scotland, UK
mark.dunlop@cis.strath.ac.uk, john.levine@cis.strath.ac.uk

ABSTRACT
This paper presents a new optimization technique for keyboard layouts based on Pareto front optimization. We used this multifactorial technique to create two new touchscreen phone keyboard layouts based on three design metrics: minimizing finger travel distance in order to maximize text entry speed, a new metric to maximize the quality of spell correction by reducing tap ambiguity, and maximizing familiarity through a similarity function with the standard Qwerty layout. The paper describes the optimization process and resulting layouts for a standard trapezoid shaped keyboard and a more rectangular layout. Fitts' law modelling shows a predicted 11% improvement in entry speed without taking into account the significantly improved error correction potential and the subsequent effect on speed. In initial user tests typing speed dropped from approx. 21 wpm with Qwerty to 13 wpm (64%) on first use of our layout but recovered to 18 wpm (85%) within four short trial sessions, and was still improving. NASA TLX forms showed no significant difference on load between Qwerty and our new layout use in the fourth session. Together we believe this shows the new layouts are faster and can be quickly adopted by users.

Author Keywords
Touch-screen; keyboard design; keyboard optimization

ACM Classification Keywords
H.5.2 User Interfaces: Input devices and strategies

INTRODUCTION
Text entry on mobile phones has always been a compromise between the space allocated to text entry and the size of the device. With finger-controlled touch screens becoming dominant in the late 00's this problem was exaggerated by the lack of precision when using relatively large blunt fingertips to tap small on-screen buttons and the lack of tactile feedback from touch screens (e.g. [13]). This combination led to higher error rates on touch screen phones than on physical keyboards [1] and many users using landscape mode to gain larger keyboards at the expense of application display space.

The Qwerty layout has been adopted almost universally on laptops and desktops despite the design constraints being far removed from the early physical typewriters that inspired the layout. Alternatives such as the Dvorak Simplified Keyboard have not been successful for many reasons [5], but largely because of the high initial learning curve when moving from Qwerty to a faster but alien layout. While there have been several faster optimized keyboard layouts for touch screens (e.g. The Opti [24], Metropolis [31] and matrix [20] keyboards), these suffer the same alienation problem as the Dvorak layout. The Qwerty keyboard has, thus, dominated on touch screen phones as pick-up-and-use usability issues have prevented the adoption of more optimal keyboards.

Bi, Smith and Zhai [2] introduced a novel approach to keyboard optimization to attempt to overcome the initial hostility of users to alternative layouts. They allowed the keys of a Qwerty layout to shuffle by at most one position from their original location to achieve a *quasi-optimized Qwerty* variant. This layout had typing speed performance between the original Qwerty layout and a fully-optimized layout while not being alien as keys were roughly where the user would expect them to be. Touch screens and finger interaction users normally focus on the keyboard area during text entry, thus moving keys slightly is less of a problem than one might expect from desktop/laptop physical keyboard use.

With modern powerful touch screen phones has come increasingly powerful error correction. Error correction

Figure 1: Triple optimized rectangular keyboard

Figure 2: Bi, Smith and Zhai's Quasi-Qwerty layout

methods attempt to correct both users' spelling mistakes and their typing errors – most commonly hitting neighbouring keys to the intended ones (e.g. [18]). Spell checking is made considerably harder when correcting typed words that are, themselves valid even if the context is wrong (e.g. [15]). As an example, the Qwerty layout has the *I* and *O* keys as neighbours, thus *in/on*, *if/of*, *for/fir*, *hot/hit* etc. are all only one key slip from each other. With smaller touch-screen phones this can be a very short physical distance, e.g. on an HTC Hero, key centres are under 4.5 mm apart. The arrangement of the characters on the keyboard can improve the performance of an error correction algorithm by, for a given language, reducing the likelihood of near-misses resulting in valid words. While it has been shown that the layout of ambiguous keyboards, for example the traditional phone 12-key pad, can considerably affect entry performance [10], we believe this paper presents the first work to adjust the layout of an unambiguous keyboard for spell correction.

In the remainder of this paper we present a triple-optimization process using Pareto front optimization that attempts to optimize for (a) speed of text entry, (b) error correction tap interpretation clarity and (c) familiarity to the traditional Qwerty layout. Initially we present the three metrics in detail then their combination through Pareto front optimization. We also present keyboard layouts generated by this process for the traditional key layout and for a slightly squarer layout that increases key sizes (figure 1). Finally, we present results from Fitts' law analysis and an initial study into pick-up-and-use usability of our optimized layout. Throughout the paper we will focus on portrait mode text entry – the normal style of interaction with a touch-screen phone and the larger challenge for text entry.

OPTIMISATION METRICS

Finger distance metric

The time taken to type a letter on the keyboard is dependent on two factors: how long it takes the user to move his/her finger to a position above the key and how long it takes to tap the key. Fitts' law [9] has been used extensively to predict the time taken by users to select spatial targets. For design, Fitts' law implies that the nearer and bigger a target is the quicker it is to tap. Fitts' law has been used to model text entry on, for example, traditional phone keypads (e.g. [27]) and stylus based keyboards (e.g. [25]) in attempts to both predict likely expert performance rates and to design faster keyboard layouts. Fitts' law calculates the time for a single key tap as:

$$T = a + b\log_2\left(\frac{D}{W} + 1\right) \qquad (1)$$

where D is the distance to the target key from the starting position and W is the width of the target key (the constants a and b are dependent on the physical characteristics of the keyboard and need to be determined empirically).

Here we constrain the optimization process in two ways:

- We fix the keyboard layout at the start of the optimization procedure: we restrict ourselves to different letter-to-key assignments and not the more general keyboard layout problem of adjusting the button sizes and positions;
- We model single finger text entry: most users of touch-screen phones use the index finger of their dominant hand as the pointer – particularly for small keys [1].

Given these constraints we can simplify from Fitts' law by only modelling the distance that the user's finger has to move to enter text. For comparing two keyboards this is a faster and simpler calculation that is as effective at stating if one keyboard is faster than the other, but without giving full predictions of typing speed. In the optimization process, all keys were modelled as the same size bar the space key which, for simplicity, we modelled as three standard sized keys beside each other on the bottom row – distances were measured to the nearest of the keys (a similar approach to [24] but with a shorter spacebar typical of mobiles).

We built a bigram weighting model of English by using the same national newspaper corpus of English text as in our previous studies [7] (with 77 317 unique words and a total of 5 171 840 occurrences). While the corpus is journalistic in nature, it has been argued that the source of the corpus is not critical to keyboard optimization [30] and our bigrams are similar to previous published ones (e.g. [28]). Our analysis calculated an occurrence count for each two-letter bigram as used in the corpus[1]. To include movement to and from the space key we also included space to give 27*27 possible letter combinations from the 26 letter alphabet. The most common letter pair was *E_* (where _ represents space) with 981 920 occurrences in our collection. The probability of any key sequence being *E_* is thus 0.033. The top key combination probabilities[2] are *E_*=0.033, *_T*=0.026, *S_*=0.022, *TH*=0.021, *HE*=0.020, *_A*=0.019. The lowest non-zero pairing was *ZX*=0.000 (1 occurrence).

We calculated the weighted average finger distance by summing the product of the Euclidian distance between letters pairs and their relative probability from the corpus:

$$M_{dist} = \langle \textstyle\sum_{\forall i,j \in \alpha} p_{i,j} \, . \, distance(k_i, k_j) \rangle$$

[1] We adjusted the text to include US and UK variants of common words

[2] Full list at http://personal.cis.strath.ac.uk/~mdd/research/chi2012/

where α is the alphabet in use (here *a...z* plus *space*), $p_{i,j}$ is the probability of the transition from letter i to j in the corpus, k_i is the key for letter i, *distance* is the Euclidian distance between the keys' centres.

To evenly balance the multiple criteria optimization process used later in this paper, it is helpful if the metrics have roughly equal ranges of values. We normalized the scores for finger distance to the range of approximately 0…1, where 1 represents the best keyboard found and 0 the worst. We initially derived a fast keyboard iteratively with several short runs of the optimizer. The normalised score was given as $M_{dist} = M_{calc} / (1.1\ M_{fast})$ where 1.1 was used to allow for better solutions in the final run. For reference the standard Qwerty layout scored 0.395 while Bi, Smith and Zhai's quasi-Qwerty keyboard scored 0.643 – confirming that their quasi-optimization process resulted in considerably less distance for a single finger to move on average.

We discuss the triple-optimized keyboards and the Pareto process in full below. However, running our Pareto optimization process resulted in over 24 000 keyboards on the final "surface". Of these, the highest scored keyboard for finger distance metric on a standard iPhone™ style layout has a distance weight of 0.908 (figure 3). Note that the top four most common bigrams (*E_*, *_T*, *S_* and *TH*) are neighbours with others being near neighbours.

Figure 3: Fastest iPhone layout keyboard[3]

The Pareto optimization process is designed to find best solutions along the Pareto front, as such it is not good at finding bad solutions as poorer ones are discarded in favour of all-round better ones. However, it is worth contrasting the best solution found with the worst recorded at the end of the search. The poorest performing keyboard on the front for finger travel distance had a weight of 0.256 (figure 4). Tapping out a common phrase with these two keyboards casually confirms that the finger moves considerably less with the best rather than the worst keyboard.

Figure 5 compares the finger travel metric for our fastest keyboard (Fig. 3) with the standard Qwerty and Quasi-Qwerty keyboards (Fig. 2).

Figure 4: Slowest keyboard on final Pareto front

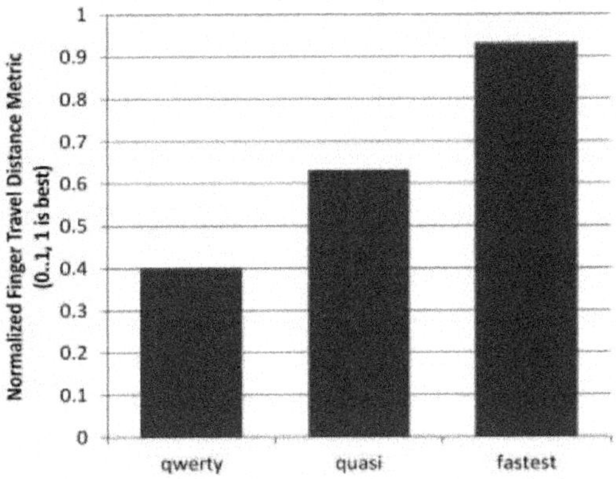

Figure 5: Finger travel distance metric comparison

Tap interpretation clarity metric (Neighbour Ambiguity)

Traditionally text entry methods can be categorized as *unambiguous*, where each key unambiguously maps to a character (e.g. laptop Qwerty keyboards), or *ambiguous*, where multiple characters are mapped to each key (e.g. the traditional 12-key phone pad). With an ambiguous keyboard the most common method of automatic disambiguation is to use a large dictionary (e.g. T9 [11] and [7]). Dictionary disambiguation offers the most common word in the language when a user types a key sequence, e.g. on a 12-key phone *hello* will be offered for *43556* as the most likely word given the keys *GHI DEF JKL JKL MNO*. Overall this works surprising well, with success rates estimated at around 95% ([10]). However, it does not cope with key combinations where two or more words are widely used, e.g. *home/good* and *he/if* are common examples that share the same keystrokes on a traditional phone. More complex approaches to disambiguation, e.g. [8, 12], attempted to solve this using more contextual knowledge. Alternatively, Gong and Tarasewich [10] investigated the best layout of miniature keypads to reduce the ambiguity of the keyboard layout itself by separating combinations that lead to multiple popular words. The best solution, of course, is a combination of both: a powerful contextual engine with an optimized layout to reduce the effort required by the context engine.

Modern powerful smart-phones and laptop/desktop spell correctors have blurred the distinction between ambiguous and unambiguous keyboards – they typically give users the impression of an unambiguous Qwerty layout but use increasingly complex automatic error correction algorithms

™ iPhone is a trademark of Apple Inc.

[3] Here we refer to iPhone-layout as a standard Qwerty key layout with 10 keys on top row, 9 middle and 7 bottom with the same tall key aspect-ratio as portrait iPhones.

to soften the solidity of the one-char-per-key rule (e.g. [4, 16, 18]). For example, typing *typung* in most desktop word processors and most touch phones will result in the word *typing* being inserted even though the user tapped the unambiguous *u* as the fourth key. Error correction has been shown to be particularly important on touch screens with small keys [18] and is seen as one of the challenges for intelligent text entry [17]. Furthermore, Allen et al. showed that, while expert touch-screen users and expert physical-keyboard users achieved roughly the same speed, both groups had higher error rates on iPhones than on mini-physical keyboard phones [1]. This implies that, although automatic error correction has come far there are still considerable problems with error correction on touch-screen mobiles.

In developing our keyboard layout one factor we wished to take into account was interpretation clarity for taps. We created a table of *bad-bigrams*, or *badgrams* for short, of keys that were ambiguous given their neighbours. This table is similar to the table used above for keyboard distance but is based on the likelihood of a one letter substitution resulting in a valid word, e.g. mistyping *for* as *fir* results in a badgram for *OI* on Qwerty keyboards. We scanned all same-length words in our corpus and assigned a frequency to each badgram found based on the more common of the two words. Summed over all words on the corpus, this resulted in *AE* being the most frequent badgram with 1 227 442 weighted occurrences (i.e. having *A* and *E* as neighbours leads to many single key tap errors giving valid words: *end* instead of *and*, *ha* instead of *he*, *been* instead of *bean* etc.). As with the bigram table, we converted to probabilities by dividing the score by the total score for all combinations to give a top badgrams[2] of *AE*=0.017, *AO*=0.017, *EO*=0.015, *ST*=0.015, *EI*=0.013, *IO*=0.012 and *AI*=0.012.

The aim of the tap clarity optimizer was to reduce the total ambiguity for keys that were adjacent in the layout, which should maximize the effectiveness of a spell corrector to correctly interpret taps. This metric is defined as:

$$M_{tap\_clarity} = 1 - \langle \Sigma_{\forall i,j \in \alpha} \begin{matrix} if \text{ neighbours}_{ij}\text{: p}_{ij} \\ else: 0 \end{matrix} \rangle$$

where α is the alphabet in use (here *a...z*), $P_{i,j}$ is the badgram probability for letters *i,j* and $neighbours_{ij}$ is true if the keys for *i* and *j* are adjacent (vertically or horizontally) on the selected keyboard, otherwise false. For Pareto optimization, this score is again normalized to approximately the range 0…1, where 1 represents the best keyboard and 0 the worst. For reference the standard Qwerty layout scored 0.559 while quasi-Qwerty scored 0.459, showing that this layout sacrificed some spell-checking clarity in making their speed gain.

Again using a standard iPhone-layout, the best found keyboard for neighbour ambiguity had a score of 0.997 (figure 6). This keyboard should be optimal for a spell checker to correctly interpret taps as single letter tap errors will most likely not result in a valid word (or at least not a common valid word). The most common badgrams are clearly separated (e.g. *AE, AO, EO, ST*). Figure 7 compares the interpretation clarity metric for this keyboard with the standard Qwerty and Quasi-Qwerty keyboards.

Figure 6: Best keyboard for spelling correction

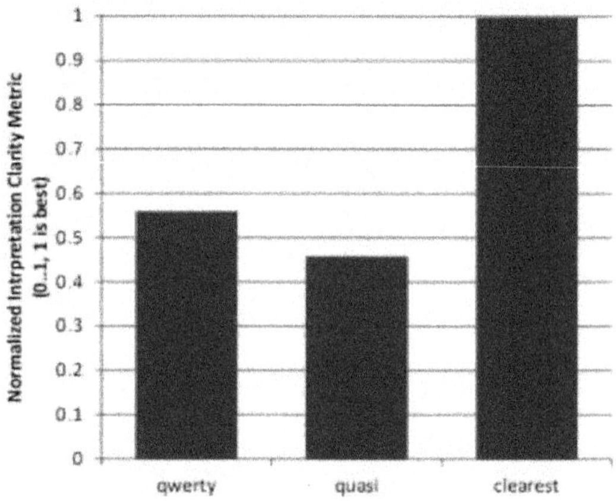

Figure 7: Comparison of Interpretation Clarity Metric

Familiarity to Qwerty metric

There is a long history of text entry research into alternative keyboards for touch screens. While achieving very promising expert user performance predictions, these layouts have had very low adoption rates as users tend to favour the familiar Qwerty layout. Bi, Smith and Zhai [2] proposal was a middle ground: they allowed keys to be moved around to optimize a layout but restricted the distance to 1 key away from the home key. We have followed their general approach but softened this rule by imposed a strong weighting against keys which move far from their Qwerty layout position. The effect being to allow keys more freedom but punish a keyboard design where many keys move from the Qwerty home location and severely punish keyboards where individual keys have moved far from their home location. The aim is that when users are typing with a finger on a touch screen, the keys they are aiming for will most often be in the proximity of where they expect it to be given their Qwerty experience but at the same time to give freedom for stronger optimization of other metrics.

Similarity between keyboards can be measured by scoring the distance of all keys to their home keys on a same-sized standard Qwerty keyboard. However, to increase familiarity of the keyboard and "punish" keys that move far from their home we experimented with different familiarity metrics based on squaring, cubing and exponential function of the Euclidean distance for each key. With experimentation, squaring the distance gave the best balance between allowing movement and keeping keys near their home locations. This function gives a distance score of 0 for a key that is in the same location as on the Qwerty layout, 1 for a key that moves to its neighbour (horizontally and a key's aspect ratio vertically, e.g. 1.7 for an iPhone), and 9 for a letter that moves three keys horizontally (given the standard layout is 10 keys wide this is a high value). However, as this metric averages the score over all keys, unlike Bi et al.'s quasi-Qwerty, it does give flexibility for individual keys to move a few keys if many of the other keys stay very close to their Qwerty location.

We calculated the familiarity metric as:

$$M_{familiarity} = \langle \sum_{\forall i \in \alpha} distance(k_i, q_i)^2 \rangle$$

where α is the alphabet in use (*a*...*z*), k_i is the location of the centre of the key on the given keyboard, q_i is its location on a same sized standard Qwerty layout keyboard, and *distance* is the Euclidian distance between these points. Again the score is finally normalized to the range 0…1 for Pareto optimization, where 1 represents the best keyboard found and 0 the worst. For reference the standard Qwerty layout scores 1.0 while quasi-Qwerty scores 0.850.

TRIPLE-METRIC OPTIMIZATION PROCESS

In designing artefacts, we often have more than one criterion that we use to evaluate the final product. For example, a motor vehicle can be judged by its fuel efficiency, its ease of handling, the comfort of the ride and so on. Often these criteria conflict: a hard suspension may help with handling but be detrimental to passenger comfort. Multi-objective optimization algorithms [29] seek to create solutions to such problems by considering the optimization process across these potentially conflicting objectives. A simple way of addressing such problems is to create a single combined objective function, where each individual objective is a component in a weighted sum. However, the difficulty of coming up with an appropriate weighting for each part of the sum and the fact that this method only returns a single solution means that this is not generally the method of choice [6]. Instead, what is needed is a method which can return multiple solutions where each solution has something about it which makes it better than other solutions according to at least one of the criteria. This leads to a need to explore solutions that are Pareto optimal. If there are 3 criteria to optimize, as in this study, and we have found a Pareto optimal artefact which has the evaluation [*x*,*y*,*z*], then this means there is no point in the solution set for which all criteria are equal or better. In other words, if we want to improve the score for one of the criteria along the Pareto front, we have to compromise by lowering the score for at least one of the other metrics. A point which is not Pareto optimal is said to be *dominated* - there is a Pareto optimal solution which is better than it in at least one dimension and no worse in the others.

The search algorithm in this work is a variant of local neighbourhood search [14] adapted for use in finding a Pareto optimal set using the above three metrics: finger travel distance, spelling interpretation clarity and Qwerty familiarity. The process starts with a randomly generated set of points that are optimized locally for different weightings of the three metrics (typically 40-50 starter keyboards are created). This initial set of keyboards is taken through 2000 iterations of improvement in which local moves are made that may, or may not, improve the solution. In each iteration each keyboard in the set has a small number of keys swapped (1 key is swapped then extra keys are swapped with a probability of 25% of continuing after each swap[4]); if the new keyboard is better on any metric then it is added to the set; if it is also at least as good on ALL metrics than an existing solution then it dominates the existing one, which is discarded. This leads to a *Pareto front* – a set of dominant solutions on a 3D surface.

The final Pareto front for optimizing the standard Qwerty keyboard is shown in Figure 8. This shows the trade-off between the different measures with high scores being achievable only at the expense of others. It also, reassuringly, shows a convex surface showing that compromise solutions are not, overall, poorer than single optimized solutions. This front is composed of over 24 000 individual keyboards (out of the 46.7 million candidate keyboards considered in the 2000 iteration run).

PROPOSED IMPROVED KEYBOARD LAYOUTS

The final compromise keyboard proposal is taken to be the keyboard that achieves best on average – the centre of the Pareto surface (i.e. keyboard nearest the 45° line through the space). All metrics were scaled in advance so the best

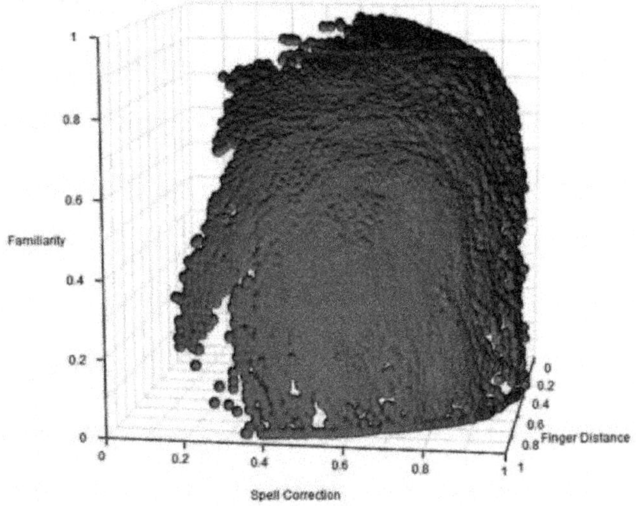

Figure 8: Pareto Front Shape

[4] This ensures that the Pareto curve optimization is, in a sense, complete as all combinations are reachable from any given initial keyboard layout.

(individual score) lies around 1 and the worst around 0 – ensuring the 45° point is a fair balance of the three metrics. This was achieved through iterative running of the Pareto optimization process. A small imbalance at this stage would result in us picking a different near-central solution. However, the solution space around the centre 45° selected keyboard was stable with only small changes being seen on solutions near the central one and a fairly smooth front shape near the centre (see Fig. 8). While varying per starter keyboard, most Pareto optimizations didn't change the suggested keyboard for the last 500+ iterations of 2000 optimization iterations, giving further confidence in stability of the solutions discussed below.

A standard Qwerty layout triple-optimized keyboard: The Sath-Trapezoidal keyboard

Using iPhone key shape (a key aspect ratio of 1.7) and a standard Qwerty layout as a starter keyboard, our triple-optimization process created the keyboard shown in Figure 9 with a score of approx. 0.69 for each metric. We will refer to this as the Sath-trapezoidal keyboard.

Figure 9: Triple optimized standard iPhone style keyboard

Table 1 summarizes the metric scores for this keyboard compared to the standard Qwerty and the Quasi-Qwerty. Overall our alternative layout achieves a considerably better finger travel distance than Qwerty and noticeably better than quasi-Qwerty. It also achieves considerably better interpretation clarity than both, but at a reduction in familiarity.

	Finger Distance	Interpretation Clarity	Qwerty Familiarity	Average score
Sath	0.694	0.695	0.694	0.694
Qwerty	0.395	0.559	1.000	0.651
Quasi-Qwerty	0.643	0.459	0.829	0.644

Table 1: Standard keyboard metrics

Given the balance of metrics and Pareto optimization process, we claim that the Sath keyboard presented here provides the best compromise between typing speed, tap interpretation for spell correction and familiarity with Qwerty to support pickup-and-use usability.

More rectangular layout: Sath-Rectangular

In the discussion so far we have focused on an "iPhone like Qwerty keyboard layout". This layout is a standard Qwerty layout from typewriter and computer use but with a higher aspect ratio – approximately 1.7 for the iPhone, when measured to include surrounding grey-space, and a slightly taller 1.75 for an HTC Hero (a relatively small Android phone). The standard Qwerty layout has a trapezoidal shape, if drawn symmetrically, with 10 keys on the top row, 9 in the middle and only 7 on the bottom row (a 10-9-7 format). Full size keyboards pad the lower rows with non-alphabetic and functional keys but there are often fewer such keys on mobiles with additional characters being entered through a secondary mode. Above we presented our results for optimization using this standard trapezoidal layout and aspect ratio.

MacKenzie states that when measuring Fitts' law distance, the size of a key should be the minimum of height and width [22]. As such these tall, thin keys have effectively the same Fitts' law functions as if they were just as high as their width but with further distances between the keys vertically. As discussed above, the small keys also tend to lead to many typing errors as the key centres are very close together – for example keys of the size found on portrait mode iPhones have been shown to be significantly slower and more error prone than larger keys [18, 19]. As such we attempted to reduce the aspect ratio of keys to make them squarer, while maintaining their height and familiarity with the original Qwerty layout. We investigated Pareto optimization starting with a more rectangular 9-9-8 profile keyboard that results in a less-tall aspect ratio of approximately 1.5 for the same screen area.

Here we started our optimization process with a Qwerty layout in which the *Q* and *A* were shifted one row down to give the starter layout *WERTYUIOP QSDFGHJKL AZXCVBNM* which has a 9-9-8 profile and a familiarity score of 0.951. Using this keyboard layout and a 1.5 aspect ratio gave an improvement over the standard 10-9-7 layout with the keyboard shown in figure 10 rating approx. 0.75 for each metric.

While a relatively small numerical improvement, the buttons in this layout also have a larger hit area which should improve typing speed and reduce miss-strikes further improving spelling performance. Using the same area as an iPhone keyboard, this layout increases the key width from 4.6 to 5.2 mm – a considerable improvement of 11% in "target size" used in Fitts' law calculations. As key

Figure 10: Optimized more rectangular keyboard layout

sizes on portrait touch-screen phones are well below research recommendations for touch screen key sizes (e.g. [26]) and have been shown to be considerably poorer than the larger keys used in landscape mode [19], this small difference may have a very significant impact on speed.

	Finger Distance	Neighbour Ambiguity	Qwerty Familiarity	Average score
Sath Trapz	0.694	0.695	0.694	0.694
Sath Rect	0.751	0.751	0.751	0.751

Table 2: Comparing standard and rectangular layouts

FITTS' LAW SPEED CALCULATIONS

The finger distance metric used above is suitable for optimization a fixed format keyboard but cannot be used to predict text entry speed. Fitts' law [9] (Equation 1) can be used to estimate the potential speed of a keyboard layout for error-free expert text entry (e.g. [28]). As such it is worth discussing here as it gives a more concrete comparison to other keyboards through use of words-per-minute estimates. Equation 2 shows the Fitts' law calculation for weighted average time to press a key. The time to press a key is logarithmically proportional to the distance to that key while logarithmically inversely proportional to width of the target key (big keys close to the starting point are fastest targets to hit). The constants a and b have to be derived experimentally for a given device, for comparison with work of others we used the figures a=0.083 and b=0.127 [2, 32] in our studies despite their being derived for stylus-based keyboarding. To calculate the average time per keystroke, a weighted average is used based on the probability of bigrams in the language, so that key combinations that are struck more commonly (e.g. moving from *e* to *space*) have a proportionally higher impact on the average than rarely used key combinations (e.g. moving from *z* to *x*). The same bigram data as used for the finger travel optimizations were used here but these were compared with the table used in [25] and found to result in very small differences in predicted times.

$$\bar{T} = \sum_{i \in \alpha} \sum_{j \in \alpha} p_{ij} \left(a + b \log_2 \left(\frac{D_{ij}}{W_j} + 1\right)\right) \qquad (2)$$

For the standard Qwerty keyboard (10-9-7) we estimated an average key tap time of 0.360 s given an aspect ratio of 1.7 and the constants a and b from above. This is equivalent to a predicted expert typing speed of 33.3 words-per-minute (wpm). Bi, Smith and Zhai used the same Fitts' constants to estimate 181.2 characters-per-minute, or 36.2 wpm, for a standard Qwerty keyboard – slightly faster than our estimate. This is predominantly due to the aspect ratio of keys – Bi, Smith and Zhai followed MacKenzie's early lead in modelling touch screen entry with square keys similar to laptop keys and not the highly stretched keys now used on touch screen phones. While the true values of a and b for finger tapping on keys below 5 mm requires to be calculated experimentally, our estimate is, we believe, unlikely to change the ordering of keyboards but will affect predicted speeds as the values of a and b used are based on studies with approximately 10 mm wide keys.

Figure 11 shows the words-per-minute estimates for our two keyboards compared with the traditional Qwerty and quasi-Qwerty (both using 1.7 aspect ratios as this matches the keyboard area of the iPhone) and, for comparison, the fastest single optimized keyboard layout we identified. This shows a predicted improvement of 10% and 11% respectively for our trapezoidal and rectangular keyboard layouts over standard Qwerty and smaller 3% and 4% predicted improvement over the quasi-Qwerty keyboard.

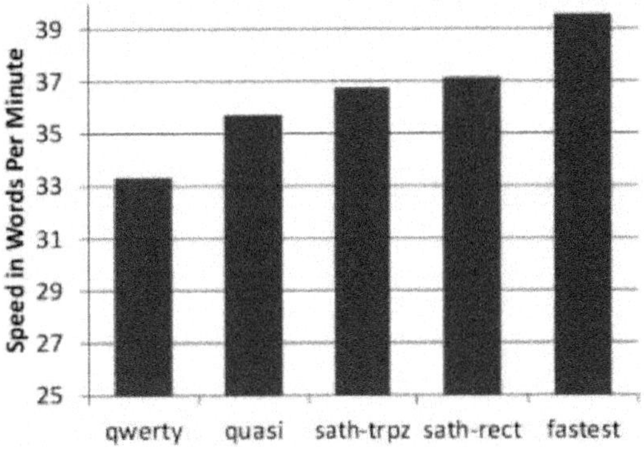

Figure 11: Comparison of keyboard typing speeds

However, as discussed above this does not fully take into account the increased key size with the rectangular keyboard (only the smaller vertical aspect ratio) nor does it take into account the improvement in error correction likely in practice given the larger keys. Fig. 12 shows that the two optimized keyboards presented here also have considerably better tap interpretation clarity that should lead to faster text entry as users will learn that they need to be less accurate on typing and still achieve corrected-error-free entry.

PAPER PROTOTYPE

To investigate the initial pick-up-and-use aspects of the new keyboard we created paper prototypes of the new keyboard layout using a slightly earlier version of our optimized rectangular keyboard. These paper prototypes were correct in size and aspect ratio for an HTC Desire and were trialled with 12 students. These users were encouragingly positive and stated that they would use the keyboard when available. The students stated that they generally found keys quickly in practice typing (though the *A* was commented on as being moved quite far). One user commented that even for two-thumbed use it felt easier as common keys were more central to the keyboard, an unintentional consequence of finger distance metric and the central space key.

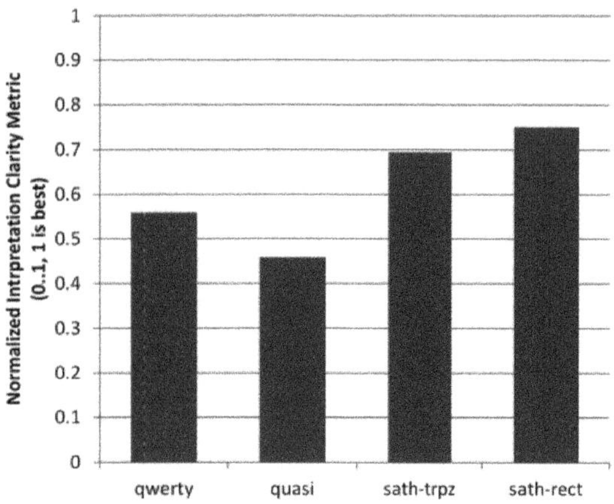

Figure 12: Comparison of keyboard interpretation clarity

INITIAL USER STUDIES

Encouraged by the paper prototype results we developed an Android implementation and ran a four day user trial with 10 regular touchscreen phones users (8 male, 2 female, mostly between 18 and 35 years old with one 36+ user) to measure their performance with rectangular-Sath over the initial learning period. Sessions lasted under 45 minutes per day in a quiet environment with subjects seated in a comfortable chair without the use of a desk.

Procedure & Equipment

Users came at the same time for four days and were asked to enter two initial warm up phrases then 17 phrases selected randomly from MacKenzie and Soukoreff [23] standard set. There were 4 task sets (68 phrases total), randomly allocated to each participant (balanced on first day with unused phrase sets per person randomly allocated on days 2-4). To assess Qwerty performance users entered some phrases using the standard Qwerty layout (first part of day 1 and second part of day 2), all other phrases were entered using rectangular-Sath (figure 1).

Phrases were presented in the web browser of an HTC Desire S and the users typed answers into a text box on the same web page before hitting "next" to move on to the next phrase. Timing information was recorded using JavaScript based on the time from first to last key press. In line with other studies, users were asked to type as quickly as possible but accurately and were allowed to use backspace to correct mistakes they spotted "immediately" but were told not to correct mistakes they noticed later and were prevented from using editing controls except backspace.

The implementation used a basic spell checking algorithm with the standard Android suggestion bar to show suggested words and highlight auto-corrections. A typed word was auto-corrected if it was not in the dictionary but a same-length dictionary word existed that was very close to the tapped locations (i.e. one tapped character was out by one key). We restricted to same length corrections to target miss-taps and not wider omitted taps, double taps or true spelling errors. The Qwerty and Sath keyboards used the same underlying code and spell corrector.

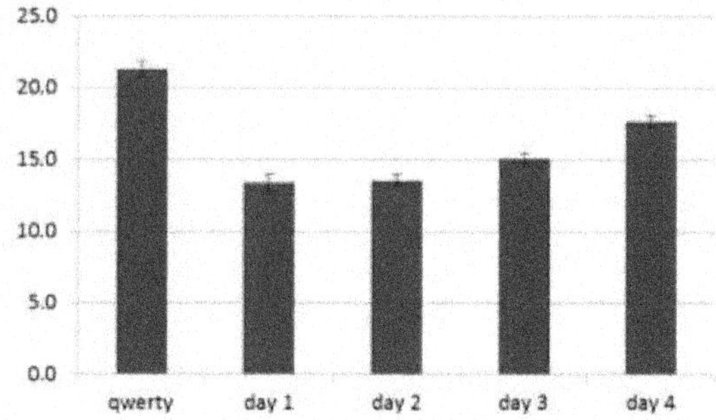

Figure 13: Words per minute speeds

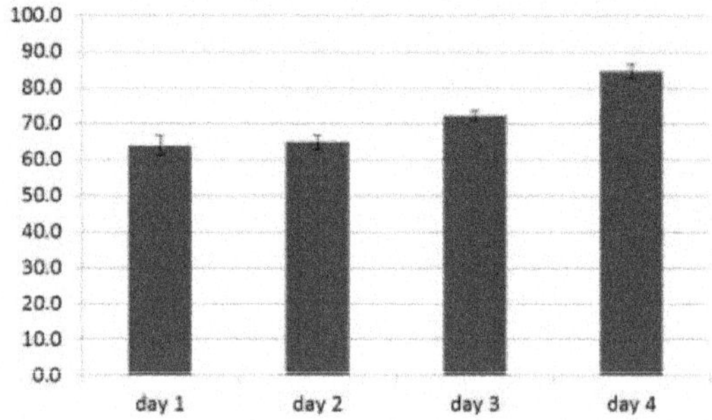

Figure 14: Percentage speed compared to Qwerty

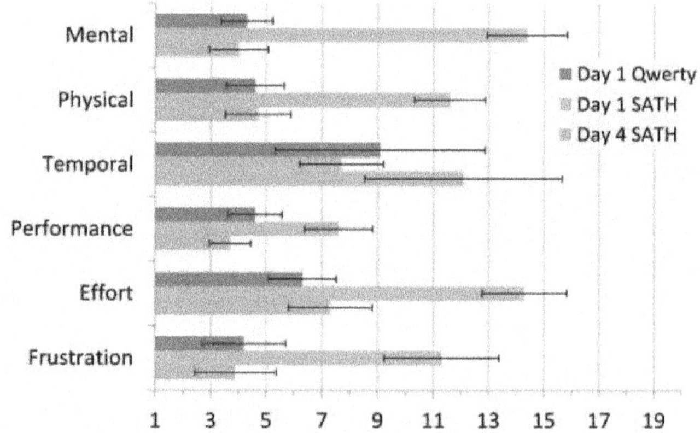

Figure 15: NASA TLX Scores

Speed results

Our users averaged 21.3 wpm (stdev 7.3) using Qwerty. Their performance dropped to 13.4wpm (6.1) when using Sath for the first time but recovered to 17.7 wpm (5.2) by the fourth day of the test (figure 13 shows the daily results – Sath speed based on Sath phrases per day with Qwerty based on all Qwerty phrases as there was no significant difference in Qwerty speed between day 1 and 2).

We also analysed speed as a percentage of the users individual Qwerty performance. This analysis shows that users dropped to 64% of their individual Qwerty speed for the first block of phrases using Sath but that this recovered to 85% on the fourth day (fig 14). For comparison average Quasi-Qwerty performance was approx. 65% of average Qwerty in word-by-word tests, while their freely optimised keyboard achieved only 45% in initial use.

Other Results

Uncorrected error rates were low throughout the study. Overall 7.9% of phrases contained a single erroneous word, with none having multiple errors. With an average phrase length of 5.6 standard words (=5 chars as used in wpm calculations), this equates to an error once per 71 words. On Qwerty tests, 5.3% of phrases were erroneous with a higher 8.8% of Sath phrases being erroneous (with no clear pattern over the four days). Errors from key positioning changes should result in same length typing errors. For Qwerty we found 3% (5 of 170) of phrases were correct-length but erroneous compared with 4% (19 of 510) of Sath phrases. All Qwerty errors were independently categorised as typos while 4 other errors were recorded with Sath – if these were excluded then Sath would have the same typo error rate as Qwerty in this initial use study (other errors were transposition of letters, spelling errors and typing the wrong, but semantically sensible, word).

NASA TLX forms were completed after each session (each block on days 1 and 2). These showed significantly higher workload for mental ($p < 0.001$, t-test, $n = 10$), physical ($p < 0.001$), effort ($p < 0.001$), and frustration ($p < 0.05$) for the new keyboard on the first day of use. However, there were no significant differences between first day Qwerty and fourth day Sath indicating that users had reduced to their Qwerty level of effort (figure 15).

At the end of the study, users were asked "if it was proven faster and less prone to spelling errors", would they adopt this keyboard. Eight of the ten users replied positively on a 7-point scale with a mean response of +1.6 (see fig. 16).

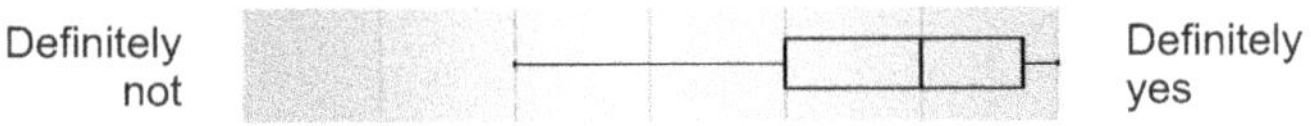

Figure 16: Adoption preference

Several users commented that it would take some time to get up to full speed on the new layout while a couple commented that they had already got used to the new layout. A couple of comments showed some users understood the design, e.g. "I liked how letters which are close to each other in a word were close on the keyboard".

Study Discussion

We observed an initial performance of 64% which, after only four short sessions, had recovered to 85% of their own Qwerty performance with users typing at nearly 18 wpm in their fourth session. While not yet outperforming Qwerty they were typing at a good speed and showed good signs of continual improvement. Given the growth shown on figures 13/14 we are confident that this study shows (a) initial use is not too painful and (b) users would most likely exceed Qwerty speed within a short period of more intensive use.

FUTURE WORK

We are currently improving the Android app to commercial quality to allow non-study usage. This will enable longitudinal trials after which we should be able to better estimate practical expert text entry speed. The constants a and b in our Fitts's law modelling are based on the best available estimates – these studies will also allow us to accurately model these for modern touch screen phones.

The Pareto curve provides a 3D surface on which all points are, in some sense, optimal given different bias on the underlying metrics. As users become familiar with the revised keyboards shown in this paper it may be possible to dynamically move forward along the front towards the origin of familiarity by building on the user's new familiarity with our keyboard. Longer trials are planned to see if users can handle a keyboard design that changes dynamically over time but in a "familiar way". We will also investigate how this impacts on their use of the standard Qwerty, for example when using a friend's keyboard or swapping to hard keyboard phone or laptop.

We picked three metrics of speed, interpretation clarity and Qwerty-familiarity as we feel any optimization should take at least these three aspects into account. Other metrics could be included as Pareto optimization is open to any number of dimensions. For example, the language models underlying our optimization are relatively simple and do not require particularly detailed corpora so it would be worth exploring optimized keyboards for other languages (another of Kristensson's challenges [17]) or even multi-lingual optimization (c.f. [3]). We are also working on optimizing for two thumbs using more detailed timing models [21].

CONCLUSION

This paper has introduced a new approach to keyboard optimization. We use Pareto Front optimization to optimize on three metrics in parallel: finger travel distance (speed of entry), tap interpretation clarity for spell correction (itself a new metric) and familiarity with standard Qwerty. Using our metrics we proposed two new Sath-keyboards that give a considerable improvement in finger travel distance by rearranging the keys on the standard layout keyboard and by also making the key layout more rectangular. In addition to the predicted improvement in speed we saw a considerable reduction in neighbour ambiguity that should lead to improved tap interpretation and spell correction. Fitts' law modelling confirmed a conservative improvement of 10-11% in terms of words-per-minute. When compared with Bi, Smith and Zhai's quasi-optimized keyboard [2] we show a small improvement in speed with a considerable improvement in the tap interpretation metric (but at a cost in familiarity). In user trials, users performed at 64% of their Qwerty speed on first use but this improved to 85% within four short trial sessions and showed strong signs of continued improvement. Moreover, the combined effect of less distance in typing and higher tap interpretation clarity should, in medium term use, see cumulative gains as users learn they can be less accurate with taps and achieve the same quality input. User studies are planned to accurately model finger-based entry on touch screens of these sizes and to study the impact of our improved layout and spell correction ability on input speeds over long term studies.

ACKNOWLEDGEMENTS

Our thanks to our pre-test and main-test subjects, Tony Fowlie who developed a preliminary keyboard as part of his honours project, Scott MacKenzie for clarifications on bigram tables and to our anonymous reviewers.

REFERENCES

1. Allen, J. M., McFarlin, L. A. and Green, T. An In-Depth Look into the Text Entry User Experience on the iPhone. In *Proc. 52nd HFES* (2008), 508-512.
2. Bi, X., Smith, B. A. and Zhai, S. Quasi-qwerty soft keyboard optimization. In *Proc. CHI 2010*, ACM Press (2010), 283-286.
3. Bi, X., Smith, B. A. and Zhai, S. Multilingual Touchscreen Keyboard Design and Optimization. *Human-Computer Interaction* (to appear 2011).
4. Clawson, J., Lyons, K., Rudnick, A., Iannucci, R. A. J. and Starner, T. Automatic whiteout++: correcting mini-QWERTY typing errors using keypress timing. In *Proc. CHI 2008*, ACM Press (2008), 573-582.
5. David, P. A. Clio and the Economics of QWERTY. *American Economic Review*, 75, 2 (1985), 332-337.
6. Deb, K. *Multi-Objective Optimization using Evolutionary Algorithms*. Wiley, 2002.
7. Dunlop, M. D. and Crossan, A. Predictive text entry methods for mobile phones. *Personal Technologies*, 4, 2 (2000).
8. Dunlop, M. D., Glen, A., Motaparti, S. and Patel, S. AdapTex: contextually adaptive text entry for mobiles. In *Proc. MobileHCI '06*, ACM Press (2006).
9. Fitts, P. M. The information capacity of the human motor system in controlling the amplitude of movement. *J. Experimental Psychology*, 47, 6 (1954), 381-391.
10. Gong, J. and Tarasewich, P. Alphabetically constrained keypad designs for text entry on mobile devices. In *Proc. CHI '05*, ACM Press (2005), 211-220.
11. Grover, D. L., King, M. T. and Kushler, C. A. *Reduced keyboard disambiguating computer* Tegic Communications, Inc., Patent US5818437 (1998).
12. Hasselgren, J., Montnemery, E., Nugues, P. and Svensson, M. HMS: A Predictive Text Entry Method Using Bigrams. In *Proc. Workshop on Language Modeling for Text Entry Methods at EACL* (2003), 43-49.
13. Hoggan, E., Brewster, S. A. and Johnston, J. Investigating the effectiveness of tactile feedback for mobile touchscreens. In *Proc. CHI '08*, ACM Press (2008), 1573-1582.
14. Hoos, H. H. and Stutzle, T. *Stochastic Local Search: Foundations and Applications*. Morgan Kaufmann, 2005.
15. Jones, M. P. and Martin, J. H. Contextual spelling correction using latent semantic analysis. In *Proc. ANLP 1997*, Association for Computational Linguistics (1997), 166-173.
16. Kristensson, P.-O. and Zhai, S. Relaxing stylus typing precision by geometric pattern matching. In *Proc. IUI 2005*, ACM Press (2005), 151-158.
17. Kristensson, P. Five Challenges for Intelligent Text Entry Methods. *AI Magazine*, 30, 4 (2009), 85-94.
18. Kwon, S., Lee, D. and Chung, M. K. Effect of key size and activation area on the performance of a regional error correction method in a touch-screen QWERTY keyboard. *International Journal of Industrial Ergonomics*, 39, 5 (2009), 888-893.
19. Lee, S. and Zhai, S. The performance of touch screen soft buttons. In *Proc. CHI 2009*, ACM Press (2009), 309-318.
20. Lewis, J. R., Kennedy, P. J. and LaLomia, M. J. Development of a Digram-Based Typing Key Layout for Single-Finger/Stylus Input. In *Proc. HFES* (1999).
21. MacKenzie, I. S. and Soukoreff, R. W. A model of two-thumb text entry. In *Proc. Graphics Interface 2002*, Canadian Information Processing Society (2002).
22. MacKenzie, I. S. and Soukoreff, R. W. Text entry for mobile computing: Models and methods, theory and practice. *Human-Computer Interaction*, 17 (2002), 147-198.
23. MacKenzie, I. S. and Soukoreff, R. W. Phrase sets for evaluating text entry techniques. In *Proc. CHI 2003*, ACM Press (2003), 754-755.
24. MacKenzie, I. S. and Zhang, S. X. The design and evaluation of a high-performance soft keyboard. In *Proc. CHI'99*, ACM Press (1999), 25-31.
25. MacKenzie, I. S., Zhang, S. X. and Soukoreff, R. W. Text entry using soft keyboards. *Behaviour & Information Technology*, 18, 4 (1999), 235-244.
26. Parhi, P., Karlson, A. K. and Bederson, B. B. Target size study for one-handed thumb use on small touchscreen devices. In *Proc. MobileHCI 2006*, ACM Press (2006), 203-210.
27. Silfverberg, M., MacKenzie, I. S. and Korhonen, P. Predicting text entry speed on mobile phones. In *Proc. CHI'00*, ACM Press (2000).
28. Soukoreff, R. W. and MacKenzie, I. S. Theoretical upper and lower bounds on typing speed using a stylus and soft keyboard. *Behaviour & Information Technology*, 14 (1995), 370-379.
29. Steuer, R. E. *Multiple Criteria Optimization: Theory, Computations, and Application*. John Wiley & Sons, New York, 1986.
30. Zhai, S., Hunter, M. and Smith, B. Performance Optimization of Virtual Keyboards. *Human-Computer Interaction*, 17, 2 (2002), 229-269.
31. Zhai, S., Hunter, M. and Smith, B. A. The metropolis keyboard - an exploration of quantitative techniques for virtual keyboard design. In *Proc. UIST'00*, ACM Press (2000), 119-128.
32. Zhai, S., Sue, A. and Accot, J. Movement model, hits distribution and learning in virtual keyboarding. In *Proc. CHI'02*, ACM Press (2002), 17-24.

Beyond QWERTY: Augmenting Touch-Screen Keyboards with Multi-Touch Gestures for Non-Alphanumeric Input

Leah Findlater[1,2], Ben Q. Lee[2] and Jacob O. Wobbrock[2]

[1]College of Information Studies
University of Maryland, College Park, MD
leahkf@umd.edu

[2]The Information School | DUB Group
University of Washington, Seattle, WA
{ benlee90, wobbrock }@uw.edu

ABSTRACT
Although many techniques have been proposed to improve text input on touch screens, the vast majority of this research ignores non-alphanumeric input (*i.e.*, punctuation, symbols, and modifiers). To support this input, widely adopted commercial touch-screen interfaces require mode switches to alternate keyboard layouts for most punctuation and symbols. Our approach is to *augment* existing ten-finger QWERTY keyboards with multi-touch gestural input that can exist as a complement to the moded-keyboard approach. To inform our design, we conducted a study to elicit user-defined gestures from 20 participants. The final gesture set includes both multi-touch and single-touch gestures for commonly used non-alphanumeric text input. We implemented and conducted a preliminary evaluation of a touch-screen keyboard augmented with this technique. Findings show that using gestures for non-alphanumeric input is no slower than using keys, and that users strongly prefer gestures to a moded-keyboard interface.

Author Keywords: Touch screen; text input; gestures

ACM Classification Keywords: H.5.2 [Information interfaces and presentation]: User interfaces - *input devices & strategies;*

INTRODUCTION
For text input on touch screens, the traditional QWERTY keyboard and geometric techniques based on it (*e.g.*, [4]) have attained the widest adoption. While these techniques focus on entering letters and full words, operations involving punctuation symbols or modifiers can be laborious. On most commercial touch-screen keyboards, for example, accessing such features requires a mode-switch to an entirely different key assignment or layout. Moreover, even though punctuation symbols such as '**.**' are more common than some letters (*e.g.*, *v*, *k*, *j*) [10], the vast majority of touch-screen text entry research only addresses alphanumeric characters. With the increased use of text and instant messaging, punctuation symbols become even more important (*e.g.*, '**#**' and '**@**' on Twitter).

We propose a multi-touch gestural approach to augment traditional ten-finger touch-screen keyboards for non-

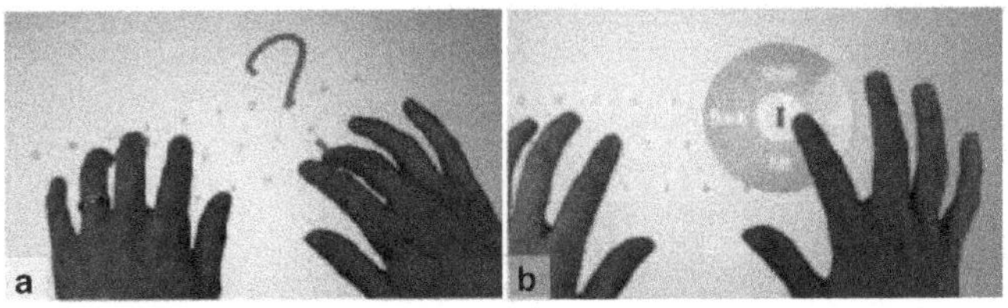

Figure 1. (a) Our multi-touch gesture technique, showing the end of the "?" gesture with all left fingers down and one right finger down; **(b)** the popup pie menu for modifier keys.

alphanumeric input (Figure 1a): the user places 4+ fingers down with one hand and gestures atop the keyboard itself with the other hand. This bimanual interaction uses active rather than passive modes, supports input with low visual attention, and does not require users to move their hands out of typing position. We envision that these gestures will *complement* rather than replace the existing mode-switched keyboard approach that is the standard for such input.

To create our gestures, we first conducted a study to elicit a set of guessable, user-defined gestures from 20 participants (based on [8,9]). The final set includes single-touch and multi-touch gestures. We then built a gesture-augmented QWERTY keyboard that incorporates the gestures and explores pie menus for those non-alphanumeric characters, such as modifier keys (Figure 1b), that were not found to be as suitable for freeform gestures. Our evaluation of the interface with 6 new participants suggests that subjective responses are positive and that, even for novice users, gestural input does *not* result in a loss in performance.

Our work is inspired by previous research in gestural text input and by augmented keyboard techniques. Although stylus-based text input is not as popular as it once was, several stylus-based techniques have included punctuation gestures, such as Palm OS's Graffiti (see [6]). However, these techniques differ considerably from our work in that they are designed for single-stroke input with a stylus rather than a finger (or fingers) and support only a single point of input rather than multi-touch. With multi-touch input devices, intuitive, efficient gestures may differ, such as using two fingers instead of one for a quotation mark. Touch-screen keyboard layouts have also been augmented with popup menus, for example, to enter multiple characters in a single stroke [3] and for diacritical marks (*e.g.*, Google's Android OS and Apple's iOS). Finally, different levels of pressure have also been used to input lowercase versus uppercase letters, augmenting traditional input [2].

The primary contributions of this paper are: (1) a set of user-defined, guessable gestures for non-alphanumeric text entry that includes single-touch and multi-touch components; (2) a multi-touch, bimanual input technique providing access to this gesture set; and (3) an evaluation demonstrating that using gestures for non-alphanumeric input is no slower than using keys, and that users strongly prefer gestures to a moded-keyboard interface.

USER-DEFINED NON-ALPHANUMERIC GESTURES

We conducted a study to elicit a guessable gesture set that includes 22 *punctuation symbols* (*e.g.*, '**: #**') and 4 *commands* (Space, Shift, Backspace, Enter).

Method

Twenty participants volunteered for this study (9 female; 11 male). They ranged in age from 19-48 ($M = 24.7$, $SD = 9.0$). Six participants had technical backgrounds, while the rest spanned domains such as social science, music, and administration. All participants reported having used a touch screen device for at least 6 months beforehand. Only one participant used an alternative to the standard QWERTY keyboard (Swype) to enter text on his device.

The study was conducted on an Apple iPad using a dynamic webpage written in JavaScript and HTML5. The webpage displayed full-screen in landscape orientation and the symbols and commands (26 in all) were presented in random order. Instructions were presented at the top of the screen, along with the buttons: "Done", "Clear" and "Skip" (if applicable); the rest of the screen was blank for drawing. For each symbol or command, participants completed three gesture trials. To compare gesture similarity with and without a visual example for the symbols, Trial 1 only gave the symbol's name (*e.g.*, "comma"), while Trial 2 additionally provided four font-varied examples (*e.g.*, '$ $ $ **$**'); for commands, Trials 1 and 2 were the same. After Trial 2, 7-point Likert scales were used to rate how easy the gesture was to draw and whether it was "a good match for its intended purpose" (following [8,9]). Finally, in Trial 3, participants were asked to switch how they drew the gesture: using multi-touch if they had previously used a single touch, or vice versa. Participants could opt to skip Trial 3 if they could not think of a reasonable gesture (*e.g.*, multi-touch for '**.**'). The webpage logged all interactions.

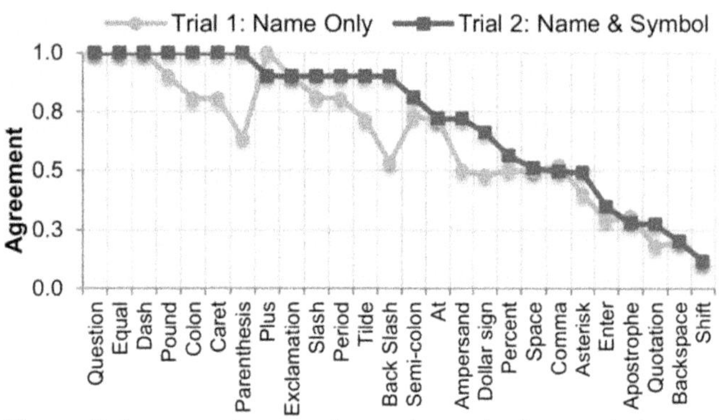

Figure 2. Agreement scores for each punctuation symbol or command: a score of 1.0 indicates perfect agreement, while 0.0 indicates that no two gestures agreed.

For each symbol and command, three members of our team independently grouped similar gestures (similar to [8,9]). Because certain symbols (e.g., '**=**') intuitively afford multiple strokes that could be applied with a *single* multi-touch gesture or *multiple* single-touch gestures, our groupings focused on the shape of the stroke rather than the number of fingers used. After groupings were completed, they were combined into a final set using a majority voting process. Agreement was calculated slightly differently from [8,9] as the count of all pairs of gestures that were deemed similar, divided by the total number of possible pairs:

$$Agreement_s = \frac{\sum_{g \in G_s} \binom{|g|}{2}}{\binom{N}{2}} \qquad (1)$$

where G is the set of groups for the symbol or command s and N is the total number of gestures drawn for s. Since N is 20 (the number of participants) in our case, the denominator is equal to 380, the total number of pairs of gestures (i.e., "N choose 2"). Agreement ranges from 0 to 1, inclusive.

Results

Figure 2 shows agreement scores; higher scores indicate more guessable gestures. Average agreement across all symbols and commands was .63 (SD = .27) in Trial 1 and .71 (SD = .29) in Trial 2, which was a significant difference ($t_{25} = 3.807$, $p < .001$). Examining Trial 1 gestures in more detail suggests that symbol names were sometimes misinterpreted (e.g., 5 participants drew a forward slash instead of a backslash).

Half the punctuation symbols and commands had agreement scores of .90 or higher in Trial 2, suggesting that selecting the most frequently drawn gesture for those cases will allow for a highly guessable set of gestures. The four commands (Shift, Enter, Space, Backspace) resulted in significantly lower agreement scores than the symbols, even in Trial 1 before participants were given visual examples ($t_{24} = 4.009$, $p = .001$). Shift, for example, had an agreement score of only .12; Figure 3 shows the diversity of gestures.

Figure 3. Some examples of the 13 different *Shift* gestures, the right-most two of which are multi-touch gestures.

To assess whether single-touch or multi-touch gestures were preferred for each symbol or command, we calculated the maximum number of fingers concurrently on the screen at any point during the gesture. In Trial 1, multi-touch gestures were made by more than one participant only for the following: 'Shift **# " : =**'. (Trial 2 results were similar.) For those symbols and the Shift command, at most half of the participants used a multi-touch gesture, from 15% of participants for Shift to 50% for '**=**'. Interestingly, when participants were asked whether they had preferred single-touch or multi-touch for the four punctuation symbols just listed ('**# " : =**'), several participants who had *initially* used single-touch stated they ultimately preferred multi-touch: preference was 65%-70% for multi-touch for all four of those symbols. Following these preferences, participants were more likely to skip Trial 3 for punctuation symbols that clearly had no appropriate multi-touch gesture (*e.g.*, 17 out of 20 participants did so for '.').

Subjective measures reflected the agreement scores (scales are 1-7; 7 = "strongly agree"). On average, gestures were rated high on ease, with punctuation symbols (M = 6.2, SD = 0.5) and commands (M = 6.0, SD = 0.4) not significantly different. However, the drawn gestures were considered to be a significantly better match for symbols (M=6.5, SD=0.2) than for commands (M=5.4, SD=0.5) ($t_{3,16}$=7.827, p = .022; *df* adjusted to account for unequal variance).

On average in Trials 1 and 2, participants took 1.2 seconds (SD = 5.6) to draw each gesture. These times ranged in Trial 2 from 0.23 seconds (SD = .33) for '.' to 2.20 seconds (SD = 0.72) for '@'. Notably, gestures for Space, while relatively high in agreement, were unreasonably slow for such a common action (M=0.95 s, SD=0.47). Most commonly, space was drawn as a horizontal bracket (']').

User-Defined Gesture Set for Non-Alphanumeric Input

Figure 4 shows the user-defined gesture set based on these results. The set contains all punctuation symbols tested, except for comma and period. These two symbols are more frequent than some letters [10] and the comma gesture conflicted with the parenthesis and apostrophe gestures; as such, we left comma and period as keys on the primary keyboard. Since the commands generally resulted in lower agreement and subjective scores than did the punctuation symbols, we recommend commands also remain as keys on the primary keyboard. (Our system also includes a popup pie menu for commands; see Figure 1b and next section.)

For the remaining symbols, we selected the most popular gesture for each symbol in Trial 1. The only potential conflict in this set is between parenthesis and apostrophe, which differ only in height: apostrophes were 1.56 cm (SD = 1.20); parentheses were 5.49 cm (SD = 1.87). Whether or not this is an issue will depend on the particular gesture recognizer used. Our data suggests that both single-touch and multi-touch gestures should be allowed for '**= # : "**'.

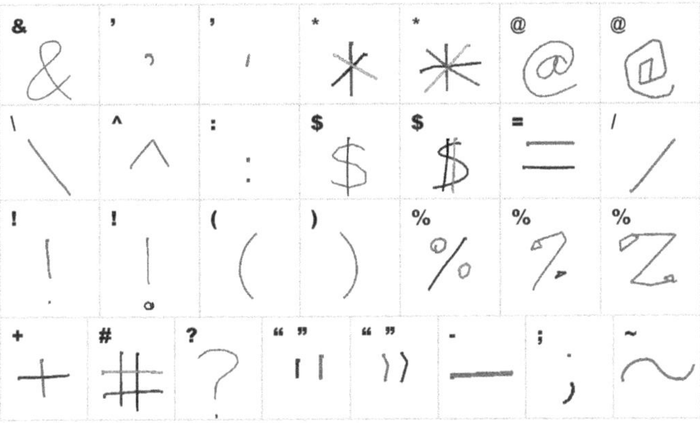

Figure 4. The final set of gestures with examples taken from study data. All are single-touch gestures, except '**# " : =**', for which we recommend multi-touch also be supported. Comma and period are not included here and remain as keys on the primary keyboard.

AN AUGMENTED QWERTY KEYBOARD

We implemented and evaluated a ten-finger touch-screen QWERTY keyboard incorporating the gesture set.

The System

Figure 1 shows screenshots of the system, built in C♯ 4.0 for a Microsoft Surface computer. The QWERTY keyboard is a standard touch-screen keyboard implementation with the same layout and key size (.09" × 0.9") as the device's native keyboard. Gesture recognition is done using a modified version of the $N Multistroke Recognizer [1], which uses template matching to classify gestures based on a library of examples. To extend the recognizer for multi-touch gestures and to reduce ambiguity in gesture recognition, we restricted the candidate template set based on the number of *concurrent* fingers and limited the possible gesture angle to be relative to the keyboard orientation. Note that we maintained $N's original invariance to gesture size.

The user invokes the gesture mode by placing 4+ fingers down with either hand (to accommodate left- and right-handed users) and draws the gesture with the opposite hand; see Figure 1a. The keyboard changes color from blue to orange to indicate the user is in gesture mode. The gesture is classified when both hands lift from the screen, and, finally, the resulting symbol is entered into the text stream. The software also includes a popup pie menu to access modifier keys *in context*, although we did not evaluate this aspect of the system in this study. This menu could contain input for which guessable gestures are not as obvious; Shift, Backspace, Control and Alt are shown in Figure 1b. The user invokes the menu by tapping and holding their finger over a key for 400 ms, then swipes to select the option they want. Lifting the finger without swiping will cancel.

Preliminary Evaluation

We conducted a preliminary study to: (1) gather subjective feedback on the gestures versus a standard moded-keyboard alternative; (2) assess the performance feasibility of the new technique—that is, determine if the gestural interface was at least on par with the moded-keyboard, even for novice users without much gesture learning.

Method

Six participants (2 female; 4 male) volunteered for this study. They were on average 29.3 years old (SD = 2.9). Five were right-handed; 1 was left-handed. All participants had been using a touch-screen device for at least 1 year and 5/6 entered text using a standard touch screen QWERTY keyboard; 1 participant used a gestural text input technique (Swype). As such, all participants had previous experience with moded-keyboards for punctuation symbols.

Study sessions lasted 30 minutes. The moded-keyboard used the same interface as the gesture condition, except that instead of gestures, two "Symbols" keys were used to toggle the key labels between alphabetic characters and punctuation symbols. (These keys were located where Shift keys are found on most keyboards.) Participants practiced entering the following 10 common symbols with each technique: '**! ? @ $ & : ; " ( )**'. After 8 practice attempts with each symbol on each of the interfaces (gestures *vs.* moded-keyboard), we asked participants to complete a more realistic task: entering pairs of words separated by one of the punctuation symbols (*e.g.*, '`toil? and`'). In the case of parenthesis and double quote, two words and two punctuation symbols were used (*e.g.*, '`with (sister)`'). The interfaces were counterbalanced and participants entered 18 of these word-pairs with each.

Findings

Although we were primarily interested in subjective responses in this evaluation because we are not seeking to replace, but rather to augment, moded designs, we first briefly examined performance. On average, participants typed at 19.7 WPM (*SD* = 5.16) with the gestures and 19.9 WPM (*SD* = 4.4) with the moded-keyboard. Uncorrected error rates [7] were also similar, at 6.3% (*SD* = 4.8) for the gestures and 6.3% (*SD* = 7.7) for the moded-keyboard. These differences were not statistically significant. The results demonstrate the feasibility of the gestural interface, even for these novice users compared to the *status quo*.

In general, reactions to the gestural input were positive. For example, when first introduced to the technique, P2 said: "This is great. It feels very seamless." Two participants also commented that the gestures were "fun" (P1, P4). This positive sentiment translated to an overall preference for the gestural interface: 5/6 participants predicted they would prefer the gestures over a moded-keyboard if both options were available on a large touch-screen device (*e.g.*, tablet). One reason for this preference was efficiency, for example:

> *"My opinion of gesture things is that there's a slightly higher learning curve but they're usually faster once the fingers know how to do them." (P1)*

The gestures were also perceived to require less visual attention than the moded-keyboard. Four participants commented to this effect, for example:

> *"[For the moded-keyboard] I always had to look down at the symbols to find where they were. With the second set [gestures] I felt I didn't have to look down really at all. If I did look down it was just to figure out if I was on the home row."* (P2)

Both interfaces also received some negative comments. The awkwardness of having to mode-switch arose with two participants, once for the moded-keyboard and twice for the gestures. The mode-switch mechanism would likely become easier with practice, but particularly so for the gestural interface since it does not require much visual attention (just putting 4+ fingers down). Future work is needed to confirm this hypothesis.

Finally, participants commented on the general difficulty of entering punctuation symbols on their touch-screen devices, which further motivates this research. P5 commented:

> *"It's one of the things that stops me from typing on the iPad because it's such a pain to get the punctuation correct."*

URLs, '@' and passwords with a lot of punctuation were cited as particularly frustrating on touchscreen keyboards.

DISCUSSION AND CONCLUSION

We have introduced a bimanual, multi-touch gestural approach for non-alphanumeric text input that is designed to *augment*, not replace, existing solutions. This technique allows for input with low visual attention and does not require users to move their hands out of typing position. To inform our design, we first created a user-defined gesture set containing single-touch and multi-touch gestures based on data from 20 participants. Although preliminary, an evaluation of the full technique suggests that users prefer the gestural input over a moded-keyboard interface. We envision this new technique will complement the moded-keyboard approach. As a side benefit, the alternate symbol keyboards can act as a "reference sheet" for novice gesture users. Future work includes a more thorough evaluation and extending the gestural interface to tablets and smaller devices. The gesture mode could be invoked for two-thumb typing, for example, by holding a single finger down.

Acknowledgements

The authors would like to thank Jon Froehlich. This work was supported in part by NSERC, Microsoft Research, and the National Science Foundation under grant IIS-0811063. Any opinions, findings, conclusions or recommendations expressed in this work are those of the authors and do not necessarily reflect those of any supporter.

REFERENCES

1. Anthony, L. and Wobbrock, J.O. 2010. A lightweight multistroke recognizer for user interface prototypes. *Proc. GI '10*, 245-252.
2. Brewster, S. A., and Hughes, M. 2009. Pressure-based text entry for mobile devices. *Proc. MobileHCI '09*, 73-76.
3. Isokoski, P.. 2004. Performance of menu-augmented soft keyboards. *Proc. CHI '04*, 423-430.
4. Kristensson, P. and Zhai, S. 2004. SHARK^2: a large vocabulary shorthand writing system for pen-based computers. *Proc. UIST '04*, 43-52.
5. MacKenzie, I.S., Soukoreff, R.W. 2002. Text entry for mobile computing: models and methods, theory and practice. *Human-Computer Interaction 17* (2), 147-198.
6. MacKenzie, I.S., Zhang, S.X. 1997. The immediate usability of Graffiti. *Proc. GI '97*, 129-137.
7. Soukoreff , R.W. and MacKenzie, I.S. 2003. Metrics for text entry research: an evaluation of MSD and KSPC, and a new unified error metric. *Proc. CHI '03*, 113-120.
8. Wobbrock, J.O., Aung, H.H., Rothrock, B. and Myers, B.A. (2005). Maximizing the guessability of symbolic input. *Extended Abstracts CHI '05*, 1869-1872.
9. Wobbrock, J.O., Morris, M.R., and Wilson, A.D. 2009. User-defined gestures for surface computing. *Proc. CHI '09*, 1083-1092.
10. Zhai, S., Hunter, M., and Smith, B.A. 2002. Performance optimization of virtual keyboards. *Human-Computer Interaction 17* (3), 89-129.

Touch Typing using Thumbs: Understanding the Effect of Mobility and Hand Posture

Hugo Nicolau
IST / Technical University of Lisbon / INESC-ID
R. Alves Redol, 9, 1000-029, Lisbon, Portugal
hman@vimmi.inesc-id.pt

Joaquim Jorge
IST / Technical University of Lisbon / INESC-ID
R. Alves Redol, 9, 1000-029, Lisbon, Portugal
jaj@inesc-id.pt

ABSTRACT

Mobile touch devices have become increasingly popular, yet typing on virtual keyboards whilst walking is still an overwhelming task. In this paper we analyze; firstly, the negative effect of walking on text-input performance, particularly the users' main difficulties and error patterns. We focused our research on thumb typing, since this is a commonly used technique to interact with touch interfaces. Secondly, we analyze how these effects can be compensated by two-hand interaction and increasing target size. We asked 22 participants to input text under three mobility conditions (seated, slow walking, and normal walking) and three hand conditions (one-hand/portrait, two-hand/portrait, and two-hand/landscape). Results show that independently of hand condition, mobility significantly decreased input quality, leading to specific error patterns. Moreover, it was shown that target size can compensate the negative effect of walking, while two-hand interaction does not provide additional stability or input accuracy. We finish with implications for future designs.

Author Keywords

Text-entry; Mobile; Walk; Thumb; Hand Posture.

ACM Classification Keywords

H.5.2 [Information Interfaces and Presentation]: User Interfaces - Input devices and strategies;

General Terms

Human factors, design, experimentation.

INTRODUCTION

Mobile devices are being increasingly used whilst walking. This new interaction context poses new challenges to mobile users since they usually compete for the same human resources that are needed to fully control electronic devices. However, interfaces are designed, developed, and evaluated for static and controlled situations, ignoring these problems. When on the move the whole body is prone to vibrations, particularly hand oscillations can hamper interaction with a mobile device [2]. This effect is worsened when the interface features small targets [8], such as virtual keys.

Studies regarding the effect of mobility report that users spontaneously reduce speed by 30-37% when performing reading tasks in a mobile device. Similarly, Bergstrom-Lehtovirta et al. [2] have shown that to maintain target selection accuracy users need to reduce speed by 26%, as compared to their preferred walking speed. Lin et al. [5] examined stylus-based tapping behavior whilst walking. Results show that walking had no effect on the time needed to select a target, yet they saw an increase towards error rates. Mizobuchi et al. [6] also focused on stylus interaction and analyzed the effects of mobility and keyboard sizes on text-entry tasks. The authors report no effect on text input speed; however, error rates tend to increase. Additionally, they saw an effect of target size: larger targets allow higher input rates and lower error rates. Although the authors also analyze the effect of walking and key size in text input, a key difference to our work lays in the fact that in their study a stylus was used and therefore, only two-handed interaction was analyzed. In our study, in addition to target size, we also considered both one-hand and two-hand interaction, in which participants use their thumbs to input text, as this is currently one of the most commonly used technique with touch screen devices.

Interaction with thumbs has been studied in target selection tasks [8], and static conditions [7], yet there is a lack of knowledge pertaining text-entry tasks whilst mobile. The study presented in this paper tries to bridge this gap by analyzing the effect of walking on text-entry performance, and secondly to understand the effects of two-hand interaction and target size. Moreover, we describe the users' typing difficulties and error patterns whilst walking, as well as their causes.

METHOD

We evaluated the participants' performance in three mobility settings: sitting, walking at average human pace (2 steps per second), and walking at 65% of average human pace (1.3 steps per second) [1]. The experiment was conducted on an indoor test track built-up at the university campus (without obstacles). In both walking conditions, we asked participants to follow a pacesetter while entering text. Although other designs could be chosen [4], we opted to keep a fixed pace rather than measure it as a dependent variable in order to ensure a comparable level of walking demand across trials. The experimenter instructed participants to stay within 2 meters of the pacesetter as he walked. If the participant fell behind by more than 4 meters, the experimenter logged a walking deviation for that trial. The pacesetter carried a mobile phone, which gave him feedback through vibration about the intended pace.

Participants

Twenty two participants, 3 females and 19 males, took part in the user study. Their age ranged from 23 to 40 with a mean of 26.5 years old. They were recruited from Campus University. None of the participants had visual or motor impairments and all of them owned a mobile phone, whereas only 15 used touch screen technology regularly. All participants were right-handed.

Procedure

At the beginning of the experiment participants were told that the overall purpose of the study was to investigate how text-entry performance was affected by walking conditions. Subjects were then informed about the experiment and how to use our evaluation application.

Before each mobility condition participants had a 5 minute practice trial to get used to the pace and text-entry task. For each mobility setting, subjects were asked to enter text with 3 hand conditions (chosen randomly) always using their thumbs: one-hand/ portrait, two-hand/ portrait, and two-hand/ landscape. For each condition participants copied seven different sentences (first two sentences were practice trials), displayed one at a time, at the top of the screen. Copy typing was used to reduce the opportunity for spelling and language errors, and to make error identification easier. Participants were instructed to type phrases as quickly and accurately as possible. Error correction (delete) was not available, since we wanted a single measure of accuracy.

Each participant entered a total of 63 different sentences, extracted from a written language *corpus*, each with 5 words, an average size of 4.48 characters per word, and a minimum correlation with the language of 0.97. Both sentences and mobility conditions were chosen randomly to avoid bias associated with experience.

Apparatus

An HTC Desire with a capacitive touch screen was used during the user study. A QWERTY virtual keyboard was used to simulate a traditional touch keyboard, where each key was 10x10mm on landscape mode, and 7x10mm on portrait mode. Letters were entered using a lift-off strategy. Neither word prediction nor correction was used. Acceleration data was captured through device's accelerometer for posterior analysis.

Design and Analysis

We used a within subjects design where each participant tested all mobility and hand conditions. In summary the study design was: 22 participants x 5 sentences x 3 hand conditions x 3 mobility settings = 990 sentences overall.

Shapiro-Wilkinson tests of the observed values for *Words per Minute (WPM)*, *Minimum String Distance (MSD) Error Rate,* incorrect characters (*Substitutions*), omitted characters (*Omissions*), and added characters (*Insertions*), showed to fit a normal distribution for all conditions. Therefore, a two-way repeated-measures *ANOVA* was used in further analysis. Greenhouse-Geisser's sphericity corrections were applied whenever Mauchly's test of sphericity showed a significant effect. Pairwise Bonferroni corrected t-tests were used for post-hoc tests.

RESULTS

Two-hand input is faster

To assess speed, we used the words per minute (*WPM*) text input measure. Overall, input speed was very similar between mobility conditions. Participants obtained an average of 24 (CI 1.4 wpm), 24.9 (CI 1.4 wpm), and 24.5 (CI 1.4 wpm) words per minute on seated, slow walking and regular walking conditions, respectively. The results show that there was no significant main effect of *Mobility* on *WPM* ($F_{2,42}$=.97, p>.1). This effect was expected since participants could not perform corrections to transcribed sentences.

Regarding hand posture, participants wrote an average of 20 (CI 0.9 wpm) words per minute with one-hand. Two-hand interaction allowed participants to reach higher input speeds: 25 (CI 1.2 wpm) and 29 (CI 1.3 wpm) words per minute with portrait and landscape positions, respectively. A repeated measures ANOVA revealed a significant main effect of *Hand Posture* on *WPM* ($F_{2,42}$=84.878, p<0.001). *Bonferroni* post-hoc tests showed significant differences between all hand conditions. As expected, writing with the two-hand landscape mode is significantly faster, followed by two-hand portrait and one-hand.

Two-hand input does not provide additional stability

In this study we measured the quality of the transcribed sentences using the *Minimum String Distance (MSD) Error Rate* (Figure 1). *Mobility* effect can be clearly seen as *MSD Error Rate* increases with amplitude of hand oscillation

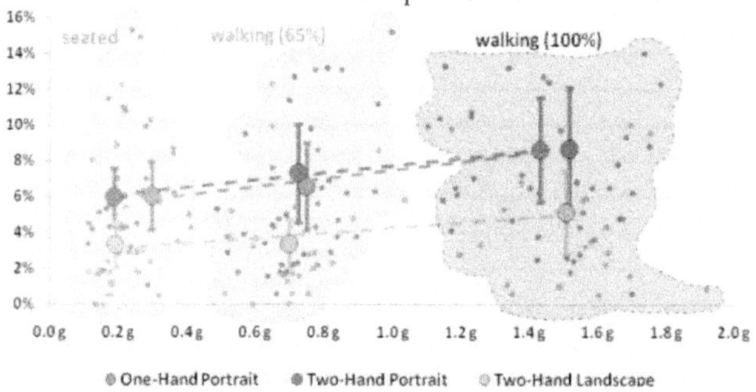

Figure 1. *MSD Error Rate by hand oscillation amplitude. Vertical bars denote 95% CI. Lines illustrate linear regression.*

(calculated as standard deviations of average accelerations [2]). Between seated and normal walking, quality of transcribed phrases decreased on average, approximately, 2.4%. Participants achieved an average *MSD Error Rate* of 5.1% (CI 1.7%), 5.7% (CI 2.3%), and 7.5% (CI 3%) on seated, slow walking, and normal walking, respectively. Results show a significant main effect of *Mobility* on *MSD Error Rate* ($F_{1.244,26.115}=4.962$, $p<.05$), with significant differences between seated and normal walking conditions.

Regarding the effect of two-hand interaction, oscillation was very similar for both portrait modes. Indeed, *MSD Error Rate* was very similar with an average of 7.1% (CI 2.5%) and 7.3% (CI 2.7%) for one-hand and two-hand, respectively, demonstrating that two-hand interaction by itself does not provide additional stability. Nevertheless, in landscape mode, accuracy increased nearly 3.4%, resulting on a significant main effect of *Hand Posture* ($F_{2,42}=16.546$, $p<.001$). This suggests that key size has a greater influence than hand grip on text input accuracy and can compensate the negative effect of mobility. No interactions between *Mobility* and *Hand Posture* were found.

Hand oscillation causes poor aiming, not finger slips

Figure 2 illustrates error types per mobility and hand conditions. We analyze only *Substitution Errors* because both *Insertion* and *Omission Errors* accounted for only a minority of error rates and there were no significant differences over conditions.

Substitution Errors significantly increased with *Mobility* ($F_{1.440,\ 30.243}=5.195$, $p<.05$) with differences between seated and normal walking conditions. Similarly, we also found a significant main effect of *Hand Posture* on *Substitution Errors* ($F_{2,42}=16.578$, $p<.001$). Differences were found between two-hand landscape (2.1%) and both one-hand (5.3%) and two-hand portrait (4.8%) conditions.

Overall, substitutions were the most common type of error and the most sensitive to mobility conditions. One could assume that due to hand oscillation the users' fingers could slip to a near key before entering the letter, resulting in a *Substitution Error*. However, on average, slips accounted for less than 10% of substitutions and were not affected by *Mobility* ($F_{2,42}=1.005$, $p>.1$). A thorough analysis revealed that 72%-92% of substitution errors are due to poor aiming, i.e. incorrect land-on target. Although participants could compensate for land-on errors, most performed quick taps as if they were typing with a physical keyboard.

Substitution errors occurred as adjacent keys in the same row.

Based on our results, we created confusion matrices for each condition. Substitution error rate per letter for one-hand portrait conditions is shown in Figure 3. When seated, the most frequent substitution errors were: E→R (4.6%), R→T (6.5%), S→D (11.5%), T→Y (4%), U→Y (4.5%), U→I (3.4%). As we can see there is a clear predominance

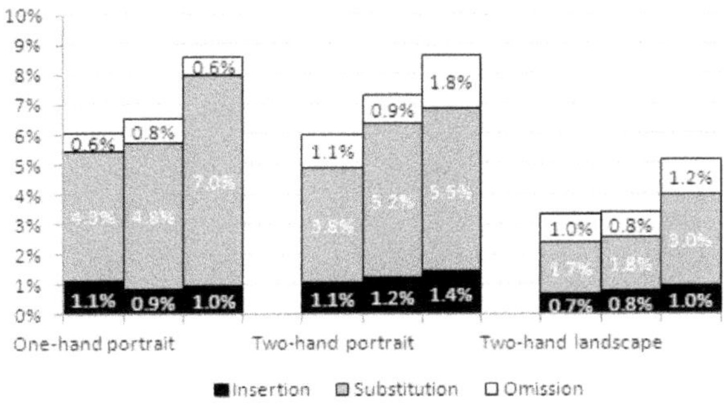

Figure 2. *Insertion, Substitution, and Omission* error rates, grouped by hand condition. Left, middle, and right bars correspond to seated, walking (65%), and walking (100%), respectively.

of same-row errors in the data, which suggests that participants found it easier to hit keys in the vertical direction than horizontally. This may be because key height was slightly higher than key width. Additionally, all errors are at a distance of one key and typically at the right. These findings need further investigation, but may be related to hand dominance. In the normal walking condition the most frequent substitution errors were: D→F (10.4%), R→T (9.3%), S→D (11.8%), T→Y (5.2%), T→R (4.6%). In this case, the highest error rate keys seem to be somewhat the more distant from the users' dominant hand (Figure 3), and once again the pattern of substitution remained the same (adjacent key). It is noteworthy that although hand oscillation increased from seated to normal walking condition, substitutions remained at a distance of one key.

Regarding the two-hand portrait condition, error rates follow the same substitution pattern. As mobility demand increase, higher error rates seem to cluster on the left side of the keyboard, suggesting that the non-dominant hand is less accurate. Frequent substitution errors were: S→A (12.6%), C→X (4.4%), E→R (3.5%), U→I (4.3%), D→F (2.7%). With the two-hand landscape posture, participants committed much fewer errors due to target size, and error rates are fairly distributed among keys.

Overall, mobility seems to increase error rate magnitude, however the substitution pattern is similar between conditions: same row errors and adjacent keys. Additionally, on one hand interaction letters are usually substituted by their right-side keys, while in two hand interaction this effect dissipates. Nevertheless, the non-dominant hand seems to have a lower accuracy, particularly when hand oscillation is higher.

Lower error rates means higher walking performance

In this user study, participants had to follow a pacesetter on mobility conditions. Walking errors were counted when users stopped or lagged behind the pacesetter by more than 4 meters. When that happened, the pacesetter waited for the participant and then resumed the pace. We found a significant main effect of mobility condition on walking

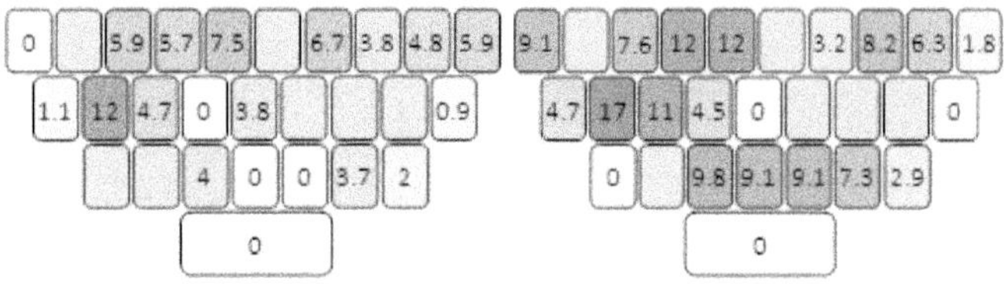

Figure 3. *Substitution* error rates per key in one-hand portrait condition whilst seated (left) and normal walking (right).

errors as participants committed significantly more errors whilst walking at a normal pace than whilst walking at slow pace ($F_{1,21}$=10.010, p<.05). Regarding hand conditions, the average number of walking errors per participant was 0.5, 0.4, and 0.3 for one-hand portrait, two-hand portrait, and two-hand landscape, respectively. Results show a significant effect of *Hand* on *Walking Errors* ($F_{1.575, 33.082}$=3.847, p<.05). Significant differences were found between landscape and both portrait conditions. This result suggests that easier text-entry methods allow for better performance on walking tasks.

Most users prefer larger keys

Regarding preference, 81.8% of participants preferred the landscape mode, with a 95% adjusted-Wald binomial CI ranging from 60.9% to 93.3%, a lower limit above the three-choice chance expectation of 33.3%. None of the participants chose this interaction mode as the least preferred, showing that generally users prefer larger keys to input text. The one-hand portrait condition shown to be the least preferred for 13 of the participants. Moreover, none chose this interaction mode as his/her preferred. Regarding the two-hand portrait condition, while it was disliked by nine users, four participants preferred this interaction mode due to convenience or input speed. Interestingly, this preference was not correlated with their performance.

DESIGN IMPLICATIONS

Do not over rely on two-hand interaction for physical stability. Future mobile text-entry solutions should not rely on hand grip to improve typing effectiveness. Data shows that two handed interaction do not decrease hand oscillation nor does it improve input quality. As an alternative, increasing key size allow users to compensate the negative effect of mobility. However, this solution is not always possible due to limited screen size.

Adjacent substitutions. Results show that substitutions are the most common type of error and usually occur on the same row and adjacent keys. Therefore, predictive text-entry methods, correction algorithms or adaptive keyboards should take into account this typing behavior. These solutions will mostly likely work for different mobility conditions, since the pattern remains unchanged.

Design for poor aiming, especially whilst mobile. Alternative modalities have been used to improve touch typing and reduce slip-based errors [3]. However, these solutions only address a minority of input errors. Future designs should focus on dealing with poor aiming. For instance, text-entry methods may automatically compensate touch locations by sensing hand tremor or increase some key sizes, thus significantly enhancing user performance.

CONCLUSION

The results described in this paper present the negative effect of walking on touch typing using thumbs. It was shown that independently of hand condition, i.e. one-hand portrait, two-hand portrait or two-hand landscape, mobility significantly decreased input effectiveness, leading to consistent substitution patterns. Moreover, two-hand interaction allowed higher input rates, however it did not provide additional physical stability or text-entry accuracy. On the other hand, when compared to portrait mode, landscape interaction can compensate the negative effects of mobility due to larger key size. Those results, in addition to the described design implications, can improve future mobile designs towards more effective text-entry solutions.

ACKNOWLEDGMENTS

This work was supported by FCT through PIDDAC Program funds. Hugo Nicolau was supported by FCT, grant SFRH/BD/46748/2008.

REFERENCES

1. Barnard, L., Yi, J., Jacko, J., Sears, A. An empirical comparison of use-in-motion evaluation scenarios for mobile computing devices. In *Int.Journal of Human-Computer Studies*, 2005, 62(4), 487-520.
2. Bergstrom-Lehtovirta, J., Oulasvirta, A., Brewster, S. The Effects of Walking Speed on Target Acquisition on a Touchscreen Interface. In *Proc. MHCI11*, 2011, 143-146.
3. Hoggan, E. and Brewster, S.A. and Johnston, J. Investigating the effectiveness of tactile feedback for mobile touchscreens. In *Proc.CHI08*, 2008, 1573-1582.
4. Kane, S., Wobbrock, J., Smith, I. Getting off the treadmill: evaluating walking user interfaces for mobile devices in public spaces. In *Proc. MHCI08*, 2008, 109-118.
5. Lin, M., Goldman, R., Price, K., Sears, A., Jacko, J. How do people tap when walking? An empirical investigation of nomadic data entry. In *Int. J. of Human-Computer Studies*, 2007, 65(9),759–769.
6. Mizobuchi, S., Chignell, M., Newton, D. Mobile text entry: relationship between walking speed and text input task difficulty. In *Proc. MHCI05*, 2005, 122–128.
7. Parhi, P., Karlson, A., Bederson, B. Target size study for one-handed thumb use on small touchscreen devices. In *Proc. MHCI06*, 2006, 203–210.
8. Schildbach, B., Rukzio, E. Investigating selection and reading performance on a mobile phone while walking. In *Proc. MHCI10*, 2010, 92-102.

WalkType: Using Accelerometer Data to Accommodate Situational Impairments in Mobile Touch Screen Text Entry

Mayank Goel[1], Leah Findlater[2,3] and Jacob O. Wobbrock[3]

[1]Computer Science & Engineering
DUB Group
University of Washington
Seattle, WA 98195 USA
mayank@cs.washington.edu

[2]College of Information Studies
University of Maryland
College Park, MD 20742 USA
leahkf@umd.edu

[3]The Information School
DUB Group
University of Washington
Seattle, WA 98195 USA
wobbrock@uw.edu

ABSTRACT

The lack of tactile feedback on touch screens makes typing difficult, a challenge exacerbated when situational impairments like walking vibration and divided attention arise in mobile settings. We introduce *WalkType*, an adaptive text entry system that leverages the mobile device's built-in tri-axis accelerometer to compensate for extraneous movement while walking. WalkType's classification model uses the displacement and acceleration of the device, and inference about the user's footsteps. Additionally, WalkType models finger-touch location and finger distance traveled on the screen, features that increase overall accuracy regardless of movement. The final model was built on typing data collected from 16 participants. In a study comparing WalkType to a control condition, WalkType reduced uncorrected errors by 45.2% and increased typing speed by 12.9% for walking participants.

Author Keywords: Touch screen; text entry; adaptive; situational impairments; mobile; virtual keyboard; walking.

ACM Classification Keywords: H.5.2. Information interfaces and presentation: User Interfaces—*input devices and strategies*.

General Terms: Human factors, design, experimentation.

INTRODUCTION

Touch screen devices have become the dominant platform for mobile computing; however, the lack of tactile feedback on these devices requires a high level of visual attention to select targets accurately. Input is particularly challenging when the user is in motion [25,26,29], a state that can be thought of as causing *situational impairments* [35]. Situational impairments may be caused by a variety of factors including vibration, divided attention, diverted gaze, body motion, awkward postures, cold temperatures, clothing, rainwater, glare, uneven terrain, ambient noise, or encumbering baggage. The challenges of situational impairments are exacerbated for mobile text entry on virtual keyboards because of the many repeated targeting actions that take place in quick succession. Researchers have explored various techniques to accommodate some situational impairments, like walking versus stationary interaction [29,36] and, to a lesser extent, adaptive techniques to *automatically* meet such needs [21,42]. Despite these advances, techniques to improve interaction in the presence of situational impairments are relatively unexplored, particularly for text entry.

Figure 1. Visualizaton of key presses with WalkType (*left*) and without WalkType (*right*) collected while users were walking during model-building, showing touch points for "N", "R" and "S". Correct key-press classifications are in green; errors are in red. In our study, WalkType (*left*) corrected 90.1% of the errors.

In this paper, we present *WalkType* (Figure 1), a system that uses a touch screen device's built-in accelerometer to increase text entry accuracy while the user is walking. Taking inspiration from image stabilization techniques of cameras to remove motion blur (*e.g.*, [5]), WalkType compensates for imprecise input by incorporating multiple features computed from the accelerometer data: displacement, acceleration, and inference about the user's movement. Additionally, WalkType uses tap location and the finger travel distance during taps to improve the user's text entry accuracy, features that increase overall accuracy regardless of movement. Previous work on adaptive text entry has largely focused on adjusting key-press probabilities based on language models [7,13,14]. To our knowledge, taking into account the user's motion through accelerometer or other sensor data has not been explored.

To design and build WalkType, we first collected touch screen typing data from 16 participants. Based on this data, we built two key-press classification models that incorporate accelerometer information. In simulations, these models improved classification accuracy over a control condition from 72.8% to 94.6% and 95.7%, respectively. While some improvement occurred for both walking and sitting, walking received an additional 4.8% increase in accuracy. The final WalkType prototype is a composite of these two models and a third more basic model that together achieved an accuracy of 97.3%.

We evaluated the final WalkType system in a controlled study with 16 participants, 5 of whom had also participated in our model-building study. Our findings show that WalkType improves typing performance for both sitting and walking, but that the benefits are greatest for walking. WalkType improved text entry speed compared to a control condition from 28.3 to 31.1 words per minute (WPM). Uncorrected error rate [37] also improved, particularly for walking, where average error rate dropped from 10.5% to 5.8% with WalkType. Finally, WalkType was highly preferred by participants, who recognized its performance benefits despite there being no visual difference between WalkType and the control interface.

The main contribution of this paper is a demonstration that accelerometer data *can* be used to improve typing performance on mobile devices when the user is situationally-impaired due to walking. This contribution comes in three parts: (1) an exploration of key-press classification models for improving mobile touch screen typing; (2) WalkType itself and its component models that incorporate accelerometer data; and (3) an evaluation of WalkType, showing that it significantly improves user typing performance over a standard touch screen keyboard, particularly while the user is walking.

RELATED WORK

We draw motivation from prior research exploring solutions to make interaction with devices easier while walking and while experiencing situational impairments. In addition, we draw on work on screen content stabilization.

Situational Impairments and Walking User Interfaces

The importance of accounting for the context in which a mobile device is used has been stressed by numerous researchers (*e.g.*, [18]). Walking has been shown to affect both input and output with mobile devices. Mizobuchi *et al.* [29] evaluated how increasing size of target buttons could improve text entry performance while walking. Lin *et al.* [25] studied the effect of walking on stylus tapping, and found that performance decreased while walking. Yesilada *et al.* [44] demonstrated that the number of errors made by an unimpaired user on a mobile device was similar to a motor-impaired desktop user. Consequently, existing techniques for motor-impaired users may be useful in accommodating situational impairments on mobile devices. Kane *et al.* [20] proposed an auto-correction system to help motor-impaired typists. Mobile devices can also impact the user's ability to read information. For example, walking has been shown to have a negative effect on both text legibility [30] and reading comprehension [1].

To address the foregoing challenges, techniques have been proposed to bridge the gap between stationary and walking interaction. For example, Brewster *et al.* [4] used audio feedback to improve touch screen interaction while standing and walking. Bragdon *et al.* [3] evaluated touch screen gestures in mobile environments, and established that gestures starting on the screen border as a reference point are not "significantly affected by the environment." Taking an adaptive approach, Kane *et al.* [21] coined the term *walking user interfaces (WUIs)* and evaluated a method to automatically enlarge soft buttons when users are walking versus stationary. Yamabe and Takahashi [42] used accelerometer information to automatically adapt the size of fonts and images while walking. Yatani and Truong [43] investigated how two-handed chorded keyboard input could improving using a stylus-based PDA while walking.

Touch Screen Text Entry and Adaptive Keyboards

A plethora of touch screen text entry techniques have been developed for both finger and stylus input. Prior work [28] provides a full review. Approaches to improve text entry performance with QWERTY keyboard layouts have been proposed, for example, using geometric pattern matching [23] and gestures [22]. Of particular relevance to our work are approaches that combine *language model* predictions with probabilities from a *touch model* (*e.g.*, [13,14]) to improve overall input accuracy. Language model predictions for the next letter to be typed have been used to resize keys, either visibly [7] or invisibly, that is, without showing the adaptation to the user [14]. (Apple's iPhone uses this approach.) Gunawardana *et al.* [14] ran a simulation study demonstrating the usefulness of key *anchoring* when the language model predictions are invisible. That is, regardless of the changing predicted letter probabilities, a center (anchor) area on the visible key always returns that letter, ensuring that a "direct hit" on the key by a user's finger provides a predictable result. We use this approach in WalkType.

As with WalkType, others have proposed techniques that use models of key-press distributions built on aggregate typing data collected from users. Most commonly, bivariate Gaussian distributions have been used to model individual keys [13,14,33]. A small number of projects have introduced models that adapt to individual typing patterns. A simulation study by Rudchenko *et al.* [33] showed that a *personalized* key-press model using bivariate Gaussian distributions for each key improved performance over an aggregate model. Adapting the location of keys based on the centroid of the user's previous key presses has also been studied for larger devices [12,16], but no performance benefits have been found in user evaluations.

Accelerometer-Based Input

Researchers have leveraged accelerometers for tasks ranging from scrolling and changing screen orientation [17], to mapping the speed of the cursor on a mobile device to the inferred degree of tilt [38]. Novel text entry techniques using an accelerometer as the primary source of input have also been proposed [19,31,34,39]. In general, these techniques have relatively high error rates and are meant for specialized contexts where touch screen keyboards may not be available. TiltType [31] and TiltText [39], for example, use combinations of tilting and button-pressing for entering letters. Our system, in contrast, uses accelerometer data as an additional source of information to improve typing on a standard QWERTY layout.

Screen Content Stabilization

WalkType derives motivation from the image stabilization techniques broadly found in digital cameras. There has been extensive research in countering user motion in image and video capture. Researchers have worked to remove effects of camera shake for images [8,24]. Similar techniques have also been used by researchers to stabilize contents of a screen. Behringer [2] addressed the problem of shaking displays in moving vehicles by dynamically shifting screen content. Similarly, *NoShake* [32] utilizes the accelerometer of a smartphone to perform content stabilization by dynamically moving screen content.

Finally, of particular relevance to walking-based situational impairments, Crossan *et al.* [6] leveraged an accelerometer to analyze in which phase of a user's gait he or she more comfortable interacting with a stylus-based PDA, and which areas of the screen are more error-prone. Although their approach is relevant to our work, Crossan *et al.* studied simpler target selection tasks than for keyboarding.

THE DESIGN OF *WALKTYPE*

WalkType uses multiple sources of information to classify a user's finger-touches as key-presses. Among these sources is data from the device's built-in accelerometer, which is used to account for extraneous movement while the user is walking. In this section, we outline WalkType and the process taken to build it, including a study to collect training data from 16 participants. In the next section, we describe a controlled study of the final WalkType system.

Model-Building

Along with accelerometer data, WalkType uses tap locations and tap travel distance to better predict the intended key. The Weka machine learning toolkit[1] was used to generate two J4.8 Decision Tree models with pruning confidence set to Weka's default (0.25). For classification, the first model used time-domain accelerometer data between taps and the second model used the pattern of accelerometer data generated from the three axes due to the phone's motion while walking. The final WalkType system combined output from both of these models along with a simple Euclidian model. Our analysis showed that this composite model performed better than individual models.

For clarity, we use the term *Euclidian model* throughout this paper to refer to a simple key-press classification model that takes as input the (x, y) coordinate of a finger-touch and returns the letter whose corresponding key's visual bounds contain those coordinates.

The models were built based on typing data collected from 16 participants (10 males, 6 females) who each volunteered for a 45-minute study session. All participants self-rated as expert computer users and intermediate to expert touch screen smartphone users. They were between 21 and 35 years of age ($M = 28.69$, $SD = 4.48$).

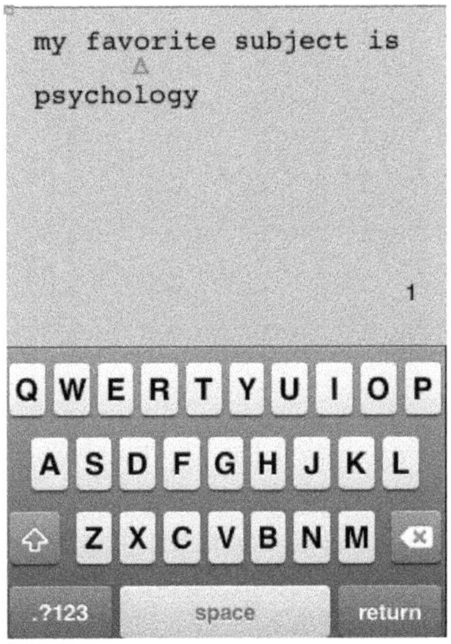

Figure 2. In *WalkType Collect*, the user was only given feedback about whether they pressed a key or not. The red triangular cursor moved forward after every key-press.

We built a custom data collection application, *WalkType Collect*, for the iPhone 3GS that records the device's movement using the on-device low-noise tri-axis accelerometer. We wanted to elicit natural typing patterns and did not want participants to be overly concerned with the accuracy of their input. Thus, we followed the approaches of Gunawardana *et al.* [14] and Findlater *et al.* [9] and created Collect's keyboard in such a way that it only gave the user feedback *that a tap had occurred*, but not where it occurred or what key had been hit. To convey this feedback, a small cursor moved under the phrase as the user typed. Figure 2 shows an example. If the user realized that they were off by a character or two while typing, they could swipe from right to left anywhere on the screen to delete one tap at a time. Participants were instructed to try to delete their tap when they knew they had made an obvious mistake or when they felt they were off by a character or two. We requested participants not to go back through the whole phrase in order to correct a supposed error. Participants were asked to enter 50 phrases in 2 postures, sitting and walking, while holding the device with both hands and typing with both thumbs. The order of postures was counterbalanced and participants were randomly assigned to orders. Short phrases of English text from MacKenzie and Soukoreff's phrase set [27] were used. Apart from these, every fifth phrase was a randomly

[1] http://www.cs.waikato.ac.nz/ml/weka

selected pangram from a list of 35 pangrams to ensure sufficient data for all letters of the alphabet.

The lack of tap-location feedback meant that users made mistakes while entering text, which added noise to our data. Thus, outliers were removed during post-processing by eliminating all taps that landed outside the Euclidean bounds of the intended key or its immediate neighbors. Figure 3 shows filtered data for one participant for the "H" key. About 2.5% taps were filtered out in this process.

Figure 3. Tap filtering for letter "H". Taps not on the intended key or its immediate neighbors are filtered out (in red).

The logs from Collect contained tap-start and tap-end locations, amount of travel while tapping, the time interval between taps, the intended key, and temporal accelerometer data. The touch-screen-based features (*tap location, tap travel* and *time elapsed* between taps) form the *base set* of classification features used in both models described in the next two subsections. We chose to include tap travel and time elapsed in this set based on observations we made while developing Collect. For tap travel, we observed that, at times, the tap-start and tap-end locations were not the same, yielding a potential feature to increase classification accuracy. For time elapsed, we observed that typing speed appeared to impact the user's input accuracy: the tendency to type the wrong key was relatively low when typing slowly compared to more quickly.

Displacement and Acceleration Model

We hypothesized that one of the major reasons for inaccuracy in typing while walking is the general movement of the phone and its displacement from a relatively stable location with respect to the user. Based on this hypothesis, the Displacement and Acceleration Model improves tap accuracy by incorporating acceleration features in all three axes, and magnitude and direction of displacement in the z-axis. To calculate these features, the data from the smartphone's on-device accelerometer was first passed through a low-pass filter to remove noise. This model also includes the base set of features.

To calculate the acceleration features, the filtered accelerometer data was resampled to 10 samples between two consecutive taps. We selected this sampling rate as it gave reasonable resolution and did not overly increase the number of attributes for the classifier. These 10 samples of (x, y, z) values constitute 30 features for the model. When dealing with accelerometer data, it is often necessary to compensate for gravitational pull on the three axes. We found this compensation unnecessary because phone orientation stays relatively constant while typing.

For the displacement magnitude and direction features in the z-axis, we first subtracted the mean acceleration from the filtered data and then double-integrated it using the cumulative sum. The direction in which the phone moved in the z-axis was also calculated. To do so, we compared the device's instantaneous acceleration with the moving mean acceleration of the device. If the instantaneous acceleration was less than the mean, we inferred that the device was moving forward. Otherwise, it was moving backward.

We conducted a 10-fold cross-validation on the WalkType Collect data to evaluate the Displacement and Acceleration Model. The model improved classification accuracy on average from 72.8% (for the Euclidian model) to 94.6%. This is a significant increase in overall accuracy (paired-samples t-test: $t_{15} = 22.23$, $p < .001$). To evaluate the benefit of the accelerometer data, we also tested this model after removing all accelerometer features. Classification accuracy dropped to 90.8% on average, which was a significant decrease (paired-samples t-test: $t_{15} = 12.95$, $p < .001$). See Figure 4 for a comparison of all models, including the Displacement and Acceleration Model.

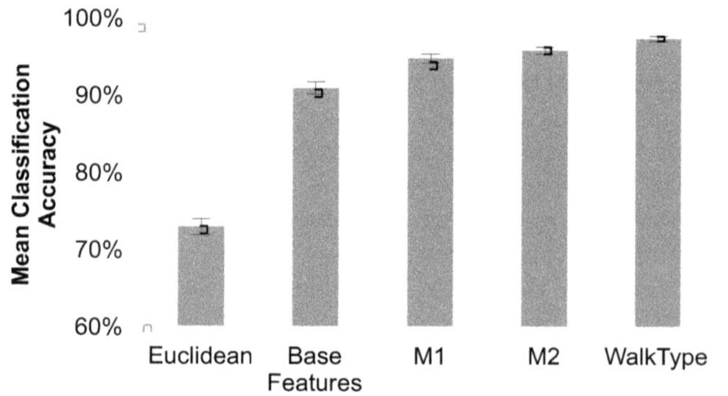

Figure 4. Classification accuracy with different models. M1 is the Displacement and Acceleration Model and M2 is the Walking Pattern Model. The difference in performance of Base Features and WalkType illustrates the benefit of the accelerometer data. Error bars show standard error.

Walking Pattern Model

In analyzing the Collect data, we observed that the phone oscillated in a largely repeatable pattern while a user was walking and typing. Figure 5 shows one such instance of the pattern in the z-axis. The Walktype Pattern Model leverages the on-device accelerometer to obtain this pattern in all three axes. In addition to the base set of classification features, it incorporates four new features per axis. Crossan *et al.* [6] observed a similar pattern and analyzed how it could be used to detect phases where the user is more comfortable performing target selection with a stylus. We use different techniques as a user's interaction with a device while typing is very different while walking.

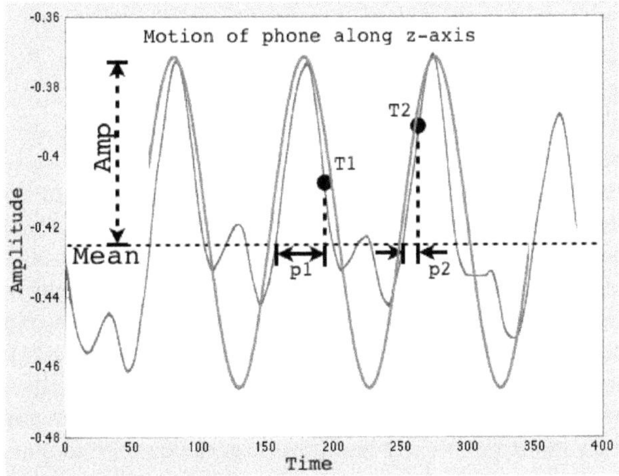

Figure 5. Motion of the phone along *z*-axis when the user is walking. T1 and T2 are two instances of taps; p1 and p2 are the elapsed times since the signal crossed the mean. The waveform in red is part of the dominant frequency wave.

To make the model adaptive to different walking speeds, we calculated the dominant frequency (*e.g.*, red wave in Figure 5) of the user's motion and its mean amplitude from all three axes. This gives us a proxy for detecting changes in the user's speed and intensity of movement. To calculate the instantaneous dominant frequency, we took the Fast Fourier Transform (FFT) of the accelerometer signal and found the frequency with the maximum amplitude. This *frequency* and *amplitude* constitute the first two features. For the third feature, the *direction* of the last mean crossing before the current tap gives a measure of the direction in which the device is moving. Finally, to pinpoint where in the pattern a tap event occurs, we use the *elapsed time* since the accelerometer signal crossed the mean value of the signal, as demonstrated in Figure 5.

These features in the *x*-axis are particularly useful in detecting the user's footstep pattern. We observed that when users' feet hit the ground, their taps tended to shift slightly towards the center of the keyboard. We also observed that a shift to the left was more common when the left foot hit the ground, and a shift to the right was more common when the right foot hit (Figure 6). When we do the analysis shown in Figure 5 on the *x*-axis data, we can detect which foot strikes the ground. If the current *x*-axis data is less than the mean, then the user's left foot has landed, and vice-versa for the right foot. Because the effect of the foot-strike on the user's accuracy would attenuate over time, we also calculated the time since the last foot hit the ground. This calculation was performed in exactly the same way as for the *z*-axis (Figure 5).

We provide the classifier with the tap location on the screen, the direction in which the phone is going in *y*- and *z*-axes, and the last foot that struck the ground. We also provide three temporal components denoting time since the last change in direction in the three axes. On 10-fold cross-validation with the Collect data, the Walking Pattern Model outperformed the Displacement and Acceleration Model with a mean classification accuracy of 95.7% compared to 94.6%, a significant difference ($t_{15} = 5.11, p < .001$).

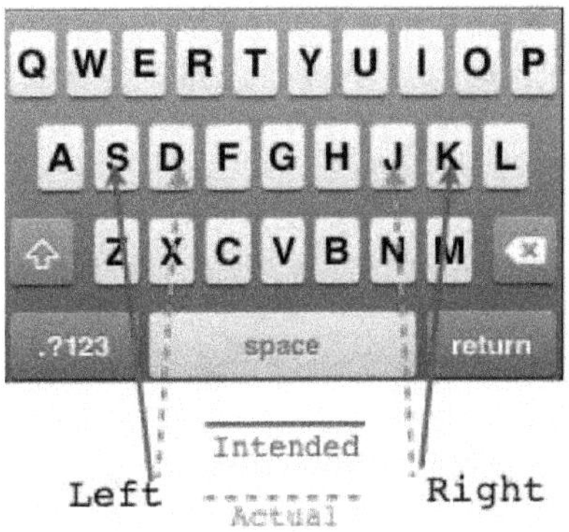

Figure 6. The Walking Pattern Model takes into account error in typing when the user's left or right foot just strikes the ground.

Combined WalkType Model

The Combined WalkType Model is a composite of the three sub-models: the Displacement and Acceleration Model, the Walking Pattern Model, and the Euclidean Model. A majority voting approach is used, whereby for each finger-touch, the key selected by at least two of the three internal models is output to the text stream. When all three models disagree, the Walking Pattern Model prevails, since it model performed the best in isolation on the WalkType Collect data. Figure 7 shows a block diagram detailing the approach. The Euclidian Model is included because, although classification accuracy was high for both of the accelerometer-based models, some keys become major sources of errors as they got masked by adjacent keys. An example confusion matrix is shown in Figure 8. Here a more frequently occurring key dominates adjacent keys, for example, "A" dominates "S". To counter this problem we combined the two models along with the Euclidean model. As mentioned earlier, the Euclidean model selects the key containing tap location. Although simple and non-adaptive, this model increases the probability of less-frequently occurring keys like "W" being correctly classified.

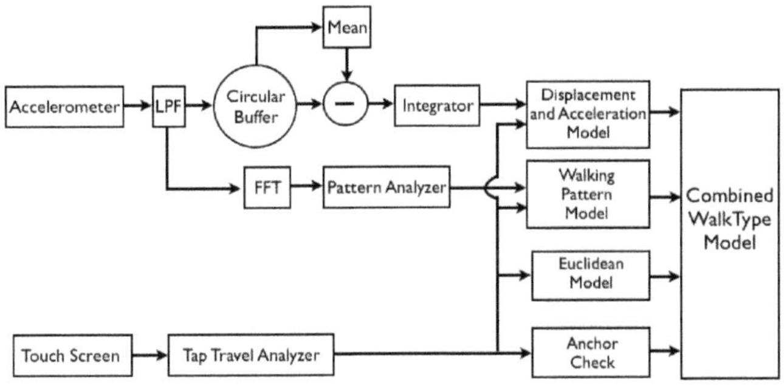

Figure 7. Block diagram of major components of WalkType's Model Building phase.

The mean classification accuracy of the Combined WalkType Model is 97%, significantly higher than both the Displacement and Acceleration Model and the Walking Pattern Model (paired two-tailed *t*-tests, respectively: $t_{15} = 6.51, p < .001$; $t_{15} = 5.94, p < .001$).

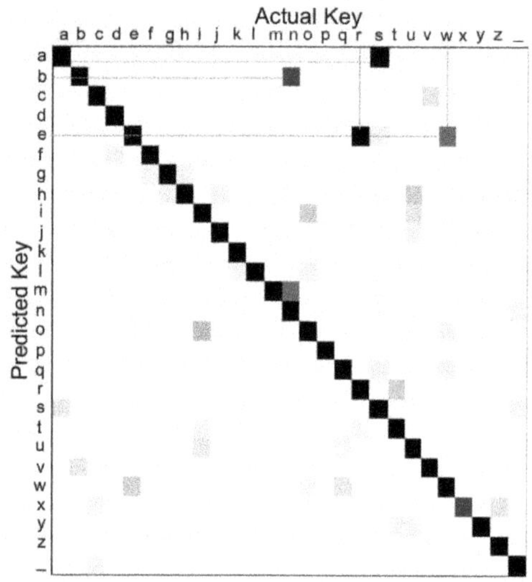

Figure 8. Frequently occurring keys dominate adjacent keys. 's' is dominated by 'a', 'r' & 'w' are dominated by 'e'.

The Combined Walktype model also incorporates key-target anchoring [14]. After incorporating the three models, there were still taps that, although clearly landing in a key's center, did not get classified correctly. Gunawardana *et al.* [14] addressed this issue in the context of adjusting key-press probabilities based on a language model. Their work demonstrated that anchoring some part of the key increases overall typing accuracy. We thus define an anchor area in the middle of each visual key; a tap within that anchor area bypasses the classification models and instead returns the visual key. We reserved the central 20% along the *x*-axis and 50% along the *y*-axis of each key as the anchor area. Introducing anchors further increased the overall accuracy of the WalkType Combined model to 97.28% (significant compared to without anchors: $t_{15} = 5.193, p < .001$).

This final model was used in *WalkType*. Referring back to Figure 4 shows the cumulative improvement in accuracy for each component within this final model. In a verification step, we confirmed that the accelerometer features are, indeed, a critical component of WalkType. Removing these features drops classification accuracy by 6.8% (SD = 2.6) on average across participants.

WalkType Online

All simulations in the previous section were run offline with Weka. The final step in the process of creating WalkType was to port the model to an iPhone 3G for online use and evaluation. To do so, we first ported the classification models generated by Weka into the iPhone and then optimized and synchronized their operations to work in real-time. The online version of WalkType first filters the accelerometer data, and then sends it to the Combined WalkType Model for classification.

EVALUATION

While the model-building phase demonstrated the potential of WalkType to improve key-press classification accuracy, the goal of our controlled evaluation was to see whether our simulation results would transfer to a real typing task. In particular, we sought to see whether WalkType would lessen the text entry performance degradation incurred by walking compared to sitting.

Participants

Sixteen participants (8 male, 8 female) ranging in age from 21 to 40 years (M = 29.7, SD = 5.7) were recruited. Five of these participants also participated in the model-building study. All participants had more than 10 years of experience with computers and self-rated as intermediate to expert computer users. Fourteen participants were near-expert touch screen smartphone users with approximately 2-3 years' worth of use. Two participants did not own touch screen smartphones and had little experience with them.

Apparatus

Participants used our custom experiment software on an Apple iPhone 3GS that has a 3.5-inch capacitive screen with 480 × 380 pixels. The application was developed using Objective-C. It recorded all of the users' screen interactions as well as movement data from the accelerometer.

Figure 9 shows a screenshot. The presented phrase appears atop the screen, wrapping onto a second line if necessary. Entered text, in dark blue for contrast, appears immediately below. When the user types a key, keystroke feedback is displayed at the top of the keyboard exactly above the position where the user tapped. Because WalkType uses finger-travel and elapsed time as features, the decision of which key was pressed occurs when the user lifts his or her finger. Accordingly, we modified the key-press feedback to occur when the finger is lifted, as opposed to when the user touches the screen, as occurs for the built-in iPhone keyboard. In the bottom-right corner of the text area, the current trial number is displayed, with a trial being equal to one phrase. Finally, the backspace functionality for the keyboard was also modified: a swipe anywhere on the screen from right-to-left backspaced one character.

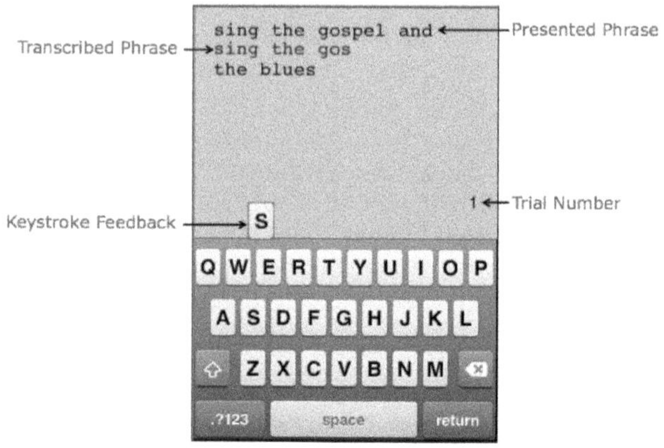

Figure 9. Testing interface showing the presented phrase, transcribed phrase, trial number and keystroke feedback.

Procedure

The procedure was designed to fit in a single 45-minute session. Each session began with an introduction to the tasks and experiment software. Participants were asked to familiarize themselves with the application and to ask any clarifying questions. This learning phase lasted approximately 5 minutes, until the user was comfortable with the system and had completed at least 5 phrases without assistance. For the walking tasks, we followed an approach similar to Kane *et al.* [21], wherein participants followed a human pacesetter, remaining within 3-5 feet. To simulate a routine and unconstrained environment, the pacesetter ensured that the walking speed was consistent at about 1.07 m/s (3.51 feet/s), a pace that comfortably accommodates a wide range of age and abilities [10]. The walking tasks were performed in a relatively quiet corridor of a university building.

For each condition, participants completed 30 test phrases, 24 of which were randomly selected from the MacKenzie and Soukoreff phrase set [27]. Apart from these, every fifth phrase was a randomly selected pangram to cover all letters in the alphabet. Participants were asked to hold the phone in both hands and type with their thumbs. We asked participants to type quickly and accurately, and to fix errors unless those errors were noticed "far behind" their current point of entry. Finally, participants were requested to complete each trial without failing to keep walking and were offered a rest period at the end of each trial.

Design & Analysis

The study was a within-subjects 2×2 factorial design. The factors and levels were:

- ***Interface***: *WalkType* and *Control*. Both interfaces used the same experiment software but the underlying key-press classification models were different. WalkType used the final combined model from the previous section, while Control was non-adaptive, using only the Euclidian model.
- ***Posture***: *Walking* and *Sitting*.

Presentation of the interfaces was counterbalanced. Within each interface, postures were also counterbalanced. With 30 trials (test phrases) in each condition, participants performed 2×2×30=120 trials each, for a total of 1920 trials in the study. Overall, we collected 57,663 key presses from 16 participants.

The main measures were speed, calculated as words per minute (WPM), and uncorrected error rate, following Soukoreff and MacKenzie [37]. Uncorrected errors represent those errors left in the transcribed text. Corrected errors, which are errors made during entry, are of less interest, as such errors slow WPM and are thus subsumed by it. Also, to evaluate whether participants could perceive any difference between the two systems, at the end of the session we asked them to rate which one of the two systems they preferred and why. To guard against any bias, participants were not initially made aware of which keyboard was Control and which was WalkType.

To calculate WPM and uncorrected error rate, we used *StreamAnalyzer* [41]. Statistical analyses were done using SPSS 19. We tested for effects of presentation order on the main measure of typing speed using a 3-way ANOVA with *presentation order* of the interfaces as a between-subjects factor and *Interface* and *Posture* as within-subjects factors. No main effect of presentation order was found, indicating that overall counterbalancing was effective. However, there was an asymmetric skill transfer: a significant interaction occurred between presentation order and *Interface* on typing speed ($F_{1,14}$ = 5.569, p = .032, η^2 = .288). The control condition benefited more when it followed WalkType than vice versa. Since this asymmetric skill transfer only injures WalkType's performance relative to the control condition, we are confident that our comparisons are still trustworthy. We present results from a 2-way repeated measures ANOVA with *Interface* and *Posture* as within-subjects factors.

For uncorrected error rate, we used the nonparametric Aligned Rank Transform [15,40] with *Interface* and *Posture* as within-subjects factors. We used this nonparametric procedure because uncorrected error rate is highly skewed toward zero and violates normality. All pairwise comparisons were protected against Type I error using a Bonferroni adjustment.

RESULTS

Speed (WPM)

Speed results are shown in Figure 10. Overall, WalkType improved typing speed regardless of whether the user was sitting or walking: on average 31.1 WPM (*SD* = 10.7) compared to 28.3 WPM (*SD* = 9.6) in the control condition. This difference was significant, as seen in a main effect of *Interface* on typing speed ($F_{1,15}$ = 6.777, p = .020, η^2 = .311). No significant main effect of *Posture* was found.

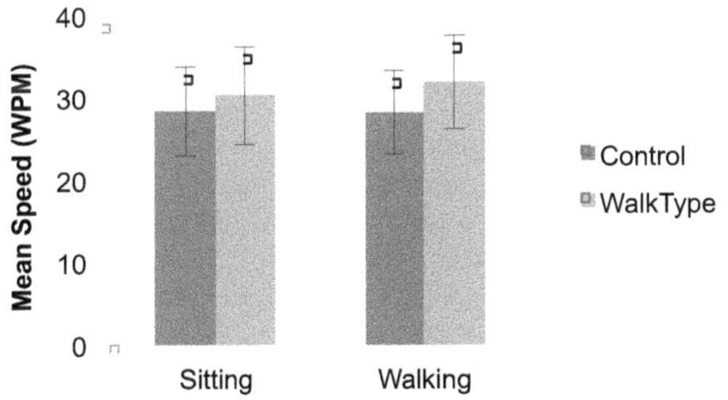

Figure 10. WalkType resulted in higher typing speeds than the control condition, particularly while participants were walking. Error bars are 95% confidence intervals.

We had expected WalkType to improve performance more for walking than for sitting, which would be seen through an interaction of *Interface* × *Posture* on typing speed. This interaction was only a trend ($F_{1,15}$ = 3.485, p = .082, η^2 = .189). Based on our hypotheses, however, we conducted pairwise comparisons of the two interfaces within each level of *Posture*. (See Games [11] for justification of pairwise comparisons on trend-level effects.)

Pairwise comparisons showed that participants benefited more using WalkType while walking than while sitting. For walking, WalkType improved typing speed by 12.9% compared to the control interface, which was a significant difference (p = .002). For sitting, in contrast, no significant difference was found between the two interfaces (p = .166).

Uncorrected Error Rate
Figure 11 shows mean error rates per condition. Mirroring the speed results, participants exhibited a marked improvement in error rate while using WalkType. A main effect was found for *Interface* on error rate, indicating that, overall, WalkType significantly reduced errors compared to the control condition ($F_{1,15}$ = 22.339, p < .001, η^2 = .598). *Posture* also significantly affected error rate, with walking resulting in increased errors compared to sitting ($F_{1,15}$ = 9.316, p = .008, η^2 = .383).

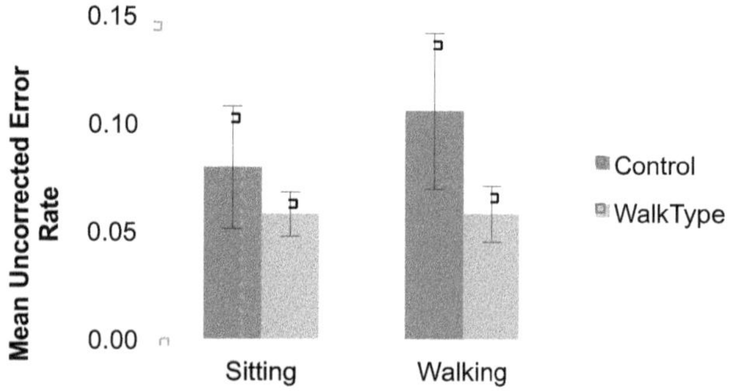

Figure 11. WalkType resulted in lower error rates than Control, especially for walking. Error bars are 95% confidence intervals.

Of perhaps more interest is how WalkType impacted errors compared to the control condition while walking. A significant *Interface* × *Posture* interaction for error rate showed that the effectiveness of the interfaces differed by posture ($F_{1,15}$ = 13.139, p = .002, η^2 = .472). Pairwise comparisons revealed that WalkType was particularly effective at accommodating the situational impairments introduced by movement. Compared to the control condition, error rates decreased from 10.5% to 5.8% with WalkType, which was a significant difference (p = .004). No significant difference in error rate was found between the two interfaces for sitting.

Preference
At the end of the study we asked participants which of the two interfaces they preferred. Preferences reflected performance results, with 14 out of 16 participants choosing WalkType over Control ($\chi^2_{(1,N=16)}$ = 7.56, p = .006).

DISCUSSION

Our goal was to develop an adaptive soft keyboard that leverages accelerometer data to compensate for the situational impairments introduced while walking. WalkType successfully improved both typing speed and error rates, particularly for users walking. On average, WalkType improved typing speed by 12.9% and reduced uncorrected error rates by 45.2% while participants were walking. Although there were no visual differences between the control interface and WalkType, participants perceived the performance benefit of WalkType and overwhelmingly preferred it to the control condition.

The Combined WalkType Model uses a majority voting approach between the three models. We also tried to combine these models into one single model with one decision tree, but the performance of the system decreased considerably because the number of features increased and became unwieldy.

The WalkType models were built using data collected both while participants were walking and while they were sitting. While experimenting with different models, we observed that using only the training data from walking further increased classification accuracy for walking, but *decreased* accuracy for sitting. Based on this finding, we combined the two datasets for the final WalkType model. However, detecting whether a user is walking or sitting and dynamically switching between different models—one trained on walking data and one trained on sitting data—would likely provide a further performance benefit.

Our analysis showed that the major source of incorrect classification was confusion between adjacent keys in the same row. We created a confusion matrix on the basis of our classification results and found that 72.8% of incorrect classifications were of adjacent keys. Further examination into whether misclassifications occurred more towards the left or right sides of the keyboard showed that misclassifications occurred about evenly in this regard. The split of same-row errors was 48.4% to the right of the intended key and 51.6% to the left. This predominance of same-row confusion shows that it was easier for users to reliably hit in the vertical direction compared to the horizontal direction. That users could do this was somewhat unexpected. While walking, most vibrations are along the y-axis, *i.e.*, the phone moves backward and forward more relative to the user. We anticipated, incorrectly, that this would lead to more inter-row misclassifications. (Thankfully, WalkType is data-driven, and thus it did not suffer for our misconception.)

Most researchers examining effects of walking on user interfaces do not use a pacesetter as we did, but either ask participants to "walk normally" or employ a treadmill [1,30,32]. Kane *et al.* [21] also used the pacesetter approach to make sure that participants walked at near constant speeds, while enabling them to be "off the treadmill" and in a natural context. Some of the features we have incorporated, such as the dominant frequency of the user's walking pattern and its amplitude, may be useful in adapting to different walking speeds. Additional testing is needed to determine how well WalkType performs with varying walking speeds and whether additional training data is needed to model that context.

During the model-building phase, we collected typing data in a condition where users were given feedback only as to whether they had hit a key, but not whether they hit the *correct* key. In comparison, in the final user study, participants saw which letters they had entered, which could have led them to more accurate typing behavior. This leads to an interesting conjecture—that training the system on more realistic data, like we collected in our evaluation, could further improve performance.

Finally, our study concentrates on the scenario where users hold the phone in both hands and type with their thumbs. It will also be interesting to explore how our models perform on data collected with users holding the phone in one hand and typing with the index finger of the other hand.

FUTURE WORK

The text entry improvements obtained by leveraging the accelerometer suggest a similar approach may be useful for mobile interaction more broadly. Stabilizing input with techniques similar to those proposed in our work, and making the device aware of users' movement patterns and gait may, for example, be useful in accounting for vibrations when users are trying to press a button or move a slider control.

Additional sensors may also be useful in further improving WalkType's classification model. We used only data from the accelerometer to infer device position and rotation. The obvious extension is to evaluate whether the built-in gyroscope would be better suited for inferring rotation.

Personalization is also a promising area of future work for WalkType. Our explorations of the WalkType training data indicate that personalized models, where the system is trained only on one user's data, may increase classification accuracy over models generated from data from all participants. A prior simulation study [33] on mobile touch screen typing data also supports this conjecture.

From our model-building data we observed that users were regularly off by a character when they tried to tap the keys on the borders of the screen, like "A", "Q", SPACE, *etc.* At times, participants' taps landed on the bezel of the device instead of on its keys. Our signal processing filtered out the vibrations caused by tapping of the screen while walking. We believe if we separate vibrations from walking and tapping, then there is potential to leverage the tapping vibrations to detect taps on the bezel and change the system's behavior accordingly, *e.g.*, by entering the most likely intended letter.

CONCLUSION

Using mobile devices in a variety of environments can lead to situational impairment due to, among other sources, vibration and divided attention. We have introduced WalkType, an adaptive system for mobile touch screen devices that leverages the on-device accelerometer to compensate for vibrations and extraneous movements caused by walking. We performed two studies with 16 participants each, first to collect the data for WalkType's model, and then to evaluate the generated models. WalkType increases users' typing speeds from 28.3 WPM to 31.3 WPM, and also reduces the number of uncorrected errors from 10.5% to 5.8% while participants are walking. While WalkType focused on touch screen text entry, its approach may be useful for mobile input in general.

ACKNOWLEDGMENTS

We thank Gaetano Borriello and Jon Froehlich. This work was supported in part by the National Science Foundation (NSF) under grant IIS-0811063. Any opinions, findings, conclusions or recommendations expressed in this work are those of the authors and do not necessarily reflect those of the National Science Foundation.

REFERENCES

1. Barnard, L., Yi, J.S., Jacko, J.A. and Sears, A. (2007). Capturing the effects of context on human performance in mobile computing systems. *Personal Ubiquitous Computing, 11* (2), 81-96.
2. Behringer, R. (2001). Stabilization of a Display in a Moving Environment. *Proc. Annual Federal Laboratory Symposium on Advanced Displays and Interactive Displays*, 131-134.
3. Bragdon, E., Nelson, E., Li, Y. and Hinckley, K. (2011). Experimental analysis of touch-screen gesture designs in mobile environments. *Proc. CHI '11.* New York: ACM Press, 403-412.
4. Brewster, S. (2002). Overcoming the lack of screen space on mobile computers. *Personal and Ubiquitous Computing, 6* (3), 188-205.
5. Canon Inc. What is Optical Image Stabilizer? Retrieved January 9, 2012 from http://www.canon.com/bctv/faq/optis.html
6. Crossan, A., Murray-Smith, R., Brewster, S., Kelly, J. and Musizza, B. (2005). Gait phase effects in mobile interaction. *Extended Abstracts CHI'05.* New York: ACM Press, 1312-1315.
7. Faraj, K.A., Mojahid, M., and Vigouroux, N. (2009). BigKey: A Virtual Keyboard for Mobile Devices. *Proc. HCI'09 Part III.* Berlin: Springer-Verlag, 3-10.
8. Fergus, R., Singh, B., Hertzmann, A., Roweis, S.T. and Freeman, W.T. (2006). Removing camera shake from a single photograph. *Proc. TOG'06.* New York: ACM Press, 787-794.
9. Findlater, L., Wobbrock, J.O. and Wigdor, D. (2011). Typing on Flat Glass: Examining Ten-finger Expert Typing Patterns on Touch Surfaces. *Proc. CHI'11.* New York: ACM Press, 2453-2462.
10. Fitzpatrick, K., M. A. Brewer, and S. M. Turner. (1982). Another Look at Pedestrian Walking Speed. *Journal of the Transportation Research Board, No. 1982*, 21-29.
11. Games, P.A. (1971). Multiple Comparisons of Means. *American Educational Research Journal*, 531–565.
12. Go, K., and Endo, Y. (2007). CATKey: customizable and adaptable touchscreen keyboard with bubble cursor-like visual feedback. *Proc. INTERACT'07.* Berlin: Springer-Verlag, 493-496.

13. Goodman, J., Venolia, G., Steury, J. and Parket, C. (2002). Language modeling for soft keyboards. *Proc. IUI'02.* New York: ACM Press, 194-195.
14. Gunawardana, A., Paek, T. and Meek, C. (2010). Usability Guided Key-Target Resizing for Soft Keyboards. *Proc. IUI'10.* New York: ACM Press, 111-118.
15. Higgins, J.J. and Tashtoush, S. (1994). An aligned rank transform test for interaction. *Nonlinear World 1* (2), 201-211
16. Himberg, J., Häkkilä, P., Kangas, P. and Mäntyjärvi, J. (2003). On-line personalization of a touch screen based keyboard. *Proc. IUI'03.* New York: ACM Press, 77-84.
17. Hinckley, K., Pierce, J., Sinclair, M. and Horvitz, E. (2000). Sensing techniques for mobile interaction. *Proc. UIST '00.* New York: ACM Press, 91-100.
18. Johnson, P. (1998). Usability and mobility: Interactions on the move. *Proc. Workshop on HCI with Mobile Devices.* Glasgow, Scotland, GIST Technical Report G98-1.
19. Jones, E., Alexander, J., Andreou,A., Irani, P. and Subramanian, S. (2010). GesText: accelerometer-based gestural text-entry systems. *Proc. CHI '10.* New York: ACM Press, 2173-2182.
20. Kane, S.K., Wobbrock, J.O., Harniss, M. and Johnson, K.L. (2008). TrueKeys: Identifying and correcting typing errors for people with motor impairments. *Proc. IUI '08.* New York: ACM Press, 349-352.
21. Kane, S.K., Wobbrock, J.O. and Smith, I.E. (2008). Getting Off the Treadmill: Evaluating Walking User Interfaces for Mobile Devices in Public Spaces. *Proc. MobileHCI'08.* New York: ACM Press, 109-118.
22. Kristensson, P. and Zhai, S. (2004). Shark: A large vocabulary shorthand writing system for pen-based computers. *Proc. UIST '04.* New York: ACM Press, 43-52.
23. Kristensson, P. and Zhai, S. (2005). Relaxing stylus typing precision by geometric pattern matching. *Proc. IUI '05.* New York: ACM Press, 151-158.
24. Kundur, D. and Hatzinakos, D. (1996). Blind image deconvolution. *IEEE Signal Processing Magazine 13* (6), 43-64.
25. Lin, M., Goldman, R., Price, K.J., Sears, A. and Jacko, J. (2007). How do people tap when walking? An empirical investigation of nomadic data entry. *International Journal of Human-Computer Studies 65* (9), 759-769.
26. MacKay, B., Dearman, D., Inkpen, K. and Watters, C. (2005). Walk 'n Scroll: A Comparison of Software-based Navigation Techniques for Different Levels of Mobility. *Proc. MobileHCI'05.* New York: ACM Press, 183-190.
27. MacKenzie, I.S. and Soukoreff, R.W. (2003). Phrase sets for evaluating text entry techniques. *Extended Abstracts CHI'03.* New York: ACM Press, 754-755.
28. MacKenzie, I.S., Soukoreff, R.W. (2002). Text Entry for Mobile Computing: Models and Methods, Theory and Practice. *Human-Computer Interaction 17* (2-3), 147-198.
29. Mizobuchi, S., Chignell, M. and Newton, D. (2005). Mobile Text Entry: Relationship between Walking Speed and Text Input Task Difficulty. *Proc. MobileHCI'05.* New York: ACM Press, 122-128.
30. Mustonen, T., Olkkonen, M. and Hakkinen, J. (2004). Examining Mobile Phone Text Legibility while Walking. *Proc. CHI'04.* New York: ACM Press, 1243-1246.
31. Partridge, K., Chatterjee, S., Sazawal, V., Borriello, G. and Want, R. (2002). TiltType: accelerometer-supported text entry for very small devices. *Proc. UIST'02.* New York: ACM Press, 201-204.
32. Rahmati, A., Shepard, C. and Zhong, L. (2009). Noshake: Content stabilization for shaking screens of mobile devices. *Proc. PerCom'2009.* Washington DC: IEEE, 1-6.
33. Rudchenko, D., Paek, T. and Badger, E. (2011). Text Text Revolution: A Game That Improves Text Entry on Mobile Touchscreen Keyboards. *Proc. Pervasive'11.* Berlin: Springer-Verlag, 206-213.
34. Sazawal, V., Want, R., and Borriello, G. (2002). The Unigesture Approach. *Proc. MobileHCI '02.* New York: ACM Press, 256-270.
35. Sears, A., Lin, M., Jacko, J. and Xiao, Y. (2003). When computers fade: Pervasive computing and situationally-induced impairments and disabilities. *Proc. HCI'03.* Marwah: Lawrence Erlbaum Associates, 1298-1302.
36. Shildbach, B. and Rukzio, E. (2010). Investigating selection and reading performance on a mobile phone while walking. *Proc. MobileHCI'10.* New York: ACM Press, 93-102.
37. Soukoreff, R.W. and MacKenzie, I.S. (2003). Metrics for text entry research: An evaluation of MSD and KSPC, and a new unified error metric. *Proc. CHI'03.* New York: ACM Press, 113-120.
38. Weberg, L., Brange, T. and Hansson, Å. W. (2001). A piece of butter on the PDA display. *Extended Abstracts CHI'01.* New York: ACM Press, 435-436.
39. Wigdor, D. and Balakrishnan, R. (2003). TiltText: using tilt for text input to mobile phones. *Proc. UIST'03.* New York: ACM Press, 81-90.
40. Wobbrock, J.O., Findlater, L., Gergle, D., and Higgins, J.J. (2011). The Aligned Rank Transform for nonparametric factorial analyses using only ANOVA procedures. *Proc. CHI'11.* New York: ACM Press, 143-146.
41. Wobbrock, J.O. and Myers, B.A. (2006). Analyzing the input stream for character-level errors in unconstrained text entry evaluations. *ACM Transactions on Computer-Human Interaction 13* (4), 458-489.
42. Yamabe, T. and Takahashi, K. (2007). Experiments in Mobile User Interface Adaptation for Walking Users. *Proc. IPC'07.* Los Alamitos, California: IEEE Computer Society, 280-284.
43. Yatani, K. and Truong, K.N. (2009). An Evaluation of Stylus-based Text Entry Methods on Handheld Devices Studied in Different Mobility States. *Pervasive and Mobile Computing 5* (5), 496-506.
44. Yesilada, Y., Harper, S., Chen, T. and Trewin, S. (2010). Small-device users situationally impaired by input. *Computers in Human Behavior* 26 (3), 427-435.

Codelets: Linking Interactive Documentation and Example Code in the Editor

Stephen Oney
Carnegie Mellon University
Pittsburgh, PA 15213 USA
soney@cs.cmu.edu

Joel Brandt
Adobe Systems
San Francisco, CA 94103 USA
joel.brandt@adobe.com

ABSTRACT

Programmers frequently use instructive code examples found on the Web to overcome cognitive barriers while programming. These examples couple the concrete functionality of code with rich contextual information about how the code works. However, using these examples necessitates understanding, configuring, and integrating the code, all of which typically take place after the example enters the user's code and has been removed from its original instructive context. In short, *a user's interaction with an example continues well after the code is pasted.* This paper investigates whether treating examples as "first-class" objects in the code editor — rather than simply as strings of text — will allow programmers to use examples more effectively. We explore this through the creation and evaluation of *Codelets*. A Codelet is presented inline with the user's code, and consists of a block of example code and an interactive helper widget that assists the user in understanding and integrating the example. The Codelet persists throughout the example's lifecycle, remaining accessible even after configuration and integration is done. A comparative laboratory study with 20 participants found that programmers were able to complete tasks involving examples an average of 43% faster when using Codelets than when using a standard Web browser.

Author Keywords: programming, example, documentation, structured editing

ACM Classification Keywords
H.5.2. [Information interfaces and presentation]: User Interfaces - Training, help, and documentation;

General Terms: Design, Human Factors.

INTRODUCTION

Instructive code examples play a central role in programmers' work practice [3,15,30]. Blocks of example code found in library documentation [15] and Web resources — such as blogs, forums, and code search engines [34] — help meet both learning and productivity needs [25]. These examples couple a concrete piece of functionality, usually implemented in 5–20 lines of code, with contextual information such as a written description of how the code works [2]. One data point suggests that when programmers are learning new libraries, as much as one-third of their code is directly taken from examples in documentation [33]. Even when a concept is well understood, programmers often choose to copy and paste examples rather than write code from scratch to save time and avoid errors [3].

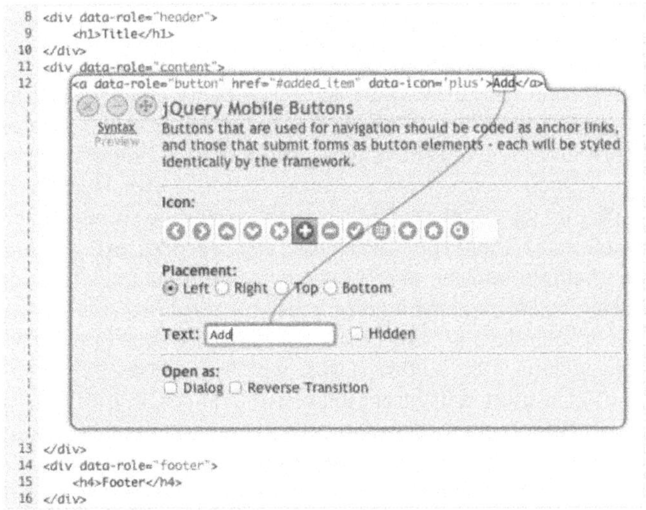

Figure 1. Codelets attach helpers to regions of code. Helpers are displayed inline with the rest of the code without obscuring it. This Codelet creates a jQuery Mobile button. Its helper is interactive and allows its user to customize the button by interacting with a form, drawing a line to illustrate which region of code each form element is changing. The user may also edit the code and the form will automatically update itself.

Blocks of example code on the Web are typically situated within a rich context. For example, jQuery Mobile's documentation[1] provides thorough descriptions of how each example functions, and often presents multiple alternative examples for a given high-level goal. Example code can even be interactive. For instance, CSSPortal's Rounded Corner Generator[2] provides a GUI for configuring parameters within an example. However, once a programmer pastes an example into her code, the rich context, alternatives, and interactions are lost. In a typical code editor, there is no notion of code provenance — example code is indistinguishable from code written by hand.

[1] jQuery Mobile is a library for developing Web pages intended for use on a mobile device. Documentation can be found at http://jquerymobile.com/demos/

[2] http://www.cssportal.com/css3-rounded-corner/

This paper begins with the insight that *a user's interaction with an example continues well after the code is pasted in her editor*. Typically, she must understand, configure, integrate, and test the example before it is useful [9]. In fact, for many programmers, interaction with an example *begins* when it is pasted. In a recent study of example use, one participant described why he copied code before understanding it by saying "I think it's less expensive for me to just take the first [code I find] and see how helpful it is at ... a very high level ... as opposed to just reading all these descriptions and text." [3]

Codelets: First-Class Examples

This paper investigates whether treating examples as "first-class" objects in the code editor — rather than simply as strings of text — will allow programmers to use examples more effectively. Prior studies suggest that examples may be difficult to use for three reasons: First, users may face difficulty in understanding how to **configure or adapt** an example to their specific needs [20]. Second, **integrating** an example into the user's code can introduce bugs (*e.g.,* if variables are not renamed properly, or a related library file is not included) [3,20]. Finally, these tasks are often **interleaved** with other coding tasks, which increases the likelihood that users will forget important contextual information [3,9]. Based on these reasons, we hypothesize that an editor can help programmers use examples more effectively if it:

- Emphasizes separate functional units in the user's code by demarcating examples.
- Maintains code provenance by linking documentation to the example code.
- Supports adaptation by allowing example authors to build structured editors or configurators that are presented inside the user's code.
- Facilitates integration by allowing an interactive example to automatically adapt to the use context.
- Makes supporting materials persistent so that users can interleave example use with other tasks.

We explore these ideas in a prototype code editor that supports the insertion of *Codelets* (see Figure 1). A Codelet is a region in the user's code that contains a block of example code and an associated interactive helper. The helper can make changes to the example code, and thus can present the user with structured editors or configurators. Additionally, the helper can inspect the user's entire code base, and so can tailor the example based on features in the rest of the code. Codelet interactions are evaluated through a comparative laboratory study with 20 participants. On average, programmers using Codelets were able to complete a programming task 43% faster ($\mu_{Codelet}$ = 12.7 minutes, $\mu_{control}$ = 22.2 minutes, $p < 0.01$).

Pragmatically, for Codelets to be effective programming tools, there must be a large collection of them available. Who will build them? Traditionally, providing rich editor interactions, such as structured editors, has been solely in the hands of the editor authors. However, the creation of examples is typically rests in the hands of library and documentation authors or other third parties. To bridge this gap, we propose an API for the code editor that allows documentation authors to create Codelets in a manner similar to how they currently author documentation. "Static" Codelets (those with helper widget that only offer static documentation) are created with a single HTML-like file. To add interactivity, the Codelet author makes calls against a JavaScript API to access the user's code and make changes to portions of the example. This means that authoring a basic Codelet is approximately the same amount of work as posting a static example on the Web. Authoring an interactive Codelet is similar in difficulty to building a Web page that is an example "configurator" (like CSSPortal's Rounded Corner Generator mentioned above).

Key Contributions

This paper makes three key contributions: First, it offers a set of code editing interactions that support example understanding and use. Second, it contributes to a theory of example usage by providing further data on what makes example use challenging — if a particular interaction is effective, it suggests that the problem it was designed to address is real. Finally, it offers an implementation technique for allowing documentation authors (or other third-parties) to create specialized code editing interactions.

SCENARIO: PROGRAMMING WITH CODELETS

Codelets help programmers by attaching "helpers" to fragments of code. We illustrate how Codelets work through a scenario. Jane is a programmer creating a Web site template for a small publishing company's online books. She decides to try a two-column layout: a sidebar column where readers can navigate to different chapters and a text column with the content of the book. Like many programmers, Jane "offloads" her memory to example code [3,5] and has stored some of her favorite site templates as Codelets. Even though she could re-create these templates from scratch if necessary, she never bothers, as it is often faster to copy example code.

Rapidly accessing examples and documentation — In her editor, Jane presses CTRL-/ to pull up her in-editor Codelet search interface (Figure 2a), searches for "column layout," and selects the first result. As soon as she does, a Codelet (Figure 2b) appears. This Codelet has two parts: a block of example code — which is inserted in the editor as usual — and a helper. Here, the helper is a piece of interactive documentation that is "linked" to the code it describes. When the helper is inserted, it "pushes" the surrounding code out of the way so that Jane can always see her entire codebase. To reduce their visual salience in the editor, helpers are indented at the same level as their surrounding code. In this case, Jane is familiar with the example she has just inserted and does not need to read the description attached in the helper. She immediately hides it by pressing ESC, knowing that she can re-display the helper later if necessary.

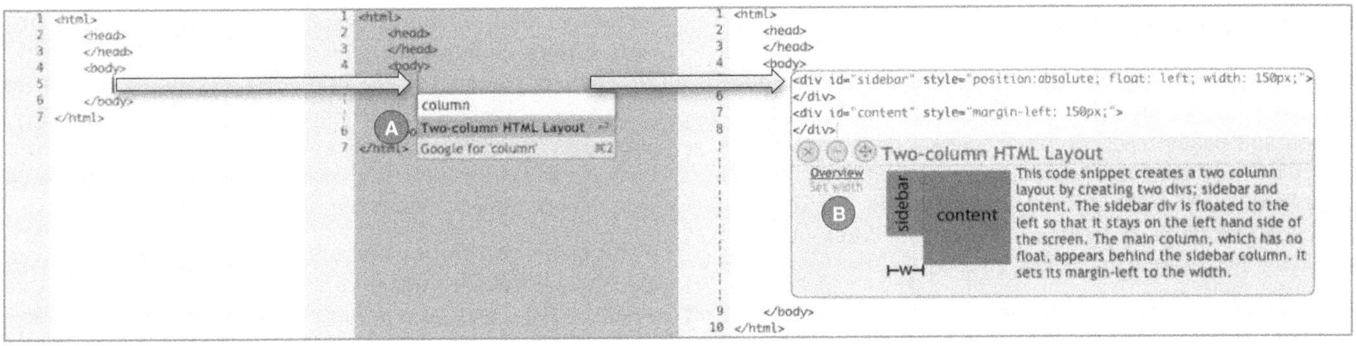

Figure 2. Our augmented editor allows Codelets to be searched for and inserted in the editor, searching for stored Codelets based on their keywords and descriptions. The search box (A) is invoked using a keyboard shortcut. If a result is selected, a Codelet (B) is inserted following the caret.

Helpers as learning tools — Jane now has a basic template. Next, she wants to add some style to her sidebar. She decides that she would like to have a border around it, preferably with rounded edges. She is not sure how to do this, and so she turns to Web search. She finds a Codelet for tuning border parameters that seems useful. After she pastes the URL into her Codelet search bar, the Codelet shown in Figure 3c appears. It contains a "builder" interface that allows her to quickly tune parameters by interacting with a standard Web form. As she experiments with different border radius values, the Codelet draws lines to indicate how changing a slider's value modifies the code. This helps her build mappings between her conceptual understanding of what she wants and the low-level CSS primitives for doing so, a major cognitive barrier faced by programmers with unfamiliar code [11,22].

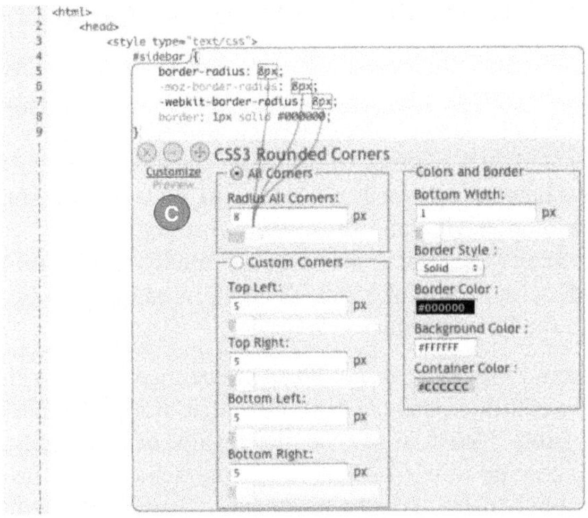

Figure 3. A Codelet inspired by CSSPortal's Rounded Corner Generator. As the developer moves the slider, it modifies the code and illustrates which parts of code are changing.

Warnings and related Codelets — After Jane finds a border radius and color she likes, she realizes that readers might not always want to see the sidebar. Ideally, they should be able to hide it when it's getting in the way. She adds a "close" button to the sidebar and decides that she wants the sidebar to animate when the user closes it by sliding off-screen to the left. She decides to do this using the "$fx" JavaScript animation library. She has never used $fx before and isn't familiar with the syntax for animations, so she decides to search for a Codelet to help her get started. When Jane adds this Codelet to her editor, it quickly pops up a yellow warning (Figure 4d), indicating that she has forgotten to include the $fx library. Jane opens the "related Codelets" list shown in Figure 4e and sees a Codelet for including $fx. She drags it into the header and a Codelet (Figure 4f) inserts the code to properly include the $fx library, suppressing the warning. Deciding she'll never need to re-invoke this helper, she destroys it by clicking the "x" in its top left corner.

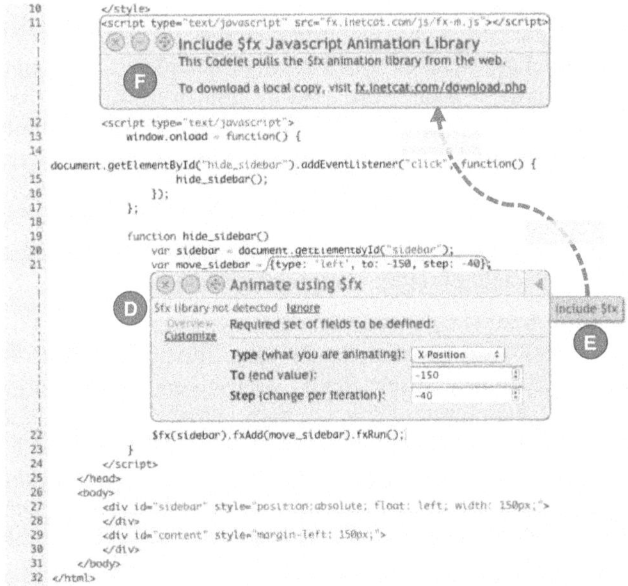

Figure 4. This Codelet displays a warning (D) after it detects the absence of a required library. On its right side (E) is a link to a Codelet for including the library. The link can be dragged into place and its Codelet (F) is inserted.

Tweaking parameters — Jane then goes back to the $fx animation Codelet and tunes the parameters of her animation, again using the helper interface to modify code. As with the Codelet for generating rounded CSS corners, she finds that experimenting is an effective way to learn how the code works [29]. After she tunes her animation, she realizes that although she animates the sidebar, the reading pane isn't re-claiming its space. In fact, she needs to animate both the sidebar and the reading pane. To animate the reading pane, she copies the code that animated the sidebar and pastes it immediately below. The attached Codelet is copied and pasted as well but Jane now feels comfortable with the $fx library, so she decides to edit her code manually rather than through the helper's interface. As she edits her code, the helper's interface updates itself automatically to reflect the parameters she has entered.

Re-invoking Codelets — After Jane finishes tuning her animations, she has a template that she's happy with. She starts filling in some content to see how it will look to a reader. When testing it, she decides to tune the borders on the sidebar once again, so that the left side isn't rounded. She re-invokes the border Codelet she had used before by holding CTRL and clicking the region of code it was tied to. She again modifies the border values until she is satisfied. Jane has quickly produced a working template using an unfamiliar library and CSS feature. In addition, her code contains interactive helpers attached to regions of code where she inserted examples. If Jane or anyone else looking at her code later wants to better understand and modify that region of code, they can re-invoke these helpers in addition to being able to modify it manually.

To understand the benefits and tradeoffs of interacting with Codelets, we built a prototype and evaluated it in a comparative lab study. We first present the results of that study, and then describe how Codelets are implemented. The implementation consists of two parts: the Codelet API with which Codelets are written and the implementation of Codelet displays in the editor.

EVALUATION

To evaluate the utility and effectiveness of programming with Codelets, we prototyped a set of Codelets for jQuery Mobile (jQM), a framework used to build websites for mobile devices. We recruited 20 participants — seven female and thirteen male. Our participants were engineers, web designers, and graduate students ages 22–45. Two participants (not included in the 20) were excluded because of a lack of programming knowledge. Eighteen of the 20 studies were conducted remotely using screen and audio sharing.

Method

Participants were first randomly split into two groups — Codelet or control. Both groups were given a code editor with a sidebar containing an output preview that they could refresh as desired. Codelet participants were first trained in how to use Codelets with a guided tutorial while control participants given a short tutorial on how to use the code editor. Each session consisted of two parts: A and B, part B being optional.

For part A, participants in both groups were asked to follow four steps to create a website using jQM. The steps were the same for both groups, but Codelets participants used jQM Codelets while control participants used the official jQM documentation, which is example-oriented. To control for search times, control participants were given links directly to relevant examples in the jQM documentation and Codelet participants were given relevant search terms. Additionally, whenever Codelet participants performed an in-editor search, the last result was always a link that initiated a Web search over jQM's documentation.

Participants that finished part A with spare time were given part B, which was oriented towards gathering qualitative results. This part asked both groups to use a Codelet-enabled editor to create a more complex website using jQM (control participants were first given a Codelets tutorial.) Part B was more freeform than part A; participants were given a goal website and the sources of three sample jQM websites that contained parts of their goal. Fourteen participants started part B and two completed it (both in the Codelet group).

Finally, all participants were asked to complete a short survey. Participants in the control group completed this survey before being exposed to Codelets. The study took approximately one hour to complete; a small gratuity was given in return for participation.

Results

Part A (Stepwise)

Part A consisted of four steps. For each step, we measured the time taken and the number of preview refreshes. Figure 5 gives an overview of the quantitative results. Participants using Codelets required significantly fewer refreshes (two-tailed heteroscedastic Student's t-test, $p < 0.05$) and took significantly less time ($p < 0.01$) than participants in the control condition. By breaking the data down into individual steps in Table 1 and below, we can gain more insight into these results.

Step 1 asked participants to create a basic jQM page. The example used by the Codelet group contained static explanatory documentation. Participants in the Codelet group performed this step significantly faster ($p < 0.01$) than the control group. Part of this effect may be the result of the Codelet group being more familiar with their code editor, having gone through a longer tutorial. The rest of this effect

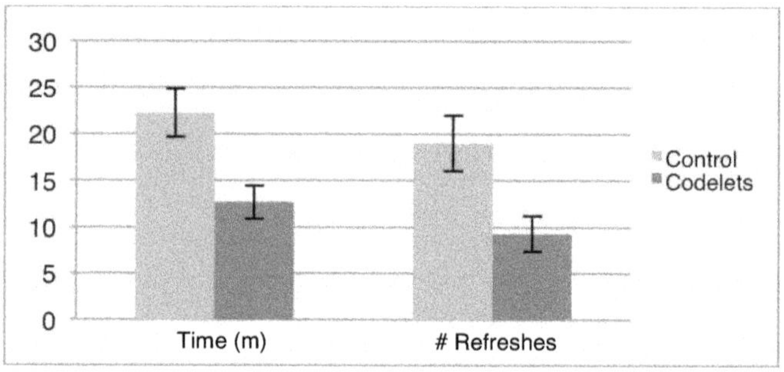

Figure 5. The overall time spent and number of refreshes in part A. Participants with Codelets completed tasks significantly faster and with significantly fewer refreshes than participants using Web examples.

	Step 1		Step 2		Step 3		Step 4	
	Time	# Refreshes	Time	# Refreshes	Time	# Refreshes	Time	# Refreshes
Codelets	2.09 (0.78)**	1.70 (0.67)	1.75 (1.22)	1.0 (0.00)**	5.57 (2.72)**	4.30 (3.59)*	3.26 (1.73)	2.3 (2.11)
Control	4.04 (1.84)**	2.90 (1.66)	2.54 (1.04)	2.44 (0.88)**	10.40 (3.91)**	8.78 (4.55)*	5.26 (3.46)	4.78 (3.63)

Table 1. Task completion time and number of refreshes used for testing during part A. Time is given in minutes, Refreshes is given as a count. Standard deviation is shown in parentheses. Columns are highlighted in green** if the difference in means is significant at $p < 0.01$, in blue* at $p < 0.05$.

can be attributed to differences in how the two groups read documentation, as described in step 2 below.

In *step 2*, the Codelet used by the Codelet group was static and contained the same example code as the official documentation used by the control group. One might expect the times for both groups to be nearly identical. However, users in the Codelet group finished this task an average of 47s faster, with fewer page refreshes.

During steps 1 and 2, participants in the Codelet group were less likely to read static documentation after example code was inserted into their document, unless they were stuck. One participant later said, "I just thought [the helper] was kind of there for newbies who want to know more about a specific feature." By contrast, in step 2, although the control group was pointed to the same example code in the documentation, they spent an average of 22s between identifying the correct example code and pasting it into the editor. The majority of this time was spent reading the documentation to be sure they were copying the correct code and double checking that they were pasting it in the appropriate place. After pasting their code, participants in the control condition spent more time "habituating" the new code — fixing indentation issues and reformatting it according to their personal preferences. The increase in the number of page refreshes in the control condition was due to the prevalence of a pattern of copying the code from the documentation, pasting it, and immediately refreshing the page to see the output. Codelet participants, by contrast, customized the example code before refreshing.

Step 3 asked participants to create jQM buttons. The Codelet group was given the interactive helper shown in Figure 1. This helper could write most of the code for them, but required them to manually set the `href` attribute in code. Participants in the Codelet group rarely expressed hesitation after realizing they had to set the `href` attribute outside of the helper and switched from interacting with the Codelet to manually editing code with little difficulty. The Codelet group finished this step nearly twice as fast as the control group, using fewer than half as many preview refreshes.

For *step 4*, participants created a new jQM page with a button, all widgets they had used before. This means that they could complete this task by copying and modifying their code from steps 1–3. The control group had the highest variance relative to task time because participants that felt comfortable with jQM copied their code from previous steps without spending time referring to documentation. In this step, only 4/10 control participants chose to refer to documentation, with 9/10 choosing to copy their own code. By contrast, only 1/10 Codelet participants copied their own code, the majority choosing to insert new Codelets. Put another way, the majority of participants preferred to insert code via Codelets rather than copying and pasting, despite having learned in the tutorial that Codelets would be been copied along with their previous code.

Part B (Freeform)
As mentioned in the "method" section, in part B, participants started with an empty document and were given three sample jQM websites. Fourteen participants spent time on the optional second part — four from the control group and ten from the Codelet group. Of these fourteen participants, thirteen chose to start developing from scratch rather than copying and pasting an example template into their code. The one participant that did not use Codelets for this task chose to start this part by copying and pasting from one of the three sample jQM websites.

Survey
When asked what was most useful about the jQM documentation 10/10 control participants cited the example code that they could copy. This indicates that examples played a crucial role in their ability to complete the task. Most Codelet participants cited the Codelets with builders and the ability to quickly insert code as the editor's most useful features.

On a nine-point Likert Scale, participants in the Codelet group rated their confidence that they could rewrite their code without any documentation higher than those in the control condition (4.63 vs. 3.80). Additionally, they rated their understanding of the code they wrote as marginally higher (7.88 vs. 7.80).

Discussion
The results from our study suggest that Codelets changed the way participants wrote code and read explanations. Whereas participants in the control group tended to read textual explanations before copying code from the jQM documentation, Codelet participants spent more time focusing on the example code. This may be because control participants are aware that by copying the example from the documentation, they will lose the surrounding explanation whereas Codelet participants always have these explanations attached to their code and can easily recall it if necessary. Alternatively, Codelet participants might have been less likely to read documentation because the documentation in Codelets is less prominent than it is in the official jQM documentation. Another possible explanation is that

participants might always be less prone to read static documentation if the code it describes is already in their project.

In our evaluation, we found two classes of Codelet users: those that tended to leave every helper open and those that never kept more than two helpers open simultaneously. Five out of the ten Codelet participants tended to leave helpers open and the usage pattern seemed to have no significant correlation with completion speed or reported programming expertise. Participants tended retain usage styles for the duration of the study. Those who preferred closing helpers said they did so to "save space" and "focus on the code." One possible design implication is that helpers could have a third state between expanded and collapsed that takes up less space than the fully expanded helper.

We also found that Codelets helped some programmers by implicitly delineating a topic or element in their code. One common mistake in the control group was to incorrectly insert code within the region of an example they had already copied. One control participant even decided to manually demarcate the range of copied examples with comments to avoid this mistake. Having Codelets attached to these regions also encapsulates them in a section that is semantically meaningful to whatever framework the programmer is using.

An interesting area for future work is to investigate learning outcomes. One participant in the control group initially started typing out their program line by line instead of copying and pasting. When asked why, they reasoned that by typing out their programs when using a new framework, it made them "learn better." This finding is consistent with prior work on example use (*e.g.*, [3]). Although the Codelet group had a slightly higher self-reported confidence in their knowledge and understanding of their code, further inquiry would be necessary to see if this is actually the case.

CODELET API

The ability to create rich editor interactions is traditionally placed solely in the hands of editor authors. However, it is unreasonable to expect editor authors or any single group to create specialized documentation for the abundance of libraries and frameworks programmers use. Codelets open the space of who can create interactive, in-editor documentation by providing an API for third parties.

This section describes the Codelet API, which is used to author individual Codelets. In the next section, we discuss the implementation of Codelet displays in the editor. To put it another way: this section explains what a documentation author would need to know to author new Codelets; the following section explains what an editor author would need to know to add Codelet support to his editor.

The Codelet API enables meaningful communication between Codelets and editors; it allows Codelets to read, interpret, and modify code; react when the programmer modifies code; and display custom interfaces and annotations in the editor. It is designed to provide a low floor — a static Codelet's implementation is approximately as complex as a static webpage — while providing a high ceiling. The Codelet API is described below, with an example Codelet implementation in Figure 6.

Overview

At a high level, Codelets are written in XML, with a top-level tag of `codelet`. Beneath this, the Codelet contains two elements: a `head` and a `body`.

A Codelet's header (lines 2–7 in Figure 6) contains meta-information about the Codelet. Its `title` property is displayed at the top of the Codelet and in search results. Codelets may optionally also have `keywords` or a short `description` (omitted in Figure 6) that are used by the editor's built-in search tool. The Codelet's `type` determines how the code snippet will be inserted and formatted in the editor. If the `type` is `block`, the snippet is meant to span one or more lines; if the `type` is `inline`, the snippet is meant to be a portion of a single line of code. Finally, the Codelet's `lang` parameter determines which parser the Codelet will use by default. In the future, the `lang` parameter may also aid in filtering search results.

The majority of a Codelet's content is in its `body` (lines 8–22 in Figure 6.) The body contains *examples, pages,* and *links* to related Codelets. An `example`, in the context of the Codelet API, is a snippet of code. A Codelet may have any number of examples, but only one example at a time will be shown in the editor. The Codelet in Figure 6 has one example, in lines 9–11.

An `example` may also contain any number of `mark` elements. *Marks* are sections of examples that are intended to be changeable (the entire example can be edited manually by the user; in addition *mark* regions are easy to change and track programmatically). Marks may be nested and can

```
01 <codelet>
02 <head>
03   <title>    Creating a var </title>
04   <keywords> create var     </keywords>
05   <type>     block          </type>
06   <lang>     javascript     </lang>
07 </head>
08 <body>
09   <example>
10     var <mark id="name" /> = <mark id="value" />;
11   </example>
12   <page>
13     Name : <input type="text" id="name_inp"/><br/>
14     Value: <input type="text" id="val_inp" />
15   </page>
16   <script src="jquery.js" />
17   <script src="widgets.js"/>
18   <script>
19     attach_input_to_mark($("#name_inp"), "name" );
20     attach_input_to_mark($("#val_inp" ), "value");
21   </script>
22 </body>
23 </codelet>
```

Figure 6. An implementation of a short Codelet. Implementation-wise, Codelets are similar to webpages, but also have a special API for interacting with the editor.

specify what values they expect. For example, a mark for a variable may specify that it will only accept characters and digits. If two marks have the same `id`, those marks will have the same value as long as the example code is in sync with its helper. The Codelet in Figure 6 has two marks: `name` and `value`. If `name` is `x` and `value` is `1`, the example code is '`var x = 1;`'

In addition to `example` elements, a Codelet may contain any number of `page` elements. *Pages* make up the content of the Codelet's helper. They are written in standard HTML and may be stylized and made interactive with CSS and JavaScript. Only one page is shown at a time but the name of every page is shown in the leftmost column of the Codelet. By splitting content into separate pages, Codelets may reduce the space taken up by their helpers. The Codelet in Figure 6 has one page, on lines 12–15. It also imports two external JavaScript files (lines 16 & 17) and includes JavaScript on lines 18–21 to make the Codelet interactive.

One feature not shown in Figure 4 is the ability to link to other relevant Codelets by adding a `link` element to the body of the Codelet with a URL (or local file path) and title for the linked Codelet. The list of related Codelets is shown in a collapsible panel on the right hand side of the Codelet, as seen in Figure 4e.

Communicating with the Editor

The above techniques can be used to create static Codelets. Authors can add interactivity to their Codelets by communicating with the editor through a JavaScript API.

Reading & Writing Code

Codelets read the user's code by calling the `get_code` function, which returns a String. This function takes a parameter to specify a scope: the entire file, the example code (which may have been modified from its original form by the user), or the code before or after the example code.

Codelets may then use provided parsers to gain semantic information about the code. The Codelet API is designed to be language-agnostic while allowing Codelets to extract semantic information about code. To balance these two needs, the Codelet API provides access to parsers and contains a set of widgets for these parsers. The default HTML parser, for example, includes functions for extracting tag names, attribute names, and attribute values from the user's code. Currently parsers exist for HTML and JavaScript, but could be included for any number of languages.

Codelets may also add *event listeners* – functions that are called when code is edited. Event listeners may be called when user's code has changed, when a mark value has changed, or when the user's code has moved to a new place. These event listeners allow Codelet helpers to update as the user modifies example code. For example, the `attach_input_to_mark` function used in Figure 6 (lines 19 & 20) automatically adds event listeners to update HTML `input` elements' values (lines 13 & 14) if the programmer edits code manually.

To write code back to editors, Codelets may change the value of marks. For instance, if the Codelet implemented in Figure 6 set `name` to `z` and `value` to `2`, its example code becomes '`var z = 2;`' Because marks may be nested, modifying marks in a given example can change code on larger or smaller scales.

Round-Tripping & Synchronization

When the user modifies a piece of code, the attached Codelet determines if any marks have changed. It does this in a "ground-up" fashion, so that if any marks are nested, it finds the lowest level on which marks may have changed. If the Codelet finds a valid change to the example's marks, then it notifies the example. If not, then the example becomes *out of sync*.

To illustrate, again, consider the example in Figure 6. If the user edits the code so that it reads '`var y = 2;`', an event is emitted showing that the mark '`name`' has the value `y` and the mark '`value`' has the value `2`. If the user edits the example to read '`z = 3;`' (removing the `var` keyword), then the example becomes out of sync. If the helper later tries to set the '`name`' or '`value`' marks, while it is out of sync, the user is presented a warning asking for permission to overwrite their code, as shown in Figure 7. Helpers may not further write code until the example comes back in sync or the programmer gives permission for that piece of documentation to overwrite their code. Note that in the above example, the keyword `var` could have been made optional by enclosing it in a mark. This allows Codelet authors to specify precisely which code is necessary and which code can change.

Annotations

Annotations are augmentations of the coding environment. Codelets provide annotations for highlighting code fragments and for drawing arrows between helpers and code fragments. To specify what should be highlighted or pointed at, annotations use mark IDs. The `attach_input_to_mark` function used in Figure 6 (lines 19 & 20) automatically adds annotations to draw lines between

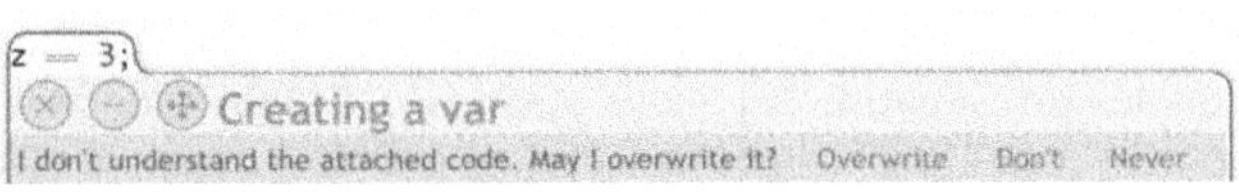

Figure 7. If the user edits the region of code attached to a Codelet so that the helper becomes out of sync with the attached code, the Codelet asks the user before the helper makes any code changes.

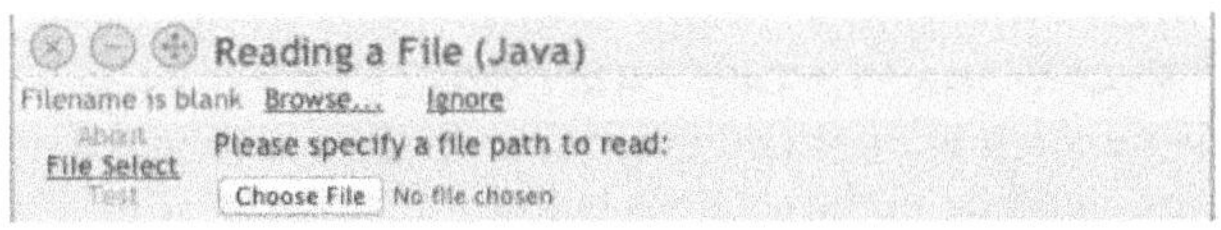

Figure 8. For consistency, Codelets have a standard mechanism for displaying warnings with text and any number of buttons. Helpers can take advantage of their semantic understanding of what their attached example code is supposed to do to display warnings even if the code is syntactically correct. This Codelet, for reading a file in Java, displays an error because the programmer has not specified a filename.

HTML `input` elements and the regions of code they manipulate, as illustrated in Figures 1 and 3.

Warnings

For the sake of consistency, Codelets have a standard mechanism for displaying warnings as yellow text in the margin of the Codelet (Figure 8). These warnings are displayed and cleared using JavaScript. Codelets do not, however, provide any standard mechanism for detecting warnings, which is left as a job for individual Codelets. This is because Codelet warnings are usually specific to the example, rather than the programming language. There are many cases where a Codelet's example may be semantically incorrect while being syntactically valid.

IMPLEMENTATION

We designed Codelets with the goal that any editor could be augmented with the ability to display Codelets. Put another way, multiple editors may be modified to be "Codelet-enabled," rather than having to create new editors from scratch. In our implementation, we augmented ACE (Ajax.org Cloud9 Editor), a code editor written for web browsers in JavaScript, HTML, and CSS.

In order for an editor to become Codelet-enabled, it must support a minimal API for communicating with the Codelets backend system. First, it must support the ability to embed custom web views that can communicate with the editor. In our implementation each Codelet is an `iframe`, or an embedded page that communicates with the editor using the API described in the previous section. Second, the editor must provide at least a minimal API for reading and modifying code. Ideally it would expose the ability to override standard copy and paste and text dragging operations so that Codelets can be copied to the clipboard as well, as they are in our implementation. Finally, the editor must provide a mechanism for choosing how its code is formatted, to allow the Codelet web views to "push" surrounding code out of the way. In our implementation, we did this by disguising the space used by any Codelet as a set of wrapped lines, preserving line numbers.

Storing Codelets in Source Files

Another implementation consideration is deciding how Codelets should be stored in source files across editing sessions. In our implementation, the editor maps Codelet locations to files, meaning that if files were shared (e.g. with a version control system) its Codelets would be lost. One could imagine other storage alternatives, such as tracking Codelets in a separate hidden file or with comments in the source code.

INTERACTIONS THAT INFORM CODELETS

This research is informed by prior work in a number of domains, outlined in the sections below.

Structured Editors

At their core, structured editors are editors that let programmers write code by directly manipulating the abstract syntax tree, with the goal of allowing programmers to focus on semantics rather than syntax [32]. Many structured editors also include interesting interaction techniques for inserting code blocks and augmenting documentation. Barista [19], for example, demonstrates the possibility of having media-rich annotations in a structured editor. Codelets and Codelet-enabled editors provide developers with some of the useful interactions possible in structured editors without the obligation to change how they edit code. Additionally, while structured editors require editor authors to build these interactions, Codelets allow third parties to build them.

Quickly Inserting Code

Autocomplete, a feature of many IDEs for typed languages, is optimal for highly localized reminder tasks, where the user is searching for a particular function and does not need documentation. Many editors — *e.g.*, Dreamweaver, Textmate, and Vim — have placeholder or snippet features that allow custom templates for often-typed code to be quickly inserted with a keyboard shortcut. Keyword Programming [23] augments this by allowing template code to be quickly inserted and customized with keywords. While quick template insertion is one feature of Codelets, our focus is on maintaining a meaningful link between the inserted code and its documentation.

Integrating Documentation into Editors

JavaDoc [21] is one of the most commonly-used editor-documentation integration mechanisms. Whereas JavaDoc is intended for documenting methods and classes statically, Codelets are oriented towards documenting examples dynamically while being tightly integrated with the code they document in the editor.

Additionally, several research projects have aimed to better integrate web resources with code editors. CodeTrail [10] and HyperSource [12] help programmers link source code and web documentation resources. While we have a similar goal, we take the approach of providing documentation tools so that framework creators can write documentation specifically for integration into the IDE. Whereas CodeTrail [10], HyperSource [12], and Blueprint [2] take advantage of the abundance of examples on the Web, Codelets focus on enabling interactive specialized documentation written especially for inclusion in code editors.

Searching for Examples

Although search was not our focus in designing Codelets, we recognize that the ability to search for useful examples is fundamental to using any example system. Example mining systems try to find example code that is useful to programmers. Prospector [24], for example, automatically mines "Jungloids," or commonly used code fragments and uses context to find relevant Jungloids.

Other projects have focused on improving API documentation design. Apatite [8] helps users learn and understand APIs by providing a new navigation interface. Jadeite [31] uses information on API usage to make its documentation easier to navigate. Additionally, it allows users of the API to add method templates that were not part of the original API. Some development recommendation systems have applied machine-learning techniques to help programmers automatically complete method bodies or find example code that is relevant to their projects [28].

Preventing Usage Errors

Codelets have an API for showing warnings when programmers might be using an API in the wrong way. This feature was inspired by the idea of code contracts. Code Contracts [16] allow API designers to programmatically enumerate assumptions they make about code that uses their API. Code contracts help prevent programmer errors by warning them about improper usage of an API, sometimes before compilation.

Unlike code contracts, the specification and warnings are given by the example documentation, meaning that the languages or libraries that Codelets use need not be augmented with code contracts.

Tools to Increase Program Readability

One main cognitive barrier to customizing examples is the difficulty of building of mappings between what the programmer wants to create and the low-level primitives of programming languages and libraries [11,22]. Knuth introduced the idea of literate programming [18], which seeks to allow programmers to write programs in an expository fashion, looking at higher-level ideas and concepts instead of always reading the low-level code.

Other research has addressed this problem by adding visualization layers over existing languages [6,7], by providing dedicated "builder" interfaces that are displayed separately from code [26], and even by designing new programming languages using HCI principles [27]. However, these techniques require either interacting with the high-level language or a low-level language (but not both), rather than building up mappings from concepts to working code. Codelets can help alleviate these problems by including custom-tailored interactions that build mappings from high-level concepts to low-level implementation details. The Codelet in Figure 1, for instance, allows programmers to customize the example code by directly editing the code or by using an interactive widget. Changes made in either representation are reflected in the other, providing users with direct feedback that has been shown to be crucial in learning to program [14].

Lowering the Cost of Writing Documentation

One of the design goals of Codelets was to allow third parties to write useful and interactive examples. While we aimed to lower the cost of writing documentation by allowing it to be written in API, we hope future tools might further lower these barriers. DocWizards [1], for instance, allows users to write documentation (in the form of wizards) by demonstration.

CONCLUSION AND FUTURE WORK

We have presented a set of techniques for better integrating examples into code editors with Codelets. The design of Codelets was guided by the insight that anyone should be able to write example code for code editors. While Codelets explore some of the possibility for this, we believe our insight opens up many avenues for interesting future research.

To start, we plan on exploring ways to better adapt examples to fit individual programmers' styles — even something as trivial as matching their naming and spacing conventions. More nuanced individual programming conventions might also be supported. We are also thinking about ways Codelets might be extended to work with examples that have code distributed in chunks across different lines or different files. For instance, a single Web snippet may require bits of HTML, JavaScript, and CSS that are not placed in a contiguous block.

Another promising area for future work is in improving in-editor search. One might, for instance, be able to point out a piece of code and perform a search for any documentation related to it. We are also exploring ways to make it easier to create Codelets by, for example, creating a tool to convert Web examples into interactive Codelets. Because Codelets also have a semantic understanding about what particular examples are for and how they have been customized, they may also help in refactoring tasks like updating code for new framework versions.

Finally, there are many interesting implications for learning. Although in our user study, Codelet participants' self-reported confidence in their knowledge of JQM was higher, it would be interesting to see what types of examples help programmers learn new libraries best. For example, comparisons may be made between static Codelets, interactive Codelets, and "tutorial" Codelets that teach programmers by build example code step-by-step.

While code examples are a valuable resource for programmers, the rich context surrounding examples is often crucial for adaptation and integration. Codelets were designed with the insight that a programmer's interaction with an example often *begins* when its code is pasted into the editor. Our evaluation of Codelets suggests that it is valuable to maintain a connection between example code and related documentation throughout the example's lifecycle.

ACKNOWLEDGEMENTS

We thank Mira Dontcheva, Brad Myers, our participants, and the many researchers at Adobe and at Carnegie Mellon who helped shape this work.

REFERENCES

1. Bergman, L., Castelli, V., Lau, T., and Oblinger, D. DocWizards: A System for Authoring Follow-me Documentation Wizards. In *Proc. UIST*, (2005), 191–200.
2. Brandt, J., Dontcheva, M., Weskamp, M., Klemmer, S.R., and Francisco, S. Example-Centric Programming: Integrat-

ing Web Search into the Development Environment. In *Proc. CHI*, (2010), 513–522.

3. Brandt, J., Guo, P.J., Lewenstein, J., Dontcheva, M., Klemmer, S.R., and Francisco, S. Two Studies of Opportunistic Programming: Interleaving Web Foraging, Learning, and Writing Code. In *Proc. CHI*, (2009), 1589–1598.
4. Brandt, J., Guo, P.J., Lewenstein, J., and Klemmer, S.R. Opportunistic Programming: Writing Code to Prototype, Ideate, and Discover. In *IEEE Software 26*, 5 (2009), 18–24.
5. Davies, S.P. Externalising information during coding activities: Effects of expertise, environment and task. In *Empi Empirical Studies of Programmers* (1993), 42–61.
6. Davis, S. and Kiczales, G. Registration-Based Language Abstractions. In *Proc. OOPSLA Onward!*, (2010), 754–773.
7. Eisenberg, A.D. and Kiczales, G. Expressive Programs Through Presentation Extension. In *Proc. AOSD*, (2007), 73–84.
8. Eisenberg, D.S., Stylos, J., and Myers, B.A. Apatite: A New Interface for Exploring APIs. In *Proc. CHI*, (2010), 1331–1334.
9. Fischer, G., Henninger, S., and Redmiles, D. Cognitive tools for locating and comprehending software objects for reuse. In *Proc. ICSE*, (1991), 318–328.
10. Goldman, M. and Miller, R.C. Codetrail: Connecting Source Code and Web Resources. In *Proc. VL/HCC*, (2009), 223–235.
11. Green, T. and Petre, M. Usability Analysis of Visual Programming Environments: A 'Cognitive Dimensions' Framework. *Journal of Visual Languages and Computing 7*, 2 (1996), 131–174.
12. Hartmann, B., Dhillon, M., and Chan, M.K. HyperSource: Bridging the Gap Between Source and Code-Related Web Sites. In *Proc. CHI*, (2011), 2207–2210.
13. Hartmann, B., Doorley, S., and Klemmer, S.R. Hacking, Mashing, Gluing: Understanding Opportunistic Design. *Pervasive Computing 7*, 3 (2008), 46–54.
14. Hoc, J.M. and Nguyen-Xuan, A. Language Semantics, Mental Models and Analogy. *Psychology of Programming* (1990), 139–156.
15. Hoffmann, R., Fogarty, J., and Weld, D.S. Assieme: Finding and Leveraging Implicit References in a Web Search Interface for Programmers. In *Proc. UIST*, (2007), 13–22.
16. Holland, I.M. and Thomas, B.M. Contracts: Specifying Behavioral Compositions in Object-Oriented Systems. In *Proc. OOPSLA*, (1990), 169–180.
17. Holmes, R., Cottrell, R., Walker, R.J., and Denzinger, J. The end-to-end use of source code examples: An exploratory study. In *Proc. ICSE*, (2009), 555–558.
18. Knuth, D.E. *Literate Programming*. CSLI Center for the Study of Language and Information, 1992.
19. Ko, A.J. and Myers, B.A. Barista: An Implementation Framework for Enabling New Tools, Interaction Techniques and Views in Code Editors. In *Proc. CHI*, (2006), 387–396.
20. Ko, A.J., Myers, B.A., and Aung, H.H. Six Learning Barriers in End-User Programming Systems. In *Proc. VL/HCC*, (2004), 199–206.
21. Kramer, D. API Documentation from Source Code Comments: A Case Study of Javadoc. In *Proc. SIGDOC*, (1999), 147–153.
22. Lewis, C. and Olson, G. Can principles of cognition lower the barriers to programming? *Empirical Studies of Programmers*, (1987), 248–263.
23. Little, G. and Miller, R.C. Keyword Programming in Java. *Automated Software Engineering* 16, 1 (2009), 37–71.
24. Mandelin, D., Xu, L., Bodik, R., and Kimelman, D. Jungloid Mining: Helping to Navigate the API Jungle. In *Proc. PLDI*, (2005), 48–61.
25. Nykaza, J., Messinger, R., Boehme, F., et al. What Programmers Really Want: Results of a Needs Assessment for SDK Documentation. In *Proc. SIGDOC*, (2002), 133–141.
26. Omar, C., Yoon, Y., Latoza, T., and Myers, B. Active Code Completion. *Ext. Abstracts VL/HCC*, (2011), 261–262.
27. Pane, J.F., Myers, B.A., and Miller, L.B. Using HCI Techniques to Design a More Usable Programming System. In *Proc. HCC* (2002), 198.
28. Robillard, M.P., Walker, R.J., and Zimmerman, T. Recommendation Systems for Software Engineering. *IEEE Software* 27, 4 (2010), 80–86.
29. Rosson, M.B. and Carroll, J.M. The Reuse of Uses in Smalltalk Programming. *ACM Transactions on Computer-Human Interaction* 3, 3 (1996), 219–253.
30. Stylos, J. and Myers, B.A. Mica: A Web-Search Tool for Finding API Components and Examples. In *Proc. VL/HCC*, (2006), 195–202.
31. Stylos, J., Faulring, A., Yang, Z., and Myers, B. Improving API Documentation Using API Usage Information. In *Proc. VL/HCC*, (2009), 119–126.
32. Teitelbaum, T. and Reps, T. The Cornell program synthesizer: a syntax-directed programming environment. *Communications of the ACM 24*, 9 (1981), 563–573.
33. Yeh, R.B. Designing Interactions that Combine Pen, Paper, and Computer. *Ph.D. thesis, Stanford University, Computer Science Department.* 2008.
34. Google Code Search. http://www.google.com/codesearch

Evaluating Interactive Support for Secure Programming

Jing Xie, Heather Richter Lipford, Bill Chu
Department of Software and Information Systems
University of North Carolina at Charlotte
Charlotte, NC, USA
jxie2, heather.lipford, billchu@uncc.edu

ABSTRACT
Implementing secure code is an important and oft-overlooked non-functional requirement. Secure programming errors are a subset of program errors that result in many common privacy and security breaches in commercial software. We are seeking to provide interactive support for secure programming in the development environment. In this paper, we have evaluated our prototype tool, ASIDE, which provides real-time warnings and code generation to reduce secure programming errors introduced by programmers. We evaluate the potential use and effectiveness of ASIDE on both novice and professional developers in two comparison user studies. Our results demonstrate that the interactive support can help address this important non-functional requirement, and suggest guidelines for such tools to support programmers.

Author Keywords
secure programming; software security; software developers

ACM Classification Keywords
D.2.6. Software Engineering: [Programming Environments-integrated environments][interactive environments]; D.2.2. Software Engineering: [Design Tools and Techniques]; H.5.2 User Interfaces: [Interaction styles]

General Terms
Human Factors; Security; Experimentation

INTRODUCTION
Software programming is a highly complex human activity, which involves cognitive processes such as reading, writing, learning, reasoning and problem solving [18]. Interactive tool support for various programming tasks has helped to successfully improve programming productivity and ease the cognitive burden on programmers [2, 8]. One example is the syntax-directed editor, which colors program tokens according to their syntactic meaning. This has become an indispensable component of any modern Integrated Development Environment (IDE). Researchers in Human Computer Interaction and software engineering have also sought to design and evaluate more usable interactive tools to help professional developers reduce general program errors. For example, Ko and Myers have developed a model for program errors [9], which later led to the design and implementation of a new approach for interactive debugging [11].

Our research is focused on a subset of program errors that can put software at risk of being attacked by malicious users, which we refer to as secure programming errors. Vulnerabilities originating from such errors in code are a major cause of security and privacy breaches in commercial software [17]. Despite their prevalence, many of these errors can be addressed with relatively simple coding practices [6].

While secure programming errors share common characteristics with general program errors, as they are often caused by developers' cognitive breakdowns [9], they are non-functional errors in that they do not interfere with the intended software logic but only surface in the face of unintended interactions. For example, one common secure programming error is to allow a user to input data that contains malicious scripts, such as with Cross-Site Scripting attacks, which may be overlooked in implementation. Therefore, current debugging tools do not help to specifically address this set of program errors. Although there is research about tools that assist software developers in implementing better non-functional requirements, little has focused specifically on software security, where such errors have unique characteristics. An additional challenge is that many programmers may not have sufficient knowledge of secure programming to understand how to mitigate such vulnerabilities.

To fill this void, we are developing an interactive tool that aims to aid programmers in implementing software with fewer secure programming errors. The current prototype, **A**pplication **S**ecurity in the **IDE** (ASIDE), is a plugin for the Eclipse Java development environment. In this paper, we present two com parison-based user studies to evaluate our approach for helping programmers to address potential security vulnerabilities in their code, examining how programmers react to and perceive the interactive secure programming support. Our results demonstrate that interactive techniques can help reduce these non-functional errors and provide guidance for the design of such tools.

CHI'12, May 5–10, 2012, Austin, Texas, USA.

RELATED WORK

Interactive tool support for software programmers in performing various programming activities has been extensively studied. One line of research is to improve programmer productivity by providing interactive code editing support. A prominent success is the incremental compilation of code in Eclipse that offers semi-immediate feedback on errors as well as provides quick fixes for common problems while programmers are editing source files [10]. Our approach is modeled after this mechanism.

Facilitating debugging through interactive support has gained attention recently through work of Ko and Myers' Whyline [11]. Hao et al. [7] proposed VIDA which continuously recommends break-points for programmers based on the analysis of execution information and the gathered feedback from a programmer during his/her conventional debugging process, increasing programmer efficiency. Murphy-Hill and Black [12] investigated an interactive code analyzer that offers refactoring advice when requested. Similarly, we hope to offer secure programming advice to programmers without interrupting their primary tasks and increase their efficiency in performing secure programming.

Little research has examined how programmers perform secure programming. One exception is Xie et al. [21], who conducted an interview study on professional developers. The results reveal a disconnect between programmers' conceptual understanding of security and their attitudes regarding their personal responsibility and practices for software security. More specifically, developers tend to rely on other processes, people, and organizations to handle software security, which may result in programmer's inadvertently introducing security errors in their code. Our goal is to examine whether an interactive tool in the IDE can bridge that gap and improve secure programming practices.

There are abundant efforts invested in educational materials and practice guidelines for promoting software security awareness and enhancing secure programming practices [6, 15]. However, many developers either do not receive such training or, as Xie et al. concluded, have not adopted such practices [21].

Current tool support for secure programming, both from tool vendors as well as within the research community, focuses on catching security errors after the program is written [3, 5, 16]. Static and dynamic analyzers work in a similar way to early compilers: developers must first run the tool, obtain and analyze results, diagnose programs, and finally fix the code if necessary. Thus, these tools tend to be used to find vulnerabilities at the end of the development lifecycle, removing programmers from the security loop. Moreover, using such tools often requires security knowledge, and thus tend to be used by experts such as security auditors. If programmers are removed from this analysis process, these tools will not help them learn about and thus prevent the security errors in the first place.

There is only limited exploration of more interactive analysis tools. For example, the commercial tool Whitebox SecurityAssist presents secure programming errors alongside the code [4]. However, the use of such an approach is unknown, and thus, we will compare against a similar approach in our studies.

INTERACTIVE SECURE PROGRAMMING SUPPORT

As has been proven successful in other areas of debugging and program understanding, we aim to examine a more interactive style of secure programming error detection and correction. Our approach rests on the belief that software developers who introduce vulnerabilities into software through writing insecure code should be included in the security loop. To that end, we conceived of the idea of integrating interactive secure programming support into the IDE by providing two key mechanisms, namely, interactive code refactoring and interactive code annotation, to address common insecure code in web applications [19]. We have developed a prototype of our approach, ASIDE, and previously evaluated the potential effectiveness of the proposed mechanisms [20] by comparing vulnerability detection on two large open source projects against the standard industry static analysis tool Fortify SCA [5]. In this paper, we complement that previous security evaluation by examining the idea from an HCI perspective: understanding the behavior and reaction of developers to providing awareness and assistance for secure programming.

ASIDE

The current ASIDE prototype is a proof-of-concept plugin for Eclipse and Java that integrates secure programming support into the programming environment. Our prototype implementation is analogous to how the incremental compiler works in modern IDEs. ASIDE works as a long running process in the background that scans a selected project for program patterns that match pre-defined heuristic rules of security vulnerabilities in the current Eclipse workspace. During the development session, it monitors developers' edits to respond to the changes in the code. Whenever a match is found, ASIDE marks the corresponding source code line using a warning icon on the left margin of the code editor and also highlights the identified vulnerable code using a dashed rectangle, shown in Figure 1.

Figure 1. ASIDE identifies vulnerable code and reminds developers through warnings.

There are numerous classes of vulnerabilities that originate from a variety of code patterns. However, for our prototype implementation we started with vulnerabilities that are caused by either a lack of input validation or output encoding, such as Cross-Site Scripting (XSS), SQL Injection, Command Injection and other injection problems. Thus, the current prototype identifies any code lines where untrusted inputs are read into the program or output to user-facing displays, such as a web browser.

In designing ASIDE, we proposed to use interactive code generation as one method to help programmers easily modify their code and prevent security vulnerabilities. However, we also wanted to examine an alternate approach, currently provided in part by a commercial tool [4], providing a detailed explanation of a warning. Thus, for this study, we implemented and evaluated two different versions of ASIDE. The first, ASIDE `CodeGen`, performs automated code generation to fix the identified vulnerable code. More specifically, `CodeGen` offers a developer a list of suggestions as a set of input types/output encoding strategies upon his/her examination of a warning through either clicking on the warning icon or hovering over the highlighted code as shown in Figure 2. Upon choosing a type from the list, `CodeGen` then automatically inserts the corresponding code segment which performs the input validation or output encoding, as illustrated in Figure 3. The developer can also choose to dismiss the warning if s/he does not wish to modify the code.

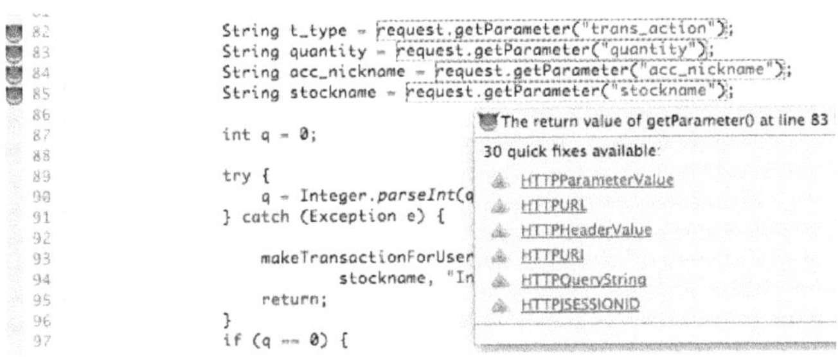

Figure 2. ASIDE CodeGen offers a list of suggestions that can be applied to address the selected warning.

Figure 3. ASIDE CodeGen generates a code segment in response to the developer's selection of an input type.

Our other alternative, ASIDE `Explanation`, instead provides only two options upon a developer's request to address the warning. When selecting "Guide Me Through", s/he will be presented with a detailed explanation, Figure 4, as to why the code is vulnerable, the consequences of not addressing the vulnerability, and the suggested remediation. Thus, `Explanation` does not automatically create code, but instead attempts to help the programmer understand the problem and address it him/her self. The other option, "Ignore this" dismisses the warning, and removes it from view.

It is our hypothesis that `CodeGen` is more effective than `Explanation` in aiding programmers, given that `CodeGen`

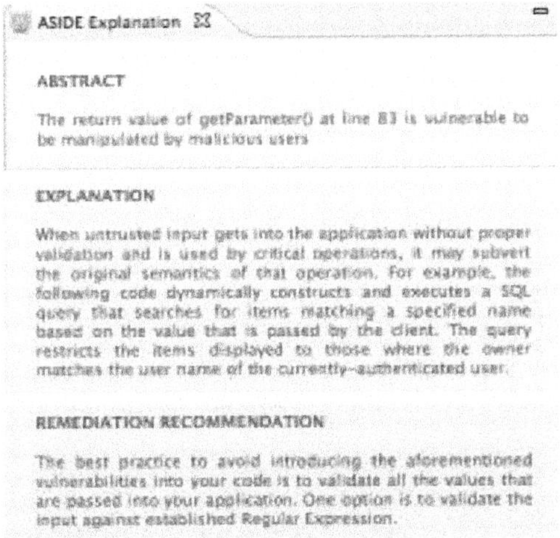

Figure 4. ASIDE Explanation provides details of the secure programming warning.

reduces a programmer's burden of creating his/her own validation/encoding routine. Furthermore, `CodeGen` provides a rich list of commonly-used, well-established input types from the security community, some of which may not be known to the developer. This, therefore, offers a chance for developers to expand their awareness of secure programming practices. However, programmers may not feel comfortable with code being generated for them, or understand how to modify that code if necessary. On the other hand, `Explanation` demands that the developer switch attention from programming to documentation reading, which may lead to ignoring the warning. Even worse, `Explanation` does not provide concrete solutions as to how to solve the problem beyond a more generic description of how to perform proper input validation/output encoding. As a result, the developer has to write the code from scratch, which may increase the developer's cognitive load and be challenging for someone without sufficient secure programming knowledge. However, `Explanation` would let the developer decide how to best incorporate the vulnerability fix into the code. Our studies examine the differences in these two approaches.

RESEARCH GOALS

ASIDE must be designed in a way that fits naturally into a developer's work environment in order to be successful. To gain an understanding of programmers' reactions towards real-time secure coding support and to evaluate whether real developers could use ASIDE effectively, we conducted a comprehensive user study on our two ASIDE prototypes. The goals of this study are:

- Do users pay attention to the warnings?
- Do users interact with warnings and how?
- How do users respond to and perceive the code generation and explanation approaches?
- Does code generation help developers produce more secure code?

Our approach aims to be useful for developers at all levels of their software development experience. However, novice programmers and expert programmers perceive and practice software development differently [1]; thus, we believe that they possess different views towards the need of tool support for secure programming. We thus performed our study in terms of two different developer populations: novice developers who are at the stage of gaining both software development knowledge and experience; and expert developers who have years of professional experience in industry.

USER STUDY I - STUDENTS/NOVICE DEVELOPERS

Participants and Procedure

For this study, we recruited 18 students from a graduate level Java-based web application development course, which was offered by our college in the Spring 2011 semester. Twelve students were male and 6 female. As part of the course, students were briefly introduced to basic secure programming techniques such as input validation and output encoding. However, project grades were assigned only based on functional requirements, not on secure programming practices.

Part of the students' course work was to build an online stock trading system incrementally over four projects throughout the semester using Java Servlet technology. Our study focused on the last increment of this project where students were asked to implement functionality including add a banking account, display stock details, make a buy/sell stock transaction, and display transaction history. Students added these functions on top of their existing work artifacts, which included static web pages, login, logout, and register functionalities.

Study Setup

We performed a controlled comparison study, where student participants were asked to come to our lab and work on their assignment for 3 hours. Participants were randomly assigned to work with either `CodeGen` or `Explanation`. Each study session took 3 hours of development and fifteen minutes of debriefing. Participants were offered a gift card as compensation for completing the study session.

The participants were first given a brief walkthrough of how the selected plugin works. In the mean time, a technical assistant helped set up the development environment and recording software on the lab machine. He also imported the participant's existing project into Eclipse and made sure it was compiled and could run on the local web server. The participant was then asked to launch the plugin before proceeding to development. Students were told to work as they wished on the assignment for 3 hours and respond to ASIDE warnings as they wanted to. The participants worked on various parts of their code and none completed the assignment during the study session.

Semi-structured Interview

Each interview lasted 10 to 15 minutes. We began by asking participants to describe their interactions with ASIDE, and the concrete actions s/he took to address the warnings and why. Next, we asked our participants to explain what they liked and disliked most about the tool that they interacted with. We also asked participants whether they thought they would likely pay attention to and fix vulnerable code without such tool support. Finally, we asked the participant whether s/he gained any knowledge from interacting with the tool.

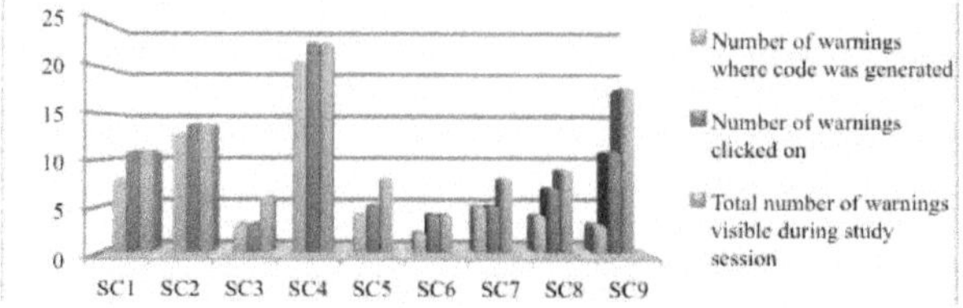

Figure 5. Metrics from students with CodeGen.

Result Analysis

For each participant, we collected a 3-hour screen recording of his/her application development and a recording of the interview. Additionally, we gathered a software log of the participant's interaction with ASIDE as a supplement to the screen recording. We analyzed the screen recording and logs, focusing on the many warnings ASIDE generated. For each warning, we analyzed how participants responded either through the tool or in their code.

The interviews provided the participants' explanations for their behavior with ASIDE. We transcribed all interviews into text, and performed open-coding on the transcripts using At.las. We identified general themes and interesting cases about their perceptions towards tool support for secure programming.

Student Participant Behavior

Figure 5 depicts the results of the 9 participants who worked with ASIDE `CodeGen`. Over all nine participants, 101 distinctive `CodeGen` warnings were generated, resulting in 11.2 warnings per participant on average. There were 83 warnings clicked on by participants (82%), or 9.2 for each participant on average.

Out of the 83 warnings clicked, 63 were addressed (76%, or 7 per participant on average) by clicking on one of the input/output types provided by `CodeGen`, leading to code being generated. The remaining warnings were deliberately dismissed by participants through the provided "Ignore this" option. All participants used `CodeGen` to generate code and none of them wrote any customized validation or encoding routines. Thus, `CodeGen`'s interactive code generation was effective in helping students write more secure code, even though they were not required to do so.

Multiple factors explain why certain warnings were not acted upon. Some of the warnings were generated when the participant wrote debugging code, which was soon deleted. Perhaps participants ignored security warnings on code that they knew was transient. Other cases have to do with a bug in the version of `CodeGen` used, which falsely warned participants of the need for output encoding. We noticed that participants learned this warning was a false positive after one or

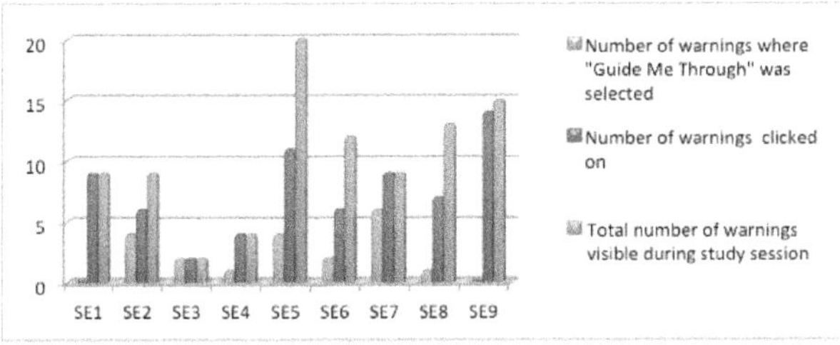

Figure 6. Metrics from students with `Explanation`.

more encounters, and then ignored those warnings thereafter. However, at least in this study, the presence of a false positive did not seem to cause the participants to not pay attention to other `CodeGen` warnings. Thus, in cases where participants encountered false positives, they were able to recognize them quickly and dismiss them.

ASIDE `CodeGen`'s code generation is designed to be intuitive and unobtrusive. In most cases, it worked just as we expected, quickly providing useful code fixes. However, in two cases the generated code caused difficulties. In both cases, the participant was validating a password string passed from the client via an HTTP request. The rule used by the validation code enforces certain restrictions on that string. However, the test data used by the students did not meet those strict restrictions (for example, one used the test string "password"). Thus, the participants were no longer able to execute and test their code because the test password failed validation. The solution would have been to create a new test password. However, this interrupted the participants' flow of development and instead both participants deleted the generated validation routine.

Figure 6 depicts an overview of results of participants using ASIDE `Explanation`. The 9 participants generated in total 93 warnings, of which 68 were clicked on (73% or 7.5 per person). In contrast to `CodeGen` warnings, 87% (59/68) of `Explanation` warnings were deliberately dismissed by clicking on "Ignore this". Throughout the sessions, only 20 warnings were examined by clicking on "Guide Me Through", which then provides the more detailed explanation. While most participants read at least one warning, none of the participants wrote any validation routines to check the identified vulnerable code.

As shown by the results, the warnings shown by ASIDE during the programming process caught participants' attention. No participant from two groups just ignored all the warnings during his/her development, and users tended to deliberately dismiss any they were not going to attend to. However, only `CodeGen` resulted in any security validation being added to the code during the session.

Student Participants Perception

Not only did students in both groups notice the warnings, they also reported welcoming the idea of being reminded of security vulnerabilities in their code in real time. Many expressed similar comments, such as:

> [SE5] Helpful, definitely helpful. It's good at the moment to use it, they come up immediately, it's not like you have to understand them later on. At the moment, if you do something wrong, it shows a warning symbol on the left.

We were concerned that warnings may divert programmers from their development flow, and thus be considered annoying. But no one reported being bothered by the warnings because they are inline with the code, not obtrusive, and do not prevent programs from being compiled.

> [SC4] No (it does not bother me). It gives me warnings so that I can write secure code.

Still we observed participants deliberately dismissing warnings rather than simply ignoring them, and leaving them on the screen.

We purposefully used the red devil-looking icon to indicate the importance of the warning, and thus to effectively attract users' attention. Two participants expressed their like of the icon because it conveyed the seriousness of the issue. However, one disliked the icon appearance, feeling that it is misleading since these warnings will not prevent programs from being compiled and thus should not be falsely presented to be as serious as compilation errors.

All but one of the participants indicated that if they were not given either `CodeGen` or `Explanation`, they would not have been aware of security vulnerabilities in their code. As one participant stated:

> [SC1] That (the warning design of `CodeGen`) was good because hadn't it prompted me, I wouldn't have realized I have to inspect those input values.

Similar to the behavior we observed with the Explanation participants, the `CodeGen` participants reported that in the absence of auto-generated code, they would not be likely to take the initiative to write their own secure code, and would prefer the code generation. The participants who used `CodeGen` all reported trusting that using the tool would make their code more secure. `CodeGen` transparently showed the regular expressions used for each data type and the code can be viewed and further edited by users. Thus most participants did report feeling like they had sufficient control over the code generation. In addition, several reported believing that the regular-expression input validation `CodeGen` used is more sophisticated than what they would come up with on their own.

> [SC8] For example, the initial code for assignment 3, assignment 2, I myself did some password validation code in JavaScript for example. Simple code, something like password length and some special characters. I mean I used such thing but this was more sophisticated because it covered everything in a simple form. If you see my code it was there are a lot of if statements for each and every condition. So this one is much simpler.

However, one participant did feel uncomfortable with the auto-generated code because he was not able to understand why the code was generated and how the generated code was impacting his existing code. One participant also worried that the code generated by CodeGen would not work in a different development environment. He tried out the code generation and thought it worked fine, but later deleted it out of concern it would not work when he later finished his assignment in NetBeans.

Participants mentioned several aspects of CodeGen that need to be improved. For instance, the most wanted feature was more information about why code was vulnerable, and what the generated code does. One participant suggested providing a demo package to explain and illustrate why certain programming practices are not secure.

Even though none of the students who worked with Explanation wrote any customized validation/encoding routines, many of them still thought it was helpful since the explanation view gave them an idea as to why the warning showed up.

> [SE5] So I realize that through out my code, there are a lot of points where possible, malicious users can take advantage of weakness in the code. So it's pretty interesting to know that, something looks so simple, someone can actually try to, find loophole and something as small as that. I didn't know these things; it's just interesting to see.

SE5 further acknowledged that he was motivated to learn more about input validation using regular expressions. Interestingly, he even took notes about what he read on the explanation view.

While some thought Explanation was useful and helpful, they complained that the explanation view did not provide a concrete example as to how to address the problem. Instead, the suggestion given was too generic and abstract. Also, the content of the explanation contained too much security jargon. Despite using graduate students who had at least brief course content on input validation and output encoding, the participants still had less security knowledge than we expected, and thus the content needed to be written for a more novice audience. These results indicate a challenge that applies to either tool: how to explain the secure programming issues and present the content in language and examples that a broad programmer population will find understandable and useful.

USER STUDY II - PROFESSIONAL DEVELOPERS

The other type of potential users our approach targets is professional software developers who are experienced with application development. Thus, in addition to studying ASIDE on novice programmers, we ran a similar comparison study on a group of expert programmers.

Participants and Procedure

We were able to recruit in total 9 professional developers through personal contacts and referrals of our personal contacts, 8 males and 1 female. The study was conducted over the course of 3 months during summer 2011. Our participants' professional experience in the software industry ranged from one year up to 20 years, with an average of 10 years. All of them had professional programming experience with developing web applications using Java technologies, although some of them do not currently directly work with Java Servlet [13] used in our study application development. Most (5/8) of our participants admitted that they do not pay additional attention or perform extra practices to ensure that the code written by them is secure. Only two participants were ever offered training by their employer on software security, but this did not include secure programming practices.

Instead of being brought into a controlled laboratory, these participants worked on one of 2 laptops provided by us at their pace and schedule during a period of up to 7 days. However, we only required them to work on the development for a cumulative 3 hours regardless of how much functionality they could implement during the given time frame. The professionals worked with either ASIDE CodeGen or ASIDE Explanation depending on the laptop they worked on, which was circulated unpredictably. They were interviewed by phone after they returned the laptops. Participants were offered the same gift cards as the previous study when they completed the study session.

We wanted to sufficiently motive the programmers to write code, not just interact with our tool. Unlike the students, they did not have intrinsic motivation to complete an assignment. Thus, to avoid priming our professional developer participants into thinking that we were only testing ASIDE, we informed them that the purpose of the study was to show students in our college how professional developers develop an application. We did require the participants to run ASIDE, and encouraged them to interact with it if they wished. But we did not provide any additional explanation of the tool. Thus, unlike the students, these participants had no brief tutorial and less priming than the students as to the purpose of the study.

Task Structure

We asked our professional developer participants to develop the same stock application as described in the students' study. However, instead of composing the application from scratch, developers were provided with a base project, which had functionality including login, logout, registration and others already implemented. Static resources such as simplified html pages were also provided along with the base project. To create other web page interfaces, the participant only needed to copy and paste code and modify. Based on the lessons from the student study that 3 hours is far from enough to complete all designated functions, we arranged the specification in a way that the functionality they were asked to implement contained the most input code, and was thus most likely to have ASIDE warnings.

Study Results

We gathered the same forms of data from the professional developer's participation as was collected from the students, namely, a 3-hour development screen recording, an interview recording, an ASIDE log and the resultant project artifact. Our results are based on 8 valid data points out of 9 professional developers participation, of which 4 worked with CodeGen and the other 4 worked with Explanation. The ninth participant failed to use ASIDE at all, which meant her data was not useful for this study and she was unable to be interviewed about ASIDE. We performed the same data analysis procedure as we did with the student study.

Professional Developer Behavior

Our four professional developer participants who worked with `CodeGen` generated in total 45 ASIDE warnings, out of which, 12 were clicked on (27% or 3 per person). This suggests that warnings were effective to at least attract some attention. However, only one participant (PDC3), as illustrated in Figure 7, used `CodeGen`'s code generation to validate the identified untrusted inputs.

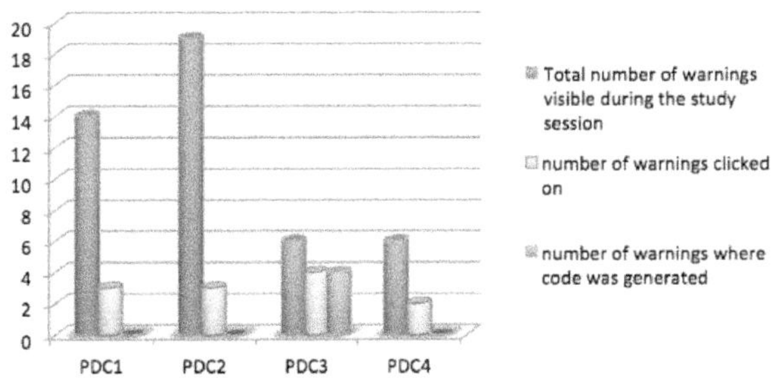

Figure 7. Metrics for *P*rofessional *D*evelopers with `CodeGen`.

Although PDC3 utilized `CodeGen` to address multiple warnings, he went through a fair amount of trouble to get everything working correctly. He selected the wrong input type and admitted during the interview that he was still not sure what the code does because he was not familiar with the ESAPI library [14] `CodeGen` uses to perform secure input validation and/or encoding. Both issues again indicate that `CodeGen` needs additional explanatory information to help users understand how it functions.

The other three participants from the `CodeGen` group neither used `CodeGen` to address the warnings nor put the effort into creating their own validation routines. A common reason given by them for not further interacting with `CodeGen` was that the given 3-hour time frame was too stringent for the development. For example, PDC2 stated:

> [PDC2] No, (I didn't take any actions to address the warnings). That's because of, that's what I said, the time, because I only had 3 hours. Had I had more time, I probably would've. I left a few comments that I should probably fix this but, I was just trying to get some of (the functionalities implemented).

As a substitute, these participants left comments in the code that indicated what needs to be done to address those warnings. Some of them added what they intended to do into the TODO list. Thus, the developers did seem to be influenced by the tool in perceiving that the validation should be added at some point, even though they chose not to address it immediately.

However, despite only being asked to implement as much functionality as they can, developers still felt compelled to achieve a functioning application at the cost of ignoring other concerns, which may also parallel the time pressures in the real world. This contrasted with the students who worked much longer than the 3 hours we observed them, and thus perhaps did not feel as much time pressure during the study.

The other four professional developer participants worked with `Explanation`. As shown in Figure 8, overall, they encountered 63 `Explanation` warnings and clicked on 14 of them (22% or 3.5 per person). All four participants interacted with `Explanation` through the "Guide Me Through" option at least once. Moreover, two participants (PDE2 and PDE4) made the effort to write customized validation routines to check identified untrusted inputs. However, these routines were far from sufficient to prevent the applications from being compromised. Thus, their attempts were not fully correct.

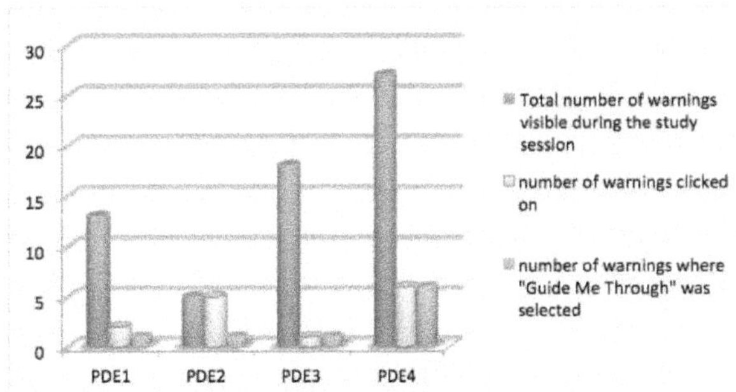

Figure 8. Metrics for *P*rofessional *D*evelopers with `Explanation`.

The two who decided not to write validation code provided several reasons. For example, PDE1 pointed out that the application he developed for the study was not realistic, and in a realistic setting other security controls in addition to just validating inputs against regular expressions (as suggested by `Explanation`) would be used and needed, such as limiting the login attempts and logging all the login attempts for later auditing. Furthermore, he failed to relate Java Servlet, the technology used in our study development, to the more current application development frameworks that he uses:

> [PDE1] The industry does not use raw servlets anymore. Instead, the industry has other technologies such as Struts, Spring MVC, and they have components that can be directly invoked and used for validation purpose.

PDE2 also reasoned that the development process in an organization setting discourages developers from addressing code that has security implications individually because the development team may have more structured countermeasures that take care of the issues.

> [PDE2] There are many ways to protect the application, even in a line of code, it looks like a security hole, but at other places we prevented it, so it will not be an issue to release this piece of code.

Professional Developer Perceptions

During the interview, all 8 participants did state that they appreciated the concept of real-time warning of secure programming issues and most acknowledged that the on-the-spot warnings made them aware of the need for input validation. For example, PDC2 left a comment in the source code about liking `CodeGen` while he was working, and another participant said that what he liked most is its ability to identify problematic areas:

> [PDE2] If Explanation didn't give me warnings, I would not pay attention to the vulnerable code.

However, ASIDE is currently a demonstration prototype, working on only one type of secure programming issue, namely, lack of input validation/encoding. Thus, several participants could not generalize the idea of integrating secure programming support in the IDE from the current prototype implementation to their professional context. These participants expressed concerns over the lack of functionality in ASIDE and questioned the feasibility of applying the approach to more mainstream frameworks. Thus, the developers' reactions were considerably more skeptical than the students' perceptions.

Discussion

The real-time detection and warning mechanism of ASIDE was universally accepted by both students and professional developers. Almost all participants responded in some way to the warnings and interacted with ASIDE, and perceived the warnings as a useful way to increase awareness of security vulnerabilities in the code. Participants also almost universally lacked detailed knowledge of secure programming practices, which meant that while they gained knowledge through using ASIDE, they also struggled to fully understand either the code generated or the explanation provided. Thus, any tool targeted at improving secure programming for developers needs to be able to be used and learned by those without little prior secure programming knowledge.

The real-time, interactive warnings were seen as sufficiently unobtrusive, and not annoying at least at the volume generated in our studies. Participants reported appreciating the instant feedback alongside the code they were currently working on. However, warnings were still deliberately dismissed when participants chose not to respond. So such warnings need to be easily removed from the view. This, however, could have negative consequences in that programmers will not be further reminded of any errors that they decided to ignore, and ASIDE does not currently provide any option of showing previously dismissed warnings. We may need to periodically remind users of unaddressed vulnerabilities, such as at the launch of the IDE, and to allow users to re-scan previous code.

Our two studies confirmed a main challenge of secure programming: as a non-functional requirement, functionality will often trump security. Not surprisingly, all participants, but particularly the professional developers, were highly motivated to get the code functionally working, and not very motivated to spend time on secure programming. While several professionals did use ASIDE to make note of places that needed later validation, as one stated:

> [PDE2] I looked at the requirements and they didn't say you have to pay attention to security problems. I just wanted to get it [the application] done.

Similar to the results of Xie et al. [21], where security was attended to only when specifically dictated by the design, clients, or regulations, PDE2 did not find security specifically addressed in the requirements specification we provided, and so focused only on the functionality.

ASIDE `CodeGen` was not as effective as expected. One important lesson was that the tool was designed with an expectation that the user had at least minimal knowledge of secure programming. We expected the tool to serve as a reinforcement and reminder of this knowledge, and as a method to reduce the burden of producing code, making secure programming easier and more efficient. But neither group had sufficient knowledge for the current prototype, which caused confusion. Without prior knowledge of code security vulnerabilities, participants were not able to gain a full understanding of the warnings and how the generated code functioned. Users need functionality that provides more awareness, explanation, and training.

Interestingly, students seemed to trust the code generated by `CodeGen`, and used it more often than the professional developers. The professionals had difficulty relating the simplistic prototype to their real-world context. Given our small user population and experimental setup, it is still not clear how or when professional developers would trust and rely on generated code for security vulnerabilities. The professional developers also related similar concerns as Xie et al. [21] noted, that there are other ways that organizations deal with such issues than the code fixes performed by or encouraged by ASIDE.

ASIDE `Explanation` was also seen as helpful, and the content of the warnings was read in some detail by most participants. However, this approach did not result in any successful secure code. No students attempted to create their own validation routines. While two professionals did, they did not get that functionality correct. Thus, explanation is not likely to be as effective as code generation in reducing warnings, particularly if the code generation technique can be augmented with more useful informational content.

The results of our study indicate that real-time warnings and code generation may be helpful for non-functional programming requirements, such as reducing secure programming vulnerabilities. The results of the studies also highlight several key design issues and necessary modifications to ASIDE.

- The increased efficiency and reduced cognitive burden do seem to be important for programmers to be willing to take the time to address security vulnerabilities while implementing functionality. Thus, automated code generation, where possible, is likely to improve software security if it is quick and easy.

- Security and secure programming are concepts with many technical details. Many programmers have little to no background in specific vulnerabilities, tools, and practices. Thus, tool interactions and explanations need to help people learn and understand how and why to use the tool. This may also be necessary so that professionals trust any advice given and code generated. At the same time, once learned, efficiency will still be critical so explanations and help should be available when needed and unobtrusive when not.

- Users do not mind real-time warnings, but do not seem to want them to persist, even if they choose to ignore them.
- Even when creating secure code is relatively easy, such as through using `CodeGen`, users still need to be motivated to make needed changes. This motivation may depend on organizational factors that encourage use amongst developers, and discourage developers from relying solely on other processes or people to handle all security concerns.

Limitations

Our studies are experimental comparison studies, on non-production applications, which has a variety of limitations. First, the participants did not work in their normal development context, which may have added confusion and modified their behavior. All participants were also unfamiliar with ASIDE, and had very little training and exposure even during a 3-hour session. While students did use their own code, all participants understood that the application was a classroom exercise, and was not going to be deployed with real users. As a result, participants may have paid less attention to ASIDE warnings as secure programming errors would have no real impact. Alternatively, the student participants may have paid more attention to the warnings because they were more aware that the study was related to ASIDE.

Our studies were also relatively small, with 27 participants across both groups of participants. While this limits the general conclusions we can make, we believe that our observations on real programming tasks are still valuable and can inform further research. Finally, ASIDE is still only a limited functionality prototype. The unsophisticated implementation may have discouraged participants, particularly the professional developers, from interacting with and exploring the secure programming support.

Despite these limitations, we believe that such a lab-based study is a good first step at understanding the potential usefulness and impact of interactive warnings and code generation. The lessons we learned will help us improve the design of the interactive mechanisms, and encourage us to continue to develop ASIDE into a more functional and deployable system that we can evaluate on a larger and more realistic scale.

CONCLUSION AND FUTURE WORK

Secure programming errors are an important non-functional class of program errors that have major impact on the overall software security of an application. We have sought to provide interactive support for programmers to reduce these errors. Our evaluations have demonstrated that real-time warnings of secure programming errors in the IDE, along with code generation to address those errors, are a potentially useful approach to improving software security. Our tool was able to be used by both novice and expert programmers on realistic programming tasks to improve their secure programming awareness and implementation.

Our results highlight several key issues in providing such interactive support, namely that programmers need easy ways of understanding and learning about secure programming and the tool functionality through interaction with the tool; that while warnings are effective at raising awareness users want to be able to easily dismiss them; and that programmers are only likely to successfully address such non-functional errors during programming if the effort and cognitive burden is sufficiently small.

We do believe that our approach can be applied to popular development frameworks such as Spring MVC, Struts, and others and are planning on expanding functionality beyond Eclipse and Java Servlet. This will enable additional evaluation on professional developers in a more realistic context to more accurately determine their behavior with such interactive support. Still, we believe our current results can inform the design of existing research and software tools currently focused on static and dynamic analysis. By providing the feedback of that analysis in a more dynamic and easy to understand way, programmers could make more successful use of such tools during development and reduce the time and effort in producing secure software.

ACKNOWLEDGMENTS

We would like to thank all our participants for being generous with their time. This work is supported by NSF Grant #501562.

REFERENCES

1. Bateson, A., Alexander, R. A., and Murphy, M. D. Cognitive processing differences between novice and expert computer programmers. *Int. J. Man-Mach. Stud. 26* (June 1987), 649–660.
2. Bragdon, A., Reiss, S. P., Zeleznik, R., Karumuri, S., Cheung, W., Kaplan, J., Coleman, C., Adeputra, F., and LaViola, Jr., J. J. Code bubbles: rethinking the user interface paradigm of integrated development environments. In *Proceedings of the 32nd ACM/IEEE International Conference on Software Engineering - Volume 1*, ICSE '10, ACM (2010), 455–464.
3. Chess, B., and West, J. *Secure programming with static analysis*, first ed. Addison-Wesley Professional, 2007.
4. Cigital. Whitebox SecureAssist. `http://www.cigital.com/solutions/secureassist/`.
5. Fortify, H. Fortify SCA. `https://www.fortify.com/products/hpfssc/source-code-analyzer.html`.
6. Graff, M. G., and Wyk, K. R. V. *Secure Coding: Principles and Practices*. O'Reilly & Associates, Inc., Sebastopol, CA, USA, 2003.
7. Hao, D., Zhang, L., Zhang, L., Sun, J., and Mei, H. Vida: Visual interactive debugging. In *Proceedings of the 31st International Conference on Software Engineering*, ICSE '09, IEEE Computer Society (2009), 583–586.

8. Kersten, M., and Murphy, G. C. Using task context to improve programmer productivity. In *Proceedings of the 14th ACM SIGSOFT international symposium on Foundations of software engineering*, SIGSOFT '06/FSE-14, ACM (2006), 1–11.
9. Ko, A. J., and Myers, B. A. A framework and methodology for studying the causes of software errors in programming systems. *J. Vis. Lang. Comput. 16* (February 2005), 41–84.
10. Ko, A. J., and Myers, B. A. Barista: An implementation framework for enabling new tools, interaction techniques and views in code editors. In *Proceedings of the SIGCHI conference on Human Factors in computing systems*, CHI '06, ACM (2006), 387–396.
11. Ko, A. J., and Myers, B. A. Debugging reinvented: asking and answering why and why not questions about program behavior. In *Proceedings of the 30th international conference on Software engineering*, ICSE '08, ACM (2008), 301–310.
12. Murphy-Hill, E., and Black, A. P. An interactive ambient visualization for code smells. In *Proceedings of the 5th international symposium on Software visualization*, SOFTVIS '10, ACM (2010), 5–14.
13. Oracle. Java Servlet. `http://www.oracle.com/technetwork/java/javaee/servlet/index.html`.
14. OWASP. ESAPI. `https://www.owasp.org/index.php/Category:OWASP_Enterprise_Security_API`.
15. SAFECode. SAFECode. `http://www.safecode.org/`.
16. SourceForge. Findbugs. `http://findbugs.sourceforge.net/`.
17. VERACODE. State of Software Security Report Volume 1, 2 and 3. `http://www.veracode.com/reports/index.html`.
18. Weinberg, G. M. *The psychology of computer programming*. Van Nostrand Reinhold Co., New York, NY, USA, 1988.
19. Xie, J., Chu, B., and Lipford, H. R. Idea: interactive support for secure software development. In *Proceedings of the Third international conference on Engineering secure software and systems*, ESSoS'11, Springer-Verlag (2011), 248–255.
20. Xie, J., Chu, B., Lipford, H. R., and Melton, J. T. Aside: Ide support for web application security. In *Proceedings of the 27th Annual Computer Security Applications Conference*, ACSAC '11, ACM (2011), 267–276.
21. Xie, J., Lipford, H. R., and Chu, B. Why do programmers make security errors? In *Proceedings of 2011 IEEE Symposium on Visual Languages and Human Centric Computing* (2011), 161–164.

Triggering Triggers and Burying Barriers to Customizing Software

Nikola Banovic[1,2], Fanny Chevalier[3], Tovi Grossman[1], and George Fitzmaurice[1]

[1]Autodesk Research
210 King St. East, Toronto,
Ontario, Canada, M5A 1J7
{firstname.lastname}@autodesk.com

[2]Dept. of Computer Science
University of Toronto, Toronto,
Ontario, Canada, M5S 3G4
nikola@dgp.toronto.edu

[3]OCAD University
Toronto, Ontario, Canada, M5T 1W1
fchevalier@ocad.ca

ABSTRACT

General-purpose software applications are usually not tailored for a specific user with specific tasks, strategies or preferences. In order to achieve optimal performance with such applications, users typically need to transition to an alternative efficient behavior. Often, features of such alternative behaviors are not initially accessible and first need to be customized. However, few research works formally study and empirically measure what drives a user to customize. In this paper, we describe the challenges involved in empirically studying customization behaviors, and propose a methodology for formally measuring the impact of potential customization factors. We then demonstrate this methodology by studying the impact of different customization factors on customization behaviors. Our results show that increasing exposure and awareness of customization features, and adding social influence can significantly affect the user's customization behavior.

Author Keywords

Adaptable interfaces; adaptive interfaces; customization; mixed-initiative; personalization.

ACM Classification Keywords

H.5.2. [Information interfaces and presentation]: User Interfaces – Graphical user interfaces.

General Terms

Human Factors, Measurement, Performance.

INTRODUCTION

One of the aims of HCI research is to design interfaces that allow users to maximize their performance while interacting with the computer. However, for complex software applications, supporting optimal efficiency while remaining universally accessible is a challenge [33]. For example, many desktop applications are designed to accommodate a broad spectrum of users and usage scenarios. These general-purpose interfaces are usually not tailored for a specific user with specific tasks, strategies or preferences. As such, the most apparent way to use software is rarely the most efficient way for any particular user. Users typically need to adapt their own behaviors if they are ever to achieve optimal performance.

In some cases, alternative enhanced behaviors are, by default, available for use. An example is preconfigured hotkeys. However, in other cases, features that would lead a user to more optimal performance are not initially accessible and first need to be customized [18].

While evidence suggests users spend a considerable amount of time personalizing the appearance of their interfaces [23] (*i.e.* customizing aesthetics), they can be reluctant to customize the functionalities to perform their tasks more efficiently [21] (*i.e.* customizing behaviors). In particular, users are reluctant to change their behavior when they are in the middle of a production process [4]. However, at some *breaking point*, a user may decide to perform a customization. This may be triggered when the perceived benefits outweigh the costs of setting up the customization. If software systems can manipulate this *breaking point*, then users could more rapidly approach optimal performance.

Although many studies look at the performance of customizable interfaces, few formally study and empirically measure what drives a user to customize. Typically, customizable interfaces are evaluated on the assumption that the user *does* choose to customize [9]. Customization factors established by Mackay [21] are probably the most thorough to date, but the identified "triggers" and "barriers" have not yet been empirically measured. In particular, it is worthwhile to explore whether such factors can be manipulated through the software application itself, to increase the customization behavior of its users, and ultimately, optimize their performance.

With these goals in mind, we present our contributions, which are both methodological and empirical. First, we describe the challenges involved in empirically studying customization behaviors, and propose a methodology for formally measuring the impact of potential customization factors. We then demonstrate this methodology by studying the impact which exposure, awareness, and social factors have on customization behaviors. Our results show that users develop different customization strategies, and that some might be more eager to customize and switch to an *enhanced behavior*. But more importantly, we also show that increasing exposure and awareness, or adding social influences, can significantly impact a user's *breaking point*. This implies that there exist customization factors which can be manipulated in software.

RELATED WORK

Our work is related to research on novice to expert transitions, personalized user interfaces, customization facilities, and customization behaviors.

Learning and Novice-Expert Transition

Grossman *et al.* [17] explicitly identified the lack of transitioning to a more expert approach as one of five main learnability problems in software. Past research looked at ways to help the user make this transition by explicitly teaching how to use an alternative approach [18, 25, 31], or even forcing the user to use the more efficient approach [16]. That body of work, however, does not focus on the customization portion of the transition.

Personalized User Interfaces

Software personalization can improve task performance and reduce workload in GUI control structures. We refer the reader to Findlater and McGrenere [12] for a detailed overview of such user interfaces.

Prior work has proposed numerous adaptive user interfaces that can improve user performance compared to static interfaces. Most adaptive approaches looked at ways to improve the performance of accessing items from a menu [6, 11, 13, 15, 29, 35], with variations on frequency-based menus [27] and split menus [14, 32] being very common. Another example in the research literature is layered interfaces [5, 10, 26, 33] which provide multiple levels of interface complexity, to match a user's skill level. Some of these adaptable interfaces also showed benefits over adaptive ones, with users performing faster [9], or showing preference for adaptable interface over adaptive ones [26].

Typically, when such techniques are evaluated, the main goal was to study the benefits of customization under the assumption that the user customized, and not whether or not the user would *choose* to customize [9]. Therefore, it still remains important to formally study what causes a user to choose to customize.

Customization Facilities

McGrenere *et al.* [26] pointed out that for some users the amount of time it took to adapt the system was an inhibitor to customization. As such, the *customization facility* should be efficient. Research has proposed to simplify customization by providing in-place customization features (*e.g.* from user's command history [19], or by selecting any GUI widget in-place and replicating it onto a command palette [34]). Neither of these two customization facilities has been formally evaluated.

Mixed-initiative incremental interfaces [1, 36], and multiple-interfaces [2] could improve the user's performance. Such interfaces provide mechanisms to prompt the users to make a customization based on user's behavior, proficiency, or current task. An example is the Adaptive Bar [7], which prompts the user to add a command to an application bar based on historical frequency of the command. The evaluation of that system showed advantage over a purely adaptable system, and also noted that novice users mostly did not customize the purely adaptable system.

Customization Behavior

Users often customize software because they wish to personalize it, improve their performance, or reduce their workload while using the software [23]. However, Mackay [21] showed that most users do not customize, and identified a comprehensive list of triggers as well as barriers to customization. However, few studies have empirically evaluated the impact of these factors on customization behaviors.

Past research has investigated user behaviors with different personalized systems. Marathe and Sundar [24] showed that customization behavior could depend on the proficiency of the user, and that power-users might be more inclined to customize to gain a sense of control over the software.

Social influence has also been identified as an important factor that could influence user customization behavior [20, 21, 37] and could encourage transition to expert use [30]. Research has shown that often there exist users within organizations that customize software and are willing to share their customizations [22], which could also be beneficial as it prevents intelligibility problems associated with local customization [8]. In our study we investigate how we can encapsulate this social influence into a mixed-initiative system in order to influence customization.

CUSTOMIZATION FACTORS

We define a user's *breaking point* as when a user decides to customize their software. The factors which Mackay [21] identified are all potential influences of a user's *breaking point*. Those factors describe the contexts and the social processes in which the user is more likely to customize. If software systems could influence this *breaking point* by manipulating those customization factors, then users could more rapidly approach optimal performance.

However, some of the customization factors listed by Mackay [21] are beyond the control of the software application (*e.g.* external factors such as job changes). Other customization factors can potentially be manipulated, which we discuss below. There, we draw parallels between these customization factors and factors that drive technology adoption in general. We refer to the factors in Unified Theory of Acceptance and Use of Technology (UTAUT) [38]: performance expectancy, effort expectancy, social influence, and facilitating conditions.

Awareness. One of the first important triggers of customization is the user's performance expectancy, or realization that there is an alternative way of performing the task, which improves the user's performance or reduces the user's workload. In order to customize software, the user must also be aware of the facilitating conditions, or the customization facility. If software could increase awareness of the mechanism for performing customizations, it could influence the user's *breaking point*.

Exposure. It is often the case that the user is aware that customization is possible, but believes that the process is too complicated. The inability of the user to determine the actual time it would take to switch from one way of performing a task to another, where the time includes the time to customize, could be a barrier to customization. On the other hand, exposing the user to the customization could change user's effort expectancy and trigger a customization.

Social influences. The social influence to perform better or simply like other users could be a strong customization trigger. Furthermore, the recommendation from a friend to customize could influence a user's perceived benefit of the customization. Integrating social cues with a software environment may allow for such triggers.

METHODOLOGY CONSIDERATIONS

As we have discussed, software customization takes place over time and is influenced by many factors. It is thus worthwhile to empirically evaluate the relative impact of these factors. Our goal is to develop a methodology where during the study, the user can freely choose between using some *default behavior* (*e.g.* using a menu), or choose to customize using a *customization facility* (*e.g.* a customization dialog box), to enable an *enhanced behavior* (*e.g.* using a hotkey). The primary dependent variable of the methodology is if and when a user chooses to customize.

However, studying a decision on behalf of the participant is challenging, as extreme care must be taken to minimize any bias of that decision process. Here we discuss the factors and process of developing our study methodology in detail.

Motivation to Customize

In order for such a study to work, there must be a reasonable motivation for the user to customize. This means that the *enhanced behavior* that the customization enables must provide real benefits in terms of task performance or workload, in comparison to the *default behavior*. Unlike real-world scenarios, where the benefits of the enhanced behavior can propagate over long periods of time, lab experiments have a limited duration. As such the benefits need to be clear and immediate, so that it is to the user's advantage to customize. In particular, the enhanced behavior should not have a steep learning curve.

Between vs. Within Study Design

Because customization behavior involves a user's decision, any exposure to the *customization facility* or *enhanced behavior* could bias the user's decision to perform future customizations. If a user is exposed to multiple conditions, their decision to customize in later conditions could be influenced by experiences from the earlier conditions [9]. Thus, a between-subject design should be used.

Task Complexity

In real-world scenarios, customization is typically a secondary task that competes for the user's resources with the user's primary task. In the past, experiments used low cognitive demand tasks which illicit customization (*e.g.* [9]) or even instructed users to customize in order to compare the benefits of different personalization approaches (*e.g.* [2]). However, in our case, we wish to evaluate the *choice* to customize, so using a low cognitive demand task may artificially bias users towards customizing. To achieve a higher degree of external validity, the study may need to include tasks that vary in cognitive load. However, due to limited duration of lab experiments, it might not be possible to test different tasks. In such cases the study should include at least a single primary task with a reasonable cognitive load.

Customization Facility

Desktop applications allow for a wide variety of customization techniques [12]. In order to study customization behaviors, it is important that the customization facility used in the experimental task generalizes well. Although some in-place customization techniques have been explored [9, 19], customizations that result in significant benefits typically have an associated cost. For example, to define a new hotkey in Microsoft Word 2007, a user needs to access a dialog, 4 levels deep in the user interface. As such, for external validity, the *customization facility* should have some associated cost.

LESSONS FROM PILOT STUDIES

Due to all of the above-noted challenges, we conducted several pilot studies, to test various methodologies and study environments. Our initial methodology was based on Grossman *et al.*'s evaluation of hotkey usage [16]. A user was shown an image and could either select an associated menu item from the top of the screen, or use a customization dialog to set up a hotkey for that item (in the original work, the hotkey was already configured and available for use). However, we found that the mental demand of the enhanced behavior, using a hotkey, was too high, and as such participants consistently chose not to customize. It was apparent that this methodology did not provide enough *motivation to customize*.

To simplify the enhanced behavior, we introduced a local tool palette as the enhanced behavior. The users could access the palette faster than the default menu bar at the top of the screen. Because it offers a visual support for successful recall of customized operations, this approach required lower mental demand, but *all* participants were customizing, and reported that it was obvious that this would improve performance. Here, it became clear that the abstract image matching task we chose did not introduce enough *task complexity*.

As such, we introduced a more involved primary task to the methodology. After running several participants, the methodology seemed to provide a good balance, as advanced users chose to customize, while less advanced users did not. We settled on this methodology for our full experiment, which we now describe in detail.

EXPERIMENT

The goal of this experiment is to compare how exposure, awareness, and social factors influence customization behavior. We looked at how these customization factors influence the *breaking point*, the amount of customization that the user is willing to perform, and how these factors compare in terms of the benefit they provide to the user.

Participants

We recruited 64 participants (34 female, ages 18-63, median=27.5). The participants were in a wide variety of occupations. All were recruited through online classifieds ads and internal existing participants lists, and compensated with a $25 gift certificate.

Apparatus

We conducted the experiment on two HP Intel Xeon computers with 3.2GHz dual-processor and 12GB RAM, running Windows 7. Both machines were equipped with a 24-inch monitor set to 1920×1200 resolution, a standard optical mouse and QWERTY keyboard. Participants performed the task in separate rooms, and the investigators monitored their progress using a VNC-based remote desktop viewer. The experimental setup required two different rooms because for one of the conditions we required participants to come in with one of their friends and take part in the study at the same time. The experimental software was implemented using Java 5 SE.

Task

Figure 1 shows an overview of the experimental GUI and task procedure.

Main task. Each participant had to recreate a reference grid of items (Figure 1.III-e) by populating a working grid (Figure 1.III-d). Each item in the reference grid consisted of the following properties: shape (triangle, star, square, circle), fill color (yellow, green, red, blue), border (solid, dashed, dotted), and a foreground image (apple, banana, basket, clock, lemon).

Populating the grid. To recreate an item, the participant had to select a cell in the working grid, and then select a command corresponding to one of the four properties. The participants added item properties one by one to the active cell using one command for each property. Different items had different number of properties that the participant had to change, resulting in some properties being more frequent than others. A correct command caused the corresponding property to be added to the item in the grid. The grid selection was then cleared so that the participant had to select a cell to be edited before performing each command. This allowed tracking of trial times. A wrong command caused a 3 second penalty and the selection was cleared. No specific order was imposed for applying the properties to the cells, with the exception that the shape always had to be added first. The participant was not required to complete an item before selecting a different cell. Figure 1.II illustrates the completion of an item made of a star shape, a banana foreground image and blue fill color. Items appeared check-marked in both grids when completed.

Command selection. To perform the commands, the participants could select from one of the application menus (*default behavior*) corresponding to the property (Figure 1.IIIa) or the command palette (*enhanced behavior)* (Figure 1.IIIc). We expected a time saving of approximately 1 second every time the palette was used instead of the menu. All commands were available from the menus, but only a subset of commands was initially available from the palette. We intentionally pre-populated the palette with some of the commands, because leaving it empty may bias users towards customization [9]. Each property menu contained 12 commands (including distracters, which were never required to be used in the study). Figure 2 shows the default palette, split into four property categories. The default palette contained all the needed shapes, and a subset of the required other properties. Each palette section also included exactly one distracter that was never needed.

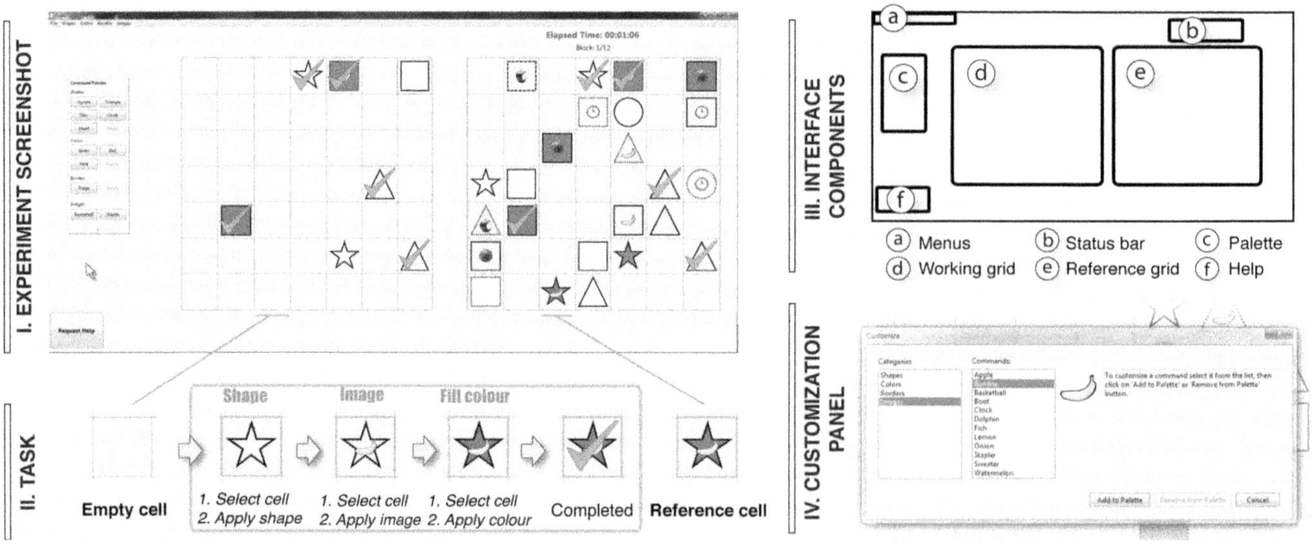

Figure 1. Experimental screenshot (I) with task (II), different components of the study interface (III), and customization panel (IV).

Customization facility. During the study the participants could customize the palette through a customization dialog (Figure 1.IV) invoked from the File menu to add or remove commands from the palette. For control purposes, the participants could customize only one command at a time. For a closer approximation to customization facilities in real software, we added a 10 second progress bar when loading the dialog.

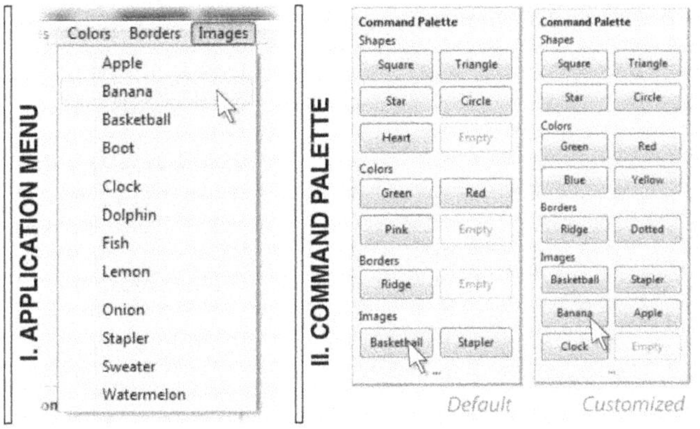

Figure 2. The application menu (I) and the default palette (II left) and a fully customized palette (II right) split into four property categories.

Procedure

Before the start of the experiment, an experimenter escorted the participants to a study room, but did not provide any verbal instructions about the task. Instead participants read the instructions once seated in the room. The instructions asked participants to perform the task as quickly and as accurately as possible. But the actual amount of time participants had to spend on the study was completely dependent on their own performance. As such, participants had an implicit motivation to complete the study efficiently.

Figure 3 shows an overview of the experimental procedure. Each participant completed 1 warm-up block and 12 study blocks. Each block consisted of a single reference grid. The set of items used to fill in the reference grid was the same across the study block, but the positions in the grid were randomly generated for each block. The participant had to execute exactly 10 correct commands in the warm-up block, and 60 correct commands in each of the study blocks. A block was completed only when all items in the grid were correctly recreated. During warm-up the participants had to use the application menu at least once, to become familiar with the default behavior.

Before the study, and after each block, the system informed users about the possibility to customize. The message was:

"All items can be accessed through the menu. The items available in the palette can be customized through the file menu."

The system provided no further instructions on how to customize. The participants were allowed to rest between blocks, with an enforced rest of at least 20 seconds.

Conditions. The experiment was a lab study with a between-subject design. The customization conditions were: *control*, *exposure*, *awareness*, and *social*. There were 16 participants in each condition. Each participant was randomly assigned to one of the four groups, but those participants who came in with a friend were only used in the *social* group. The conditions were as follows:

- *Control* – this condition provided only the mention of the existence of the customization feature (*i.e.* minimal awareness of the functionality).
- *Exposure* – this condition models high exposure to the customization feature. Participants in this group were forced to practice customizing one command during the warm-up, and then accessing that command from the palette. This was the only group that was ever instructed on how to customize. We included this condition because it provides the exposure through experiencing the customization facility.
- *Awareness* – this condition increases the awareness of the customization feature. Participants received a notification messages informing that customizing a specific command enables faster access (Figure 4). We chose this approach as it is similar to many past mixed-initiative systems.
- *Social* – this condition adds a social component to the raised awareness condition. In this condition, two friends completed the study at the same time in separate rooms. The participants received a similar message as for the *awareness* condition, but the message was crafted so that it said that the friend customized a command and was completing the task faster (Figure 4). The message was provided regardless of the friend's activity. This approach allowed us to test the impact of social influences on customization behavior.

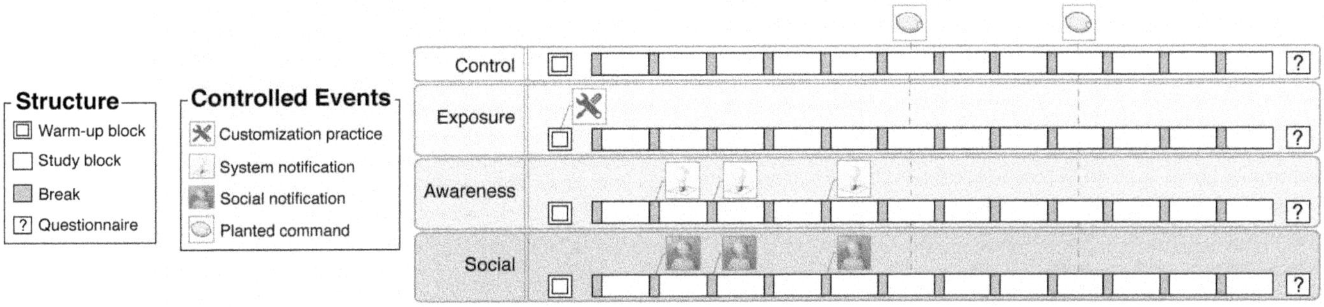

Figure 3. Overview of the experimental procedure for the four conditions.

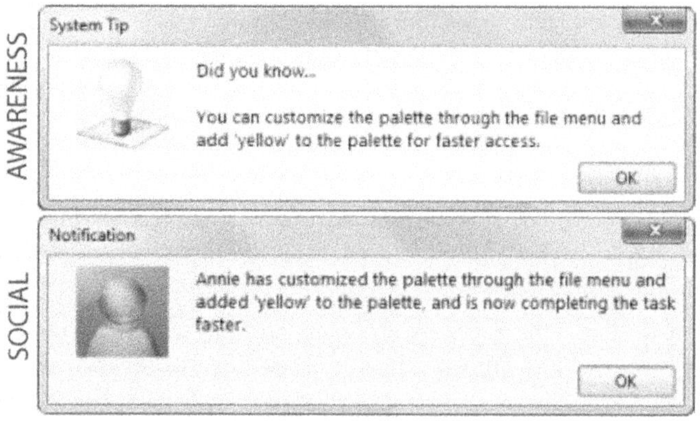

Figure 4. Awareness and social notification messages.

The participants in the *awareness* and *social* groups received notifications during the rest time after the first, second, and fourth grid. In the first message the system proposed the most frequent command that the participant had not customized at that point, in the second message it proposed the most frequent command that the participant had customized, and in the third message it proposed the next most frequent command that the user had not customized. If all commands were already customized, an arbitrary command was chosen.

Design

Each participant completed 12 grids × 60 commands each = 720 commands. The frequencies of commands were computed based on 30 random drawings from a Zipfian distribution of exponent 1 (relative frequency 1/rank) [39]. The frequencies were rounded to produce 7 frequencies (12, 6, 4, 3, 2, 2, 1). There were 14 commands that participants used in the experiment (2 assigned to each frequency). The command to frequency assignment was counterbalanced across participants, with each command mapped to a frequency once. The participant did not know the command frequencies upfront, but they became apparent as they were the same every block.

We also included one *planted* command, which only appeared twice across the entire study, to see how participants would respond to a command that would not be beneficial to customize. The *planted* command (lemon image) replaced one of the regular image commands in the 6th and 9th grids.

Additionally, the items in the grid had different properties and each item belonged to one of the four groups: items consisting of a shape only, a shape and 1 property, a shape and 2 properties, and a shape and 3 properties. The following default properties were assigned to a shape: white fill color, solid black border, and no foreground image. The participant never had to select any of the default properties as they were prepopulated on the item once a shape was added to the grid. The warm-up grid contained 4 items, one in each group, and a set of 24 items were used during the study, with 6 objects in each group.

Measures

We measured the performance time for individual commands, and the total study time, as defined below:

- *Command Time* - the average time between cell selection (click on a grid cell) to command execution (click on a command in a menu or in the palette). Only correct commands were considered.
- *Study Time* - the time it took to complete all trial grids (not including breaks).

We also measured when the participants first customized and the extent of customization which occurred:

- *Breaking Point* - the block in the experiment when the participant decided to customize the first command.
- *Customization Magnitude* - the number of customizations the participant performed in different blocks in the experiment.

Participant expertise levels. To provide additional insights into the data, we classified users as power or non-power users. To do so, participants completed a post-experiment questionnaire asking about their demographics, computer usage (*e.g.* amount of hours, type of tasks), and customization behavior. The customization behavior questions asked about the amount of customization (if any) and the type of customization the user would perform (e.g. personalizing Gmail account look, customizing Word command ribbon, modifying Word templates, creating Excel macros, etc.). This was done to account for different levels of customization experience [28]. Three of the authors performed data coding on participant's responses. The participants were grouped in two categories: power users (30 participants) and non-power users (34 participants). There was substantial agreement between the coders (Fleiss' κ=0.635). The split between power users and non-power users across conditions was relatively balanced (min=6, max=10, median=8).

RESULTS

In this section we present the results of our experiment. Unless otherwise stated, we analyzed parametric participant data (such as time to complete the study) with one-way and two-way ANOVAs. Type II ANOVA was used when data was mildly unbalanced. The pair-wise comparison was done using a Tukey's test. Non-parametric data, such as number of customizations we analyzed using a Kruskal-Wallis test and pair-wise comparison was done using a Mann-Whitney's U test. We used Fisher's exact test when comparing categorical data (*e.g.* number of participants that customized and those that did not).

Performance Time

One of the important design considerations in our methodology was to ensure that customization would benefit the user (*motivation to customize*). Accessing items from the command palette (mean=1.366s) was indeed faster than accessing an item from the menu (mean=3.226sec) ($F_{1,55}$=422.99, p<.001, η^2=0.13). Additionally, in all groups, participants who customized at least once completed the study faster than those who did not ($F_{1,56}$=23.47, p<.001, η^2=0.42), with average completion times of 38.59min and 49.03min respectively (Figure 5). It is also interesting to note that there was a difference in study completion times between conditions ($F_{3,56}$=4.26, p=.0087, η^2=0.23), where users in the *social* group completed the study faster than the *exposure* (p<.05) and *awareness* (p<.005) groups. Thus, the social factor might have influenced them to work faster.

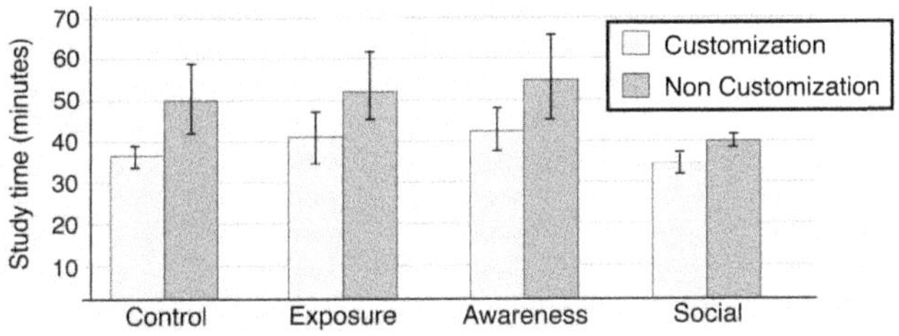

Figure 5. Study completion time per group and customization. The error bars represent 95% confidence interval.

Customization Strategies

Participants demonstrated different strategies, but at the high level, we looked at: (1) strategies of those that did not customize and (2) strategies of those that did customize. Across the 64 participants, 46 customized and 18 did not. Some users in the *control* group (N=3) chose to use only menus (1.1), but the majority of non-customizers used both the menu and the command palette (1.2). One participant who did not use the palette stated after the experiment that she prefers to "get into the flow" with one particular way of performing a task and dislikes switching.

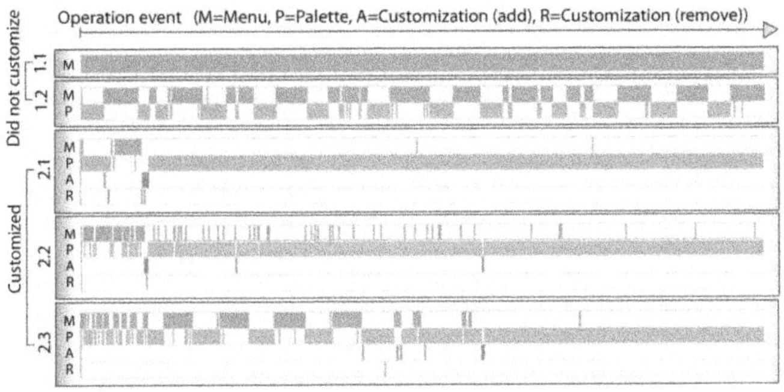

Figure 6. Examples of customization strategies of actual participants that did not customize (1.1 and 1.2) and those that customized study software (2.1, 2.2, and 2.3).

Strategies of those participants that customized can further be classified into: (2.1) early customization, (2.2) sparse customization and (2.3) later customization. The early customizers and late customizers tended to customize most of the commands in quick succession (usually within a single block), differing only in the time when they first started customization. The sparse customizers customized early in the experiment, but took time to customize all of the commands that they did, before switching to almost exclusively using the palette. Figure 6 shows examples of these customization strategies from actual participants.

Customization Behavior Between Conditions

We now look at the actual customization behaviors between groups. Figure 7 shows the number of participants that customized in the four conditions. In comparison to the *control*, the number of users who customized increased by 62.5% in the *exposure* and *awareness* conditions, and by 50% in the *social* condition. Despite the observable trend, the data only represents a single sample per user, and the difference did not reach statistical significance.

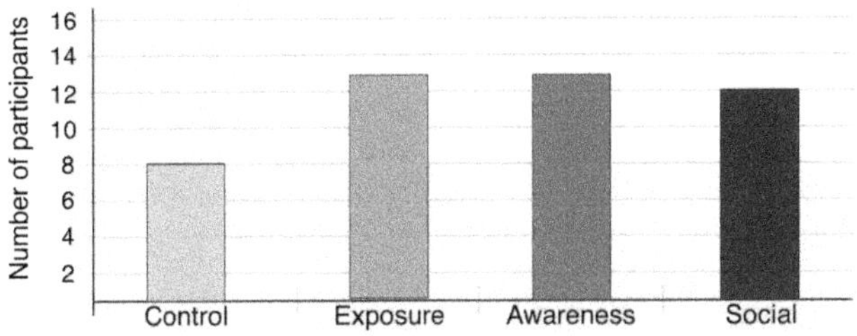

Figure 7. Number of participants out of 16 that customized study software by condition.

In the *control* group, 6 out of 8 power users and 2 out of 8 non-power users customized. This suggests that the study design, to a degree, resembles the real difference in customization behavior between power and non-power users [23]. We found a similar trend in the *awareness* group, and the difference in number of those who customized between non-power users (4 out of 7) and power users (9 out of 9) approached significance (p=.0625). We did not find significant difference between number of power and non-power users who customized in the other two groups. This may indicate that exposure and social factors are more effective for non-power users.

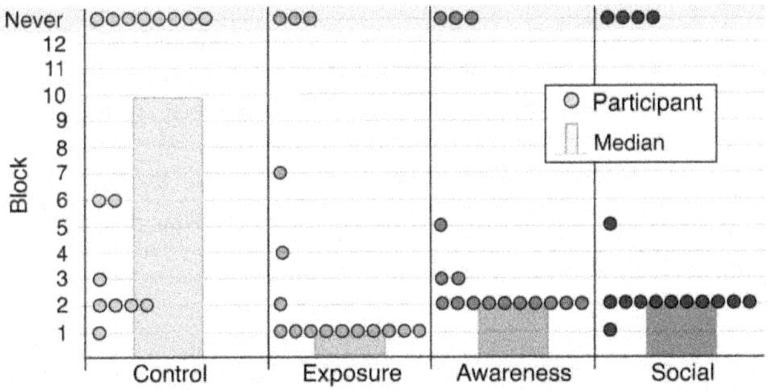

Figure 8. Median breaking point block per condition. Participants who did not customize are also included.

Breaking point. There was a significant difference between the breaking point between conditions ($\chi^2_{(3)}$=11.17, p=.0108) (Figure 8). Participants in the *control* group took longer to decide to customize than the *exposure* group (U=198, Z=2.76, p=.005, r=0.69). The *awareness* and *social* groups also appeared faster to customize than *control* and the difference approached significance (U=173, Z=1.81, p=.0652, r=0.45 and U=171.5, Z=1.764, p=.0696, r=0.44 respectively). The participants in the *exposure* group also first customized earlier than *awareness* (U=73.5, Z=2.14, p=.0329, r=0.54) and *social* (U=76, Z=2.06,

p=.0380, r=0.52) groups. This was likely because exposure occurred before the first block, whereas the awareness and social messages appeared before the second block. Overall, this provides empirical data that the evaluated factors can influence a user's *breaking point*.

Customization magnitude. Out of the 46 participants who customized at least one command, the percentage of those who customized all 7 of the commands was 57.45% (N=27). Some participants (N=17, 9 power users, 8 non-power users) removed some of the distractor commands from the palette. This is different from other studies that reported that participants rarely remove features [10]. This indicates that some users, not only switched to the *enhanced behavior*, but also tried to further improve their performance.

In order to further analyze the magnitude of customization, we grouped blocks in distinct periods in the experiment: start (blocks 1-4), middle (blocks 5-8), and end (blocks 9-12).

For all groups except control, most of the customizations occurred in the start period of the experiment (p<.05) (Figure 9). In the *control* group, the start and middle periods were not significantly different. This means that *exposure*, *awareness*, and *social* conditions can help users customize more items earlier, when customization has the most value.

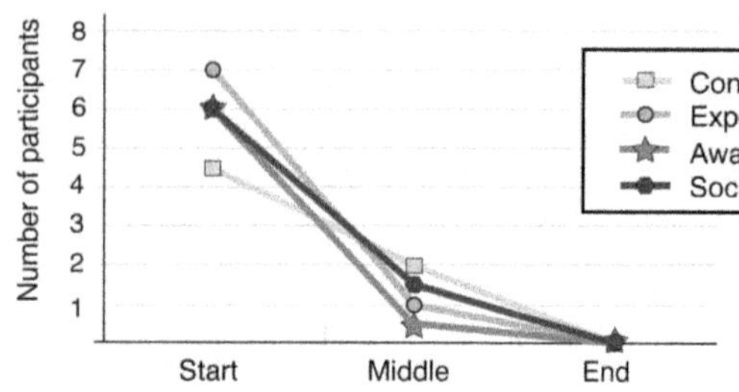

Figure 9. Median number of customizations by period and condition. The values do not include participants that have not customized.

Some participants also customized the *lemon*. The percentage of users that customized the *lemon* command in the middle period was: 0% in the *control* group, 25% in the *exposure* group, 0% in the *awareness* group, and 6.25% in the *social* group. The differences approached significance (p=.0652). One other participant from the *awareness* group (6.25%) customized *lemon* in the end period. This could mean that some participants (mostly in the *exposure* group) acted impulsively and simply repeated the learned action to customize without considering the value of customization.

Subjective Results

After the experiment we asked the participants about how much impact the assigned condition had on their strategy (*e.g.* "During the study you have received number of notifications about what your friend was doing. To which extent did this impact your strategy?"). Responses were measured on a scale from 1 to 7, where 1 was very low impact and 7 was very high impact. The mean results were 4 in *exposure* and *awareness*, and 5 in *social*. The differences were not significantly different (p=.452). However, the open-ended questions highlighted some interesting differences between conditions.

The participants in the *exposure* group saw the training as a means to raise their awareness of the customization facility. However, none of them commented that exposure helped them in realizing that customization was easy to perform:

"If it had not been for the information I derived during the warmup period, I wouldn't have customized my palette to the elements that appeared most often." –$P12_{exposure}$

"Once I found out I can customize, I thought about when it is best to customize and when it was not." –$P16_{exposure}$

For some users, exposure did not trigger customization because they were unsure of the benefits of the enhanced behavior:

"At first I didn't bother [to customize], as I didn't see it as a factor, thinking that there would be so many grid boxes to replicate that choosing customizations would just take up space and cost time." –$P8_{exposure}$

For participants in the *awareness* group, raising the awareness of customization facility was enough to trigger customization:

"At first I was unaware of the ability to customize the palette. After I received that advice from the system, I realized the advantage of having all the most commonly used commands on the palette and quickly added them." –$P14_{awareness}$

However, the content of the message was less useful to some power users. They were able to understand the benefit of the *enhanced behavior* even before the notification:

"The tips were never particularly important, only the knowledge I could customize, which I did at a later while with my own decisions." –$P11_{awareness}$ (power user)

However, non-power users found this information helpful:

"It was as if the system was giving clues as to what was going to be needed to do the next task." –$P5_{awareness}$ (non-power user)

Most participants felt that the social message increased their awareness of the customization facility. It also made them perform the task faster in order to compete with their friend.

"I didn't even think about seeing if I could customize the palette until I noticed that my friend was doing it. It sent me in the right direction." –$P15_{social}$

"I get very easily competitive, so seeing that he was performing tasks faster made me want to do better myself. Seeing that the customizations helped his strategy made me take the time to make my own customizations to enable me to work to my full capacity to complete the task." –$P16_{social}$

The social message could have also been a tipping point for some, as it increased their confidence that they would be able to learn how to use the customization facility.

"At first I did not want to change the option. I figured it would take too much work. But when I saw that my friend changed it, I thought I might as well try it once." –P10 social

"During the first round I was not adventurous enough to spend time discovering how to use/customize the pallet. After seeing my friend had, I decided to attempt to customize my own, and discovered it was a fairly simple process." – P1 social

However, for some participants in both *awareness* and *social* groups, the notifications had little impact. In fact some chose to disregard the messages thinking the content had no importance, while for others the messages added negative pressure, and may have inhibited customization:

"I didn't want to get stressed out by what he was doing. I really didn't care what he was doing to be honest!" –P5 social

"I didn't want to waste time [finding out how to customize]. I tend to be rather competitive, so it just added extra pressure to perform. [My friend] is competitive too, so I like to beat him if I can." –P7 social

DISCUSSION

Through our analysis, we have identified that the factors we tested have a significant influence on users' customization behavior. In this study, this was mainly manifested in changing when a user chose to customize. While not significant, it also seemed to influence whether or not a user chose to customize. These are encouraging results.

The analysis revealed only subtle differences in the impact of the three test conditions. Larger scale studies, with more participants, may be required to more accurately measure the relative impact of these factors. Most prominent was that in the *social* condition, users performed the task significantly faster than in other conditions. This could be due to competition rather than benefits of customization. Even so, in addition to changing the customization behavior this approach could be used to increase user performance.

We also found that the factors might have a different effect on power and non-power users. In the *control* group, only 25% non-power users customized, and in the *awareness* group, only 57%. On the other hand, in the *exposure* and *social* conditions, more non-power users customized (80% and 78% respectively). This may indicate that awareness is a weaker influence for non-power users.

In an actual application, exposure to the customization facility could be achieved through occasional enforced training. But it could also be combined with social influences, where the system notifies the user about her friend's or colleague's behavior and offers to guide her through the customization process.

It was interesting to note that some participants chose not to customize even in the test conditions. While we expected this behavior in the *control* group, we found various reasons for such behavior in other groups. In the *exposure* group this could be due to participants being overly reluctant to changing their behaviors [4]. Providing a rationale for customization might help [3], but it remains unclear how behavior of such users could be changed, and more research is required. In the *awareness* and *social* groups some participants did not customize simply because they chose to disregard the messages. As such, other techniques to expose users to awareness and social factors, besides system messages, should be explored. An ambient display of such information, which a user would not be as rushed to dismiss, could be one potential solution [25].

The *social* condition might have an adverse effect on some users, as the pressure to perform faster could inhibit their willingness to explore customization options. Future research should explore how social factors affect users with different personalities. However, as users were under time pressure in the lab study, it remains an open question if such adverse effects would occur in a more relaxed setting.

A secondary contribution of our work is that we show how sensitive customization studies are to the particulars of the study methodology. Small changes made after each of our pilots had large effects on user behaviors. Our experiences, and our methodology considerations discussion, provide important lessons for future customization studies.

In summary, each of the factors we tested impacted customization behaviors, and some trade-offs between the techniques appeared. In order to design successful customization facilities, designers should consider the strengths and weaknesses of these factors. However, some of these influences could potentially work together (*e.g.* social influence on top of a mixed-initiative system) to remedy some of the weaknesses and enhance the strengths.

CONCLUSION AND FUTURE WORK

In this paper we demonstrated a methodology for personalization studies which require a user choice. We then used this methodology to design and execute a user study. The results of the study exposed different customization strategies and differences in how users respond to increased exposure and awareness, and social influences. We showed that these three factors can decrease the time to the *breaking point*, and that software can in fact control such factors in order to change user behavior.

Based on these findings we proposed directions in which future research can improve customization facilities. While our results may generalize beyond the specific facility and enhanced behavior from our methodology, the factors should be evaluated against different customization approaches [12]. Also, our findings provide grounding for follow-up field studies with more complex and real-world software applications to test whether our results would extend to such systems. As we discussed, lab studies have inherent challenges when running studies that involve user choice. It would be interesting to develop field study methodologies to test how closely our results would be replicated in actual usage scenarios. Nevertheless, our findings provide insights into customization factors and allow for more focused field studies of customization factors that can be controlled by software.

REFERENCES

1. Brusilovsky, P. and Schwarz, E. User as student: towards an adaptive interface for advanced web-based applications. *User Modeling*, (1997), 177-188.
2. Bunt, A., Conati, C., and McGrenere, J. Supporting interface customization using a mixed-initiative approach. In *Proc. IUI '07*. ACM (2007), 92-101.
3. Bunt, A., McGrenere, J., and Conati, C. Understanding the Utility of Rationale in a Mixed-Initiative System for GUI Customization. In *Proc. UM '07*. (2007), 147-156.
4. Carrol, J. M., and Rosson, M. B. Paradox of the active user. In *Interface thought: Cognitive aspects of human-computer interaction*. Cambridge (1987).
5. Clark, B., Matthews, J. Deciding Layers: Adaptive Composition of Layers in a Multi-Layer User Interface. In *HCI International*, Volume 7, July 2005.
6. Cockburn, A., Gutwin, C., and Greenberg, S. A predictive model of menu performance. In *Proc. CHI '07*. ACM (2007), 627-636.
7. Debevc, M., Meyer, B., Donlagic, D., and Svecko, R. Design and evaluation of an adaptive icon toolbar. User Mod. and User-Adap. Inter., 6, 1, (1995), 1-21.
8. Dourish, P., Lamping, J., and Rodden, T. Building bridges: customisation and mutual intelligibility in shared category management. In *Proc. GROUP '99*. ACM (1999), 11-20.
9. Findlater, L. and McGrenere, J. A comparison of static, adaptive, and adaptable menus. In *Proc. CHI '04*. ACM (2004), 89-96.
10. Findlater, L. and McGrenere, J. Evaluating reduced-functionality interfaces according to feature findability and awareness. In *Proc. INTERACT'07*. Springer-Verlag (2007), 592-605.
11. Findlater, L. and McGrenere, J. Impact of screen size on performance, awareness, and user satisfaction with adaptive graphical user interfaces. In *Proc. CHI '08*. ACM (2008), 1247-1256.
12. Findlater, L. and McGrenere, J. Beyond performance: Feature awareness in personalized interfaces. Int. J. Hum.-Comput. Stud. 68, 3 (March 2010), 121-137.
13. Findlater, L., Moffatt, K., McGrenere, J., and Dawson, J. Ephemeral adaptation: the use of gradual onset to improve menu selection performance. In *Proc. CHI '09*. ACM (2009), 1655-1664.
14. Gajos, K. Z., Czerwinski, M., Tan, D. S., and Weld, D. S. Exploring the design space for adaptive graphical user interfaces. In *Proc. AVI '06*. ACM (2006), 201-208.
15. Greenberg, S. and Witten, I. Adaptive personalized interfaces: A question of viability. Behav. Inf. Tech. 4, 1, (1985), 31-45.
16. Grossman, T., Dragicevic, P., and Balakrishnan, R. Strategies for accelerating on-line learning of hotkeys. In *Proc. CHI '07*. ACM (2007), 1591-1600.
17. Grossman, T., Fitzmaurice, G., and Attar, R. A survey of software learnability: metrics, methodologies and guidelines. In *Proc. CHI '09*. ACM (2009), 649-658.
18. Krisler, B. and Alterman, R. Training towards mastery: overcoming the active user paradox. In *Proc. NordiCHI '08*. ACM (2008), 239-248.
19. Kurlander, D. and Feiner, S. A history-based macro by example system. In *Proc. UIST '92*. ACM (1992), 99-106.
20. Mackay, W.E. Patterns of sharing customizable software. In *Proc. CSCW '90*. ACM (1990), 209-221.
21. Mackay, W.E. Triggers and barriers to customizing software. In *Proc. CHI '91*. ACM (1991), 153-160.
22. MacLean, A., Carter, K., Lövstrand, L., and Moran, T. User-tailorable systems: pressing the issues with buttons. In *Proc. CHI '90*. ACM (1990), 175-182.
23. Marathe, S.S. Investigating the psychology of task-based and presentation-based UI customization. In *Proc. CHI EA '09*. ACM (2009), 3129-3132.
24. Marathe, S. and Sundar, S.S. What drives customization?: control or identity?. In *Proc. CHI '11*. ACM (2011), 781-790.
25. Matejka, J., Li, W., Grossman, T., and Fitzmaurice, G. CommunityCommands: command recommendations for software applications. In *Proc. UIST '09*. ACM (2009), 193-202.
26. McGrenere, J., Baecker, R.M., and Booth, K.S. An evaluation of a multiple interface design solution for bloated software. In *Proc. CHI '02*. (2002), 164-170.
27. Mitchell, J. and Shneiderman, B. Dynamic versus static menus: an exploratory comparison. SIGCHI Bull. 20, 4 (April 1989), 33-37.
28. Mørch, A. Three levels of end-user tailoring: customization, integration, and extension. In *Computers and design in context*. MIT Press (1997), 51-76.
29. Page, S.R., Johnsgard, T.J., Albert, U., and Allen C.D. User customization of a word processor. In *Proc. CHI '96*. ACM (1996), 340-346.
30. Peres, S.C., Tamborello II, F.P., Fleetwood , M. D., Chung, P., and Paige-smith, D. L. Keyboard shortcut usage: The roles of social factors and computer experience. *Hum. Fact. & Ergo. Soc., 48*. (2004), 803-807.
31. Scarr, J., Cockburn, A., Gutwin, C. and Quinn, P. Dips and ceilings: understanding and supporting transitions to expertise in user interfaces. In *Proc. CHI '11*. ACM (2011), 2741-2750.
32. Sears, A. and Shneiderman, B. Split menus: effectively using selection frequency to organize menus. ACM Trans. Comput.-Hum. Interact. 1, 1 (1994), 27-51.
33. Shneiderman, B. and Plaisant, C. Designing the User Interface: Strategies for Effective Human-Computer Interaction (4th Ed.). Pearson Addison Wesley (2004).
34. Stuerzlinger, W., Chapuis, O., Phillips, D., and Roussel, N. User interface façades: towards fully adaptable user interfaces. In *Proc. UIST '06*. ACM (2006), 309-318.
35. Tsandilas, T. and schraefel, m.c. An empirical assessment of adaptation techniques. In *CHI EA '05*. ACM (2005), 2009-2012.
36. Thomas, C.G. and Krogsæter, M. An adaptive environment for the user interface of Excel. In *Proc. IUI '93*, ACM (1993), 123-130.
37. Twidale, M.B. Over the Shoulder Learning: Supporting Brief Informal Learning. *Comput. Supported Coop. Work 14, 6* (December 2005), 505-547.
38. Venkatesh, V., Morris, M.G., Davis, F.D., and Davis, G.B. User Acceptance of Information Technology: Toward a Unified View. *MISQ (27:3)*, 2003, 425-478.
39. Zipf, G. *Human behavior and the principle of least-effort*. Addison-Wesley (1949).

Brainstorming for Japan: Rapid Distributed Global Collaboration for Disaster Response

Michael Muller† and Sacha Chua‡
† IBM Research, One Rogers Street, Cambridge, MA, USA 02142
‡ IBM Global Business Services, 3600 Steeles Ave., East Markham, ON, Canada M6P2P5
michael_muller@us.ibm.com sachac@ca.ibm.com

ABSTRACT
Tragic events struck northern Japan in March-April 2011. This note presents a case study of rapid distributed brainstorming for disaster response, involving 275 contributors from 23 countries within a three-day period, conducted among the staff in a multinational company. Factors that appear to have contributed to the success of this brainstorming include: Social media that could be easily appropriated; and employee familiarity with large-scale brainstorming. The formation of this "flash-community" joins other CHI reports to point toward a new genre of rapid large-scale responses to disasters through social media.

Author Keywords
Disaster response; emergency management; social media; online community; virtual team.

ACM Classification Keywords
H.5.3 [Information interfaces and presentation]: Group and organization interfaces – Collaborative computing;

七転八起
Fall down seven times, get up eight.
-- Japanese proverb

INTRODUCTION
The people of northern Japan suffered a series of cascading disasters beginning 11 March 2011: an earthquake leading to a tsunami, followed by human and technological emergencies on a massive scale. More than 13,000 people were killed, and more than 300,000 people were displaced. Damage from the tsunami led to a crisis at the Fukushima nuclear plant. Millions of Japanese, nationwide, were without power. A series of secondary and tertiary problems resulted in a months-long crisis for Japan, with spreading societal, commercial, and financial impacts around the world.

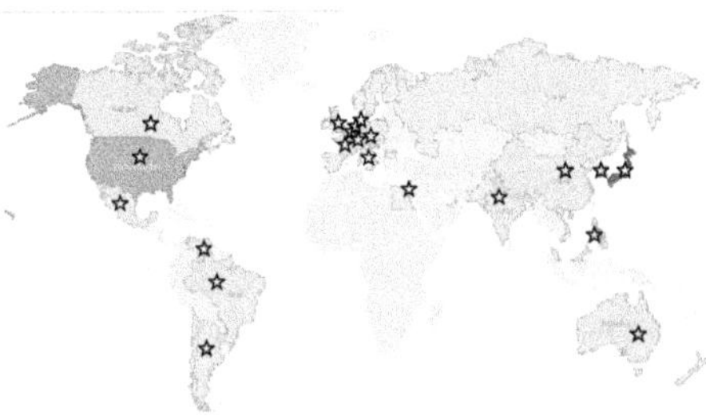

Figure 1. Employees participated from 45 countries. Darker colors indicate more participants. Stars show the 23 countries from which employees made visible contributions. A few smaller countries are omitted for visual clarity.

Many people, nations, and organizations around the world responded with food, supplies, money, and people's time, labor, and expertise. This note describes one response in detail: the use of social media to develop ideas for response by employees in IBM, a multinational company. We intend this note as a "case," rather than as a formal CHI analysis. We will tell the story of the collaboration, connect that story to Related Work in CHI, CSCW, and related fields, and close with proposed topics for future research.

Palen et al. called for a vision of Information and Communication Technology (ICT) to support public engagement during emergencies [7]. In this work programme, they have documented ways in which "people are developing new practices for emergency responding, using ICT to address problems that arise from information dearth and geographical dispersion" in online communities that are defined in social rather than geographic terms [11]. They called for new designs and services that can increase citizen participation ([7]; see also [1]). Carver and Turoff argued for systems that support creativity and improvisation during emergencies [2]. Online communities are already doing this kind of work, often in a voluntary manner whose motivation has been described as "altruistic" [5,11]. Among these communities, online forums appear to be key resources [8]. In this note, we expand the scope of online communities and forums, and their types and manners of participation or contribution during emergencies.

BRAINSTORMING FOR JAPAN
Like many people and organizations of good will, IBM acted to support the citizens and government of Japan in the early hours of 12 March, contributing technology, services, and consultation. After several weeks of intense relief work,

managers at IBM began to discuss longer-term responses and proposals. They decided to convene a voluntary brainstorming activity for employees called the Japan Forum.

Using IBM Connections, a commercial social media product, the managers created an online community for the brainstorming. In the discussion forum of that community, they posed four topics for discussion; the large response by employees allowed them to expand this list to seven topics.

Brainstorming at IBM

Employees were accustomed to conducting remote, online, asynchronous brainstorming sessions (forums) for small groups (10-500 employees during a customer engagement), medium sized groups (500-10,000 employees discussing a market segment, in some cases with client participation), and company-wide discussions (100,000 or more employees, business partners, and clients, working on new business concepts [4]). Common attributes were as follows:

- Forums were conducted in environments which supported tree-structured text-based discussions.
- Each forum addressed assigned topics.
- To create a sense of urgency, each forum had defined date/time limits. In the medium and large groups, these limits were enforced by the software, which did not allow participants to log in before or after the specified time. In the smaller, informal sessions conducted on IBM Connections, the limits were indicated but not enforced.
- Each forum had open registration to all employees and contractors. The larger forums had open registration for business partners and/or customers. The contents of the forum could be observed by anyone who had registered.
- At least 95% of participants in each of the forums were volunteers. A small core team established the problem(s)-to-be-addressed, and members of the core team moderated the forum as it took place. Often, an extended team of subject-matter experts was invited to participate; their participation was not mandatory. Any member of a forum was able to invite colleagues to join, and in practice many of the participants were in this peripheral group of completely voluntary, socially-invited contributors.

Participation was thus a dynamic activity, driven by personal interest and passion. In the Discussion, we will return to themes of interest, practice, and volunteering.

Post-forum analysis was typically done by staff with specific skills. For the smaller- and medium-sized forums, the analysts were usually members of the marketing team who had organized the forum. For the company-wide forums, a team of specialists would work for hundreds of staff-hours on many thousands of contributions.

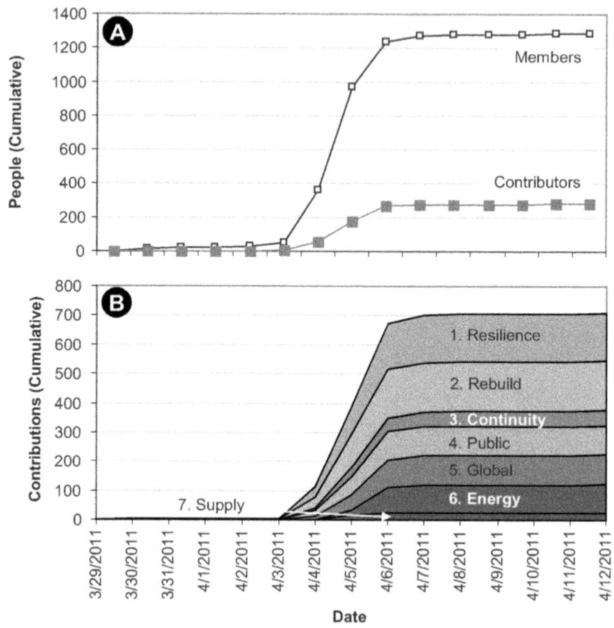

Figure 2. A. Growth of members and contributors during the forum. B. Growth of contributions in each of the seven discussion topics.

Conducting the Japan Forum

The Japan Forum was begun in the manner of a customer engagement. People in diverse organizations, who had a shared interest in emergency response, were informed of the forum, and were invited to recruit their colleagues. As we will show, the urgency of the situation led to a much larger response than a typical 100-person customer-engagement forum, with interesting outcomes.

The planners initially proposed four discussion topics: (1) Increasing resilience of Japan to future problems; (2) Leveraging technology in rebuilding; (3) Continuity planning; and (4) Addressing public perceptions. Three additional topics were added during the forum: (5) Engaging global support; (6) Managing energy consumption; and (7) Improving health and food supply chains.

Quantitative Results

Participation and Contribution. The Japan Forum was announced via an email appeal to several thousand employees, and it was featured on the IBM intranet homepage. At least some of the recipients informed additional employees. The day before the official beginning of the Forum, 47 people had registered. Four days later, at the conclusion of the Forum, 1250 people from 45 countries had registered (Figure 1). Among them, 275 people (20%) from 23 countries had made at least one contribution, for a total of 701 discussion responses (range: 1-68 responses/ person, median=1), during the three days of the Forum. The timeline of contributions is shown in Figure 2, which includes post-forum analytic contributions during the weeks after the conclusion of the forum.

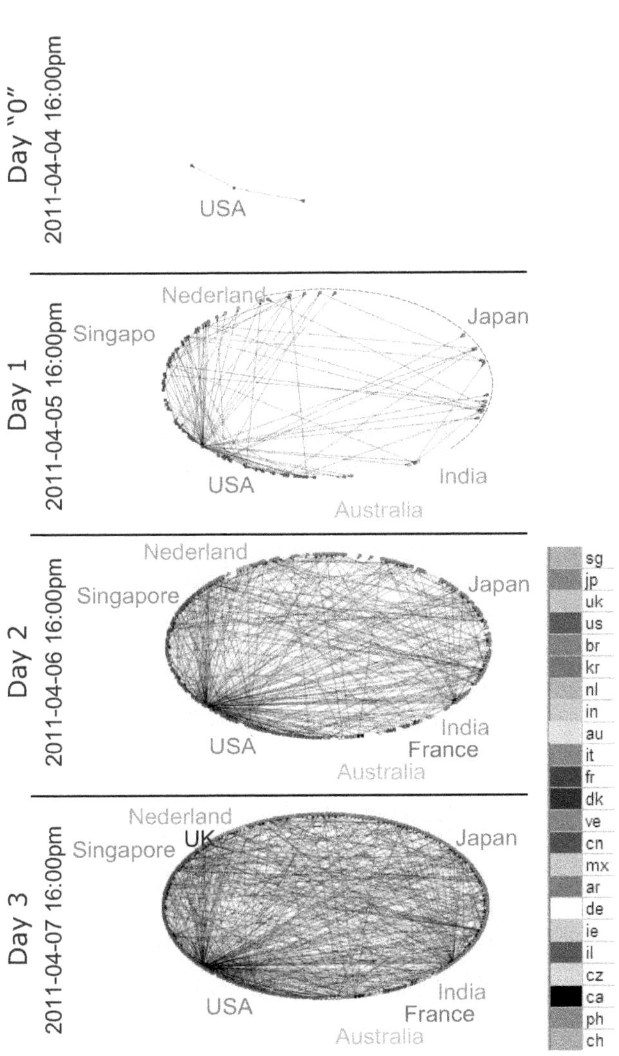

Figure 3. Growth of social network among the contributors, from "day 0" (the day before the brainstorm), to the end of the third day of the brainstorm. Country codes are from internet domain conventions (e.g., http:// ftp.ics.uci.edu/pub/ websoft/wwwstat/country-codes.txt, accessed 2011-12-20).

Participation followed a long-tail distribution, with 135 people (52%) making more than one contribution, and only 37 people (14%) making 5 or more contributions. We note that 78 contributors (30%) wrote responses on more than one day. Thus, participation was global, with more than a quarter of the participants showing sustained interest.

Lurking. Like most commercial systems, IBM Connections recorded only active participation, with no record (other than membership) of the 1011 non-contributing participants (i.e., "lurkers"). We assume that they took an active interest, because they took the time to join the community – an effort that was as voluntary as contributing. See [6] for a discussion of how lurkers transport information from a lurked resource into active use outside of that resource.

Social Network Analysis. Except for the organizers who proposed the topics, each of the visible participants created a response to another person's contribution. These response relationships allowed us to calculate the social network connecting contributors, across the three active days of the forum. Figure 3 shows the dramatic increase in social network connections across the three days of the forum.

Qualitative Results

Employees' contributions in the brainstorm contained rich ideas. In this note, we can only summarize what was discussed. We organize our report of the contents of the forum according to the conventional analysis of emergency management into four phases [3]: Responding (21.52% of contributions), Recovering (43.81%), Preventing (10.53%), and Preparing (49.23% -- note that 25.08% of contributions involved more than phase, so the percentages add up to more than 100%):

Responding. Brainstorming about how to *respond* to the current emergency involved many ideas, including:

- expanding available modeling tools to address the current conditions (e.g., using weather forecasting tools to predict radiation spread)
- repurposing existing technology for early sensing of tremors (e.g., accelerometers, disk shock-protectors)
- monitoring and modeling disease outbreaks
- managing electronic health care records during wide-scale technology outages
- providing telemedicine in the absence of power grids and reliable communication infrastructures

Recovering. While much of Japan's power generation was offline for safety checks, employees brainstormed about how to use the remaining power effectively:

- optimizing power usage at personal level and at regional level through "smart" utility management techniques
- improving power efficiencies in data centers
- using impact models to prioritize and schedule the needed rolling power outages

Information technology resources were limited, and therefore part of the "Recovering" discussion considered:

- developing more resilient networking for cities
- providing rapid-recovery for city records
- expanding these capabilities to businesses, as needed

Preventing. While earthquakes and tsunamis cannot be prevented, damage from those events can be minimized:

- providing rapid-recovery for city records
- "hardening" and strengthening existing networks and storage redundancies by simulated emergency testing

Preparing. Because of history, Japan as a nation has committed many resources to planning for future emergencies. Employees attempted the challenging task of adding to what the Japanese have already considered:

- studying best practices from other regions
- developing simulations to test resource resilience and social response

These and other ideas are currently under discussion as a kind of portfolio of potential joint work between the government of Japan and IBM; details remain confidential to both parties. This is a typical interim outcome from these kinds of corporate brainstorms, because of the substantial resources required to implement ideas of this scale. We regret that we cannot provide further details at this time.

RELATED WORK AND CONCLUSION

In [1], panelist Tiantian Wang noted the need to determine "What constitutes the disaster community?" What kind of entity was the Japan Forum? If it was an online community of interest or community of practice (e.g., [10]), its four-day duration was unusually brief. If it was a virtual team (e.g., [9]), it managed to be highly effective without a manager, an assignment, a task list, or a reward structure.

Based on the IBM experiences with forums [4], we suggest that this kind of limited-duration, low-commitment idea-generation collaboration is a distinct genre of online collaboration. Its distinguishing characteristics appear to include the brief timeframe, the brainstorming atmosphere of innovative thinking [2], and the ability of volunteers to make small contributions with very low cost-of-contribution [11].

This genre extends the space of online communities that form during and after emergencies and disasters [1,2,7,8]. Most research about "disaster communities" [1] has focused on people who are directly affected by the emergency. Our experiences expand the space of action for remote volunteers from assistants/translators for people facing the emergency (e.g., [11]) to autonomous actors who collectively create new knowledge as a distinct type of contribution.

Implications for Design

Based on our case study, we suggest that systems and services to support this kind of volunteerism should allow people to join with a very low cost-of-commitment [11], and should recognize volunteers as participants whether they make visible contributions or act invisibly as engaged readers [6]. There appears to be no need for recognition, incentives, or rewards to motivate participation [4,11]. We speculate that the forums might be strengthened through a parallel community space that was designed for sociality [8,10], in addition to informational contributions.

Future Research Directions

In future research, we plan to conduct interviews to understand participants' motivations. We also plan to ask them about what additional information they would find useful. We hope to offer forums outside of the enterprise setting, to test replication on the broader internet.

In summary, we have described a case in which a group of volunteers was able to organize quickly to develop creative solutions in the service of other people who were facing an emergency. We showed the breadth of volunteerism, the large volume of ideas generated, and the growth of social connectedness that took place in a matter of days. We used this case to propose a distinct genre of remote collaborative contribution during crises, and we sketched some potentially important attributes. We used this analysis to propose implications for design and future research directions.

ACKNOWLEDGMENTS

We thank John Gordon for patient discussions about the business implications of this work.

REFERENCES

1. Bedford, D., & Faust, L., 'Role of online communities in recent responses to disasters: Tsunami, China, Katrina, and Haiti,' *Proc. ASIST 2010*.
2. Carver, L., & Turoff, M., 'The human and computer as a team in emergency management information systems,' *CACM 50*(3), 33-38, 2007.
3. FEMA, *Guide for all-hazard emergency operations planning*, 1996, http://www.fema.gov/pdf.plan/slg101.pdf (accessed 2011-12-29).
4. Helander, M., Lawrence, R., Liu, Y., Perlich, C., Reddy, C., & Rosset, S., 'Looking for great ideas: Analyzing the Innovation Jam,' *Proc. KDD 2007*.
5. Kaniasty, K., & Norris, F., 'In search of altruistic community: Patterns of social support mobilization following Hurricane Hugo,' *Am. J. Com. Psych. 23*(4), 447-477, 1995.
6. Muller, M, Shami, N.S., Millen, D.R., & Feinberg, J. (2010). 'We are all lurkers: Consuming behaviors among authors and readers in an enterprise file-sharing service,' *Proc GROUP 2010*.
7. Palen, L., Anderson, K.M., Mark, G., Martin, J., Sicker, D., Palmer, M., & Grunwald, D., 'A vision for technology-mediated support for public participation and assistance in mass emergencies and disasters,' *Proc. Vis. Comp. Sci. 2010*.
8. Palen, L., Hiltz, S.R., & Liu, S.B., 'Online forums supporting grassroots participation in emergency preparedness and response,' *CACM 50*(3), 54-58, 2007.
9. Powell, A., Piccoli, G., & Ives, B., 'Virtual teams: A review of current literature and directions for future research,' *DATABASE Adv.Info. Sys. 35*(1), 6-36, 2004.
10. Preece, J., *Online communities: Designing usability, supporting sociability*, Wiley, 2000.
11. Starbird, K., & Palen, L., '"Voluntweeters": Self-organizing by digital volunteers in times of crisis,' *Proc. CHI 2011*.

Designing Social Translucence Over Social Networks

Eric Gilbert
School of Interactive Computing & GVU Center
Georgia Institute of Technology
gilbert@cc.gatech.edu

ABSTRACT
Social translucence is a landmark theory in social computing. Modeled on physical life, it guides designers toward elegant social technologies. However, we argue that it breaks down over modern social network sites because social networks resist its physical metaphors. In this paper, we build theory relating social translucence to social network structure. To explore this idea, we built a tool called Link Different. Link Different addresses a structural awareness problem by letting users know how many of their Twitter followers already a saw link via someone else they follow. During two months on the web, nearly 150K people used the site a total of 1.3M times. Its widespread, viral use suggests that people want social translucence, but network structure gets in the way. We conclude the paper by illustrating new design problems that lie at the intersection of social translucence and other unexplored network structures.

Author Keywords
social networks; social translucence; design; cmc; twitter

ACM Classification Keywords
H.5.3 [Group and Organization Interfaces]: Asynchronous interaction - Web-based interaction;

INTRODUCTION
Social translucence [22] is a landmark theory in social computing. In essence, it describes ways to build social technologies that support social life. Social translucence argues that we should make online social behavior *visible* to facilitate *awareness*, ultimately creating social spaces where we feel *accountable* to one another. Erickson & Kellogg model the theory on social processes we see in real, everyday life. For example, they share a story where authors gather in a room to arrange the chapters of an edited book ([22], pgs. 62–63). It works because the room affords visibility: if I try to move a chapter somewhere that upsets the book's delicate balance, you can intervene because you see me moving it. Typically, we have to carefully design social media to afford what this room affords effortlessly.

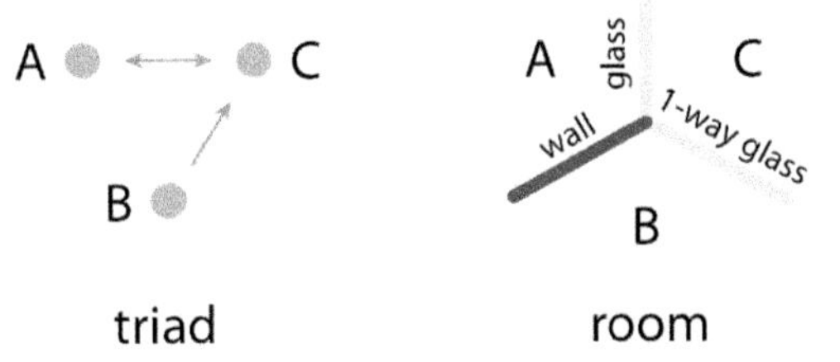

Figure 1. A hypothetical room mirroring a social media triad.

Early social media resembled real-life places like this room. Chat clients evoke conference rooms. Forums recall café bulletin boards. However, today many of the internet's most popular sites (e.g., Facebook, Twitter, Google+) don't look like rooms at all. Rather, they revolve around the concept of social networks. To illustrate, consider an ordinary group of three people on Twitter. We've depicted their relationships in Figure 1. *A* and *C* follow each other, and *B* follows *C*. Now, picture the room you would have to build to mirror Twitter's constraints. You need to keep *A* and *B* separate, so you might build a wall between them. *B* should see *C*, but not the other way around, so put one-way glass between those two. At first glance, it seems like you don't need anything between *A* and *C*, but you should keep them separate so *A* doesn't wander over, permitting *B* to see *A*.

This room is unlike anything you would find in everyday life. And it's just three people. What would it look like with four, five or six? It becomes hard to imagine such a room. The complexity grows so quickly because social networks disrupt sight lines in complex ways. Consequently, the metaphors around physical space so central to social translucence simply break down in the context of social networks.

This paper aims to bridge the gap, offering a new way to think about social translucence in the era of networks. We build a theory relating specific structures within complex social networks to the problems they cause for social translucence. Using it, we work through an awareness problem arising from one of these structures, the triad $A \leftarrow B \rightarrow C$. Here, *A* has difficulty sharing new information with *B* because she cannot know what *B* already heard from *C*. We designed a tool called Link Different to address this problem on Twitter. When someone wants to share a link with their followers, Link Different reports how many of them already saw the link via someone else they follow. Deployed openly on the web for two months, nearly 150K people used Link Different 1.3M+ times in total. We think these orders of magnitude speak volumes: people still want social translucence's cues, but network structure gets in the way.

We begin by reviewing social translucence and its descendent systems, as well foundational work on social networks. Next, we introduce Link Different and the sharing behavior of its users. Finally, we conclude the paper by extending the theoretical work behind Link Different, arguing that new social computing problems lie at the intersection of social translucence and various unexplored network structures.

LITERATURE REVIEW

First, we review the theory of social translucence. We also consider some of the many systems architected around it. Because our approach connects social translucence with social network structures, we conclude this section with a summary of fundamental social network research.

We focus on social translucence because it provides specific design guidance that we can overlay on social networks. However, theoretical alternatives exist. For example, the venerable CHI paper "Beyond Being There" [34] argues that we shouldn't try to replicate the affordances of real life in social technologies—a central tenet of social translucence. This tension deserves resolution, with new work perhaps arising by adopting an alternative theoretical lens.

Social Translucence

Comprising three major papers [21, 22, 23], the theory of social translucence aims to take what we do so naturally in real social life and map it onto online social media. (However, the term "social media" didn't exist at the time and doesn't appear in those papers.) Erickson & Kellogg write:

> The difficulty of digital communication and collaboration stands in stark contrast to our ability to communicate and collaborate with one another in the physical world . . . We have evolved an exquisite sensitivity to the actions and interactions of others. Whether it is wrapping up a talk when the audience starts fidgeting, or deciding to forego the grocery shopping because the parking lot is jammed, social information like this provides the basis for inferences, planning, and coordination of activity. [22] (p. 60)

(Hereafter, we refer to Erickson & Kellogg as "E&K.") This is the yardstick against which E&K argue we should measure our social technologies. Despite being published more than ten years ago, we can see technologies still catching up with the vision. For example, the recently launched startup Localmind lets users ask "how crowded the bar is, or how long the line to the club is" from afar [42]. Presumably, you might choose to stay home if the club line is too long, recalling E&K's jammed grocery store parking lot.

Unless explicitly designed into systems, most social information remains hidden inside databases. E&K propose three guiding principles for bringing it to the forefront, which we referred to at the beginning of the paper: *visibility*, *awareness* and *accountability*. Each gives rise to the next, and visibility is the most basic. Social translucence argues that we should make collective activity visible to everyone in a space. Of course, privacy is an issue, and this is where the word "translucence" takes on particular importance. Rather than build a totally transparent system (e.g., publish GPS coordinates), a system should abstract away from raw data without sacrificing too much useful social information (e.g., publish neighborhoods). In addition, constraints act on visibility. For example, our ability to see things decays as we move farther away from them. Social software can model this, for instance, by providing greater resolution to people nearby.

Awareness arises from visibility. Having seen the social cues floating around me, I absorb them, and use them to decide what to do next. Furthermore, my social and cultural expectations come to bear on my newfound awareness. For example, suppose I see you methodically cleaning up files in our shared code repository. I become *aware* that soon you will reach my files, and social customs dictate that I release my lock on the files so you can do your work. Finally, out of this distributed social awareness comes a second-order effect: accountability. As E&K put it, "I know that you know that I know."

As we alluded earlier, social translucence has been very influential in social computing and CSCW, attracting over 1,000 citations since its publication a decade ago [30]. Across a wide variety of application areas, many systems have used it to guide design (e.g., [7, 9, 11, 24, 36, 46, 47]). Most work has focused on small groups. For example, [11], [24] and [36] use social translucence to abstract away from raw presence data in experimental IM clients. In [7], the theory provides a way to visualize abstract histories of presence among distributed workgroups. A notable exception to the small-group trend is WikiDashboard [46], which employed social translucence to make behind-the-scenes Wikipedia activity visible.

Particularly relevant to the present work, [9] built and field-tested a "directed content sharing" tool called FeedMe. While browsing RSS feeds in Google Reader, FeedMe recommends people who might also be interested in an article and lets you to share it with them via email. FeedMe uses social translucence to show you how many other FeedMe recommendations the target person has received. We take FeedMe as a point of departure. Where FeedMe allowed point-to-point sharing via email, we ramp the idea up to social media at scale on Twitter. To the best of our knowledge, the system we present in this paper is the first to connect social translucence and large-scale social networks.

Social Networks

Studied by sociologists for decades [38], social networks silently structure social life. The literature is simply too vast to cover here, but we attempt a very brief overview of fundamental work. Social networks start out simply: I become friends with you, you become friends with someone else, and so on. Friendships often form by way of homophily (i.e., shared interests and tastes) [43] and a process called preferential attachment [5], whereby people prefer to connect with those who are already well-connected. Over time, a complex, organic structure emerges. Via a network's macroscopic structural properties and dynamics, you can tell who is popular [6], who will have good ideas [17] and who in a company will get promoted [16].

It is important to note that social networks differ from *social network sites* [13]. Social networks are a concept. Social network sites (SNSs), on the other hand, revolve around social networks, using them as a central design element. SNSs

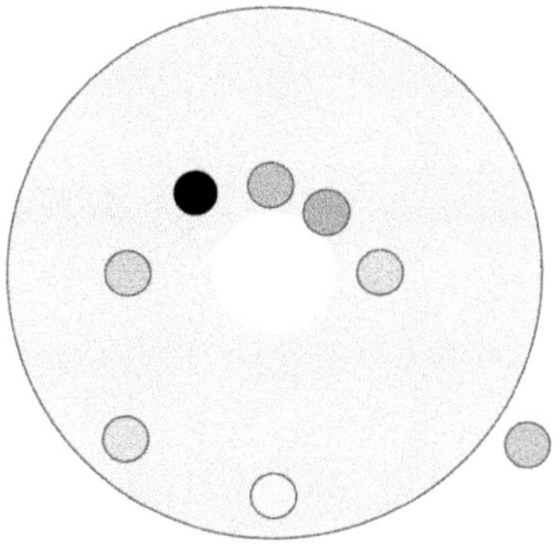

Figure 2. Babble's "social proxy," used to signal activity in a chat room. Avatars, represented by simple abstract circles, move to the center to signal interest in chatting. Reproduced from [21].

like Twitter, Facebook and Google+ are important: they can provide us with new social capital [20], answers to questions [44], and sometimes a sense of well-being [15].

We add to this growing literature by considering the design of SNSs as a function of embedded social network structures. We believe this is the first work to do this. In the next section, we consider how traditional social translucence cues interact with micro-structures called triads.

SOCIAL TRANSLUCENCE & SOCIAL NETWORKS

E&K often draw analogies between physical space and digital space. Consider, for example, the system discussed by E&K in *Social Translucence*, the chat program Babble. In Babble, we all enter the same digital space to chat. Your avatar moves to the center of the room to signal your interest in talking, and the geometry of Babble's circular design forces it into proximity with other avatars (see Figure 2). The parallels between physical space and online conversational space are direct and apparent. E&K explicitly connect digital social spaces with physical ones via an architecture metaphor:

> As designers of communication and collaboration systems, we find ourselves taking inspiration from work in the areas of architecture and urban design. This is not surprising, since, like architects and urban designers, we are concerned with creating contexts that support various forms of human-human interaction. [22] (p. 61)

As we discussed before, early social media resembled physical spaces. Chat rooms can be thought of as digital conference rooms—the insight made by Babble. You could argue that email distribution lists resemble neighborhood association meetings and therefore build affordances that mimic those meetings. In real life, as in these technological metaphors, social signals are tied to the space. For example, in real life, if I move, then everybody nearby notices me moving. If someone addresses our group, but I'm idly looking out the window, then everybody else can infer that I'm bored. The physics of everyday life affords these things.

However, modern social media—especially some of the most popular sites—often do not reflect everyday physical life. Rather, they rest on the primacy of social networks. Social networks do not have physical analogs. On Twitter, you follow diverse people who share things you find interesting. Those people follow who they want, and so on. Social signals—the

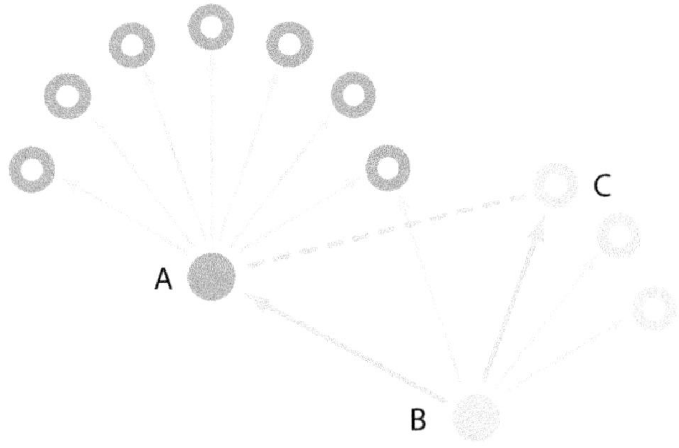

Figure 3. A fragment of a directed social network like the attention networks found in Twitter. Highlighted in gold is a triad that gives rise to a *triadic awareness problem*. B follows A and C, but A does not follow C. Consequently, A does not know what B has heard from C.

building blocks of visibility, awareness and accountability—are not tied to a specific digital space. Rather, social signals *flow through* networks. Whereas E&K envisioned digital "architecture" (i.e., rooms and spaces), today networks structure many aspects of online social life.

Of course, they also permit a scale of social media unthinkably large for 2000, when social translucence was first introduced. Twitter has at least 38 million active users; imagine them all in the same chat room. (Where "active" is defined, for the sake of argument, as following at least 16 people [18].) Networks let us carve up our attention, looking at a select group of people rather than at everyone. This is probably a prerequisite for scale.

Yet while the underlying architecture may have changed, we are still social creatures attuned to social cues. We want social information so we can act appropriately. We want to know who's interested in what we say. We want to know whether our audience is bored and looking out the window or hanging on our every word. We want rich social cues that also respect privacy. We think the spirit of *Social Translucence* remains the same. Only the landscape has changed.

A Triadic Awareness Problem

What does this mean for design? As we discussed earlier, we believe social translucence breaks down because of fundamental structural differences between physical space and social networks. Therefore, we adopt a structural perspective in this paper. Our major theoretical claim is that different structures embedded within complex social networks give rise to different social translucence design problems.

We will work an example end-to-end in this paper. However, we revisit this broader claim—that network structures unlock design problems—in our *Discussion* section as it suggests new open problems for social computing. Now, we introduce a particular *triadic awareness problem*. A triad is a small fragment of a social network: three people and the ties that bind them. They can exhibit various shapes. Let us consider the directed attention networks like the ones that underly Twitter and Google+. Given three people—call them A, B and C—each relationship can take on one of four

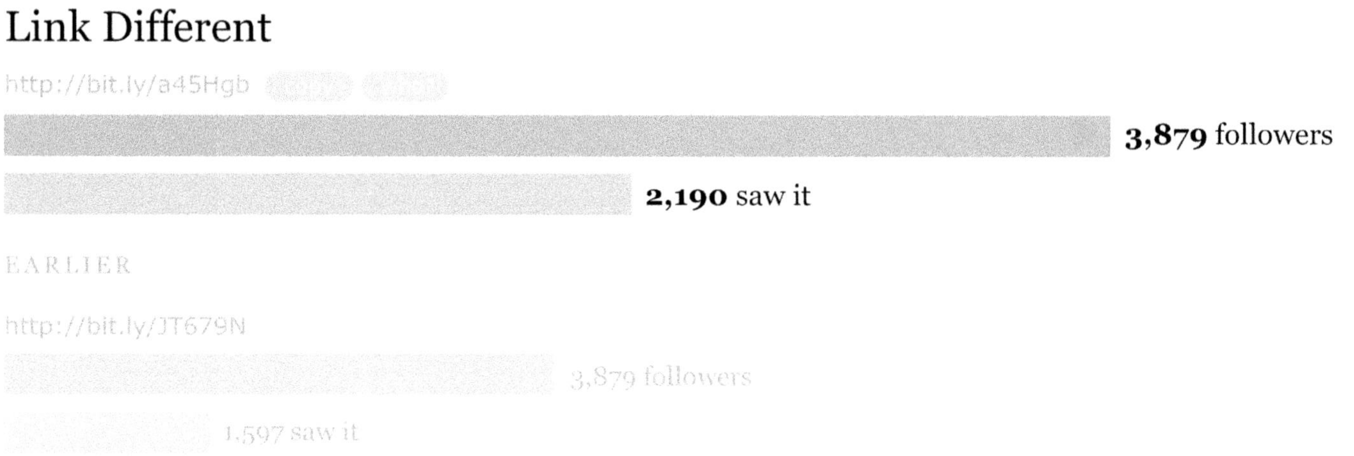

Figure 4. The Link Different web interface. When a user visits a webpage, she can use the Link Different bookmarklet to compute how many of her Twitter followers have already seen it from someone else they follow. Link Different displays the information as simple bar charts and includes some recent history. Users can also copy the link and view a random sample of followers who already saw it.

states: absent, left-directional (Twitter's "following"), right-directional (Twitter's "followed by") or bidirectional. $64=4^3$ possible triads emerge from the multiplicative combination of pairwise ties. For example, a triad might be fully closed, $A \leftrightarrow B \leftrightarrow C \leftrightarrow A$ or some less-connected variant, like $A \leftrightarrow B \leftarrow C$. (See [19] for background on triads and [28] for their recent use in social media research.)

A triadic awareness problem arises from a certain triad, the one shown in gold in Figure 3: $A \leftarrow B \rightarrow C$. (The arrows indicate attention flowing in that direction.) Set in the context of Twitter, this triad means that B follows both A and C, but A does not follow C (or vice versa). However, because A is not listening to C, this presents a problem. If A wants to share novel information with B, then she has to estimate whether B already heard it from C.

In practice, however, this problem is orders of magnitude harder than what we just described. A must estimate whether B already heard her information from C *or from anybody else B follows*. Furthermore, A has followers other than B and must estimate that same thing for each of them. Let us assume that the average active Twitter user follows 100 people and has 100 followers—probably a conservative estimate [3]. Then A has to estimate novelty for 100 followers, each of whom follows 100 people. Therefore, a typical scenario involves roughly 100^2=10,000 triadic awareness problems. All this complexity arises from a simple question: "What have your followers already heard?"

Contrast what we just described with a space like a chat room. There, A simultaneously listens to B and C. In fact, we might consider a chat room a special theoretical case: the fully closed triad $A \leftrightarrow B \leftrightarrow C \leftrightarrow A$. In a chat room, everyone can talk and listen to everybody else. (They may not always talk to and listen to everyone, but it is always possible.) Social networks purposely dissect this idea. A and C *choose* not to pay attention to each other; they don't want social translucence's visibility. Like in Figure 1 at the beginning of the paper, networks disrupt visibility (and hence, awareness and accountability) between people.

Figure 5. Link Different bookmarklet installed in Chrome. While visiting a webpage, users click it to run Link Different on the page's URL.

LINK DIFFERENT

The theory we have developed suggested a need for a tool to solve the triadic awareness problem on social network sites. This is why we developed Link Different. Link Different is a web-based application that lets Twitter users know how many of their followers already saw a link from someone else they follow. We built Link Different to enhance the common practice of link-sharing on Twitter. Recent estimates suggest that at least 25% of all tweets contain a link to somewhere else on the web [45]. We focused on links, rather than more general concepts like "newsworthy topics" (e.g., how Google News groups stories) for tractability reasons which we explain shortly. Link Different is designed to support a scenario like the following:

> Sue takes a break from the report she's writing to browse the *New York Times*. She reads a fascinating article about the Chinese economy's rising service sector. Having built a Twitter following based in part on her economics expertise, she goes to share the story on Twitter. But then Sue notices its publication date: *yesterday*. News flies fast on Twitter, and she sees the distinct possibility that her followers already saw this article from someone else. She brings the URL to Link Different. Link Different provides her with a simple bar chart showing the proportion of her followers who already saw the *New York Times* piece from somebody else they follow. Sue chooses to share it after seeing that only 22% of her followers saw the story already.

People interact with Link Different via a bookmarklet they install in their browser. Much like bit.ly's bookmarklet [12], users install a small snippet of Javascript in their browser's bookmarks bar (see Figure 5). While visiting some page on the web and considering sharing it on Twitter, users can click the bookmarklet to have Link Different operate on the their

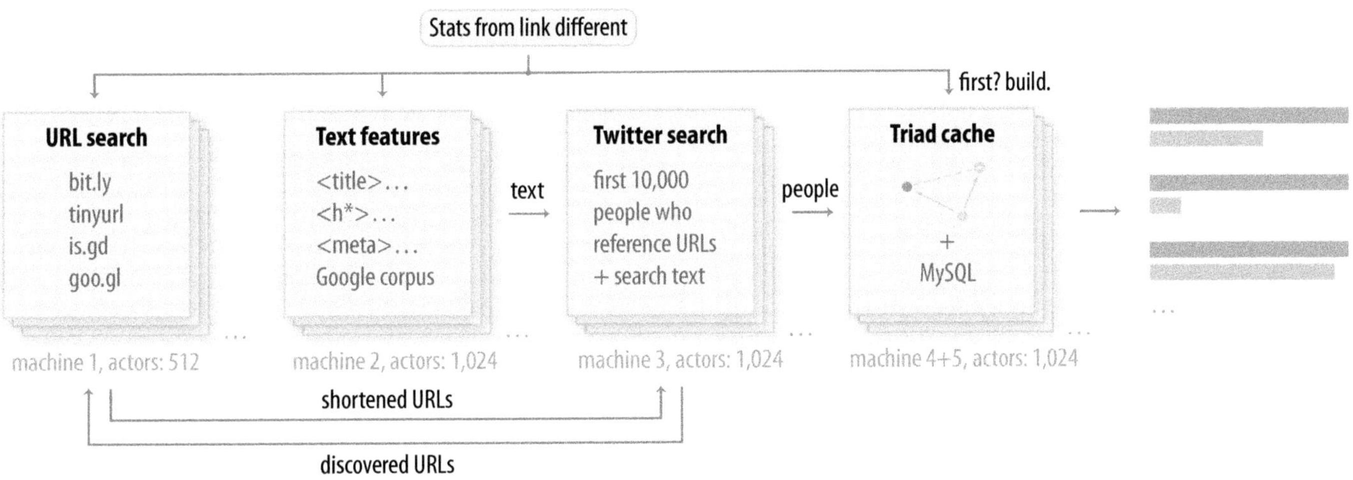

Figure 6. Link Different's server-side architecture. The application is distributed across five load-balanced machines, each running its own pool of parallel Scala actors. URLs and textual features get passed to a Twitter search to find references to the target webpage. The first 10,000 people to reference the target page are compared to the triad cache, which we build when someone uses Link Different for the first time.

page's URL. To get access to the bookmarklet, people first have to authenticate Link Different's Twitter app—something they do once at sign-up. (We explain the reason behind authentication in the *Implementation* section.)

When a user clicks the Link Different bookmarklet, a new tab opens, bringing them to a page like the one in Figure 4. We modeled this interaction on bit.ly's behavior when shortening URLs. After Link Different finishes its crawl of the user's Twitter network, Figure 4's simple bar charts appear. The top one shows the total number of followers, while the one below it shows how many followers already saw it from someone else they follow. In Figure 4, slightly more than half of the user's followers have seen it already. Link Different also shows a recent history in gray. We pursued a very simple design, hiding the complexity of the distributed Twitter crawl in the server-side software.

Link Different automatically shortens the link for users, using bit.ly's API, and it also provides a copy button to let users quickly put the shortened link on their clipboard. After our release, we received many tens of requests from users asking for a feature to let them know *which* followers had seen the link already. The logic behind many of these requests seemed to be that different followers are differentially important, and our users might be willing to bother some as long as a few others benefitted. In response, we added the "who?" button. It reveals a random sample of up to 50 followers who already saw the link, sorted by their number of followers—a proxy for their status on Twitter.

Implementation

Link Different's user interface is simple HTML, CSS and jQuery [39] served by PHP. Link Different's server-side architecture, on the other hand, is a parallelized distributed system. Figure 6 presents an overview. To ensure acceptable response times with potentially thousands of concurrent users, Link Different is distributed among five high-end machines (e.g., Quad-core i7, 16GB+ RAM, etc.) that interact with each other via message passing. The software is written in Scala and uses its actor and message-passing implementations [32]. That is, the components broken down in gray boxes in Figure 6 operate in parallel with one another, responding to requests from other components when they have available time and resources. The Link Different architecture makes thousands of HTTP requests every time a user clicks the Link Different bookmarklet, yet its distributed design means that most people receive responses within 10 seconds. (This is admittedly long by web standards, but we considered it acceptable for a research prototype.) Also, Twitter granted us a whitelisted IP address, providing Link Different with 20,000 API requests per hour, per user—the reason we require users to authenticate our Twitter app.

A historical quirk in Twitter's design substantially complicates the Link Different implementation. Since Twitter limits tweets to 140 characters (an artifact of Twitter's early text message focus), people have an incentive to shorten their URLs to save characters in their tweets. A number of services sprung up to serve this need, such as bit.ly, the most popular URL shortener [1]. Moreover, many of these shortening services provide their users with personalized click-through statistics. They do this by creating custom short-URLs for every person (e.g., http://bit.ly/AB4fgT for you and http://bit.ly/6kyk90 for me), each resolving to the same long-URL via HTTP redirects. This means that for a popular article on the web, say a *New York Times* article, thousands of short-URLs often exist. Link Different needs to track all of these. While bit.ly and tinyurl APIs permit discovering all short-URLs (and luckily account for nearly 90% of short-URLs [1]), other services do not.

Therefore, in addition to pushing the Link Different user's long-URL through various shorteners, we also perform Twitter searches on key textual information from the webpage. Our goal is to find references to the target article not discovered via the URL search. We extract text within the `title`, `header` (i.e, `<h1>`, `<h2>`, `<h3>` and `<h4>`) and `meta` tags. Every possible tri-gram phrase is used as input to its own Twitter search. In addition, we use the Google 1T corpus [14] to compute normalized TF-IDF statistics [25] for each uni-, bi- and tri-gram from the page's non-HTML text. The Google 1T corpus has baseline frequencies for phrases on the web, and computing these statistics uncovers a page's most descriptive phrases. The phrases scoring in the top decile become inputs for their own Twitter searches. For all these searches (a typical page creates around 500), any tweet containing a URL is queued for inspection by the "URL search" process. If they resolve to Link Different's target, then the person tweeting the URL is a candidate. We consider up to 10,000 Twitter users as candidates in our server's final stage. (An alternative to our textual approach, one taken by the recently acquired BackType [4], is to catalog and index every URL on the Twitter firehose. While it would greatly simplify Link Different, we did not have resources to build something at this scale.)

The "URL search" and "Text features" searches ultimately generate candidate Twitter users who could be parts of triads similar to the example in Figure 3. To find the subset that belong to these triads, we cache all people who could be *C*s in a Figure 3 triad. The first time someone clicks the Link Different bookmarklet, we build a triad cache in parallel with the ongoing search described above. A distributed crawl is initiated, where we build an index mapping every *C* to a list of *B*s that follow *C*. We store this cache in a MySQL database. Here, we traded space for time, as the average Link Different user requires roughly 1K of cache space. However, as a result, for every candidate Twitter user returned via searches, we can use our index to do a constant-time lookup, retrieving every one of our user's followers who follows the candidate. After removing duplicates by adding them to a set data structure, we arrive at the number of followers who already saw this link from someone else they follow.

Limitations

Link Different's user interface is very simple. It does not let you explore *who* mentioned a link to your followers, nor *when* they saw it. It cannot tell you whether your followers actually clicked on the link they saw from someone else, only that it appeared in their Twitter streams. People would almost certainly welcome this deep information. Furthermore, it would be interesting to extend Link Different to operate on stories rather than links. For example, when a major event happens (e.g., the Super Bowl), various outlets cover it. We can envision users welcoming the opportunity to explore concepts rather than simple URLs. Link Different's text searches might be the beginning of an approach.

Moreover, Link Different makes probabilistic tradeoffs in its server implementation. There is no guarantee that the "saw it" number is precise. For performance reasons, we traded off precision for response time. Deeper indexing strategies might resolve these inconsistencies.

WEB FIELD STUDY

We chose to evaluate Link Different as an open field study on the web. Other approaches also make sense, such as an in-depth, but small-*N* field study like the one in [9]. Yet, we were primarily interested in establishing a new theoretical claim: that this triadic awareness problem exists and people struggle with it. Rather than showing that a technology solves a problem we know to exist, in this paper we want to study whether the problem exists at all. For this reason, we chose to open Link Different up to any Twitter user on the web.

After finalizing the Link Different build, we "launched" it by sending short email messages describing the project to a handful of well-known technology blogs. We were fortunate enough to have one of them cover Link Different [41]. Often, one of the biggest hurdles for a release—especially for an academic lab—is getting the initial word out, and this helped us overcome it. Simultaneously, the blog coverage meant that we did not have to rely on our existing online networks, such as Twitter, Facebook and internal email lists. For example, this sidesteps validity threats due to snowball samples originating with a technology's creators [10]. After the initial coverage, Link Different primarily spread virally through Twitter. During its two months online, 144,232 unique people used Link Different 1,343,322 times in total. The blog coverage drove an initial burst of visitors to the site, but via HTTP referrer headers [29] we found that 84% of Link Different's usage came from our users discussing Link Different on Twitter.

Sharing Behavior

After releasing Link Different, we found that we were generating very interesting data about conformity and novelty effects on social media sharing. Although not our intention, you can view the simple Link Different interface as a prompt to this question: "Now that you know what proportion of your followers have already seen your link, do you still want to share it?" We realized that viewing sharing behavior as a function of the proportion of followers who have already seen the link may yield new insight into conformity and novelty in social media.

Because Javascript cannot copy text to the clipboard across browsers, Link Different uses a snippet of Flash code to let users copy the bit.ly link. Rather than load this code upfront, we use jQuery to load it dynamically into the page when the user clicks the copy button. Via this mechanism, our web server logs recorded when a user decided to copy a link and when they didn't. Presumably, when they use the copy button, they intend to share it on Twitter.

To verify this *copy-as-proxy* idea, we randomly sampled 5,000 instances where a user copied a link and 5,000 where they did not (out of the 1,343,322 total events). Our goal was to estimate how often a copy click leads to sharing and how often a non-click entails not sharing. If consistent, we can use the copy click as a proxy for sharing without having to crawl every tweet ever made by everyone who used Link Different—something we simply did not have the resources to accomplish. Over 90% of copy clicks lead to sharing and over 90% of non-clicks lead to not sharing. Therefore, for the remainder of this discussion, we will use copy-click data as a proxy for sharing data.

From our 1,343,322 events, we computed the proportion of links shared as a function of a moving 2% "already seen" window. Figure 7 illustrates the results. For example, the leftmost bar in Figure 7 says that people shared links 42% of the time when only 0-2% of their followers had seen the link from

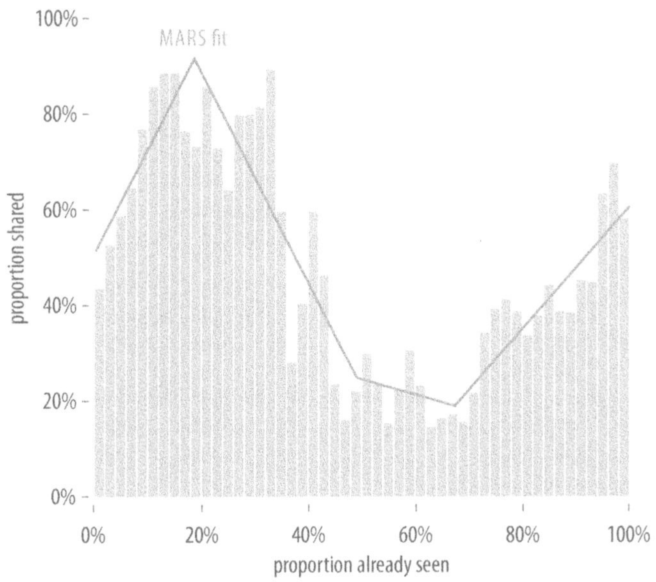

Figure 7. The proportion of links shared (y-axis) as a function of the proportion depicted in the Link Different interface (x-axis). Given a stimulus of how many followers already saw a link, the graph shows the likelihood of sharing it. The orange line plots a Multiple Adaptive Regression Splines (MARS) fit, uncovering four different regions.

someone else. We chose a 2%-wide window because it was the smallest integer to produce 99% confidence intervals of ±1% using the Agresti-Coull confidence interval technique for proportions [2]. Other window sizes could presumably change Figure 7's shape slightly.

It would be nice to abstract away from some of the noise in Figure 7. Therefore, we used R's MDA library [33] to compute a Multiple Adaptive Regression Splines (MARS) fit of our data. In essence, the technique iteratively converges on a piecewise linear fit, uncovering regions with fundamentally different shapes. It learns these regions from data. The orange line in Figure 7 shows the MARS fit. It uncovers four segments, each modeled as a line with a different slope. From left to right, they have slopes (i.e., β-weights), 3.86, -4.46, -2.23 and 1.9. This model fits the data reasonably well, with an Adj. $R^2 = 0.445$. While some regions in Figure 7 are distinctly curvilinear, the MARS decomposition provides an abstract layer over which we can reason and potentially build theory—something we attempt in the *Discussion* section.

Limitations

The analysis performed above does not tell us about how often people share based on what they estimate their followers have already seen. Presumably, this calculation is part of everyday sharing behavior on social media sites. It would be interesting and insightful to look into how sharing varies as a function of *perceived* novelty.

Word-of-mouth Twitter referrals drove visitors to Link Different. While blog coverage started it, this is a snowball sample nonetheless. Snowball samples arise when one participant refers another, who refers another, etc. A concern is that the participant pool is biased—or, in this context, that it follows the path of least resistance. Researchers often use snowball sampling to recruit difficult-to-reach populations [27], and you could argue that this is one. In any case, we make no claims that we have a random, representative sample, even of social media users. We revisit this issue shortly in the *Discussion* section.

DISCUSSION

We worked from theory to uncover a problem we suspected to exist on sites backed by social networks. We built Link Different to examine this idea, a strategy we might call a "technology probe" [37] at internet scale. We were honestly surprised by the response from Twitter. Within hours, our servers hit their memory limits and we rushed to deploy an optimized architecture (the one depicted in Figure 6). While we firmly believe social media research does not have to spread virally to show value, we should also embrace it when it happens—something other authors have also argued recently [8]. That is, word-of-mouth adoption is sufficient (and welcome), but not necessary. In this case, we think the widespread, rapid and voluntary adoption of Link Different speaks to the scale and reality of this triadic awareness problem.

That said, we were lucky. The press could have just as easily ignored us. A release strategy based on an authoritative blog linking to your project is risky at best. Like other authors, we have struggled with getting the word out in other projects. We can offer no conclusive strategies or advice. Simply put, this time it worked. Furthermore, viral adoption has its downsides. For example, we cannot claim that we recruited even a random *Twitter* sample, let alone a random sample. We attracted those people willing to experiment with a new tool. This is what we meant when we said "the path of least resistance" earlier. Like a river, Link Different probably found its way via referrals to the people who were most inclined to use it. While 100K+ users is quite high for an academic project, you could reframe the number the following way. Very conservatively, Twitter has 38 million active users. Do only 0.4% of them (i.e., 150K/38M) face the triadic awareness problem? Also, probably not. We think it is wise to not test the total numbers of users statistic too rigorously. However, we do claim that the widespread and voluntary response suggests a deep problem lurking under the network.

Users' sharing behavior surprised us. When we built Link Different, we hypothesized that sharing was strictly inversely proportional to novelty. We would have expected a graph that started high on the left and went primarily down from there. Rather, we find a bimodal distribution, with curious points at the leftmost and rightmost ends. The likelihood of sharing starts at around 40% when almost no one has already seen your link, steadily rising to over 80% when 16-18% of your followers haven't seen it. One way to interpret this is that perhaps we do not want to share things that *no one* seems to be interested in, and we wait until a bigger (but still small) fraction of people see it to finally share the link. From there, the data does what we would expect, moving steadily down through the next two MARS segments. Then it goes back up again. This truly surprised us. At around 72%, sharing behavior starts to track steadily up from its low points in the 40-60% range, finally peaking when almost everyone has seen it (the high bars in the 94-100% range). Perhaps an interpretation is that sharing with people who already know about it is valued because it serves to signal that you too are "in the know."

These data provide a starting point for asking questions about whether sharing behavior depends on the genre of the link shared. Also, does it vary as a function of follower counts or time on the site? These are all interesting questions, and we look forward to follow-up research.

Social Translucence Over Social Networks

We built Link Different around a theoretical idea for designing social network sites: small structures embedded within social networks unlock social translucence design problems. Specifically, we employed a method where we started with a triad and looked for where social translucence breaks down over it. With Link Different, we looked at one triad and built a system to solve a an awareness problem that arises from it. The response from Twitter suggests the scope of the problem.

We believe this extension of social translucence has depth. If you count the members of a triad as interchangeable (i.e., the *A*, *B*, *C* labels have no real meaning), then directed social networks have 16 non-isomorphic triads ([26], pgs. 141–142). (In network/graph theory, "isomorphism" means you can turn one graph into another by relabeling the nodes/vertices.) This gives us 16 structures over which we can examine where social translucence breaks down. Intersecting any one of these structures with a social translucence design trait (i.e., visibility, awareness and accountability) could yield new insight into problems in today's social media. In other words, this means 48=16·3 new design spaces.

In Table 1, we have mapped out six problems we feel likely to exist over certain triads. This is the start of work in this space, and much research needs to be done cataloging and assessing triadic social translucence problems. We offer Table 1 as a sample of what this approach might produce. For example, in Table 1's first example design problem, we highlight tensions that arise from Granovetter's "forbidden triad" [31]. In his words, "if strong ties *A–B* and *A–C* exist, and if *B* and *C* are aware of one another, anything short of a positive tie would introduce a 'psychological strain' into the situation." (You have to allow for mapping his labels to ours and letting his "strong tie" be our "bi-directional.") So how does *B* carry on a simultaneous conversation with *A* and *C* without drawing attention to the forbidden triad? In a simultaneous conversation between the three, *B* would reference both *A* and *C*, but *C* would notice that *A*'s replies never mention him. While this triad occurs relatively infrequently in natural social networks [35], the sheer scale of modern social media sites suggests millions of these triads exist on the internet today. This also highlights an interesting point: design problems are conditioned upon the baseline probabilities for how often particular triads occur in social networks.

In Table 1's fourth example, we see a problem Twitter addressed a few years after it launched. In Twitter's early days online, *A* could see *B*'s conversation with *C*, even though *A* doesn't follow *C*. But since *A* doesn't follow *C*, she never saw *C*'s replies. Twitter solved this with software changing how it routes messages: *A* now only sees *B*'s conversation with *C* if she also follows *C*, cutting *A* out of the conversation entirely.

Triad	Trait	Example design problem
1. 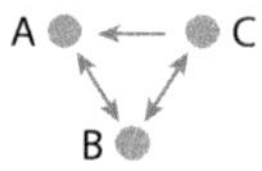	Visibility	When chatting with A and C, how does B not highlight the "forbidden triad?"
2. 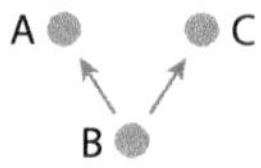	Visibility	B hears something from A relevant to C. How does B bring it to C's attention?
3. 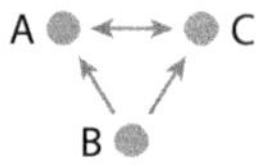	Awareness	Are A and C always aware that B hears everything they say to one another?
4. 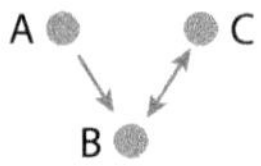	Awareness	A can hear what B says to C, but not what C says back. * addressed by Twitter.
5. 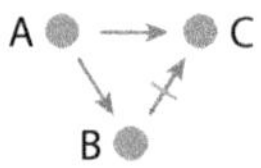	Awareness	A followed C because B did. Now B severed the tie. Does A still want to follow?
6. 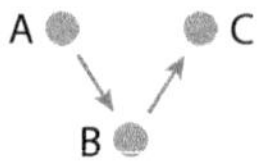	Accountability	B can take credit for what C says, since A only hears C through B.

Table 1. Six triads and potential social translucence design problems that arise from them. We argue that design problems arise from specific structures, although more work needs to be done establishing prevalence and importance.

Other solutions exist, but we highlight this case to show a real-world occurrence of a triadic design problem. You can also consider the structural dynamics in triads and its role in design (i.e., how ties change over time). We take a first step in this direction with Table 1's fifth design problem.

What about bigger structures? In this paper, we have exclusively considered triads, leaving out higher-order structures connecting four, five or even six people. Higher-order structures may yield their own insights, but perhaps at the cost of greater conceptual complexity. The complexity of such structures rises roughly as the square of the number of people in them, so we must carefully choose what structures designers should consider. In other words, the bigger the structure, the harder it is to reason about. In any case, we need more work cataloging where social translucence breaks down over specific structures within networks.

Social translucence offers fundamental theoretical guidance for social media designers: *who-sees-what*, *who-knows-what* and *who-knows-that-I-know*. We argue that it is out of these building blocks that bigger theories about designing social media emerge [40]. We need to know as much as we can about the lower levels of design (i.e., their structural properties) to support higher-level problems, such as starting a new community. We think Link Different highlights the significance of structural design problems underlying today's social media.

Limitations & Future Work

We hope to see new work pick up where we left off. Link Different's user interface could benefit from extensions permitting deeper inspection of the social connections behind sharing. The server implementation could be extended to handle more complex stories, not just URLs. While we find the study of sharing behavior in this paper fascinating, it is just a start. It presents as many questions as answers.

We hope future work finds traction with the new theory in this paper. That said, what we have presented here is just the beginning. We need more work to uncover which problems occur in the real world and which matter most. We envision both theoretical work that extends this research, as well as more practically oriented systems work establishing the parameters of particular problems.

CONCLUSION

We believe this work addresses a fundamental issue for modern social media: providing social cues over social networks. The theory we would normally turn to—social translucence—breaks down because social networks resist social translucence's physical metaphors. In this paper, we built theory relating social translucence to social network structure, updating social translucence for the era of social networks. Based on the widespread and viral response we got when we applied it, we think this approach has the potential to uncover other problems lurking in social media today.

ACKNOWLEDGEMENTS

We would like to thank the comp.social lab and Amy Bruckman for reviewing early drafts of this work. Leslie Gilbert came up with the hypothetical example used in the introduction. Both Yahoo! and Google helped support the work.

REFERENCES

1. D. Aamoth. "When It Comes To URL Shorteners, bit.ly Is Now The Biggest." *TechCrunch*. http://tcrn.ch/aqGvUh. Retrieved September 23, 2011.
2. A. Agresti and B. Coull. Approximate Is Better Than "Exact" for Interval Estimation of Binomial Proportions. *The American Statistician*, 52:119–126, 1998.
3. C. Arthur. "Average Twitter User has 126 Followers, and Only 20% Go via Website." *The Guardian*. http://bit.ly/3AiLy. Retrieved September 23, 2011.
4. BackType. http://backtype.com. Retrieved September 23, 2011.
5. A. Barabási and R. Albert. Emergence of Scaling in Random Networks. *Science*, 286(5439):509–512, 1999.
6. P. S. Bearman, J. Moody, and K. Stovel. Chains of Affection: The Structure of Adolescent Romantic and Sexual Networks. *American Journal of Sociology*, 110(1):44–91, July 2004.
7. J. B. Begole, J. C. Tang, R. B. Smith, and N. Yankelovich. Work Rhythms: Analyzing Visualizations of Awareness Histories of Distributed Groups. In *Proc. CSCW*, pages 334–343, 2002.
8. M. S. Bernstein, M. S. Ackerman, E. H. Chi, and R. C. Miller. The Trouble with Social Computing Systems Research. In *Proc. EA CHI*, pages 389–398, 2011.
9. M. S. Bernstein, A. Marcus, D. R. Karger, and R. C. Miller. Enhancing directed content sharing on the web. In *Proc. CHI*, pages 971–980, 2010.
10. P. Biernacki and D. Waldorf. Snowball Sampling: Problems and Techniques of Chain Referral Sampling. *Sociological Methods & Research*, 10(2):141–163, 1981.
11. J. Birnholtz, L. Reynolds, E. Luxenberg, C. Gutwin, and M. Mustafa. Awareness Beyond the Desktop: Exploring Attention and Distraction with a Projected Peripheral-vision Display. In *Proc. GI*, pages 55–62, 2010.
12. Bit.ly. Bit.ly tools. https://bitly.com/pages/tools. Retrieved September 23, 2011.
13. d. boyd and N. Ellison. Social Network Sites: Definition, History, and Scholarship. *Journal of Computer-Mediated Communication*, 13(1):210–230, 2008.
14. T. Brants and A. Franz. Web 1T 5-gram Version 1. *Linguistic Data Consortium, Philadelphia*, 2006.
15. M. Burke, C. Marlow, and T. Lento. Social Network Activity and Social Well-being. In *Proc. CHI*, pages 1909–1912, 2010.
16. R. Burt. *Structural Holes: The Social Structure of Competition*. Harvard University Press, August 1995.
17. R. S. Burt. Structural holes and good ideas. *American Journal of Sociology*, 110(2):349–399, September 2004.
18. N. Carlson. "How Many Users Does Twitter Really Have?" *Business Insider.* Retrieved September 23, 2011.
19. D. Cartwright and F. Harary. Structural Balance: A Generalization of Heider's Theory. *Psychological Review*, 63(5):277, 1956.
20. N. Ellison, C. Steinfield, and C. Lampe. The Benefits of Facebook "Friends:" Social Capital and College Students' Use of Online Social Network Sites. *Journal of Computer-Mediated Communication*, 12(4):1143–1168, 2007.
21. T. Erickson, C. Halverson, W. Kellogg, M. Laff, and T. Wolf. Social Translucence: Designing Social Infrastructures that Make Collective Activity Visible. *Communications of the ACM*, 45(4):44, 2002.
22. T. Erickson and W. Kellogg. Social Translucence: An Approach to Designing Systems that Support Social Processes. *TOCHI*, 7(1):59–83, 2000.
23. T. Erickson, D. Smith, W. Kellogg, M. Laff, J. Richards, and E. Bradner. Socially Translucent Systems: Social Proxies, Persistent Conversation, and the Design of "Babble". In *Proc. CHI*, pages 72–79, 1999.
24. J. Fogarty, J. Lai, and J. Christensen. Presence Versus Availability: The Design and Evaluation of a Context-Aware Communication Client. *International Journal of Human-Computer Studies*, 61(3):299–317, 2004.
25. W. B. Frakes and R. Baeza-Yates. *Information Retrieval: Data Structures and Algorithms*. Prentice Hall, 1992.
26. O. Frank. Triad Count Statistics. *Discrete Mathematics*, 72(1-3):141–149, 1988.
27. O. Frank and T. Snijders. Estimating the Size of Hidden Populations Using Snowball Sampling. *Journal of Official Statistics*, 10(1):53–67, 1994.

28. S. Golder and S. Yardi. Structural Predictors of Tie Formation in Twitter: Transitivity and Mutuality. In *Proc. IEEE SocialCom*, 2010.

29. Google Analytics. http://google.com/analytics. Retrieved September 23, 2011.

30. Google Scholar. http://scholar.google.com/scholar?q=social+translucence. Retrieved September 23, 2011.

31. M. S. Granovetter. The strength of weak ties. *The American Journal of Sociology*, 78(6):1360–1380, 1973.

32. P. Haller and M. Odersky. Scala Actors: Unifying Thread-based and Event-based Programming. *Theoretical Computer Science*, 410(2-3):202–220, 2009.

33. T. Hastie and R. Tibshirani. http://cran.r-project.org/web/packages/mda. Retrieved September 23, 2011.

34. J. Hollan and S. Stornetta. Beyond Being There. In *Proc. CHI*, pages 119–125, 1992.

35. P. Holland and S. Leinhardt. A Method for Detecting Structure in Sociometric Data. *American Journal of Sociology*, 76(3):492–513, 1970.

36. G. Hsieh, K. P. Tang, W. Y. Low, and J. I. Hong. Field Deployment of IMBuddy: A Study of Privacy Control and Feedback Mechanisms for Contextual IM. In *Proc. UbiComp*, pages 91–108, 2007.

37. H. Hutchinson, W. Mackay, B. Westerlund, B. B. Bederson, A. Druin, C. Plaisant, M. Beaudouin-Lafon, S. Conversy, H. Evans, H. Hansen, N. Roussel, and B. Eiderbäck. Technology Probes: Inspiring Design for and with Families. In *Proc. CHI*, pages 17–24, 2003.

38. M. O. Jackson. *Social and Economic Networks*. Princeton University Press, 2008.

39. jQuery. http://jquery.com. Retrieved September 23, 2011.

40. R. E. Kraut and P. Resnick. *Evidence-Based Social Design: Mining the Social Sciences to Build Online Communities*. MIT Press, 2011 (forthcoming).

41. F. Lardinois. “Don’t Bore Your Twitter Followers: Link Different” *ReadWriteWeb*. http://rww.to/qQ2IBr. Retrieved January 13, 2012.

42. Localmind. http://foursquare.com/app/localmind. Retrieved September 23, 2011.

43. M. Mcpherson, L. S. Lovin, and J. M. Cook. Birds of a feather: Homophily in social networks. *Annual Review of Sociology*, 27:415–444, 2001.

44. S. Paul, L. Hong, and E. Chi. Is Twitter a Good Place for Asking Questions? A Characterization Study. In *Proc. ICWSM*, 2011.

45. L. Rao. “Twitter Seeing 90 Million Tweets Per Day, 25 Percent Contain Links.” *TechCrunch*. http://tcrn.ch/by1ZrB. Retrieved September 23, 2011.

46. B. Suh, E. Chi, A. Kittur, and B. Pendleton. Lifting the Veil: Improving Accountability and Social Transparency in Wikipedia with Wikidashboard. In *Proc. CHI*, pages 1037–1040, 2008.

47. M. Svensson, K. Höök, J. Laaksolahti, and A. Waern. Social Navigation of Food Recipes. In *Proc. CHI*, pages 341–348, 2001.

A Longitudinal Study of Facebook, LinkedIn, & Twitter Use

Anne Archambault
Microsoft Corporation
Redmond, Washington USA
annea@microsoft.com

Jonathan Grudin
Microsoft Research
Redmond, Washington USA
jgrudin@microsoft.com

ABSTRACT
We conducted four annual comprehensive surveys of social networking at Microsoft between 2008 and 2011. We are interested in how these sites are used and whether they are considered to be useful for organizational communication and information-gathering. Our study is longitudinal and based on random sampling. Between 2008 and 2011, social networking went from being a niche activity to being very widely and heavily used. Growth in use and acceptance was not uniform, with differences based on gender, age and level (individual contributor vs. manager). Behaviors and concerns changed, with some showing signs of leveling off.

Author Keywords
Social networking; Facebook; LinkedIn; Twitter; Enterprise

ACM Classification Keywords
H.5.3 Group and Organization Interfaces

INTRODUCTION
We conducted four annual in-depth surveys of attitudes and behaviors around social networking sites in Microsoft, a large technology company. In May 2008, MySpace was the largest site worldwide, with over 100 million users. Today it has 30 million. Facebook, LinkedIn, and Twitter increased from 75 to 600 million, 20 to 100 million, and 2 to 200 million, respectively. How did this unprecedented technology shift play out in an organizational setting? Our survey data are a unique longitudinal window into one company through an interesting time.

Social networking with family and friends is widespread. Their use in marketing and publicity is growing. Organizational benefits from employee use are less clear. Some organizations ban the use of public sites such as Facebook, although blocking employee access via smart phones is difficult. Organizations that allow access may reveal how the use of social networking sites can be beneficial or distracting in such a setting.

New communication and collaboration technologies often encounter initial organizational resistance. Email, instant messaging, and employee blogging were first used mainly by students and consumers to support informal interaction. Managers, who focus more on formal communication channels, often viewed them as potential distractions [4]. A new communication channel initially disrupts existing channels and creates management challenges until usage conventions and a new collaboration ecosystem emerges.

Email was not embraced by many large organizations until the late 1990s. Instant messaging was not generally considered a productivity tool in the early 2000s. Slowly, employees familiar with these technologies found ways to use them to work more effectively. Organizational acceptance was aided by new features that managers appreciated, such as email attachments and integration with calendaring.

Many organizations are now wrestling with social networking. About half of U.S. companies reportedly block sites or have restrictive policies [9, 17]. Echoes of past email and IM debates rage in the trade press [6]. Change could come more quickly this time: People are accustomed to using new technologies, adoption is less expensive, work-life boundaries are eroding, and the use of these technologies by successful people in government and entertainment is discussed in the media.

In 2008, two years after Facebook became available, the size of its Microsoft "group" indicated that it was used by over one-third of all employees. How were they using it? How much if any was for work purposes? How did use or attitudes vary with role or age? Whether using such sites at home or work, employees are learning what they can provide and are developing skills in using them.

Different social networking sites have been popular at different times and in different countries [16]. Over half of the Microsoft employees are in North America. The others are distributed around the world. In 2008, we found some use of Plaxo and international use of Orkut, Bebo, QQ, and other sites, but it was minimal and has diminished [10]. The primary sites from 2008 to 2011 were LinkedIn, Facebook, MySpace, Twitter, and Live Spaces. Live Spaces was a commercial product endorsed for internal use. An internally-developed microblogging tool was released in 2010 but does not figure prominently in the data.

Today, over 80% of our employees and over 10% of the world population are active Facebook users. Most joined during the three years spanned by our study. Past experience with new technologies indicates that employers who can trust employees not to misuse them can benefit from employee use. The nature of potential benefits and the optimal approach to realizing them are unpredictable. Should employees use external sites that include non-employees? How will social networking tools that are restricted to an organization's intranet fare? Will people visit and update multiple sites? Will integrated tools that span external and internal social networking be embraced?

Surveys of the public and analyses of public feeds are useful but do not reveal organizational behavior. Snapshots of use in one organization at one point in time provide insights, but longitudinal studies of a relatively stable population can reveal dynamics in greater detail.

Many of the 90,000 employees at Microsoft are early adopters—but the rest of the world is catching up. When the study began in early 2008, Facebook and Twitter had been available to non-students under two years. There was no published research on enterprise social networking use.

The history of adoption of earlier communication technologies provided strong grounds for hypothesizing that attitudes and behaviors would begin conservatively and evolve to show more acceptance of social networking site use for work purposes. The literature discussed next emerged in the course of our study, but did not motivate it.

LITERATURE REVIEW

The media and the research literature focus mainly on Facebook and Twitter use by the general population. Facebook data are not public, so most research is in the form of surveys and interviews. A partial exception is the Burke et al. [1] examination of social capital, which used Facebook server logs as well as two surveys of volunteers from a general population of Facebook users, conducted 8 months apart. The Twitter API provides streams from users who do not opt out, enabling collection and analysis of large-scale samples [e.g., 7, 12, 14]. These reports have some validity as single snapshots of the general population.

Many of the organizational use studies are of prototypes, notably the Beehive, BlueTwit, and Timely systems built, used, and studied at IBM [e.g., 5, 8, 19]. Researchers interview employees and analyze usage logs. These systems generally have relatively low organizational uptake and a limited active lifespan, but are considerably more informative than more limited tests of prototype systems. Companies such as Deloitte and CA Technologies report high uptake of internal systems, but details are unavailable.

The most relevant studies examine employee use of widely-used social networking sites. These are discussed next.

Turner et al. [18] surveyed members of a small company about their full range of communication channels and interviewed 23 of them, in May 2008 and May 2009. Not surprisingly, use of IM, blogs, Facebook, LinkedIn and Twitter reportedly increased over the year.

Zhao and Rosson [21] recruited eleven heavy users of Twitter at a large IT company in late 2008, using personal contacts and 'snowball' referrals. Heavy users may not be typical, but they can identify useful features and today's heavy user might (or might not) be tomorrow's average user. Twitter was used in their organization for 'life updates' or personal status, for sharing information with friends or colleagues in real time, and as 'personal RSS feeds' to monitor trusted external sources for news or links.

In early 2009, Zhang et al. [20] studied one organization's use of Yammer, a Twitter-like tool, typically restricted to employees, that has unlimited post length. They report categories of use similar to Zhao and Rosson: to broadcast status, usually group or business unit rather than personal; questions or directed messages for real-time interaction; and items of interest (an employee becomes an "intermediary RSS feed" relaying information from outside). 1.5% of employees (458) used Yammer, almost all of them over 30 years old. About 25% were also active Twitter users. With such limited adoption, even enthusiastic users had difficulty finding value in Yammer. Some followed specific individuals; other followed everyone in the company who posted to Yammer. Hashtag use was rare, perhaps because of the low volume of use.

In the spring of 2009, Ehrlich and Shami [5] compared uses of Twitter and BlueTwit, a Twitter-like internal IBM tool that allows posts of 250 characters. BlueTwit had been available for a year and adopted by one third of 1% of IBM employees. 34 employees who actively used both BlueTwit and Twitter were identified and studied. On average, they tweeted 561 times over four months, or four times a day. 57% of the tweets were from the five heaviest users, who averaged 18 in a day. (In contrast, Zhao and Rosson's heaviest user posted four times a day). The authors found less status posting and more information or comments directed to specific individuals than is reported in studies of the general Twitter-using population. (This is consistent with what we heard from power tweeters, a small minority of employees.)

The use of the Facebook-like Beehive application deployed at IBM was affected by its restriction to employees. Absent are the tensions that arise when 'friends' include colleagues, social friends, and family. Absent also are privacy concerns that arise with public sites [3]. Nine months after deployment, employees were using Beehive to share personal information, to promote themselves by describing skills and accomplishments, and to campaign for projects. Beehive was not being used to find information or get quick answers to questions.

In mid-2008, 10% of IBM employees had Beehive profiles. Facebook and Twitter had been in corporate use for about two years. A year later, in their organization, Turner et al. [18] found the norm to be once-a-week use of Facebook and Twitter. They predicted that corporate use of Twitter would thrive, which as we will see remains uncertain.

Finally, a report on the first of our four surveys, conducted with Meredith Skeels, was published in 2009 [16]. As a contrast to the Beehive use, we found that in mid-2008, 49% of employees had Facebook profiles, 52% had LinkedIn profiles, and 6% had Twitter accounts. About 20% were daily users. Those who reported using the sites for work identified the creation and strengthening of weak ties as a key benefit. Tension arose from having contacts from different groups: colleagues, managers, external friends and professionals, family members, and so on.

METHOD

On four occasions a year apart, 1000 of the approximately 90,000 full-time Microsoft employees were randomly selected from the company address book and emailed an invitation to take a survey on communication technologies. The invitation was worded ambiguously to avoid discouraging non-users of social networking sites. Those invited once were subsequently excluded, due to possible behavioral influence from taking the survey. As an incentive, participants were entered in a drawing for a digital appliance. The surveys closed in May of the years 2008 through 2011. This paper addresses the evolution of behaviors and attitudes over the years.

Most published organizational studies are "snapshot" studies of heavy users recruited by word of mouth or examining system logs. These studies of early adopters of quickly-evolving technologies have value. Different things are learned by examining representative samples over time.

Our survey covered demographic information (age, gender, role in company), behavior, and attitudes toward social networking sites. People were asked their level of agreement or disagreement with statements such as 'I think social networking software (Facebook, MySpace, LinkedIn, Friendster, etc.) can be useful for personal socializing/networking,' and '...can be useful for networking within Microsoft.' We asked which sites were used, how frequently, and the frequencies of a broad range of activities, such as posting a picture or inviting people in different categories to connect. Open-ended questions let respondents discuss thoughts, experiences, and concerns (if any) with social networking software use.

We also recorded in-depth interviews with 46 employees selected to provide a range of ages, roles and levels in the company, geographic locations, and attitudes (positive or negative) toward the usefulness of social networking software for work. Most were survey respondents who indicated a willingness to follow up. A few were developing prototypes of internal social networking tools. Others were active users identified through distribution list activity or referrals. We followed internal email discussion lists that cover social networking tools and technologies, which primarily attract heavy users and evangelists.

Most interviews were conducted in the informant's office, lasted about an hour, and were recorded with permission. Eleven geographically distant employees, who worked in Asia, Europe, South America, and North America, were interviewed by phone or during visits.

We asked for their professional background, prior experience with social networking sites, and current use: how, when and why they started using a system, when they access it, how their use evolved, and what if anything they felt it is useful for. We covered family members, former schoolmates, and work colleagues, asking them to approximate the number of different connections. If they posted information, we asked what they posted or avoided posting. We asked them to speculate about the future of social networking.

For most interviews, including all in the first year, we typed up notes and where they did not coincide, referred back to the recordings. With early interviews and free text survey data, Atlas.ti was used for open coding. A list of themes gradually stabilized; the same themes recurred in subsequent interviews and fewer new themes emerged. Interview analysis is described further in our report on the first survey [16]. In subsequent interviews we noted some new themes emerging. However, this paper focuses mainly on the trajectories found in the annual survey data.

RESULTS

The survey response rates were relatively high, ranging from 42% to 45% of the 1000 invited. Respondents seemed representative: 45% were from the headquarters region, as are 45% of employees 23.0% were female, and as of this writing, 23.8% of employees are women. We asked employees to place themselves in one of five age ranges. In 2008 the mode was 26-35, in subsequent years 36-45, reflecting the aging employee base, which now averages 38.4 years. The major product development roles—developer, tester, and program manager—are roughly equally represented and comprise about 45% of our sample. Sales, marketing, and product support were about 32%. Other roles were much less numerous. Roughly 1% were executive level, 27% served in managerial or supervisory positions, and 70% were individual contributors.

We had large samples and are only generalizing our results to Microsoft population. The 95% confidence intervals for the results reported range from ±2% to ±4%. For example, the rise in daily use of LinkedIn from 6% in 2010 to 15% in 2011 is highly reliable, with 95% confidence that the first is no higher than 8% and the second no lower than 13%. (Table 1 and Figure 1). The earlier rise from 4% to 6% was probably real, but not noteworthy. The discussion focuses on significant changes that seem particularly interesting.

Pattern of Overall Increased Use

Table 1 covers the five most frequently used sites. Some other sites were frequently used by employees in particular regions, but overall their use was much lower.

Percent of all employees	Facebook				LinkedIn				Twitter				MySpace				Live Spaces			
	2008	2009	2010	2011	2008	2009	2010	2011	2008	2009	2010	2011	2008	2009	2010	2011	2008	2009	2010	2011
Never Used	36	23	13	12	41	33	22	18	**88**	**68**	**44**	**39**	48	61	56	61	53	50	51	60
Only Read	16	7	6	4	7	5	3	2	6	11	15	12	21	13	14	15	8	7	5	4
Have Profile and Use	46	67	78	82	**49**	**58**	**71**	**77**	5	18	36	40	**25**	**15**	**17**	**9**	32	36	36	28
Use Daily+	**17**	**29**	**41**	**52**	**4**	**6**	**6**	**15**	**2**	**6**	**10**	**11**	4	1	0	1	5	4	3	3
Use Several Times / Day	**5**	**8**	**14**	**20**	1	1	0	4	1	3	4	5	1	0	0	0	1	1	0	0
Had Profile, Don't Use	3	4	3	**2**	3	5	3	**3**	1	3	5	**6**	6	10	13	**15**	7	6	8	**8**

Table 1. The five most frequently used sites. Daily+ is daily plus several times in a day. Bold items are emphasized in the discussion.

The sharp increase in reported use of social networking sites from 2008 to 2011 is unsurprising, but the details provide a richer picture. In 2008, slightly more employees had LinkedIn profiles than Facebook profiles (49% vs. 46%), but fewer used LinkedIn daily. In 2011, 82% reported using Facebook, which may be reaching a ceiling. Through 2010, the dominant mode of Facebook use was 'Occasional,' but in 2011, over half reported using it daily and 20% several times a day. LinkedIn use rose slowly until 2011, when more employees reported joining LinkedIn than Facebook in the previous year. Although the survey was completed before LinkedIn garnered attention by going public, daily use of LinkedIn rose 250% and surpassed daily Twitter use, which may have plateaued in 2011. Figure 1 depicts the daily use of the three most active sites.

Employee Twitter profiles increased 8-fold over three years, but its ubiquity in the media led us to expect more than 11% of employees to report daily use. Moreover, Twitter is experiencing greater churn (bottom row of Table 1). 13% of Twitter profiles have been abandoned (46% of employees created a Twitter profile, 6% discontinued use). In contrast, Facebook lost 2% and LinkedIn 4%. MySpace use declined rapidly, with 62% of users abandoning it. Live Spaces, once promoted internally, lost 22% of its users after being rebranded and de-emphasized.

In 2008, 5% of employees claimed to know nothing about social networking sites. In 2011, only 1% did. In 2008, 61% reported that they had been using social networking sites for 0-2 years; by 2011 that had fallen to 26%. Those reporting more than 5 years' use rose from 9% to 32%.

Basic Attitudes Toward Social Networking Site Uses

Attitudes were assessed by asking about four uses of social networking: for fun, for personal socializing and networking, for networking with external professional contacts, and for internal networking within the company. Table 2 shows data from the five point scale, after merging strongly disagree and disagree, strongly agree and agree.

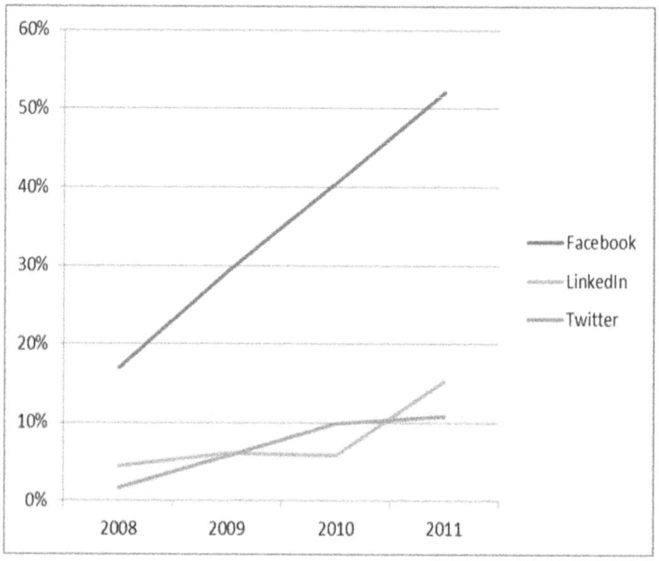

Figure 1: Percent of employees who are daily users.

More people now see benefits in all categories. Most saw personal benefits early; 80-90% agreement may be a ceiling. Utility for external professional networking rose, with only a quarter of the employees still unconvinced. But for internal networking, about 20% of employees remain convinced it is not useful. 30% are neutral, and half see it as beneficial—relatively weak support. Of course, contrasted with email, which took decades to attain broad acceptance, a 13% rise to majority support in three years is significant.

Interviews revealed sources of skepticism about internal use. One executive we interviewed considered social networking to be a diversion, a "productivity killer!" An individual contributor who worked within yards of his teammates saw no use for it. Some employees distant from headquarters were concerned that upper management might disapprove of its use. We interviewed young overseas employees, active users of social networking outside work, who seemed surprised by even the *idea* of using it at work.

A common source of uneasiness about internal use was that people's social networks transcend company boundaries, limiting what can be said on work topics [16]. Nevertheless, only one in five remained negative. The 28% who reported being neutral in 2011 could be persuaded by the positive majority of their colleagues, some of whom in interviews described building and strengthening weak ties with colleagues and getting quick answers to questions, benefits also reported in the literature.

In early 2010, a microblogging tool accessible within the Microsoft corporate firewall was released. By May, 2011, 21% of the employees reported having a profile. This launch may have opened minds to internal possibilities. It could help explain the jump in sentiment favoring internal networking [Table 2].

Access Control and Concerns about Use

Figures 2 and 3 show a steady increase in the use of access control settings and a modest rise in concerns about social networking sites. Some privacy concerns arose in interviews and in responses to open-ended survey questions. Social networking sites had few access control features in 2008. Facebook added them slowly, given its underlying conviction that sharing is good. The account of our first survey [16] goes into considerable detail about employees struggling with the diversity of their friends. Some mused about creating multiple aliases, but no one we interviewed had done so. People are not keen to expend energy on managing access control, but do report more use of available tools. In response to queries about concerns with social networking, most report them to be minor.

A Gender Difference

Women only comprise a quarter of the workforce, but men and women occupy the same roles. Contrary to some stereotypes, there are only 20% more male developers, testers and program managers. Executives are disproportionately male, but women are otherwise roughly equally represented in management and supervisory positions. 10% more women are in the 36-45 age range, with 5% more men in each of the 25-35 and 46-55 spans.

In 2011, women surveyed were proportionally more likely to report being daily Facebook users, 56% vs. 51% of men.

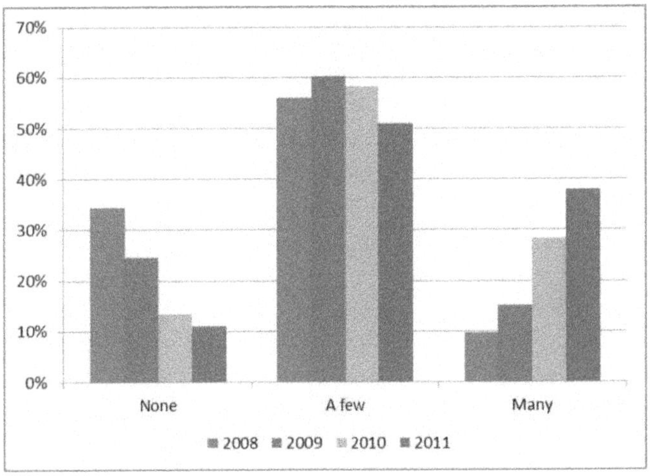

Figure 2. Changes to access control settings.

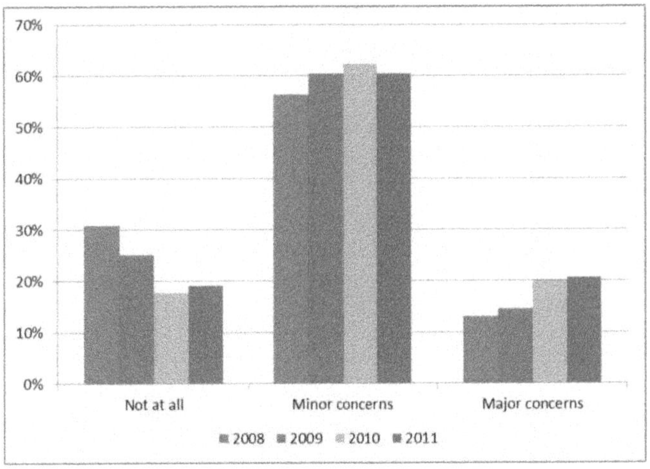

Figure 3. Concerns about social networking site use.

A higher proportion of women than men (5% to 11%) agreed that sites were useful for each category in Table 2.

Use of access controls and concern about networking sites show an inverse gender pattern. The genders are equal in that about 10% ignore access control settings altogether and 20% express no concerns. However, 46% of women report setting many access controls versus 35% of men, yet only 13% of women have major concerns about the sites, versus 23% of men. Men do less to control how they appear and worry more about the consequences.

Percent of employees	Disagree				Neutral				Agree			
	2008	2009	2010	2011	2008	2009	2010	2011	2008	2009	2010	2011
Fun?	7%	5%	4%	5%	22%	18%	13%	12%	72%	77%	83%	83%
Personal socializing?	5%	4%	2%	3%	12%	8%	7%	7%	83%	88%	91%	90%
External professional?	14%	11%	8%	9%	25%	22%	20%	19%	61%	66%	72%	72%
Internal networking?	24%	23%	21%	21%	38%	32%	33%	28%	38%	46%	46%	51%

Table 2. Social networking sites are good for…

Age

In 2008, Facebook and LinkedIn use varied with age, but not the same way. Facebook use was inversely correlated with age, as you would expect. In contrast, LinkedIn was not aimed at students and did not appeal to young employees. Use showed an inverted-U pattern, rising with age until the 36 to 45 age range, then dropping.

In [16], we described LinkedIn's appeal to professionals in the 25 to 40 age range. It is a self-updating address book they will own if they change jobs. It enables them to track college classmates who have dispersed and friends from high school who are no longer seen in the summer and holidays. It is a free, professional website for marketing yourself without drawing your employer's attention to a future job search. Its greatest appeal for some was as a way to connect with people met at an event, much more effective than business cards that sit untouched in a drawer. An invitation to connect is minimally intrusive or presumptuous; it can be ignored or accepted, but if accepted does create a link that can be used.

As seen in Table 3, the LinkedIn pattern is much less pronounced in 2011. Daily LinkedIn use is flat, rising among older employees. There could be several factors: roles differ with age, senior employees may make more use of LinkedIn groups, or older employees may search for people with a long employment history, which is more likely to be found on LinkedIn than Facebook.

The Facebook use pattern also evolved. In every age category, 84-87% of employees have profiles. Now, frequent use falls off with age. Note that 41% of the 25-and-under employees report using Facebook several times a day. Will this also spread to older age categories? Email use once exhibited a similar pattern, heavy use by young employees and occasional use or none at all by their elders.

Individual contributors and managers

The attitudes of managers towards social networking were a surprise. In 2008, proportionally fewer rated social networking sites useful for internal networking (32% vs. 40% of individual contributors) but more saw value for external professional networking (71% vs. 59%). Both groups became more favorable, but by 2011 managers were proportionally *more* positive about internal networking potential: 58% vs. 50% of individual contributors. We interviewed executives, some positive and some negative toward social networking, but the survey sample was too small to analyze.

		< 26	26-35	36-45	46-55
Facebook	Created Profile	85%	87%	84%	84%
Facebook	Uses Daily	70%	59%	47%	42%
Facebook	Several Times / Day	41%	22%	17%	16%
LinkedIn	Created Profile	74%	78%	83%	81%
LinkedIn	Uses Daily	15%	14%	14%	23%

Table 3. Employee Facebook and LinkedIn use by age in 2011.

Correlated with this, by 2011 more of the younger age groups saw utility for fun and personal life, but the oldest group saw the greatest potential for the work-related uses.

Range of Uses of Social Networking Sites

For 20 different activities, we asked people whether or not they engaged in them on social networking sites and if so, how often. Every activity saw increased use, most dramatically between 2008 and 2010. For example, in 2008, 19% of employees reported using sites to keep in touch with external friends on a weekly basis and 25% never had. Two years later, 56% reported keeping in touch with external friends at least weekly on these sites, and only 14% reported never doing so. In a company of 90,000 employees, about 10,000 had done this for the first time. Between 2008 and 2010, each of the 20 activities was used *for the first time* by 5,000 to 20,000 employees.

In 2011, the overall growth in activity continued, but some activities plateaued or declined in frequency. For example, 'connect with new family members online' gained in frequency from 2008 to 2010, but declined in 2011, perhaps because people had run out of family members who had not yet connected but were willing to do so.

DISCUSSION

Social networking sites will be used

Some organizations, like some countries, try to block access to Facebook, Twitter, and other social networking sites. On a recent visit, an IT architect at a tech company that blocks access observed that employees there used smart phones to circumvent the ban. With a laugh, he mused about whether the company might arrange with local telecoms to black out the area.

We also met with representatives of a major manufacturing company that blocked Facebook and Twitter but years ago had approved LinkedIn, which it saw as a repository of web pages. LinkedIn has added interactive features, supporting activities that led to the others being banned. However, employees now rely on LinkedIn, so banning it was not being considered. "The camel's nose is in the tent."

In the past, some countries and organizations that blocked Internet access found that it put them at a competitive disadvantage. This may be repeated with social networking tools, as organizational use of the sites matures.

We did not find universal consensus regarding the value of social networking to enterprises. The skeptical 20% have not wavered appreciably, and it is easier to show a potential for distraction [7] than to prove a productivity benefit from a communication channel that may be only used for minutes a day to strengthen ties and get quick answers.

Given the intense pressure to produce productivity impacts, studies will be produced, but they are unlikely to be definitive. It was impossible to prove that previous communication technologies increased productivity. In the 1990s, organizational theorists still argued that email reduced productivity. In the 2000s, leading analysts recommended that organizations block IM [4]. Yet these tools were eventually deemed mission-critical in most organizations, despite the absence of conclusive studies.

The rapid rise of managerial belief in workplace benefits suggests that acceptance could come quickly this time. The well-publicized frustration of the Obama team over the inability to use such tools when they arrived in the White House in 2009 revealed that an effective team was really *using* the tools, not posturing to attract the youth vote. One spokesperson described the transition as "like moving from an Xbox to an Atari." This news led our customers to inquire about social networking software. Widespread reports that social media have driven events in the Middle East, some of which appear credible, contribute to a sense that social media can aid serious undertakings.

Even when the tools are used for non-work purposes, employees develop skills and insights into what the tools can do. For example, when a question posted on a social network draws a quick answer, the effectiveness of the medium for Q&A is demonstrated, whether or not the question is work-related. Morris et al. [13] brought in experienced users with real problems that required search. They were asked to simultaneously post a query to their social networks and look for the answer with their search engine. More often than not, the answer came back more quickly from the social network. There is a collective cost to their network in fielding queries, but this illustrates a possible benefit beyond strengthening ties.

Many employees we interviewed felt strongly that social networking helps them work more efficiently. "I can't recall how I did this job without LinkedIn," said a recruiter. One external informant works for a company that blocks social networking sites and issues employees a phone that also blocks them. So he carries two phones and engages in communication over which the company has little control.

External sites vs. internal tools

A great tension over using public sites at work is that they span the firewall [16]. Many people we interviewed first networked with family or friends (including colleagues from previous jobs), then added current work colleagues. As a result, accessing the site inevitably introduces non-work distractions, and posting to such sites constrains or puts at risk work-related discussions.

Possible solutions, each with challenges:
(i) Find an external tool that supports subgroups.
(ii) Acquire an internal tool that only connects employees.
(iii) Acquire a tool that aggregates different sites, one of which is restricted to employees.

Internal tools are exemplified by the IBM Beehive and BlueTwit prototypes. Yammer is a commercial offering that restricts communication to people inside a corporate firewall, although it is externally hosted. Internal tools face challenges in achieving critical mass of use and coexisting with popular external tools. The IBM studies described use by under 2% of employees for the microblogging tools and about 10%, after years of promotion, for Beehive. Prototype development ceased; more limited networking features were added to existing products.

How many employees who actively use Facebook or Twitter will adopt another tool with similar functionality? Few with a public site that includes work colleagues may be willing to set up and manage another. But if they do, their experience will facilitate using it effectively.

People we interviewed raised these issues. They would like to be able to direct some posts to work colleagues—this emerged repeatedly—but they have limited bandwidth for creating and managing multiple groups. The access control features Facebook has slowly added remain limited and may never be simple enough to use effectively. And the question of data security would remain.

There may be opportunities for internal tools that aggregate feeds from public tools. For example, Deloitte's D Street, an internal Facebook-like site built on SharePoint, is reportedly used actively by 75% of the large, distributed company. Integrated with other internal tools, it was introduced with a support team that will custom design features for workgroups, and with a tolerance for including discussion of non-work activities (such as hobbies) within the firewall. It includes an aggregator that accesses external social networking sites [15].

The conflict between proprietary and mass-market solutions is a recurrent thread in the history of communication tools. Consider instant messaging. A closed system could insure security but require that IM-savvy users learn a new interface. Prying employees away from familiar clients is difficult. The U.S. military developed a highly secure communication system, used in war games, but in Desert Storm, young soldiers under pressure opted to use the unsecure commercial IM they used every day. This led the military to inquire into having security features added to commercial clients (personal communication).

Several people we interviewed mused that it would be nice to have distinct Facebook or Twitter profiles for work and for social purposes. Only one was taking steps to try it. Facebook was initially developed for students with few demands for online social compartmentalization. It has added grouping features, but creating and maintaining multiple groups requires time and effort, and must then be remembered. A work colleague who is also a friend—which group is she in, or is she in both? Can I easily post to everyone I want to? In addition, employers must overlook the risk of hacker attacks through these sites and grow comfortable with external hosting of business information.

Major platform developers can provide IT departments with the tools to build D-Street-like integrated solutions. For social network sites to do the same would require a major investment in integrating with other enterprise systems.

What does the success of LinkedIn tell us?

Survey data informed by some interviews directed attention to the related and possibly countervailing issue of information overload on one channel. As the size and diversity of my network grows, as my audience becomes more diverse, posting items of interest to a small subset is less appealing. Any given communication may seem odd to a subset of my network. Use of a site for strengthening ties diminishes when it becomes a public broadcast channel.

This creates an opportunity for specialized, differentiated tools. Almost all of the 77% of Microsoft employees with LinkedIn profiles also have Facebook profiles. LinkedIn serves a different function for them. The spike in daily use in 2011 could be a harbinger. Should Facebook allow alternative views, one of them professional? Would that be confusing? Do people prefer to conduct different activities in different places? More niches may develop that carve off social networking activity. An enterprise client that provides access to an internal social networking site and to LinkedIn, Facebook, Twitter, and others could succeed.

Twitter and microblogging

The lack of a significant rise in Twitter adoption in 2011 was unexpected. In each of the two previous years use had doubled. In this section we provide some background and explore possible contributing factors.

Sites such as Friendster, Orkut, Bebo, and Plaxo helped prepare people for the public release of Facebook in 2006. Twitter, also released in 2006, had fewer widely-used antecedents. It did not support photos, games and other popular features. Its open platform allowed applications to be built on it, but each had to attract a user base. Twitter's broadcast nature was critical to its success. It appealed to people in media and public relations. Adoption by celebrities provided sensational visibility by 2009.

In 2011, Twitter profiles increased from 36% to 40% and daily use from 10% to 11% of Microsoft employees. At that pace, it will take a long time to reach existing LinkedIn and Facebook levels, and the latters' use is still rising.

What might explain Twitter's slow growth despite its high visibility? Its limited functionality? Twitter is less well-defined: Some consider it to be a broadcast medium, others use it to interact with friends. Facebook (and to some extent LinkedIn) have been redesigned to promote real-time or several-times-per-day communication, invading Twitter's niche. The internally-developed Microsoft microblogging tool could be a factor: Only 2% of employees report using it daily and another 8% occasionally, which might draw enough work-related Q&A and status messaging to lower the incentive to use Twitter.

A 2009 Nielsen Online report put Facebook's retention rate at 70% and Twitter's closer to 40%, but the analysis relied on web access and ignored the growing use of phones and aggregators [12]. We found minimal abandonment of Facebook and LinkedIn. Twitter's 13% abandonment would be inconsequential if adoption was still doubling, but it is significant when adoption rises 10% in a year. Interviews discussed below revealed some resistance to microblogging, but the nature of the objections suggested that there is potential for growth if microblogging potential is realized and a critical mass of use is attained.

A decade ago, some weblogs were for friends and families, such as LiveJournal blogs, while others focused on journalism, public education, and self-promotion. Some 'A-list bloggers' in the second camp argued that the former were not "real blogs." Microbloggers show the identical pattern. Some tweet to close friends and family, others seek a large audience.

Our interviews indicated that social network sites undermine both forms of blogging. Many LiveJournal blogs were relatively heavy-duty ways to share ephemeral news. LiveJournal use has declined. We interviewed 'serious' bloggers who also reported a decline in blog posting, not always by plan, as their tweets and status updates increased.

Which use is appropriate at work? A few people we interviewed couldn't see why a serious person would be attracted to Twitter, which they saw as just a way to post casual notes to fill idle moments. One young program manager used Twitter enthusiastically to follow trends outside work, but saw no place for it at work: "For broad messages, the broader they are at work, the more careful you have to be about what you say... precise, specific. I don't really see Twitter being built for that... Email is bad enough... if they had Twitter that would just be insane."

Others reported benefits from sharing information, getting quick answers to questions, and strengthening ties. One recruiter used the full range of social networking tools and was enthusiastic about their value for engagement and sharing information, but her "worry-wart side" felt that "we as professionals have learned some lessons about email... things you don't say... I don't know that everyone has made that leap of understanding about microblogging yet."

Yammer users studied by Zhang et al. [20] mostly followed colleagues. Microblogging has a lower barrier to entry than blogging; celebrities and politicians who could not credibly blog can microblog. The publicity given to the tweeting of Oprah, Shaq, and Sarah Palin did not enhance the perception that it is a serious medium. Public relations, marketers, and journalists saw the potential of microblogs as they had for blogs [4], notably for live coverage of events. But this is of professional interest to a narrow band of employees in most organizations.

The opportunity for microblogging lies in the fact that many employees were unaware of useful features, such as the use of hashtags to signal topic and enable searching, or the capability of directing tweets at an individual in a publicly visible and searchable stream using the @mention convention. The potential for these features was expounded on by a heavy user of Twitter in 2009 for whom search had been transformed:

“Searchability is really the biggest power of it. It gives you the pulse of ***now***, what’s being talked about ***now***, what’s trending right now, information about the information, and if you’re able to act on that and do something, it’s really powerful.” He extended it to the organization, “tapping into knowledge management, the hot topic in the organization.”

For him, search had shifted from seeking static web information to cutting a path through a dynamic, constantly-flowing tweet-stream. He set up feeds on topics of interest, some short-term, such as discussion of cultural activity in a city he planned to visit.

Recall the study in which social networks bested search engines [13]. The drawback, that querying friends interrupts them, does not apply to searching. Subsequent to this 2009 interview, search engines began including coverage of social networking feeds. Twitter’s search was itself described as the world’s fastest-growing search engine [2].

Employees described the use of social networking sites for marketing. Some Twitter searches today yield a string of commercial ads; others yield people tweeting conversationally about a topic. This evolution could affect perceptions and uses of the medium.

To summarize, a key finding is that non-tweeters were unaware of potential uses of the medium. As this changes, microblogging use could increase. We recorded slowing growth, but use could reach a critical point after which adoption would increase more rapidly.

Burnout? The limits of social networking

Mass media oscillate between hype and disparagement. Some argue that Facebook is anti-social: "I used to respond immediately to friend requests. But in the past six months I'm tired. I'm just tired." [11]. What do the data tell us?

Our quantitative data provide no evidence of significant burnout. MySpace was abandoned, but overall use of social networking continues to expand, with very little abandonment of today’s leading sites. However, some active users we spoke with are reassessing, claiming to have discovered limitations of social networking tools.

“No one plans anymore. It feeds into some bad personality traits… People tend to lose the sense of commitment being important because there might be something better that hasn’t been posted yet. So people are much more cagey about things.”

“Twitter gives you a fake sense of connection with somebody that isn’t real… If you don’t talk with someone for three months and then you pick up the phone and call them, that’s how you fill the gap in, you don’t know what they’ve done at all, you have to do all the hard work yourself. Where if you’ve been on Twitter you might not see them for a year, when you do see them again, it’s not like you haven’t seen them for a year ‘cause hey, you know what they did yesterday, you know what they did two weeks ago, you know what vacation they went on six months ago, so you *think* you know what they’ve been up to, and you *think* you know what they’re feeling, but you don’t actually. You just know the little message that they send and it’s completely out of context.”

The insight may not seem startling, but it can strike a person as a revelation: Social networking sites can create ties and strengthen weak ties, but only to a certain degree. In the end, one is interacting with crafted online personae of other people. There is a point after which use does not further strengthen a bond, and over-reliance on social networking for communication could weaken a strong tie without those involved realizing it.

Understanding this could drive some people away from social networking sites. It might enable others to engage appropriately, by setting accurate expectations about what can and cannot be achieved through interacting online.

CONCLUSION AND DIRECTIONS

In 2008 we set out to examine public social networking sites as perceived and used by 90,000 Microsoft employees. Historically, new communication technologies encountered resistance that slowly dissipated. Social networking sites typically span company firewalls; despite their speed of adoption around the world, many organizations block their use. We set out to see how they are used in an organization that permits use, and how that shifted over three years.

Microsoft is not a typical organization, despite its diverse and aging workforce. It has a high proportion of early-adopting technology users. Its publicized relationship with Facebook may affect attitudes and behaviors. Our findings are an existence proof of some behaviors and an indication of developments to look for in other organizations.

Use of social networking sites by professionals in our organization expanded dramatically. Much of it is personal, but employees have come to see its value for work. Facebook and LinkedIn have near-universal adoption. Co-existence with them seems a requirement for internal tools. Tight integration could allow employees one-stop shopping. Search engines within such tools could compete with standard search engines that increasingly mine social network sites. An ongoing challenge, as work-life boundaries erode, is to gracefully span the firewall.

Frequency of Facebook use by the youngest cohort continues to grow. What are the implications for the future of social networking in the enterprise? An unexpectedly high use of LinkedIn continues to be centered on 25-45 year olds, although age differences have declined. We saw Twitter expansion slow in 2011 after two years of strong growth. But microblogging could reach a critical mass and resume rapid growth or it could be integrated into established platforms and applications.

We recorded a modest increase in the use of access controls and in concern about sites. Women were somewhat more likely to be heavy users, more likely to use access controls, and less likely to express major concerns.

Generational differences and accommodation were evident. We spoke to one veteran recruiter who has a conservative side; she remarked that she didn't want to see pictures of her pastor drinking on Facebook sites. She uses social networking sites heavily when recruiting students. How did she feel about Facebook pictures of job applicants drinking?

"It's that's degree of judgment. Unless you're talking about 'you just got released from jail' I'm probably OK with most of it. Would I walk away from a student with a beer bong in his mouth? No. You know, I mean, whatever, that's what college is about, right?"

Interviewer: What if it's a marijuana bong?

"Yeah, that one, it's like, maybe it's a poor judgment, you don't post that on your Facebook page… But I hired creatives for years, that's what makes people creative."

Attitudes change. It is a unique period of transformation.

ACKNOWLEDGMENTS

Gina Venolia assisted with survey preparation. Meredith Skeels collaborated in the first survey and the 2009 paper.

REFERENCES

1. Burke, M., Kraut, R. & Marlow, C. 2011. Social capital on Facebook: Differentiating uses and users. *Proc. CHI 2011,* 571-580. ACM.
2. Carr, A. July 8, 2010. Twitter now the world's fastest growing search engine. *Fast Company.* http://www.fastcompany.com/1667617/twitter-isworlds-fastest-growing-search-engine
3. DiMicco, J.M., Millen, D.R., Geyer, W., Dugan, C., Brownholtz, B. & Muller, M. 2008. Motivations for social networking at work. *Proc. CSCW 2008*, 711-720.
4. Efimova, L. & Grudin, J. 2008. Crossing boundaries: Digital literacy in enterprises. In C. Lankshear & M. Knobel (eds.). *Digital Literacies: Concepts, policies, practices.* New York: Peter Lang.
5. Ehrlich, K. & Shami, N. S. 2010. Microblogging inside and outside the workplace. *Proc. ICWSM 2010.* IEEE.
6. Finley, K. 2010. To block or not to block Facebook and social media in the workplace. ReadWrite Enterprise. http://www.readwriteweb.com/enterprise/2010/07/cisco-security.php
7. Gaudin. S. July 22, 2009. Facebook use cuts productivity at work. Computerworld. http://www.computerworld.com/s/article/9135795
8. Geyer, W., Dugan, C., Brownholtz, B., Masli, M., Daly, E. & Millen, D.R. 2011. An open, social microcalendar for the enterprise: Timely? *Proc. CHI 2011,* 247-256.
9. Half, R. 2009. Technology. Whistle-but don't tweet-while you work. http://rht.mediaroom.com/index.php?s=131&item=790
10. Helft, M. July 7, 2010. Facebook makes headway around the world. *New York Times.*
11. Hesse, M. Status symbol: Facebook is ubiquitous, but is it really an antisocial network? *Washington Post,* July 23, 2010.
12. Leahul, D. 2009. Twitter users abandon website after one month. *BrandRepublic.* http://www.brandrepublic.com/News/901752
13. Morris, M.R., Teevan, J. & Panovich, K. A 2010. Comparison of information seeking using search engines and social networks. *Proc. IWCSM 2010.* IEEE.
14. Naaman, M., Boase, J. & Lai, C.H. 2010. Is it really all about me? Message content in social awareness streams. *Proc. CSCW 2010,* 189-192. ACM.
15. Romeo, P. Aug. 13, 2009 & Aug. 4, 2010. Personal communications.
16. Skeels, M. & Grudin, J. 2009. When social networks cross boundaries: A case study of workplace use of Facebook and LinkedIn. *Proc. GROUP 2009*, 95-104.
17. Sophos. August 21, 2007. 50% of employees blocked from accessing Facebook at work. http://www.sophos.com/pressoffice/news/articles/2007/08/block-facebook.html
18. Turner, T., Qvarfordt, P., Biehl, J.Y., Golovchinsky, G., & Back, M. 2010. Exploring the workplace communication ecology. *Proc. CHI 2010,* 841-850.
19. Wu, A., DiMicco, J. & Millen, D.R. 2010. Detecting professional versus personal closeness using an enterprise social network site. *Proc. CHI 2010,* 1955-1964.
20. Zhang, J., Qu, Y., Cody, J. & Wu, Y. 2010. A case study of micro-blogging in the enterprise: Use, value, and related issues. *Proc. CHI 2010*, 123-132. ACM.
21. Zhao, D. & Rosson, M.B. 2009. How and why people Twitter: The role that micro-blogging plays in informal communication at work. *Proc. GROUP 2009*, 243-252.

Breaking News on Twitter

Mengdie Hu [†*], **Shixia Liu** [‡], **Furu Wei** [‡], **Yingcai Wu** [§], **John Stasko** [†], **Kwan-Liu Ma** [§]
[†] Georgia Institute of Technology, GA, USA
[‡] Microsoft Research Asia, Beijing, China [§]University of California at Davis, CA, USA
[†] {mengdie.hu, stasko}@cc.gatech.edu [‡] {shliu, fuwei}@microsoft.com [§]{ycwu, ma}@cs.ucdavis.edu

ABSTRACT
After the news of Osama Bin Laden's death leaked through Twitter, many people wondered if Twitter would fundamentally change the way we produce, spread, and consume news. In this paper we provide an in-depth analysis of how the news broke and spread on Twitter. We confirm the claim that Twitter broke the news first, and find evidence that Twitter had convinced a large number of its audience before mainstream media reported the news. We also discover that attention on Twitter was highly concentrated on a small number of "opinion leaders" and identify three groups of opinion leaders who played key roles in spreading the news: individuals affiliated with media played a large part in breaking the news, mass media brought the news to a wider audience and provided eager Twitter users with content on external sites, and celebrities helped to spread the news and stimulate conversation. Our findings suggest Twitter has great potential as a news medium.

Author Keywords
Social media; Twitter; breaking news; opinion leaders

ACM Classification Keywords
H.5.m [Information Interfaces and Presentation]: Miscellaneous;

General Terms
Human Factors;Verification

INTRODUCTION
Microblogs play an increasingly important role in our social life and are gradually transforming the ways we communicate. One striking example is how the news of Osama Bin Laden's death leaked through Twitter. On the night of May 1st, 2011, US President Barack Obama addressed the nation at 11:35 pm EST and announced that Osama Bin Laden had been killed. However, as later noted by multiple sources [2, 7, 1], millions of people had already learnt of the news before the White House announcement thanks to Twitter. The person credited with breaking the news is Keith Urbahn, an aide for former US Defense Secretary Donald Rumsfeld, who tweeted at 10:24 pm that he had heard of the death of Osama Bin Laden from a reliable source. The tweet quickly went viral and produced numerous retweets and discussions. Only after 21 minutes did the major TV channels ABC, CBS, and NBC report the news, which prompted even more Tweets. Twitter later reported that from 10:45 to 12:30 pm that night the highest ever sustained rate of Tweets occurred, with an average of 3000 tweets per second [3].

*This work has been done when the author was visiting Microsoft Research Asia.

The mainstream media's reaction to the significance of the Osama Bin Laden story was very mixed. While some claimed that this was a turning point and Twitter would completely reshape the landscape of journalism [7, 5], others dismissed Twitter as merely spreading rumors which no one believes until confirmed by the mainstream media [11]. To understand the real role Twitter played, we extracted Tweets about Osama Bin Laden posted in a two-hour time window during and after the breaking of the news and examine whether Twitter convinced its audience. We also study how the news spread from a few sources to the public through identifying key players at different stages of the news flow. In addition, we analyze links included in Tweets to see what kind of content was shared during discussions of the news.

The results of our study complement a number of recent works on microblogging behaviors and information diffusion on Twitter. Java et al. [8] surveyed people's intentions in using Twitter and found most people either use Twitter to talk about daily life with friends or to seek and share information. Kwak et al. [9] examined the topology of Twitter and concluded that Twitter is closer to an information network than a social network. Wu et al. [14] studied how news flow from mass media to the public on Twitter in the context of media communication theories and found that instead of acquiring information directly from mass media, most people rely on an intermediate layer of opinion leaders, which our study confirms. Soon after the Osama Bin Laden story emerged, a startup company named SocialFlow charted a follower network graph of Keith Urbahn to examine how his Tweet spread [1] and identified @brianstelter as a key person in helping spread the news. Our study goes beyond a single Tweet to identify the key user groups in advancing the story. Also of revelance are studies on linking online news in other forms of social media such as blogs [10, 13]. Our results are consistent with the high-level findings of these works that social media draws from news events and impacts mass media in turn. It is possible for us to adopt their techniques of linking media posts through phrase variations in our future work.

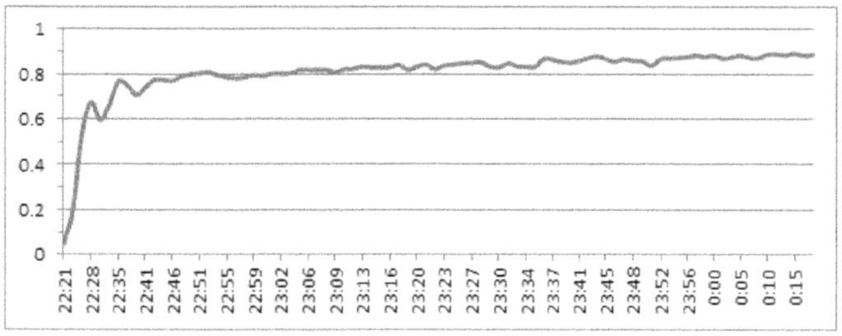

Figure 1. Percentage of Tweets sounding certain.

DATA

Our data comes from a Twitter database maintained by our collaborators at Microsoft. Due to the huge volumes of data on Twitter, they employ a sampling method to obtain only a portion of the data. This method periodically collects Tweets for approximately 40 consecutive seconds in every two minutes, and randomly samples roughly 30% of all Tweets during those 40 seconds. Although the data that we worked on is incomplete, we argue that because of its large size and the systematic sampling strategy, we were able to infer general trends and significant disruptions on Twitter through the sampled data.

Since we are interested in the "breaking" of the news, we decided to focus on May 1st 10:20pm to May 2nd 0:20am EST, which covers both the first rumors of the news and President Obama's speech. We were able to collect 614,976 Tweets containing the string "laden" posted during those two hours. We are aware that we miss many Tweets related to our subject matter that do not contain the term "laden". We argue that the vast majority of the missed Tweets are non-English, and since we are primarily interested in analyzing English Tweets they do not pose a big problem. We also miss some English Tweets that address the event but do not include the string "laden", but we believe the much larger "laden" set can generalize for the missed English Tweets. There also exist Tweets that contain "laden" but are unrelated to the event, but we believe the ratio is extremely low, since 98.52% of the Tweets in our dataset contain the string "bin" and 54.66% contain the string "osama" or "usama".

DID TWITTER BREAK THE NEWS?

First, we wished to confirm the claim that @keithurbahn was the person who broke the news on Twitter. We examined all Tweets between 10:20 pm and 10:45 pm (when three major TV channels announced the news) and found that the most mentioned Twitter users during those 25 minutes were @jacksonjk, @keithurbahn, and @brianstelter who were mentioned 3370, 1177, and 593 times respectively. @keithurbahn tweeted at 10:24 pm: "So I'm told by a reputable person they have killed Osama Bin Laden. Hot damn." @jacksonjk, a CBS News producer, tweeted 8 minutes later: "House Intelligence committee aide confirms that Osama Bin Laden is dead. U.S. has the body." @brianstelter, a New York Times reporter, retweeted both their Tweets and helped spread the news. These findings support the claim that Keith Urbahn wrote the first Tweet about Osama Bin Laden's death that made an impact on Twitter.

DID TWITTER CONVINCE ITS AUDIENCE?

Twitter may have broken the news first, but the question remains whether its users believed these early Tweets or if they viewed them as mere rumors. To find the answer, we trained a classifier to learn certainty in the tone of Tweets and classified all English Tweets in our dataset as "certain", "uncertain", or "irrelevant". We assumed that if people expressed doubts or reservation then they were uncertain about this event. On the other hand if they made a statement about this event as if it was a fact then they had high confidence in it being true. So "Rumor, Bin Laden dead. Don't know for sure" indicates the author was uncertain about the event, while "They caught Osama Bin Laden!" infers the author was fairly sure the event was true. Through labeling each Tweet certain or uncertain and calculating the percentage of certain Tweets, we could gain an impression on the overall confidence of Twitter users. We do run the risk of overestimating confidence since people sometimes make statements about things even though they consider them rumors. We do not claim that the percentage of certain Tweets directly translates to the percentage of Twitter users convinced by the news. Rather, we look for changes in percentage of certain Tweets which indicates shifts of confidence among Twitter users.

We selected 300 Tweets posted before the "breaking news" Tweet, immediately after it and at the end of the dataset. Two researchers familiar with the dataset individually labeled each Tweet and they agreed on 235 Tweets (78.3%). Of the 235 Tweets, 54.9% were certain, 42.1% were uncertain, and 3.0% were irrelevant. We used the 235 Tweets to train two binary classifiers. The first classifier determines whether a Tweet is relevant and the second classifier classifies the relevant Tweets as either certain or uncertain. The Support Vector Machine (SVM) technique was used with bag-of-words as features. We estimated the performance of the classifiers with a 5-fold cross-validation scheme [6] and reported 75.8% overall confidence.

Figure 1 shows the percentage of certain Tweets among all English Tweets collected. We found certainty started very low and drastically rose to over 50% following @keithurbahn's Tweet. Then it gradually increased to nearly 80% by 10:45 pm. After 10:45 pm when ABC, CBS, and NBC "officially" announced the death of Osama Bin Laden on TV, certainty rose to over 80% and remained steady. The certainty analysis suggests that a large percentage of Twitter users expressed confidence in the early Tweets. While it is difficult to explain why users were so confident without interviewing a large number of them, we have some speculation that their trust is partially due to the professional identities of the authors of the early Tweets. @brianstelter is a well-known New York Times reporter with tens of thousands of followers. And while @keithurbahn and @jacksonjk did not have so many followers, their public profiles described their jobs. It is unlikely that an aide for formal Defense Secretary Donald Rumsfeld or a CBS News producer would spread groundless rumors of something so important and risk jeopardizing their reputation. Indeed we found that 29.91% of Tweets mentioning @keithurbahn contain the word "Rumsfeld" and 18.61% of Tweets mentioning @jacksonjk contain the word "CBS".

mainstream media	26
media people	18
news aggregators	3
political figures and organizations	4
real-life celebrities	15
twitter celebrities	16
popular blogs	6
"Osama Bin Ladens", "Jesus Christs"	4
odinary users	5

Table 1. Number of Twitter accounts among the top 100 under each category.

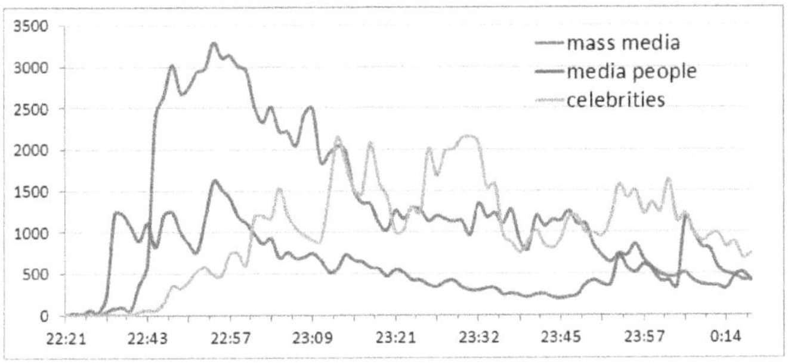

Figure 2. Number of Tweets per minute mentioning a Twitter account from one of the categories.

WHO GENERATED THE BUZZ?

After the news was "broken", Twitter users eagerly engaged in discussions. To find out who generated the biggest reactions among Twitter users, we identified the 100 users most mentioned in the two hours. Unsurprisingly, @CNN, @CNNEE (CNN in Spanish), and @nytimes (the New York Times) topped the list. @jacksonjk, who was among the first to report the news, ranked 4th. The 5th place went to @BarackObama. Together the 100 users were mentioned in 111,325 Tweets, which accounts for 18.10% of the total Tweets. This finding echoes the observation of Wu et al. [14] that on Twitter a great portion of all information consumed is generated by a small number of elite users.

We further manually grouped the top 100 users into categories (see Table 1). We found that 47 media-related accounts, with 26 accounts for mass media, 3 for automatic news aggregators, and 18 for media people (individuals employed by major news organizations, such as reporters and news anchors). The 26 mass media accounts were mentioned in 5.84% of all Tweets and the 18 media people were mentioned in 3.36% of all Tweets. This finding suggests that the media people had a strong voice of their own independent from their employers. We also found that 31 of the top 100 accounts belonged to celebrities, whether in real life or only on Twitter (we treated 100,000 followers as a cutoff line for Twitter celebrities). Together these people were mentioned in 4.53% of all Tweets. Given the political nature of the subject matter, and the fact that few of the celebrities were known to be heavily involved in politics, this figure is quite high. The strong presence of celebrities is in line with the literature on social influence on Twitter [14].

To further understand the difference between categories, we charted the aggregated mention trend for three groups: mass media, media people, and celebrities. As shown in Figure 2

cnn.com	4105	M	go.com	875	M
msn.com	2596	M	bbc.co.uk	826	M
nytimes.com	2569	M	wsj.com	788	M
twitpic.com	2560	U	facebook.com	750	U
yfrog.com	1689	U	whitehouse.gov	729	M
globo.com	1545	M	huffingtonpost.com	619	M
twitlonger.com	1257	U	aljazeera.net	597	M
youtube.com	1257	U	yahoo.com	587	M
tumblr.com	1148	U	google.com	568	M
reuters.com	1083	M	foxnews.com	560	M
tmi.me	1068	U	uol.com.br	551	M
lockerz.com	984	U	blogspot.com	541	U
mashable.com	930	M	globovision.com	540	M

Table 2. The most linked sites and the number of times they were mentioned. The sites are labelled as either a Mass Media site (M) or a site for sharing user-created content(U).

we found that the mention patterns for the three groups were very distinct. Media people were mentioned first, which is what we would expect knowing some of them were among the first to spread the news. Around 22:45 mass media exploded with reports and instantly caught the attention of Twitter users. Celebrities tagged behind, but because of their large amount of loyal followers they gradually overtook mass media in the number of mentions. These findings suggest that the three groups influence Twitter users in different ways. While media people and the mass media compete to be the first to report the news, celebrities use their social influence to help spread the news and stimulate discussions.

WHAT DID PEOPLE SHARE?

We are also interested in the content that people share in their Tweets, represented by links. Examining URLs included in Tweets we found 9.69% of all Tweets in our dataset contain links. Most of the links were shortened with a Tweet-shortening service. We traced every link back to its destination web page. Then we examined both the web pages and their top level websites. Table 2 lists the 26 websites, which accounts for 58.83% of all valid links. We classified the sites into mass media sites (the M group) and sites hosting user-generated content (the U group). The M group contains mainstream media sites such as cnn.com as well as sites like huffingtonpost.com which hosts curated news and blogs and enjoys high readership and reputation. Whitehouse.gov, which was not really a media site, was placed in this bin because of its authority and popularity. The U group contains Tweet-shortening services, picture and video sharing sites, social network sites, and blog services. All of the sites in the U group host uploads by everyday users. We argue that in general content from the M group comes from a small number of "elite" sources, while content from the U group is produced by the common people.

We found that among the links that point to one of the top 26 sites, 64.07% of links point to a site of the M group, and 35.93% of links point to a site from the U group. This finding suggests that mass media still provides the majority of content that people share, especially in the context of news event and political discussions. On the other hand a significant number of users are also eager to share content created by themselves or other users. We also examined the web pages shared over

615 times (which means over 0.1% of Tweets in our dataset linked to that web page) and found six of them. All six web pages originated from mass media sites. The most popular one, linked by Twitter users for more than 2000 times, points to a video clip of Obama's speech on MSNBC.MSN.com. It seems that while ordinary users created plenty of content, their work had a limited reach. The content consumed by the most people is still created by mass media.

DISCUSSIONS

Our certainty analysis on Tweets suggests that Twitter convinced many of its audience of Osama Bin Laden's death before confirmation came from mass media. We speculate this is because the people who posted the news were politicians and journalists, who were authorities on the subject matter. Our findings suggest that individuals in media related professions can play critical roles in breaking and spreading news on Twitter, since they enjoy high reputation and access to the news sources, and they could take advantage of the speed and reach of Twitter. It seems that news organizations have also noted this tendency. In November 2011, the Associated Press issued a warning to its staff members that they should file any breaking news to the wire before putting it out on social media [4].

Through our examination of the 100 most mentioned users on Twitter, we discovered a high concentration of attention on a very small subset of users and found three key user groups who influenced their audience in different stages of the news cycle. This could be interpreted through the lens of the two-step flow of communication theory, which Wu et al. discussed in length in [14]. The theory suggests most people acquire information not directly through mass media, but through an intermediate layer of "elite users", also known as "opinion leaders", who filter and interpret the information from mass media based on their own values. Wu et al. found significant evidence of the two-step flow of information on Twitter, and they identified celebrities as the most important group of opinion leaders. Our findings agree with the claim that information flow from mass media to celebrities, who voice their reactions on Twitter and pass their opinions to their followers.

Our analysis on user attention and links suggests that mass media is still at the core of reporting. Even though mass media may not be the fastest in breaking news, people still trust the content it produces more than other sources.

Our study confirms Twitter's rising potential in news reporting and identifies key players in the breaking, spreading, and consuming of information on Twitter. We recognize that our study is limited to a single case. The Osama Bin Laden story is significant because it is among the earliest reports of Twitter breaking news before mass media. At the moment reports of social media breaking news are still rare and anecdotal [12], so it is hard to reach a general conclusion from a single case study. However, the set of methods we presented in this paper could be applied to study other situations, and we believe as social media plays an increasingly important role in our news generation and consumption, studies of this kind will become more and more valuable. The findings of the case study could also be applied to several research areas such as news event detection and tracking. For those interested in reporting early development of news stories, our result suggests that it should be important to monitor Twitter accounts of journalists. Furthermore, those trying to spread information on Twitter or to influence public opinion should target one of the "opinion leader" groups such as celebrities.

CONCLUSION

In this paper, we present a study of the role of microblogs in breaking and spreading news by analyzing how Osama Bin Laden's death leaked through Twitter. We identify three groups of "elite users" who played key roles at different stages of the news cycle. Certainty analysis shows that the people who broke the news were able to convince many Twitter users before confirmation came from mass media. We speculate this is due to their professional identity as politicians and journalists. Our results confirms Twitter's rising potential in news reporting and our method could be applied to study other cases of social media breaking news.

ACKNOWLEDGMENTS

We thank the reviewers and the associate chairs for their helpful feedback.

REFERENCES

1. Breaking Bin Laden. `http://blog.socialflow.com/post/5246404319/breaking-bin-laden-visualizing-the-power-of-a-sing`
2. How the Bin Laden Announcement Leaked Out. `http://mediadecoder.blogs.nytimes.com/2011/05/01/how-the-osama-announcement-leaked-out/`.
3. Twitter: Last night saw the highest sustained rate of Tweets ever. From 10:45 - 2:20am ET, there was an average of 3,000 Tweets per second . `http://twitter.com/#!/twitterglobalpr/status/65125115272249344`.
4. Associated Press reporters told off for Tweeting. `http://www.bbc.co.uk/news/technology-15772243`.
5. Twitter just had its CNN moment. `http://www.businessinsider.com/twitter-just-had-its-cnn-moment-2011-5`.
6. Geisser, S. *Predictive Inference: An Introduction*. CRC Press, 1993.
7. Lessons from the Osama bin Laden coverage. `http://www.guardian.co.uk/technology/2011/may/09/lessons-from-bin-laden-coverage`.
8. Java, A., Song, X., Finin, T., and Tseng, B. Why we twitter: understanding microblogging usage and communities. In *Proc. WebKDD/SNA-KDD '07*, ACM (2007), 56–65.
9. Kwak, H., Lee, C., Park, H., and Moon, S. What is twitter, a social network or a news media? In *Proc. WWW '10*, ACM (2010), 591–600.
10. Leskovec, J., Backstrom, L., and Kleinberg, J. Meme-tracking and the dynamics of the news cycle. In *Proc. KDD '09*, ACM (2009), 497–506.
11. Why All the Hyperventilating About Twitter 'Breaking' Bin Laden's Death Is Total Nonsense. `http://adage.com/article/mediaworks/twitter-broke-news-bin-laden-s-death-nonsense/227327/`.
12. 10 news stories that broke on Twitter first. `http://www.techradar.com/news/internet/10-news-stories-that-broke-on-twitter-first-719532`
13. Tsagkias, M., de Rijke, M., and Weerkamp, W. Linking online news and social media. In *Proc. WSDM '11*, ACM (2011), 565–574.
14. Wu, S., Hofman, J. M., Mason, W. A., and Watts, D. J. Who says what to whom on twitter. In *Proc. WWW '11*, ACM (2011), 705–714.

The Twitter Mute Button: A Web Filtering Challenge

Jennifer Golbeck
Human-Computer Interaction Lab
College of Information Studies
University of Maryland
College Park, MD 20742
jgolbeck@umd.edu

ABSTRACT
The microblogging service Twitter has become an important, and sometimes primary, source of information for many users. As a forum for sharing news and discussing events, it can provide instant access to the latest updates, but this is not always welcome. In the case of television shows or live sporting events, for example, tweets about them may reveal spoilers to users in different time zones or who are delaying their viewing until later. More broadly, because Twitter is a broadcast medium, users may often want to temporarily or permanently hide content about a very specific given topic.

In this paper, we describe the unique challenges to HCI, social computing, and computational linguistics posed by the task of building an interface that blocks all tweets about a specific event or topic. We illustrate some of the challenges through a pilot experiment run for three major television events: the 2009 NFC Championship football game, the 2010 mid-season finale of the show Glee, and the 2010 season premiere of the show 24. While simple techniques achieve very high recall ($> 98\%$), spoilers still make it through the filter and precision is extremely poor. We conclude with a description of challenges to the community in implementing this new and increasingly important feature.

Author Keywords
twitter, computational linguistics, filtering

ACM Classification Keywords
H.5.2 Information Interfaces and Presentation: Miscellaneous

General Terms
Human Factors

INTRODUCTION
"Why do people insist on talking about the plot line of '24' when those of us on the West Coast haven't seen it yet?"

"Really, guys? We're going to tweet Glee spoilers? It's fine. I didn't want to watch it on tivo tomorrow or anything... nope... not me.".

"@user9452636 pls Stop spoiling 24 for those of us at work and who have it tivo'd....I'm too addicted to twitter to shut it off"

Twitter has evolved to serve many purposes. The 140-character microblog posts (called "tweets") can describe mundane details of people's lives, like what they had for lunch, but the service has also become a platform for politics [1, 2], disaster response and recovery [10, 11], and a useful backchannel at events [8].

Twitter has also become a widely used medium for real time conversation and information sharing about events. As an example, consider television shows and sporting events. Twitter backchanneling can provide a rich supplement to the user's viewing, allowing them to discuss, receive clarification, share thoughts, and discover a community of people with similar interests. However, it also introduces a problem of spoilers to viewers/users who are waiting to watch the program and do not want to see tweets about it ahead of time. Indeed, in our data collection for these experiments, we discovered the tweets included above that complain about this exact phenomenon.

Right now, the only reliable solution for users who wish to avoid tweets about a given event or topic is to avoid Twitter all together. Of course, this has the negative side effect of disconnecting them from all the other information they may receive. As Twitter becomes an increasingly prominent information source for users, the strategy of total avoidance becomes less tenable. The solution is a selective "mute" button that will block all tweets related to a specific topic of event.

Potential solutions lie in methods already used in the HCI, social computing, and computational linguistics (CL) communities. Although these researchers have studied Twitter before, we describe a unique and difficult challenge: identify and block every tweet on a given topic. This is harder than it may sound at first. While CL techniques may seem a natural fit, and there is much existing work on using them with Twitter (e.g. [4, 12, 9]), the goodness of solutions to this problem is not well-measured by traditional IR or CL metrics. Recall must be nearly 100% lest an important spoiler (like the score of a football game) makes it through to the user. Precision, on the other hand, can be relatively poor because a large number of false positives will not necessarily have a significant impact on the perceived quality of the filter. Combine this with the fact that tweets are exceptionally short with no more than 140 characters and that recognizing patterns in the content often requires specific domain knowledge for human users to identify it.

Though the challenge is daunting, we believe there is a large and growing need for an interface tool that allows users to selectively and effectively filters information on a given topic. In this paper, we discuss the challenges that are faced by HCI, social, and CL researchers who want to build such a tool and we present a pilot study that attempts to filter tweets about three events.

BACKGROUND AND RELATED WORK

Classification of tweets into 'allowed" and "disallowed" categories, as is done with spam filtering, is initially an attractive option for the problem at hand. Previous work [5] has shown that tweets can be classified as spam or non-spam, and [9] present a technique that classifies tweets into high level categories like News, Opinions, and Private message. However, for the specific problem we present here, classification alone is not likely to be effective. Spam tends to have similar characteristics - particularly links to pages whose content is longer and fits well-established patterns of spam. Broad categories like News vs. Opinions also have differentiating characteristics. On the other hand, classifying tweets as about or not about a much narrower topic, like a specific television show, is much more difficult. As discussed below, our pilot study shows difficulty blocking tweets that are very specific to the content of the programs . Content like quotes from a show, comments about characters that presumes a deep background among the readers or results of sports plays given in abbreviations and numbers may be meaningful to others with appropriate background, but they do not clearly indicate the topic in a way that a classifier could recognize. Indeed, some tweets could be about nearly anything and it is only through context and background knowledge that human readers are able to correctly classify them.

When looking specifically at spoilers posted in text, [3] presents an approach for detecting them in movie reviews. However, this technique worked on full reviews, not the very limited text of tweets. Furthermore, our goal is to detect not just spoilers, but any text about a given topic or event, and thus spoiler detection alone will be insufficient. That said, we discuss the use of some of their techniques, like latent Dirichlet allocation, in the Discussion section of this paper, as these methods are likely to be important components for a Twitter mute button.

PILOT STUDY: FILTERING TELEVISION TWEETS

To illustrate the potential challenges and successes of a technique to filter tweets on a given topic, we present a prototype Twitter mute button and test its effectiveness on tweets posted during three televised events. We keep the approach simple here, using a basic "bag of words" approach. While other algorithms and approaches will certainly lead to better precision, the recall challenges - which are critical to this application - are likely to remain. Our efforts here are not to present *the* solution to this problem, but rather to show some possible approaches to the problem with their benefits and drawbacks.

Methodology

Data Set

We use a subset of the Twitter corpus collected in [7] via the Twitter streaming API. Our subset of the data spans November 10, 2009 to February 1, 2010. This includes 96,369,325 tweets from 9,139,986 unique users.

We chose three events that happened in this time span which highlight the type of event about which one might want to block tweets in his or her Twitter stream:

- The 2009-2010 NFC Championship playoff game between the New Orleans Saints and the Minnesota Vikings, which began at 6:40pm EST on January 24, 2010, to an average of 57.9 million US viewers.
- "Sectionals", the mid-season finale for the first season of the television show "Glee", which aired at 8pm EST on December 9, 2009 to just over 8.1 million US viewers
- The season premiere of the seventh season of the television show "24", a two-hour episode that aired at 9pm EST on January 11, 2010 to 12.6 million US viewers

For each event, we collected all the tweets on our corpus made between when the program started to air and ending one hour after the show ended.

We also limited the language of the tweets to English so we could competently create a ground-truth dataset (although our technique will work for any and/or multiple languages). To do this, each tweet minus any hash tags, mentions, and links, was passed to the Google Translate API for language detection. Any tweets detected as English with certainty > 0.05 were kept.

We randomly selected 10,000 tweets from the set for each event. These were then reviewed by one researcher with expertise on the given show and one Amazon Mechanical Turk worker. After taking a qualifying test, mTurk workers saw ten tweets at a time and marked them as being about the show or not. Since the purpose of this exercise is to catch *every* tweet that might be related to the program in question, all tweets that were marked relevant by at least one coder were included in the set of tweets about the show.

There were 79 tweets about "24", 185 about "Glee", and 1,223 about the NFC Championship game.

Tweet Blocking

The core of our pilot approach is to automatically create a word blacklist for each pattern. We describe that process below. Once the list is built, we look for blacklisted words within tweets. We used pattern matching so that any time the string of a blacklisted word appears in a tweet, even if it is part of a larger word, the tweet is blocked. This is necessary in the Twitter environment where words often appear embedded in hash tags, joined with other words (e.g. "glee" in the hastag #totalGleeFail).

Blacklists are built automatically. Because sporting events and television programs are different, we use slightly different approaches with the same theme.

For television shows, we compiled a list of actor and character names from the Internet Movie Database (IMDB). The first and last names of all the characters were included individually on the list. On one hand, this will certainly lead to many false positives, as people will mention others by name who coincidentally have the same name as a character. On the other hand, there is no option but to block tweets in this way. For example, among the 79 tweets identified as about "24", five of them could only be identified by the first names of the characters discussed (e.g. "About dang time Jack...").

In addition, the name of the show was blocked.

For sporting events, we followed the same process but we used the names of players and coaches instead of actors. The names of the teams, their stadiums, and the sporting event taking place were also blacklisted. Finally, we blocked names of positions (e.g. quarterback) and events within the game (e.g. penalty, touchdown). All of this data was automatically pulled from the structured Wikipedia pages on the topic.

From these lists, we eliminated any single letters (which often appeared as initials) and and two-letter words, including "St." and "Dr". Punctuation was also removed. Because we used the block list words as patterns to match, such short strings were so likely to appear in many words as to make the system essentially a full Twitter block. We removed stop words from this list (e.g. "of", "from", "a").

Results

Catching Identified Tweets

Using this method, we blocked all but 1 of the tweets about "24" (1.26%). The missed tweet contained no spoilers:

@user678805 first season was classic. I quit after the 3rd!

For Glee, we missed six tweets (3.24%):

1. Lol "Im going to hug you now"
2. I love it, the show is all about energy and connection. The music is quite fitting.
3. Hey Mr Shue, you forgot your keys... "No I didnt..."
4. aren't you guys dating? "...sex is not dating..."
5. OMFGG THE SEASON'S OVER IN 8 MINUTESSS ¡333333333
6. @user364884 you would think that she would FINALLY be happy!!

None of these contain explicit spoilers, and for someone who had not seen the episode, many would appear out of context. However, the third tweet beginning "Hey Mr Shue" uses a nickname for a character that was not picked up by our character name filters.

We also missed twenty tweets about the NFC Championship game (1.64%), ten of which are shown below as examples. Even though this gives us over 98% accuracy in catching tweets, there are some major spoilers in this list. Some tweets reveal the score or that the game is about to go to overtime.

1. Damnnn that was a nice spin move lol
2. big stop
3. they are hitting the shit out of fave damn
4. This is gonna be a shoot out! me like very much :)
5. MIN 14 - NO 7 - 1min 1qtr
6. Wow this looks like it could be a damn shoot out...and I want see but the last half of it..:(
7. 7-7.lets go
8. Last team in 20 min then its over! Thank god! I hate all cheerleaders.
9. This bout to be a #ShootOut
10. Wow. Two drives, two TDs. 7-7. This is going to be fun!

False Positives

Because we cast a very wide net in an attempt to block 100% of tweets that were identified as being part of our event, there was a high level of false positives. For "Glee", 2,987 of 9,805 tweets that were *not* about were blocked (30.5%). For 24, we blocked 6,815 out of 9,920 (68.7%). For the NFC Championship, 6,166 out of the 8,788 marked negatives were blocked, 70%. These rates are very high. For some users, such rates would be acceptable if all spoilers were blocked, as it still allows them to see some information on Twitter while the block is in place. For other users, these rates may be far too high.

Pilot Experiment Discussion

Our results show that for television programs, we can achieve a very high level of accuracy in catching tweets about the show being blocked. The proportion of false negatives ranges widely between our sample shows. While no spoiler tweets made it through our filter in this case, the false negatives we found suggest that this may be possible in another dataset. We believe our social filtering would likely help this in a full implementation, and we discuss several techniques for boosting our performance in other ways below.

On the NFC Championship game, while we still had a high rate of catching tweets about the game (> 98%), there were major spoilers to be found in the tweets we missed. Indeed, a simple score (7-7) posted during an important game, a misspelling, or a colloquial term (e.g. "Gooooooaaaaallll!" with any number of each letter) will be very difficult to catch without causing all tweets to be blocked. Indeed, we would essentially need to block all numbers to account for message discussing players by number or revealing scores.

Before discussing applications of CL, there is a straightforward social approach that we believe belongs in a Twitter mute button. When a user has a tweet blocked when the filter is active, it indicates they may be tweeting about the event or topic. Thus, blocking all additional tweets from that user may be an effective way of blocking other related content. We were unable to test that here because the dataset we had to work with has users anonymized and is not a full record of tweets from the given period. Although we were unable to apply social filtering, we believe it will be an important component of a working Twitter mute system.

From the CL perspective, our pilot uses the most straightforward path to creating blacklists - simple bags of words.

While we believe this will remain a critical component of any strategy that tries to block all tweets on a given topic, more advanced techniques like modifications of TF-IDF and query expansion that identify additional blacklist words for a given topic, latent Dirichlet allocation, and machine learning approaches may help identify words or patterns of text that will increase recall and improve precision over what might be expected from our pilot results.

As we progress with this work, data will also be a challenge. Because tweets are so short, many of them are needed to start detecting patterns in word use. Thus, to test any of these methods, we will need an even larger dataset than what is currently available.

CONCLUSIONS

In this paper, we present a challenge for identifying and blocking every message about a specific topic posted on Twitter. This will prevent users from seeing content they find objectionable, such as spoilers for events like sports and television shows, while still retaining access to the rest of the information stream. We discuss some of the challenges for computational linguistic and social techniques and illustrate these through a pilot study run with three events.

Using a corpus of data from the Twitter streaming API, we selected a large sample of tweets from three events - the season premiere of "24", the mid-season finale of "Glee", and the NFC Championship football game. Our results show that simple, automated blocking strategies can detect nearly all tweets about a specific topic, but that they are not enough to block all spoilers and that the rate of false positives may be unacceptable for some users.

While we focused on the television application here, this problem is representative of a much wider range of filtering challenges. A technique that is successful in the television domain could also be used for parental filtering and blocking discussions about broader topics like religion or politics, hashtag games, etc.

Moving forward with this work, we see it as a challenge for researchers in HCI, social computing, and computational linguistics that can be standardized. Obtaining a large dataset with anonymized but consistent social information will provide the groundwork. Then, identifying representative events and topics and creating ground truth classification of tweets about each of those will provide a basis for judging the quality or improvement offered by any given technique. From there, we will have standard measures by which new approaches can be tested and evaluated. Not only will this help solve a problem that we believe is becoming increasingly important - selective filtering of short user-generated content - but it may also inspire the development of new algorithms and uses for social and textual data on the web that will have applications in other areas.

CONCLUSIONS

REFERENCES

1. Golbeck, J., Grimes, J., and Rogers, A. Twitter use by the u.s. congress. *Journal of the American Society for Information Science and Technology 61* (2010), 16121621.
2. Golbeck, J., and Hansen, D. Computing political preference among twitter followers. In *Proceedings of the 2011 annual conference on Human factors in computing systems*, CHI '11 (2011).
3. Guo, S., and Ramakrishnan, N. Finding the storyteller: automatic spoiler tagging using linguistic cues. In *Proceedings of the 23rd International Conference on Computational Linguistics*, COLING '10, Association for Computational Linguistics (Stroudsburg, PA, USA, 2010), 412–420.
4. Jansen, B., Zhang, M., Sobel, K., and Chowdury, A. Twitter power: Tweets as electronic word of mouth. *Journal of the American society for information science and technology 60*, 11 (2009), 2169–2188.
5. Lee, K., Caverlee, J., and Webb, S. The social honeypot project: protecting online communities from spammers. In *Proceedings of the 19th international conference on World wide web*, WWW '10, ACM (New York, NY, USA, 2010), 1139–1140.
6. Neustaedter, C., Tang, A., and Tejinder, J. K. The role of community and groupware in geocache creation and maintenance. In *Proceedings of the 28th international conference on Human factors in computing systems*, CHI '10, ACM (New York, NY, USA, 2010), 1757–1766.
7. Petrović, S., Osborne, M., and Lavrenko, V. Streaming first story detection with application to twitter. In *Human Language Technologies: The 2010 Annual Conference of the North American Chapter of the Association for Computational Linguistics*, Association for Computational Linguistics (2010), 181–189.
8. Ross, C., Terras, M., Warwick, C., and Welsh, A. Enabled backchannel: Conference twitter use by digital humanists. *Journal of Documentation 67* (2011), 214–237.
9. Sriram, B., Fuhry, D., Demir, E., Ferhatosmanoglu, H., and Demirbas, M. Short text classification in twitter to improve information filtering. In *Proceeding of the 33rd international ACM SIGIR conference on Research and development in information retrieval*, SIGIR '10, ACM (New York, NY, USA, 2010), 841–842.
10. Starbird, K., and Palen, L. "voluntweeters": self-organizing by digital volunteers in times of crisis. In *Proceedings of the 2011 annual conference on Human factors in computing systems*, CHI '11, ACM (New York, NY, USA, 2011).
11. Vieweg, S., Hughes, A. L., Starbird, K., and Palen, L. Microblogging during two natural hazards events: what twitter may contribute to situational awareness. In *Proceedings of the 2010 annual conference on Human factors in computing systems*, CHI '10 (2010).
12. Yerva, S., Miklós, Z., and Aberer, K. It was easy, when apples and blackberries were only fruits. In *CLEF 2010 (Notebook Papers/LABs/Workshops)*, Citeseer (2010).

'Timid Encounters': A Case Study in the Use of Proximity-Based Mobile Technologies

Christian Licoppe
Département Sciences Economiques et Sociales,
Télécom ParisTech
46 rue Barrault 75013 Paris, France
christian.licoppe@telecom-paristech.fr

Yoriko Inada
Département Sciences Economiques et Sociales,
Télécom ParisTech
46 rue Barrault 75013 Paris, France
yoriko.inada@telecom-paristech.fr

ABSTRACT
We report a comparative ethnographic study of a proximity-based mobile "video game" (Dragon Quest 9) in Japan: the Nintendo DS game terminals may 'recognize' one another and allow players to exchange game resources when they are close to one another. Because different communication infrastructures are available, situations of encounter are shown to be potentially seamful and to support multi-layered participation frames. Our observations show a variety of encounter formats, among whom 'timid' encounters are the most characteristic of the kind of sociality which may develop in urban public places turned into proximity-sensitive "hybrid ecologies" The normative order which governs such encounters is marked by a tension between the minimality expected of encounters with strangers in urban spaces, and the concern for identification and focused interaction that derives from being engaged in proximal digital communication. These empirical observations and framework of analysis offer insights for the design and the understanding of proximity-based mobile technologies.

Author Keywords
Proximity; gaming; mobility; encounters; hybrid ecology; locative media; public space.

ACM Classification Keywords
H.5.m. [Information interfaces and presentation]: Miscellaneous;

INTRODUCTION
The development of ubiquitous computing (Weiser, 1991) has stimulated a growing interest in the organization of activities, particularly collaborative ones, accomplished in complex ecologies, where a variety of digital resources, often based on different types of network infrastructures, intersect each other and are simultaneously available. This strand of research, centered on computer-supported collaborative work (CSCW), has focused on the way the 'seamlessness' or 'seamfulness' of actual situations of use can support collaboration (Chalmers & Galani, 2004), and how people are able to creatively combine 'assemblies' of artefactual resources and rely upon these in order to support new experiences of sociality adjusted to these complex ecologies (Hindmarsh et al, 2005). The development of locative media seems to go one step further with respect to the traditional version of ubiquitous computing. Their availability is constitutive of 'hybrid ecologies' in which different forms of access to a particular place (e.g. through embodied presence, and through various screens and terminals) are somehow articulated (Crabtree & Rodden, 2008). This perspective leads to a complete reshaping of our understanding of what has been dubbed 'virtual practices' and understood as actions performed online by a de-contextualized user engaging with his networked computer, a kind of practice perhaps best epitomized by online multiplayer games. Recent ethnographic work on the use of games such as that of World of Warcraft in China is pushing towards a reconsideration of how such online games are played: 'on screen' collaborative actions and co-present interactions are meshed in a way that can only be understood by taking into account the particular 'hybrid cultural ecology' of the internet café or *wang ba* (Lindtner et al., 2008).

Early examples of the uses of locative media concerned various games combining online actions and urban mobilities that led to the construction of 'playful urban spaces' (de Souza, Silva & Hjorth, 2009). Early studies showed how location awareness could support sociality in specific ways, and how the mutual knowledge of proximity made face-to-face encounters relevant (Licoppe & Inada, 2006; 2010). More recently, the idea that various forms of location awareness might support specific forms of cooperation and sociality has led to the notion of 'location-based social networks' (de Souza, Silva & Frith, 2010) and an interest concerning their use in urban public spaces to produce 'digital cityscapes' (de Souza, Silva & Sutko, 2010). It has also made relevant a phenomenological orientation in which researchers try to bring together the articulation of the corporeal experience of mobility, sociality and the location-informed engagement of players with their mobile terminal into a single embodied experience, such articulation work being constitutive of the way players or more generally mobile users may inhabit together 'hybrid ecologies' (Richardson, 2010; Richardson & Wilken, 2010).

We can extend this argument to public settings other than the street. As soon as people are equipped with handheld connected digital devices, then any kind of public space, be it the street, the museum or the internet café, becomes a 'hybrid cultural ecology'. However, the focus of CSCW research on the way such ecologies support collaboration in general masks a sensitive issue regarding the specific kind of sociality that could be developing in urban spaces *qua* public places. Public places are where strangers can meet one another. The city as a public place is a 'world of strangers' (Lofland, 1973) where strangers are ceaselessly experiencing 'traffic encounters' (Hannerz, 1980). Public places are settings in which strangers 'appear' all the time and where such 'appearances' have therefore to be socially managed in acceptable ways. The normative rules that govern the patterns of such encounters with strangers are an integral part of the 'interaction order' that is constitutive of relations in public (Goffman, 1963; 1971). As this author has shown, strangers collaborate to move, interact and recognize each other through gaze and embodied resources with an orientation towards minimality and the avoidance of singularizing the other, as in the case of 'civil inattention'. Moreover, individuals in public places always constitute a potential audience for any events that might occur there (Lofland, 1998). The forms of collaboration that develop in urban public settings are generally marked by a particular form of 'laconic urbanity' (Joseph, 1993) in which requests for help are, for instance, framed so as to require only limited commitments.

The question is: what happens when urban public places become 'hybrid ecologies'? What kind of sociality is supported by these 'hybrid ecologies', and what kind of interaction order and public-sphere relations? How do we orient to strangers and how do we 'encounter' them in such connected settings? Will the urban hybrid ecologies of the future be as 'democratic' as the megalopolis of the 20th century, in the sense of treating all individuals as equivalent in innumerable traffic encounters? What kind of public place might the digital cityscape, 'augmented' with pervasive computing, become?

If we want to understand the use of mobile media in urban hybrid ecologies and the distinctive but culturally-shaped way we experience the latter as places, we need detailed ethnographies of their use and of the kind of sociality between strangers and interaction order that evolve around the availability of location-sensitive shared resources. This paper aims to provide such a case study, through the ethnographic observations we made of the use of Dragon Quest 9 in Japan. Dragon Quest 9 is a 'proximity game' (Soderlund, 2010) in which the proximity of players becomes a resource in the gameplay. The game scenario provides incentives for players to approach one another, leading them to meet and gather in urban spaces. When this occurs, traditional public places, such as malls, stations or parks, become crowded with groups of players, many of whom are not acquainted with one another (to varying degrees, as we will see), in an ecology which provides them with many different resources to become mutually perceptible and to interact together: those of co-presence (voice, gaze, gestures, etc.), but also those originating from digital networks, available either through a game terminal or a mobile phone. The way players articulate such resources to produce distinctive patterns of relations in public prefigures the kind of interaction order that may develop in public places as hybrid ecologies.

FIELDWORK

We began by studying exchanges posted on several forums used by Japanese players (Mixi & Shirabata. We were able to discuss online with ten players, and interview twelve players we recruited there. We also gathered and studied systematically the players' electronic discussions on forums three months before our ethnographic fieldwork and one month after, for the purpose of documenting some of the phenomena we were investigating. We did the fieldwork in Japan in two waves, in 2009 and 2010. This involved going to the players' gathering spots to observe the way they convened in urban public spaces. We tried to visit each meeting two or three times each so as to gain a sense of their variability. Each of these observations allowed us to observe in detail the behavior of a dozen of players each times, and to discuss informally with the meeting organizer and two or three players present on the average. The places we went to in Japan were: Akihabara and Odaiba Fuji TV in Tokyo, and the train station and the Apita commercial mall in Shizuoka, a town about 200 km from Tokyo on the Tokyo-Osaka *Shinkansen* line. In all these places we tried to talk informally with the players and organizers. One of us (Y.I.) also purchased a DS terminal with the French and Japanese versions of the game, enabling him to play in both countries. This was to allow us to familiarize ourselves with this form of play and to acquire thereby a direct experience of proximity-mediated game encounters.

.

ENCOUNTERS IN DRAGONQUEST 9

Dragon Quest 9 as a 'proximity game'

Dragon Quest is a game for Nintendo DS terminals. It was initially a Dragon Quest game where players perform quests, fight monsters and gain experience points that enable them to reach higher levels. The ninth version of the game is different in that it has three additional features in the game scenario that exploit the possibility for terminals to 'recognize' and connect to one another through a Wi-Fi connection when within twenty or thirty meters of each other, thereby turning the game into a 'proximity game' (Soderlund, 2010).

First, players who are within about 20 meters of each other may engage into multi-player gameplay. Second, when within the same range, players may 'appear' on each other's screen: a window pops up on the screen with the name of the other player's game character and description. When this occurs, the player may go to the place in the game called 'Rikka's Inn', where the other player's avatar appears. By clicking on it, the player's profile and tag message appear. During the event, some of the resources of the player who has just appeared may get transferred to the initial player. This is the case of maps, for example, some of which are rare and essential to make progress in the game and to reach higher levels. Japanese players call such mediated encounters '*surechigai tsushin*'. '*Tsushin*' means 'communication' or 'transmission' and carries here a connotation of exchange or transaction. '*Surechigai*' is a substantive form of the verb '*surechigau*' which combines '*sureru*', 'to rub' and 'chigau', 'to differ'. It is ordinarily used to refer to a situation in which the paths of two persons come close (metaphorically in a situation of 'rubbing off with one another') before diverging further on. There is a constraint on the number of *surechigai tsushin* one can experience: the gameplay only allows three connections of this type at any one time. The screen needs to be refreshed before allowing three more to occur, and so on. '*Surechigai tsushin*' is a crucial feature of the game experience that combines corporeal mobilities and digital actions in a way that may reshape urban experiences. In 2009, a Japanese user might experience ten or more such events during his commute to the center of Tokyo.

Third, there are specific incentives in the gameplay for users to assemble in groups. These go beyond the mere fact that in such gatherings there may be many opportunities for *surechigai tsushin* and exchanging rare game resources. For instance, the game narrative involves an inn ('Rikka's Inn' in Japan) whose cellar and first floor, which usually remain hidden, may appear when there are several players close by whose avatars have entered the inn.Within these new rooms, players can find additional resources to make further progress. So the game design in many ways invites players to make a strategic use of spatial proximity and its potential serendipitous translation into the event of *surechigai tsushin*.

URBAN ENCOUNTERS IN 'HYBRID ECOLOGIES'

Dragon Quest 9 players may 'appear' in several different ways in urban public spaces, because as one plays the game, such settings are experienced as hybrid ecologies, in which different infrastructures for access and communication are made available.

Co-present traffic encounters

Players may appear by just passing one another independently of any screen event, in a way which is indistinguishable from the traffic encounters with equivalent and anonymous strangers that are a commonplace feature of the experience of the modern city. Such encounters unfold as the paths of mobile and anonymous strangers cross. The spatial proximity and visual availability of the strangers who appear thus makes a possible interactional involvement relevant, but within the bounds of an overarching concern of the participants to preserve their 'personal territories' (Goffman, 1971), their right to remain inattentive and not to be interrupted, and thus their enjoyment of a certain freedom compared to the forms of obligation that the presence of other individuals might produce. So there is constant tension between the way a sudden proximity may make an interaction relevant and the way the urban denizen expects to benefit in such places from 'minimal hospitality', which implies a 'right to tranquility' (Joseph, 1999: 123). One common way to manage this tension is by exerting 'civil inattention', which Goffman argues is a characteristic feature of interactions in public places: an exchange of gaze to manage the embodied encounter that acknowledges the mutual proximity but evades any further involvement and singularization of the encounter and its participants (Goffman, 1963).

Such urban encounters perform city dwellers as mobile and anonymous bodies, endowed with perceptive, expressive and interactional capacities, categorizable as strangers with apparently equal rights and obligations regarding the management of proximities and encounters. Such subjects are usually expected to treat one another on an equal footing and anonymously, in a way that obliterates singularity, that is, all that might connect the person to a singular identity and make that particular identity relevant. The kind of urbanity that is routinely deployed in these public spaces, the enactment of which constitutes a background expectation of proper behavior, performs participants as anonymous and category-less strangers: '*by passing from the neighborhood to the city, the definition of urbanity is supposed to rid itself of problems of identity*' (Joseph, 1993).

Surechigai tsushin

Proximity-based technologies introduce new issues into the organization and management of interactions in public places. They hybridize the random screen-based 'pop-up' of another player with urban traffic encounters with strangers, precisely because the digital 'appearance' only occurs when the paths of the mobile users meet, so that co-present identification and recognition may become possible and, as we will see below, a relevant concern. *Surechigai tsushin* in Dragon Quest 9 may be considered as a paradigmatic example of this type of hybrid encounter. When the 'random encounter' players and these come close to one another, the name of the game character of the one may appear on the game terminal of the other, as in Figure 1. This is not necessarily reciprocal, and the function is activated on the DS game terminals of two player whose terminal has been 'entered' by the other has no way of knowing from the game whether his own character has 'appeared' to others, including those who have 'appeared' to him.

Moreover, players who have activated their terminal in the 'random encounter' mode may elect to make available one particular map in such mediated encounters. The map will be transferred to the resources of the players encountered without any action being required of any of the participants of such mediated encounters. The player on the receiving end will simply receive a notification that he has been given a map.

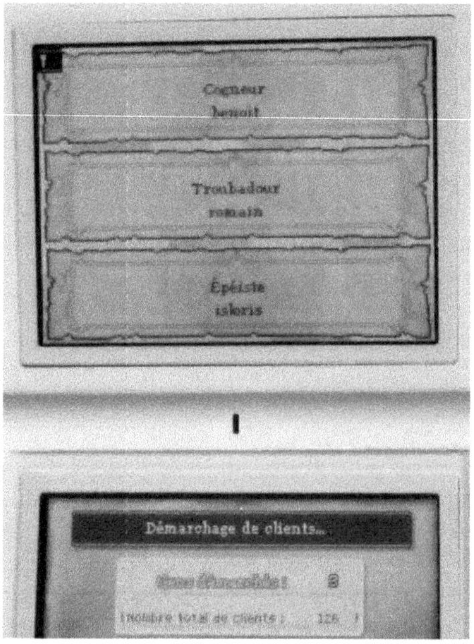

Figure 1. The game terminal interface showing three 'encountered' players

So it is part of the game's attraction that other players may pop up randomly on one's terminal as players get close to one another, and that one's urban mobility may be directly rewarded by screen-mediated encounters and gifts of game resources, on the basis of serendipitous proximities. We did a trial run in Shibuya with our own terminal and experienced rapidly three such 'apparitions' of players. Connecting to their avatars in Rikka's Inn we got their tag messages, which typically ran like: '*Hello, I am called X (the game name)! I am a legendary brave man well known in Saitama*'; '*Hi, I live in Tokyo and I am a kaji-tetsudai. My name is X*'; '*I ... I ... am called X. I am zero year old. I am a slow life of the blue sky who lives in the neighborhood*'. It is remarkable how in these three examples we picked up randomly, the players interweave descriptions related to the gameplay (the name of their avatar and some of its qualities), with references to the place they live, which points towards a world of physical and embodied presence. The design of such tag messages marks an a priori orientation of players towards the hybrid character of *surechigai tsushin*.

Recently, CSCW and ubiquitous computing research have emphasized the need to look at the uses of these technologies outside the laboratory, in ecologies that are unavoidably heterogeneous, 'seamful' and messy (Bell & Dourish, 2007). The dual concepts of 'seamfulness' and 'seamlessness' try to capture this (Chalmers & Galani, 2004). In our case, the seamfulness of the Dragon Quest game experience is related to what Goffman calls 'evidential boundaries' (Goffman, 1974): onscreen events are not visible outside the screen and are generally not made available to other players nearby. Moreover, when a game encounter occurs on screen there are often no cues to identify which of the individuals nearby is the player who has just 'appeared' on one's screen, though such an appearance would make such an identification relevant. So there is a potential evidential boundary separating what goes on on screen and in co-presence. In such a potentially seamful situation, players are confronted with a potential choice. The first is to ignore or elude the possibility of recognizing the 'encountered' player 'in real life'. This would accomplish the situation as seamful and as unfolding in channels of activity that are maintained as separate. The other possibility is to try to identify the nearby player who has popped up on one's game terminal among crowds of anonymous passers-by and potential fellow players. In this case, the player who looks around engages in an effort to make the situation seamless and to align what goes on in his/her screen with what is happening in his/her immediate urban surroundings. This shows that seamfulness and seamlessness are not just abstract qualities of a given situation and the hybrid ecology in which it unfolds. They constitute a collaborative and situated practical accomplishment. Furthermore, the fact that several heterogeneous infrastructures co-exist is a dynamic resource in the production of collective behavior in hybrid ecologies.

In the case of Dragon Quest 9, the heterogeneity of the situation of play is even greater, because players have other resources to interact during and around *surechigai tsushin* events, particularly in Japan. Japanese Dragon Quest 9 players interact through various internet-based social media, and particularly three forums, *Shirabata*, *Koryakukan* and *Mixi*. Because the use of mobile internet is widespread in Japan, players can interact continuously on their mobile phones on these forums, not only before and after encounters, but also during them. It is frequent to see players switch from their game terminal to their mobile phone and back, or to hold a terminal in each hand (Figure 2).

Figure 2. A player with the game terminal in his right hand and his mobile phone in the other

The mobile internet communication infrastructure introduces new seams in the *surechigai tsushin* situation, and the possibility of even more fragmented and multi-layered participation frames.

A crucial tension in *surechigai tsushin* events

There is one dimension of the proximity encounters which the concepts of 'seams' or evidential boundaries do not describe well, though. The availability of proximity-sensitive digital communication makes relevant a particular tension in situations of play in public settings, a tension that is related to the issues of identification and recognition. Digital communication infrastructures rely on unique identifiers. Whether such identifiers lean more towards the 'technological' side (e.g. IP addresses, Bluetooth identifiers, etc.) or towards the 'human' side (e.g. handles, tags, pseudonyms, avatars, etc.), they all share the property of singularizing the participants of a digital communication event while at the same time allowing them to preserve their real life anonymity: there are no direct links between such identifiers and the usual cues for recognition 'in the real life' that might give their identity away. However, such identifiers constitute participants to such digital communication events as relationally singular. They are made unique with respect to one another by the very communication event they have engaged in and the way it relies on singular identifiers.

With regard to sociality in public places, when people just talk or chat on their mobile phone with others at a distance, there is a complete separation between the persons one may see and talk to in one's surroundings and the remote conversationalist(s). The issue of being able to identify or recognize the remote participant is generally irrelevant. However, this is no longer the case when the digital communication is triggered by proximity, as in the case of Dragon Quest 9 and similar proximity-based mobile social technologies. Then the 'real life' identification of the person with whom one is exchanging digitally becomes not only possible - because there is a good chance that he or she is close enough -, but also an issue.

Membership categorization analysis can help clarify the problem. In an event such as *surechigai tsushin*, players are affected by the mobility of fellow players they are unacquainted with. Furthermore, different sets of categories and category-bound activities, with differing rights and obligations, are enacted *simultaneously*. Once another player 'enters' one's game space and occupies part of one's screen with his avatar name and tag message, a first set of relational paired categories becomes relevant (Sacks, 1992): the two people are constituted as Dragon Quest 9 'players', and more specifically 'paired players', bound by the *surechigai tsushin* event. This makes relevant various category-bound activities (i.e. playing the game and more specifically giving or receiving game resources such as maps) and some types of mutual obligation (such as acknowledging the 'gift' and thanking the other player for it), which require for their achievement identification and mutual recognition on one communication channel or another (i.e. in co-presence or through mobile internet websites).

Surechigai tsushin events occur mostly in urban public spaces and are triggered by spatial proximity. Therefore, in addition to the category of '(paired) players', they make relevant a second category, usually related to traffic encounters, that of 'paired mobile strangers', and a specific set of rights and obligations, such as the obligation to manage tactfully the mutual and embodied proximity, and the 'right to tranquility' or to keep to oneself, which, as we have discussed above, is characteristic of public space urbanity in industrialized megalopoli. So one should avoid anything that goes beyond the minimal kind of acknowledgement characteristic of 'civil inattention', including any kind of engagement that might singularize the passing stranger and make him/her different from all the strangers one passes on an everyday basis.

There is therefore a potential tension that is inherent to the *surechigai tsushin* event itself. As a proximity-triggered digital encounter between fellow players, it implies an orientation towards acknowledging the exchange and identifying the other participant, something which spatial proximity makes possible in real life. As a specialized kind of traffic encounter with mobile strangers in a large city, its tactful management implies an orientation towards avoiding any kind of singularization of the event and its participants, from mutual ignorance to civil inattention. This makes it particularly interesting to make an ethnographic study of the way players manage this potential tension in public places where they may meet and assemble.

OCCASIONAL GATHERINGS AT THE SHIZUOKA STATION

We will now describe a typical type of urban settings in which players arrange to meet in Japan and in which assembled groups of more or less acquainted players equipped with proximity-sensitive game terminals and mobile internet communication resources mingle with crowds of mobile urban denizens. Beyond the particulars of the Dragon Quest 9 gameplay, we are interested here in understanding the kind of interaction order that is supported by public places when these become hybrid ecologies. In the perspective we develop here, places, the kinds of social encounters that unfold there and the interaction order through which the management of such encounters is made accountable are mutually constitutive. This definition is in line with the approach of some geographers such as Doreen Massey for whom places can only be understood as 'articulated moments in networks of social relations and understandings' (Massey, 1994), that is, as sites of 'throwntogetherness' (Massey, 2005). Indeed, in order to understand what an augmented public place might be, we must understand how strangers are thrown together in its hybrid ecology, and how they manage their proximity socially and turn it (or not) into various forms of encounters by relying on the many seams and multiple communication infrastructures of the situation.

The hybrid ecology of the Shizuoka gatherings

Because the gameplay gives players many incentives to meet, groups of players who live in the same area and interact on internet-based social media have taken to organizing regular meetings in various places. Unlike the Akihabara case, these are not permanent urban fixtures. They are planned and announced on player forums and newsgroups accessible through mobile internet. They mostly take place in malls, in or nearby train stations, or in food courts in busy commercial areas. This particular choice of location reflects how Japanese players establish a strong relationship between proximity-based game encounters and everyday urban mobilities. Meeting places are chosen at the intersection or in the immediate vicinity of well trodden urban paths. Such a choice allows players to come by in the course of their own activities, either because it is on their everyday commute in the case of a station, or because they can drop by for a few minutes while doing family shopping in the case of malls.

This is in marked contrast with what can be observed for instance in France from our preliminary observations. French players convene in public gardens and refuse to gather in stations or commercial places. The choice of parks ties the game activity with the sphere of leisure more than that of mobility practices, and the defiance expressed towards other kinds of public places favored by the Japanese players displays a concern with preserving players' meetings from contamination by other commercial or institutional interests, which is markedly different.

The meetings at Shizuoka station particularly highlight this Japanese orientation towards articulating game and mobility practices. The 'organizer' usually announces meetings on the three forums mentioned above, and any player is free to join. Those who regularly participate in such gatherings are often able to recognize one another by sight and to identify each other by their game handles and/or forum aliases, when the two differ. However, they do not usually exchange their real names or mobile phone numbers, maintaining a relatively tight boundary between game-related sites of communication and their other activities as individuals.

Figure 3. The start of the meeting at Shizuoka station, with the core group of regulars.

In a typical meeting of this type, players are immersed in a public place where many non-playing strangers come and go, and where known and unknown players may make their physical presence acknowledged (e.g. by getting close to the group, sometimes even engaging into a face-to-face conversation, etc.) or not (e.g. by doing *surechigai tsushin* while avoiding getting noticed). They may also communicate by relying on public or semi-public mobile internet resources. We observed and interviewed participants at one such meeting at Shizuoka station (Figure 3) and we also had online discussions with a few of them.

'Brave' engagements and 'timid' encounters at Shizuoka station

In this section we will discuss various forms of encounters with unknown players and the way players present on the site may exploit the layered resources and the seamfulness of the situation in different ways to produce distinctive participation frames. At one end of the continuum is the case depicted in figure 4. An unknown player, accompanied by a friend, has been informed of a meeting on one of the forums on which it has been announced. He walks into the group of players gathered there (it is recognizable as a group of Dragon Quest players because the meeting has been announced for this time and place, and all those standing there have a DS terminal in hand) and addresses them verbally in order to perform *surechigai tsushin* and exchange game resources. In this configuration, two channels of interaction at least (e.g. co-presence and the game itself) have been opened and somewhat aligned, since the physical appearance of the player who has manifested his presence can now be linked to his game handle. On the basis of his physical appearance, he has become recognizable for future co-present encounters as the owner of a particular character, even if his 'real' name remains unknown. When the co-presence of players is managed thus, the incoming person makes his 'visit' a shared encounter between players and the event is accomplished as a seamless whole.

Figure 4. A newcomer 'bravely' addressing the organizer and joining in to exchange maps

At the opposite end of the spectrum, we have the case of a lady in her late thirties who had gone to do some shopping with her husband and young son around Shizuoka station. She was already aware through the forum that a meeting was to take place at the station and took the opportunity of her presence there to connect her game terminal while eating with her family at a nearby fast food restaurant, thereby gaining access, through *surechigai tsushin*, to the game space of several of the players gathered there. As her unknown character popped up on the screen of some of the players assembled, none of them noticed or discussed it explicitly. When her meal was over, she left her family and got closer to the group, sitting for a few minutes next to the small Shinto monument visible at the left of Figure 4, at which point she became 'visible' to the ethnographers, who, unlike the players, were actively scanning the scene for a suitable candidate to account for the 'apparition' of the unknown character. Then her husband and son joined her and they disappeared into the station together without providing any visible cue that she had participated in the meeting other than the fact that she was holding a game terminal in her hand. She thus displayed another mode of engagement in the meeting, with two separate participation statuses. One the one hand, she behaved as a ratified and active participant in a game encounter, and on the other hand, she displayed a very loose participation status with respect to the co-present encounter. This falls somewhat in between Goffman's categories with respect to the management of co-presence: while she was more engaged than a simple passerby, as demonstrated her particular form of displacement, which took her around the boundaries of the group of players, she was no more engaged than a bystander, because she did not provide any further visible form of orientation towards the gathering as such. Players have a term to describe players displaying such behavior, which, incidentally, is considered perfectly admissible and legitimate. They call them 'timid' players. 'Timid' players exploit the 'evidential boundaries' of the situation in order to maintain a separation between game and co-present encounters, together with a distinct set of rights and obligations. In a 'timid' encounter, the situation is accomplished as seamful.

The degree to which this may be done is a collaborative accomplishment, whatever the looseness of the relationship between the 'timid' player and the standing group of regulars may be. For the latter, remarking that a new character has popped up on their screen is always a possibility, a kind of 'safe topic' in their ongoing and open state of interaction. Though they often do not mention such events, they occasionally do so. Such 'noticings' turn the *surechigai tsushin* event with the unknown player into a public matter of discussion within the group. However, they rarely try to look around to spot a person they can link the new character to, unless the character is related to a player they are 'acquainted' with (in the sense of interacting regularly with him/her through one medium or another). This is not just passive indifference, for they often justify themselves for not doing so (c.f. below), but an active indifference, akin to civil inattention, which somehow 'resists' a normative orientation towards acknowledging digital interactions in co-presence. 'Timid' encounters are a collaborative accomplishment which displays a particular format of civil inattention, adapted to, and characteristic of urban places augmented as hybrid public places. However, this does not exhaust the possibilities of exploiting the evidential boundaries of the situation to produce even more layered participation frames.

Though it may happen, such behavior is less observable in France, where unacquainted players getting to talk together besides their "on screen encounters" seems the norm rather than the exception. This makes French gatherings noisy affairs with respect to Japanese ones. This may be due in part to cultural factors but it also depends a lot on the particular ecology achieved when French players meet in a public garden. They appear as a tight bundle of players, sharply separated from ordinary strollers. Within the boundaries of such a gathering, it is therefore 'normal' to assume that any other person in the vicinity will be a fellow players, non-players being the rare exception besides those who may have accompanied a player. This makes the norm of not addressing strangers in urban public places less relevant. It also makes it more difficult to sustain "timid encounters" in French gatherings, for such conduct precisely plays on the possibility of behaving plausibly like a non-playing stranger while being close. So the spatial distribution of players and non-players in the vicinity of gatherings is a crucial factor to understand the kind of interaction order which emerge in such gatherings

Layered 'timid' encounters and fragmented participation frames

By definition, "timid encounters" are elusive. We observed one such event "physically" in Shizuoka, but also found repeated instances of after the fact acknowledgement of "timid encounters" in forums. A typical case is the one in which two players who have occasionally exchanged on a forum make arrangements to perform *surechigai tsushin.* This 'rendezvous' of sorts, is of a special nature, as we will see, for it does not necessarily involve meeting or talking in person. For now, let us discuss in more detail a typical example in which the participants publicly discuss their encounter on a forum using their mobile internet access. From a co-present perspective, they are strangers who do not know one another's real name, have never met in person, and are unable to recognize one another visually. But from a mobile internet perspective, they are electronic acquaintances: they 'talk' together and know each other's pseudonym, which singularizes them. Finally, within the game, they are strangers all over again, for they have never met in it before and are unaware of the names of the characters they use.

We will now look more closely at part of their electronic conversation, which encompasses their strange kind of 'rendezvous'.

1. Rick (September 04) 18:40: *Tonight I am going to Aeon Hamamatsu Ichino at 20:00. Since I have many things to do I will communicate with you via forum or messenging. Won't Sugimaro be there?*

2. Baba (Sept 04) 19:31: *Great! I will also go to Ichino around 20:30 or 21:00. It would be nice if we could do a surechigai. I think I will stay mostly in the food court. I hope it will work well.*

3. Rick (Sept 04) 20:27: Baba-*san, It's OK ! I am already having a drink in the food court* (^□^)ノ

4. Baba (Sept 04), 21:19: *Rick-san, I've arrived. I'm coming after going around for a while.*

5. Rick (Sept 04), 23:30: *Baba-san. Hello. We have probably done surechigai easily. You are 55 happy-san aren't you?*

6. Baba (Sept 06), 12:17: *Rick-san. Thanks a lot for the other day. I think we probably have been able to do the surechigai. I have seen someone who might have looked like Rick-san, but I was not brave enough to go and greet you. I would like to play again another time.*

The arrangements for their encounter start with 'co-location work' . Rick announces he will go soon (in about one hour) to a place known to be a meeting place for players, and that he will be available only through the mobile internet channel, because he has other things to do (Message 1). Baba responds by announcing she will also go to the mall at about the same time (Message 2). She also evokes a possible game encounter in a way that may be heard as a proposal, and then indicates a more precise location in the mall (the food court), thus going one step further in arranging for such a possibility: being together in the mall might not be enough to ensure the possibility of a game encounter, but being co-present in the food court in the mall probably would be, because of the implied proximity. Rick then announces he is currently in the food court (Message 3), to which Baba replies she has arrived in the mall but has things to do before joining him (Message 4), which projects the game encounter in the future. Messages 3 and 4 show how players use mobile internet resources on the move to manage practical arrangements and adjust the tempo and timing of their encounter through mobile messaging.

The next message by Rick (Message 5) takes place two hours later. It starts with a greeting. We may wonder why the greeting, since they were already talking like this way before. This is made retrospectively clear by what immediately follows, i.e. a hypothetical claim that they may have entered each other's screen. So the greeting can be read as oriented towards a change in the mode of presence of Baba, through her likely 'apparition' on the screen of Rick's terminal. Rick then ends the message by an identity check, which tries to verify whether the character who has entered the gameplay is indeed Baba's. This explains retrospectively why he evokes the game encounter with Baba only as a very likely hypothesis: he has no independent way other than Baba's direct confirmation to connect the game character who has appeared with the forum pseudonym 'Baba'. Such identification work is needed to align what happens on the screen with the online conversation.

Message 5 is left unanswered for more than a day, and the issue is only evoked in the post scriptum of Baba's next message, the main body of which discusses something else (Message 6). It first indicates that she has seen, and therefore looked for and noticed, someone who might have been Rick, and then immediately provides an excuse for not engaging in co-present interaction with him (she was not 'brave' enough, she says). Such an excuse is oriented to and made relevant by a more general principle, left implicit here, which states that when two persons who are mutually acquainted are spatially very close, their acknowledgement of the fact through gaze or speech is expected (Licoppe & Inada, 2010). Message 6 therefore shapes retrospectively the encounter as a refined type of 'timid encounter', in which the participants avoid physically acknowledging their mutual co-presence, and therefore elect to remain strangers at that level, while acknowledging their proximity through mobile messaging.

RELEVANCE FOR THE DEVELOPMENT OF UBIQUITOUS COMPUTING AND GAME DESIGN

It has been suggested that the design of technologies to be used in the public place should be sensitive to the potential number of encounters that these technologies might mediate. One should 'design for scalability' (Hindmarsh et al., 2005), and this is true of proximity-based technologies which are resources to prompt encounters between users. This would require that the gameplay and its functionalities be adjusted to the intensity of the flux of encounters between users at a given place and time, i.e. design orientations that are sensitive to the existence of 'hot' places, in which many 'encounters' may occur on a regular basis (as was the case of Tokyo for Dragon Quest 9 users in 2010), and of 'cold' places, in which users rarely 'encounter' other users (such as Paris in 2011).

Our study gives an indication of how this could be done innovatively by exploiting the fact that our sense of place goes way beyond mere location. How we experience locations as places of a certain type is deeply related to the kind of people who may or may not gain access to a given setting and the kind of encounters and interaction order that the local ecology supports. In the Dragon Quest 9 case, we have seen that the types of 'places' or locales in which players met can evolve and are sensitive to : a) the number of players one can and expects to connect with there; b) expectations regarding the likelihood that one might be acquainted to the players gathered there (which contrasts the Akihabara case, in which one expected to meet only unknown players, with the Shizuoka station case, in which a subgroup of 'regulars' were already strongly acquainted and most players had previously conversed in game-relevant internet forums c) the proportion between players and non-players and the ways those may potentially spatially mix or remain segregated (for instance, 'timid encounters' are a relevant possibility mostly in situations in which players are not segregated from non players).

Proximity game plays have already been made sensitive to the number of connections in a given area, that is roughly to the density of players in a given area (Soderlund, 2010). But such a notion of distributed game play might be enriched by making the game play sensitive to other local features, such as the degree of acquaintance with nearby players. One way to achieve this would be to implement some text mining applications regarding the digital communication infrastructures used by the players in order to make available within the game system information such as the fact that players A and B, 'present' in a given area, have already exchanged messages, and with what frequency. Then one could collect these in order to obtain the distribution of mutual acquaintance between players in a given area and make the game play sensitive to the fact that a given user is in an environment of players he is previously acquainted with or not. The same idea could be extended to the probability of presence of non users by exploiting the Bluetooth and Wi-Fi inter-platform connectivity of terminals; in that case the game play could be made sensitive to the fact that the player is surrounded by players only, or in the midst of a mix of players and non players. This would make the game play more sensitive to features of hybrid ecologies essential to the way we experience them as places. It would thus lead to hybrid ecologies meshing more tightly digital resources and experiences (the proximity game) and the 'physical world' (i.e. the way we experience particular locales as 'places' in which we are thrown together in, and which we collectively inhabit).

CONCLUSION

Proximity-based games such as Dragon Quest 9 are a particular case of location-sensitive playful practices. When played in urban environments, proximity games produce a particular form of urban space, shaped as a 'hybrid ecology' through the complex kinds of encounter and collaboration they support. Game encounters mix spatial proximity and digital connectivity in a way that involves several 'seams' and 'evidential boundaries', that is, many resources for the management of multiple identities and the construction of layered participation frames. 'Seams' are not an a priori quality of the situation of play but a potentiality that still has to be accomplished practically: players dynamically orient towards the seamlessness or the seamfulness of the situation on a moment-to-moment basis. Finally, the existence and use of multiple communication infrastructures adds degrees of complexity to the forms of engagement into play, as shown with the example of mobile internet communication resources in Japan.

Playing such games in the street raises the question of how such 'playful urban spaces' may also constitute public places, in which participants must openly manage encounters with strangers. In this case, encounters involve two types of unknown persons: urban traffic encounters with non-playing strangers, as in any kind of modern city, and game encounters with (unknown) players. In the latter case, the encounter may preserve the anonymity of the participants, but require that they connect through digital identifiers and pseudonyms. Such forms of connection and interaction therefore unavoidably singularize their participants. Singularization raises issues of potential identification and recognition, and creates a potential tension with respect to the urban traffic encounters in which every participant is supposed to be equivalent to any other, and in which identification is usually avoided. We think this tension is a very general phenomenon, more generally characteristic of the spread of ubiquitous computing in urban spaces and of hybrid ecologies as public settings.

In our case study, game encounters or *surechigai tsushin* make the identification 'in real life' a relevant concern for the players involved, and such a normative orientation provides meaningfulness to some of the participation frames the players orient to. The behavior of 'timid players', who come to experience game encounters while trying to elude visual or verbal recognition, and also the fact that they are characterized as such on the basis of their particular behavior, provides an example of the consequences of such a tension. It also constitutes a kind of complex form of civil inattention that is specifically adapted to hybrid ecologies in which numerous digital encounters randomly occur, and in which players and non players mingle. Such a form of 'hybrid civil inattention' could therefore become a specific feature of mediated encounters in large and heavily 'augmented' cities with proximity-based mobile resources. The kind of public place and interaction order assembled players produce in each case seems highly sensitive not only to cultures of urban public places, but also to two significant factors: a) the way players and non-players can be expected either to mingle or remain more or less segregated in a given public place b) expectations regarding the likelihood of prior mutual acquaintance between players gathered there.

We think that all this is much more general, not specific to the Dragon Quest 9 case. Through this case study, we get a glimpse of the kind of interaction order that may appears to characterize an augmented city whose denizens are highly connected in a location-sensitive way. Such an interaction order is not as 'democratic' as the public order in the twentieth century megalopolis, in which, from Simmel to Goffman, passers-by are performed as noticeable but equivalent strangers through civil inattention. It does not revert to the city of earlier times, which was a mix of neighborhoods organized along some form of categorical membership, for instance types of trade or regions of origin. Urban places as hybrid ecologies for proximity-sensitivity passer-by appear as the loci of dense fluxes of mobile denizens in which traffic encounters occur simultaneously at several levels, that of anonymous equivalent mobile bodies, and that of suddenly (through the event of their proximity) and categorically paired individuals through their communication in digital networks, singularized by this connection event, allowing multiple forms of encounter and layered participation frames.

REFERENCES

1. Bell, G., & Dourish, P. Yesterday's tomorrows: notes on ubiquitous computing's dominant vision. *Personal & Ubiquitous Computing* 11, 2 (2007), 133-143.
2. Chalmers, M. & Galani, A. Seamful Interweaving: Heterogeneity in the Theory and Design of Interactive Systems. *Proc. ACM DIS 2004*, ACM Press (2004), 243-252.
3. Crabtree, A., & Rodden, T. Hybrid Ecologies: Understanding Cooperative Interaction in Emerging Physical-Digital Environments. *Personal and Ubiquitous Computing* 12 (2008), 481-493.
4. De Souza e Silva, A., & Frith, J. Locative Mobile Social Networks: Mapping Communication and Location in Urban Spaces. *Mobilities* 5, 4 (2010), 485-505.
5. De Souza e Silva, A., & Hjorth, L. Playful urban spaces: A historical approach to mobile games. *Simulation & Gaming* 40, 5 (2009), 602-625.
6. Goffman, E. *Behavior in Public Places*. Free Press, New York, USA, 1963.
7. Goffman, E. *Relations in Public. Microstructure of the Public Order*. Harper & Row, New York, USA, 1971.
8. Goffman, E. *Frame Analysis. An Essay on the Organization of Experience*. Harper & Row, New York, USA, 1974.
9. Hannerz, U. *Exploring the City: Inquiries towards an Urban Anthropology*. Columbia University Press, New York, USA, 1980.
10. Hindmarsh, J., Heath, C., Von Lehn, D. & Cleverly, J. Creating Assemblies in Public Environments: Social Interaction, Interactive Exhibits and CSCW. *Computer Supported Creative Work* 14 (2005), 1-41.
11. Joseph, I. L'espace public et le visible. *Architecture & Comportement* 9, 3 (1993), 397-401.
12. Joseph, I. Activité située et régimes de disponibilité. *Raisons Pratiques* 10 (1999), 157-172.
13. Licoppe, C., & Inada, Y. (2006). Emergent Uses of a Location Aware Multiplayer Game : The Interactional Consequences of Mediated Encounters. *Mobilities* 1, 1 (2006), 39-61.
14. Licoppe, C., & Inada, Y. Locative media and cultures of mediated proximity: the case of the Mogi game location-aware community. *Environment and Planning D: Society and Space* 28, 4 (2010), 691-709.
15. Lindtner, S., Nardi, B., Wang, Y., Mainwaring, S., Jing, H. & Liang, W. A Hybrid Cultural Ecology: World of Warcraft in China. *Proc. CSCW'08*, ACM Press (2008), 371-382.
16. Lofland, L. *A World of Strangers. Order and Action in Urban Public Space.* Waveland Press, Prospect Heights, USA, 1973.
17. Lofland, L. *The Public Realm. Exploring the City's Quintessential Social Territory.* Aldine de Gruyter, NY, USA, 1998.
18. Richardson, I. Ludic Mobilities: The Corporealities of Mobile Gaming. *Mobilities* 5, 4 (2010), 431-447.
19. Richarson, I., & Wilken, R. Haptic Vision, Footwork, Place Making: A Peripatetic Phenomenology of the Mobile Phone Pedestrian. *Second Nature* 2 (2009), 23-39.
20. Sacks, H. *Collected Lectures*. Cambridge University Press, Cambridge, UK, 1992.
21. Soderlund, T. Proximity Gaming: New Forms of Wireless Gaming. In A. de Souza e Silva & D. Sutko (Eds). *Digital Cityscapes. Merging Digital and Urban Playspaces,* Peter Lang, New York, USA (2010), 217-230.
22. Weiser, M. The computer for the 21st century. *Scientific American* 285 (1991), 94-104.

Characterizing Web Use on Smartphones

Chad C. Tossell, Philip Kortum
Dept. of Psychology
Rice University
{chad.tossell,pkortum}@rice.edu

Ahmad Rahmati, Clayton Shepard, Lin Zhong
Dept. of Electrical & Computer Engineering
Rice University
{rahmati,cws,lzhong}@rice.edu

ABSTRACT
The current paper establishes empirical patterns associated with mobile internet use on smartphones and explores user differences in these behaviors. We apply a naturalistic and longitudinal logs-based approach to collect real usage data from 24 iPhone users in the wild. These data are used to describe smartphone usage and analyze revisitation patterns of web browsers, native applications, and physical locations where phones are used. Among our findings are that web page revisitation through browsers occurred very infrequently (approximately 25% of URLs are revisited by each user), bookmarks were used sparingly, physical traversing patterns mirrored virtual (internet) traversing patterns and users systematically differed in their web use. We characterize these differences and suggest ways to support users with enhanced design of smartphone technologies and content.

Author Keywords
Web browsing; Smartphone; Revisitation; Mobile Web

ACM Classification Keywords
H.5.4 [Information Interfaces and Presentation]: Hypertext/Hypermedia - User issues;

General Terms
Design, Human Factors, Measurement

INTRODUCTION
The web is a resource for information, communication, and entertainment used by over two billion people worldwide [13]. This ubiquity has led to a large amount of research examining how it is used. Most of the work has focused on understanding behaviors associated with the PC. Now, smartphones are becoming pervasive and making the web accessible in most personal and professional environments [19]. There is even evidence that users spend more time on these devices compared to PCs [20].

Although a substantial amount of research has characterized web use on PCs, there are several reasons why these studies may not apply to web use associated with smartphones. First, internet resources can be accessed through native applications as well as a browser. Second, smartphones are smaller and have different input and display functionalities. Finally, smartphones provide continuous access to the internet in almost any setting. These factors could lead to the development of new patterns of behaviors and routines associated with use of the web on smartphones.

The goal of the present study is to understand the dynamics of these behaviors. We describe users' visiting and revisiting patterns to internet resources through both their smartphone browsers and native applications along with physical locations where their smartphones are used. We update previous work applied to the PC and establish empirical patterns for internet use on smartphones by analyzing naturalistic and longitudinal data logged from user interactions in the wild. User differences are explored along with the influence of experience, physical location traversing, the type of content accessed and user revisiting strategies to provide targeted design recommendations for mobile internet use with smartphones.

BACKGROUND
The web has been a primary focus of human-computer interaction (HCI) research since the 1990s. PC-based studies have developed an understanding of user goals [17], browsing strategies [4], tasks [3], search behaviors [36], revisitation of websites [32], and differences between groups (e.g., novice-expert [12]) among a number of other efforts. Some of the earliest HCI studies of the web used a logs-based approach [4,32]. Internet browsers were instrumented with logging technologies to collect naturalistic usage data instead of observing users completing tasks constructed by researchers. In particular, user recurrence to web content has been a central focus. The first study that examined these behaviors found that PC users visited a small total number of unique websites (i.e., vocabulary); however, the revisitation frequency to this set was high [4] resulting in a revisitation rate of 61% [32]. Shortly after, a similar study (N = 23) resulted in a 58% revisitation rate to web content [32]. From these data, characterizations were developed to understand patterns of web navigation.

Because of the changing dynamics of the web, these revisitation studies on the PC have been revisited [24]. Cockburn and McKenzie [5] collected data for 119 days and found that internet behaviors were even more repetitive. Users visited an even smaller number of sites than older PC studies and reaccessed these sites very frequently. They reported a revisitation rate of 81% from 17 computer science (CS) students. More recently, Obendorf and his colleagues [24] captured web data from a slightly larger and more diverse set of users (N = 25, 64% CS students) to obtain a much lower revisitation rate of 46%. One reason for this large gap between revisitation rates in these studies, they stated, was due to the changing nature of the web. For instance, instead of users reaccessing the same web pages repeatedly, users visit new pages within frequently accessed domains. These studies of recurrent behaviors on the web have been important in understanding different user types and designing better user interfaces for web navigation including history systems [4,24].

Using the Web on Smartphones

As mentioned above, several factors likely drive differences between internet use on PCs and smartphones. Smartphones offer users two primary ways to access resources on the internet. Similar to the PC, users can get to the internet through a web browser. Many web sites that are opened on smartphone browsers automatically display a version of the site that is optimized for smaller screens, though there are usually options to view the full site. Additionally, native applications provide access to mobile content designed specifically for the device. These applications are factory installed or installed by users via an application store (e.g., the Apple AppStore). The combination of more powerful mobile devices and optimized applications and web content has made using internet resources more efficient [22,35].

Still, there are noted usability challenges with the mobile web that apply to current-generation devices. Long download times for page loading appear to be a primary problem [28]. These delays can result in sharp usage decline and considered the largest HCI concern in web usability [21]. Other challenges with using the web on smartphones result from the size of the device. Text optimized to fit on small screen interfaces can be difficult to read [7] and awkward text entry is even more problematic for efficient web use [22,35].

Despite these problems, users access the web frequently through their smartphones. One in four smartphone owners prefer accessing the internet through their smartphones over the PC [27]. Many in this group (33%) have discontinued web connectivity at their residences because of smartphone accessibility. Even with connectivity, users still frequently choose to access the internet at home through their smartphones over their PCs [23].

Smartphones are also widely accessed on-the-go in diverse contexts [33]. Without smartphones, PC users access the internet when they have opportunities to stay at a stationary location for a defined period of time; conversely, smartphone users go online whenever they get the urge [8]. Context drives the nature of these interactions. For instance, smartphone users often access the web in between planned activities [11]. Though smartphone users reported accessing their phones in a small cluster of locations, the nature of the location can inform user needs [18]. Interruption is often expected during these interactions [1]. Nevertheless, technological and usability advances has made computing on these devices more similar to larger computers. For instance, data from Google search logs revealed that users' iPhone searching behaviors are more similar to PCs compared to previous-generation mobile phones [15].

Additonally, individuals use their smartphones to extend and complement their computing on other devices. 75% of the domains visited on users' smartphones were also visited on their PCs [16]. Many times they optimize what they do on their PCs or laptops as opposed to their smartphones. For instance, users choose to compose longer emails on a PC, but use their smartphones for shorter messages [19]. Mobile internet use is generally directed and shorter (e.g., fact finding) rather than the less-directed (e.g., browsing) whereas the reverse has been found for the stationary web [6]. More recent research has shown that this could be a function of user goals in a particular location and not necessarily the technology being used [18].

We build on this research by contributing characterizations of internet use on smartphones, focusing on recursive behaviors similar to PC-based studies. Since there are two ways to access the internet on these devices—via native applications and a browser—our first interest is to describe how both are used. The roles of experience and the task on visit and revisit patterns are explored to this end. We also examine user variability to distinguish mobile users for enhanced design of smartphone systems and content.

METHODS

The logging methodology applied in this study has been previously discussed in detail [31]. However, we briefly describe our data collection and analysis procedures below.

Data Collection

The 24 students (M = 19.2 years old) that participated in our study were not previous smartphone owners and only 8% were CS students. Fourteen of the students were male. They were given iPhones to use for an entire year if they agreed to use it as their only mobile phone. We also provided free unlimited data plans along with unlimited text messaging and 450 phone minutes/month. The instrumented iPhones ran iOS 3.1.3 and were logged continuously for a period of one year. All interactions were recorded unobtrusively and strict privacy constraints were maintained throughout. For instance, all data were attached to participant numbers for anonymity, no content of communications data were collected, and encryption was applied to avoid unwanted eavesdropping. During the study period, we intentionally withheld from introducing novel interfaces, artificial tasks, and researcher-participant meetings in order to decrease participant reactivity. We gave no instructions about how to use the iPhone and two meetings were scheduled to record items such as their bookmarks and answer questions to help interpret the log data.

For this study, we examined web logs along with native application interaction logs. The custom logger recorded every URL visited on the users' browsers, as well as application usage. Both of these logs included the date, time, Cell ID (location), and duration of the interactions.

Data Analysis

Since our interest is internet usage, we analyzed only those native applications that require the internet for their primary functionalities. The native applications with functions that largely do not depend on the internet were manually removed (see Table 1). For instance, the camera application on the iPhone does not require the internet to take pictures or view photos, however it can be used to send pictures over email. Since it is reasonable to assume that cameras are largely used offline, we did not consider this application or similar ones in our analysis. We call the internet-connected native applications that are examined "native internet applications" (**NIAs**) hereafter. Browser use is removed from NIA analysis and presented separately for comparative purposes.

Removed		Kept	
SMS	Voice Phone	Email	Maps
Non-Web Games	Camera	Facebook	Weather
Settings	iPod	Web Games	News

Table 1. Some NIAs and categories of NIAs analyzed along with several we removed.

We organized our web browser logs by sessions. Sessions are defined as when the browser was launched and then closed instead of an arbitrary time delta. Within these sessions, visits to sites (i.e., domains) and pages (i.e., full URLs) were recorded.

Revisitation rates were computed to understand recursive behaviors associated with visiting NIAs and content via web browsers. For enhanced precision [see 24], we present rates separately for NIAs, sites (i.e., domains), and full URLs (i.e., pages) using the below equation.

Revisitation rate = (total visits – unique locations) / total visits

where unique locations is the total number of distinct NIAs, sites or pages accessed by each user. In addition to virtual revisitation on the internet, we also examine physical (location) revistation with the same equation. The value of unique locations here is the number of unique Cell IDs recorded by our logger from each participant's phone use. Total visits account for all visits across these Cell IDs for each participant. Other behavior rates of interest are described below.

RESULTS

Over the entire year, NIAs were accessed much more than browsers. A total of 2,080 unique NIAs were launched across 225,151 visits. In contrast, 7,672 URLs were accessed through browsers accumulating 112,083 total visits. In general, browsers provided access to a wider variety of resources more sporadically while a steady set of NIAs were used more frequently. We first describe visits and revisits to the former and compare with previous PC-based studies. Following this, we characterize NIA and physical location traversing before we explore user differences.

Browser Visits

We were surprised that not all users relied on their browser, even with free service. Users averaged 3.86 browsing sessions per day (*Median* = 3, *SD* = 10.84). Half of our users launched their browsers less than three times per day. The lowest volume user averaged eight browsing sessions per *month*. He, along with four others, stated a preference for browsing on the computer, low information needs requiring the web, and a heaver reliance on voice phone and SMS. The user that relied on Safari the most launched Safari an average of 11 times per *day*. Clearly, there was large variance in browsing use among our participants.

Search was consistently relied upon within browsers. Users issued over 17,500 searches across the entire study period resulting in a 56% query rate (i.e., number of browsing sessions that consisted of at least one search). Users did not vary much in their volume of searches (*M* =53.3%, *SD* = 7.2%) and use of Google. Less than .1% of all queries were conducted outside of Google.com. Most browsing sessions with search (85%) contained less than four queries. According to our users, two reasons for the relatively low number of queries per search session compared to PCs was due to low time for navigating and long page loading times. This was also apparent in the typical length of smartphone web browsing sessions. Browsing sessions were generally under two minutes (*M* = 105.86 sec., *Median* = 96 sec., *SD* = 40.84 sec.) and consisted of a small number of unique sites (*M* = 2.18, *Median* = 1.5 *SD* = 2.88) and total pages (*M* = 6.07, *Median* = 3, *SD* = 3.58) visited per session.

Table 2 shows the differences between browser use on smartphones and PCs. Pages (i.e., full URLs) were not revisited very often (25.3%). Just over 60% of all pages were visited once and 15% were visited twice. Interestingly, these numbers are extremely similar to results obtained from the PC 15 years ago (60% and 19% respectively [33]). Revisitation rate variances were much smaller compared to previous work on the PC [23]. Page revisitation rates were all under 50% (13% to 41%). The site revisitation rate of 90.3% also yielded relatively low variance (86% to 97%).

Compared to PCs, browsers on smartphones are accessed less frequently, for shorter durations, and to visit fewer pages. One reason for the distinction in overall use is the increased reliance on NIAs as mentioned above resulting in lower browser use. Additionally, users did not access static pages repeatedly leading to a substantially lower page

	PC Studies	iPhone
Mean URL visits per day/user	7.6 - 258.5 [24]	0.4 - 20
Site vocabulary	84 – 2,127 [24]	27 – 543
Mean session duration	476.4 sec. [36]	105.9 sec.
Page visits/session	17.7 [36]	6.1
Query rate	12.5% [36]	56.3%
Queries/session	4.3 [36]	2.1
Site revisitation rate	70% [24]	90.3%
Page revisitation rate	45.6% [24]	25.3%

Table 2. Browser comparisons between platforms.

revisitation rate than previously reported. Instead users relied on search at a much higher rate compared to the PC.

Nature of the Task

We also found a greater distinction between page and site revisitation rates compared to the PC. The full URL (page) revisitation rate was much lower than the site revisitation rate indicating that users access a small number of sites to view different pages [see 24]. For instance, Google was the most visited site followed by a number of blogs and the Rice.edu institutional site. The site revisitation rate for Google was high because all search results pages were within the same domain. However, most search results pages were unique because of different query terms (and thus unique URLs). Similarly, blogs were revisited often across users and yielded a long tail (Figure 1). In contrast, there were more sub-top level pages visited within institutional sites such as the Rice.edu domain (e.g., registrar.rice.edu, dining.rice.edu) and News sites.

The highest ranking pages in Figure 1 were mostly top-level (e.g., home) pages that provided users access to sub-level content within the same site. Since only 9% of all pages were revisited more than 5 times, we manually categorized these pages as (1) log-in pages, (2) subsequent home pages after a log-in, (3) a top-level page (e.g., http://google.com, http://www.espn.go.com), or (4) other. Many were indeed in the first three categories (62%) thus demonstrating how these top-level sites were used as a gateway to other content, often within the same site (substantiated by the high site revisitation rates). The top five sites for each user accounted for a minimum of 22.3% of page visits to a maximum of 91.8% of all page visits with a mean of 73.4%. These top sites, such as Google.com, Rice.edu, and Wikipedia.org, were reaccessed frequently to provide users portals to new or changing information.

Temporal Patterns and Revisitation Strategies

Fragmented browsing across interruptions also resulted in page revisiting. Many short-term page revisits (accessing the same URL within a period of three days) occurred via a page being reaccessed across adjacent web browsing sessions. We found that 21% of all page revisits were due to the loading of a page prevously closed with the browser. Our logger did not record the page visit if it did not load completely. Thus, many users retrieved this information intentionally to continue a previous navigation sequence. Roughly a quarter of these revisits were continued after an interruption such as a text message or voice phone call. The other three quarters of these type of revisits were after the phone display was turned off for some period of time. A few users reported using small periods of free time to access a page for viewing later, perhaps a strategy developed to deal with long page loading times.

Longer-term revisits generally occurred through navigating from top-level pages accessed through search. 37% of sites revisited after three days and 25% of all page revisits after three days occurred through search. All users but one accessed sites in their top three (e.g., neoseeker.com, craigslist.org) via Google consistently throughout the entire

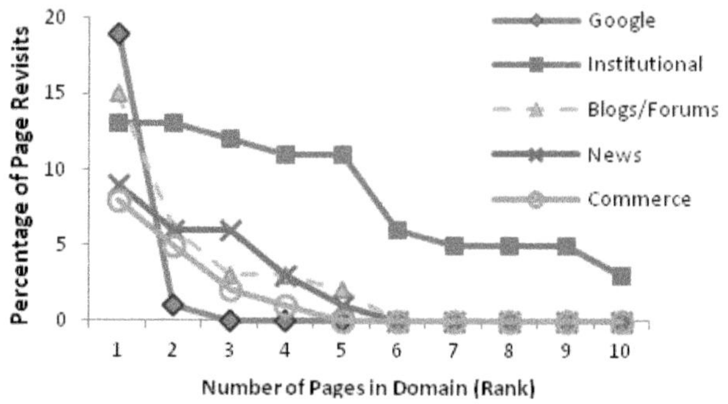

Figure 1. Page revisits by type of site [after 24].

study. Additionally, we asked users, via an open-ended question, to report some of their common strategies for revisiting web pages that they have not been to in two weeks. Every user mentioned the use of search. 50% of our users stated that they use other windows to access sites on a recurring basis. These users assign particular sites or pages to other windows and switch to targeted windows when the content is needed, though most mentioned difficulty in maintaining this strategy. Typing in an address within the URL address bar was mentioned by only one user.

Bookmarks were not used frequently. We recorded the number of bookmarks that were added. 83% of users did not add any bookmarks in Safari. Three users only added one or two bookmarks throughout the entire year. One user added more than two (i.e., 9). Additionally, only two users added bookmarks to their springboards (one linked a single page while the other linked two pages). Based on these data, it did not appear bookmarks or adding icons to springboards constituted primary methods for revisiting. However, 54% of the sites visited also were installed as an NIA (e.g., Google Mobile, Rice, etc.) which appeared to supplant other types of bookmarking to some degree.

Use of Native Internet Applications

Table 3 shows aggregate statistics similar to those reported for the browser above. User vocabularies and visit patterns were diverse. For instance, one user added only 10 native applications to his smartphone over the course of the 12-month study. Conversely, another user installed over 451 native applications. Users also uninstalled a surprisingly large number of applications (M = 82.25, *Median* = 43.34, SD = 29.85). Users were more similar to each other, however, in their revisitation of NIAs. The high revisitation rate of 97.1% was driven by a high number of visits to a set

	Mean	SD	Min	Max
Visits/Active Day	17.40	8.30	1.00	36.00
Vocabulary	124.63	106.17	31.00	475.00
Revisitation Rate	0.97	0.02	0.91	0.99
Hours/Active Day	2.02	1.21	0.26	4.69
NIAs Visited Once	33.00	41.43	0.00	185.00
% Search App Use	0.002	0.004	0.00	0.02
% Visits in Top 10	60.39	13.15	32.39	89.84

Table 3. Summary and variance statistics for NIA use.

of NIAs such as the five most frequently accessed across our users: Mail, Facebook, Maps, Words with Friends and Weather. These five NIAs made up more than 50% of all visits. NIAs that could be used to issue internet searches were installed by 91% of our users. Google Mobile was most common,though one user installed Bing as well. These applications were not used very often; across the entire length of the study, they were accessed an average of 6.2 times over the entire year (*Median* = 5.5, *SD* = 4.97). Similar to sites, NIAs were accessed for dynamic content; dissimilarly, information searches were not issued frequently off-the-browser.

Also similar to sites, NIAs were used for brief periods of time (*M* = 137.29 sec., *Median* = 62 sec., *SD* = 207.29 sec.). As can be seen by the large difference between the mean and median, this distribution is positively skewed with most NIAs being used for roughly one minute. Of course, the large standard deviation also reflects the fact that durations of NIA use are heavily task dependent and largely a function of what NIAs were installed by each user. For instance, NIAs such as Pandora were used for longer periods of time compared to others (e.g., Weather). Across all NIAs, many were operated independently; 59% of iPhone activations (i.e., the display was turned on) were for the use of one NIA alone before the display was turned off.

From an aggregate perspective, NIAs were visited more than twice the amount of sites. Longitudinally, however, the distinctions between NIA and site visits appeared to be driven by experience. Figure 2 shows sites and NIAs were accessed at similar levels for the first three months of the study. Geometric means are used in these figures to reduce

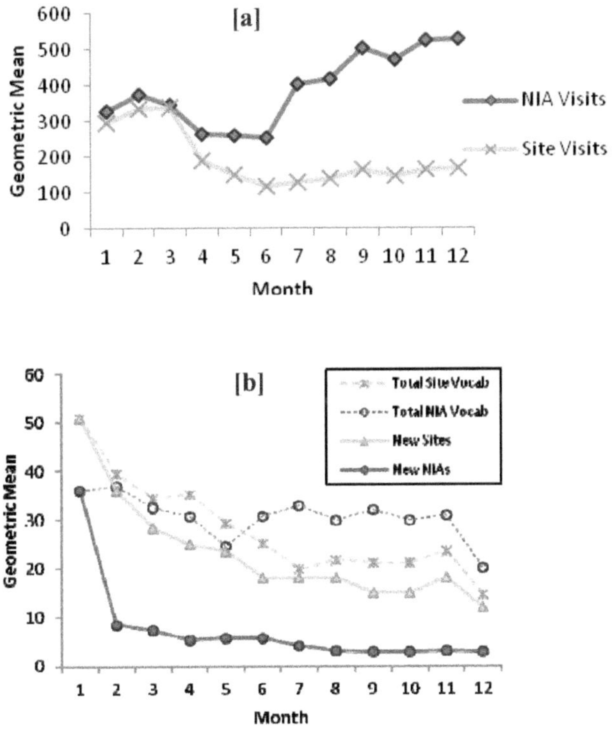

Figure 2. Number of (a) visits, (b) total vocab and new content accessed through NIAs and the browser by month.

the influence of extreme use within each month on our summary statistics. Months 4-6 were during the summer break. Within this period, all internet use decreased; browsing decreased more dramatically compared to NIAs. After the summer, browser use increased modestly compared to the use of NIAs which sharply increased. Users generally reported the low summer use was due to decreased school-related activity along with being closer to friends and family they usually corresponded with online.

New NIAs were not installed and accessed as frequently as sites. New content was visited more than twice as much on sites (*M* = 27.33, *Median* = 25, *SD* = 10.94) compared to NIAs (*M* = 10.04, *Median* = 9.5, *SD* = 9.69). Instead, a more steady set of NIAs were accessed regularly by our users. The installation of new NIAs dropped more sharply after the first month. By the third month, users averaged under eight visits to new NIAs per month. Figure 2b shows how the distinctions between total vocabulary and new content for each modality changed as a function of experience. The small number of new NIAs accessed accumulated with time and by six months NIA vocabularies exceeded site vocabularies. Browsers were continually used to access new content and these new sites generally made up most of users' overall vocabularies within a given month. The sites that were revisited were revisited very frequently resulting in 3-5 sites that were generally revisited heavily for each user and a long tail of unique sites not revisited after one or two visits.

We asked our users about their methods for visitng new sites and new NIAs on their smartphones. In an open-ended question collected after data logging concluded, users described why they used their browser more to access new domains compared to NIAs. 79% stated they did not want to take the time to install an NIA that they perceived would not be used again. Most of these users reported that they used their browser to get quick information and were unable to predict their information needs to install an appropriate NIA ahead of time. One user stated this clearly, "sometimes Google knows what I need better than I do." Five users mentioned that installing NIAs was more like shopping whereas accessing new content on the web browser was more obligatory for information needs.

Visiting and Revisiting Physical Locations

Though smartphones are used in more diverse contexts compared to PCs, we found that users frequently revisit the same places to interact with their phones (*Location Revisitation Rate* = 90.6%). The 24 participants in our study revisited a small set of physical locations at about the same rate as virtual locations (e.g., sites, reported above at 90.3%) though the variance between users was higher for physical locality revisiting (*SD* = 8.63%, *Min* = 61.3%, *Max* = 96.2%). Of course, the level of granularity of our location measurement is coarse; users could be accessing their phones in a number of settings within a given radius and still record under the same Cell ID. Still, the localities we captured reveal physical traversing following patterns similar to web localities. Indeed, the distribution of visits and revisits to places is similar to those for sites and NIAs (Figure 3). Most locations are visited once; however, a majority of smartphone interactions occur within a small subset of places. The high revisitation rate reflects a large number of visits to users' top three to five locations similar to NIA and site revisit rates. Location rates were higher during the academic year compared to summer months, most likely because 91% of our users lived on campus during the former time period.

User Differences in Accessing the Internet

Until now, we have described empirical patterns of behavior associated with internet use via smartphones and the physical locations where users interacted with their smartphones. In this section, we examine the large user variance reported above to characterize smartphone users in their visiting patterns. To this end, we developed NIA-to-site indices. These measures were computed for each user with the following equation:

NIA-to-site index = (NIA visits – site visits) / (NIA visits + site visits)

Positive values reflect greater use of NIAs compared to sites on the browser. Negative values show greater use of the browser relative to NIAs. A score of zero reflects that users accessed both NIAs and sites via their browser at the same proportion. As Figure 4 shows, our users varied greatly in their reliance on each modality. An inverse correlation was also found between overall internet use and NIA-to-site indices (r = -.61, p = .001). Thus, most participants visited NIAs; however those that used the internet more via their smartphone also more frequently accessed sites via their browsers. For clarity and reasons we explain more in detail below, we call users lower in NIA-to-site indices **Pioneers** because, while they visited NIAs (i.e., "native territory"), they also frequently accessed new information on the web. Those with higher indices we call **Natives** because they largely avoided exploring the web on their browsers, but accessed resources native to the device. We keep the index as continuous to avoid strict compartmentalization of users into two user types. We instead imply that users at each end of the spectrum can manifest behaviors at the other extreme, though perhaps not as frequent.

Pioneers' larger reliance on their web browsers resulted in higher site (r = -.54, p < .01) and page (r = -.44, p = .02) revisitation rates. There was not a significant correlation between NIA-to-site index values and NIA revisitation rates (r = .09, p = .69). Interestingly, however, we found that Pioneers revisited physical locations at a higher rate though not quite reliable at a .05 alpha level (r = -.26, p = .10) and used their phone in more unique localities across the entire study period (r = -.29, p = .08). We expect that with a larger sample size these p-values would reach statistical significance. Still, these results provide some evidence that Pioneers' and Natives' unique traversing patterns in virtual space (i.e., the web) manifest similarly in the real world.

When the browser was accessed, Natives tended to use it in conjunction with NIAs and for quick searches. As NIA-to-

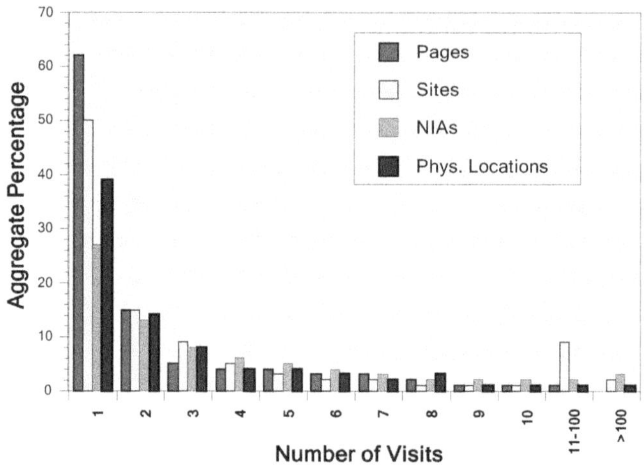

Figure 3. Aggregate percentages of pages, sites, NIAs and physical locations (Cell IDs) by their number of visits.

site indices increased, the proportion of browsing sessions that consisted of only one URL that loaded before the session ended increased as well (r = .51, p = .01). 63% of these followed access to another NIA. For instance, many of these browser visits occurred directly following the Mail NIA suggesting that Natives were following a link in an email message. Interestingly, Natives also yielded higher query rates (proportion of browsing sessions that included at least one search) when they did access their browser (r = .41, p = .02). The strength of this correlation increased when we removed browsing sessions that directly followed use of another NIA (r = .55, p < .01). In other words, when Natives launched Safari from their springboards there was a high probability that a search would be issued.

Pioneers accessed their browser more from their springboard and in isolation of other NIAs. This led to different browsing patterns. As NIA-to-site indices decreased, users tended to access more pages per session (r = -.39, p = .03) leading to each session lasting for longer periods of time (r = -.37, p = .04). Though they yielded fewer sessions with queries (lower query rates), Pioneers averaged more queries per browsing session (r = -.37, p = .04). Thus, when Pioneers used search they tended to search more within the same session. This resulted in more new content consumed reflected by higher unique site vocabularies per session (r = .69, p < .001). Clearly, Pioneers relied on their web browsers for repeated visits to pages and then ventured to explore new information.

Natives used NIAs differently than Pioneers. First, they tended to spend less time on each NIA launch, though not quite significantly different (r = .30, p = .06). They did not differ from Pioneers in the installation of new NIAs. Thus, since Natives and Pioneers yielded similar NIA revisitation rates and vocabularies, it appears differences in use of NIAs is influenced by other factors. Indeed, the coarse location revisitation rates we report above highly correlate with NIA revisitation rates (r = .63, p < .001) suggesting external stimuli likely prompt routine (or habitual [25]) use of NIAs. Still, user differences characterized here show differences in how NIAs are accessed. Natives accessed more NIAs

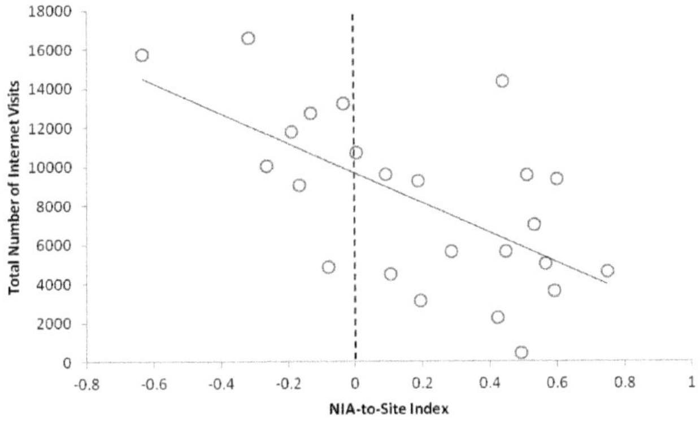

Figure 4. Scatter plot of total visits by NIA-to-site index values.

once without any revisits (r = .41, p = .02). Interestingly, Pioneers uninstalled more NIAs (r = -.34, p = .04). Natives use NIAs briefly and leave unused NIAs deserted on their springboards. Pioneers, on the contrary, spent more time on each NIA when launched and uninstalled more NIAs.

Experience

We also explored how experience with the iPhone influenced use of the browser relative to NIAs. We considered that one reason NIA-to-site indices were so low was due to high early browser use. Recall that all of our users were not previous smartphone owners. We thought that computer experience could have transferred to users' smartphone use and led to higher web browsing early in the study. Thus, we assessed differences in NIA-to-site indices between the first and second halves of the study. We found that 20 of the 24 users' difference scores were positive showing an increase in NIA use over browser use during the second half of the study. The mean of these difference scores (M = 1.56, SD = 2.43) was significantly greater than zero ($t(23)$ = 3.14, p = .01). Thus, users' reliance on NIAs relative to their browsers increased with experience; however, this was not the case for every user. Query rates on the browser also increased with experience. Using a similar approach using difference scores, we found that the second half of the study consisted of 5% more sessions that contained at least one search. This increase also yielded a mean difference score reliably greater than zero ($t(23)$ = 2.17, p = .04).

Taken together, use of the phone over time led to increased reliance on NIAs and a greater use of search on the browser. The iPhone seemed to afford users to optimize both modalities by accessing NIAs for repeated use of favorite content and browsers for searching for and use of new and fleeting information.

DISCUSSION

The goal of this study was to characterize web interactions with smartphones using a deliberately naturalistic and longitudinal methodology. Indeed, because our logger unobtrusively collected interaction data from ecologically-valid environments over a substantial period of time, we submit the behaviors examined in this study were particularly realistic. At the broadest level we found differences between technologies—the PC and the smartphone—in how the internet was accessed and differences between users in how the latter was used. We discuss both findings in turn before we provide design recommendations.

Using the Web on Smartphones

Clearly, the web browser is not as fundamental to smartphone use as it has appeared to be with PCs. The *highest* frequency user in the current study averaged fewer URL visits per day (20) compared to the *lowest* frequency user in the most recent PC study published in 2008 (24.9). This difference between platforms was both because the browser was accessed less often and, when it was accessed, it was for shorter periods of time. Indeed, smartphone browsing sessions were roughly three times shorter than PC browsing sessions in both duration and pages visited.

Revisitation patterns were also dissimilar. Page revisitation rates were much lower than previous PC-based studies. Many of these revisits were continued after an interruption or to a top-level portal only to get to targeted (new) content. We see the former as a unique characteristic of mobile browsing. The latter reflects the lack of browser use to revisit static content. Though pages were not revisited often, sites were revisited at levels much higher than any previous PC study. Clearly, a small set of domains provide users access to a much larger number of diverse pages suggesting designers should surface these portals when the browser is accessed (as discussed below).

The distinction between computing platforms in volume of use became more pronounced with experience as browser use gave way to higher NIA activity. NIAs consumed most visits to the internet, especially after users became more experienced with their devices. These visits were short and concentrated to a relatively stable vocabulary of NIAs that were frequently revisited. When our users first received their smartphones, they seemed to apply mental models developed from computer use and relied heavily on their smartphone browser for touring a large number of sites and accessing these sites often. However, instead of bookmarking these sites within their browsers, users installed NIAs that "stuck" to their vocabularies for longer periods of time. In a sense, this emphasis on a new type of bookmarking (installing NIAs to springboards) has afforded iPhone users to optimize their devices. NIAs were used more frequently to access a stable set of resources in particular contexts. Web browsers became a tool that afforded searching for and consuming new and dynamic information with low likelihood of repeated visits. Adding the former required users to predict their information and entertainment needs while the latter was used more ad hoc. The clear message to web designers is to point users to installing the NIA to increase the probability of revisits.

Even with these links to install an NIA, our study suggests that it is difficult for new NIAs to become part of users' "active" vocabularies. Not all NIAs that are installed are used frequently. Many are removed after one visit or deserted on a springboard and not accessed more than a few times (recall Figure 3). Interestingly, the mean vocabulary rates for NIAs within each month did not increase much across the entire length of this study, though new NIAs were installed. This suggests total NIA vocabularies are somewhat fixed for users; as new NIAs are added, others are either uninstalled or left on springboards with low likelihood of revisits. Of course, there was large user variance in most aspects of internet use on smartphones confirming that personalization based on each user's unique usage patterns and contextual needs is an important design strategy for mobile space.

Different Types of Smartphone Users

Indeed, previous studies have found differences between smartphone users at several orders of magnitude [9]. Here, we characterize these differences building on a growing line of empirical research in HCI. Catledge and Pitkow [4] described differences between PC web users based on browsing patterns. One type, "Serendipitous Browsers" did not yield repeated sequences of URL visits. "Searchers", in contrast, were repetitive in short navigation sequences. Teevan et al. [34] labeled users at these extremes as "Filers" and "Pilers". Filers designated explicit locations to organize their electronic information. Pilers, on the other hand, were unstructured and used different search strategies to retrieve their electronic information. Extending findings in education, Ford [10] found that "Holists" issued more exploratory searches and valued serendipitous encounters with new information. In contrast, "Serialists" follow a linear pattern to learning and navigate on the web in a more sequential manner. White and Drucker [36] similarly described PC users as "Explorers" and "Navigators". The former prefers undirected browsing and discovery of new information. The latter prefers rapid access to target information and performed more directive searching to desired content.

We now characterize mobile users at two ends of a similar behavioral continuum. At one end, "Pioneers" relied on their browsers more and these interactions yielded visits to more diverse content, longer sequences of URLs per session, more searches within each browsing session and higher rates of revisiting across modalities. This larger consumption seemed to reflect that these users "settle" on a small subset of favorite resources on the browser very frequently. However, they also continue to pioneer in these browsing sessions with search and visiting of new content for more sundry reasons. This behavioral pattern manifested somewhat in NIAs as well; perhaps exploring more within NIAs reflected by longer visits and clearing out room on their springboards for new NIAs. Pioneers also revisited physical locations at a higher rate and used their iPhones in more unique localities. Clearly, these users are most similar to "Serendipitous Browsers", "Holists", "Explorers" and "Pilers" in that they consume more diverse amounts of information, interact for longer sequences when on the web and traverse in more localities in the real world.

On the other end, Natives did not access the internet as much and did not venture outside of "native territory" to visit as much new content. They are most similar to "Searchers", "Filers", "Serialists" and "Navigators" in this regard and because they rely on shorter navigation sequences using search when on their browsers. Web browsers were sparingly used to discover new information; though it was used directly after another NIA. Natives yielded web sessions shorter in terms of both pages visited and duration. Similarly, NIA launches from their vocabularies were for shorter durations as well.

How can these user differences be explained more theoretically? First, we submit these distinctions reflect patterns explained by differing cognitive styles identified in previous learning and HCI studies [see 37]. Because stable behavioral differences, similar to differences between *holists* and *serialists*, manifested across virtual and physical traversing in our study, our smartphone users differed because of how they varied along this cognitive spectrum. Second, these differences between users could have manifested because of the types of contexts visited and user goals within those settings [See 18]. Natives seemed to actively use their smartphones more as tools to accomplish short information needs. Pioneers seemed to use their smartphones actively and passively for both utilitarian and hedonic reasons. Pioneers may have developed more habitual routines as they revisit more of the same locations to access their phones [26]. Since they do not visit more physical locations, perhaps they compensate by traversing more on the web to content previously settled on along with additional explorations. This hypothesis should be tested in additional research. Finally, our results could be driven by an interaction between these two factors.

Design Implications

Our study suggests several ways to support smartphone users. Even though we direct these recommendations toward users at each end of the continuum, we purport that each suggestion would be beneficial for all users. Indeed, users along the entire spectrum can display both types of behavioral patterns and gain from enhanced designs.

We think **Pioneers** could benefit from capabilities previously reported for similar types of users [e.g., 36] along with several suggestions for mobile space:

- **Optimize content for mobile browsing and NIAs**: Content designers should not ignore designing a usable mobile site for web browsers. Many new smartphone users rely heavily on their browsers to access the internet and find information to be bookmarked via installing the NIA. Additionally, the mobile browser continuously provides a vehicle for many users at all experience levels to access new content with low likelihood of revisiting. Optimized content for mobile browsing should assume users are new and provide clear "knowledge-in-the-world" to support first-time interactions along with clear links to add bookmark through installing the NIA, adding the site tag to a springboard, or the top browser bar.
- **Better design of mobile browsers:** Most certainly, our study suggests that the real estate used for the URL address bar can be better exploited for personalized

access to favorite content. Since many of the sites and pages revisited were Top-Level Pages (e.g., home pages), designers should surface these portals to avoid unneeded typing, searching, and page loading. For instance, the Google search bar could double as the URL address bar for pasting URLs and for autocomplete functionality to revisit pages. The free space on the top browser bar (no longer occupied by the URL address bar) could be used to access top-level sites based on each user's most visited sites or adaptable for users to add and edit based on their perceived needs. For sites with a short tail (such as the institutional sites in Figure 1), these personalized buttons could display a menu with the most visited sub-level sites when selected.

- **More intelligent springboards:** We submit, based on our findings, that springboards can be designed more effectively to support discovering new NIAs. This could take several forms. For example, user profiles could be developed from NIA and browsing history to provide suggestions based on content visited. Smartphone designers could give users the option to designate one springboard page for recommender capabilities. This springboard may allow users to try NIAs before they permanently install or buy applications. In other words, a recommender system would install suggested NIAs for trying out instead of relying on the user to browse, install, and try out the app for him- or herself. Most users had room on their springboards for such a capability. We recommend, especially for Pioneers, a Springboard page designated for "Try-before-you-buy" NIAs already installed based on previous usage. Part of this springboard space could be used for browser access. For instance, an auto-bookmark mechanism to provide links to a top-level site from a user's unique history could be leveraged similar to the Windows Start Menu. Perhaps even a static top-level page with links to sub-level resources would be beneficial for more efficient interactions.

Natives could also benefit from design features to help them get to desired information more quickly:

- **Predictive systems:** More predictive capabilities are needed to attenuate mobile HCI problems mentioned above such as page loading and awkward text entry. Activity gathered from other devices can be useful to this end [16]. According to our study, each user's history of web use on their smartphones could provide ways to predict likely site destinations. Most overall internet use was dominated by a relatively small set of sites and NIAs. Using contextual information and most frequented sites to preload pages (e.g., top-level pages) would be beneficial to avoid long page loading delays.

- **Web search from the springboard**: When Natives accessed their browsers, it was usually for quick searches. Queries were conducted most often on the web. It may be beneficial to offer a vehicle to search from the springboard. For instance, instead of capabilities to "search your iPhone" from the springboard, it may be more useful to have a "search the web" bar right on the springboard main pages.

- **Identify Springboards**: Across the entire study, NIA vocabs were generally higher than what could fit on one springboard page. Natives did not uninstall NIAs much compared to Pioneers. Also, they used more NIAs just once. Taken together, it seems like springboards could be designed to more effectively support revisits. Perhaps one way to do this is giving users options to identify each springboard. Another way might be to set up reminder for NIAs previously installed that have not been used over a period of time. This reminder could alert NIAs to this resource and perhaps encourage increased usage.

Limitations

Of course, these findings should be generalized with caution because of several limitations in the current study. Foremost, our small sample size does not represent the entire range of the millions of smartphone users around the world. However, the number of users analyzed here is roughly equivalent and perhaps more diverse than many of the previous studies that have informed our research. Second, we only examined the use of iPhones. Future research should assess how our results generalize to other devices. Third, the PC studies are slightly older and we suspect current PC web use has changed (at least for smartphone owners). It is unclear how use of a smartphone with a PC impacts the latter. Future studies should assess intra-user differences across PC and smartphone platforms.

CONCLUSION

Bearing these limitations in mind, this study contributes an empirical characterization of web use on smartphones. We established behavioral patterns associated with browsing, NIA use and physical locations where smartphones were used to build on previous descriptions of user differences. Indeed, we found these differences were stable across virtual and physical location visiting with smartphones.

ACKNOWLEDGMENTS

We appreciate the tremendous efforts of Amy Buxbaum, Beth Herlin, Wen Xing and Louis Fornage. We also thank Michael Byrne, David Lane, Jeff Zemla and all reviewers for their feedback on earlier versions of the current paper. This research was supported by NSF IIS/HCC 0803556.

REFERENCES

1. Abowd, G.D. & Mynatt, E.D. Charting past, present, and future research in ubiquitous computing. *ACM Trans. on Computer-Human Interaction,* 7, 2000, 29-58.

2. Bales, E. *et al*. Planning, apps, and the high-end smartphone: exploring the landscape of modern cross-device reaccess. In K. Lyons et al. (Eds.): *Pervasive 2011, LNCS 6696, pp. 1-18*. Berlin: Springer.

3. Byrne, M., John, B., Wehrle, N.S. & Crow, D.C. The tangled web we wove: A taskonomy of www use. *In Proc. CHI 99,* ACM Press (1999), 544-551.

4. Catledge, L.D. & Pitkow, J.E. Characterizing browsing strategies in the world wide web. *In Proc. WWW 1995,* ACM Press (1995), 1065-1073.
5. Cockburn, A., McKenzie, B. What do web users do? An empirical analysis of web use. *International Journal of Human-Computer Studies*, 54(6), 2001, 903-922.
6. Cui, Y. & Roto, V. How people use the web on mobile devices. *In Proc WWW'08,* ACM Press (2008), 905-914.
7. Duchnicky, R.L. & Kolers, P.A. Readability of text scrolled on visual display terminals as a function of window size. *Human Factors,* 25, 1983, 683-692.
8. Ericsson Consumer Labs. From apps to everyday situations, 2010. http://www.ericsson.com
9. Falaki, H. et al. Diversity in smartphone usage. *In Proc MobiSys 2010*. ACM Press (2010). 179-194.
10. Ford, N. *et al.* Information seeking and mediated searching. *JASIST,* 53, 2002, 728-735.
11. Gallette, D.F., *et al.* When the wait isn't so bad: The interacting effects of website delay, familiarity, and breadth. *Info. Systems Research,* 17(1), 2003, 20-37.
12. Holscher, C. & Strube, G. Web search behavior of internet experts and newbies. *Computer Networks,* 33, 2000, 337-346.
13. Internet World Statistics, 2011. Retrieved May 2011: http://www.internetworldstats.com/stats2.htm
14. Kaikkonen, A. Full or tailored mobile web-where and how do people browse on their mobiles? *In Proc. of Mobility '08*, 1-10.
15. Kamvar, M., Kellar, M., Pater, R. & Xu, Y. Computers and iPhones and mobile phones, oh my! A logs-based comparison of search users on different devices. *In Proc. WWW 2009*. ACM Press.
16. Kane, S.,*et al.* Exploring cross-device web use on PCs and mobile devices. *Human-Computer Interaction – INTERACT 2009*, Springer (2009), 722-735.
17. Kellar, M., Watters, C. & Shepherd, M. A field study characterizing web-based information-seeking tasks. *American Society for Information Science and Technology,* 58(7), 2007, 999-1018.
18. Lee, I., Kim, J. & Kim, J. Use contexts for the mobile internet: A longitudinal study monitoring actual use of mobile internet services. *International Journal of Human-Computer Interactions,* 18, 2005, 269-292
19. Matthews, T., Pierce, J. &Tang, J. No smartphone is an island: The impact of places, situations, and other devices on smartphone use. *IBM Technical Report #RJ10452,* 2009.
20. Newark-French, C. Mobile apps put the web in their rear-view mirror, 2011. http://blog.flurry.com
21. Nielsen, J. User interface directions for the web. *Communications of the ACM*, 42(1), 1999, 65-72.
22. Nielsen, J. Mobile Usability, 2009. http://www.useit.com/alertbox/mobile-usability.html
23. Nylander, S., Lundquist, T. & Brännström, A. At home and with computer access – why and where people use cell phones to access the internet. *In Proc. CHI 2009,* ACM Press (2009), 1639-1642.
24. Obendorf, H., Weinreich, H., Herder, E. & Mayer, M. Web page revisitation revisited: Implications of a long-term click-stream study of browser usage. *In Proc. CHI 2007*, ACM Press (2007), 597-606.
25. Oulasvirta, A., Rattenbury, T., Ma, L. & Raita, E. Habits make smartphone use more pervasive. *Pers Ubiquitous Computing,* Published online: 16 June 2011.
26. Perry, M., O'hara, K., Sellen, A., Brown, B. & Harper, R. Dealing with mobility: Understanding access anytime, anywhere. *ACM TOCHI,* 8(4), 2005, 323-347.
27. Pew Research Center. *Internet and American Life Project,* 2010. http://www.pewinternet.org
28. Roto, V. & Oulasvirta, A. Need for non-visual feedback with long response times in mobile HCI. *In Proc. WWW 2005*. ACM Press (2005). 775-781.
29. Sellen, A.J., Murphy, R. & Shaw, K.L. How knowledge workers use the web. *In Proc. SIGCHI 2002*. ACM Press (2002). 227-234.
30. Selvidge, P. Examining tolerance for online delays. *Usability News*, 5(1), 2003. http://psychology.wichita.edu/surl/usabilitynews/51/delaytime.htm.
31. Shepard, C., Rahmati, A., Tossell, C.C., Zhong, L. & Kortum, P. Livelab: Measuring wireless networks and smartphone users in the field. *ACM Sigmetrics Performance Evaluation Review, 38(3),* 2011, 15-20.
32. Tauscher, L. & Greenberg, S. How people revisit web pages: Empirical findings and implications for the design of history systems. *International Journal of Human Computer Studies*, 47(1), 1997, 97-138.
33. Taylor, C.A. *et al.* Always on: A framework for understanding personal mobile web motivations, behaviors, and contexts of use. *Int'l Journal of Mobile HCI,* 1(4), 2009, 24-41.
34. Teevan, J. *et al.* The perfect search engine is not enough: A study of orienteering behavior in directed search. *In Proc CHI,* ACM Press (2004): 415-422.
35. Tossell, C.C., Kortum, P., Shepard, C., Rahmati, A. & Zhong, L. Performing common tasks on handheld mobile computers. *In Proc. of HFES* (2010).
36. White, R.W. & Drucker, S.M. Investigating behavioral variability in web search. *In Proc. WWW 2007*, ACM Press (2007), 21-30.
37. Witkin, H.A. *et al.* Field-dependent and field-independent cognitive styles and their educational implications. *Review of Educational Research,* 47, 1977, 1-64.

Narratives of Satisfying and Unsatisfying Experiences of Current Mobile Augmented Reality Applications

Thomas Olsson
Tampere University of Technology, Unit of Human-Centered Technology
Korkeakoulunkatu 6, 33720 Tampere, Finland
thomas.olsson@tut.fi

Markus Salo
University of Jyväskylä, Department of Computer Science and Information Systems
Mattilanniemi 2, 40100 Jyväskylä, Finland
markus.t.salo@jyu.fi

ABSTRACT
Over the last few years, mobile applications demonstrating Augmented Reality (AR) – such as Layar, Junaio and Google Goggles – have been introduced to consumers. We conducted an online survey to explore the user experience (UX) of early stage mobile AR applications available in the market in spring 2011, covering both location-based AR browsers and image recognition AR applications for object-based interaction. We identify various types of experiences such applications have evoked by qualitatively analyzing 84 users' narratives of their most satisfying and unsatisfying experiences. The results highlight, for example, experiences of awareness of surroundings, empowerment, positive surprise, amazement and fascination from the novelty value, as well as some examples of immersion and social connectivity. The analysis indicates that the applications have not yet reached their potential in evoking a multifaceted user experience that is characteristic especially to AR. This work helps in understanding the experiential design potential in mobile AR and points out UX issues to further focus on in design.

Author Keywords
Mobile augmented reality; mixed reality; location-based service; object-based interaction; end user application; user experience; evaluation; online survey; user narration.

ACM Classification Keywords
H.5.2 [Information Interfaces and Presentation]: User Interfaces – User-centered design; H.5.1[Information Interfaces and Presentation]: Multimedia Information Systems – Artificial, augmented, and virtual realities.

General Terms
Human Factors.

INTRODUCTION
According to the broad definitions of Augmented Reality (AR), it combines real and computer-generated digital information into the user's view of the physical and interactive real world so that they appear as one environment [12,28]. AR integrates digital information with the tangible surrounding reality it relates to, for example by visually superimposing content on top of the view of the real world. Hence, AR could allow the user to access, manipulate and create location- and object-based information with an interaction paradigm that is intuitive and based on similar tangible interactions that occur in interacting with the physical world [22].

As result of active prior research and development of enabling technologies like computer vision and mobile computing and sensor technologies, we have lately seen mobile applications with AR features to penetrate to the day-to-day activities of consumers. With the recent introductions of mobile applications such as Layar[1], Junaio[2], Google Goggles[3], ShopSavvy[4], we are witnessing AR-related technologies to become exploitable for purposes of, for example, browsing location-based content, entertainment and gaming, as well as identifying products and objects while mobile. The current publicly available mobile AR-like applications can be roughly classified into two common approaches: *AR browsers* and *image recognition-based AR* applications. Both types rely heavily on the visual modality in providing digital information related to real-world objects and locations. AR browsers explore the augmented world through the camera view ("magic lens" [1]), usually visualizing points of interest based on the GPS location and magnetometer orientation. In addition to Layar and Junaio, good examples of AR browsers of today are Wikitude[5] and Sekai Camera[6]. Image recognition-based AR connects surrounding objects, products, and other physical targets with related digital information with the help of visual recognition of QR codes, barcodes, or other graphic markers. Product-related

[1]www.layar.com, [2]www.junaio.com,
[3]www.google.com/mobile/goggles,
[4]www.shopsavvy.mobi, [5]www.wikitude.org,
[6]www.sekaicamera.com

applications (e.g. ShopSavvy[7], pic2shop[8], and StickyBits[9]) represent a notable share of such AR applications but Google Goggles as a general image-based search application is probably the most used. Such object-related and marker-based applications can also be seen as a visual interface for physical browsing [18], and "Internet of Things" [3].

Despite the technical differences between these approaches, from the user's perspective 1) the ways of interaction are very similar, 2) both augment the visual physical world in real time by utilizing the real world to access digital content related to locations or objects, and 3) both provide augmented content that is interactive. AR browsers provide an overall picture of the surrounding digital information, whereas image recognition AR allows the same but on a narrower, object-based scale. Considering the similarities from the user's point of view, in this paper we consider the two technological approaches as one entity.

The current AR applications can be disparaged as rather simple demonstrators of AR (e.g. not truly 3D content, imprecise alignment). Nevertheless, being the 1st generation of publicly available applications that utilize visual AR elements in the context of location- and object-based services, they provide a fruitful ground to conduct user research on a large scale. Our research explores the various elements of user experience of mobile AR by gathering subjective descriptions of end users' most satisfying and unsatisfying experiences. To further justify our research, user experience research is only in its infancy when considering the recent AR applications and, in fact, AR related technologies in general [8,22].

THEORETICAL BACKGROUND AND RELATED WORK

Offering a stimulating and pleasurable *user experience* (UX) is becoming a central goal and design strategy in design of technology products and services. UX is regarded as a comprehensive concept describing the subjective experience resulted from the interaction with a technological product or service [13]. UX depends on contextual factors like social setting, cultural influences, and user's other activities. The nature of the experience with technology can be, for example, pragmatic, emotional, symbolic, aesthetic, meaning-related or visceral [6,11]. Emotional elements are easily underutilized in design although emotions play a surprisingly great role in use of technology: they initiate behavior and motivate decisions; they allow focusing on interesting things as well as make people discard the unsatisfying [7].

In the following, we present a few UX-related frameworks relevant in contemplating the results of this study. Jordan [14] describes various types of pleasure in use of products: 1) physio-pleasure (related to body and senses), 2) psycho-pleasure (related to the mind and emotions), 3) socio-pleasure (related to relationships and status), and 4) ideo-pleasure (related to values and attitudes). Desmet [5] discusses the matter from a perspective of emotional reactions, identifying 5 categories: 1) surprise emotions & amazement, 2) instrumental emotions (e.g. disappointment, satisfaction), 3) aesthetic emotions related to intrinsic pleasantness (e.g. disgust, attracted to), 4) social emotions (e.g. indignation, admiration), and 5) interest emotions (boredom, fascination) arising from, e.g., challenge. Finally, Hassenzahl [11] has distinguished between two main perceptions of product quality: *pragmatic* and *hedonic*, which create the abstract consequences (i.e. experiences) in the user: *appeal*, *pleasure*, *satisfaction*. Pragmatic quality refers to the product's ability to support achievement of behavioral goals (e.g. usefulness, usability, appropriateness). Hedonic quality is divided into three dimensions: 1) stimulation (e.g. enabling personal growth), 2) identification (e.g. expressing and building one's identity through the product) and 3) evocation (provoking memories and emotions). Overall, all of these three frameworks describe the *types of user experience*, however from slightly different standpoints and levels of abstraction.

Methodologically, evaluating the subjective emotional user experience can be carried out with, for example, interviews and subjective agreement statements, but also probing and diary methods, such as the *critical incident technique* (CIT) [10]. CIT allows gathering users' perspectives as stories of the most significant experiences that have occurred during the use of a product. Storytelling in general has been regarded as an effective way to get a holistic view of the user experience [9,19]. For a user it is relatively easy to remember single remarkable experiences with the product without needing to engage in intensive cognitive reflection. Furthermore, storytelling methods also enable related contextual information like physical context, temporal context, task context, social context, and the technical and information context influencing the described event [15] to be recorded. Similar approaches of users reporting their momentary and episodic experiences remotely are utilized in *day reconstruction method* [16] and *experience sampling method* [21], from which we also draw inspiration.

What comes to related work on user experience of AR, very little research exists. The survey paper by Dünser et al. [8] shows that only approx. 10% of AR-related papers published 1992-2007 included some sort of user evaluation. Moreover, even those had limited to evaluating early prototypes, mostly looking into perception and cognition issues and user task performance (see e.g. [20]). More importantly, to the best of our knowledge, academic publications about user research on the aforementioned applications are so far virtually non-existent (excluding our prior publication [24]).

Finally, location-based service (LBS) is an important underlying theme of the current AR applications. The

[7]www.shopsavvy.mobi, [8]www.pic2shop.com, [9]www.stickybits.com

design targets are partially similar as in the current AR applications: for example including finding something or someone, proximity-based notifications and location-based communication. Regarding LBS, user research has been rather numerous. In addition to evaluating demonstrators of LBS technology, there has been research on users' needs and requirements [27], user acceptance and adoption [4], and user experience aspects [23]. As an example, Chang et al. [4] point out that adoption rates of location-aware services suffer from worry of security & privacy issues and quality of information. Other related concepts are object-based interaction, Internet of Things and physical browsing [3]. For example, linking social content with physical products has been seen as a viable way for users to receive ratings or other user-created information about products and thus help in decision-making [17]. However, because of the extent of these fields, we leave further discussion out of the scope of this paper.

OBJECTIVES AND METHODOLOGY

This paper addresses the question "What kinds of experiences have been present in interaction with current publicly available mobile AR-like applications?" We aim to gather qualitative insight on 1) the characteristics of experience that have taken place, 2) what features of the applications have had an influence on the experiences, and 3) under what kind of contextual factors have they occurred. The research question was approached with an extensive online survey for the users of current AR applications. In this paper we focus merely on the users' narratives of their most satisfying and unsatisfying experiences. Other parts of the survey, e.g. perceived strengths and weaknesses of the most used applications, have been published in another paper [24].

Survey Design and Dissemination

In the most central part of the survey we asked users to freely describe 1) the *most satisfying* and 2) the *most unsatisfying* single experience with the AR application that they had used the most. The most satisfying experiences were expected to reveal aspects like what kind of experiences users have regarded as the most pleasing or interesting, what features of the applications are appreciated, and what is the overall potential of AR in creating a rich, delightful UX. The most unsatisfying experiences were expected to support this by shedding light on what kind of experiences users have found most inconvenient and highlighting the central hindrances in the applications that cause them. The most satisfying experiences being our primary interest, and to avoid respondent fatigue during the entire 15-minute survey, it was not compulsory to report the most unsatisfying experience. This was also suggested by several pilot respondents, both fellow researchers and end users. The verbatim instructions for the respondents are presented next (similar instructions for the most unsatisfying experience).

> Think of the personally *most satisfying and unsatisfying* experiences or moments you have had with the application. Take a few minutes to be sure to come up with the most crucial experiences that you also remember well. If it is very hard for you to come up with the most unsatisfying one, it is ok to skip that.
>
> First, please consider the **most satisfying** one. We would like you to verbalize your experience as diversely as possible from your personal perspective. For example, you can consider the following things: **1)** what happened and what was the overall situation in which the experience occurred, **2)** how you felt about it or otherwise reacted to it, and **3)** what aspects when using the application do you think caused your feelings or reactions.

To measure the various contextual elements in the described situation, a set of Likert-statements regarding the context was applied from Partala & Kallinen [26]. After the experience narratives the respondents were asked to respond to UX-related subjective agreement statements operationalized from the experience categorization by Desmet [5,6], as well as our earlier findings on users' expectations [23] (statement #6 relating to intuitiveness and #7 to transparency). Such quantitative data from the statements was expected to support the qualitative insights from the experience narratives by looking into the diversity of experiences that have taken place overall. Here as well, the focus was on the respondents' most used application.

To ensure understandability of terminology and appropriate formulation of the questions, the survey was piloted first with 10 fellow researchers, all experts in empirical user research, and after that with 5 pilot respondents as representatives of end users.

To reach the target group of AR application users, the survey call was spread through various web channels, such as specific AR related groups in Facebook and LinkedIn, well-known AR related blogs (Games Alfresco, Augmented Times, Augmented Planet), and a few email lists consisting of students and university staff members from the field of information technology. Furthermore, Layar, Wikitude, Junaio and Stickybits kindly announced the survey link through their Facebook and Twitter feeds, which all reach thousands of relevant persons.

At the front page the concept of augmented reality was explained in layman's terms and a requirement for participation was declared: the respondent had to have used AR application(s) to such a degree that one can point out and describe one's experiences of them. The survey was informed to take about 15 minutes and that 50EUR Amazon.com gift cards would be raffled among the respondents. The survey was open for approximately a month during spring 2011.

Narrative Analysis

Analysis of the experience narratives was based on data-driven, theory-independent coding (grounded theory approach). First, common themes were interpreted from the data (open coding), iteratively constructing a hierarchy of categories in which each narrative could be classified. After this, each narrative was categorized into one or several categories. We argue that by not limiting the analysis on a specific UX framework, we could identify more relevant and a greater extent of different kinds of experiences.

The analysis aimed at identifying three underlying elements from each narrative: 1) goal or activity the user was engaged in, 2) characteristics of the experience that occurred, and 3) features of the application that evoked or catalyzed the experience. As the narratives were user-created, they often involved several different themes, which resulted in classifying each narrative to several categories (especially regarding the experience categories). The analysis was carried out with NVivo software, which provides a flexible way to construct, examine and revisit the themes and categorize the data. The categories were originally interpreted by one researcher but iterated in collaboration between two researchers. The same two researchers independently placed each narrative to the identified categories. Appropriate measures of inter-rater reliability are presented in the Results section.

Respondents

The survey page was visited 2277 times, and we received 95 responses, of which 90 could be included in the analysis (some of them were flawed or evident acts of mischief). 74 of the respondents were male, 15 female and one preferred not to report their gender. The mean age was 31 years, ages ranging from 16 to 65 years (median 28). The respondents represented a total of 18 nationalities, for example American (7), Dutch (7), German (6), Austrian (4), and Finnish (27, probably explained by the research team being located in Finland). 13 respondents preferred not to report their nationality. 43 respondents had completed an undergraduate degree and 41 had a master's degree or higher, meaning that in general the respondents were relatively highly educated.

The respondents were asked 8 Likert statements about their general attitudes to technology and experiences with it, which generally showed a high level of technological orientation. For example, they agreed strongly with statements about being active in using mobile services and other new technology. In this sense, the overall profile of the respondents is in line with our target of gathering user perspectives from early adopters who are technologically adept enough to understand the principles and possibilities of AR. It is important to understand how the first adopters of a new technology value it and what are the issues that they see to stand in the way of making it more widespread.

RESULTS

We first shortly describe background information about the used applications and contexts of use. The main contribution, i.e. the qualitative analysis of the most satisfying and unsatisfying experiences, is first introduced by a brief analysis of the users' activities and contextual factors related to the experiences. Finally, we shortly report the statistics about the subjective statements with regard to the respondents' overall UX.

Applications and Usage Statistics

Most respondents had been using several applications that match with our definition of an AR-like application (on average, 2.8 different applications per respondent). The question regarding the most used application highlights especially Layar (35 selections as the most used application), Google Goggles (22) and Junaio (16). Other responses included e.g. Stickybits (2), Nokia Point&Find, ShopSavvy and Pic2shop. All of the most used applications can be considered as representatives of an AR application that builds around location- or object-based information. Other, less used, applications represented a wide range: other utility-oriented AR browsers like SekaiCamera, Acrossair and FlightRadar24Pro, 3D augmentation (e.g. Argon), shopping-related (e.g. pic2shop, StickyBits, ShopSavvy), AR-gaming (e.g. Pandemica), and translation applications (e.g. WordLens).

The majority had used their most used application for a rather long time already. 73% had obtained their most used application already "3 months ago or more", 16% "1-3 months ago", and only 4% "1-4 weeks ago" and 4% "Less than a week ago" (3% "hard to say"). Additionally, over half reported having used the application on at least a weekly basis after installing it: 19% "Daily", 36% "Weekly", 24% "Monthly", and 18% "Less frequently than monthly" (3% hard to say).

With regard to the contexts of use, almost all had used the application in densely populated areas such as city centrums and campus areas or industrial areas, but sparsely populated or rural areas had also been the context for roughly 25% of the respondents. Outdoors use was very frequent as expected (78% had used) but indoors use was also common, e.g. at home (62%), at office (38%), in shops (31%), or at events & exhibitions (7%). Expectedly, the gps-based applications were more used outdoors whereas the marker- and object-based mostly indoors.

Activities and Contexts in the Experience Narratives

The users' activities taking place in the reported most satisfying and unsatisfying experiences were identified as part of the qualitative analysis. They included many practical use cases typical to the AR applications in question, and the categories were also very similar in both the satisfying and unsatisfying experiences (Table 1). The 'other' category in Table 1 includes e.g. just playing around, testing 3D features, and showing off. All in all, the activities include both very goal-oriented and explorative use. The activities are further exemplified by the user quotes in the upcoming sections.

The user's activity in the narrative	☺	☹
Identifying objects and acquiring additional information about them	16	16
Navigation and finding points of interest	13	7
Entertainment and art	10	0
Exploring the surroundings	8	7
Acquiring specific location-related information	6	0
Creating or utilizing own content	5	0
Work- and study-related activities	3	6
Shopping & price comparison	3	0
Translation	3	0
Other	6	6
Not able to identify	16	26

Table 1. Users' activities in the narratives of most satisfying (☺) and most unsatisfying (☹) experiences (# of cases).

The contextual factors related to the described experience were queried with six statements [26]. As shown in Table 2, the social context rarely had any influence on the experience, the reported experiences had occurred in both familiar and unfamiliar environments, and busyness was rarely present. The activity performed with the application was not considered especially critical in most cases. The need for the information had high variance (Std 2.1 in both), which consolidates the observation in the previous section about applications having been used both for a specific need and just for exploration and passing time. Interestingly, the distributions were highly similar in both types of experiences: in pairwise comparisons only the item about *technical problems* showed statistically significant difference between the most satisfying and unsatisfying experiences ($p<0.001$, Mann-Whitney U-test for independent samples). The 1-7 scales were treated as ordinal for methodological hygiene (non-Gaussian distributions). This was surprising as the *importance* and *need for information* were also expected to play a role here.

Statement and scale *Median*	☺	☹	*Sig.*
Other people influenced the experience… (1: not at all, 7: very much)	2.0	1.0	-
The environment that I was in was… (1: very unfamiliar, 7: very familiar)	5.0	6.0	-
I was… (1: in a big hurry, 7: not busy at all)	5.0	5.0	-
The activity I was doing was for me… (1: not at all important, 7: very important)	4.5	4.0	-
I was in need of the information that the application could possibly offer… (1: not at all, 7: very much)	4.0	4.0	-
Technical problems (e.g. malfunction) were involved in this event… (1: not at all, 7: very much)	2.0	5.5	***

Table 2. Medians of the contextual statements, significance of possible statistical difference between the satisfying and unsatisfying experiences. N_1=78–84, N_2=56–61.

Characteristics of Experiences and Related Application Features

In the following, we first characterize and categorize the most satisfying experiences and analyze which features of the application had evoked or catalyzed the experience in question. This is followed by a similar description and analysis of the unsatisfying experiences.

Satisfying Experiences

Altogether 84 narratives of satisfying experiences were included in the analysis: six responses were omitted because of vague or missing data or respondent not wanting to highlight any single experience. The descriptions were on average 157 characters long (max 579, min 10, median 125). The reported experiences had taken place relatively long ago, 37% at least 3 months ago and 26% 1-3 months ago, and only 19% less than 2 weeks ago. As a measure of inter-rater agreement, a Cohen's Kappa (considered as a conservative measure of agreement) coefficient of 0.74 was obtained, indicating a very high level of agreement.

The characteristics of experiences analyzed from the narratives demonstrate various instrumental and pragmatic experiences, fascination, interest and surprise experiences, and a few aesthetic and social experiences as well. 3/84 narratives did not contain enough information to allow identifying any specific experiences. On the other hand, a good number of narratives contained plenty detail that allowed us to identify several different types of experience from each of them.

The most instrumental and pragmatic experiences relate to sense of efficiency in carrying out information acquisition tasks (analyzed from 16 narratives), empowerment with new possibilities (26) and awareness of surroundings (27). The efficiency category includes aspects of saving time, money and effort, and feeling helped by technology in information acquisition tasks. Such experiences were often attributed to easiness of interaction, acquiring content that is related to the current location and perceived usefulness of the application in various tasks. Empowerment includes feelings of powerfulness and being provided with novel possibilities, tools and ways of creating, finding and utilizing information (functionalities one has not had access to before). These were also largely arisen from the usefulness of the application's functionality in general or in specific tasks, and content being location-based and thus relevant in the situation. However, this seemed to be also explained by the novelty value of AR (e.g. merging physical and virtual realities, new interaction paradigm), collaboration features and collectively created content. Experience of awareness relates to being educated about one's immediate surroundings (locations and objects), and finding novel aspects of already familiar environments. Again, the utility values and merging of realities mostly explain this experience. The first text box on the next page presents a few excerpts of the respondents' narratives representing the aforementioned categories of experience.

"I was with a friend and we could not make out what was written in German on the back of a parked truck ... I whipped out my Android phone, fired up the app, pointed the camera at it and within a minute we knew what we were reading. Pretty handy!" (Indian male, 25, Google Goggles)

"... It was very satisfying because I could stand on the line of Hadrian's Wall, seeing the forts and towers spread off into the distance - but with the little markers hanging above them, telling me what each turret was." (British male, 32, Layar)

"I was in urgent need of ATM ... so I used junaio to find one. And for my luck it was just other side of the street which I just happened to miss. Well luckily to junaio I saved time, got me in better mood and I was fascinated about technology which can work as your eyes" (Finnish male, 23, Junaio)

"I actually was able to identify a (fairly obscure) person in a photo that I had no information on at all -- quite a remarkable achievement, based on purely visual information." (American male, 55, Google Goggles)

"... when you need to find information fast that relates to your immediate location..." (British male, 40, Layar)

A good number of narratives demonstrated experiences of fascination or general interest on the technology (example quotes shown in the upper text box on the right). These mostly resulted from the novelties in technology and the uncommon way of interaction. These types of experiences include examples from positive amazement (14 narratives) to general excitement and interest (9). Especially the first-mentioned were often related to the first time of use, thus attributed especially to the charm of novelty in AR. The respondents used terms such as "cool", "clever", "magic", "wow effect", "unique", and showed general interest towards engaging in the new world augmented with virtual elements. Some experiences of fascination and excitement were explained by the wide potential in utilizing and commercializing AR. Partly related to these, a few explicit mentions of feelings of getting immersed into the mixed reality were identified (3).

Experiences of surprise arose both from the functionality (11) and information content (6). These include aspects of delightful surprise arising from finding very useful, momentarily relevant or unexpectedly great amount of content, and the application performing much better than expected and actually tackling the dubious things promised in the application description (esp. highlighting Google Goggles). Examples in the text box mid-right.

A few narratives contained social aspects (7), demonstrating e.g. real time collaboration, remote social connectedness, altruism, or shared experience in situ. Finally, 14 narratives showed experiences of mediocre pleasure or gratitude. Such almost neutral experiences did not show as much excitement as the aforementioned, and had arisen from the practical help and interesting information provided by the application, overall usefulness, easiness of the way of interacting, and helping in work or business. Examples are shown in the text box lower right.

"Moved to rural area and used the tweet plug-in to locate people close to me. When I launched it I found an old school friend I hadn't seen in like 15 yrs., all because I recognized their picture ... The feelings were excitement and thought it was trick..."(Caucasian female, 38, Layar)

"The first time my experiment worked and I had result on my phone, I felt confused and powerful. It was possible for me to visualize any information around me that could not be seen by the naked eye ... Old philosophic questions came up; what is real and reality? How we know what we see is real? That all was amazing!" (Dutch male, 32, Junaio)

"When I first time saw how an AR application can add content to a live picture. It was great to understand how big opportunities there are in AR field." (Finnish female, 28, StickyBits)

"Experience the existence of a truly 3D virtual world around me. The satisfaction of being surrounded, and having the possibility to really walk around the objects, made the virtual environment very real." (Dutch male, 37, MoMA AR exhibition)

"Using Google Goggles to solve a sudoku that would have otherwise been left unsolved. This experience certainly surprised me, because Goggles worked so well and I wasn't expecting it to." (Finnish male, 23, Google Goggles)

"... Then I tried google goggles and it translated the text for me. It was very surprising that it worked so well." (Finnish male, 25, Google Goggles)

"When I first used the application I was positively surprised. I felt the application did what the description promised and the information provided was useful." (Finnish male, 23, Google Goggles)

"Desperately wanting an item but hating the price at a local store. Used Shopsavvy and found it for over 90% off. That was a fab day and allowed me to get something I really wanted, save a lot of money, and not be guilty about it! ..." (American female, 38, ShopSavvy)

"Playing with Biggar, a world-sized augmented reality art piece that is interactive. It was exciting to see it change live due to inputs of users from around the world." (Male, 30, Layar)

"Being lost in a foreing city, hungry and no idea where to eat. Layar helped me find restaurants close to my location and I was able to get more information and reviews from google without even closing the app ... I was really happy and thankful because I didn't have to walk around in search of a restaurant. It saved time and time is worth a lot, I think that's the reason for my happy reaction." (German female, 26, Layar)

"Creating new AR cases for our clients is every time very satisfying." (German male, 26, Junaio)

"I was able to help someone to get to the hospital, using Layar to point them the right direction." (Portuguese male, 23, Layar)

Unsatisfying Experiences

With regard to unsatisfying experiences, we included 65 narratives in the analysis. As this part of the survey was not compulsory, 17 left this empty. Six were omitted because of too vague or unspecific narrative or mentions of having had no bad experiences. A Cohen's Kappa coefficient of

0.64 was obtained, indicating a good inter-rater agreement. The descriptions were on average 134 characters long (max 559, min 12, median 114). These experiences were slightly more recent than the satisfying ones: 22% at least 3 months ago, 25% 1-3 months ago, 11% 3-4 weeks ago, and 34% less than 2 weeks ago. However, no statistical significances were found with regard the recentness of most unsatisfying vs. satisfying experiences.

The reported unsatisfying experiences are much more homogeneous than the satisfying ones, mostly limited to manifesting different grades of dissatisfaction: explicitly mentioned frustration or strong irritation (5), disappointment from not completing one's task or meeting one's goal-oriented expectations (27), and general dissatisfaction resulting from, e.g., small functionality problems or other limitations (25). The aforementioned categories include aspects of not finding what looking for, expectations not being met, doing things in vain, not having hardware powerful or robust enough, poor overlay and mixing of realities, and application not being useful, usable or efficient enough in the activities it was used for. A few examples of such narratives below.

> *"Barcode scanning ... due to the poor camera it was really difficult to get a hit indoors even with lights on. Experience is frustrating when the barcode isn't recognized even after multiple attempts."* (Finnish male, 26, Google Goggles)
>
> *"... when the software didn't recognize anything from a well-known scenery."* (male, 25, Google Goggles)
>
> *"90% of the use is unsatisfying. Usually GG does not recognize the items or context that I'm trying to picture. I see its potential as a tool to search information on something that can't be easily described in words. So far it's failing in that. If I shoot a street view, I don't need more pictures of streets. I want location based information and list of shops, POI, etc. that can be found from the direction I'm looking at."* (Finnish male, 28, Google Goggles)
>
> *"Expecting to have information available but it isn't there. I guess this is failed expectations. ... I believe I want to see AR succeed the way I want it to and it's not there by a long shot."* (American male, 51, Layar)

Other unsatisfying experiences manifested being flooded with information (2), and asocial and alone (3), e.g. as results of not having enough content or other users available to make real use of the application. Examples of these in the text box on the right. In addition, there were 3 narratives where clearly a deficiency of the application has been expressed but the resulted experience remains unclear, and one that mentioned that every single experience so far have been unsatisfying.

Subjective Statements about Overall Experiences

In the end of the survey, the respondents were presented statements about how often they have experienced various things while using the selected application. In Figure 1, the statements have been reordered from the originally randomized order. As shown in Figure 1, the respondents

> *"In general, apps like Wikitude are not helpful when they're flooded with virtual billboards for pizza restaurants and real estate agents. If AR is used like this, it will just be noise."* (American male, 55, Layar)
>
> *"Encountering content that is not yet finished. Arriving in a Layar to 'score' the world. But there wasn't any content anywhere. Felt like I was totally alone, the only user in an empty augmented world."* (Dutch male, 37, Layar)
>
> *"Barcode leads to incorrect or too unspecific results to make it useful. I have also been harassed by shop staff for taking 'photos' of barcodes."* (35, Amazon pricecheck)
>
> *"I cannot pinpoint one particular example, sometimes the location is not accurate enough and points close to me are not where they should be."* (Austrian male, 27, Wikitude)

agreed that they felt knowledgeable about their surroundings rather frequently, which is well in line with the findings from the narratives. Most often, the respondents felt stimulated by the AR information, felt it playful to interact with it, and were positively surprised by it (statements 2-4). The element of surprise largely corresponds with the experience narratives. However, playfulness and stimulation were not explicitly mentioned as central elements of the most satisfying experiences but apparently such experience have been present in the application usage over time.

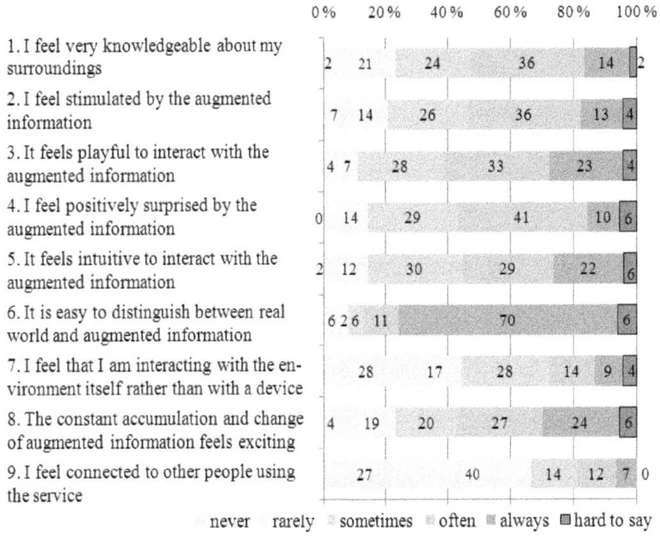

Figure 1. "In general, how often do you experience the following when using the application?" (N=90).

As the integration of virtual and real worlds currently remains at rather austere level, the augmented content seemed very easy to distinguish from the real world (statement 6). Nevertheless, feeling of interacting with the environment instead of a device had been present surprisingly often, although almost one third had never experienced such an immersive experience with the application. Related to stimulation as well, augmented information and its constant accumulation (statement 8) provided excitement quite often. However, social connectedness has not been emphasized in the experiences although in many applications the content is largely created by other users.

DISCUSSION AND CONCLUSIONS

We first summarize the results and the contribution of the paper, after which the identified experiences are reflected to prior frameworks and studies of user experience. Finally, we discuss the central take-away lessons, methodological reliability issues, and share ideas for future work.

Summarizing the Findings and Contribution

The contribution of the paper is the understanding of early adopters' most satisfying and unsatisfying experiences with current consumer targeted mobile AR applications. We have identified experience categories that either could be targeted at (satisfying) or should be avoided (unsatisfying) in designing novel mobile AR service concepts as well as specific features. The paper illustrates central UX concepts and issues in the domain of mobile AR, but they can also be considered with other emerging mobile and ubiquitous technologies.

Most often the satisfying experiences showed pragmatic and instrumental aspects of *efficiency* in information acquisition, *empowerment* with novel and unequalled tools and ways of utilizing information, and *awareness* of the digital content related to one's immediate surroundings. *Strong amazement*, *general excitement* and *surprise* seem to have been the most frequent emotionally oriented satisfying experiences. A few narratives demonstrated experiences of *immersion* in the mixed reality, and a few others *social* experiences. All in all, the most satisfying experiences that users reported are mostly explained by the instrumental utility value and usefulness of the application's content in various information acquisition activities. The interaction and interface specific to AR seems to have contributed mostly to the experiences of *awareness* and *immersion*. The charm of novelty in terms of AR as a new concept and the new functionalities mostly explains emotional experiences of *fascination* and *amazement*. As most AR content is location-based, it was often regarded relevant in the situation, which further facilitated experiences of awareness, empowerment and surprise. Finally, some applications' performance and content exceeding the users' expectations created positive experiences of surprise.

The most unsatisfying experiences highlight mostly different grades of instrumental dissatisfaction: from *frustration* to *disappointment* and *general dissatisfaction*. Altogether, the unsatisfying experiences show less variance and interesting aspects with regard to our general research agenda of exploring the UX of AR applications. The unsatisfied experiences are mainly results of inadequately performing technology (e.g. hardware deficiencies) or instrumental expectations not being met. As many of the applications are rather immature both regarding extent of functionalities and usability, the probable experiential challenges fall in the minority (e.g. issues related to relevance, reliability and liveliness of content, interacting with AR, or AR causing physical risks in the surroundings).

The agreement statements mostly consolidate the experience narratives, especially considering experiences of awareness and surprise. However, the statements also brought up experiences of playfulness, intuitiveness of interaction and stimulation from content to be present when using the applications. Such experiences – and probably many others – were clearly not dominant enough to be highlighted as a "critical incident". Finally, regarding the contextual factors in satisfying vs. unsatisfying experiences only the item about presence of technical problems showed a statistically significant difference. In other words, with regard to such a novel technology, at least the most remarkable experiences seem to originate mostly from the product itself instead of the contextual factors.

Reflection to Prior Work and UX Frameworks

On one hand, especially the most satisfying experiences represent a surprisingly good number of different situations where AR applications have been used, but on the other hand, the overall diversity of different types of experiences is surprisingly low. When reflecting to our earlier research on potential users' expectations of AR-related technologies [23], we can see that especially the pragmatic experiences like increased awareness, efficiency and empowerment largely correspond with the expectation studies. However, there are several characteristics of experience that have been expected but are missing in this data: for example, experience of *inspiration* (encouraged, cognitively stimulated and eager to try new things), *playfulness & entertainment* (joy, amusement and playfulness), *liveliness* (constantly acquiring new and updated content that is socially constructed), *creativity* (self-expressive and artistic feelings in mixing digital with the real), and *intuitiveness* (naturalness and human-likeness in interacting with AR).

The results can be further examined in the light of various general UX frameworks. Regarding the appraisal theory of product emotions by Desmet [5], our findings of the abstract product features that explain experiences are very similar. The *charm of novelty* seemed to largely explain the surprise emotions and amazement – especially as many of the satisfying experiences were rather old and related to the first-time use. The *motive compliance* (product satisfying a goal) partly explained the instrumental emotions, such as disappointment and general satisfaction. The interest emotions like fascination are partly explained by the *challenges and promise* in AR. Nevertheless, aesthetic emotions like attraction or disgust are more or less non-existent in the data, which is almost the case of social emotions like admiration as well. Furthermore, considering the framework by Hassenzahl [11], this data covers the *pragmatic* aspects very well. *Stimulation* is covered to some extent by amazement and surprise. However, *identification* and *evocation* appear in only few narratives although the premise for them is high: an AR application could be used to communicate and build one's identity, e.g., by creating content in it, and the location-related content could easily evoke related memories.

Design Considerations

From an experiential point of view, current AR-like applications leave much to desire – but at the same time space and potential for design. The aforementioned limitations in the diversity of the identified experiences could be interpreted to further confirm that the current AR applications exhibit low technical maturity and are still in their infancy. For example related to the most unsatisfying features, the applications' experiential and emotion-related weaknesses do not emerge and become highlighted because the weaknesses in functionality and usability (i.e. "hygiene factors") are so dominant in causing bad experiences. Regarding satisfying experiences, although the applications were used rather frequently, the narrations showed only few cases where the use has been somehow playful, innovative, collaborative, or fooling around. In addition, the social and collaboration elements in the applications are clearly too limited to create of a sense of community or provide social values. Such aspects could, however, foster and ensure the creation of content that is useful and semantically rich.

Many of the identified experiences are rather common and generic by nature, meaning that the most AR specific features (e.g. related to AR interaction and visualization of content) affect them rather little. Many of the satisfying experiences were largely resulting from location-based features and content instead of being characteristic to AR per se. Hence, there is much design potential in catalyzing experiences of, e.g., immersion, intuitiveness and awareness, which can be considered more typical of AR.

In long term, the overall value and UX of the applications is most probably not as dependent on the functionalities provided as they are on the richness, relevance, aesthetics and trustworthiness of the content. As mobile AR competes with mobile web browsers and other location-based services in *acquiring surrounding digital information*, the content is a critical design factor. It has to truly take advantage of AR instead of being merely aggregated from web services (e.g. 3D and animated augmentations, high contextual relevance, and tangible interactivity).

Methodological Considerations and Future Work

Regarding reliability of the methodology, some issues of bias need to be highlighted in order to assess the overall utility of the results. First, regarding the choice of method, we can question if some of the experience categories in prior research are perhaps too implicit, unconscious or not dominant enough (e.g. aesthetics or inspiration) for a user to identify them in the first place or to consider them important enough for highlighting them as a *critical incident*. The UX statements implied that the diversity of experiences in AR is actually greater than those identified in the narratives. CIT excelled in elicit strong pragmatic experiences like awareness or dissatisfaction but other methods might be needed to look into to the less dominant, transient or unconscious experiences. In addition, limiting the number of narratives asked per respondent to 1+1 might also have led people to report the clearly strongest experiences, thus concealing the less dominant ones.

Second, such retrospective evaluations are naturally exposed to possible memory and retrieval bias. A memory of a past experience might not contain all the subtleties, especially after longer periods of time. Nevertheless, measuring the remembered experience is important and valid in the sense that the decisions about future use or application purchases are made based on memories as well. UX is known to be time-dependent and we gathered many narratives about incidents from several months ago. Nevertheless, we regard this justifiable as a research approach and valid for others to learn from: 1) the approach allowed us to gather a good number of subjectively *most meaningful* experiences about a domain that is little known. Gathering momentary experiences over a certain period of use would have been more laborious for the users and most probably would have contained more irrelevant narratives for both the AR development and UX research. Many of the narratives represented the first time use, which is critical for the user's understanding of AR as a concept; 2) the reported critical experiences are significant for the users in assessing the goodness and value of the application as well as AR as a technology in general; 3) the applications in question have not developed radically during this time so that the experiences of today would be totally different.

The generalizability of the results slightly suffers from the low response rate (2277 visits on survey page vs. 93 respondents). The amount of respondents did not allow statistical analysis regarding, for example, correlation between the experience categories and application features evoking them. Although our intention was to attract early adopters and there is little knowledge of the overall target population, we assume that our respondents represent a slightly biased set of the current users such applications: very high technology orientation and education, uneven nationality distribution, some respondents being developers as well, respondents being self-selected. Considering the above-mentioned, the numeric results should not be looked too closely or generalized to AR application users overall. After all, in such explorative research it is more important to pay attention to the diversity and richness of the data.

With regard to future research, the question of what is particular to the experiences of AR is not fully addressed yet, and it deserves further research. In addition, we are planning a field study with diary and interviewing methods for the same target group but focusing on how the UX of AR applications has changed over time. Despite many very unsatisfying experiences, most reported to be still using their application, which brings up the question of what elements in the applications have maintained their interest.

ACKNOWLEDGMENTS
We thank Kaisa Väänänen-Vainio-Mattila, Lauri Frank, Antti Hautamäki, Heli Väätäjä, Eija Kaasinen, Markus Makkonen, Seppo Risku, Minna Kynsilehto, Tuomas Vaittinen, and Charles Woodward for their insightful comments in planning the survey and finalizing the paper.

REFERENCES
1. Azuma, R.T. Tracking requirements for augmented reality. *Communications of the ACM* 36, 7 (1993), 50-51.
2. Barba, E., MacIntyre, B., Rouse, R., Bolter, J. Thinking inside the box: Making meaning in a handheld AR experience. In *Proc. ISMAR 2010*, IEEE (2010), 19-26.
3. Barthel, R., Hudson-Smith, A., Jode, M., Blundell, B. Tales of things. The Internet of 'old' things: collecting stories of objects, places and spaces. In *Proc. Internet of Things*, IEEE (2010).
4. Chang, S.E., Hsieh, Y., Lee, T., Liao, C., Wang, S. A user study on the adoption of location based services. In *Proc. APWeb/WAIM Workshops* (2007), 276-286.
5. Desmet, P. *Designing emotions*. Dissertation, Delft University of Technology, 2002.
6. Desmet, P. & Hekkert, P. Framework of product experience. *International Journal of Design* 1, 1 (2007), 57-66.
7. Desmet, P., Porcelijn, R., van Dijk, M. Emotional design; Application of a research-based design approach. *Knowledge, Technology & Policy* 20, 3 (2007), 141-155.
8. Dünser, A., Grasset, R., Billinghurst, M. A survey of evaluation techniques used in augmented reality studies, In *Proc. ACM SIGGRAPH 2008*, ACM Press (2008).
9. Geven, A., Schrammel, J., Tscheligi, M. Narrations and storytelling as methodological key elements for studying user experience. In *Proc. NordiCHI COST294-MAUSE*, ACM Press (2006), 79-83.
10. Gremler, D. The critical incident technique in service research. *Journal of Service Research* 7, 1 (2004), 65-89.
11. Hassenzahl, M. *The thing and I: understanding the relationship between user and product.* In Funology: From Usability to Enjoyment, Blythe, M. et al. (Eds). Kluwer Academic Publishers, 2003, pp 31-42.
12. Höllerer, T. & Feiner, S. *Mobile Augmented Reality*. In Karimi, H. & Hammad, A. (Eds), Telegeoinformatics: Location-Based Computing and Services, Taylor & Francis Books Ltd, 2004.
13. ISO FDIS 9241-210:2009. Ergonomics of human system interaction - Part 210: Human-centred design for interactive systems. International Organisation for Standardisation, ISO (2009).
14. Jordan. P.W. *Designing pleasurable products*. CRC Press, 2002.
15. Jumisko-Pyykkö, S. & Vainio, T. Framing the context of use in mobile HCI. *International Journal of Mobile Human-Computer Interaction* 2, 4, (2010), 1-28.
16. Kahnemann, D., Krueger, A., Schkade, D., Schwarz, N., Stone, A. A survey method for characterizing daily life experience: The day reconstruction method. *Science 3* 306, 5702 (2004), 1776-1780b
17. Karpischek, S. & Michahelles, F. my2cents – Digitizing consumer opinions and comments about retail products. In *Proc. Internet of Things*, IEEE (2010).
18. Kindberg, T. Implementing physical hyperlinks using ubiquitous identifier resolution. In *Proc. World Wide Web*, ACM Press (2002), 191-199.
19. Korhonen, H., Arrasvuori,J., Väänänen-Vainio-Mattila, K. Let users tell the story: Evaluating user experience with experiencer. In *CHI Extended Asbtracts*, ACM Press (2010), 4051-4056.
20. Kruijff, E. Swan, E., Feiner, S. Perceptual issues in augmented reality revisited. In *Proc. ISMAR 2010*, IEEE (2010), 3-12.
21. Larson, R., & Csikszentmihalyi, M. The experience sampling method. *New Directions for Methodology of Social and Behavioral Science* 15, (1983), 41-56.
22. Olsson, T., Ihamäki, P., Lagerstam, E., Ventä-Olkkonen, L., Väänänen-Vainio-Mattila, K. User expectations for mobile mixed reality services. In *Proc. ECCE'09*, ACM Press (2009), 177-184.
23. Olsson, T., Lagerstam, E., Kärkkäinen, T., Väänänen-Vainio-Mattila, K. Expected user experience of mobile augmented reality services: A user study in the context of shopping centers. *Journal of Personal and Ubiquitous Computing*, Online first (2011).
24. Olsson, T. & Salo, M. Online user survey on current mobile augmented reality applications. In *Proc. ISMAR 2011*, IEEE (2011), 75-84.
25. Paay, J. & Kjeldskov, J. Understanding the user experience of location-based services: five principles of perceptual organizations applied. *Journal of Location Based Services* 2, 4 (2008).
26. Partala, T. & Kallinen, A. Understanding the most satisfying and unsatisfying user experiences: emotions, psychological needs, and context. *Accepted to Interacting with Computers*.
27. Vaittinen, T., Kärkkäinen, T., Olsson, T. A diary study on annotating locations with mixed reality information. In *Proc. Mobile Ubiquitous Multimedia 2010*, ACM Press (2010), Article No. 21.
28. Vallino, J. Interactive augmented reality. Dissertation, University of Rochester (1998).

Exploring User Motivations for Eyes-free Interaction on Mobile Devices

Bo Yi[1], Xiang Cao[2], Morten Fjeld[3], Shengdong Zhao[1]

[1]Dept. of Computer Science
National University of Singapore
{yi-bo, zhaosd}@ comp.nus.edu.sg

[2]Microsoft Research Asia
Beijing, China
xiangc@microsoft.com

[3]t2i Lab, Dept. of Applied IT
Chalmers University of Technology
morten@fjeld.ch

ABSTRACT

While there is increasing interest in creating eyes-free interaction technologies, a solid analysis of why users need or desire eyes-free interaction has yet to be presented. To gain a better understanding of such user motivations, we conducted an exploratory study with four focus groups, and suggest a classification of motivations for eyes-free interaction under four categories (*environmental, social, device features, and personal*). Exploring and analyzing these categories, we present early insights pointing to design implications for future eyes-free interactions.

Author Keywords

Eyes-free; user motivation; mobile devices.

ACM Classification Keywords

H.5.m [Information Interfaces and Presentation (e.g., HCI)]: Miscellaneous;

INTRODUCTION

Interaction with and through mobile devices tends to rely primarily on users' visual attention. However, visual attention is a limited resource and is often heavily taxed by contextual factors in mobile environments. Researchers and designers have recently tried out alternative modalities such as acoustic and haptic to assist interaction with mobile devices and minimize the reliance on visual attention, also known as eyes-free interaction [1, 2, 4, 8, 9].

When designing such interactive systems, an important principle, as argued by Alan Cooper [3], is to satisfy the needs and desires of the user. It emphasizes that we perform tasks in order to achieve specific goals. Applying this principle to the design of effective eyes-free interaction requires an understanding of user motivations in order to provide the best way to support eyes-free interaction. While many innovative systems with eyes-free interaction capabilities have been introduced [1, 2, 4, 9], there is a lack of systematic investigation into the fundamental user motivations that drive the need and desire for eyes-free interaction.

In this paper, we present a user-centered exploration of user motivations in choosing eyes-free technologies for mobile interaction. To assure a wide range of user feedback, we held four focus groups with twenty-two participants in total and identified ten typical user motivations for eyes-free interaction, classified into four categories (environmental, social, device features, and personal) as defined by the intersection of two dimensions (contextual vs. independent; physical vs. human).

We present contributions intended to increase understanding of eyes-free interaction in the following two aspects: 1) From a user's perspective, we systematically examine motivations for eyes-free interaction on mobile devices, and further describe a categorization for them; 2) By exploring the characteristics of these motivations, we establish high level design implications for satisfying users' needs and goals.

METHOD

In order to collect user motivations for eyes-free interaction in an open-ended fashion, we chose to use focus groups, which are particularly suitable for early exploration in identifying new problems and assessing users' needs [5].

Participants

Twenty-two participants (indexed P1-P22; 13 male and 9 female) from a diverse background (14 students from different disciplines: computer science (8), biology (3) and Chinese studies (3), 8 working professionals from different industries: banking (1), telecommunications (4), education (2), and IT (1)) were recruited for our focus groups. Average age was 26.7 years (SD=7.40). All participants had more than 5 years of experience in using mobile devices. Each focus group had 5 or 6 participants.

Procedure

Four focus groups were conducted. Each of them lasted approximately 90 minutes with the following five steps. 1) The moderator introduced the purpose of this research. (~5 mins); 2) The moderator introduced the concept of "eyes-free" with the demonstration using two tasks: volume change in HTC G2 and text typing in Dopod C750 (~5 mins); 3) Participants performed a self-introduction and discussed their first impression of eyes-free interaction (~15 mins); 4) In the main discussion participants freely discussed three themes: a) situations where visual interaction is not suitable, b) experience of using eyes-free interaction and c) expectations of eyes-free technologies (~1 hour); 5) Summary and debriefing (~10 mins).

Analysis

Each focus group was filmed; the recordings were transcribed and coded based on the Grounded Theory [7] by the two experimenters. The following measures were taken to minimize the influence of less logical statements that often occur in focus groups towards the validity of motivation categorization: 1) Participants were encouraged and guided by the moderator to reflect on and verbalize the underlying logical meaning behind their statements; 2) During the coding phase, less logical statements that were not backed up by other statements were not used as evidence.

A CATEGORIZATION OF MOTIVATIONS

Via clustering and merging, ten motivations for using eyes-free interaction in mobile context (identified as M1 to M10) emerged from the focus groups. We identified the properties of each motivation and found that they were related to specific settings and originated in either the physical or human realm. Based on this observation, the ten motivations were categorized along two orthogonal dimensions as shown in Table 1.

	Physical	Human
Contextual	***Environmental*** **M1**: Enable operations under extreme lighting conditions (e.g. [2]) **M2**: Improve safety in task-switching (e.g. [2])	***Social*** **M3**: Foster social respect (e.g. [1]) **M4**: Avoid interruption to social activities (e.g. [1]) **M5**: Protect private information (e.g. [4])
Independent	***Device Features*** **M6**: Enable operation with no/small screen (e.g. [9]) **M7**: Enable multitasking on same device (e.g. [4])	***Personal*** **M8**: Entertainment **M9**: Serve desire for self-expression **M10**: Lower perceived effort

Table 1. Categorization of user motivations for using eyes-free interaction: based on two dimensions (contextual vs. independent; physical vs. human) we sorted all motivations into four categories (environmental, social, device features, and personal).

The first dimension is the context dependency, which can be either contextual or independent. The second dimension is the realm, which can be either physical or human. Crossing these two dimensions results in four categories: environmental, social, device features, and personal. Now, we present, examine, exemplify, and discuss the ten motivations (M1 to M10) by category.

Environmental (contextual + physical)

In many environments interaction with mobile devices is interfered with or prevented by the characteristics of that environment.

As participants indicated, extreme lighting conditions are a major source of interference to visual perception (M1) [2], which can be either too bright or too dark. In the former situation, participants complained that overly bright situations, such as direct sunlight, often make the screen unreadable, *"It's hard for me to read the text while walking in bright light. So I have to try to find a place without so much light."* (P3) In the latter situation, one participant mentioned her experience when working in a dark room for film development: *"I often needed to answer calls or wanted to switch the music, but I was developing photographs in a dark room where the light from the screen was not allowed."* (P5)

Another motivation frequently mentioned is improving safety in contexts where switching visual attention between the device and the physical environment poses safety concerns (M2) [2]. For example, it is hazardous to switch visual attention between a mobile device and the road while driving. Nonetheless, such simultaneous usage is often unavoidable: *"Everyone knows it's dangerous to use mobile phones while driving, but I just want to use it. I think it's a part of my life."* (P8)

Social (contextual + human)

As indicated by Palen et al. [6], using mobile devices has become a part of social norms. However, in some situations overtly using a mobile device is socially inappropriate (M3 and M4), while some other situations raised privacy concerns (M5).

In some social settings, openly interacting with mobile devices is unanticipated and sometimes unacceptable. For instance, while talking with others, frequently playing with mobile phones is impolite and may leave a bad impression on the other party. Nonetheless, sometimes attending to the mobile device is necessary (e.g. an urgent message). In that case, users can be motivated to use eyes-free interaction to reduce the perceived interference between mobile interaction and the surrounding social activities to maintain social respect (M3) to others [1], *"When I was doing a presentation, a phone call came and I felt the vibration. I couldn't take it out because it was impolite. So I just reached into the pocket and pressed the end button."* (P10)

In other situations, users may voluntarily desire to pay more attention to the surrounding social activity, such as when attending a lecture. In that case, avoiding the interruption to the social activities (M4) can motivate users to adopt eyes-free interaction [1]. For example, one participant described such a situation where eyes-free interaction can facilitate quick responses – *"I often text messages in class. But in math class, sometimes I had to copy the formulas written by the teacher so that I couldn't pay attention to the received messages. So sometimes I missed some appointments."* (P3)

Besides maintaining social relationships, users may also be motivated to use eyes-free interaction for protecting privacy. More specifically, interaction relying on visual feedback has the danger of leaking private information to others in social contexts (M5) [4]. Eyes-free interaction is expected to reduce this risk by hiding the user input (e.g. the operation of pressing buttons) and/or the device output (e.g. displayed visual information). As one participant indicated, *"I am always worried that my password could be seen by others when I am in a queue."* (P11)

Device Features (independent + physical)

Sometimes, users would like to use eyes-free interaction with their mobile devices due to the physical constraint of the devices themselves. In order to overcome inconveniences (M6 and M7) caused by device constraints, users are motivated to adopt eyes-free interaction.

Participants mentioned two types of inconveniences related to eyes-free interaction on mobile devices. On one hand, devices designed with small or even no screens (M6) make interaction using visual feedback difficult and/or irrelevant [9]. For example, *"There is no screen on my iPod shuffle. But I can operate it very well just with the audio feedback."* (P2) On the other hand, interruptions can happen while performing multiple tasks on the same mobile device (M7) [4], which can motivate users to use eyes-free interaction to reduce the interruption: *"When talking with my customers on the phone, I have to frequently check my schedule in my phone to make appointments. So I have to frequently suspend the phone conversation to look at the screen. It's very inconvenient."* (P20)

Personal (independent + human)

In addition to achieving practical goals, eyes-free interaction is also motivated by personal factors. In this category, the motivations (M8, M9, and M10) are more intrinsic to the users themselves and not necessarily dependent on devices or contexts.

Some participants indicated that they would like to use eyes-free interaction just because they thought it was fun to use (M8). The joy is generated from the unusual experience and the resulting sense of accomplishment. As one participant said, *"I can experience very different things when I am using eyes-free interaction. I think I am very good if I can succeed."* (P17)

Several participants also indicated that their desires for self-expression (M9) made them take the initiative to use eyes-free interaction. One participant said, *"It's cool to show my friends that I can use my phone without using my eyes. I think they envied me and I felt proud."* (P10)

Interestingly, participants mentioned that sometimes they used eyes-free interaction even when it was possible to visually focus on the mobile devices. An underlying reason may be that some users perceived the cognitive/physical effort for eyes-free interaction (M10) to be lower than for visual interaction. For example, one participant mentioned, *"When I enter the library, I need to switch my phone to silent mode. But it's troublesome to take the phone out. So I like to do it in my pocket without looking at the phone."* (P4)

DISCUSSION

Although our investigation has covered a variety of different motivations, this is meant to be a list of representative motivations instead of an exhaustive one. We expect the categorization suggested will help to identify more user motivations in the future. Still, we believe this list provides a solid initial basis for discussion of design insights for the diversity of motivations, the concurrency and shifting of motivations, and related design implications.

Diversity of Motivations

Our results have shown that there is a diversity of motivations for eyes-free interaction, ranging from environmental constraints to personal intentions. Designing a single eyes-free solution to cover all those motivations is challenging and perhaps undesired, but it is essential for designers to be aware of this diversity. Much research has focused on eyes-free interaction widgets, which are more or less designed as a general technique (e.g. earPod [9]). However, in order for such inventions to be widely adopted by users, mechanisms to adapt and customize them to various user motivations may be key.

By exploring the diversity of motivations, we also surprisingly find that personal intentions may play an important role in motivating eyes-free interaction. On one hand, this reveals future potential innovations such as the design of eyes-free systems for entertainment. On the other hand, perhaps more significantly, it highlights the role of enjoyment when designing eyes-free interaction.

Concurrency and Shifting of Motivations

It is important for designers to understand how multiple motivations can play a joint role. That is, frequently a small number of motivations are not independent and may all be in effect concurrently during an activity.

In our study, concurrency of motivations is observed in two aspects. First, as a kind of basic demand, it is quite common for users to mix M10 together with other motivations. For example, participants who reported to be in outdoor environments with bright sunlight also complained that the small screen influenced their operations and that they expected eyes-free interaction to require less effort.

"Sometimes when I am walking (M2) in bright daylight (M1), I have to search for someone's contact information in my phone. I have to make too much effort (M10) to recognize the text in the small screen (M6)." (P19)

Second, if the user is in a specific context, different motivations related to the contextual dimension often complement one another. For example, in social activities, the need to avoid interrupting social activities often complements the need to foster social respect.

"My friend was supposed to present at a seminar. But he was late and his professor asked me about his whereabouts, I wanted to send a message to get my friend to contact his supervisor immediately. But I had to focus on the chat with the professor (M4) and I didn't want to be rude (M3)." (P8)

Besides the concurrency of motivations for the same user and device, there are cases when the user, while attempting to complete a task, is exposed to different situations consecutively, each of them requiring eyes-free interaction but with different motivations, which we call "shifting". For example, as one participant mentioned, *"When I am driving, typing text may be dangerous (M2). But after I arrive at the destination and talk with others, typing text could be impolite (M3)."* (P14) In both situations, the task was the same (typing text), and both had the need for eyes-free interaction, but the motivations were different (M2 vs. M3).

Design Implications

Based on the observations and analysis of user motivations, we highlight three groups of implications for the design of eyes-free interactions in mobile usage.

Make the interaction method adaptive to changing motivations: As discussed above, the user may want to use eyes-free interaction with different motivations at different times. In this case, a single interaction method may not satisfy different motivations unless dynamic adaptation occurs. We notice that motivations often vary together with changes in the contextual settings. So designers could leverage context-aware technologies to facilitate such adaptive interaction methods. For example, by detecting the change in contextual settings, non-visual reminders could change from vibrations in a meeting room (e.g. M3 and M4) to audio cues while driving a car (e.g. M2).

Seamlessly integrate with social activities: During social activities, eyes-free interaction demands more social responsibility (e.g. M3, M4, and M5). So designers need to think about the social impact of interaction methods they design for eyes-free interaction. Ideally, eyes-free interaction should be subtle and socially acceptable. One possible solution is embedding eyes-free interaction into commonplace objects and socially acceptable behaviors such as rotating a finger ring [1].

Minimize cognitive/physical workload: Although eyes-free interaction reduces reliance on visual attention, it is still possible to cause a high cognitive/physical workload due to the uses of cognitive/physical resources from other modalities [8]. Thus, designers need to carefully design the interaction method so that users can finish the eyes-free interaction with a minimal cognitive/physical cost. Beyond the desire for perceived convenience (e.g. M10), it is also relevant to more critical issues such as safety (e.g. M2).

CONCLUSION

We adopted a user-centered approach to explore motivations for eyes-free interaction on mobile devices via focus groups. Based on context dependency (*contextual or independent*) and realm (*physical or human*) we developed a four-category classification of motivations. We analyzed user motivations and sorted them into the four categories. We then discussed issues of diversity, concurrency and shifting of motivations, followed by design implications for eyes-free interactions in mobile device usage.

Our work provides a different view of eyes-free interaction from the user's perspective and helps to reveal insights and relationships among motivations. By enhancing the understanding of the motivations behind eyes-free interactions, we hope that better eyes-free interfaces can be created in the future.

ACKNOWLEDGMENTS

This project is funded by the National Research Foundation (NRF) and managed through the multi-agency Interactive & Digital Media Programme Office (IDMPO) hosted by the Media Development Authority of Singapore (MDA) under Centre of Social Media Innovations for Communities (COSMIC). We thank Erik Tobin, anonymous reviewers, and all members in the NUS HCI lab for their help.

REFERENCES

1. Ashbrook, D., Baudisch, P. and White, S. Nenya: subtle and eyes-free mobile input with a magnetically-tracked finger ring. In *Proc. CHI 2011*, ACM (2011), 2043-2046.
2. Brewster, S., Lumsden, J., Bell, M., Hall, M. and Tasker, S. Multimodal 'eyes-free' interaction techniques for wearable devices. In *Proc. CHI 2003*, ACM (2003), 473-480.
3. Cooper, A. *The inmates are running the asylum*. SAMS publishing, 2004.
4. Li, K. A., Baudisch, P. and Hinckley, K. Blindsight: eyes-free access to mobile phones. In *Proc. CHI 2008*, ACM (2008), 1389-1398.
5. Morgan, D. L. *The focus group guidebook*. Sage Publications, Inc, 1998.
6. Palen, L., Salzman, M. and Youngs, E. Going wireless: behavior & practice of new mobile phone users. In *Proc.CSCW 2000*, ACM (2000), 201-210.
7. Strauss, A. L. and Corbin, J. M. *Basics of qualitative research: Techniques and procedures for developing grounded theory*. Sage Publications, Inc, 1998.
8. Vazquez-Alvarez, Y. and Brewster, S. A. Eyes-free multitasking: the effect of cognitive load on mobile spatial audio interfaces. In *Proc. CHI 2011*, ACM (2011), 2173-2176.
9. Zhao, S., Dragicevic, P., Chignell, M., Balakrishnan, R. and Baudisch, P. Earpod: eyes-free menu selection using touch input and reactive audio feedback. In *Proc. CHI 2007*, ACM (2007), 1395-1404.

Protecting Artificial Team-Mates: More Seems Like Less

Tim Merritt and Kevin McGee
NUS Graduate School for Integrative Sciences & Engineering
National University of Singapore
{timothy.merritt,mckevin}@nus.edu.sg

ABSTRACT
Previous research on conversational, competitive, and cooperative systems suggests that people respond differently to humans and AI agents in terms of perception and evaluation of observed team-mate behavior. However, there has not been research examining the relationship between participants' protective behavior toward human/AI team-mates and their beliefs about their behavior. A study was conducted in which 32 participants played two sessions of a cooperative game, once with a "presumed" human and once with an AI team-mate; players could "draw fire" from a common enemy by "yelling" at it. Overwhelmingly, players claimed they "drew fire" on behalf of the presumed human more than for the AI team-mate; logged data indicates the opposite. The main contribution of this paper is to provide evidence of the mismatch in player beliefs about their actions and actual behavior with humans or agents and provides possible explanations for the differences.

Author Keywords
CSCP; CASA; team-mate

ACM Classification Keywords
H.5.2 Information Interfaces and Presentation: Miscellaneous

General Terms
Human Factors, Experimentation

INTRODUCTION
There is much interest in the development of artificial partners in various contexts including work as well as play. Considerable effort has been directed at designing team-mates to have human-like characteristics and capabilities of cooperation toward shared goals, taking risks, responding to social cues, etc. Various research has explored how people respond to human and computer team-mates, with results that vary according to the context – in some cases findings suggest that people treat computers the same as humans as proposed by Media Equation research [21, 16], while other more recent research suggests that various factors influence the social treatment of media and computer agents [26]. The Media Equation research claims that minimal social cues result in equal social responses, yet other research claims that the beliefs about the identity of a partner being human or agent leads to very different social responses [3].

As artificial agents fill more roles in our lives, it is important that we examine how the *beliefs* about team-mate abilities and characteristics impact behaviors in cooperative tasks. This has significant implications for any situation in which artificial agents can potentially fill roles in place of human partners (e.g., human-robot interaction, video games, copilot scenarios, etc). With a more clear understanding of the rationale and motivation for coordinated actions, developers can begin to look at whether (and how) it may be possible to compensate for such beliefs. The underlying question is, how does the perception of team-mate identity affect the attitudes and expectations of cooperative behavior from a team-mate and does this impact the way players engage in cooperative behavior?

RELATED WORK
Work that has tried to answer this question includes research focused on human responses and behavior in conversational, competitive, and cooperative interactions. Of particular interest is the research that has directly compared the human responses to computers with their responses to other humans, which provides clear insights into differences that may arise. Some of these examples of comparative work involve mild deception – participants are told that their partner is a human or a computer when in fact it is otherwise. This is usually done so that the stimuli for the experimental conditions are of otherwise equivalent interactions.

Conversational Interactions
There has been considerable attention in the research that has examined how people respond to conversational agents compared to other humans either in person or represented as an avatar in a mediated environment. Studies that explored the influence of perceived ethnicity of an on-screen conversational partner and social responses suggest that people react more positively to avatars and agents that seem similar to them [17]. Similarly, research that compared the experiences of interviewing a prospective human or computer team-mate suggests that there is no difference in the feeling of presence or social presence related to the partner identity [18]. In a more simple, goal-oriented text-based context, however,

interacting with computer partners resulted in more interpersonal stress than text interactions with another human [6].

In terms of effects on behavior, there are also a mix of studies suggesting similarities and differences according to the identity of the partner. In [15] participants responded with reciprocal matching in conversations with humans as well as computers. However, in [19] children interacted with embodied conversational agents differently than with humans suggesting that they perceived the computer agent as an "at risk" listener and they adjusted their speech to ensure the computer could understand them. Researchers examining conversational differences related to the Desert Survival Game suggests that people engage more in attempts to establish an interpersonal relationship when they think they are interacting with another human [23].

Competitive Interactions

Research that has looked at responses to competitive interactions and the role of perceived identity of the competitor suggests that people have a very different experience depending on whether they believe they are interacting with a computer or another human. Results from competitive game-based studies suggest that there is more positive affect in interactions with humans because of an increase in social cues and potential for communication [5], which has been attributed to an "appetitive motivation" for social interaction that people seek out with other humans [20], whereas interactions with computer competitors often result in higher levels of aggression due to a lack of human communication [28]. In research focused on more action oriented games, results suggests that there is greater arousal with a human competitor due to more engrossed play [11] and higher reported sense of presence, flow, and enjoyment when playing against another human due to a greater sense of social presence [27].

Cooperative Interactions

In terms of research on the effects of partner identity and cooperative play, there is further evidence to suggest that people react very differently when they perceive their partner as either a computer or another human including differences in partner preference, perceptions of game events, and even differences in behavior.

For players engaged in a dyadic drumming exercise, computer partners were preferred because they were perceived as more consistent and predictable than human players [2] yet in other research on cooperative games, team-mates presumed to be other humans were preferred, and interactions with them resulted in more enjoyment [12] and higher levels of arousal [10] than with computer team-mates.

The perception of game events and judgment has been shown to be affected by the perception of team-mate identity, with computer team-mates being blamed unfairly, and their skill being assessed inaccurately [14]. Another study examined how the perceived identity of the team-mate affected the participants' perception of cooperation and risk-taking by two different team-mates – participants claimed that the presumed human team-mate cooperated more and took more risks on their behalf compared to the computer team-mate, however, in both situations they were actually controlled by the same computer algorithm [13]. Going beyond perception, results from a well known study involving an iterated Prisoner's Dilemma game suggest that people honor commitments more to a human than a computer due to an imagined social contract [8]. A more recent study on brain imaging [22] has provided further support with results suggesting that there are differences in brain activity depending upon the identity of a partner who treats them unfairly – suggesting that there is a neurological basis for treating others differently depending upon whether the other is perceived to be another human or not.

RESEARCH PROBLEM

Previous research has examined responses to presumed human and computer team-mates including differences in social expectations, enjoyment, and perceptions in cooperative games, however, aside from the few examples of differences in cooperation in the turn-based Prisoner's Dilemma game, there has not been adequate focus on examining how the manipulation of team-mate identity corresponds to differences in player *behavior* and *interpretations* of game events. The main contribution of this paper is provide evidence that players behave differently in the real-time cooperative game context taking quantitatively more protective actions to help AI team-mates compared to presumed human team-mates – and to provide possible explanations for these differences.

STUDY

In order to examine this, a study was conducted, in which 32 participants played a real-time, goal-oriented, cooperative game. The game allows (but does not require) players to take actions to protect their team-mates – specifically, players can "draw gunfire" towards themselves (and away from their team-mates). During the study, all participants were familiarized with the game and then played the game twice: once with an AI team-mate and once with a "presumed" human team-mate (i.e., an AI team-mate that they believed was a human team-mate). Thus, the team-mate performance and behaviors were *objectively* identical for both cases – and in both cases, the team-mate "drew gunfire" an equal amount of the time. Participants answered questions related to the game sessions as well as questions focused on their attitudes, beliefs, and feelings about team-mates in general.

Participants

The 32 participants who took part in the study included 23 female and 9 male students between the ages of 19 and 24 with an average age of 20.7 years. Participants were briefed on the concept of cooperative game play and were asked to fill out a small questionnaire and consent form. When asked to rate their experience and skill level with interactive digital games, the results were fairly evenly distributed: 9.4% claimed to be *novice*, 25% claimed to have *little experience (less than average)*, 50% claimed to have *average experience*, 15.6% claimed to have *much experience (more than average)*, and no participants claimed to be *expert*.

In terms of experience with cooperative games, 93.8% reported having played interactive digital games involving human team-mates, and similarly, 93.8% had played interactive digital games involving computer team-mates. A large majority (87.5%) reported that they enjoy interactive digital games.

Cooperative game: Capture the Gunner

For the study, a game called *Capture the Gunner* was used (see Figure 1). This is a simple cooperative game which can be played with either a human or with a computer team-mate.

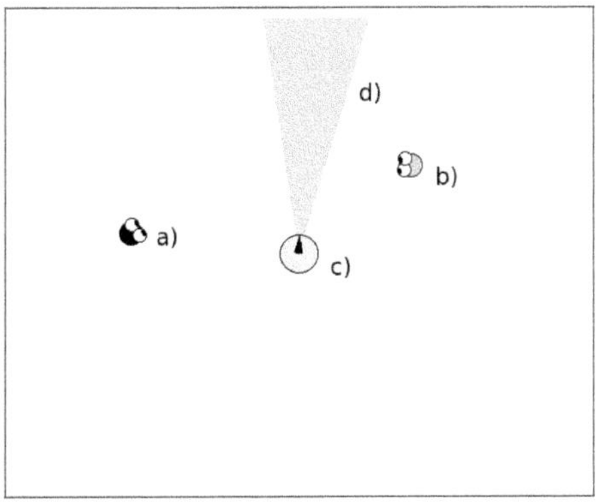

Figure 1. Capture the Gunner game elements: a) human-controlled avatar b) computer-controlled agent c) gunner d) gunner's field of view (FOV)

The game consists of a human-controlled avatar and a computer-controlled agent that, together, must evade bullets and cooperate in order to "capture" (touch) the gunner, which is rotating and firing within its "field of view" from the middle of the game space. At each level, both players must touch the gunner (though, not necessarily at the same time); once this occurs, the game proceeds to the next level, with the gunner rotating faster as described in [1], however, for the present study, an additional feature of the explicit action of "drawing fire" was used as explained in [12].

Drawing Fire

Players can protect their team-mate by "drawing fire": attracting attention of the gunner and encouraging the gunner to shift focus from their team-mate and becoming the actively targeted player. This can be done by moving into the field of view of the gunner or, the more explicit way of drawing attention of the gunner requires the player to press the "W" key while in the field of view of the gunner, which is described to the participants as a metaphor for "yelling" at the gunner. The "yell" action causes the player's avatar to blink yellow for two seconds to indicate the elevated attempts to draw attention. The AI team-mate is programmed to draw attention in both ways at regular intervals.

Gunner Behavior Algorithm

The game is designed so that the gunner is a challenging and somewhat unpredictable opponent that can be influenced by player actions.

The gunner has two actions that it can perform: rotating to target the players – and firing bullets to strike the players. The gunner seeks out both players equally at the beginning of each level. It rotates until one of the players is in its field of view, at which point it begins firing at that player. Every three seconds, a dice roll is made (not visible to the players), which results in the gunner choosing either to stay with the current target, or to pursue the other player using odds that begin at 50/50. The players can influence the likelihood of being targeted by positioning their avatar in the gunner's field of view and performing the "yell" action. With each yell event, the odds shift 10% in favor of targeting the player who has yelled. This shift in odds is not visible to the player, who is told that the yelling action is a more explicit way to draw the attention of the gunner to protect their team-mate. The participants are simply told that "yelling" will likely raise the desire for the gunner to target them.

Study Session Protocol

Participants arrived at a private testing room, did not meet any other participants, and were assured that their comments would be kept anonymous and not revealed to other human participants. Each participant was briefed on the game, read a description of the game objectives and explanation of the "yell" feature, which was identified as an explicit way of attracting attention of the gunner. The participants then watched a short video twice, once with an explanation of how the gunner is captured and then another viewing of the video was accompanied with more attention to the "yell" events that occurred at various times in the video. In order to avoid confusion and to ensure the participants were comfortable and proficient with drawing fire, during the practice session, the participants were guided through pressing the "W" key during two levels of the game.

Participants played the game for three sessions. The first session was identified as the practice session with an AI team-mate lasting approximately four minutes to familiarize the participants with moving their avatar, completing at least two levels, and pressing the "W" key to activate the yell feature in both levels. This was followed by two sessions of five minutes each, one with an AI team-mate and another with a PH ("presumed human") team-mate. At the start of each session, the researcher reminded the participant that they could press the "W" key if they desired and the researcher motioned to the "W" on the keyboard and ensured that the participant placed their finger on the key to be ready to press the key during the game session as desired. This aimed to remind the participants and to ensure that participants would be able to press the key without having to find it during the game. During the five-minute sessions, the participants were told to do as well as possible and achieve the highest level they could within the allotted time. If the team lost on any level, the game was reset to the first level and the participant was asked to continue playing until the five minutes of the session had elapsed. The order of these sessions was alternated to minimize the effects of order of exposure such that half of the participants were exposed to the PH team-mate first and half were exposed to the AI team-mate first.

The PH team-mate was actually controlled by the computer using the same AI algorithm in both sessions, yet the participants were told that there was a human participant who joined through the network controlling the team-mate. The mild deception was to ensure that any differences in the ways that the participants described or reacted to the team-mate could be attributed to whether they believed the team-mate was computer-based or human. The purpose was not to see whether or how easily humans can be led to believe they are coordinating with other humans (e.g., variant Turing test). Using the same artificial team-mate throughout the study also ensured that the participant's team-mate would perform at a consistent level across all play sessions, the importance of which is noted in [10].

Measures

The participant response to the game was measured in two different ways: logged game events and self-reporting.

Game event measures

Various game events were logged to a text file during each game session to track in-game behaviors, which resulted in two text files per participant, one for each of the two team-mate conditions to allow for later comparisons. These measured events included the following: highest level achieved, how many times each player touched the gunner first, number of deaths (participant avatar/agent), and number of yell events (participant avatar/agent).

The logging of the yell events was intended to capture the intentional protective attempts to draw fire that players make for their team-mate. The less explicit method of drawing fire by entering the field of view is not used as a comparison because it provides little insights into the actual player behavior and intentions. In previous analysis of player behavior, neither entering the field of view nor the total amount of time spent in the field of view correlated with the intentions of the player to protect the team-mate. For example, a common reason for a player to be in the field of view is because the gunner actively scanned and locked on to the player. Players often remain in the field of view while the gunner tracks them even during their attempts to flee. The total number of times a team-mate enters the field of view is also a problematic data point that does not capture the user intentions accurately. For example, while fleeing the gunner, players often escape and are re-targeted as they are moving away, which increases the total number of times that they have entered the field of view, yet it represents the opposite of protecting the other by drawing fire and is merely an attempt at self-protection. Considering these limitations, the more explicit draw fire action was selected for the focus of this research.

Self-report measures

After both sessions had been completed, the participants were asked to answer forced selection, Likert-type scale, and open-ended questions that focused on comparing the two game sessions. Additional questions focused on the participants' beliefs, stereotypes, and experiences with human and AI team-mates in their past as well as opinions about interactions between team-mates in short video clips and hypothetical scenarios involving team-mates.

Q1: Self Evaluation of Protective Behaviors "Which team-mate did you protect the most? (Human / AI) Why?"

Q2-4: Stereotypes In order to explore the preconceived opinions, stereotypes, and beliefs about human and AI team-mates, three 5-point Likert-type scale questions focused on the degree to which the participant would agree with statements about typical behaviors and characteristics of a team-mate. The three questions were posed about human as well as AI team-mates resulting in six questions in total, which are as follows:

- Q2: (Human/AI) team-mates can adapt according to the situation.
- Q3: (Human/AI) team-mates are helpful.
- Q4: (Human/AI) team-mates are very understanding.

These questions focused on the stereotypes held by the participants and were posed to the participants after all games had been played and after they were asked to make judgments about their protective behaviors in the game to ensure that the behaviors and thoughts about the behaviors would not be affected.

Q5: Personal Pressures In order to explore the social pressures related to playing games with human and AI team-mates, a 5-point Likert-type scale question asked the participants how much they agree with the statement about the pressures to act in the game. The question was posed about human as well as AI team-mates resulting in two questions in total.

- Q5: With a (Human/AI) team-mate I feel pressure to try as hard as I can to win.

Q6-11: Explaining Observed Behaviors In order to explore differences in how players interpret the behavior of AI and human team-mates, participants were asked to watch six short video clips of the game being played, after each video, they were asked to explain in their own words, what one of the team-mates was trying to do. In three of the videos, the participant was told that both team-mates were controlled by human players and they were instructed to focus on one player identified by the researcher. The other three videos were copies of the first three videos, however, the participants were told that one of the team-mates was a human and one was an AI team-mate. The participants were told they should focus on the AI team-mate. Participants were permitted to watch the video clips more than once if desired. The content of the videos are briefly described:

- Q6 (PH) & Q9 (AI): Team-mate of focus touched the gunner, then proceeded to activate "yell" events continuously until the other team-mate completed the second touch. This was intended to demonstrate a deliberate attempt to protect the team-mate.
- Q7 (PH) & 10 (AI): Team-mate of focus touched the gunner, then passed through the field of view without

signaling. This was intended to demonstrate a more ambiguous attempt to protect the team-mate.

- Q8 (PH) & 11 (AI): Team-mate of focus touched the gunner, then avoided the field of view for the remainder of the video. This was intended to demonstrate a deliberate attempt to avoid protecting the team-mate and to avoid the gunner.

RESULTS

The main result of this study is that participants engaged in more protective signaling events for their AI team-mates compared to the PH ("presumed human") team-mate. Surprisingly, however, this stands in contrast to the self-reported feedback in which the participants claimed to have protected the PH team-mate the most. Additional self-reported feedback indicates various stereotypes, feelings and attitudes toward human and AI team-mates with more emotional descriptions of intention for human team-mates and AI team-mates being judged more critically. Taken as a whole, the results suggest that perceived identity is a moderator for protective behavior in cooperative games and that the reflections about this behavior are not perceived objectively by players. In the remainder of this section, these results are presented in more detail.

Preliminary Analysis

Before examining the differences in the subjective ratings of the participants toward their team-mates and logged in-game behaviors, statistical analyses were conducted to rule out any confounding effects of the order of exposure to the AI or PH team-mate. There were no significant effects of order for any of the dependent measures including subjective responses and game outcomes. In light of previous research that suggests experience moderates social responses to technology [7], MANOVAs were conducted to detect any possible effects of demographic variables of age, gender, and self-reported experience on all the dependent measures, and there were no significant interactions or main effects.

Logged Data

Paired samples T-tests were used to compare the logged data during both game sessions. Among the logged data, there was a statistically significant difference in the number of times the player "yelled" when playing with the AI and human team-mates, with the participants signaling more to protect their AI team-mates than they did for human team-mates. Various data were shown to have statistically significant correlations, which provides additional insights into the player behaviors.

Protective signaling

The results from a paired-sample T-test revealed that when people played with the AI team-mate, they drew fire more in the game ($M=13.22$, $SD=10.98$) than when they played with the PH team-mate ($M=9.88$, $SD=9.65$), $t\ (31)=2.236$, $p<0.05$.

Paired samples T-tests were used to compare the other logged data during both game sessions, which revealed that any differences in highest level achieved, number of times the participant touched the gunner before the team-mate, and the number of deaths of participant or team-mate were all non-significant as shown in Table 1. This confirms that the AI performed in an equivalent manner for all sessions.

Correlations in Behavioral Data

Further analysis of the logged data suggests that behaviors of signaling, making the 1st touch on the gunner, and deaths of the players are related in various ways, providing insights into typical player behaviors. These correlations are now briefly described.

- The amount of participant signaling in both conditions is positively correlated. This suggests that those who signal frequently, generally do so in both conditions. $r(30) = .671, p<.001$.
- The amount of participant signaling in both conditions was negatively correlated with the number of deaths by the participant. This suggests that those who signal more frequently, die less often. In the PH condition $r(30) = -.458, p<.01$ and in the AI condition $r(30) = -.465, p<.01$.
- The amount of participant signaling in the PH condition is positively correlated with team-mate signaling, $r(30) = .467, p<.01$. This means that when playing with the PH team-mate, participants usually mirror the team-mate signaling behavior.
- The number of 1st touch events by the participants in both conditions is positively correlated, $r(30) = .509, p<.01$. This suggests that those who frequently make the first touch, will do so in both conditions.
- The number of 1st touch events by the team-mate in both conditions is positively correlated, $r(30) = .525, p<.01$. This suggests that players who enable their team-mate to make the first touch frequently, will do so in both conditions.

Self-evaluation of protective behavior

Q1 explored the effects of team-mate identity on the perception of the amount the team-mate protected their team-mates. A large majority of participants (71%) indicated that they protected the presumed human team-mate more than the AI team-mate.

A review of the open-ended feedback explaining their selections provides additional insights into the priorities and concerns participants had for their team-mates. Those who claimed they protected the presumed human the most provided explanations that can be grouped into four common explanations. The most commonly stated reason (36.4%) involved claims that their team-mate *needed more protection*. 22.7% claimed that the *ease of providing protection* to the presumed human team-mate guided their actions. Another 22.7% noted that they protected the presumed human more out of a *sense of obligation or duty*, and the remaining 18.2% claimed that they protected the presumed human more due to a *sense of empathy* with their team-mate.

Logged game event	Mean	SD	Diff.	t	df	p
Highest level achieved with PH team-mate	7.31	2.306	-0.688	-1.278	31	0.211
Highest level achieved with AI team-mate	8.00	2.423				
# of 1st touch events by participant with PH team-mate	10.25	3.724	-0.344	-0.550	31	0.586
# of 1st touch events by participant with AI team-mate	10.59	3.387				
# of 1st touch events by PH team-mate	17.13	5.621	-0.156	-0.166	31	0.869
# of 1st touch events by AI team-mate	17.28	5.262				
Deaths of participant avatar with PH team-mae	6.75	2.489	-0.094	-0.225	31	0.824
Deaths of participant avatar with AI team-mate	6.84	2.737				
Deaths of PH team-mate	0.53	0.671	-0.094	0.682	31	0.500
Deaths of AI team-mate	.44	0.619				
"yell" events by participant with PH team-mate	9.88	9.648	-3.344	-2.236	31	0.033
"yell" events by participant with AI team-mate	13.22	10.983				
"yell" events by PH team-mate	17.06	4.819	-1.188	-1.574	31	0.126
"yell" events by AI team-mate	18.25	4.593				

Table 1. Table of means of logged game events showing the differences between game sessions with PH and AI team-mates.

In contrast, those who claimed that they protected the AI team-mate more gave only one of two reasons why they protected the AI team-mate more, which focused on either the perceived *needs of the team-mate* or the *ease of offering protection*. Approximately 55% of those who claimed to have protected the AI team-mate more cited the needs of the team-mate as reasons. Of those, two of the participants noted that the AI team-mate lacked a sense of understanding about the participants' intentions, which made it necessary for them to protect it more than the presumed human. The remaining 33% explained that protecting the AI team-mate was easier for them in some way and gave no other indication about their motives or feelings otherwise. One participant (12%) did not provide a reason for their selection.

Stereotypes

Q2-4 explored the opinions and stereotypes participants have for human and AI team-mates. Participants rated humans more favorably in various dimensions. The items that resulted in statistically significant differences are now presented:

Q2 asked the participants to rate their belief in team-mates adapting according to the situation. The results suggest that participants believe more strongly that human team-mates can adapt according to the situation (M=4.28, SD=.581) than an AI team-mate (M=3.25, SD=.672). Results from a paired-samples T-test showed that the difference was statistically significant $t(31)=6.777$, $p<0.001$.

Q3 asked the participants to rate their belief in helpfulness of team-mates. The results suggest that participants believe more strongly that human team-mates are more helpful (M= 4.03, SD=.740) than an AI team-mate (M=3.47, SD=.718). Results from a paired-samples T-test showed that the difference was statistically significant $t(31)=3.241$, $p<0.01$.

Q4 asked the participants to rate their belief in how understanding team-mates are, with results that suggest participants believe more strongly that human team-mates are more understanding (M=3.69, SD=.738) than an AI team-mates (M=2.84, SD=.954). Results from a paired-samples T-test showed that the difference was statistically significant $t(31)= 3.425$, $p<0.01$.

Personal pressures

Q5 asked the participants to rate the pressure they feel to try as hard as they can to win the game with human and AI team-mates. The results suggest that participants feel more pressure to try as hard as they can to win when playing with a human team-mate (M=4.38,SD=.609) than with an AI team-mate (M=2.97, SD=.861). Results from a paired-samples T-test showed that the difference was statistically significant $t(31)=7.411$, $p<0.001$.

Observed behaviors

Q6-11 explored how the identity of the team-mate results in differences in evaluations of observed behaviors. The explanations given for the presumed human team-mate usually involved positive evaluations, offering more than one possible explanation, and reflected beliefs that the team-mate brings emotion, thought, and intention to their actions. The explanations given for the equivalent behaviors when participants thought they were AI team-mates were much more simple, critical, and were often more condemning of the team-mates actions. The results for the three videos are now provided including examples of the contrasting explanations.

Q6&9 presented participants with a video clip in which the team-mate activated the "yell" frequently drawing fire continuously for their team-mate. Explanations about the presumed human team-mate discussed intentions, while the explanations for the behavior of the AI team-mate were critical, expressed doubt and an unwillingness to project more complex interpretations.

Participant 13 explained what the presumed human team-mate was trying to do:

> P13: I think that initially he was trying to be safe, then tried to help the team-mate when he could, he has some confusion though and doesn't know right away what to do.

In their description of the AI team-mate in an identical video, the description changes:

> P13: Its actions have no strategy, it is just doing what it is supposed to do, like, under a computer generated command.

Q7&10 presented participants with a video clip in which the team-mates made a more ambiguous attempt to protect the team-mate. The contrast between the explanations for the presumed human and AI team-mate videos followed a similar trend with more thoughtful explanations provided for the presumed human team-mate and more negative and critical explanations for the AI team-mate. Participant 6 explained the behavior of the presumed human:

> P6: The black player is hesitant at the start, he took quite a while to do it [touch the gunner].

The explanation for the identical video when the team-mate was presumed to be an AI agent resulted in a very different explanation:

> P6: The AI seems broken, it looks as if the AI is moving around and it seems to just go after the gunner and doesn't think of the team-mate.. like he is playing by himself!

Q8&11 presented participants with a video clip in which the team-mates avoided the field of view of the gunner and did not make any attempts to protect the team-mate. There are notable differences in the explanations of this video clip, with the explanations of the presumed human focusing on selfish attitudes and intentions, while the explanations when the team-mate was a presumed AI team-mate claimed that the AI was broken, ineffective, or not focused on the goal. The explanations by participant 19 followed this format, with the explanation of the human team-mate involving notions of care and intentions:

> P19: He wants to hurry and finish and take the back seat. After he touched, he didn't really care about the team-mate anymore

This was contrasted by their explanation that faulted the AI team-mate for the same clip:

> P19: This computer doesn't know what he is doing – totally not helping at all!

DISCUSSION

The protective behavior of the participants differed significantly for their team-mates with 33.8% more yell events on average (13.22) when they believed their team-mate was an AI agent than when they believed their team-mate was another human (9.88). Surprisingly, the participants overwhelmingly (71%) claimed to have protected the presumed human team-mate more.

Considering the difference in behavior and the self-reported measures, the discussion will include explanations for the difference in the participants' protective behavior and the incongruent claim about their behavior. The most plausible explanation for difference in amount of protective acts performed involves the following two factors: 1) participants relied on stereotypes and attended to the greater expected need for protection that is characteristic of AI team-mates, protecting them more, 2) when actually performing the protective acts, the participants attended more to aspects of fairness involved in their altruistic actions resulting in a mirroring of the actions of presumed human team-mate (tit for tat), yet with the AI team-mate, the participant engaged in protective acts quantitatively more because they were not concerned with the level of reciprocity from their team-mate. Instead, they tried to protect the team-mate as much as they could, resulting in more protective acts.

In reflection, when participants considered how much they protected their team-mates, they claimed to have protected the human team-mates more than the AI team-mates because the protective acts performed for the presumed human team-mate were likely more memorable and therefore, seemed like quantitatively *more*.

In this section we discuss the proposed explanation in more detail, review possible competing explanations for the results as well as possible limitations of the study.

More protection for AI team-mates

The proposed explanation for the significantly greater amount of protective acts for the AI team-mates is due to the greater perceived need to protect AI team-mates and the complexities of altruistic acts performed for other humans that results in more attention to fairness rather than game outcomes.

AI team-mates need more protection

Participants engaged in cooperative play with two team-mates, which were objectively the same, yet were explained as being either controlled by another human or controlled by a computer. The participants could not communicate with their team-mates, they could not see or hear their team-mate, nor could they use any other modes to understand their team-mate or confirm their assumptions. Typically, when people engage in social activities, the channels of communication permit a process of person perception, in which the actors try to infer the mental states, intentions, abilities, and feelings of the other by examining facial expressions, vocalizations, or gestures. In the present study, the participants could only make these judgments based on the observed on-screen behaviors and their expectations based on stereotypes they held about typical qualities and limitations of their team-mates.

Responses to the questions regarding adaptability and understanding resulted in human team-mates being rated significantly higher than AI team-mates. This suggests that participants expected that when interacting with typical AI team-mates, they would be less able to adapt according to the situation and would be less understanding in the cooperative game, thus likely to need more help. Additional open-ended feedback suggests that given the negative stereotypes, the participants expected less from the AI team-mates, which resulted in a perception bias when evaluating their team-mates' behaviors. When participants explained the behaviors of team-mates in video clips, they drew conclusions very quickly about AI team-mates and usually made more negative assessments, whereas the explanations for identical behavior by presumed human team-mates reflected a delay judgment and expectations that behaviors were part of a larger strategy.

In the feedback from those who claimed to have protected the AI more during the game, the responses often described a lack of communication or understanding by the AI team-mates, which made the participants feel that more protection was needed. In [19], findings suggested that AI partners are considered "at risk" partners that need more "hand-holding" as conversational partners, requiring more explicit and deliberate actions to ensure that the human is understood. The results from the present study suggest that participants held similar beliefs and expectations about AI team-mates and took more explicit protective actions for them.

Complexity of Altruism

The findings suggest that when cooperating with presumed human team-mates, players expected and cared about the reciprocity of protective actions, however when playing with AI team-mates, this was less important – participants seemed to be driven more by utility, which led to more protective actions on their behalf.

In the CTG game, the act of signaling (yelling) to the gunner is a protective and altruistic act that reduces the danger presented by the gunner for one's team-mate, however, this protection comes at the expense of increased danger brought on by the gunner focusing more on the player who has signaled. Players were told that their team-mates would engage in the signaling behaviors during the game and thus some expectation of reciprocity was established with the participants. The logged data confirms that the team-mate signaling was the same for both conditions. The positive correlation for the signaling behaviors in the PH condition suggest that participants mirrored the behavior of their team-mate, employing a tit-for-tat strategy. The signaling behaviors in the AI condition reflected significantly more protection for the team-mate, which suggests that the tit-for-tat strategy was not followed as closely when playing with the AI team-mate. This seems to support related research that suggests that in games involving humans, people attend more to fairness and scrutinize the choices of their team-mate, however when cooperating with an AI team-mate, there is less concern for being treated unfairly and choices are made more objectively [22]. Research from behavioral economics and game theory, well summarized in [9], suggests that altruism is complex, often resulting in irrational behavior, such as the strong aversion to being in "last place." The authors of this paper propose that a similar behavioral mechanism resulted in participants mirroring the presumed human behavior but only to the point that the altruistic acts satisfied the tit-for-tat expectation to some degree.

When the team-mate is an AI agent, the open-ended feedback suggests that the players cared less about reciprocating acts of altruism and engaged in signaling because they felt it was the most effective thing to do. In fact, in both conditions, the logged game events show a negative correlation between signaling and deaths of the participant, not just their team-mate. Signaling was linked to less casualties for the participant and was actually a more effective strategy! A common topic in self-reported feedback is that the participants felt that the game with the AI team-mate is akin to playing alone. Any success or failure is theirs alone and altruistic acts for the AI team-mate are effectively self-serving acts that further their own goals.

Claims of protective behavior

The fact that participants signaled more for the AI team-mate, yet claimed to have signaled more for the human team-mate is, at first, a surprising result. However, in research on brain imaging, studies suggest that the perception of agency (belief that something is alive) results in higher self-reported altruism [24]. This suggests a biological explanation in which the protective behavior done to help the presumed human team-mate activates different parts of the brain – for every altruistic act of protection, the brain is stimulated more. Other research in brain imaging suggests that people get more of an emotional payoff from altruistic acts from other humans compared to computers [4]. The findings of this paper seem to support that the acts of altruism *felt different* when participants thought they were playing with another human compared to an AI team-mate.

Competing explanations

There are some possible competing explanations for the results of our study, some of which are now discussed including a possible disconnect in the protective behavior and the achievement of team goals, as well as a possible reconstruction bias.

One possible explanation for the difference in the amount of protective action could be a disconnect in the protective actions and the team goals. The results for Q5 suggest that participants felt it was more important to try as hard as they could to win when playing with a human compared to an AI team-mate. One explanation for this result could be that when playing with a human team-mate, the participant felt that the optimal strategy was not to perform protective actions, but instead focus on offensive strategies. Although the logged data suggests that taking protective actions was the optimal survival strategy, perhaps for the participants, taking protective actions did not seem to be the optimal strategy to reach higher levels in the game. In addition, any differences between the number of times the participants touched the gunner first were found to be non-significant. This suggests that the offensive actions were similar in both conditions.

A possible explanation for the mismatch between the participants' claims and the actual amount of protective actions taken on behalf of the team-mates could be due to a reconstruction bias. Since the participants played the game for two sessions of five minutes, with questions following the game play, it is possible that the participants were at a loss when trying to remember how many protective acts they took for each team-mate and therefore, reflected upon what they thought they "should have" done in the game. Protective acts might have been considered by the participants as what they "should have done" for another human and thus, they could have adjusted their recollection of the actual events to fit. This is difficult to measure, and rule out, requiring an examination into real-time measures of brain activity during game play sessions. As previously noted in [24], however, evidence suggests a neurological basis for a difference in self-reported altruism due to differences in perceptions of identity. That study indicated differences in thought patterns according to observed behavior of others, yet suggests that a similar effect could be measured for actions carried out by one's self. Aside from monitoring brain activity, eye-tracking technologies could be used to measure the differences in selective focus on protective events as they unfold.

Limitations

There are several aspects of this study that present possible limitations that should be discussed and evaluated. These include the recording of game play, the breadth and granularity of logged data, and the design of the game. We now discuss how these might affect the validity of the contribution.

The game play screen was not video-recorded and the nuanced differences in the player behaviors are not captured. Players may have engaged in different strategies when playing with their presumed human and AI team-mates. While the fine details of the game play have not been captured, the logged data has served to ensure that both conditions offered the participants team-mates that performed identically. The difference between the "yell" events by the AI and PH team-mate was not significant (p=0.126), however, this curious result suggests that participant actions resulted in small differences in the opportunities for the team-mate to draw fire. The video recording of the gameplay would also become more important if the study was focused on matching biosignals to events in the game as the experience unfolds over time. This was not the scope of this study, however, in future work, matching the player emotions to altruistic acts would be of great interest to take the current research further.

In lieu of video recorded sessions, another possible limitation is that the logged data could have been more extensive in order to capture more of the player styles and strategies. However, capturing more data points requires additional analysis that does not always yield useful information. For example, the time spent in gunner's field of view may at first seem useful, however, capturing the player's intention from this data point is not possible because there are times that players flee from the gunner and their intentions is to protect themselves, while in other instances, spending time in the field of view carries the opposite intentions – to protect their team-mate. The logged game events were chosen and refined to provide the most clear insights into the intentions and actions of the participants, and to avoid confusing or useless data.

Another possible limitation of this study is related to the design of the game. It is possible that the game was overly simple and does not reflect the typical games that are encountered in the market. While it is true that the graphics and aesthetic appeal of the game are quite simple, the game has been rated as highly enjoyable in previous research [12] and provides a clear and measurable mechanism to measure protective behavior in a cooperative game experience. While the findings presented in this paper are valid and important, future research could examine cooperative game contexts that are more complex.

CONCLUSION

Participants played a real-time cooperative game, once with an AI team-mate and once with a presumed human team-mate. Logged data from the game sessions revealed that participants engaged in the protective act of "drawing fire" more for the AI team-mate than the presumed human team-mate. Surprisingly, the participants claimed that they protected the presumed human team-mate more. Additional evidence gathered through self-reported feedback suggests that participants had very different beliefs and opinions about typical human and AI team-mates in general, which suggests that they expected the AI team-mates to need more protection. The protective acts in the game when played with presumed human team-mates resulted in more attention to fairness, and expectations of reciprocity, yet with AI team-mates, the protective actions were performed as needed and out of utility. In reflection, participants had exaggerated perceptions about their protective behaviors, resulting in claims that they protected the presumed human team-mate more. The findings suggest that the altruistic acts seemed like quantitatively more with the presumed human team-mate because they took place in what felt like a social context.

While research on the media equation might suggest that it is social cues that are inviting social responses, this study complicates that model by examining the rationale and motivation for cooperative responses depending upon the beliefs about the ontology of team-mates. The findings in the present paper reflect the complexity of the human relationship with technology discussed in [25]. In the current climate, technology is becoming ever more pervasive, with agents taking up more roles and helping people with the challenges they face, this research serves as a reminder of how expectations, emotions, and social pressures play a significant role in the experience resulting in differences in how people perceive the world and perceive their own actions.

ACKNOWLEDGMENTS

This work was supported by National University of Singapore AcRF grant "Understanding Interactivity" R-124-000-024-112. We thank the reviewers for their comments.

REFERENCES

1. Abraham, A. T., and McGee, K. AI for dynamic team-mate adaptation in games. In *Proc. CIG '10* (Aug. 2010), 419–426.

2. Beaton, B., Harrison, S., and Tatar, D. Digital drumming: a study of co-located, highly coordinated,

dyadic collaboration. In *Proc. CHI '10*, ACM Press (2010), 1417–1426.

3. Blascovich, J. A theoretical model of social influence for increasing the utility of collaborative virtual environments. In *Proc. CVE '02*, ACM Press (2002), 25–30.
4. Fehr, E., and Rockenbach, B. Human altruism: economic, neural, and evolutionary perspectives. *Curr. Opin. Neurobiol. 14*, 6 (Dec. 2004), 784–790.
5. Gajadhar, B., de Kort, Y., and IJsselsteijn, W. Influence of social setting on player experience of digital games. In *Proc. of CHI EA '08*, ACM Press (2008), 3099–3104.
6. Hayashi, Y., and Miwa, K. Cognitive and emotional characteristics of communication in Human-Human/Human-Agent interaction. In *Proc. CogSci '09*, Springer-Verlag (2009), 267–274.
7. Johnson, D., and Gardner, J. The media equation and team formation: Further evidence for experience as a moderator. *IJHCS 65*, 2 (2007), 111–124.
8. Kiesler, S., Sproull, L., and Waters, K. A prisoner's dilemma experiment on cooperation with people and human-like computers. *J. Pers. Soc. Psychol. 70*, 1 (Jan. 1996), 47–65.
9. Kuziemko, I., Buell, R. W., Reich, T., and Norton, M. I. "last-place aversion": Evidence and redistributive implications. *National Bureau of Economic Research Working Paper Series* (July 2011), 17234+.
10. Lim, S., and Reeves, B. Computer agents versus avatars: Responses to interactive game characters controlled by a computer or other player. *IJHCS 68*, 1-2 (January 2010), 57–68.
11. Mandryk, R. L., Inkpen, K. M., and Calvert, T. W. Using psychophysiological techniques to measure user experience with entertainment technologies. *Behav. Inform. Technol. 25*, 2 (Apr. 2006), 141–158.
12. Merritt, T., Chuah, T. L., Ong, C., and McGee, K. Choosing human team-mates: higher enjoyment and preference for human vs. AI team-mates in cooperative games. In *Proc. FDG '11*, ACM Press (2011).
13. Merritt, T., Ong, C., Chuah, T., and McGee, K. Did you notice? artificial Team-Mates take risks for players intelligent virtual agents. vol. 6895 of *Lecture Notes in Computer Science*. Springer, 2011, ch. 37, 338–349.
14. Merritt, T. R., Tan, K. B., Ong, C., Thomas, A., Chuah, T. L., and McGee, K. Are artificial team-mates scapegoats in computer games. In *Proc. CSCW '11*, ACM Press (2011), 685–688.
15. Miwa, K., and Terai, H. Analysis of human-human and human-computer agent interactions from the viewpoint of design of and attribution to a partner. In *Proc. CogSci '06*, Springer-Verlag (2006), 597–602.
16. Nass, C., Fogg, B. J., and Moon, Y. Can computers be teammates? *IJHCS 45*, 6 (December 1996), 669–678.
17. Nass, C., Isbister, K., and Lee, E. Truth is beauty: Researching embodied conversational agents. In *Embodied conversational agents*, J. Cassell, J. Sullivan, S. Prevost, and E. Churchill, Eds. MIT Press, Apr. 2000, 374–402.
18. Nowak, K. L., and Biocca, F. The effect of the agency and anthropomorphism of users' sense of telepresence, copresence, and social presence in virtual environments. *Presence-Teleop. Virt. 12* (Oct. 2003), 481–494.
19. Oviatt, S., and Adams, B. Designing and evaluating conversational interfaces with animated characters. In *Embodied conversational agents*, J. Cassell, J. Sullivan, S. Prevost, and E. Churchill, Eds. MIT Press, Apr. 2000, 319–345.
20. Ravaja, N., Saari, T., Turpeinen, M., Laarni, J., Salminen, M., and Kivikangas, M. Spatial Presence and Emotions during Video Game Playing: Does It Matter with Whom You Play? *Presence-Teleop. Virt. 15* (August 2006), 381–392.
21. Reeves, B., and Nass, C. *The media equation: how people treat computers, television, and new media like real people and places*. Cambridge U. Press, 1996.
22. Sanfey, A. G., Rilling, J. K., Aronson, J. A., Nystrom, L. E., and Cohen, J. D. The neural basis of economic Decision-Making in the ultimatum game. *Science 300*, 5626 (June 2003), 1755–1758.
23. Shechtman, N., and Horowitz, L. M. Media inequality in conversation: how people behave differently when interacting with computers and people. In *Proc. CHI '03*, ACM Press (2003), 281–288.
24. Tankersley, D., Stowe, C. J., and Huettel, S. A. Altruism is associated with an increased neural response to agency. *Nat. Neurosci. 10*, 2 (Jan. 2007), 150–151.
25. Turkle, S. *The Second Self: Computers and the Human Spirit*. The MIT Press, Sept. 2005.
26. von der Pütten, A. M., Krämer, N. C., Gratch, J., and Kang, S.-H. "it doesn't matter what you are!" explaining social effects of agents and avatars. *Comput. Hum. Behav. 26*, 6 (Nov. 2010), 1641–1650.
27. Weibel, D., Wissmath, B., Habegger, S., Steiner, Y., and Groner, R. Playing online games against computer- vs. human-controlled opponents: Effects on presence, flow, and enjoyment. *Comput. Hum. Behav. 24*, 5 (Sept. 2008), 2274–2291.
28. Williams, R. Aggression, competition and computer games: computer and human opponents. *Comput. Hum. Behav. 18*, 5 (Sept. 2002), 495–506.

Online Gaming Motivations Scale:
Development and Validation

Nick Yee, Nicolas Ducheneaut, Les Nelson
Palo Alto Research Center
3333 Coyote Hill Road, Palo Alto, CA
[nyee, nicolas, lnelson]@parc.com

ABSTRACT
Understanding gaming motivations is important given the growing trend of incorporating game-based mechanisms in non-gaming applications. In this paper, we describe the development and validation of an online gaming motivations scale based on a 3-factor model. Data from 2,071 US participants and 645 Hong Kong and Taiwan participants is used to provide a cross-cultural validation of the developed scale. Analysis of actual in-game behavioral metrics is also provided to demonstrate predictive validity of the scale.

Author Keywords
Online games; player motivations; taxonomy; scale development; scale validation; cross-cultural.

ACM Classification Keywords
H5.m. [Information interfaces and presentation (e.g., HCI)]: Miscellaneous;

INTRODUCTION
Research in gameplay motivations across multiple fields has shown repeatedly that it is myopic to treat gamers as a monolithic group [1,4,10]: different people play games for very different reasons. Therefore, having a validated motivations taxonomy and a robust measure of those motivations would provide a crucial theoretical and methodological bridge between players and in-game behaviors and outcomes. This taxonomy and measurement tool could, for example, help in examining the links between demographics, motivation, engagement, retention, and learning or behavioral outcome.

Understanding player motivations is an important topic for CHI because gaming-related mechanisms are being implemented in many non-gaming applications, such as: location tracking (e.g., foursquare), news aggregation (e.g., Google News), and exercise monitoring (e.g., fitbit). Others have made the bolder claim that enterprises will have to design gaming mechanisms into everyday business to fully engage the gamer generation [6], In fact, Gartner has predicted that by 2014, more than 70% of Global 2000 organizations will have at least one gamified application [2]. Thus, understanding gamer psychology, and specifically their motivations for playing, is valuable even outside the context of games.

Many player and motivation taxonomies have been proposed, but most of these were not developed using statistical methods and do not provide a means for quantitative assessment (see for instance [4]). One exception in the domain of online gaming motivations is Yee's motivation taxonomy [10], based on a factor analytic examination and restructuring of Bartle's player taxonomy of MUD players [1]. Yee's research identified 10 motivations that fall into 3 higher-level categories related to: achievement, social, and immersion motivations. Given that current gamification efforts draw inspiration from online games (including both Facebook games and role-playing games like World of Warcraft), an existing taxonomy grounded in online gaming is a good starting point for our current research effort.

While Yee's research provided both a taxonomy and survey instrument for assessment, it suffers from 3 weaknesses:

1. Although Yee's taxonomy identified 3 higher-level motivation factors, his 39-item survey instrument assesses the underlying 10 components without providing a direct means of assessing the 3 high-level factors. Given that these factors parsimoniously capture many different motivations, it is important to construct and validate a shorter survey instrument that can directly assess them.
2. Yee's taxonomy was derived using an English-speaking participant sample, and it is unclear whether the factor analysis results would be consistent in other cultures. A replication in a non-Western culture would provide much-needed evidence of the applicability of the motivation taxonomy to other cultures.
3. And finally, Yee's research does not provide data on predictive validity--how well the self-report survey measures correlate with actual in-game behaviors. After all, just because a survey scale has high internal reliability doesn't mean it actually measures anything meaningful [8]. Data showing meaningful correlations with in-game behavioral metrics would provide evidence for predictive validity.

The current study attempts to resolve these 3 weaknesses by: 1) constructing and validating a survey measure of the 3 high-level motivation factors via factor analysis, 2) replicating the factor structure in a non-Western culture, and 3) examining the predictive validity of the scale in terms of correlations with in-game behavioral metrics.

STUDY ONE - SCALE DEVELOPMENT

We first describe how the revised scale was constructed and the initial validation of the scale using exploratory factor analysis.

Scale Construction

First, strong inventory items in each of the 10 components from Yee's 39-item scale were selected via factor loading. Then, in several intermediate pilot surveys (each with N > 300), we tested variants of these inventory items and iteratively selected items that had high factor loadings. In creating variants, we attempted to create shorter, more direct inventory items. For example, the item "How important is it to you that your character is as optimized as possible for their profession or role?" was revised to "Optimizing your character as much as possible". We also avoided items that were semantically similar. Finally, we streamlined the response options. Thus, while the original inventory items varied in using "how much", "how often", "how interested", and "how important" question stems, the revised items are all framed using "how important are these gameplay elements when you play online games". Thus, the response options are identical for all inventory items--a 5-point Likert scale ranging from 1 (Not Important At All) to 5 (Extremely Important). In the final iteration of this process, we selected 12 items (4 for each factor) as the final inventory set to be tested in this study (see Table 1).

Participants

To collect data for scale validation, we recruited *World of Warcraft* (WoW) players in the US to participate in an online survey version of the scale by posting announcements in high traffic websites and forums dedicated to WoW. Altogether, 2,071 WoW players participated in the survey. Of the participants, 1,358 were male, 709 were female, with an average age of 29.95 (SD = 9.20).

Exploratory Factor Analysis

To examine the underlying factor structure of the revised scale, we conducted an exploratory factor analysis (EFA)--a statistical procedure that examines the covariances among a set of variables to identify latent factors.

Kaiser's Meyer-Olkin measure of sampling adequacy was .78, while Bartlett's Test of Sphericity was significant at $p < .001$. These two measures indicate that the data set was appropriate for factor analysis.

We conducted an EFA in SPSS 18 using principal factors analysis. Given that most psychometric factors are mildly correlated, we used an oblique rotation. Three factors emerged with eigenvalues greater than 1. Examination of the scree plot also suggested a solution with 3 factors. Together, these 3 factors accounted for 59.3% of the overall variance. In Table 1, we report the pattern matrix.

Item	Soc.	Imm.	Ach.
Chatting with other players	**0.73**		
Being part of a guild	**0.70**		
Grouping with other players	**0.67**		
Keeping in touch with your friends	**0.60**	0.11	
Learning about stories and lore of the world		**0.78**	0.12
Feeling immersed in the world		**0.73**	0.11
Exploring the world just for the sake of exploring it		**0.60**	-0.14
Creating a background story and history for your character		**0.54**	-0.13
Becoming powerful			**0.73**
Acquiring rare items		0.13	**0.68**
Optimizing your character as much as possible		-0.12	**0.67**
Competing with other players			**0.55**
% of Variance	23.9%	21.4%	13.9%
Cronbach's α	.77	.75	.74

Table 1. Factor loadings. For ease of reference, we sort the items using their factor loadings with the primary loadings bolded, and exclude any factor loadings less than .10.

The pattern matrix shows that the scale items loaded onto 3 factors that correspond to Immersion, Social, and Achievement motivations respectively. The factor loadings are high; most are over .60. None of the cross-loadings are higher than .2. Finally, the scale items within each factor all have Cronbach α's above .70. Together, these findings suggest that the revised scale has a good factor structure and good internal reliability. In terms of inter-factor correlations, the Social factor was correlated with the Immersion and Achievement factors at .09 and .24 respectively. The Immersion factor was correlated with the Achievement factor at -.21.

Factor	Gender Means (SD)	Gender Differences	Age Corr.
Achievement	Male = .14 (.83) Female = -.27 (.91)	$t = 10.08$ $p < .001$	$r = -.27$ $p < .001$
Social	Male = -.05 (.88) Female = .09 (.90)	$t = -3.43$ $p < .005$	$r = -.13$ $p < .001$
Immersion	Male = -.07 (.89) Female = .13 (.87)	$t = -4.70$ $p < .001$	$r = -.01$ $p = .64$

Table 2. Gender and age differences.

For completeness, we report the gender and age differences related to the motivation factors in Table 2. We note that these differences are consistent with those previously reported [10].

STUDY TWO - CROSS-CULTURAL VALIDATION

To validate the scale cross-culturally, we recruited participants from Hong Kong (HK) and Taiwan (TW). These two non-Western cultures were selected because they share the same server pools (in Taiwan) and share a written language (traditional Chinese script).

Scale Preparation

To localize the scale, a bilingual translator first translated the scale into Chinese (traditional script). We then piloted the translated instrument with several WoW players in the two locations for idiomatic fluency and made several revisions. Finally, a different translator back-translated the scale into English to ensure the two English scales were comparable.

Participants

To collect data for the study, we recruited WoW players from HK and TW to participate in the online survey version of the scale by posting announcements in high traffic websites and forums dedicated to WoW. Altogether, 645 players participated in the study--406 from TW, 239 from HK. 514 participants were male, 128 were female. The average age was 23.59 (SD = 5.16).

Confirmatory Factor Analysis

To verify that the 3-factor structure replicates in a non-Western culture, we conducted a confirmatory factor analysis (CFA)--a statistical procedure that compares the fit of the data with a factor model specified by the researcher, or in essence, the opposite of the EFA procedure.

We conducted a CFA with Amos 18. In the specified CFA model, the three motivation factors were included as latent variables, each hypothesized to have a direct effect on the 4 corresponding measured scale items. Unique measurement errors were hypothesized to have a direct effect on each measured scale item. Finally, the 3 latent factors were hypothesized to co-vary with each other.

Maximum likelihood estimation was used for the analysis. The chi-square statistic of the model was significant (χ^2 [51] = 140.88, $p < .001$) as is expected from the large sample size. In these scenarios, goodness of fit indices provide a more meaningful assessment. We report here the common set of indices recommended: CFI = .95, SRMR = .04, and RMSEA = .05. All these values fall within the range of current recommendations for good model fit [3]. Thus, data from HK and TW were consistent with the 3-factor structure identified in the US data. More importantly, this implies that the factor structure of motivations we have identified is not simply an artifact of Western culture, and has some level of cross-cultural applicability.

STUDY THREE - PREDICTIVE VALIDITY

To examine predictive validity of the scale, we collected behavioral metrics within WoW and examined the correlations between the self-report and behavioral data.

Behavioral Metrics in WoW

The context of WoW and the availability of in-game metrics via the Armory have been described in the CHI literature [9]. Of particular relevance to our research goal is the existence of hundreds of in-game goals known as *achievements*. For example, there are achievements for exploring every zone within a continent, and achievements for killing a dungeon boss within a short amount of time. More importantly, these achievements are grouped into 6 categories and an aggregate achievement score is provided for each. These behavioral categories are automatically calculated and compiled by the game and require no additional coding on our part. These achievement categories map on to very different aspects of gameplay within WoW:

- Quests: Individual, easy, goal-based missions.
- Exploration: Systematic geographical exploration.
- PvP: Competitive, player-vs-player activity.
- Dungeons/Raids: Team-based collaboration with large rewards.
- Professions: Non-combat crafting skills.
- World Events: Thematic, seasonal, story-based events.

Our first hypothesis is that each of the motivation factors has a significant impact across this set of in-game behavioral categories.

To examine whether the relationships between the motivation factors and in-game behaviors are aligned with theory, we leveraged the behavioral expectations of the motivation factors from Yee's original work [10]. We hypothesized that the Achievement factor would correlate positively with Dungeons/Raids and PvP (related to Yee's Advancement and Competition components respectively). We hypothesized that the Social factor would correlate positively with Dungeons/Raids, suggested by Yee's Teamwork component. And we hypothesized that the Immersion factor would correlate positively with Exploration, as suggested by Yee's Discovery component.

Data Collection

From the data sets already collected, we randomly sampled 500 participants from the US region, as well as 500 participants from the HK and TW region for behavioral data collection. In the online survey, participants were asked to list their active characters. On average, each participant had 2.79 active characters (*SD* = 1.51). We used an XML scraper to collect data from the Armory for each character over a 6-month period and used the most recent character snapshots for the following analysis.

To generate a player-level metric across characters, we calculated the score ratio for each achievement category (i.e., = category achievement score/total achievement score) across all of a player's characters. This allowed us to avoid confounding achievement scores with character levels.

Results

We calculated the factor score for each motivation factor and conducted a multivariate regression using these factor scores to predict the in-game achievement category ratios, controlling for gender and age. The multivariate tests were significant for the Achievement (F = 19.95, $p < .001$), Social (F = 11.61, $p < .001$), and Immersion (F = 3.38, $p < .01$) factors. Thus, it is clear that the self-report data has a significant relationship with the set of in-game behavioral metrics. The individual regression coefficients are shown in Table 2. Our hypothesized correlations are all supported by the data. In addition, we note that the Achievement factor is strongly negatively correlated with Professions, Exploration, and Quests. In hindsight, it makes sense that activities that do not lead directly to functional rewards are not appealing to Achievement-oriented players. The same is true of the negative correlation between Quests and the Social factor. Given that quests are now designed to be completed alone, it is not surprising in hindsight that Social-oriented players find quests less appealing.

Category	ACH	SOC	IMM	Adj R^2	p
Quests	**-.21**	**-.16**	**.10**	.13	< .001
Exploration	**-.21**	**-.09**	**.09**	.17	< .001
PvP	**.14**	-.05	**-.07**	.18	< .001
Dungeons	**.28**	**.18**	**-.10**	.30	< .001
Professions	**-.19**	**-.14**	.06	.25	< .001
World Event	**-.11**	.03	.05	.11	< .001

Table 3. Standardized beta coefficients and significance of regression models. Bolded coefficients are p < .01.

CONCLUSION

Data provided in this paper show that online gaming motivations can be parsimoniously captured using a 3-factor model. Our assessment tool for this model was validated in both a Western and non-Western culture using rigorous statistical methods. And finally, self-report data using this measure is significantly correlated with actual in-game behavioral metrics. Together, this data demonstrates the robust validity and reliability of the developed scale.

On the other hand, there are several weaknesses that should be mentioned. First, we only collected data from players of one online game. However, the concordance between the current findings and the earlier work (using a broader online gaming sample) provides moderate assurance that these factors generalize more broadly than just WoW. Nevertheless, future research should attempt to validate this scale with players of additional online games. Secondly, the behavioral correlations with the Immersion factor were not particularly strong. Future studies should examine whether this is an artifact of WoW lacking good in-game variables relating to Immersion, or whether the subjective nature of the Immersion items are poorly captured by behavioral metrics in general. Finally, validating the scale in other cultures would help us understand how universal the 3-factor structure is.

As we mentioned in the introduction, game-related mechanisms have been predicted to slowly permeate many application categories. We believe that the development of a robust and well-validated scale is an important foundation in understanding why players play, what mechanisms may work better for different demographic segments, and variances in learning or behavioral outcomes.

Beyond this usage, leveraging the scale to understand a player's profile before they start using a game (or game-like) system opens the possibility of tailoring their experience to better match their motivations – and such personalization has been a topic of interest at CHI for many years [5,7]. In fact, our in-game data shows that this process could even be automated to infer player motivations directly from their in-game behaviors, raising the possibility of dynamically tailoring a player's experience over time and without explicitly asking them for information. Such personalization, dynamic or otherwise, would most likely increase the efficiency of many of the game-like systems starting to appear at CHI and elsewhere.

ACKNOWLEDGEMENTS

This research was sponsored by the Air Force Research Laboratory.

REFERENCES

1. Bartle, R. Hearts, Clubs, Diamonds, Spades: Players Who Suit MUDs. *The Journal of Virtual Environments 1*, (1996).
2. Gartner. Gartner Newsroom Press Release. 2011. http://www.gartner.com/it/page.jsp?id=1629214.
3. Hu, L. and Bentler, P. Cutoff criteria for fit indexes in covariance structure analysis: Coventional criteria versus new alternatives. *Structural Equation Modeling 6*, (1999), 1-55.
4. Lazarro, N. Why We Play Games: Four Keys to More Emotion Without Story. *GDC*, (2004).
5. Mackay, W. Triggers and Barriers to Customizing Software. *Proceedings of SIGCHI 1*, (1991), 153-160.
6. Reeves, B. and Reed, L. *Total Engagement: Using Games and Virtual Worlds to Change the Way People Work and Businesses Compete*. Harvard Business School Press, 2009.
7. Riecken, D. Personalized Views of Personalization. *Communications of the ACM 43*, (2000), 26-28.
8. Slater, M. How colorful was your day? Why questionnaires cannot assess presence in virtual environments. *Presence: Teleoperators and Virtual Environments 13*, (2004), 484-493.
9. Yee, N., Ducheneaut, N., Nelson, L., and Likarish, P. Introverted Elves and Conscientious Gnomes. The Expression of Personality in World of Warcraft. *Proceedings of CHI 1*, (2011), 753-762.
10. Yee, N. Motivations for Play in Online Games. *Journal of CyberPsychology and Behavior 9*, (2007), 772-775.

Experimental Investigation of Human Adaptation to Change in Agent's Strategy through a Competitive Two-Player Game

Kazunori Terada
Gifu University
Yanagido 1-1, Gifu, Japan
501-1193
terada@gifu-u.ac.jp

Seiji Yamada
National Institute of Informatics / SOKENDAI
2-1-2 Hitotsubashi, Chiyoda, Tokyo, Japan 101-8430
seiji@nii.ac.jp

Akira Ito
Gifu University
Yanagido 1-1, Gifu, Japan
501-1193
ai@gifu-u.ac.jp

ABSTRACT
We conducted an experimental investigation on human adaptation to change in an agent's strategy through a competitive two-player game. Modeling the process of human adaptation to agents is important for designing intelligent interface agents and adaptive user interfaces that learn a user's preferences and behavior strategy. However, few studies on human adaptation to such an agent have been done. We propose a human adaptation model for a two-player game. We prepared an on-line experimental system in which a participant and an agent play a repeated penny-matching game with a bonus round. We then conducted experiments in which different opponent agents (human or robot) change their strategy during the game. The experimental results indicated that, as expected, there is an adaptation phase when a human is confronted with a change in the opponent agent's strategy, and adaptation is faster when a human is competing with robot than with another human.

Author Keywords
Human-Agent Interaction; human adaptation to an agent; two player game; appearance; intentional stance.

ACM Classification Keywords
H.5.2 [Information Interfaces And Presentation]: User Interfaces - Theory and methods;

General Terms
Experimentation; Human Factors.

INTRODUCTION
Human-Agent Interaction, Human-Robot Interaction and embodied conversational agents have been extensively studied in the HCI community. It is important to experimentally investigate the human adaptation process to construct an agent model to use when a user confronts an agent. Such a model enables us to adequately design an agent's appearance and behavior based on its influence on user adaptation [6, 8]. Although there have been many studies that have focused on the influence of an agent's appearance and behavior on humans [7, 5, 3], few have investigated human adaptation to an agent.

We believe human adaptation to change in an agent's behavior strategy is especially significant in various human adaptations. Because intelligent agents that learn a user's preference and behaviors have been developed, and most constantly change their behaviors through learning. To maintain successful interaction, a user needs to recognize and adapt to the agent's change in strategy.

We experimentally investigated human adaptation to change in an agent's behavior strategy through a simple two-player game. We prepared a modified matching-pennies game. A participant and an agent play the game through the on-line experimental system. The independent variable is the opponent agent's appearance including a bear-like robot and a human. The opponent agent changes its behavior strategy during the game. We carefully observed the behaviors of the participant to the change in the agent's strategy and investigated how different agent appearances influence human adaptation by using two different opponent agents.

Komatsu and Yamada proposed the *Adaptation Gap*[4], which describes the difference between an agent model and a user model before/after actual interaction, and conducted various experiments to understand human adaptation. Their focused sign $(+, 0, -)$ of adaptation gap's value AG, and made the following assumptions, "$AG < 0$: most people would be disappointed by the agent and would stop interacting with it and $AG > 0$: most users would continue interacting with it".

Gajos et al. [2] also studied human adaptability to an adaptive user interface. They prepared a simple adaptive user interface equipped with strategies, and conducted experiments to determine the relationship between a user's predictability on behaviors of the adaptive user interface and its accuracy in such an environment. They observed that improvement in the system's accuracy had a stronger effect on user's performance and satisfaction than the improvement in predictability.

MODEL OF HUMAN ADAPTATION TO AGENT

Model of human adaptation phase
We modeled the process of human adaptation to an agent's change in strategy in terms of exploitation and adaptation

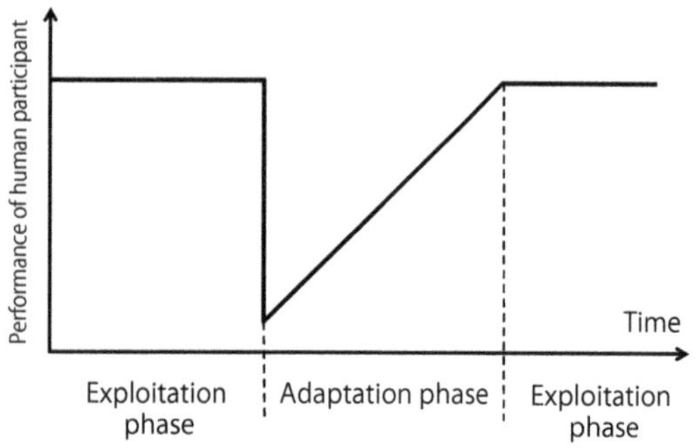

Figure 1. Player's performance in adaptation and exploitation phases.

phases. We focused on the adaptation phase in a competitive two-player game because adaptation to an agent's change in strategy is critical in a competitive situation. Figure 1 shows a simplified performance profile of a player in this two-phase framework. In a competitive two-player game, a player needs to identify the opponent's behavior strategy and decide his/her behavior strategy based on it. However, estimating the opponent's strategy based only on observed behavior is an ill-posed inverse problem because different strategies sometimes produce the same behavior. Therefore, probing an agent's strategy by actively changing player's strategy is more effective for quickly estimating than just waiting without changing strategy: the *adaptation phase*.

The player's performance in the adaptation phase increases according to improvement in estimation accuracy; therefore, performance in this phase can be approximately modeled as a linear function of time not as a step function. Once the player identified the opponent's strategy, he/she purely executes actions according to the current strategy and exploits the opponent as long as the opponent's strategy is stable in time: the *exploitation phase*. These two phases are repeated alternately.

The length of the adaptation phase differs depending on the complexity of the opponent's strategy. A more complex strategy requires a longer adaptation period because more probing steps are needed to identify the opponent's strategy. The gradient of the adaptation phase in Figure 1 indicates *adaptation speed*.

Different adaptation to different opponents

The appearance of an agent affects its modeling of cognitive ability and behavior. Dennett [1] proposed three stances, "intentional", "design", and "physical", as a criterion for an observer to model an object. Physical stance is the most concrete and concerned with the domain of physics. At this level, we are concerned with such things as mass, energy, and velocity. More abstract is the design stance, which is the domain of biology and engineering. At this level, we are concerned with such things as purpose, function, and design. Intentional stance is the most abstract and concerned with the domain of human/agent's minds. At this level, we recognize objects in terms of the belief, thinking, and intention.

With an artificial agent, we often recognize it as having intention (an intentional stance) as well as just being a machine (a design stance). Various factors, such as human-like appearance and life-like autonomy, lead a human to an intentional stance. Thus, we assigned a human opponent player and a robot player as independent variables for our experiments and investigated the change in human adaptation depending on whether the opponent is human or a robot. We expected a participant to construct a simpler and deterministic strategy model for a robot opponent and a more complicated and probabilistic model for a human one. Hence, we also expected human adaptation to a human opponent to be faster than to a robot opponent. As described in the next section, this expectation is hypothesized and verified by observing adaptation speed in an experiment with human participants.

EXPERIMENTS

The above-mentioned model of human adaptation to an agent leads to the following hypotheses:

H1: An adaptation phase exists when a human is confronted with a change in the opponent's strategy.

H2: Adaptation is faster when a human is competing with a robot than with a human.

The two hypotheses were tested through an experiment with human participants.

Penny-matching game with bonus round

A repeated penny-matching game with a bonus round was created for validating the hypotheses. The penny-matching game is a zero-sum game and is played between two players, players A and B. Each player has a penny and must secretly turn the penny to heads or tails. The players then reveal their own choices simultaneously. If the pennies match (both heads or both tails) player A keeps both pennies and gets to keep player B's penny (+1 for A, -1 for B). If the pennies do not match (one heads and one tails), player B keeps both pennies (-1 for A, +1 for B). While this game has no pure strategy Nash equilibrium, the unique Nash equilibrium of this game is in mixed strategies: each player chooses heads or tails with equal probability.

We modified the game rules so that players are able to use a deceptive strategy. The penny-matching game was played repeatedly. One game consists of six rounds, and ten games were played in the experiment. The payoff of the sixth round in every game is increased twenty times: the bonus round. A reasonable strategy for this game is to strive to win the bonus round and abandon the other five rounds because of the large payoff gap. A player is able to trap the opponent by making a series of choices during the normal five rounds so that the opponent's prediction of the player's sixth choice will be wrong. Note that the unique Nash equilibrium of the penny-matching game with a bonus round is still a mixed (random) one even though the bonus round is added.

The agents used as opponents in our experiment used only the two strategies (straightforward and deceptive) listed in Table 1. The two strategies are realized with two series of uniform and alternate choices. Uniform and alternate choices in the first five rounds were suggestive of the opponent; i.e., those exposed to the obvious trapping choices are forced to

round		1	2	3	4	5	6
payoff		1	1	1	1	1	20
straightforward	uniform	●	●	●	●	●	●
	alternate	●	○	●	○	●	○
deceptive	uniform	●	●	●	●	●	○
	alternate	●	○	●	○	●	●

Table 1. Two strategies (straightforward and deceptive) in penny-matching game with bonus round used in experiment. Black and white circles represent heads and tails, respectively. Only difference between straightforward and deceptive strategy is choice in sixth round.

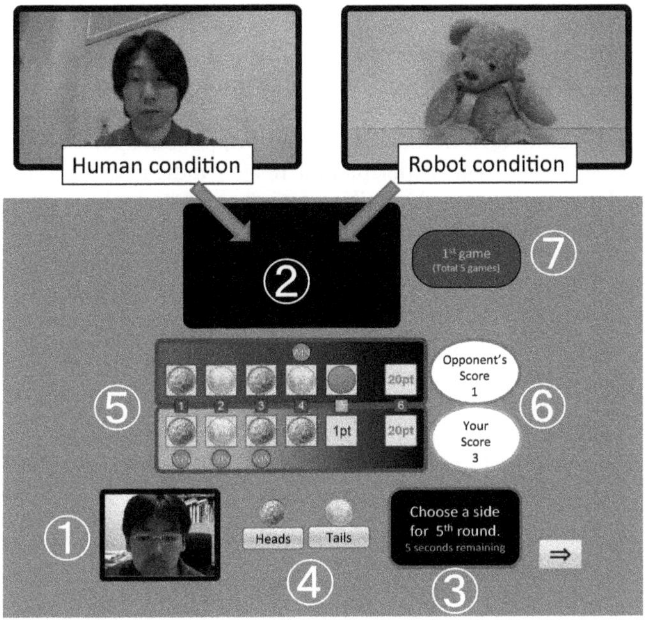

Figure 2. Interface of on-line experimental system: 1) participant's face, 2) opponent agent's appearance, 3) remaining time, 4) choice buttons, 5) histories of both players' choices, 6) scores for both players, and 7) game number.

anticipate that the opponent's sixth choice will be either deceptive (violating regularity) or straightforward (keeping regularity).

Experimental setup and measurement

The game was implemented with JavaScript and HTML and played in a Web browser (Firefox). Figure 2 shows the game interface. A Flash video of the opponent (robot or human) is displayed at the top of the interface. The bear-like robot moves its head and arms randomly in the video. The behavior of the human was recorded when he played the game in advance. The agents' behaviors, such as choosing a side of the coin, are automatically controlled by JavaScript program. Participants were told that the opponent is online. To make the participants believe the game is online, the participants' faces captured using a web camera mounted on the monitor were displayed at the bottom of the interface. Participants were instructed to click the button corresponding to his/her choice within 10 seconds for every round. Scores for both players are shown in the interface. The choices of both players remain displayed so that the participant is able to recognize the opponent's strategy. Before the main experiment, all participants played five games only for training.

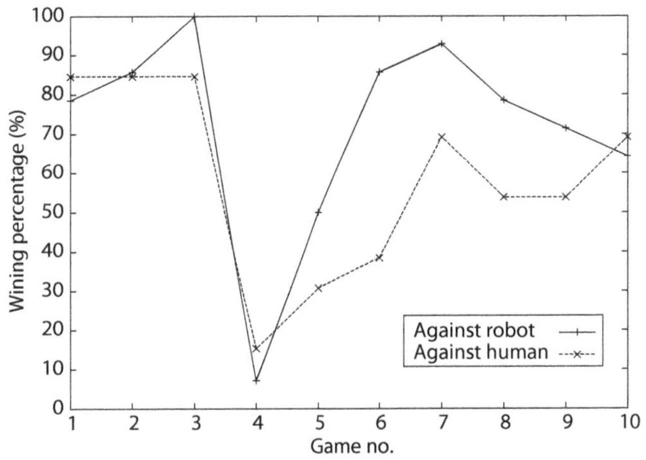

Figure 3. Percentage of participants who won sixth round of ten games.

A single-factor two-level between-subject experimental design was used. Twenty-eight graduate and undergraduate students participated in the study. Participants were randomly assigned to either a robot or human opponent condition and were seated in front of a desktop computer. Participants were informed that the point of the experiment was to access the usability of an online game system.

A total of eight series of choices including another four series beginning from tails equivalent to the four series shown in Table 1 were used. The agents used a straightforward strategy, one of the four series of straightforward strategy was randomly selected, in the first three games and a deceptive one for the rest. This is the change in agent's behavior strategy during the game, and observing human adaptation to it is our aim of the experiment.

The outcomes of the sixth round for all ten games were recorded because the participants' expectation of their opponents' strategies, i.e., which strategy, straightforward or deceptive, did they expect, was of interest. Winning the sixth round against an agent indicates that the participants expectation of the agent's strategy is correct.

RESULTS

The percentages of the participants who won the sixth round for all ten games are shown in Figure 3. Almost all the participants lost the fourth game because the agents changed their strategy from straightforward to deceptive. After the fourth game, the winning percentage with both opponent agents gradually recovered to the level of the third game. A chi-square test was conducted to investigate whether the winning percentages of the fourth to tenth games were different from that of third one (see Table 2). The results indicate that at least two games were required to adapt to the change in strategy of both agents. The gradual increase in the winning percentage after the opponent's strategy changed indicates the existence of the adaptation phase, confirming hypothesis **H1**.

The differences between recovery speeds of the winning percentage between those playing against the robot and those against the human agent (plotted on the graph in Figure 3)

Game no.	4	5	6	7	8	9	10
Against robot condition	**24.26, p<.01**	**19.33, p<.01**	2.15, n.s.	1.04, n.s.	3.36, n.s.	**4.67, p<.05**	**6.09, p<.05**
Against human condition	**14.29, p<.01**	**7.34, p<.01**	**5.60, p<.05**	0.85, n.s.	2.80, n.s.	2.80, n.s.	0.85, n.s.

Table 2. Chi-Square values (df=1) and significance levels for the winning percentages of fourth to tenth games compared with that of the third one.

were statistically confirmed. Table 2 indicates that those who played against a human agent required one more game for adapting to their opponent's change in strategy than those who played against a robot. This implies that participant's adaptation speed against a human is significantly slower than against a robot, confirming hypothesis **H2**.

DISCUSSION

The participants did not equate the robot to the human in terms of adaptation speed against the opponent's change in strategy. While the strategy equally changed in the fourth game for both opponents, what caused the inequality in participant's adaptation speed is the difference in the video the participants watched. Slow adaptation of the participants who played against the human indicates that they were cautious but not optimistic against the opponent's strategies after the strategy change in the fourth game. This is because the human appearance made the participants anticipate another change in the human opponent's strategy, and the robot appearance gave the participants the impression that its strategy was stable. The behavior of the designed artifacts, including robots and computers, is governed by laws such as mechanical, algorithmic, or structural constraints; therefore, the input-output relations of the artifacts are stable. This prototypical concept of artifact's regulated behavior might make the participants expect the simpler and less complicated strategy of the robot.

There are two causes for the gradual increase in the winning percentage in the adaptation phase: 1) Each participant changed his/her strategy just once in the adaptation phase (during games 5 to 7) and the timings of the changes varied across the participants. 2) Each participant changed his/her strategy plural times to find the most suitable strategy. To investigate these causes, we compared the number of strategy changes in the adaptation phase in two conditions. The average number of strategy changes by the participants was 1.07 under an "against robot" condition and 1.57 under an "against human" condition was 1.57, so there was a marginally significant difference ($t(26) = 1.919$, $p = 0.066$). This suggests that strategy changes by the participants were one-shot deterministic under an "against robot" condition bat indecisive and exploratory under an "against human" condition.

We consider the drop of winning percentage in the eighth game could be accounted for by meta-adaptation. Our game design requires at least two levels to be adapted. The first is adaptation for regularity of the agent's choice in the first five rounds. The second is adaptation for strategy change in the fourth game. The third, which was beyond our expectations, is an adaptation for periodic change in an agent's strategy. Participants might think the agent's strategy changes once every three games and so expect to change again in the seventh game.

Not only the appearance but also the behavior of the agents differed between the two videos. We did not separate the appearance and motion factors in our experiment. Investigating which factor contributes to the change in human adaptation speed to an agent is for future work.

CONCLUSION

We theoretically modeled and experimentally investigated human adaptation to an agent. We conducted a penny-matching game with a bonus round in a web browser for investigating how humans adapt to an opponent agent's change in strategy. The experimental results indicated there is an adaptation phase when a human is confronted with a change in the opponent agent's strategy, and adaptation is faster when a human is competing with robot than with another human. Although this experiment might be just a preliminary stage, we strongly believe this work provided a significant case study and will be inspiration for practical design of an agent and its interaction with a human.

REFERENCES

1. Dennett, D. C. *The Intentional Stance*. Cambridge, Mass, Bradford Books/MIT Press, 1987.
2. Gajos, K. Z., Everitt, K., Tan, D. S., Czerwinski, M., and Weld, D. S. Predictability and accuracy in adaptive user interfaces. In *CHI'08* (2008), 1271–1274.
3. Kiesler, S. Fostering common ground in human-robot interaction. In *RO-MAN'05* (2005), 729–734.
4. Komatsu, T., Kurosawa, R., and Yamada, S. How does the difference between users' expectations and perceptions – about a robotic agent affect their behavior? *Int. Journal of Social Robotics* (2011), 1–8.
5. McQuiggan, S. W., Rowe, J. P., and Lester, J. C. The effects of empathetic virtual characters on presence in narrative-centered learning environments. In *CHI'08* (2008), 1511–1520.
6. Tinwell, A., and Grimshaw, M. Bridging the uncanny: an impossible traverse? In *Proceedings of the 13th International MindTrek Conference: Everyday Life in the Ubiquitous Era*, MindTrek '09 (2009), 66–73.
7. Vugt, H. C. V., Bailenson, J. N., Hoorn, J. F., and Konijn, E. A. Effects of facial similarity on user responses to embodied agents. *ACM Tran. on Computer-Human Interaction 17* (May 2008), 7:1–7:27.
8. Yee, N., Bailenson, J. N., and Rickertsen, K. A meta-analysis of the impact of the inclusion and realism of human-like faces on user experiences in interfaces. In *CHI'07* (2007), 1–10.

Through the Azerothian Looking Glass:
Mapping In-Game Preferences to Real World Demographics

Nick Yee[1], Nicolas Ducheneaut[1], Han-Tai Shiao[2], Les Nelson[1]

[1]Palo Alto Research Center
3333 Coyote Hill Road, Palo Alto, CA
[nyee, nicolas, lnelson]@parc.com

[2]University of Minnesota, Twin Cities
200 Union St, Minneapolis, MN
shiao003@umn.edu

ABSTRACT
Examining how in-game behavior preferences map onto real world demographics provides important empirically-derived insights into how to match game-based mechanisms to target demographic segments. Using behavioral and demographic data from 1,037 World of Warcraft players, we use multiple regressions to provide this mapping. Given current interest in "gamifying" applications, we believe these findings are relevant for both gaming and non-gaming research.

Author Keywords
In-game behaviors; gamification; player demographics.

ACM Classification Keywords
H5.m. [Information interfaces and presentation (e.g., HCI)]: Miscellaneous;

INTRODUCTION

Research in online games hints at a fascinating irony in their "massively multiplayer" social dynamics—that their affordances and scope shape a culture of being "alone together" [2] and that it is precisely the disparity in motivations for playing that causes tensions to emerge among players [1]. This research underscores a crucial point about gamers; they play the same game for very different reasons.

Studying this intersection between in-game preferences and real world demographics using quantitative methods has historically been a challenge. Most game companies closely guard their server data for marketing and competition reasons. And access to in-game data alone does not reveal the player demographics without an additional survey component. Nevertheless, as more and more applications incorporate gaming mechanisms to enhance user engagement and behavioral outcomes, it is important to gather empirical data on how in-game preferences are related to real world demographics. Just as some examples of this "gamification" trend, game-based mechanisms have been implemented in chemotherapy compliance (e.g., Remission), loyalty reward programs (e.g., My Starbucks Rewards), and finding protein folding solutions (e.g., Foldit). Indeed, this trend is expected to permeate even corporate business applications and Gartner [3] has predicted that by 2014, 70% of Global 2000 companies will have at least one gamified application.

Empirical data linking in-game preferences with real world demographics would provide insight into 3 issues relevant to CHI at different stages of game and gamified application development:

1) In designing and developing game-based elements, which game mechanisms should be prioritized given a target audience? Quantitative data would allow us to provide a framework for this mapping.

2) Given the variety of options and choices within a game, can we dynamically emphasize different game elements to a user given their demographic? This dynamic tailoring would allow us to maximize engagement with different users.

3) And finally, after a game or gamified application has been deployed, how might adding or removing a game mechanism impact a community at the demographic level? Again, an empirical mapping would allow predictive modeling of how different demographic segments might react to the change (in terms of retention and new players).

Previous research in this area has tended to rely on self-report data, linking demographics with player motivations [4,5,6,9] (although the Virtual World Exploratorium [7] and the PARC PlayOn group [2] are notable exceptions). Without in-game data, it is difficult to assess how well those findings generalize to actual in-game behaviors. Nevertheless, this research in player motivations is consistent in finding that men are more driven by achievement motivations [6,9]. Data on the other motivation factors are more mixed. For example, two studies found women to be more engaged with social factors [6,9], while another two studies found that women were less likely to be motivated by social interaction [4,5]. It is worth noting, however, that the former studies emphasize in-game socializing, while the latter studies emphasize real-world socializing—a distinction that may have contributed to the different findings.

It is also worth noting that there are even fewer data points on age differences in gaming motivations since most studies have used small or college-based samples. [9] is an exception, finding that younger players are more achievement-oriented, and that age in fact explains more variance than gender does.

For this paper, we conducted a study that paired behavioral data from the online game *World of Warcraft* (WoW) with self-report demographic data to directly examine the links between in-game preferences and real world demographics. We also included additional demographic variables beyond gender and age to provide a broader demographic profile mapping, such as marital and child status, regular playing times, and number of days spent playing. Given that past research provides few consistent anchor points (beyond the gender and age differences in achievement), it is more sensible to approach the behavioral mapping as open research questions. Thus, while we expect male and younger players to prefer achievement-oriented activities, we do not make any specific hypotheses regarding social or immersion factors.

METHOD

WoW is a popular online role-playing game set in a fantasy context. Since the dynamics and game-play of WoW have been previously described in the CHI literature [2,8], we will only emphasize aspects of WoW that are particularly relevant to our study.

There are two reasons why in-game data from WoW is unique. First, Blizzard (the developers of WoW) have decided to release in-game data to third-parties via a web portal known as the Armory. The Armory provides over 3,500 variables for each active character. Second, behavioral variables in WoW are provided in meaningful hierarchies and categories. This is in contrast to systems like Second Life where the sandbox nature of the environment makes it difficult to create a set of meaningful behavioral variables. Thus, in Second Life, the system only captures raw metrics such as distance moved and number of other avatars within a certain radius—metrics that are difficult to map to meaningful behaviors. In WoW, on the other hand, many meaningful behaviors are captured. For example, the Armory provides variables on hugs given and deaths by falling from high places.

Achievement Categories

Furthermore, WoW has an internally-defined mapping of in-game actions into 6 high-level achievement categories. These categories provide parsimonious metrics of in-game preferences. These categories are:

- **Quests:** Goal-based missions that have been designed to be completed by individual players without much difficulty or unexpected complications. Quest completions provide small rewards.
- **Exploration:** Systematic geographical exploration of the game world that provides no functional reward.
- **PvP:** Competitive, player-vs-player activity. Can be 1-on-1 duels or group-based battles.
- **Dungeons/Raids:** Team-based collaboration that requires moderate to high time investment, contains moderate to high risk, but provides large rewards.
- **Professions:** Non-combat crafting skills that individual characters can develop and master to produce usable goods and equipment.
- **World Events:** Thematic, seasonal, story-based events that provide cosmetic rewards. For example, a lunar New Year event provides quests for a brocade-style dress and decorative fireworks.

While these achievement categories do not cover all aspects of in-game behaviors (e.g., no chat data is processed), they nevertheless cover a broad selection of in-game preferences. For example, these categories cover both collaborative and competitive activities, combat and non-combat activities, and individual and group-based activities.

Participants

To collect data for this study, we used an online survey to recruit participants and gather demographic information, followed by extracting Armory and in-game data for those participants' characters in WoW. The study was advertised in high traffic websites and forums dedicated to WoW (e.g., WoW Insider). Altogether, 1,037 WoW players participated in the study, of which 762 were male and 273 were female. The average age was 27.03 (SD = 8.21). Participants were asked to list their active characters. Each player had on average 2.79 characters (SD = 1.51).

Real World Demographic and Play Pattern Variables

The following demographic variables were collected in the self-report surveys. We specify the numeric codings as they are used for the regression analysis reported later. The demographic variables were: 1) gender, coded as male (1), female (0), 2) age, 3) marital status, coded as single/divorced/widowed (0) and partnered/married (1), 4) child status, coded as no (0) and yes (1).

Additionally, play pattern variables were derived from a LUA-based script deployed within the game client. Every hour, the script runs a "/who" command for characters in our study and notes whether the character was observed online. The script was deployed from 03/2010 to 09/2010. This data allowed us to map out the playing patterns of players over the 6-month period (and including the career data accumulated prior to the study period). We created 4 daily time segments (keyed to server time) and calculated the ratios for these 4 segments: 1) midnight (12am-6am), morning (6am-12pm), afternoon (12pm-6pm), and evening (6pm-12am). Thus, a 0.80 in evening would mean that over the course of 6 months, a player spent 80% of their playing time in the evening hours. And finally, we calculated a "unique days played" variable based on this data.

In-Game Behavioral Variables

A scripted XML collection tool was used to collect the relevant Armory variables on a daily basis. To create a player-level aggregate variable across their characters, we added up the achievement category scores and total scores across characters, and then divided the category total by the full total for each category. In this way, we derived 6 category ratios for each player. For example, a 0.25 in the Quest category would mean that across all of a player's characters, 25% of their achievements are in the Quest category. Since players who spend more time playing have completed more achievements (correlation between days played and total achievement score is $r = .45$, $p < .001$), these ratios avoid any confounds with character level and time spent playing the game.

RESULTS

To examine the relationship between the achievement category ratios and the real-world demographics and play pattern variables, we conducted a series of multiple regressions using the achievement ratios as the dependent variables. The regressions allow us to precisely see the unique contribution of each variable, as well as the overall significance of each model. The latter is an indicator of how well in-game preferences can be predicted on real world demographics alone. For each regression, we use a table to concisely present the significant standardized coefficients. Complete results (including the non-significant findings) are presented in a web appendix.

We found that older players and players with less playing time preferred quests in WoW (Table 1). Given that quests do not need to be scheduled and can be completed alone, it makes sense that players with less flexible schedules and less playing time would prefer them. Similar to earlier research on playing "alone together" [2] illustrating a multi-tier approach to social engagament, WoW also provides a casual path alongside its more time-intensive raiding option.

Variable	Beta	t	p
Age	0.27	7.16	0.00
Days Played	-0.16	-4.31	0.00
Adj. $R^2 = 0.9$, F[1016] = 11.57, p < .001			

Table 1. Multiple Regression results for Quests

In terms of the Exploration category (Table 2), we found that this activity was preferred by female players, by older players, and by players who often play in the morning. The gender and age coefficients are consistent with the earlier reported gender and age effects on the appeal of goal-oriented achievement in games. Given that exploration in WoW does not directly lead to functional rewards, this pattern makes sense. Again, WoW illustrates that it is possible to build game mechanisms for very different demographics side by side via branching options.

Variable	Beta	t	p
Gender	-0.10	-3.12	0.00
Age	0.28	7.47	0.00
Time: Morning	0.10	2.94	0.00
Adj. $R^2 = 0.13$, F[1016] = 17.27, p < .001			

Table 2. Multiple regression results for Exploration

For PvP, we found a preference for this activity by male players, by younger players, by those who have children, and by those who play in the evenings. This finding is largely consistent with previous research showing that competitiveness is correlated with younger players and male players [9]. The "children" correlation was unexpected. By itself, having children is negatively correlated with the PvP ratio ($r = .09$, $p < .001$). But since older players are more likely to have children and older players are less competitive, we need to control for the effect of age to examine the unique contribution of having children. In this case, the multiple regression revealed that having children actually increases the interest in PvP.

Variable	Beta	t	p
Gender	0.23	7.79	0.00
Age	-0.30	-8.43	0.00
Child Status	0.10	2.71	0.01
Time: Evening	-0.08	-2.28	0.02
Adj. $R^2 = 0.18$, F[1016] = 23.85, p < .001			

Table 3. Multiple regression results for PvP

In terms of Dungeons and Raids, the aspect of the game with the least flexible demand on time, we found that this activity is preferred by male players, by younger players, by players who are single and don't have children, and who concentrate their playing time in the evenings. We begin to see a bifurcation with younger players and male players preferring competitive, hack-and-slash activities, and older and female players preferring non-combat activities. We will continue to see this split with the remaining achievement categories.

Variable	Beta	t	p
Gender	0.19	6.65	0.00
Age	-0.28	-7.86	0.00
Marital Status	-0.07	-2.11	0.03
Child Status	-0.08	-2.23	0.03
Time: Morning	-0.10	-3.13	0.00
Time: Afternoon	-0.12	-3.82	0.00
Time: Evening	0.08	2.53	0.01
Adj. $R^2 = 0.22$, F[1016] = 33.13, p < .001			

Table 4. Multiple regression results for Dungeons/Raids

We found a preference for Professions among female players, older players, players who play in the mornings and afternoons, and players who play fewer days. Like Quests, we find a profile for older, more casual gamers here.

Variable	Beta	t	p
Gender	-0.20	-6.95	0.00
Age	0.36	10.26	0.00
Time: Morning	0.06	2.03	0.04
Time: Afternoon	0.14	4.52	0.00
Time: Evening	-0.09	-2.77	0.01
Days Played	-0.09	-2.55	0.01
Adj. $R^2 = 0.23$, $F[1016] = 34.42$, $p < .001$			

Table 5. Multiple regression for Professions

And finally for World Events, we found a preference for this activity among female players, and players with more playing time.

Variable	Beta	t	p
Gender	-0.23	-7.71	0.00
Days Played	0.18	4.99	0.00
Adj. $R^2 = 0.13$, $F[1016] = 18.45$, $p < .001$			

Table 6. Multiple regression for World Events

We present the overall gender and age correlations with the achievement categories in Table 7.

Variable	Qu.	Expl.	PvP	Dung.	Pro.	W. Ev.
Gender	-.05	**-.16**	**.29**	**.26**	**-.29**	**-.28**
Age	**-.25**	**.33**	**-.32**	**-.39**	**.40**	**.18**

Table 7. Correlations between gender, age, and achievement category ratios. Gender was scored as Male (1), Female (0).

CONCLUSION

The multiple regression results inadvertently hint at why WoW may be such a successful game—the game caters to very different players with different demographic and engagement profiles without forcing a particular play style onto players. Overall, the findings begin to trace out a bifurcated mapping between in-game preferences and demographics. We found that male players, younger players, and players with more time to play prefer competitive and high reward activities, which tend to have fairly inflexible time demands. On the other hand, female player, older players, and players with less time to play prefer non-combat activities that have more flexible demands on time.

Our findings also directly address the 3 design issues relevant to CHI that we mentioned in the introduction. First, these findings help designers prioritize game elements given a target audience. For example, games for younger players should emphasize rewards and competition. Second, the significant regression models show that it is possible to predict game preferences based on demographics alone. Thus, a game tutorial, knowing that the user is male, can emphasize the leader board to increase initial engagement. And third, our findings provide a framework for understanding how enhancement or removal of a game component might impact the player base at a demographic level. For example, enhancing PvP would likely increase retention of younger players.

Several weaknesses bear mentioning. First, our study only focused on one game. Future studies should further examine this mapping in other games. Second, we relied on a convenience sample, and further work will be required to understand how generalizable these findings are. And finally, our reliance on public data feeds meant that we did not have access to all possible in-game variables, such as the rich information in chat logs.

While it is easy to ask players what they enjoy via a survey, it is important to observe what players actually do in a game to make empirically-driven design decisions. Given the interest in gamifying applications, we believe our findings provide an important mapping between in-game preferences and real world demographics.

ACKNOWLEDGEMENTS & WEB APPENDIX

This research was sponsored by the Air Force Research Laboratory. A web appendix listing the detailed methods and regression results is available at: http://www.nickyee.com/wmap.html.

REFERENCES

1. Bartle, R. Hearts, Clubs, Diamonds, Spades: Players Who Suit MUDs. *The Journal of Virtual Environments 1*, (1996).
2. Ducheneaut, N., Yee, N., Nickell, E., and Moore, R.J. Alone Together? Exploring the Social Dynamics of Massively Multiplayer Games. *CHI*, (2006), 407-416.
3. Gartner. Gartner Newsroom Press Release. 2011. http://www.gartner.com/it/page.jsp?id=1629214.
4. Jansz, J., Avis, C., and Vosmeer, M. Playing The Sims2: an exploration of gender differences in players' motivations and patterns of play. *New Media & Society 12*, (2010), 235-251.
5. Lucas, K. and Sherry, J. Sex Differences in Video Game Play: A Communication-Based Explanation. *Communication Research 31*, (2004), 499-523.
6. Williams, D., Consalvo, M., Caplan, S., and Yee, N. Looking for Gender: Gender Roles and Behaviors Among Online Gamers. *59*, (2009), 700-725.
7. Williams, D., Poole, S., Contractor, N., and Srivastava, J. The Virtual World Exploratorium. *Communication Methods and Measures*, (in press).
8. Yee, N., Harris, H., Jabon, M., and Bailenson, J. The Expression of Personality in Virtual Worlds. *Social Psychological and Personality Science 2*, (2011), 5-12.
9. Yee, N. Motivations for Play in Online Games. *Journal of CyberPsychology and Behavior 9*, (2007), 772-775.

Diversity among Enterprise Online Communities: Collaborating, Teaming, and Innovating through Social Media

Michael Muller*, Kate Ehrlich*, Tara Matthews†, Adam Perer*, Inbal Ronen‡, and Ido Guy‡
IBM Research
*One Rogers Street, Cambridge, MA, USA 02142 {michael_muller, katee, adam_perer}@us.ibm.com
†650 Harry Road, San Jose, CA, USA 95120, tlmatth@us.ibm.com
‡Haifa University, Mount Carmel, Haifa, Israel, {inbal, ido}@il.ibm.com

ABSTRACT
There is a growing body of research into the adoption and use of social software in enterprises. However, less is known about how groups, such as communities, use and appropriate these technologies, and the implications for community structures. In a study of 188 very active online enterprise communities, we found systematic differences in size, demographics and participation, aligned with differences in community types. Different types of communities differed in their appropriation of social software tools to create and use shared resources, and build relationships. We propose implications for design of community support features, services for potential community members, and organizations looking to derive value from online groups.

Author Keywords
Communities; Online communities; Teams; Virtual Teams; Idea Labs; Communities of practice

ACM Classification Keywords
H.5.3 Group and organizational interfaces/CSCW

General Terms
Design, Human factors

INTRODUCTION
There is a growing body of research into the adoption and use of social software in an enterprise including studies of blogs [10,15,16,46], microblogs [11,30,48], wikis [14,34], shared bookmarks [25], shared files [40,43,45] and social network sites [8,40], adding to earlier studies of email [32]. However, there is much less known about how these technologies are adopted and used by groups in general and by communities in particular [22,36,39].

About a decade ago, online communities engaged in knowledge- and information- sharing largely through discussions and conversations [44]. The advent of social software augments traditional community technologies, adding blogs, wikis, and social file-sharing services that offer other forms of collaborative engagement and information sharing [10,11,14,25,34,37,41,43]. At the same time, social software tools have become increasingly meshed in a broader social media environment, so that a tool aimed to support enterprise communities may appear in the same software suite as a tool for virtual teams (e.g., [36,39]) and a tool for enterprise social networking (e.g., [8]). The new structures and use patterns add to the diversity that has already been studied among online communities (see Related Work, below). The new capabilities allow us to discover the types of collaborations that are currently taking place in tools aimed to support communities, and to explore new classifications that reflect these appropriations.

Although most studies of online communities have been conducted with public internet communities, studies of social software tools tell us that enterprises provide a different context for interaction [10,11,27,28,34,41]. With respect to communities, we suggest there are several critical differences. Firstly, an enterprise provides a shared context in addition to the context of the community, which can contribute to a level of trust and common ground [8,24]. Secondly, enterprise communities are likely to be business-focused, leading to different content and perhaps styles of discussion [24,36]. Thirdly, companies, which require authenticated access and use of real names, eliminate anonymity and provide greater transparency [8].

Our goal is to delineate different patterns of tool use as a way of understanding the different functions and practices of enterprise communities. In this paper, we report on five emergent structures and usage patterns when enterprise groups appropriate an online communities application. Specifically, the study described in this paper examined the patterns of use of social software in enterprise online communities across five different types of communities: Communities Of Practice (COPs), Teams, End-user technical support, Idea Labs, and Recreation. We will also consider the implications of this new diversity in structure and usage for the design of metrics and services.

RELATED RESEARCH

Online communities form in response to many human and organizational needs, including sharing information, pursuing passions, building skills, working toward shared goals, finding sociality, engaging in commerce, and curiosity [1,2, 4,6,9,13,18,19,24,26,33,35,37,44]. Researchers from different disciplines have provided many ways of analyzing communities by attributes or by types.

Types of Communities

Lazar and Preece considered communities in terms of their social attributes, supporting technology, and relationship to physical communities [1]. Wenger considered more functional aspects, similar to the *attributes* of Lazar and Preece, such as communities of practice, formal work-groups, project teams, and informal networks [44]. Several researchers pursuing specific theoretical agendas have provided analyses that dealt with social network analysis variables [17], division of labor [5], and social qualities [18].

Several researchers described communities in terms of what members were seeking, such as knowledge platforms, networking with fellow enthusiasts, and finding solutions to problems [20]; or interest, relationship, fantasy, and transaction [13]; or educational opportunities, professional opportunities, or topical interests [6].

Business-oriented researchers focused on factors that shape the community, such as the source of initiative in business-oriented communities [35]; or types of sponsoring organization [7]. Marketing typologies have taken a more pluralistic position, organizing their analyses in terms of customer goals, business (provider) goals, governance models, and demographics [26,33]. Other business researchers have focused on technical aspects, such as discussion-based, task-based, virtual worlds, or "hybrid" [42].

The development of global virtual teams has also suggested new ways of organizing people and resources in enterprises [23,35], with unique aspects of coordination and timeframe that may affect the success of those teams [36,39].

Many of these reports relied on interviews, surveys, or inspections of internet community webpages. By contrast, our analysis is narrower but also deeper. We used data from a production "Communities" application in IBM, the internal deployment of IBM's Connections product. We observed quantitatively how a workforce appropriated the Communities application in their daily work.

Social Software

Online communities have traditionally relied on communication and discussion technologies such as electronic bulletin boards, real-time chat, email message archives and perhaps members' individual web pages. However, contemporary social software suites afford additional shared authoring via blogs and wikis and information sharing via shared bookmarks [25], shared files [31,43], and wikis [14]. Groups form unique combinations of these tools, depending on their goals, tasks, timeframes, and work dynamics [22].

"Landscape Analysis": Community Usage and Patterns

In a preliminary, unpublished study, we used methods based on [3] to perform a "landscape analysis" of the use of the Communities application during April 2010. This analysis showed great diversity of community configurations, and many overlaps among the names and descriptions that organizers gave to their communities. One of many examples occurred around the concept of communities of practice: similar configurations carried names or labels such as "community of interest," "center of excellence", and "network". We also became aware that workgroup teams had begun to use the Communities application, sometimes in configurations of as many as 140 teams.

Employees and organizations were appropriating the Communities application in unanticipated ways. Similar results, across a more diverse set of enterprise social media, were provided in [23]. Our landscape analysis showed an enormous diversity in community types and characterizations.

Research Questions

The initial observations from our "landscape analysis" led us to believe that online enterprise communities required a different typology from the ones previously used. Thus, our first goal was to develop a typology. Secondly, the focus of social software on sharing information and developing relationships led us to ask the following research questions:

RQ1: Do different types of communities differ in their *Human Capital* – i.e., number of people, participation rate?

RQ2: Do different types of communities differ in their *Intellectual Capital* – i.e., what they share with each other, and which social software tools they use in that sharing?

RQ3: Do different types of communities differ in their *Relational Capital* – i.e., the relative contribution made by people, and the connections they make through the tools?

RESEARCH SETTING

The study took place in IBM, a global multinational company that had been using, and encouraging the use of a suite of social software tools called "IBM Connections Communities" that can include discussion forums, blogs, wikis, shared bookmarks, shared files, feeds and activities. Employees who participate in these Communities come from diverse corporate organizations, including Sales, Marketing, Consulting, Development (hardware and software), Support, and Research. Participation is in general voluntary, with two exceptions: (a) People in certain teams may have been "strongly encouraged" to participate in specific communities; (b) Some community *leaders* included their community work in their job responsibilities.

Community Roles

The Communities application differentiates participants in terms of "owners" and "members". There is no upper or lower bound on the number of owners or members in a community; in practice, some communities in the company-wide dataset have only one member (probably failed experiments), and a few communities have 20,000 or more members. Many communities have an associated "leadership team" of owners who may share responsibilities in initiating and managing the community.

Owners have additional access rights, including the ability to change the role of members and to add members or owners directly. They can also delete any entry, and customize the community's website.

Community Tools and Media

The default tools in a community are shared bookmarks, shared feeds, and shared discussion forums. Bookmarks of internet or intranet pages with descriptive tags can be shared with the rest of the community. Feeds are RSS feeds whose output is public. Discussion forums allow users to start a thread with a topic on which other users can respond. Blogs allow authorship of blog entries, on which other users can comment. Wikis allow collaborative editing of web pages. Files, such as documents and presentations, can be uploaded by a user, and shared with other members of the community. Activities [30] allow a more structured set of shared materials, including collaborative task management.

Initiating a Community

Any employee may create a community by clicking on a "Start a Community" button in the Communities application. The community creator specifies the name of the community and its level of privacy (public or private), and provides a description and optional tags. The Communities application provides no data field for a "community type", although some owners may include "CoP", "Network", "Circle", "Team", or "Idea Lab" in the title and/or text description of their community or provide some indication of the function of the community in the description.

The content of all public communities, including the membership list, is visible to any employee, although only community members have permission to create content. The membership list includes members and owners under their real names, along with basic contact information and job function. Further information on any member is available from their general profile, which is public to all employees.

Study Timeframe

The Communities application has been in operation since April 2007. At the time of our study (July, 2011), there were approximately 25,000 communities with membership open to any employee, and just under 10,000 additional communities whose contents were visible to all employees, but which required the permission of an owner for membership (i.e., for privileges to create content in the community). There were also an estimated 25,000 fully private communities that were inaccessible to our analysis. Over 75% of employees had joined at least one community over the four years in which the service had operated.

DATA COLLECTION

Communities

To reduce the overwhelming diversity of community descriptions that we had encountered in the landscape analysis, we targeted the top 250 public communities as defined by the total number of contributions of any type during the 2 months prior to the data collection for our study. Since our focus was on the use and appropriation of technology by community members, we wanted communities that were mature enough to have reached a stable set of behaviors, and active enough to provide us with sufficient data for analysis and that we might ask people about their *recent* activities and experiences (see Self-Reported, below). We removed communities that could subsequently not be found (e.g., deletion or change-of-name) or which were duplicates (n = 18), or in which the content was generated by software rather than humans (n = 16). We also omitted communities in which there was no English content (n = 17), or for other technical reasons (n = 11), leaving us with a corpus of 188 communities.

In those 188 communities, 96,877 employees from 107 countries had joined at least one community; 31,159 people (32%) had joined more than one community in the dataset. Among the 96,877 members, 12,190 (13%) from 74 countries had made at least one contribution to at least one community; among the contributors, 2053 (17%) had made contributions to more than one community. The number of members per community ranged from 10 to 8750 people (mean = 828, median = 192). The duration of membership ranged from 1 to 1206 days (mean = 190, median = 88).

There were 1078 employees who served as owner in at least one community in our sample. The number of owners per community ranged from 1 to 49 (mean = 6.57). The number of communities per owner (in the role of owner) ranged from 1 to 10 (mean = 1.15).

Community Type

Consistent with our earlier landscape analysis, the 188 communities studied in this paper were created by diverse employees in many different organizations. Some appeared to be large communities of practice for employees with a common discipline, but who were embedded in teams whose majority of members had a different discipline (e.g., [24,27]). Other communities appeared to be large, multi-country teams with executive leadership and a specific mission, such as selling to financial customers. Other communities appeared to be focused on solving specific problems in a relatively short time-frame (e.g., [28]). Informal interviews had convinced us that different types of communities might have different needs. We therefore focused our investigation on a quantitative study of the diversity among communities, with a goal of understanding which *types* of communities were present. Future research will provide an analysis of success factors associated with types of communities.

Our earlier landscape analysis suggested several major categories of communities. We pursued those categories in our quantitative study. As part of a larger survey, we asked the community owners to choose from the following choices to describe their community: *Community of Interest, Community of Practice, Center of Excellence, Team, Idea Lab,* and *Recreation*. Surveys were sent to 1296 owners. We received 469 responses (36% response rate) representing 162 communities (86% of the communities).

Three researchers independently coded each community based on the owners' responses; we resolved the few disagreements through discussion. We created a combined category, COP (Community of Practice), because the owners seemed to have difficulty distinguishing between Community of Practice, Community of Interest and Center of Excellence. Additional analysis revealed that several communities were providing technical support (e.g., [47]). Although this community-type had not been offered as a choice in the survey, we added it to the coding protocol. In summary, we used the following community types:

- **COP**. A group of people with a common interest or practice who share information and/or network. Typical COPs in our study tended to focus on well-defined methods for notifying members of events and content. There was little evidence of "deliverables" (work products) or other team-like attributes.
- **Team**. Communities working on a shared goal for a particular client, project, or business function. Typical teams in our study tended to focus on particular clients, industries, or products, with well-defined "deliverables" and deadlines. (Teams have previously been thought of as an *alternative* structure to communities [36,39,42]. In the Communities application, teams adopted the technology and language of communities, so we include them as a *type of community* in our analysis.)
- **Technical Support**. Providing technical support for a particular technology. Typical Tech Support communities in our study tended to focus on the technology itself, rather than a product based on the technology, or a client who used the technology.
- **Idea Lab**. Communities in which members brainstorm around a set of questions or issues for a limited period of time, usually as part of a client engagement. Typical Idea Labs in our study tended to have a very tight focus in terms of topic (i.e., a specific client) and timeframe (24 to 72 hours in duration).
- **Recreation**. Communities devoted to recreational activities unrelated to work.

Three coders examined the owner reports and the community itself to assign a unique type to each community. Cronbach alpha measuring the level of agreement between the 3 coders was 0.84 ($F = 11.53$, $p < 0.001$). Coders resolved the few cases of uncertainty by discussion.

Shared Resources

The data in each community were extracted by crawling the Communities database through a published Application Program Interface (API). This is a common method used for large-scale studies of social media usage within an organization [8,0,11,12,14,15,25,29,40]. For each community, we extracted

- a list of owner and member IDs
- a count of all bookmarks, feeds, and files
- a count of all forum entries (topics and responses)
- a count of each activity entry (summarized as a "root" object or as a response to that root)
- a count of each blog entry (posts vs. comments)
- a count of each wiki (original pages vs. revisions)

Each data item included a timestamp, and the ID of the person who created or modified the item. (From a privacy perspective, we note that the contents of all of these communities were visible to any employee, and we never associated any data result with personal information.)

Self-Reported Community Participation

Beyond the formal data (community type and contents), we were also interested in the experiences of the owners and members of the communities. As part of a larger survey, we asked a stratified sample of members to rate their Visit Frequency – i.e., how often did the respondent visit the community? (Scale of *0/never* to *5/daily.*)

1342 members completed the survey (19% response rate). However, 51 members did not provide the community name or the name could not be resolved, and therefore their responses could not be used. An additional 170 members reported never visiting the community they were responding to. We omitted these data, leaving a sample of 1121 responses for 156 communities (83% communities).

RESULTS

Our results center around the question of how different types of communities use technology and whether there are similar or different patterns of usage depending on the type of community (COP, Team, Technical support, Idea Lab, Recreation). For these business communities, we organized our analysis in terms of the business concepts of Human Capital, Intellectual Capital, and a newer concept, of Relational Capital.

Unless stated otherwise, all analyses were done using SPSS GLM, with LSD tests between levels of each effect ($p<.05$). Any results reported in this paper achieved at least that level of significance. To guard against non-normality, we confirmed our analyses with log-transformed data. The results were in substantial agreement.

Human Capital

Counting People

We use the term *Human Capital* to refer to the people in the communities. In this analytic category, we differentiate the roles and activities of members and owners within a community.

Table 1 shows the mean number of *members* and *owners* for each type of community. *Participation rate* represents the proportion of unique people, out of the total community membership (including both members and owners), who made at least one contribution to the community – i.e., it is a summary measure of the visible or "public" signs of participation. By contrast, *visit frequency* is people's self-reports of how often they visited the community, including view participation – the invisible or "non-public" aspect of participation ("lurking") [38]. We also include a calculation of the *age* of the community, which can be an important explanatory variable.

The communities differed with respect to the number of owners and members, with COPs and Tech Support communities the most populous; these results were significant ($p<.02$) in a simple ANOVA. However, the community differences for members became non-significant when we included age as a covariate. We considered age, because communities that are in existence for a longer period may have an opportunity to gain more members ("more days, more people"). By this age-corrected analysis, there are no differences in overall size of the communities. The number of owners, however, is generally not affected by age, because owners are usually assigned when the community is formed.

We considered three explanations for the large number of owners of COPs. First, this effect may reflect a greater effort required for running a COP. Alternatively, these findings may reflect the tendency for COPs to fall outside of the formal team structure of workplaces [24,44]. Leaders were, in effect, volunteering their time to keep the COPs vital, and may have deliberately shared the workload for the community in order to protect time and energy for their primary jobs. A third possibility is that COPs could have a more diverse membership, with a social need to include people with different backgrounds among the leadership. These hypotheses may become future research topics.

Visible and Invisible Participation

Communities also differed in terms of participation rate (percent of people making visible contributions) and in terms of Visit Frequency; these effects remained robust (p<..01), even with community age as a covariate. Idea Labs, which are primarily venues for quick brainstorming [28], have the highest participation (50%), but this is not significantly different from Recreation communities or Teams. Teams had significantly greater participation rates than COPs, but were not significantly different from Tech communities. Future research should explore the nature of

	COP	Team	Tech	IdeaLab	Rec
N.	91	73	16	5	3
Members ***	1154.82	416.47	1086.13	259.20	76.67
Owners ***	8.43	5.14	4.19	4.60	1.33
Part. Rate ***	21%	37%	31%	50%	44%
Visit Freq. ***	2.95	2.80	2.78	1.27	1.00
Age (days) ***	571.49	382.96	494.56	53.00	455.00

*** $p < .001$

Table 1. Human Capital results for each community type: Mean numbers of people and relevant ratios.

these Tech communities, which seem to have some attributes relating to both Teams and COPs.

Overall, these communities are large (average size = 828 people), well established (all except Idea Labs, have been in operation for over a year) and have a higher participation rate than the 10%, which has been reported for online communities (e.g., [21]). These data confirm that communities with a high level of activity are likely to spread the work of contributing over several people rather than concentrating in just a few people.

Now that we have a preliminary idea of how many people use each type of community, and with what degree of participation, it is time to look at the materials they share with one another in the communities.

Intellectual Capital

We use the term *Intellectual Capital* to refer to the structured and unstructured knowledge that is created in communities. Companies are often concerned to catalogue this knowledge for retrieval and re-use. We analyze the Intellectual Capital of a community as the mass of contributions that the owners and members share with one another. These contributions could take the form of bookmarks, feeds, forum discussions, blogs, files, activities, and wikis. We discovered that some wikis were automatically updated through RSS feeds, so we have excluded them from our analyses of *human* actions related to the shared contents of the communities.

Use of any of the types of shared objects in a community was optional. With all of these choices, which types of objects were used in each type of community?

Invoking the Tool (Resource) Types

Table 2 shows the percentage of communities in each type, which made use of each of the resource types. Differences within each row were tested via a 2x5 chi-squared test.

Some resources, like bookmarks, and forums, appear to have achieved a ceiling effect, in which nearly all of each

	COP	Team	Tech	IdeaLab	Rec.
Bookmarks	88%	89%	88%	80%	100%
Feeds*	67%	53%	50%	0%	33%
Forums	96%	92%	100%	100%	100%
Activities	28%	30%	25%	0%	33%
Blogs**	75%	58%	63%	0%	33%
Files***	93%	99%	63%	80%	100%
Wikis*	90%	88%	75%	100%	33%

* $p<.05$, ** $p<.01$, *** $p<.001$ – differences within each row

Table 2. Intellectual Capital results for each community type: Percentage of each community type that contained at least one of each type of shared resource.

community type used that resource. Forums were used by a larger percentage of authors than any other tool (Anova and least-significant difference, $p<.001$). Feeds were used in all community types except Idea Labs, which typically involve an active brainstorm of only 1-3 days. We assume that Idea Labs are not used long enough to warrant a feed, whose value tends to grow over time.

Blogs had the same pattern as feeds: zero use in Idea Labs, and perhaps for the same reason. The files feature was used in most of the communities, with the partial exception of the Tech communities. As will be seen, the Tech communities put most of their effort into the forums, so perhaps files were too cumbersome for their relatively light-contribution-cost style of collaboration. Finally, although wikis were used in most of the communities in all types except Recreation, many communities populated their wikis via an automated mechanism. We refrain from over-interpreting the wikis results until a future time when we understand communities' use of the automatic features better.

These results show that communities made use of the rich features of contemporary social media, going well beyond the traditional discussion forum patterns of past communities. The next questions are about the extent of usage of these resources within each type of community.

Using the Tools (Resources)

Table 3 shows the contributions per resource type, in each type of community. As a first analysis, we have counted user-created entries at the lowest level. Thus, we count each forum topic, and each forum response, and we report the total. Similarly, we count each blog post and each blog comment, and we report the total. We do the same for the tree-structured (thread-structured) contents of the activities. For wikis, we count each original page, and each revision, and report the total. Of course, different metrics schemes are possible, such that a discussion topic would be reported as a single data item, no matter how many responses accrued to it. We hope to explore and compare these different ways of counting social resources in a future paper.

Because these data are *usage-sensitive*, they provide a somewhat different picture from the preceding data, which were based on whether a resource type was used at all.

Unlike the Human Capital analyses, the analyses of the number of shared resources were complex to think about. From the perspective of an organization, one of the important aspects of a community of any type is its productivity – i.e., *how many of each type of resource does each type of community contain*? We provide a summary of the number of each type of resource, for each type of community, in Table 3A.

However, from the perspective of a researcher, a more important question is to compare the shared resources in proportion to the *opportunity for those resources to be produced* – i.e., are there differences in the creation of certain type of resources among the community types? We address this question via a summary of the number of each type of resource in each type of community, *divided by the number of people in the community* (i.e., where each person represents an "opportunity" to contribute a resource), in Table 3B. Because many people were non-contributors ("lurkers"), these results tended to be relatively small numbers.

For the organization-oriented analyses, we conducted a separate analysis of variance for the data in each row of Table 3A. We also conducted analyses of covariance, using the age of the community and the number of people in the community. Forums and files were the principal differentiators of community types. There was significantly more forum activity among Tech and Recreation communities than COPs, Teams, and Idea Labs. Among files, there were more items in COPs and Teams than among Idea Labs and Recreational communities.

These results make it clear that different types of communities steward different configurations of shared resources. An organization might want to consider what kinds of outcomes it hopes to "harvest" from its communities, and it might want to select the type(s) of communities to initiate based on those "harvesting" goals.

A researcher may be more interested in the number of resources weighted by the opportunity to create a resource. Each person in a community represents an "opportunity" to create a resource in that community. Therefore, the data in Table 3B are expressed as resources/persons.

The results are rather different from the organizational perspective of Table 3A. Forums are again a significant differentiator, but in the population-weighted analysis of Table 3B, the Recreation communities produce far more forum items *per person* than the other types of communities. Wikis were also a differentiator in this representation; however, as we noted above, some of the wikis were populated by an automated process, so we will not attempt to interpret these results until we have more fully investigated that process and its rationale.

A	COP	Team	Tech	IdeaLab	Rec.
Bookmarks	75.56	34.03	37.19	4.80	5.00
Feeds	4.21	2.12	1.94	0.00	0.67
Forums**	313.26	257.34	859.13	113.00	817.33
Activities	31.74	34.30	43.25	0.00	0.33
Blogs	76.82	48.12	52.81	0.00	1.67
Files***	39.80	39.71	21.00	0.80	5.67
Wikis	133.37	140.49	102.50	6.00	0.67
Total[a]	541.40	415.63	1015.31	118.60	830.67

B	COP	Team	Tech	IdeaLab	Rec.
Bookmarks	0.275	0.425	0.078	0.102	0.981
Feeds	0.017	0.023	0.007	0	0.011
Forums***	0.781	2.202	1.803	1.448	13.412
Activities	0.152	0.387	0.151	0	0.003
Blogs	0.309	0,612	0.114	0	0.028
Files	0.302	0.567	0.071	0.017	0.094
Wikis***	0.694	1.649	0.244	0.100	0.011
Total[a***]	1.837	4.034	2.225	1.566	13.630

* p<.05, ** p<.01, *** p< .001 – differences within each row
[a.] Excludes Wikis

Table 3. Intellectual Capital results for each community type. (A) From a researcher's perspective: Mean contributions divided by the number of people in each community. (B) From the organization's perspective: Mean contributions per tool per community type.

Again, we have found different patterns of production of shared resources in different types of communities. We also note that there was a nearly significant difference for files (weighted by community size), and we speculate that, in a larger sample, Teams might have had significantly higher scores in the per-person production of files.

In summary, different community types are associated with different patterns of resource type utilization (Table 2), different patterns of shared resource production (Table 3A), and different per-person patterns of shared resource production (Table 3B). The different community types appear to use different types of collective resources.

Relational Capital

We propose the term *Relational Capital* as a measure of the opportunity for one person to interact with another person through the resources that we described in the preceding subsection, potentially leading to stronger social ties. We are studying several different algorithms for measuring interaction opportunities in social media (e.g., [29]); Relational Capital is our candidate metric for communities. For this paper, we will use a method based on combinatorics within a discussion thread (or equivalent structure). Suppose UserA creates a new forum topic, and UserB writes a response, and UserC writes a response to UserB, and UserA also writes a response to UserB. We now have a thread containing items written by a total of three people. We assume that each of the three people has interacted (responded to) the others, and thus we can compute a combinatoric estimate of "interaction opportunities" for each unique pair among the *k* users among three people of 3 x 2 / 2 = 3 interaction opportunities (i.e., using the combinatoric of *k* [*k* -1] / 2).

	COP	Team	Tech	IdeaLab	Rec.
Forums***	972.35	466.24	4027.44	561.20	1838.33
Activities	222.26	132.78	126.00		1.00
Blogs	27.20	36.91	15.25		0
Wikis	77.52	78.09	323.83	0	0
Total*	1299.33	714.20	4492.52	561.2	1839.33

* p<.05, ** p<.01, *** p< .001 – differences within each row

Table 4. Relational Capital for each community type, for the types of shared resources that support a thread-like structure of responses. Each entry is a count of the pairwise opportunities for one person to interact with a colleague.

We analyzed Relational Capital in forums (above), blogs (through blog-post and blog-comment), activities (through their node-and-leaf structure [30]), and wikis (through their linear revision sequences). For each of these resources, we identified the root item for each thread; we found the associated items within the thread; we counted the number of unique authors of those items; and we calculated the per-thread relational capital based on the above formula.

Table 4 presents a summary of the calculated interaction opportunities. While each of the four media potentially supports the creation of relationships through post-and-response, these community types carry most of their sociality in the forums. The Tech communities show the greatest development of pairwise connections in the forums, significantly more than COPs or teams.

This result appears to be similar to the Intellectual Capital results. However, that result was based on the *number of items* of each type, whereas the Relational Capital results were based on the *relationships of the persons* who had created those resources. In principle, it would be possible for a single person to create a large number of resources within a single thread (high *Intellectual Capital*). However, if no one else created a resource in the same thread, then the Relational Capital would be very low.

DISCUSSION

Out of the 35,000 public and invitational communities in an enterprise Communities application, we selected 188 of the most active communities for detailed study. Our initial landscape analysis had shown us that the Communities application was being used in diverse ways. For a first in-depth analysis, we pre-selected four types of communities for comparison. In the course of coding the 188 communities, we discovered a fifth type of community, and added that to our classification, resulting in categories of

Communities of Practice, Idea Labs, Recreational Communities, Teams, and Technical Support communities.

We examined the five types of communities for differences, using three conceptual lenses: Human Capital (people and participation), Intellectual Capital (shared resources), and Relational Capital (interaction opportunity). We found highly significant differences through each of those conceptual lenses.

Each of the three lenses provides its own distinct emphasis. The view based on Human Capital showed significantly more owners in COPs than other communities, and a trend toward more members as well. Despite the smaller number of people in Idea Labs, their intense time-constrained brainstorming process produced the highest participation rates. And yet the COPs, Teams, and Tech communities had the highest overall visit frequency.

The view based on Intellectual Capital showed differential patterns of feature use, with a surprisingly high productivity of forum entries in the Tech communities. We also noted different patterns depending on whether we took an organizational view (emphasizing the resource available to the company) vs. a research view (emphasizing the contributions normalized for community size and age).

Finally, the view based on Relational Capital showed differential accumulation of social connections among employees in different types of communities.

These results provide new ways of thinking about typologies of online enterprise communities. Previous research categorized communities in terms of broad distinctions, such as networking vs. knowledge-sharing vs. solution-finding [20] or relationships vs. "fantasies" vs. transactions [13,35] or types of opportunities sought by members [6] or by community sponsors [7,26,33]. Our analyses show specific categories of enterprise activities (similar to [44]), and suggest new features to support those categories (see Implications for Design, below). Other typologies focused on the technological features in each category of community [42]. Our analyses show that, even with the same technologies available in all communities, owners and members will make differential use of those resources to achieve strikingly different organizational forms and outcomes.

Limitations

Our study involved the technology-informed workforce at IBM, which has been an early adopter of enterprise social software. Other companies, such as Microsoft, MITRE, and Yammer, are also pursuing enterprise social software, and the space of commercial products in this area is growing. We therefore think that our results will become increasingly useful to other companies, and the growing body of researchers who study social software in organizations.

Our selection strategy focused on the most active communities. This may have biased our sample toward more successful communities. We plan to test our results on new samples based on the largest communities and the longest-active communities.

We have used the word "communities" because the users themselves chose that word – perhaps because it was suggested by the name of the application. We note that IBM Connections Communities provides a richer feature set than earlier discussion-only communities, and thus may eventually require a new analytic category.

Implications for Design

Community Metrics. We found that different types of communities comprise different numbers of people; seem to require different extents of effort from their leaders; make use of different resources; and support different configurations of relationships (see also [24]). These results suggest that future research into success metrics for communities should analyze each community type separately.

Community Design. It may be useful to develop templates for different types of communities, so that a new community can achieve a faster launch by assembling the right configuration of resources, with appropriate goals for that type of community. This kind of support could be important for community-founders who are not technically savvy, and/or who want to accomplish a particular work goal, rather than to explore and configure a technology. Our preliminary landscape analysis showed that there was much more diversity than the five categories that we studied in this paper. Therefore, the community-templating service should be flexible and customizable, to allow users to appropriate the Community technology to innovate new genres. The Idea Labs provide a strong example: These communities made novel use the discussion forums, transforming the Communities application from the intended use for long-term, informal exchanges in a COP, into a brief-duration, highly-focused problem-solving environment [28] – without changing a single line of source code.

Community Recommendation Service. Different types of communities offer different benefits [2,6, 13,20,24]. People looking for opportunities to contribute (or for resources to "consume") may need advice about how to choose communities to join. The different qualities of the different community types could become features for a community-recommendation service similar to [12], which could be valuable for new employees or employees with new job responsibilities.

Organizational Design. Organizations may want to use the information in this paper to choose the community types that they need to achieve certain objectives (e.g., [7,35,44]). An organization that values file-based resources, for example, might foster Teams and COPs. By contrast, an organization that wanted to create discussions or greater connections among its workers, might focus its resources on creating Tech support and Recreation communities. Organizations concerned about low-sized, under-performing communities might use our three families of metrics to find highly-similar communities that could be combined to reach a form of critical mass for community vitality.

Implications for Theory

As social applications become more important for getting work done, there is a need to understand the abstract qualities of different types of social applications, and the different configurations of those applications that can support business, governmental, non-profit, and civic organizations. Earlier work to distinguish types of communities used interview, survey, or inspection data. Different analyses have focused on business needs [1,7,26,35], human strivings [19,31,37,38,44], social motivations [2, 20], and technologies [41].

We add to that literature with a more quantitative investigation that begins to integrate several of the conceptual domains of the former analyses, combining human action (Human Capital), business needs as expressed through shared resources (Intellectual Capital), and social dynamics (Relational Capital). Our work can contribute precision regarding types of communities, which can be used in conjunction with broader models of Collaboration Personas [22] and other explorations of the organizational adoption of social media [10,11,14,16,34,38,43,45]. Stronger methods for classifying communities can clarify agendas for determining organizational benefits (e.g., [29]), and crucial attributes of successful communities.

Our work points toward new investigations into large-scale enterprise COPs and enterprise virtual teams [36,39]. Previous work suggested that COPs could become vibrant information exchanges among a large percentage of members of a "minority discipline," using an online venue for sharing aspects of their practice [2,24,44]. Comparing COPs and Teams, our results suggest a less participative pattern in COPs, in which a small percentage of people make the COP contributions. We had previously thought of COPs as diffuse networks of co-contributing practitioners [24,27], but our results suggest a small active core and a larger group of non-public participants [38].

We were surprised that Teams made such strong use of the Communities application. The IBM Connections product contains an "Activities" application that was intended for collaborative task management [30], and that permits a more formal structuring of a group's shared resources. We would have expected virtual teams to prefer the task-focused, knowledge-curatorial affordances of Activities. Yet there were no significant differences in the use of the Activities features within Communities. Furthermore, we found that virtual teams had a higher participation rate in the Communities application than COPs, for whom it had been designed. We do not yet understand why Teams chose the Communities application. Our findings may show that, in enterprises, the distinction of teams vs. communities [36, 39] may be blurring. Perhaps the less formal *social* affordances of Communities were more important than the more formal *structured* capabilities of Activities (see [39] for review of social needs in virtual teams). Future research should re-examine concepts of virtual teams and communities in the context of the new enterprise social media.

Summary and Contributions

We have shown three lenses through which to analyze the differences among social software entities in organizations, and we have applied those lenses to show systematic differences among active, productive groups in an enterprise online communities application. Our work may inform the design of online communities, the design of services for people seeking online communities, and the design of organizations. We hope that our work will contribute to on-going efforts to describe and model the organizational use of online communities, and of collections of social software for use by collaborative groups.

ACKNOWLEDGMENT

The work of some of the authors was partially supported by the EU-FP7 project ROBUST (grant no. 257859).

REFERENCES

1. Armstrong, A., & Hagel III, J., Real profits from virtual communities. *Mckinsey Quart, 3,* 126-141, 1995.
2. Bogdan, C., & Bowers, J., Tuning in: Challenging design for communities through a field study of radio amateurs, *Proc Communities & Technologies 2007*, Springer, 439-461.
3. Bos, N., Zimmerman, A., Olson, J., Yew, J., Yerkie, J., Dahl, E.,, & Olson, G., From shared databases to communities of practice: A taxonomy of collaboratories, *JCMC 12*(2), 652-672, 2007.
4. Bressler, S. E., & Grantham, C. E.,. *Communities of commerce: Building Internet business communities to accelerate growth, minimize risk, and increase customer loyalty*. McGraw-Hill, 2000.
5. Butler, B., Sproull, L., Kiesler, S., & Kraut, R., Community effort in online groups: Who does the work and why? In Weisband, S., & Atwater, L, (eds.), *Leadership at a distance: Research in technologically supported work*, Earlbaum, 2008.
6. Carlén, U., Typology of online learning communities, *Proc. Int. Conf. Net Learning 2002.*
7. Denison, T., Hardy, G., Johanson, G, Stillman, L., & Schauder, D., Community networks: Identities, taxonomies and evaluations, *Proc Elec. Netwk. 2002.*
8. DiMicco, J., Millen, D.R., Geyer, W.G., Dugan, C., Brownholtz, B., & Muller, M. (2008), Motivations for social networking at work, *Proc. CSCW 2008.*
9. Dubé, L., Bourhis, A., & Jacob, R., Towards a typology of virtual communities of practice, *Int. J. Info, Knowl. Mgmt. 1*, 69-93, 2006.
10. Efimova, L., & Grudin, J., Crossing boundaries: A case study employee blogging, *Proc. HICSS 2007.*
11. Ehrlich, K. & Shami, N.S. 2010. Microblogging inside and outside the workplace. *Proc. ICWSM '10.*

12. Freyne, J., Jacovi, M., Guy, I., & Geyer, W., Increasing engagement through early recommender intervention, *Proc. RECSYS 2009.*

13. Hagel, J., & Armstrong, A., *Net Gain: Expanding markets through virtual communities*, Harvard Business School Press, 1997.

14. Holtzblatt, L.J., Damianos, L.E., & Weiss, D., Factors impeding wiki use in the enterprise: A case study, *Proc. CHI 2010.*

15. Huh, J., Jones, L., Erickson,T., Kellogg, W.A., Bellamy, R.K.E, & Thomas, J.C., BlogCentral: the role of internal blogs at work, *CHI 2007 Extended Abstracts.*

16. Jackson, A., Yates, J., and Orlikowski, W . (2006). Corporate Blogging: Building community through persistent digital talk. *Proceedings of HICSS.*

17. Jones, Q., & Rafaeli, S., Time to split, virtually: 'Discourse architecture' and 'community building' create vibrant virtual publics. *Elec. Mrkts, 10*(4), 214-223, 2000.

18. Komito, L., The net as a foraging society: Flexible communities. *Info. Soc. 14,* 97-106, *1998.*

19. Lazar, J., & Preece, J., Classification schema for online communities, *Proc. AISAC 1998.*

20. Liu, C.-C., Identifying the value types of virtual communities based on the Q method, *Int. J. Web Based Commun. 7*(1), 2011.

21. Ludford, P.J., Cosley, D., Frankowski, D., & Terveen, L., Think different: Increasing online community participation using uniqueness and group dissimilarity, *Proc. CHI 2004.*

22. Matthews, T., Whittaker, S., Moran, T., Yuen, S. (2011). Collaboration personas: A new approach to designing workplace collaboration tools. *Proc. CHI 2011.*

23. Matthews, T., Whittaker, S., Moran, T., Yuen, S., Judge, T. (2011), Productive interrelationships between collaborative groups ease the challenges of dynamic and multi-teaming, *CSCW Journal* Special Issue on Collective Intelligence in Organizations. DOI: 10.1007/s10606-011-9154-y.

24. McDermott, R. (1999). Learning across teams: The role of communities of practice in team organizations. *Knowledge Management Review*, May/June 1999.

25. Millen, D.R., Feinberg, J., & Kerr, B., Social bookmarking in the enterprise, *Proc. CHI 2006.*

26. Mittilä, T. and Mäntymäki, M., Classification of Online Communities. *Proc. Frontiers of e-Business Research 2003.* http://www.ebrc.info.

27. Muller, M., & Carey, K., Design as a minority discipline in a software company: toward requirements for a community of practice, *Proc. CHI 2002.*

28. Muller, M., & Chua, S., Brainstorming for Japan: Rapid distributed global collaboration for disaster response, *Proc. CHI 2012.*

29. Muller, M.J., Freyne, J., Dugan, C., Millen, D.R., & Thom-Santelli, J., Return On Contribution (ROC): A metric for enterprise social software. *Proc. ECSCW 2009.*

30. Muller, M.J., Geyer, W., Brownholtz, B., Wilcox, E., & Millen, D.R., One-hundred days in an activity-centric collaboration environment based on shared objects, *Proc. CHI 2004.*

31. Naaman, M., Boase, J., & Lai, C.-H., Is it really about me? Message content in social awareness streams, *Proc. CSCW 2010.*

32. Orlikowski, W., Learning from Notes: Organizational issues in groupware implementation, *Info. Soc. 9*(3), 237-250, 1993.

33. Plant, R., Online communities, *Tech. Soc. 26*, 51-65, 2004.

34. Poole, E.S., Grudin, J., A taxonomy of wiki genres in enterprise settings, *Proc. WikiSym 2010.*

35. Porter, C.E., A typology of virtual communities: A multi-disciplinary foundation for future research, *JCMC 10*(1), 2004.

36. Powell, A., Piccoli, G., & Ives, B., Virtual teams: A review of current literature and directions for future research, *DATABASE Adv. Info. Sys. 35*(1), 6-36, 2004.

37. Preece, J., *Online communities: Designing usability, supporting sociability*, Wiley, 2000.

38. Preece, J. and Maloney-Krichmar, D., Online Communities. In J. Jacko and A. Sears, A. (Eds.) *Human-Computer Interaction Handbook*, Erlbaum, 596-620, 2003.

39. Sarker, S., & Sahey, S., Understanding virtual team development: An interpretive study, *JASIS 3*, 247-285, 2002.

40. Shami, N.S., Muller, M., & Millen, D.R., Browse and discover: Social file sharing in the enterprise, *Proc. CSCW 2011.*

41. Skeels, M.M., & Grudin, J., When social networks cross boundaries: A case study of workplace use of Facebook and linkedin, *Proc. GROUP 2009.*

42. Stanoevska-Slabeva, K., & Schmid, B.F., A typology of online communities and community supporting platforms, *Proc HICSS 2001.*

43. Voida, S., Edwards, W.K., Newman, M.W., Grinter, R.E., & Ducheneaut, N. 'Share and share alike: Exploring the user interface affordances of file sharing, *Proc CHI 2006.*

44. Wenger, E., McDermott, R., & Snyder, W., *Cultivating communities of practice: a guide to managing knowledge.* Harvard Business School Press, 2002.

45. Whalen, T., Toms, E.G., & Blustein, J. (2008). Information displays for managing shared files, *Proc CHIMIT 2008.*

46. Yardi, S., Golder, S.A., Brzozowski, M., Blogging at work and the corporate attention economy, *Proc. CHI 2009.*

47. Yardi, S., & Poole, E.S., Please help!: Patterns of personalization in an online tech support board, *Proc. C&T 2009.*

48. Zhang, J., Qu, Y., Cody, J., & Wu, Y. 2010. A case study of micro-blogging in the enterprise: use, value, and related issues. *Proc. CHI 2010.*

Homeless Young People on Social Network Sites

Jill Palzkill Woelfer and David G. Hendry
The Information School
University of Washington
Seattle, WA 98195-2840
{woelfj, dhendry}@uw.edu

ABSTRACT
This paper reports on the use of social network sites (MySpace and Facebook) by homeless young people, an extraordinary user population, made so in part by its vulnerability. Twenty-three participants of diverse ethnicities, 11 women and 12 men (mean age, 21.7 years), were interviewed in same-sex discussion groups of four participants each. The interviews consisted of questions about the uses, benefits, and harms of social network sites and how people present themselves online. Qualitative analysis of the discussion group transcripts shows how young people explore their identities, cultivate and exploit social ties, experience interpersonal tensions, manage incompatible audiences, and respond to shifting affiliations and transitions. From this analysis, implications for social intervention and technical design are presented, focused on maintaining ties with pro-social family and friends and with maintaining separation between communication spheres of incompatible audiences. This work contributes to the growing literature on vital, deeply human experiences that have become associated with social network sites.

Author Keywords
Homeless young people; vulnerability; social network sites; Facebook; MySpace; social and technical design

ACM Classification Keywords
K.4.2 Social Issues: Miscellaneous

General Terms
Design

INTRODUCTION
By late 2010 about half of all American adults, age 18 and over, used social network sites, almost doubling the 2008 estimate [7]. Empirical work has shown social network sites to be associated with many vital human experiences, including, for example: adolescent socialization and parent-teen conflict [10], identity exploration and formation among emerging adults [10,19,1], intimacy and life relationships [8], and major life transitions in American society such as moving from high school to college [10,13], and college to the workplace [4,25]. Impression management, that is, how one negotiates the representation of self for different audiences – some distinct and separate – is one major theme of much of this work [3,6,14,15,16,26]. While the specific platforms, cultural practices, and the particular meanings of social network sites may change [3], their use today may be of enduring significance, and, with great current potential for individual development and social improvement.

In this paper we add to this literature by reporting findings on the use of social network sites by a population with extraordinary needs, namely homeless young people. Our prior work has shown that homeless young people use social network sites and, like college students who transition into the workforce, face challenges with impression management [28]. For example, in one telling report a MySpace profile was "used simultaneously to advertise sexual services and to communicate with drop-in staff" [9, p. 775]. Without moral interpretation, we note that the profile served two "conflicting social spheres" [2], a systemic challenge with social network sites [6].

Relatedly, recent HCI research and design has investigated the use of technology by homeless adults living in urban environments [17,18,24]. In one landmark study it was found that technology, especially the mobile phone, was used by homeless adults to stay connected with friends and family and with members of service-based organizations such as caseworkers [18]. A second field study of homeless adults similarly found technology to be an important but non-obvious tool for creating and tapping into social networks, for obtaining resources for survival and for social involvement [24]. In contrast to these studies, which have largely focused on older homeless adults aged 40-60 [17, 24] or homeless mothers aged 20-53 [18], in this paper we focus on homeless young people, aged 18-30, a group at a markedly different developmental stage than older adults.

Perhaps like anyone who is homeless, homeless young people have extraordinary needs, arising at least in part from their vulnerability, needs that may lead to extraordinary experiences with social network sites. Nevertheless, we shall also see that homeless young people garner ordinary benefits from and encounter ordinary challenges with social network sites. We shall see, moreover, that the idea that "extra-ordinary needs are only exaggerated ordinary needs" [21, p. 8] may very well apply to this population of users.

BACKGROUND

Homeless Young People

Homelessness among youth, aged up to 30, is a pressing problem with lasting social and economic consequences. By one estimate, as much as 1% of the U.S. population, that is, about 3 million people, is both young and homeless at some point in the year [27]. As such, the psycho-social factors of homeless young people have been studied extensively in the social sciences [e.g., 11]. This research reveals that homeless young people are a heterogeneous mix of ages, genders, races and ethnicities, and many suffer mentally and physically from the long term effects of abuse, neglect and chronic stress.

Many homeless young people come from poverty and dysfunctional family backgrounds. Youth have likely experienced many problematic encounters with adults, such as school personnel and police officers, and institutions, such as foster care. These encounters, in turn, leave homeless young people wary of adults and institutions. Moreover, youth often lack basic life skills: cooking and healthy eating, knowing when to seek out health care, how to reduce stress, and so forth. Managing mental health, substance abuse, or chronic health issues can be extremely difficult when alone and on the streets. Individual and structural features of homelessness have profound effects on the process of emerging adulthood [27], the very time that social network sites may be of particular benefit [19].

Homeless Young People and Social Network Sites

We can expect to see features of these homeless life circumstances surface in the use of social network sites; for example, tensions related to family. At the same time, like college students, the use of social network sites might impact a homeless young person's future opportunities, which are often limited as time on the street increases.

The analysis of social networks, both face-to-face and mediated, is a key research tool for discovering knowledge about homeless young people [27,22]. One finding, important for the methodological framing below, is that when young people enter homelessness they may either, one, rapidly loose connections with home and take on connections with risk-taking street youth; or, two, maintain connections with home and never fully embrace street life. In the first case, face-to-face social networks can increase long-term risks when, for example, an individual joins the street economy and begins selling drugs – the potential for physical harm, substance abuse or incarceration increase. On the other hand, in the second case, mediated social networks can provide protective, pro-social support when, for example, a homeless young person receives emotional support from a caring teacher from high school. In brief, social network sites might help youth, on the move and away from home, sustain or re-establish home-based, protective ties. Yet, in tension with this protective role, social network sites, by their convenience for representing ties, for following people, and so forth, might speed the transition into street life or deepen entrenchment.

This picture, however, is overly simple because street-based networks, either face-to-face or mediated, might have pro-social effects (e.g., emotional support) while, on the other hand, some ties to home-based networks might bring about risk-taking behaviors (e.g., substance abusing parents). Accordingly, studies have been conducted that seek to identify correlations between particular self-reported ties on social network sites and drug and sex-related risk-taking behaviors [22,23]. Findings have shown that, on the one hand, positive correlations were found between home-based, pro-social ties and reductions in sexual and drug-related risk-taking behaviors. Here, pro-social ties were defined as communicating with such roles as *family member* or *friends that young people knew before becoming homeless* that were also *substance-non-using*. On the other hand, a positive correlation was also found between certain "friends" roles and increases in sexual and drug-related risk-taking behaviors. Here, "friends" roles include *friends from the street* or *friends who young people have met online* who are *substance-using* [22]. These findings suggest that the availability and utilization of certain kinds of ties, the essential feature of social network sites, may go some substantial way toward improving the welfare of homeless young people – a result of great potential importance.

Research Framing and Questions

From this background, we make three framing propositions. First, homeless young people, like most young people in America, use social network sites. Second, as an extraordinary group of users, homeless young people are likely to exhibit extreme needs for social network sites, yet needs with possible relevance to all users. Finally, social network sites, when used to promote and engage protective, pro-social ties, might be a crucial tool for improving the welfare of homeless young people and for helping them to escape homelessness. Accordingly, in this research we investigated the experiences that homeless young people have with MySpace and Facebook, seeking to identify opportunities for social and technical design. Specifically, we ask: With whom and how do homeless young people communicate within social network sites? How might social network sites influence the quality of relationships?

METHOD

Procedure

The procedure was based on a 2008 study of identity development, emerging adults, and MySpace, where same-sex discussion groups were employed [19]. In the present study, we followed the interview protocol from the 2008 study closely. One exception was that we adjusted the discussion questions so that participants could respond to their use of both MySpace and Facebook.

The procedure consisted of two main phases. In the first phase, participants were asked to complete a background questionnaire, consisting of demographic questions, how access to the Internet is obtained, use of social network sites, circumstances of homelessness, how homelessness might be ended, and similar things. The demographic and technology-related questions were largely drawn from Rice [22]. Then, the group discussion proceeded, with the discussion structured around 12 thematic questions, with specific sub-questions [19, Appendix 1].

One male and one female moderator, the authors, respectively moderated the discussion of same-sex groups of four participants. Following [19], the main rationale for this procedure was to promote free discussion consistent with the exploratory nature of the research. Additionally, since some questions explored impression management and other gender-related topics, we expected same-sex groups to position participants to speak frankly and expansively. To equalize participation, a well-known problem of group interviews, the moderators sought to follow up with all individual participants. Indeed, we found the discussions to be generally lively and inclusive, with participants building upon and contrasting each other's points and stories.

In February–April 2011, participants were recruited by familiar and trusted agency staff during a drop-in for homeless young people at our collaborating organization in the University District (U-District), a few miles north of downtown Seattle. Youth attending the drop-in were invited to participate in a research study and once four youth volunteered, staff brought them to a quiet nearby room where the group discussion took place. In order to protect participants' identities, and following approved human subjects protocols, all participants gave verbal assent only of their willingness to take part in the research. All participants received a gift card worth $15.

The interviews ranged in length from 53–84 minutes. The interviews were audio-recorded and the audiotapes were transcribed resulting in a corpus of 71,007 words.

Participants

Twenty-four homeless young people, twelve women and twelve men, aged between 18 and 30 years participated in this study. One woman did not complete the group interview and her data was not analyzed, leaving 23 participants. See Table 1 for the distributions of ages (M=21.7 years), ethnicities, and educational achievement. In summary, this sample comprises emerging adults, generally beyond the 11th grade, who are or have recently been homeless, and who use social network sites.

Concerning homeless status, even with attending a drop-in for homeless youth, six participants indicated they were *not* homeless. Of these, four had recently moved into housing; the two others indicated: "have places to stay," and "couch surfin'." Two participants indicated they had jobs, which were: "the streets, panhandler" and "state unemployment."

Two participants used MySpace only, eight participants used both MySpace and Facebook, and 13 participants used Facebook only. The majority of participants (69.5%) used MySpace or Facebook at least once every couple of days, for a range of topics, with music and media being the most common. Seven participants indicated that they had more

DEMOGRAPHICS	n	%
Age		
18-20	8	34.8
21-23	12	52.2
24-26	2	8.7
26-28	0	0
29-30	1	4.4
Gender		
Male	12	52.2
Female	11	47.8
Ethnicity		
Mixed Race	10	43.5
White	8	34.8
Amer. Indian	1	4.4
Asian	1	4.4
Black	1	4.4
Latino	1	4.4
Pac. Islander	1	4.4
Education		
8th grade or <	1	4.4
9-10th grade	2	8.7
11-12th grade	16	69.6
13-14th grade	3	13.0
No response	1	4.4
SNS USE		
MySpace	10	43.5
Facebook	21	91.3
Both	8	34.8

WHAT DO YOU TALK ABOUT ON SOCIAL NETWORK SITES?	n	%
Music	19	82.6
Movies or television	15	65.2
Videos	14	60.9
Drinking/drugs/partying	13	56.5
Work	13	56.5
Love/relationships	12	52.2
Place to stay	12	52.2
School	11	47.8
Sex	9	39.1
Nothing	1	4.4
CIRCUMSTANCES		
Consider self homeless?		
Yes	17	73.9
No	6	26.1
Currently have a job?		
Yes	2	8.7
No	21	91.3
WHERE DO YOU GET ONLINE?		
Public library	17	73.9
Youth service agency	9	39.1
Where you are staying	7	30.4
Friend/associate's home	7	30.4
Internet café	6	26.1
My cell phone	4	17.4
School	2	8.7
Nowhere	1	4.4
Work	0	0.0

HOW OFTEN DO YOU USE SOCIAL NETWORK SITES?		
Several times a day	7	30.4
Once a day	2	8.7
Once every couple of days	7	30.4
About once a week	3	13.0
Less than once a week	3	13.0
Never	1	4.4
WHO DO YOU COMMUNICATE WITH USING SOCIAL NETWORK SITES?		
Parents (including foster or step family)	11	47.8
Brothers, sisters, cousins or other family members	17	73.9
Friends or associates you know from home	19	82.6
Case workers, social workers or staff at youth agencies	7	30.4
Friends or associates you know from the streets	20	87.0
Friends or associates you met online	10	43.5
Boss or employer at your job	2	8.7
Potential employers, looking for work	3	13.0
Others	9	39.1

Table 1. Self-reported participant characteristics.

than one profile on MySpace, Facebook, or both. One participant responded that he "never" used social network sites, contradicting his other responses on the questionnaire and statements during the group interview. For obtaining access to the Internet, as might be expected, public libraries and youth service agencies were most common.

Concerning network sizes, participants indicated that they ranged from less than 10 to 1,000. This data should be interpreted cautiously since it is self-reported and many participants hedged their estimates as uncertain. Moreover, since about 1/3 of the participants had both MySpace and Facebook profiles or maintained multiple profiles, inaccuracies may have compounded. That said, removing five responses which were vaguely stated (e.g., "less than 37") and taking the lower number in ranges (e.g., "400-450"), the mean of the 11 remaining responses was 240 friends (Range = 14-1,000).

Data Analysis and Reporting

For interpretive analysis and reporting, which departs significantly from the 2008 study [19], we established an analytic stance that would allow us to show both the extraordinariness and ordinariness of homeless young people and social network sites. This stance was shaped by two over-arching principles. First, to appreciate the extraordinariness of experience, we decided to present relatively rich and coherent portraits of the participants, a method of reporting used in prior work [29]. We did this to emphasize the *individual* as a whole, and to work with a reporting style that allowed us to bring forward something of the ambiguity, nuance, and tensions that arise through the use of social network sites by this population of users. Second, to characterize the ordinariness of experience, we decided to connect the portraits to accounts of uses of social network sites by emerging adults in college or the workplace. We did this to show how the accounts in the portraits relate, either by commonality or by difference, to accounts published in the literature.

From this analytic stance, we followed a four-step process, iteratively and synthetically.

Step # 1 – Selection criteria. We decided on three criteria for selecting participants' accounts. First, we sought accounts which covered the space of communications between the participants and roles within the home-based and street-based categories. Recall that these categories came from prior work [22]. Second, we sought accounts which showed the double-edged nature of the home-based and street-based categories; that is, we selected accounts that appear to be pro-social and risk-related within each of these categories. Third, for representativeness across all 23 participants, we sought accounts that covered the diversity of participants' ethnicities, circumstances, and activities.

Step #2 – Read transcripts. The two authors independently read the transcripts from all six discussion groups. One author generally sought to find accounts related to pro-social and risk-related ties. The other author generally sought to uncover accounts that fit into themes from the social network literature. The accounts were extensively discussed and the transcripts were read repeatedly.

Step #3 – Write portraits. Portraits, using pseudonyms, were drafted and extensively revised. For writing style, we sought to convey a little about the participants' appearance and background. Lengthy quotations were used, partly to allow readers to judge our interpretations. Portraits were examined for satisfying the selection criteria, and eight portraits were selected and edited for concise reporting.

Step #4 – Identify themes from the social network literature. Five themes from the literature were identified. Then, the portraits were connected to those themes and the correspondences between the portraits and the themes were characterized, thus providing a means to illuminate and examine the extraordinary and the ordinary.

THE PORTRAITS

Bernie: Family, Tech Savvy and Survival

Bernie, aged 21, reported being homeless on and off since age 15. Yet, she was the first girl in her family to attend college and wanted to continue her studies. Like many young homeless women, Bernie wore oversized clothes, hiding her frame, and making her seem physically larger. Bernie described growing up in a:

> [H]obo crack grubby town [where] like girls were constantly getting on MySpace and meeting dudes online. And you know bad sh*t would happen to them.... [My family was] a military old school Hispanic family.... I was raised where the cooks [women] would cook, my dad and the dudes would go and sit down and eat, and when they were done eating...the kids and [women] ate last.... And then I [turned 15] like screw this.

A "MySpace fanatic" at 15, she enjoyed meeting up with friends in chat rooms. However, her independent spirit led to conflict with her parents, especially her father.

> They just thought I was going to explode with all these bad things when I was 15...because when you are 15 you are a woman.... And I remember...this girl got raped in the woods by my house because she met someone off the Internet, but I mean keep in mind the girl was like 15 and the dude was 48.... my mom...was getting really, really paranoid and my parents would panic because I would go on the computer and then they would assume I am going out and doing drugs and whoring it up.... And so...my dad took my computer out of my room and put it outside on the porch.

Bernie retaliated by way of her father's computer.

> ...I ended up taking my father's computer and I hacked it. And I changed all his passwords and everything.... I remember when I found out [my father's password]...I found out my dad is so stupid, so ridiculously stupid. I mean the worst he could ever do was: One, have one password for everything; or two, have that password also be the same password to all [his] credit card numbers.... And then it takes like 5 minutes to get on the computer, download a key log app...and anything you type I will know everything.

Having moved to Facebook, Bernie still enjoyed social network sites. However, she noted that spending too much time on the computer was a problem.

> I think the computer can be really time-consuming and I feel like it can really inhibit...someone...from developing their social skills...having interactions...getting more knowledge. Like you know I get more knowledge on the streets.... And you know I can be academically smart, because Thank God I was a nerd, but at the same time like I am thrusted [sic] outside with nothing but the clothes on my back I can survive because Thank God I got off of the f*cking computer.

Lulu: Facebook for Friends and Life

Lulu, aged 25, had a young son. She did not consider herself homeless because she was not sleeping outside at the time of the group interview. However, like Bernie, Lulu was also from a Hispanic family and had been "homeless off and on since [she] was 15." Seemingly fun-loving and confident, Lulu gave other participants "high-fives" and self-reported that she was popular. Multi-tasking, she used her mobile phone to text throughout the group interview.

Lulu resisted moving from MySpace to Facebook, but made the switch once all her friends had switched.

> I don't see a lot of my friends everyday because some of them are downtown, some of them live like in [the] surrounding [area] and like I'm here [in the U-District] everyday…. It's just to me it [Facebook; mobile phone] brings us closer because we don't see each other all the time and we get to talk to each other and make jokes and you know really find out how and what each other is doing on a daily basis. Even though we are not together all the time we know what each other is doing all the time, and it makes us closer you know. That's how I feel.

When asked if Facebook had changed anything about her life, Lulu said:

> Facebook is life-changing. I found my birth mom on Facebook last week…. Facebook is amazing. I owe about 21 years of my life's search to Facebook….. I went down and saw her…. two days later…. There wasn't any disappointment [meeting my mom] because I mean when you look for somebody that long, no matter the fact that they are alive, you know, is really what it was for me is that she was alive, you know, yeah I got to see her, and I have two brothers and a sister too that I met….

This revelation prompted a response from Mary.

> Oh that is amazing dude. I wish I knew…but like I have no idea who my parents were. I would never be able to, but I think it's really neat when people can actually find their true kin because I have never met my real family. And I was like abandoned when I was a baby…and like I grew up in a city orphanage…but if I could find my parents I think that Facebook would be a cool way to meet them, because you could like ask them a bunch of questions…and not have that terrifying staring at your parents kind of judgment look, like whoa what kind of person did you grow up to be.

To which Lulu, who was also abandoned, said:

> I think that's the best part about my thing was there was no way she could look at me and judge me for anything, because, you know, because of what she did…she made her own choices.

Finally, Lulu summed up her experience.

> I love Facebook. …you know, if there was a person that I could write and say 'Thank you for making Facebook' I would…. I almost called Oprah…. I mean like it's crazy to find somebody you searched for your whole life on Facebook. You know, like it doesn't happen to everybody.

Jazz: Multiple Selves

Jazz was 21 and had just found housing after being homeless for three and a half years. Jazz told us she is attracted to girls and reported her race as White. She is tall and thin with short hair, an affable grin, and a gift for training animals, such as cats and rats. Jazz, like Bernie, was fluent with technology, and had used PageRage to change the background of her Facebook profile to "a half-naked elf lady leaning up against this snow tiger."

Jazz had a mobile phone in her pocket that she checked throughout the discussion. She had four unique Facebook pages for herself, one that she had created for her cat. She had one page just to communicate with her parents "who kept messaging [her] and stuff and [she] didn't want to be in contact with them." Jazz created the other pages after her phone was stolen and during a recent stay in the hospital, recovering after being badly beaten on the street.

> And other ones [Facebook pages] are just because like my phone got stolen, and one of my accounts was lined up with my phone, and I tried to access it using someone else's phone. And I was trying to get in touch with somebody while I was in the hospital and it ended up locking me out of Facebook. So I had to make a new one to get in touch with everybody again…. So now I have got three Facebooks. And then recently I decided to make one for my cat.

On Facebook, Jazz had friended both case workers and family. These ties, in combination, were life-changing.

> Like [service agency and staff names] are all on my site. …and thanks to them being on my Facebook they were able to get a hold of my sister when I was in the hospital which is how my family found me and why I am no longer homeless.

Connecting with her sister was important for Jazz who had a rocky relationship with other members of her family, particularly her parents. Recounting events prior to leaving home and her hospitalization, she said:

> My dad unfriended me…. He pissed me off, so I put a comment on my Facebook. It was nothing horrible, but I wanted to see what was going to happen. And I put on my Facebook – this really kind of sucks, I want to move out, and I blocked both my parents and my little brother from that comment. I didn't realize that by blocking that comment I would block them from my whole page…. And so a week later he [Jazz's father] was all like 'Oh, did you notice that I unfriended you?' And I was like all 'Dude, I didn't realize that by blocking one comment that it would completely block them.'

Although Jazz apologized, her father refused her recent friend request. Indeed, lately she had been focusing her efforts on her cat's Facebook site, which her good friends knew was the best way to contact her.

Mary: Street Friends

Mary, aged 19 and Asian, described herself as being into the rave scene when she was in high school. She said that, in the past, her activities on social network sites had "caused a lot of problems" for her since she had made friends with strangers and had been incautious when giving out personal information. Mary is currently trying to transition off the street, and when responding to a question about posting negative comments, she said:

> You know like saying 'You suck.'…I hate people who say that, but a lot of my friends are like 'You suck [Mary]'…because I'm not like kickin' it like I used to, because I'm just like I am trying to stay out of trouble now.

However, Mary noted that through these interactions, Facebook helped her determine which friends to keep close and which ones to hold at arms-length.

> So…like it just kind of helps you realize who is your friend and who is really not your friend…. You know, based by people's comments and how they interact with you on Facebook…. [S]o then I know not to hang out with them on [the main street in the U-District] really. I'm like I don't need to hang out with you anymore, but yeah sure you can still be on my Facebook.

Sheri: Multiple Profiles for Different Audiences

Sheri was 18, and self-reported as Mixed Race. Like six other participants, Sheri reported having more than one profile on either Facebook or MySpace.

> Well, I do it because I have different audiences of people, like my family is very, very straight edged, like it is ridiculous. My family is huge and kind of my aunts and uncles and my grandma and grandpa and everything. Everyone is like military, except for me and my one cousin. The rest of them are like straight edged, they go to church every day, on time every day, they are over in the military doing their little military stuff, they come back, their house is perfect. Me and my cousin are the only black sheeps [sic], so there are a lot of things that go on in my day to day that would give my grandmother a heart attack and kill her, like no joke. She would just freak out. So I have my family page, which is where I keep track of all my family and my relatives and stuff, and then I have my friend page, which is where you actually get to see more real stuff, because my friends actually know everything, well most everything.

Sheri was wearing a black leather jacket, and a collar around her neck with a leash attached. She said that multiple profiles might help people "express themselves in a way that they feel is safe," saying of her own life experience:

> Okay well so I am a pagan and most of my family is Christian. So I have my Christian profile, which not really Christian but my family profile, which is really tame laid back. I mean I do have a sweet softie side of me, I just don't put it out there that much, and so it has got like a fairy for the background, this really awesome heart music that I've never listened to around any of my friends because they would laugh at me. And then there is like my street profile,…it has got like angry hard rock on it, this like vampire leg it is like half torn apart – it is pretty awesome, pretty sick, pretty wicked – and it is like because I feel safe because they [my friends] all don't really care.

Along with the different profiles that Sheri had created for family and friends, Sheri could also see that multiple profiles could be useful for communicating with employers.

> Oh and my family page is also my business page…. So if like a business like looks me up my actual legal name is on my family page, where my street name is on my friend page.

Marvin: Friends with Everyone and a Better Life

Marvin was 23. He reported that he was Mixed Race. In response to whether he considered himself homeless, he wrote: "I have been homeless since the age of six, in the streets of [major Midwestern US city], and I've honestly never had a place of my own." Marvin, neat in appearance and matter of fact in conversation, said that he had also spent time in a Midwestern state.

Unlike the majority of participants, who tried to limit their Facebook friends to people they had met in person, Marvin was open to being friends with anyone who asked. In response to another participant's statement about limiting friends, Marvin said:

> I can't do that…. I try to be a person who tries to keep everybody as friends, everybody…. I try not to bump nobody or anything. I try to be friends with everyone…. If somebody like offers to add me as their friend I am like 'OK, so who are you and where are you from and what is your name?' Important…. Even if I don't recognize who they are…I will always try to get to know them…. I try to talk…. I don't grade nobody.

In contrast to Jazz and others, Marvin was unaware that it was possible to have more than one Facebook page. In any case, he said that he did not want to maintain separate pages in order to partition friends and family. Among his Facebook friends were his mother who lived in another state on the west coast, his father, his brother in a southern state, his sister and other family members, as well as local case workers and service agencies. He had also recently found an old girlfriend.

> There is this girl I know in [a Midwestern state]…. I actually consider her my best friend besides my mom.

The emotional support provided by all these people and the ability to easily communicate with them were part of Marvin's plan for transitioning out of homelessness.

> I am trying to change my life and get myself off the street so I can have a better life…. Most of the case managers that I have like that are on my Facebook…I like them and I like keeping in contact with them to let them know how I am doing and how I have been or what I am doing and what I am up to.

Roger: Facebook is like Crack

Roger was 23 and reported his race as White, and "slept in shelters, churches, and in doorways, under bridges in a tent and some nights I just stay up." Roger considered social network sites to be "crazy, mind-blowing, [and] time-consuming," and somewhat of a distraction, but also a good way to connect to others.

Roger had one MySpace account for friends and two Facebook accounts, one for friends and a second for family. He knew his niece and nephew only through his family account on Facebook. He thought that the separation was important to the way that he was perceived by others, and in opening up future opportunities. Roger could envision the positive and negative uses of social network sites.

> Like say if you're on the streets and you meet a bunch of street people and 'Boom!' you have all these street people hitting you up [i.e., wanting to be friends on your Facebook page] and you're like, 'Oh, this does not look good.' But like if you're in the communication world… You know like resources that you could probably use like, 'Oh, this guy's a geologist. Oh, I'm going to do something with geology one day.' 'Boom!' that day comes and I'm like 'Hey, contact him.'… You know, that if you already know somebody or he can help you network with somebody else that knows. So there's like a little system going on there. So I think that's really cool…

Similarly, in another example, Roger was using Facebook to stay in touch with his grandmother, who might provide a bus ticket to her home. On the other hand, while being drunk, Roger had angered both his mother and father by confronting his parents' mutual male friend, Tom, after seeing Tom on his mother's Facebook page. Roger asked Tom for his phone number, called, and belligerently told him to stay away from his mother, "a married woman."

Learning about the confrontation from Tom, Roger's mother urged Roger to "get help" with his drinking.

Roger was so concerned about eradicating traces of his homeless life that he had recently tried to delete his Facebook profile, as he worried that it gave the wrong impression of his character. However, he had found that:

> I realized you can't actually delete your Facebook account.... I deleted one, set up another one to just add family and that was gonna be it. And then one day, I just like typed in the old address, and it brought up my whole old account.... They never actually deleted it. It never gets deleted. It's always there...it just deletes it from your friends being able to see it. But like it stays in the system, so you can just log back on.

When another participant remarked that he knew how to permanently get rid of a Facebook account, Roger said:

> Oh, you gotta show me that. I want to do the permanent [delete], 'cause I keep going back on. And it's like crack. It's like I keep going back. I need to get rid of it [my friend Facebook page] altogether. No going back.

Chip: Skateboarding and Couchsurfing

Chip, 21, reported that he was White. Although he participated in service agency programs for homeless youth, he did not see himself as homeless. Rather, Chip was "couchsurfin' from house to house and week to week," meaning that he was intermittently sleeping at different friends' and associates' places. He was very interested in skateboarding, in composing music and lyrics, and in working as an emcee (i.e., a master of ceremonies who selects and mixes recordings live at dance clubs).

He said that in November 2010 he created a Facebook account because a beta release of MySpace, which he had used in high school, performed poorly. Like several other participants, Chip liked to keep up with the music community on MySpace and felt that Facebook was less suited to this pursuit. Chip communicated with over 400 friends – some he had known since kindergarten – through MySpace and Facebook. However, of all his family members, he had friended only one of his brothers.

Chip would think carefully about each one of his posts and wanted to avoid work-related repercussions.

> I'm pretty professional on the Internet, honestly. You can put anything on the Internet, but employers are starting to investigate more on their employees' personal life [sic].

Having acquired and maintained a large network of people who shared his interests, Chip imagined that he might draw on his network to facilitate a skateboarding trip.

> You can set up a really good network if you're couchsurfing, or if you are trying to cross down from the high Northwest corner of the United States and go all the way down...to Southern California. You could send out, 'Hey, I'm looking for a couch [to sleep on tonight] and I'm in so-and-so'.... You have certain friends that live along the route, you know, it could help.

Chip had engaged in discussions and worked on his musical compositions via Facebook.

> I talk a lot [on Facebook].... I've edited three or four songs just on Facebook. So it's kind of, it makes foot traffic non-existent anymore. You don't have to take it [a song] over to somebody, 'Hey, listen to this tape or listen to this.' It's like all you have to do is you type your lyrics and it's saved, and...you can send it wherever. So it's all kind of like a storage place....

Chip, however, could see a downside to online storage.

> I just don't feel it's secure enough.... You're able to type whatever you want. But when it takes you a month to write a decent song, you don't want it jacked [stolen] in like two seconds. 'Copy, Paste, Boom!' How are you supposed to protect yourself? 'Cause...you're trying to let your scene or your community around you know what's going on, but you're not wanting to leave yourself vulnerable.

DISCUSSION

With the eight portraits now presented, the next step is to position them in the literature. Given the exploratory goals of this study, the reporting style of the portraits, and the small sample, we cannot report on the generalizability of the portraits. That said, the aim here is to show how the extraordinary and ordinary aspects of experience in these portraits relate to the uses, benefits, and concerns which are experienced at least to some degree by most if not all users of social network sites. The following five themes come from our reading of the literature on social network sites.

Exploring Identity

Like emerging adults in general, homeless young people are in a period of change, exploration, and experimentation with various roles [27,19], some of which play out online. Chip, for example, had built a social network that might support him as a couchsurfer and was using Facebook to explore his interests in skateboarding and music. However, identity explorations can also potentially lead to family conflict, a particularly salient issue for homeless young people [11]. We saw that Bernie's conflict with her family was associated with her use of social network sites, partly motivated by her rejection of the traditional female role that her family expected. Finally, Sheri provides an example of the balance that can be struck when identity is explored online. By maintaining two profiles, Sheri felt that she could *safely* explore the darker side of her identity with like-minded friends while also portraying herself elsewhere in a manner expected to be favorable to her family and to potential employers.

Cultivating and Exploiting Social Ties

Like a college graduate who uses social ties to cultivate and identify opportunities for dating or jobs [12,13], the social networks of homeless young people can be exploited for opportunity but, even more, for human well-being. Jazz, for example, was re-united with her family because of two unrelated ties. When Jazz was hospitalized, a caring case manager, the first tie, happened to find Jazz's sister, the second tie, which allowed the case manager to reach Jazz's mother. This contact, in turn, led to some kind of reconciliation and shelter for Jazz. In a different vein, but still related to social ties, Lulu used Facebook to find her birth mother after being abandoned as a child, saying "Facebook is life-changing." These are deeply human events, suggesting high stakes indeed. At the same time, many of the participants in the study reported ordinary uses of Facebook. Chip, for example, kept in touch with friends from grade school, posted music, and found couches. And, Lulu kept her friends in touch with things in her life.

Interpersonal Tensions, Brought Online and Amplified

As social network sites are used to maintain existing social ties [13,4] and as a means for achieving offline ends [3], we would expect that pre-existing social tensions, and accords, would be reified online. We see Marvin, for example, tapping into a harmonious relationship with a past girlfriend and supportive relationships with case managers. At the same time, many of the participants spoke of interpersonal tensions that can arise with the use of social network sites – "drama" was a common term for it, which, incidentally, has been recently analyzed as an emic, youth-centered concept [20]. Roger, for example, illustrated how impulsive use, in his case while drunk, can lead to communication failures. Additionally, by trying to control access to content, Jazz inadvertently offended her father, which appeared to lead to an escalating communication failure or at least exacerbated existing tensions. The usability of privacy controls, a notoriously difficult technical problem [5], would appear to be implicated in this breakdown. Finally, the conflict around computers, and specifically social network sites in Bernie's family, is noteworthy. In this study no claim, of course, can be made that social network sites cause interpersonal tensions. Nevertheless, it may be the case that at times they provide a catalyst that amplifies pre-existing tensions [10]. Moreover, the need to repair communication breakdowns, or resolve drama, appears to be a very common challenge for participants of this study.

Managing Audiences, Adjusting Profiles

Like college graduates transitioning into employment and seeking to manage their audiences [4,25], or a college athlete who will be publically scrutinized [14], we have seen that homeless young people come to adjust their profiles and structure their online identities. Perhaps for reasons similar to Sheri, discussed above, seven of the participants had reported that they had multiple profiles. One participant used the term "decoy" for her profile that was meant for family and employers. Jazz achieved similar ends by using a cat, that is, her pet to veil her identity from her family. One likely account is that these participants, like many people, have faceted, incompatible, identities [6] and are seeking a means to achieve *pseudonymity*, a phenomena documented in a study of relatively older users (aged 24-57) with multiple profiles [26]. For homeless young people, "real" and "street" names (cf. *nom de plume*) may provide a particular opportunity for online pseudonymity and thereby avoid the undesirable convergence of multiple social groups [2,15]. It should be noted, however, that the use of multiple profiles is a violation of Facebook's terms of service. In a different vein, to avoid an undesirable imputation of a social identity, young people adjusted their profiles by deleting friends that portrayed undesirable ideas and activities, a strategy that has been reported among new employees just out of college [4]. Finally, in responses to the questions "who do you communicate with when using [social network sites | email]," participants indicated that they would more often communicate with employers by email than social network sites (48% vs. 13%), suggesting tactical awareness for impression management, consistent with other conceptual and empirical work [6].

Shifting Affiliations and Transitions

For many homeless young people, breaking face-to-face and online ties with street friends is a key component of transitioning off the street into mainstream society [27]. When this transitional process occurs it is both emotionally and practically difficult, as can be seen in Mary's portrait, where she is drawn to make excuses for *not* "kickin' it" and trying to stay out of trouble. Perhaps indicative of this process is Roger's belief that his ties to street friends will undermine his future prospects; thus, prompting him to delete his Facebook page. In another kind of example, a participant told of warning off "old friends," saying she would broadcast messages such as "so I'm going to be in town the next couple of days and just if you see me please, please try to turn the other cheek…." Here, Facebook is being used as a "virtual-physical" tool [see 3] to create social distance, a striking contrast to its use for arranging offline social gatherings [1]. The literature contains reports on the social awkwardness of unfriending and declining friend requests and of the anxiety of unwelcomed messages from past lovers [3]. However, the social transitions undertaken as homeless youth struggle to rejoin mainstream society are *radical*. Perhaps similar to a divorcee who separates from former in-laws or a recovering alcoholic who separates from drinking buddies, a homeless young person must separate from an entire group, once looked to for pleasure, for support, and even for survival.

SOCIAL INTERVENTION AT LIBRARIES AND DROP-INS

This study suggests implications for social intervention that apply particularly to homeless young people. To begin, consistent with theory and supporting the largely quantitative studies cited in the background [22,23], this qualitative study shows the potential harms as well as the potential opportunities for improved welfare. Clearly, the character and meaning of social network site ties are crucial, as are the planned and opportunistic purposes to which they are put. Given this over-arching point, namely the double-edged nature of social network sites, we now draw out the following three opportunities for social design.

Encourage young people to seek out and to keep ties with pro-social family and friends (Jazz, Marvin, Roger). While serious interpersonal tensions may exist between a young person and family members or a long break in contact may seem to be a daunting obstacle, life experiences of either party may lead to the possibility for some degree of reconciliation. At that point, the existence of social ties may become critical. Thus, people invited to be friends by a homeless youth might be encouraged to accept those requests, to be there, in case a youth reaches out for understanding, forgiveness, or help. This, of course, may be easier said than done. One participant, for example, sadly reported that his grandparents declined his friend request, possibly because they did not want their social ties to see his social ties and activities. This illustrates the challenge that young people face when family and friends come together [2]. For these kinds of cases, opening a one-to-one communication channel may be a practical approach [6].

Encourage young people to reflect upon their ties and the impressions that are created through social identity (Bernie, Lulu, Mary, Chip, Roger). Homeless young people, in general, can be expected to maintain ties with street youth because those ties may be important for survival or be socially desirable [24]. At the same time, when transitioning off the street, those ties may come to reflect a dissonance between a desired, future identity and a current, but unwanted, identity. To resolve such dissonance, these ties may need to be broken and put aside. For youth that are ready, librarians or case managers might create a "terms of use agreement," similar to what a college athlete might agree to [14], and a mentor might work with youth to check for conformance as part of the process for leaving the street. This process, of course, is likely to be fraught with difficulties as young people reconsider who to keep close and who to keep at arms-length. In brief, the difficult work that must be done offline must also be done online.

Encourage young people to consider how their audiences can be separated and engaged independently (Jazz, Sheri). This study has shown something of how some young people manage evidently faceted, incompatible, identities [6]. We have seen attempts at *pseudonymity*, by the use of multiple, unlinked profiles. Given that any effort to keep facets of one's identity separate comes with the threat of disclosure, we are unsure of the effectiveness of multiple profiles. In this study several participants spoke about family members, including younger siblings, finding out more about them than desired. Given the stigma associated with homelessness and life on the street, one might expect some youth to experience a good deal of anxiety about unwelcomed access to social ties. Accordingly, there is a need to help young people use social computing tools to keep incompatible, or at least different, audiences separate. This is all the more important given the potential benefits of keeping in touch with pro-social family. Strategies for regulating boundaries between the private and the public [16], appropriately adapted, appear highly applicable.

Social practice and technology (tools and infrastructure) interpenetrate and reciprocally interact; if this interaction stance is granted, these social interventions should also raise challenges for technical design. We present three: (1) *Tenuous connections* – When a person is not connected with everyday institutions (e.g., home, school, workplace) has a group identification which is stigmatized, yet lives spatially, in the built world, and makes contact with service agencies, how might the person's living circumstances be represented in social network sites? (2) *Radical transitions* – How might social media be designed to support the distancing and breaking of social ties that were once trusted and intimate but which have come to hold the possibility for emotional or physical harm? (3) *Pseudonymity* – How might social media be designed to support unlinked, incompatible identities, and how might subsequent risks of information leakage and disclosure be mitigated?

CONCLUSION

What is at stake when youth or emerging adults who are experiencing homelessness use social network sites? We know from our collaborating organization that a pressing concern is developing policy that addresses this question. That said, the key to this question is that life is very difficult when a good deal of one's time is spent securing safety, food, and shelter, under conditions of chronic stress, often without basic life-skills for interacting with society's institutions, and when physical and mental health and substance abuse problems are common. Taken all together, and in general, these psycho-social factors make homeless young people vulnerable [11,27]. A violation of a civility law, an indiscretion, a communication failure, or an unlucky setback can have serious consequences, often far more severe than would be experienced by a young person with stable family, or family-like, relations [28].

The stakes may indeed be similarly high when homeless young people use social network sites because this condition of vulnerability stays with the individual. Yet, we do not think that too much needs to be made of this admittedly somewhat paternalistic point. No matter what one's age or socio-economic standing, whether middle school student or politician, social network sites can lead to an embarrassment, a damaged relationship, or a lost job.

Nevertheless, in American society homeless young people are more vulnerable than most people. Indeed, this vulnerability makes homeless young people an extraordinary user group, as the elderly are in some circumstances [21]. The opportunities for social intervention and the questions for technical design show how the specific needs for homeless young people might be addressed and, in turn, potentially benefit many people. Given this, and our current findings, further work is needed to investigate the design of policies and social interventions for supporting homeless young people's access to and use of social computing technologies.

ACKNOWLEDGMENTS

Sincere thanks to the participants for talking about their uses of social network sites and to the CHI reviewers for helping us to improve the presentation of this work. This paper is based upon work supported by the National Science Foundation under Grant No. 1018008.

REFERENCES

1. Barkhuus, L., and Tashiro, J. Student socialization in the age of Facebook. In *Proc. CHI 2010*, ACM Press (2010), 133-142.
2. Binder, J., Howes, A., and Sutcliffe, A. The problem of conflicting social spheres: Effects of network structure on experienced tension in social network sites. In *Proc. CHI 2009*, ACM Press (2009), 965-974.
3. Brubaker, J. R., and Hayes, G. R. SELECT * FROM USER: Infrastructure and socio-technical representation. In *Proc. CSCW 2011*, ACM Press (2011), 369-378.
4. DiMicco, J. M., and Millen, D. R. Identity management: Multiple presentations of self in Facebook. In *Proc. GROUP 2007*, ACM Press (2007), 383-386.
5. Egelman, S., Oates, A., and Krishnamurthi, S. Oops, I did it again: Mitigating repeated access control errors on Facebook. In *Proc. CHI 2011*, ACM Press (2011), 2295-2304.
6. Farnham, S. D., and Churchill, E. F. Faceted identity, faceted lives: Social and technical issues with being yourself online. In *Proc. CSCW 2011*, 259-368.
7. Hampton, K. N., Goulet, L. S., Rainie, L,. and Purcell, K. *Social Network Sites and our Lives*. Pew Research Center, Washington, D.C., 2011.
8. Hancock, J. T., Toma, C., and Ellison, N. The truth about lying in online dating profiles. In *Proc. CHI 2007*, ACM Press (2007), 449-452.
9. Hendry, D. G., Woelfer, J. P., Bauer, T., Fitzer, T., and Champagne, M. How to integrate digital media into a drop-in for homeless young people for deepening relationships between youth and adults. *Children and Youth Services Review, 33*, 5 (2011), 774-782.
10. Horst, H. A. Families. In *Hanging Out, Messing Around, and Geeking Out*, M. Ito (Ed.). MIT Press, 2010, 149-194.
11. Kidd, S. A., and Davidson, L. "You have to adapt because you have no other choice": The stories of strength and resilience of 208 homeless youth in New York City and Toronto. *Journal of Community Psychology*, *35*, 2 (2007), 219-238.
12. Lampe, C., Ellison, N. B., and Steinfield, C. A Face(book) in the crowd: Social searching vs. social browsing. In *Proc. CSCW 2006*, ACM Press (2006), 167-170.
13. Lampe, C., Ellison, N. B., and Steinfield, C. A. Changes in use and perception of Facebook. In *Proc. CSCW 2008*, ACM Press (2008), 721-730.
14. Lampe, C., and Ellison, N. B. Student athletes on Facebook. In *Proc. CSCW 2010*, ACM Press (2010), 193-196.
15. Lampinen, A., Tamminen, S., and Oulasvirta, A. "All my people right here, right now": Management of group co-presence on a social networking site. In *Proc. Group 2009*, ACM Press (2009), 281-290.
16. Lampinen, A., Lehtinen, V., Lehmuskallio, A., and Tamminen, S. We're in it together: Interpersonal management of disclosure in social network services. In *Proc. CHI 2011*, ACM Press (2011), 3217-3226.
17. Le Dantec, C. A., Farrell, R. G., Christensen, J. E., Bailey, M. Ellis, J. B., Kellogg, W. A., and Edwards, W. K. Publics in practice: Ubiquitous computing at a shelter for homeless mothers. In *Proc. CHI 2011*, ACM Press (2011), 1687-1696.
18. Le Dantec, C. A., and Edwards, W. K. Designs on dignity: Perceptions of technology among the homeless. In *Proc. CHI 2008*, ACM Press (2008), 627-636.
19. Manago, A. M., Graham, M. B., Greenfield, P. M., and Salimkhan, G. Self-presentation and gender on MySpace. *Journal of Applied Developmental Psychology 29*, 6 (2008), 446-458.
20. Marwick, A., and boyd, d. (2011). "The Drama! Teen conflict in networked publics." Presented at the *Oxford Internet Institute Decade in Internet Time Symposium.*
21. Newell, A. F. Chapter 1 - Extra-ordinary human-computer interaction (pp. 3-18). In *Extra-ordinary Human-Computer Interaction*. Cambridge University Press, New York, 1995.
22. Rice, E. The positive role of social networks and social network technology in the condom-using behaviors of homeless young people. *Public Health Reports*, *125*, (2010), 588-595.
23. Rice, E., Milburn, N. G., and Monro, W. Social network technology, social network composition, and reductions in substance use among homeless adolescents. *Prevention Science 12*, 1 (2011), 80-88.
24. Roberson, J., and Nardi, B. Survival needs and social inclusion: Technology use among the homeless. In *Proc. CSCW 2010*, ACM Press (2010), 445-448.
25. Skeels, M. M., and Grudin, J. When social networks cross boundaries: A case study of workplace use of Facebook and LinkedIn. In *Proc. GROUP 2009*, ACM Press (2009), 95-104.
26. Stutzman, F. D., and Hartzog, W. Boundary regulation in social media. In *Proc. AOIR* 2009, Milwaukee.
27. Whitbeck, L. B. *Mental health and emerging adulthood among homeless young people*. Psychology Press, New York, 2009.
28. Woelfer, J. P., and Hendry D. G. Homeless young people's experiences with information systems: Life and work in a community technology center. In *Proc. CHI 2010*, ACM Press (2010), 1291-1300.
29. Woelfer, J. P., and Hendry, D. G. Homeless young people and living with personal digital artifacts. In *Proc. CHI 2011*, ACM Press (2011), 1697-1706.

Supporting the Social Context of Technology Appropriation: On a Synthesis of Sharing Tools and Tool Knowledge

Sebastian Draxler[1], Gunnar Stevens[1], Martin Stein[1], Alexander Boden[1], David Randall[2]

(1) University of Siegen
Hölderlinstrasse 3, 57068 Siegen
{prename}.{lastname}@uni-siegen.de

(2) Manchester Metropolitan University
All Saints, Manchester, M15 6BH
D.Randall@mmu.ac.uk

ABSTRACT
There is an increasing spread of flexible software applications that can be modified by adding components (sometimes called plug-ins or add-ons). A popular example in the software development domain is Eclipse, a flexible development environment that can be extended with literally thousands of different plug-ins. However, searching, installing and configuring new plug-ins requires complex overhead work that is only weakly addressed by existing support mechanisms. Recent research has highlighted the related practices of learning about new plug-ins and tailoring software tools as being highly cooperative, situated, socially embedded, and often connected to particular work situations. Based on an empirical study in small software enterprises, we develop an understanding of appropriation as a social and collaborative activity. We then suggest design principles for appropriation support that are grounded in the practices we have found in the field, and present a prototypical implementation of the concept that extends existing mechanisms of sharing tools and tool-knowledge.

Author Keywords
Appropriation; tailorability; learning; ad-hoc; peer-to-peer; help giving; workplace learning; software development

ACM Classification Keywords
H.5.3 **[Group and Organization Interfaces]:** Computer Supported cooperative Work

INTRODUCTION
Today, tailorability is an important part of software development. We have conducted a study on tailorability in the context of the Eclipse IDE, one of the most popular development environments that is widely used by software developers [6]. Eclipse provides support for a broad variety of programming languages, connectors to other software engineering tools such as bug trackers, as well as project management functionalities (just to name a few). All these functionalities are provided by a huge number of available plug-ins, which can extend and adapt Eclipse to virtually any software engineering project [20]. However, this flexibility also leads to problems for practitioners, who often need to deal with a considerable overhead in finding, selecting, installing and configuring the right plug-ins for a task at hand—always at risk of breaking their installations due to possible incompatibilities between plug-ins [27].

As a consequence, discovering new features has become an inherent and non-trivial part of the daily work of software developers [6]. This task can be time-consuming, confusing and involves a number of decisions concerning compatibility issues etc. Our data clearly shows that Eclipse users struggle with the necessary overhead work of managing their installations, keeping them up-to-date and reconfiguring them for new tasks. Hence, there is a strong case for understanding how people go about finding the plug-ins they need, what problems and constraints they have to deal with, and what kinds of support they rely on. In companies, appropriation is shaped to large extents by individual activities as well as by the formal structure and demands of the organization [1]. Yet, in its very nature, appropriation is a highly social activity which is embedded in particular work-related situations and carried out mostly between peers or colleagues. Cooperative appropriation may be performed in numerous different and elegant ways. Examples are asking colleagues for help, purposefully discussing new tools, casually sharing tools over coffee breaks, using email or newsgroups to ask for help, or relying on Twitter for information about new tools [5, 20, 21].

As we will show in this paper, individual aspects of software appropriation like tailoring, configuration sharing or informal learning are covered well in the literature. However, the connections between these aspects are not well understood. At the same time, existing solutions for sharing and managing tools and configurations provide only fragmented support for the diverse facets of technology appropriation. Based on the example of Eclipse, we present a novel, lightweight approach that is based on a holistic understanding of appropriation as an entangled, cooperative process of searching, becoming aware, installing, configuring, and learning how to use new tools. This approach is meant to overcome the fragmentations in the current design of appropriation support systems, filling a gap between solutions for general file sharing, specialized platforms for mass-distribution and configuration, as well as knowledge management approaches.

RELATED WORK

Our work is grounded in the Marxian tradition of understanding appropriation as the social process of incorporating objects into one's life, including changes to the objects, caused by the changing modes of using it [5, 28]. Configuring and sharing artifacts is seen as closely related to organizational learning in this tradition, and appropriation is understood as a holistic concept that includes adoption, tailoring, configuration sharing, tool awareness and informal learning. In this section, we want to give a brief survey of these inter-related aspects.

Sharing tools at work

In both CHI and CSCW, studying data sharing practices has a long tradition [11]. Since peer-to-peer networks have become a mass-phenomenon, a special focus in HCI has been on music sharing [3], addressing political and legal issues (like impacts on the music industry and digital right management), as well as hedonic issues (like socializing, intimacy, or expressing identity and personal experiences e.g. by creating mix-tapes) [3,32].

From a technical viewpoint, Voida et al. [33] analyzed the different systems people use in practice for file sharing (like e-mail, shared folders, version control systems or peer-to-peer networks). By classifying these systems, they developed a scheme of categories (including scope, addressing, distribution, visibility and notification) that should be considered by the design of sharing tools in general. While such general principles are valuable, we will argue that the specific demands and pragmatics of sharing tools and customizations in the work context remain important. In the case of customizations the shared object is a hybrid one, since not only the files need to be shared (or copied), but also the contextualized information how to use the customized tool. Therefore, a technological solution to address this issue has to deal with knowledge sharing as well as pure file sharing.

With regard to customization sharing, several important studies from the 1990s showed that local social networks play an important role for adaptation and adoption of software in organizations [8,19,34]. Within these networks, an informal division of labor exists where small groups of *lead users* create sophisticated customizations. These customizations are further adapted by *translators* to the needs of less experienced *users*, who usually do not adapt tools themselves, but profit from their colleagues' configuration work [19].

As noted by Mackay, local work practices become objectified by the customizations and diffuse through the sharing practices: *"The exchange of customization files provides another example of how users in an organization share information about their preferred ways of interacting with software"* [19]. However, Pipek [24] pointed out that the forms of usage and the use conventions are only partially manifested in the tailored artifact. In order to foster the collaborative appropriation and the negotiation of conventions, he argues for providing built-in mechanisms for recording and annotating usage, as well as use-discourse infrastructures to share these annotations with others.

In addition, as customizations affect the work within the group, Wulf [34] argues that groupware systems should include a means for collaborative tailoring. However, because of the complexity and subtle interplay between individualization and group preferences, it remains an open research topic how general demands of collaborative tailoring can be realized adequately.

Kahler [16] further elaborates Wulf's line of thought with regard to the special case of sharing individual customizations. He suggests technical as well as organizational means of support, including push and pull mechanisms (like sending tailored artifacts by email [18] or by a built-in notification system as well as providing common repositories for configuration sharing [15]), enabling the annotation of configurations and allowing to test the modifications in an exploration environment [35]. Furthermore, he suggests raising the awareness of tailoring activities and fostering a tailoring culture by encouraging cooperation among colleagues as well as between users and local experts, and by recognizing tailoring efforts as important part of cooperative work with computers.

Finding new tools and learning how to use them

As indicated, appropriating new technologies refers not only to the physical installation of new tools but also to organizational 'learning', and specifically to transformations of work practices and the acquisition of new competencies [4]. As Lave and Wenger [17] have shown, such processes are often embedded in everyday work situations. Informal interaction within *communities of practice* turned out to be an important driver for knowledge exchange in this regard. The related learning processes have been outlined in an *apprenticeship* model that describes how apprentices learn from a master or colleague by peripherally participating in their practices.

Twidale has demonstrated how important these aspects are in the context of "informal technical help giving between colleagues" [30]. Stressing the importance of the specific situation and the collaborative nature of learning activities, he showed how knowledge sharing could be understood flexibly and contingently. In contrast to the apprenticeship model that usually discerns fixed roles ("masters" and "apprentices"), Twidale discovered that actors tend to switch between these roles in practice. One example would be a student working in a software company. One the one hand, he could be seen as an apprentice learning about software development practices. On the other hand, in some situations he may also be seen as a master, introducing new technologies to his colleagues that he learned about in University. Such forms of learning therefore could often be better characterized as *peer learning*, instead of *apprentice learning*. Furthermore, Twidale observed that sitting together in front of a computer in order to work together and discuss work issues often determines a starting point and defines the context of the learning situation. Such forms of "over-the-shoulder-learning" [30] are important for the diffusion of work practices in an organization, as it enables people to discover and become aware of unknown tools or features in their social surroundings, and observe how to use them.

Similar issues have been studied by Murphy-Hill and Murphy [21]. They analyzed peer interaction in collocated and remote pair programming settings[1] according to related situated discovering and learning processes. Among other aspects, they identified sequences of *peer observation* and *peer recommendation*. In the first case, one programmer observes a colleague using a programming tool or feature that he/she was not familiar with. In the second case, the programmer is observed by a colleague and gets a suggestion with regard to a new tool or feature.

Such situations could be characterized as special cases of the over-the-shoulder-learning [30] that lead to the discovery of new tools and/or initiated learning processes about how to use these tools. In comparison to other information sources like internet forums or following Twitter, practitioners reported a preference for the local peer interaction because they valued the opinions and advice from colleagues' more. If possible, organizations should therefore support discussions about tools as a regular part of informal work communication as well as of regular team meetings. Furthermore, the results of Murphy-Hill and Murphy indicate a need for system design "*to make existing tools and environments more discoverable and distributed collaboration more effective.*" [21].

Discussion

At the technical level, sharing tools and configurations is similar to file sharing in general [33]. However, there are also important differences with regard to the related pragmatics. As tools have to be configured in order to match the individual needs or the IT infrastructure of the company, it is insufficient to share relevant files only. One also has to share the information how tools can and should be configured and used. As we have shown, such processes are often accompanied by forms of informal learning that are focused by concepts such as *legitimated peripheral participation* [17], *over-the-shoulder learning* [30] or *peer interaction* [21]. However, such concepts are hardly supported by general purpose sharing solutions like Napster or Dropbox that just support users specifying "*the what, with whom*, and *how* of sharing" [33, p. 2].

Even in the case of specialized platforms for software distribution (like Apple's App Store, the Firefox add-ons page or the Eclipse Marketplace), these aspects are only weakly supported. Rating and commenting functionalities are practically anonymous, making trustful interactions hard to establish. As a result, the features provided by these platforms do not have the same impact as recommendations from known persons or colleagues [23,25]. Also the existing configuration and installation managers that are integrated in some applications (like Firefox add-on manager or Eclipse update manager) primarily focus on the single user, and arguably neglect the sharing of tools and tool expertise within personal social networks.

In summary, we have identified a lack of support for the appropriation of new tools in situations where a large number of alternatives of varying use and relevance are possible. Current systems especially fail to address the social dimension of appropriation and fail to take into account the close interrelation between the physical sharing of tools, and the highly social and situated activity of sharing tool expertise. These shortcomings on the technical level also reflect shortcomings on the conceptual level. In particular, holistic concepts that provide theoretical accounts for the integration of configuration sharing and knowledge sharing features have been introduced just recently covering only parts of the issue [21]. Hence, there is a need for further research that takes the complex interrelations between informal learning and collaborative tailoring into account. In the following sections, we present such an approach and demonstrate how it can be realized in the case of Eclipse.

METHODOLOGY

Our work adopts the combination of ethnographic studies of work practice and participatory design as outlined in the concept of Co-realization [12] and Design Case Studies [26]. As noted by Hartswood et al. [12] knowing "what exists" can inform design, but cannot replace the practical experience of designing and using the actual artifact. In particular, the realization and appropriation of socially embedded software leaves ontic and epistemic traces that cannot be fully anticipated [26]. It has been suggested that design research comprises both retrospective and prospective elements [1]. Prospectively, the purpose of theoretical and empirical knowledge is to sensitize and inspire design. Retrospectively, analytic work should make explicit *"what shows up [...] as having been all along already implicit in that tradition [which is created by the ontic and epistemic traces of the realization process]"* [2]. The purpose of retrospective analysis is further to clarify and elaborate the general lessons learned that are worth remembering. So prospection and retrospection follow a different logic, but taken together, they constitute the iterative design process [26]. Here, retrospectively, we discuss a design project, where we developed a plug-in solution for Eclipse that is able to support collaborative appropriation. The design realization followed an iterative, participatory approach that was mainly organized in three cycles:

[1]Pair programming is an agile development technique where two software developers synchronously work together in front of one computer.

Cycle 1: Concept Design

In the first cycle we studied the Eclipse appropriation practices in five organizations (3 small and medium enterprises, 1 large enterprise and 1 research institute). In 2 small and medium enterprises, we conducted participative observation for more than two weeks. We furthermore interviewed at least 3 developers in each organization. In addition, we conducted an online survey in which 138 persons participated. As part of this survey, 76 Eclipse installations were sent in to be analyzed. The findings of these studies are partially published in [5,27]. Their results show that appropriation is an important prerequisite for Eclipse users in order to get their work done, and that local social networks of colleagues are a hugely important source for support in this regard.

We then developed a first design concept enabling users to browse the Eclipse installations of their colleagues. We evaluated the concept at the research institute in a small team of 8 developers, who are located at the same floor. Following a Wizard of Oz approach, we manually collected information about all Eclipse installations in the team. Based on the installed plug-ins, we derived suggestions for interesting tools for the team members. The value of the suggestions was assessed by the participants, followed by interviews that aimed to identify possible collaborative appropriation features within Eclipse. We further developed a first demonstrator to illustrate the general idea.

Cycle 2: Interaction Design

In Cycle 2 we focused on improving the interaction with the demonstrator. Initially, we conducted a 3-hour Participatory Design workshop with 6 students who regularly used Eclipse. Additionally, we presented the existing demonstrator to 7 Eclipse users from 2 of the small and medium enterprises and the research institute. As a preliminary evaluation of the interaction concept, we presented screenshots of the user interface to the practitioners. Later, the participants explored the demonstrator by themselves. The user tests were followed by interviews to get an insight into user perceptions of the tool. These interviews followed the Laddering technique, took about one hour each, and included discussions about the general impression of the design, areas for improvement, motivational aspects and possible use scenarios. The usability of the new interface design was also evaluated by 5 of the previous participants in form of follow-up interviews. This part of the evaluation included open explorative tasks as well as 'solving' tasks such as plug-in searches, browsing user configurations and commenting on a plug-in. The specification of these tasks was informed by our previous empirical study and the participatory discussion about meaningful use scenarios.

Cycle 3: Field trials

In Cycle 3, we developed a fully functional prototype that is stable enough to be used in practice. This stable version is currently being evaluated at the research institute, where 8 users have integrated the plug-in into their daily working environments. The feedback of the users is being used to continuously improve the prototype.

DESIGN PRINCIPLES

This section describes the major design principles we have identified, based on the ongoing ethnographic and evaluative work conducted. As described above, this process consisted of stages such as realizing and discussing prototypes and designing sketches with users, conducting field studies and surveys, as well as analyzing related work in the literature. As our understanding of appropriation practices reached a saturated level [9], we elaborated a system of related issues that designers of supportive systems for collaborative appropriation might consider. In the following, we present the most essential parts of this design space analysis.

Facilitating collaborative appropriation

"[...] especially one person in the project was extremely experienced in using Eclipse. It would have helped me a lot to know which [tools] he was using. I just would have used the tool[s] he used and wouldn't have had to worry about it." (Participant of an interview study, beginning cycle 2, translated by authors)

In the software industry, technology often follows rapid innovation cycles that make it hard for practitioners to keep up to date in their relevant fields. Furthermore, tool competencies often vary among team members in software companies with regard to different degrees of expertise (see e.g. [19]), but also with regard to the different specializations of team members (as we observed in our fieldwork). The dynamics and diversity of technology-related knowledge can also be seen in the working environment. For example, in our online survey the average Eclipse installation consisted of 418 plug-ins combined into 42 assembly units (so called Eclipse features), the average age of a plug-in version was not older than 6 months [5,27]. In addition, even among colleagues no installation was identical to the other.

In line with existing literature [16,19,21,30], our fieldwork shows that tool adoption emerges mainly from ad-hoc circumstances in everyday work [5,27]. Even when people were not actually working together on a common task, we observed developers sometimes 'having a look' at a colleague's machine to understand which tools he used for his daily work. If something attracted attention, communication was initiated about further explanations, help was taken and given, and customizations were shared with each other.

Support for collaborative appropriation should exploit this diversity, as it allows people to learn from each other. In particular, it should support the situated and social nature of appropriation in the context of modifying tools and learning new features in interaction with colleagues. In addition, design has to recognize the fact that appropriation is an important part of the 'work to make things work', but it is usually not the primary work objective [1]. Hence, the overall challenge is to facilitate situated appropriation, without distracting users from their primary work.

Based on our observations, supporting collaborative appropriation should consider the following design issues:

- **Workplace integration:** Supporting the interleaving of work and appropriation [30], a solution should be seamlessly and consistently integrated into the work context.
- **Sharing scope**: With regard to the scope of sharing, the most promising granularity is the organization, the group and the team that works closely together or has at least some personal contact.

With regard to tasks that should be supported, we identified three major areas:

- **Searching tool knowledge:** Features are needed for supporting users in finding the right information about the tool that might solve the problem at hand, and/or persons who are willing and competent to give advice in the given case.
- **Appropriation awareness:** In order to facilitate serendipitous situations of discovering new artifacts by chance, opportunities for social interaction in the sense of a "tickets-to-talk" approach [29] should be provided.
- **Peer installation:** In order to support the exchange and tools between colleagues, a solution for installing tools that are already in use by peers is needed.

While some of these design issues may sound self-evident, they are disregarded by existing tools for appropriation support and customization sharing. For example, sending customizations via emails (as suggested by [18]) is detached from ordinary work and involves the overhead of collecting the relevant files (or related links to repositories). Similarly, using shared file systems as local repositories (as suggested by [15]) introduces extra burdens with regard to administrating and maintaining the repository. While the more recent integration of marketplace features in applications (like the Firefox built-in add-on manager or the currently released plug-in for accessing the Eclipse marketplace) is a step in the right direction for satisfying the needs of appropriation, these solutions do not support the sharing of tools and tool knowledge within the local context of a team or company, but rely on external repositories or error-prone and clumsy file copying.

Workplace integration

In order to reduce any extra efforts and preserve the work context, appropriation features should be closely integrated into the ordinary working environment and be easily accessible in a casual manner. The integrated features especially allow the interleaving of work and learning from others by reducing the overhead for both the help-giver and the help receiver by 'looking over the *virtual* shoulder' [30]. In order to be perceived as an integral component, the additional features should conform to the general *look & feel* of the working environment. Further a lightweight solution is needed that avoids additional burdens of configuring the system and/or maintaining extra information.

Sharing scope

With regard to the sharing scope that specifies what data should be shared with whom, we can distinguish three design alternatives in general: public, selective and subnet [33]. Examples of public sharing solutions are websites, blogs or Twitter, where the content is published on the Internet for a public audience. Examples of selective systems are Emails, where providers intentionally select the persons the information should be shared with. An example of a subnet solution is the possibility to share pieces of music and whole playlists in the media player iTunes. It restricts the public audience to persons in the same network (typically colleagues or friends).

With regard to the pragmatics of collaborative appropriation, the drawback of the *selective* scope is that it is only appropriate for intentional interaction where the provider knows in advance which person the information is relevant to. This sharing mechanism facilitates serendipitous situations only weakly. In addition, the selective mechanism excludes newcomers who are not yet well connected to established local networks. The selective mechanism is therefore inappropriate for promoting the learning processes of newcomers within the community of practice [17].

In contrast, sharing information with the general public audience allows others (even strangers or people one is only weakly connected to) to become aware about one's activities. Hence, the public sharing mechanism enables a legitimate peripheral awareness [17] of appropriation activities. Yet, the public scope is too broad and lacks a common work context that is important for trust building and initiating peer-interaction [5,21]. We therefore recommend providing features that make appropriation activities publicly visible within the scope of the organization and its work groups. Technically, this could be realized by a subnet solution. Although the benefits of subnet sharing are well known and used by some tools like iTunes, to our knowledge no tool sharing solution exists so far which has adopted this sharing mechanism with regard to software tools and configurations.

Searching tool knowledge

"I think this [used browsing tools] would be interesting for our company, since (...) we do work in quite different projects. On the other hand, we are talking about a small group in whose competences I trust—unlike a web portal such as the plug-in community, which contains all [Eclipse] plug-ins, but I don't know who rated or commented these. That is just useless." (Participant of an interview study, translated by authors)

In order to support the searching within the local context, we explored the concept of being able to browse the tools installed by colleagues. As illustrated by the transcripts above, all users stated that a browsing feature would be really helpful for them. In addition, the users recognized that this feature is not only relevant for appropriation, but also addresses a general problem in cooperative work: namely identifying hidden conflicts that are related to using different tools and configurations [24]:

"I would have been interested in my colleague's [Eclipse] installation, since I need to be able to get and run the code that he produces. It would be useful to compare and match different Eclipse configurations [...]" (Participant of an interview study, translated by authors)

As tool knowledge only partially manifests itself in the plug-ins a user has integrated so far, such features as 'browsing' and 'comparing tool configurations' should be supplemented by a means to document and discuss configuration settings, best practices etc. [19]. Knowledge additionally should be made persistent as the appropriation of new tools happens irregularly and often casually as a kind of invisible work. For example, our study revealed that people often could not remember when and how they did modifications to their Eclipse installations, even in case they viewed these modifications as highly important (and sometimes struggled to replicate them in case of re-installations or updates). Hence, we believe that there is a need for a local memory that makes tool-centric knowledge persistent and easily retrievable, and that provides information on who has created the information, and how he or she can be contacted.

In addition, the system should increase the visibility of others' tool expertise and provide cues for becoming aware of what kind of tools the colleagues are usually working with. The cues should make use of automatic recordable information like which tools a person has installed, and how long they have been installed. However, the automatic collected data alone does not necessarily qualify practitioners to offer help to their colleagues, so cues should also consider user-controlled information, e.g. in a way as outlined by one of our participants:

"... the system should somehow visualize that one has done a lot of annotations, as this implies and shows others that one is experienced." (Participant of an interview study, translated by authors)

Appropriation awareness

"Probably it would be useful to be able to send messages like 'I solved all our problems by...' if I discovered something new. [...] The question would also be, if I get informed if someone else installed or likes something." (Participant of an interview study, cycle 2, translated by authors)

In the literature, awareness is mainly studied from the perspective of coordinating activities (e.g. [13,22]). In our case, we are more interested in a second, often neglected aspect of awareness about the work activities of colleagues, that of casual 'looking over the shoulder' [21,30]. Observing work practices and noticing individual tool modification activities in a team allows for legitimate peripheral participation and supports the learning and enculturation of newcomers [17].

Existing research results show that awareness support systems are especially useful in the context of distributed work, as the knowledge about each other's context decreases with distance [22]. However, the evaluation of our design concept in the first cycle shows that even small co-located teams would benefit from such support. As indicated in the transcript above, appropriation awareness is especially useful if the people work on different projects and profit from the each other's specific competences.

To reduce overhead, we argue that an information notification mechanism should be integrated, so that users do not have to fall back to communication channels like email *"to make sure that their indented recipient knows that a new file is available"* [33]. Such a mechanism should support both sending explicit messages as well as providing notifications that are implicitly triggered by tailoring activities. The last issue is related to Wulf's concept of informing groupware users of someone else's tailoring activities by an integrated notification system [34]. The major motivation is to support serendipitous situations of *peer observation* and *peer recommendation.* This means that the notification system should not just inform users about conflicting activities, but also support them in sharing information about newly discovered tools or solved problems within the work context.

Technically, awareness features could be realized as an awareness pipeline [7] that grants users fine grained control of the implicitly triggered notifications as well as the filtering of received events. As users want to spend as little extra time as possible with appropriation work, the design of sophisticated but complex configuration options has to adhere to the principle of proportionality. Hence, the design of a lightweight solution should take into account that notifications about tailoring activities will only sparsely be triggered as users do not modify their working environments daily. In addition, design should take into account that the default appropriation activities should be visible in the subnet in order to foster collaborative appropriation (see above).

Peer installation

"If you start using software, it helps to see how colleagues are using it. It helps to get a first overview, and to configure the [Eclipse] environment in a way that enables you to work with it." (Participant of an interview study, translated by authors)

Studies conducted in the 1990's [15,18,19] mainly focused on the sharing of self-created customizations. However, today it is easy to distribute customizations world wide. Instead of creating own solutions, users nowadays have the opportunity to look for existing solutions that relate to their problem and share the adopted solution with others.

Our fieldwork indicated that Eclipse users follow this trend, as they made intensive use of the growing market of freely available tools. The practitioners regularly modified their working enviroment by downloading new plug-ins and exchanged them with colleagues. However, the intention to exchange plug-ins was typically not planned in advance, but emerged in peer-interaction situations, where one observed an interesting feature in use by a colleague. Acquiring the relevant feature, however, requires knowledge of:

- Which plug-in implemented the feature in question?
- Does the plug-in in question depend on other plug-ins?
- What plug-ins need to be transfered, which have already been installed, in which version, and will this create conflicts?
- Were are the plug-in's files stored?

In principle, the Eclipse installations of peers contain all the requireded information and files to answer these questions and to (semi-)automize the task. However, we are not aware of any solutions that support the exchange of tools in the peer interaction situations we observed in our study. Instead, users are forced to carry out clumsy and error-prone workarounds as outlined above.

Based on this observation, we conclude that there is a need for supplementing existing solutions with features supporting peer-installation in situations of peer observation as well as peer recommendation [21]. We therefore decided to provide peer-installation features that support users in installing plug-ins and features observed on someone else's installation, as well as in recommending useful features to other users.

THE COLLABORATIVE APPROPRIATION PROTOTYPE

In order to support workplace integration and facilitation of appropriate methods, described above, we adopted the general sharing experience idea of iTunes. Like the music sharing feature is directly integrated into iTunes, the suggested features should be integrated directly into Eclipse. In order to realize this seamlessly, the prototype was implemented as an Eclipse plug-in. It uses the native Eclipse user interface, and relies on typical Eclipse interaction concepts. The user interface consists of different so called views (e.g. to show other peers) and editors (e.g. to comment a plug-in), typical elements of the Eclipse interaction concept, which consistently integrate the appropriation features into the work context (see Figure 1 for an overview).

Also like iTunes, our prototype is realized as a lightweight peer-to-peer solution, where users do not need to configure anything apart from activating the sharing and setting a nickname (optionally users can provide a picture, full name as well as their location). Technically, the prototype uses a simple JXTA peer-to-peer architecture that supports subnet visibility [10]. The network connections between the users' installations are established automatically if the prototype is installed on their machines, as the peers broadcast their availability. The communication infrastructure allows users to browse each other's Eclipse installation within the subnet to foster the coincidental nature of just meeting someone in the office. In contrast to iTunes, our prototype optionally caches information about users, the tools they installed as well as their comments and ratings (see below). Thus, tool information can be browsed even when the people are currently offline.

Realizing search and annotation features

In order to support *looking over the virtual shoulder* [31] we implemented an Eclipse view that allows users to in-

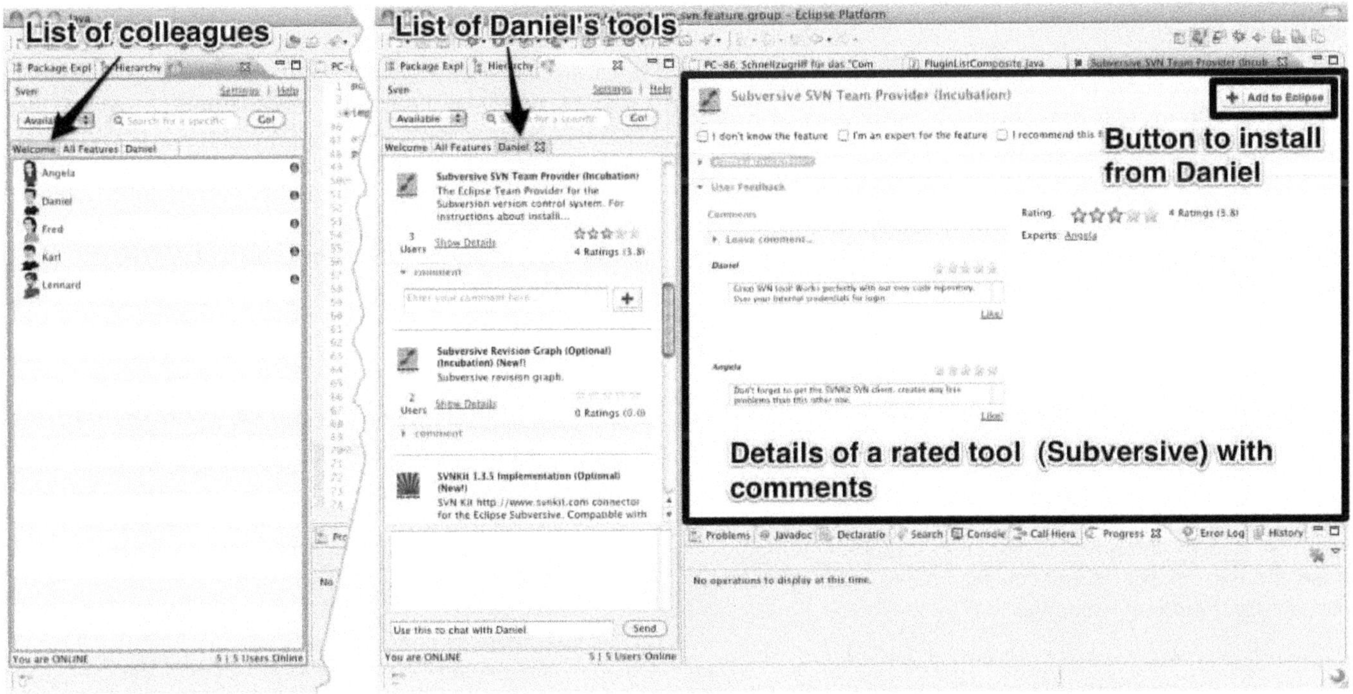

Figure 1: Integration of collaborative appropriation within the work context. Left: List of Eclipse users within the local network. Right: List of tools used by a colleague and a detail view showing the stored tool knowledge.

spect what tools are used in the local context. Like a Skype contact list, this view consists of all (cached) users in the subnet including name, picture and presence information (see Figure 1 on the left). By clicking on an entry, the view changes its appearance and shows the plug-ins used by the colleague (Figure 1 on the right gives the example of the plug-ins used by Daniel). Information in the list of tools includes the tool's icon as well as the name and parts of the description. From our usability study we know that this usually enough information for Eclipse users to decide if the tool is worth further exploration. If a user wants to have further information, he/she can click on an entry. This opens a detail view (see Figure 1 black rectangle on the right) that gives additional information including comments and ratings of other users (see below).

In general, these user interface elements enable users to explore the diverse Eclipse installations used in the subnet and look for tools that might be helpful for them. This is especially useful, as the experience in the group usually varies. To enhance the browsing experience, we further implemented different ways to filter and sort the results. For example, the user can search for keywords. This inverts the navigation, as the user can find a consultant by searching for a tool's name and therefore get help even without knowing in advance who is an expert on a particular topic. Further, it is possible to hide the tools that are used by both the user and his colleagues in the same version in order to enhance the awareness about differences in the configuration.

The list of tools can be sorted either alphabetically in order to simplify search, or by popularity in order to show potentially interesting tools. Currently, we measure popularity by calculating the average rating given by users (see below) and by the number of colleagues who use the plug-in, if multiple plug-ins show the same average rating. In addition, it is possible to exclude tools from the result set that have not been rated or received bad ratings.

To capture and maintain a shared memory of the tool knowledge, we adopted the common concept (used for example by commercial marketplaces like Amazon) to allow customers to annotate and rate the products that are provided on the platform. We provided rating and commenting in the detail view (see Figure 1 right). During design workshops, we introduced several different ways of annotating, namely, comments, rating, tags, and categories. However, free comments and ratings were perceived as the most useful ways of sharing knowledge and experiences and have therefore been included in the prototype.

As illustrated by the quote below, it is important to understand the reasons for using such features as well as necessary configuration information:

"I would add tool related information [annotations]. For example information that is important for the initial configuration [of a tool]. Team members can benefit from this information as it will save time and money..." (Participant of an interview study, beginning of cycle 2, translated)

An important factor here is common work context. Colleagues, for instance, need to know what kind of pitfalls might occur when installing new plug-ins, or may find it useful to know that particular plug-ins are both useful and easy to install. Figure 1 (details box) presents an example of the different pragmatics. In this case one of participants used the implemented annotation feature to provide an instruction on how to configure the *SVN tool* in order to access the company's new source code revision control system.

Generally, restricting annotation features to the local organization has the effect that users are not forced to make knowledge explicit that could be taken for granted in the shared work context. This prevents the general problem of 'sticky information' [14] and allows users to focus on more specific comments that are valuable for the local context. For example, formulations and instructions are highly beneficial for the local context, but do not make much sense without it. In their pragmatics, local annotations therefore differ from information that is targeting a public audience (like official help manuals or a users' review published on Amazon).

The shared work context also has an effect on the pragmatics of reading comments. In our fieldwork, for example, users often preferred to ask certain persons when seeking advice. Trust is often enabled by specific knowledge of the capabilities and characteristics of colleagues. The system allows for such filtering and, if in doubt, supports to ask the author supplementary questions, to clarify some information or get additional advice.

Realizing awareness features

In order to raise awareness of the infrequent appropriation situations, the system sends notifications to local peers in cases of users tailoring their installations, or when they comment or rate tools (see Figure 2 for an example). By sending notifications to all colleagues, we provide a solution for the lack of peer interaction in non-collocated settings and increase their visibility at the team level of peer interaction, as the users do not need to be working in the same room or building to discover that a colleague is using a new or interesting tool.

Figure 2: Notification example of a tool (SWT Designer) that was commented and rated by the user Bart.

The notifications (we used Figure 2 as example) provide the user with different kinds of information:

- *Tool Awareness:* Users become aware of the tool itself (SWT Designer) and are able to look up more detailed information about it by clicking the corresponding link in the notification.
- *Peer information:* Users become aware of the fact that a colleague (Bart) has installed the tool. They can contact him or check his profile by clicking the corresponding link in the notification.
- *Additional context:* Users become aware that their colleague has provided comments to specify a certain work context, tasks, pitfalls or practices that have proven to be beneficial.

Notifications enable the user to navigate to relevant objects (a tool that might be interesting and a person who may be an experienced user) by clicking the corresponding link.

Realizing peer installation features

In order to support users to share tools, we implemented a peer install feature. It makes use of the circumstance that the users' installations hold all needed information and files for the exchange of plug-ins. Instead of forcing the user to switch to an external marketplace or to copy files manually, the user can install a tool from a colleague's installation by clicking a single button (see Figure 1 upper right corner). The functionality behind this button calculates the plug-in's dependencies, detects possible version conflicts, and identifies all the files that need to be transferred. As all needed files are stored on the colleague's machine, the prototype does not need an internet connection. Instead, all relevant files are copied using the peer-to-peer infrastructure and are afterwards installed on the local machine. To calculate dependencies between plug-ins, we used Eclipse's internal provisioning mechanism (P2), which is also used by the default mechanism to update and install plug-ins from market places. By reusing this functionality, the installation process using the prototype does not differ from the installation from any other source.

EVALUATION

So far, we have conducted a limited evaluation in the research institute mentioned above. Even so, useful feedback has been obtained through workshops and usage tests during all phases of the design process. Users were generally positive and were particularly enthusiastic about the opportunity to browse each other's installations and be aware of each other's customization activities. The peer installation is more efficient and preferred over the clumsy and error-prone solution of copying files, and users do not feel distracted by additional appropriation features. In other words, the system acts to significantly reduce overheads in terms of time. It also has the valuable function of preventing installation crashes since one person's experiences can be easily propagated to others and necessary tools and plug-ins are provided. However, certain limitations are also becoming apparent.

One of the limitations that has become evident is the absence of a feature that can draw a connection between a user interface element and the underlying tool. For example a new Eclipse user needs help with a certain user interface element or functionality. However since Eclipse plug-ins are integrated so deeply it is not clear what tool/plug-in delivers this functionality and therefore he can't use the prototype to find an experienced user who uses the same tool. The same is true if a user wants to recommend certain functionalities but does not know which plug-ins contribute these. In a future version, we plan to adopt the approach of the Eclipse plug-in spy, a functionality which reveals the plug-in that is responsible for a certain user interface element by pressing a shortcut key.[2]

Another issue is the overly mechanistic implementation of the *subnet*, which needs to be more flexible than we have provided for. Changes in team membership; the involvement of external members (such as consultants to an organization) and casual sharing with outsiders (friends, university colleagues, and so on) are currently not well supported. In addition, the prototype does not yet support the sharing of configuration settings many Eclipse users have expressed a wish for.

CONCLUSION

Tailoring flexible software products is an increasingly important and common aspect of organizational work. As our study showed, Eclipse users have to deal with complex overhead work for maintaining and extending their working environments to the emerging needs of the daily work. This is a real problem that thousands of Eclipse users encounter regularly in their daily work. While over one thousand additional tools for Eclipse exist, it is hard to find relevant and useful ones. Furthermore, the users have to work out which conflicts may occur, what version of a tool is necessary, and what the tool can be used for.

In the case of Eclipse, the related sharing and learning practices turned out to be highly cooperative, situated, and grounded in the context of particular work situations. We have argued that because these issues are seldom addressed together, existing solutions only partially support the full context of appropriation. In other words, they largely fail to provide adequate appropriation support in organizations. Hence, there is strong evidence that better solutions for collaborative appropriation are needed and that we have to support all the related facets of finding, sharing and learning in order to support appropriation in practice.

Drawing on a detailed understanding of appropriation practices, we have presented design principles for supporting the social and collaborative aspects of appropriation. These principles were implemented in form of a prototype that addressed different aspects we have found to be important in the context of organizations:

[2] Cf. http://www.eclipse.org/pde/incubator/spy/

- Appropriation awareness within the organization helps to systematically uncover customizations that are interesting for others.
- The active search for tools and tool expertise help to decide what to use and whom to ask, based on the people within the organization rather than relying on anonymous market places.
- Peer installation of customizations supports sharing customizations with colleagues in a safe way, without having to search for dependencies and without having to work with files directly.

Right now, the prototype is tested 'in the wild' in form of a long-term study. Early results are positive, though they are subject to the limitations we mentioned above. Right now it is too early for a summative evaluation of how the prototype is being used in practice. As many issues of appropriation support can only be studied in long-term field trials (due to the relatively rare and unconscious occurrence of appropriation), we plan to conduct further evaluations and iterate our design accordingly.

REFERENCES

1. Balka, E. and Wagner, I. Making things work Proc. of CSCW'06, (2006), 229–238.
2. Brandom, R. Tales of the Mighty Dead. Cambridge Univ Press, 2002.
3. Brown, B., Sellen, A.J., and Geelhoed, E. Music sharing as a computer supported collaborative application. Proc. of ECSCW'01, (2001), 179–198.
4. Dourish, P. The appropriation of interactive technologies. JCSCW 12, 4 (2003), 465–490.
5. Draxler, S. and Stevens, G. Supporting the Collaborative Appropriation of an Open Software Ecosystem. JCSCW 20, 4 (2011), 403-448.
6. EvansData. 3rd Annual Eclipse Global Enterprise Survey Research Findings. Evans Data Cooperation, 2007.
7. Fuchs, L., Pankoke-Babatz, U., and Prinz, W. Supporting cooperative awareness with local event mechanisms. Proc. of ECSCW (1995), 247–262.
8. Gantt, M. and Nardi, B.A. Gardeners and gurus: patterns of cooperation among CAD users. Proc. of CHI'92 (1992), 107-117.
9. Glaser, B.G. and Strauss, A.L. The discovery of grounded theory.. Aldine Transaction, 2007.
10. Gong, L. JXTA: A network programming environment. IEEE Internet Computing 5, 3, 88-95.
11. Greif, I. and Sarin, S. Data sharing in group work. ACM TOIS 5, 2 (1987), 187–211.
12. Hartswood, M. et al. Co-realization, Co-Evolution and artifacts, (2008), 59–94.
13. Heath, C. and Luff, P. Collaboration and control. JCSCW 1, 1 (1992), 69–94.
14. Von Hippel, E. " Sticky information" and the locus of problem solving: Implications for innovation. Management science, (1994), 429–439.
15. Kahler, H. More Than WORDs. Journal of Universal Computer Science 7, 8 (2001), 826–847.
16. Kahler, H. Supporting collaborative tailoring. Department og Communication, Journalism and Computer Science, 2001.
17. Lave, J. and Wenger, E. Situated learning: Legitimate peripheral participation, 1991.
18. MacLean, A. et al. User-tailorable systems: pressing the issues with buttons. Proc. of CHI'90, (1990), 175-182.
19. Mackay, W.E. Patterns of sharing customizable software. Proc. of CSCW'90, ACM (1990), 209-221.
20. Murphy, G et al. How Are Java Software Developers Using the Eclipse IDE? IEEE Software 23, 2006, 76-83.
21. Murphy-Hill, E. and Murphy, G Peer interaction effectively, yet infrequently, enables programmers to discover new tools. Proc. of CSCW'11, (2011), 405–414.
22. Olson, G.M. and Olson, J.S. Distance matters. Human-computer interaction 15, 2 (2000), 139–178.
23. Ozakca, M. and Lim, Y.-K. A study of reviews and ratings on the internet. CHI '06 extended abstracts, ACM (2006), 1181–1186.
24. Pipek, V. From tailoring to appropriation support University of Oulu, Oulu, 2005.
25. Rogers, E.M. Diffusion of Innovations, 5th Edition. Free Press, 2003.
26. Rohde, M. et al.. Towards a paradigmatic shift in IS Proc. of DESRIST'09, (2009), 15.
27. Stevens, G. and Draxler, S. Appropriation of the Eclipse Ecosystem. Proc. of COOP (2010).
28. Stevens, G., Pipek, V., and Wulf, V. Appropriation Infrastructure. JOEUC, 22, 2 (2010), 58–81.
29. Svensson, M.S. and Sokoler, T. Ticket-to-talk-television Proc. of NordCHI'08 (2008), 334–343.
30. Twidale, M. Over the Shoulder Learning: Supporting Brief Informal Learning. JCSCW 14, 6 (2005), 505-547.
31. Twidale, M.B. Interfaces for Supporting Over-The-Shoulder Learning. Proc. of HICS, (2000), 33–37.
32. Voida, A., et al. Listening in: practices surrounding iTunes music sharing. Proc. of CHI'05, (2005), 191–200.
33. Voida, S. et al. Share and share alike. Proc. of CHI'06 (2006), 221–230.
34. Wulf, V. Mechanisms for conflict management in groupware. Advances in Human Factors/Ergonomics 20, (1995), 379–384.
35. Wulf, V. Exploration environments. Interacting with Computers 13, 2 (2000), 265–299.

ReticularSpaces: Activity-Based Computing Support for Physically Distributed and Collaborative Smart Spaces

Jakob E. Bardram; Sofiane Gueddana; Steven Houben; Søren Nielsen
The Pervasive Interaction Technology Laboratory
IT University of Copenhagen, Rued Langgaardsvej 7, DK-2300 Copenhagen, Denmark
{bardram,sgue,shou,snielsen}@itu.dk

ABSTRACT
Smart spaces research focuses on technology for multiple displays and devices for collocated participants. In most approaches, however, users have to cope with heterogeneous interfaces and information organization, as well as a lack of support for collaboration with mobile and remote users outside the smart space. In this paper, we present *ReticularSpaces*; a multi-display smart space system built on the principles of activity-based computing. The focus of *ReticularSpaces* is to support: (i) unified interaction with applications and documents through *ReticUI*, a novel distributed user interfaces design; (ii) management of the complexity of tasks between users and displays; (iii) mobile users in a local, remote or 'nomadic' settings; and (iv) collaboration among local and remote users. We describe the motivation, design, and architecture of *ReticularSpaces*, and report from a preliminary feasibility study. The study shows that participants found *ReticularSpaces* useful and effective, but at the same time reveals new areas for research on smart environments.

Author Keywords
Distributed User Interfaces, Multiple Display Environments, Smart Spaces, Collaboration, Nomadic Computing

ACM Classification Keywords
H.5.2 INFORMATION INTERFACES AND PRESENTATION: User Interfaces—*User interface management systems*

INTRODUCTION
Technological advances in recent years have led to a myriad of interactive devices and displays, ranging from tiny embedded displays and mobile handhelds to larger and more static tabletops and wall displays. Research into Smart Spaces and Distributed User Interface (DUI) technology seeks to exploit this technology trend by setting up infrastructures that allow users to engage in new forms of seamless digital interaction, which is less tied to specific computing devices, locations or hardware setup, but instead enable tightly integrated

CHI'12, May 5–10, 2012, Austin, Texas, USA.

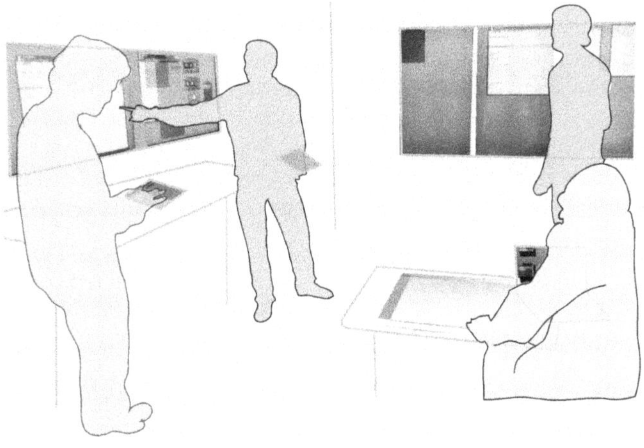

Figure 1. ***ReticularSpaces*** **deployed in a smart room including wall-based, tabletop, desktop, laptop, and tablet displays. Nomadic users can bring devices to the space, which is then automatically added to the smart space setup. Users in other locations can join collaborative sessions from remote displays.**

group interaction on multiple shared devices and displays. Research on Smart Spaces, such as iLand [16], Gaia [11], Interactive Workspaces / iRos [12] and Impromptu [8] have initiated research into the underlying infrastructures and interaction technologies for such reactive environments. These systems demonstrate how users may utilize new kinds of interaction techniques for using multiple collocated and shared displays and devices.

There is, however, still a set of core research challenges, such as spanning tasks over a large amount of devices or dealing with multiple users, locations and documents [17]. Previous approaches have focused mostly on extending existing personal computing operating systems and user interfaces to work in a collocated device and display sharing setup. This leads to a set of challenges. First, when smart space technology *extends legacy* personal computing operating systems and user interfaces, it implies that users face an interface design and metaphor designed for personal information management at a desk, which in no way is designed to work across multiple computers in the smart space setup. Second, users have *no structured support* for managing large amounts of information, exchange documents or organize flows of tasks between collaborators and devices. None of the existing smart space technologies support users in managing their information according to work tasks, and there is a significant overhead in configuring smart spaces to fit different workflows. Third, the challenge of *reconfiguration* of smart space technology is amplified when mobility is added to the smart space setup, since one of the intrinsic properties of mobile users is that they dynamically join and leave both local and remote collaborative sessions. Most research systems lack support for a dynamic engagement of nomadic users. Fourth, few smart space environments have built-in support for *remote collaboration*, but rely on external tools for awareness, coordination, and communication. This constantly requires an additional effort from users to manually configure collaborative sessions and invite people to join as needed.

In general, the use of legacy user interfaces, and the lack of support for tasks, mobility and collaboration therefore still make this technology disruptive and complex. To address these challenges, we propose the *ReticularSpaces* infrastructure (Figure 1), a new and integrated smart space technology which is based on the principles of *activity-based computing* [3] as the overall design approach. *ReticularSpaces* supports:

1. A *unified interaction paradigm* for handling activities, applications, resources, documents, and services across a distributed displays environment.
2. A *peer-to-peer and event-based architecture* to manage the complex flow of distributed activities and documents between users, displays and devices.
3. Support for *mobile and nomadic* users moving in and out of the smart space environment.
4. Support for *communication, collaboration and awareness* among local and remote users

This paper presents the motivation, design, and technical implementation of the *ReticularSpaces* system, including its distributed user interface and infrastructure architecture. We also report the results of a preliminary feasibility study that was performed in a laboratory setting. We conclude the paper by discussing the lessons learned from implementing and evaluating the *ReticularSpaces* system.

RELATED WORK

Existing smart space research systems can be organized in a taxonomy as illustrated in Figure 2. The four horizontal categories address whether a smart space supports; (i) a user interface (UI) specifically designed for smart space interaction; (ii) document, information, task, and workflows management; (iii) multiple users, in terms of synchronous and asynchronous collaboration; and (iv) mobility, specifically in terms of moving user sessions across devices ('roaming') in multiple locations, and context-aware adaptation as the user moves between multiple locations and hence contexts.

Prior research proposed techniques to transfer digital elements across display boundaries [2, 15]. These approaches were extended to included the relocation of input devices, windows, documents and even applications in a smart space environment. *Aris* for example, provides techniques that support the redirection of windows and input between private devices and public screens [7]. Both the window and input redirection can be used either separately or combined with each screen visualized on an iconic map. Although users can share their content and engage in collaborative work, they are faced with traditional user interfaces which are not designed for smart space setup.

iLand proposed to move beyond legacy interfaces and provided an interface, specially designed for smart spaces, which is integrated in the architectural space and furniture of a smart room [16]. The system allowed users to transfer documents or windows between different screens by moving a physical object between them. Users can also engage in collaborative interactions by replicating their display to computer-enhanced tables and chairs. This allows users to interact simultaneously on multiple displays: users can make remote annotations at the wall display from one of the interactive chairs or manipulate an artifact at the table. The iLand system provided a *unified* interface enabling collocated and synchronous group collaboration.

Impromptu was designed specifically to support collocated collaborative interaction in smart spaces. Smart space users can exchange application windows by replicating them, e.g. for problem solving, or by sharing them on public displays, e.g. for discussion or reflection [8]. To improve collaborative smart space experiences, Impromptu integrates special collaboratives tools, such as tele-pointers, screen sharing and instant messaging, into the smart room technology. However, there is currently no support for asynchronous data access or remote and nomadic collaboration.

Other research approaches extended smart room technology to include dynamic user membership and mobile devices. *IRos* is a suite of systems that can be used to create applications for multiple devices with the ability to integrate portable devices in smart space interaction [12]. It supports the redirection of input with *PointRight* [13], replication of content with *Multibrowse* [12], and asynchronous exchange of documents with *DataHeap*. In iRos, information can thus be accessed across multiple displays and by mobile users that are dynamically added or removed as they join or leave the smart space.

Focusing specifically on nomadic computing, *XICE* supports dynamic engagement. It allows users to easily extend their mobile device input and output by *annexing* smart space wall and table displays [1]. Hence, XICE support basic device roaming. In a multi-user setup, XICE allow for several people to annex the same screen, but not to merge their displays and inputs into one shared collaborative surface. *Gaia* builds on the same annexation principle, but treats each user as a physical object that triggers the addition of information into a smart space [11]. Data are directly linked to the user, thereby becoming available whenever they enter a new active space. The system also supports multiple displays by rebinding whole applications to any display or device. User context is used to organize data and make information that is relevant to the current context easily accessible.

Outside smart space research, Activity-Based Computing (ABC) supports complex information and task management, and has been successfully applied to several areas, including desktop computing [5, 18] and pervasive computing in hospitals [3,

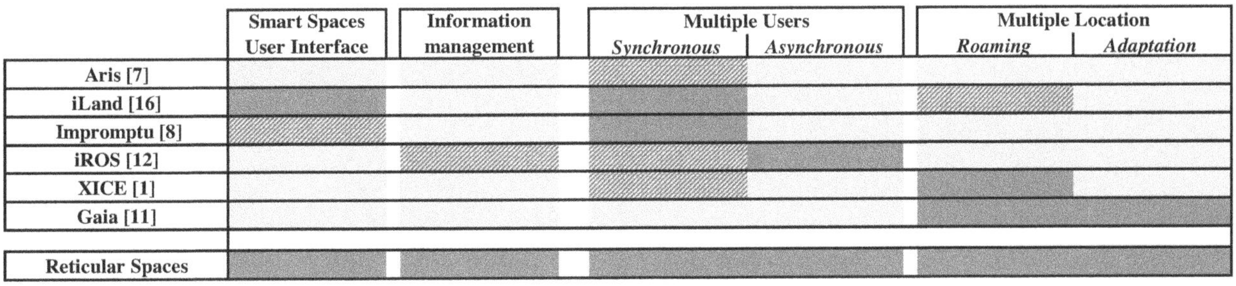

Figure 2. Research systems support for smart spaces challenges (limited support is dashed).

4]. ABC proposes to aggregate relevant resources into activities and provides a set of principles that describe how activities can be used [3]. Recently, Clinical Surfaces [4] used the ABC approach to allow clinicians to manage, access, and move patient data across a distributed multi-display environment covering a whole hospital. Based on the ABC principles of 'activity-centric resource aggregation' and 'activity suspend/ resume', Clinical Surfaces aggregates medical information in working contexts and dynamically presents information and tasks relevant for a user context.

Compared to previous research on smart space technology, *ReticularSpaces* presents an integrated approach to a unified UI design, information and task management, collaboration, and nomadic computing that builds on the activity-based computing approach and principles. Compared to previous work on ABC, *ReticularSpaces* extends the research on distributed multi-display environments for hospitals to a generic approach for general-purpose smart space technology.

RETICULAR SPACES – APPROACH AND CONCEPTS

The goal of *ReticularSpaces* is to provide a novel smart space infrastructure and UI that unifies task and information management with support for mobility and collaboration in a distributed user interface environment. The principles of activity-based computing (ABC) [3, 6] works as the unifying concepts and metaphors. Thus, *ReticularSpaces* extends the use of activity-based computing to a multiple display environment. This section describes the overall approach and concepts of *ReticularSpaces* with respect to providing a uniform information and task management, remote and local collaboration and mobility support. The technical description of the UI software technology and underlying infrastructure of *ReticularSpaces* is presented in the following sections.

Unified Information and Task Management

Unified information management in *ReticularSpaces* is based on the ABC principle of 'Activity-centric Resource Aggregation'. This principle states that all documents, resources, services, etc. that are relevant for a human activity, should be organized into a corresponding 'Computational Activity', or just 'Activity'. Unified task management is based on the ABC principle of 'Activity Resume/Suspend', which states that activities have multiple participants, which each can resume and suspend an activity and thereby work on it.

ReticularSpaces implements these ABC principles into an ontology illustrated in Figure 3. Each *activity* is composed of a

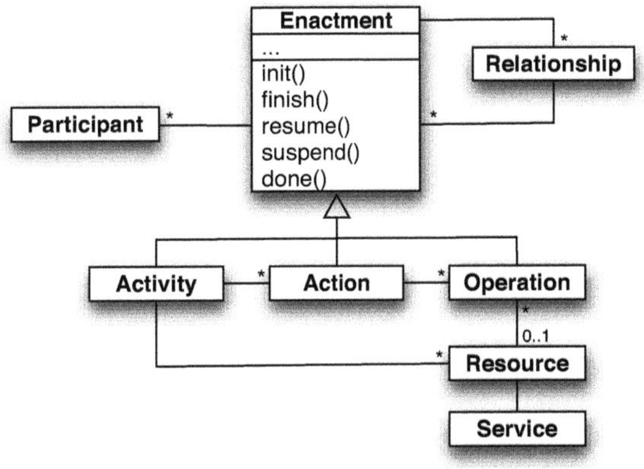

Figure 3. The ABC Ontology used in *ReticularSpaces*.

set of *actions*, each again holding a set of *operations*. Each operation points to a *resource*, such as a document, a picture, html page, etc. Resources can also be external *services*, such as a device, like a printer, which can be accessed through an operation. Each activity has a list of *participants*, and only participants can access (resume/suspend) the activity, and its actions and operations. *Relationships* allows users to organize activities, actions, and operations in different workflow structures. Such structures could be simple association links showing which activities are related, as well as more complex workflow constraints specifying which activities has to be done before another activity can be resumed. Because of the overlapping properties between activities, actions and operations, they are abstracted into an *enactment*.

Shared Activities and Collaboration Tools

Since an activity (and its actions and operations) can have several participants, they are by default shared and collaborative. This is the ABC principle of 'Activity Sharing'.

Asynchronous activity sharing happens when participants take turn in resuming and working on an activity. Since *ReticularSpaces* maintains state information about the work done in activities, one participant can take over working where the previous participant left the work. By using an *activity log*, users can get a log over past events including log entries entered by other participants. Hence the activity log also works as a medium for leaving activity specific messages to each other.

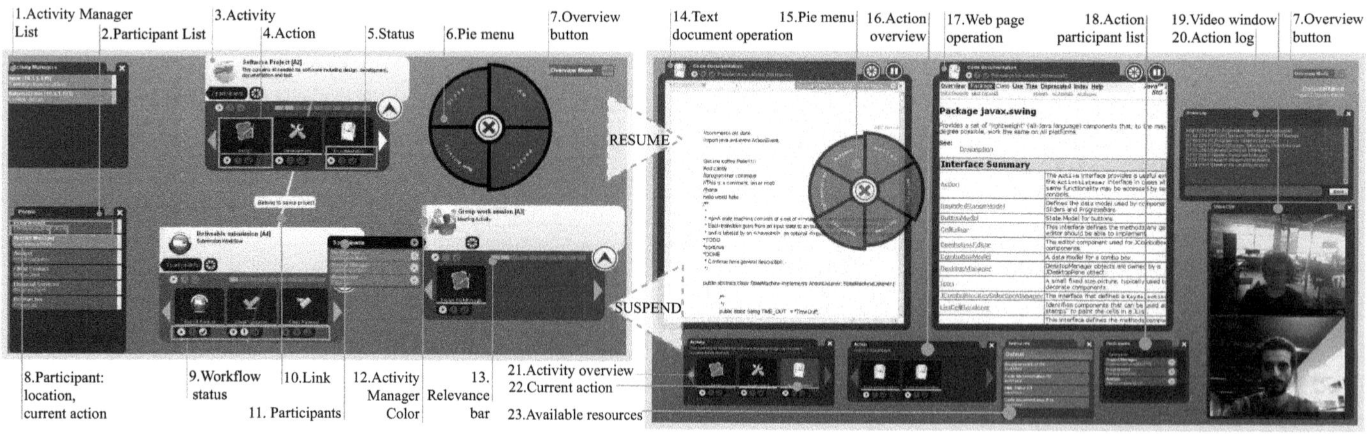

Figure 4. The *ReticUI* user interface. The *Activity View* (on the left) shows a list of activity managers available, a list of users in this smart space room, and the set of activities that are relevant in this context. Each activity (the while box) can be expanded to show its list of actions and participants. Workflow relationships between activities are shown as lines with a text label. The *Action View* (on the right) is displayed when a user resumes an action. This view shows the action's operations and the resource each operation links to, such as a text document or a web page. The action view can show various overview panels as shown at the bottom of the view. From left to right these are overviews of: all actions in the overall activity; operations in this action; available resources; and the participants. On the right side the collaboration windows are shown, including (from the top); the action log and the remote video feeds. Users can switch between the two views by suspending and resuming an action. All user interaction works by multi-touch gestures and pie menus.

If two or more participants resume the same activity simultaneously from multiple displays – either collocated in the smart space or remotely – they engage in *synchronous activity sharing*. Due to the shared state management this entails that the view on the displays are synchronized (as in a desktop sharing setup) and appropriate communication channel like text, voice, and video are established if needed. Since the activity log is updated in real time, it works as an instant messaging system in this case. The activity as such hence work to mediate a collaborative space and since an activity knows it list of participants, automatic session management is achieved.

Mobility and Context-Awareness

ReticularSpaces supports nomadic work and mobility by implementing the ABC principle of 'Activity Roaming'. This principle states that a participant should be able to suspend an activity on a device in one location and then later resume it on a display in another location. The activity is resumed in the same state (and hence looks the same) as when suspended, since the activity maintain state information.

ReticularSpaces has build-in support for location tracking using active badges. Similar to ClinicalSurfaces [4], this information is used in context-aware adaptation of the UI to show the most relevant activities for the set of users in a specific location. Hence, a wall display in a smart space will mainly show the activities that are relevant for the people in the room, which typically are the activities they participate in. The 'relevance' mechanism is rather flexible and can be extended to also include the collocation of e.g. objects, devices, and non-users. The list of participants of an activity will also show their location information, which helps provide an awareness of the whereabouts of participants in an activity.

Location of users is also used to provide context-aware voice and video connectivity in a synchronous activity sharing session. If the participants are in different places, then an audio and video link is automatically established – something that is not needed if they are collocated. If they move to the same location, the communication link is removed.

As we shall described below, the architecture of *ReticularSpaces* is a peer-to-peer architecture where each device can store activity information in a local *activity manager*. In order to share local activity information, *ReticularSpaces* allow displays to mount activity managers as they are discovered. Hence, if a user with a laptop enters a smart space, all devices will discover the activity manager of each other. The user can then, for example, go to the public display and mount his own activity manager, thereby getting access to activities and data on his own laptop. Access to an activity manager can be secure and password protected. When leaving the smart space again, the user's activity manager is automatically unmounted.

RETICUI: AN ACTIVITY-BASED UI FOR SMART SPACES

Designed to unify the user experience in a smart spaces, *ReticularSpaces* provides the *ReticUI* user interface (UI) as shown in Figure 4. *ReticUI* consists of two views; the Activity View and the Action View. Both views are zoomable and panable, and are thus designed to be used on any display size, even very large wall-based displays. Contextual pie menus are used consistently to allow for users to access them across a large wall-based display. The displays do not, however, support rotation, and when used on a tabletop display, the user should be situated in 'front of' the table.

Activity View

The activity view is the default view that is shown on a display. This view initially shows a list of people and activity manager in the same location as the display; the default activity manager is always the local one. Users can access a display and mount an activity manager by clicking its icon and entering a PIN code. The activity view will then display activities, from this activity manager, that are relevant for the current context. The current implementation of the relevance algorithm finds the activities that people in the room participate in, but the architecture is open for implementing more advanced relevance algorithms. The degree of relevancy is show in the green relevance bar. In Figure 4, three activities are shown which are related to a software company, and Figure 5 shows an activity in detail. Since several activity managers can be mounted on a display, the left border of an activity is marked by a color reflecting which activity manger it belongs to. By clicking the black arrow, the activity expands to show its list of actions beneath it, and by clicking the 'participants' label, the list of participants are shown to the left of the activity. By using the small '+' and '−' buttons, a participant can add or remove participants to the activity.

Workflow relationships between activities are shown as lines with a text label. Workflow status for both the overall activity and for each of the actions are revealed by the three small icons beneath each activity or action; the 'play' icon indicate if this activity/action can be resumed; the '!' icon indicates if this activity/action is required (i.e., has to be done), and the 'checkmark' icon indicates whether the activity/action has been done. The description of the activity-based workflow features of *ReticularSpaces* is, however, outside the scope of this paper.

Figure 5. The activity as shown in the activity view. Each activity has an icon, a name, an ID, a description, a set of participants, a list of actions, and a workflow status. Each action has an icon, a name, and workflow status. The color bar beneath each action indicates its status (resumed/suspended).

Action View

When a user clicks an action icon, *ReticUI* shows the action view (Figure 4, right). The primary purpose of this view is to show the action's operations and the resources they link to. Since work is done at the level of operations, the action view is where the user is working with the resources in the action. Resources can be text documents, images, files, or web pages, as shown in Figure 4. A resource can also be an external service, like a printer or a video camera, in which case the operation will show a user interface suited for this service. Operations can be created, copied, and deleted, and can be marked as done, which is then reflected in the overall workflow status. Like activities and actions, operations can be resumed and suspended. Suspended operations in an action cannot be accessed. The action view has a set of auxiliary panels that provide meta information to the user. At the bottom, from the left in Figure 4 is shown: the activity panel showing an overview of the activity that this action is part of; the action panel showing an overview of this action and its operations; a list of available resource in this activity (resources are managed on the level of the activity); and a list of participants involved in this activity, including their current work activity, status, and location. On the right-hand side of the activity view are two collaboration panels: the action log showing both a history of events happened in this action and text entries from users; and the video window showing video feeds from participants currently having this action resumed – in this case two other users also participate. As mentioned above, this video link is context-aware and is only established if the users are not collocated.

As the action view is zoomable and panable, the view consists of a large canvas on which numerous operations are displayed. Zooming and panning is done with standard pinch-to-zoom and drag-to-pan gestures. The overview button is used on single-touch devices to zoom out and show all operations.

By using state synchronization between devices that are part of a synchronous activity sharing session, the action view is kept synchronized across the participating displays. This applies for the placement, size and content of the operation windows. This entails that a user working on a large, high resolution display may move operations into places where participants using smaller devices cannot see them. However, by using the zoomable canvas, users are always able to zoom out, get an overview of all operations and zoom in and focus on an area appropriate for them. Note that there is no 'zoom mode' in *ReticUI*; all functionality, buttons, icons, and pie menus work regardless of zoom level. Since the auxiliary panels work as personal toolboxes for a user, they are neither zoomable or synchronized during an activity sharing session.

ARCHITECTURE

The software architecture of the *ReticularSpaces* system is illustrated in Figure 6. The system consists of two main components; the *ReticUI* user interface component and an underlying infrastructure consisting of a set of Activity Managers. In addition to these two components, the infrastructure is able to connect to external services, like location tracking systems, RFID readers, and other domain-specific services.

The *ReticularSpaces* infrastructure is a peer-to-peer, event-based distributed system. Peer-to-peer means that a copy of the infrastructure – the Activity Manager – is deployed on all devices participating in the system setup. Communication, data sharing, and event propagation takes place directly between the devices participating in the smart space setup. *ReticularSpaces* hence do not use a centralized server, but one device can act as a 'super-peer' and de-facto work as a server, if needed. Event-based means that the infrastructure supports a Model-View-Controller (MVC) architecture [10] based on subscribe-notify type of interaction, rather than the more traditional request-response model. Event-based architectures are used in user-interface technology when updating user interface components based on events from e.g. input devices. As *ReticularSpaces* is a distributed user-interface system, it similarly rely on an extended event-based style of programming now running distributed across a network. Hence, the

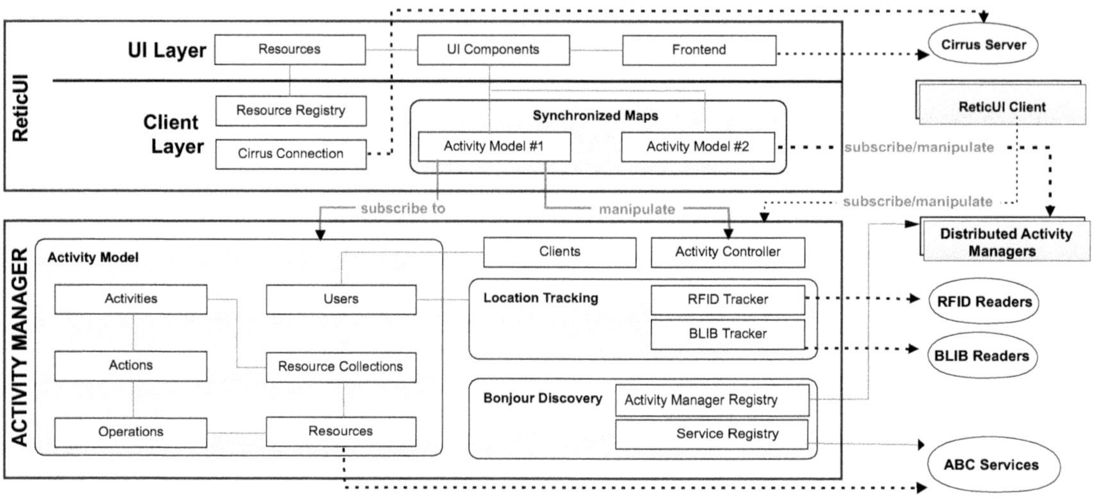

Figure 6. The software architecture of *ReticularSpaces* consisting of the *ReticUI* UI component (shown in Figure 4) and the Activity Manager infrastructure. The *ReticUI* connects to a local or remote Activity Manager, and Activity Managers can connect to each other in a distributed peer-to-peer fashion. Activity Managers and other application-specific services are discovered on the network using mDNS/Bonjour service discovery.

ReticularSpaces architecture essentially implements a distributed Model-View-Controller (dMVC) architecture [9, 14].

The main components of the Activity Manager are the Activity Controller and the Activity Model. The activity model organizes data into the ABC ontology shown in Figure 3. The activity controller holds all data on users, devices, activities, resources, etc. The activity model and the activity manager are based on the Aexo framework, which implements a distributed model-view-controller architecture [9]. A *ReticUI* client can register to one or more activity managers and by using the distributed event-based mechanisms in Aexo, the client maintains a synchronized copy of the activity model from each manager. Updates to the local activity model then again updates the *ReticUI* accordingly, using a local observer pattern. The activity controller provides an interface for external clients, including the *ReticUI*, to control the activity manager and the activity model. It provides mechanisms for managing users, clients, services, and other activity managers.

Each activity manager announces itself on the network using Bonjour (mDNS) and activity managers can hence automatically discover each other. Discovered activity managers are registers in the Activity Manager Registry and listed in the Activity Manager List in the *ReticUI* (shown on the left hand side of Figure 4). From this list the user can then select which activity manager he wants to 'mount' and thereby connect to. These mechanisms of activity manager discovery and mounting is used to set up and maintain the peer-to-peer topology of activity managers in a smart space.

Similarly, external services can be discovered and registered in an activity manager. For example, location tracking of users is done by having location tracking services discovered and registered as a service to an activity manager. These services then update the data model with location information about users and devices.

A domain-specific service can be associated with a resource. When an action is resumed, automatic service discovery of domain-specific services linked to the resources of the action's operations are initiated. When the operation is resumed, the service is asked to also resume working. A service can be a virtual service such as a web service, or a physical device such as a scanner or a printer. The *ReticUI* client is just handed an URI pointing to the service, and uses this URI to fetch and show any data coming from that service. This flexible mechanism separates domain-specific data from the *ReticularSpaces* infrastructure itself and routes data to/from the *ReticUI* directly to/from independent services. This mechanism account for the dynamic addition, removal and network relocation of devices.

The *ReticUI* client holds a synchronized replication of the activity data model for each of the activity managers to which it has registered. On top of this, the *ReticUI* implements the different UI components shown in Figures 4. *ReticUI* is designed to work across all types of devices and displays in a smart space. As such, the goal of *ReticUI* is to provide a homogeneous user experience in manipulating and displaying data elements like activities, actions, operations, resources, and services.

For each type of domain-specific resource that *ReticularSpaces* handles, *ReticUI* provides a corresponding resource view component that is able to render the resource inside the operation windows in the action view. For example, in order to show HTML resources, an HTML resource render (i.e., a web browser) is needed. Domain-specific resource components are loaded on runtime and registered in the Resource Registry of *ReticUI*. When an action, its operations and associated resources are resumed, the corresponding UI resource components are looked up in the resource registry. This is based on the type of a resource. And since a resource just points to a service, the UI resource component knows how to connect to a service, and render and manipulate data from this service. For example, the service shown in Figure 4 shows a action view with a text resource, which is pointing to a shared text document residing on a server. Note that sharing of resources is not part of the architecture, and resources will normally reside on servers external to *ReticularSpaces* .

As discussed above, support for collaboration is a core part of *ReticularSpaces*. Synchronized action view and real-time update of the activity log is supported by a distributed state synchronization mechanism. This is implemented via the distributed MVC architecture of Aexo, which maintains synchronization of the distributed activity models. This implies that any update to an activity model on one client will be synchronized on all clients connected to the same activity manager, and updates to an activity model will in turn cause an update of the user interface. Hence, support for synchronized views while collaborating is a built-in feature of the distributed MVC architecture. Video conferencing is based on an external video server, acting like any other external service in the system; when resuming an action with a 'video resource' the video UI component connects to the video server and starts streaming video content to and from it.

The *ReticularSpaces* architecture is implemented using different technologies. The Activity Manager is implemented in Java on top of the Aexo distributed event system, using a RESTful[1] protocol for event distribution and XML for serializing the activity model. The *ReticUI* is implemented in Adobe Flex AIR[2], and the video server is using the Adobe RTMFP Cirrus server[3]. Location tracking is done by the BLIP Bluetooth location tracking system[4], and the RFID tagging is done using the WaveTrend activity RFID technology[5]. Resources are handled using uniform resource identifies (URI) and MIME types.

FEASIBILITY STUDY

In order to evaluate the *feasibility* of the *ReticularSpaces* approach and verify the *stability* of the system before moving into larger scale field experiments, the system was deployed as a smart space environment in a research lab as shown in Figure 1. The goal of this study was to expose users to the design of this new smart space technology and assess its perceived usefulness. To focus on the features specific to our complex system, we conducted a feasibility study rather than comparing it with previously implemented systems. Essentially, we were interested in evaluating the following question: "Does *ReticularSpaces* effectively support interaction with multiple displays and devices, involving multiple users distributed across multiple locations?"

Participants and Setup

12 participants (mean age 27) were recruited to participate in the experiment. The setup consisted of two large interactive wall displays, a multitouch tabletop display, two tablet computers, and a notebook. The smart space itself containing the large wall displays and the tabletop display functioned as a meeting room, while the mobile devices (i.e., the laptop and tablets) moved in and out of the smart space or were used in the hallway, another meeting room, and a remote office.

Method

As both the system as well as the concept of a smart space environment were completely new to most users, we used a scenario-based approach to guide participants in interacting with *ReticularSpaces*. After a short 15 min. introduction to the basic functionality and design rationale of the system, participants completed 5 scenarios in groups of 2 using the think-aloud method. Scenarios were randomized per group of 4 participants using latin square. The first scenario was excluded from randomization, as it included basic notions required to complete other scenarios. Completing all scenarios took approximatively one hour for each group. During the completion, participants were observed by one researcher while being guided through the scenario by another researcher. After each scenario, participants filled in a 5-point Likert scale questionnaire, and a semi-structured interview was conducted with them after completing all scenarios. During the interview, participants elaborated on their questionnaire results and answered open questions related to the user experience.

Scenarios

Five scenarios were designed to represent real situations that occur in a typical software development company. The first two scenarios were focused on information management: (1) create a presentation at office before presenting it at the conference room and sharing it with the team; and (2) collaborate on completing a project delivery by taking turns in performing actions, such as "submit deliverable' and "validate submission'. In the remaining three scenarios, participants were introduced to different collaborative setups: (3) working asynchronously on the code of a software project while communicating code changes; (4) starting a group meeting remotely on a mobile device before arriving into the conference room thereby changing from remote to local settings; and (5) moving to a conference room and move work from a tablet computer to the wall display, while discussing shared artifacts with a remote colleague. Scenario 4 is shown in Figure 7 as an example.

Focus of the experiment

Questionnaires and interviews focused on the following four areas:

Activity-Based computing. The usefulness of the basic concepts of activity-based computing such as a the main components of an activity (activity, action and operation), the suspending and resuming of activities, the management (activity creation, templates and relations), and the activity workflow features.

Distributed Interaction. The usefulness of activity roaming across different locations, different devices, and access to distributed resources such as documents.

Asynchronous Collaboration. The usefulness of the notion of multiple participants, the action log, and the sharing of activities.

[1] http://www.ics.uci.edu/~fielding/pubs/dissertation/rest_arch_style.htm
[2] http://www.adobe.com/products/air/
[3] http://labs.adobe.com/technologies/cirrus/
[4] http://www.blipsystems.com/
[5] http://www.wavetrend.net/

Scenario 4 – *Late for a meeting, the project manager (PM) resumes the meeting activity on his tablet PC, while walking down the hallway. The activity view of* ReticUI *shows the shared documents and automatically establishes a video link with his colleagues in the meeting room, allowing him to announce that he is on his way. Arriving in the meeting room, the video connection is automatically stopped. Meanwhile, a remote colleague (RC) sitting in his office notices that his colleagues are currently working on their common project in the meeting room. She decides to join them. When she resumes the action, a video link is established connecting her with the meeting room, and her colleagues fill her in on their discussion. RC starts adding text to one of the shared documents, and her colleagues in the meeting room see the text appear in their screens. Then, while discussing two version of a diagram, PM place them along each other from his tablet, which update documents layout on all displays. Afterward each team member start to work on different parts of a document thereby being highly focused on their individual tasks. To ask a question without interrupting others, RC uses the action log and type it in a chat message. PM notices the question on the wall display and answers it with a chat message from his tablet. After the meeting, back to his office, PM resumes the meeting activity and all resources are restored as suspended in the smart room.*

Figure 7. Scenario 4 focusing on remote group meeting.

Synchronous Collaboration. The usefulness of real-time collaborative instant messaging, video conferencing and synchronous activity sharing, as well as the usefulness of the list of participants while collaborating.

Results

Figure 8 provides an overview of the quantitative results of the questionnaire. The results from the interviews are discussed in the 'Discussion' section.

Activity-Based Information Management

In general, the activity-based concepts were perceived as very useful ($Q3$: μ= 4,2; $\tilde{x}$= 4; σ= 0.72). Restrictions of workflows on action level (with the action view) was seen as a good approach to deal with distributed work that requires some order ($Q4$: μ= 4,25; $\tilde{x}$= 4; σ= 0.63). Participants reported that sharing documents easiness was average ($Q1$: μ= 3,6; $\tilde{x}$= 4; σ= 1,165). Work management was also rated with an average score ($Q2$: μ= 3,5; $\tilde{x}$= 3; σ= 0.79). We anticipated that this average score was caused by a learning curve and this was confirmed during the interviews.

Distributed Interaction

The fact that participants were able to access activities and their resources on several devices simultaneously was considered very valuable ($Q7$: μ= 4,5; $\tilde{x}$= 4.5; σ= 0.52). The location roaming ($Q5$: μ= 4,6; $\tilde{x}$= 5; σ= 0.49) and device roaming ($Q6$: μ= 4,4; $\tilde{x}$= 5; σ= 0.79) were also found highly useful.

Asynchronous Collaboration

In general, participants found the action log very valuable both for leaving messages related to the action log ($Q8$: μ= 4; $\tilde{x}$= 4; σ= 0.58) as well for automatic logging ($Q9$: μ= 4,1; $\tilde{x}$= 4; σ= 0.2).

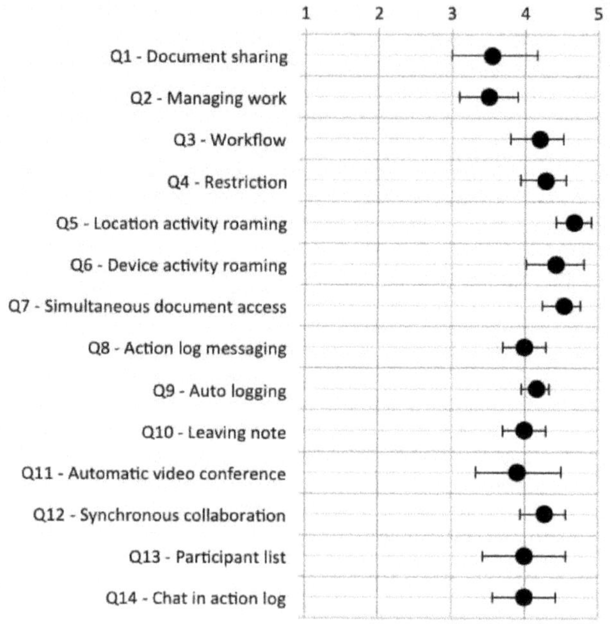

Figure 8. The results of the questionnaire. Scores are on a 5-point Likert scale from 1 (not useful) to 5 (very useful).

Synchronous Collaboration

Overall, participants found the system very useful for synchronous collaboration ($Q12$: μ= 4,3; $\tilde{x}$= 4; σ= 0.62). The display of the list of participants was also considered useful ($Q13$: μ= 4; $\tilde{x}$= 4; σ= 1,13) as it could be a starting point for collaboration. The use of the action log as an additional real-time communication channel was also appreciated as useful ($Q14$: μ= 4; $\tilde{x}$= 4; σ= 0.85). Finally, most participants agreed that automatic video conferencing is a good way to support collaboration with a remote person ($Q11$: μ= 3,9; $\tilde{x}$= 4; σ= 1,13).

DISCUSSION

The purpose of *ReticularSpaces* is to unite information management, co-located and remote collaboration and mobility into a new activity-based smart space environment. In this section, we discuss these features based on the results of the study questionnaires and interviews.

Activity-based Information and Task Management

One of the key challenge that we addressed in *ReticularSpaces* is unifying task and information management in smart spaces into a new activity-based UI metaphor, *ReticUI* . By introducing a homogeneous interface that allows for a seamless transition between synchronous and asynchronous work, *ReticularSpaces* can support dynamic and multi-device smart space environments. Information can easily be accessed, moved and shared between smart space users but also between devices. In the interviews, several participant expressed their appreciation for this unified interface and argued that the integration between individual and collaborative work, as well as between collocated and remote participants felt "natural".

During interviews, the activity-based organization of work in our system was considered especially valuable for managing large amount of information. One participant referred to this type of interface as a "project-based interaction with information and users". However, several users were confused that they did not need to save documents, as everything is automatically synchronized, and explained that this may be due to different habits. Clearly the new paradigm implies a learning curve, but we observed that participants became familiar with the approach before the end of evaluation sessions. In the interviews, one participant explained that he found this organizational approach of *ReticularSpaces* much more natural then traditional computing systems.

Our activity-based approach also introduces workflow relationships and constraints that helps build and manage complex flows of tasks. The study showed that this approach can greatly aid different roles in complex collaborative set-ups but that the current implementation was too limited. Some participants expressed concerns regarding the scalability of this feature if it were to be used in large and complex organizations. A remaining issue for future work in the UI design is thus the interactive visualization and construction of such activity-based workflows. *ReticUI* represents workflow steps simply as successive action visualized with a status bar. Participants pointed out that even though workflow status is shown in the UI, it is hard to grasp the overall logic and organization of a workflow, specially in large or complex projects. But in general the results of the study provide evidence that activity-based computing is a valuable approach for a unifying design concept for smart space technology.

Activity-mediated Collaboration

Another core goal of *ReticularSpaces* is to introduce the smart space environment as a technology for collaborative work among both co-located and remote users. Beside support for an interface and information management model that supports multi-device co-located and remote collaboration, *ReticularSpaces* also provides a set of tools to directly support collaboration and awareness.

For example, the list of users provides an overview of all users, and shows what activity (and action) they are currently engaged in as well as their current location. Several of the study participants argued that this is an excellent mechanism for starting a new collaboration session, as location can be an important factor for collaboration. For example, when an employee working from home sees that several other colleagues are having a discussion in the meeting room, this might trigger him to quit his ongoing activity and remotely join the discussion. Additionally, the list of an activity's participants is very helpful to understand who is currently engaged in the activity.

The use of the action log for posting notes in asynchronous communication was also found useful. In the interviews, participants suggested several applications for this asynchronous communication channel, such as task delegation, communicating changes in the shared action, or requesting updates to a document. For synchronous communication, the seamless transformation from an individual activity to real-time synchronous activity sharing was perceived as very useful. Furthermore, the use of automatic video conferencing as an additional communication channel for remote collaboration was reported to be a very strong feature, because it eliminates the need to start separate communication applications and establish the relevant collaboration sessions with all participating users. As one user put it:

> — *"The integrated collaboration is really useful. Even in cases when you are sick at home, you can still fully participate in meetings without the need for you and your colleagues to setup many tools."*

ReticularSpaces uses location information to maintain an audio-video communication channel only when users are engaged in a remote collaborative setting. The link is thus only established when remote participant joins the activity and is removed when she leaves. During the interviews, some participants argued that automatic video is a good approach because video adds a layer of trust to the collaboration. However, some participants also mentioned that there might be privacy issues when using an automatic video connection.

The study also showed that instant messaging in the action log can work as a real-time communication back channel used for aside or less intrusive communication that supplements the video communication. By attaching communication channels to shared structure that also holds users' documents and tasks, these features of *ReticularSpaces* hence introduce an efficient approach for collocated and remote collaboration.

Mobility and Context Awareness

One of the critical differences between *ReticularSpaces* and most of previous work is the integration of *mobility* into the smart room environment. A user can simply walk in and out of a smart room while carrying his work with him. In *ReticularSpaces*, mobility is implemented through activity roaming and activity suspend/resume. This allows a user to suspend, move, and resume an activity between locations and/or devices, or even allow for simultaneously work on several devices. This feature was really appreciated by the participants of the user study. Most of our participants mentioned these features as the best of the system. During the interviews, one participant suggested that *ReticularSpaces* might be able to solve a common challenge in meeting rooms:

> — *"You can simply prepare your work at your office, walk into the conference room, wirelessly mount your device to the room, present your work and afterwards share the presentation with the room display with people interested in having it. This kind of interaction and information sharing is currently a big problem at our company."*

By using location tracking, only activities that are relevant to the active participants are presented on the displays in the smart room. This mechanism allows for a scalable activity visualisation as it implicitly deals with cluttering but also provides integrated and fluid support for mobile users as they walk in and out of smart rooms.

CONCLUSION

ReticularSpaces is a multi-display smart space system that uses the principles of activity-based computing to offer: a novel unified UI named *ReticUI* for smart space technology; support for management of complex tasks; an extension of smart space interaction to mobile users; and collocated and remote activity-mediated collaboration.

In this paper, we presented the motivation, design, and architecture of *ReticularSpaces*, and reported from a preliminary feasibility study. The study showed that participants found the system and approach very useful, while at the same time uncovered a set of challenges to be addressed in future research on smart space technology. Future work will refine *ReticularSpaces* design and prepare it for a large scale field study.

REFERENCES

1. R. Arthur and D. R. Olsen, Jr. Xice windowing toolkit: Seamless display annexation. *ACM Transactions on Computer-Human Interaction*, 18:14:1–14:46, August 2011.
2. T. Bader, A. Heck, and J. Beyerer. Lift-and-drop: crossing boundaries in a multi-display environment by airlift. In *Proc. of AVI 2010*, pages 139–146, New York, NY, USA, 2010. ACM.
3. J. E. Bardram. Activity-based computing for medical work in hospitals. *ACM Transactions on Computer-Human Interaction*, 16(2):1–36, 2009.
4. J. E. Bardram, J. Bunde-Pedersen, A. Doryab, and S. Sørensen. Clinical surfaces — activity-based computing for distributed multi-display environments in hospitals. In *Proc. of INTERACT 2009*, pages 704–717, Berlin, Heidelberg, 2009. Springer-Verlag.
5. J. E. Bardram, J. Bunde-pedersen, and M. Soegaard. Support for activity-based computing in a personal computing operating system. In *Proc. of SIGCHI*, pages 211–220. Press, 2006.
6. J. E. Bardram, J. Bunde-Pedersen, and M. Soegaard. Support for activity-based computing in a personal computing operating system. In *Proc. of CHI 2006*, pages 211–220, New York, NY, USA, 2006. ACM Press.
7. J. T. Biehl and B. P. Bailey. Aris: an interface for application relocation in an interactive space. In *Proc. of GI 2004*, pages 107–116, Waterloo, Ontario, Canada, 2004. Canadian Human-Computer Communications Society.
8. J. T. Biehl, W. T. Baker, B. P. Bailey, D. S. Tan, K. M. Inkpen, and M. Czerwinski. Impromptu: a new interaction framework for supporting collaboration in multiple display environments and its field evaluation for co-located software development. In *Proc. of CHI 2008*, pages 939–948, New York, NY, USA, 2008. ACM.
9. J. Bunde-Pedersen. *Distributed Interaction for Activity-Based Computing*. PhD thesis, Computer Science Department, University of Aarhus, Denmark, 2009.
10. E. Gamma, R. Helm, R. Johnson, and J. Vlissides. *Design patterns: elements of reusable object-oriented software*. Addison-Wesley Longman Publishing Co., Inc., Boston, MA, USA, 1995.
11. C. K. Hess, M. Román, and R. H. Campbell. Building applications for ubiquitous computing environments. In *Proc. of Pervasive 2002*, pages 16–29, London, UK, 2002. Springer-Verlag.
12. B. Johanson, A. Fox, and T. Winograd. The interactive workspaces project: Experiences with ubiquitous computing rooms. *IEEE Pervasive Computing*, 1:67–74, April 2002.
13. B. Johanson, G. Hutchins, T. Winograd, and M. Stone. Pointright: experience with flexible input redirection in interactive workspaces. In *Proc. of UIST 2002*, pages 227–234, New York, NY, USA, 2002. ACM.
14. N. Marquardt and S. Greenberg. Distributed physical interfaces with shared phidgets. In *Proceedings of the 1st international conference on Tangible and embedded interaction*, TEI '07, pages 13–20, New York, NY, USA, 2007. ACM.
15. J. Rekimoto. Pick-and-drop: a direct manipulation technique for multiple computer environments. In *Proc. of UIST 1997*, pages 31–39, New York, NY, USA, 1997. ACM.
16. N. A. Streitz, J. Geißler, T. Holmer, S. Konomi, C. Müller-Tomfelde, W. Reischl, P. Rexroth, P. Seitz, and R. Steinmetz. i-land: an interactive landscape for creativity and innovation. In *Proceed. of CHI 1999*, pages 120–127, New York, NY, USA, 1999. ACM.
17. L. Terrenghi, R. May, P. Baudisch, W. MacKay, F. Paternò, J. Thomas, and M. Billinghurst. Information visualization and interaction techniques for collaboration across multiple displays. In *Extended Proc. of CHI 2006*, CHI '06, pages 1643–1646, New York, NY, USA, 2006. ACM.
18. S. Voida, E. D. Mynatt, and W. K. Edwards. Re-framing the desktop interface around the activities of knowledge work. In *Proceedings of the 21st annual ACM symposium on User interface software and technology*, UIST '08, pages 211–220, New York, NY, USA, 2008. ACM.

Regional Undo/Redo Techniques for Large Interactive Surfaces

Thomas Seifried[1], Christian Rendl[1], Michael Haller[1], Stacey D. Scott[2]

[1]Media Interaction Lab
University of Applied Sciences Upper Austria
Hagenberg, Austria
mi-lab@fh-hagenberg.at

[2]Collaborative Systems Lab
University of Waterloo
Waterloo, Canada
s9scott@uwaterloo.ca

ABSTRACT

When multiple users are simultaneously sharing a workspace, it is not always clear what should happen when a user invokes an undo action. In this paper we explore different user interfaces for undo/redo for co-located collaborative workspaces, such as large interactive whiteboards. A preliminary study revealed that users expect neither a global nor personal undo, but rather a regional undo. We propose and evaluate three automatic regional undo/redo techniques (clustering, workspace, field of view) designed for a large interactive whiteboard. The results of the evaluation showed that an undo technique based on users' field of view was most preferred, while the content-based clustering technique produced most errors. We conclude with potential improvements to the developed techniques, and propose a set of design recommendations for implementing regional undo/redo on large interactive surfaces.

Author Keywords

Undo; co-located collaboration; interactive surfaces; interactive whiteboard; large displays; multi-user input;

ACM Classification Keywords

H.5.2 [Information Interfaces & Presentation]: User Interfaces - Graphical user interfaces; H.5.3 [Information Interfaces & Presentation]: Group and Organization Interfaces - Computer Supported Collaborative Work;

General Terms

Design, Human Factors.

INTRODUCTION

Undo/redo is a very common application operation familiar to most users. It provides a simple method to correct errors, to recover a former document state and it is also a safe way to learn software features in a trial-and-error approach [7]. Therefore, undo/redo is seen as an essential functionality [29], which virtually every desktop application provides. On such single-user systems undo is quite simple to implement and it is quite clear what users expect when they select the undo functionality. In contrast, the undo action on a multi-user interface is more complex – not only from a technical [20], but also from a user interaction perspective (e.g., awareness problems, feedback).

When multiple users are working on a document at the same time, it is not always clear what happens if one user invokes an undo action. Historically, this problem has been mainly addressed in the field of *distributed* collaborative environments. Due to the fact that interactive surfaces are becoming larger and larger, the same problem is occurring in *co-located* collaborative setups. Moreover due to advances of input technology, many of these large interactive surfaces also provide a *multi-user* experience, which again makes it more complex to address the undo/redo problem.

Figure 1: Collaborative *(left)* and individual *(right)* work on a large interactive display.

Figure 1 depicts a scenario on a large interactive wall-display, where multiple users can either work close together *(left)* and share the same region, or work individually *(right)*. In both cases, the undo/redo action should make sense to each person. A *global undo* [27] introduces significant issues for solving the undo/redo problem on a large screen, because the person on the right side would not be aware of what is happening if the pair on the left side triggered an undo action. A *personal undo*[1] [1], on the other hand, may also make undo highly cumbersome. If, for example, the pair on the left shares the same sketch on the board, they may consider it as their collective creation and may perform an undo action not just for their own personal strokes (Figure 2), but for the entire sketch. In this case, the system should allow them to also undo strokes that have been produced by their collaborator.

[1] *Personal* undo is a synonym to *local* or *user* undo.

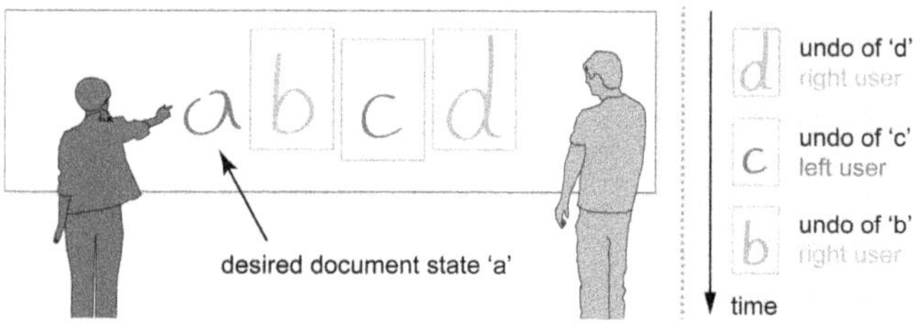

Figure 2: A personal undo action requires a close collaboration of all users to get back to the desired status.

In this paper, we address these challenges. To understand user expectations of undo/redo actions performed on a large interactive display, we conducted a background study. Based on the results of this study, we present the design and implementation of several *regional undo techniques* that provide different solutions to meet the users' expectations. Finally, we discuss the results of the user evaluation of the presented techniques.

RELATED WORK

Undo/Redo has been a focus of research for many years and has primarily been studied for single-user [27] and distributed multi-user [1] systems. However, a classification scheme has yet to be established. To reduce confusion about the terms in this paper we propose a new classification scheme, and structured the discussion of the related work using this scheme. Undo/redo concepts can be described using three main categories: undo/redo *model*, *method* and *interface*.

The *undo model* refers to algorithms and data structures behind undo/redo actions and is most relevant for the technical implementation. In general, undo models can be split into two groups: models that only allow actions to be undone sequentially, namely *linear* undo models, and undo models which can undo arbitrary actions from the past, namely *non-linear* undo models. *Non-linear* undo models can be further divided into models for single-user [2, 5, 28, 29, 30] and multi-user applications [3, 20, 21, 22, 25, 24, 26]. While the data structure used to store "undoable" actions is different for many undo models, most models facilitate a so-called *history list,* which holds a linear, chronologically sorted list of all undoable actions. In order to support synchronous collaborative work a non-linear multi-user undo model is necessary as described by Sun [25, 24]. However, the undo model is not the focus of this work and more detailed information about algorithms and data structures can be found in the referenced work. In our software prototype, we implemented a *non-linear (selective)* undo model based on Sun's *AnyUndo* [25].

The second category constitutes the *undo method*, which defines the general behavior of undo in an application, e.g. *global* [1, 27], *personal* [1], *selective* [3, 20] or *regional undo* [20]. Generally speaking, the undo method defines the way actions are selected for undo. For example in personal undo, users only undo actions that have been invoked by themselves, or in regional undo, users only undo actions in a certain area on the screen. The offering of *personal*, *selective* or *regional undo* in an application requires *a non-linear* undo model that can selectively undo actions from history.

Finally, the *undo/redo interface* describes the concrete user interface for an undo method. This includes both interaction as well as visualization. Research in this area mainly focused on history visualizations as proposed in [8, 13, 14]. Nevertheless the invocation of undo and feedback can also pose an issue, especially in a co-located multi-user environment. Furthermore, Choudhary and Dewan identified general requirements for multi-user undo [7] which should be considered in the design of an undo interface. In this paper we focus on different *undo interfaces* within the *regional undo* method.

Regional undo has thus far received little attention. Prakash and Knister [20] introduced *regional undo/redo* as a possible side-effect of their *selective* undo approach for a distributed text editor. They pointed out that designing a user interface for *regional undo* might be much more complicated than for *global* or *personal undo*, because the location of text regions may change over time. Li et al. [15] approached this problem by using arbitrary regions in text documents to choose actions for *selective undo*. Moreover, a technique called "region transformation" modifies regions according to later executed actions. Nevertheless, in this paper we focus on sketched content on large interactive surfaces which is quite different to word processing in text editors. Meng et al. [17] and Nakamura et al. [19] presented methods to filter actions in a textual history visualization based on specific regions in a document. In both papers, additional user interface dialogs were introduced which considerably limit the usability for most undo use-cases. In contrast, we aim to simplify the user interaction by embedding *regional undo* directly into the document without additional dialogs.

As Abowd et al. [1] have claimed, undo is highly related to user expectations. There has been some previous work that has examined user expectations related to undo functionality, but these have focused on single-user [6] or distributed [10] settings. Yet, no one has investigated user expectations in a co-located, collaborative work setting, which we believe may introduce key differences in user expectations of undo functionality. Therefore, we conducted a background study to capture user expectations in a co-located whiteboard setting.

UNDERSTANDING USERS' EXPECTATIONS

To gain a better understanding of how users perceive undo/redo actions, we conducted a background study. The primary goal of this study was to find out which of the undo/redo models (global-, personal- or regional undo) matches user expectations. 23 unpaid volunteers (17 males, 6 females) were recruited from the local university. The participants' ages ranged from 20 to 32 years (M=24.3, SD=3.4). All participants were daily users of computers, with an average daily usage of 8.5 hours (SD=2.5). Only

13% of them had worked with an interactive whiteboard before; none had used it for synchronous co-located collaboration.

Apparatus

The study was conducted on a large (4.5m×1.2m) interactive whiteboard (IWB), operated by three Hitachi CP-A100 projectors with a total resolution of 3072×768. The system was capable of handling simultaneous multi-user input by using Anoto digital pens (ADP-301) (Figure 3) [9].

Figure 3: The first study was conducted to determine expectations of undo in co-located collaborative work.

A very simple (freehand) drawing application was used on the IWB, whereby all graphical user interface elements were hidden to reduce clutter.

Procedure

Each participant was accompanied by two study confederates [16] to provide a multi-user experience with three people per group. The confederates were not allowed to express any opinions and were also not interviewed to minimize influence on the participants' answers. The same people acted as confederates for each trial.

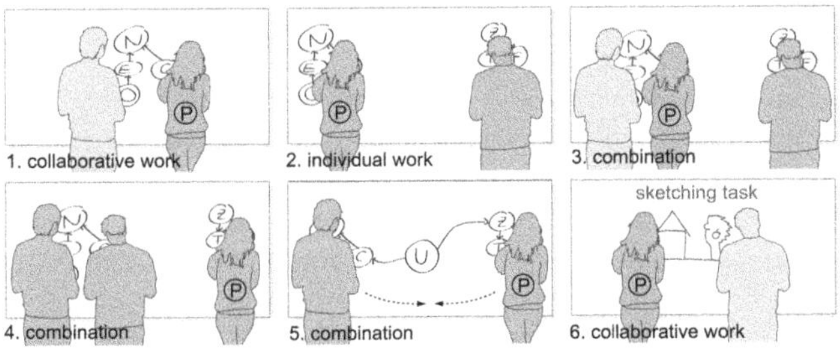

Figure 4: Six scenarios were conducted in the background-study. The participant is highlighted with "P".

At the beginning, each participant was asked to complete a pre-test questionnaire soliciting demographic data. Prior to data collection the goal and procedure of the experiment was introduced to the participants. Each participant had to perform six tasks; every task was designed to imitate a different scenario of co-located work on the IWB: individual work, collaborative work, and combinations of both (Figure 4).

After each task, participants were asked to explain verbally what they would expect to change on the IWB, if they invoke a first and a second undo action. Additionally, each participant concluded a task by completing a short post-trial questionnaire. For each task the whole screen was cleared. Five tasks were to draw a simple directed graph (Figure 3) and one task to draw a sketch. Each participant and confederate was provided with instructions printed on a sheet of paper, containing the steps to construct the graph or sketch (e.g., *node "E" depends on node "N"*).

For individual working scenarios, the participants' instructions contained all necessary information to finish the graph, but for collaborative ones they contained only half of the information. Due undo granularity was not subject of this study and to keep the results comparable, the participant were told that one step on the instruction sheet will be undone by a single undo action. According to the recorded verbal answers the experimenter recreated a resulting graph, representing the expected result of each undo step, which was used for analysis.

Design

The study was a within-subjects design and the order of the tasks was counterbalanced. The resulting (partly undone) graphs were matched with the anticipated results of *global* undo, *personal* undo and *regional* undo. To highlight differences between the undo methods, the tasks were designed so that the anticipated result of each method was different if possible. The results of the sketching task were not included into the accumulated results because the same collaborative setting (group work) was also represented in a graph drawing task and the results were the same.

Results

The study indicates that regional undo meets the expectations of the users in most cases (cf. Figure 5). In 86% of all cases it produced the results the participants were expecting. Personal undo (47%) and global undo (22%) would have been much less expected. In 5% of all cases the expectation could not be applied to any known undo method.

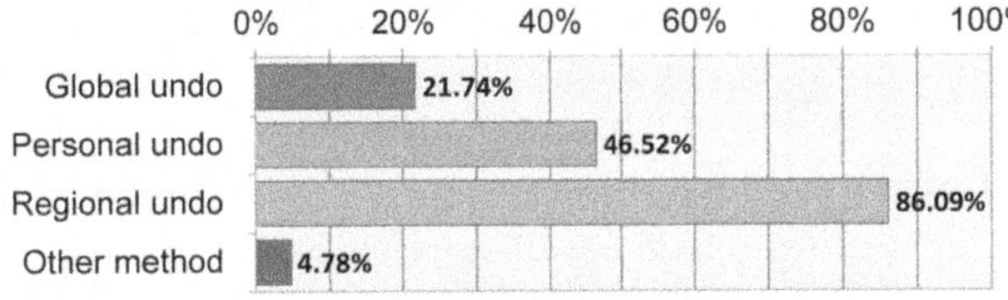

Figure 5: Regional undo meets the expectations most.

The observation of the participants also showed that the expected behavior of undo depends on the type of work (Figure 6). When working on a common task, users expect undo to affect the collective work of the group. When working on an individual task, users expect undo to be applied to their own work. These results also apply even if others are working on the same interactive space. No participant expected that an undo action would have any effect on other graphs except their own graphs as long as they do not change the focus of their current work. Also, awareness of the other people's actions in the interactive surface seems to be an important factor. Users reported that they were not aware of the other people's actions when they were working on another task, even when they were quite close to each other like in Figure 3. Therefore, it was impossible for them to anticipate the effects of their undo actions on other people's work. Furthermore, most participants reported that such behavior would be socially inacceptable.

Figure 6: Users expect that undo only affects their current workspace, which might either be a collaborative one or not.

The controlled nature of the study and the strong focus on collaborative work might have exaggerated the results. So, one might argue that personal undo would meet the expectations well enough in a real world scenario. While this might be true for correcting errors in most cases, for other uses of undo (trial-and-error, restore document state) it causes problems (as described in Figure 2). Moreover in some cases personal undo does not work at all. If users leave the collaborative session access to their undo-steps will be lost. Also technical limitations of the current system can trigger this problem, for example if the system loses track of the user or if users switch input devices which are used to identify users.

REGIONAL UNDO/REDO

The results of the background study suggest that most users expect *regional undo* once they are working on large interactive surfaces. This means, the spatial "reach" of undo-redo actions should be limited to a certain area of the surface. This may be due to the user's mental separation of the whole display into separate workspaces, but also due to the lack of awareness of what other users are doing elsewhere on the large surface.

But regional undo/redo can be implemented in several different ways. In general, a regional undo/redo technique consists of the following three steps: First, the definition of a region, second, the selection of a region, and finally the undo/redo action itself within that region. Although each of those steps needs to be considered, the way a region is defined is a strong distinction for regional undo techniques.

Defining Regions

In the context of regional undo, we use the term "region" as a two-dimensional area with distinct boundaries of arbitrary shape, which is ultimately limited by the boundaries of the display. Therefore, a region can be defined in many ways. Figure 7 depicts a conceptual framework of how we can define regions for the undo/redo actions. The simplest approach is to use already visible boundaries. Those predefined regions could be system-related, e.g., boundaries of the screen, or defined by the application, e.g., by showing pages or other elements that visually separate the screen. If there are no pre-defined regions, a user could create them on demand by explicitly defining regions.

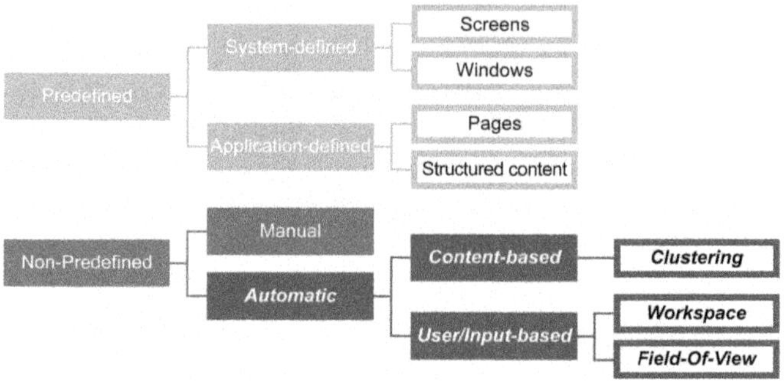

Figure 7: A conceptual framework for defining regions.

In the following sections, we will briefly describe different regional undo/redo techniques based on the described framework, but we will focus on *automatic techniques* due to their higher complexity.

Pre-defined Regional Undo/Redo

In many cases, the display or the application already provides a physical or virtual region. For example in a multi-projector setup, each projection screen may be visually separated from each other (if not edge-blended). Furthermore, the application itself can provide pre-defined virtual regions. Editors, for example, often mimic the real world by providing pages. Such physical and virtual boundaries are already good candidates for an undo/redo region as they are easy to understand. We also have a similar experience if we work with multiple applications on the desktop PC, where every application has its own undo/redo history.

Manual Regional Undo/Redo

A very simple way of defining an undo/redo region is to define it manually as described by Li et al. [15]. In this case, users can create any desired size of a region on which they would like apply an undo/redo action. An explicit visual feedback of the undo/redo region is not necessary since it is defined by the users themselves. This technique can be easily implemented in many applications. If the application features some kind of selection (e.g., a lasso or marquee tool), manual regional undo can utilize those features and can be applied to the selected region.

The disadvantage of this technique is that it requires a two-step approach, namely *selecting the region* and *triggering the undo/redo action*. This might be okay if a user wants to restore a certain document state on a certain area, but it will be very cumbersome and time-consuming for small corrections. An alternative implementation of a manual regional undo would be a visual overlay or magic lens that provides quicker access. However, this would introduce additional visual clutter.

AUTOMATIC UNDO/REDO TECHNIQUES

For applications with no explicit visual regions (e.g., a large sketching surface), regional undo techniques are more complex. In this case, we have to find a way how to detect regions automatically. In the following sections, we explore three different techniques that facilitate the spatial organization of content in the application and/or the users' location.

Automated Clustering Undo/Redo Technique

Instead of defining the region manually, a clustering technique groups currently visible items into clusters defining an undo/redo region. The idea behind this content-based regional undo/redo technique is to mimic the human's perception that items belong together if they are in spatial proximity [12]. With this technique, regional undo is executed in the region next to the undo/redo button the user pressed (Figure 8).

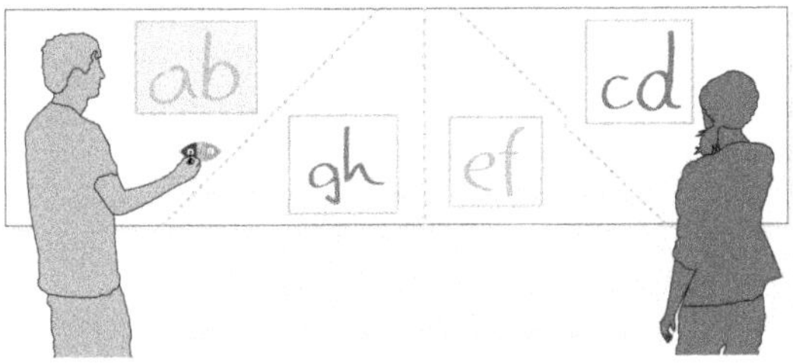

Figure 8: In the clustering technique, items in close proximity are grouped together and define an undo/redo region. Once a user selects an undo action, the cluster closest to the invoked tool palette (containing the undo button) will be chosen.

As depicted in Figure 9, our implementation of the clustering results in rectangular boxes containing associated content. We used an axis-aligned bounding box approach for the automated clustering technique. Once the distance between two items is under a certain threshold (in our case 11.7 cm or 80 px) they are grouped automatically into a new cluster. These clusters are calculated for every item on the screen. If a user selects an undo action, the cluster closest to the invoked user interface element (containing the undo button, see Figure 8) is chosen.

Figure 9: Upon selection of the undo-button on the digital tool palette (left), users get visual feedback of the undo/redo region (middle). The feedback disappears once the undo action has occurred (right).

By automatically generating undo/redo regions, the required effort to perform an undo action is reduced. In contrast to the later described techniques, this only provides temporary visible feedback about the region (see Figure 9). If this feedback would be permanent, the visual structure of an application would change and may also put too much emphasis on undo/redo functionality.

Workspace Undo/Redo Technique

This technique is based on the idea that users occupy a certain workspace on a large interactive surface (Figure 10). The background study showed that users would not expect that their actions have an effect outside their current work area. Therefore in this technique the undo/redo region is defined by the users' workspace. Although each user occupies a single workspace, collaborative work is still supported as such workspaces may overlap if two or more users are working in the same area.

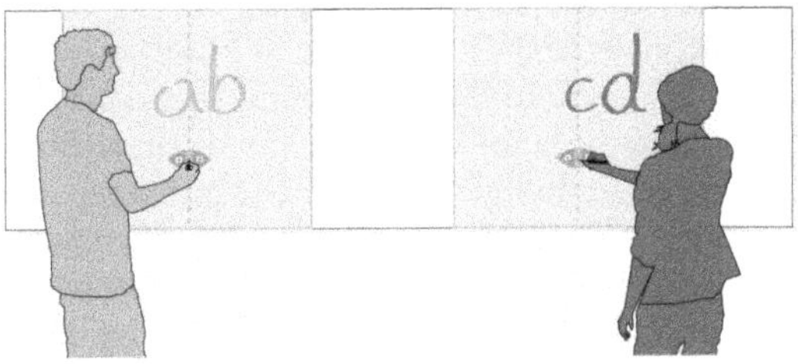

Figure 10: The workspace technique facilitates the users' workspace for regional undo.

We also simplified the workspace region by expanding it to the full height of the surface, because people usually do not work individually on top of each other on a vertical display. This simplification also allows placement of unobtrusive feedback to the top or bottom of the workspace and hence a way to inform the user about the extents of the workspace. In our implementation a bar (Figure 11) is displayed on top of the screen indicating the width of the workspace. The initial size is 75 cm which has been derived from guidelines for an ergonomic workspace [11]. The location of the workspace is controlled by the user interface element that contains the undo/redo buttons. This element is always at the center of the workspace. In our implementation the undo/redo buttons are incorporated to the users' digital tool palette which can be freely moved to any location on the display. Hence the workspace is relocated accordingly.

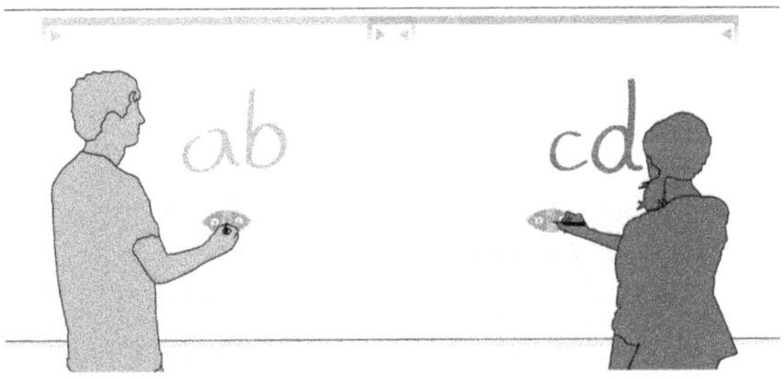

Figure 11: In our implementation, workspaces are visualized by color-coded bars on top of the screen. Inward arrows clarify overlapping workspaces. Positioning the bars at the top of the workspace limits the visual clutter during work.

Alternatively, the whole workspace can be manually repositioned by dragging the workspace bar to a different location. Moreover they can be manually resized by using the arrow-shaped handles (see Figure 11). In both cases the bar will show a lock symbol to indicate that the position of the digital tool palette will not affect the location of the workspace anymore.

In contrast to the cluster regions in the automated clustering technique, this technique provides areas for permanent visual feedback. Yet it introduces minimal clutter, because it is usually located in the periphery visual field of a user and users rarely interact near the boundaries of such large displays [9]. Despite this it still provides good feedback for changes of the workspace - since the human eye is highly sensitive to motion in the peripheral visual field.

Field-Of-View Undo/Redo Technique

The field of view (FOV) technique is based on the area a user physically sees. In the background study, we observed that the awareness is an important factor in setting users' expectations of undo/redo actions. Furthermore, users did not expect that an undo/redo action would affect an area far from their current location. Therefore, the undo/redo region is formed around the user's field of view (Figure 12).

Figure 12: The personal field of view defines the undo region. A tangible tool palette facilitates triggering of undo/redo actions and allows the user to move freely.

This also gives users the ability to simply change the undo/redo region by moving their body. To support "free" movement of users, undo/redo-actions are triggered by a mobile interface (Figure 12, *right*). This enables users to step back from the whiteboard to enlarge their field of view and still be able to trigger undo/redo. Hence, no direct input is necessary on the interactive surface.

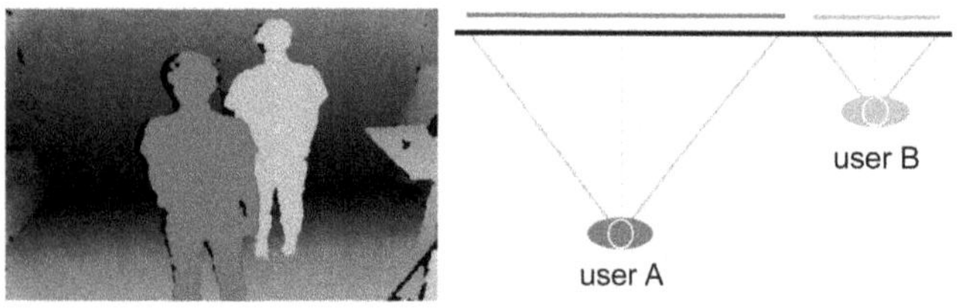

Figure 13: Users in front of the interactive surface are identified and their position tracked using Microsoft Kinect (left). Depending on the distance to the surface the width of their visual field is estimated (right).

Our implementation of this technique uses an approximation of the field of view by tracking users in front of the large interactive surface. As depicted in Figure 13, users are identified and their position tracked by using a Microsoft Kinect; one Kinect is able to capture the entire 4.5 meters in front of the IWB. Depending on the distance between the user and interactive surface we estimate the area visible to the user (we assume a field of view of 125°). An input device is mapped to a tracked user upon the first interaction on the IWB by comparing the users' location to the received input coordinates. Similarly to the workspace technique, the approximated visual field is only applied in the horizontal direction. Moreover, the extents of the region are visualized by a bar on the top of the display. Users can either use a digital or tangible tool palette to trigger an undo action (our tangible tool palette is shown in Figure 12, *right*).

In theory, visual feedback should not be necessary in an optimal implementation of this technique. But accurate eye-tracking would be necessary to calculate the precise visual field, which would require additional hardware and calibration for each user.

EVALUATION

We conducted an initial experiment to evaluate the proposed automatic regional undo/redo techniques. In the study, we mainly focused on qualitative data to gain insights on the expectations for each technique. Overall the objectives of this study were:

1. to measure the users preference,
2. to understand the users preference,
3. to observe which technique is less prone to errors (errors in the sense of undo/redo-actions leading to unexpected results), and
4. to find triggers for such unexpected undo results in our regional undo techniques.

Participants

In total, 18 unpaid volunteers (15 males, 3 females) participated from local software engineering companies (14 employees) and the university (4 employees). Participants performed the study in pairs (nine pairs in total). Their age ranged from 22 to 44 years (M=29.2, SD=5.7). All participants were daily computer users, with an average daily usage of 8.6 hours (SD=2.0). No participant reported using an interactive whiteboard frequently, but 56% had used one before, and 17% had used one for synchronous co-located collaboration at least once. 17 participants reported having a technical background. Finally, 95% of participants used undo/redo regularly, with 50% of them using it frequently.

Apparatus

The study was conducted in the same room and used the same hardware as the background study. A similar sketching application was used, with the addition of the regional undo/redo techniques described above. It also provided a digital and tangible tool palette to trigger undo and redo actions.

Tasks

All participants performed three different tasks that were designed to represent typical use cases for co-located work on an IWB. Each task consisted of two parts covering major undo use cases: error-correction and recovering a former document state. In the first part participants had to write text on the IWB. After each word we analyzed the written strokes with handwriting recognition software using Microsoft's built-in Ink Analyzer. Participants could only continue with the task when a word was recognized correctly. In the second part the participants were told to undo actions until they reach a specific (former) document state.

The quality of the recognition software was intentionally reduced with an average error probability of 60% per word to ensure that every participant had to call undo multiple times during one trial. At the beginning, users were informed about the error-proneness of the handwriting recognition software, so that participants did not feel discouraged or embarrassed during the study.

Task 1 – Individual work, change of location: Each participant had to write a short sentence at a pre-defined location on the IWB (four words with 35 letters on average). Upon completion, participants then had to switch places and undo their partner's entire sentence. This sequence was then repeated with a different sentence (Figure 14).

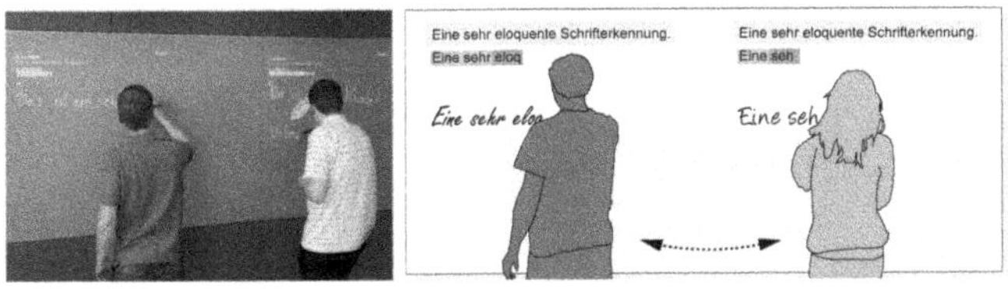

Figure 14: Individual work, change of location after completion of sentence.

The objective of this task was to test the regional undo techniques focusing on an individual working scenario. We also wanted to find out how well the techniques performed when participants changed locations.

Task 2 – Collaborative work, turn-taking: Similar to the first task, participants had to transcribe a sentence. In contrast to task 1, the participants had to complete this task together, each taking turns to write successive words in the sentence.

Figure 15: Collaborative work, turn-taking after each successive word.

The sentences were also longer in this task (11-13 words with 66 letters on average). Once the sentence was completed, the participants had to clear the whole sentence by using undo (Figure 15).

This task was designed to mimic a turn-taking collaborative working scenario. Such a scenario is common in collaborative work, especially during discussions (e.g., when creating a to-do list). Moreover, the length of the chosen sentences in this task ensured usage of a large area on IWB.

Task 3 – Collaborative work, synchronous work: In the final task, participants had to collaboratively recreate a single tag-cloud consisting of 14 words. The words in the tag-cloud were presented in three steps, with each step revealing more words. Participants were instructed to maintain the predefined spatial arrangement of the tag-cloud. Once completed, participants were asked to clear the whole tag-cloud (Figure 16).

The objective of this task was to encourage synchronous collaborative work on a single artifact. This scenario emulates common collaborative work activities, where the group members divide the task into sub-tasks. This usually appears when content needs to be created quickly under time pressure.

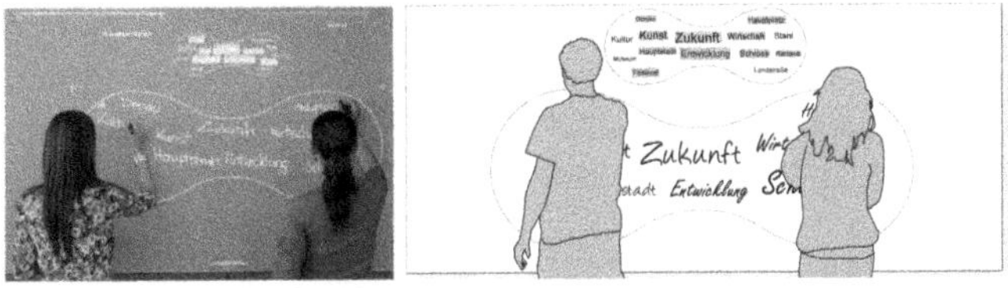

Figure 16: Collaborative and synchronous work.

The tasks were designed to challenge the limits of the different regional undo techniques. Therefore, participants experienced pros and cons of each technique to give them an impression how well each technique performs.

Design

The study used a 3 (task) × 3 (technique) within-subject design. In each session, a pair of participants performed three tasks (individual, collaborative turn-taking, collaborative synchronous), with each undo/redo technique (clustering, workspace, FOV). To minimize learning effects, the presentation order of the tasks was counterbalanced using a 3×3 Latin-square design. Similarly, the order of techniques within each task was also counterbalanced. Sentences (tasks 1 and 2) and tag-cloud words (task 3) were different for every trial in a session.

Procedure

Participants were first welcomed and provided an overview of the study and its goals. Participants then completed a pre-test questionnaire gathering demographic data. The sketching application, the study tasks, and the three different undo techniques were then explained to the participants. They were then given a 5-minute training session to familiarize themselves with the system, to practice writing in the system, and to practice the three undo techniques. Following this training session, they performed the three tasks, each with every undo technique. After completing a task with each technique participants were asked to complete a post-trial questionnaire. After completing all tasks, participants completed a post-study questionnaire regarding all executed tasks and techniques. The study was concluded with an informal interview to capture general experiences and feedback from participants. In total, each session lasted for approximately one hour.

Data Collection

Relevant data was captured through software logging, observation, questionnaires, and interviews. Participants' system interactions were captured in computer log files, including all undo/redo actions. In all sessions, observational field notes were taken by two researchers present in the room, focused on counting and classifying unexpected behavior of undo (i.e., undo errors). Undo errors were counted if an undo action was followed by an instant correction, or were clearly not expected (e.g. undone action was not part of the incorrect word). Furthermore the observers also took short notes what might have caused this undo error. The undo error rate was calculated by dividing the number of counted undo errors with the total amount of undo sequences executed by the participants. The sequence of subsequent undo actions was captured by software logging. Ratings and feedback were captured with questionnaires using 7-point Likert-scale questions, and general feedback and experiences with the informal interview.

Results

Overall, the participants rated the FOV technique highest (M=6.16, SD=0.98). As depicted Figure 17 (top), half of the participants even gave the highest rating. The workspace techniques' rating was lower (M=5.33, SD=1.37), whereas the clustering technique got the lowest rating (M=4.16, SD=1.33) with almost 40% of the participants rating the clustering technique negatively (1-3).

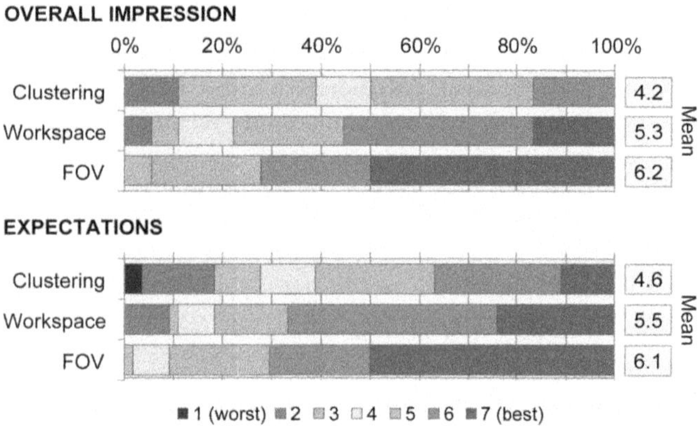

Figure 17: Participants' ratings on overall impression (top) and how well each technique met the expected behavior (bottom).

This also reflects the accumulated ratings of how well the undo technique met the expectations of the participants (Figure 17, bottom). Participants reported that the FOV technique matched their expectations the most, while the clustering technique matched their expectations the least.

Unexpected Undo Behavior - Undo Errors

Log file analysis revealed that, on average, 20.96 (SD=8.29) undo sequences occurred per trial resulting in an average error rate of 3.2% (SD=5.2%). The undo error measurements were analyzed using a repeated-measures ANOVA test with Bonferroni corrections for pair-wise comparisons. For all tests an alpha level of 0.05 was used. The ANOVA test showed significant main effects for both the *Task* ($F_{2,16}$ = 6.399, $p < 0.01$) and the *Technique* ($F_{2,16}$ = 6.275, $p < 0.01$). The assumption of sphericity was not violated. Post-hoc analysis showed that the clustering technique produced a significantly higher error rate than all other techniques (*Workspace*: $t(8)$ = 3.33, $p < 0.05$; *FOV*: $t(8)$ = 2.39, $p < 0.05$). The *clustering* technique's error rate of 5.1% (SD=2.1%) was twice as high as from the *workspace* (M=2.2%, SD=1.6%) or *FOV* technique (M=2.2%, SD=2.8%). No significant difference was found between workspace and *FOV* technique.

These results are consistent with participants' feedback on the error-proneness of the techniques (Figure 18). Interestingly, even though the actual and perceived error-proneness of the workspace and FOV technique were similar, participants' clearly favored the FOV technique, as indicated by their high ratings of this technique when ask how well each technique met their expectations (Figure 17).

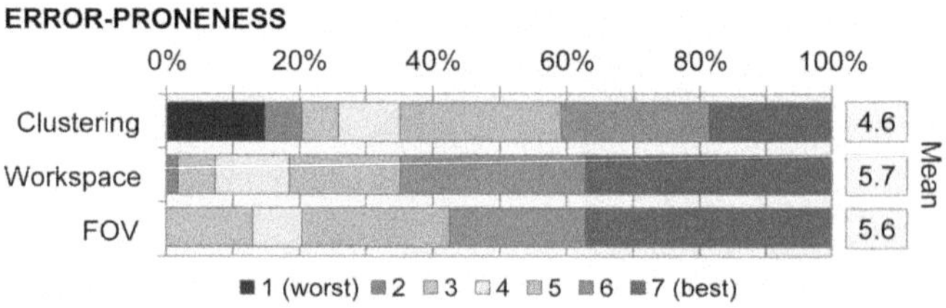

Figure 18: Ratings on the error-proneness of each evaluated regional undo technique (overall).

Causes of Errors

There were several reasons why the different undo techniques occasionally led to undesirable results. Causes of error with the clustering technique were (in total 26 errors):

1. *Ambiguous clusters / too large clusters (occurred 23 times):* Sometimes the calculated clusters did not match the expectations of the participants. For example, this happened during task 3 when participant were simultaneously working on the tag-cloud. Due to the close proximity between the words the whole tag-cloud was recognized as a single cluster, but participants expected separate undo regions.
2. *Cluster selection error (3 times):* If there were multiple clusters recognized, sometimes participants triggered an undo/redo action on a different cluster then they intended. For example, this often happened when they kept the digital tool palette static and reached for it to trigger undo, but the tool palette was closer to another cluster.

Causes of error with the workspace technique were (in total 11 errors):

1. *Incorrect workspace position (5 times):* Sometimes, the position of the workspace was unexpected because the participants placed their digital tool palette not in the center of their actual work area and hence inappropriate actions were undone.
2. *Locked workspace (3 times):* The participants' workspace was manually set to a specific position on IWB. Occasionally, they forgot to unlock it before triggering undo from a new position.

3. *Overlapping workspaces (3 times):* The workspaces of both participants sometimes overlapped when they were working individually but in close proximity. This occasionally resulted in contents of the other user being erroneously undone.

The main causes for errors with the FOV technique were (in total 10 errors):

1. *Incorrect position (5 times):* Sometimes, the position of the calculated field of view was unexpected, for example, when a participant changed their viewing angle without changing their body position.
2. *Unexpected size (4 times):* For some participants the calculated field of view was too large when standing close to the board.
3. *Overlapping field of view (1 time):* Similarly to the "overlapping workspaces" error described above, the field of view of participants overlapped when participants were working in close proximity, which occasionally led to content of the other user being erroneously undone.

DISCUSSION

Although the FOV is equally prone to errors as the workspace technique, participants preferred the FOV technique. Post-study interviews suggest that participants felt to control the FOV technique took less effort. One participant described the main advantage of the FOV over the other techniques: "The region is always there where I need it". Moreover, participants reported that they were able to more quickly become aware of the results of an undo action because, as another participant described, "it must be somewhere close to me". Despite the users' clear preference toward the FOV technique, all techniques produced some undesirable results. Therefore, we propose following improvements to reduce undo errors.

Improving Automatic Regional Undo/Redo Techniques

Our implementation of the FOV technique only tracked the position of a body. This implementation provided reasonable control over the undo region, however, tracking head [4] and, in particular, eye movement, would improve this technique. This may reduce errors of incorrect position and possibly also those of size. But FOV tracking depends on additional hardware that may not be available or feasible for every setup. In such cases improved clustering or workspace based techniques are also reasonable.

Clustering: The results of the study indicated that participants expected more fine-grained clustering, like in [18]. One way to address this would be to use lattice grouping to provide different levels of clusters [23]. Such approach, however, would also increase the complexity of cluster selection. Furthermore, an ideal clustering technique would need to comply with the way people structured content in their mind, like described in Gestalt laws of grouping [12]. Despite this, the lack of persistent visual feedback is clearly an open problem in this technique. Also it could be easily done by showing the boundaries of clusters all the time, it would change the visual structure of an application and may also put too much emphasis on undo/redo functionality.

Workspace: Another potential improvement would be to combine clustering and workspace techniques. Visualization of the workspace was highly appreciated by participants. The main sources of undesirable undo behavior resulted from the workspace size not matching participants' expectations and the need to manually modifying its location. Locking its position was especially problematic. Combining the workspace and clustering techniques would enable the size of a workspace to be automatically adjusted, based on nearby clusters.

Regional Undo/Redo Design Recommendations

Summarizing we propose the following design recommendations which are based on the lessons learned from development of our regional undo/redo techniques and user feedback from both user studies:

- **Visualize extents of regions:** The position and extents of an undo region must be clear to the user. Therefore, it is essential to visualize them.
- **Minimize users' effort:** Regional undo/redo should require as little user effort as possible (in comparison to global or personal undo), especially when a user wants to correct a mistake.
- **Minimize visual overhead:** Though undo is a valuable feature, it is not the main application functionality and, thus, visual overhead should be minimized.
- **Provide additional manual control:** Automatic regional undo techniques can handle most undo cases. When users experience limits, however, manual control of the undo region should be provided. Automatic and manual regional undo can easily be combined, for example by enabling undo/redo on a user selection. But manual controls must be clear and simple to use.

LIMITATIONS

This paper is a first step exploring the area of undo/redo on large interactive surfaces. Hence, the tasks included in the evaluation were intentionally contrived to present opportunities to test the limits of the techniques under study in an efficient manner. However, these tasks were designed to emulate aspects of common collaborative work scenarios on an IWB. While we recognize that different types of collaborative work activities may occur, especially during long work processes, we feel the included tasks provide a good starting point for understanding at least the common usage scenarios of undo/redo on an IWB. However, further study is warranted in a more naturalistic setting with real task groups performing real-world tasks. We also limited our focus to text input on an IWB, because this activity often produces errors. Nevertheless, IWBs are frequently used for digital drawing. We believe, however, that study results will also apply to those use cases. Furthermore only a limited set of commands (*add* and *remove*) were used in this study. Further study is necessary for commands with a larger impact on the visual structure such as movements or automatic sorting. Moreover, as this work is mostly focused on vertical displays further study is warrant for tabletop displays.

CONCLUSION AND FUTURE WORK

In this paper, we investigated undo and redo for co-located collaborative work on large vertical surfaces, supporting both collaborative and individual work. We first conducted a background study, which showed that regional undo, which only applied undo/redo actions to localized content, was most consistent with users' expectations in such an environment. Thus, we developed several regional undo techniques (clustering, workspace, and FOV) that each provide different potential regional undo solution. We then evaluated the developed techniques in an initial user study. The study revealed that users strongly preferred the FOV technique, while making significantly more errors with the clustering technique compared to either the workspace or FOV technique (which produced similar error rates). Based on the study results, and lessons learned in developing the evaluated techniques, we suggest improvements to these techniques, and recommendations regarding the design of regional undo techniques on large interactive surfaces.

In the future, we are interested in exploring regional undo techniques in mixed co-located and distributed cooperative work scenarios. We also plan to investigate the use of large-scaled eye tracking for refining the FOV technique. There are also additional topics related to undo/redo that were not discussed in this paper. For example, undo granularity is an important design consideration to providing effective undo functionality [1]. Finally, we plan to investigate the question, if regional undo, in general, can be substituted by a different method of undo, such as an "intelligent" group undo where the systems recognizes group or individual work regardless of regions on the display.

REFERENCES

1. Abowd, G. D. and Dix, A. J. Giving undo attention. *Interacting with Computers*, 4 (1992), 317-342.
2. Archer, Jr., J. E., Conway, R. and Schneider, F. B. User Recovery and Reversal in Interactive Systems. *ACM Trans. on Programming Languages and Systems*, 6 (1984), 1-19.
3. Berlage, T. A selective undo mechanism for graphical user interfaces based on command objects. *ACM Trans. on Computer-Human Interaction*, 1 (1994), 269-294.
4. Bezerianos, A., Dragicevic P. and Balakrishnan, R. Mnemonic Rendering: An Image-Based Approach for Exposing Hidden Changes in Dynamic Displays. In *Proc. UIST 2006*, 159-168.
5. Cass, A. and Fernandes, C. Using Task Models for Cascading Selective Undo. In *Proc. TAMODIA 2006*, Springer (2007).
6. Cass, A. G., Fernandes, C. S. T. and Polidore, A. An empirical evaluation of undo mechanisms. In *Proc. NordiCHI 2006*, ACM (2006), 19-27.
7. Choudhary, R. and Dewan, P. A general multi-user undo/redo model. In *Proc. ESCSW 1995*, Kluwer Academic Publishers (1995), 231-246.
8. Grossman, T., Matejka, J. and Fitzmaurice, G. Chronicle: capture, exploration, and playback of document workflow histories. In *Proc. UIST 2010*, ACM (2010), 143-152.
9. Haller, M., Leitner, J., Seifried T., Wallace, J., Scott, S., Richter, C., Brandl, P., and Gokcezade, A., The NiCE Discussion Room: Integrating Paper and Digital Media to Support Co-Located Group Meetings. In *Proc. CHI 2010*, ACM (2010), 609-618.
10. Hazemi, R. and Macaulay, L. User requirements for undo support in CSCW. In *Proc. of the HCI'95*, Cambridge University Press (1995), 181-193.
11. ISO, EN ISO 14738, Anthropometric requirements for the design of workstation machinery
12. Koffka, K. *Principles of Gestalt Psychology*, Harcourt, 1935.
13. Kurlander, D. and Feiner, S. *A history of editable graphical histories*, MIT Press, Cambridge, MA, USA, 1993, 405-413.
14. Kurlander, D. and Feiner, S. A Visual Language for Browsing, Undoing, and Redoing Graphical Interface Commands. *Visual Languages and Visual Programming*, Plenum Press (1990).
15. Li, R. and Li, D. A Regional Undo Mechanism for Text Editing. In *Proc.IWCES 2003*.
16. McGrath, J. *Groups: Interaction and Performance*, Prentice-Hall, Englewood, NJ, 1984
17. Meng, C., Yasue, M.; Imamiya, A. and Mao, X. Visualizing Histories for Selective Undo and Redo. In *Proc. APCHI 1998*, IEEE (1998), 459-464.
18. Mynatt, E. D., Igarashi, T., Edwards, W. K. and LaMarca, A. Flatland: new dimensions in office whiteboards. In *Proc. CHI 1999*, ACM (1999), 346-353.
19. Nakamura, T. and Igarashi, T. An application-independent system for visualizing user operation history. In *Proc. UIST 2008*, ACM (2008), 23-32.
20. Prakash, A. and Knister, M. J. Undoing actions in collaborative work. In *Proc. CSCS 1992*, 273-280.
21. Ressel, M. and Gunzenhäuser, R. Reducing the problems of group undo. In *Proc. SIGGROUP* 1999, 131-139.
22. Ressel, M., Nitsche-Ruhland, D. and Gunzenhäuser, R. An integrating, transformation-oriented approach to concurrency control and undo in group editors. In *Proc. CSCW 1996*.
23. Saund, E., Fleet, D., Larner, D. and Mahoney, J. Perceptually-supported image editing of text and graphics. In *Proc. UIST 2003*, 183-192.
24. Sun, C. and Chen, D. Consistency maintenance in real-time collaborative graphics editing systems. *ACM Trans. on Computer-Human Interaction*, 9 (2002), 1-41.
25. Sun, C. Undo any operation at any time in group editors. In *Proc. CSCW 2000*, 191-200.
26. Sun, D. and Sun, C. Operation context and context-based operational transformation. In *Proc. CSCW 2006*, 279-288.
27. Teitelman, W., Goodwin, J. and Bobrow, D. Interlisp reference manual. *Xerox Palo Alto Research Centers*, 1978.
28. Vitter, J. US & R: A new framework for redoing. *IEEE Software*, 1 (1984), 39-52.
29. Yang, Y. Undo support models. *International Journal of Man-Machine Studies*, 28 (1988), 457-481.
30. Zhou, C. and Imamiya, A. Object-based nonlinear undo model. In *Proc. COMPSAC 1997*, IEEE (1997), 50-55.

Tangible Remote Controllers for Wall-Size Displays

Yvonne Jansen
Université Paris-Sud / INRIA

Pierre Dragicevic
INRIA

Jean-Daniel Fekete
INRIA

{jansen, dragice, fekete}@lri.fr

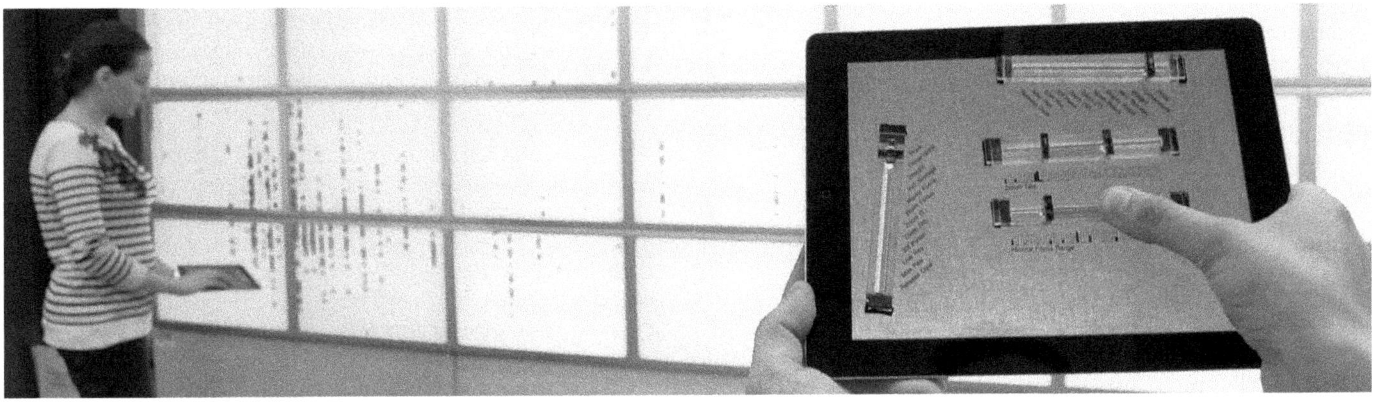

Figure 1. Two users performing dynamic queries on a scatterplot using tangible remote controllers.

ABSTRACT
We explore the use of customizable tangible remote controllers for interacting with wall-size displays. Such controllers are especially suited to visual exploration tasks where users need to move to see details of complex visualizations. In addition, we conducted a controlled user study suggesting that tangibles make it easier for users to focus on the visual display while they interact. We explain how to build such controllers using off-the-shelf touch tablets and describe a sample application that supports multiple dynamic queries.

Author Keywords
Wall-size displays; tangible user interfaces; visual exploration.

ACM Classification Keywords
H.5.2 : User Interfaces—*Input devices and strategies.*

General Terms
Design, Human Factors, Experimentation.

INTRODUCTION
Wall-size displays (WSDs) have applications in a wide range of domains but interaction with WSDs raises different issues than in desktop environments. Despite the wealth of solutions that have been proposed so far, the search for effective interaction techniques remains a challenge.

Previous work has mainly focused on input issues without considering the types of tasks that might be actually carried out on a WSD. These tasks are likely to be essentially *visual* in nature, since they will benefit the most from moving from desktop environments to high-resolution WSDs. Examples are visual exploration tasks such as in information visualization, and they constitute the main motivation for this work.

Since a key benefit of high-resolution WSDs is the ability to get an overview of complex visuals from a distance and see details up-close, it is important to support locomotion. For users to be able to comfortably carry out visual tasks, interaction devices must also be easy to operate eyes-free.

In this article we discuss five such requirements and how well they are supported by existing WSD interaction techniques. We present a categorization of techniques that uncovers a promising area in the design space that combines mobility and tangibility. Here we propose to explore the use of customizable tangible remote controllers such as illustrated in Figure 1 for carrying out visual exploration tasks on WSDs.

We explain how to build such devices using multitouch tablets and capacitive tangible controls. Since there is a practical cost in building and employing such controls (e.g., they must be carried around), they must provide clear benefits compared to similar solutions based on touch or pen input alone [25, 23, 7]. We report on a controlled user experiment taking the slider as an example to show that tangible controls can indeed facilitate interaction with vertical displays.

We finally illustrate our approach with a prototype system that lets users explore multidimensional datasets on a high-resolution WSD by performing multiple dynamic queries with tangible range sliders [1].

BACKGROUND

Here we discuss the requirements for interaction techniques to conveniently support visual exploration tasks on large displays, and how well they are met by existing approaches. We then motivate the use of tangible remote controllers, and discuss previous evaluations of tangible user interfaces to show why more studies are needed to validate our approach.

Requirements for Interaction Techniques

We derive the five following requirements for WSD interaction techniques in a context of visual exploration:

R1 *Little visual attention*: the interaction devices should demand as little visual attention as possible. For example, a scientist who is tuning the parameters of a simulation should be able to observe the results directly on the large display without having to constantly switch her attention between the display and the input device.

R2 *Little visual clutter*: since the primary focus of the task is the visual information displayed, the technique should not require too much visual feedback on the WSD. For example, a pop-up menu can occlude the data being visualized and disrupt the exploration process or disturb other users.

R3 *Mobility*: the technique should allow for locomotion. This is especially important on high-resolution WSDs, where users can get an overview of a complex visualization when standing at a distance, while moving towards the screen provides them with previously illegible details [3, 5].

R4 *Task-specificity*: the appropriate input technique depends on the task. Input devices for WSDs have been categorized by their degree of guidance into 3-D, 2-D and 1-D [24], and guidance should best match the number of degrees of freedom of the task [4]. Although scientific visualization applications exist that need 3-D positional input, most information visualization applications heavily rely on 2-D object selection and 1-D dynamic queries [1].

R5 *Genericity*: while devices and techniques should be ideally targeted towards applications, many visual exploration applications exist depending on the domain. For practical reasons we therefore need to access a wide range of applications with the same technology and interaction styles.

There is a natural tension between task-specificity and genericity, which on standard desktop computers has been partly addressed by the use of a generic input device (the mouse) and a set of logical tools that are half-way between generic and specific (GUI widgets). But it is not clear yet how this tension should be addressed in WSD environments.

Approaches to Large Display Interaction

We discuss existing approaches for WSD interaction with respect to our requirements. We classify them according to their *input range* and the *type of input* they involve (Table 1). The first two types of input are from [24]. We focus on manual input; other modalities can be quite useful as they often allow for mobility and in some cases eyes-free operation, but they are best used as complements to manual input for tasks that require a minimum amount of input bandwidth.

Mid-Air Interaction Techniques

Mid-air or freehand techniques are techniques where the user's hand is free to move in 3-D space [24] (Table 1 top row).

The large majority of these techniques support mobility (Table 1 right column). They combine hand or handheld device tracking with interaction techniques such as ray-casting and hand posture recognition to let users perform tasks such as selecting objects or panning-and-zooming (e.g., [33, 24]). Other mid-air techniques need to be operated from a desk [22] (Table 1 mid column) and sensing technologies also exist that only work close to the display [2] (Table 1 left column).

Mid-air interaction supports mobility (R3) – although techniques such as ray casting are not well-suited to up-close interaction – but it is inherently limited in accuracy and often subject to fatigue. Eyes-free operation is possible (R1) but most mid-air techniques require additional visual feedback on the display (R2). Although pointing is the most common task, a large design space exists for techniques that are more task-specific, especially 3-D tasks for which mid-air input is particularly well-suited. For precise 2-D or 1-D input, however, other approaches exist that seem more adequate.

Surface-Based Interaction Techniques

In surface-based techniques, the hand's motion is constrained by a 2-D surface [24] (Table 1, second row).

A first type of approach uses the WSD itself as the constraining surface (Table 1 left column), and this mostly includes pen-based and touch interaction. A problem is that users need to move in front of objects to select them, and although a number of reaching techniques have been proposed (e.g, [18, 6]), touch- and pen-based input unavoidably require users to be close to the display (R3).

A second type of approach uses horizontal constraining surfaces separate from the wall, such as a desk and a mouse (e.g., [16]) or touch-sensitive tabletops (Table 1 center column). But this type of approach, as well as solutions such as chair-mounted touch tablets [29], restricts locomotion (R3).

A third type of approach uses handheld surfaces such as PDAs and touch tablets (e.g., [7, 23, 25]) (Table 1 right column). Users are free to move around as if they were using a remote controller (R3). This approach opens up a wide range of possibilities, such as deporting the application's widgets to the handheld device, eliminating the need for visual feedback on the wall (R2). However, this also implies switching users' focus from the display to the input device, something which should be best avoided for visual exploration tasks (R1).

Fixed Physical Controls

Physical controls such as buttons, sliders and knobs are widely used in everyday life and can be useful in WSD environments as well (Table 1 third row). Physical controls can be placed at a fixed location, either at a distance from the display (e.g., control boards or mixing consoles, see Table 1 center column) or on the display's structure (e.g., buttons on Smartboard displays, see Table 1 left column). However, the best solution for mobility are remote controllers (Table 1 right column).

Input type		Input range: Up-close	Input range: Fixed in the room	Input range: Mobile
	Mid-air	depth sensing [2]	desktop hand tracking [22]	laser & hand pointing [33], gyroscopic mice, hand gestures [24]
	Surface	touch and pen-based [18, 6], touch devices as magic lens [27]	desktop mice [16], horizontal touch displays, chair-mounted tablets [29]	remote control with touch devices [25, 23], point & shoot with touch devices [7]
	Physical controls	display-integrated controls	control boards	classical remote controllers
	Tangible	sticky or magnetic props [32] and controls [21]	configurable control boards [14, 31, 32], props [13, 20] and controls [34] on an horizontal display	**tangible remote controllers**

Table 1. Classification of interaction techniques for WSDs by input range and input type, with examples of previous work.

One simple example are hand-held devices used to navigate in slides during presentations, and a more sophisticated version could be devised for navigating in visualizations.

One advantage of physical controls is that they provide richer tactile feedback than flat 2-D surfaces and therefore they might be easier to find and operate eyes-free (R1). In addition, continuous controls such as sliders or knobs are especially well-suited to 1-D tasks since they are path constrained [24] (R4). But despite the fact that some controllers exist that are programmable, classical remote controllers are not flexible enough to accommodate a wide range of tasks (R5).

Tangible Interaction Techniques

Tangible user interfaces (TUIs) employ physical rather than virtual objects for interacting with applications [13]. In contrast with the previous category, most tangibles are reconfigurable in space (R5). Although TUIs have been rarely used with WSDs, we include in our classification techniques that can potentially be employed (Table 1 bottom row). We make a distinction between physical *props*, i.e., objects that can be moved around and whose primary purpose is to specify positions and orientations, and *controls*, i.e., objects with moving parts such as buttons and sliders that are usually fixed.

Most existing TUI systems are not mobile (R3) (Table 1 center column). Early systems involve application-specific props [13, 20]. Systems with generic controls have also been proposed that include configurable control boards [14, 32] and hybrid systems [34] where controls are laid out on horizontal touch displays. Hybrid systems have the advantage of supporting both 2-D surface and tangible interaction (R4), and allow dynamic control relabelling (R2, R5).

Other techniques have been designed for vertical surfaces, and include sticky or magnetic props and controls [21]. These, like other techniques on the left column of Table 1, have the drawback of requiring close-up interaction (R3).

So far no system combining tangible interaction and mobility has been proposed for wall interaction (bottom right cell in our taxonomy), but hybrid tangible systems have started to be built for touch-phones and tablets. We review them in more detail in the next section.

Tangible Remote Controllers

Based on the previous requirements and classification of techniques, we propose to use tangible remote controllers to perform visual exploration tasks on a WSD. Remote controllers fully support mobility (R3) and compared to early PDA-based systems [25, 23], tangible controls should be easier to acquire and operate when the display requires full user attention (R1).

Technically speaking, we propose a hybrid solution similar to SLAP [34]. Compared to a display-less configurable control board approach [14], this approach supports flexible relabeling (R2, R5) and 2-D positional input. Both phone and tablet form factors are commercially available, the latter being especially suited to input-rich applications.

Like GUI widgets, tangible controls can be built that are between generic and task-specific (R4, R5). Since widgets are already widely used in desktop applications – including in information visualization applications – this approach can facilitate both the porting of existing applications to WSDs and knowledge transfer among end users.

Tangibles have already started to be combined with portable touch devices. With the introduction of the iPhone and iPad, the do-it-yourself community developed tutorials on how to build tangible add-ons for touch tablets such as styli, props and knobs[1]. One of them, the Fling Joystick[2], is commercially available. Yu et al. also recently proposed TUIC [36], a capacitive marker design relying either on spatial markers, or on time-multiplexed active markers that are detected by a distinctive tap pattern produced by micro-controllers.

Our tangible remote controller prototype uses a similar technology. However, with the exception of the Fling Joystick and Clip-On buttons [35], existing systems require the tablet to lie flat so that the tangibles do not glide off it, which defeats the mobile nature of tablets (R3). Also, no previous system has been designed to be used as remote controllers. In isolation, these augmented tablets are of limited use since tangibles and visual output from applications compete for the same (limited) space. Using them with WSDs is, we believe, a more compelling application, but it poses technical and design problems that we address in this article.

[1] http://labs.teague.com/?p=579
[2] http://tenonedesign.com/fling

Previous Evaluations of TUIs

Our approach can be evaluated in different ways. Concerning mobility, commercial touch phones and tablets are designed to support it, so provided controllers stick to the display and can be conveniently carried when unused, tangible systems built with these devices should inherently support mobility. A less clear claim is that tangibles bring advantages compared to similar approaches that use touch only (right column second row in Table 1). Since studies have been already carried out on general-purpose TUIs, we first review them.

Fitzmaurice and Buxton [12] devised a task where various tangible objects had to be manipulated to match their virtual counterparts on a screen. Baseline conditions involved multiple pens & pucks or a unique pen & puck (time multiplexing). Although tangibles were found to be more effective, touch input was not tested.

Tuddenham et al. [30] repeated the study including a direct touch condition. Tangible props outperformed direct touch but in contrast to the original study, input and output spaces coincided so there was no eyes-free component to the task.

Chipman et al. [9] compared a physical slider used with a non-dominant hand to a mouse-operated scrollbar and a mouse-wheel for a scrolling and selection task. They found the slider to outperform the scrollbar, which proves the superiority of two-handed input but not of tangible input per se.

One of the SLAP widgets [34], the rotary knob, was evaluated in a task where subjects had to reach back-and-forth between buttons placed near a video player requiring sustained attention and a knob placed far away. The tangible knob was found to outperform its touch counterpart. However, these results cannot be easily generalized to our setup where the user is free to move the tablet with respect to the visual display.

Overall these studies provide some support for the idea of augmenting remote controller tablets with tangibles, but they apply to situations that significantly differ from ours. Tuddenham's study involves an interactive table where input and output coincide, a very different setup from ours which requires operating a hand-held device while observing visual feedback on a wall display. The SLAP widgets study did separate input and visual output, yet its setup differs from ours since it lacked a physical frame of reference and the controls could not be moved with respect to the display, both of which can make touch input harder. Also, Fitzmaurice and Tuddenham evaluate compound actions for which tangibles are known to be especially suited and SLAP evaluates a touch widget that is known to be difficult to operate eyes-free [28]. We therefore propose a new study to address these concerns.

Another contribution of our study lies in clean performance metrics. Tuddenham and Fitzmaurice only measure overall error and completion time. Device reacquisition is not controlled for and reacquisition time is only inferred by comparing global user idle times per trial. We set out to determine not only if tangibles are more effective overall but also when and why. We therefore measure control acquisition performance and control operation performance separately, as well as how subjects allocate their visual attention.

TANGIBLE REMOTE CONTROLLER PROTOTYPE

In this section we present the design of our remote controller prototype. Similar to recent work [36], we lay out tangible widgets on off-the-shelf capacitive touch tablets, as these are now widely available and support wireless communication necessary for WSD interaction. In addition, they provide 2-D touch and display capabilities.

In contrast to previous work, we specifically designed our system to be used as a remote controller for WSDs. This involves technical requirements, some of which directly derive from our general requirements for WSD techniques.

Because users need to be able to move with the remote controller and operate it in any orientation (R3), the tangible controls should stick to the screen and be kept small to save screen real estate. Users should be able to control as many applications as possible (R5), hence tangible controls should be kept generic and ideally mimic widgets that are commonly found in existing GUI toolbars (see Figure 2). Additionally the remote controller should be fully reconfigurable since users might need to control different applications or might need different control sets depending on the current task (R4). This requires support for dynamic control reassignment, and also requires tangibles to be easy to remove and to replace on the tablet surface.

We explain how to build a tangible remote controller that addresses these requirements. We focus here on the hardware aspects; remote communication with WSD applications and mechanisms for mapping controls to applications will be discussed in the section Sample Application.

Capacitive Sensing Design

Our tangible controls are tracked using capacitive sensing. Most multi-touch tablets use *mutual capacitance* between row and column electrodes to detect touch: each row / column crossing exhibits a baseline capacitance that increases when a conductive object gets close enough [26]. Small conductive items such as metal paper clips typically produce small changes which cannot be discriminated from the sensor noise, whereas bigger objects like scissors or human bodies produce measurable changes. On a capacitive tablet, a touch event is typically produced when the capacitance exceeds a threshold.

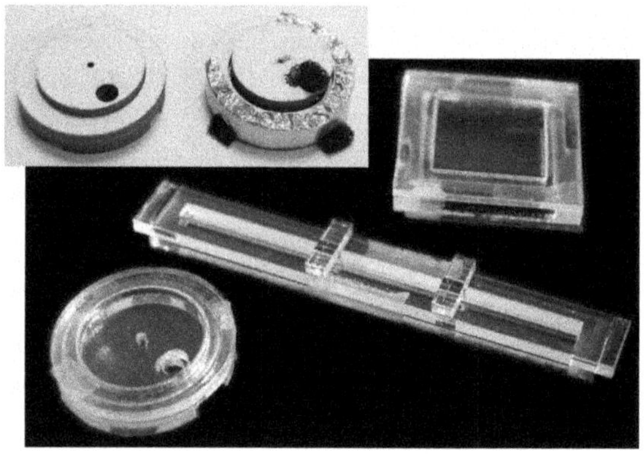

Figure 2. Cardboard/copper control prototypes and acrylic controls.

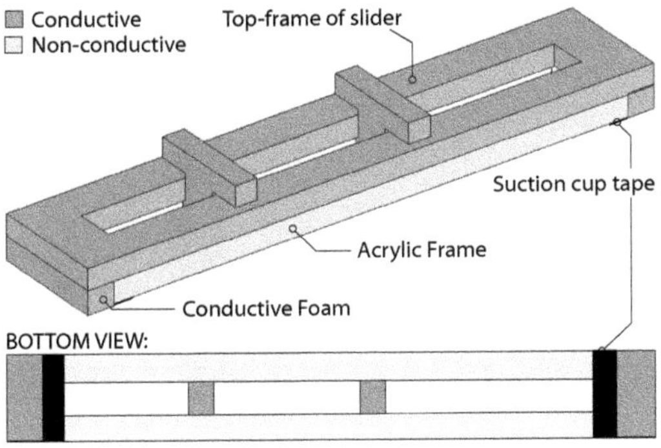

Figure 3. The making of the tangible range slider.

Accordingly, tangibles can in principle be designed so that they are constantly tracked as in vision-based systems. However, most tablets do not give access to raw input, making the detection of small tangibles impossible or unreliable. Also, the number of simultaneous touches that can be tracked is limited, which limits the number and complexity of tangibles that can be used. We therefore chose to have our tangibles detected and tracked only *while touched*. This allows to fit more controls and works well in practice, since our tangibles stick to the tablet and their moving parts are unlikely to move unless they are touched.

To have tangibles detected and tracked only when touched, we used non-conductive bodies with a conductive coating that forwards user touch to the capacitive screen (see Figure 3). For rapid prototyping we experimented with electrostatic bags, graphite spray paint, copper tape and conductive foam (see Figure 2). For a more finished looking we used conductive ink based on carbon nanotubes[3] or PEDOT:PSS[4].

Marker Design

We use capacitive markers so that the tablet can track the geometry (position and/or orientation) of tangible controls and their moving parts. We opted for passive rather than active markers since an active design would require more space for electronics and batteries [36]. We decided against encoding individual control IDs in order to save space for the markers. Once a control has been placed on the tablet, its type, location and orientation are registered. Since controls stick in place, their identity and the identity of their moving parts can be subsequently retrieved from the position of touch events.

Since it might be useful to let users interact with the available tablet surface in addition to operating the tangible controls, we need to discriminate between tangible operation and actual touch events. Our current prototype uses Apple iPads whose current API (iOS 4.3.2) only exposes information on touch location and the radius of its major axis. We therefore use a marker encoding scheme that uses distance between single touch points and their major axis radii. For sliders we use two 3×10 mm feet, while buttons and knobs use three 5×5 mm feet. This proved enough to allow reliable detection of tangibles without false positives and false negatives.

[3]http://www.nano-lab.com/nink.html
[4]http://www.clevios.com

Body Design

The body of our tangible controls has been built from laser-cut non-conductive material such as cardboard and acrylic (Figure 2). Our final prototypes are built from transparent acrylic to allow visual information to be displayed underneath as in SLAP Widgets [34]. All controls are based on a fixed frame, which is entirely coated with conductive ink such that users are free to touch them wherever they prefer while preserving their transparency. The frames are directly connected to the feet to forward touch events. Moving parts are also coated with conductive ink and each part, i.e., button plate, inner knob, and slider thumbs, creates its own touch event. Figure 3 illustrates the mechanism for the range slider.

In contrast to previous systems like TUIC [36] we need to support mobile use and therefore require that the controls stick to the tablet. They should also be easy to remove and reposition and not require special modifications to the tablet. Consequently, we decided against magnets [21] as they require a ferromagnetic backing of the tablet. Suction cups as used by the Fling Joystick are better suited but take up considerable space or restrict the tangibles to the edge of the screen. Instead we use suction cup tape, i.e., a film containing microscopic craters on its surface that act as suction cups[5]. We found that two to three small surfaces of about 20 mm^2 are enough to provide a tight grip on tablets while being easy to remove without leaving traces.

COMPARISON OF TOUCH VS. TANGIBLE SLIDERS

Because tangibles have a practical cost – they need to be built and carried around – their benefits need to be clearly demonstrated to justify their use. Although intuition and common sense suggests that tangible controls should always outperform touch, some studies show that it is not always the case [19]. In fact, it is hard to build reliable and effective tangible controls, and other negative results likely exist that have never been published due to reporting bias. Other studies suggest that touch devices can be operated very effectively, so the need for augmenting them with tangibles is unclear. For example, Buxton et al. [8] informally observed that users quickly learned to find touch controls using tablet edges and operate them eyes- and error-free.

We set out to determine whether tangible controls provide benefits when using a tablet as a remote controller. Our goal was to keep the experiment design as simple as possible to make our findings independent from the task and get a better understanding of the causes of differences in performance.

We chose to examine interaction using a single control and opted for a slider because it is widely used and is neither too simple nor too complex. We decided to test it on a low-level tracking task, a task upon which we believe depends the performance of many higher-level visual exploration tasks, and added a secondary task to test control acquisition. Furthermore, since we were not interested in user locomotion per se, we used a simplified setup where subjects stood in front of a wall-mounted display (see Figure 4).

[5]www.inventables.com/technologies/suction-cup-tape

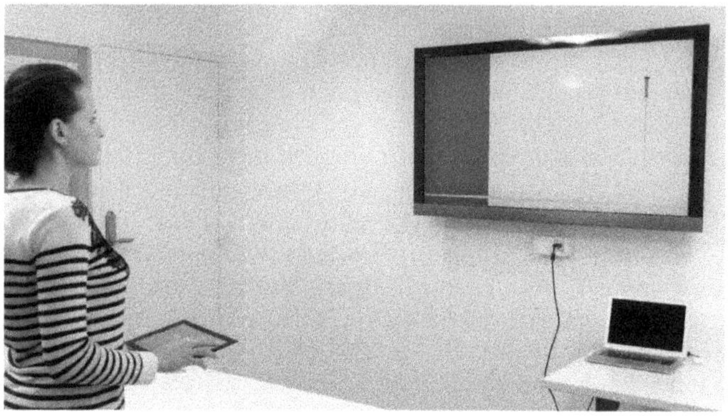

Figure 4. The experimental setup.

Design

A repeated measures full-factorial within participants design was used. One factor was the input technique, i.e., *touch* or *tangible* input. A second factor was the task, i.e., either pure tracking (*tracking*) or tracking with a secondary task that forced subjects to release and reacquire the slider (*tracking + reacquisition*). 12 participants were randomly assigned to one of four groups according to a balanced latin square 2 x 2 design. So the experiment consisted of:

$$\begin{array}{ll} & 12 \text{ participants} \\ \times & 2 \text{ techniques} \\ \times & 2 \text{ tasks} \\ \times & 4 \text{ repetitions} \\ = & 192 \text{ trials} \end{array}$$

Each trial took 90 seconds, summing up to about 35 minutes including training for each participant.

Apparatus

We ran the experiment on a MacBook Air connected to a 121×68 cm (1920×1080 pixels) display mounted on a wall at a 125 cm height (bottom edge), and communicating wirelessly with an iPad 2. A table prevented subjects from getting closer than 230 cm. In the touch condition, the iPad displayed a virtual slider of 1.2×9.5 cm with an active touch area of 1.2×8.0 cm (the thumb jumped to the touch position). In the tangible condition, a 1.2×9.5×0.6 cm physical slider (1.2×0.4 cm thumb size), designed as explained in the previous section, was placed on top of the virtual slider. As shown in Figure 5, the two sliders had a similar appearance.

Task

The primary task for this experiment was loosely designed after the tracking task used by Fitzmaurice and Buxton [12]. Participants held the tablet, stood in front of a wall-mounted display and had to continuously readjust the slider to track a target presented on the vertical display. The display showed a larger slider with both the current thumb position and the desired position (the *target*) (see Figure 4). A red bar connected the two to highlight the error. Subjects were instructed to keep this error as small as possible at all times.

The target followed a precomputed 1-D path among four different paths whose order was randomized within each block.

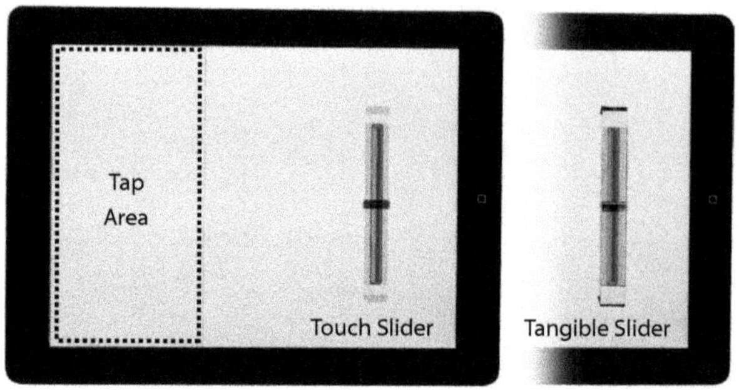

Figure 5. Top view of the tablet with the touch and the tangible slider.

Like in [12], the target moved at a constant speed, "darted off" at random intervals and changed direction when it reached an extremum. We used a target speed of 0.15 units per second, a dart-off distance of 0.3 units and a dart-off interval between 2 and 4 seconds. A *unit* equals the slider's total range.

During the *tracking + reacquisition* task, the left side of the vertical display lit up red — which we refer to as the *tap stimulus*, see Figure 4 — at pre-defined random intervals between 2 and 6 seconds (about 20 times per trial). When this happened, subjects were instructed to tap the corresponding area of the tablet as soon as they could, then promptly return to the tracking task. The tap area was large enough to allow for confident eyes-free acquisition and its only purpose was to have participants release then reacquire the slider's thumb. In case the tap stimulus was ignored (which rarely occurred during the experiment), each new tap stimulus was queued and displayed immediately after the reacquisition of the slider.

Subjects were told to be as fast and accurate as possible throughout the experiment and that the tracking and tapping tasks were equally important. They were instructed to stand, hold the tablet in their non-dominant hand, and perform the taps with the index finger of their dominant hand in order to enforce the need for releasing the slider. Subjects could otherwise hold the tablet and use the slider as they wished.

Subjects were given an initial practice session of 90 seconds per technique with the *tracking + reacquisition* task. They were warned that holding the tablet could yield fatigue and were allowed to rest between trials. Subjects were videotaped during the experiment and upon its completion, were given a questionnaire and were asked to comment on the techniques.

Participants

7 male and 5 female unpaid volunteers participated in the experiment. 58% own a mobile phone with a touch screen (no interaction with gender). All agreed to be videotaped.

Measures

Our three main dependent variables were:

- *Tracking Error*, the distance between the thumb and target as a percentage of the slider range, averaged over samples.
- *Reacquisition Time*, the average time between the moment the subject taps the left area of the tablet and the first subsequent touch event within the slider's active area.

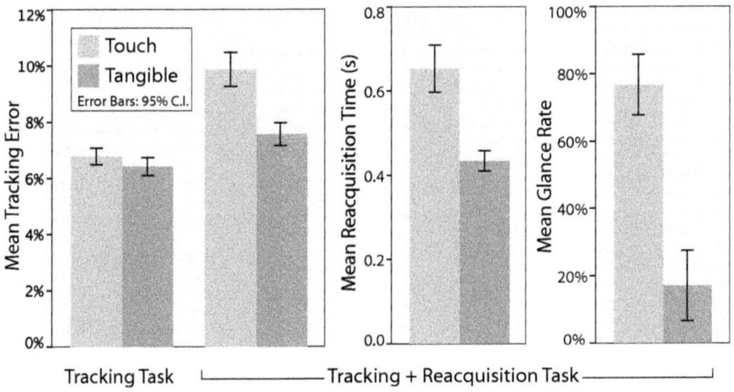

Figure 6. Results for our three measures, averaged across trials.

- *Glance Rate*, the number of times the subject looked at the tablet as a percentage of the number of tap stimuli. Glances were accompanied with a clear downward head motion and were counted by viewing video recordings.

We additionally included the two following measures:

- *Tap Reaction Time*, the average time between the onset of the tap stimulus on the vertical display and the moment the subject taps this area on the tablet.
- *Misacquisitions*, the average number of times the subject misacquires the slider per tap stimulus.

A *misacquisition* was defined as a touch event that occurs i) outside the slider's active touch area, ii) at a distance less than 80 pixels to this area, iii) between a tap action and a reacquisition, iv) 200 ms or more before the reacquisition. These criteria were determined from event and video logs and effectively discriminated between misacquisitions and accidental touches (e.g., a different finger touches the tablet during a successful reacquisition or the left hand touches the tablet).

Hypotheses

We conjectured that the tangible slider would be faster to reacquire and that we would hence observe lower tracking errors overall during *tracking + reacquisition* tasks than using touch. We also speculated that users would be more confident and therefore would look less often at the tablet. However, we did not expect the tangible slider to bring much benefit while users operate them, hence we supposed there would be no measurable difference between the techniques in the pure *tracking* task. Therefore, our hypotheses were:

- For the *tracking + reacquisition* task:
  H1. The tangible condition yields a *lower tracking error* than the touch condition.
  H2. The tangible slider is *faster to reacquire* than the touch-operated slider.
  H3. The tangible condition yields *less glances* to the tablet than the touch condition.
- For the pure *tracking* task:
  H4. Input technique has no effect on tracking error.

Results

All data were analyzed using a repeated measures ANOVA. Since only the *Tracking Error* measure provides data for the two task conditions, we only report on the main effect and interactions for this measure. All other measures are specific to the *tracking + reacquisition* task condition.

Tracking Error

We found a significant main effect for technique on *Tracking Error* ($F_{1,8}$ = 29.2, p = .001). An overall means comparison shows it was smaller with tangible (M_{tangible} = 7.0%) than with touch (M_{touch} = 8.3%). The interaction between technique and task is also significant ($F_{1,8}$ = 22.82, p = .001).

For the pairwise comparison the effect is only significant under the tracking + reacquisition task ($F_{1,8}$ = 31.8, $p < .001$), which supports our hypothesis H1. The averages are plotted in Figure 6 left. When comparing the two techniques under the tracking task, the effect is not significant but shows a trend ($F_{1,8}$ = 3.5, p = .098), which weakly supports our hypothesis H4. All the following analyses are reported for the condition *tracking + reacquisition* only (see Figure 6).

Reacquisition Time

Analysis of variance showed a significant effect for technique on *Reacquisition Time* ($F_{1,8}$ = 14.6, p = .005). Means were lower for tangible control (M_{tangible} = 0.43s, M_{touch} = 0.65s), supporting our hypothesis H2.

Glance Rate

The analysis for *Glance Rate* also showed a significant effect for technique ($F_{1,8}$ = 34.2, $p < 0.001$). Overall means were much lower for tangible (M_{tangible} = 17%) than for touch (M_{touch} = 77%), supporting our hypothesis H3.

Tap Reaction Time

We found no effect on *Tap Reaction Time* ($F_{1,8}$ = 2.5, p = .154) for technique.

Misacquisitions

The analysis of variance for the number of misacquisitions per tap stimulus also showed a significant effect for technique on *Misacquisitions* ($F_{1,8}$ = 25.2, p = .001). Overall means were much lower for tangible (M_{tangible} = 0.7%) than for touch (M_{touch} = 18%).

Strategies

Subjects used 3 types of strategy for managing their attention:

- 7 subjects looked at the tablet at almost every tap / reacquisition under the touch condition (average glance rate of 88%) and almost never looked with the tangible (1.6%),
- 3 subjects tried not to look at the tablet under both techniques (32% for touch and 0.72% for tangible),
- 2 subjects consistently looked at the tablet under both techniques (103% for touch and 95% for tangible).

Most subjects who switched their attention to the tablet at each reacquisition did so while acquiring the tap area. During the touch and tracking + reacquisition condition, two subjects held the iPad in front of them for a few seconds then renounced, and one subject did so during a whole 90s trial.

In the tangible condition, two subjects reported using their whole hand to find the slider's thumb. Some subjects reported using a strategy consisting in using the edge of the iPad as a frame of reference [15], especially for the touch condition.

User Feedback

When asked about their preference, 10 subjects replied they preferred the tangible slider and 2 subjects reported having no preference. Subjects' comments and answers to our questionnaire were consistent with our objective measures.

Two subjects commented that the iPad was too heavy to hold for such a long period of time (despite the breaks). 7 subjects commented negatively on the feeling provided by the touch screen while operating the slider (especially after extensive use) and/or commented positively on the feeling provided by the tangible slider: "the screen was a bit sticky", "after doing the task for a while I felt that the surface of the iPad was too sticky in a way", "at one point my finger was getting sweaty and it was not that easy to move the slider"; "no (less) friction with the tangible slider.", "the slider was more slippery", "less friction, faster to slide", "sliding felt a little easier than touch input because it was 'on rails' ".

Discussion

Our findings strongly suggest that using a tangible rather than a virtual slider on a touch device facilitates interaction with a vertical display that requires visual attention. The tangible slider was faster to reacquire (about 2/3 the time needed for a touch slider), which yielded a significantly smaller tracking error in the dual-task condition. This is despite the fact that the active area of the touch slider spanned the whole height of the slider and thus was larger than the physical thumb. At the same time, subjects could have used their hand like an area cursor to first find the physical thumb, then switch to a precise grip based on the tactile information they got.

Most importantly, users looked much less often at the tablet when they were using the physical slider (17% of the time versus 77%). Note that no critical event could be missed if subjects briefly switched their attention down, and they could easily catch up with the tracking task as they looked back at the target. Despite the relatively low cost of looking down, most subjects did so only when this was necessary to prevent frequent misacquisitions (the number of misacquisitions negatively correlate with the glance rate, $R = -0.708$, $p = .005$).

Although most subjects reported feeling more effective when they could maintain their visual attention on the vertical display, it is likely that they kept looking at the display also because it was simply more natural and comfortable. One subject did report feeling uncomfortable switching back and forth between the two displays in the touch condition and mentioned neck discomfort at the end of the experiment.

User feedback further suggests that operating the tangible slider once acquired provides a better user experience compared to dragging on the iPad's touch surface. As for performance, we did not expect the tangible slider to be more effective to operate once acquired, but we did find a trend in the pure tracking task that deserves further examination.

Overall these findings provide another strong case for the use of tangibles. And yet, although our tangible underwent several iteration cycles and its design has been validated by our experiment, it still does not measure up to commercial physical controls. One subject felt the slider was "flimsy" and did not move smoothly enough and another felt its resistance was too low. Tracking errors also occurred, mainly due to a misplacement of the tangible slider. This is because the virtual slider had to be at a fixed position for the purpose of the experiment, but in practice it would align itself to the tangible.

Despite providing useful findings, our controlled experiment has a number of limitations that we hope to address in future work: it only tests sliders (other potential controls are buttons, rotary knobs, etc.), does not capture the manipulation of multiple controls, uses a low-level tracking task instead of a real-world visual exploration task, and does not perfectly mimic interaction with an actual WSD environment (which includes locomotion). Furthermore, it focuses on acquisition and manipulation of controls and does not provide any information on how easy it is to lay them out on the tablet and map them to functions, as we illustrate in the next section.

SAMPLE APPLICATION

We built a prototype system to explore how a tangible remote controller can be used to interact with an actual application on a WSD (see Figure 1). We chose the information visualization system ivtk [11] because it contains a large number of GUI controls to perform visual exploration tasks (see Figure 7). Our system runs on a 5.5m x 1.8m WSD of 32 screens of 30" each, controlled by a 18-computer cluster [5].

The WSD server runs a modified version of ivtk that allows the external control of its GUI elements through TUIO [17]. Upon connection ivtk sends an interface description of the GUI controls for its current visualization as an XML stream to the tablet. Each GUI control is given a TUIO ID that is listed in the description and then used by the tablet to send update events to ivtk.

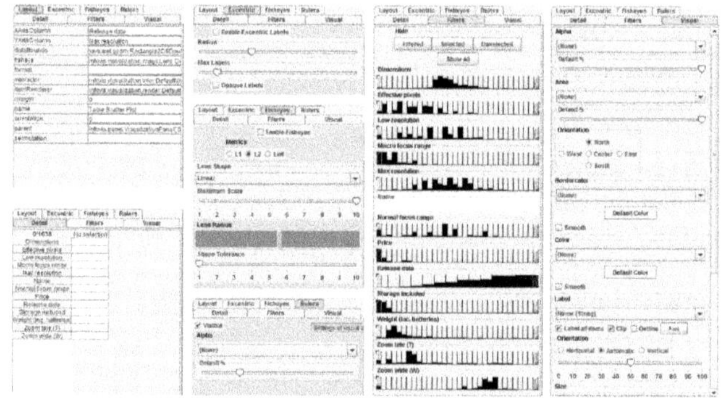

Figure 7. Widgets in ivtk for configuring and navigating in a scatterplot.

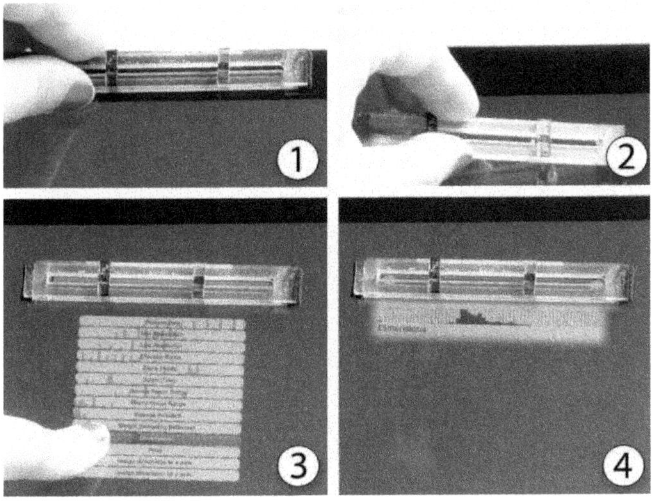

Figure 8. Mapping a tangible range slider to a dynamic query axis.

Adding and Mapping Tangible Controls

In this section we focus on end-users who are experts and already know the application's functionalities. When such a user starts the system, the WSD shows an overview of the dataset and the tablet screen is initially empty.

To start exploring the data the user can take one of the tangible controls available (e.g., from a desk or from the edge of the tablet, see Figure 8-1) and stick it to the tablet's screen. A menu then pops up and shows which functions are available that are compatible with the control (see Figure 8-3). Our current prototype gives users access to any of the dataset dimensions necessary for visual variable mapping and dynamic queries [1]. A larger number of functions would require the use of hierarchical menus. Once assigned, the control displays its function and possibly additional visual information through the display (Figure 8-4).

The user can then operate the physical control or add new ones. Each new control only shows those functions that are not already mapped to a control. In a multi-user setting, the TUIO client keeps track of controls that are already mapped and notifies all connected tablets about changes.

Remapping Existing Controls

Each physical control can be reassigned to another function by pulling the mapping menu with a swipe gesture. This support for dynamic remapping of tangible controls allows users to make only those functions available that are of immediate interest to them for the task at hand. For example, users searching in a multidimensional dataset typically start with the most discriminant attributes (e.g., price and location when searching for a house), then progressively refine their search with secondary attributes [10]. A dynamic query control can therefore be mapped to a new attribute once the user is fully satisfied with the settings for the current attribute.

Such a remapping mechanism lies somewhere between fully temporal multiplexing mechanisms where a single control is used to access many functions and fully spatial multiplexing schemes where each function has a physical counterpart [12]. Although full spatial multiplexing is often the most effective (e.g., mixing consoles), it can require an amount of space that is unrealistic for mobile usage.

In some cases, a specific configuration will be used intensively over a period of time. In the house search scenario, for example, the user might end up with too many or too few results that depend on attributes for which she has no clear preference (e.g., less rooms vs. smaller garden vs. no parking lot). In that case, the user might need to go back-and-forth between these attributes to filter them and observe how this affects the results. Given the findings from our user study, we expect tangible controls to facilitate this type of task.

Building Custom Control Boards

Because controls can be freely laid out on the tablet surface, users can experiment with different spatial layouts and chose the ones that are the most meaningful to them. Although applications already exist that let users customize the layout of toolbars, they require specific interaction techniques and mode switches that are arguably not as natural to end users as simply moving physical controls around.

For example, on Figure 1, the topmost and leftmost sliders are used to change the attributes of the X and Y axes of a scatterplot, and are laid out in a way that maximizes the degree of compatibility between actions and visual responses [4]. Tangible controls can also be grouped by function to leverage spatial memory or to facilitate their concurrent control.

Support for Locomotion

Finally, our controller is wireless and portable, and can therefore be operated from any location in the room, depending on users' needs and on what they deem the most comfortable. This includes sitting on a chair and resting the controller on their lap or on a table, although rich visualizations on ultra high-resolution WSDs typically encourage users to move forward to see more details [5].

In addition to "locomotion-based zoom and pan", our remote controller is compatible with location-aware interaction techniques [33] and can be sequentially combined with a number of surface interaction techniques. For example, a user operating tangible controls on a tabletop [34] might need to perform selections on a touch-sensitive wall while keeping access to some of the parameters she was controlling. With our system she could move some of the tangibles on the tablet and carry the tablet with her as she walks to the wall.

Future Extensions of this Prototype

Our information visualization control system is an initial prototype that has been developed for exploration purposes and to illustrate the feasibility of the approach. We plan to add extensive support for ivtk functionalities and support non-expert use by adding two mapping modes: one that shows the most important functions on the iPad as virtual widgets on top of which can be added tangible controls, and one where the complete list of functions is displayed in a dedicated scrollable area of the tablet. We also plan to add support for object selection and search, two other fundamental task in visual exploration, by allowing users to use any free area on the tablet for 2-D pointing and by building a tangible mini-keyboard.

CONCLUSION AND FUTURE WORK

Tangible remote controllers have unique properties that make them well-suited to visual exploration tasks on high-resolution WSDs. With respect to our requirement R1, they demand little visual attention, especially compared with touch-only solutions. Our user experiment confirms that, at least for sliders and for low-level tracking tasks, tangible controls are easier to operate when users' attention is focused on a vertical display.

With respect to our other requirements: R2) tangible remote controllers require no external visual feedback and therefore preserve information that is of immediate interest to users; R3) they support user locomotion; R4) tangible controls can come in different flavors, although most of them are especially suited to 1-D tasks like dynamic queries. Two other key tasks are object selection (through 2-D pointing) and search (through text input) and we plan to support them in the future.

Finally, R5) our tangible controls are modeled after GUI widgets and are generic. They make it possible to deport to the tablet GUI widgets from existing applications, which can facilitate porting and user knowledge transfer. Tangible remote controllers can also be customized by end-users, who can choose the controls that are relevant to their task and lay them out in a way that is meaningful to them.

We already mentioned some avenues for future work. First of all, our experiment provided us with useful findings but more studies must be conducted to generalize and refine our results. Also, our information visualization control system is currently only a prototype for illustrating the approach. We are currently improving it in order to conduct observational studies on end users, including in collaborative settings.

REFERENCES

1. Ahlberg, C., Williamson, C., and Shneiderman, B. Dynamic queries for information exploration: an implementation and evaluation. In *Proc. of CHI'92*.
2. Balali Moghaddam, A., Svendsen, J., Tory, M., and Branzan Albu, A. Integrating touch and near touch interactions for information visualizations. In *Proc. of CHI EA '11*.
3. Ball, R., and North, C. The effects of peripheral vision and physical navigation on large scale visualization. In *Proceedings of graphics interface 2008*, Canadian Information Processing Society, 9–16.
4. Beaudouin-Lafon, M. Instrumental interaction: an interaction model for designing post-wimp user interfaces. In *Proc. of CHI'00*.
5. Beaudouin-Lafon, M. Lessons learned from the wild room, a multisurface interactive environment. In *Proc. of IHM '11*.
6. Bezerianos, A., and Balakrishnan, R. The vacuum: facilitating the manipulation of distant objects. In *Proc. of CHI'05*.
7. Boring, S., Baur, D., Butz, A., Gustafson, S., and Baudisch, P. Touch projector: mobile interaction through video. In *Proc. of CHI '10*.
8. Buxton, W., Hill, R., and Rowley, P. Issues and techniques in touch-sensitive tablet input. In *ACM SIGGRAPH Computer Graphics*.
9. Chipman, L. E., Bederson, B. B., and Golbeck, J. A. Slidebar: analysis of a linear input device. *Behav. Inf. Technol. 23* (2004).
10. Elmqvist, N., Dragicevic, P., and Fekete, J.-D. Rolling the dice: Multidimensional visual exploration using scatterplot matrix navigation. *IEEE TVCG 14*, 6 (2008), 1141–1148.
11. Fekete, J.-D. The InfoVis Toolkit. In *Proc. of InfoVis'04*.
12. Fitzmaurice, G. W., and Buxton, W. An empirical evaluation of graspable user interfaces: towards specialized, space-multiplexed input. In *Proc. of CHI'97*.
13. Fitzmaurice, G. W., Ishii, H., and Buxton, W. A. S. Bricks: laying the foundations for graspable user interfaces. In *Proc. of CHI'95*.
14. Greenberg, S., and Fitchett, C. Phidgets: Easy development of physical interfaces through physical widgets. In *Proc. of UIST '01*.
15. Hinckley, K., Pausch, R., and Proffitt, D. Attention and visual feedback: the bimanual frame of reference. In *Proc. of the 1997 symposium on Interactive 3D graphics*, I3D '97.
16. Johanson, B., Fox, A., and Winograd, T. The interactive workspaces project: Experiences with ubiquitous computing rooms. *IEEE Pervasive Computing 1* (2002), 67–74.
17. Kaltenbrunner, M., Bovermann, T., Bencina, R., and Costanza, E. Tuio: A protocol for table-top tangible user interfaces. In *Proc. of GW'05*.
18. Khan, A., Fitzmaurice, G., Almeida, D., Burtnyk, N., and Kurtenbach, G. A remote control interface for large displays. In *Proc. of UIST '04*.
19. Kratz, S., Westermann, T., Rohs, M., and Essl, G. Capwidgets: Tangible widgets versus multi-touch controls on mobile devices. In *Proc. of CHI'11EA*.
20. Kurtenbach, G., Fitzmaurice, G., Baudel, T., and Buxton, B. The design of a gui paradigm based on tablets, two-hands, and transparency. In *Proc. of CHI '97*.
21. Leitner, J., and Haller, M. Geckos: combining magnets and pressure images to enable new tangible-object design and interaction. In *Proc. of CHI '11*.
22. Malik, S., Ranjan, A., and Balakrishnan, R. Interacting with large displays from a distance with vision-tracked multi-finger gestural input. In *Proc. of UIST '05*.
23. Myers, B. A., Stiel, H., and Gargiulo, R. Collaboration using multiple pdas connected to a pc. In *Proc. of CSCW '98*.
24. Nancel, M., Wagner, J., Pietriga, E., Chapuis, O., and Mackay, W. Mid-air pan-and-zoom on wall-sized displays. *Proc. of CHI'11* (2011).
25. Rekimoto, J. A multiple device approach for supporting whiteboard-based interactions. In *Proc. of CHI '98*.
26. Rekimoto, J. Smartskin: an infrastructure for freehand manipulation on interactive surfaces. In *Proc. of CHI'02*.
27. Sanneblad, J., and Holmquist, L. E. Ubiquitous graphics: combining hand-held and wall-size displays to interact with large images. In *Proc. of AVI '06*.
28. Smith, G. M., and schraefel, m. c. The radial scroll tool: scrolling support for stylus- or touch-based document navigation. In *Proc. of UIST '04*.
29. Streitz, N. A., Geissler, J., Holmer, T., Konomi, S., Müller-Tomfelde, C., Reischl, W., Rexroth, P., Seitz, P., and Steinmetz, R. i-land: an interactive landscape for creativity and innovation. In *Proc. of CHI '99*.
30. Tuddenham, P., Kirk, D., and Izadi, S. Graspables revisited: multi-touch vs. tangible input for tabletop displays in acquisition and manipulation tasks. In *Proc. of CHI'10*.
31. Ullmer, B., Ishii, H., and Jacob, R. Tangible query interfaces: Physically constrained tokens for manipulating database queries. In *Proc. of INTERACT'03*.
32. Villar, N., and Gellersen, H. A malleable control structure for softwired user interfaces. In *Proc. of TEI'07*.
33. Vogel, D., and Balakrishnan, R. Distant freehand pointing and clicking on very large, high resolution displays. In *Proc. of UIST '05*.
34. Weiss, M., Wagner, J., Jansen, Y., Jennings, R., Khoshabeh, R., Hollan, J. D., and Borchers, J. SLAP widgets: bridging the gap between virtual and physical controls on tabletops. In *Proc. of CHI'09*.
35. Yu, N., Tsai, S., Hsiao, I., Tsai, D., Lee, M., Chen, M., and Hung, Y. Clip-on gadgets: expanding multi-touch interaction area with unpowered tactile controls. In *Proc. of UIST'11*, 367–372.
36. Yu, N.-H., Chan, L.-W., Lau, S. Y., Tsai, S.-S., Hsiao, I.-C., Tsai, D.-J., Hsiao, F.-I., Cheng, L.-P., Chen, M., Huang, P., and Hung, Y.-P. TUIC: enabling tangible interaction on capacitive multi-touch displays. In *Proc. of CHI'11*.

Gesture Coder: A Tool for Programming Multi-Touch Gestures by Demonstration

Hao Lü*
Computer Science and Engineering
DUB Group, University of Washington
Seattle, WA 98195
hlv@cs.washington.edu

Yang Li
Google Research
1600 Amphitheatre Parkway
Mountain View, CA 94043
yangli@acm.org

ABSTRACT
Multi-touch gestures have become popular on a wide range of touchscreen devices, but the programming of these gestures remains an art. It is time-consuming and error-prone for a developer to handle the complicated touch state transitions that result from multiple fingers and their simultaneous movements. In this paper, we present Gesture Coder, which by learning from a few examples given by the developer automatically generates code that recognizes multi-touch gestures, tracks their state changes and invokes corresponding application actions. Developers can easily test the generated code in Gesture Coder, refine it by adding more examples and, once they are satisfied with its performance, integrate the code into their applications. We evaluated our learning algorithm exhaustively with various conditions over a large set of noisy data. Our results show that it is sufficient for rapid prototyping and can be improved with higher quality and more training data. We also evaluated Gesture Coder's usability through a within-subject study in which we asked participants to implement a set of multi-touch interactions with and without Gesture Coder. The results show overwhelmingly that Gesture Coder significantly lowers the threshold of programming multi-touch gestures.

Author Keywords
Multi-touch gestures, programming by demonstration, state machines, decision trees, Eclipse plug-in.

ACM Classification Keywords
H.5.2 [User Interfaces]: Input devices and strategies, Prototyping. I.5.2 [Design Methodology]: Classifier design and evaluation.

INTRODUCTION
An increasing number of modern devices are equipped with multi-touch capability—from small consumer gadgets, such as mp3 players [5], mobile phones [10] and tablets [18], to large interactive surfaces, such as tabletops [17] and wall-size displays [20]. Depending on the desired action, multi-touch gestures come at a great variety. For example, a user might pinch with two fingers to zoom or possibly swipe with two fingers to go forward or backward in a web browser [19]. As these examples imply, multi-touch gestures are intuitive, efficient, and often have physical metaphors. Two-finger pinch-to-zoom, for example, is analogous to the physical action of stretching a real world object using two fingers.

Clearly, multi-touch gestures are beginning to play an important role in modern user interfaces, but they are often difficult to implement. The challenge lies in the complicated touch state transitions from multiple fingers and their simultaneous movements.

To program a set of multi-touch gestures, a developer must track each finger's landing and movement change, which often results in spaghetti code involving a large number of states. For example, it is nontrivial to develop simple touch behaviors in a note-taking application that features one-finger move-to-draw, two-finger pinch-to-zoom, and two-finger move-to-pan gestures. To decide when to draw on the screen, a developer must track 1) if more fingers land after the first finger touches the screen, and 2) if the amount of movement of the first finger is significant. Once the second finger lands, the developer must analyze the relative

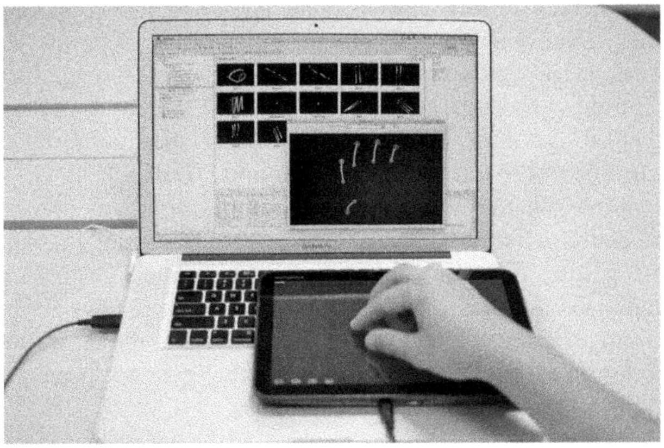

Figure 1: Gesture Coder lets the developer easily add multi-touch gestures to an application by demonstrating them on a target device. In this figure, the developer is demonstrating a five-finger-pinch gesture on a tablet device connected to the Gesture Coder environment.

* This work was done while the author was an intern at Google Research.

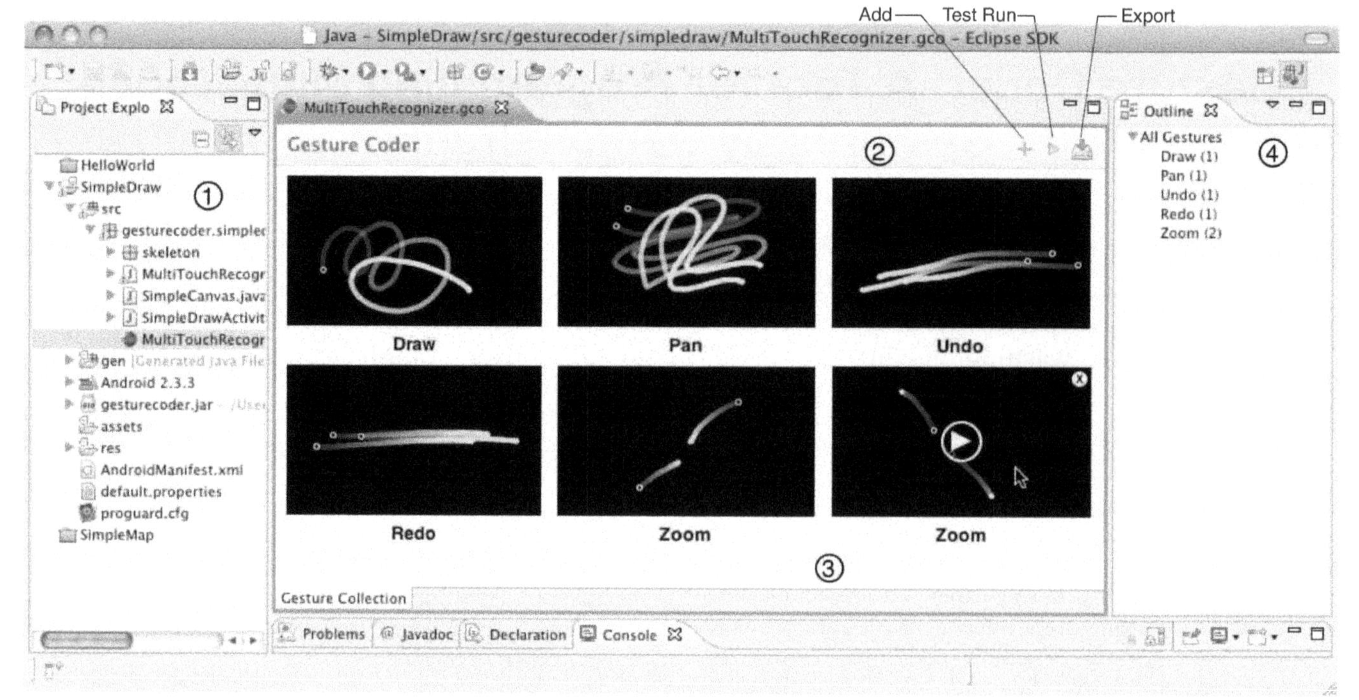

Figure 2: The Gesture Coder interface includes (1) Eclipse's Project Explorer through which the developer can add a Gesture Coder file to the project; (2) the Gesture Coder toolbar, which contains the buttons for adding gesture examples, testing the learned recognizer, and exporting source code; (3) the Gesture Collection view, a compendium of all the gesture examples; and (4) the Outline view, which categorizes the examples and shows the number available for each gesture.

movement between the two fingers to determine if the user is pinching or panning. Our study shows that many experienced developers cannot implement interaction of this kind in a short time.

Although substantial work has been done on gesture recognition [26,27], it is insufficient to address multi-touch gestures for two reasons. First, prior work was primarily concerned with classifying gestures based on their trajectories that are generated with a single finger or stylus. In contrast, multi-touch gestures are produced with multiple fingers. The number of fingers involved and the relative spatial relationship among them are often more important than their absolute movement trajectories. Second, prior work largely treats gestures as a shortcut for triggering a discrete, one-shot action [4]. In contrast, a multi-touch gesture is often employed for direct manipulation that requires incremental and continuous feedback [24]. For example, when a user pinches to zoom, the target size must be continuously updated as the fingers slide, not just when the gesture ends. In other words, multi-touch gestures can comprise a series of repetitive movements, each of which might trigger an action. This demands more frequent communication between the UI—the gesture processing component—and the application logic.

Several existing toolkits provide a set of built-in recognizers, each of which deals with a common multi-touch gesture, e.g., a pinch recognizer [28]. However, this approach is limited because developers must still deal with the low-level details of multi-touch input when creating custom gestures. Also, there is little support for handling the coexistence of multiple gestures. To do so, developers must combine multiple recognizers manually and resolve potential ambiguity. Gesture specification languages such as [12] attempt to keep developers from the programming details, but they require learning a new language and can be too complicated to be practical.

In this paper, we describe Gesture Coder, a tool for programming multi-touch gestures by demonstration. Instead of writing code or specifying the logic for handling multi-touch gestures, a developer can demonstrate these gestures on a multi-touch device, such as a tablet (see Figure 1). Given a few sample gestures from the developer, Gesture Coder automatically generates user-modifiable code that detects intended multi-touch gestures and provides callbacks for invoking application actions. Developers can easily test the generated code in Gesture Coder and refine it by adding more examples. Once developers are satisfied with the code's performance, they can easily integrate it into their application.

The paper offers the three major contributions.

- a set of interaction techniques and an architectural support for programming multi-touch gestures by demonstration that allow developers to easily demonstrate, test, and integrate the generated code into their application;
- a conceptualization of multi-touch gestures that captures intrinsic properties of these gestures and enables effective machine learning from one or a small number of gesture examples; and

- a set of methods for training multi-touch gesture recognizers from examples and generating user-modifiable code for invoking application-specific actions.

In the rest of the paper, we first provide a walkthrough of Gesture Coder using a running example. We then examine the intrinsic properties of multi-touch gestures from which we derived a conceptualization of this type of gestures. We next present the algorithms for learning from examples and generating the code to recognize multi-touch gestures. We then move to our evaluation of Gesture Coder's learning performance and usability. Finally, we discuss the scope of our work as well as related work and conclude the paper.

USING GESTURE CODER: AN EXAMPLE

To describe how developers can create multi-touch interactions using Gesture Coder, we use the context of a hypothetical, but typical, development project. The project description is based on our current implementation of Gesture Coder as an Eclipse plug-in compatible with the Android platform [1]. Developers can invoke Gesture Coder and leverage the generated code without leaving their Android project in Eclipse. Although Gesture Coder's current implementation is tied to a specific platform, its general approach is applicable to any programming environment and platform that supports multi-touch input.

Assume a developer, Ann, wants to implement multi-touch interactions as part of her drawing application for a tablet device. The application should allow the user to draw with one finger, pan the drawing canvas with two fingers moving together, and zoom with two fingers pinching. In addition, panning and zooming should be mutually exclusive; that is, only one can be active at a time. These are typical interactions for a multi-touch drawing application [7].

Demonstrating Gestures on a Multi-Touch Device

Ann first connects a multi-touch tablet to her laptop where she conducts the programming work via a USB cable. She then adds a Gesture Coder file to her project using Eclipse's Project Explorer, which opens the Gesture Coder environment (see Figure 2).

In the background, Gesture Coder launches a touch sampling application on the connected device remotely and establishes a socket connection with it. The touch sampling application, running on the tablet device, will capture touch events and send them to Gesture Coder.

To add an example of multi-touch gestures, Ann clicks on the Add button in the Gesture Coder toolbar (see Figure 2.2). This brings up the Demonstration window, which visualizes multi-touch events that the developer produces on the tablet in real time and that appear as gradient-yellow traces, similar to each example in the Gesture Collection view (see Figure 2.3). The traces serve to verify if the gesture has been performed correctly. The developer can then name the gesture example and add it to the collection

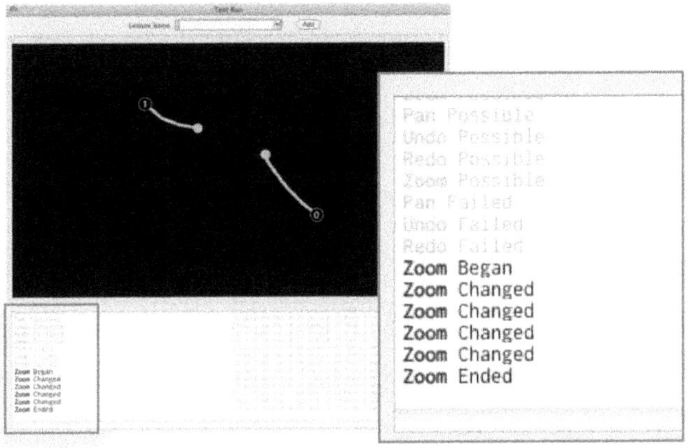

Figure 3: Gesture Coder's Test window with a magnified view of the Console output.

of examples, which are portrayed as thumbnails. Hovering over the thumbnail brings up the Play and Delete buttons. When the developer clicks on the Play button, Gesture Coder animates the trace in real time, essentially providing a playback of the captured example. In our hypothetical project, Ann adds examples of five gesture types: Draw, Pan, Zoom, Undo, and Redo.

Testing the Generated Recognizer Anytime

After adding a few examples, Ann wants to find out if Gesture Coder can detect these gestures correctly. She begins this process by clicking on the Test Run button in the Gesture Coder toolbar; this brings up the Test window (see Figure 3). Similar to demonstrating an example, the Test window visualizes simultaneous finger movements as Ann performs a multi-touch gesture on the connected tablet.

As Ann tries different gestures, the Test window displays recognition results in real time in its Console, including the gesture type, its state, and the probability distribution of all the target gesture types. Ann can then verify if Gesture Coder has correctly recognized her gesture.

If Ann finds that Gesture Coder has incorrectly recognized the gesture that she just performed, she can correct the error without leaving the Test window by simply typing the name of the intended gesture. This action generates a new example for learning. She can then keep testing the revised recognition.

Integrating Generated Code into Developers' Project

Once Ann is satisfied with the recognition results, she clicks on the Export button from the Gesture Coder toolbar. This exports the recognizer as a Java class in Ann's drawing application project.

To use the generated class MultiTouchRecognizer (see Figure 4), Ann first instantiates a recognizer object from it and lets recognizer handle all the low-level touch events received by the multitouchUI, a View object in Android. The recognizer class takes low-level touch events and invokes

```
// Instantiate the recognizer class generated by Gesture Coder.
recognizer = new MultiTouchRecognizer(multitouchUI);

// Add app-specific actions in response to each gesture stage.
recognizer.addGesturePinchListener(
  new GestureSimpleListener () {
    @Override
    public void onBegan (GestureEvent event) {
      // Init.
    }
    @Override
    public void onChanged (GestureEvent event) {
      // Zoom.
    }
```

Figure 4. A code snippet for using the generated recognizer.

an appropriate callback. It encapsulates the details of recognizing and tracking the state transition of each gesture.

Similar to Apple iOS's touch framework, the lifecycle of a gesture in Gesture Coder can involve six possible stages: Possible, Failed, Began, Changed, Cancelled, and Ended. A developer can add a callback for each gesture stage that will be invoked when the stage becomes active.

Every gesture starts as Possible when the user input starts, that is, when the first finger lands. A gesture is Failed when it can no longer be a possible match with the user input. A gesture is Began when it becomes recognized and Changed whenever there is a new touch event while the gesture remains recognized. A recognized gesture is Cancelled when it no longer matches the user input or Finished when the user has finished the input.

MULTI-TOUCH GESTURES

Before diving into the details of how the underlying system works, we first discuss multi-touch gestures that we intended to address. The research community and industry have used "touch gesture" broadly to refer to various interaction behaviors on the touch screen or surface of a touch-sensitive device. Overall, touch gestures tend to fall into one of the following two categories.

A large body of work was concerned with gestures that have a predefined trajectory or shape, e.g., recognizing handwriting symbols for text entry or gesture shortcuts for invoking commands [4,26], or detecting the crossing over a series of targets to trigger a specific action [14,27]. These gestures are often produced with a single finger or the stylus. The interaction behaviors associated with this type of gesture are one-shot—an action is triggered only when the gesture is finished.

The second category of gestures refers to those for direct manipulation of interfaces, e.g., tapping to activate, swiping to scroll, pinching to zoom, or twisting to rotate, which are more prevalent in commercial products. These gestures may involve more than one finger and typically do not concern the exact trajectory of the finger movement. For example, when panning a map with two fingers, the absolute trajectory of the fingers can be arbitrary. In addition, the interaction behaviors associated with these gestures often require frequent communication with application logic to provide incremental feedback, an important property of direct manipulation interfaces [24]. We focus on this type of gestures, especially those involving the use of multiple fingers.

Conceptualizing Multi-Touch Gestures

We here form a conceptualization of multi-touch gestures, which defines the scope of our work and serves as a basis for our learning algorithms. Apple introduced a definition of multi-touch gestures [9]: "comprising a chord and a motion associated with chord, wherein a chord comprises a predetermined number of hand parts in a predetermined configuration." This definition effectively captures many existing multi-touch gestures. However, it has two shortcomings.

First, the definition does not clarify what motion can be associated with the fingers (chord). By analyzing existing gestures, we found the absolute trajectories of the fingers often do not matter, but *the change of the spatial relationship* between the fingers usually does. For example, the two-finger pinching gesture is determined solely on the basis of whether the distance between the two fingers has changed. Although this definition does not exclude complicated trajectories to be associated with each finger, we have not seen such gestures. In fact, when multiple fingers must move in a coordinated fashion, the type of motion that a finger can perform is fundamentally bounded by a physical limitation—at some point, the motion is no longer humanly possible. In addition, because these gestures are used primarily for direct manipulation, they often consist of *a sequence of repetitive motions*, which generates incremental changes of the same nature.

The second shortcoming is that the definition leaves out gestures that have multiple finger configurations (or multiple chords) such as double-tap. Although only a few cases of multi-touch gestures have *multiple finger configurations*, we argue that these emerging gestures can be useful, since using different finger configurations can effectively indicate a mode switch, which is an important problem in modern interfaces. In addition, even a gesture defined for a single-finger configuration can incur multiple finger configurations during interaction. For example, imperfect finger coordination can cause the number of fingers sensed for a two-finger pinch gesture from beginning to end as 1, 2 and 1. The duration of the single-finger stages could be short.

As a result, we propose a new framing for multi-touch gestures based on the previous definition:

Definition 1. *A multi-touch gesture consists of a sequence of finger configuration changes, and each finger configuration might produce a series of repetitive motions. A motion is repetitive when any of its segments triggers the same type of action as its whole.*

In Gesture Coder, a *finger configuration* primarily refers to the number of fingers landed and their landing orders, and a *motion* refers to the continuous finger movement. In the next section, we discuss how this framing enables Gesture Coder to learn recognizers from a few examples.

ALGORITHMS

In this section, we discuss the underlying algorithms that enable Gesture Coder to generate a gesture recognizer from a set of examples. We first derive a generic computational model for detecting multi-touch gestures, and then discuss how to automatically create such a model for a specific set of gestures by learning from a collection of examples.

Deriving a Computational Model for Detecting Gestures

Based on our conceptualization, a multi-touch gesture involves a sequence of finger configuration where each configuration might have a continuous motion associated with the fingers. Each gesture can have a different finger configuration sequence and a different set of motions. Given a set of multi-touch gestures, their sequences are well represented by a state machine, which takes primitive touch events and triggers application actions associated with each state transition.

State Transitions Based on Finger Configurations

A finger configuration such as the number of fingers on the touchscreen determines what motion can be performed. As a result, we treat each configuration as a state and the landing or lifting of a finger triggers the transition from one state to another.

If we use the order of a finger touching the screen to represent the finger, we can represent each finger configuration as a set of numbers (the orders). We can then describe the possible transitions for a two-finger-tap gesture as two sequences: $\{\}\rightarrow^{+1}\{1\}\rightarrow^{+2}\{1,2\}\rightarrow^{-2}\{1\}\rightarrow^{-1}\{\}$ or $\{\}\rightarrow^{+1}\{1\}\rightarrow^{+2}\{1,2\}\rightarrow^{-1}\{2\}\rightarrow^{-2}\{\}$, depending on which finger first lifts up (see Figure 5a). In our representation, $+i$ and $-i$ denote the landing and lifting of the ith finger respectively. We assume without loss of generality that no two events will occur at exactly the same time. Otherwise, we can always treat them as two sequential events with the same timestamp.

Multiple gestures can be captured in the same state machine. For example, the state machine in Figure 5b captures both one-finger-tap and two-finger-tap gestures, denoted as T1 and T2 respectively. Each state keeps a set of possible gestures when the state is reached, e.g., both T1 and T2 are possible at the beginning.

State Transitions Based on Motions and Timeouts

So far, we have addressed only gestures that are not concerned with time and motions. However, many gestures contain motions, such as two-finger-pinch, while others, such as press-and-hold, rely on timing.

To represent timing and motion in gestures, we introduce two event types in addition to finger landing and lifting. The *Move* event occurs when the fingers start noticeable movement; the *Timeout* event takes place when the fingers have remained static over a specific period. For example, the two-finger-pinch gesture can have a transition sequence $\{\}\rightarrow^{+1}\{1\}\rightarrow^{+2}\{1,2\}\rightarrow^{move}\ldots\rightarrow^{move}\{1,2\}\rightarrow^{-2}\{1\}\rightarrow^{-1}\{\}$, and the press-and-hold gesture can have $\{\}\rightarrow^{+1}\{1\}\rightarrow^{timeout(1sec)}\{1\}\rightarrow^{-1}\{\}$. As the latter sequence indicates, the Timeout event takes a parameter to specify the duration. A Timeout event can also invalidate a gesture. For example, the double-tap gesture will not be recognized if the time interval between two taps is longer than a specified time window (see Figure 5c).

Figure 5d shows a larger example, a state machine that enumerates all the possible transitions of a set of six gesture types: one-finger tap, two-finger tap, one-finger press-and-hold, one-finger double-tap, two-finger move (to pan), and a two-finger pinch (to zoom). When two gestures have the same event sequence, such as, two-finger panning and zooming, they are indistinguishable if we rely only on their event sequence (e.g., the panning and zooming gestures in Figure 5d). In this case, we must look at the difference of motions under each finger configuration for these gestures. For example, at the two-finger state, we detect if the observed motion satisfies one of the two-finger gestures each time that a Move event occurs. If it does, a state transition takes place.

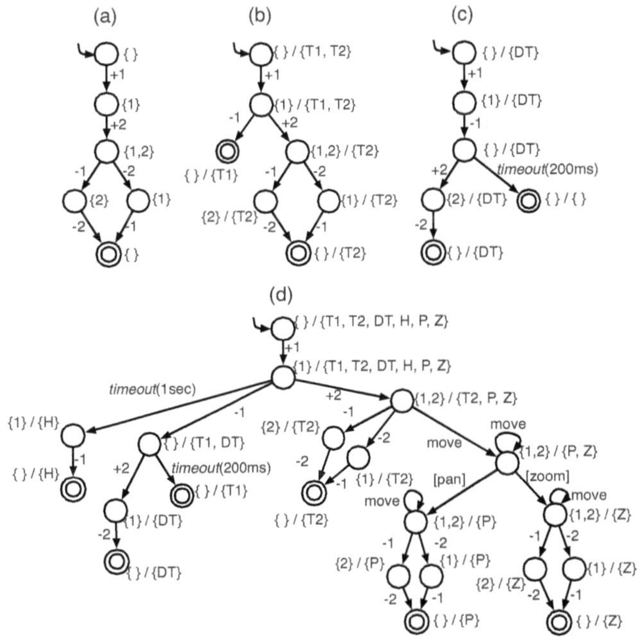

Figure 5: State machines that recognize (a) two-finger tap; (b) one-finger tap and two-finger tap; (c) double-tap; (d) T1: tap with one finger; T2: tap with two fingers; DT: double-tap; H: press-n-hold; P: two-finger move (to pan); and Z: two-finger pinch (to zoom).

In the figure, the state machine transitions to zooming if the distance between two fingers varies more than a certain threshold or to panning if the centroid of the two fingers travels over a certain distance. Because only one gesture can be active at a time, the one that is satisfied first is activated. Consequently, the result of motion detection can condition a state transition.

Consistency with Existing Implementation Practice

Our model is an abstraction of the current practice for implementing multi-touch gestures. After analyzing the implementation of several typical multi-touch interaction behaviors, such as pinching to zoom or moving to pan, we found developers tend to use a large number of hierarchical, conditional clauses (e.g., the If-Then-Else statement) to track these states and trigger transitions.

It is time-consuming and error-prone to implement such a model manually—an assertion that we confirmed in our user study. When we asked highly experienced programmers to implement multi-touch interactions, many could not capture these behaviors in the required time (45 minutes in our study). These results argue strongly for the need for a tool like Gesture Coder, which automatically learns such a model from gesture examples.

Automatically Learning the Model from Examples

Our learning algorithm consists of two stages: 1) learning a state machine that is based on the event sequences in the examples (e.g., a series of finger configuration changes) and 2) resolving the ambiguity in the learned state machine using motion differences. The second stage involves learning one or multiple decision trees. Before an example is used for learning, we preprocess the example by applying noise filtering, such as low-pass filtering.

Learning a Coarse State Machine from Event Sequences

This stage establishes the state machine's skeleton by identifying the transitions triggered by events such as finger configuration changes. A multi-touch gesture example consists of a sequence of discrete events. For example, Figure 6b denotes Zoom as a series of Move events after two fingers touch the screen, and the sequence finishes as two fingers lift. The nature of learning in this stage is to automatically create a state machine that can model event sequences of target gesture examples.

Our learning process begins by seeding the hypothetical state machine with a single node that serves as the starting state (see Figure 6d). It then iteratively applies the state machine to each training example and expands states and transitions if the machine fails to capture the example.

Assume we want to learn a state machine that can detect one-finger move (to draw), two-finger pinch (to zoom) and two-finger move (to pan) (see Figures 6a, b and c), which can be three basic interactions for a multi-touch drawing pad. When our learning algorithm examines an example, it

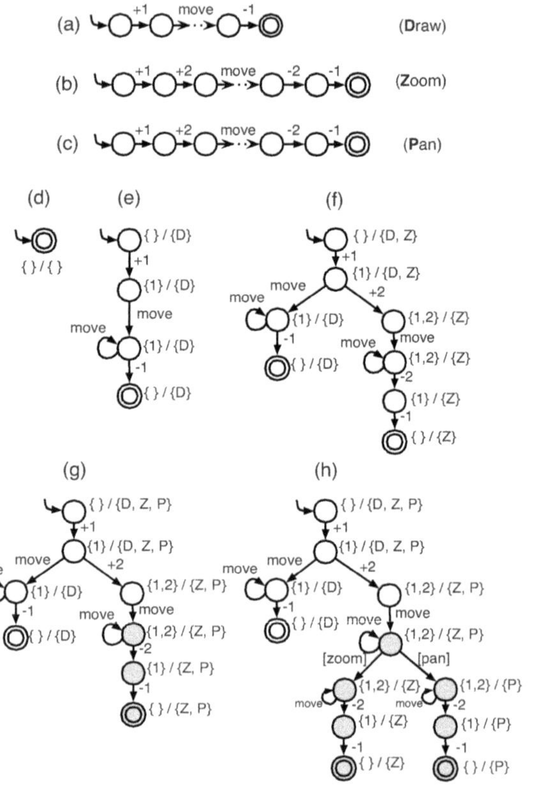

Figure 6: Learning a state machine from examples.

selects a path in the state machine that can maximize the alignment with the example's event sequence. If the state machine cannot fully absorb the sequence, it expands accordingly. For example, Draw's starting node (see Figure 6a) matches that of the state machine. However, the state machine must expand to accommodate the rest of Draw's sequence (see Figure 6e). When there are consecutively occurring events of the same type (e.g., a sequence of Move events), the learning algorithm abstracts them as a single loop transition.

Similarly, to capture Zoom in Figure 6b, our learning algorithm expands the state machine as shown in Figure 6f. However, the third gesture Pan (see Figure 6c) will not cause the state machine to further expand, because the event sequence of Pan is the same as that of Zoom and thus the state machine can fully absorb it. As a result, the state machine learned in this phase can distinguish Draw from Zoom and Pan, but cannot tell the difference between Zoom and Pan (Figure 6g).

Resolving Ambiguity by Learning Motion Decision Trees

Because event sequences alone might be insufficient for modeling all the target gestures, our learning algorithm automatically looks into motions associated with each finger configuration to seek motion differences between ambiguous gestures. In the previous example, we identified the need to resolve the ambiguity in Figure 6g by determining if the motion is Zoom or Pan; that is, we must generate the state machine illustrated in Figure 6h.

We here employ a binary decision tree [21], which takes finger motion and outputs a probability distribution over possible gestures. We chose this method partially because decision trees are easy to convert to user-modifiable code.

Having a large amount of data is critical to learning. Based on Definition 1, for a given gesture, we can consider each Move in the motion series as primitive motion with the same nature, e.g., each Move in the scaling motion is also a scaling. The motion's repetitive nature offers an effective way to extract many training samples from a single example. For example, for a motion that has a sequence of *N* segments, we acquire *N* samples instead of one. This makes our approach practical.

By analyzing existing multi-touch gestures, we extracted an initial feature set for our decision tree learner, including translation, rotation, and scaling. Richer motion can be built on top of these transformation primitives. Translation is defined as the change of the centroid of multiple fingers along both X and Y axes. Rotation is defined as the average angular change of each finger relative to the centroid. Scaling is defined as the average change of the distance between each finger and the centroid. These constitute the feature vector for each sample.

To train a decision tree, we use the standard C4.5 algorithm [21] from the Weka toolkit [25]. During the training, we bound the depth of the decision tree to avoid overfitting. A learned decision tree outputs a probabilistic distribution of possible gestures upon each Move event occurrence.

Invoking Callbacks

In a traditional state machine, an action is often triggered when a transition takes place. We use the same style to invoke callbacks.

As discussed earlier, there are six callbacks for each gesture, which correspond to six stages: Possible, Fail, Begin, Changed, Cancel, and End. When the arriving state has more than one available gesture, the state machine invokes these gestures' onPossible callbacks. For example, given a state {D, Z} in Figure 6, we invoke both gestures' onPossible. When a gesture's probability increases above a given threshold for the first time, its onBegan is invoked and its onChanged is invoked thereafter as long as its probability remains above the threshold.

If a gesture becomes unavailable in the arriving state, there are three situations. If the gesture's onBegan has never been invoked, the gesture's onFailed will be invoked. If the arriving state is an end state (see Figure 6), its onEnded will be invoked. Otherwise, onCancelled will be invoked.

Generating Code

Once we learn the state machine as well as the decision trees for evaluating conditions on Move transitions, it is straightforward to transform the learned model into executable code. We briefly discuss the process in the context of generating Java source code.

The first step is to encode the states into integers. Then the transitions are translated into a function that takes a state and a touch event and returns a new state. This function consists of a large Switch-Case statement. Each entry of the Switch-Case statement corresponds to one state in the state machine. The possible gestures under each state are represented as arrays, which update the probability distribution after each transition. Decision trees are translated into If-Then-Else statements.

IMPLEMENTATION

We implemented Gesture Coder as an Eclipse Plugin in Java, using SWT for its user interface and Android SDK [1] to communicate with Android-powered touch devices. We have also developed a separate Android application to send the touch events from the connected touch device to the development machine through a TCP socket.

EVALUATION

We evaluated both the performance and usability of Gesture Coder. We analyzed performance in terms of recognition accuracy and speed using a set of gestures collected from users in a public setting. We investigated usability through a laboratory study with eight professional programmers.

Evaluating Gesture Recognition Performance

To evaluate the Gesture Coder's recognition performance, we collected 720 gesture examples from 12 participants at a cafeteria. These participants were passers-by whom experimenters recruited on the scene, including three children who wanted to play with the tablet, three elders who have never used multi-touch devices, and two foreign tourists seeking a translator. The experimenters asked each participant to perform four times for each of a set of 15 target gestures that we selected from a set of existing multi-touch gestures (see Table 1), on a Motorola Xoom Multi-Touch Tablet (10'1" capacitive screen with 1280x800 resolution and 160dpi), running Android 3.0. During data collection, the tablet remained blank. The touch traces displayed on a laptop connected to the tablet through a USB cable.

The experimenter explained all the gestures to a participant before the actual tasks, and prompted the participants for each gesture. Because no application was associated with the gestures, for gestures such as 1-Finger-Scroll, the experimenters gave participants more specific instructions such as "scroll to the left" rather than just "scroll."

Our aim was to examine how the accuracy of our recognition algorithm changes with the number of available examples and target gestures to recognize. Hypothetically, the more available examples, the better the performance. The more target gestures, the more difficult it is for a recognizer to recognize them correctly. Our experimentation was based on the following procedure.

Along the spectrum of recognition complexity, we randomly selected k different target gestures from the set in Table 1 and repeated (for each k) 100 times to compute the average. Based on our data, k was varied from 2 to 15, where the 2-gesture case is the simplest and the 15-gesture one the hardest.

Given a k, we then conducted a 12-fold cross validation across users. To simulate real system use, each time we trained on the data of 1 participant (as the developer) and tested on the data of the remaining 11 participants (as the users). Notice that our cross validation is different from a typical leave-one-out approach, which would train on 11 participants and test on the remaining 1. Consequently, our cross validation uses a more challenging learning condition.

Given a selected developer, we varied from 1 to 4 the number of developer-supplied examples available for training, m. We then used a trained model to recognize all the gesture examples from the 11 users. Figure 7 shows the average accuracy with m from 1 to 4 and k from 2 to 15.

Overall, our algorithm was effective and achieved over 90% accuracy for simple cases where only two gestures were to be recognized. When there were 4 gestures—the number in many existing multi-touch applications—our algorithm achieved about 80% accuracy.

1. 1-Finger-Move	10. 2-Finger-Rotate (CW or CCW)
2. 1-Finger-Tap	11. 2-Finger-Swipe (up, down, left, or right)
3. 1-Finger-DoubleTap	12. 4-Finger-Vertical-Swipe (up or down)
4. 1-Finger-TripleTap	13. 4-Finger-Horizontal-Swipe (left or right)
5. 1-Finger-Hold	14. 5-Finger-Rotate (CW or CCW)
6. 1-Finger-Hold-And-Move	15. 5-Finger-Pinch (scale up or down)
7. 1-Finger-Swipe (up, down, left, or right)	
8. 2-Finger-Move	
9. 2-Finger-Pinch (scale up or down)	

Table 1: The 15 gestures used in evaluating Gesture Coder's recognition performance.

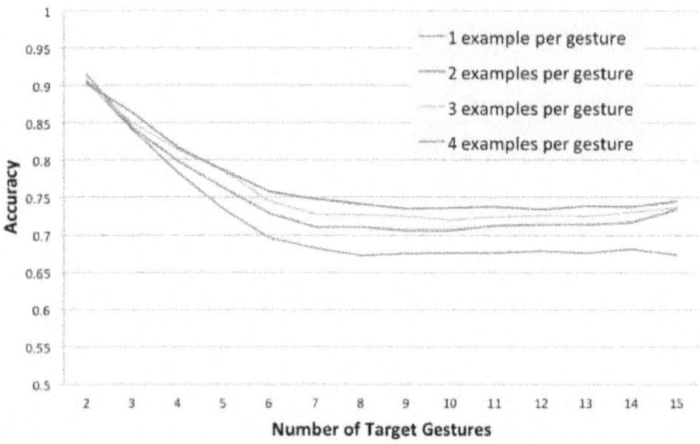

Figure 7: The accuarcy varies as the number of training sample and the complexity of recogniton task changes.

The results largely confirmed our hypotheses. When the number of target gestures to recognize increases, accuracy decreases (see Figure 7). However, performance soon became stable and did not drop further even with more target gestures involved.

The level of accuracy achieved is reasonable for rapid prototyping but seems unsatisfactory for production use. This experiment allowed us to quickly examine the learning algorithm at a large scale with 67,200 recognizers learned. However, it in fact underestimated the performance that Gesture Coder would achieve in real use. In actual product development, a professional developer, not random passers-by, would provide examples, which would yield much higher quality training data than what we acquired in the cafeteria. In addition, a developer will have the opportunity to refine recognition iteratively with demonstration and testing in Gesture Coder. In our cross validation, when the person's data used in training had a poor quality, it could seriously hurt the recognition rates. By playing back some of the collected traces, we found messy and incorrect samples from several participants.

Our evaluation demonstrated that Gesture Coder can learn effectively with a large corpus of data. We expect improved recognition rates with more training data, which is often available in an iterative development-testing process. Figure 7 already shows such a trend that recognition rates improved when more examples became available.

In terms of speed, under the most complex condition (15 gestures and 4 examples per gesture), the average training time was 28ms, and the average prediction time was 0.1ms. We obtained the performance data on a MacBook Pro with Quad-Core Intel Core-i7 2.0GHz CPU and 8GB RAM.

Laboratory Study

To evaluate the Gesture Coder's usefulness and usability, we compared it with a baseline condition in which developers implement multi-touch interactions based on touch events dispatched by the platform. We chose not to use an existing toolkit as a baseline condition for several reasons. Most existing toolkits provide built-in recognizers for a limited set of predefined gestures. A developer has to start from scratch and deal with raw touch input when the toolkit does not support a gesture. Existing toolkits are designed such that each predefined gesture has its own built-in recognizer. Thus, when multiple gestures are involved, the developer must manually combine the outcome of each individual recognizer, which can be nontrivial.

We conducted a laboratory study with 8 professional programmers (all males, aged from 20 to 50 with a mean age of 30). All the participants were familiar with the Java programming language, the Eclipse environment, and the Android platform. They had varied experience in programming touch interactions: two participants had multi-touch experiences, five had programmed only single-touch interactions; and one had never programmed touch interactions.

Study Setup

We asked each participant to implement a realistic application with and without Gesture Coder in Eclipse and we counterbalanced the order of the two conditions across participants. We grouped the participants according to task. Participants in the first group had to implement a Drawing application for tablets. Participants in the second group were assigned a Map navigation application for mobile phones. Our goal was to examine both conditions with two multi-touch applications that embody a set of typical multi-touch interaction behaviors in a feasible timeframe for a laboratory study.

The Drawing application requires five gesture behaviors: one-finger move to draw, two-finger move to pan the canvas, two-finger pinch to zoom, three-finger leftward swipe to undo, and rightward swipe to redo. The Map application requires five gesture behaviors: one-finger move to pan the map, one-finger double-tap to zoom in 2x, one-finger triple-tap to zoom out 2x, two-finger pinch to zoom the map continuously, and two-finger vertical move to tilt the viewing angle. We instructed participants not to worry about ideal solutions and corner cases, but to implement a solution that they considered "good enough" for a demonstration.

We implemented the skeleton code for each application as an Eclipse Android project, which includes all the application logic, such as rendering the map at a certain scale, except the part regarding detecting gestures and invoking application logic. The participants had to integrate their gesture recognition code with the skeleton code via exposed methods. These methods were designed in such a way that participants needed to pass only simple parameters such as finger locations.

We gave participants a tutorial on the tools that they could use in each condition and then asked them to do a warm-up task. After a participant became comfortable with the condition, we demonstrated the application to be implemented and clarified the gestures involved in the application and the methods exposed by the skeleton code. We then let the participants work on the task for 45 minutes as we observed their screen from a different monitor.

Results

All the participants finished their tasks using Gesture Coder within a mean of 20 minutes (std=6). However, none of the participants could complete the task within 45 minutes in the baseline condition (Gesture Coder is not available).

After the study, we asked participants to answer a questionnaire about Gesture Coder's usefulness and usability using a 5-point Likert scale (1: Strongly Disagree and 5: Strongly Agree). Participants overwhelmingly thought Gesture Coder was useful (seven Strongly Agreed) and easy to use (six Strongly Agreed). In contrast, all participants responded negatively to the baseline condition.

We observed that participants tended to implement the gestures incrementally in the baseline condition. For example, they first implemented a one-finger-move gesture and then tested it before moving to the next gesture. They had to constantly come back to modify the previously implemented gestures. In contrast, with Gesture Coder, participants tended to demonstrate all the gestures at once and then test the performance. Interestingly, however, when integrating the generated code with the skeleton code, they tended to handle one gesture at a time. Yet, participants never had to come back to modify previously implemented gesture behaviors. One participant even noted that Gesture Coder is "much more scalable." In the baseline condition, participants all did heavy debugging using console output that they injected in their code to verify gesture behaviors. In contrast, with Gesture Coder, participants relied primarily on its more efficient testing support. All the participants strongly agreed that the ability to test on the fly is useful.

Two participants were confused about how to demonstrate arbitrary movement. One commented, "It took me awhile to wrap my head around arbitrary gestures like single-finger panning." Such confusion was partially due to our insufficient explanation of Gesture Coder during the study. For this special case, explicit specification of a random motion could be more efficient than demonstration.

DISCUSSION AND FUTURE WORK

Assuming repetitive motions lets Gesture Coder effectively learn and detect the motion of many useful multi-touch gestures. However, training based on individual motion segment does not allow the capture of a motion's global features, such as its shape trajectory of a motion. However, as discussed earlier, global geometrics such as shape trajectories are less important for multi-touch gestures.

There are several opportunities for improving Gesture Coder. In addition to training with higher quality and more training data, we could improve recognition performance by tuning parameters such as motion segment length and the threshold for the low-pass filtering of touch motion. Because our framework is extensible, we could easily add more features such as the contour of finger touches to our model or plug other motion classifiers into the framework. Finally, developers can fine-tune recognition to handle more complicated situations by modifying the generated Java code or adding constraints such as the absolute location of a gesture on the screen.

RELATED WORK

Multi-touch gestures are employed in various applications on a range of devices, e.g., [10,17,18]. To support the implementation of these gestures, Apple iOS's SDK provides a gesture framework [28] that supports six predefined gestures with one recognizer for each gesture. Similar frameworks can be found on other platforms, e.g., [1]. However, even with these frameworks, developers still need to deal with low-level touch events when they want to implement custom gestures or combine multiple recognizers.

Higher-level specification languages can hide low-level programming details in creating multi-touch gestures [12,13,23], but these languages can lead to complex specifications and are hard to scale when the number and complexity of gestures grow. In addition, learning a new language is a nontrivial burden on developers. In contrast, with Gesture Coder, developers can create multi-touch gestures without programming or specification; they need only demonstrate a few gesture examples.

Although several previous tools (e.g., [6,16,22]) allow users to create gesture recognizers using examples, none of them deals with the types of multi-touch gestures that we focus on. In addition, Gesture Coder provides unique support for integrating the generated recognizer with application code, which is not available in these previous tools.

Gesture Coder employs a programming by demonstration (PBD) approach, which has been successfully applied in prior work, e.g., [8,11,15]. Gesture Coder adds to the family of PBD systems by addressing a new problem. It contributes a set of methods for inferring target touch interactions from examples and for generating developer-modifiable code that can be easily integrated with the developer's application.

Extensive work has been done on recognizing gestures from the trajectories generated with a single finger or stylus [2,3,26,27]. However, prior work is insufficient to address multi-touch gestures, which employ features such as the number of fingers involved and the relative spatial relationship among them, instead of absolute movement trajectories. In addition, prior work mostly treats gestures as a shortcut for triggering a discrete, one-shot action [4]. In contrast, multi-touch gestures are often employed for direct manipulation that requires constant communication with application logic [24].

CONCLUSION

We presented Gesture Coder, a tool for programming multi-touch gestures by demonstration. It automatically generates developer-modifiable code by learning from examples demonstrated by the developer. The code can be easily integrated into an application.

REFERENCES

1. Android. http://www.android.com.
2. Anthony, L. and Wobbrock, J.O. A lightweight multistroke recognizer for user interface prototypes. *Proc. GI 2010*, 245-252.
3. Appert, C. and Bau, O. Scale detection for a priori gesture recognition. *Proc. CHI 2010*, 879-882.
4. Appert, C. and Zhai, S. Using strokes as command shortcuts. *Proc. CHI 2009*, 2289-2298.
5. Apple iPod Nano 6th Generation. http://www.apple.com/ipodnano/.
6. Ashbrook, D. and Starner, T. MAGIC: a motion gesture design tool. *Proc. CHI 2010*, 2159-2168.
7. Brushes. http://www.brushesapp.com/.
8. Cypher, A., ed. *Watch What I Do: Programming by Demonstration*. MIT Press, 1993.
9. Elias, J.G., Westerman, W.C., and Haggerty, M.M. Multi-Touch Gesture Dictionary. US Patent, 2007.
10. Google Nexus. http://www.google.com/nexus/.
11. Hartmann, B., Abdulla, L., Mittal, M., and Klemmer, S.R. Authoring sensor-based interactions by demonstration with direct manipulation and pattern recognition. *Proc. CHI 2007*, 145-154.
12. Hoste, L. Software engineering abstractions for the multi-touch revolution. *Proc. ICSE 2010*, 509-510.
13. Kin, K., Hartmann, B., DeRose, T., and Agrawala, M. Proton: Multitouch Gestures as Regular Expressions. *Proc. CHI 2012*.
14. Kurtenbach, G. and Buxton, W. User learning and performance with marking menus. *Proc. CHI 1994*, 258-264.
15. Lieberman, H., E. *Your Wish Is My Command: Programming by Example*. Morgan Kaufmann, 2001.
16. Long, Jr., A.C. Quill: a gesture design tool for pen-based user interfaces. Doctoral Dissertation, University of California, Berkeley, 2001.
17. Microsoft Surface. http://www.microsoft.com/surface/.
18. Motorola Xoom. http://developer.motorola.com/products/xoom/.
19. OS X Lion: About Multi-Touch gestures. http://support.apple.com/kb/HT4721.
20. Perceptive Pixel Multi-Touch Collaboration Wall. http://www.perceptivepixel.com.
21. Quinlan, J.R. *C4.5: programs for machine learning*. Morgan Kaufmann, 1993.
22. Rubine, D. Specifying gestures by example. *ACM SIGGRAPH Computer Graphics 25*, 4 (1991), 329-337.
23. Scholliers, C., Hoste, L., Signer, B., and De Meuter, W. Midas: a declarative multi-touch interaction framework. *Proc. TEI 2011*, 49-56.
24. Shneiderman, B. Direct manipulation: a step beyond programming languages. *Computer 16*, 8 (1983), 57-69.
25. Weka. http://www.cs.waikato.ac.nz/ml/weka/.
26. Wobbrock, J.O., Wilson, A.D., and Li, Y. Gestures without libraries, toolkits or training: a $1 recognizer for user interface prototypes. *Proc. UIST 2007*, 159-168.
27. Zhai, S. and Kristensson, P.-O. Shorthand writing on stylus keyboard. *Proc. CHI 2003*, 97-104.
28. iOS developer library. http://developer.apple.com/library/ios/.

Proton: Multitouch Gestures as Regular Expressions

Kenrick Kin[1,2] **Björn Hartmann**[1] **Tony DeRose**[2] **Maneesh Agrawala**[1]
[1]University of California, Berkeley [2]Pixar Animation Studios

ABSTRACT
Current multitouch frameworks require application developers to write recognition code for custom gestures; this code is split across multiple event-handling callbacks. As the number of custom gestures grows it becomes increasingly difficult to 1) know if new gestures will conflict with existing gestures, and 2) know how to extend existing code to reliably recognize the complete gesture set. Proton is a novel framework that addresses both of these problems. Using Proton, the application developer declaratively specifies each gesture as a regular expression over a stream of touch events. Proton statically analyzes the set of gestures to report conflicts, and it automatically creates gesture recognizers for the entire set. To simplify the creation of complex multitouch gestures, Proton introduces *gesture tablature*, a graphical notation that concisely describes the sequencing of multiple interleaved touch actions over time. Proton contributes a graphical editor for authoring tablatures and automatically compiles tablatures into regular expressions. We present the architecture and implementation of Proton, along with three proof-of-concept applications. These applications demonstrate the expressiveness of the framework and show how Proton simplifies gesture definition and conflict resolution.

Author Keywords
Multitouch; UI framework; Regular expressions; Conflict detection; Gesture tablature editor

ACM Classification Keywords
D.2.2 Software Engineering: Design Tools and Techniques; H.5.2 Information Interfaces & Presentation: User Interfaces

INTRODUCTION
Multitouch application developers frequently design and implement custom gestures from scratch. Like mouse-based GUI frameworks, current multitouch frameworks generate low-level touch events (e.g., *touch-down, touch-move, touch-up*) and deliver them to widgets or objects in the scene. A *multitouch gesture* is a sequence of low-level events on scene objects such as *touch1-down-on-object1, touch1-move, touch2-down-on-object2, ...* Unlike mouse gestures which track the state of a single point of interaction, multitouch gestures often track many points of contact in parallel as they each appear, move and disappear. Writing robust recognition code for sets of multitouch gestures is challenging for two main reasons:

Gesture Regular Expression

$$D_1^c M_1^c{*}\left(D_2^a (M_1^c | M_2^a){*}U_2^a M_1^c{*} \,\middle|\, D_2^a (M_1^c|M_2^a){*}D_3^a(M_1^c|M_2^a|M_3^a){*} \ldots\right.$$
$$\left.\left(U_3^a(M_1^c|M_2^a){*}U_2^a M_1^c{*} \,\middle|\, U_2^a(M_1^c|M_3^a){*}U_3^a M_1^c{*}\right)\right){*}U_1^c$$

panCamera() zoomCamera()

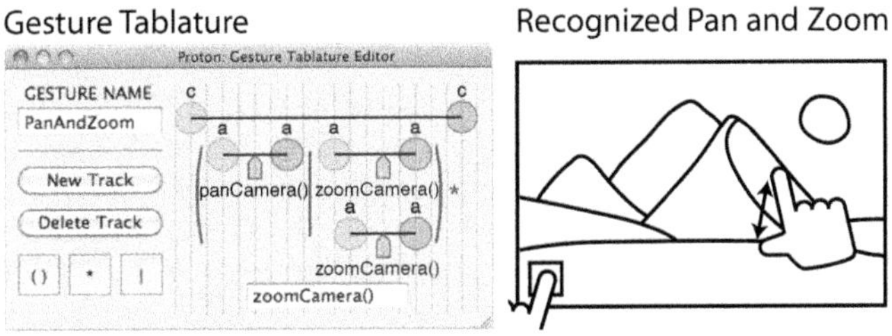

Figure 1. Proton represents a gesture as a regular expression describing a sequence of touch events. Using Proton's gesture tablature, developers can design a multitouch gesture graphically by arranging touch sequences on horizontal tracks. Proton converts the tablature into a regular expression. When Proton matches the expression with the touch event stream, it invokes callbacks associated with the expression.

1) Multitouch gesture recognition code is split across many locations in the source. Today, developers must write separate callbacks to handle each low-level touch event for each scene object. Implementing a gesture requires tracking the sequence of events that comprise the gesture across disjoint callbacks. Consider a gesture in which the user must simultaneously touch two scene objects to connect them as nodes in a graph. The developer must maintain the state of the gesture across callbacks for each object and communicate this state via messages or global variables. Such *stack ripping* [1] results in complicated and hard-to-read "callback soup." Breaking up gesture code makes it difficult to not only express a gesture, but also to understand and modify the gesture later.

2) Multiple gestures may be based on the same initiating sequence of events. Consider two gestures, one for rotating and one for scaling objects in a 2D scene. Both gestures require the first touch to fall on an object to select it, while the motion of a second touch indicates the transformation. At the level of touch events, the two sequences are identical and the developer must write disambiguation logic to resolve this conflict within the respective callbacks. Yet, such gesture conflicts may not even be apparent until a user performs one of the gestures at runtime and the application responds with an unintended operation. In large applications that support many gestures, identifying and managing such gesture conflicts can be extremely difficult.

These two sources of complexity – splitting gesture recognition code across callbacks and conflicts between similar gestures – make it especially difficult to maintain and extend multitouch applications.

To help alleviate these issues, we present *Proton*, a new multitouch framework that allows developers to declaratively specify the sequence of touch events that comprise an entire gesture using a single regular expression. Proton automatically manages the underlying state of the gesture; the developer writes one callback function that is invoked whenever the stream of input events matches the gesture's regular expression. To provide visual feedback over the course of a gesture, the developer can optionally define additional callbacks that are invoked whenever the input stream matches expression prefixes. Our approach significantly reduces splitting of the interaction code as developers do not have to manually manage state or write a callback for every touch event.

Declaratively specifying gestures as regular expressions also allows Proton to statically analyze the gesture expressions to identify the conflicts between them. Instead of having to extensively test for such conflicts at runtime, our static analyzer tells the developer exactly which sets of gestures conflict with one another at compile time. The developer can then choose to write the appropriate disambiguation logic or modify the gestures to avoid conflicts.

Complex regular expressions can be difficult to author, read, and maintain [5]. In regular expressions that recognize multitouch events, the interleaving of multiple, simultaneous touch events in a single event stream exacerbates this complexity. To help developers build gesture expressions, Proton offers *gesture tablature*, a graphical notation for multitouch gestures (Figure 1). The tablature uses horizontal tracks to describe touch sequences of individual fingers. Using Proton's tablature editor, developers can author a gesture by spatially arranging touch tracks and graphically indicating when to execute callbacks. Proton automatically compiles the gesture tablature into the corresponding regular expression.

Our implementation of Proton makes two simplifying assumptions that limit the types of gestures it supports. First, it does not consider touch trajectory in gesture declarations. We focus on gestures defined by the sequencing of multiple touch events and the objects hit by those touches. As in current multitouch frameworks, the developer may independently track the trajectory of a touch, but our system does not provide direct support. Second, Proton focuses on single users who perform one gesture at a time. However, each gesture can be complex, using multiple fingers and hands, and may include temporal breaks (e.g., double-taps). We discuss an extension to multi-user scenarios, but have not yet implemented it.

We demonstrate the expressivity of Proton with implementations of three proof-of-concept applications: a shape manipulation application, a sketching application and a unistroke text entry technique [43]. Using these examples, we show that Proton significantly reduces splitting of gesture recognition code and that it allows developers to quickly identify and resolve conflicts between gestures. Proton increases maintainability and extensibility of multitouch code by simplifying the process for adding new gestures to an existing application.

RELATED WORK

The regular expressions used by Proton are closely related to finite state machines: regular expressions describe regular languages; finite state machines accept such languages [39]. We briefly summarize prior research on modeling user input as state machines and formal languages. We then describe related work on multitouch event-handling, declarative specification of multitouch gestures and techniques for handling input ambiguity.

Modeling Input with State Machines & Formal Languages

Since Newman's pioneering work on Reaction Handler [30], researchers have modeled user interactions using formalisms such as state machines [2, 14, 15, 29], context-free grammars [6, 16, 17] and push-down automata [33]. These formalisms are used as specification tools, e.g., for human factors analysis [6]; to describe interaction contexts [18, 37]; and to synthesize working interface implementations [33]. A recurring theme in early work is to split user interface implementation into two parts: the *input language* (the set of possible user interface actions); and the *application semantics* for those actions. The input language is often defined using state machines or grammars; the semantics are defined in a procedural language.

Proton takes a conceptually similar approach: it uses regular expressions as the underlying formalism for declaratively specifying sequences of touch events that comprise a gesture. Callbacks to procedural code are associated with positions within the expression. Proton goes beyond the earlier formalisms by also providing a static analyzer to detect conflicts between gestures as well as a graphical notation to further simplify the creation of gestures.

Multitouch Event-Handling

With the recent rise of multitouch cellphones and tablet computers, hardware manufacturers have created a variety of interaction frameworks [3, 12, 28] to facilitate application development. These frameworks inherit the event-based callback [32] structure of mouse-based GUI frameworks. While commercial frameworks usually support a few common interactions natively (e.g., pinch-to-zoom), implementing a new gesture requires processing low-level touch events. Open-source multitouch frameworks similarly require developers to implement gestures via low-level event-handling code [8, 10, 13, 31, 41]. Lao et al. [23] presents a state-transition diagram for detecting multitouch gestures from touch events. This diagram serves as a recipe for detecting simple gestures, but the developer must still process the touch events. Many frameworks are written for specific hardware devices. Kammer et al. [19] describe the formal properties shared by many of these frameworks. Echtler and Klinker [9] propose a layered architecture to improve multitouch software interoperability; their design also retains the event callback pattern. However, none of these multitouch frameworks give developers a direct and succinct way to describe a new gesture.

Describing Gestures Declaratively

Researchers have used formal grammars to describe multitouch gestures. CoGesT [11] describes conversational hand gestures using feature vectors that are formally defined by a context-free grammar. Kammer et al. [20] present GeForMT, a formal abstraction of multitouch gestures also using a context-free grammar. Their grammars describe gestures at a high level and do not provide recognition capabilities. Gesture Coder [24] recognizes multitouch gestures via state machines, which are authored by demonstration. In contrast, Proton allows developers to author gestures symbolically using the equivalent regular expressions.

In multitouch frameworks such as GDL [21] and Midas [35] developers declaratively describe gestures using rule-based languages based on spatial and temporal attributes (e.g., number of touches used, the shape of the touch path, etc.). Because these rule-based frameworks are not based on an underlying formalism such as regular expressions, it is difficult to reason about gesture conflicts at compile time. The developer must rely on heavy runtime testing to find such conflicts. In contrast to all previous techniques, Proton provides static analysis to automatically detect conflicts at compile time.

Handling Input Ambiguity

Mankoff et al. [25, 26] present toolkit-level support for handling input ambiguities, which arise when there are multiple valid interpretations of a user's actions. Mediators apply resolution strategies to choose between the different interpretations either automatically or with user intervention. More recently Schwarz et al. [36] present a framework that tracks multiple interpretations of a user's input. The application's mediator picks the most probable interpretation based on a likelihood metric provided by the developer. Proton borrows this strategy of assigning scores to interpretations and applying the highest scoring interpretation. In addition, Proton statically analyzes the gesture set to detect when ambiguities, or conflicts, can occur between them. Such compile-time conflict detection can aid the developer in scoring the interpretations and in designing the gestures to reduce ambiguities.

A MOTIVATING EXAMPLE

We begin with a motivating example that demonstrates the complexity of implementing a custom gesture using Apple's iOS [3], which is structurally similar to many commercial multitouch frameworks. We later show how writing the same example in Proton is significantly simpler, making it easier to maintain and extend the interaction code.

As the user interacts with a multitouch surface, iOS continuously generates a stream of low-level touch events corresponding to *touch-down, touch-move* and *touch-up*. To define a new gesture the developer must implement one callback for each of these events, *touchesBegan()*, *touchesMoved()* and *touchesEnded()*, and register them with objects in the scene. For each touch event in the stream, iOS first applies hit-testing to compute the scene object under the touch point and then invokes that object's corresponding callback.

It is the developer's responsibility to track the state of the gesture across the different callbacks. Consider a two-touch rotation gesture where both touches must lie on the object with the pseudocode on the following column.

The gesture recognition code must ensure that the gesture begins with exactly two touches on the same object (lines 5-10), that rotation occurs when both touches are moving (lines 11-14) and that the gesture ends when both touches are lifted (lines 15-19). Counting touches and maintaining gesture state adds significant complexity to the recognition code, even for simple gestures. This state management complexity can make it especially difficult for new developers to decipher the recognition code.

```
iOS: rotation gesture
 1: shape.addRecognizer(new Rotation)
 2: class Rotation
 3: gestureState ← possible /*gesture state*/
 4: touchCount ← 0
 5: function touchesBegan()
 6: touchCount ← touchCount + 1
 7: if touchCount == 2 then
 8:    gestureState ← began
 9: else if touchCount > 2 then
10:    gestureState ← failed
11: function touchesMoved()
12: if touchCount == 2 and gestureState != failed then
13:    gestureState ← continue
14:    /*compute rotation*/
15: function touchesEnded()
16: touchCount ← touchCount − 1
17: if touchCount == 0 and gestureState != failed then
18:    gestureState ← ended
19:    /*perform rotation cleanup*/
```

Suppose a new developer decides to relax the rotation gesture, so that the second touch does not have to occur on the object. The developer must first deduce that the gesture recognition code must be re-registered to the canvas containing the object in order to receive all of the touch events, including those outside the object. Next the developer must modify the *touchesBegan()* function to check that the first touch hits the object, and set the gesture state to failed if it does not. While neither of these steps is difficult, the developer cannot make these changes without fully understanding how the different callback functions work together to recognize a single gesture. As the number of gestures grows, understanding how they all work together and managing all the possible gesture states becomes more and more difficult.

USING PROTON

Like iOS, Proton is an event-based framework. But, instead of writing callbacks for each low-level touch event, developers work at a higher level and declaratively define gestures as regular expressions comprised of sequences of touch events.

Representing Touch Events

A touch event contains three key pieces of information: the touch action (down, move, up), the touch ID (first, second, third, etc.) and the type of the object hit by the touch (shape, background, etc.). Proton represents each event as a symbol

$$E_{T_{ID}}^{O_{Type}}$$

where $E \in \{D, M, U\}$ is the touch action, T_{ID} is the touch ID that groups events belonging to the same touch, and O_{Type}

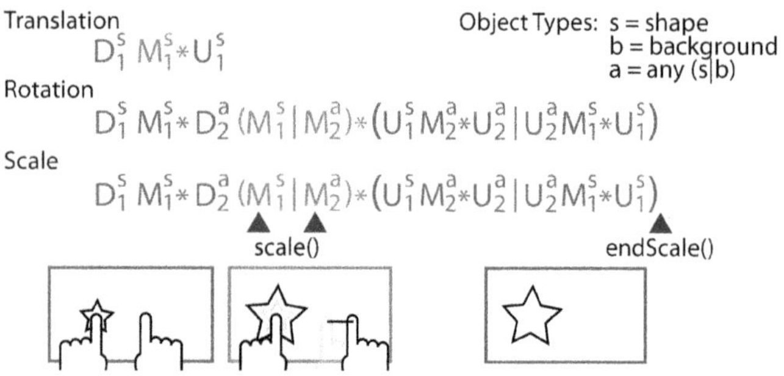

Figure 2. Regular expressions for translation, rotation and scale gestures. The thumbnails illustrate the user's actions corresponding to the colored symbols for the scale gesture.

is the type of the object hit by the touch. For example, D_1^{star} represents *first-touch-down-on-object-star* and M_2^{bg} represents *second-touch-move-on-object-background*. As we explain in the implementation section, Proton works with the multitouch hardware and hit-testing code provided by the developer to create a stream of these touch event symbols.

Gestures as Regular Expressions

The developer can define a gesture as a regular expression over these touch event symbols. Figure 2 shows the regular expressions describing three shape manipulation operations:

Translation: First touch down on a shape to select it (red symbol). The touch then moves repeatedly (green symbol). Finally, the touch lifts up to release the gesture (blue symbol).

Rotation: First touch down on a shape followed by a second touch down on the shape or canvas (red symbols). Then both touches move repeatedly (green symbols). Finally, the touches lift up in either order (blue symbols).

Scale: First touch down on a shape followed by a second touch down on the shape or canvas (red symbols). Then both touches move repeatedly (green symbols). Finally, the touches lift up in either order (blue symbols).

Describing a gesture as a regular expression both simplifies and unifies the gesture recognition code. The Proton pseudocode required to implement the general rotation gesture (with a second touch starting on a shape or background) is:

```
Proton: rotation gesture
   /*indices:1  2    3   4    5       6  7   8   9  10   11*/
1: gest : D1s M1s* D2a (M1s|M2a)* (U1s M2a* U2a|U2a M1s* U1s)
2: gest.addTrigger(rotate(), 4)
3: gest.addTrigger(rotate(), 5)
   /*compute rotation in rotate() callback*/
4: gest.finalTrigger(endRotate())
   /*perform rotation cleanup in endRotate() callback*/
5: gestureMatcher.add(gest)
```

Instead of counting touches and managing gesture state, the entire gesture is defined as a single regular expression on line 1. Unlike iOS, Proton handles all of the bookkeeping required to check that the stream of touch events matches the regular expression. The developer associates callbacks with

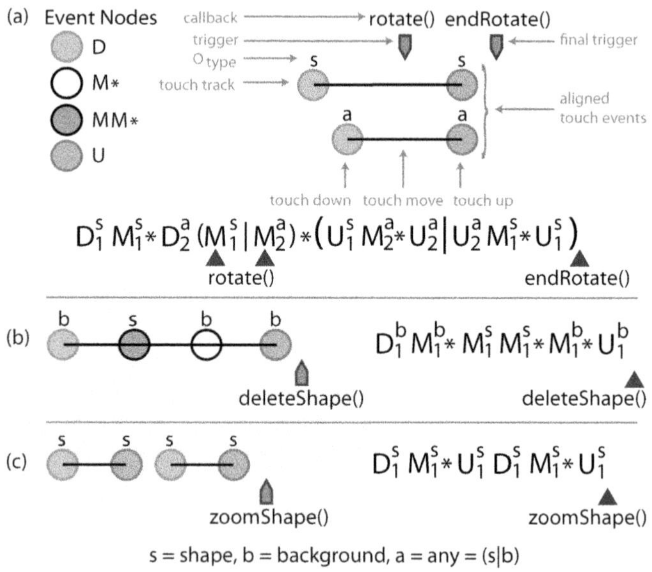

Figure 3. (a) Tablature for a two-touch rotation gesture. (b) Tablature for a strikethrough delete gesture. (c) Tablature for double tap zoom.

trigger locations within the expression. The second parameters in lines 2 and 3 create triggers at the 4th and 5th symbols of the expression. The application invokes the *rotate()* callback each time the event stream matches the regular expression up to the trigger location. In this case the match occurs when the two touches are moving; the callback can provide on-screen feedback. The location for the final trigger (line 4) is implicitly set to the end of the gesture expression.

To change a gesture's touch sequence the developer simply modifies the regular expression. For example, to require users to place the second touch on a shape, the developer need only change the regular expression so that the second touch down must occur on a shape rather than a shape or background. In iOS, making this change requires much deeper understanding of the state management in the gesture recognition code.

Gesture Tablature

When a gesture includes multiple fingers each with its own sequence of touch-down, touch-move and touch-up events, the developer may have to carefully interleave the parallel events in the regular expression. To facilitate authoring of such expressions, Proton introduces *gesture tablature* (Figure 3). This notation is inspired by musical notations such as guitar tablature and step sequencer matrices. Developers graphically indicate a touch event sequence using horizontal *touch tracks*. Within each track, a green node represents a touch-down event, a red node represents a touch-up event and a black line represents an arbitrary number of touch-move events. Vertical positions of nodes specify the ordering of events between touch tracks: event nodes to the left must occur before event nodes to the right, and when two or more event nodes are vertically aligned the corresponding events can occur in any order.

Using Proton's interactive tablature editor, developers can create independent touch tracks and then arrange the tracks into a gesture. We believe that this separation of concerns facilitates authoring as developers can first design the event sequence for each finger on a separate track and then consider how the fingers must interact with one another. Developers can also graphically specify trigger locations and callbacks. Proton converts the graphical notation into a regular expression, properly interleaving parallel touch events. Finally, Proton ensures that the resulting regular expressions are well formed.

For example, Figure 3a shows the tablature for a two-touch rotation gesture where the first touch must hit some shape, the second touch can hit anywhere, and the touches can be released in any order. Proton converts the vertically aligned touch-up nodes into a disjunction of the two possible event sequences: $(U_1^s M_2^a{*} U_2^a | U_2^a M_1^s{*} U_1^s)$. Thus, Proton saves the developer the work of writing out all possible touch-up orderings. We describe the algorithm for converting tablatures into regular expressions in the implementation section.

Proton inserts touch-move events between touch-down and touch-up events when converting tablature into regular expressions. To indicate that the hit target must change during a move, the developer can insert explicit touch-move nodes. Consider a strikethrough gesture to delete shapes that starts with a touch-down on the background, then moves over a shape, before terminating on the background again. The corresponding tablature (Figure 3b) includes a gray node with $O_{Type} = s$ indicating that at least one move event must occur on a shape and a white node with $O_{Type} = b$, indicating that the touch may move onto the background before the final touch-up on the background. Developers can also express multiple recurring touches (e.g., a double tap), by arranging multiple touch tracks on a single horizontal line (Figure 3c).

A *local trigger* arrow placed directly on a touch track associates a callback only with a symbol from that track (Figure 1). A *global trigger* arrow placed on its own track (e.g., *rotate()* in Figure 3a) associates the callback with all aligned events (down, move or up). A final trigger is always invoked when the entire gesture matches. To increase expressivity our tablature notation borrows elements from regular expression notation. The developer can use parentheses to group touches, Kleene stars to specify repetitions and vertical bars to specify disjunctions. Figure 1 shows an example where the user can place one touch on a button and perform repeated actions with one or two additional touches.

Static Analysis of Gesture Conflicts

Gesture conflicts arise when two gestures begin with the same sequence of touch events. Current multitouch frameworks provide little support for identifying such conflicts and developers often rely on runtime testing. However, exhaustive runtime testing of all gestures in all application states can be prohibitively difficult. Adding or modifying a gesture requires retesting for conflicts.

Proton's static analysis tool identifies conflicts between gesture expressions at compile time. Given the regular expressions of any two gestures, this tool returns the extent to which the gestures conflict, in the form of a longest prefix expression

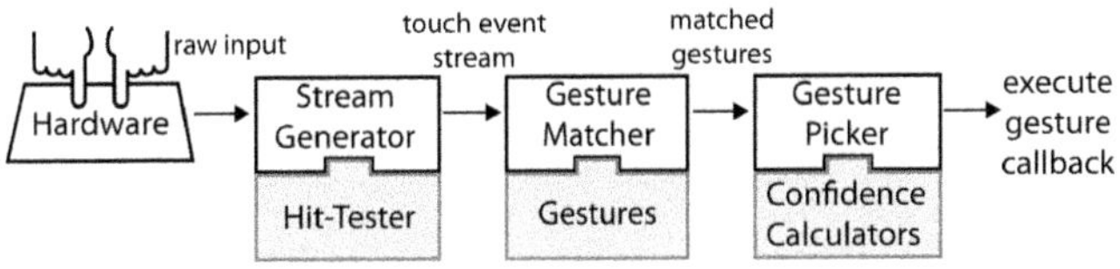

Figure 4. The Proton architecture. The application developer's responsibilities are shown in blue.

that matches both gestures. For example, when comparing the translation and rotation gestures (Figure 2), it returns the expression $D_1^s M_1^s{*}$, indicating that both gestures will match the input stream whenever the first touch lands on a shape and moves. When the second touch appears, the conflict is resolved as translation is no longer possible.

Once the conflict has been identified the developer can either modify one of the gestures to eliminate the conflict or write disambiguation code that assigns a confidence score to each interpretation of the gesture as described in the next section.

IMPLEMENTATION

The Proton runtime system includes three main components (Figure 4). The *stream generator* converts raw input data from the hardware into a stream of touch events. The *gesture matcher* compares this stream to the set of gesture expressions defined by the developer and emits a set of candidate gestures that match the stream. The *gesture picker* then chooses amongst the matching gestures and executes any corresponding callback. Proton also includes two compile-time tools. The *tablature conversion algorithm* generates regular expressions from tablatures and the *static analysis tool* identifies gesture conflicts.

Stream Generator

Multitouch hardware provides a sequence of time-stamped touch points. Proton converts this sequence into a stream of touch event symbols (Figure 5 Left). It groups touches based on proximity in space and time, and assigns the same T_{ID} for touch events that likely describe the path of a single finger. Proton also performs hit-testing to determine the O_{Type} for each touch. It is the developer's responsibility to specify the set of object types in the scene at compile-time and provide hit-testing code.

When the user lifts up all touches, the stream generator flushes the stream to restart matching for subsequent gestures. Some gestures may require all touches to temporarily lift up (e.g., double tap, Figure 3c). To enable such gestures, developers can specify a timeout parameter to delay the flush and wait for subsequent input. To minimize latency, Proton only uses timeouts if at least one gesture prefix is matching the current input stream at the time of the touch release.

Gesture Matcher

The gesture matcher keeps track of the set of gestures that can match the input stream. Initially, when no touches are present, it considers all gestures to be possible. As it receives new input events, the matcher compares the current stream against the regular expression of each candidate gesture. When a gesture no longer matches the current stream the

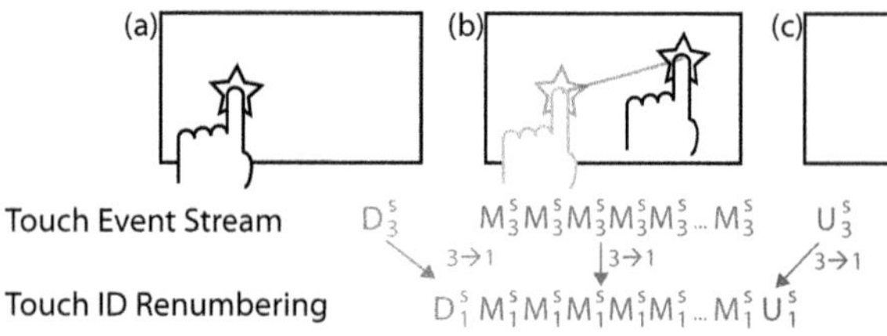

Interaction	Gesture
Translation	$D_1^s M_1^s * U_1^s$
Rotation	$D_1^s M_1^s *$ ~~$D_2^a (M_1^s \mid M_2^a) * (U_1^s M_2^a * U_2^a \mid U_2^a M_1^s * U_1^s)$~~
Scale	$D_1^s M_1^s *$ ~~$D_2^a (M_1^s \mid M_2^a) * (U_1^s M_2^a * U_2^a \mid U_2^a M_1^s * U_1^s)$~~
⋮	⋮

Figure 5. Left: Proton generates a touch event stream from a raw sequence of touch points given by the hardware. (a) The user touches a shape, (b) moves the touch and (c) lifts the touch. The gesture matcher renumbers unique T_{ID}s produced by the stream generator to match the gesture expressions. Right: The gesture matcher then sequentially matches each symbol in the stream to the set of gesture expressions. Translation, rotation, and scale all match when only a single finger is active, (a) and (b), but once the touch is lifted only translation continues to match, (c).

matcher removes it from the candidate set. At each iteration the matcher sends the candidate set to the gesture picker.

In a gesture regular expression, T_{ID} denotes the touch by the order in which it appears relative to the other touches in the gesture (i.e., first, second, third, ... touch within the gesture). In contrast, the T_{ID}s in the input event stream are globally unique. To properly match the input stream with gesture expressions, the matcher first renumbers T_{ID}s in the input stream, starting from one (Figure 5 Left). However, simple renumbering cannot handle touch sequences within a Kleene star group, e.g., $(D_1^a M_1^a * U_1^a)*$, because such groups use the same T_{ID} for multiple touches. Instead we create a priority queue of T_{ID}s and assign them in ascending order to touch-down symbols in the input stream. Subsequent touch-move and touch-up symbols receive the same T_{ID} as their associated touch-down. Whenever we encouter a touch-up we return its T_{ID} to the priority queue so it can be reused by subsequent touch-downs.

The gesture matcher uses regular expression derivatives [7] to detect whether the input stream can match a gesture expression. The derivative of a regular expression R with respect to a symbol s is a new expression representing the remaining set of strings that would match R given s. For example, the derivative of $abb*$ with respect to symbol a is the regular expression $bb*$ since $bb*$ describes the set of strings that can complete the match given a. The derivative with respect to b is the *empty set* because a string starting with b can never match $abb*$. The derivative of $a*$ with respect to a is $a*$.

The matcher begins by computing the derivative of each gesture expression with respect to the first touch event in the input stream. For each subsequent event, it computes new derivatives from the previous derivatives, with respect to the new input event. At any iteration, if a resulting derivative is the empty set, the gesture expression can no longer be matched and the corresponding gesture is removed from the candidate set (Figure 5 Right). If the derivative is the *empty string*, the gesture expression fully matches the input stream and the gesture callback is forwarded to the gesture picker where it is considered for execution. If the frontmost symbol of a candidate expression is associated with a trigger, and the derivative with respect to the current input symbol is not the empty set, then the input stream matches the gesture prefix up to the trigger. Thus, the matcher also forwards the trigger callback to gesture picker. Finally, whenever the stream generator flushes the event stream, Proton reinitializes the set of possible gestures and matching begins anew.

One Gesture at a Time Assumption: The gesture matcher relies on the assumption that all touch events in the stream belong to a single gesture. To handle multiple simultaneous gestures, the matcher would have to consider how to assign input events to gestures and this space of possible assignments grows exponentially in the number of gestures and input events. As a result of this assumption Proton does not allow a user to perform more than one gesture at a time (e.g., a different gesture with each hand). However, if the developer can group the touches (e.g., by location in a single-user application or by person [27] in a multi-user application), an instance of the gesture matcher could run on each group of touches to support simultaneous, multi-user interactions.

Supporting one interaction at a time might not be a limitation in practice for single-user applications. Users only have a single locus of attention [34], which makes it difficult to perform multiple actions simultaneously. Moreover, many popular multitouch applications for mobile devices, and even large professional multitouch applications such as Eden [22], only support one interaction at a time.

Gesture Picker

The gesture picker receives a set of candidate gestures and any associated callbacks. In applications with many gestures it is common for multiple gesture prefixes to match the event stream, forming a large candidate set. In such cases, additional information, beyond the sequence of touch events, is required to decide which gesture is most likely.

In Proton, the developer can provide the additional information by writing a *confidence calculator* function for each gesture that computes a likelihood score between 0.0 and 1.0. In computing this score, confidence calculators can consider many attributes of the matching sequence of touch events. For example, a confidence calculator may analyze the timing between touch events or the trajectory across move events. Consider the conflicting rotation and scale gestures shown in Figure 2. The confidence calculator for scale might check if the touches are moving away from one another while the confidence calculator for rotation might check if one finger is circling the other. The calculator can defer callback execution by returning a score of zero.

The gesture picker executes confidence calculators for all of the gestures in the candidate set and then invokes the associated callback for the gesture with the highest confidence score. In our current implementation it is the responsibility of the developer to ensure that exactly one confidence score is

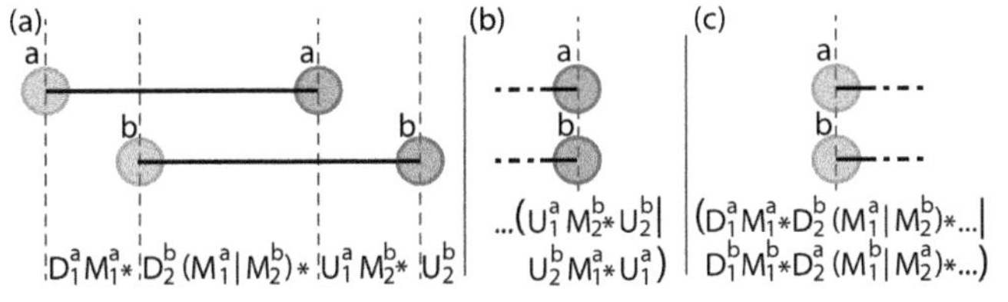

Figure 6. Our tablature conversion algorithm sweeps left-to-right and emits symbols each time it encounters a touch-down or touch-up node (vertical dotted lines). We distinguish three cases: (a) non-aligned nodes; (b) aligned touch-up nodes; (c) aligned touch-down nodes.

highest. We leave it to future work to build more sophisticated logic into the gesture picker for disambiguating amongst conflicting gestures. Schwarz et al.'s [36] probabilistic disambiguation technique may be one fruitful direction to explore.

One common use of trigger callbacks is to provide visual feedback over the course of a gesture. However, as confidence calculators receive more information over time, the gesture with the highest confidence may change. To prevent errors due to premature commitment to the wrong gesture, developers should ensure that any effects of trigger callbacks on application state are reversible. Developers may choose to write trigger callbacks so that they do not affect global application state or they may create an undo function for each trigger callback to restore the state. Alternatively, Proton supports a *parallel worlds* approach. The developer provides a copy of all relevant state variables in the application. Proton executes each valid callback regardless of confidence score in a parallel version of the application but only displays the feedback corresponding to the gesture with the highest confidence score. When the input stream flushes, Proton commits the the application state corresponding to the gesture with the highest confidence score.

Tablature to Expression Conversion

To convert a gesture tablature into a regular expression, we process the tablature from left to right. As we encounter a touch-down node, we assign the next available T_{ID} from the priority queue (see Gesture Matcher subsection) to the entire touch track. To emit symbols we sweep from left to right and distinguish three cases. When none of the nodes are vertically aligned we output the corresponding touch symbol for each node followed by a repeating disjunction of move events for all active touch tracks (Figure 6a). When touch-up nodes are vertically aligned we emit a disjunction of the possible touch-up orderings with interleaved move events (Figure 6b). When touch-down nodes are vertically aligned we first compute the remainder of the expressions for the aligned touch tracks. We then emit a disjunction of all permutations of T_{ID} assignments to these aligned tracks (Figure 6c). We output the regular expression symbols (,), |, or $*$ as we encounter them in the tablature. If we encounter a global trigger we associate it with all symbols emitted at that step of the sweep. If we encounter a local trigger we instead associate it with only the symbols emitted for its track.

Static Analysis Algorithm

Two gestures conflict when a string of touch event symbols matches a prefix of both gesture expressions. We call such a string a *common prefix*. We define the regular expression that describes all such common prefixes as the *longest common prefix expression*. Our static analyzer computes the longest common prefix expression for any pair of gesture expressions.

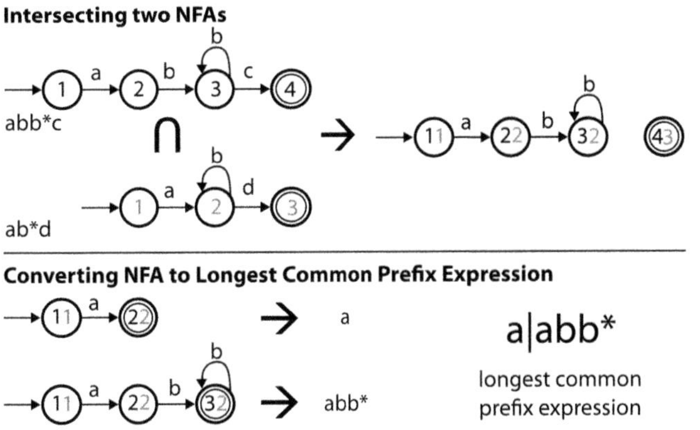

Figure 7. Top: The intersection of NFAs for the expressions $abb{*}c$ and $ab{*}d$ does not exist because the start state 11 cannot reach the end state 43. Bottom: Treating states 22 and 32 each as end states, converting the NFAs to regular expressions yields a and $abb*$. The longest common prefix expression is the union of the two regular expressions.

To compute the longest common prefix expression we first compute the *intersection* of two regular expressions. The intersection of two regular expressions is a third expression that matches all strings that are matched by both original expressions. A common way to compute the intersection is to first convert each regular expression into a non-deterministic finite automata (NFA) using Thompson's Algorithm [42] and then compute the intersection of the two NFAs. To construct the longest common prefix expression we mark all reachable states in the intersection NFA as accept states and then convert this NFA back into a regular expression.

We compute the intersection of two NFAs [39] as follows. Given an NFA M with states m_1 to m_k and an NFA N with states n_1 to n_l, we construct the NFA P with the cross product of states $m_i n_j$ for $i = [1, k]$ and $j = [1, l]$. We add an edge between $m_i n_j$ and $m_{i'} n_{j'}$ with transition symbol r if there exists an edge between m_i and $m_{i'}$ in M and an edge between n_j and $n_{j'}$ in N, both with the transition symbol r. Since we only care about states in P that are reachable from its start state $m_1 n_1$, we only add edges to states reachable from the start state. Unreachable states are discarded. Suppose that m_k and n_l were the original end states in M and N respectively, but that it is impossible to reach the cross product end state $m_k n_l$. In this case the intersection does not exist (Figure 7 Top). Nevertheless we can compute the longest common prefix expression. We sequentially treat each state reachable from P's start state $m_1 n_1$ as the end state, convert the NFA back into a regular expression, and take the disjunction of all resulting expressions (Figure 7 Bottom). The NFA to regular expression conversion is detailed in Sipser [39].

APPLICATIONS

To demonstrate the expressivity of our framework, we implemented three proof-of-concept applications, each with a variety of gestures.

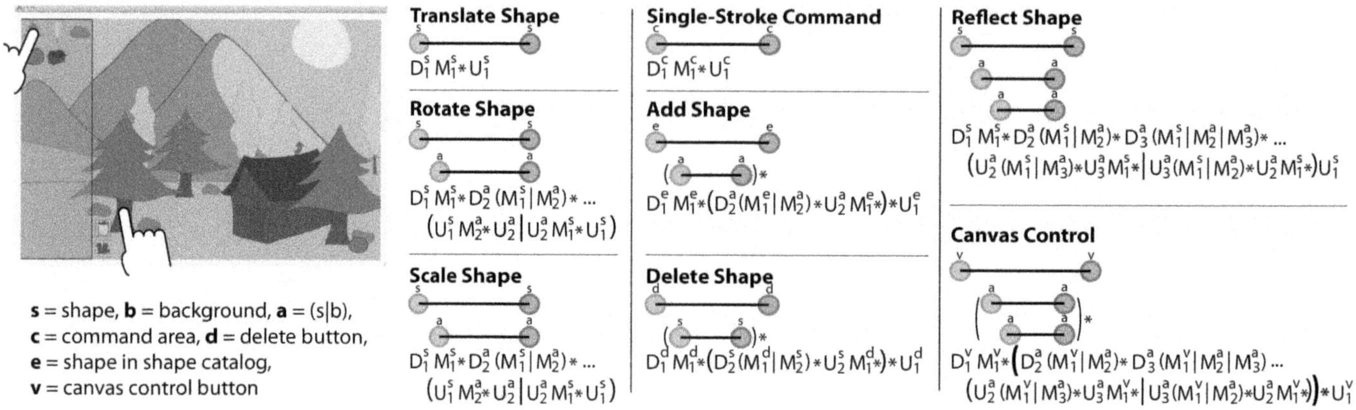

Figure 8. The shape manipulation application includes gestures for 2D layout, canvas control, and shape addition and deletion through quasimodes.

Application 1: Shape Manipulation

Our first application allows users to manipulate and layout shapes in 2D (Figure 8). The user can translate, rotate, scale and reflect the shapes. To control the canvas the user holds a quasimode [34] button and applies two additional touches to adjust pan and zoom. To add a shape, the user touches and holds a shape icon in a shape catalog and indicates its destination with a second touch on the canvas. To delete a shape, the user holds a quasimode button and selects a shape with a second touch. To undo and redo actions, the user draws strokes in a command area below the shape catalog.

Succinct Gesture Definitions

We created eight gesture tablatures, leaving Proton to generate the expressions and handle the recognition and management of the gesture set. We then implemented the appropriate gesture callbacks and confidence calculators. We did not need to count touches or track gesture state across event handlers.

Many of our tablatures specify target object types for different touches in a gesture. For example, the Delete gesture requires the first touch to land on the delete button and the second touch to land on a shape. Proton enables such quasimodes without burdening the developer with maintaining application state. Target object types do not have to correspond to single objects: the Rotate, Scale and Reflect gestures allow the second touch to land on any object including the background. We also specified the order in which touches should lift up at the end of a gesture. While the Rotate and Scale gestures permit the user to release touches in any order, modal commands require that the first, mode-initiating touch lift up last. Finally, we specified repetitions within a gesture using Kleene stars. For example, the second touch in the Delete gesture is grouped with a Kleene star, which allows the expression to match any number of taps made by the second touch.

Static Analysis of Gesture Conflicts

Proton's static analyzer reported that all six pairs of the shape manipulation gestures (Translate, Rotate, Scale and Reflect) conflicted with one another. Five of the conflicts involved prefix expressions only, while the sixth conflict, between Rotate and Scale, showed that those two gestures are identical. We wrote confidence calculators to resolve all six conflicts.

The static analyzer also found that all shape manipulation gestures conflict with Translate when only one touch is down. We implemented a threshold confidence calculator that returns a zero confidence score for Translate if the first touch has not moved beyond some distance. Similarly, Rotate and Scale only return a non-zero confidence score once the second touches have moved beyond some distance threshold. After crossing the threshold, the confidence score is based on the touch trajectory.

Application 2: Sketching

Our second application replicates a subset of the gestures used in Autodesk's SketchBook application for the iPad [4]. The user can draw using one touch, manipulate the canvas with two touches, and control additional commands with three touches. A three-touch tap loads a palette (Figure 9a) for changing brush attributes and a three-touch swipe executes undo and redo commands, depending on the direction.

In this application, the generated expressions for Load Palette and Swipe are particularly long because these three-touch gestures allow touches to release in any order. We created tablatures for these gestures by vertically aligning the touch-up nodes and Proton automatically generated expressions containing all possible sequences of touch-up events (Figure 9b).

Proton includes a library of predefined widgets such as sliders and buttons. We used this library to create the brush attribute palette. For example, to add color buttons into the palette, we created new instances of the button press widget, which consists of a button and corresponding button press gesture. We gave each button instance a unique name, e.g., $redButton$, and then assigned $redButton$ as the O_{Type} for the touch events within the expression for the button press gesture.

We also implemented a soft keyboard for text entry. The keyboard is a container where each key is a button subclassed from Proton's built-in button press widget. We associated each key with its own instances of the default button press gesture and callback. Thus, we created 26 different buttons and button press gestures, one for each lower-case letter. Adding a shift key for entering capital letters required creating a gesture for every shift key combination, adding 26 additional gestures.

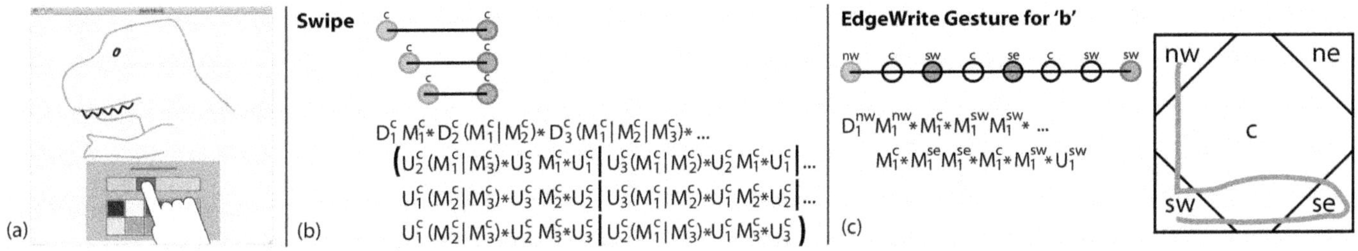

Figure 9. (a) In the sketching application's palette, the user adjusts brush parameters through predefined widgets. (b) Aligned touch-up nodes for the swipe tablature generate all six touch-up sequences. (c) EdgeWrite gestures change hit targets multiple times within a touch track.

Application 3: EdgeWrite

Our third application re-implements EdgeWrite [43], a unistroke text entry technique where the user draws a stroke through corners of a square to generate a letter. For example, to generate the letter 'b', the user starts with a touch down in the NW corner, moves the finger down to the SW corner, over to the SE corner, and finally back to the SW corner. Between each corner, the touch moves through the center area c (Figure 9c, Left). We inserted explicit touch-move nodes (gray and white circles) with new O_{Type}s into the tablature to express that a touch must change target corner objects as it moves. The gesture tablature for the letter 'b' and its corresponding regular expression are shown in Figure 9c, Right.

Our EdgeWrite implementation includes 36 expressions, one for each letter and number. Our static analyzer found that 18 gestures conflict because they all start in the NW corner. The number of conflicts drops as soon as these gestures enter a second corner; 9 conflicts for the SW corner, 2 for SE, 7 for NE. Our analyzer found that none of the gestures that started in the NW corner immediately returned to the NW corner which suggests that it would be possible to add a new short NW–NW gesture for a frequently used command such as delete. Similarly the analyzer reported conflicts for strokes starting in the other corners. We did not have to resolve these conflicts because the callbacks execute only when the gestures are completed and none of the gestures are identical. However, such analysis could be useful when designing a new unistroke command to check that each gesture is unique.

Performance

Our research implementation of Proton is unoptimized and was built largely to validate that regular expressions can be used as a basis for declaratively specifying multitouch gestures. While we have not carried out formal experiments, application use and informal testing suggest that Proton can support interactive multitouch applications on current hardware. We ran the three applications on a 2.2 GHz Intel Core 2 Duo Macintosh computer. In the sketching application with eight gestures, Proton required about 17ms to initially match gestures when all the gestures in the application were candidates. As the matcher eliminated gestures from consideration, matching time dropped to 1-3ms for each new touch event. In EdgeWrite, initial matching time was 22ms for a set of 36 gestures. The main bottleneck in gesture matching is the calculation of regular expression derivatives, which are currently recalculated for every every new input symbol. The calculation of derivatives depends on the complexity (e.g., number of disjunctions) of the regular expression. We believe it is possible to significantly improve performance by pre-computing the finite state machine (FSM) for each gesture [7].

FUTURE WORK

We have demonstrated with Proton some of the benefits of declaratively specifying multitouch gestures as regular expressions. Our current implementation has several limitations that we plan to address in future work.

Supporting Simultaneous Gestures

Proton currently supports only one gesture at a time for a single user. While this is sufficient for many types of multitouch applications, it precludes multi-user applications. One approach to support multiple users is to partition the input stream by user ID (if reported by the hardware) or by spatial location. Proton could then run separate gesture matchers on each partition. Another approach is to allow a gesture to use just a subset of the touches, so a new gesture can begin on any touch-down event. The gesture matcher must then keep track of all valid complete and partial gestures and the developer must choose the best set of gestures matching the stream. The static analyzer would need to detect conflicts between simultaneous, overlapping gestures. It currently relies on gestures beginning on the same touch-down event. A revised algorithm would have to consider all pairs of touch-down postfix expressions between two gestures.

Supporting Trajectory

Proton's declarative specification does not capture information about trajectory. While developers can compute trajectories in callback code, we plan to investigate methods for incorporating trajectory information directly into gesture expressions. For example, the xstroke system [44] describes a trajectory as a sequence of spatial locations and recognizes the sequence with a regular expression. However, like many current stroke recognizers [38] this technique can only be applied after the user has finished the stroke gesture. We plan to extend the Proton touch symbols to include simple directional information [40], computed from the last two positions of the touch, so the trajectory expressions can still be matched incrementally as the user performs the gesture.

User Evaluation

Although we validated Proton with three example applications, we plan to further investigate usability via user studies. We plan to compare the time and effort to implement custom gestures in both Proton and an existing framework (e.g., iOS).

A more extensive study would examine how developers build complete applications with Proton.

CONCLUSION

We have described the design and implementation of Proton, a new multitouch framework in which developers declaratively specify the sequence of touch events that comprise a gesture as a regular expression. To facilitate authoring, developers can create gestures using a graphical tablature notation. Proton automatically converts tablatures into regular expressions. Specifying gestures as regular expressions leads to two main benefits. First, Proton can automatically manage the underlying gesture state, which reduces code complexity for the developer. Second, Proton can statically analyze the gesture expressions to detect conflicts between them. Developers can then resolve ambiguities through conflict resolution code. Together these two advantages make it easier for developers to understand, maintain and extend multitouch applications.

ACKNOWLEDGMENTS

This work was supported by NSF grants CCF-0643552 and IIS-0812562.

REFERENCES

1. Adya, A., Howell, J., Theimer, M., Bolosky, W. J., and Douceur, J. R. Cooperative task management without manual stack management. *Proc. USENIX 2002* (2002), 289–302.
2. Appert, C., and Beaudouin-Lafon, M. SwingStates: adding state machines to the swing toolkit. *Proc. UIST 2006* (2006), 319–322.
3. Apple. iOS. `http://developer.apple.com/technologies/ios`.
4. Autodesk. SketchBook Pro. `http://usa.autodesk.com/adsk/servlet/pc/item?siteID=123112&id=15119465`.
5. Blackwell, A. *SWYN: A Visual Representation for Regular Expressions*. Morgan Kauffman, 2000, 245–270.
6. Bleser, T., and Foley, J. D. Towards specifying and evaluating the human factors of user-computer interfaces. *Proc. CHI 1982* (1982), 309–314.
7. Brzozowski, J. A. Derivatives of regular expressions. *Journal of the ACM 11* (1964), 481–494.
8. De Nardi, A. Grafiti: Gesture recognition management framework for interactive tapletop interfaces. Master's thesis, University of Pisa, Italy, 2008.
9. Echtler, F., and Klinker, G. A multitouch software architecture. *Proc. NordiCHI 2008* (2008), 463–466.
10. Fraunhofer-Institute for Industrial Engineering. MT4j - Multitouch for Java. `http://www.mt4j.org`.
11. Gibbon, D., Gut, U., Hell, B., Looks, K., Thies, A., and Trippel, T. A computational model of arm gestures in conversation. *Proc. Eurospeech 2003* (2003), 813–816.
12. Google. Android. `http://www.android.com`.
13. Hansen, T. E., Hourcade, J. P., Virbel, M., Patali, S., and Serra, T. PyMT: a post-WIMP multi-touch user interface toolkit. *Proc. ITS 2009* (2009), 17–24.
14. Henry, T. R., Hudson, S. E., and Newell, G. L. Integrating gesture and snapping into a user interface toolkit. *Proc. UIST 1990* (1990), 112–122.
15. Hudson, S. E., Mankoff, J., and Smith, I. Extensible input handling in the subArctic toolkit. *Proc. CHI 2005* (2005), 381–390.
16. Jacob, R. J. K. Executable specifications for a human-computer interface. *Proc. CHI 1983* (1983), 28–34.
17. Jacob, R. J. K. A specification language for direct-manipulation user interfaces. *TOG 5*, 4 (October 1986), 283–317.
18. Jacob, R. J. K., Deligiannidis, L., and Morrison, S. A software model and specification language for non-WIMP user interfaces. *TOCHI 6*, 1 (1999), 1–46.
19. Kammer, D., Freitag, G., Keck, M., and Wacker, M. Taxonomy and overview of multi-touch frameworks: Architecture, scope and features. *Workshop on Engineering Patterns for Multitouch Interfaces* (2010).
20. Kammer, D., Wojdziak, J., Keck, M., and Taranko, S. Towards a formalization of multi-touch gestures. *Proc. ITS 2010* (2010), 49–58.
21. Khandkar, S. H., and Maurer, F. A domain specific language to define gestures for multi-touch applications. *10th Workshop on Domain-Specific Modeling* (2010).
22. Kin, K., Miller, T., Bollensdorff, B., DeRose, T., Hartmann, B., and Agrawala, M. Eden: A professional multitouch tool for constructing virtual organic environments. *Proc. CHI 2011* (2011), 1343–1352.
23. Lao, S., Heng, X., Zhang, G., Ling, Y., and Wang, P. A gestural interaction design model for multi-touch displays. *Proc. British Computer Society Conference on Human-Computer Interaction* (2009), 440–446.
24. Lu, H., and Li, Y. Gesture Coder: A tool for programming multi-touch gestures by demonstration. *Proc. CHI 2012* (2012).
25. Mankoff, J., Hudson, S. E., and Abowd, G. D. Interaction techniques for ambiguity resolution in recognition-based interfaces. *Proc. UIST 2000* (2000), 11–20.
26. Mankoff, J., Hudson, S. E., and Abowd, G. D. Providing integrated toolkit-level support for ambiguity in recognition-based interfaces. *Proc. CHI 2000* (2000), 368–375.
27. MERL. DiamondTouch. `http://merl.com/projects/DiamondTouch`.
28. Microsoft. Windows 7. `http://www.microsoft.com/en-US/windows7/products/home`.
29. Myers, B. A. A new model for handling input. *ACM Trans. Inf. Syst. 8*, 3 (1990), 289–320.
30. Newman, W. M. A system for interactive graphical programming. *Proc. AFIPS 1968 (Spring)* (1968), 47–54.
31. NUI Group. Touchlib. `http://nuigroup.com/touchlib`.
32. Olsen, D. *Building Interactive Systems: Principles for Human-Computer Interaction*. Course Technology Press, Boston, MA, United States, 2009, 43–66.
33. Olsen, Jr., D. R., and Dempsey, E. P. Syngraph: A graphical user interface generator. *Proc. SIGGRAPH 1983* (1983), 43–50.
34. Raskin, J. *The Humane Interface*. Addison Wesley, 2000.
35. Scholliers, C., Hoste, L., Signer, B., and De Meuter, W. Midas: a declarative multi-touch interaction framework. *Proc. TEI 2011* (2011), 49–56.
36. Schwarz, J., Hudson, S. E., Mankoff, J., and Wilson, A. D. A framework for robust and flexible handling of inputs with uncertainty. *Proc. UIST 2010* (2010), 47–56.
37. Shaer, O., and Jacob, R. J. K. A specification paradigm for the design and implementation of tangible user interfaces. *TOCHI 16*, 4 (2009).
38. Signer, B., Kurmann, U., and Norrie, M. iGesture: A general gesture recognition framework. *Proc. ICDAR 2007* (2007), 954–958.
39. Sipser, M. *Introduction to the Theory of Computation*, 1st ed. International Thomson Publishing, 1996, 46,70–76.
40. Siwgart, S. Easily write custom gesture recognizers for your tablet PC applications, November 2005. Microsoft Technical Report.
41. Sparsh UI. `http://code.google.com/p/sparsh-ui`.
42. Thompson, K. Regular expression search algorithm. *Communications of the ACM 11*, 6 (1968), 419–422.
43. Wobbrock, J. O., Myers, B. A., and Kembel, J. A. Edgewrite: A stylus-based text entry method designed for high accuracy and stability of motion. *Proc. UIST 2003* (2003), 61–70.
44. Worth, C. D. xstroke. `http://pandora.east.isi.edu/xstroke/usenix_2003`.

Bootstrapping Personal Gesture Shortcuts with the Wisdom of the Crowd and Handwriting Recognition

Tom Y. Ouyang *
MIT CSAIL
ouyang@csail.mit.edu

Yang Li
Google Research
yangli@acm.org

ABSTRACT
Personal user-defined gesture shortcuts have shown great potential for accessing the ever-growing amount of data and computing power on touchscreen mobile devices. However, their lack of scalability is a major challenge for their wide adoption. In this paper, we present Gesture Marks, a novel approach to touch-gesture interaction that allows a user to access applications and websites using gestures without having to define them first. It offers two distinctive solutions to address the problem of scalability. First, it leverages the "wisdom of the crowd", a continually evolving library of gesture shortcuts that are collected from the user population, to infer the meaning of gestures that a user never defined himself. Second, it combines an extensible template-based gesture recognizer with a specialized handwriting recognizer to even better address handwriting-based gestures, which are a common form of gesture shortcut. These approaches effectively bootstrap a user's personal gesture library, alleviating the need to define most gestures manually. Our work was motivated and validated via a series of user studies, and the findings from these studies add to the body of knowledge on gesture-based interaction.

Author Keywords
Gesture-based interaction; search; mobile computing.

ACM Classification Keywords
H.5.2 [Information Interfaces and Presentation]: User Interfaces. H.3.3 [Information Storage and Retrieval]: Information Search and Retrieval.

General Terms
Human Factors, Algorithms.

INTRODUCTION
With the ever-growing complexity of mobile devices like the Android [1] and iPhone [11], there is a pressing need for faster and more natural ways to access all of the diverse functions that are available to mobile users today. Gesture shortcuts on the touchscreen represent one promising new modality for confronting this problem. Imagine being able to draw a quick star to launch Google Sky Maps (an application for exploring stars, planets, and constellations) or a fast cursive "NY" to open your browser to The New York Times (as illustrated in Figure 1). These gestures can be quick to draw, easy to remember, and require very little cognitive load on the user.

Figure 1: When a user draws a gesture in Gesture Marks, the system shows a list of matches based on: 1) a library of learned gestures from the user, 2) gestures from other users—the crowd, and 3) a built-in handwriting recognizer.

A system that supports user-defined gesture shortcuts often employs a template-based approach [19], in which a new gesture is matched against a set of known gestures defined by the user. Compared to prior work that uses built-in, system-defined shortcuts, e.g., those based on letters [14,21], this approach enables a richer unconstrained gesture vocabulary and allows users to easily create their own personal shortcuts. A new gesture can be added to the library in an on-line manner without expensive retraining, and it can immediately contribute to future recognition. Furthermore, because such a system can continually learn from the user's gestures over time, it allows the gesture

* This work was done while the author was an intern at Google Research.

language to adapt to the particular drawing or handwriting style of the user instead of the other way around.

However, despite the appeal and promise of user-defined gesture shortcuts, the main challenge is their scalability. It is not practical for a user to define custom gesture shortcuts for every target they might visit, e.g., accessing a large corpus such as the web. To address this challenge, our goal is to find ways to alleviate users from the burden of having to define gesture shortcuts manually.

To this end, we first conducted an exploratory study to find out whether there are any intrinsic properties or commonalities in gesture shortcuts, both within one individual as well as across individuals. The study revealed two important findings. First, we found a major portion of gesture shortcuts that users defined were character-based and mnemonically associated with the target, e.g., "NY" for The New York Times website. Second, there was a significant overlap in the gestures defined by different users for the same target, e.g., many users drew a plus symbol for Google+. These findings motivated us to develop Gesture Marks, a novel system that allows users to access applications and websites on their phone using natural unconstrained gesture shortcuts without necessarily having to define them beforehand.

Our major contribution is a novel approach for bootstrapping personal gesture shortcuts, using a combination of crowdsourcing and handwriting recognition. It alleviates the effort of defining gesture shortcuts and makes gesture-based interaction more scalable. The novelty of the system is two-fold. First, Gesture Marks leverages the "wisdom of the crowd". It infers what a user intends to access with a gesture by looking at how the gesture is commonly used by others. Second, it combines this template-based gesture recognizer with a robust cursive handwriting recognizer that can infer the user's target even when there is no matching target in the gesture library. The handwriting recognizer effectively captures the long tail of gesture shortcuts, ones that are rare or specific to an individual user. Since each gesture usage is recorded by Gesture Marks, the results of these gesture-based interactions all contribute to the user's personal library of gesture shortcuts. A validation study that we conducted showed that crowd-defined gestures and handwriting recognition effectively bootstrapped the gesture shortcut library of each individual user.

This paper focuses on applications and websites because these are two classes of targets that are likely to be shared between users, thus allowing us to better study the commonality in gesture shortcuts across the user population. However, we believe that many of the ideas presented here can be extended to other types of targets such as music and phone settings.

In the remainder of the paper, we first describe an exploratory study where we analyze the types of gestures people draw, and develop a set of guidelines based on our findings. We next present Gesture Marks, a novel gesture interface we designed and implemented based on those guidelines. We then present a set of evaluations on our system, and finally conclude with discussions of future and related work.

EXPLORING USER-DEFINED GESTURE SHORTCUTS

We conducted an exploratory study to investigate the types of gestures people tend to draw. In particular, we analyzed whether there were any visual or semantic patterns in gesture shortcuts defined by the same individual, and whether these patterns hold across individuals. We then used the findings to inform the design of a user-defined gesture shortcut system.

Data Collection Procedures

We collected gesture shortcut samples from 26 Android phone users for their personalized applications and websites. We asked these users to install a data collection tool that we developed on their Android phone. The tool automatically extracted a set of targets for which participants were asked to define gesture shortcuts. These targets consisted of 20 applications randomly selected from their device and the top 20 websites sampled from their browsing history based on visit count. The selection of these targets approximates the actual usage model of applications and websites for each user.

Participants were prompted with one target at a time, and they could not see any previous gestures they had already drawn. To make sure our gestures were representative of actual usage, participants were allowed to skip targets they did not recognize and would have no intention of using in real life. Each participant was prompted with the list of targets twice. For each round, we randomized the order of the occurrence of these targets. The procedure allowed a total of two gesture samples per user per target. Since the targets were personalized, different participant could have different sets of targets.

Results & Analyses

We collected a total of 1,970 gestures spanning 407 different targets from 26 users. Our analysis of this data revealed three important findings.

Frequency of Handwriting versus Drawing Gestures

First we analyzed what types of gestures people tended to draw for different types of targets. We labeled all of the gestures we collected as either *handwriting* or arbitrary *drawings* and calculated the frequency for each (see Figure 2). As we can see, a majority (72%) of the gestures people drew consisted of alphanumeric characters, i.e., letters and numbers. The rest (28%) were arbitrary drawings, e.g., boxes, stars, and birds. There was a larger percentage of non-handwriting gestures for applications (40%) than for websites (14%). One possible reason for this is that application icons, which users are constantly exposed to, inspired them to use drawing-based gestures.

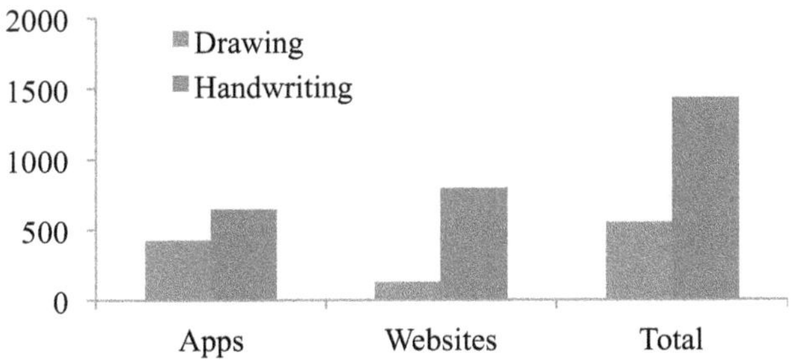

Figure 2: The frequency of arbitrary drawing gestures versus handwriting gestures.

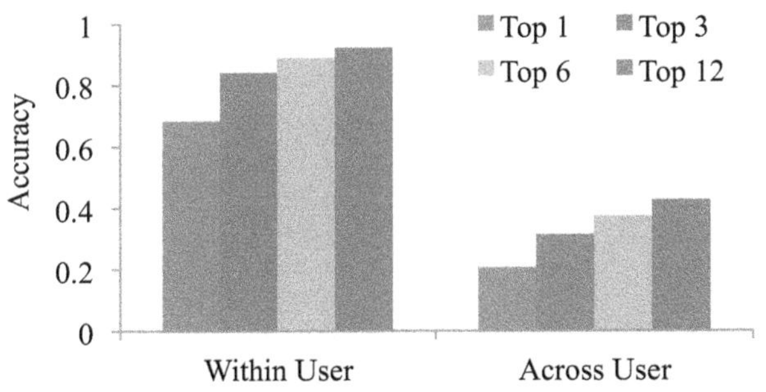

Figure 3: (left) Within-user similarity-based prediction accuracy and (right) across-user accuracy.

Consistency of Gesture Shortcuts Within Each User

Next we analyzed the consistency of gesture shortcuts created by *the same user*. The consistency here measures how well the visual similarity between two gestures predicts the likelihood that they both map to the same target.

To this end, we first split the gestures from each user into two halves, with each half containing one of the two examples for each target (assigned randomly). We then trained a template-based gesture recognizer on the first half and measured how well it can predict the intended targets for the gestures in the second half. The recognizer employs an appearance-based distance metric [17], so the result is an estimate for how often visually similar gestures map to the same target. We then repeated the experiment in reverse: training on the second half and testing on the first.

The accuracy results for this within-user cross validation analysis are shown in Figure 3 (left). We found that for a large majority of the shortcuts (68%), it is possible to predict the destination of a gesture by looking only at the most similar gesture (the nearest neighbor) drawn by the same user. One important reason that the accuracy was lower than that reported on previous gesture datasets [15,19,20] is the mapping ambiguity from gestures to targets. We frequently observed instances where the same user drew similar gestures for different targets (e.g., an "M" gesture for both Maps and Music), in which case it is impossible to determine the exact meaning of the gesture. In contrast, no such ambiguity needed to be addressed in previous experiments.

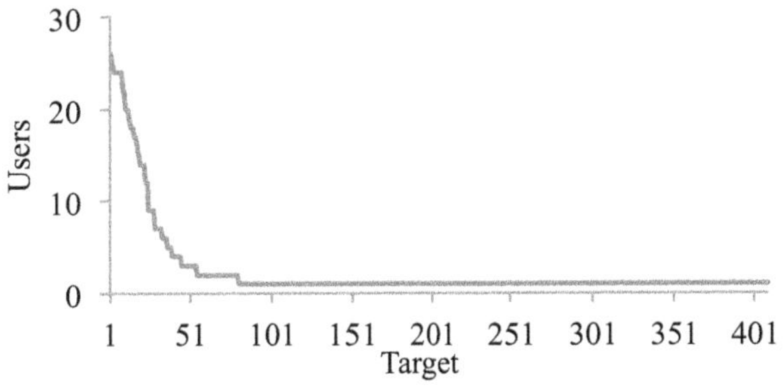

Figure 4: The number of users who defined gestures for each target obeys a power law

If we look at the top 12 nearest matches, the maximum number of targets that can be shown on the lower portion of our prototype interface (see Figure 1), the accuracy increases to 92%. With more gesture repetitions per target we may expect to see even higher accuracy.

Consistency of Gesture Shortcuts Across Users

Finally we analyzed whether there was any similarity in gesture shortcuts created by *different users*. We performed a similar analysis as in the within-user case before, except here there was no overlap between the users in the training and test sets. We are now measuring how well we can predict the target for a given gesture using only data from the other users.

We performed a total of 26 cross validation tests, one for each user, and the final accuracy results are shown in Figure 3 (right). The recognizer was able to predict the correct destination 21% of the time if we only look at the top match, and 42% of the time if we look at the top 12 matches. Notice that both the accuracy of the recognizer and the consistency of gesture shortcuts across users contributed to this result.

As expected, the accuracy was lower than in the within-user case, due in part to the following reasons. First, a large majority of the targets had gestures from only one user (see Figure 4). In such cases, it was impossible to predict what the user intended since there was no training data matching the target from any of the other users. Second, there was more mapping ambiguity because with multiple users, it was even more likely that some of them would assign different meanings to the same gesture.

However, the result is still encouraging given that our data was from only 26 users. As the system accumulates more and more gestures from the user population, this sparsity issue should become less of a problem. For example, if we repeat the same test but limit our dataset to only those shortcuts with gestures from 4 or more users (a total of 45 targets with 1146 gestures), the accuracy increases to 36% for the top 1 match and 77% for the top 12 matches. The mapping ambiguity issue can be addressed by taking into account of the popularity of gestures, e.g., the number of users who used the gesture, and the personal preferences and usage history of each user.

Discussions for Creating a Gesture Shortcut System

Based on these findings, we developed the following guidelines for creating a gesture shortcut system.

1. It should be able to predict the target for a gesture based on the targets of similar gestures from the same user.

The results in Figure 3 (left) show that visual similarity to the user's own gestures is a remarkably informative metric for predicting the target of a new gesture. This confirms previous work [20] that uses a template-based approach to recognize user-defined gesture shortcuts. A template-based gesture recognizer is also essential for non-handwriting input, where the number of gesture classes is unbounded and the number of training examples per class can be very low.

However, it will be impractical to expect users to define a gesture for every target they want to visit beforehand. In fact, the overhead for specifying user-defined gesture shortcuts has been the main challenge for its adoption in the real world. Thus, based on the findings from the study, we add two important bootstrapping and refinement mechanisms.

2. It should be able to take advantage of gestures drawn by other users.

The results in Figure 3 (right) show that there was significant predictive power from gestures drawn by other users, even in this study where the number of users is small and gestures per target were extremely sparse. In a real world setting where the number of users is continually expanding, we would expect the predictiveness of cross-user gestures to be even higher. This implies that even before a user defines any gesture shortcuts, there is the possibility to interpret the user gesture by looking at what other users drew.

3. It should be able to recognize handwriting gestures even when there are no matching templates.

Since handwriting gestures are used so frequently (see Figure 2), incorporating handwriting recognition into the system allows it to effectively recognize these gestures even when they have never been defined before by any user. This is especially useful for rare targets or targets that are specific to a given user.

GESTURE MARKS

Based on the findings and guidelines derived from the exploratory study, we designed and implemented Gesture Marks, a system that allows the user to use unconstrained gesture shortcuts to access applications and websites. Here we describe how users interact with the system.

Querying Based on Multiple Sources

Gesture Marks is implemented as an alternative Android home screen. When the user draws a gesture query on the screen, Gesture Marks interprets it based on three sources: 1) a library of learned gestures from the user; 2) gestures from other users; and 3) a built-in handwriting recognizer. The system then displays the best matches in a list view below (see Figure 1). The user chooses the correct target

Figure 5: Defining a new gesture shortcut drawn from the home screen.

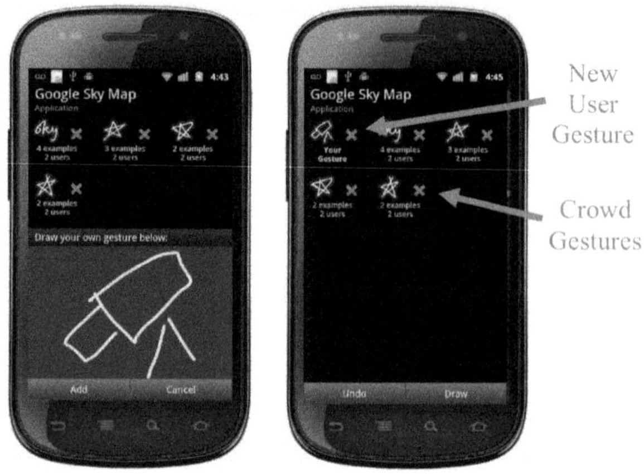

Figure 6: Defining a new gesture shortcut from the gesture explorer view

from the list, which launches the website or application. Meanwhile, the system learns the new association between the user drawn gesture and the target for future queries.

Defining Gestures As a By-Product of Finding Targets

The intended target might not always be in the list of matches when the user draws a gesture query (see Figure 5 left). If this happens the user can manually define the gesture by clicking on the Manual Selection button. This opens a list of all apps and visited websites, as well as a search box for text queries (see Figure 5 right). The gesture just drawn by the user is shown in a miniaturized version on the upper left. When the user chooses the intended target, Gesture Marks asks her whether she would like the system to learn the definition for future queries before launching it.

Exploring Gestures from Others

The user can also perform a long finger press on any target to bring up a screen that shows all of the gestures assigned to that target (see Figure 6). Here she can explicitly define a new gesture shortcut by drawing it in the gesture panel on the bottom. She can also see what popular gestures other people have used for the target. Each crowd gesture is shown with its popularity metrics including the number of gesture examples and the number of unique users. If the user dislikes any of the gestures, she can remove it by

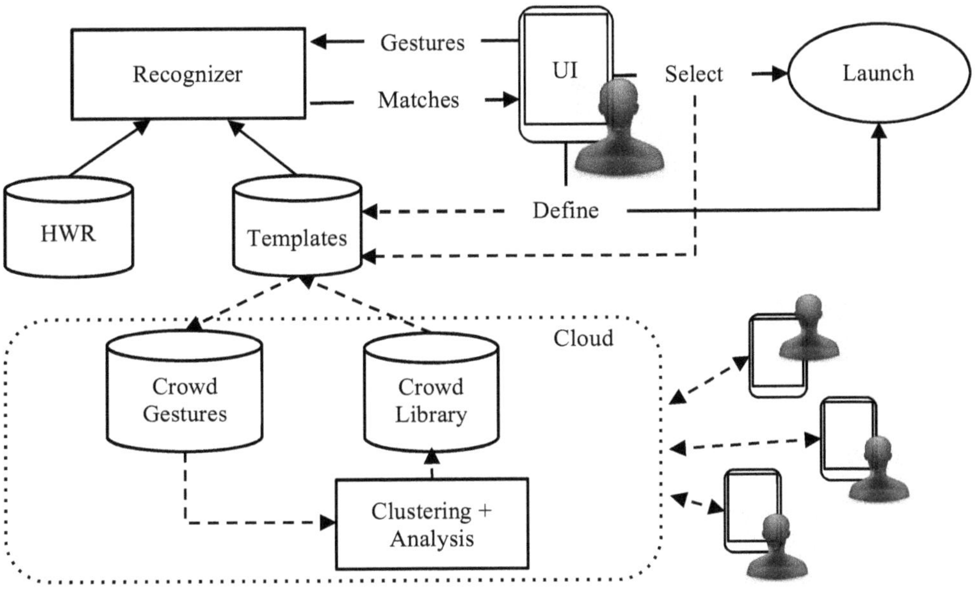

Figure 7: The Gesture Marks System Architecture.

clicking on the X next to it, which informs the system not to use this gesture for the target in the future.

THE SYSTEM ARCHITECTURE

This section presents the Gesture Marks architecture, shown in Figure 7. When the user draws a gesture, it is processed by both an extensible template-based gesture recognizer and a built-in handwriting recognizer. The resulting matches are presented to the user, who can either select one if the correct target is in the list or define the target manually. In either case, the new gesture is learned by the system. In addition, each gesture is recorded in the crowd-based gesture library, which clusters, analyzes, and shares the gesture shortcuts among the user population.

Inferring Shortcuts with Gesture Matching

Gesture Marks employs a template-based recognizer that infers the target of a user gesture by matching it against a library of collected gesture shortcuts. Every time the user draws a gesture and selects a match, the system stores the new gesture shortcut in the user's library that is both maintained on a server in the cloud and cached locally on the device. The recognition performance thus improves over time as the system accumulates more examples from the user for each target. Furthermore, since the gestures are cached, matches can be shown instantly for favorite shortcuts even if the connection to the Gesture Marks server is slow or inaccessible.

In addition, the system leverages the "wisdom of the crowd" by harvesting gesture shortcuts from the entire user population. It then recommends relevant gestures to individual users based on their installed applications and browsing history.

Gesture Matching

An important component of the recognizer is how it matches an input gesture against a set of learned gesture shortcuts. We adapted an appearance-based matching algorithm that had been applied successfully to the domain of sketch recognition on pen-based tablets [17] and tailored it to our domain - mobile touchscreen devices. Since this recognizer focuses on vision-based features instead of temporal stroke patterns, it naturally overcomes many common gesture recognition challenges such as stroke order differences and over-tracing (drawing over a previously drawn region). The performance of the recognizer is competitive with prior approaches [14,19,20] on recognizing single-stroke gestures. Furthermore, our recognizer also naturally handles multi-stroke gestures at no additional cost. A more detailed discussion on the implementation and evaluation of this recognition approach is available in [17].

Gesture Clustering

In order to facilitate fast retrieval and shortcut analysis, the server first clusters together similar gestures for each target. This is done using an agglomerative clustering algorithm [7] that produces a hierarchy of progressively larger clusters. Each cluster can then be described by 1) its center: the gesture that has the minimum average distance to each of the other members of the cluster; and 2) its diameter: the maximum distance between any two gestures in the cluster. We stop growing clusters when the diameter reaches a predetermined threshold, chosen empirically based on analysis of the similarity scores from the previous exploratory study.

Online Clustering

As new gestures are added to the server, they need to be incorporated into the cluster hierarchy to be used effectively. To accomplish this task Gesture Marks employs a scalable distributed agglomerative clustering algorithm that first splits the data into partitions, and then clusters each partition independently. It then merges the clusters generated across multiple partitions by keeping only their respective cluster centers.

Gesture Cluster Analyses

The server records a set of statistics for each gesture cluster such as the number of gestures in the cluster and the number of unique users who provided gestures for the cluster. These statistics allow the system to more effectively evaluate the popularity of each cluster. Currently our simple model is to rank the clusters based on the number of users, and to use the number of gestures only when there is a tie. As the system collects more usage statistics, one area for future work is exploring more sophisticated models for predicting the popularity of a gesture cluster.

Combining Crowd and User's Own Gestures

Gesture Marks uses the same representation and matching algorithm for both gestures drawn by the user as well as gestures drawn by the crowd. However, since the user's own gestures are more likely to be relevant than those from others, we add a bias to the system so that it slightly favors these user gestures. This bias was determined empirically based on analysis of the similarity scores from the exploratory study.

Inferring Shortcuts with Handwriting Recognition

As we discussed earlier, a significant portion of gesture shortcuts were based on characters. We employ a handwriting recognizer in Gesture Marks so that these types of gestures can be recognized even if they have never been seen before by the system. While handwriting recognition is not our main contribution, it is an important component in our gesture bootstrapping approach and we discuss it in detail here for readers to better understand how our system can be implemented.

Touch-screen handwriting gestures have many special properties, such as finger-based input, limited drawing area, limited computational resources, and a language model consisting of quick mnemonic shortcuts instead of complete dictionary words. To address these challenges, we developed a specialized handwriting recognizer for Gesture Marks that has the following important properties:

- It is tailored to finger-based input and trained on letters and words collected on touch screen smartphones.
- It uses a language model that is specially designed for mobile shortcut navigation.
- It supports natural multi-stroke letters as well as mixed cursive handwriting.
- It does not require character level labels for training.
- It is fast enough to run in real time on a smartphone.

In order to support natural cursive handwriting, our recognizer needs to accomplish two tasks: character segmentation (i.e., determining where one character ends and the next begins) and recognition (i.e., inferring the identity of each segmented character). We will discuss both of these in turn.

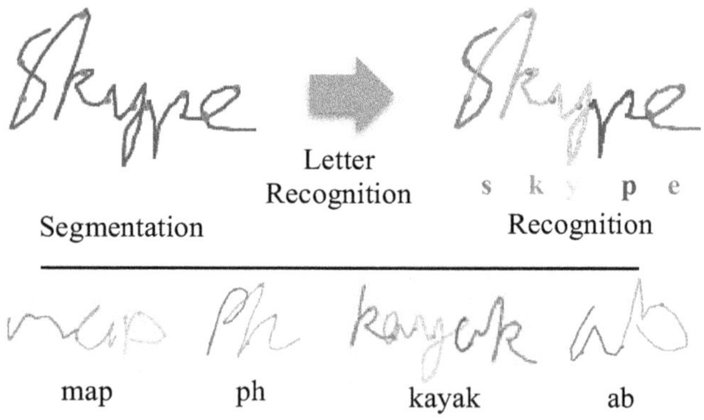

Figure 8: (top) An illustration of the segmentation and recognition approach in our handwriting recognizer. (bottom) Examples of handwriting gestures our system recognized correctly as well as their inferred character segmentations.

Character Segmentation

In the case of cursive handwriting a single character may be drawn with multiple strokes and a single stroke may contain multiple characters (we define each stroke as the sequence of points drawn by the user between a touch-down and touch-up event). Our approach to segmentation starts by splitting all of the strokes in the gesture at points that correspond to local minima and maxima in the y-axis. The result of this splitting process is a sequence of stroke fragments as shown in Figure 8.

The next task for the recognizer is to determine how the individual stroke fragments combine to form the characters in the word. We accomplish this task by applying our character recognizer (described in the next section) on all possible groups of up to k temporally contiguous stroke fragments (in our implementation we empirically set $k = 5$). Next we determine which of these groups most likely correspond to intended characters. Let $\boldsymbol{G}$ be a sequence of n groups $\{G_1, G_2, \ldots, G_n\}$ and $\boldsymbol{L}$ be a sequence of character labels $\{L_1, L_2, \ldots, L_n\}$ representing one possible labeling for the groups in $\boldsymbol{G}$. Then the word score for the sequence is defined as:

$$W(\boldsymbol{G}, \boldsymbol{L}) = \sum_{i=1}^{n} \log(f(G_i, L_i))\, n_f(G_i)$$

where $f(G_i, L_i)$ is the character score for assigning group G_i the label L_i and $n_f(G_i)$ is the number of fragments in group G_i (this is needed to prevent the system from biasing interpretations that contain fewer groups). We use beam search to find the n-best sequences that maximize W.

Recognition

We build a letter recognition model that employs the same visual feature images that we use for similarity based gesture matching. We also incorporate a set of additional features that capture the temporal pattern of the candidate group. These consist of the position, direction, and curvature of the gesture at n equally spaced touch points sampled along the path of the gesture. Finally, we add a set of geometric features such as the number of fragments, the number of strokes, the aspect ratio, and relative size of the candidate group compared to the complete gesture.

We use a support vector machine (SVM) [4] with a linear kernel to classify each group, based on the set of features listed above. We chose the linear kernel because it allows for efficient constant time classification, and only requires that we store a weight vector for each class rather than the full set of support vectors.

The training data for the SVM consists of both positive examples (correctly segmented characters) as well as negative examples (mis-segmented fragments). Training is done via an efficient linear SVM algorithm based on gradient descent in the dual space [9]. In order to produce probability estimates we fit a sigmoid function over the SVM decision values.

Training using Forced Alignment

One important feature of our handwriting recognition approach is that it does not require character level labels for the words in the training set. This means that the developer does not need to manually label the beginnings and endings of all the characters in the word (e.g., that fragments 1-2 in Figure 8 form an "s", etc.). She only needs to provide the whole word label (e.g., "skype").

To extract and learn character models from these partially labeled words we employ an EM based approach [6] that is similar to the forced alignment process in natural language transcription. During training the recognizer first builds a letter model using only the isolated character examples in the training set. Next, it applies this character model to the whole words in the training set, inferring the correct segmentation as the one that maximizes the word sequence score W. This process relies on the fact that since we know the whole word label, we can force the system to only consider those character sequences where the labeling $\boldsymbol{L}$ matches the ground truth.

Once we have the approximate character boundaries, we can re-train our letter model with these inferred cursive characters in addition to the isolated characters from before. We can then use this updated character model to refine the approximate character boundaries even further, repeating the process across multiple iterations until performance on a validation set ceases to improve.

The Language Model

To improve accuracy and speed we limit the space of possible word interpretations to the set of partial words and initials found in the targets on the user's device. For example, these would include "a", "an", "b", "bi", "ab", etc., for the target Angry Birds. The result of the handwriting recognition process is a ranked list of word predictions, each of which is mapped to one or more targets (e.g., "ma" to both Maps and Market).

Combining Predictions

Our system generates predictions using a combination of two distinct methods: template-based gesture matching and handwriting recognition. We need to merge the two sets of predictions to build the final list of targets presented to the user. Unfortunately, this is not a trivial task because we cannot compare the results of the two recognizers directly. The former is a similarity distance and the latter is a word sequence score.

In this initial implementation of our system, we employed a simple but robust approach to combining these two sets of predictions. This method relies only on the rank of a given target in either prediction list. We assign a rank score to each target as $rs = 1/r_g + 1/r_h$, where r_g is the rank of the target given by the gesture similarity recognizer and r_h is the rank given by the handwriting recognizer. This ensures that the system presents the user with high-ranking matches from both gesture similarity matching and handwriting recognition, and favors most those that are ranked highly by both.

EVALUATIONS

We conducted a user study to understand how users interact with our system. The goals of the study were to learn:

- How often the system is able to correctly predict the destination for a gesture.
- The sources contributing to the correct prediction: crowd gestures, user's own gestures, or handwriting recognition.
- How the prediction accuracy and the role of each source evolve as users use the system.

Experimental Procedures

For this study we asked 22 participants (4 female) to use our system to launch a series of targets (websites and applications) using gestures. Their ages ranged from 19 to 35 (mean = 29) and their occupations included engineers, students, researchers, and business analysts. First, users were asked to pick out a set of 40 targets that they use most frequently from a list of 80 popular applications and websites. The list contained the most common targets from the previous exploratory study.

Next, the system prompted the users with each of the selected targets in random order, asking them to draw a gesture to launch the target in question. The system then tried to predict the intended target of the gesture using its combined template and handwriting recognizer, displaying a set of 8 best matches to the user. If the correct target was in this list, the participant was asked to click on it, and the system moved on to the next target.

The goal of the evaluation was not to test how well users could guess the most popular gesture for a given target, so we asked users to draw whatever gesture made sense to them. If the system did not predict the correct target among its list of top 8 matches, the participant was told to select the target manually from the full list of applications and websites. The series of targets was repeated 4 times, to simulate users revisiting the same target.

To guarantee that the conditions across users remained constant, we fixed the crowd-based gesture library to contain only the gestures collected before the start of the study. We also fixed the list of applications and websites for this study to match the 80 most popular targets found in the first exploratory study (a total of 50 apps and 30 websites). The resulting crowd-based library contained a total of 414 gesture clusters covering the set of 80 targets in the study. Of course, in the real world users will have a much wider range of targets they may wish to visit, including less popular links for which there are fewer crowd-based gestures. However, in a real world deployment the crowd-based gesture library will also be much larger than the one used during the study, and will be continually expanding over time. Note that while users were prompted to draw gestures for their 40 selected targets, the system predictions spanned the whole 80 targets.

Experimental Results

In this section we present the results of our evaluation, looking at prediction accuracy, the contribution of each source to the correct prediction, and user impressions while using our interface.

Prediction Accuracy

We first wanted to analyze how often our system was able to predict the correct target for the user's gesture in the list of top 8 matches. In Figure 9, the "Manually Defined" line shows the number of gestures that the subject had to define manually because the system did not display it in the list, over each of the 4 repetitions. It shows that the users needed to manually define only 23% percent of the targets in the initial round. This means that the system was able to predict the correct target based on the user's gesture 77% of the time, even before it had seen any of the user's own gestures for the targets. By the final repetition, users manually defined less than 1% of their gestures, while the system correctly predicted the target over 99% of the time.

Contribution of Each Source to the Correct Prediction

For the cases where the system did predict the correct target to a gesture query, we also recorded the rank given by both the template-based recognizer and the handwriting recognizer. Furthermore, in the template-based case we recorded whether the correct match came from the user's own gesture library or the crowd's. Figure 9 plots how frequently each of the 3 sources (user gesture, crowd gesture, or handwriting) ranked the correct target the lowest (i.e., was the most informative). This was done for each of the 4 repetitions. In the event of a tie we applied partial counts, e.g., 1/2 to the handwriting recognizer and 1/2 to the user gestures.

At the beginning (during the initial round), because users had not drawn any gestures, the contribution of the user's own gestures (the red plot in Figure 9) was zero.

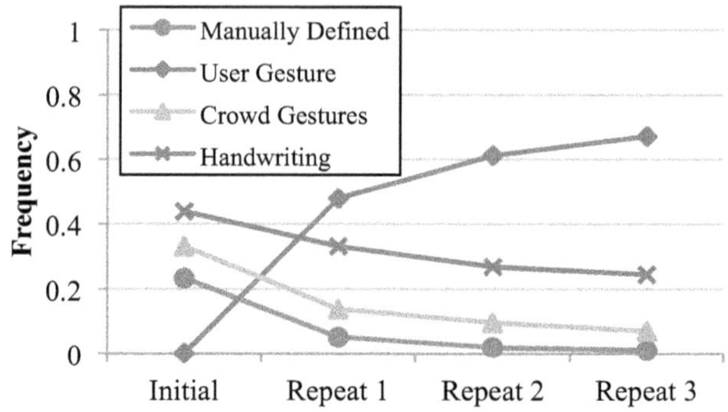

Figure 9: Frequency that each source was the most informative for the correct prediction.

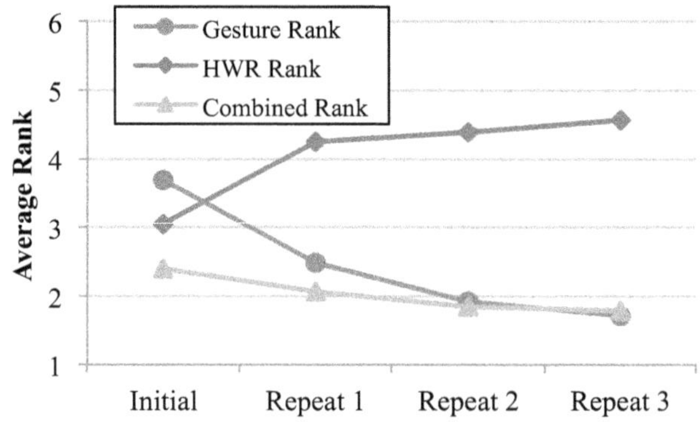

Figure 10: The average rank of the correct target using only gesture similarity, only handwriting, and the average final combined rank (lower means the correct target is closer to the top choice and more accurate).

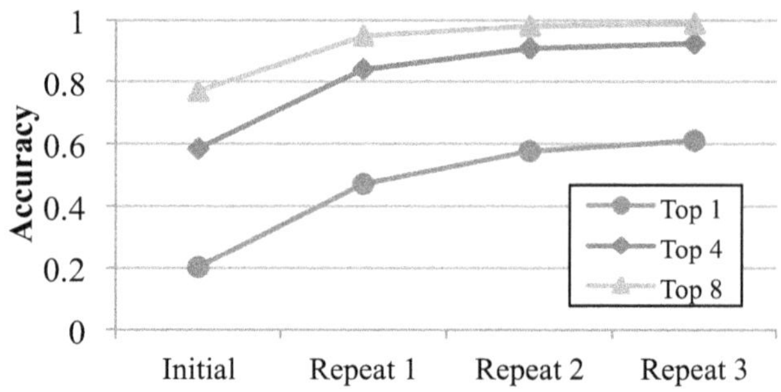

Figure 11: The prediction accuracy when considering the top 1, 4, and 8 matches.

Handwriting recognition and crowd gestures were the major contributors. Handwriting recognition gave the correct target with the lowest rank 44% of the time, while crowd gesture matching did so 33% of the time.

In the second repetition, the most useful source was already the user's own gestures, as all the gestures drawn in the initial round were recorded as templates. This source ranked the correct target the lowest 48% of the time. By the last repetition, this frequency increased to 67%. This suggests that users rapidly converged to a small set of possible gestures for a majority of the targets, and that our system was capable of quickly and effectively learning these gesture patterns.

Gesture Rank

In addition to looking at which source was the most informative, we also examined the average rank given to the correct target using only the template-based recognizer, only the handwriting recognizer, and using the combination of the two. Figure 10 plots these average ranks across the 4 rounds of the study. We can see that especially in the earlier rounds, the combined rank is noticeably lower than the rank from either gesture similarity or handwriting recognition alone. This demonstrates that there is significant benefit in combining the two sources. Furthermore, we found that the gesture rank and combined rank both converged to about 1.7 by the last repetition, meaning that the system was no longer relying on the handwriting recognizer at this stage and that the correct match was frequently ranked first or second in the list.

Interestingly, we also discovered that the average rank provided by the handwriting recognizer actually got slightly worse with each repetition. We suspect that one reason for this is due to the fact that users became faster and messier as they revisited the same targets, and became more confident as they noticed that the system could accurately recognize their particular handwriting or drawing style. As we can see from Figure 9, this accuracy was mostly due to the visual similarity to the user's own previously provided gesture examples.

Prediction Ranking

Finally, we also analyzed how often the system predicted the correct target in the top 1, 4, and 8 matches. This helps us understand how the system would perform in a different interface that provides a smaller list of predictions. The results in Figure 11 show that in the initial round our system was able to predict the correct target as the first choice 20% of the time and include it in the top-8 list 77% of the time. These numbers increase to 61% and 99% respectively by the last repetition. Note that one reason why the top-4 and top-8 accuracies are significantly higher than top-1 is likely due to mapping ambiguity, where a user draws the same gesture for multiple targets. By displaying multiple predictions, the system can retrieve all of the targets that map to a given gesture.

User Feedback

We asked all of the participants in the study to answer a survey afterwards about their experience using Gesture Marks. We asked users to rate whether they thought the system would be useful for them, whether it was accurate in predicting the intended target for a gesture, and whether it became more accurate with use. All of the ratings were on a 5-point Likert scale with 1 for "strongly disagree" and 5 for "strongly agree". A majority of users agreed that Gesture Marks would be useful (median=4) and was accurate (median=4), and strongly agreed that the accuracy improved with use (median=5).

Users mentioned in their comments that they liked the speed and accuracy of the system, and it's ability to handle arbitrary gestures: *"I liked that it learned quickly about what I wanted it to display, even if I picked something wacky"*, *"liked -- got pretty accurate as time progressed. intuitive, simple to use."*, and *"I really like the simplicity in this program that allows you to access applications and websites that on a regular task may take you some time to find amongst all your apps."*

Several users also mentioned that they might have trouble remembering custom gesture for a large number of targets. One user came up with a solution to the recallibility problem by using the gestures to specify categories of targets: *"i tend to use the gesture for a category of things, like m (as in mail) for gmail and other mail apps."* Another user liked that fact that he could filter the list of targets quickly using a single letter.

One common criticism for Gesture Marks was that handwriting gestures did not work for some abbreviations such as "kyk" for Kayak or "m" for Gmail, since the language model employed by the handwriting recognizer only matched partial words or initials.

RELATED WORK

There is a long history of gesture and sketched based interfaces in the HCI community. Touch gestures have been used for searching mobile devices [14] and for creating custom shortcuts to invoke commands [2,8,12,13], bypassing the standard hierarchical menu structure with a quick and natural gesture.

Search with alphabet-based gesture shortcuts leverages the mnemonic relationship between gestures and targets (e.g., [14]), alleviating the effort for both defining and recalling gestures. However, they are limited because they are constrained to only character-based gestures, do not adequately adapt to a particular user's drawing style, and can be less efficient for accessing a large corpus such as the web. Other systems allow users to associate an alphabet gesture with a specific task (e.g., [12,21]), but the process of manually defining gesture mappings or learning larges sets of predefined ones can be tedious.

In contrast, Gesture Marks addresses these problems with gesture shortcuts using the following features. 1) It allows arbitrary drawing gestures in addition to handwritten characters. 2) It supports mixed cursive handwriting that is based on a language model tailored for shortcuts. 3) It contains a crowd-based gesture library that records, analyzes, and shares popular gestures among the user population. 4) It adapts to the user over time by learning his or her particular drawing or handwriting style.

Although substantial work [14,15,19,20] has been conducted on gesture recognition, little effort has been devoted to the situation when little or no data is available, or on how to continuously improve recognition over time. In our work we explored both of these challenges and contributed two bootstrapping approaches based on the "wisdom of the crowd" and handwriting recognition.

Morris et al. [16] elicited a set of gestures for interactive surfaces and revealed that participants preferred gestures authored by larger groups of people. Similarly, our crowdsourcing component is built on the assumption that popular gestures tend to be preferred by users. In contrast to their work, Gesture Marks automatically learns and dynamically evolves these gestures as users interact with the system instead of relying on researchers to manually distill a favorable gesture set from the users.

Handwriting recognition is a well-studied area of research that has been used in many mobile platforms such as the Palm Pilot, Apple Newton, and Microsoft Windows Mobile. Previous work on handwriting recognition has focused mainly on isolated characters [3,5] or complete lines of text consisting of dictionary words [10,18]. In contrast, Gesture Marks employs its own specialized handwriting recognizer that is tailored to the types of gestures people draw on touch screen devices. It also uses a dynamic language model that is customized for the set of targets available on each individual's device.

CONCLUSIONS AND FUTURE WORK

This paper presented Gesture Marks, a novel approach to touch-gesture interaction that allows a user to access applications and websites using natural gestures without having to define them beforehand. Our initial study contributed new knowledge on user-defined gesture shortcuts. It investigated the types of gestures people tend to draw and analyzed the visual and semantic consistency of gesture shortcuts, both from the same user and across users. We presented two approaches for bootstrapping user-defined gesture shortcuts, leveraging gestures drawn by the crowd and employing a specialized handwriting recognizer. An evaluation showed that our system was able to achieve a high level of accuracy even before a user had defined any of his or her own gestures, and was able to quickly learn a user's drawing patterns over time.

This paper focused on navigating applications and websites because these are two types of targets that are very likely to be shared across users. For more personal information like contacts, crowd-based gestures may become less useful. In that case the system will need to rely more on user-defined gestures and handwriting recognition. In the future we intend to support these and other types of targets such as phone settings and music tracks. We will also start to deploy Gesture Marks extensively to more participants for longitudinal studies, to find out how the system and user behaviors evolve over a longer period of time.

REFERENCES

1. Android. http://www.android.com/.
2. Appert, C. and Zhai, S., Using strokes as command shortcuts: cognitive benefits and toolkit support. In *CHI 2009*, 2289-2298.
3. Bahlmann, C., Haasdonk, B., Burkhardt, H., On-Line Handwriting Recognition with Support Vector Machines; A Kernel Approach. In *IWFHR 2002*, 49-54.
4. Boser, B., Guyon, I. M., and Vapnik, V.N. 1992. A training algorithm for optimal margin classifiers. In *COLT 1992*, 144-152.
5. Connell, S.D., and Jain, A.K. Template-based online character recognition. In *Pattern Recognition 2001*, 1-14.
6. Dempster, A, pp., Laird, N. M., Rubin, D. B. Maximum likelihood from incomplete data via the EM algorithm. *Journal of the Royal Statistical Society* 1977, 1-38.
7. Guha, S, Rastogim R, and Shim, K. CURE: an efficient clustering algorithm for large databases. In *SIGMOD 1998*, 73-84.
8. Guimbretiere, F. and Winogra, T., FlowMenu: Combining Command, Text and Parameter Entry. In *UIST 2000*, 213-216.
9. Hsieh, C., Hsieh, K., Chang, C., Lin, S., S. Keerthi, and S. Sundararajan. A dual coordinate descent method for large-scale linear SVM. In *ICML 2008*, 408-415.
10. Hu, J., Gek, Brown, M. Writer independent on-line handwriting recognition using an HMM approach. In *Pattern Recognition 2000*, 133-147.
11. iPhone. http://www.apple.com/iphone/.
12. Kristensson, P.O. and Zhai, S. Command strokes with and without preview: using pen gestures on keyboard for command selection. In *CHI 2007*, 1137-1146.
13. Kurtenbach, G. and Buxton, W. The limits of expert performance using hierarchical marking menus. In *CHI 1993*, 482-487.
14. Li, Y. Gesture Search: A Tool for Fast Mobile Data Access. In *UIST 2010*, 87-96.
15. Li, Y. Protractor: A Fast and Accurate Gesture Recognizer. In *CHI 2010*, 2169-2172.
16. Morris, M.R., Wobbrock, J.O. and Wilson, A.D. Understanding users' preferences for surface gestures. In *Graphics Interface 2010*, 261-268.
17. Ouyang, T and Davis, R. A Visual Approach to Sketched Symbol Recognition. In *IJCAI 2009*, 1463-1468.
18. Plamondon, R. and Srihari, S.N. Online and off-line handwriting recognition: a comprehensive survey. In *PAMI 2000*, 63-84.
19. Wobbrock, J.O., Wilson, A.D., and Li, Y. Gestures without libraries, toolkits or training: a $1 recognizer for user interface prototypes. In *UIST 2007*, 159-168.
20. Anthony, L., Wobbrock, J.O. A Lightweight Multistroke Recognizer for User Interface Prototypes. In *Graphics Interface 2010*, 245-252.
21. Zhai, S. and Kristensson, P.O. Shorthand writing on stylus keyboard. In *CHI 2003*, 97-104.

Habit as an Explanation of Participation in an Online Peer-production Community

Donghee Yvette Wohn[1], Alcides Velasquez[1], Tor Bjornrud[1], Cliff Lampe[2]

[1]Michigan State University
409 Communication Arts
East Lansing, MI 48824
{wohndong, velasq24, bjornrud} @msu.edu

[2]University of Michigan
4388 North Quad
Ann Arbor, MI 48109
cacl@umich.edu

ABSTRACT
User activities in peer-production communities have mainly been examined under the assumption that individuals are rational individuals who are always cognizant of what they are doing and why. We argue that not all use is the same; while some behaviors are governed by conscious motivations, others may be a habitual response that is developed out of routine. We take a more granular approach to explaining what people are doing in online communities and how motivations and habits explain their use of specific features. In the context of the peer-production community Everything2 we employ both server log data and self-report, finding that habit is a non-conscious-driven behavior that is more associated with less cognitively-demanding tasks than content production.

Author Keywords
Habit; online community; motivations; computer supported collaborative work

ACM Classification Keywords
H.5.3. Group and Organization Interfaces

General Terms
Human Factors, Theory, Verification

INTRODUCTION
In this paper, we introduce the concept of *habit* as an important psychological construct that helps predict sustained user participation in online communities. Habit is an automated cognitive heuristic that helps people make decisions about system use without having to incur the cost of conscious decision processing on a regular basis. By creating a heuristic of use, habit may be a more salient concept to explain sustained use than motivation, which involves conscious choice and may be more prevalent at the inception of online community participation.

Previous research has shown that the way people participate in peer-production communities is not monolithic. For example, on Wikipedia researchers have identified multiple types of activities in both editing [37] and administration [19]. Activities can range from simply reading the content of others, to posting original content, interacting with other users, or administering content through rating or editing. We take a granular approach to explaining what people are doing in online communities because the activities that users engage in can range from passive consumption of content to active production of content. Previous studies that have taken a more nuanced look at the different types of behaviors within online communities [8,33] have found that conceptualizing activities in online communities in a uniform manner may not paint an accurate picture of user behavior.

It is important to understand what contributes to sustained user participation in peer-production communities, which often have social or economic value. For example, Wikipedia provides information freely and broadly, but has been shown to be losing editors over time [34]. Previous research has tried to explain and understand why people consume and contribute to websites with user-generated content. Some have used theoretical frameworks, including cost and benefit paradigms [12,30], social psychological explanations [5,10], and social learning theory [7,22], to study participation. Others have examined the issue from more of a design perspective, reporting that specific features of the media [33], characteristics of the content [3,6], or design elements can motivate people to participate [29]. Much of the research has focused on explaining participation of new users [7,22] though more recent studies have looked into motivations of long-term users [23].

Despite the different approaches that scholars have taken to study these communities, the one thing that they have in common is the underlying assumption that users *consciously* choose why and how they want to use the site. In other words, it is expected that users are rational beings in that they actively make their decisions. However, to what extent is this presupposition true? Could it be that some of our behavior online is more or less conducted without much thinking?

The concept of habit as an individual user characteristic has not been studied in depth in information system use, though early organizational theorists proposed habit as an essential aspect in decision making along with emotion and cognition, and have related it to the concept of organizational routines [11]. We distinguish habits as properties of an individual and routines as a property of a group or organization. Recently, media researchers have started to suggest that conscious motivations are more salient when someone is just beginning to use a system, but gradually become co-mingled with habit [21]. We adapt this focus on habit from media research as a potential explanation for why users participate in social media.

We also shift the focus from how much time people spend in online communities to how much time they are spending on individual activities. In the context of the peer-production community Everything2.com, we employ both server log data and self-reports, we present how habit predicts different uses of the website.

EXPLAINING HABIT

Habit is a routine that individuals engage in with little conscious knowledge, awareness, or intention [1,39]. For example, putting on one's seatbelt may have been something that first-time drivers pay much attention to, but veteran drivers will probably buckle their seatbelt without much thought. Habits can also govern media use [21]. If you think about what you do when you first turn on the computer, you will probably realize that there is a pattern in terms of which websites you visit.

Early definitions of habit have described of the concept in terms of frequency of past behavior [39]. However, further research, concept, and measurement refinements have conceptualized habit as not necessarily defined in terms of frequency of past behavior, but in terms of the automaticity of behaviors triggered by specific cues [36], that can also be performed at the same time as other activities [25].

In this paper, we define habit as an automatic responses that is triggered by an environmental stimulus [4,36]. In other words, habits are "sequential, repetitive, motor, or cognitive behaviors elicited by triggers, that, once released, can go to completion without constant conscious oversight" [14]. So the inside of the car can be the environmental stimulus to trigger putting on the seatbelt, whereas a browser or computer screen can act as a stimulus to trigger habitual Internet surfing behavior. These behaviors are almost reflexive in the sense that the individual isn't thinking about why he or she is doing it or how.

Behaviors that are considered habitual do not require continuous attention to be performed, as cognitive resources are freed to deal with other unrelated thoughts [39]. This idea of cognitive overload has been the underlying explanation of psychological theories of peripheral information processing [9,28]. Basically, these theories argue that sometimes people carefully consider information based on the strength of the argument, while other times they rely on cognitive "shortcuts," or heuristics, to make a judgment [24]. In this sense, habits respond to the efficiency in which cognitive resources are used, as the brain does not have to make the same decision each time a behavior is performed.

Although habit is a type of non-conscious behavior, they are not unrelated to conscious behavior, such as goals—in other words, an individual's behavior can still be habitual even when there is an underlying motivation to accomplish a task. For example, one may have the goal of driving to work; habit may cause the person to take the same route every day without giving it much thought. At the same time, habits are not permanent: a different stimulus—such as a traffic accident—could take an individual out of the habit and pursue different behavior. Thus, habits can act in parallel with conscious intentions and motivations as predictors of a behavior.

HABIT AND MEDIA USE

Many studies of why people use media have been guided by social learning or uses and gratifications [7,23]. Uses and gratifications is the notion that people have certain needs and use media to fulfill those needs [17]. The majority of uses and gratifications studies identify motivations and look at the linear relationship between motivations and time spent using a particular medium—such studies include early research on television [32] to more recent research on social network sites [16]. These studies report a small but significant relationship between motivations and time spent on the site: an overview of several uses and gratifications studies shows that motivations explain less than 30% of the variance, with most studies reporting less than 10% [20].

The notion of habit as a construct to help understand media use runs in parallel to the uses and gratifications paradigm, but many of the studies on habitual media use have been qualitative in nature. In one of the earliest studies, Greenberg [15] identified habit as one of the seven television viewing motivations of children and adolescents. Krendl and Lasky [18] conducted a content analysis of adolescents' open-ended responses to television's influences on their lives and found that 52% of those who mentioned negative effects referred to television viewing as a "habitual dedication established by routine rather than by conscious choice." Rosenstein and Grant [31] examined individuals' television viewing patterns between weekdays and weekends; the similarity in the patterns suggested that habit plays a significant role in viewing behavior. Adams [2] reported data from focus groups, also supporting the role of habit in television viewing. Despite this evidence, habitual media use has been a topic of controversy among mass communication scholars because of the general trend in the social sciences of focusing on behavior involving more complex cognitive processes [21].

Why is it important to consider habit in our studies of how people use media, including social media and online communities? In the case of online behavior, recent studies show that when asking questions to people who have already been using a certain medium, habit is a larger predictor of time spent using the medium than motivations. In many cases, habit accounts for 40-50% of the variance in time spent on the Internet [20] or playing social games [35].

Thus, for designers or administrators who are trying to create and maintain a system that is trying to keep users engaged in the long run, understanding how habits are formed and how habits affect future use may greatly supplement what can be learned just by looking at user motivation and even provide explanations for behavior that is less affected by motivation. There is little literature in the CHI community about habitual behavior, but the few studies that do exist suggest that habit is an extremely important factor in usability. For example, a large-scale study on password use reports that users' choice of passwords are strongly influenced by habit [13]. Habit can also pose difficulties for users switching mobile phone models [40].

RESEARCH QUESTIONS

Many uses and gratifications studies have used motivations to explain how much time users spend using a particular media [16,27]. However, scholars who have added habit strength to their models have found that habit significantly adds to the variance explained by motivations in terms of how much time a user spends using a media [20]. The first question, therefore, is to see if habit indeed increases explanatory power in terms of users' time spent on the site.

RQ1: Does habit help explain the overall amount of time spent on the site?

Habit is reliant on the repetition of positive reinforcements; previous satisfactory experiences enhance the tendency to repeat a behavior and create habits. The strength of the habit, however, depends on the persistence of environmental features [24]. Habit is strongly dependent on the stability of the context in which the behavior is performed. In stable environments where performance times, locations and other contextual features are persistent; repeated behaviors tend to become habitual as these environmental cues trigger associated behaviors.

Our second research question is to see if use of specific features in an online community is associated with habit and if cue-dependent activities are more associated with habit than those that are not:

RQ2: What is the relationship between past behaviors on Everything2 and habit strength?

Also of interest is if habit can be a predictor of how a user perceives they will use the site in the future—in other words, how habit affects individuals' intention in terms of how they want to use the specific features in the future—and if there is any difference between what habit predicts and what current motivations predict. Ouellete and Wood [25] suggest that once habits have been established, intentions become antecedents of habitual behavior. Furthermore, conscious motivations and attitudes become less salient as habits form. In addition, even if habit is able to explain future behavior, does it apply to all behavior? It could be that habit predicts intention for certain behaviors but not others.

RQ3a: How do motivations predict general intention to visit the site in the future?

RQ3b: How does habit predict general intention to visit the site in the future?

RQ4a: How do motivations predict intention to use specific features?

- Read others' content?
- Write content?
- Communicate with other users?
- Vote on others' content?

RQ4b: How does habit predict intention to use specific features? (Same features as above).

METHOD

About Everything2

The research questions outlined above were tested in the context of Everything2. Founded in 1999, Everything2 is a wiki-style online community where members can interact with one another through many different modes of communication, centered around series of topical write-ups. Everything2 has an active user base of about 3,000 contributing members, and receives approximately 590,000 unique visitors and 1.2 million page views in one month as of September, 2011.

Everything2 is structured as an encyclopedia, much like Wikipedia, so content is in the form of articles, even though on Everything2 these articles can include creative writing content and more personal diary-like entries. Any one topic on Everything2 is called a "node" and individual user contributions to that topic are called "Write-ups". Unlike other wikis, users maintain ownership of their contributions, and contributions may *not* be edited by other users. Different social features on Everything2 allow users to give feedback through voting systems, reputation systems, as well as through private messaging. Users can also use messaging to engage in personal conversations that are more social in nature. Upvotes are positive evaluations that users can assign to the Write-ups of other users. Downvotes are similar to Upvotes, but only differ in that they are negative evaluations. All votes are +/- assignments, and users may only vote once on each Write-up. Users are limited in the number of votes they may assign within a given timeframe. This time frame, and size of a user's voting pool depends on many factors such as amount of contribution to the site and/or administrator status.

These features were made available to users to facilitate community building and management of site-content. Furthermore, there are editorial actions and voting actions that other members of the community may take to highlight and edit which Write-ups become seen on the first page of Everything2, as well as which Write-ups are viewed first on a typical node.

Participants

An online survey of registered users of the site Everything2.com was conducted in order to answer the research questions in this study. The online survey was conducted on the website Survey Gizmo over a three-week period during the summer of 2011.

A banner inviting users to participate in a study was viewable on the top of the front page of Everything2 once users had logged-in. The banner remained viewable on each page of the site until users had accepted to participate on the survey, or declined the invitation by clicking on a "No thanks" link. To prevent duplicate survey entries from the same user, after clicking on either link the banner would no longer be shown on Everything2.com pages served to that user's IP address.

A total of 148 registered users answered the online survey. Participants' average age was 33.2 (*S.D.*= 10.85). 77.3% were males and 22.7% were females. Participants were from 18 different countries, 61.8% of which were from the United States, and 79.9% had English as their first language.

Survey Measures

The survey questionnaire included items assessing participants' habit strength for using the site and their motivations. The measurements of each of these variables were constructed using multi-item additive indices that assessed different aspects of each variable. The questionnaire also asked users about their intentions to use specific features of the site during the next two months.

We examined six motivations incorporating constructs from existing uses and gratifications scales [20]: social, status, enjoyment, self-reactive, novelty, and monetary. The items were prefaced with "Using E2, how likely are you to..." which users answered on a 7-point Likert-type scale from "Very unlikely" to "Very likely." Table 1 reports the reliability scores for the scales of each of the variables, as well as their means and standard deviations. All scales showed a reliable score with a Cronbach's α above .70.

The definition of habit in terms of automaticity, as well as the characterization of this type of behavior in relation to its defining dimensions, has also derived on the development of operational definitions of the concept. We used the Self-Report Habit Index (SRHI), which measures the degree of habitual behavior perceived by an individual, which encompasses different dimensions of the construct [36]. We used eight items from the Self-Report Habit Index. One item ("Using Everything2 is something that expresses my personal style") was deleted because it lowered the reliability of the scale. The scale was very reliable and showed a normal distribution among survey participants (M=4.0, SD=1.58, Cronbach's alpha=.95) Users rated the

"Using Everything2, how likely are you to..."
Social (M=4.97, SD=.14, α=.83)
Feel you belong to a group
Contribute to the community
Stay in touch with other users
Provide information to others
Status (M= 4.64, SD=1.28, α=.87)
Communicate with like-minded people
Impress other users
Feel important
Help other users
Encourage other users
Enjoyment (M=5.25, SD= 1.07, α =.84)
Cheer yourself up
Get a good laugh
Be entertained
Play
Relax
Self-reactive (M=4.83, SD=1.21, α=.78),
Forget about your problems
Relieve boredom
Feel less lonely
Find a way to pass time
Novelty (M=5.27, SD=1.13, α=.84),
Get new information
Learn how to do things
Learn about things you can learn elsewhere
Generate new ideas
Monetary (M=4.90, SD=1.35, α=.83).
Avoid spending
Interact with others without spending money
Have fun without spending much
Save money
Engage in an activity that does not require costs

Table 1. Survey scales for motivations.

following items on a 7-point Likert-type scale from "Strongly disagree" to "Strongly agree":

"Using Everything2.com is something..."

- I do automatically
- I do without having to consciously remember
- That makes me feel weird if I do not do it
- I do without thinking
- That would require effort not to do it
- I start doing before I realize I'm doing it
- I would find it hard not to do
- I have no need to think about doing

Another question we asked was how often people used specific features in the past month. Users were asked to rate the frequency of their behavior in the past month on a 5-point Likert-type scale from "never" to "very frequently."

We also asked users to report their intention to use specific features in the next two months. We asked, "Considering your usage of Everything2.com, how frequently do you intent to perform the following actions during the next two months?" which they answered on 5-point Likert-type scale from "never" to "very frequently." Users reported on their intention for visiting the website, contributing Write-ups, reading other users' Write-ups, using the private messaging feature, Upvoting others' Write-ups, and Downvoting others' Write-ups. Means and standard deviations are reported in Table 2.

Self-reported use of features in past month	
Contribution to Write-ups	M=2.10, SD=1.34
Upvoting	M=3.55, SD=1.55
Downvoting	M=2.48, SD=1.34
Messaging	M=3.37, SD=1.47
Intention to use specific features in next two months	
Intent to…	
Visit website	M=4.05, SD=.87
Contribute Write-up	M=2.42, SD=1.06
Read others' Write-ups	M=4.05, SD=.89
Use private messaging	M=3.15, SD=1.22
Upvote others' Write-ups	M=3.44, SD=1.25
Downvote others' Write-ups	M=2.43, SD=1.03

Table 2. Self-reported past use and intent for future use on a 5-point Likert-type scale

Other descriptive questions included Membership length (self-report of how long they were a member of the site), average time spent on the site, gender, age, country, English proficiency, primary username, and any additional account usernames. For time spent on the site, we asked users how many hours and minutes they spend on the site on a typical weekday (M=1.17 hours, SD=1.40) and typical weekend (M=1.32, SD=1.40) and averaged the time (M=1.24, SD=1.29). We used the usernames to extract their behavioral data from the servers, but once the behavioral data was matched with their self-report, their user names were discarded.

Log Data

Behavioral activity was measured using server-log data directly from Everything2. Metrics for each respondent were calculated from the 30 days prior to their survey participation until the end of survey data collection. Survey responses of usernames were then matched against the entire list of Everything2 usernames. Usernames on Everything2 are unique to each account. A long-standing member of the Everything2 community reviewed participant responses and corrected assumed typographical errors. Accounts that could still not be matched after this processing were discarded.

We summed the total votes users gave to other Write-ups, including both positive and negative votes. The total number of Write-ups contributed to the site was also summed. Number of Write-ups also included any Write-ups that later were deleted by administrators. We also looked at how many messages users sent. A message addressed to multiple users was only considered as a single message. Contribution activities were measured covering their activities in the month prior to launching the survey (July 8th, 2011 to September 9th, 2011). Ranges, means, and standard deviations of user activity are reported in Table 3.

	Min~Max	Mean (SD)
Activity during entire membership		
Account age (days)	14~4,799	2,487.99 (1,544.18)
No. of Write-ups	0~ 1,846	244.58 (394.67)
No. of Votes	0~180,367	16,541 (31, 880)
Messages sent	0~40,153	4,225.59 (7,266.32)
Activity one month prior to survey		
No. of Write-ups	0~47	2.3 (5.73)
No. of Votes	0~2,465	155.60 (392.26)
Messages sent	0~1,777	144.49 (317.28)

Table 3. Log data of user activity

RESULTS

Explaining Time Spent on Site

First, we tried to replicate previous studies [20,35] that have reported a significant effect of habit in terms of increasing explanatory power of time spent on the site. We ran three Ordinary Least Squares (OLS) regressions with a self reported measure of time spent on the site as the dependent variable in each model: the first model used motivations as the independent variables; the second model used habit only as the independent variables; the third combined both sets of independent variables.

It is important to note that habit, when it is activated, is more or less a non-conscious *neurological* process. In other words, engaging in a habitual behavior does not mean that the individual is oblivious as to what is going on, only that the individual is not actively thinking about it. Because habits are associated with goals, habits and motivations are not mutually exclusive, which is why we would want to ultimately include both in the same model.

As can be seen in Table 4, status and monetary outcomes are the two motivations that positively and significantly explain why people spend time on the site—people who seek status or want to avoid spending money are more likely to report higher habit.

On its own, habit was also a strong predictor: people who use the site in a habitual manner are more likely to spend more time on the site. In addition, the second model with habit as the sole predictor of time spent on the site (F(4, 138)=8.63, p<.001) explained more variance of time spent on the site than model 1, which just had motivations. This suggests that time spent on the site is more driven by habit than by conscious motivations.

	Just Mot.	Just Habit	Both
Membership length	-.160	-.138	-.152
Age	-.091	-.068	-.095
Gender	.097	.062	.075
Mot: Social	.043		-.076
Mot: Status	.295*		.306*
Mot: Enjoyment	.068		.073
Mot: Self Reactive	.100		-.008
Mot: Novelty	-.198		-.131
Mot: Monetary	.199*		.174
Habit		.441***	.294**
Adjusted R^2	.165***	.171***	.224***

*p<.05, **p<.01, ***p<.001

Table 4. OLS regressions explaining average time spent on the site with Motivations (Mot) and Habit

The third model adding habit into the same model as motivations ($F(10, 138)=5.27$, p<.001) explained 22% of the variance in time spent on the site. Although the change in adjusted R^2 when adding habit to the model with motivations was not as large as those reported in the use of Internet [20] or social games [38], it was still significant (F change=11.48, df change=1, p=.001). This suggests that both motivations and habits should be considered when explaining how much time users are spending on online communities.

Relationship Between Past Use and Habit

Results of RQ1 provided a cross-sectional glimpse of how motivations and habit strength can explain time spent on the site. To see how use of past features is associated with habit (RQ2), we ran a Pearson's product-moment correlation between use of three different activities (Writing, Voting, sending messages) and the self-reported habit scale. This would enable us to get a sense of what recent *actual* behaviors are associated with users' *perception* of their habitual behavior.

We had two measures of past behavior. The first was a measure of quantity, based on behavioral data of the most recent month of activity obtained from the server logs. We only looked at the most recent month of activity because habit builds gradually over time; thus activities from a long time ago may not reflect habitual behavior. The server data included how many Write-ups users wrote in the past month, how many times they voted, and how many messages they sent.

The second measure was self-reported behavior of perceived frequency of use of specific features in the past month: we asked "How often did you use the following features in the past month?" which users rated on a 5-point scale from "never" to "very frequently."

As can be seen in Table 5, use of different features on the site had different degrees of association with habit strength. The self-report data and behavioral data from the servers were all significantly correlated at a moderate level, suggesting that an individual's perception of how often they are engaging in a behavior is related to how much they performed the behavior. The correlation between self-report and behavioral was strongest for Write-ups, followed by message-sending. In terms of relationships between different features, messaging was strongly correlated with giving Upvotes, implying that these two features may be linked with the same underlying motive of communication.

However, when examining the correlations between habit strength and features use, we found that the number of Write-ups recorded in the server did not have a significant association with habit strength (p=.120) yet the self-reported frequency of Write-ups was significantly correlated. Similarly, the correlation between habit strength and messages was also stronger for frequency than the actual number of messages sent.

	1)	2)	3)	4)	5)	6)	7)
1) Habit	-						
2) No. of Write-ups (server)	.131	-					
3) No. of Votes given (server)	.344***	.559***	-				
4) No. of Messages sent (server)	.223**	.325***	.348***	-			
5) Frequency of Write-ups (self-report)	.312***	.561***	.481***	.375***	-		
6) Frequency of Upvotes (self-report)	.388***	.255**	.331***	.260**	.342***	-	
7) Frequency of Downvotes (self-report)	.191*	.211*	.325***	.193*	.232***	.668***	-
8) Frequency of Messages sent (self-report)	.433***	.268**	.303***	.426***	.426***	.637***	.493***

*p<.05, **p<.01, ***p<.001

Table 5. Correlation of use of features in past month and current habit strength

	Write-ups	Read	Message	Upvotes	Downvotes	Future visit
Gender	.022	-.109	-.117	.002	.089	-.060
Membership Length	-.341	-.077	.054	.072	.153	-.087
Hours spent per week	.185	.151	.252***	.147	.229*	.318***
Motivations						
Social	.378**	.027	.331**	.408**	.098	.164
Status	.144	-.099	.222*	.050	.128	-.157
Enjoy	-.067	.330**	-.048	-.013	.041	.056
Self Reactive	.020	-.149	-.030	-.031	-.172	.023
Novelty	-.083	.315**	.000	.152	.110	.256**
Monetary	.030	-.069	-.024	-.093	-.119	-.203**
Habit	.088	.211*	.282***	.203*	.153	.478***
Adjusted R^2	*.410****	*.289****	*.611****	*.388****	*.162***	*.518****

$^{*}p<.05$, $^{**}p<.01$, $^{***}p<.001$

Table 6. Motivations and habit predicting intent to use specific features

This suggests that habit is less affected by how much an individual engages in the behavior and more associated with the individual's perception of how frequently he or she engages in the behavior. These results were consistent with prior research looking at the relationship between frequency and habit [25]. For example, Person A and Person B may have each posted three of Write-ups during the past month, but A may perceive the posting to be frequent, whereas B posted all three posts on the same day and did not perceive it as being frequent. Thus A's posting behavior may be more associated with habit than B's.

Relationship Between Habit and Intention of Future Use

To see how current habit strength explains intention of future use, a series of OLS regression models were employed for general use of the site and specific features. In these models, the independent variables included several control variables—gender, self-reported membership length, self-reported time spent on the site per week, and motivations.

Table 6 displays the results of the regression analyses. The variables in the top row—intention to use that feature—are the dependent variables for all of the models, while the variables in the first column are the independent variables.

Addressing RQ3 regarding general activity, habit was the largest predictor for intention to visit the site in the future (next two months). Individuals with stronger habit strength were more likely to report a greater frequency of future visits. The novelty motivation (e.g., seeking information) also positively predicted intention for future visits. The monetary motivation is negatively associated with future visits, suggesting that people who use the site to save money are less likely to visit in the future. None of the other motivations were statistically significant.

When we looked at the specific features instead of the broad concept of visiting the site (RQ4), we found that habit played a role in predicting future intent to read, send messages, and make positive evaluations through Upvotes. There was no significant relationship between intent to write and habit (β=.088, p=.338). This suggests that habits are more likely to inform behavior that is more passive, than behaviors that require more active participation and/or creativity. Intention to Downvote (β=.088, p=.143) was also not influenced by current habit. The fact that habit informs intent to Upvote but not Downvote seems conflicting, but looking at the motivations, we see that Upvotes are strongly influenced by social motivations. This could imply that users are more careful about giving a negative vote and that a positive vote is more of a social support signal than an evaluation of the quality of the content. This could mean that positive evaluations that people make in social information systems may not reflect what they think about the content, but rather be more of an evaluation towards the person—for example, when people "like" others' content on Facebook, is it about the person or the content, or both?

Intent to write was only explained by social motivations. This may partially explain as to why sites that do not support multiple channels of social interaction—such as Wikipedia—are waning in terms of contribution. Social motivations predict intention to produce Write-ups, exchange private messages, and Upvote content—the coefficients were above .3, suggesting not only a significant, but fairly strong effect. However, social motivations do not show up when looking at the more general dependent variable of visiting the website. Similarly, enjoyment and novelty motivations only predicted intention to read. The separate regressions for specific features unveiled patterns that were somewhat different from the regression predicting the more general act of visiting the website.

These results suggest that when we are measuring activity online, generic measurements may cancel out any significant or strong effects that certain variables may have and that it is important to take a more granular approach in segmenting different uses rather than looking at site activity as a whole. This seemingly discrepant pattern between what variables predict specific features as opposed to which variables predict generic use is consistent with research that has taken more nuanced direction in the context of social network site use [33].

DISCUSSION

In this paper, we introduced the concept of *habit* in understanding the use of systems, and asked about the role this concept plays in explaining sustained use of information systems. This concept may help explain why people continue use of these types of mediated interaction environments over time. Although findings suggest that conscious motivations still play an important role in choosing which sites to use and how to use them, evidence supports that habit is also important when examining the different ways in which users continue participation in peer-production communities.

We found that the average time that users perceive they spend on the site is not only associated with their conscious motivations, but also with their sense of the automaticity of their use. This indicates that we should not see use of a system as being a wholly conscious decision based on motives for every instance of use. Rather, cognitively efficient processes inherent in habit seem to play a role in spending time on a site, even when accounting for motivations.

Habit was more strongly related to perceptions of how frequently users contributed with specific features on the site than with the actual number of times they contributed. This may be an artifact of how we measured behavior—which only takes into account the end product, whereas user perception would account for all times the participant engaged in that type of use. It could also be a typical instrument bias effect. This suggests that habit strength may be better detected through frequency of log-ins and session durations rather than the sum of individual feature use.

Habit seems to play a different role in production vs. consumption uses. Namely, consumption of content, in terms of reading on the site and anticipating future visits to the site, are both strongly related to the habit variable. Previous work has shown that people have different motivations for using a site [23] and express those motivations as different types of uses [26]. For those users who engage in more passive uses in peer-production communities, it could be a more straightforward media consumption relationship. In other words, habit plays a stronger role when there is less cognitive effort in making that behavioral choice, such as when users consume content rather than produce it.

Users may expend more effort when producing a Write-up on Everything2, given that it is a sole-authored work and may be deleted if it does not meet community standards. Because authoring requires focused cognitive energy, this focus may not trigger the automaticity inherent in habit. As described in the review of habit, it is activated when it is cognitively efficient to depend on a heuristic, rather than making a conscious choice for every task.

Messaging, a social type of use, is a form of content creation that is associated with both habit and social motivation. While habit did not predict intention to write, we see in Table 3 that messaging is strongly correlated to producing Write-ups. It could be that uses like Upvoting and messaging are socially oriented, thus moderating the relationship between habit and the more intensive Write-up behaviors.

Habit does play a role in producing content, but the content most likely to be produced out of habit is relatively lightweight contribution like ratings or messages. For example, voting also requires some cognitive activity but is not necessary—theoretically, voting involves reading and evaluating, but technically, it only involves one click of the mouse. The different patterns in Upvoting and Downvoting also suggest that voting—in particular, Upvoting—may not be an artifact of careful consideration. It could be that the social cost of Downvoting, being higher than Upvoting, gives users pause because there are social consequences of the action, kicking them out of habit mode and into conscious thought. It makes sense that reading—which is dependent on the environmental cue of an existing Write-up—is more susceptible to habit than writing.

Implications for practice and design

Online communities depend on the sustained contributions of members to exist, which is why it is of key importance to understand not only what drives people to participate and contribute to these sites, but especially why they sustain their participation over time.

While some communities are purposefully designed for short-term contributions, most others intend to persist over time. Wikipedia, for example, has existed for over ten years, and intends to maintain its activity into the foreseeable future. Although such systems can try to rely on a continuous supply of new users, if any efforts are being made on trying to retain old users, our results suggest that creating various means of social interaction—such as private messaging and voting—may contribute to retention, as these features are strongly associated to habit strength, and also to future contribution of content. Additional opportunities may include building faux-social interactions such as those induced by social bots, into the design of the system, although additional research is required to see whether or not users differentiate different types of computer-mediated interactions.

Extrapolating more generally on the construct of habit strength, another implication for design is the importance of context stability, which is required to build a habit. System designers who are constantly changing their interface or site structure may be making it difficult for users to develop a habit. When experimenting with new designs, it may be better to segment users and retain a more stable design for users who are logged in.

LIMITATIONS

The primary limitation of our study is that our measure of habit was a self-report. Although self-report has been shown in numerous studies to be strongly correlated to habitual behavior [36], there are individual differences in terms of how aware one is that one's behavior is a habit. Especially since the Self Report Habit Index requires one to think about past behavior, there is always room for error in terms of how accurate people's recollection is.

We tried to triangulate results through self-report and behavioral data. However, in terms of explaining how behavior is associated with habit, we realize that there are many other factors, such as frequency of the behaviors and types of feedback that users received regarding their behaviors that were not taken into account in this study.

Although our sample was normally distributed in terms of habit strength, it may be susceptible to seasonal effects in contribution, as those who visit and contribute to the community during summer may differ than those in other seasons. It is also unclear how non-response bias affects our results. For example, less attached users may be less likely to answer a survey about the site, and it is reasonable to expect this group would have different habits regarding Everything2.

We cannot make causal claims about whether time spent on the site and use of different features affect habit, or if habit affects use.

CONCLUSION

In this paper, we introduce the concept of *habit* as a form of online community use that is not driven by conscious mental processes, but rather as a cognitively efficient way of making use choices. We find that people s self-reports of habitual use of a peer-production online community helps explain time people spend using an online community. Habit and motivation were found to be co-present in association with many types of online behaviors. Since online peer-production communities involve a rich, heterogeneous set of possible uses, different combinations of motivation and habit may help explain that ecology of behavior.

We found that habit explains passive use of the site such as reading, and social uses such as messaging and voting, but not active contribution of new content. While writing can contribute to habit formation, habit does not necessarily predict writing. Consequently, while habit may not explain all use choices in peer-production communities, it does seem to be importantly related to lower cognitive tasks that are essential for the sustainable operations of those systems.

ACKNOWLEDGMENTS

We wish to thank the users of Everything2 for their participation in this research. This work was supported by NSF grant IIS-HCC-0812429.

REFERENCES

1. Aarts, H., Verplanken, B., and Knippenberg, A. Predicting behavior from actions in the past: Repeated decision making or a matter of habit? *Journal of Applied Social Psychology 28*, 15 (1998), 1355-74.
2. Adams, W.J. How people watch television as investigated using focus group techniques. *Journal of Broadcasting Electronic Media 44*, 1 (2000), 78-93.
3. Arguello, J., Butler, B., Joyce, E., et al. Talk to me : Foundations for successful individual-group interactions in online communities. In *Proc. CHI 2006* (2006), 959-68.
4. Bargh, J.A. and Chartrand, T.L. The unbearable automaticity of being. *American Psychologist 54*, 7 (1999), 462-79.
5. Beenen, G., Ling, K., Wang, X., et al. Using social psychology to motivate contributions to online communities. *Journal of Computer-Mediated Communication 10*, 4 (2005).
6. Burke, M., Joyce, E., Kim, T., Anand, V., and Kraut, R. Introductions and requests : Rhetorical strategies that elicit response in online communities. In *Proc. Communities and Technologies 2007,* Springer (2007), 21-39.
7. Burke, M., Marlow, C., and Lento, T. Feed me: motivating newcomer contribution in social network sites. In *Proc. CHI 2009*, ACM Press (2009), 945-54.
8. Burke, M., Marlow, C., and Lento, T. Social network activity and social well-being. In *Proc. CHI 2010*, ACM Press (2010), 1909-12.
9. Chaiken, S., Liberman, A., and Eagly, A.H. Heuristic and systematic information processing within and beyond the persuasion context. In J.S. Uleman and J.A. Bargh, eds., *Unintended Thought*. Guilford Press, 1989, 212-52.
10. Cheshire, C. and Antin, J. The social psychological effects of feedback on the production of Internet information Pools. *Journal of Computer-Mediated Communication 13*, 3 (2008), 705-27.
11. Cohen, M.D. Reading Dewey: Reflections on the study of routine. *Organization Studies 28*, 5 (2007), 773-86.
12. Farzan, R., DiMicco, J.M., Millen, D.R., Brownholtz, B., Geyer, W., and Dugan, C. When the experiment is over: Deploying an incentive system to all the users. *Symposium on Persuasive Technology*, (2008).
13. Florencio, D. and Herley, C. A large-scale study of web password habits. In *Proc. WWW 2007*, (2007), 657-65.
14. Graybiel, A.M. Habits, rituals, and the evaluative brain. *Annual Review of Neuroscience 31*, 1 (2008), 359-87.

15. Greenberg, B.S. Gratifications of television viewing and their correlates for British children. In J.G. Blumler and E. Katz, eds., *The Uses of Mass Communications Current Perspectives on Gratifications Research.* Sage, 1974, 71-92.

16. Joinson, A.N. Looking at, looking up or keeping up with people?: Motives and use of Facebook. In *Proc. CHI 2008*, ACM Press (2008), 1027-36.

17. Katz, E., Blumler, J.G., and Gurevitch, M. Utilization of mass communication by the individual. In J.G. Blumler and E. Katz, eds., *The uses of mass communications: Current perspectives on gratifications research.* Sage, 1974, 19-32.

18. Krendl, K.A. and Lasky, K. Influences of television: Views from the next generation. *Communication Research Reports 6*, 2 (1989), 100-105.

19. Kriplean, T., Zachry, M., Borning, A., and Mcdonald, D.W. Enabling social translucence for Wikipedia. *Science And Technology*, (2010), 529-30.

20. LaRose, R. and Eastin, M.S. A social cognitive theory of Internet uses and gratifications: Toward a new model of media attendance. *Journal of Broadcasting Electronic Media 48*, 3 (2004), 358-377.

21. LaRose, R. The problem of media habits. *Communication Theory 20*, 2 (2010), 194-222.

22. Lampe, C. and Johnston, E. Follow the (slash) dot: effects of feedback on new members in an online community. In *Proc. GROUP 2005*, ACM Press (2005), 11-20.

23. Lampe, C., Wash, R., Velasquez, A., and Ozkaya, E. Motivations to participate in online communities. In *Proc. CHI 2010*, ACM Press (2010), 1927-36.

24. Orbell, S. and Verplanken, B. The automatic component of habit in health behavior: Habit as cue-contingent automaticity. *Health Psychology 29*, 4 (2010), 374-383.

25. Ouellette, J.A. and Wood, W. Habit and intention in everyday life: The multiple processes by which past behavior predicts future behavior. *Psychological Bulletin 124*, 1 (1998), 54-74.

26. Panciera, K., Priedhorsky, R., Erickson, T., and Terveen, L. Lurking? Cyclopaths? A quantitative lifecycle analysis of user behavior in a Geowiki. In *Proc. CHI 2010*, (2010), 1917-26.

27. Papacharissi, Z. and Rubin, A.M. Predictors of Internet Use. *Journal of Broadcasting Electronic Media 44*, 2 (2000), 175-96.

28. Petty, R.E. and Cacioppo, J.T. The effects of involvement on responses to argument quantity and quality: Central and peripheral routes to persuasion. *Journal of Personality and Social Psychology 46*, 1 (1984), 69-81.

29. Priedhorsky, R., Jordan, B., and Terveen, L. How a personalized geowiki can help bicyclists share information more effectively. In *Proc. WikiSym 2007*, ACM Press (2007), 93-98.

30. Rashid, A.M., Ling, K., Tassone, R.D., Resnick, P., Kraut, R., and Riedl, J. Motivating participation by displaying the value of contribution. In *Proc. CHI 2006*, ACM Press (2006), 955-58.

31. Rosenstein, A.W. and Grant, A.E. Reconceptualizing the role of habit: A new model of television audience activity. *Journal of Broadcasting Electronic Media 41*, 3 (1997), 324-44.

32. Rubin, A.M. Television uses and gratifications: The interactions of viewing patterns and motivations. *Journal of Broadcasting 27*, 1 (1983), 37-51.

33. Smock, A.D., Ellison, N.B., Lampe, C., and Wohn, D.Y. Facebook as a toolkit: A uses and gratification approach to unbundling feature use. *Computers in Human Behavior 27,* 6 (2011), 2322-29.

34. Suh, B., Convertino, G., Chi, E.H., and Pirolli, P. The singularity is not near: slowing growth of Wikipedia. In *Proc. WikiSym 2009*, ACM Press (2009), 1-10.

35. Sung, J., Bjornrud, T., Lee, Y., and Wohn, D.Y. Social network games: Audience traits. In *Proc. CHI EA 2010*, ACM Press (2010), 3649-54.

36. Verplanken, B. and Orbell, S. Reflections on past behavior: A self-report index of habit strength. *Journal of Applied Social Psychology 33*, 6 (2003), 1313-30.

37. Welser, H.T., Cosley, D., Kossinets, G., et al. Finding social roles in Wikipedia. In *Proc. iConference 2011*, ACM Press (2011), 122-29.

38. Wohn, D.Y. The role of habit in social network game play. *Communication Research Reports 29,* 1 (2012), 74-79.

39. Wood, W., Quinn, J.M., and Kashy, D.A. Habits in everyday life: Thought, emotion, and action. *Journal of Personality and Social Psychology 83*, 6 (2002), 1281-1297.

40. Yamashita, A.F., Barendregt, W., and Fjeld, M. Exploring potential usability gaps when switching mobile phones: an empirical study. In *Proc. of the 21st British HCI Group Annual Conference on People and Computers*, British Computer Society (2007), 109-116.

Evaluating Compliance-Without-Pressure Techniques for Increasing Participation in Online Communities

Mikhil Masli and Loren Terveen
GroupLens Research
Department of Computer Science and Engineering
University of Minnesota, Minneapolis, MN, USA
{masli, terveen}@cs.umn.edu

ABSTRACT
Social psychology offers several theories of potential use for designing techniques to increase user contributions to online communities. Some of these techniques follow the "compliance without pressure" approach, where users are led to comply with a request without being subjected to any obvious external pressure. We evaluated two such techniques – *foot-in-the-door* and *low-ball* – in the context of Cyclopath, a geographic wiki. We found that while both techniques succeeded, low-ball elicited more work than foot-in-the-door. We discuss design and research implications of applying these (and other such techniques) in online communities.

Author Keywords
Increasing participation; social production; online communities; compliance; foot-in-the-door; low-ball

ACM Classification Keywords
H.5.3 Information Interfaces and Presentation: Group and Organizational Interfaces

General Terms
Human Factors, Design

INTRODUCTION
A large body of literature from social psychology suggests techniques that may be used to motivate people to contribute to these communities. One set of these techniques is known as *compliance without pressure* [12]: these techniques are designed to increase compliance to requests in the absence of any obvious sources of pressure. Two of the most popular techniques are:

- *Foot-in-the-door* (FITD): Once a person performs a small request, he/she is more likely to perform a subsequent, larger demand [12].
- *Low-ball* (LB): Once a person commits to a request, he/she is more likely to perform it at a later stage, even if its cost is increased [8].

While these techniques have been evaluated extensively in several offline contexts, there has been very little evaluation in the world of computer-mediated communication [16, 17], and none in online social production communities.

We evaluated FITD and LB techniques in the context of Cyclopath[1], an online geographic wiki that offers route-finding services for cyclists in the metropolitan area of Minneapolis-St. Paul, Minnesota, USA. We carried out a work campaign in which we requested Cyclopath users to contribute information to the map in the form of tags with the goal of improving the map for the next cycling season. We conducted a field study and a follow-up survey and found that LB succeeded in eliciting more contributions than the control condition, while FITD had limited success.

This paper is organized as follows. We first survey relevant related work and explain the motivation to carry out empirical evaluation in the online context. Second, we describe our field experiment, its results and their interpretation using theories from social psychology. Third, we describe our follow-up survey, and conclude with implications for design and future research.

RELATED WORK

Social Production Communities
Social production communities [2, 14] let loosely-connected users work together to produce information and artifacts of value [10]. Collaborative filtering systems like MovieLens[2] and Amazon leverage users' ratings of items (movies, consumer products, etc.) to enable personalized recommendations. Q&A sites like Yahoo! Answers and Stack Overflow form knowledge economies, where users spend points to ask or boost the priority of questions and earn them for answering. Wikis take user-provided content to its logical end: anyone can add, edit, or delete anything. Wikipedia is among the top 10 most popular sites on the Web, and smaller wikis are ubiquitous. Because of the significant value produced by online communities, ensuring that they receive adequate member participation is an important research topic.

[1]cyclopath.org
[2]www.movielens.org

Compliance Without Pressure

Compliance without pressure techniques are designed to lead people to comply with requests without any obvious source of external pressure. Researchers from social psychology and marketing have developed several techniques that fall under this category, e.g. FITD, LB, *door-in-the-face* [7], *that's-not-all* [3] and *bait-and-switch*. FITD is one of the oldest and the most popular of them with well over a hundred studies devoted to it over the last 50 years [4]. LB has also been found to be one of the most effective of these techniques [21, 22]. Because of their effectiveness, FITD and LB are interesting candidate solutions to the problem of under-contribution in online communities, and we thus chose to investigate them.

Several theories have tried to explain why and how FITD and LB work (or not). The most popular explanation for the success of the FITD technique is Bem's self-perception theory [1], which postulates that when a person is induced to comply with a smaller request, he/she is more likely to comply with a subsequent, larger request because of perceiving himself/herself as the type of person that does such tasks. Alternative theories including those citing psychological reactance, conformity to existing social norms including reciprocity and cognitive dissonance [11] have also been used to explain both successes and failures of the FITD technique. The LB effect has been generally explained using the theory of commitment [8], which says that people generally tend to stick to their commitments when acting in public view. We elaborate on these techniques in a later section in this paper while interpreting the results of our field experiment.

While compliance-without-pressure techniques may have potential to increase participation in online communities, if users perceive these techniques as manipulative, their use could negatively impact long-term member satisfaction and commitment. Accordingly, in this work, along with evaluating how successful FITD and LB are in an online social production context, we also evaluate the extent to which they are harmful and discuss the pragmatic issues designers of online communities might face when employing some of them.

NEED FOR EMPIRICAL EVALUATION

This research focuses on empirically evaluating the techniques of FITD and LB in the context of an online social production community. Is this necessary? Could we not merely assume findings from the offline settings of social psychology? Online communities have several key differences that makes them unique, and justify the need for an empirical evaluation of proven offline techniques:

1. **Anonymity on the Internet**. Psychological phenomena like cognitive dissonance, considered one of the factors behind the FITD and LB effects, as well as the LB effect itself have been shown to be more effective in public situations [5, 32], where visibility is higher (and consequently, anonymity is lower). However, since obtaining an identity on the Internet is cheap [13], online communications have a higher degree of anonymity than offline situations. Hence, it is not clear if online social production communities are public (contributions are shared) or private spaces (people can work from the confines of their homes), thereby raising questions over the effectiveness of the FITD and LB techniques.

2. **Nature of online communication**. Email and similar modes of communication are used most often by online social production communities to interact with their members, as it is the norm on the Internet. These modes are fundamentally not as personal as face-to-face or telephone communication – modes used by most studies of compliance in offline situations. Further, due to problems of email overload, it easy to ignore incoming messages. These reasons affect any interventions that use email as the underlying mode of communication.

Although online communities are different from their offline counterparts in some respects, they are similar in many others. Indeed, the social sciences have provided design inspiration and specific techniques that Computer Supported Cooperative Work (CSCW) designers and researchers have used to create more effective online communities [28]. Researchers have successfully applied theories and models like the Collective Effort Model [23, 25], goal-setting [25] and social comparison [20] to address the problem of under-contribution. Closer to this work, the FITD technique has been shown to be effective over email [16, 17].

Drawing inspiration from these successes, our research extends prior work in significant ways:

- We empirically evaluate the FITD and LB techniques in the context of an online social production community using a live field experiment and a follow-up survey.
- We demonstrate that the LB technique is largely successful in eliciting a higher quantity of contributions, while the FITD technique receives mixed results.
- Based on what we learned from our studies, we discuss the advantages and limitations of employing these (and similar) techniques in real-world online social production communities.

RESEARCH PLATFORM

Cyclopath went live in the summer of 2008. As of May 17, 2011, Cyclopath had 3,232 registered users and visits from 69,754 different IP addresses. Cyclopath has served as an excellent research platform for prior research on user behavior in social production communities, including studying efficient ways of eliciting contributions [29], user lifecycles [27] and specialization of contributions [26].

Like any wiki, users contribute information to Cyclopath in sets of edits called revisions. When a user makes the desired edits in the Cyclopath interface (e.g. add a point) and clicks "Save Changes", they are saved as a single revision associated with the username of the user (if the user is logged in), IP address and a time-stamp (see [30] for a more in-depth description). All revisions are publicly visible and revertible (via the Recent Changes list). So far, the Cyclopath map has seen 12,949 revisions (11,258 by 699 registered users and 1,691 anonymously).

Each revision may contain edits to points, blocks, regions, notes and tags. Blocks (roads and trails like the *Kennilworth Trail*) are useful for route-finding, points help define route endpoints (e.g., from *CS Building* to *Lagoon Theater*), tags enable more customized route requests (e.g., a route that is more *scenic*, but less *bumpy*), and notes supplement blocks included in a route with subjective information useful for evaluatint the route (e.g., "icy during the winter").

Prior work in Cyclopath suggests that many notes contain potential tags [33]. If extracted, these tags could provide more options for users to customize their routes. Further, this task could be performed by any person, regardless of his/her familiarity with the note or the area on the map where the note was applied (just like the task of fixing intersections [29]). Hence we chose to ask Cyclopath's users to do the task of extracing tags from notes. Prior to the start of our experiment, users had added 6,373 tags (applied to 4,312 blocks and points) and 8,405 notes (applied to 6,084 blocks).

EXPERIMENT DESIGN

Hypotheses and Variables

We conducted a field study in Cyclopath during winter 2010-11. Like bike-riding (at least, in colder climates), Cyclopath use is seasonal – it sees over 150 route requests per day and over 100 revisions per week during the summer and only about a third of those numbers during the winter. This made winter a good time for our field study – any effects we observe are primarily due to our manipulation and not the general motivations that drive contributions during summer. As a part of our field study, we requested Cyclopath users to contribute tags to the resource.

Our experiment design was guided by two hypotheses:

H1. The FITD technique will result in higher compliance for the contribution request than the request being presented alone.

H2. The LB technique will result in higher compliance for the contribution request than the request being presented alone.

We measured compliance using two outcome (dependent) variables:

- **Response:** Whether the user responded at all and the number of responses per user (we allowed users to respond multiple times, as described later) to the target request.
- **Quantity of Work:** The amount of work done by the user in response to our request, measured in terms of number of tag-applications to blocks and points, and number of new tags introduced into the tag vocabulary.

Method

Partitioning Users

We partitioned users into three groups – FITD (953 subjects), LB (953 subjects), and a control group (951 subjects). However, since participation on Cyclopath is highly unequal (like most voluntary online activities), we took care to ensure that user experience levels were more-or-less evenly distributed among the three groups, i.e. not all highly experienced users (measured by the number of prior revisions made) were assigned to the same group. Specifically, we ordered users in descending order by the number of revisions they saved and stepped through this list assigning users to control, FITD and LB groups in a cyclic fashion.

Procedure

General structure. All communication with users was conducted via email. We presented both experimental groups (FITD and LB) with their *initial contacts* on December 9, 2010 at 5 pm. We then followed this up with the *target request* (the real request for which we wanted compliance) to all groups, via email 6 days later[3], on December 15, 2010 at 5 pm.

It is important to note here that essentially, we are comparing 3 techniques of eliciting work: "simply asking users to do work" (control) and two "enhanced ways of asking users to do work" (FITD, LB). We could have evaluated other, intermediate techniques like Freedman and Fraser's *familiarity-only* (related to FITD) [12] and *commitment-but-no-increase-in-cost* (related to LB) as well. However, in this paper, we have explicitly chosen to evaluate FITD and LB in their entirety and not part-by-part.

The following paragraphs detail the initial contact and the target request for the various groups (the control group received no initial contact).

Initial contact – FITD. We sent email to the subjects in the FITD group asking them to do the initial (small) task of extracting just one tag from a single note, with the subject line "A tiny favor: Cyclopath needs your help!". The key passage was: *Would you spare a minute to help this campaign? All we are asking you to do is to read the following note and extract only one meaningful tag (one or two word label) from it.* The email also contained the note itself (we thought that once the subject eyeballed it, the task of extracting one tag would seem trivial), a sample note-tag pair, and a link to an interface to submit the tag. This link launched a simple HTML-based interface where the subject could re-read the note and enter the tag he/she extracted (see Figure 1(a)). For example, a subject extracted the tags *"Dirt path"* from the note *"dirt path connects to Arcade beware of curb"*. Since the initial FITD contact had to be short and easy, we limited subjects to just one attempt at it: if a subject clicked the link again, the system would display a message saying he/she has already completed the task. After the subject submitted the tag from the HTML interface, he/she was thanked.

Initial contact – LB. We asked the subjects in the LB group (with the same subject line) to agree to extract one tag from a single note, explicitly asserting that this task should take only a minute to complete. The key passages were: *Would you spare a minute to help this campaign? All we are asking you to do is to read a note and extract only one tag (single word label) from it (this should just take you a minute)* and

[3]Prior research suggests that a short (near-zero) delay between the initial and the target requests when both originate from the same requester can tend to counteract the FITD effect [4, 19].

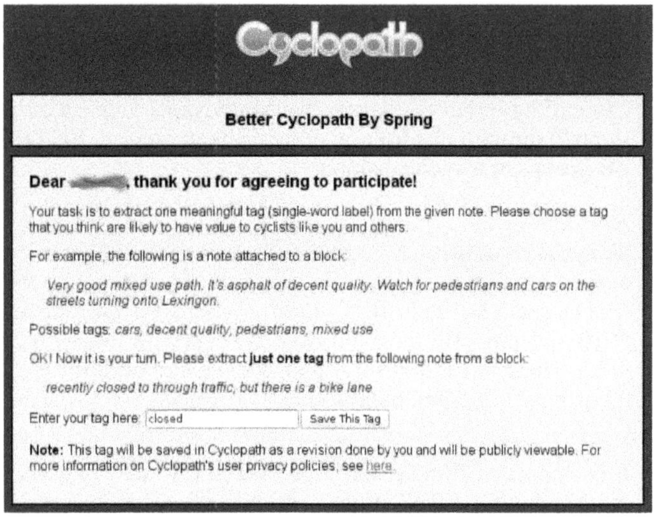

(a) FITD Interface

(b) LB Interface

Figure 1. Initial contact. We designed simple HTML-based interfaces for the FITD subjects to perform their small task, and for the LB subjects to express their commitment.

If you agree now, we'll contact you with specific instructions in near future, after we have heard from more people. The email also contained a sample note-tag pair and a link to an interface to express commitment. This link launched a simple HTML-based interface (similar to the FITD interface) where the subject was thanked for agreeing (see Figure 1(b)).

Target request – all groups. Our target request to all three groups was to extract as many tags as possible from a given set of notes. To avoid any biases resulting from subjects' self-selection, this email request was sent to every subject in the FITD and LB groups, regardless of their response to the initial contact. Crucially, for the FITD and LB conditions, we needed to explain why we were asking for more work than in the original request. Our explanation was that Cyclopath had miscalculated the amount of work required of each user and that more work per user was needed in order to analyze all notes by spring time[4]. The key passage in this email was: *You will be presented with a area on the map. Read any notes you find on blocks in this area and extract around 2-3 potentially useful tags (one or two word labels) from each note. This should take you 15-20 minutes.* The link in the email

[4]This argument was also included in the email sent to the control group for uniformity, though not framed as an "excuse".

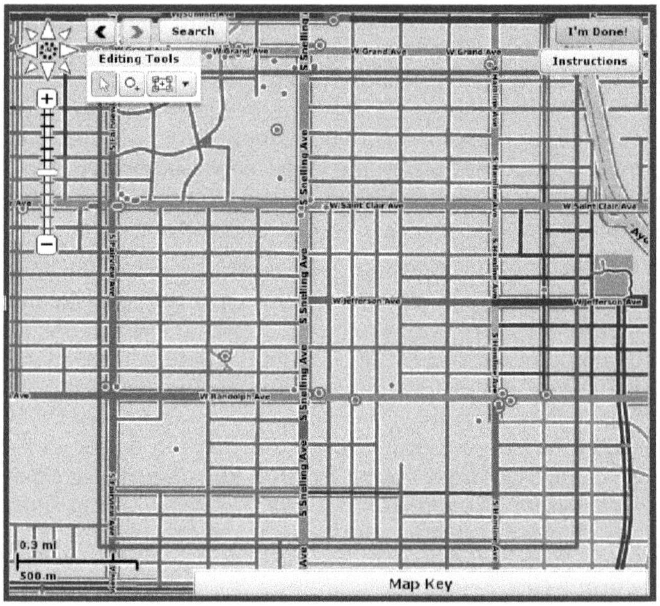

Figure 2. Target request. Each subject could perform as many experimental trials as he/she wishes. The blue box showing the area the subject was asked to work in, with the "I'm Done" button to end the trial at the top right.

launched an experimental trial (the procedure as well as the code for conducting trials was adapted from [29]):

1. *Begin trial.* The subject begins the trial by clicking on the link provided in the email.

2. *Select viewport.* The system chooses a viewport (100 km^2 area) randomly on the map, ensuring that there are at least 5 notes available to extract tags from.[5]

3. *Display viewport.* The map pans and zooms to the selected viewport, and highlights it with a blue box. An instruction dialog box pops up that details the task to be done, with brief instructions on how to do it and links to help (see Figure 2). All blocks and points with notes were highlighted with a purple halo.

4. *Subject does work.* The subject is now free to use the system. Although we explicitly asked the subject to work in the assigned area, the system did not restrict him/her in any way – the subject was free to make edits anywhere on the map.

5. *End trial.* The subject clicks a button labeled "I'm Done", which results in the completion of one trial. The subject can now either leave Cyclopath, use it for other purposes, or start another trial.

We recorded when the subjects started and finished the trials, the number of trials requested, and everything they did as a part of those trials.

[5]This was to ensure that there was *some* work available to do. Further, at the outset of our analyses, we also verified that there were no statistically significant differences in the number of notes available per user and per trial among the three groups.

Group	Response
FITD	11.4% (109)
LB	12.7% (121)

Table 1. Response to the initial contact. Response rates are low, but typical of contributory behavior in social production communities.

Group	Response	Trials per subject
Control	6.14% (58)	0.22 (205)
FITD	5.14% (49)	0.10 (92)
LB	7.35% (70)	0.29 (272)

Table 2. Response to the target request. The numbers in parantheses are the respective absolute counts. There are no statistically significant differences between the three groups of subjects.

Results

We took a snapshot of the database on January 16, 2011. By this date, 190 users completed 597 trials. We removed 28 trials from our analyses – 15 were unusually long (over 2 hours[6]) and 13 were done by 6 users who were not in any of our groups (these users joined Cyclopath after the experiment started). This left us with 569 trials by 177 subjects. We present our results organized by our outcome variables.

Response

Initial contact response. Table 1 shows the response to the initial contact. Out of the 953 subjects in the FITD condition to whom we sent the initial contact emails, 109 (11.4%) completed the short task. Out of the 953 subjects in the LB condition to whom we sent the initial contact emails, 121 (12.7%) responded.

Target request response. Table 2 shows how subjects responded to the target request. We see no significant differences among groups in the response rates, or the number of trials per subject. However, we found interesting differences in the quantity of work done, as described in the following sub-section.

Quantity of Work

Metrics. When a tag that does not already exist in the system is applied to a new map feature, a new tag is introduced into the tagging vocabulary. We call such an action "creating a tag." On the other hand, if an existing tag is applied, it is merely re-used, i.e., a new connection is added between the existing tag and the map feature to which it is applied. We call such an action "applying a tag." Naturally, when a tag is created, it is also applied to some map feature (e.g., a block), resulting in a tag application. We counted the number of tag applications (split into tag applications on blocks and points) and the number of new tags added, per user and per trial.

Work done per user. LB subjects applied more tags on average (about 3 times) than FITD or control subjects. These results were statistically significant. We performed statistical tests (for p-value computations) on $log(1 + x)$-transformed variables to account for the non-normality (long-tail nature) of the data and compensate for counts of zero. We first did a one-way analysis of variance (ANOVA) on the number of tag applications ($F(2, 2854) = 2.78, p = .06$), then did post-hoc pairwise comparisons using Tukey's HSD test (the difference between LB and control groups was marginally significant, $p = .06$). On an average, LB subjects also created nearly thrice as many tags as control subjects (ANOVA: $F(2, 2854) = 2.70, p = .07$, then Tukey's HSD: LB vs. control: $p = .08$). Table 3 summarizes the number of tag applications and new tags added per user by subjects from the three groups.

[6]The median length of a trial was 1.5 minute. We hypothesize that the unusually long trials represent cases where the subject forgot to click the "I'm done" button, remembering only much later. Consequently, we could not idenfity, with reasonable confidence, the parts of the trial that were done as a response to the target request.

(a) Tags created per user.

Group	Total	Mean	SD	p
Control	70	0.07	0.65	
FITD	99	0.10	1.05	
LB	193	0.20	1.64	*

(b) Tags applied per user.

Group	Total	Mean	SD	p
Control	542	0.57	5.07	
FITD	571	0.60	6.05	
LB	1702	1.79	18.07	*

Table 3. Tagging work done per user in response to the target request. * indicates statistical significance at the 0.1 level when compared with control.

(a) Tags created per trial.

Group	Total	Mean	SD
Control	70	0.34	1.08
FITD	99	1.08	2.43
LB	193	0.71	2.54

(b) Tags applied per trial.

Group	Total	Mean	SD
Control	542	2.66	7.20
FITD	571	6.23	13.11
LB	1702	6.25	13.79

Table 4. Tagging work done per trial in response to the target request.

Work done per trial. We see evidence of the success of the LB technique at the per-trial level too. The average LB trial produced more than twice as many tags (6.25) as the average control trial (2.66). Table 4 summarizes these comparisons. Looking back at Table 2, we see that the average FITD subject did fewer trials than the average control subject. This explains why there is a significant difference between the FITD and control groups in terms of work done per trial, despite there being none in terms of work done per user.

Summary of results. Our results suggest that the LB technique significantly increased the quantity of work subjects put in (hypothesis H2). The FITD technique, on the other hand, is not as successful – an average FITD trial produced more work than a control trial, but on an average, FITD subjects did no more work than control subjects ($0.57 \approx 0.60$) (hypothesis H1). There also was evidence that the LB technique fared better than the FITD technique.

Discussion – Why these results?

We have just described an empirical investigation of the FITD and LB techniques of compliance-without-pressure in the context of an online social production community, Cyclopath. Why did we obtain the results we saw? What aspects of our procedure caused these results, and what aspects produced opposing forces? Answering these questions is important for crafting recommendations concerning the use of these techniques for designers of online communities. We now refer back to relevant social psychological theories to make sense of our results.

Why did LB succeed?

The LB effect is theoretically simpler: it is generally explained by the theory of commitment. The seminal work on the LB effect [8] attributed its success to the development of commitment to the task in the minds of the person as a consequence of the initial contact. Further research [6] has shown that commitment to the requester, not the task, is actually responsible for the increased likelihood of compliance to the target request. In our case, either is possible: task commitment, since we explicitly asked LB subjects to agree to the task of extracting a tag from a note, or requester committment, as Cyclopath is a community resource, and people tend to care for the communities they are a part of.

Why did FITD meet with limited success?

There have been several attempts at explaining the FITD effect (or the lack of it) using a variety of psychological processes and theories [4]. Based on these theories, we speculate on the following reasons behind our results.[7]

Self-perception not strong enough. The self-perception theory [1] is the most popular explanation for the success of the FITD effect. The reasoning is that, when a person is induced to comply with the smaller request, he/she infers from this behavior that he/she is the kind of person that does such tasks and supports the cause behind the request; this self-perception later causes him/her to comply with the larger request. However, if a weak FITD effect is observed (as our results indicate), then we can hypothesize that the inferential process of self-perception triggered by the smaller request did not take place or was not strong enough.

Reactance as a result of excessive requesting. Psychological reactance may also undermine the FITD effect – the subject may simply feel badgered and pressured by the repeated requests and refuse the second, larger request. Our results showed a significant difference in the work done per trial, but no difference in the work done per user between the FITD and control groups. This is because although the number of subjects from the FITD group who responded to the target request is about the same as that from the control group, the FITD group completed fewer trials than the control group (see Table 2). A possible hypothesis for this behavior is that some FITD subjects might have either felt badgered by the repeated requesting or felt that they have "already done their part" when they complied with the smaller request.

Reciprocity: Cyclopath did not return the favors asked. Expectation of reciprocity may actually work against the processes driving the FITD effect. If the subject, after complying with the smaller request, expects the requester to give something in return, then the fact that he/she instead comes back with a larger request has the potential of inviting a refusal on the part of the subject. On the other hand, had the subject turned down the initial contact, then the norm of reciprocity would drive him/her to comply with the target request even if it is larger. Indeed, 21 subjects who did not respond to our initial request did respond to the target request. Whether reciprocity was the reason for this behavior is worthy of investigation.

Conformity to norms: Was the target request not to be done? Another factor that might affect compliance is the knowledge of existing social norms. For example, if the subject learned that the norm is that the larger request is not complied with, then he/she also might refuse. However, in this study, Cyclopath saw nearly 500 revisions to the map after the target request was sent out: so, if any norm was present, it was the norm of contributing.

Consistency needs. The cognitive dissonance theory [11] stipulates that people have a need to appear consistent and resolve any dissonances in their selves as soon as possible, even if it means making irrational decisions. In the FITD context, when a subject is presented with the larger request, he/she behaves consistently with his/her prior behavior in a similar context, i.e., the compliance to the initial smaller request. Although social psychologists have developed a scale to measure the preference for consistency [15], any conclusion we draw here would be about the people who use Cyclopath, and not the design of the system itself.

We conducted a follow-up study to investigate which of these processes may have affected our results.

FOLLOW-UP STUDY

Research Questions

We designed a follow-up study to address the following research questions that we constructed from analyzing the results of our field study:

RQ-FITD. Why did the FITD technique meet with limited success? Possible reasons include:

- FITD subjects did not perceive themselves to be the type of people who respond to requests from community sites like Cyclopath (self-perception).
- FITD subjects did not feel motivated enough to comply with the target request because they felt that they had already done their part when they responded to the initial contact (reactance).
- FITD subjects felt that the repeating requesting behavior from Cyclopath was badgering them (reactance).

[7]Burger's review [6] of about 100 FITD studies clearly points out that the degree to which each of the psychological processes known to enhance/reduce the FITD effect operate depends on the specific procedures used in the intervention. Hence, one must exercise caution while generalizing any speculations we make regarding how strongly they operated in our case.

FITD group statements:

About whether the subject would respond to initial request:
- *"I would do the task because it was requested by Cyclopath."*
- *"I would do the task because it is small and easy."*
- *"I would do the task regardless of who requested it."*

About how the subject would feel after responding to the initial request were presented:
- *"I have done my part towards helping Cyclopath."*
- *"I am the type of person who typically responds to requests for help from community sites."*

About the target request:
- *"Asking me to do something else after only a week has gone by is too often."*
- *"I've already done my part when I responded to the earlier request."*
- *"(If I hadn't done the task from the earlier request) I will do this one since I haven't done the task from the earlier email."*
- *"I'm the type of person that helps Cyclopath whenever called upon."*

LB group statements:

About whether the subject would respond to initial request:
- *"I would commit to such a request because it was requested by Cyclopath."*
- *"I would commit to such a request because it is small and easy."*
- *"I would commit to such a request regardless of who requested it."*

About the target request:
- *"This is unfair, Cyclopath just increased the amount of work it asked me to do."*
- *"I'm a person of my word: I agreed to help, so I'll do it now."*
- *"I'm the type of person that helps Cyclopath whenever called upon, so I would do this one too."*

Control group statements:

About the target request (in addition to statements for the FITD group):
- *"It is too much of a favor to ask on the part of Cyclopath."*
- *"I typically do not respond to such requests."*

General statements:

About perceived norms:
- *"If Cyclopath sent the above email to all registered users, how many people do you think (other than you) would respond to this request?"*
- *"It would be bother me if few people did the requested task."*

Figure 3. Follow-up survey items. Each experimental group was presented with a different set of scenarios and items. Subjects rated each item (except the first of the general statements) on a 7-point Likert scale.

- FITD subjects who turned down the initial contact felt obligated to comply with the target request on the grounds of reciprocity (reciprocity).

RQ-LB. Why did the LB technique succeed in eliciting more contributions? Possible reasons include:

- LB subjects complied with the target request because they felt a sense of commitment towards the task of extracting tags from notes (task commitment).
- LB subjects complied with the target request because they felt a sense of commitment towards Cyclopath (requester commitment).

Method

We sent out a survey on April 13, 2011 to subjects from all the groups. In the survey, subjects were asked to imagine scenarios similar to the experimental procedure of our field study; e.g., the FITD group was presented with the scenario: *Imagine this: You receive an email from Cyclopath asking you to do a task. The task is an easy one: you're asked to read a 20-word note, and create a single meaningful tag for it (a 1-2 minute task). What would your response be?* We took this approach (of asking people to imagine) instead of relying on subjects' memories of their experimental experience for two reasons: First, the interval between the start of the experiment and the survey was about 4 months, and it was unlikely that subjects would accurately remember their experiences over such a large interval. Second, this approach made it possible for us to administer the survey even to those who had not participated in the experiment.

Note that for subjects who participatedin the field study, we assigned them a survey consistent with their experience in the field study, i.e. FITD-relevant items be presented only to the FITD group, and so on. Users who registered after the start of the experiment (and hence were not assigned to any group) were randomly assigned to one of the three groups for the purpose of the survey.

Subjects were asked to rate several statements on a 7-point Likert scale (1-completely disagree to 7-completely agree) with regards to each scenario. Figure 3 lists some of the items.

Results and Discussion

We received 148 responses to our survey by April 20, 2011, a week after it was launched. Out of these, 43 (29%) of the users were among those who had participated in the previously described field study, whereas 105 (71%) were new. There were no statistically significant differences in the responses of these two sets of users. Table 5 presents the most important results. Our survey results showed some condition-specific patterns and some general population-wide patterns.

We observed general ideological patterns across all groups: respondents said they would do the requests because they came from Cyclopath ($M \geq 5.13, 1.23 \leq SD \leq 1.38$ in all cases) and would not do so in general ($M \leq 3.13, 1.58 \leq SD \leq 1.73$ in all cases). Moreover, respondents from the control group disagreed with the statement that the task requested of them (the target request) was too much of a favor ($M = 2.64, SD = 1.15$)! This shows users' general commitment to the Cyclopath community and can be a powerful motivation to contribute whenever requested.

FITD. Respondents from the FITD condition agreed with the statement that they would perform the task requested in the initial contact because it was small and easy ($M = 5.42, SD = 1.54$) – a verification of the FITD design. Further, we saw that FITD respondents agreed with the fact that they felt that they had *done their part towards helping Cyclopath* ($M = 5.47, SD = 1.16$) and that asking them to do something more after just a week had passed by was too often ($M = 4.62, SD = 1.32$). This is an indication that a likely reason for the lower-than-expected contributions to the FITD target request was that people felt that they were badgered.

The results also seem to indicate that this reason outweights the self-perception effect: contributions from the FITD group in the field study were lower despite FITD respondents in the

Group	Survey Item	Mean (M)	Std. Dev. (SD)
FITD	Initial contact: How would you respond?		
	I would do the task because it was requested by Cyclopath.	5.53	1.23
	I would do the task because it is small and easy.	5.42	1.54
	I would do the task regardless of who requested it.	3.13	1.73
FITD	Initial contact: How would you feel after you did it?		
	I have done my part towards helping Cyclopath.	5.47	1.16
	I am the type of person who typically responds to requests from community sites.	4.70	1.65
FITD	Target request: How would you respond?		
	Asking me to do something else after only a week has gone by is too often.	4.62	1.32
	I'm the type of person that helps Cyclopath whenever called upon.	4.43	1.39
LB	Initial contact: How would you respond?		
	I would commit to such a request because it was requested by Cyclopath.	5.57	1.35
	I would commit to such a request regardless of who requested it.	2.65	1.58
	I would commit to such a request because it is small and easy.	4.98	1.50
LB	Target request: How would you respond?		
	This is unfair, Cyclopath just increased the amount of work it asked me to do.	4.47	1.50
	I'm a person of my word: I agreed to help, so I'll do it now.	4.63	1.50
Control	Target request: How would you respond?		
	I would do the task because it was requested by Cyclopath.	5.13	1.39
	I would do the task regardless of who requested it.	3.00	1.63
	It is too much of a favor to ask on the part of Cyclopath.	2.64	1.15

Table 5. Results of our follow-up survey.

survey agreeing that after doing the task requested during the initial contact, they would feel like they are the type of people that would respond to requests for help from community sites ($M = 4.70, SD = 1.65$).

We did not find any statistically significant evidence for reciprocity; however, one respondent said, *"yeah if you help us back, this ain't a one-way street buddy"* as a response to how he/she would feel after responding to the initial contact.

LB. Respondents from the LB group verified the LB design by agreeing to the statement that they would commit to the request in the initial contact because it was small and easy ($M = 4.98, SD = 1.50$). Further, they also agreed to the statement that they would contribute to the target request because they were *persons of their word* ($M = 4.98, SD = 1.50$); in other words, committed to doing the task requested.

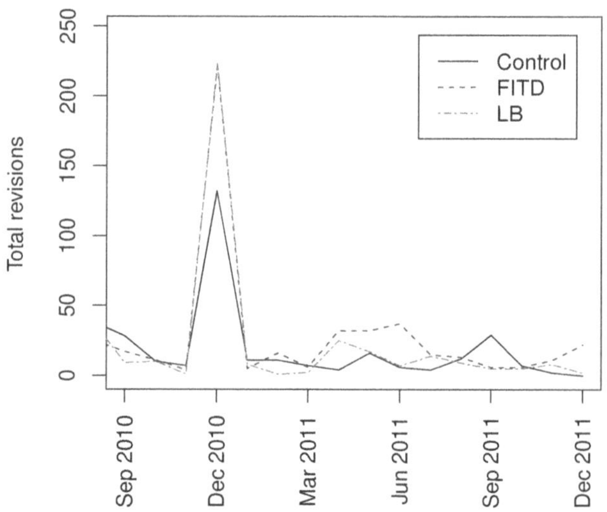

Figure 4. One-shot Effect. Our intervention saw a burst of activity just after the experimental emails were sent out (Dec, 2010), which dropped off steeply soon after. Note that the activity of Cyclopath's most prolific contributor has been excluded from this figure.

IMPLICATIONS AND SUMMARY

We believe this work is useful to both researchers and practitioners designing interventions to increase community participation. The success of the LB technique showed that an intervention as subtle as requesting prior commitment produced large, significant increases in participation. This low-cost-high-returns mechanism is potentially of great use to large scale campaigns such as WikiProjects and crowd-sourcing initiatives. However, care should be taken while applying theories from social psychology to online communities: there are subtleties and points of caution that must be considered.

Compliance-without-pressure in the online world. Earlier in the paper, we outlined how features such as anonymity and the loose, detached nature of online communication (as opposed to the more involved face-to-face) motivated the need for an empirical evaluation of the FITD and LB techniques. Looking at our results in the light of these premises, we see that the LB technique succeeded due to a heightened feeling of commitment despite the relative anonymity associated with the online community. However, FITD only produced limited success because it was very easy for subjects to simply close their browsers if they felt badgered by the repeated requesting. Thus, differences between online and offline interactions must be carefully considered before planning any intervention using a compliance-without-pressure technique.

Short versus long-term effects. We have seen in the past that interventions that try to boost member participation succeed in doing so only while they are active, and that participation drops to pre-intervention levels once it is withdrawn [29]. Our FITD and LB interventions fell within the same category. We saw a burst of activity (measured as number revisions saved) immediately following the initial contact and the target request, which dropped off steeply soon after (Figure 4). The self-perception effect, one of the explanations for the success of the FITD technique, is one of the most likely processes that could have caused long-term effects, whereas psychological reactance would work against any. In our case, we did not see any evidence for self-perception, which is consistent with our understanding of why our work campaign produced a one-shot effect.

While the failure to cause a long-term increase in participation levels is a limitation of the techniques we evaluated, we believe that they have utility in one-shot interventions. Online social production communities do require one-shot bursts of member participation at times – e.g, if a WikiProject in Wikipedia wishes to categorize several hundred articles into a hierarchical structure, or if a geographic open content community like FixMyStreet[8] needs to identify all potholes in a locality as a part of a neighborhood campaign.

That said, research efforts should try to focus on producing long-term increases in participation. In other words, researchers must try to devise techniques that enable the community to support itself. One way of tackling this issue is to employ the powerful and ubiqutous norm of reciprocity, an approach we are currently exploring.

Member satisfaction and retention. From past research, we know that although users can be manipulated into behaving in a particular manner, they tend to detect the manipulation and become less satisfied with the system [9]. This reduces the value of perhaps the greatest asset of an online community: the trust and commitment of its members.

Similarly, in the context of our study, we must consider the possible effects on member satisfaction of implementating the type of compliance-without-pressure techniques we studied. Our users certainly felt that the repeated emailing was excessive (in case of FITD), and that increasing the cost of the requested task was unfair (LB) (Table 5). From an online community designer's perspective, users might be viewed as *workers* – in which case they can be manipulated to achieve maximum throughput – or as *community members* – in which case they must be carefully preserved and nurtured. Recognizing the strengths of the community (e.g., existing levels of user commitment) is critical: if apparently effective in the short term, techniques like FITD and LB might do more long term damage to users' perceptions of and commitment to a community. After all, the tangible product of a group activity is not the only outcome that matters; in the long run, users will continue to participate only if their needs are met [18, 24]. Finally, since there are so many online communities, users who are not satisfied with one are likely to leave it in favor of an alternative, more attractive one that serves the same purpose.

Limitations and future work. An alternative explanation for the LB effect is the role of time: people tend to discount how busy they are or how much effort is needed when they make a commitment in the future [31]. LB studies that vary the amount of time between the initial contact and the target request are required to test this explanation.

Our study used a simple survey to conduct the qualitative follow-up to the field experiment. A limitation of post-hoc surveys are that they are presented out-of-context. Although we tried to mitigate this problem by making the survey as standalone as possible, better qualititative information could be collected if the survey was interwoven into the field experiment itself.

Summary. We described an evaluation of the compliance-without-pressure techniques foot-in-the-door (FITD) and low-ball (LB) in the context of an online social production community, using a field experiment and a follow-up survey. We found that despite the subtlety in its manipulation, the LB technique elicited nearly 3 times more participation. However, while both techniques managed to produce an increase in contribution, this was short-lived. These findings are applicable to both researchers and designers who create interventions to boost participation in online communities. However, more research is needed to look into other techniques (like the norm of reciprocity) that may yield lasting effects.

ACKNOWLEDGEMENTS

We thank the members of GroupLens Research, the Cyclopath team, the Cyclopath user community, and our reviewers. We also thank Dr. Reid Priedhorsky, Katie Panciera, Jason Weaver, Dr. Donald Ross Jr., Dev Oliver, and Ginny Sims for providing valuable feedback and guidance on research and writing. This work was supported in part by the National Science Foundation grant IIS 08-08692.

REFERENCES

1. Bem, D. Self-perception: An alternative interpretation of cognitive dissonance phenomena. *Psychological review 74*, 3 (1967), 183–200.
2. Benkler, Y. *The wealth of networks: How social production transforms markets and freedom*. Yale Univ Pr, 2006.
3. Burger, J. Increasing compliance by improving the deal: The that's-not-all technique. *Journal of Personality and Social Psychology 51*, 2 (1986), 277.
4. Burger, J. The foot-in-the-door compliance procedure: A multiple-process analysis and review. *Personality and Social Psychology Review 3*, 4 (1999), 303.
5. Burger, J., and Cornelius, T. Raising the Price of Agreement: Public Commitment and the Lowball Compliance Procedure. *Journal of Applied Social Psychology 33*, 5 (2003), 923–934.
6. Burger, J., and Petty, R. The low-ball compliance technique: Task or person commitment. *Journal of Personality and Social Psychology 40*, 3 (1981), 492–500.
7. Cialdini, R., et al. Reciprocal concessions procedure for inducing compliance: The door-in-the-face technique.

[8] www.fixmystreet.com

Journal of Personality and Social Psychology 31, 2 (1975), 206.

8. Cialdini, R., et al. Low-ball procedure for producing compliance: Commitment then cost. *Journal of Personality and Social Psychology 36*, 5 (1978), 463–476.
9. Cosley, D., et al. Is seeing believing?: How recommender system interfaces affect users' opinions. In *Proc. CHI*, ACM (2003), 585–592.
10. Cosley, D., et al. Using intelligent task routing and contribution review to help communities build artifacts of lasting value. In *Proc. CHI* (2006).
11. Festinger, L. *A theory of cognitive dissonance*. Stanford University Press, 1957.
12. Freedman, J., and Fraser, S. Compliance without pressure: The foot-in-the-door technique. *Journal of Personality and Social Psychology 4*, 2 (1966), 195–202.
13. Friedman, E., and Resnick, P. The social cost of cheap pseudonyms. *Ann Arbor 1001* (1999), 48109–1092.
14. Gilbert, E., and Karahalios, K. Using social visualization to motivate social production. *IEEE Transactions on Multimedia 11*, 3 (2009), 413.
15. Guadagno, R., et al. When saying yes leads to saying no: Preference for consistency and the reverse foot-in-the-door effect. *Personality and Social Psychology Bulletin 27*, 7 (2001), 859.
16. Guéguen, N. Foot-in-the-door technique and computer-mediated communication. *Computers in Human Behavior 18*, 1 (2002), 11–15.
17. Guéguen, N., and Jacob, C. Fund-raising on the web: the effect of an electronic foot-in-the-door on donation. *CyberPsychology & Behavior 4*, 6 (2001), 705–709.
18. Hackman, J. The design of work teams. *Handbook of organizational behavior 315* (1987), 342.
19. Harari, H., et al. Faculty Helpfulness to Students. *Personality and Social Psychology Bulletin 6*, 3 (1980), 373.
20. Harper, F., et al. Social comparisons to motivate contributions to an online community. *Persuasive Technology* (2007), 148–159.
21. Hornik, J., et al. Comparison of three inducement techniques to improve compliance in a health survey conducted by telephone. *Public Health Reports 105*, 5 (1990), 524.
22. Joule, R. Tabacco deprivation: The foot-in-the-door technique versus the low-ball technique. *European Journal of Social Psychology 17*, 3 (1987), 361–365.
23. Karau, S., and Williams, K. Social loafing: A meta-analytic review and theoretical integration. *Journal of personality and social psychology 65*, 4 (1993), 681.
24. Kraut, R. Applying social psychological theory to the problems of group work. *HCI models, theories and frameworks: Toward a multidisciplinary science* (2003), 325–356.
25. Ling, K., et al. Using social psychology to motivate contributions to online communities. *Journal of Computer-Mediated Communication 10*, 4 (2005), 00–00.
26. Masli, M., et al. Task specialization in social production communities: The case of geographic volunteer work. In *Proc. ICWSM* (2011).
27. Panciera, K., et al. Lurking? cyclopaths? A quantitative lifecycle analysis of user behavior in a geowiki. In *Proc. CHI*, ACM (2010), 1917–1926.
28. Preece, J. *Online communities*. Wiley & Sons, 2001.
29. Priedhorsky, R., et al. Eliciting and focusing geographic volunteer work. In *Proc. CSCW*, ACM (2010), 61–70.
30. Priedhorsky, R., and Terveen, L. Wiki Grows Up: Arbitrary Data Models, Access Control, and Beyond. In *Proc. WikiSym*, ACM (2011).
31. Roy, M., et al. Underestimating the duration of future events: Memory incorrectly used or memory bias?. *Psychological Bulletin 131*, 5 (2005), 738.
32. Tedeschi, J., et al. Cognitive dissonance: Private ratiocination or public spectacle?. *American Psychologist 26*, 8 (1971), 685.
33. Torre, F., et al. bumpy, caution with merging: an exploration of tagging in a geowiki. In *Proc. GROUP 2010*, ACM (2010), 155–164.

Social Desirability Bias and Self-Reports of Motivation: A Study of Amazon Mechanical Turk in the US and India

Judd Antin
Yahoo! Research
4401 Great America Pkwy.
Santa Clara, CA 95054
jantin@yahoo-inc.com

Aaron Shaw
Department of Sociology
University of California, Berkeley
Berkeley, CA 94720
adshaw@berkeley.edu

ABSTRACT
In this study we extend research on online collaboration by examining motivation to do work on the crowdsoucing service Amazon Mechanical Turk (MTurk). We address a challenge to many existing studies of motivation in online contexts: they are based on survey self-reports, which are susceptible to effects such as social desirability bias. In addition we investigate a second challenge to the extant research on motivation in the context of MTurk: a failure to examine potential differences between MTurk workers (Turkers) from different parts of the world, especially those from the US and India, MTurk's two largest worker groups. Using a survey technique called the list experiment, we observe distinct profiles of motivation and patterns of social desirability effects among Turkers in the US and India. Among US Turkers, we find that social desirability encourages over-reporting of each of four motivating factors we examined. The over-reporting was particularly large in the case of money as a motivator. In contrast, among Turkers in India we find a more complex pattern of social desirability effects, with workers under-reporting "killing time" and "fun" as motivations, and drastically over-reporting "sense of purpose." We conclude by discussing these results and proposing implications for future research and design.

Author Keywords
motivation; social desirability; crowdsourcing; Amazon Mechanical Turk; distributed work

ACM Classification Keywords
H.5.2 Information Interfaces and Presentation: Misc.

General Terms
Human Factors, Experimentation

INTRODUCTION
As online collaboration and user-generated content have become commonplace on the web, motivations for online participation have become an important area of study. Over more than 20 years, researchers have explored motivations for participating in a wide variety of online collaborative systems, such as open-source software [19] and Wikipedia [35]. This research has produced many insights that illuminate both theory and design. However, in this paper we highlight a specific weakness in much of this literature: a failure to assess potential bias in self-reports of online motivations.

Many studies on motivation rely on survey-based techniques in which participants explicitly state their motivations. Surveys, however, are vulnerable to a variety of response effects [15] – among them *social desirability bias*, or the tendency to respond in ways that participants believe would appear desirable to others. Because of the lack of attention to potential social desirability bias in self-reports of online motivation, there is very little evidence about whether such biases exist or how they may influence existing results.

In this study we examine the potential for social desirability bias in the context of Amazon's Mechanical Turk (MTurk). Part online community and part online labor market, MTurk attracts workers (Turkers) from all parts of the world. However, the vast majority of visits to MTurk come from just two nations: the United States and India [2]. Although there is likely to be significant within-group variation, in this study we acknowledge the potentially significant contrasts between the two countries and treat them as distinct subpopulations. Theories from cultural psychology and related fields suggests that motivation may vary as a result of the specific socio-cultural, economic, and political environment in which individuals live and work. As a result, we examine both motivational profiles and patterns of social desirability separately for Turkers in the US and in India.

We employ a quasi-experimental survey technique called the list experiment which mitigates social desirability bias. Comparing the results of the list experiment to traditional agreement statement-style questions, we find significant evidence of social desirability bias among both US and India Turkers. Furthermore, our results suggest different patterns of both motivation and social desirability effects between the two groups. These findings contribute to the existing literature in two ways. First, we demonstrate that self-reports of motivation *can* be subject to social desirability bias. In doing so we highlight prior studies' failure to consider the possibility for bias, the need to investigate potential biases in existing findings about online motivation, and the potential for non-optimal design decisions based on inaccurate findings. Secondly, we reveal interesting dynamics around expectations and perceptions of desirable motivations for performing crowdsourcing work in two distinct participant populations. These dynamics provide further evidence that computer-mediated crowdwork cannot wash away differences between the participants in online collaborative systems, despite the tendency of some researchers and media reports to treat them as a single population, homogenized through the abstraction of distributed work.

MOTIVATIONS FOR ONLINE PARTICIPATION

Not long after computing and networking technologies began to develop in the 1960's, the ideologies and social structures of open collaboration around computing and code began to form [38]. Especially since the advent of open-source software, collaborative content, and social media, there has been significant interest in the question of what motivates people to participate in these systems. The literature on motivations spans a wide variety of socio-technical systems and practices – open source software [19], Wikipedia [35], blogging [26], photo-sharing [29], and question-answering [32], just to name a few.

Research across online contexts has consistently found that factors such as fun, a belief in ideologies of knowledge production, the desire for social connection, and knowledge development are important motivators for online participation. Most studies of online motivation have relied on self-reports, employing surveys with variations of traditional agreement statement-style questions. However, online surveys are susceptible to response effects that can skew results [15]. In this study we focus on one such response effect – *social desirability bias* – and document its effects on survey self-reports of motivation among participants in a specific crowdsourcing system.

SURVEYS & SOCIAL DESIRABILITY

Social desirability bias refers to "the tendency of people to deny socially undesirable traits or qualities and to admit to socially desirable ones" [30]. The theory of social desirability bias suggests it is primarily the result of two underlying social psychological processes. First, providing what individuals believe to be socially desirable responses is a form of impression management [8] — an effort to mold one's public image and to construct a favorable presentation of self based on expectations, norms, and beliefs about a given context. Secondly, providing socially desirable answers can be a form of self-deception [27]. In this respect, social desirability is often an attempt to deny one's "true" attitudes, or mask an underlying belief by expressing a contradictory one. Importantly, answers influenced by social desirability bias should not be considered as merely lies. Social desirability is often subtle, unconscious, and based on implicit attitudes which individuals are not aware of or able to express [28]. Social desirability bias in survey studies is a problem primarily because it can produce inaccurate results which misrepresent the "true" prevalence of attitudes and behaviors. In addition to biasing mean values, social desirability bias can also create spurious or suppressed correlations, mediations, moderations, or other statistical relationships [7]. Because of its potentially wide-ranging influences, social desirability bias should be a real concern, especially for research that relies on survey self-reports.

Researchers have found social desirability bias in survey responses on many controversial topics such as immigration, affirmative action, and racial prejudice.[1] However, the effects of social desirability are not limited to hot-button, divisive issues. For example, Adams and colleagues found that social desirability influenced self-reports of physical activity [1]. Several studies have documented pervasive biases in behavioral and attitudinal scales commonly used in organizational behavior research [25, 22]. A large meta-study also found evidence of widespread social desirability effects in scales used for marketing research [16].

Self-Reports of Online Motivation

Few studies have directly examined social desirability effects in self-reports of motivation, and to our knowledge none have done so in online contexts. As a result, little is known about whether social desirability can influence reports of motivations to participate online, and if it can how prevalent or strong the bias may be. Many online systems are designed on the basis of survey studies documenting users goals and motivations. If these studies misrepresent user motivations because of social desirability bias, the result may be non-optimal design decisions which reduce user satisfaction, present barriers to engagement and collaboration, and potentially disenfranchise users.

Survey self-reports of motivation are likely subject to social desirability bias for at least two reasons. First, there are often socially desirable connections between motivations and activities. For example, we may expect that an individual who makes a charitable donation should be motivated by altruism and look favorably upon such behavior. On the other hand, a man who volunteers primarily to meet women may be looked upon unfavorably. Social norms and stigmas can provide powerful cues about the motivations that should normatively be attached to a given activity. Secondly, one's motivation is often interpreted as a signal of other characteristics. For example, in the absence of other information, individuals may ascribe positive characteristics to the charitable altruist and negative characteristics to the date-seeking volunteer.

There is some evidence that, compared to face-to-face interviews, online surveys may be less susceptible to social desirability effects [15]. Computer-mediated interactions can introduce social distance that mitigates social desirability concerns in some contexts. However many users still actively engage in impression management in computer-mediated communication [14]. Furthermore, self-deception effects are likely to be relevant across interaction mediums. As a result, we contend that the presence and character of

[1] For a review of the literature on social desirability we recommend [5].

social desirability bias within online environments is long overdue for empirical investigation.

In sum, our first research question concerns a pervasive and crucial phenomenon that remains largely overlooked:

RQ1: Can self-reports of online motivation be subject to social desirability bias?

MOTIVATION TO PARTICIPATE ON MTURK

The setting for our research is Amazon Mechanical Turk (MTurk).[2] MTurk is a service which allows "requesters" to distribute small chunks of work to thousands of workers around the globe. In exchange for a few minutes or seconds of a worker's effort on what Amazon calls Human Intelligence Tasks (HITs), Turkers earn small payments which typically range from a few cents to a few dollars.

Dedicated Turkers can earn a significant amount of money by completing HITs. Indeed, MTurk itself highlights the money-making possibilities by prominently inviting visitors to "Make money by working on HITs" on the service's homepage. According to an informal study, however, most Turkers earn less than $10 per week [10]. So, monetary incentives remain an essential but complex part of the motivational landscape of MTurk [21]. Especially for long-term Turkers there are also likely to be important non-monetary motivations.

Several studies have examined non-monetary motivations for doing work on MTurk, as well as the potential interactions between monetary and non-monetary motivations. Synthesizing a variety of previous studies on crowdsourcing markets, Kaufmann and colleagues [12] suggest a motivational model that includes "enjoyment-based motivations" (e.g. fun, passing time, interest), "community-based motivations" (e.g. social interaction, community identification), and "social motivations" (e.g. ideology, social approval). In the same study cited above, Ipeirotis [10] finds that sizable proportions of Turkers reported that fun, killing time, and the feeling that MTurk is a fruitful way to spend time were important motivators. Similarly, Buhrmester and colleagues suggest that intrinsic task enjoyment forms a substantive part of many Turkers' motivation [3]. Several recent studies have confirmed this suggestion, finding evidence that framing an MTurk task as benefiting a non-profit group [33] or as advancing scientific progress [4] interacts with monetary reward to motivate Turkers.

MTurk in the US and India

Our primary purpose in this study is to examine the potential for social desirability effects in self-reports of motivation on MTurk. Any serious attempt to do so must begin with an understanding of who Turkers are, and a rejection of the unsupported assumption that Turkers should be considered as a single, homogeneous group. MTurk attracts workers from all over the world, but the vast majority of visits to the site come from just two countries: the United States and India. As of December 2011, 40.8% of MTurk traffic was traced to IP addresses in the United States, while 35.7% of traffic was traced to addresses in India. [2]. In a study conducted in 2010, Ipeirotis [10] estimated that 46.8% of Turkers reside in the US, while 34% reside in India. A meta study by Ross and colleagues also documents what they describe as a trend moving from "a primarily moderate-income, US-based workforce towards an increasingly international group with a significant population of young, well-educated Indian workers" [34]. These results do not directly indicate the amount of work done by Turkers who hail from each country. However, they are a strong indicator that Turkers from the US and India make up the vast majority of the worker population.

The diversity of MTurk workers contrasts with popular images of crowd-sourcing. According to some media and academic portrayals, phenomena such as online labor markets, crowd-sourcing, and social search represent – at least theoretically – the fulfilment of techno-futuristic fantasies in which globalized, distributed human intelligence is rendered quickly and cheaply available through the click of a few buttons [39]. Reality, however, has not borne out these fantasies of commoditized brainpower. Rather than the seamless integration of person and machine, the global spread of computer-mediated communication has consistently revealed the difficulties of designing socio-technical systems in the face of the incredible diversity of human experience.[3] Empirical comparisons between different practices of human computation and the motivations of sub-populations of "human computers" can complement studies focused primarily on system design or evaluation [31].

Cross-cultural research in psychology[4] underscores the importance of cultural differences for conceptions of self, society, motivation, action, and emotion [20]. For our purposes, the most salient aspect of this research is the suggestion that individuals *both* understand the same action differently *and* explain their reasons for pursuing a particular action differently. Based on the extensive laboratory and field evidence supporting cross-cultural psychological differences, comparable patterns likely exist among distinct sub-populations of participants in online communities, crowd-sourcing platforms, and related phenomena.

Findings from studies comparing the experience of workers across national and cultural settings suggest that crowd-sourcing workers from different national groups might face unique pressures and employ unique self-presentation strategies in the context of their particularly atomized and alienated workplace interactions. Ethnographies examining the motivations of IT sector workers in India, for example,

[2] See `http://www.mturk.com`.

[3] A vast body of research has documented the challenges of designing socio-technical systems for users with diverse socio-cultural backgrounds. One useful high-level entry point is James Scott's work on "high modernist" utopias [36].

[4] We adopt the narrow usage of the term "cross cultural" to refer to nationality which is common in the field of cultural psychology. In the sociological or anthropological sense, nationality is considered to capture only a small part of an individual's socio-cultural identity.

depict a distinct environment in which such workers enact a complex set of identities. Business Process Outsourcing (BPO) workers in India encounter culturally specific forms of prejudice and respond in culturally specific ways [24]. We anticipate that crowd-sourcing workers in India may engage in similarly distinct behaviors when compared with workers in the US.

The potential for distinct patterns of motivation and social desirability bias among Turkers is even more likely in light of the fact that so much crowd-sourcing work – and especially the paid variety – is perceived in the United States as undesirable, undignified, or both [23]. Furthermore, the power dynamics of a paid labor market introduce an added dimension of inequality between researchers and their subjects: researchers surveying workers in the context of a paid crowd-sourcing platform are, if only briefly, their subjects' employers, creating an environment in which seemingly unobtrusive questions may prove sensitive. Given these circumstances, we anticipate finding social-desirability bias among both workers from the US and India, but that the character of the bias will vary between the two groups.

In addition to the theoretical arguments presented above, support for considering US and India Turkers as distinct sub-populations can be drawn from existing studies of what Turkers from the two countries actually do on the site. For example, research has illustrated that Turkers from different countries tend to produce different quality results participate at different rates and times, as well as with different attitudes and abilities that reflect their social and cultural context [37, 13, 34, 10]. Furthermore, the two populations provide distinct responses to survey questions about their motivations for working on MTurk, confront distinct work and employment conditions, and bring very different sets of skills and experiences to bear on their MTurk tasks [10, 13, 34, 37]. So, while dividing our analysis on the basis of country-of-origin captures differences in socio-cultural, political, and economic factors only at a high level of abstraction, even this abstract classification is associated with significantly different patterns of participation.

In sum, there is ample support for considering the two sub-populations of Turkers separately could yield distinct patterns. Our second research question addresses this issue:

> **RQ2: Is there evidence of similar or distinct profiles of social desirability effects in reports of motivation across MTurk's two primary sub-populations?**

METHODS

Social desirability is a problem in survey self reports because participants must select specific answers to explicit questions. Researchers have primarily examined two general techniques for mitigating social desirability bias in experiments and surveys: (1) the use of additional survey instruments which measure individual participants' susceptibility to social desirability, and (2) survey and interview techniques which mitigate potential bias through indirect questioning, the use of so-called "proxy" subjects, and other

Condition Name	N US	N India
Agreement Statements	194	156
List Experiment Control	184	159
List Experiment "Sense of Purpose"	183	152
List Experiment "to Kill Time"	181	142
List Experiment "Fun"	179	152
List Experiment "Make Extra Money"	189	137

Table 1. Condition Descriptions and Sample Sizes

creative techniques [27]. In this study we employ a type of indirect questioning called *the list experiment* (See, e.g. [18]). The list experiment asks each participant to report only *how many* he selects from a list of possible choices. Some participants will un-problematically select all of the potential choices (e.g. 4 out of 4) or none of them, but others will select 1, 2, or 3 out of 4. In the latter case, the list experiment provides an opportunity for the respondent to express support for his "true" attitudes without explicitly naming them: there is no way for anyone to determine exactly which items were chosen (if any). As a result of this freedom from the actual or implied judgment of others, responses to the list experiment are comparatively free of the pressure of others' actual or imagined judgment. A variety of studies comparing traditional survey questions to the list experiment have demonstrated the effects of social desirability bias and the list experiment's ability to mitigate it. For example, such comparisons revealed social desirability bias in responses to questions about racial attitudes in the American South [18], attitudes about immigrants and immigration [11], and the prevalence of vote buying in Nicaragua [9].

To assess motivations for doing HITs on MTurk, we asked survey questions using traditional agreement statements and the list experiment. First, we asked randomly selected participants to make a binary choice to agree or disagree with four motivation statements. We selected statements on the basis of a variety of prior survey research on motivations for doing work on MTurk. For a summary of this research, we suggest [12]. The four statements were: "I am motivated to do HITs on Mechanical Turk..." (1) "to kill time," (2) "to make extra money," (3) "for fun," and (4) "because it gives me a sense of purpose." List experiment participants were randomly assigned to one of five groups. In a control group participants were shown a list of all 4 motivations described above and given the following instructions: "How many of the following would you say is a motivation for you when you do HITs on Mechanical Turk? Please respond only with a number between 0 and 4." In the four treatment groups, participants were shown a list of only *three* motivations – each of the four motivations was absent in one group – and asked to respond with a number between 0 and 3. In each treatment condition, the mean response tells us how many of the 3 motivations participants selected. The mean in the control condition describes selection of the same three motivations plus a single additional motivation. Therefore, the difference in means between each treatment group and the control can be attributed to the addition of that single item to the list. For example, if participants in the control condition selected an average of 2.8 out of 4 items, while participants in a treatment condition selected 2.4 out of 3 items, all things being equal we can estimate that, in the absence of social desirability bias, 40% (i.e. 2.8 – 2.4) of participants would select the 4th item. Because of the indirect manner of calculating this value, the final result of the list experiment should be interpreted as an estimate or expected value for the proportion of people who would select a motivation in the absence of social desirability bias.

The general lack of social presence in the MTurk user interface makes it a conservative test for social desirability bias effects in online collaborative settings. Social desirability bias is magnified by the actual or perceived presence of others when answering questions. In the context of MTurk, however, there are few user-to-user interactions or signs of social presence. This reduced social presence in a computer-mediated context should make social desirability effects less likely [15]. If we observe social desirability effects among MTurk workers nonetheless, it will increase our confidence about observing them in other contexts with greater social presence.

Data Collection & Sample

A secondary benefit of our focus on MTurk is that it is possible to collect survey responses from Turkers using the service itself [17]. In July 2010 we recruited 1200 US-Based Turkers into our study, and in November 2010 we recruited 1216 India-based Turkers. Recruitment of specific or random users is not possible on MTurk, so our sample is composed of individuals who chose to respond to our request for survey responses. Participants were paid 5 cents for completing the survey, which took approximately 30 seconds to complete. Each user within each of the two sub-population samples was randomly assigned to one of six experimental conditions and restricted to participating only once.[5] In addition to questions about motivation, in each condition we asked users about their gender, age, education level, and frequency of completing HITs. Although random assignment should eliminate the potential influence of other individual differences between participants, we nonetheless followed the method used in [11], and included these co-variates in a series of OLS regression models to assess potential influences of demographic differences between conditions. No significant differences were found across conditions which suggests that, within the US and India samples, random assignment successfully mitigated the potential counfounding effects of demographic factors. Our analysis directly compares results across treatment (list experiment) and control (agreement-statement) groups *within* the samples of US and India Turkers.

We do not conduct hypothesis tests for significant differences between US and India Turkers because the list experiment provides only group-level (rather than individual-level) data. As a result it is not possible to systematically compare the two samples. However, we do present the results from the two groups side-by-side and make descriptive observations between them.

[5]To enforce condition assignment, country location restrictions, and the single-use restriction we employed a third-party service called CrowdFlower (`http://crowdflower.com`).

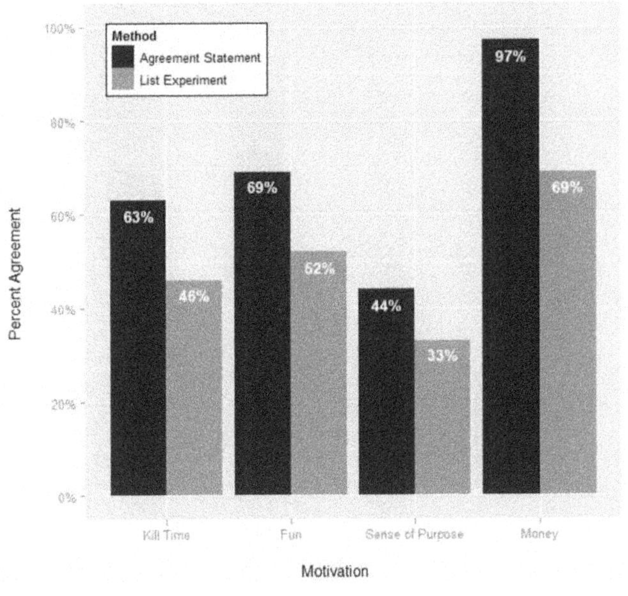

Figure 1. The proportion of US participants who selected each motivation using agreement statement-style questions or the list experiment. N = 1132.

RESULTS

Out of 1200 US responses, 68 (5.6%) were removed because they were invalid or incomplete, leaving a final valid sample of 1132. A higher proportion of responses in the India sample were invalid. Out of 1216 India responses, 318 (26%) were removed, leaving a final valid sample of 898. The higher rate of low quality work provided by India Turkers is consistent with prior research [13, 37]. Rates of invalid responses between conditions were not significantly different from random in either of the two samples (For the US sample, $\chi^2 = 5.84, p = 0.32$; For the India sample, $\chi^2 = 6.68, p = 0.25$). Invalid-response rates were also consistent across conditions for the combined samples $\chi^2 = 8.32, p = 0.14$). Table 1 illustrates sample sizes in each of the six conditions for both US and India sub-populations. Examining first the US sample, a comparison of the two survey methods showed that a smaller percentage of respondents said they were motivated by each factor in the list experiment compared to the agreement statements. Figure 1 provides a visual representation of these results.

		Gender		Education	
	Age	Female	Male	College Degree	Graduate Degree
US	32.7(11.6)	60.7%	39.3%	51.6%	14.2%
India	29.3(8.9)	36.2%	63.8%	84.1%	53.6%

Table 2. Age, gender, and educational level among respondents in the US and India samples. Age is reported as mean with s.d. in parenthesis.

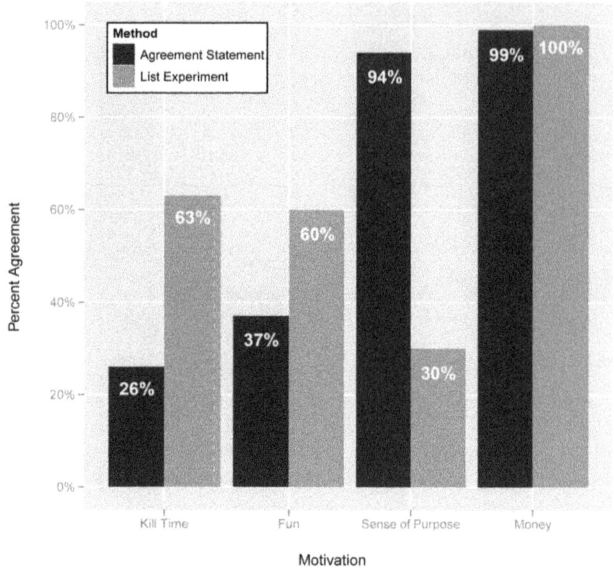

Figure 2. The proportion of India participants who selected each motivation using agreement statement-style questions or the list experiment. N = 898.

Pearson's chi-square tests showed significantly *smaller* proportions among US participants in the list experiment for "killing time" ($\chi^2 = 10.19, p < .01$), "fun" ($\chi^2 = 10.89, p < .001$), and "money" ($\chi^2 = 53.82, p < .001$), and a moderately significant difference for "sense of purpose" ($\chi^2 = 3.47, p = .06$). The differences in proportions between the two methods were also quite large: 17% for both "killing time" and "fun," 11% for "sense of purpose," and 28% for "money."

The India sample showed a substantially different pattern. Figure 2 provides a visual representation of these results. Pearson's chi-square tests showed significantly *larger* proportions of agreement among India participants in the list experiment for "killing time" ($\chi^2 = 40.71, p < .001$) and "fun" ($\chi^2 = 16.04, p < .001$) and significantly *smaller* proportions in the list experiment for "sense of purpose" ($\chi^2 = 132.83, p < .001$). There was no significant difference between the two techniques for "money" ($\chi^2 = .38, p = .53$). Again, the differences in observed agreement between the two methods was large: 37% for "killing time," 23% for "fun," and a remarkable 64% for "sense of purpose."

Several aspects of our findings are notable. First, social desirability bias appears to encourage US Turkers to over-report the number of factors that motivate them. Participants in the agreement-statement condition from the US sample reported an average of 2.7 out of 4 motivations, while participants in the list experiment conditions reported only 2.1 out of 4 motivations on average. So, across conditions most US Turkers still reported being motivated by at least two factors, and each of four the motivations remained salient for a sizable proportion of our sample. However, accounting for the effects of social desirability, in each case that proportion was reduced.

We also found evidence of social desirability bias in our sample of Turkers in India, but the results do not suggest a uniform pattern. Participants in the agreement-statement condition over-reported "sense of purpose" and under-reported "killing time" and "fun." Results suggest no social desirability effects in reporting of money as a motivator. In contrast with the US sample, workers in the India sample reported approximately the same number of average motivations across the agreement-statement and list experiment conditions – 2.6 out of 4 compared with 2.5 out of 4 respectively. As with the US sample, all motivations were salient for at least some India participants, regardless of the measurement method used.

Examining MTurk's two key sub-populations separately allows us to observe potential differences in motivational profiles and social desirability biases between the two. The differences we observe are likely the result of a number of factors, including (but not limited to) gender, age, and class. However, building on the research discussed above, we argue it is likely that macro-scale socio-cultural, political, and economic factors, as captured broadly by nationality (India or US) also help to account for observed differences between the two groups. The specific causes, mechanisms, and implications of these patterns merit further investigation and comparison.

Figure 3 illustrates the degree to which agreement statements over or under-reported agreement with each motivation compared to the theoreticaly more accurate value obtained from the list experiment. Within the US sample, agreement statements modestly over-reported three of the four motivations compared to the list experiment: "killing time" (36% over-reported), "fun" (32% over-reported), and "sense of purpose" (33% over-reported). The magnitude of over-reporting was largest in the case of "money" as a motivation (40% over-reported). So, more than for other types of motivations, social desirability appears to encourage individuals to say that money is a motivator even though that may not be the case.

Turkers in India showed larger and more variable social desirability effects compared to US Turkers. Within the India sample, agreement statements under-reported 2 motivations — "killing time" (–142%) and "fun" (–62%), and dramatically over-reported "sense of purpose" by almost 200% compared to the list experiment. Results showed no social desirability bias related to money as a motivator, as effectively all participants in both conditions agreed that it was an important motivator.[6] So, in the case of Turkers in India, social desirability appears to encourage individuals to over-state the importance of "sense of purpose" as a motivator, and under-state the importance of both "killing time" and "fun."

[6]Values for the list experiment conditions are estimates based on the tabulation of the responses across each permutation of answers (see the Methods section, above). The point estimate in this case was actually 103%, but since this is an artifact of the mathematical procedure, we report the maximum possible value of 100%.

DISCUSSION

The recent rise of computing metaphors such as the "cloud" and the "crowd" have, perhaps, encouraged a stereotype of the faceless and undifferentiated Internet user. Similar views are particularly prominent in the case of crowdsourcing work which itself tends to be comparatively featureless, repetitive, and unskilled. However, the robust evidence of diversity in opinions, perspectives, and backgrounds among users testifies to the failure of large-scale socio-technical systems to abstract out the foundations of online and offline life. In this study we turn a particular spotlight on the diversity of workers on MTurk, investigating whether Turkers from different countries might be influenced by distinct economic, socio-cultural, and political environments, and thus express different motivations and social desirability effects for doing work on the site.

Demographic differences between the samples of US and India Turkers likely contribute to the variations in reported motivation and social desirability bias we observe across the two groups. As we discussed above, while random assignment *within* each national group assures that demographic attributes were also distributed randomly across the list experiment and survey conditions, the nature of the MTurk platform and our study design made it impossible to ensure random distribution *across* the two groups. As a result, we cannot identify the precise cause(s) of the differential presence of social desirability bias across MTurk workers in the US versus those in India. However, while the nature of our experiment precludes explicit statistical comparison between national groups, treating them as distinct sub-populations does allow us to observe the different contours of the data.

While social desirability did not alter the rank-order of motivations between the agreement-statement and list experiment conditions, the consistent over-reporting of motivation in the US sample is an important finding in itself. The apparent proportional consistency of the bias does not diminish its importance. In the context of a multivariate analysis of these results, the inaccuracy of survey responses could produce spurious or suppressed correlations, mediations, moderations, and other statistical relationships (see [7]).

This finding is suggestive of our participants' desire to appear highly motivated to others, as well as their belief that clearly articulating those motivations is socially desirable. The finding that at least some US Turkers over-state their motivation is particularly interesting given (largely unsubstantiated) media reports suggesting that many Turkers are individuals with lots of discretionary time (e.g. stay-at-home parents, security guards) For these Turkers and others, social desirability pressure may come from an expectation that behavior should be well-reasoned, from the tendency to ascribe positive characteristics to highly motivated individuals, and from the desire to express intrinsic interest in work (even rote side-work). Economic theories of rational choice as well as social psychological theories such as the theory of planned behavior rely on similar assumptions that human action is (or normatively should be) intentional and

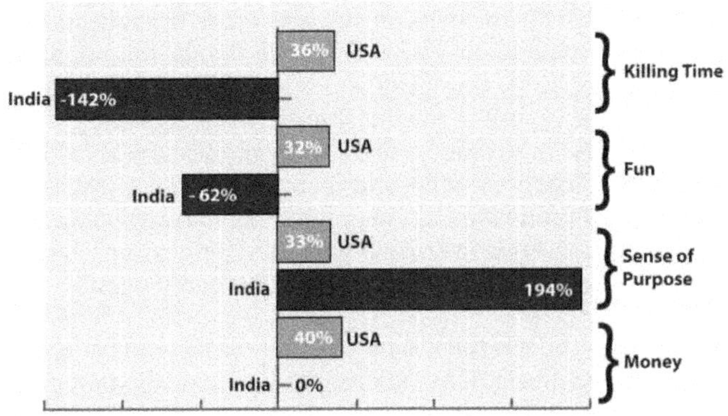

Figure 3. The degree of over or under-reporting of each motivation using traditional agreement statements, compared to the list experiment conditions. For example, compared to using the list experiment estimate as the "expected value," US participants over-reported that "killing time" was a motivation by 36%.

thoroughly considered. An individual is assumed to have established preferences, as well as known desired goals or outcomes for her behavior. While many scholars have argued that these normative models are incomplete and inaccurate, their prevalence in education and popular culture may have created social pressure among US Turkers to appear well-reasoned and highly motivated.

Again, our findings provide no direct information about why we should observe such distinct patterns of over- and under-reporting in the India sample, but previous research suggests potential explanations. Transnational IT work in India involves complex negotiations of identity as well as strategies of self-presentation that attempt to disguise experiences and values perceived to be inconsistent with foreign employers' or clients' desires [6, 24]. This may explain respondents' perception that "sense of purpose" is more desirable than "killing time" or "fun," even though the latter two appear to be important to many. Here again, our results may signify a form of self-deception in which some India participants attempt to mask their genuine motivations for doing work with the motivation they believe is socially "correct." The relatively high status sometimes accorded to BPO and call-center work in India may likewise contribute to the perception that workers who want to kill time or have fun are insufficiently serious and dedicated about their (desirable) jobs.[7] Requesters in the U.S. or elsewhere may ultimately find these sorts of motives inoffensive.

The Almighty Dollar (or Rupee)?

The over-reporting of monetary motivation among the US workers in contrast to workers in India raises particularly interesting questions in the context of MTurk. Upon its release in 2004, some reports painted MTurk as a "virtual sweatshop" [23], assuming that most HITs would be completed by workers in the developing world for whom even a few dollars could be a lot of money. However, according to web-tracking firm alexa.com, as of December

[7]Note also the higher average education level of the workers in our India sample versus the US sample.

2011 nearly 50% of visits to the site were from users in the United States [2]. Our research builds on popular press reports [23] and prior studies [10, 21] that have illustrated the complex relationship between monetary and non-monetary motivations in crowdsourcing work. Our contribution is to provide strong evidence not only that both types of motivation are important, but that participants' motivations are often in tension with their perceptions about the motivations that others would look favorably upon.

In addition, our results indicate that money may be a motivator for fewer US Turkers than previously thought. The presence of an especially strong social desirability effect for reports of monetary motivation also suggests that US Turkers believe that money is the reason they *should* complete HITs. In the context of an online labor market like MTurk, workers shape their responses to conform with imagined expectations they attribute to job requesters (even researchers) or to the creators of MTurk who promote money-making as the primary reason to the use the service.[8] Alternatively, they may be influenced by the popular perception that crowdsourcing is an undesirable, "low class" form of labor [23], and likewise assume the popular belief that it would be undesirable to cast such labor as a fulfilling, fun, or personally satisfying way to spend one's time. However, given prior studies showing that task framing interacts with monetary motivation [33, 4], it is likely that the specific type of task, the beneficiary of the work, and other contextual factors would moderate these issues. Further research is necessary on this issue.

LIMITATIONS, IMPLICATIONS & CONCLUSION

Our study is subject to a number of important limitations. First, as we noted earlier, our data does not allow us to make structured statistical comparisons between US and India sub-populations. Demographic differences between the two samples probably account for at least part of the differences we observe; however, it is unlikely that gender or age alone (for example) could explain the differences. Furthermore, factors such as gender and age are inextricably tied to the socio-cultural, economic, and political foundations of crowd-work in India and the US. Macro-scale conditions also inform the types of people to whom crowd work is available and attractive.

Secondly, we note that our study is limited only to the unique socio-technical context of MTurk, and it would be inappropriate to generalize our findings beyond this context. Furthermore, our method is more descriptive than explanatory, which limits the ability of our findings to contribute to theories of social desirability in online motivation. Only through in-depth examination in mixed-methods studies will we learn how accurate our estimates are or how they may generalize to other crowd-sourcing and online collaborative systems.

[8]Half of the MTurk website's landing and login page is dedicated to workers, and the largest, boldest, and blue-est typeface is reserved for the phrase "**Make Money** by working on HITs" (See: http://mturk.com; original emphasis).

We believe, however, that our findings strongly inform RQ1: reports of online motivation *can* be subject to social desirability bias. This finding demands that more attention be paid to the issue of social desirability in other contexts. Our findings also suggest that survey results in other online settings, especially those with greater social presence and a wider array of potentially sensitive topics at stake, could reflect some degree of social desirability bias in the reporting of online motivation. With respect to RQ2, the cross-national comparison indicates that the precise contours of social desirability depend on the context of interaction, the task at hand, and the populations involved. In a future study we intend to expand this methodology to search for social desirability bias in other online contexts such as open-source software and Wikipedia, and to include additional motivations that would be relevant in those contexts.

Many prior studies have used non-survey techniques such as behavioral/experimental tasks and qualitative interviewing to assess motivation. These methods, however, generally do not allow researchers to capture as large or as diverse a sample as surveys do. Despite this important benefit of surveys, our results cast a shadow of doubt on prior studies which have used direct questions to assess motivation in MTurk. For example, Ipeirotis' study [10] found that "very few Indian workers participate on MTurk for 'killing time'." Our results suggest this result is likely due to social desirability bias, and in fact that the majority of Turkers in India are at least partly motivated by "killing time." Likewise, accounting for the effects of social desirability, our results suggest that 60% of Turkers in India do HITs at least partly because they think it's fun, while only 20% reported fun as a motivation in Ipeirotis' study.

While it would be premature to suggest specific design implications on the basis of this work, dynamics such as the interaction of "fun," "killing time," and "sense of purpose" in India highlight the importance of identifying potential social desirability effects for design. For example, on the basis of a survey study Amazon might reasonably make decisions about how to message to potential Turkers and how to provide feedback about their participation. With inaccurate information similar to what was provided in our agreement statement conditions, designers might choose to highlight money-making and the meaningfulness of crowd-work at the expense of fun and killing time. In addition, believing that only a small portion of India Turkers are motivated by fun, designers might shun the integration of game-like features. However, such decisions might at best fail to capitalize on opportunities to enhance user satisfaction, and at worst alienate Turkers who perceive a motivational mismatch.

This speculative example illustrates the importance of this topic for the HCI community. Our results strongly suggest that future studies of motivation in online environments should take account of potential social desirability bias. The list experiment is just one method for doing so, and techniques for addressing social desirability bias and other response effects have been under development for more than 30 years [27]. In addition, the different patterns of motivation and bias across US and India Turkers underscore the importance of cross-national and cross-cultural studies of online motivation. As socio-technical systems become more global, designers must seek to facilitate social interaction and collaboration across national as well as cultural boundaries, strive to understand the differential foundations of motivation for participation, and consider how those motivations may influence divergent patterns of activity.

We also add further evidence that monetary incentives represent just one part of a complex motivational array behind paid work. Incentive systems that rely solely on paying users for content, ignoring other key motivations such as fun and providing a sense of purpose do so at their peril. Likewise. collaborative systems that seek to engage workers or collaborators from diverse backgrounds may benefit from context-specific adaptations to sub-populations with divergent attitudes about money or employment. While we used national boundaries as a proxy for macro-scale cultural differences, there are numerous sub-groups within both the US and India. As a result, studies of any popular socio-technical system such as Wikipedia, open-source software, or even Facebook would benefit from explicitly identifying and comparing important sub-populations and their perspectives on motivation and activity.

Finally, we provide another example case in which asking users to explicitly state their motivations can produce inaccurate and incomplete data [28]. Interviews, interactive games, and other behavioral data will provide complementary information that can be used to better understand the stated and unstated preferences of participants in online systems. A program of rigorous and creative research will be necessary to develop a thorough understanding of motivation in online contexts and inform the intelligent design of incentive systems.

Despite the immense popularity of crowdsourcing and other forms of online collaboration, it is likely that current systems are only beginning to realize their potential. Efforts to expand the reach of online collaboration to previously under-served and under-represented populations are already underway [13]. Understanding the path forward for designing effective and engaging systems of online collaboration — including crowd-sourcing systems — will depend on developing clear, accurate, and nuanced views of users and their motivations. As researchers and practitioners inform ongoing development with investigations of user motivation, it will be essential to consider social desirability and other response effects in order to maximize the transformative potential of online collaboration.

ACKNOWLEDGMENTS

Many thanks to Wayne Lutters and the many anonymous reviewers whose commentary significantly improved this paper. An earlier version of this work also benefited from the feedback of discussants at a 2011 CSCW Horizons session.

REFERENCES

1. S. A. Adams, C. E. Matthews, C. B. Ebbeling, C. G. Moore, J. E. Cunningham, J. Fulton, and J. R. Hebert. The effect of social desirability and social approval on Self-Reports of physical activity. *American Journal of Epidemiology*, 161(4):389 –398, Feb. 2005.

2. Alexa.com. mturk.com - traffic details. http://alexa.com/siteinfo/mturk.com, Dec. 2011.

3. M. Buhrmester, T. Kwang, and S. D. Gosling. Amazon's mechanical turk. *Perspectives on Psychological Science*, 6(1):3 –5, Jan. 2011.

4. D. Chandler and A. Kapelner. Breaking monotony with meaning: Motivation in crowdsourcing markets. *University of Chicago mimeo*, 2010.

5. T. J. DeMaio. Social desirability and survey measurement: A review. In C. F. Turner, E. Martin, and N. R. C. U. P. on Survey Measurement of Subjective Phenomena, editors, *Surveying subjective Phenomena*, volume 2, pages 257–282. Russell Sage Foundation, June 1984.

6. S. Derné. Cultural conceptions of human motivation and their significance for culture theory. In D. Crane, editor, *The Sociology of Culture: Emerging Theoretical Perspectives*, pages 267–287. Blackwell, Cambridge, MA, 1994.

7. D. C. Ganster, H. W. Hennessey, and F. Luthans. Social desirability response effects: Three alternative models. *The Academy of Management Journal*, 26(2):321–331, June 1983. ArticleType: research-article / Full publication date: Jun., 1983 / Copyright 1983 Academy of Management.

8. E. Goffman. *The presentation of self in everyday life.* Doubleday, NY, NY, 1973.

9. E. Gonzalez-Ocantos, C. K. de Jonge, C. Melndez, J. Osorio, and D. W. Nickerson. Vote buying and social desirability bias: Experimental evidence from nicaragua. *American Journal of Political Science*, Forthcoming.

10. P. Ipeirotis. The new demographics of mechanical turk. `http://behind-the-enemy-lines.blogspot.com/2010/03/new-demographics-of-mechanical-turk.html`, Mar. 2010.

11. A. L. Janus. The influence of social desirability pressures on expressed immigration attitudes*. *Social Science Quarterly*, 91(4):928–946, 2010.

12. N. Kaufmann, D. Veit, and T. Schulze. More than fun and money . worker motivation in crowdsourcing a study on mechanical turk. In *Proceedings of the Seventeenth Americas Conference on Information Systems*, Detroit, MI, 2011.

13. S. Khanna, A. Ratan, J. Davis, and W. Thies. Evaluating and improving the usability of mechanical turk for low-income workers in india. In *Proceedings of the First ACM Symposium on Computing for Development*, ACM DEV '10, pages 12:1–12:10, New York, NY, USA, 2010. ACM.

14. S. Kiesler, J. Siegel, and T. W. McGuire. Social psychological aspects of computer-mediated communication. *American Psychologist*, 39(10):1123–1134, 1984.

15. S. Kiesler and L. S. Sproull. Response effects in the electronic survey. *Public Opinion Quarterly*, 50(3):402–413, Sept. 1986.

16. M. F. King and G. C. Bruner. Social desirability bias: A neglected aspect of validity testing. *Psychology and Marketing*, 17(2):79–103, Feb. 2000.

17. A. Kittur, E. H. Chi, and B. Suh. Crowdsourcing user studies with mechanical turk. In *Proceeding of the twenty-sixth annual SIGCHI conference on Human factors in computing systems*, pages 453–456, Florence, Italy, 2008. ACM.

18. J. H. Kuklinski, M. D. Cobb, and M. Gilens. Racial attitudes and the "new south". *The Journal of Politics*, 59(2):323–349, May 1997.

19. K. R. Lakhani, R. G. Wolf, J. Feller, B. Fitzgerald, S. Hissam, and K. R. Lakhani. Why hackers do what they do: Understanding motivation and effort in Free/Open source software projects. In *Perspectives on Free and open Source Software*. MIT Press, Cambridge, Mass, 2005.

20. H. R. Markus and S. Kitayama. Culture, self, and the reality of the social. *Psychological Inquiry*, 14:277–283, Oct. 2003.

21. W. Mason and D. J. Watts. Financial incentives and the "performance of crowds". *SIGKDD Explor. Newsl.*, 11(2):100–108, 2009.

22. A. Meade, A. Watson, and C. Kroustalis. Assessing common methods bias in organizational research. In *22nd Annual Meeting of the Society for Industrial and Organizational Psychology, New York*, 2007.

23. K. Mieszkowski. "I make $1.45 a week and i love it". `http://www.salon.com/tech/feature/2006/07/24/turks/index_np.html`, Sept. 2007.

24. K. Mirchandani. Practices of global capital: Gaps, cracks and ironies in transnational call centres in india. *Global Networks*, 4(4):355–373, 2004.

25. R. H. Moorman and P. M. Podsakoff. A meta-analytic review and empirical test of the potential confounding effects of social desirability response sets in organizational behavior research. *Journal of Occupational and Organizational Psychology*, 65(2):131–149, 1992.

26. B. Nardi, D. J. Schiano, M. Gumbrecht, and L. Swartz. Why we blog. *Communications of the ACM*, 47(12):41–46, 2004.

27. A. J. Nederhof. Methods of coping with social desirability bias: A review. *European Journal of Social Psychology*, 15(3):263–280, 1985.

28. R. Nisbett and T. Wilson. Telling more than we can know: Verbal reports on mental processes. *Psychological Review*, 84(1):231–259, 1977.

29. O. Nov, M. Naaman, and C. Ye. Motivational, structural and tenure factors that impact online community photo sharing. In *Third International Conference on Weblogs and Social Media (ICWSM 2009)*, San Jose, CA, 2009.

30. D. L. Phillips and K. J. Clancy. Some effects of "social desirability" in survey studies. *The American Journal of Sociology*, 77(5):921–940, Mar. 1972.

31. A. J. Quinn and B. B. Bederson. Human computation: A survey and taxonomy of a growing field. In *Proceedings of ACM CHI 2011 Conference on Human Factors in Computing Systems*, 2011.

32. S. Rafaeli, D. R. Raban, and G. Ravid. How social motivation enhances economic activity and incentives in the google answers knowledge sharing market. *International Journal of Knowledge and Learning*, 3(1):1 – 11, 2007.

33. J. Rogstadius, V. Kostakos, A. Kittur, B. Smus, J. Laredo, and M. Vukovic. An assessment of intrinsic and extrinsic motivation on task performance in crowdsourcing markets, 2011.

34. J. Ross, L. Irani, M. S. Silberman, A. Zaldivar, and B. Tomlinson. Who are the crowdworkers?: shifting demographics in mechanical turk. In *Proceedings of the 28th of the international conference extended abstracts on Human factors in computing systems*, pages 2863–2872, Atlanta, Georgia, USA, 2010. ACM.

35. J. Schroer and G. Hertel. Voluntary engagement in an open Web-Based encyclopedia: Wikipedians and why they do it. *Media Psychology*, 12(1):96, 2009.

36. J. Scott. *Seeing Like a State: How Certain Schemes to Improve the Human Condition Have Failed*. Yale University Press, New Haven, CT, 1998.

37. A. Shaw, J. Horton, and D. Chen. Designing incentives for inexpert raters. In *The 2011 ACM Conference on Computer Supported Cooperative Work (CSCW, 2011)*, Hangzhou, China, 2011.

38. S. Weber. *The Success of Open Source*. Harvard University Press, Apr. 2004.

39. J. Zittrain. Ubiquitous human computing. *Philosophical Transactions of the Royal Society A*, 366:3813–3821, 2008.

Deploying MonoTrans Widgets in the Wild

Chang Hu[1,2,3], Philip Resnik[1,3,4] Yakov Kronrod[3,4], Benjamin B. Bederson[1,2,3]
[1]Computer Science Department, [2]Human-Computer Interaction Lab,
[3]Institute for Advanced Computer Studies, [4]Department of Linguistics,
University of Maryland
{changhu, bederson}@cs.umd.edu, resnik@umiacs.umd.edu, yakov@umd.edu

ABSTRACT
In this paper, we report our experience deploying the MonoTrans Widgets system in a public setting. Our work follows a line of crowd-sourced monolingual translation systems, and it is the first attempt to deploy such a system "in the wild". The results are promising, but we also found out that simultaneously drawing from multiple crowds with different expertise and sizes poses unique problems in the design of such crowd-sourcing systems.

Author Keywords
Monolingual; translation; translation interface; human computation; distributed human computation; wisdom of crowds; crowd-sourcing; machine translation;

ACM Classification Keywords
H.5.m [Information interfaces and presentation (e.g., HCI)]: Miscellaneous;

General Terms
Design, Human Factors, Experimentation

INTRODUCTION
Crowd-sourced monolingual translation [3][7] is a method to obtain translation without bilingual translators, but instead via the collaboration of two crowds of monolingual people coupled by machine translation systems. Our previous experiments with crowd-sourced monolingual translation have shown that significant quality improvement over machine translation alone is possible [3][4]. However, no such system has been deployed to large crowds of users in everyday use.

Encouraged by our initial success, we take the monolingual system a step further and deploy it "in the wild". By doing so, we hope to identify the real-world challenges to building a crowd-sourced monolingual translation system – or, more broadly, a crowd-sourcing system that draws expertise from multiple different crowds.

In our previous experimentation attempting to deploy the MonoTrans2 system [4] to the public, we identified several problems with its standalone, integrated interface design, the main problem being that complicated tasks are not well suited to casual use. The MonoTrans2 UI was designed to show all possible tasks for a collection of sentences (usually from the same book page). While this provides users with ample context and the freedom to choose among the available tasks, understanding, selecting and then performing those tasks became so complicated that it was unrealistic to expect significant engagement with casual users. In our previous experiments, even recruited users who were fully committed to using the MonoTrans2 UI expressed confusion over this task model. This high entry barrier for casual users became an even more significant problem when MonoTrans2 was built as a standalone website without an existing user base.

We have addressed the task complexity and the user population problems with our new MonoTrans Widgets design (Figure 1). To address the task complexity problem, we simplified the MonoTrans2 system into widgets, small, embedded web pages with a single, short task. To further alleviate the user population problem, we chose to draw from an existing, sizable and stable user base that we know and have access to, the users of the International Children's Digital Library (ICDL www.childrenslibrary.org). The MonoTrans Widgets system has a goal directly related to the ICDL users: translating children's books, so the books can be viewed in more languages on ICDL, and this goal gives the ICDL users a strong motivation to help. However, the widget approach has a price. Compared to the earlier designs, there is room for only minimal context, – putting translation quality at stake. The ICDL user population is unevenly distributed, with a majority of English speakers, adding a further challenge.

In this paper, we present our experience deploying

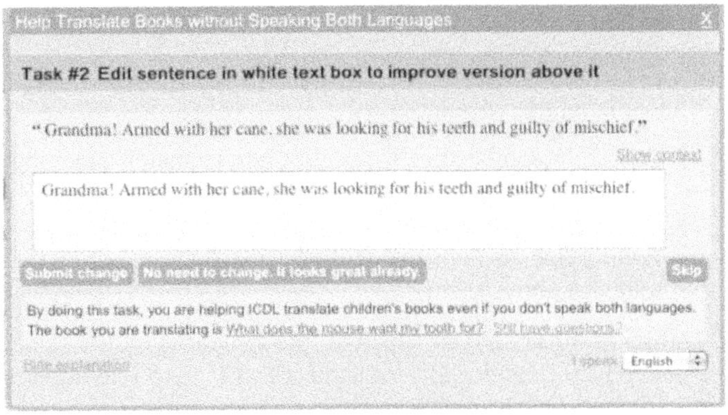

Figure 1. One of the MonoTrans Widgets with explanation message expanded

MonoTrans Widgets "in the wild", including quantitative results about translation quality. We also discuss general design lessons from this process. Because most prior works assume no imbalance between multiple worker populations that are simultaneously involved, our lessons involving multiple crowds of different sizes may be especially useful for such real-world scenario.

BACKGROUND

The idea of embedding a small task into users' web browsing experience is not new. Anyone who has an online account may have encountered reCAPTCHA [1], and thus contributed to the crowd-sourced OCR project.

Providing users with short, self-contained tasks ("micro-tasks") that encourage quick completion is one of the most adopted crowd-sourcing approaches, because fine task granularity is crucial to solicit answers from a large crowd [5]. Micro-tasks are capable of supporting complex tasks, as shown by various designs [6][8]. In particular, bilingual translation can be done via Mechanical Turk[8]. However, since MonoTrans breaks down the task of translation further between two crowds and into multiple steps, the effectiveness of micro-tasks still needs to be studied.

The concept and first prototypes of crowd-sourced monolingual translation were proposed in the Language Grid system [7] and MonoTrans [3]. The MonoTrans Widgets system described in this paper is the latest member of the MonoTrans system family [3][4], whose members all implement similar iterative protocols. The same as its ancestor MonoTran2, the MonoTrans Widgets system implements an asynchronous iterative protocol in which the source and the target language speakers take edit or attach extra information to the translation together [4]. However, MonoTrans Widgets cannot provide users with nearly as rich context as MonoTrans2 does.

DESIGN OF MONOTRANS WIDGETS

MonoTrans Widgets support the same types of tasks as MonoTrans2 [4], with each one tailored into a customized widget. In total, there are six types of tasks:

Target language speaker tasks:

1) *Edit*: Edit sentence in white text box to improve version above it
2) *Identify errors*: Highlight incorrect parts of the sentence below
3) *Vote*: Click to pick the best sentence

Source language speaker tasks:

4) *Edit*: Edit sentence in white text box to match meaning of version above it
5) *Paraphrase*: Say the highlighted part in a different way
6) *Vote*: Click to pick the sentence that best matches the sentence above them

Unlike MonoTrans2, in which all the sentences on the same book page and all related tasks are available simultaneously, MonoTrans Widgets only present one task to the user at a time. Within a task, minimal context is provided. Users can optionally see the previous and the next sentences. They cannot see background images in picture books as in MonoTrans2.

In this case, the system (rather than the user) chooses the task. Doing this right turns out to be a surprisingly subtle problem. This is because the system simultaneously organizes multiple crowds (speakers of different languages) that participate in multiple book translations (each involving a language pair), and that language distribution is very uneven among current ICDL users. It is further complicated because the system does not require logins (thus no user IDs) and needs to be efficient since many tasks are performed (i.e., no complex database analysis per task assignment).

There are two steps in the task assignment algorithm: task type selection and sentence prioritization. When a new user (as implied by server session) starts using MonoTrans Widgets, the initial task type is selected from a predefined random distribution. The user is then given tasks of the same type, with a probability to be given a different type after each task.

Once the task type is selected, the system chooses a sentence for the users to perform the task on. Sentence prioritization is independent of task type. Each sentence is assigned a priority based on the following two conditions:

1) How close the sentence is to being "finished".[1]
2) How difficult it is to get source or target language speakers. This is a crucial adjustment to the multiple-crowd-multiple-language issue described above.

Based on our a priori knowledge of the language distribution in ICDL, a higher priority is given to sentences whose source and/or target language is less common. If both the source and the target languages are uncommon, the sentence receives an even higher priority.

The highest priority sentence translating from or to the user's language is assigned to every first-time user. After that, sentences that follow within the same book are assigned in sequence until the user has seen the last sentence of the book. Then the newly prioritized sentences are assigned in the same way.

DEPLOYMENT OF MONOTRANS WIDGETS

We deployed the MonoTrans Widgets to the International Children's Digital Library (ICDL), which has about 10,000 unique daily visitors. In addition to English, the widgets were translated into Spanish, French, German, Japanese and Chinese and placed on every book reader page in ICDL as a link on the top of the page with the text "Help Translate

[1] "Finished" is itself subtle to define. Here we use the operational definition that a sentence is finished being translated if (a) there have been at least two rounds of editing between the target and the source language speakers, and (b) the translation candidate with the most rounds has been voted for at least three times. Notice that this definition pertains the order in which sentences are worked on, and does not affect translation quality *per se*.

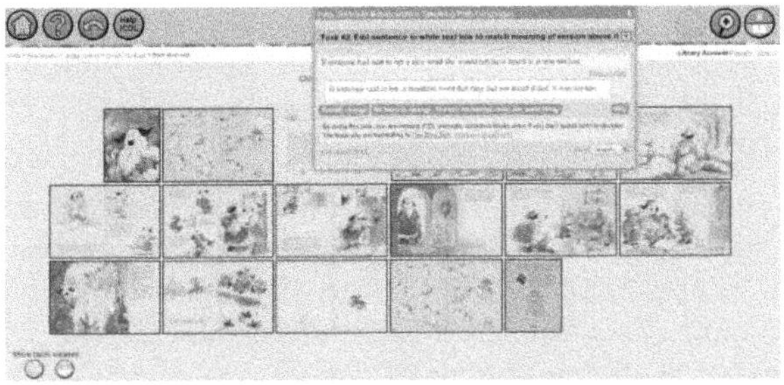

Figure 2. The widget as shown on ICDL web page

Books without Speaking Both Languages". When users click on the link, a widget is displayed as an embedded frame with instructions and a task (see Figure 2). Users can also switch to other languages within the widget.

Deploying on ICDL brings the MonoTrans Widgets about 1,000 daily visitors. This user population is very different from the participants in our previous experiments because they are not hired or directly recruited, and in general they do not routinely take part in translation of children's books.[2]

In the first 21 days after deployment, 27,858 users visited the MonoTrans Widgets, and there were 6,358 widget task submissions.

QUANTITATIVE EVALUATION

Among the 10 children's book translations being translated through the MonoTrans Widgets, we selected one English book (for translation into Spanish) and one Spanish book (for translation into English) to conduct an evaluation on translation quality. The English book contains 30 sentences, and the Spanish book contains 24 sentences. These books are intended for 6-9 year olds. While more sentences in these books were edited because there are more English and Spanish speakers in ICDL, the books were not cherry-picked by their translation quality.

Both books were translated from the language in which they were originally published. The initial machine translation (also the baseline) was done using the Google Translate Research API [9]. The books were deployed in the MonoTrans Widgets system for 14 days (Sep 5 to Sep 18, 2011), during which there were 3,678 submissions (including edits, votes, error identifications, and explanations) from 739 IP addresses. On average, each sentence completed 1.1 round-trips between the English speakers and the Spanish speakers. For each submission, the average time spent was 126 seconds.

Independent to the MonoTrans Widgets system, two native bilingual evaluators were recruited to assess translation quality for fully automatic output of Google Translate (evaluation baseline) and for output of MonoTrans Widgets (using Google Translate as the translation engine). In the evaluation, the evaluators were not aware of how translations were done, and the sentences were presented to them randomly. For each output (translation) paired with its corresponding source sentence, the evaluator's task was to rate the translation's fluency and accuracy on a 5-point scale, where fluency of 5 indicates complete fluency and accuracy of 5 indicates complete preservation of meaning [2]. The evaluation results are shown in figures 3 and 4.

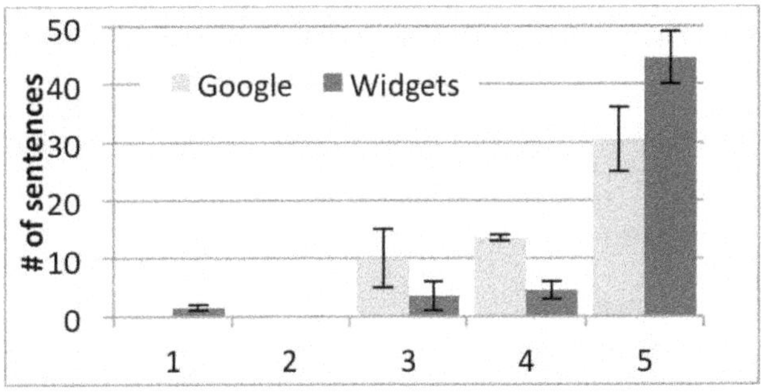

Figure 3. Fluency distribution of edited sentences with two bilingual evaluators (1=worst, 5=best)

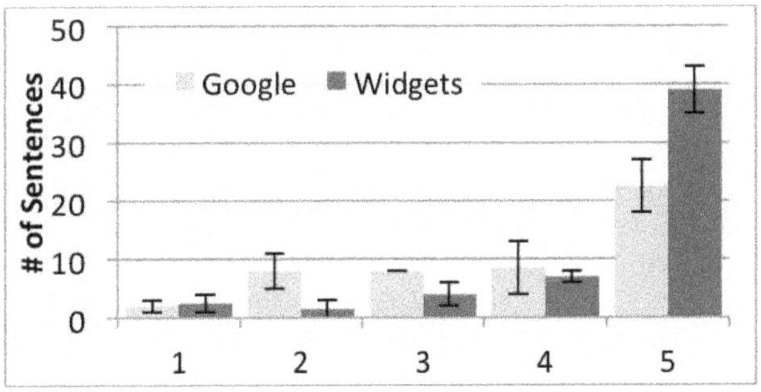

Figure 4. Accuracy distribution of edited sentences with two bilingual evaluators (1=worst, 5=best)

A pairwise t-test was run between scores given by the evaluators to corresponding translations by the two systems. All the evaluators rated the MonoTrans Widgets translation statistically significantly higher quality than the Google Translate translation. (Table 1)

On the very conservative criterion that a translation output is considered high quality only if both bilingual evaluators rated it a 5 for both fluency and accuracy, Google Translate produced high quality output for 31% of the sentences, and MonoTrans Widgets improved this percentage to 52%.

Evaluator	Fluency	Accuracy
B1	.047	.035
B2	8.9e-4	.025

Table 1. T-test p values for fluency & accuracy scores

These results are well aligned with our previous results with MonoTrans2 in that both systems, with only monolingual people involved, significantly improved translation fluency and accuracy over machine translation alone.

[2] Due to the no-login design, we cannot guarantee that this user population does not overlap with our previous participants.

Language	Population Size
English	10, 120
Spanish	1, 431
German	170

Table 2. Number of MonoTrans Widgets users by browser language (Sep 5-Sep 18, 2011)

DESIGN LESSONS

During the deployment of MonoTrans Widgets, we learned some important design lessons, which we believe can be helpful to designers of other crowd-sourcing systems.

Favor the smallest crowd: In a crowd-sourcing system that involves multiple crowds, task assignment should favor the smallest crowd, because it is often the bottleneck of throughput.

Early in the deployment, we observed a disproportionately low throughput for German-Spanish tasks. The reason turned out not to be the German or the Spanish speakers, but the English speakers: On ICDL, English speakers are the majority, followed by the Spanish speakers, and the German-speaking population is very small (Table 2). Initially, our system did not prioritize tasks by speaker population, and since Spanish speakers were overwhelmed by English-Spanish tasks that the English speakers were performing, no Spanish speaker was available for any Spanish-German task. The lesson here is that since there are always "more than enough" English speakers and not enough German speakers, some Spanish speakers should be allocated to collaborate with the German speakers first.

Prepare for scanning: In a system where users quickly browse some tasks before committing to finishing one, task viewing should have low overhead.

We observed that there is a roughly 2:1 skipping/submitting ratio with the MonoTrans Widgets.[3] For every task viewed, the system needs to perform task assignment (whose major overhead is sentence prioritization). We optimized this process by pre-calculating and caching sentence priority scores, and this allowed quicker scanning performance.

Context versus complexity: More context can usually help users understand the task, but it also requires more screen space, and more reading on the users' side. In our case, MonoTrans widgets' ability to obtain significant improvement over machine translation implies that it is possible to deploy with little task context[4].

Difficulty of doing controlled experiment "in the wild": Unlike controlled experiments, deploying to ICDL did not allow us to select only the monolingual users. For this paper's purpose, we designed the widgets to only show tasks in one language. This design guaranteed users to be effectively monolingual.

Nevertheless, deploying to a specific user population did help the MonoTrans Widgets avoid some quality control issues. For example, there was very little spam or irrelevant user input. This will need to be taken into account when deploying to other user populations.

CONCLUSION

In this paper, we presented our study of deploying MonoTrans Widgets "in the wild". By introducing micro-tasks, MonoTrans Widgets were able to be deployed to the ICDL web site, and to be used by its many daily visitors. A comparison to machine translation showed that the MonoTrans Widgets can obtain significantly improved quality with little context provided to the users. We also discussed design lessons that may be valuable to other crowd-sourcing system designers in general.

ACKNOWLEDGMENTS

This research is supported by NSF contract #BCS0941455 and by a Google Research Award.

REFERENCES

1. von Ahn, L., Maurer, B., McMillen, C., Abraham, D., and Blum, M. reCAPTCHA: Human-Based Character Recognition via Web Security Measures. *Science 321*, 5895 (2008), 1465 -1468.
2. Dabbadie, M., Hartley, A., King, M., et al. A hands-on study of the reliability and coherence of evaluation metrics. *Workshop at the LREC 2002 Conference*, (2002), 8.
3. Hu, C., Bederson, B.B., and Resnik, P. Translation by iterative collaboration between monolingual users. *Proceedings of Graphics Interface 2010 on Proceedings of Graphics Interface 2010*, 39-46.
4. Hu, C., Bederson, B.B., Resnik, P., and Kronrod, Y. MonoTrans2. *Proceedings of the 2011 annual conference on Human factors in computing systems - CHI '11*, (2011), 1133.
5. Law, E. and von Ahn, L. Human Computation. *Synthesis Lectures on Artificial Intelligence and Machine Learning 5*, 3 (2011), 1-121.
6. Little, G., Chilton, L.B., Goldman, M., and Miller, R.C. Exploring iterative and parallel human computation processes. *Proceedings of the ACM SIGKDD Workshop on Human Computation*, ACM (2010), 68-76.
7. Morita, D. and Ishida, T. Designing Protocols for Collaborative Translation. In *Principles of Practice in Multi-Agent Systems*. 2009, 17-32.
8. Zaidan, O. and Callison-Burch, C. Crowdsourcing Translation: Professional Quality from Non-Professionals. *Proceedings of the 49th Annual Meeting of the Association for Computational Linguistics: Human Language Technologies* (2011), 1220-1229.
9. Documentation – University Research Program for Google Translate - Google Research. 2009.

---

[3] In the first 21 days, there were 11,672 skipping action and 6,358 task submissions.

[4] We do realize that the evaluation results are not directly comparable to those of MonoTrans2 because of different translation material and participants. For a direct comparison, the books in the MonoTrans2 experiment are currently being translated with MonoTrans Widgets.

A Quantitative Explanation of Governance in an Online Peer-Production Community

Chandan (Dan) Sarkar,[1] Donghee Yvette Wohn,[2] Kurt DeMaagd [4]
Media and Information Studies
Michigan State University
East Lansing, MI 48824
{sarkarch,wohndong, kdemaagd}@msu.edu

Cliff Lampe [3]
School of Information
University of Michigan
105 S. State St.
Ann Arbor, MI 48109
cacl@umich.edu

ABSTRACT
In this paper, we examine how user ratings of content produced for an online community are taken into account by administrators when they decide whether to delete content. Incorporating about 10 years of server data from the online peer-production community Everything2, we looked at how specific features of voting predicted deletion of posts. We found that not all types of voting are the same: negative voting of users was the strongest factor explaining deletion of a Write-up. Receiving a positive vote from a member with higher status decreases the chances of deletion, while receiving a positive vote from a user with neutral status has a very little effect on the deletion of content.

Author Keywords
Online community; moderation; user voting; feedback; online governance; content editors; decision-making.

ACM Classification Keywords
H.5.3. [Information interfaces and presentation]: Group and Organization Interfaces.

INTRODUCTION
Online peer-productions communities are based on user-generated content and emergent social systems that help govern user behavior in those sites [1]. Wikipedia, Flickr, YouTube and other content-based sites have varying rules and norms about evaluating user-generated content, but in general, users can often provide feedback about the value of the content to those who have the ability to delete that content. Deletion privileges are usually reserved for site administrators, with notable exceptions, like Wikipedia.

Some online communities have a role for users who evaluate and delete content. We are interested in whether or not editors' deletion of articles is informed by feedback provided by other users when such information is available, or if they make decisions independently of that feedback. *Research Question: What is the relationship between user feedback on content and editorial deletion decisions?* Decision-making processes are an integral part of online community governance [1,8]. Understanding these processes and how they are associated with governance structure has broader implications for design, infrastructure, and sustainability for online communities.

COMMUNITY GOVERNANCE
Preece [8] explains that the process of community self governance is basically a process of decision making that involves decision makers (administrators or editors) and policies and norms association with decision making. One of the most important decisions that are made in peer-production communities is the decision on whether or not content should be retained or deleted.

In the context of peer production communities such as Wikipedia or Usenet, researchers have studied how content policies are enforced [3,4]. Kollock and Smith [4] described global and local-level guidelines within Usenet to describe the administrative governance. In these communities, there are a variety of governance structures, ranging from tight control of content quality in the case of most open source projects, to the more distributed deletion authority of Wikipedia [3, 10]. Wiki structure communities such as Wikipedia, also function following the *Iron Law of Oligarchy*— in which power structure and decision making rest on a small group of individuals [5]. Although some scholars argue that Wikipedia policy-making is becoming more de-centralized over time still policy-making is being performed by a core small group of content editors [3].

All these studies show that this small group is responsible for decision-making, but we don't know how their decisions are informed—in particular, if they take into consideration the opinions of the users. If indeed editors' decisions to delete content are informed by general users' opinions, then we would expect that positive feedback from other users would affect preservation of the content while negative feedback from other users would predict deletion.

METHOD
Everything2
To understand how feedback from users in the form of ratings informs administrator deletion behaviors, we analyzed data from the server logs of the peer-production

community, Everything2.com. This site has been studied by the authors in other work [7] and two of the authors have been long-term participant-observers of the site.

Everything2 started in 1999 as an open source encyclopedia, but has evolved over time to include more personal journaling and creative writing. Everything2 is a reasonable case to study for the research question due to following reasons: it has a heterogeneous set of users, a large corpus of articles, and the administrators granted us access to server level data. Everything2 has an active user base of about 3,000 contributing members, and receives approximately 590,000 unique visitors and 1.2 million page views per month as of September, 2011.

The primary contribution of authors on Everything2 is a "Write-up", similar to an article on Wikipedia in that it's an original contribution of content. However, each "Write-up" is solely owned by one author, and only administrators may edit or delete it.

There are three different types of feedback that users can provide to others' Write-ups through the system. The first is page-views, which can be a measure of how much attention the Write-up is garnering. Page-views are a measure of traffic—the online version of people voting with their feet. Although it is ambiguous as to why people are choosing to view that content.

The second type of feedback is a more direct measure of valence: voting. Registered users who have contributed content can rate Write-ups with an Up-vote (positive feedback) or Down-vote (negative feedback). Users are allocated with a fixed number of votes per day and can only vote once per Write-up. These votes are anonymous.

The third type of feedback is one that can only be provided by registered site members who have a certain amount of experience on the site. Known as a "Cool," this is the same as an up-vote in terms of positive valence, but is more exclusive in that there are fewer members (with high status) who can grant it.

While registered users of the site can provide feedback about content, only a small group of users, known as "content editors", can delete content. Users do not have permission to delete their own content, though editors often do so, on request. Consequently, all deletion decisions are made by these content editors.

By default, the system informs authors when their content has been deleted. The administrators can choose to "cloak" a deletion however so the user is not informed. Content editors on the site can also leave a small message as to why the content was deleted, but they have a large amount of discretion as to whether and when to do so.

Analysis

We collected all 36,925 Write-ups that had been deleted from the site over its ten-year history. Server logs were used to select 37,000 non-deleted Write-ups with similar aggregated length distributions of deleted Write-ups. The non-deleted Write-ups were selected randomly using repeated measures through a computer script until a match in aggregated length is obtained between the samples. We then collected the total number of Up-votes, Down-votes, page views, words (length) for each of the Write-ups.

We wanted to see if the three types of feedback factors outlined above contributed to the likelihood of a Write-up being deleted or not. Our research question was explored using the Hazard model (COX proportional Hazard model with time dependent covariates) [2]. This method is similar to binary logistic regression in that it is used to predict a categorical dependent variable, but takes into account the probability that the case would survive. In other words, for our data, Write-ups that are currently not deleted have the probability of being deleted in the future; the model takes into consideration this probability (future censoring). This analysis is used when the dependent variable is affected by time and future likelihood of change [6] and is fairly robust in dealing with time dependent explanatory variables [9]. We only matched length between deleted and non-deleted Write-ups because Hazard model will account the influence of covariates over time on non-deleted Write-ups.

In our case, the outcome variable (Write-ups deleted/ not deleted) is exponential in distribution and associated with censoring, since non-deleted Write-ups could be deleted in the future. Moreover, our covariates (Up-votes, Down-votes, Cools, Page-views) are likely to be affected over time, as the longer the Write-up sustains in the community, the more Cools and Votes it would likely receive over time. As Write-ups have been on the site for different amounts of time, we used rate instead of total number in terms of measuring our independent variables to reduce the influence of time on covariates (to some extent). For example, instead of total Up-votes, we looked at the rate of Up-votes, as it is likely that Write-ups which are posted on the site for a longer period will have increased levels of voting in general. Rate was determined by dividing the total numbers of instances by how long the Write-up had been on the site (lifespan of Write-up). For deleted Write-ups, lifespans (time to events) were measured by subtracting posting time from deletion time. For non-deleted Write-ups, lifespan (time to events) was measured by subtracting posting time from server log captured time. The predictor variables we used in our model are described in Table 1.

The length of the Write-up was added to account for potential proxies for users' responses to a Write-up. Length is likely a signal of quality to users, even though quality will obviously vary. Finally, we included the ratio of positive/negative votes in our model since it may not be the rate of Up-votes or Down-votes but the proportion that may have affected editors' decisions. The outcome variable is categorical (deleted or not deleted). Non-deleted Write-ups include Write-ups not yet deleted but could be deleted in future outside your study time and Write-ups that will never be deleted.

Variables	Explanation
Rate of Up-votes (*M*=.79, *S.D.*=.14)	No. of Up-votes per Write-up /Write-up lifespan
Rate of Down-votes (*M*=.56, *S.D.*=.06)	No. of Down-votes per Write-up/ Write-up lifespan
Rate of Cools (*M*=.14,*S.D.*=.73)	No. of Cools per Write-up / Write-up lifespan
Rate of Page-views (*M*= .05, *S.D.*=.74)	No. of Page views per Write-up/ Write-up lifespan
Votes Ratio (*M*=.007,*S.D.*=.14)	No. of Up-votes /No. of Down-votes
Write-up Length (*M*=42.5, *S.D.*=129.20)	Length of Write-up in words

Table 1: Predictor Variables

RESULTS

Table 2 shows the results of the Hazard Rate Analysis. The EXP(B) column represents the Hazard, or odds ratio. Due to the large sample size, statistical significance should be examined with the effect size as indicated by the odds ratio.

The interpretation of this model is similar to Logistic Regression. In this case, the hazard's ratio for the rate of Page-views is 1.00, which suggests that the variable in the model has no effect on the deletion of Write-ups over time. On the other hand, the Hazard ratio for rate of Down-votes is 1.126, implying that a single unit increase in Down-vote (Rate of Down-vote) will increase the probability of a Write-up being deleted over time by 12.6% {(1.126-1)*100%} at the $p<.001$ significance level). Clearly, a strong correlation is present between Down-votes and deletion of Write-ups. The Hazard ratio for Cools is .301, suggests that for every single unit increase in Cool (Rate of Cools) on a Write-up, the probability of deleting a Write-up will *decrease* by 232%. This suggests that the positive evaluations made by experienced high status users are being taken into more account by content editors when deciding whether or not to delete a Write-up.

The Hazard ratio for Up-votes is 1.005. This suggests that for a single unit increase in Up-vote (Rate of Up-votes) the probability of deleting a Write-up will marginally increase by 0.5%. The result is counter intuitive, but the effect size was very small, so this should be taken into consideration when interpreting the data. One possible explanation could be that content editors did not pay attention to ordinary members' voting behavior for making their decision. The Hazard ratio of Write-up Length is .996, suggests that for every single word increase in length the probability of deleting a Write-up will *decrease* by 0.4%.The chi-square difference between null model and full model is significant at $p<.001$, suggesting that the effects size of the covariates explaining the deletion of the Write-ups event is significant. The coefficients of Rate of Up-votes, Rate of Down-votes and Rate of Cools are more than twice than the corresponding standard errors, confirms the time dependencies of the covariates.

	β	Wald	SE	EXP(B)
Rate of Page-views	.000	.012	.911	1.000
Rate of Up-votes	.005	47.287	.001	1.005*
Rate of Down-votes	.119	66.097	.015	1.126*
Rate of Cools	-1.200	9652.976	.012	0.301*
Votes Ratio	-.760	1.235	.684	0.467
Write-up Length	-.004	897.595	.000	0.996*

**p< .001(Chi Square difference between null and full model is significant at p<.001*, one-degree of freedom(df=1) chi-square distribution of covariates explains time proportionality of the hazard ratio)*

Table 2: Hazard Model Predicting Deletion of Write-up

DISCUSSION

In this paper we show that deletion decisions by editors within a peer production community are being informed by users' action. While there is some relationship between user feedback and editorial deletions, it's clear that editors' decisions are only slightly guided by that feedback. While some editors do use feedback as a guide what to delete, they are not obligated to base their judgments on votes. Positive votes had a statistically significant but practically meaningless effect on deletion. The ratio of Up-votes to Down-votes did not end up being statistically significant, but we still suspect that the relationship between up-votes and down-votes is telling in this process. Page-views had no effect on editorial deletion decisions. The length of the Write-up was statistically related to the survival of a Write-up, but the low coefficients suggest they are not key factors in editorial decisions.

The strongest predictor that a Write-up would not be deleted was the presence of "Cools". Cools are given to Write-ups by experienced members of the site, suggesting that editors placed more importance on the opinions of these experienced, or high-status members. It could be that informing editorial decisions would be helped by applying stronger signals of the rater—such as expertise or credibility—than simple ratings. The study shows that quality of Write-ups has very slight positive influence on editors not deleting a Write-up. In general, while features of the content and the feedback the content has received from other users appears to be informing editorial deletion decisions, those variables are only explaining part of that decision-making process. Content editors are still clearly making autonomous decisions on Everything2 about what content to keep. This may be positive, in that these members are experienced users who may have a better global sense of how to govern content on the site than an aggregate of votes on content could provide. On the other hand, it may create disgruntled users who think their opinions are not reflected in editorial decisions.

IMPLICATIONS FOR PRACTICE

Sustained management of peer-production communities is dependent on positive relationships between administrators and users who provide feedback on the quality of content. If the user-base sees these editors as ignoring their feedback, then they may become frustrated, members may feel that their voices are not being acknowledged. This may lead to a decrease in participation and eventually members may leave the community. Understanding how site administrators incorporate user feedback into their content deletion decisions can inform the development of better tools to communicate that information. For example, "Cools" were strong signals of quality, which may have helped administrators make decisions. Such signals could be added as design elements to be used as feedback by trusted members. Tools that aggregate these types of feedback cues could reduce the efforts of peer-production administrators in incorporating them into their practices.

LIMITATIONS

Although we found some correlations between administrators' decisions on deletions of user-generated content and user ratings, additional methods of collecting data might like interviews or content analysis would add more depth to these findings. A limitation of our study is that we were unable to look at how other channels of communication such as messaging or chatting may have affected content editors' decision to delete content. Votes are anonymous. It is not possible for editors to distinguish who made the Vote before deletion. On the other hand Cools are not anonymous. Editors can distinguish whether Cools applied to a Write-up are from editors or higher status members. In our sample, 1116 distinct users submitted Cools. We did not account separately for Cools submitted by editors and non-editors separately as editors are also users and contributors in the community. Never the less this may added slight bias in our results for Cools, though only 1.76% of the Cools were from content editors in our sample. In addition, our data are derived from a snapshot of user behavior, thus we cannot determine causality, nor account for users' and administrators' beliefs or opinions regarding their participation.

CONCLUSION

In this paper we have looked at how voting behaviors as feedback in an online community over a period of 10 years supports the editorial decision making process. This study supports the notion that positive feedback from higher status members positively affects administrators' decision making about not deleting a Write-up while receiving a negative feedback from an ordinary user significant increases likelihood of deletion. These findings suggest that more nuanced feedback cues and the providers of the feedback are important for online community leaders who need to plan ways to encourage members to participate, and to retain them in their ongoing social structures.

ACKNOWLEDGMENTS

The authors wish to thank the administrators and users of Everything2.com. This work was supported by NSF grant IIS-HCC-0812429.

REFERENCES

1. Ackerman, M.S., Swenson, A., Cotterill, S., and DeMaagd, K. I-DIAG: from community discussion to knowledge distillation. *Communities and Technologies*, (2003), 307–325..
2. Cox, D. R. and Oakes, D. *Analysis of Survival Data.* Chapman and Hall, London, England, 1984.
3. Forte, A., Larco, V., and Bruckman, A. Decentralization in Wikipedia Governance. *Journal of Management Information Systems 26*, 1 (2009), 49-72.
4. Kollock, P. and Smith, M. Managing the virtual commons□: Cooperation and conflict in computer communities. In S.C. Herring (ed.) *Computer-Mediated Communication: Linguistic, Social, and Cross-Cultural Perspectives*, (1996), 109-128..
5. Konieczny, P. Governance, organization, and democracy on the Internet: The iron law and the evolution of Wikipedia. *Sociological Forum 24*, 1 (2009), 162-192.
6. Kraut, R., Wang, X., Butler, B., Joyce, E., and Burke, M. Beyond information: Developing the relationship between the individual and the group in online communities. *Information Systems Research*, In Press (2010).
7. Lampe, C., Wash, R., Velasquez, A. and Ozkaya, E. Motivations to participate in online communities. *Proceedings of the SIGCHI conference on Human factors in computing systems*,(2010),1927-1936, ACM, Atlanta, Georgia, USA.
8. Preece, J. Sociability and usability in online communities: Determining and measuring success. *Information Technology 20*, 5 (2001), 347-356.
9. Singer, J. D. and Willett, J.B. *Applied Longitudinal Data Analysis: Modeling Change and Event Occurrence*. Oxford University Press, 2003.
10. Viégas, F.B., Wattenberg, M., and Mckeon, M.M. The hidden order of Wikipedia. International conference on Online communities and social computing, (2007), 445–454.

Identifying Usability Issues via Algorithmic Detection of Excessive Visual Search

Corey Holland
Department of Computer Science
Texas State University
San Marcos, TX 78666 USA
ch1570@txstate.edu

Oleg Komogortsev
Department of Computer Science
Texas State University
San Marcos, TX 78666 USA
ok11@txstate.edu

Dan Tamir
Department of Computer Science
Texas State University
San Marcos, TX 78666 USA
dt19@txstate.edu

ABSTRACT
Automated detection of excessive visual search (ES) experienced by a user during software use presents the potential for substantial improvement in the efficiency of supervised usability analysis. This paper presents an objective evaluation of several methods for the automated segmentation and classification of ES intervals from an eye movement recording, a technique that can be utilized to aid in the identification of usability problems during software usability testing. Techniques considered for automated segmentation of the eye movement recording into unique intervals include mouse/keyboard events and eye movement scanpaths. ES is identified by a number of eye movement metrics, including: fixation count, saccade amplitude, convex hull area, scanpath inflections, scanpath length, and scanpath duration. The ES intervals identified by each algorithm are compared to those produced by manual classification to verify the accuracy, precision, and performance of each algorithm. The results indicate that automated classification can be successfully employed to substantially reduce the amount of recorded data reviewed by HCI experts during usability testing, with relatively little loss in accuracy.

Author Keywords
Human-computer interaction; eye tracking; visual search; usability; usability testing.

ACM Classification Keywords
H5.2. User Interfaces: Evaluation/methodology; H5.2. User Interfaces: User-centered design.

General Terms
Algorithms; Experimentation; Human Factors; Theory; Performance.

INTRODUCTION
Usability refers to the ease with which users can make use of a system for its intended purpose, and is arguably the most important quality of any system meant for human interaction. The ISO 9241 standard defines usability as "the extent to which a product can be used by specified users to achieve specified goals with effectiveness, efficiency and satisfaction in a specified context of use" [1].

Unfortunately, usability testing is often an expensive and time consuming process, requiring careful manual review and analysis of users' interaction with applications [2]. As a result, despite the integral nature of usability to the success of an application, usability testing is often neglected as part of the development process [3].

The primary shortcoming of usability testing is its qualitative nature, as described by several usability practices and guidelines [4]. By identifying and standardizing usability metrics, usability may be evaluated quantitatively, a process which lends itself to automation. In this way, usability testing itself can be made more usable, by reducing the time and effort spent evaluating an interface.

In this paper, we consider the efficacy of eye movements as an indicator of software usability. Specifically, we explore a number of techniques for the automated segmentation and classification of usability recordings of eye movement data. Through quantitative analysis of basic eye movements (fixations and saccades) and the patterns they produce (scanpaths), we attempt to accurately and precisely locate time intervals in which the user experiences difficulty with a software interface.

There are a number of eye movement types identified by varying characteristics; of these, however, fixations and saccades are of particular importance to the field of human-computer interaction [5]. Fixations occur when the eye is held in a relatively stable position such that the fovea remains centered on an object of interest, providing heightened visual acuity. Saccades occur when the eye globe rotates quickly between points of fixation, with very little visual acuity maintained during rotation [6].

Various sources have described the usability implications of eye movements [7]; however, usability evaluation based on eye movements generally makes use of only scanpath (a sequence of fixations and saccades) and fixation density overlays [8, 9], discarding a wealth of information that may be gained from the complete eye movement record.

Visual search occurs naturally as a means of obtaining information about our surroundings, and there are two primary types of information processing that occur during visual search, parallel and serial [10]. Parallel search, exemplified in Figure 1, occurs when the target object is distinguishable from distractor objects by a single basic feature (color, motion, orientation, etc.), allowing parallel processing of objects and near constant reaction time. Serial search, exemplified in Figure 2, occurs when the target object is defined by more than one basic feature, requiring attentional shifts between objects until the target is located. Poor interface layout, individual interface component sizes, coloring, and other usability/design issues may lead to prolonged or excessive visual search. For the purposes of this paper and the corresponding research, *excessive visual search* (ES) is defined as *any onscreen search interval not directly related to task completion*.

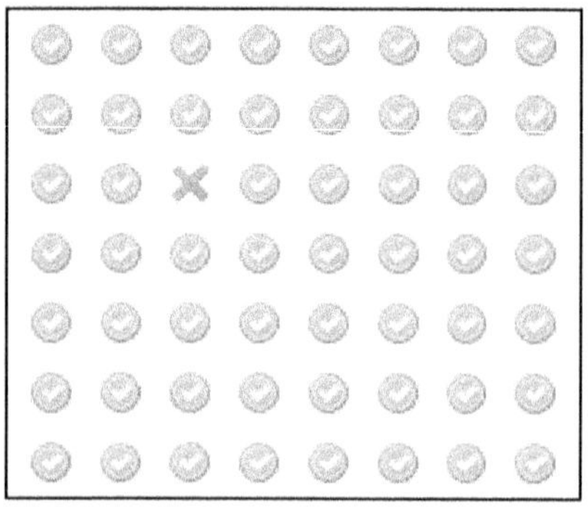

Figure 1. Parallel search example. Find the .

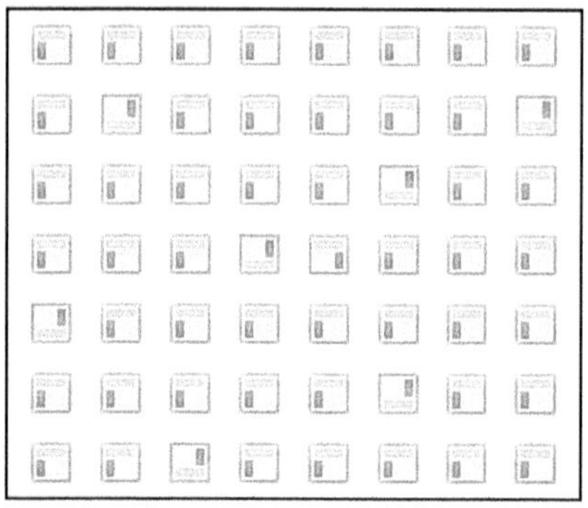

Figure 2. Serial search example. Find the .

While there has been a substantial amount of research on visual search [11, 12] and its implications on usability [13], to the best of our knowledge there has been very little progress in the automated identification of excessive visual search. In previous work, we described and evaluated several techniques for the automated classification of excessive visual search under mouse/keyboard based event segmentation. In this paper we describe several previously considered techniques for the automated classification of excessive visual search [14-16], present a variety of novel eye movement based segmentation methods, and provide an objective evaluation of the various segmentation and classification algorithms as compared to that of manually classified excessive search intervals across an expanded data set.

We begin by defining visual search and its properties, exploring previous research on its applicability to the field of human-computer interaction, and providing a general description of the way it may be identified by automated analysis. We then present an overview of five segmentation algorithms used to divide the eye movement recordings into distinct intervals, along with seven classification algorithms used to identify intervals of excessive search. Finally, we present the methodology used to verify the accuracy of each algorithm, a description of our manual classification process, and a discussion of the results.

PREVIOUS WORK

Eye tracking was first employed as a usability metric in the 1950s by Fitts, et al. in their study of aircraft pilot behavior during landing procedures [17], and has since been utilized to analyze the usability of software applications, web pages, questionnaire formats, driving and navigation systems, and handheld devices. Jacob and Karn [18] survey 21 usability studies incorporating the use of eye movement metrics as a primary usability metric.

A common trend among these studies is the noted use of fixation count and duration as primary indicators of software usability. Eye movement metrics are often considered with little attempt to detect problem areas of a recording, instead attempting only to identify that usability problems exist within it [19, 20]. It is this problem in particular that we attempt to address in the current work.

Poole and Ball [7] provide a thorough summary of a variety of quantitative eye movement metrics (including the characteristics of fixations, saccades, scanpaths, blink rate, and pupil size) and their implications towards the usability of a given interface. For instance: fixations indicate areas of interest within an interface, and in the context of visual search short fixations and fixation clustering across a region may indicate difficulty identifying a target; regressive saccades and re-fixations are indicative of difficulty processing a target, often due to poor design or increased complexity; and increased pupil size is often indicative of cognitive effort and fatigue. A scanpath is an aggregate of fixations and saccades directed from one target of interest to the next.

According to [21]: "In a search task, an optimal scan path is viewed as being a straight line to a desired target, with relatively short fixation duration at the target." This ideal, however, is often not the case, and visual search occurs frequently during the course of human-computer interaction due to the non-uniformity of basic tasks and the complex design patterns of modern user interfaces.

IDENTIFYING EXCESSIVE VISUAL SEARCH

The graphical user interface employed by the vast majority of modern software applications presents interface elements of a diverse range of colors, sizes, and dimensions. As a

Algorithm	Metrics	Region	Threshold
SEG-MK	Mouse/keyboard events	N/A	N/A
SEG-E	Eye position	Square	200 pixels
SEG-EC	Eye position	Circular	275 pixels
SEG-F	Fixation centroid	Square	75 pixels
SEG-FC	Fixation centroid	Circular	175 pixels

Table 1. Segmentation algorithms.

result, eye movements tend to follow a serial visual search pattern, with search time dependent on the number of distractor elements within the interface [10].

Due to the serial nature of visual search within an interface, usability issues in the design and implementation may be identified through analysis of excessive visual search [21]. While automated analysis cannot interpret the placement or quality of individual interface components in the same manner as a human observer, the quantitative properties of eye movements make it possible to identify intervals of excessive visual search within an eye movement recording. Automated identification of excessive search intervals makes it possible to reduce manual inspection of usability recordings, ignoring less relevant sections of the recording and focusing the attentions of a human observer on intervals of poor usability.

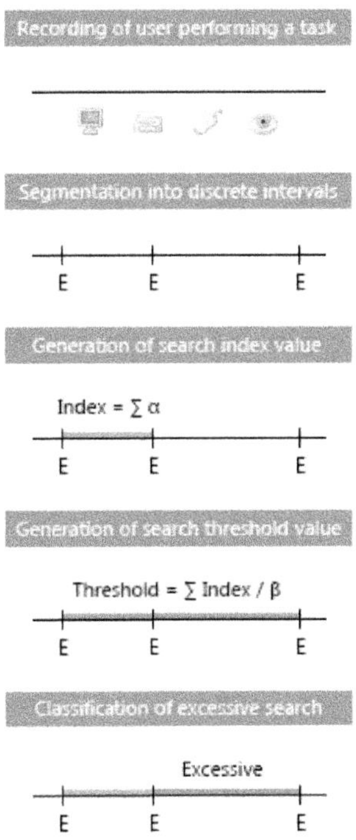

Figure 3. Automated detection of visual search. E represents mouse, keyboard, or eye movement events. α and β are variable metrics involved in classification.

Visual search leading directly to task completion, idle search behavior, and off-screen behavior are not considered excessive. Then, excessive visual search is identified according to the following basic algorithm, as shown in Figure 3, where specific eye movement metrics and threshold values vary:

1. The eye movement recording is parsed and divided into distinct intervals.
2. An index value is generated for each interval based on the characteristics of specific eye movement metrics within the interval.
3. A threshold value is generated, either empirically or as a function of the average index.
4. The intervals with an index above or below the threshold are classified as excessive visual search.

Presented in this work, segmentation algorithms attempt to identify and define distinct intervals of visual search (i.e. the scanpaths that make up a given search task), and classification algorithms attempt to identify the type of visual search being experienced. Threshold values are empirically selected via manual inspection of performance data to provide greater accuracy, though these values may vary with application domain and environment.

SEGMENTATION ALGORITHMS

Each recording is segmented into a set of unique time intervals considered to be candidates for ES according to a number of discrete events. Several segmentation methods are developed using different metrics and summarized in Table 1.

Mouse/Keyboard Segmentation

The mouse/keyboard segmentation method (SEG-MK) uses mouse/keyboard events to segment the eye movement recordings, as these represent conscious decisions by the user and imply that the user's target has been found. Our first excessive search classification algorithms have been developed using this segmentation method, and as such it is used as a baseline for comparison with subsequent methods. That is, the classification algorithm thresholds were set and fixed using the SEG-MK segmentation method, and during the development of subsequent segmentation methods these thresholds were not changed.

Algorithm	Metrics (per interval)	Threshold
ES-F	Fixation count	> Average
ES-S	Average saccade amplitude	> Average
ES-P	Average pupil dilation	< Average
ES-SL	Total saccade amplitude	> Average
ES-SA	Convex hull area	> Average
ES-SAI	Convex hull area × Inflection count	> Average
ES-SAID	Convex hull area, Inflection count, Duration	> Average, > 5 Inflections, > 4 Seconds

Table 2. Classification algorithms.

Eye Movement-based Segmentation

While mouse/keyboard events provide an acceptable segmentation of the recording timelines for automated classification, use of this technique requires access to an additional layer of information. As well, it is our hypothesis that more detailed segmentation methods may improve the accuracy of the presented algorithms.

To further investigate, an eye movement based segmentation method (SEG-E) is developed using only the raw eye movement data to define event intervals as follows:

1. Mark the first/current point in the eye movement recording as the reference point.
2. Continue through the eye movement record until a point that is more than D units horizontally or vertically from the reference point is found.
3. Mark this new point as the current reference point and add it to the event list.
4. Repeat steps 1-3 until all points in the eye movement record have been examined.

Essentially, this defines a rectangular region of interest and allows for a certain amount of overlap as the user's attention shifts between elements. For our purposes, all off-screen points were ignored and D was empirically set to 200 pixels. Nevertheless, this parameter is application dependent.

An additional segmentation method (SEG-EC) is derived from the SEG-E variant, using the Euclidean distance between points for comparison to D, essentially defining a circular region of interest. For this purpose, all off-screen points are again ignored, and in the current experiments D is empirically set to 275 pixels.

Fixation Based Segmentation

To examine whether additional accuracy could be gained by considering only fixation points, rather than the raw eye movement data, providing the segmentation that is based on strictly defined points of attention. The eye movement based algorithms are modified to use the fixation points filtered by an I-VT algorithm [22].

In comparison to the raw eye movement signal, fixations are often more directly indicative of attention and interest. Fixation based segmentation followed the basic algorithm described previously for SEG-E, with the primary difference being the data set to which the algorithm is applied. In comparison, SEG-E and SEG-EC operate on the raw eye movement signal, while the fixation based algorithms (SEG-F and SEG-FC) operate on the fixations identified within the raw eye movement signal.

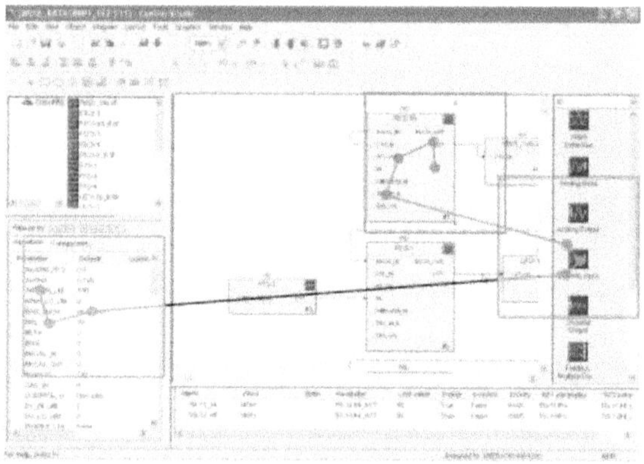

Figure 4. Fixation based segmentation (ES-F). Fixations represented by dots, saccades represented by lines, and logical segments separated by color.

This results in two further segmentation methods: SEG-F, shown in Figure 4, using rectangular regions of interest with a threshold D of 75 pixels; and SEG-FC, using circular regions of interest using a threshold D of 175 pixels. A velocity threshold of 30°/sec is employed for the velocity threshold algorithm (I-VT).

CLASSIFICATION ALGORITHMS

Seven classification algorithms are presented as described previously in [14, 16] and summarized in Table 2. The ES-F, ES-S, ES-P, and ES-SL algorithms rely on basic attributes of the human visual system, while the scanpath based algorithms ES-SA, ES-SAI, and ES-SAID incorporate more advanced aspects of visual search.

Fixation Based Algorithm

The fixation based algorithm (ES-F) uses the fixation count of each interval as its index value, and the average fixation count as the threshold. Search intervals with a fixation count above the threshold are classified as ES.

Saccade Based Algorithm

The saccade based algorithm (ES-S) uses the average saccade amplitude of each interval as its index value, and the average across all intervals as the threshold. Search intervals with an average saccade amplitude above the threshold are classified as ES.

Pupil Based Algorithm

The pupil based algorithm (ES-P) uses the average pupil dilation of each interval as its index value, and the average of average pupil dilations as the threshold. Search intervals with average pupil dilation below the threshold are classified as ES.

Scanpath Length Algorithm

The scanpath length algorithm (ES-SL) uses the total saccade amplitude of each interval as its index value, and the average across all intervals as the threshold. Search intervals with saccade amplitude above the threshold are classified as ES.

Scanpath Area Algorithm

The scanpath area algorithm (ES-SA) uses the area of the convex hull formed by fixation points within each interval as its index value, and the average across all intervals as the threshold. The area of the convex hull is indicative of the total search area, with smaller values indicating efficient search behavior. Search intervals with a convex hull area above the threshold are classified as ES.

Scanpath Area/Inflections Algorithm

The scanpath area/inflections algorithm (ES-SAI) uses the area of the convex hull formed by fixation points multiplied by the number of times the scanpath changes direction (inflections) for each interval as its index value, and the average index value across all intervals as the threshold. Inflections of the scanpath are indicative of attention shifts, with larger inflections counts suggesting increased visual search. Search intervals with an index value above the threshold are classified as ES.

Scanpath Area/Inflections/Duration Algorithm

The scanpath area/inflections/duration algorithm (ES-SAID) uses multiple index values for each interval: the area of the convex hull formed by fixation points, the inflection count, and the total duration of the interval. Longer intervals between subsequent mouse/keyboard events can indicate difficulties in locating the next target, therefore increasing the probability of the ES. Search intervals with a convex hull area above the average, an inflection count greater than 5, or duration of more than 4 seconds are classified as ES. Threshold values were selected empirically.

METHODOLOGY

Software

Usability testing is performed on the DeltaV process control software, utilizing an interface similar to common diagram editing applications (such as Microsoft Visio), as part of a related but separate study for developing methods of objective usability evaluation. Screen recordings and their corresponding scanpath/input event overlays are viewed for manual classification of visual search with Tobii Studio. All algorithms and data analysis are implemented and performed in MATLAB.

Apparatus

Usability testing is conducted with the Tobii X120 eye tracker running at 120Hz. DeltaV is run on a Dell Optiplex 745 with 4 GB of RAM, and displayed on a 19 inch flat panel monitor with a resolution of 1280×1024. A velocity threshold (I-VT) of 30°/sec is used to reduce the eye movement data into the fixations and saccades [22].

Participants

A total of 14 student volunteers and 12 experienced users have participated in the usability testing. Due to the substantial amount of time required for manual classification, randomly selected recordings from 21 of these subjects are used.

Manual Classification

Four basic user behaviors are considered during the manual classification: task completion (TC), in which the user is performing the operations necessary to complete a given task; excessive visual search (ES), in which the user is experiencing prolonged difficulties finding the interface components necessary for task completion; idle (IL), in which the user is waiting for the interface to respond after a specific action is performed; and off-screen (OS), in which the user is reading task-related instructions presented outside the boundaries of the computer monitor.

Manual classification of the task recordings was performed by a trained research assistant using superimposed eye movement traces to build a classification baseline. A full and thorough description of the manual classification process is described in [15].

Procedure

Participants are given a series of 15 tasks to complete in the process control application, during which screen recordings, eye movement records, and input logs are generated and synchronized for each task. All tasks are performed within the same user interface and follow a uniform procedure: 1) delete component; 2) add component; 3) make connections between components; 4) transfer changes to controller simulator; 5) change component value; 6) change interface view; 7) save changes and exit. Tasks are similar to each other with specific interface components varied to reduce learning effects.

ES intervals are then manually classified for the recordings (chosen arbitrarily from unique subjects with a uniform distribution of trials) according to the previous description of manual search classification. The automated ES classification algorithms are subsequently run using the various segmentation methods with the eye movement recordings and input logs of the manually identified recordings. ES intervals generated by the automated analysis are compared to those provided by manual classification to determine the percentage of automatically identified search intervals that were correctly identified as excessive and the percentage of ES intervals missed or erroneously identified.

To determine the relative performance of the different segmentation/classification algorithms, each algorithm was then run separately across all eye movement records and computation times were measured in seconds.

RESULTS

Note that in all the figures, an asterisk (*) indicates statistical significance of $p < 0.05$ and a dagger (†) indicates statistical significance of $p < 0.001$, as determined by a one-way ANOVA test between the algorithms of a particular group. For the segmentation algorithms, the comparison is performed across all classification algorithms, and vice versa, where $F(6, 140)$ for segmentation algorithms and $F(4, 100)$ for classification algorithms. For example, the label "ES-F *" indicates that there is a significant main effect in the values produced by the ES-F algorithm when compared across segmentation algorithms.

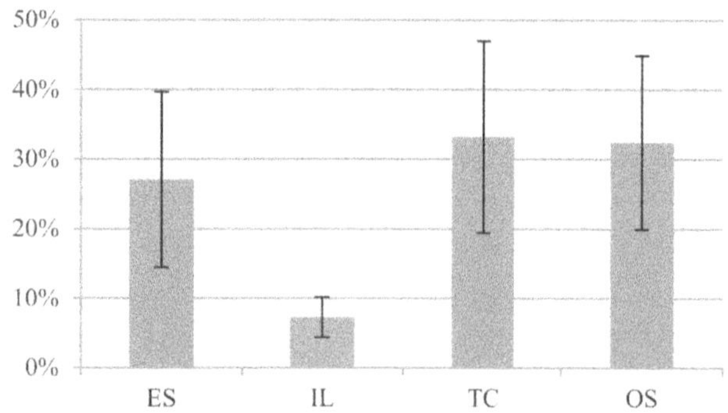

Figure 5. Manual Search Behavior.

Manual Classification

Figure 5 presents a summary of the relative distribution of search behavior identified during manual classification. Across the 21 eye movement recordings, task completion and offscreen behavior comprise roughly one third of the recording time each, while excessive visual search and idle search constitute the remaining duration. The amount of idle search is relatively low, occurring only when the interface is unresponsive, and often resembling excessive search behavior. The overall amount of non-task completion behavior is substantial, on average leaving 67% of the recording time as irrelevant. The difference in time between different behaviors was statistically significant, $F(3, 80) = 24.01$, $p < 0.001$.

Automated Classification of Excessive Visual Search

Average Percent of Total Time Classified

$$Percent\ of\ Total = \frac{total\ classified\ time}{total\ recording\ time} \quad (1)$$

Figure 6 presents a summary of the average percent of total time classified by each algorithm. Assuming correct identification of ES intervals, a lower percent of total time classified as ES indicates more precise identification. Averaged across all classification algorithms, segmentation by mouse and keyboard events (SEG-MK) on average marks the smallest amount of the total recording time as ES (M = 47%, SD = 8%), while segmentation based on fixations (SEG-FC) marks the largest (M = 54%, SD = 12%). Across all segmentation algorithms, pupil based classification (ES-P) on average marks the smallest amount of the total recording time as ES (M = 31%, SD = 14%), while classification based on scanpath length (ES-SL) marks the largest (M = 64%, SD = 6%).

Average Percent Correctly Classified

$$Percent\ Correct = \frac{correctly\ classified\ time}{total\ manual\ time} \quad (2)$$

Figure 7 presents a summary of the average percent of time correctly identified as excessive search by each algorithm. Averaged across all classification algorithms, segmentation by mouse and keyboard events (SEG-MK) has the highest average percent of correctly identified intervals (M = 55%, SD = 8%), while segmentation based on fixations (SEG-FC) has the lowest (M = 45%, 13%). Across segmentation algorithms, scanpath based classification (ES-SL) has the highest average percent of correctly identified intervals (M = 64%, SD = 5%), while pupil based classification (ES-P) has the lowest (M = 25%, SD = 16%).

Average Percent Error

$$Percent\ Error = \frac{misclassified + unclassified\ time}{total\ recording\ time} \quad (3)$$

Figure 8 presents a summary of the average percent of time erroneously classified by each algorithm. Averaged across all classification algorithms, eye movement based segmentation (SEG-EC) has the lowest average percent error (M = 31%, SD = 4%), while fixation based segmentation (ES-FC) has the highest (M = 35%, SD = 2%). Across all segmentation algorithms, fixation based classification (ES-F) has the lowest average percent error (M = 26%, SD = 3%), while pupil based classification (ES-P) has the highest (M = 36%, SD = 2%).

Average Computational Performance

Recording times did not exceed 4.8 minutes (M = 2.6 minutes, SD = 1.0 minutes). Segmentation algorithms did not exceed 3.5 seconds per recording (M = 1.3 seconds, SD = 0.7 seconds), and classification algorithms did not exceed 1.0 seconds per recording (M = 0.3 seconds, SD = 0.2 seconds).

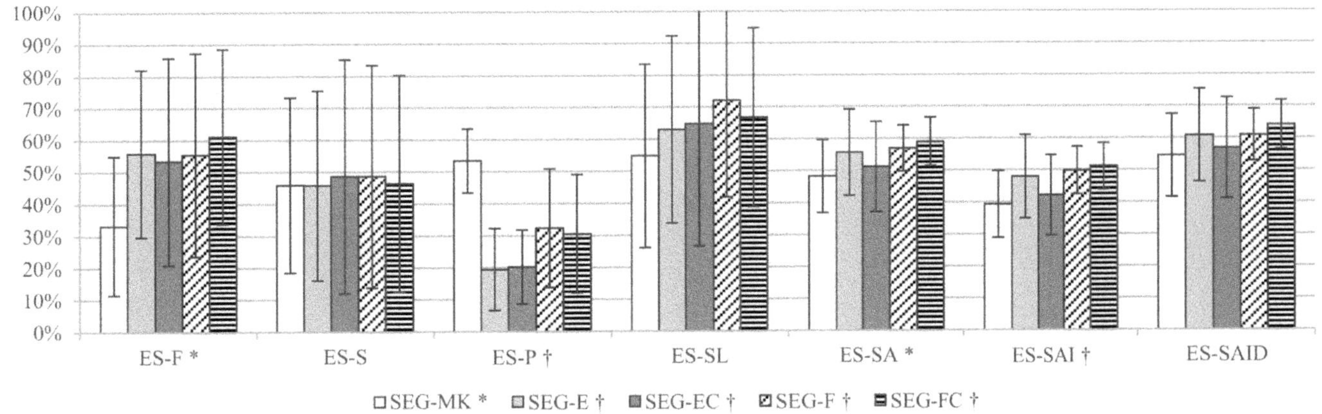

Figure 6. Average Percent of Total Time Classified.

DISCUSSION

Segmentation Algorithms

Of the various segmentation methods, segmentation by mouse and keyboard events (SEG-MK) provides the most stability, with less fluctuation in the results obtained between algorithms. Classification algorithm thresholds are set using the SEG-MK algorithm, which may account for its relative stability; it is likely that the accuracy of the various segmentation methods could be improved by modifying these thresholds. Mouse/keyboard events represent a conscious action by the user, often directly related to task completion. This leads to some amount of overlap in behavioral intervals, and increases the likelihood that any given interval contains at least some amount of task completion behavior.

Eye movement based segmentation (SEG-E and SEG-EC) obtains the best results overall, often having a higher percent of correctly identified intervals and a lower error than the other segmentation methods. Eye movement based segmentation defines intervals according to approximated regions of interest, allowing the users' attention to determine the logical segments of the recording. In general, SEG-E outperforms SEG-EC; this may be due to the fact that user interface elements (i.e. buttons, menus, controls, etc.) are often rectangular.

Fixation based segmentation (SEG-F and SEG-FC) shows the least accuracy of the considered segmentation methods, generally having a higher percent of total time classified, a lower percent correct, and a higher percent error than the opposing segmentation methods. Inaccuracy in the fixation based segmentation methods may be due, in part, to inaccuracies inherent in the I-VT algorithm used to identify fixations and the reduced specificity caused by the merging of individual data points into discrete fixations/saccades.

Eye movement based segmentation (SEG-E) may be the most useful algorithm, relying solely on the eye movement record without the need for extraneous information such as input events or application state. In general, the SEG-E algorithm surpasses all segmentation algorithms with the exception of SEG-EC in classification accuracy, and provides the highest accuracy of all considered algorithms when paired with the ES-SAID classification algorithm.

Classification Algorithms

Of the classification algorithms, fixation based classification (ES-F) obtains the best results using eye movement based segmentation (SEG-EC), with an average of 53% of total time classified, 60% correctly classified, and 25% erroneously classified. Saccade based classification (ES-S) obtains the best results using eye movement based segmentation (SEG-EC), with an average of 49% of total time classified, 52% correctly classified, and 29% erroneously classified. Pupil based classification (ES-P) obtains the best results using segmentation by mouse and keyboard events (SEG-MK), with an average of 53% of total time classified, 52% correctly classified, and 39% erroneously classified. Classification based on scanpath length (ES-SL) obtains the best results using eye movement based segmentation (SEG-EC), with an average of 65% of total time classified, 69% correctly classified, and 28% erroneously classified. Classification based on scanpath area (ES-SA) obtains the best results using eye movement based segmentation (SEG-E), with an average of 56% of total time classified, 65% correctly classified, and 32% erroneously classified. Classification based on a combination of scanpath area and inflections (ES-SAI) obtains the best results using eye movement based segmentation (SEG-EC), with an average of 42% of total time classified, 53% correctly classified, and 31% erroneously classified. Classification based on a combination of scanpath area, inflections, and duration (ES-SAID) obtains the best results using eye movement based segmentation (SEG-E), with an average of 61% of total time classified, 73% correctly classified, and 31% erroneously classified.

Classification based on a combination of scanpath area, inflections, and duration (ES-SAID) may be the most useful algorithm, averaging the highest percent correctly identified and an error rate somewhere between the other algorithms. The ES-SAID algorithm, in its current state, could be used

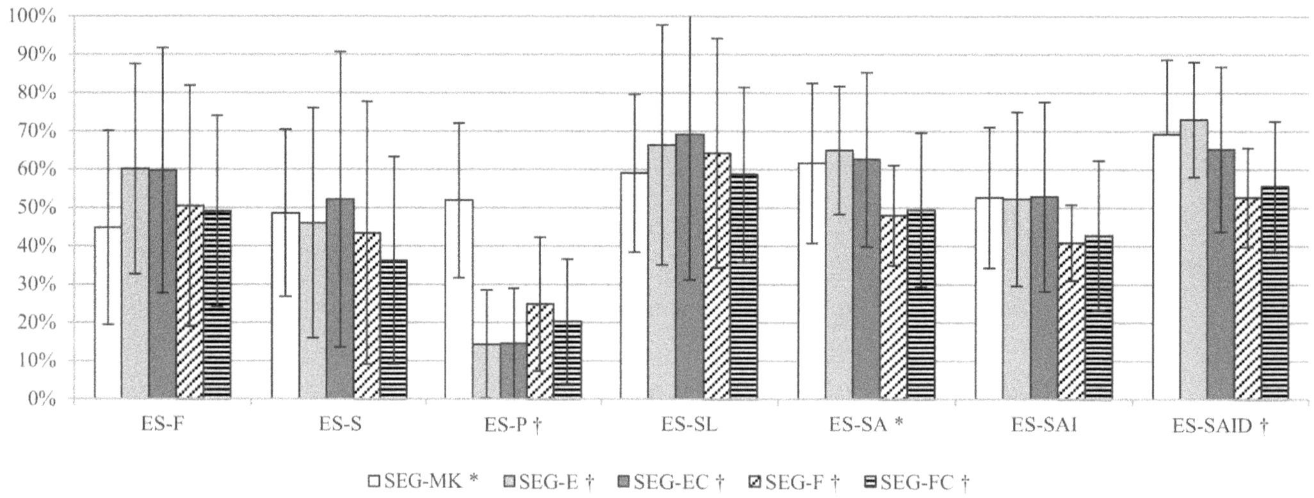

Figure 7. Average Percent Correct.

to discard irrelevant sections of recording with little loss of relevant data, substantially reducing the time required to review recorded data.

Pupil based classification (ES-P) is clearly the least effective of the considered algorithms, averaging the lowest percent correctly identified and the highest error rate. While pupil diameter is indicative of cognitive effort, it is also susceptible to the influence of light, fatigue, and emotion [7] . As such, it seems to be a poor indicator from which to draw conclusions about usability in the context of this work.

Of the basic eye movement metrics, fixation count seems to be the most reliable indicator of excessive search behavior, with a greater number of fixations indicating more extensive visual search and processing among distractor elements in the interface. Average saccade amplitude is less indicative of excessive search, as this reflects similarly the extent of visual search and processing, but is also largely affected by the size and location of interface elements. Scanpath length and area indicate the overall span of attention within the interface, and are more accurate indicators of excessive search than the basic metrics. Scanpath inflections indicate shifts in user attention and scanpath duration indicates the extent of processing; applying these in conjunction with scanpath area provides greater accuracy than any individual metric for the identification of excessive visual search.

Peculiarities

Throughout the course of manual classification, we have noticed several eye movement patterns indicative of excessive visual search. Difficulty selecting an interface element (often due to size) generally results in a scanpath concentrated within a small region, with long fixation durations and small saccade amplitudes. Difficulty finding interface elements (often text within a list/menu) generally results in vertical scanning of a localized screen region, with short fixation durations, slightly larger saccade amplitudes, and an increased number of vertical inflections. Difficulty understanding the interface layout (due to non-intuitive design or unclear instructions) often results in extensive scanning across multiple regions of the screen, with large saccade amplitudes, slightly longer fixation durations, and erratic inflections. In addition, while its classification as excessive search is debatable, there are a number of occurrences of what could be deemed habitual search, these are immediately preceded and followed by off-screen behavior and generally consist of 3-7 short fixations not necessarily related to task completion. It should be noted that while these are the most prevalent indicators of excessive visual search, they should not be considered comprehensive.

Classification error as defined in the previous section is a combination of the unclassified excessive search intervals and the intervals misclassified as excessive search. Several factors contribute to this error. The most substantial of these may be the accuracy of segmentation; manual classification is a relatively fine-grained approach, defining intervals of excessive search at the millisecond level, while automated segmentation provides a much coarser separation. As such, the intervals defined by manual and automated classification are not exactly equivalent. In this sense, a certain amount of error is unavoidable, but can be reduced by improving the accuracy of segmentation. Additionally, excessive search is not clearly defined by a single eye movement pattern, and as a result it is difficult to pinpoint excessive search intervals using only a single metric (as is illustrated by the relatively high accuracy of the ES-SAID algorithm, which employs a combination of metrics).

Limitations

The primary limitation of this technique is the inherent cost of suitable eye tracking equipment. Unfortunately, automated classification of excessive visual search does not yet provide the level of accuracy and precision necessary to eliminate the need for a trained human observer. As such,

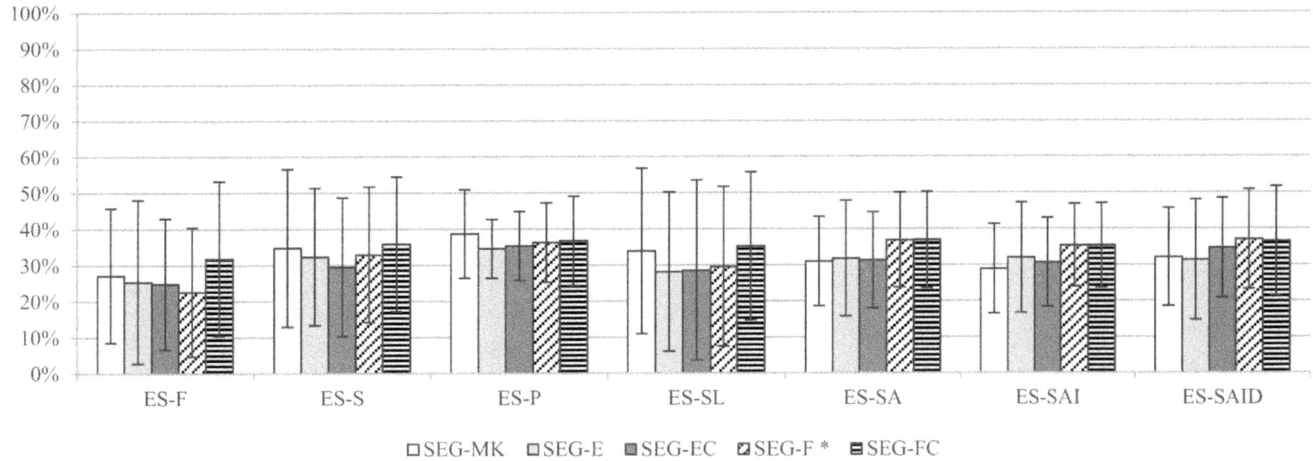

Figure 8. Average Percent Error.

the cost of eye tracking equipment must be compared to the possible time savings that may be obtained by its use. However, as eye tracking becomes more ubiquitous, and novel methods of producing cheap eye tracking equipment receive more attention [23, 24], this limitation will inevitably be resolved.

Another issue is the applicability of the usability problems identified in the process control interface to the usability of software interfaces in a more general context. For instance, an excessive amount of time spent reading a control list within a process control interface would not necessarily be considered an excessive amount of time while reading the contents of a web browser. In general, however, these metrics are valid for many applications in which direct user manipulation is the primary context of use (i.e. diagram editing, photo editing, etc.), though this assertion is currently untested.

Unfortunately, the time, effort, and training required for manual classification is extremely prohibitive, and, as such, it was only possible to obtain manual classification data from a single source in the current work. This issue may have introduced some amount of bias or inaccuracy into the performance comparison, as manual inspection is at least partially subjective and may vary from person to person. Despite this, the strictest adherence to formulaic inspection of usability recordings was employed to ensure similarity in the manual intervals produced.

Applications

The current paper focuses on the identification of intervals of excessive visual search within the recording, allowing software developers to more easily inspect areas of concern; however, the range and scope of possible applications is much wider. Based on classification statistics and assuming accurate classification it may be possible to provide further diagnostics. For example, the percentage of intervals classified as excessive visual, or a related measure, may be applied to determine the overall usability of the interface according to pre-defined thresholds; or similarly, it may be possible to determine the type and degree of usability issues within an interval based on the scanpath characteristics displayed. These are areas of active research, however, and are beyond the scope of this paper.

CONCLUSION

The primary shortcoming of usability testing is its qualitative nature, requiring detailed and time consuming analysis by a trained observer. In our experience, each minute of recorded data required approximately one hour of manual review. With average recording times of 3 minutes per subject, this equates to roughly 63 hours spent on manual classification of the 21 usability recordings considered in this paper. In comparison, automated classification with the ES-SAID algorithm is able to correctly identify an average of 73% of the excessive search intervals while discarding roughly 40% of the total recording time across the 21 recordings in less than 5 minutes. This is a substantial improvement, providing a potential savings of roughly 25 hours spent on manual classification.

In this paper we have described several previously considered techniques for the automated classification of excessive visual search, presented a variety of novel eye movement based segmentation methods, and provided an objective evaluation of the various segmentation and classification algorithms across and expanded data set. The results indicate that automated classification of excessive visual search may be employed to substantially reduce the amount of recorded data reviewed during usability testing.

Of the considered algorithms, the segmentation algorithm SEG-E and classification algorithm ES-SAID provided the most accurate detection of excessive visual search, confirming that eye movement based segmentation is able to provide more accurate search intervals than segmentation based purely on mouse/keyboard events. This was accomplished by defining search intervals according to variable regions of interest across the screen using the recorded eye gaze signal, and identifying excessive visual search through a combined analysis of attentional span (scanpath area), attentional shifts (inflection count), and processing complexity (scanpath duration).

Future research in this area will likely involve improvements and innovations in both segmentation and classification, the eventual goal being to detect not only when usability problems occur, but to provide further analysis of the location and reason for these problems within the interface. In addition to this, we hope to develop more complex algorithms for the automated detection of additional search behaviors, such as task completion and idle search.

REFERENCES

[1] A. A. Witold, *et al.*, "Consolidating the ISO Usability Models," presented at the 11th International Software Quality Management Conference and 8th Annual INSPIRE Conference, 2003.

[2] J. Rubin and D. Chisnell, *Handbook of Usability Testing: How to Plan, Design, and Conduct Effective Tests*, 2 ed. New York, NY: Wiley, 2008.

[3] L. Vukelja, *et al.*, "Are engineers condemned to design? a survey on software engineering and UI design in Switzerland," presented at the 11th IFIP TC 13 international conference on Human-computer interaction, Rio de Janeiro, Brazil, 2007.

[4] J. S. Dumas and J. C. Redish, *A Practical Guide to Usability Testing*: Intellect Books, 1999.

[5] R. J. Leigh and D. S. Zee, *The Neurology of Eye Movements*, 4 ed.: Oxford University Press, USA, 2006.

[6] A. Duchowski, *Eye Tracking Methodology: Theory and Practice*, 2nd ed.: Springer, 2007.

[7] A. Poole and L. J. Ball, "Eye tracking in human-computer interaction and usability research: current status and future prospects," in *Encyclopedia of Human-Computer Interaction*, C. Ghaoui, Ed., ed: Idea Group, 2005, pp. 211-219.

[8] L. J. Ball, *et al.*, "Applying the Post-Experience Eye-Tracked Protocol (PEEP) Method in Usability Testing," *Interfaces*, vol. 67, pp. 15-19, 2006.

[9] M. C. Russell, "Hotspots and hyperlinks: using eye-tracking to supplement usability testing," *Usability News*, vol. 7, 2005.

[10] J. M. Wolfe, "What Can 1 Million Trials Tell Us About Visual Search?," *Psychological Science*, vol. 9, pp. 33-39, 1998.

[11] J. Shen, *et al.*, "Distractor ratio influences patterns of eye movements during visual search," *Perception*, vol. 29, pp. 241-250, 2000.

[12] I. D. Gilchrist and M. Harvey, "Refixation frequency and memory mechanisms in visual search," *Current Biology*, vol. 10, pp. 1209-1212, 2000.

[13] A. J. Hornof and T. Halverson, "Cognitive strategies and eye movements for searching hierarchical computer displays," in *SIGCHI conference on Human factors in computing systems*, Ft. Lauderdale, Florida, USA, 2003, pp. 249-256.

[14] O. V. Komogortsev, *et al.*, "Eye movement driven usability evaluation via excessive search identification," in *14th International Conference on Human-Computer Interaction*, 2011.

[15] O. Komogortsev, *et al.*, "EMA: Automated eye-movement-driven approach for identification of usability issues," in *Design, user experience, and usability. Theory, methods, tools and practice*. vol. 6770, A. Marcus, Ed., ed: Springer Berlin / Heidelberg, 2011, pp. 459-468.

[16] O. Komogortsev, *et al.*, "Aiding usability evaluation via detection of excessive visual search," presented at the 2011 ACM SIGCHI Conference on Human Factors in Computing Systems (CHI), Vancouver, BC, Canada, 2011.

[17] P. M. Fitts, *et al.*, "Eye movements of aircraft pilots during instrument-landing approaches," *Aeronautical Engineering Review*, vol. 9, pp. 24-29, 1950.

[18] R. Jacob and K. Karn, "Commentary on Section 4. Eye Tracking in Human-Computer Interaction and Usability Research: Ready to Deliver the Promises," in *The Mind's Eye: Cognitive and Applied Aspects of Eye Movement Research*, ed: Elsevier, 2003, pp. 573-607.

[19] F. T. W. Au, *et al.*, "Automated usability testing framework," presented at the Proceedings of the ninth conference on Australasian user interface - Volume 76, Wollongong, Australia, 2008.

[20] M. Ivory and A. Chevalier, "A Study of Automated Web Site Evaluation Tools," University of Washington, Department of Computer Science2002.

[21] J. H. Goldberg and X. P. Kotval, "Computer interface evaluation using eye movements: methods and constructs," *International Journal of Industrial Ergonomics*, vol. 24, pp. 631-645, 1999.

[22] O. V. Komogortsev, *et al.*, "Standardization of Automated Analyses of Oculomotor Fixation and Saccadic Behaviors," *IEEE Transactions on Biomedical Engineering*, vol. 57, pp. 2635-2645, 2010.

[23] W. Sewell and O. Komogortsev, "Real-time eye gaze tracking with an unmodified commodity webcam employing a neural network," in *28th of the international conference extended abstracts on Human factors in computing systems*, Atlanta, Georgia, USA, 2010, pp. 3739-3744.

[24] J. S. Agustin, *et al.*, "Low-cost gaze interaction: ready to deliver the promises," presented at the Proceedings of the 27th international conference extended abstracts on Human factors in computing systems, Boston, MA, USA, 2009.

An Evaluation of How Small User Interface Changes Can Improve Scientists' Analytic Strategies

Radu Jianu
Brown University
jr@cs.brown.edu

David H. Laidlaw
Brown University
dhl@cs.brown.edu

ABSTRACT
Subtle changes in analysis system interfaces can be used purposely to alter users' analytic behaviors. In a controlled study subjects completed three analyses at one-week intervals using an analysis support system. Control subjects used one interface in all sessions. Test subjects used modified versions in the last two sessions: a first set of changes aimed at increasing subjects' use of the system and their consideration of alternative hypotheses; a second set of changes aimed at increasing the amount of evidence collected. Results show that in the second session test subjects used the interface 39% more and switched between hypotheses 19% more than in the first session. They then collected 26% more evidence in the third than in the second session. These increases differ significantly ($p < 0.05$) from near constant control rates. We hypothesize that this approach can be used in many real applications to guide analysts unobtrusively towards improved analytic strategies.

Author Keywords
Visual Analytics; Analytic Biases; Persuasive Technology

ACM Classification Keywords
H.5.2 User Interfaces: Misc

General Terms
Experimentation, Human Factors, Measurement

INTRODUCTION
This paper provides experimental support for the hypothesis that we can use subtle changes in the interfaces of visual analysis systems to influence users' analytic behavior and thus unobtrusively guide them towards improved analytic strategies. We posit that this approach may facilitate the use of visual analytics expertise to correct biases and heuristics documented in the cognitive science community.

Specifically, we report results from a controlled study in which subjects were asked to complete three analysis sessions using a system consisting of a visualization and an analysis support module. Two sets of non-functional changes were made to the analysis support interface before the second and third sessions. These changes were designed to improve three hypothesized or observed analytic deficiencies: analysts' excessive reliance on memory, inability to consider hypotheses in parallel, and insufficient search for evidence. Our quantitative results show that the interface changes succeeded in alleviating these deficiencies. Compared to a control group, our test subjects used the support module more, they switched among hypotheses more often, and they collected more evidence per hypothesis. Our data not merely show that changes in interfaces translate into different user behavior, but demonstrate that we can leverage interface design and cognitive principles in controlled ways to overcome known analytic deficiencies.

Our work was motivated by extensive cognitive science research showing that human thinking is subject to heuristics and biases that often lead to suboptimal decision making [22]. Recent visual analytics efforts suggest that visualization and interfaces can offer support against such cognitive biases and heuristics, possibly by leveraging the expertise of cognitive science and intelligence communities [21, 32, 20, 35]. However, to the best of our knowledge, few concrete attempts have used visual analytics techniques to align *descriptive analysis* (i.e., what people actually do to derive a solution) to *normative analysis* (i.e., rational strategies of deriving the best solution). Here, we evaluate a potential solution inspired by previous work in the fields of behavioral economics and human-computer interaction (HCI): *libertarian paternalism* [36, 38] and *persuasive technology* [17] are similar concepts that advocate designing choice layouts and computer interfaces so that they *nudge* users towards decisions that are in their best interest.

Contributions: We hypothesize that subtle changes in visualization interfaces can be used in controlled ways to guide users towards more normative analysis and provide quantitative evidence that supports this hypothesis. We also present qualitative observations on analytic strategies, biases, and heuristics that our subjects used in their tasks.

Roadmap: Next, a related work section summarizes existing research that we build on and extend. We then describe a user-study that validates our hypothesis and summarize its results. We end with a discussion and concluding remarks.

RELATED WORK
This section shows how our work relates to and is motivated by existing research.

Guiding user's choices
Thaler and Sunstein's work [38, 36] in the field of behavioral economics popularized the term *choice architecture* — how a

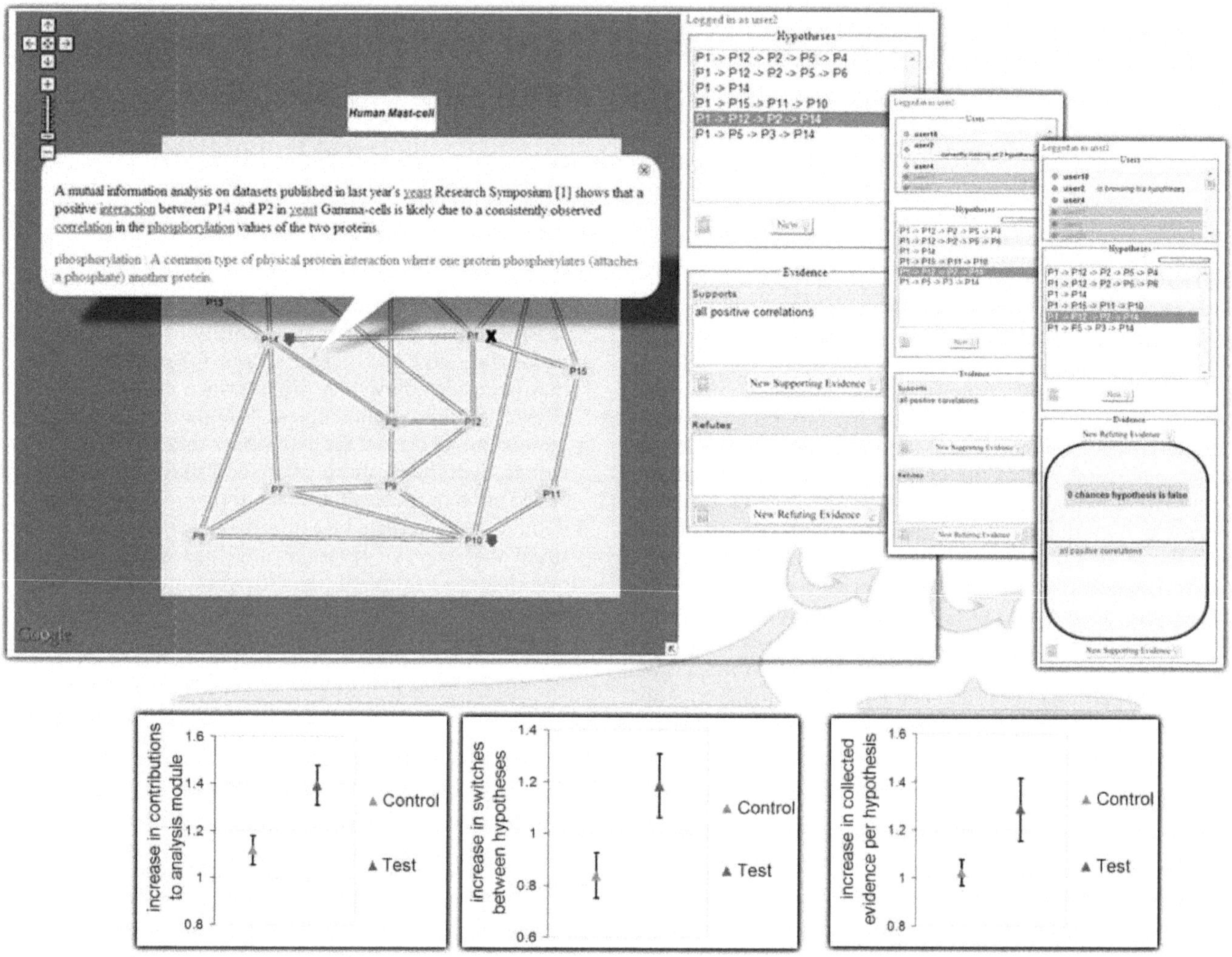

Figure 1. By making subtle, non-functional changes in the interface of an analysis support module (top) we generated statistically significant changes in users' analytic behavior in a visual problem-solving task. A first set of changes nudged subjects to increase their use of the analysis module by 39% **(lower left,** $p = 0.02$**) in an attempt to support our subjects' working memory. It also caused them to switch among hypotheses** 19% **more often (lower center,** $p = 0.03$**), indicating more consideration of alternative hypotheses. A second set of changes then led subjects to gather** 26% **more evidence per hypothesis (lower right,** $p = 0.01$**). These three increases compare to smaller or negative variations in a control group** (+15%, −17%, −2%)**.**

set of choices is presented to a consumer — and the concept of *libertarian-paternalism* — designing choice architectures that "nudge" consumers towards decisions that are in their own interest (paternalistic) while unrestricting choice (libertarian). A similar concept was proposed in the HCI domain by Fogg [17] who defines *persuasive technology* as "interactive information technology designed for changing users' attitudes or behavior". We build on these previous approaches and demonstrate empirically how the nudge paradigm can further the visual analytics agenda.

Sunstein and Thaler as well as Fogg motivate their approaches with two arguments, which they support with experimental evidence. First, any choice architecture or computer interface necessarily influences decision-making behavior, whether intentionally or not. Second, as already shown, research indicates that people's choices and behaviors are not always aligned with their goals. From a visual analytics perspective, this means that even if analysts' objective is to select the optimal course of action based on available data, cognitive biases and heuristics can steer them towards suboptimal results.

Both approaches have inspired scientific results that validated their feasibility and provided inspiring design models for the analysis nudges presented here. Thaler and Benartzi [37] use an array of cognitive effects such as *mental discounting* or *default options* to persuade employees of a company to increase their contributions to their retirement plans. In the technological realm, the enhanced speedometer [27] changes its appearance based on the current speed limit (when known), encouraging users to stay within speed limits, while the smart sink [2] augments a normal sink with visual cues that make energy consumption apparent.

In their work, Sunstein, Thaler and Fogg discuss potential nudging opportunities. These can generally be explained by Gray's *soft constraints* hypothesis [19] – humans abide by hard constraints that define all possible paths of action, but also by soft constraints which are preferred modes of action given a decision environment. An example of soft constraint is the *least effort decision strategy* and maps well to the *default nudge* (i.e. people tend to opt for default sets of choices). Other nudging examples proposed are: decisional inertia, mental discounting, social effects, motivational display of information (statistics, graphical).

Finally, the three authors address ethical questions raised by influencing choice or behavior. Their consensus is that influencing behavior through design is unavoidable. Thaler's view is that libertarian paternalism should ensure that people can easily avoid the paternalist option. Fogg proposes an evaluation of gains and losses of developers, distributers and users of a system to determine its ethicality. Subsequent papers impose additional ethical constraints and guidelines for avoiding coercion and deception, and advocating openness and unobtrusiveness [29].

Analytic biases and heuristics

Our work is motivated by extensive cognitive science research demonstrating that people are prone to a range of analysis biases and heuristics that can lead to analysis errors [22]. A specific manifestation of such effects occurs in the context of hypothesis-driven analysis. For example, *satisficing* [33] limits analysis to a hypothesis that is good enough, a *confirmation bias* conditions us to confirm hypotheses rather than disconfirm them [40], and people often fail to to consider alternative explanations [7]. Many such studies have been conducted with naive subjects, but research shows that biases and heuristics also occur in scientific and clinical settings, with similar error-inducing effects [13, 4, 31]. Several results suggest however, that experts, while not immune to such biases and heuristics, may be better equipped to overcome them [14, 25].

Evidence suggests that users can be helped to overcome biases and heuristics and instead use normative analysis, a change that usually yields improved analytic performance. For instance, subjects conditioned to pursue alternative hypotheses and disconfirming evidence reached solutions to a scientific puzzle more often [13]. Analogies and subsequent unexpected findings lead to consideration of multiple hypotheses and novel findings [14]. Medical students using hypothesis-driven analysis outperformed those using a data-immersion approach [16]. Finally, multiple-attribute utility theory can reduce the *prominence* effect (i.e. basing a decision on one attribute deemed most important) [22]. These results support our goal of guiding users towards normative analysis practices.

Related work in visual analytics

The paper "Illuminating the path" [39] introduced the field of visual analytics (VA) as "the science of analytical reasoning facilitated by interactive visual interfaces". The work presented in this paper extends the VA research agenda, concentrating on designing interfaces and visualizations that support the aggregation of data insights into cohesive scientific theories.

Our work is tangential to VA results on understanding the sense-making process [6, 30, 23, 5] and draws on position papers that argue for leveraging the expertise of cognitive science and intelligence communities [21, 35]. In our evaluation we use a system inspired by a range of efforts to design analysis support interfaces that let users store, annotate, and browse analysis artifacts such as hypotheses or evidence [8, 41, 18, 42, 15]. Such VA efforts improve analysis by supporting memory and attention span and enabling more diverse data queries. However, they do not provide support against decision biases and heuristics, a further cognitive limitation. Our work thus complements current VA research by using interface design to create a link between observed analytic deficiencies and corrected behavior.

Perhaps closest to our work is that of Savikhin et al. [32] demonstrating experimentally that a targeted visual representation can induce normatively correct decisions in an otherwise biased economic choice task. We extend this result by linking it to the more general nudging approach proposed by Sunstein, Thaler and Fogg, by exploiting interface design in general, and by providing an experimental validation for a high-level analytic task.

METHODS

We conducted a controlled user study to test the hypothesis that small changes in a visualization system's interface can be used to produce targeted modifications in users' analytic workflows. This section presents the design of this study. We start with an overview description of the methodology used and continue with an in-depth presentation of each aspect of the study.

Study overview

Subjects completed an analysis task inspired by a real scientific problem using a visualization and an analysis-support interface (Figure 1, top). Each subject performed three such analysis sessions at one-week intervals. Each session lasted roughly one hour.

Thirty-six subjects, mostly undergraduate and graduate students, were divided into two groups: 21 test and 15 control subjects. The control group solved all three tasks using the same analysis-support interface. Conversely, test-group subjects were given slightly different versions of the analysis-support interface in each session. Specifically, two sets of interface nudges were added to the analysis system before the second and third sessions. We hypothesized that, while changes between sessions would be observed in both groups due to task-learning effects, the test group would exhibit additional effects due to the interface nudges.

The analysis task was inspired by the proteomic domain: finding causal paths in protein interaction networks to explain the interdependency of pairs of proteins that are not directly connected. None of the subjects was familiar with the task or background material beforehand and all received a 20-minute tutorial at the beginning of the study.

Our test system was instrumented to log users' interactions automatically. Subjects were also asked to distill their analysis in a written questionnaire at the end of each of the three analysis sessions. We analyzed the datasets both quantitatively, to look for support for our nudging hypothesis, and qualitatively, to gain insight into how subjects approached their task.

Task description

Subjects were asked to solve three artificially constructed analysis tasks inspired by workflows of proteomic researchers studying protein signaling pathways.

Proteins are functional molecules within cells that interact with one another to form complex causal pathways that determine the response of cells to events. Such protein interactions are the object of intense scientific research because understanding these cellular pathways would let researchers devise efficient drugs to influence a cell's behavior without causing unwanted side effects. Proteomicists often use visualizations of interaction networks to understand changes in protein activation patterns measured in experiments. A distinct class of experiments is *knockout experiments*: here researchers deactivate particular proteins and compare protein activation levels before and after the removal.

Our subjects were given network visualizations that were said to depict protein interactions documented in recent publications. Figure 1 shows one of three distinct networks that subjects were asked to analyze. The networks were manually created and laid out. The familiar Google Maps user interface was used to display the network images and offer basic interaction. Clicking on nodes or edges opened information bubbles referring to these particular elements. Interactions were described by fictional, brief paper abstracts detailing the particulars of each interaction and the context in which it was discovered. The sizes of the three networks – node and edge count – were: $(18,30),(16,29),(15,27)$.

Subjects were told that a knockout experiment had been performed on a specific type of cell. They were informed that a protein was removed from the cell and that researchers subsequently observed changes (positive or negative) in the levels of several proteins. These changes were marked on the network with arrows. Finally, subjects were asked to use the available information to determine network paths likely to have produced those changes and to rank them in order of plausibility. This network task represents a visual, complex, and open-ended implementation of causal reasoning tasks that have been typical choices of cognitive studies [40].

Our networks used proteomic terminology but introduced fictitious proteins, interactions and interaction mechanisms. Thus, the probability of a regulation chain was determined by the logical consistency of the evidence presented. The key rules that subjects were expected to extract from the evidence and use in their analysis were: the probability of a depicted interaction is lower if it was documented in species and cells other than those investigated in the knockout experiment; a correlation between two proteins should be treated as an edge with uncertain directionality; interactions could describe direct or inverse regulation mechanisms; and the edges sequence in a solution path should justify the sign of the observed change. These assumptions, along with a general description of protein signaling, were illustrated in a 20-minute tutorial (text and video) and were clarified on request. Moreover, essential terms were highlighted in all evidence text and in-situ explanations were displayed upon mouse clicks (Figure 1).

The order in which the three networks were presented to users was alternated to minimize the chance of network differences influencing the global result. Thus, in the test group, six subjects solved the networks in order $1,2,3$, seven subjects solved them as $2,3,1$, and the remaining six solved them as $3,2,1$. A similar division was used for the control group.

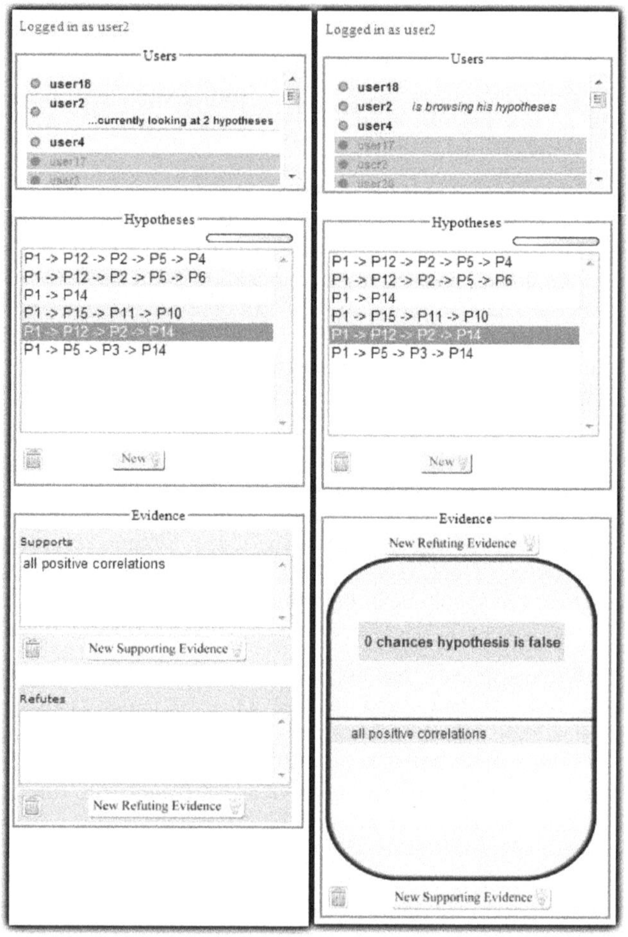

Figure 2. The two modified analysis interfaces include three evaluated nudges: a box lists online users actively interacting with the analysis module (left), a color gradient (white to gold) shows recently analyzed hypotheses (left), a redesigned, larger evidence box asks users to commit to the implications of a hypotheses lacking associated evidence (right).

Analysis interface and evaluated nudges

In addition to the protein network viewer, an analysis support interface augmented the experimental environment (Figure 1). As noted in Section 3.1, control subjects used the same base analysis interface in all three sessions. Test subjects started with an identical interface but then used upgraded versions in the second and third sessions. These versions, obtained by incrementally including two sets of evaluated nudges in the base interface, are shown in Figure 2.

The base analysis module contained three lists where users stored their hypotheses, confirming, and disconfirming evidence. Hypotheses were entered into the system as noncyclical network paths by clicking on sequences of nodes. Evidence was entered by typing free text in a pop-up box. Selecting hypotheses would highlight their corresponding paths on the visualization and display their associated evidence, thus allowing subjects to revisit and compare hypotheses. Subjects were familiarized with these features in the tutorial video at the beginning of the study.

Three nudges were designed to alleviate three analytic deficiencies. First, we assumed that subjects would rely on their working memory rather than use the analysis system. Second, based on cognitive science studies, we assumed that subjects would have trouble considering multiple hypotheses in parallel. Third, we hypothesized that subjects would gather mostly confirming evidence for their hypotheses, and ignore the aspect of disconfirming evidence. The results of our initial session one runs caused us to adjust our last assumption: subjects were gathering approximately equal amounts of confirming and disconfirming evidence but in overall small amounts. We refined the design of our last nudge to target this issue better.

As noted, the **first nudge** (Figure 2, left) aimed to increase users' reliance on the interface. Our design assumed that if subjects knew other users were actively interacting with the module, they would do so as well. To test this, a section listing online users was added to the base analysis module. As users interacted with the module, this was reflected in a status message (e.g., "user is browsing hypotheses", "user has entered evidence"). Fake user-bots ensured that a nudge factor was present at all times. This design was inspired by research on conformity effects and motivational factors for online contributions. Specifically, humans change behavior to match that of others [10, 3, 9] to gain social approval [11], or because they extract information from observing what others do [34, 24]. In addition, visibility encourages users of social networks to increase their online contributions [1, 28, 28].

The **second nudge** aimed to encourage users to compare and contrast hypotheses in parallel rather than sequentially. Initially we planned to evaluate this nudge by itself but ultimately merged it with the first to make the length of the study manageable. The design involved assigning hypotheses recency scores that decayed over time but increased with interactions targeting a hypothesis (e.g. selection, adding evidence). Recent hypotheses were highlighted in the hypotheses list by using a color gradient based on the recency score. Finally, thresholding this score allowed us to determine the number of a user's active hypotheses, display this in the user status (Figure 2, left), and sort users based on the number of active hypotheses. This offered a visual and status reward. A user could trick the system by quickly switching between hypotheses, but this was taken into account in data analysis (see Results section) and we observed just two instances of it. The first two nudges were integrated into the analysis interface before the second session.

Finally, the **third nudge**, deployed in the last session, aimed to have test subjects gather more evidence for their hypotheses. To that end we changed the evidence collection section (Figure 2, right). First, the evidence-collection area was made more visually interesting and distinct. Second, if no confirming or disconfirming evidence had been entered for a hypothesis, the evidence boxes would read "0 chances that hypothesis is false" or "hypothesis is unlikely". This essentially required subjects to commit to extreme cases — something people are known to avoid [12]. Third, a change introduced unintentionally while implementing the design was that the evidence boxes in this nudge were larger than in the base interface.

We hypothesize that this nudge could be restricted to disconfirming evidence only, in which case it could potentially alleviate confirmation biases [40]. As noted, our subjects did not exhibit a confirmation bias in the early stages of the study, so that we resorted to testing the more general case of increasing the amount of total evidence.

User pool

Our study included a total of 36 subjects. Of these, 16 were women and 20 men. Six of them were young professionals, 18 were undergraduates, and 12 were graduate students. Twenty-six of the subjects were active in sciences, while 10 were humanities students. None of the subjects had previous experience with proteomic analysis. Thus, all subjects relied solely on the tutorial provided at the beginning of the study.

Subjects were randomly distributed in control (15) and test (21) groups such that the two groups had similar distributions of gender and age (undergraduate, graduate or postgraduate). Subjects were compensated for their participation.

User study limitations

Ease of hypothesis elicitation: A pilot run showed us that free-text specification of hypotheses would have produced considerable variability in what users entered as hypotheses. To be able to compare results across subjects we limited hypotheses to paths of connected proteins. This interaction mode, reinforced by the tutorial video, gave subjects an easy "recipe" for generating hypotheses: any network path was a valid hypothesis.

Lack of motivation: Our study did not involve monetary incentives to encourage subjects to provide valid solutions. This limitation affected a small data portion. Two users created random entries to pass time and were excluded from the analysis, two users were observed texting/browsing, and eight sessions (not users) were shorter than average. This data of potentially lower quality amounts to less than 10% and is evenly distributed over experimental groups and sessions. Generally, users were engaged, their assessment of evidence consistent with other users and over sessions, and their final reports detailed. Also, the qualitative analysis suggests deliberation in most datasets (e.g., preliminary browsing of a path's evidence, verifying evidence after entering a hypothesis, re-routing paths).

Unforeseen problem-solving strategies: A few early subjects copied the network on paper and annotated each interaction and protein. This strategy is not scalable to real protein interaction networks and it does not capture the exploratory nature of analysis. To avoid this, we instructed the rest of the subjects not to use such exhaustive analysis strategies.

Task misunderstanding: Instead of constructing short paths that linked the knockout protein to each changing protein, two subjects looked for long paths that linked the knocked-out protein and all arrow proteins (i.e proteins with changed levels) together. We retained these results because the subjects used this interpretation consistently in all three sessions.

Variation in analysis times: We urged users to spend approximately 60 minutes on each session. Several subjects, however, insisted on finishing earlier. Moreover, a few datasets showed prolonged intervals of inactivity and several users were observed to take web-browsing or texting breaks. In our analysis we eliminated intervals with no activity and normalized all measurements by the time spent on the task.

Small number of subjects: Our sample size (21 test, 15 control subjects) was relatively low for the open-ended tasks our study involved. However, we note that the trends in the data became apparent with as few as six users in each group and changed very little throughout the experiment.

Effect of change not captured: Our study does not capture the amount by which interface changes amplify the saliency of our nudges. It may well be that nudges are less observable and effective if they are introduced into the first system release.

RESULTS

Here we describe quantitative and qualitative results from our user study. All data and analyses are available online [43].

Data preparation and analysis

Thirty-two subjects completed all three sessions while four completed only the first two for a total of $28 \times 3 + 4 \times 2 = 104$ datasets. Four of the subjects, two from each group, solved the tasks on paper using exhaustive annotation of the networks. Three additional users also switched to this approach in the final session. All these data were discarded from the analyses leaving $104 - 4 \times 3 - 3 \times 1 = 89$ datasets from 13 control subjects and 19 test subjects.

We measured and analyzed three quantitative indicators to support our nudging hypothesis. First, we recorded the number of hypotheses and evidence entered into the system as a proxy for the degree to which subjects relied on the interface to trace their analysis. This number was normalized by the time, in minutes, subjects spent on each session. Second, we measured the number of times a subject switched between hypotheses and normalized it by the number of hypotheses, as an indicator of the degree to which hypotheses were analyzed in parallel during analysis. Third, we recorded the number of evidence items collected and divided it by number of hypotheses.

The normalizations address three issues. First, users did not spend fixed amounts of time on tasks. Time normalization lets us compare subject's results over multiple sessions. Second, hypothesis count varied between sessions and we meant to capture if a subject analyses all explanations in parallel (i.e. a user exploring all of five hypotheses ranks higher than one exploring the last five of fifteen). Normalizing switches by hypothesis count achieves this. Third, a similar discussion applies to evidence over hypotheses.

In the case of hypotheses switches, we ignored hypotheses selections lasting less than 5 seconds because we observed that users sometimes cycled rapidly through hypotheses as a method of gauging progress. We also ignored switches occurring in the last part of the analysis while subjects were filling in the answer questionnaire. We found that by default most users did a comparative analysis of hypotheses at the very end. Our nudge however was designed to encourage users constantly to consider alternatives.

In a second phase we also made a qualitative analysis of our subjects' workflows. Our goals were to understand the dominant analytic strategies and behavioral patterns, and to verify the degree to which biases and heuristics were applied.

Quantitative support for nudging hypothesis

The premise of our experiment was that interface nudges would cause test subjects to change their behavior between sessions differently from how control subjects' behavior evolves naturally due to learning or boredom. Figures 3-5 demonstrate the validity of our premise by contrasting the relative changes in performance measures between consecutive sessions in both experimental groups. As expected, change was negligible in control subjects (means of triangles are close to one), but was significant for test subjects when a nudge was present (means of black squares greater than one). However, test group behavior was constant whenever performance measures were not specifically targeted (e.g. change in contributions between last two sessions). This suggests that subjects were responding not simply to interface changes but to nudges targeting particular performance measures.

Test subjects contributed 39% more hypotheses and evidence items to the analysis module in the second session than in the first. This compares to an increase of only 15% in the control group (Figure 3). A t-test found this difference to be statistically significant ($t(29) = -2.07, p = 0.02$). Contributions remained close to constant between the second and third sessions in both the control and test group (Figure 3). This conforms to the expected behavior since no nudge targeting contributions was added between these sessions.

The difference in switches between hypotheses was an increase of 18% in test subjects versus a decline of 17% in control subjects (Figure 4). The difference was significant, as indicated by the t-test ($t(25) = -1.89, p = 0.03$). The first two nudges were both added before the second session. Thus, we assign either of the observed changes not to any single nudge but to all interface changes made between the first two sessions.

The amount of evidence collected per hypothesis remained fairly constant between *all* consecutive sessions in the control group with a decrease of 2% (Figure 5). Test subjects however, gathered on average 24% more evidence per hypothesis

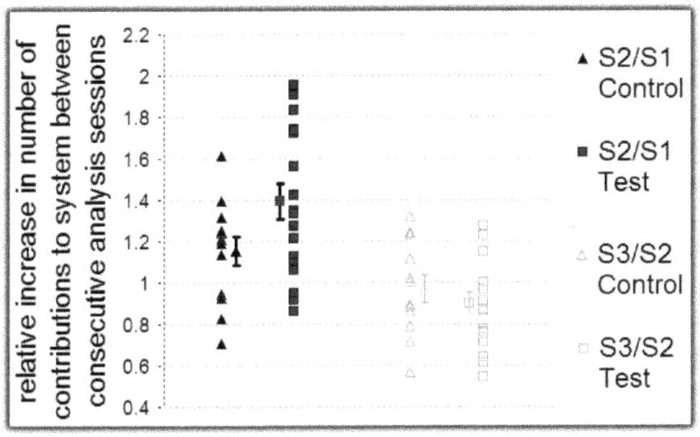

Figure 3. Changes between the first two sessions (black) caused test subjects (squares) to increase the number of hypotheses and evidence items entered into the analysis system by an additional 24% over the control subjects'(triangle) relative increase. The interface changes before the third session had no significant impact on this performance measure (gray).

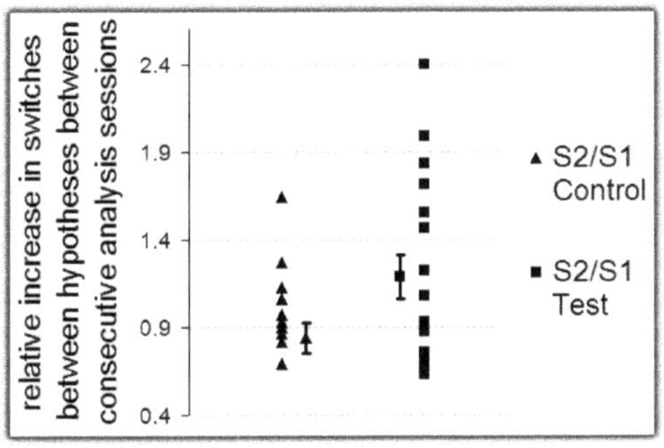

Figure 4. Changes between the first two sessions caused test subjects (squares) to switch between hypotheses an additional 35% more than than the control subjects'(triangle) relative increase.

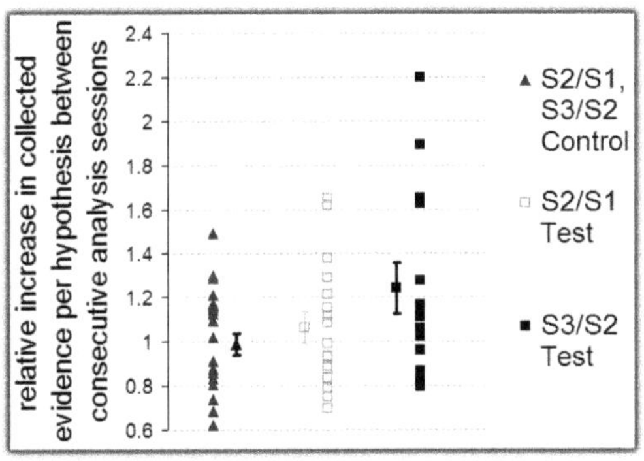

Figure 5. Changes between the last two sessions (black) caused test subjects (squares) to gather 24% more evidence for their hypotheses as opposed to a constant evidence/hypotheses ratio (-2%) between all consecutive control sessions (triangles). Changes in the test group before the second session (gray) produced non-significant changes in evidence collection as compared to the control group.

in the third condition than the second. This difference was also found to be statistically significant ($t(38) = -2.28, p = 0.01$).

We note that since we included both last nudges in a single session we cannot attribute any changes observed between the last two sessions to one specific nudge. However, the changes and the fact that they conformed to our expectations remains an important contribution.

Qualitative analysis of subjects' workflows

We logged subject's interactions (e.g., protein and interaction browsing, hypothesis creation, evidence addition) and analyzed the collected data using a time-line viewer. This let us assess users' workflows qualitatively to extract common strategies and to determine the extent to which users relied on analytic biases and heuristics. The following paragraphs summarize our conclusions.

Observed workflows: More than half our subjects started with an initial exploration of the network. This exploration was not hypothesis driven and typically lasted between three and six minutes. Subjects then moved on to a hypothesis-driven analysis, trying to connect arrow proteins to the knock-out protein (Figure 1). We could discern two strategies for entering hypotheses. Most subjects would pick a candidate path, do a pre-evaluation of its likelihood, enter it into the system if it was plausible, and then follow with a second pass to summarize and document evidence. These users would often revisit hypotheses and compare them. A few subjects added hypotheses without prior exploration and then summarized evidence in a following pass. Generally, they did not reevaluate those hypotheses again until a final pass when they decided on a global likelihood ordering.

Observed biases and heuristics: We also analyzed the data in terms of biases and heuristics documented in cognitive science literature. In particular we looked for confirmation bias, *single-attribute analysis* (i.e. focusing on a single most prominent attribute and using that to rank options), *conjunction fallacies* (i.e a specific condition is deemed more likely than an ecompassing general one), and inabillity to operate with varying degree of probabilities. Our findings are interesting because they show that some of these effects are not as dominant in a close to real analysis setting as cognitive science suggests and because they describe potential scenarios that trigger such behavior.

A first interesting finding was that confirmation bias is not dominant. In fact, subjects gathered slightly more disconfirming evidence than confirming evidence. Moreover, several users gathered almost exclusively disconfirming evidence, while others pruned paths that had strong negative evidence. Also, one subject would copy entire sections from the information bubbles and enter it directly as confirming evidence, but would always carefully summarize negative evidence. This suggests that she recognized the higher diagnostic value that the disconfirming evidence would have in her final ranking.

A known heuristic that we did find in several datasets was *single-attribute analysis*. We noticed several cases in which subjects added complicated paths before shorter, more intuitive ones. On closer inspection we found that they had selected a single attribute (e.g. cell type) and were using it to include or discard paths from their analysis.

We also noticed an inability to operate with varying degrees of probability. Several subjects seemed to postpone the consideration of paths involving a complex probability judgment (e.g. multiple interactions with associated uncertainty) and instead concentrate on paths that allowed a binary decision.

Our network setup was well suited to discovering *conjunction fallacies* since short paths should be more likely candidates for analysis than longer paths. In general, our subjects seemed aware of this principle. In fact, most new hypotheses abided by this rule. Additionally, several subjects added the short length of a path as positive evidence. However, we noticed that subjects' analytic strategies tricked them into the conjunction fallacy in a significant number of cases. We observed three main scenarios leading to this.

First, the favored method of expanding a set of hypotheses was to modify an existing one by rerouting part of its path. At the very least, subjects often used interactions that they were already familiar with. Most subjects avoided picking completely new routes, especially in network areas where they had already done some analysis. Such small changes to initially short paths lead subjects to analyze increasingly longer paths. Ultimately, subjects spent considerable time on long paths that were less likely than unexplored shorter options.

Second, subjects occasionally considered longer paths linking together multiple arrow proteins more likely than short paths from the knockout protein to each of those arrow proteins. We hypothesize that users were looking for good unifying stories, a known cognitive tendency. Interestingly, one of the subjects confessed that he was aware of the conjunction fallacy but that the "story was too good" to be irrelevant.

The third reason for multiple instances of conjunction fallacy was tied to the network layouts. The way paths were visually displayed had an impact on which ones were chosen for analysis. Most subjects preferred paths that described fairly continuous visual arches, or that were symmetric with ones they had already looked at. Sharp-angled paths were usually selected last even if they were shorter than already analyzed hypotheses. Another effect observable in several datasets was that symmetrical paths were more often compared to each other than to other hypotheses.

DISCUSSION

Here we discuss the broader impact of our contributions, alternative methodologies, and open questions.

Significance

Some of the findings reported in this paper may seem unsurprising. That interface design can alter analytic workflows is evident, as is the fact that online visibility is correlated with increased online activity [28]. However, our study data shows more than that interface changes translate into different user behavior. Our contribution lies in demonstrating that interface elements can be leveraged in controlled ways to unobtrusively correct users' strategies: our subjects' deficiency in supporting their hypotheses with evidence was observed in the first session and alleviated by a redesigned analysis-support module in the third session. We believe this approach is valuable because it has the potential to correct and improve users' strategies without having to rely on coercive or obtrusive elements such as pop-up messages or help agents.

Design guidelines

Our work aimed to provide experimental support for the nudge paradigm in the visual analytics domain rather than introduce specific design guidelines. We tried to approximate real analysis rather than use small, toy tasks and used high level nudges to demonstrate that nudging can be applied in practice. However, the nudge design space warrants more exhaustive exploration because it can be a tool for improving users' analytic strategies and help us understand how interfaces unintentionally shape exploratory and analytic patterns. To generate actual design guidelines we envision a follow-up study involving crowd sourcing, many users, and small tasks to quantify the nudging potential of particular interface elements.

A few design guidelines, however, can be distilled from our work. First, collaborative elements and conformity triggers can nudge users to change their behavior. We hypothesize that artificial *model-analysts*, such as in our experiment, may nudge users towards desired behaviors. Second, visual rewards, such as our recency score, may encourage users to consider options in parallel. Third, messages in text areas, perhaps in conjunction with box size, may be used to prompt for content. Finally, our qualitative analysis of users' workflows indicates that ways of automatically suggesting hypotheses may alleviate some of the observed conjunction fallacies and that subjects would benefit from support for multiple attribute analysis. Both such mechanisms need to be domain specific and are beyond the scope of our work.

General considerations

The data distributions may suggest that nudges, rather than uniformly targeting all subjects, tend to be particularly effective for a subgroup and less so for the rest. As seen in Figures 3-5, measurements obtained from test subjects appear to form two clusters: one with values similar to those measured in the control group, and one with distinctively higher values. These clusters do not correlate with the order in which networks were presented to users. However, the data gathered as part of this study is insufficient to test this hypothesis.

The analytic biases and heuristics targeted in our study were chosen because they are amply documented in the cognitive science literature. It is likely that one or more of these effects do not appear or are beneficial in some areas or settings. In fact *naturalistic decision making* [26], a distinct research area, models situations (e.g., crisis control, time-sensitive operations) in which heuristics are an efficient analytic strategy. The aim of this study was not to eliminate a specific set of biases and heuristics but to demonstrate that if such effects are identified we can use interface elements to reduce their occurrence.

Our study did not replicate some biases documented by cognitive science. Most notably, people are thought to be unable to elicit many hypotheses and to be biased towards gathering confirming evidence. Instead, our subjects generated many hypotheses and showed no confirmation bias. We see two possible explanations for this. First, our study limitations may be responsible: the ease of generating hypotheses and subjects' lack of motivation led them to pursue many hypotheses and not be attached to favored ones. Another explanation is that people can switch from every-day thinking to an analysis mode in which normative principles are more carefully observed. Research by Dunbar [14] hints at this hypothesis.

This latter possibility supports our choice of analysis task. Shorter, more focused tasks like those used in cognitive experiments can be applied to large numbers of users and provide clean data. However, the extent to which they apply to exploratory scientific analysis is far from clear. As noted in the related work section, several studies indicate that there are observable differences between laboratory settings and real scientific or clinical situations.

Ideally our study had tested domain experts in their field of research. However, experts are scarce and the variability in the problems they solve is high. Thus, quantitative studies in real-life scientific settings are difficult to organize. Our choice of task and users approximates a real analytic scenario and lets us collect sufficient data for quantitative testing with the drawback of leaving some questions about result generality unanswered. Can domain experts, who generally follow well established workflows, be nudged as easily as our subjects? Will a high familiarity with an analysis system cause expert subjects to overlook interface nudges?

Similarly, scientific analysis often involves large data and complex visualizations. Our tasks are small by comparison and do not capture some exploratory aspects of data analysis. However, our study focused not on modeling exploratory processes inherent to real analysis but on understanding how users search for evidence and aggregate it into hypotheses. We believe our setup distilled the deliberative aspect of analysis and made results easier to compare across subjects.

CONCLUSION

We presented results from a quantitative user study showing that controlled changes in the interface of an analysis system can be employed to correct deficiencies in users' analytic behavior. Specifically, we altered the design of a basic analysis tool over three analysis sessions to produce three changes in our subjects' analysis. First, subjects were nudged to increase their reliance on the analysis-support module that accompanied the visualization. Second, subjects were nudged to analyze hypotheses in parallel rather than sequentially. Third, subjects were nudged to gather more evidence for their hypotheses. The significance of our work is threefold. First, we show how even the simplest design decisions shape users' analytic behavior. Second, we advance visual analytics by introducing and validating an approach that leverages interfaces to correct analytic biases and heuristics reported by cognitive science. Third, we provide a short overview of analysis workflows and biases and heuristics that our subjects used on a scientifically inspired analysis task.

ACKNOWLEDGMENTS

This work was supported by NIH grant AI072073.

REFERENCES

1. Ames, M., and Naaman, M. Why we tag: motivations for annotation in mobile and online media. In *Proceedings of the SIGCHI Conference on Human factors in Computing Systems*, ACM (2007), 980.
2. Arroyo, E., Bonanni, L., and Selker, T. Waterbot: exploring feedback and persuasive techniques at the sink. In *Proceedings of the SIGCHI Conference on Human factors in Computing Systems*, ACM (2005), 639.
3. Asch, S. Studies of independence and conformity: a minority of one against a unanimous majority. *Psychological monographs 70*, 9 (1956), 1–70.
4. Ben-Shakhar, G., Bar-Hillel, M., Bilu, Y., and Shefler, G. Seek and ye shall find: Test results are what you hypothesize they are. *Journal of Behavioral Decision Making 11*, 4 (1998), 235–249.
5. Bier, E., Card, S., and Bodnar, J. Entity-based collaboration tools for intelligence analysis. In *Visual Analytics Science and Technology, 2008. VAST'08. IEEE Symposium on*, Ieee (2008), 99–106.
6. Bodnar, J. Making sense of massive data by hypothesis testing. In *International Conference on Intelligence Analysis* (2005), 2–4.
7. Bruner, J., and Potter, M. Interference in visual recognition. *Science 144*, 3617 (1964), 424–425.
8. Canas, A., Carff, R., Hill, G., Carvalho, M., Arguedas, M., Eskridge, T., Lott, J., and Carvajal, R. Concept maps: Integrating knowledge and information visualization. *Lecture Notes in Computer Science 3426* (2005), 205.
9. Chartrand, T., and Bargh, J. The chameleon effect: the perception-behavior link and social interaction. *Journal of Personality and Social Psychology 76*, 6 (1999), 893–910.
10. Cialdini, R., and Goldstein, N. Social influence: Compliance and conformity. *Annual Psychology Review 55* (2004), 591–621.
11. Deutsch, M., and Gerard, H. A study of normative and informational social influences upon individual judgment. *Journal of Abnormal and Social Psychology 51*, 3 (1955), 629–636.
12. DuCharme, W. Response bias explanation of conservative human inference. *Journal of Experimental Psychology 85*, 1 (1970), 66–74.

13. Dunbar, K. Concept discovery in a scientific domain. *Cognitive Science 17*, 3 (1993), 397–434.
14. Dunbar, K. What scientific thinking reveals about the nature of cognition. *Designing for science: Implications from Everyday, Classroom, and Professional Settings* (2001), 115–140.
15. Eccles, R., Kapler, T., Harper, R., and Wright, W. Stories in geotime. *Information Visualization 7*, 1 (2008), 3–17.
16. Elstein, A., and Schwarz, A. Clinical problem solving and diagnostic decision making: selective review of the cognitive literature. *Stroke 33* (2002), 493–6.
17. Fogg, B. Persuasive computers: perspectives and research directions. In *Proceedings of the SIGCHI Conference on Human Factors in Computing Systems*, ACM Press/Addison-Wesley Publishing Co. (1998), 225–232.
18. Gotz, D., Zhou, M., and Aggarwal, V. Interactive visual synthesis of analytic knowledge. In *Proceedings of the IEEE Symposium on Visual Analytics Science and Technology* (2006), 51–58.
19. Gray, W., and Fu, W. Soft constraints in interactive behavior: The case of ignoring perfect knowledge in-the-world for imperfect knowledge in-the-head. *Cognitive Science 28*, 3 (2004), 359–382.
20. Green, T., Ribarsky, W., and Fisher, B. Visual analytics for complex concepts using a human cognition model. In *Visual Analytics Science and Technology, 2008. VAST'08. IEEE Symposium on*, IEEE (2008), 91–98.
21. Green, T., Ribarsky, W., and Fisher, B. Building and applying a human cognition model for visual analytics. *Information Visualization 8*, 1 (2009), 1–13.
22. Hastie, R., and Dawes, R. Rational choice in an uncertain world. *Journal of the Indian Academy of Applied Psychology* (2003), 107.
23. Kang, Y., Gorg, C., and Stasko, J. Evaluating visual analytics systems for investigative analysis: Deriving design principles from a case study. In *Visual Analytics Science and Technology, 2009. VAST 2009. IEEE Symposium on*, IEEE (2009), 139–146.
24. Kenrick, D., Maner, J., Butner, J., Li, N., Becker, D., and Schaller, M. Dynamical evolutionary psychology: Mapping the domains of the new interactionist paradigm. *Personality and Social Psychology Review 6*, 4 (2002), 347.
25. Klayman, J., and Ha, Y. Confirmation, disconfirmation, and information in hypothesis testing. *Psychological Review 94*, 2 (1987), 211–228.
26. Klein, G. A recognition-primed decision (rpd) model of rapid decision making. *Decision Making in Action: Models and Methods* (1993), 138–147.
27. Kumar, M., and Kim, T. Dynamic speedometer: dashboard redesign to discourage drivers from speeding. In *CHI'05 Extended Abstracts on Human Factors in Computing Systems*, ACM (2005), 1576.
28. Nov, O. What motivates Wikipedians? *Communications of the ACM 50*, 11 (2007), 64.
29. Oinas-Kukkonen, H., and Harjumaa, M. Towards deeper understanding of persuasion in software and information systems. In *First International Conference on Advances in Computer-Human Interaction*, IEEE (2008), 200–205.
30. Pirolli, P., and Card, S. The sensemaking process and leverage points for analyst technology as identified through cognitive task analysis. In *Proceedings of International Conference on Intelligence Analysis*, vol. 2005 (2005), 2–4.
31. Rodgers, R., and Hunter, J. The discard of study evidence by literature reviewers. *The Journal of Applied Behavioral Science 30*, 3 (1994), 329.
32. Savikhin, A., Maciejewski, R., and Ebert, D. Applied visual analytics for economic decision-making. In *IEEE Symposium on Visual Analytics Science and Technology, 2008. VAST'08* (2008), 107–114.
33. Simon, H. Rationality as process and as product of thought. *The American Economic Review 68*, 2 (1978), 1–16.
34. Stangor, C., Sechrist, G., and Jost, J. Social influence and intergroup beliefs: The role of perceived social consensus. *Social Influence: Direct and Indirect Processes* (2001), 235–252.
35. Stasko, J., Gorg, C., and Liu, Z. Jigsaw: supporting investigative analysis through interactive visualization. *Information Visualization 7*, 2 (2008), 118–132.
36. Sunstein, C., and Thaler, R. Libertarian paternalism is not an oxymoron. *U. Chi. L. Rev. 70* (2003), 1159.
37. Thaler, R., and Benartzi, S. Save More Tomorrow: using behavioral economics to increase employee saving. *Journal of political Economy* (2004), 164–187.
38. Thaler, R., and Sunstein, C. *Nudge: Improving decisions about health, wealth, and happiness*. Yale Univ Pr, 2008.
39. Thomas, J., and Cook, K. Illuminating the path: The research and development agenda for visual analytics. *IEEE Computer Society* (2005).
40. Wason, P. Reasoning about a rule. *The Quarterly Journal of Experimental Psychology 20*, 3 (1968), 273–281.
41. Wright, W., Schroh, D., Proulx, P., Skaburskis, A., and Cort, B. The Sandbox for analysis: concepts and methods. In *Proceedings of the SIGCHI conference on Human Factors in computing systems*, ACM New York, NY, USA (2006), 801–810.
42. Yang, D., Rundensteiner, E., and Ward, M. Nugget discovery in visual exploration environments by query consolidation. In *Proceedings of the sixteenth ACM conference on Conference on information and knowledge management*, ACM New York, NY, USA (2007), 603–612.
43. Experimental data. `http://graphics.cs.brown.edu/research/sciviz/nudge`

Mouse Tracking: Measuring and Predicting Users' Experience of Web-based Content

Vidhya Navalpakkam
Yahoo! Research
nvidhya@yahoo-inc.com

Elizabeth F. Churchill
Yahoo! Research
echu@yahoo-inc.com

ABSTRACT
Previous studies have used mouse tracking as a tool to measure usability of webpages, user attention and search relevance. In this paper, we go beyond measurement of user behavior to *prediction* of the resulting user experience from mouse patterns alone. Specifically, we identify mouse markers that can predict user frustration and reading struggles at reasonably high accuracy. We believe that mouse-based prediction of user experience is an important advance, and could potentially offer a scalable way to infer user experience on the web. In addition, we demonstrate that mouse tracking could be used for applications such as evaluating content layout and content noticeability; we apply this in particular to advertisements. More generally, it could be used to infer user attention in complex webpages containing images, text and varied content, including how attention patterns vary with page layout and user distraction.

Author Keywords
Mouse tracking; web pages; user experience; reading online; attention; distraction; frustration; measurement; prediction; content effectiveness

ACM Classification Keywords
H.5.2 Usability, Accessibility and User Experience

INTRODUCTION
The conventional approach to studying user attention on the web has been through tracking eye-gaze[24]. The pros of this approach are that it offers a direct measure of users overt attention or what they are looking at, it provides detailed data at millisecond resolution, and offers insights into how people consume pages and why they fail to click certain elements (e.g., you cant click what you dont see). The cons are that it is not scalable, it is slow, expensive and does not track user behavior in their natural state at home or work (e.g., behavior may be somewhat different in the lab settings).

In recent years, focus has turned to whether mouse tracking could offer a scalable alternative to eye tracking for measuring usability of webpages, user attention and search relevance. Mouse tracking applications promise the ability to estimate the relevance of search results in the presence or absence of clicks[16, 19] for improving search relevance estimation, to study web usability design [1] and to determine preferred reading regions that help in inferring which portions of long documents receive more user attention[?, 2, 4]. Such applications illustrate the potential of mouse tracking, although to date most applications have focused on measuring user attention in webpages that contain mainly text.

In this paper, we attempt to go beyond measurement of user behavior to generating *predictions* about user experience of web page content from mouse movement patterns alone. We ask: Do users' mouse movements correlate with the user experience of web page content? Can mouse tracks be used to detect user reading struggles or distraction? In addition, we test whether mouse tracking can reveal the distribution of user attention in the face of complex content settings, for example with pages that contain both text and multimedia content such as images and display advertisements (ads). Given most previous work has focused on simple pages containing mostly text, e.g., search engine results pages, our work aims at understanding whether mouse tracking could offer a potentially scalable approach to studying user attention and experience on the web where, increasingly, mutlmedia content is the norm.

Our study makes the following contributions. We find that mouse movement patterns offer rich signals that can predict whether the reading experience of the user is pleasant or not significantly better than chance. More generally, mouse tracking could be used to infer user attention in complex webpages containing both text and multimedia content such as images and display ads, including how attention patterns vary with page layout and user distraction. In addition, we demonstrate that mouse tracking could be used for applications such as evaluating effectiveness of display advertisements (ad layout and ad noticing). In the next sections we describe the related work, our experiments and findings in more detail.

RELATED WORK
Several studies have analyzed eye-mouse coordination, to test whether the mouse could be used as a weak proxy for gaze. For search results pages, the mouse sometimes leads the eye horizontally (which is rare), follows the eye vertically (which is more common), and is often parked at an interesting position (e.g., book marking snippets of information, or indicating a result that has been carefully examined) [26]. Similar to the book marking behavior, in an interactive task where users had to select menu items, the mouse was used to tag interesting targets in menus that were looked at before [7]. Incidental mouse usage has also been observed, where the mouse

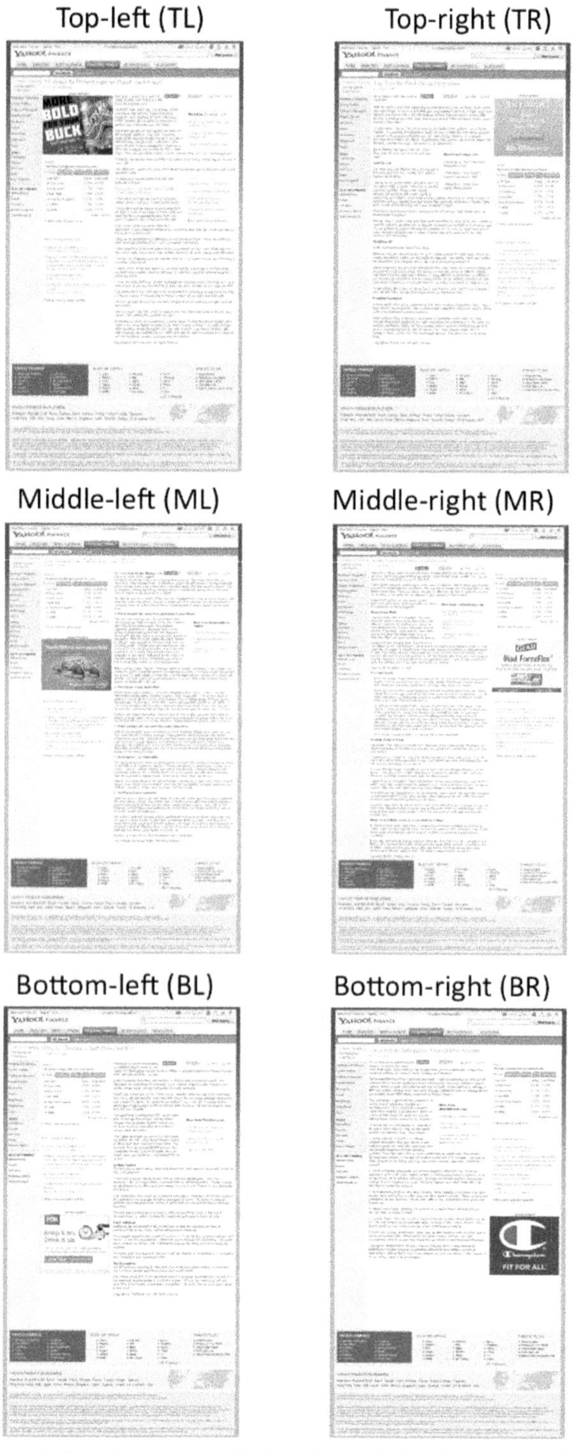

Figure 1. Sample web pages in Experiment 1. Participants saw six article pages from Yahoo! Finance. The pages were heterogeneous and contained rich content with many page elements, including display advertisements (ads), textual content, market watch, mortgage rates, related article links, navigation menu, header and footer. Each page was paired with an ad randomly selected from six popular brands. The ad could appear at one of six different positions on the page, as shown in this figure.

is used for clicking somewhere on page or manipulating the web browser and is less correlated with eye gaze [26].

In a recent study [13], Guo & Agichtein show that with reasonable accuracy (77%), one can predict when and whether eye gaze and mouse position are coordinated and within 100 pixels of each other. This is a promising step towards predicting eye gaze from mouse position. In this paper, we adopt a different approach. Instead of analyzing whether the mouse position is correlated with eye gaze, we ask to what extent is the mouse position sensitive to user task conditions.

Some studies have shown that eye-mouse-attention are correlated while web browsing [6, 25]. According to one study, 35% users moved their mouse while reading web pages [22]. This suggests that the mouse might indicate user focus of attention, and might be used to classify user behavior as reading, skimming, scrolling, thinking, interacting with menus.

Hornbk and Frkjr [?] analyzed the reading behavior of long documents in more detail and explored the effect of different document visualization techniques. They observed by looking at scrolling behavior that documents are sometimes read linearly, sometimes parts are skipped, and sometimes parts are read multiple times. Atterer & Lorenzi [2] use the above ideas to implement a browser plugin that does heatmap visualization and shows the display time beside the browser scrollbar. In another study, Arroyo & colleagues [1] proposed mouseTrack, a usability tool for monitoring and visualizing mouse tracks on web pages, that helps testing webpage design.

A recent study [19] proposed a novel method to perform remote eye tracking at a large scale using mouse tracking. This approach highlighted the search snippet at the current mouse position and blurred the rest of the page. By controlling page visibility using the mouse, this study was able to measure the amount of attention devoted to the different search snippets as a function of position on page, and search relevance. This approach offers a promising way to measure how long users dwell on the page element given that they notice it. One limitation is that due to the distortion of the display resulting in a loss of peripheral visual information, this method does not tell us whether users will notice the page element in the first place.

The above studies show that there has been a big thrust towards investigating whether the mouse can serve as a weak proxy for eye gaze, which is known to be a strong indicator of user attention. These studies identify different types of eye and mouse coordination behavior by computing the Euclidean distance between them in X and Y coordinates. Our approach fundamentally differs from these previous approaches: instead of analyzing distance measures and asking whether the mouse can act as a weak proxy for gaze, we directly investigate whether the mouse is sensitive to task conditions and user attention. In other words, instead of multiple sequential inferences between task/attention → eye gaze, and eye gaze → mouse that lead to increased noise thereby limiting this approach, we directly investigate the relationship between task/attention → mouse.

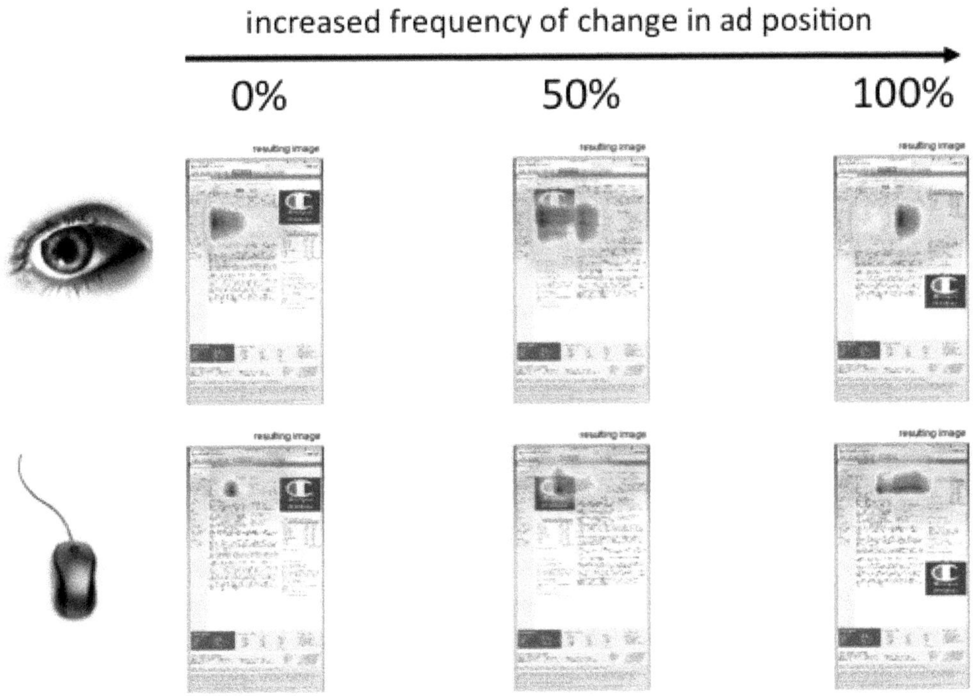

Figure 2. Gaze heatmaps (top) vs. mouse position heatmaps (bottom). As the ad position changes from being fixed at the top-right (frequency of change 0%; leftmost column) to randomly varying across 6 positions on each display (frequency of change 100%; rightmost column), the eye and mouse activity shift from being focused on the top-left to the center of the page.

Apart from web related applications, mouse tracking has also been used to reveal real-time unfolding of underlying cognitive processing in simple language comprehension and decision making tasks. Hand motions, tracked by a mouse, wireless remote or position sensor, have been used to track the evolution of users' commitments to different choice alternatives. For example, Spivey et al. [28] showed that when users were shown a candle on the top-left and a candy on the top-right and asked to 'click the candle' by moving the mouse from the bottom center of the screen, mouse movements were continuously attracted towards the incorrect option before selecting the correct alternative. The amount of attraction towards the incorrect option increases with ambiguity, and similarity between the alternatives. In other words, slow and arched mouse trajectories indicate ambiguity in state of mind during decision-making [12, 20, 10].

Similar effects have been observed with choosing between true and false statements [21, 8], between male and female when shown a sex-typical (masculine male) or sex-atypical face (feminine male) [9], for race categorization [11] and simple perceptual decision-making tasks [27]. These findings suggest that hand movements, such as those tracked by a mouse, are intertwined with mental processing, and therefore, movements that are sampled fast enough could potentially reveal the real-time unfolding of user mental state.

These cognitive studies in language comprehension and decision-making deployed simple, uncluttered displays with a few choice alternatives (mostly 2). It is not known whether mouse movements can reveal the user mental state in more realistic and cluttered display settings such as web pages that contain plenty of text, images and other content.

In this paper, we explore the extent to which mouse tracking can inform us about whether users are attentive to certain content, and what their experience is. Our approach differs from previous work in the following ways: 1) instead of focusing on whether the mouse position correlates with eye gaze (which correlates with attention), we focus on whether the mouse position is sensitive to different task conditions; 2) we consider complex web pages that contain multimedia content including text and images (e.g., display advertisements or ads); 3) we test whether the mouse can inform us about ad noticing and good ad positions on page; 4) we investigate whether the mouse is sensitive to saliency which is known to be an important driving factor of visual attention [18]; 5) we study how the mouse behaves when the user is distracted; and finally, 5) we go beyond measurement of user behavior to prediction of user experience — we identify mouse markers that predict whether the user is distracted, and finds the experience unpleasant.

EXPERIMENT 1 — ATTENTION ON WEB PAGES

Design. The experiment consisted of 3 treatments. Across all treatments, the ad could appear at one of 6 positions on the page top-left, top-right, middle-left, middle-right, bottom-left and bottom-right. Each treatment used a within-participant randomized design with 1 factor, namely the ad position on page. In the 1st treatment, the ad always appeared on the top right of the page. In the 2nd treatment, the ad appeared on the top right in 50% of the displays, and randomly appeared at one of the 5 remaining positions in the other 50% of the displays. In the 3rd treatment, the ad could randomly appear at any position on the page. Thus, the frequency of changing ad position varied from 0 to 50 to 100% between the 3 treatments.

Each participant saw 6 articles from Yahoo! Finance, that were paired with a different ad, and could appear at any of the 6 different page positions. The template of the web pages was fixed except for changes in ad position and reading content. Examples are shown in Fig. 1. A pre-study survey showed participants several ads and asked them to express their level of agreement on whether the ads were familiar, entertaining, effective, interesting, attractive, informative, professional, and whether users were willingness to purchase. 15 ads were shown out of which the top scoring 6 ads were selected. These ads belonged to familiar brands such as Disney, Intel, Glad, Purwater, Champion sports and Brisk drink. These ads were selected to be of similar familiarity and aesthetic appeal.

Apparatus. We recorded participants' gaze patterns during task performance using a Tobii 1750 eye tracker (50Hz sampling frequency), with a 17" LCD monitor, set at resolution 1024×768, at roughly 85 cm viewing distance. Mouse position was also sampled at 50 Hz. We collected a log of eye and mouse movements.

Participants. There were 90 participants aged 19-60, with normal vision (acuity: 20/20 vision, no color blindness) or corrected vision (glasses, contact lenses to restore normal acuity). Participants were randomly assigned to one of the 3 treatments, resulting in 30 participants per treatment.

Procedure. The study began with a 5-point calibration procedure followed by the task-instruction screen. This was followed by 6 reading articles paired with an ad. Participants were instructed to read the articles as they normally would while consuming online content. At the end of the study, participants participated in a Usability Measurement Inventory survey and provided feedback on their user experience. The survey consisted of 21 questions including questions on likelihood of recommending the site to friends; whether the site was mentally stimulating, enjoyable, informative and whether the content was clear; on frequency of usage; whether the experience was frustrating, or disruptive to the way users like to read etc. Answers were provided on a five-point scale (1=strongly agree, 5=strongly disagree).

Data analysis and metrics. The raw mouse and eye tracks were obtained from Tobii 1750 eye tracker. These were tuples of the format: (x, y, t) indicating the x,y coordinate of the mouse/eye and the corresponding timestamp. We parsed these to obtain the (x,y,t) where t is relative to when the page loads. We further parsed the eye tracking data to obtain eye fixations (brief pauses in the eye) and saccades (abrupt jump in eye position) using standard algorithms described in [5]. We extracted measures such as the number of eye fixations, dwell time per fixation, total dwell time, saccade length, amount of re-reading (%fixations that revisit previously read content), saccade length of re-reading (distance by which the eye travels while re-reading). We followed a similar procedure for parsing mouse tracks: we record a mouse visit on a page element (e.g., ad) when the instantaneous mouse position of the mouse lies within that element. We obtain the following measures: number of mouse visits per element, dwell per visit, total dwell time by mouse, distance travelled by the mouse between successive visits, % of mouse revisits to previously read content, distance travelled by the mouse during the revisits.

Results

Attention heat maps

Participants interacted with each page for around 100-120 seconds. Gaze heat maps are a popular way to visualize attention on a page[24]. Fig. 2 visualizes the impact of changing ad position on page. The leftmost column shows the results from treatment 1, where the ad position is fixed at the top-right (frequency of change in ad position 0%). We find that the eye and mouse activity is focused on the top-left of the page, away from the ad. The middle column shows the results from treatment 2, where the ad appears at the top-right on 50% displays, and appears randomly at one of the remaining 5 positions in the other displays (frequency of change in ad position 50%). Here, we find that the eye and mouse activity are still focused on the top-left of the page, and in addition, a weak bias occurs towards the center of the page. The rightmost column shows the results from treatment 3, where the ad position changes randomly on every display (100% frequency of change in ad position). A clear center bias emerges in both the eye and mouse activity, as participants focus their attention away from possible ad positions, and try to focus on where the content is most likely to appear.

Two aspects of the data are striking. First, ad avoidance — participants tend to focus away from the ad, to where the content appears. Second, the similarity between eye and mouse heatmaps — although the mouse heatmap is much sparser, it captures the main trend in eye-gaze which is a shift in attention from top-left to the center of the page as the ad position changes from the top-right to anywhere on the page.

Impact of changing ad layout

We analyzed the data quantitatively to extract various gaze and mouse metrics. Gaze metrics included the number of eye fixations, dwell time per eye fixation, and total gaze time on ad versus content. Mouse metrics were analogous to the gaze metrics, and included the number of mouse visits, dwell time per mouse visit and the total mouse time on ad versus content.

Results show that changing the ad layout frequently impacts the way people engage with the content and with the ad. The right panel of Fig. 3 shows that when the ad position changes frequently, It is noticed 70% sooner by the eye (33 vs. 10 seconds on average), and 60% sooner by the mouse (15 vs. 6 seconds on average) compared to when the position is fixed on the page. These observations are consistent with the ad avoidance issue discussed earlier. When the ad position is fixed, participants tend to avoid the ads and notice them later; but when the ad position changes randomly between displays, it becomes hard to avoid the ads, leading to faster noticing of ads. Based on these results, it is tempting to think that

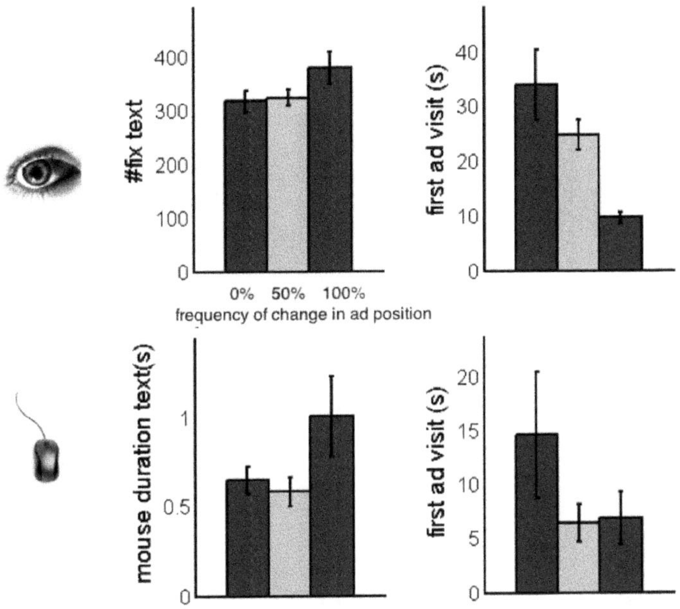

Figure 3. Impact of changing ad layout on eye and mouse movement patterns. When the ad layout changes frequently, it leads to faster noticing of the ads, and comes at the cost of increased processing of the textual content on the page.

changing the ad layout is a desirable strategy for the publisher and advertiser, as it leads to sooner and better ad noticing. However, this strategy comes at a cost.

Time to comprehend the content, as measured by the total time spent by the eye and mouse on the textual content of the page, increases as seen in Fig. 3, left panel. Participants perform 27% more eye fixations, and mouse-dwell 40% longer on the text. This suggests that participants have to *work harder* to process the content when the ad position changes unpredictably, possibly due to increased distraction from the ad. This is further supported by a post-study survey where participants indicate that changing the ad frequently disrupts the way they like to read articles, indicating a negative impact on user experience.

Thus, both the eye and mouse visit the ad sooner and spend more processing the content when the ad position changes frequently.

Attention on ad versus content

We focus on the 3rd treatment for subsequent analysis, as it offers more interesting insights by varying the ad position randomly between displays. We find that participants spend little time on the ad — there are much fewer eye fixations on the ad than content (paired t-test, $t(27)=7.88, p<<0.01$), and the dwell time is lower on the ad ($t(27)=7.82, p<<0.01$), resulting in less than 2% time on ad ($t(27)=9.11, p<<0.01$).

Mouse metrics showed similar patterns, although the differences were smaller than with gaze. The number of mouse positions, the dwell time per position, and total mouse time are significantly lower for the ad than the content (paired t-test results are $t(27)=5.26$, $p<<0.01$; $t(27)=3.82$, $p<<0.01$; $t(27)=8.09$, $p<<0.01$ respectively). Thus, both the eye and mouse show less attention on the ad than the content. Although we find ad avoidance, we do not find any evidence for ad blindness — participants notice the ad, although for much less time than the content.

Ad noticing

For each ad, we determined the time to first eye fixation, and the time to the first mouse visit. We find a strong correlation between how soon the eye and mouse visit the ads (r^2=0.60). Some ads are visited within 25 seconds, while other ads are visited after 50 seconds. Why is there a huge variation in ad noticing? Saliency, discussed below, offers some clues.

Effect of saliency

Several studies have shown that eye gaze is sensitive to saliency [18, 3, 14]. Salient events such as abrupt visual onsets, moving stimuli, and salient image regions such as those with higher color contrast, luminance contrast are known to attract the human eye [30]. All things being equal, salient events draw attention sooner [29, 18]. Thus we hypothesized that salient ads may be fixated earlier by the eye and mouse.

To test this, we used the saliency model of human visual attention[17] to compute the visual saliency of ads used in our study. For each webpage, we computed the corresponding saliency map, and determined what fraction of the page salience is the ad. We call this ad salience. We found a negative correlation between ad salience and the time taken by the eye to first visit the ad (r^2=0.21). Ads with high visual contrast, such as the Champion ad with a big white C on a blue background on a white page (Fig. 1 rightmost column), are salient and visually catchy, and noticed sooner. Ads with low visual contrast, such as the Pur ad with a white background on a white page (Fig. 1 fifth column), are not salient and noticed later. This confirms our hypothesis that the eye is drawn to salient ads sooner than non-salient ads.

Is the mouse sensitive to saliency as well? To test this, we repeated the above analysis using the mouse data. Surprisingly, like eye gaze, the mouse also shows that some ads are visited much sooner than others, and that this is negatively correlated with ad salience (r^2=0.52). To our knowledge, this is the first demonstration that the mouse is sensitive to subtle aspects of attention such as saliency.

Effect of ad position

So far, we have shown that the mouse can tell us much about user attention on page, such as how soon and how well the ad is attended. This prompts us to ask whether the mouse can help us determine which ad positions on page are more effective in drawing attention.

In this study, each brand ad could appear at any of six possible positions on page: top, or middle or, bottom and left or right. We pooled the data by ad position and determined the number of eye fixations, the dwell time per fixation, and the total time on ad as a function of its position. Results are shown in Fig. 4. A 1-way repeated measures ANOVA shows a main effect of ad position on #fixations on ad ($F(5,145)=21.28, p<<0.01$), dwell time per fixation ($F(5,145)=26.37, p<<0.01$), and total time on ad ($F(5,145)=22.08, p<<0.01$). In particular, the number of fixations on the ad is at least 67% higher when it

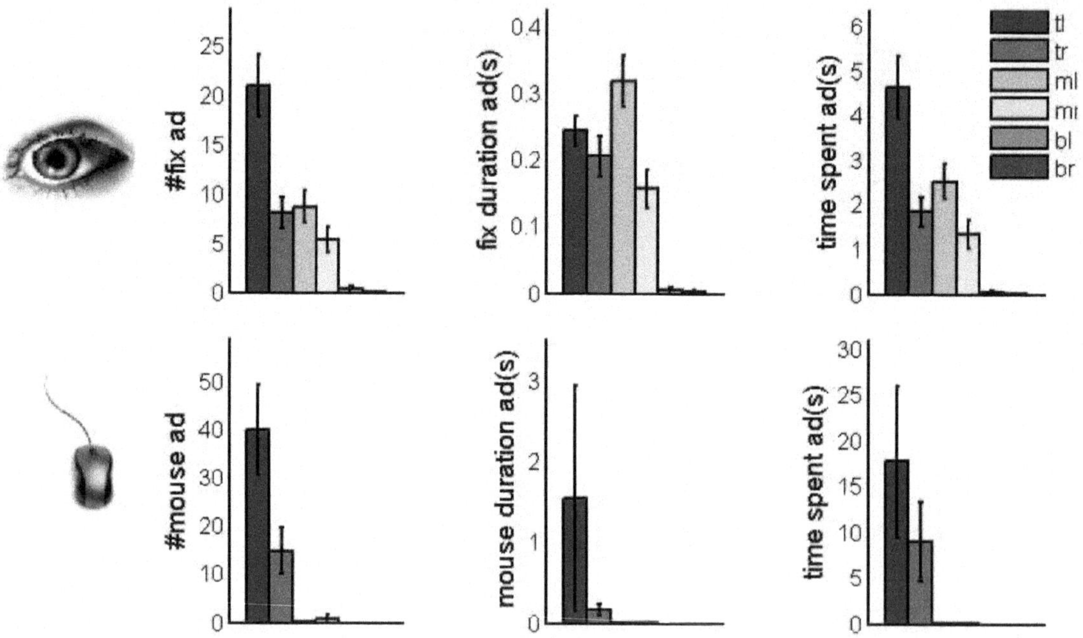

Figure 4. Impact of ad position on eye and mouse movement patterns. When the ad appears at the top of the page, it draws more eye fixations and mouse visits than when the ad appears at the middle or the bottom page positions. When the ad appears at the left of the page, it draws more eye fixations and mouse visits than when it appears at the right. Similar preference for top and left positions is observed with the time spent by the eye and mouse on the ad (per visit, and compounded over all visits).

appears at the top left than at other page positions. Similarly, the ad is noticed at least 77% longer.

Further analysis shows that the top position gets double the number of fixations as the middle position, which receives 35 times more fixations than the bottom position (top: 14.4+-1.3, middle: 7.1+-1.2 , bottom: 0.2+-1.2). Similarly, time on ad also decreases from top to mid to bottom (top: 3.2+-0.3s, middle: 1.9+-0.3, bottom: 0.02+-0.3). we also find that they left ad position draws double the number of fixations and dwell time as the right (#fixations on the left: 10+-1.2, right: 4.5+-1.2; dwell time on the left: 2.5+-0.3s, right: 1.1+-0.3s). These findings demonstrate that the ad is noticed better at certain page positions than others.

To test whether the mouse is sensitive to ad position, we repeated the above analysis on the mouse data. We analyzed the number of mouse positions on the ad, dwell time per position and the total mouse time on ad as a function of ad position on page. The results are strikingly similar to that of gaze. We find that the top ad position draws the mouse more often and for longer time than the middle or bottom (#mouse visits decrease from 27.4+-3 at top to 0.5+-3 at mid and 0+-3 at bottom, and mouse dwell decreases from 13.3+-2.7 at top to 0+-2.7 at mid and 0+-3 at bottom). Similarly, the left ad position is better than right (#mouse visits decrease from 13.5+-3 at left to 5.3+-3 at right, and mouse dwell decreases from 6+-2.3 to 3+-2.3). This shows that the mouse can be used to infer good ad layouts.

EXPERIMENT 2 — EFFECT OF DISTRACTION

So far, we have shown that mouse tracking can enable measurement of user attention on webpages, including the distribution of attention on ad versus content, and in evaluating ad noticing and ad layouts. Next we ask whether most tracks can enable prediction of user mental state, such as whether the user is distracted or frustrated and struggling to read. To test this we design another experiment.

Design. The experiment consisted of a within-participant randomized design with 3 factors: no distraction, medium distraction and high distraction created by presenting no graphics, static graphics and animated graphics. Each participant saw 3 essays (from the Test of English Language Fluency), that were randomly paired with one of the graphic types. Each essay consisted of 300-400 words, followed by 5 factual/theme-based multiple-choice questions, and 2 subjective questions where participants were asked to rate their user experience on a scale of 1-5 for interestingness and pleasantness (e.g., 1 for least pleasant and 5 for most pleasant).

Apparatus. We recorded participants' gaze patterns during task performance using a Tobii 1750 eye tracker (50Hz sampling frequency), with a 17" LCD monitor, set at resolution 1024x768, at roughly 85 cm viewing distance. We collected a log of eye and mouse movement.

Participants. There were 20 participants aged 19-60, with normal visual acuity. Participants were paid $1 for every correct answer (5 questions per essay x 3 essays). During data cleaning, 3 participants were excluded due to poor calibration (inability to maintain stable head position, 2 participants), or

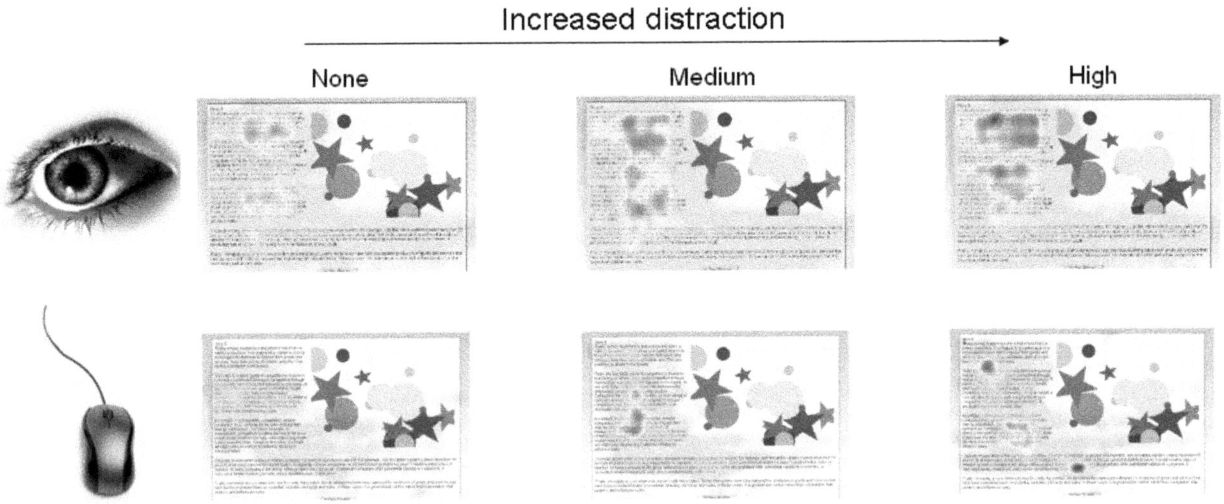

Figure 5. Impact of distraction on eye and mouse movement patterns. Both eye gaze and mouse position heatmaps show higher activity on the textual content as the level of distraction increases, indicating that users had to work harder to comprehend the content under distraction.

outliers in fixation duration or number of fixations (3 standard deviations, 1 participant).

Procedure. The study began with a 5-point calibration procedure followed by the task-instruction screen. Participants were instructed to read the articles as they normally would while consuming online content. The instruction was followed by one practice essay paired with animated graphics to help participants familiarize themselves with the task, types of graphics and the format of the questions in the reading-comprehension test. Next, participants saw the 3 essays randomly paired with no, static or animated graphics. At the conclusion of the study, participants were paid based on their performance.

Results

Effect of distraction

As the distraction level increases, we found that participants struggle to read the text. The average dwell time on page is around 140 seconds, but participants take longer to comprehend the text under distraction (at least 25ms more per word). They also perform more eye fixations, of longer durations, and with increased revisits to previously read content. The gaze patterns were analyzed in our previous paper[23]. Here, we focus on mouse behavior.

Is the mouse behavior different under distraction? Fig. 5 shows increased eye gaze and mouse activity on the reading content as the level of distraction increases, consistent with the hypothesis that users struggle to read under distraction. To test this quantitatively, we analyzed ten different mouse related metrics, that were analogous to the gaze related metrics. These included six metrics on the text the number of mouse positions, dwell time per position, total time the mouse spent on the text, the distance between successive mouse positions, how frequently the mouse revisits previously visited content (%re-reading by mouse), and the length of these the visits (in pixels). In addition there were four metrics on the ad the number of mouse positions, dwell time per position,

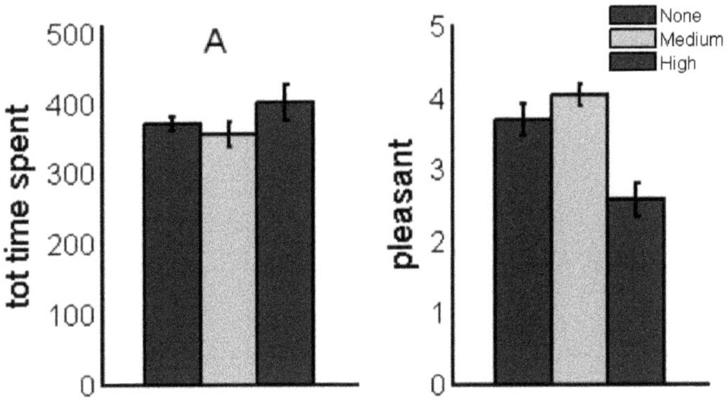

Figure 6. As the level of distraction increases from none to medium to high, the total dwell time on the page (measured in milliseconds/word) increases. This is accompanied by a significant drop in the reported pleasantness scores.

total time spent by the mouse on the ad, and the time to first visit the ad. We analyzed how these metrics varied with distraction. Results are shown in Fig. 6.

Although none of these metrics showed any strong differences (1-way repeated measures ANOVA shows $p>0.05$), we found that as the distraction level increases from none to high, the mouse spends an a average of 25% more time processing the text, with 27% more mouse positions on the text and 26% longer dwell time per position, and 10% more mouse revisits to previously read content, which tends to be nearby than farther away. Also, we found that ads are visited 40% sooner as well as rejected 77% sooner under high levels of distraction. These trends are similar to those observed in gaze patterns, although none of these differences are significant.

Predicting user experience

Next we ask a more ambitious question. Can the mouse reveal the user's mental state, if so to what extent? As a first step, we test whether we can we infer when and whether the user is distracted and struggling to read. In this study, at the end of reading each article, participants reported their experience on a 5-point scale (1 being not at all pleasant, and 5 being very pleasant). We collapsed the 5-point scale to a binary measure of whether user experience was pleasant or not (ratings>3 denoting somewhat pleasant and very pleasant are considered 'pleasant', and the rest are considered 'not pleasant').

We fed all ten mouse related metrics as inputs to a decision tree classifier, with a binary output variable indicating whether the user experience was pleasant or not. We used a 'leave one out' cross validation procedure. Results show that the mouse can predict pleasantness experience 15% better than chance. The most predictive mouse metrics are the mouse dwell time on text (per visit) at 75%, the time to first graphic visit at 73%, the number of mouse visits on text at 70%, and the time on graphic at 67%. In simpler words, longer and frequent mouse visits on text, and quick visitation and rejection of graphics by mouse are strong predictors of an unpleasant user experience. This demonstrates that the mouse can signal not just user attention on page, but also the net user experience.

In a previous study, we asked a related question — whether gaze patterns could predict the pleasantness of user experience. We found that under high levels of distraction, participants noticed the graphic earlier and rejected it quicker; and they spend more time processing the text, indicated by increased number of eye fixations, more time on text, and increased number of revisits to previously read content. Using a similar approach as above (decision tree classifier with gaze metrics), we found that we could predict user experience up to 80% accuracy (20% above chance). The most predictive metrics were the amount of revisits to previously read content at 75% and time to first visit on the graphic at 70%.

These findings show that both eye gaze and mouse patterns contain surprisingly rich information about the user state, such as whether the user is distracted and struggling to read.

DISCUSSION

The conventional approach to studying user attention in complex web pages (containing images, text and varied content) uses eye tracking as the main methodology. Eye tracking offers rich detail about overt attention at the millisecond resolution. But it is expensive, not scalable, and involves lab settings that may not reflect the natural environment of consumption of the user. In order to understand user attention in natural settings, previous studies have focused on whether the mouse can act as a weak proxy for gaze, which in turn is a proxy for attention. Thus, several recent studies have focused on analyzing eye mouse coordination behavior, and in attempting to predict eye gaze from mouse position. While this is a promising direction, it is limited as the eye and mouse are often not correlated (few people read with their mouse).

Previous work on mouse tracking has focused on 2 aspects of to users' activities on the Internet — 1) as a tool to understand web page usability, and 2) to understand users' behavior when presented with pages of search engine results. The latter has received more attention recently, in the form of studies that have focused on, for example, analysis of eye-mouse coordination behavior, prediction of eye gaze from mouse movement, using mouse tracks to estimate / improve search relevance and studies of mouse movements immediately prior to web page abandonment. The web pages considered in these studies have contained mostly text. However, increasingly, the majority of web pages that users encounter when surfing the Internet present heterogeneous content, containing a mixture of images (display ads, pictures), text and other content. In this paper, we ask: What can mouse tracking tell us about user attention when dealing with web pages filled with multimedia content?

Our approach fundamentally differs from previous work. Instead of an indirect, multi-step approach of understanding how mouse position relates to eye gaze and how eye gaze relates to attention, we use a direct, one-step approach of understanding how mouse position relates to attention, and how it is affected by various task conditions such as different levels of distraction, and different page layouts. We find that this approach is fruitful, and we report the 3 main findings: 1) not only can mouse tracks be used to measure user attention, but they can also be used to predict the overall experience of the user, such as whether the user is frustrated and is struggling to read; 2) mouse tracking can reveal the focus of user attention on the page, including how user attention changes due to distraction and with changes in page layout; 3) mouse tracking can serve as a novel tool to evaluate ad content impact (and potentially effectiveness, where content retention is the goal) by providing information on the speed and intensity of content noticing, and offering insights into what forms of content layout draw more attention in the form of mouse dwells.

It is known that there is variability in mouse usage; passive users don't move the mouse much except to click and scroll, active users follow the eye with the mouse and some others use the mouse to track content as they consume it. Yet we find in our study that mouse tracking can capture important trends in user attention. For example, in the first study, as the content (the display ad) position changes from being fixed at the top right of the page to appearing anywhere on the page, eye gaze patterns shift from being focused on the top left of the page to the center of the page. Interestingly, mouse patterns show a similar trend, although the mouse heatmaps are sparser than the eye gaze heatmaps. In the second study, as the amount of user distraction (due to the image) increases, we find that users have to work harder to comprehend the reading content. This extra effort is reflected in the corresponding eye gaze heatmaps which show increased eye fixations and longer dwell time on the reading content. Again, we find a corresponding pattern with mouse tracks.

Despite the wide variability in mouse usage between users, it is impressive that the mouse movement patterns capture the main trends in attention and its distribution in pages containing multimedia content. We speculate that with enough users and at large scale, otherwise sparse mouse heatmaps may begin to resemble the high density eye gaze heatmaps obtained from a few users. We did not find significant differences between active and passive users on the main findings in this study. Future work will explore this issue in detail at larger scale.

We demonstrate potential applications for mouse tracking using display ads as an example. We show that the mouse is sensitive to subtle aspects of attention such as the visual catchiness of the content, or visual saliency [18]. For example, ads with high visual contrast such as a big white logo on a blue background are visually salient and are noticed sooner by the eye and mouse. On the other hand, ads with low visual contrast such as small gray logo on a white background are not salient and are noticed later by the eye and mouse. In addition to providing insights on ad noticing, mouse tracking can be used to evaluate good ad layouts that draw more mouse dwells (and eyeballs). These findings suggest that mouse tracking could serve as a valuable tool to evaluate ad effectiveness (ad noticing, ad layout) in a scalable way.

Finally, we go beyond measurement of user behavior to *prediction* of the end user experience — we demonstrate that mouse movement patterns can predict whether the experience of a user is perceived as pleasant or not. Like eye gaze, we found that the mouse is also sensitive to user distraction. We found that early visits on the distractor image, quick rejection of the distractor image, longer mouse dwell time on text, and increased number of mouse positions on text are the most informative mouse related signals that can predict user distraction and frustration significantly better (+15%) than chance. These findings show that mouse movement patterns contain useful signals about the user mental state and experience, such as whether the user is struggling to read and is therefore frustrated. We believe that such mouse-based prediction of user experience is an important advance, and could potentially offer a scalable way to infer user experience on the web. Potential applications of this include designing adaptive interfaces that perform online detection of user reading struggles and tune the interface to minimize the struggle and enhance the pleasantness of user experience.

To summarize, in this paper, we demonstrate that mouse tracks can provide valuable information about user attention and experience in complex webpages containing both images and text. The current findings are from lab studies involving 20 to 90 participants. Future work will involve testing these findings at larger scale, and in determining differences due to age, gender and other factors, which are beyond the scope of this paper. The findings reported in this study are obtained from users consuming content via desktop PCs using a mouse. While this is currently the most popular way of consuming content, newer technologies such as touch screens and track pads are increasingly becoming popular. Thus another interesting direction for future work will be to explore whether and how mouse tracks on touch screens and track pads relate to user attention and experience.

CONCLUSION

The state-of-the-art in mouse tracking involves measurement of user behavior to understand web page usability, search relevance and page abandonment. In this paper, we go beyond measurement of user behavior to *prediction* of the resulting user experience from mouse patterns alone. Specifically, we identify mouse markers that can predict user frustration and reading struggles significantly better than chance. In addition, we demonstrate that mouse tracking could be used for applications such as evaluating ad layout and ad noticing. More generally, it could be used to infer user attention in complex webpages containing images, text and varied content, including how attention patterns vary with page layout and user distraction. These findings suggest that mouse tracking could potentially offer a scalable way to infer user attention and experience on the web.

Acknowledgements

We thank Michael Bartholomew, Lisa Guy and Prasad Kantamneni for providing us with the data for experiment 1. We thank Justin Rao and Malcolm Slaney for helping with experiment 2. We also thank Fernando Diaz for useful discussions.

REFERENCES

1. E. Arroyo, T. Selker, and W. Wei. Usability tool for analysis of web designs using mouse tracks. In *CHI'06 extended abstracts on Human factors in computing systems*, pages 484–489. ACM, 2006.
2. R. Atterer and P. Lorenzi. A heatmap-based visualization for navigation within large web pages. In *Proceedings of the 5th Nordic conference on Human-computer interaction: building bridges*, pages 407–410. ACM, 2008.
3. N. Bruce and J. Tsotsos. Saliency based on information maximization. *Advances in neural information processing systems*, 18:155, 2006.
4. G. Buscher, R. Biedert, D. Heinesch, and A. Dengel. Eye tracking analysis of preferred reading regions on the screen. In *Proceedings of the 28th of the international conference extended abstracts on Human factors in computing systems*, CHI EA '10, pages 3307–3312, New York, NY, USA, 2010. ACM.
5. G. Buscher, E. Cutrell, and M. Morris. What do you see when you're surfing?: using eye tracking to predict salient regions of web pages. In *Proceedings of the 27th international conference on Human factors in computing systems*, pages 21–30. ACM, 2009.
6. M. Chen, J. Anderson, and M. Sohn. What can a mouse cursor tell us more?: correlation of eye/mouse movements on web browsing. In *CHI'01 extended abstracts on Human factors in computing systems*, pages 281–282. ACM, 2001.
7. A. Cox and M. Silva. The role of mouse movements in interactive search. In *Proceedings of the 28th Annual Meeting of the Cognitive Science Society*, pages 1156–1161, 2006.
8. N. Duran, R. Dale, and D. McNamara. The action dynamics of overcoming the truth. *Psychonomic bulletin & review*, 17(4):486–491, 2010.
9. J. Freeman and N. Ambady. Motions of the hand expose the partial and parallel activation of stereotypes. *Psychological Science*, 20(10):1183–1188, 2009.

10. J. Freeman, R. Dale, and T. Farmer. Hand in motion reveals mind in motion. *Frontiers in Psychology*, 2, 2011.
11. J. Freeman, K. Pauker, E. Apfelbaum, and N. Ambady. Continuous dynamics in the real-time perception of race. *Journal of Experimental Social Psychology*, 46(1):179–185, 2010.
12. J. Goldberg, M. Stimson, M. Lewenstein, N. Scott, and A. Wichansky. Eye tracking in web search tasks: design implications. In *Proceedings of the 2002 symposium on Eye tracking research & applications*, pages 51–58. ACM, 2002.
13. Q. Guo and E. Agichtein. Towards predicting web searcher gaze position from mouse movements. In *Proceedings of the 28th of the international conference extended abstracts on Human factors in computing systems*, pages 3601–3606. ACM, 2010.
14. J. Harel, C. Koch, and P. Perona. Graph-based visual saliency. *Advances in neural information processing systems*, 19:545, 2007.
15. K. Hornbæk and E. Frøkjær. Reading patterns and usability in visualizations of electronic documents. *ACM Transactions on Computer-Human Interaction (TOCHI)*, 10(2):119–149, 2003.
16. J. Huang, R. White, and S. Dumais. No clicks, no problem: using cursor movements to understand and improve search. In *Proceedings of the 2011 annual conference on Human factors in computing systems*, pages 1225–1234. ACM, 2011.
17. L. Itti and C. Koch. A saliency-based search mechanism for overt and covert shifts of visual attention. *Vision research*, 40(10-12):1489–1506, 2000.
18. L. Itti and C. Koch. Computational modelling of visual attention. *Nat Rev Neurosci*, 2(3):194–203, Mar 2001.
19. D. Lagun and E. Agichtein. Viewser: enabling large-scale remote user studies of web search examination and interaction. In *Proceedings of the 34th international ACM SIGIR conference on Research and development in Information*, pages 365–374. ACM, 2011.
20. J. Magnuson. Moving hand reveals dynamics of thought. *Proceedings of the National Academy of Sciences of the United States of America*, 102(29):9995, 2005.
21. C. McKinstry, R. Dale, and M. Spivey. Action dynamics reveal parallel competition in decision making. *Psychological Science*, 19(1):22, 2008.
22. F. Mueller and A. Lockerd. Cheese: tracking mouse movement activity on websites, a tool for user modeling. In *CHI'01 extended abstracts on Human factors in computing systems*, pages 279–280. ACM, 2001.
23. V. Navalpakkam, J. Rao, and M. Slaney. Using gaze patterns to study and predict reading struggles due to distraction. In *Proceedings of the 2011 annual conference extended abstracts on Human factors in computing systems*, pages 1705–1710. ACM, 2011.
24. J. Nielsen and K. Pernice. *Eyetracking web usability*. New Riders Pub, 2009.
25. B. Pan, H. Hembrooke, G. Gay, L. Granka, M. Feusner, and J. Newman. The determinants of web page viewing behavior: an eye-tracking study. In *Proceedings of the 2004 symposium on Eye tracking research & applications*, pages 147–154. ACM, 2004.
26. K. Rodden, X. Fu, A. Aula, and I. Spiro. Eye-mouse coordination patterns on web search results pages. In *CHI'08 extended abstracts on Human factors in computing systems*, pages 2997–3002. ACM, 2008.
27. J. Song and K. Nakayama. Hidden cognitive states revealed in choice reaching tasks. *Trends in cognitive sciences*, 13(8):360–366, 2009.
28. M. Spivey, M. Grosjean, and G. Knoblich. Continuous attraction toward phonological competitors. *Proceedings of the National Academy of Sciences of the United States of America*, 102(29):10393, 2005.
29. A. Treisman and G. Gelade. A feature integration theory of attention. *Cognitive Psychology*, 12:97–136, 1980.
30. J. Wolfe and T. Horowitz. What attributes guide the deployment of visual attention and how do they do it? *Nature Reviews Neuroscience*, 5(6):495–501, 2004.

Evaluating the Benefits of Real-time Feedback in Mobile Augmented Reality with Hand-held Devices

Can Liu[1,2,3] Stéphane Huot[2,3] Jonathan Diehl[1] Wendy E. Mackay[3,2] Michel Beaudouin-Lafon[2,3]
{can.liu , jonathan.diehl}@rwth-aachen.de {huot , mackay , mbl}@lri.fr

[1] RWTH Aachen University 52056 Aachen, Germany
[2] Univ Paris-Sud & CNRS (LRI) F-91405 Orsay, France
[3] INRIA F-91405 Orsay, France

ABSTRACT
Augmented Reality (AR) has been proved useful to guide operational tasks in professional domains by reducing the shift of attention between instructions and physical objects. Modern smartphones make it possible to use such techniques in everyday tasks, but raise new challenges for the usability of AR in this context: small screen, occlusion, operation "through a lens". We address these problems by adding real-time feedback to the AR overlay. We conducted a controlled experiment comparing AR with and without feedback, and with standard textual and graphical instructions. Results show significant benefits for mobile AR with feedback and reveals some problems with the other techniques.

Author Keywords
Augmented Reality; Hand-held Devices; Real-time Feedback.

ACM Classification Keywords
H.5.1 Information Interfaces and Presentation: Multimedia Information Systems—*Artificial, augmented, and virtual realities*

INTRODUCTION
Augmented Reality (AR) techniques have been used to assist workers in complex tasks such as assembly [7] or maintenance [3] by overlaying localized instructions onto physical objects with a Head Mounted Display (HMD). But casual users may also need guidance when using common appliances: *"How do I set this washing machine for this cloth?"* While the use of a HMD is impractical for daily activities, recent smartphones can be used for "Mobile Augmented Reality" applications and provide in-place guidance anywhere and for everyone (Fig. 1).

Manipulating objects while following instructions is an "Alternating Attention" task [6] that requires to switch between two complementary sub-tasks. In our context, notes and instructions are usually made of plain text or pictures to be interpreted before operating the device. Text instructions

Figure 1. Hand-held AR instructions for entering a code on a keypad.

require an additional level of interpretation than pictures to map the descriptions to actual objects. Conversely, pictures provide a better spatial mapping to retrieve physical objects but require annotations to convey additional information, e.g., how to operate a control, which value to use for a setting. In both cases, when instructions are long or complex, repeatedly switching between sub-tasks can be highly demanding for the user as it requires memorizing instructions, visually finding the objects of interest, retrieving the next instruction, etc.

For such tasks, AR techniques combine the advantages of text and pictures as they ease the localization of physical objects by displaying additional "in-place" information [3]. This should improve user performance by reducing task switching and alternating attention. However, occlusions from the AR layer and the user's hand while interacting with physical objects may offset this benefit. This is even more likely with hand-held devices, due to their small size.

In order to take full advantage of mobile AR for instruction tasks, we propose to provide real-time feedback of actions in the physical world directly in the AR layer. Combining instructions and real-time status of physical objects on top of the camera input, e.g., the status of a button or the position of a knob, solves the occlusion problem and should enable interaction through the device screen, thus minimizing task-switching. After discussing related work, the rest of this paper presents a mobile AR prototype with feedback (AR+F) and a study that assesses the advantages of this approach.

RELATED WORK
The benefits of AR for assisting operational tasks have been evaluated in different contexts. Feiner et al. demonstrated the concept in their early KARMA system [1]. Tang et al. compared the efficiency of a HMD-based AR system in an object-assembly task with printed manual and overlaid instructions

on a LCD display [7]. They found that AR instructions reduce error rate and cognitive effort, suggesting that AR assists mental transformation and minimizes attention switching. In the context of vehicle maintenance, Henderson and Feiner showed that a HMD AR system helps to retrieve the object of interest and also assists the psychomotor phase of procedural tasks better than static 3D instructions on a monitor [3].

Using mobile devices for see-through AR in operational tasks has received less attention. Hakkarainen et al. describe a mobile AR system for assembly tasks [2] that displays sequences of image in adjusted real-world perspective. AAR [5] uses a similar approach by displaying pre-rendered animations on a location-tracked tablet-PC to learn a complex machine.

Providing real-time AR feedback of physical actions in the real world has received little attention so far. Apart from Kotranza et al's Mixed-Reality medical learning system where students receive real-time feedback about their actions [4] and Henderson and Feiner's work [3], we are not aware of other similar work in Mobile AR nor of any empirical study about the effectiveness of this approach.

In summary, most studies have focused on specialized tasks with expert or specialized users and with specific devices (HMD). While they demonstrate the potential of AR, its benefits for everyday manipulation of physical appliances by casual users with standard mobile devices, with or without real-time feedback, remain to be demonstrated.

AR WITH REAL-TIME FEEDBACK PROTOTYPE

Providing real-time feedback in mobile AR applications raises technical issues that require state-of-the-art technologies in ubiquitous computing and computer vision, whether the manipulated objects and the mobile device are connected or not. We can expect such technologies to be available on mobile phones in the near future. In the mean time, and since our primary objective is to evaluate and understand the benefits of this approach, we built an ad-hoc prototype based on a generic controller that communicates with a mobile device.

We use a JLCooper CS-10[2] MIDI control station (Fig. 2) that features controls commonly found on physical appliances (buttons, knobs, sliders and a jog wheel). The mobile application runs on a HTC Desire mobile phone running Android 2.3. We use the NyARToolkit[1] for tracking fiducial markers attached to the control panel. Data from the controller (the values of the controls) is transmitted in real-time to the mobile application through the MIDI and OSC protocols.

When the mobile phone recognizes a marker, it displays an AR layer on top of the real-time camera image with outlines of the physical controls and in-place instructions to perform the task, e.g. a value to enter or a button to press. The user can move the controls while looking through the phone. A color overlay provides real-time visual feedback: if the user is expected to set slider 3, a red bar indicates the value to dial (Fig. 2c&d). Once she moves the correct slider to the correct value, the bar turns blue (Fig. 2d). If she uses the wrong control, its outline turns purple.

[1] `http://nyatla.jp/nyartoolkit/wiki/index.php`

ASSESSING MOBILE AR FOR OPERATING INSTRUCTIONS

We conducted a controlled experiment to assess the benefits of hand-held mobile augmented reality instructions for manipulating physical devices, with or without real-time feedback. Participants were asked to perform tasks of variable difficulty using our prototype. In addition to *Augmented Reality* (AR) and *Augmented Reality + Feedback* (AR+F), we also tested *Text* and *Picture* instructions as control.

Based on previous studies and our experience with the prototype, our hypotheses are:

- *H1:* With respect to speed, (a) AR+F outperforms AR; (b) AR+F and AR outperform Text and Picture; (c) Performance differences increase with task difficulty.
- *H2:* AR techniques are less error-prone and facilitate the correction of errors.
- *H3:* AR+F instructions are preferred to Text, Pictures and AR instructions by users.

Participants. We recruited twelve men and four women, all right-handed, age between 24 and 44. None of them had any experience with augmented reality applications, but four were frequent users of surface controllers, e.g., mixing consoles or guitar amplifiers, and nine owned a smart phone.

Apparatus. Settings were performed on the controller of our prototype and the instructions were displayed on a HTC Desire mobile phone (display: 3.7 inches, resolution: 480×800 px, weight: 135 g, dimensions: $119 \times 60 \times 11.9$ mm), running Android 2.3. Text and Picture instructions were displayed with standard Android widgets and AR techniques were performed with our prototype. We used 10 buttons, 6 knobs and 8 faders of the controller, which was covered with white paper to hide the other controls and display AR markers (Fig. 2).

Design and Procedure

The experiment is a [4×3] within-subject design with two factors: TECHNIQUE (*Text*, *Picture*, *AR*, *AR+F*) and DIFFICULTY (*Easy*, *Medium*, *Hard*). A trial is a "setting" task requiring participants to set the controls on the panel as instructed by the corresponding TECHNIQUE on the mobile device, in any order. Once done, participants are asked to press a hardware button on the device. In case of failure, they are asked to continue the trial and correct the setting until they succeed or a timeout occurs. At the end of the trial, the participants reset the controller and rest in a default position in front of the panel before starting the next trial.

Instructions for each Technique.
– *Text* instructions are displayed with a control-value pair on each line (Fig. 2a), as in mobile note-taking apps. To avoid a potential order effect inherent to linear presentations, the order of lines is randomized across participants.
– *Picture* instructions are presented with a 1024×537 pixels image of the expected setting (Fig. 2b). The picture is initially fully visible and participants can pan and zoom to get a better view of the controls.
– *AR* displays vector graphics on top of the camera input and highlights every control of the panel (Fig. 2c). Controls that must be set appear in red together with the target value.

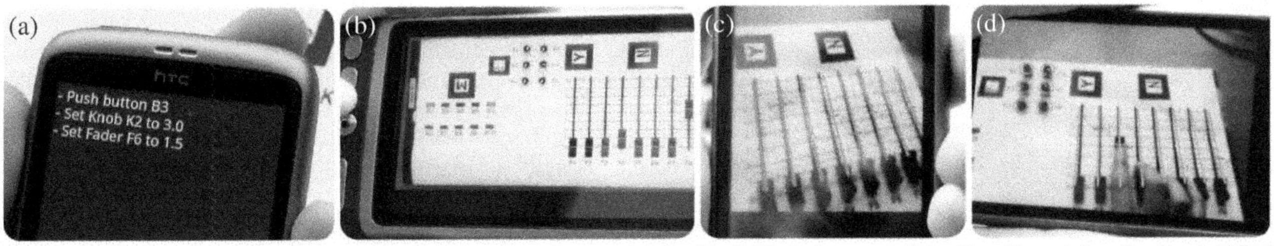

Figure 2. Setting instructions methods: a) Text. b) Picture. c) Augmented Reality (AR). d) Augmented Reality with real-time Feedback (AR+F).

– *AR+F* is similar to *AR* but updates in real-time as controls are manipulated by the user (Fig. 2d): the current value of the manipulated control is displayed next to it and the overlay turns blue once set to the correct value.

Settings and Difficulty. Each setting task includes three types of controls – buttons, knobs and sliders – and its difficulty is determined by the total number of controls to manipulate. For each type of controls, the range of possible values is (i) 0 or 1 for buttons, (ii) 1 to 5 for knobs and (iii) 1 to 7 for sliders, both with a 0.5 interval for the latter two.

To ensure that the number of controls to manipulate in a setting is the only parameter affecting difficulty, the following rules are used to randomly generate each setting: (i) each control is used at most once; (ii) the number of controls of each type is balanced; (iii) the values of continuous controls are balanced (same number of low, medium and high values).

We conducted an informal pilot study with two participants and six difficulty levels (3, 6, 9, 12, 15, 18 controls) to validate these rules and determine appropriate difficulty levels for the study. It suggested that settings with the same number of controls are equivalent in terms of performance and that three levels of difficulty are sufficient: 3 controls for *Easy*, 9 for *Medium*, 18 for *Hard*, with timeouts of 2, 4, and 6 minutes.

Finally, to avoid learning effects, we generated several random settings for each difficulty level and counterbalanced these settings across participants so that none of them perform the same setting twice during the experiment.

Procedure. Trials are grouped into blocks according to TECHNIQUE and each TECHNIQUE × DIFFICULTY condition is replicated twice. The four techniques are introduced to the participants at the beginning of the experiment. Participants perform practice trials with a low difficulty level until they feel comfortable with each technique and the control panel. Then, they perform one *recall* trial prior to each new TECHNIQUE. The presentation order for TECHNIQUE and DIFFICULTY is counterbalanced across participants using a Latin square. This design results in (4 × TECHNIQUE) × (3 × DIFFICULTY) × (2 replications) × (16 × PARTICIPANT) = 384 measured trials.

Each session lasted about 40–50 minutes, after which participants where asked to rank each technique in general and for each difficulty level.

Data Collection. We collected: (i) *TrialTime*, the trial completion time; (ii) *ReactionTime*, the time from the appearance of the instructions to the first action of the participant on the controller; (iii) *Errors*, the number of errors by trial, i.e. the number of times a wrong setting was validated during a trial.

Results and Discussion

We removed 3.03% outliers (trials with a total time greater than two standard deviations from the mean) and performed a full-factorial analysis TECHNIQUE×DIFFICULTY×Random(PARTICIPANT) with the REML technique for repeated measures and Tukey HSD for post-hoc tests.

H1: Which Technique Performs Best?

We found a significant effect of TECHNIQUE ($F_{3,45} = 45.61$, $p < 0.0001$) and DIFFICULTY ($F_{2,30} = 299.83$, $p < 0.0001$) and a significant TECHNIQUE×DIFFICULTY interaction effect ($F_{6,90} = 27.59$, $p < 0.0001$) on *TrialTime*. As expected, *TrialTime* increases with DIFFICULTY and all difficulty levels are significantly different (*Easy* = 11.8s, *Medium* = 28.4s, *Hard* = 56s). For TECHNIQUE, *AR+F* (23.9s) is significantly faster than all other techniques, and *Text* (43.9s) is significantly slower (*AR*= 29.4s and *Picture*= 31.1s). This result supports most of *H1a&b* as *AR* outperforms *Text* but not *Picture*.

The small difference in performance between *AR* and *Picture* could be explained by the screen resolution and the graphical occlusions by the hand that hinder manipulation while looking through the device's screen, reducing the potential benefit of displaying in-place instructions. In fact, we observed that participants were using *AR* in a similar way to *Picture*: (i) they held the AR display over the panel for an overview and moved it for a close-up look at several controls in order to memorize the values; (ii) they moved the AR display aside to interact with the controls directly; (iii) they moved it back to learn the next set of controls. By contrast, *AR+F* allows to set the controls while keeping the attention focused on the on-screen instructions thanks to its real-time feedback, thus increasing performance by reducing the division of attention.

The TECHNIQUE×DIFFICULTY interaction effect provides a more interesting insight into the performance of each technique according to task difficulty (*H1c*). As shown in Fig. 3, *TrialTime* increases sharply with difficulty for *Text*, more slowly for *AR+F*, with *AR* and *Picture* in between. This is confirmed by a TECHNIQUE×Random(PARTICIPANT) ANOVA, with significant effects of TECHNIQUE for each DIFFICULTY level:

- At the *Easy* level, only *Picture* is performing slower than other instruction methods. This is likely due to the time required to find the controls to set in the picture, compared with reading and memorizing three textual instructions or skimming through the panel with the AR techniques;
- At the *Medium* level, the performance of *Text* drops significantly and *AR+F* performs faster than *Picture*. *Text*, *Picture* and *AR* require more attention switches because instructions are more difficult to memorize (nine controls). Also, *Text* probably makes it more difficult to keep track of the instructions in the list while switching attention;

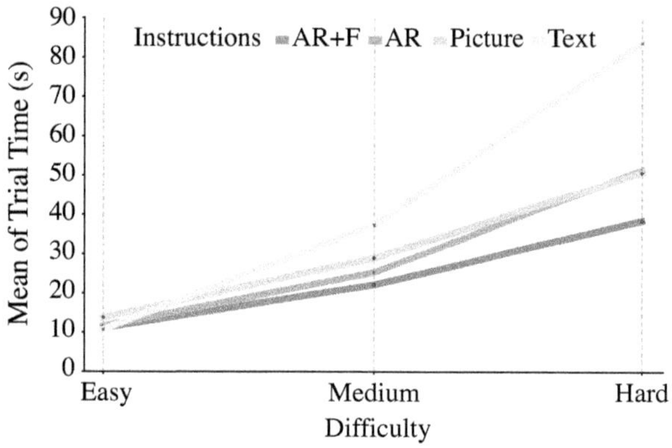

Figure 3. Mean of *TrialTime* for each TECHNIQUE by DIFFICULTY.

- At the *Hard* level, these differences are exacerbated. *Text* is by far the slowest technique, *Picture* and *AR* have similar performance, and *AR+F* is the fastest (Fig. 3).

H2: Are AR Techniques Less Error-Prone?

13.4% of trials had at least one error. A nominal logistic ANOVA model for TECHNIQUE×DIFFICULTY∼*Errors* shows significant effects for TECHNIQUE ($\chi^2 = 11.39, p = 0.0098$) and DIFFICULTY ($\chi^2 = 30.62, p < 0.0001$). We observe an increase in error rate with DIFFICULTY, however post-hoc tests are only significant for *Hard* (26.6%) against *Medium* (11.7%) and *Easy* (3.12%). For TECHNIQUE, the only significant difference is between *Picture* (21.9%) and *AR+F* (5.2%). Error rates for *Text* and *AR* are 15.6% and 12.5% respectively.

These results partially support *H2*: while *AR+F* and *AR* have fewer errors, not all differences are significant. Also, we do not find any effect of TECHNIQUE or DIFFICULTY on the number of errors per trial that were not successful on the first attempt. So we cannot conclude about error recovery. In fact, assessing error recovery would have required a specific error correction task. Finally, we observe that error rate alone cannot explain the difference in performance among techniques since it does not exhibit the same effects as *TrialTime*. This supports our assumption that alternating between subtasks is the most influential performance factor.

H3: Do Participants Prefer AR Techniques?

Participants were asked to rank the instruction methods (1 to 4) for each difficulty level and overall. A nominal logistic ANOVA model for TECHNIQUE×DIFFICULTY∼*Rating* shows a significant effect of TECHNIQUE ($\chi^2 = 233.61, p < 0.0001$) and a significant TECHNIQUE×DIFFICULTY interaction effect ($\chi^2 = 46.81, p = 0.0104$). In fact, *AR+F* was ranked as the preferred technique by all participants overall and by most of them for each difficulty level. It was followed by *AR*, *Picture* and *Text*, except at the *Easy* level where *Text* was often ranked 3rd, explaining the interaction effect.

Participants preferred *AR+F* mainly because it does not require to switch between the device and the panel: the interactive feedback solves the occlusion problem with *AR*. In fact, ten users never looked at the panel with *AR+F* and four only occasionally, while only two looked at it all the time. For *AR*, participants mostly raised the issue of graphical occlusion, but also explained that without interactive feedback, the size of the screen and the resolution of the camera image impaired precise manipulation when not looking at the panel. Some participants also felt unnatural to set the controls through the screen with both AR techniques, but this was balanced by the benefits of real-time feedback for *AR+F*.

Overall, these ratings and comments are consistent with our quantitative analysis. Participants' preferences match their performance, and their comments support the same explanations that led to our hypotheses.

CONCLUSION AND FUTURE WORK

We presented a prototype and a user study to evaluate the performance of AR on mobile phones for daily operational tasks. We simulated a technique – AR+Feedback – that adds real-time feedback to the AR overlay and compared it with Text, Picture and AR without real-time feedback for task instructions. The results show that the conventional AR approach performs almost as well as pictures, and that AR+Feedback significantly improves task performance and user experience. More studies are needed to explore real-time AR feedback for hand-free operations with a HMD, or in comparison with other kinds of dynamic instructions, e.g., Text and Pictures with real-time feedback. However the present work provides valuable insights to incorporate feedback to mobile AR systems.

This work leads to a new way for AR to go out of professional domains and reach a larger audience. We will apply and test this concept with more use cases and other types of tasks. We also plan to develop further prototypes to improve the connection between mobile devices and physical objects.

ACKNOWLEDGEMENTS

We thank Clément Pillias, Pierre Rossinès, Theophanis Tsandilas and David Bonnet for their help and suggestions, the anonymous reviewers for their feedback, and our participants for their time and efforts.

REFERENCES

1. Feiner, S., Macintyre, B., and Seligmann, D. Knowledge-based augmented reality. *CACM 36* (1993), 53–62.
2. Hakkarainen, M., Billinghurst, M., and Woodward, C. Augmented assembly using a mobile phone. In *MUM '08*, ACM (2008), 84–87.
3. Henderson, S. J., and Feiner, S. K. Augmented reality in the psychomotor phase of a procedural task. In *ISMAR '11*, IEEE (2011), 191–200.
4. Kotranza, A., Scott Lind, D., Pugh, C., and Lok, B. Real-time in-situ visual feedback of task performance in mixed environments for learning joint psychomotor-cognitive tasks. In *ISMAR '09*, IEEE (2009), 125 –134.
5. Quarles, J., Lampotang, S., Fischler, I., Fishwick, P., and Lok, B. A mixed reality approach for merging abstract and concrete knowledge. In *VR '08*, IEEE (2008), 27 –34.
6. Sohlberg, M. M., and Mateer, C. A. *Introduction to Cognitive Rehabilitation: Theory and Practice.* Guilford Press, 1989.
7. Tang, A., Owen, C., Biocca, F., and Mou, W. Comparative effectiveness of augmented reality in object assembly. In *CHI '03*, ACM (2003), 73–80.

How Do We Find Personal Files?: The Effect of OS, Presentation & Depth on File Navigation

Ofer Bergman
Bar-Ilan University
Ramat Gan, 52900 Israel
oferbergman@gmail.com

Steve Whittaker
University of California at Santa Cruz
1156 High Street, Santa Cruz, CA 95064, USA
stevejohnwhittaker@gmail.com

Mark Sanderson
RMIT University
GPO Box 2476, Melbourne 3001, Victoria, Australia
mark.sanderson@rmit.edu.au

Rafi Nachmias
Tel Aviv University
Ramat Aviv, Tel Aviv 69978, Israel
nachmias@post.tau.ac.il

Anand Ramamoorthy
Universiteit Ghent
9000, Ghent, Belgium
valvilraman@yahoo.co.in

ABSTRACT
Folder navigation is the main way that computer users retrieve their personal files. However we know surprisingly little about navigation, particularly about how it is affected by the operating system used, the interface presentation and the folder structure. To investigate this, we asked 289 participants to retrieve 1,109 of their own active files. We analyzed the 4,948 resulting retrieval steps, i.e. moves through the hierarchical folder tree. Results show: (a) significant differences in overall retrieval time between PC and Mac that arise from different organizational strategies rather than interface design; (b) the default Windows presentation is suboptimal – if changed, retrieval time could be reduced substantially and (c) contrary to our expectations, folder depth did not affect step duration. We discuss possible reasons for these results and suggest directions for future research.

Author Keywords
Personal information management; files; navigation.

ACM Classification Keywords
H.5.2 User Interfaces: Evaluation/methodology, User-centered design.

INTRODUCTION
Most information retrieval research has focused on *public* data sources such as databases, libraries and the web, developing various theories and methods for retrieving such public information. Yet we all retrieve our *personal* files many times a day, predominantly using navigation. Personal file navigation (*navigation* for short) is a two-phase process [3]. First, users manually traverse their organizational hierarchy until they reach the folder in which the target file is stored. Second, they locate the file within that folder. Surprisingly little is known about this process; more specifically, how it is affected by the operating system used, the interface presentation and the folder depth. Our large scale quantitative study aims to deepen our understanding of navigation.

Industrial and research efforts have predominantly focused on search when addressing personal information retrieval. Much novel desktop search technology has been developed over the last few years; e.g., Google Desktop, Microsoft Windows Search, and Macintosh Spotlight. According to its advocates, desktop search promises to minimize users' organizational problems. Search reduces the need to manually organize personal information, which is automatically indexed by the search engine. Search has other potential advantages: it allows flexible and efficient ways to query one's personal information [6, 13]. Despite its promise, however, various studies still show a strong preference for navigation over search for accessing personal information when both are available [1, 5, 12, 15]. Moreover, the use of improved search engines has been shown to have little effect on this preference [3]. Bergman et al. [3] show that regardless of search engine quality, there is a strong preference for navigation.

It therefore seems that manual file organization and navigation remain critical Personal Information Management (PIM) behaviors that demand further study. While previous studies have looked at how we manually *organize* personal files [2, 7-12], less attention has been paid to retrieval; i.e., how people exploit these structures to *access* that information. To better understand navigation, we therefore conducted a large scale study testing for the effect of folder structure on file navigation [4]. In that study, we found folder structures to be shallow (files were retrieved from a mean depth of 2.86 folders), with small folders (a mean of 11.82 files per folder) containing many subfolders (M = 10.64). Navigation was largely successful and efficient with participants successfully accessing 94% of their files and taking, on average, 14.76 seconds to do so. Retrieval time and success depended on folder size and depth, indicating shallow but broad structures to be adaptive. Finally, a linear regression model identified an optimization point in this trade-off, leading us to recommend that users avoid storing more than 21 files per folder and create an additional level of subfolders instead.

However, there are still fundamental questions that can be asked about navigation, namely: does the *operating system* affect navigation – do Mac users navigate to files more quickly than PC users? There are also questions of *presentation*. There are multiple ways to present file information in a folder, e.g. details, icons, list, thumbnails, etc. Windows 7 currently presents the details view by default, but is this optimal for navigation in terms of retrieval time? Finally, in our earlier study, we did not test the effect of *folder depth* on step duration; i.e., the time it takes to navigate a single step down the folder tree. We assumed that folders that are higher in the file hierarchy would be retrieved more quickly because of greater familiarity. Higher levels should be more familiar because they are accessed more often. But is there empirical evidence for this assumption?

To the best of our knowledge, the effect of OS, presentation, and familiarity on file navigation have never been evaluated. In what follows, we report a large-scale study where our research questions were:

1. Does the operating system type affect retrieval success and retrieval time?
2. Does the folder's visual presentation affect retrieval time? If so, which of the views leads to shorter retrieval times?
3. Does folder depth affect step duration?

METHOD

To increase external validity, we collected data from large numbers of users who retrieved their own files on their computers. The requirement for lightweight, non-intrusive data collection led us to a procedure in which we recruited users and videotaped their screens as they accessed personal files from their own computers. We did not install software on people's machines to record organization and retrieval behaviors. Installation is error prone, and pilot interviews showed that users were concerned about its intrusiveness and potential implications for their privacy.

Research shows that users tend to access recent information items most frequently, regardless of whether these are files, web pages or emails [8-10]. We therefore videotaped participants navigating to files in their Recent Documents list; i.e., personal files that they had recently spontaneously retrieved and opened from their own computers, as part of their everyday computer use. There are a number of other important benefits to this approach. Focusing on recent files meant that users were trying to access files that we were confident were present on their disks and that were definitely retrievable by the user. It also allowed us to identify active files without having to manipulate or access participants' file systems, avoiding encroaching on their privacy.

Participants

Participants were 289 everyday computer users: 158 males, 131 females. The majority of participants were students and employees at a UK university. Participants' ages ranged from 16 to 64 years ($M = 26.44$, $SD = 9.63$). The majority of participants were Windows OS users (246: 181 XP, 62 Vista, 3 Windows 2000) and 43 used a Mac OS X operating system. We excluded 7 Linux users because their small number did not allow for reliable statistical comparisons.

Procedure

Participants used their own computers for the retrieval task. The tester printed out the participants' Recent Documents list, asking them to navigate to each file (the target) in that list in order. Participants were asked to click on the target file once but not open it. We did this to preserve users' privacy as target files might contain sensitive information. Participants were asked to close all open folders before each navigation task, so that all retrievals started from the desktop. Participants were asked to skip a file in the list if they had already navigated to that target folder during a previous access task. We did this to prevent access to these items being primed because that folder had already been accessed. We asked our participants to access only files saved on their computer and to avoid retrieving files on external drives and email attachments that hadn't been saved as files on their hard drive.

Retrievals and Time Measurements

Our study includes 1,109 valid retrievals. Of the initial set of 1,158 recorded retrievals, we excluded 4%, mostly because they were interrupted by external events such as phone calls or instant messenger alerts. Recordings of user interactions were made using a high definition digital video camera (with 1,080 horizontal scan lines) with a fixed rate of 25 frames per second, making each frame 40 milliseconds (0.04 seconds) long. We measured retrieval time by manually analyzing the videos frame-by-frame.

Retrieval Time was measured from the first mouse movement made by a participant in the navigation, until the moment when participants either clicked on the target file (in successful retrievals) or announced that they could not find it (indicating retrieval failure).

Step Duration – We use the term 'step' for each folder opened in the navigation process. Altogether, we measured 4,948 steps. Step duration was measured from the time a folder was opened until the time the user: (a) clicked on a subfolder to continue the navigation sequence, (b) reverted to a parent folder (if the relevant item was not found), (c) clicked on the target file, or (d) said, "I give up." Because step duration distribution was not normally distributed, we normalized it to Z scores for all statistical tests.

RESULTS

Does the operating system type affect retrieval success and retrieval time?

Table 1 shows the effect of operating system on retrieval success and time. A Mann-Whitney test showed no significant differences regarding retrieval success (row a); however, an independent sample t test indicates that Mac retrievals were significantly faster than PC retrievals (row b). As Table 1 shows, this difference cannot be explained by a difference in step duration (as no significant difference was found in the step duration t test. See row c). Instead, this difference in retrieval time seems to be the result of different organizational strategies. Row d shows that Mac users stored their target files higher in the hierarchical tree than PC users. Mac users also had smaller folders (row e) containing more subfolders (row f). Our previous research [4] showed that folder depth and size are positively correlated with retrieval time. Therefore, it seems that Mac users use a slightly different storage strategy: keeping their folders shallower and smaller than PC users, and compensating for that with broader hierarchies.

	PC *N=246, 980 retrievals, 4,469 steps*	**Mac** *N= 43, 129 retrievals, 479 steps*	**Statistical Test**
a. Success rate	93%	96%	U=1.17 p>0.05
b. Retrieval time	17.27 (16.23)	12.56 (13.61)	t(1107)=3.15, p<0.001**
c. Step duration	3.3 (5.26)	3.13 (4)	t(4945)=.67, p=0.5
d. Folder depth	2.93 (1.87)	2.35 (1.63)	t(1030)=3.26, p<0.001**
e. Folder Size	25.05 (52.3)	19.04 (29.59)	t(3907)=2.24, p<0.001**
f. # of subfolders	8.85 15.67	10.73 40.42	t(2614)=1.97, p<0.05*

Table 1: The effect of OS on success rate, retrieval time, step duration, folder depth, folder size and number of subfolders in folder, showing Means and (Standard Deviations).

Does the folder's visual presentation affect retrieval time? If so, which view leads to shorter retrieval times?
There were 9 possible visual presentations of participant folders: 6 for Windows (Tiles, Icons, Details, Thumbnails, List and FilmStrip) and 3 for Mac (Icons, List and Columns). For a total of 4,209 steps, we were able to determine the visual presentation from the videos. Table 2 shows the effect of visual presentation on retrieval time.

Two one-way ANOVAs show a significant difference between the presentation groups for both PC F(5,3792) = 19.08, p<0.001 and Mac F(2,408)=11.24, p<0.001. Table 2 shows that *Icons* is the view that leads to the fastest step durations for both PC and Mac groups of presentation types. To test whether *Icons* led to significantly shorter step durations than the Windows default view (which was *Tiles* in Windows XP and *Details* in Windows 7), we conducted post hoc LSD tests. Both LSD comparisons were significant (and could not be explained by a difference in folder size or folder depth). On average, steps that used the *Icons* view instead of the *Details* view were 1.78 seconds faster. This means that if Microsoft were to change its default from *Details* to *Icons*, we might expect a reduction in average file retrieval time of 41%.

	No. of steps tested	**Step duration – *M* (*SD*)**
MS Icons	874	2.6 sec. (3.22 sec.)
MS Tiles	1,620	3.13 sec. (4.16 sec.)
MS List	313	3.21 sec. (4.73 sec.)
MS Details	609	4.38 sec. (8.88 sec.)
MS Thumbnails	345	5.45 sec. (7.91 sec.)
MS FilmStrip	37	5.5 sec. (5.38 sec.)
Mac Icons	229	2.22 sec. (2.01 sec.)
Mac List	123	3.57sec. (3.71 sec.)
Mac Columns	59	3.81 sec. (4.53 sec.)

Table 2: The effect of visual presentation on step duration.

Does folder depth affect step duration?
It is well known in cognitive psychology and HCI that familiarity reduces performance time [14], so we expected folder depth to increase step duration. Shallower folders should be more familiar as they are accessed more often. With an average of 10 subfolders in each folder, we can estimate that almost 100% of navigations pass through the main repository (e.g., My Documents), 10% pass through each of its subfolders, 1% of navigations involve its sub-subfolders, etc. To test this question, we conducted a regression analysis. Our data showed that step duration is positively correlated with folder size and folder size tends to decrease with depth [4]. We therefore partialled out the size effect using a stepwise regression. Results of the regression model (R^2= 0.09, p<0.01) show that folder depth did not significantly affect step duration when the effect of size was partialled out (see Table 3).

Factor	**Coefficient**	***SE***	***t***	***p***
Constant	2.05	0.07	27.61	<0.01
Size	0.03	0.002	16.78	<0.01
Depth	0.009	0.006	1.54	>0.05

Table 3: Regression model using size and depth to predict step duration.

DISCUSSION AND CONCLUSIONS

The results of our large-scale study are threefold:

(a) Mac users retrieve their files significantly faster than PC users. This difference seems to arise from the fact that Mac users deploy more sophisticated organizational strategies. Unlike PC users, they keep their files closer to the root directory by using small folders that branch sideways with a higher percentage of subfolders. The reasons for this behavioral difference between PC and Mac users should be investigated in future research.

(b) Visual folder presentation affects the time it takes users to complete a step. The *Icons* view led to significantly faster retrieval than *Details*, which is currently the Windows default view. Our results indicate that changing the Windows default from *Details* to *Icons* would reduce retrieval time by 41%. However, there may be other usability considerations, e.g., the *Details* view adds information about the files and allows effortless transformation to chronological sorting.

(c) Folder depth had no effect on step duration, after partialling out the effect of folder size. This is a rather surprising result. A possible explanation is a ceiling effect (as these files were taken from the Recent Documents list making their retrieval paths highly primed). A more interesting possibility is that users see navigation paths as single conceptual entity, rather than consisting of a combination of elements broken down into each of the folders along the paths. This may be similar to physical navigation in which some (typically new) paths are remembered as a combination of turning points, while other (typically more familiar) paths may be remembered as a single entity (e.g. "the way home"). Future research could test whether file navigation involves a step-wise cognitive process ("OK I got this far, where to now?") or a holistic one, where the entire path is viewed as a single entity.

We also wanted to test for the effect of sorting on step durations; however, in only 2% of the steps was the sorting changed from the default alphabetical one, which was not enough for a valid statistical comparison.

Directions for future research include investigation of the effect of file presentation on step duration in a laboratory setting, tracking both eye and mouse movements. Controlled research involving eye tracking could investigate why some presentations lead to shorter duration time by manipulating file icon size, spatial order and the details of information added to them. These studies could in turn lead to informed design of new presentations with shorter retrieval time. Other research could investigate the effect of screen size on retrieval time. In our own work, we intend to further investigate the familiarity result by controlling folder familiarity, or using independent methods to measure it.

ACKNOWLEDGMENTS

This research was partially funded by the European Union Marie Curie Grant, PERG-GA-2009-248997.

REFERENCES

1. Barreau, D. K. and Nardi, B. A. Finding and reminding: File organization from the desktop. *SIGCHI Bulletin 27*, 3 (1995), 39-43.
2. Bergman, O., Beyth-Marom, R. and Nachmias, R. The project fragmentation problem in personal information management. In *Proc. CHI 2006*, ACM Press (2006), 271-274.
3. Bergman, O., Beyth-Marom, R., Nachmias, R., Gradovitch, N. and Whittaker, S. Improved search engines and navigation preference in personal information management. *ACM Transactions on Information Systems 26*, 4 (2008), 1-24.
4. Bergman, O., Whittaker, S., Sanderson, M., Nachmias, R. and Ramamoorthy, A. The effect of folder structure on personal file navigation. *Journal of the American Society for Information Science and Technology 61*, 12 (2010), 2426–2441.
5. Boardman, R. and Sasse, M. A. "Stuff goes into the computer and doesn't come out": A cross-tool study of personal information management In *Proc. CHI 2004*, ACM Press (2004), 583-590.
6. Cutrell, E., Dumais, S. T. and Teevan, J. Searching to eliminate personal information management. *Communications of the ACM, 49*, 1 (2006), 58-64.
7. Gonçalves, D. and Jorge, J. A. An empirical study of personal document spaces. In *Proc. DSV-IS'03* (2003), 46-60.
8. Hardof-Jaffe, S., Hershkovitz, A., Abu-Kishk, H., Bergman, O. and Nachmias, R. How do students organize personal information spaces? In *Proc. Educational Data Mining 2009* (2009), 250-258.
9. Hardof-Jaffe, S., Hershkovitz, A., Abu-Kishk, H., Bergman, O. and Nachmias, R. Personal information space organization strategies in learning context. *Special Issue of Journal of Digital Information on the Social and Psychological Aspects of Personal Information Management 10*, 5 (2009), 1-16.
10. Henderson, S. and Srinivasan, A. An empirical analysis of personal digital document structures. In *Proc. HCI International 2009* (2009), 394-403.
11. Jones, W., Phuwanartnurak, A. J., Gill, R. and Bruce, H. Don't take my folders away! Organizing personal information to get things done. In *Ext. abstracts CHI 2005*. ACM Press (2005), 1505-1508.
12. Kirk, D., Sellen, A., Rother, C. and Wood, K. Understanding photowork. In *Proc. CHI 2006,* ACM Press (2006), 761-770.
13. Russell, D. and Lawrence, S. Search everything. In W. Jones and J. Teevan (Eds.), *Personal information management*. University of Washington Press (2007), 153-166.
14. Shneiderman, B. and Plaisant, C. *Designing the user interface.* Addison-Wesley Publ. Co., Reading, 2010.
15. Teevan, J., Alvarado, C., Ackerman, M. S. and Karger, D. R. The perfect search engine is not enough: A study of orienteering behavior in directed search. In *Proc. CHI 2004*, ACM Press (2004), 415-422.

Look & Touch: Gaze-supported Target Acquisition

Sophie Stellmach and Raimund Dachselt
User Interface & Software Engineering Group
University of Magdeburg
Magdeburg, Germany
{stellmach, dachselt}@acm.org

ABSTRACT

While eye tracking has a high potential for fast selection tasks, it is often regarded as error-prone and unnatural, especially for gaze-only interaction. To improve on that, we propose *gaze-supported interaction* as a more natural and effective way combining a user's gaze with touch input from a handheld device. In particular, we contribute a set of novel and practical gaze-supported selection techniques for distant displays. Designed according to the principle *gaze suggests, touch confirms* they include an enhanced gaze-directed cursor, local zoom lenses and more elaborated techniques utilizing manual fine positioning of the cursor via touch. In a comprehensive user study with 24 participants, we investigated the potential of these techniques for different target sizes and distances. All novel techniques outperformed a simple gaze-directed cursor and showed individual advantages. In particular those techniques using touch for fine cursor adjustments (*MAGIC touch*) and for cycling through a list of possible close-to-gaze targets (*MAGIC tab*) demonstrated a high overall performance and usability.

Author Keywords

Gaze input; mobile touch interaction; selection; target acquisition; gaze-supported interaction

ACM Classification Keywords

H.5.2 Information Interfaces and Presentation: User Interfaces - Evaluation/methodology – Input devices and strategies

General Terms

Design, Human Factors

INTRODUCTION

The diversity of display setups is increasing and with that is the need for more efficient means to interact with them. While traditional mouse input works excellent for pointing tasks in desktop environments, it does not apply well for situations in which the user is standing in front of a powerwall or sitting on a couch to interact with a large-sized television set.

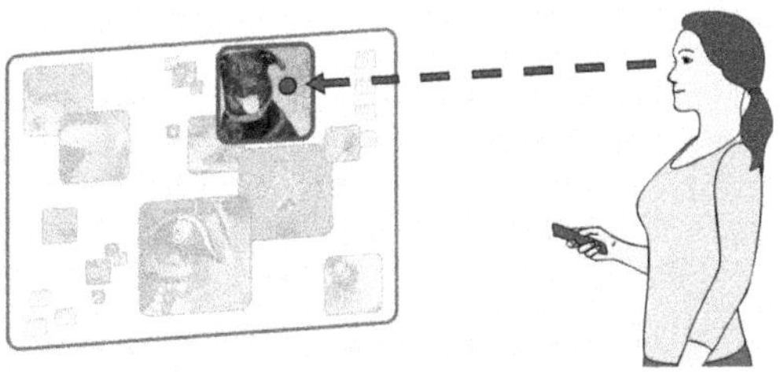

Figure 1. Basic idea: Gaze-supported interaction in combination with a handheld touchscreen and a distant display.

Regardless of the specific interaction setup used, the selection of targets is one of the fundamental tasks that need to be supported in any application. Gaze is a promising input modality to bridge the gap between a user and a distant display as illustrated in Figure 1. In this respect, it can even be a more efficient means for pointing tasks than traditional input devices [4, 21, 24].

Even though target acquisition seems to be a simple process which basically involves positioning a cursor and confirming a selection, it imposes several challenges when using eye gaze. Among them are *inherent inaccuracies* caused by the physiological nature of our eyes and by measurement errors of the tracking systems which lead to *jitter* and *offsets* [17, 23]. Thus, for more precise selections it is essential to address these two problems. Jittering can, for example, be compensated by stabilizing the gaze cursor (e.g., [28]). Offsets are difficult to handle as the degree of the offset is usually not known. Common solutions for gaze interaction include:

- *Large-sized* or *magnified* graphical user interfaces (GUIs) [2, 13, 14, 20],
- A combination of *gaze and manual (mouse) input* to perform exact positioning manually [7, 27],
- Invisibly *expand targets in motor space* [16],
- *Intelligent* algorithms to estimate the object of interest [17, 18, 23].

In this paper, we focus on the first two approaches as they provide high flexibility for diverse settings. They neither require any changes of conventional GUIs, nor substantial a priori knowledge about the distribution of items.

Beside accuracy issues, the *Midas touch* problem [11], the unintentional execution of actions, is often described as one of the major challenges for gaze-based interaction. The combination of gaze with other input modalities can solve these problems [5, 18, 22, 24]. Nevertheless, up to now dwell time activations are mostly used for gaze-based selections (e.g., [9,

10, 15]). This especially supports people who are not able to use their hands to interact with a digital system, for example, because of disabilities or because their hands are busy.

To alleviate the stated problems, this work aims at supporting precise target acquisition in a natural way while still maintaining sufficient task performance. In this context, eye movements may serve well as a supporting interaction channel in combination with other input modalities, such as speech, hand and body gestures, and mobile devices. We call this type of interaction *gaze-supported interaction*. For this work, we propose to conveniently use eye gaze in combination with touch input from a handheld device following the principle *gaze suggests* and *touch confirms*. Note that we do not aim at replacing or beating the mouse, but instead motivate gaze-supported interaction for diverse display setups. This may include public screens or large projection walls, for which we see a particularly high potential for this type of distant interaction. Another specific goal of this work is to support accurate selections even of *small* and *densely positioned* targets.

In this paper, we contribute a set of practical and novel gaze-supported selection techniques using a combination of gaze and touch input from a handheld touchscreen. The techniques utilize principles such as target expansions and separating coarse and fine positioning of a selection cursor by means of gaze vs. manual touch input. We carefully investigated the design space and developed five solutions which were tested and compared in a comprehensive user study. In particular those techniques using touch for fine cursor adjustments (*MAGIC touch*) and for cycling through a list of possible close-to-gaze targets (*MAGIC tab*) resulted in very promising results with respect to their overall performance and perceived usability.

The remaining paper is structured as follows: First, we discuss how gaze has been used for target acquisition tasks in previous work. Based on that we elaborated five gaze-supported selection techniques that are described in the *Design* section. These techniques have been tested by 24 participants which we report in the *User Study* section. The paper concludes with a discussion of the results from the user study and an outlook to future work.

RELATED WORK

In general, gaze input has a high potential for fast pointing tasks and may even outperform traditional selection devices such as a mouse [4, 21, 24]. In the following, we will investigate gaze-based selections in combination or in context with (1) target expansions, (2) a manual input device, (3) distant displays, and (4) a supportive modality.

Target Expansions for Gaze-based Selections

One way to ease gaze-based target selections is to magnify the display either locally at the point-of-regard [2, 8, 13, 14, 16, 20, 22] or globally [1, 3, 9]. Empirical evidence shows that eye pointing speed and accuracy can be improved by target expansions [2, 16, 20]. In this respect, Ashmore et al. [2] describe different types of dwell activated fisheye lenses that either follow the user's gaze at all times (*eye-slaved*) or remain fixed at a fixated position. They point out that users would find it irritating if the lens is active at all times. Fono and Vertegaal [8] use eye input with either dwell time or a key for zoom activation. The latter was preferred by users over automatic activations. Kumar et al. [13] present *EyePoint*: a combination of gaze and keyboard input for selecting GUI elements. For this, they introduce the concept of *look-press-look-release*. On pressing a keyboard button, the viewed region is enlarged. Different keys on the keyboard are assigned to various actions, such as single click, mouse over, and double click. However, the magnified view is based on a screen capture. Thus, no dynamics (e.g., an animation) are possible during this mode. Hansen et al. [9] present *StarGazer*: a 3D interface displaying groups of keyboard characters for gaze-only target selections (in this case gaze typing) using continuous pan and zoom. The point-of-interest moves towards the center of the screen while zooming and thus provides a better feedback for more precise selections. Skovsgaard et al. [20] use a local zooming lens to gradually increase the effective size of targets. They distinguish between discrete and continuous zooming tools for step-wise zooming. While their zooming tools improve hit rates, it takes longer to perform a selection compared to the non-zooming interface.

Gaze & Manual Input

Zhai et al. [27] present the MAGIC (i.e., *Manual And Gaze Input Cascade*) pointing technique, a combination of mouse and gaze input for fast item selections. The idea is to warp the cursor to the vicinity of the user's point-of-regard prior to moving the mouse. Then the cursor can be manually positioned using the mouse for more precise selections. Drewes and Schmidt [7] point out that the problem of this technique is *overshooting*: the cursor is only set to the gaze position after a mouse timeout and after the mouse is then moved again. Thus, the mouse is already in motion when the pointer is positioned which is difficult to coordinate. Zhai et al. [27] acknowledge this problem and propose to dampen the cursor movement based on the initial motion vector and distance to the previous cursor position. Instead, Drewes and Schmidt [7] use a touch-sensitive mouse button. Thus, when touching the mouse key (and before performing any mouse movement), the mouse pointer is set to the gaze position.

Gaze & Distant Displays

Several studies indicate that gaze *can* be faster than mouse input [9, 11, 13, 24]. In this respect, gaze-based input is acknowledged a particularly high potential for a more convenient interaction with high-density information on large (e.g., public) displays [1, 7, 9, 19, 26]. However, a main issue remains for accuracy versus speed. Kumar et al. [13] report, for example, that while task completion times were similar for gaze and mouse conditions, error rates are usually much higher for gaze input. San Agustin et al. [19] present a gaze-based navigation of a *digital bulletin board*. If messages lie on top of each other, the user can look at them and they will get separated from each other. Yoo et al. [26] combine gaze data (head orientation) and hand gestures for the interaction with large-sized displays. A 3D push-and-pull gesture is used to control the zoom for different applications, such as a geographical information system.

Gaze-supported Selection

Ware and Mikaelian [24] compare three gaze-supported selection techniques: a button press, gaze dwell, and an on-screen button to confirm a selection. Although dwell time and button activations resulted in similar completion times, dwell-based activations were more error-prone. Salvucci and Anderson [18] also use a button press for confirming a gaze-based selection for which they report errors due to a *leave-before-click* issue. This means that the gaze was already fixating a new target when pressing the button. After all, Ware and Mikaelian [24] conclude that eye tracking can be used as a *fast selection* device, if the target size is sufficiently large. Monden et al. [17, 25] present three gaze-supported selection techniques in combination with a mouse. First, when clicking the mouse, the closest item to the current gaze position is selected. This is especially useful for selecting small-sized targets, however, it has no advantage for closely positioned objects. Second, the cursor position can be manually adjusted with the mouse. Third, the first two approaches were combined and showed to be the fastest technique, even beating mouse input.

So far, few researchers have investigated a combination of gaze with a mobile touch-enabled device for interacting with distant displays (e.g., [7, 22]). As indicated by Stellmach et al. [22], it is very important to design the interaction with the mobile device in a way that the need to switch the user's visual attention between the distant and local (mobile) display is minimized. In this respect, Cho et al. [6] compare tilt, button, and a click wheel (as on the Apple iPod) input for exploring image collections. While participants found tilt most interesting to use, buttons offered the most control.

DESIGN OF GAZE-SUPPORTED SELECTION

For the design of gaze-*supported* target selection techniques, the first design decision is the choice of an additional input modality. In this work, we decided to use a small touch-enabled device, because smartphones are very commonplace and easy to use. It can be held in the user's hand and combined with his/her direction of gaze. For this, we assume that the eyes are tracked to deliver gaze positioning information with respect to a distant display. In addition, the handheld display allows for confirming a selection and for additional functionality addressing the problems of small targets and targets being too close to each other to be easily selected with gaze input only. Moreover, for advancing gaze-supported selection in combination with a mobile touch display, we elaborated the following design goals:

- Possibility to interact with standard GUIs
- Possibility to select *small* and *closely positioned* targets
- Prevent performing involuntary actions (*Midas Touch*)
- Subtle gaze interaction - should not overwhelm the user
- Support of *eyes-free* interaction with the mobile device
- One-handed interaction: hold mobile device in one hand and interact with the thumb only (based on [22])

Considering these design goals, we envisioned and investigated different approaches for combining gaze and touch-enabled input. We thereby distinguish between three basic gaze-supported selection types that are further discussed in this paper (specific variants in italic):

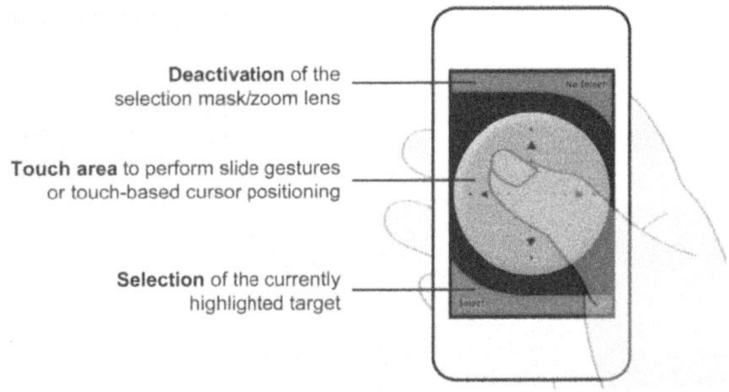

Figure 2. Interface prototype for the mobile touch device.

- Gaze-directed cursor (basic selection)
- Gaze-supported manual selection: *MAGIC touch* and *tab*
- Gaze-supported expanded target selection: *Eye-slaved* and *semi-fixed zoom lens*

All types use a different combination of touch and gaze, but follow the underlying principle *gaze suggests* and *touch confirms*. The basic interaction vocabulary – besides gaze for cursor positioning – is briefly outlined here: On mobile touch-enabled devices held in one hand, the simplest way of interaction is to tap a particular button which is typically used for confirming a selection, changing modes or activating other functions. Another one is to use a sliding gesture for controlling a numeric value such as a zoom factor. Next, the thumb can be positioned and dragged around continuously within a particular area, which can often be used for panning and positioning tasks. More complex gestures are not easy to be performed with a single finger in eyes-free operation and are therefore not further considered here (cf. design goals five and six). Finally, built-in sensors such as accelerometers can be employed to recognize tilting or rotating the device. Since this is continuous input, too, it can be used for zooming, panning or adjusting other values.

Using these basic interaction techniques and combining them with gaze allowed us to contribute novel gaze-supported selection techniques. To help preventing involuntary actions, the mobile touch device is used to issue a selection event (*touch confirms*), thus avoiding the Midas Touch effect (cf. design goal 3). For this, we developed an interface prototype that is shown in Figure 2. For our current prototype, we use virtual buttons on the mobile device to confirm selections as they offer more control compared to tilt input [6]. Further details (including the terms *selection mask* and *zoom lens* used in Figure 2) are discussed in context with the individual selection techniques in the following.

For each technique, we provide a brief description first. Then, we go into detail about the specific mapping of interaction methods to the envisioned functionality as we have used it for our implementation. Finally, we briefly discuss particular advantages and disadvantages of each technique. Please note that we explicitly aim for diverse techniques that can be later combined in a *complex interaction set* benefitting from their particular advantages.

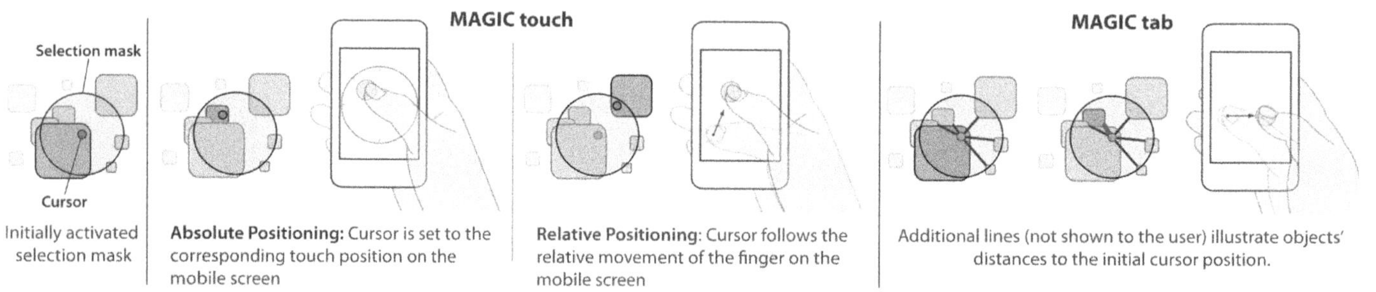

Figure 3. Manual gaze-supported selection: Initial situation (left), MAGIC touch – Absolute and relative adjustment of the cursor within the selection mask (middle) and MAGIC tab – Slide gesture to iterate through an item collection to select a target (right).

Gaze-directed Cursor

A *gaze-directed cursor* is the most basic technique, depicting an icon at the user's point-of-regard (*gaze suggests*). Internally it is represented by a single gaze position (in contrast to area cursors [12]). This is a common approach for substituting mouse with gaze input (e.g., [13, 25]). Different zones on the mobile display can be used for supporting toggle and multiple item selection (similar to Shift or Ctrl keys).

Interaction design. The user simply touches the mobile screen (anywhere) to highlight currently viewed objects. When releasing the touchscreen, the currently highlighted item is selected. If the user does not want to select an item, he/she can simply look at a void spot or look away from the distant display and lift the finger from the touchscreen.

Discussion. An advantage of this pointing technique is that it is easy to adapt to common mouse-based interfaces. However, the pointing is imprecise as it does not take inherent eye tracking inaccuracies into account. As mentioned before, jittery gaze movements can be compensated by stabilizing the gaze cursor (e.g., [28]). However, the offset problem remains.

Gaze-supported Manual Selection

As presented by Zhai et al. [27], the idea of MAGIC pointing is to roughly position the cursor based on a user's gaze position and then let the user make manual fine adjustments with the mouse. We adapt this concept to touch input and further extend it. For that, we first define a selection mask in whose proximity more precise selections can be performed using the mobile touch device (see Figure 3, left). As with the previously described technique gaze suggests the target, but here touch allows for fine adjustments before confirming the selection. Once the selection mask is activated (e.g., after a touch on the mobile device), the cursor does not follow the gaze anymore. For performing the manual fine selection, we contribute two variations: *MAGIC touch* and *MAGIC tab*, which are described in the following.

MAGIC touch. The cursor can be manually moved according to the touch position on the mobile screen. For this purpose, a representation of the selection mask is shown on the mobile screen (see Figure 3).

Interaction design. We propose a differentiation between *absolute* and *relative* positioning. This means, if the mobile screen is only briefly touched in the circular *touch area* (see Figure 2), the cursor will jump to the respective absolute position within the selection mask on the distant display. On the other hand, if the finger is dragged across the touchscreen, the cursor will move according to the relative movement from the initial touch position (see Figure 3, middle). This aims at supporting the user in keeping the view on the distant screen instead of switching his/her attention to the mobile device for manual cursor positioning.

Confirming a selection. The user can activate the selection mask by touching the mobile screen. As illustrated in Figure 2, the selection mask can be deactivated without performing a selection by touching the *no selection* area at the top of the mobile screen. Analogous, a selection can be confirmed by touching the *selection* area at the bottom of the mobile screen. Furthermore, large targets can be *directly* selected without the need to activate the selection mask first. This is achieved by looking at the target and touching the *selection* area immediately.

MAGIC tab. The cursor remains at the center of the selection mask and does not move. Items intersecting the selection mask can be discretely cycled through by using, for example, a continuous sliding gesture on the touchscreen. Another interaction option includes tilting the device to the left or right to browse through the collection of intersected items. Thus, *MAGIC tab* is similar to using the *tab button* on a keyboard.

Interaction design. The closest item to the user's point-of-regard when activating the selection mask is automatically highlighted (see Figure 3, right). For going through the other objects intersecting the selection mask, we suggest using a *horizontal slide gesture* (to the left or right). If the user performs such a gesture and does not release the touch, the list is further passed through. Confirmation of an item's selection is again done via touch on a virtual button as described for MAGIC touch (subsection *Confirming a selection*). In addition, we propose a *vertical slide gesture* to alter the size of the selection mask from very small (1 px) to a maximum value (100 px). This helps in confining the number of selectable items. Concerning the order of highlighted items, the sliding direction could indicate a clockwise or counterclockwise selection. Alternatively, items could be cycled through according to their distances to the mask's center.

Discussion. With the MAGIC techniques gaze is no longer required after activating the selection mask and control is entirely handed over to manual fine selection. An advantage of the MAGIC techniques is that, despite inaccurate gaze tracking, small and closely positioned targets can be selected. *MAGIC touch* allows for fine tuning the cursor position with the finger. *MAGIC tab* is decoupled from the size and distance of targets, because candidate objects are discretely highlighted one after each other. This may have a disadvantage for the selection of an item from a larger group of close targets as more objects need to be cycled to reach the desired target. The possible manual change of the selection mask's size alleviates this problem. In addition, the order in which the items are stored in the list may not be clear to the user at all times. We propose to sort them according to the distance to the center of the selection mask. While this has the advantage that items close to the current cursor position are highlighted first, it may have the disadvantage that items with a similar distance are positioned at opposite sides and that their highlighting order may confuse the user.

Gaze-supported Expanded Target Selection

A local zoom lens can be activated at the current gaze position to faciliate target selections. We refer to this approach as *gaze-supported expanded target selection*. The lens activation can be done via a manual command, e.g., by pressing a button, issuing a touch event, or performing a gesture. Within the magnified area the user can select items more accurately with his/her gaze. Inspired by the gaze-based fisheye lenses from Ashmore et al. [2], we contribute two variations, which are illustrated in Figure 4 and described in the following.

Eye-slaved zoom lens. The lens follows the user's gaze. Thus, the cursor remains always at the center of the lens.

Interaction design. After activating the zoom lens by tapping on the touch device, the user can move the lens based on his/her gaze position. A target can be selected in the previously described way by touching the selection area at the bottom of the mobile screen (*touch confirms*). To decrease jittery movements because of the target expansions, the gaze cursor is further stabilized (i.e., by increased filtering). The magnification level can be altered using a *vertical slide gesture* on the mobile screen (i.e., moving the finger up results in a higher magnification).

Semi-fixed zoom lens. A zoom lens is activated at the user's point-of-regard, and the cursor can be freely moved within the lens using eye gaze. The lens does not move itself until the user looks beyond its boundary. In this case, the lens is dragged towards the current gaze position.

Interaction design. Similar to the *eye-slaved zoom lens*, a *vertical slide gesture* can be used to change the magnification level. Furthermore, we suggest a rate-based control for moving the lens while looking outside its border: the further the distance between the gaze position and center of the lens, the faster the lens will move.

Discussion. The proposed zoom lenses have the advantage of improving the visibility of small targets. However, a local magnification may not necessarily improve pointing accuracy, if the cursor speed remains at the same level. This means that the cursor movement may become more jittery when further zoomed in. Thus, target expansions may facilitate gaze-based target selections, but do not entirely overcome eye tracking inaccuracies (e.g., *offset* problems).

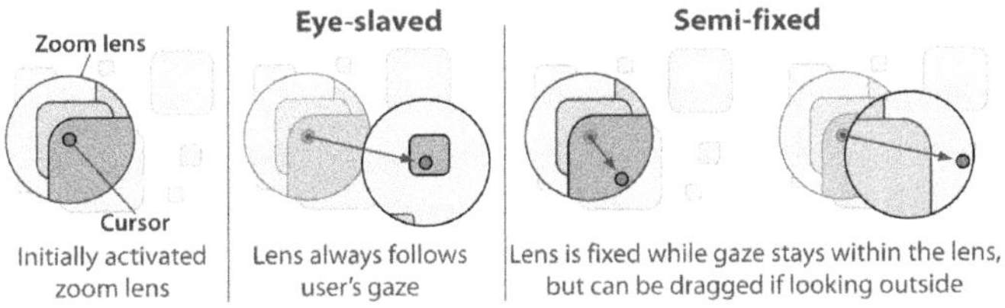

Figure 4. Initial situation (left) and variations of the gaze-supported expanded target selection - *eye-slaved* and *semi-fixed* zoom lens.

USER STUDY

We conducted a user study testing the five described gaze-supported selection techniques for different selection conditions. In particular, we were interested in the performance and suitability of each technique with regard to different target sizes and distances, which were both used as independent variables. Tasks ranged from selecting targets from an abstract grid of items to a more realistic desktop-like setting. This aims at better assessing the suitability of the developed techniques for different situations and how they can be further enhanced. Besides investigating the performance of each technique, we put a particular emphasis on qualitative user feedback for gaining better insights, identifying potential problems, and possible solutions for them.

Design. We used a within-subjects design with five interaction conditions:

C	Gaze-directed cursor
$\mathbf{M}_{tch}$	MAGIC touch
$\mathbf{M}_{tab}$	MAGIC tab
$\mathbf{Z}_{es}$	Eye-slaved zoom lens
$\mathbf{Z}_{sf}$	Semi-fixed zoom lens

We decided to test C, the two M and the two Z conditions together in a counterbalanced order to prevent the influence of order effects. This was done since $\mathbf{M}_{tch}$ and $\mathbf{M}_{tab}$ are very similar and belong to the same selection type (i.e., gaze-supported manual selection) and $\mathbf{Z}_{es}$ and $\mathbf{Z}_{sf}$ respectively (i.e., gaze-supported expanded target selection).

Participants. Twenty-four paid volunteers (14 male, 10 female) participated in the study, aged 22 to 31 (Mean (*M*) = 26.3) with normal or corrected-to-normal vision. In an initial questionnaire we asked participants about their background and to rate several statements on a 5-point Likert scale from 1 - *Do not agree at all* to 5 - *Completely agree*. Based on this, participants stated that they mainly use mouse and keyboard for computer interaction (M=4.79, Standard Deviation (*SD*)=0.50). While participants are interested in novel input devices (M=4.33, SD=0.80), many participants do not frequently use multitouch devices (such as smartphones) (M=3.50, SD=1.58). Finally, while all participants use computers on a daily basis, only eight had already used an eye tracker for interaction before.

Apparatus. For gathering gaze data we use a Tobii T60 table-mounted eye tracker: a binocular eye tracker is inte-

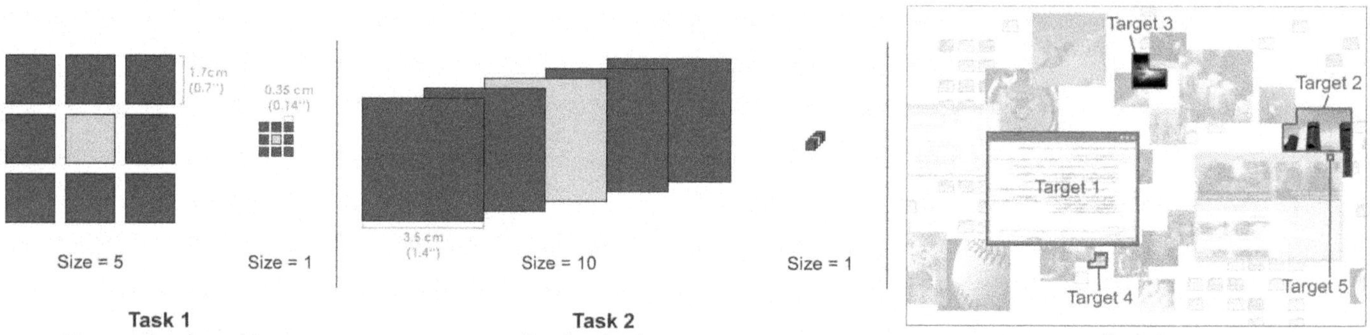

Figure 5. Schematic exemplary illustrations for the three task blocks T1, T2, and T3. Sizes and distances varied among the runs for T1 and T2. For T3, five targets had to be selected in the same order from a scene resembling a cluttered desktop interface.

grated in a 17-inch TFT flat panel monitor with a resolution of 1280x1024, a 0.5° accuracy, and sampling rate of 60 Hz. The gaze position is stabilized using the *speed reduction* technique [28]. Based on initial tests before the user study, we use a ratio of 8% of the current with 92% of the previous gaze position. The described gaze-supported selection techniques have all been implemented as suggested in the respective *Interaction design* paragraphs. We use a similar system setup for the gaze-supported multimodal interaction as proposed by [22]. We use Microsoft's XNA Game Studio 3.0 (based on C#) for the creation of a test environment allowing for the selection of targets on the Tobii display (cf. Figure 5). An iPod Touch is used for the interaction on a mobile touchscreen. The GUI on the iPod is designed according to the screen prototype illustrated in Figure 2.

Procedure. The user study started with a brief introduction and an initial questionnaire about participants' background (see subsection *Participants*). Participants were seated approximately 60 cm from the eye tracker display and were instructed to sit fairly still without restricting their movement. For each selection technique the same procedure was followed. First, a 9-point eye tracker calibration sequence was performed. Then, one selection technique at a time was described and the user could directly play around with it. The participant could test the technique until s/he felt sufficiently acquainted with it (usually less than 5 minutes). Three task blocks had to be completed in the same order with each selection technique. An overview is presented in Figure 5. The overall task was to select a single target from a set of given objects, whereby the alignment and size of objects and their distances differed among the task blocks:

- T1 Non-overlapping 2D items aligned in a grid
  (3 sizes x 4 distances = 12 runs)
- T2 Overlapping 2D items aligned in a row
  (3 sizes x 4 distances = 12 runs)
- T3 Desktop mockup: Overlapping items varying in size
  (5 differently sized targets = 5 runs)

For task block T1 and T2, the object sizes and distances varied. The sizes differed from 10 (large) to 5 and 1 (small). The distances ranged from 1 (large distance) to 0.5, 0.25 and 0 (objects touch each other). The size and distance values are based on an internal virtual unit. Based on the Tobii T60's screen resolution, a size of 10 equals 3.5 cm (1.4"). Thus, assuming a distance of 60 cm to the eye tracker screen, the visual angle of targets ranged between 3.3° (size 10) to 0.3° (size 1). Item sizes and distances were differed across runs but not within the same run (see Figure 5). The same order was used for alternating target sizes and distances: First, all large targets (size=10) were tested with differing distances to distractors; then, this was repeated for the other target sizes as well. At the beginning of each run, participants needed to look at the center of the screen and touch the mobile device to confirm readiness. This was meant to improve the comparability between selection times. Targets had always the same distance to the screen center, however, they were positioned at alternating corners depending on the respective run.

For task block T3, a prototype was used that should resemble a desktop environment containing windows and icons. Participants had to select five targets as illustrated in Figure 5. The targets always had to be selected in the same order, starting with the largest (target 1) and finishing with the smallest and most difficult one (target 5).

Measures. Our quantitative measures included logged target acquisition times and error rates (an error is issuing a selection without the target being highlighted). Furthermore, as previously pointed out we aimed for substantial user feedback for a better assessment of the individual selection techniques. An *intermediate questionnaire* was handed out after T1-T3 have been completed with a single selection technique. The *intermediate questionnaires* consisted of three types of questions, for which all quantitative questions were based on 5-point Likert scales from 1 - *Do not agree at all* to 5 - *Completely agree*:

- Q1 Six general usability questions (see Figure 8) that were the same for all techniques
- Q2 Several questions concerning the particular selection technique - the number of questions differed from 5 to 7 depending on the respective technique
- Q3 Two questions asking for qualitative feedback on what the users particularly liked and disliked about the tested selection technique

In the *final questionnaire*, participants had to rate how they liked each selection technique, answer some concluding

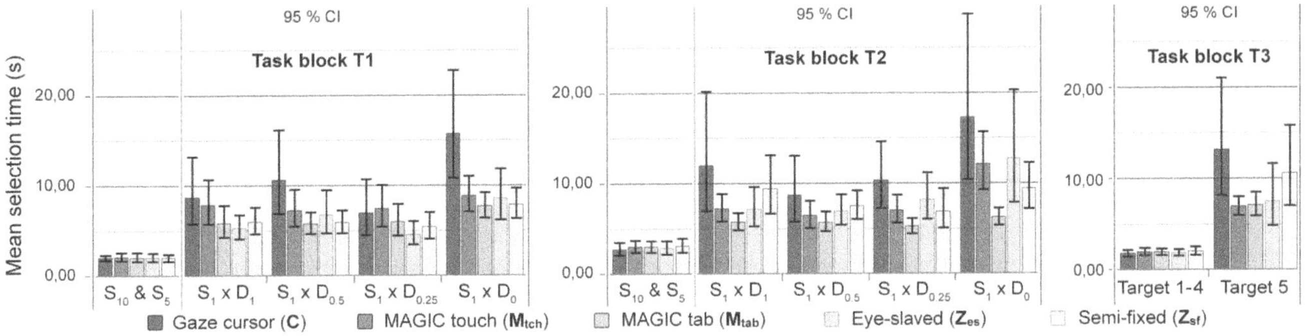

Figure 6. Overview of mean target acquisition times for the three task blocks. Results are summarized for S_{10} and S_5 (no significant differences).

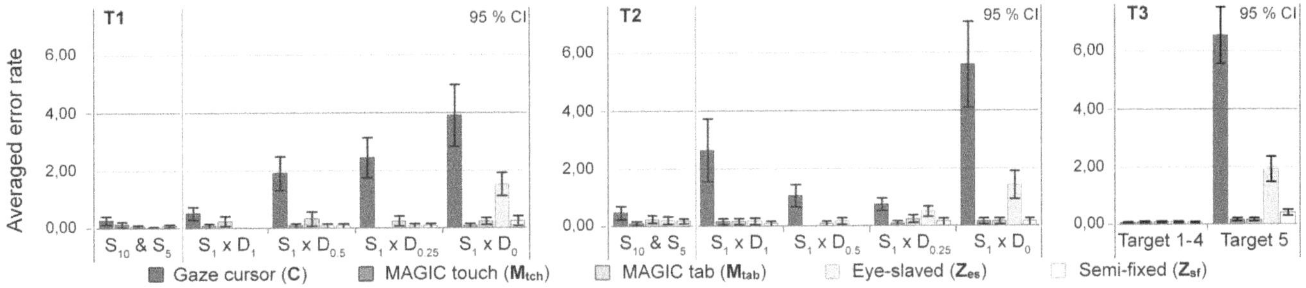

Figure 7. Overview of the averaged error rates for the three task blocks. Results are summarized for S_{10} and S_5 (no significant differences).

questions on the potential of gaze-supported selections, and give concluding qualitative feedback. On average, each session took about 120 minutes with instructions, carrying out the described procedure, and completing the questionnaires.

RESULTS

For the evaluation, we were particularly interested in qualitative feedback about how the developed gaze-supported selection techniques were experienced by the participants. The quantitative measures such as *target acquisition times* and *error rates* give a good indication about the practicality of these techniques. A repeated-measures ANOVA (Greenhouse-Geisser corrected) was used to investigate differences in task completion times and usability rankings. Post-hoc paired samples t-tests with a Bonferroni correction were used to further investigate which particular values differed significantly (pairwise comparisons).

Target Acquisition Times and Error Rates

Mean selection times and error rates are shown in Figure 6 and 7 with error bars indicating 95% confidence intervals (CI). They will be further discussed in the following based on the independent variables *distance* (D_1, $D_{0.5}$, $D_{0.25}$, D_0), *target size* (S_{10}, S_5, S_1), and *selection technique*. The influence of D and S on the mean selection times for T1 and T2 are summarized in Table 1.

For T1 and T2, different **target sizes** (S) had a *highly significant* impact on the selection times for all techniques (cf. Table 1). Selection times were significantly worse for S_1 than for S_5 and S_{10} for each selection technique. Large targets (S_5 and S_{10}) on the other hand could be quickly selected with all five techniques with no significant performance differences. Therefore, we accumulated values in Figure 6 and 7 for S_5

	T1	T2
C	$F_D(3,216)=4.50$, **p=0.004**	$F_D(3,180)=3.40$, **p=0.036**
	$F_S(2,72)=41.21$, **p<0.001**	$F_S(2,60)=23.92$, **p<0.001**
$\mathbf{M}_{tch}$	$F_D(3,216)=0.27$, p<0.81	$F_D(3,216)=7.11$, **p=0.001**
	$F_S(2,72)=31.33$, **p<0.001**	$F_S(2,72)=52.77$, **p<0.001**
$\mathbf{M}_{tab}$	$F_D(3,216)=0.81$, p=0.40	$F_D(3,216)=5.14$, **p=0.003**
	$F_S(2,72)=20.12$, **p<0.001**	$F_S(2,72)=36.19$, **p<0.001**
$\mathbf{Z}_{es}$	$F_D(3,216)=6.13$, **p=0.001**	$F_D(3,213)=5.04$, **p=0.013**
	$F_S(2,72)=29.02$, **p<0.001**	$F_S(2,71)=21.59$, **p<0.001**
$\mathbf{Z}_{sf}$	$F_D(3,216)=0.84$, p=0.47	$F_D(3,210)=3.80$, **p=0.04**
	$F_S(2,72)=40.43$, **p<0.001**	$F_S(2,70)=13.25$, **p<0.001**

Table 1. Overview of the influence of target distances (D) and sizes (S) on the mean selection times. Significant results are printed in bold.

and S_{10}. Selection of small targets using **C** was very difficult and partly not realizable. In fact, on average only 81.5% of the participants managed to select a target of S_1. As a result, selection times for **C** were significantly worse than for all other techniques for S_1, except in comparison to $\mathbf{Z}_{es}$ for T2. In addition, $\mathbf{M}_{tab}$ performed significantly faster than the other techniques for S_1 in T2. A dependence between increased **error rates** and decreased target sizes exists for **C** and in an alleviated way for $\mathbf{Z}_{es}$ (see Figure 7). The error rates for $\mathbf{M}_{tch}$, $\mathbf{M}_{tab}$, and $\mathbf{Z}_{sf}$ do not significantly differ with respect to S.

While the mean selection times and error rates were not significantly influenced by varied **distances** (D) for S_{10} and S_5, D had a significant effect on the task completion time for the smallest target size S_1 both for T1 ($F(4,384)=20.95$, $p<0.001$) and T2 ($F(4,288)=12.33$, $p<0.001$). This was es-

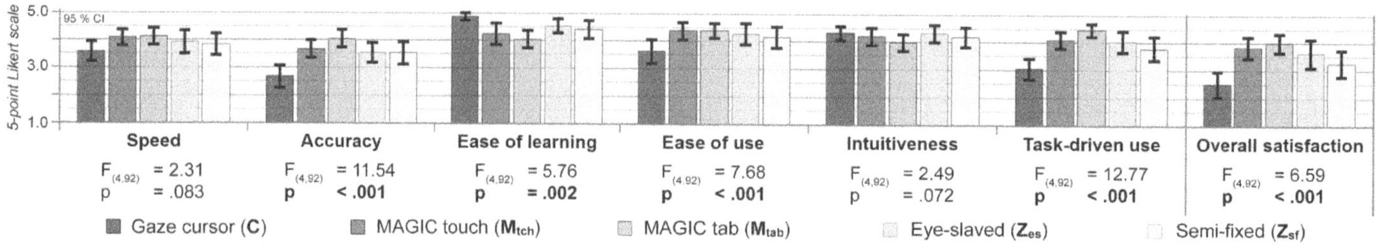

Figure 8. User-ranked gaze-supported selection techniques based on six usability factors and the overall satisfaction.

pecially the case for **C** and $\mathbf{Z}_{es}$ (cf. Table 1). As shown in Figure 6, for S_1 mean selection times did not significantly vary between different distances for $\mathbf{M}_{tch}$, $\mathbf{M}_{tab}$, and $\mathbf{Z}_{sf}$. **Error rates** significantly increased for **C** with a decreasing distance for very small target sizes and in an alleviated way for $\mathbf{Z}_{es}$. The error rates for $\mathbf{M}_{tch}$, $\mathbf{M}_{tab}$, and $\mathbf{Z}_{sf}$ remained relatively stable for varied distances.

For task T3, selection techniques significantly differed for the five targets (see Figure 6 and 7, right) with respect to target acquisition time (F(4,440)=3.32, p=0.04) and error rate (F(4,440)=9.27, p<0.001). Selecting target 5 was considerably harder than the other targets: a significant increase in target acquisition time occurred for all selection techniques. However, the error rates for $\mathbf{M}_{tch}$, $\mathbf{M}_{tab}$, and $\mathbf{Z}_{sf}$ remained fairly constant, while there was a significant increase for selecting the smallest target (5) with **C**, t(108)=3.56, p<0.05 (cf. Figure 6). In addition, selecting target 5 with **C** was significantly slower than with $\mathbf{M}_{tch}$ (t(107)=3.13, p=0.02) and $\mathbf{M}_{tab}$ (t(107)=3.15, p=0.02).

Quantitative User Feedback

For each selection technique, users rated how satisfied they were with different usability aspects (Q1 in the intermediate questionnaires), such as how *intuitive* the technique felt and whether tasks could be achieved as anticipated (*task-driven use*). The results are summarized in Figure 8. **C** received significantly lower ratings for task-driven use, accuracy, and ease of use which reflects the low task performance of **C** (high selection times and high error rates). On the upside, users assessed **C** significantly easier to learn. No significant differences occurred among $\mathbf{M}_{tch}$, $\mathbf{M}_{tab}$, $\mathbf{Z}_{es}$, and $\mathbf{Z}_{sf}$. Finally, Figure 8 (on the right) presents how participants rated the individual selection techniques in the final questionnaire after having tested each of them. **C** was assessed significantly worse than the other gaze-supported selection techniques. Although the other techniques were rated very similar, MAGIC tab received the best overall rating.

Qualitative User Feedback & Discussion

In the following, we discuss the gaze-supported selection techniques based on the user feedback to Q2 and Q3 (intermediate questionnaires) and the previously presented results. In general, the combination of gaze- and touch-based input for the interaction with a distant display was found very useful (M=4.63, SD=0.56). As one participant summarized well: *A prolonged working with the eyes will be wearisome, if the gaze input demands high precision and concentration from the user. The MAGIC and zoom lens techniques ease this and make gaze input more comfortable.* In this regard, precise and fast selection of small targets was particularly wearisome for **C**, $\mathbf{Z}_{es}$, and $\mathbf{Z}_{sf}$, as participants sometimes had to look at a location near or beside a target to actually select it. This is reflected by high selection times and error rates especially for **C**, which partly prevented users from selecting a small target at all. Participants preferred the MAGIC techniques (M=4.58, SD=0.57), for which a rough gaze cursor position is sufficient and manual fine adjustments can be made. Seven participants mentioned that this gave them more control.

Mobile touchscreen. Although participants liked the virtual buttons on the touchscreen to confirm a selection (M=3.76, SD=0.90), this was sometimes error-prone. Especially for $\mathbf{M}_{tch}$ some users accidentally hit the selection button when trying to manually position the cursor. Instead, a selection could, for example, be performed with a double tap, and the selection mask could be deactivated by looking away from it for a specific amount of time.

Gaze-directed cursor. Although the gaze-directed cursor **C** was not suitable for the selection of small targets (high selection times and error rates), 19 participants emphasized its high potential for very easy, fast, and intuitive selections of large objects (also see Figures 6 and 7). Participants appreciated that items are highlighted as long as touching the display (M=4.38, SD=0.63).

MAGIC touch and tab. In general, the idea to manually position the cursor precisely via touch for $\mathbf{M}_{tch}$ and $\mathbf{M}_{tab}$ was found very good (M=4.06, SD=0.85), because it is more relaxing for the eyes (mentioned by 8 participants). In this respect, the MAGIC techniques were assessed very positively with respect to several usability aspects that are listed in Figure 8. The high grade for task-driven use can be explained by consistently low error rates for $\mathbf{M}_{tch}$ and $\mathbf{M}_{tab}$. Furthermore, the selection mask was found very helpful to confine the cursor movement or the amount of selectable targets respectively (M=4.08, SD=0.93).

MAGIC touch. The current implementation of the relative (M=3.63, SD=1.18) and absolute cursor positioning (M=3.29, SD=1.37) was not particularly liked by participants. The relative cursor movement was sometimes too fast, which led to overshooting problems. This was especially a problem for very small targets, which 14 participants described as tedious. The absolute positioning was regarded as most suitable for quickly selecting large targets.

MAGIC tab. Participants liked the discrete selection of targets very much (M=4.42, SD=0.70), as it was fast and precise. Particular advantages of $\mathbf{M}_{tab}$ include its robustness against inaccurate gaze data, its suitability to select small targets, and that it is more relaxing for the eyes. However, the task performance is affected by the amount of targets intersecting the selection mask. Hence, it is important that users can easily narrow down the amount of selectable items, as this was criticized by participants. The size of the selection mask changed too slowly and was therefore considered as less useful (5 participants). In general, the slide gestures were described as slow and imprecise (9 participants), because they were sometimes not immediately recognized due to the current implementation. In addition, five participants complained that the tab order was unintuitive. It was not clear where the target was in the item collection and whether going forward or backward would be faster to reach it. Instead of using slide gestures, backward and forward buttons may offer more control. It was also suggested that the selection could be based on the gesture's direction to perform more systematic selections, for example, by flicking the cursor towards a desired target and snapping the cursor to it. However, this may cause problems if objects are positioned behind or close to each other. Another idea is to automatically adapt the initial size of the selection mask depending on the current context, for example, based on the number, size, and distance of targets.

Gaze-supported zoom lenses. The combination of an enlarged view and a slowed movement of the cursor/lens are considered helpful for selecting small targets more precisely. However, they do not overcome eye tracking inaccuracies completely, which becomes apparent for small and closely positioned targets (see Figure 6). In addition, participants liked the vertical slide gesture to adjust the zoom level (M=3.80, SD=1.01). However, especially for the zoom lens techniques it showed that users desired more possibilities for *customization*, for example, of the lens size, the maximum zoom level, and the lens speed. This is reflected in highly diverging ratings in the questionnaires. For example, the decreased speed, although preferred by several users, received an overall moderate rating (M=3.46, SD=1.25). In this respect, five participants explained that they found the *lens speed* too *slow* and three *not slow enough*.

Eye-slaved. While $\mathbf{Z}_{es}$ was on the one hand described as fast and intuitive (by three users), it was also characterized as distracting, laborious, and imprecise, because it does not take eye tracking inaccuracies into account. Participants liked that the cursor was always at the lens's center (M=3.96, SD=1.06) and that the lens immediately moved according to the gaze (M=4.04, SD=1.21).

Semi-fixed. $\mathbf{Z}_{sf}$ was found less irritating than $\mathbf{Z}_{es}$ (four participants), however, it was considered imprecise (8 participants). It was positively mentioned that $\mathbf{Z}_{sf}$ provides more stability (M=3.58, SD=0.95) while still being flexible to be panned if the user looks outside the lens (M=3.79, SD=1.19). However, seven users particularly disliked the way the $\mathbf{Z}_{sf}$ lens moved, because users had to look away from the lens to move it and look back to see if the desired target has been reached. Thus, it was suggested that the lens should already move when looking at the lens's border from within so that there is no need to leave the lens with the gaze.

Combination of techniques. All in all, each selection technique has its unique advantages as described above. Even though **C** achieved the lowest performance and overall user rating, it was assessed very positively for the selection of large targets. In this respect, a seamless integration of the proposed selection techniques into one complex interaction set seems highly promising to cater for diverse selection contexts. While large targets can be selected with a simple gaze-directed cursor (**C**), smaller items could be quickly selected with a *gaze-supported zoom lens* and/or manual selection (*MAGIC*) technique. Providing more customization features for the zoom lenses, a user could dynamically adjust how fast the lens follows the gaze and with that a smooth transition between $\mathbf{Z}_{es}$ and $\mathbf{Z}_{sf}$ could be achieved. The lenses could then be advanced by allowing the user to move it via touch or select items within the lens using $\mathbf{M}_{tch}$ or $\mathbf{M}_{tab}$.

In summary, the combination of gaze- and touch-based input for the interaction with a distant display was perceived as very promising. However, since this study was restricted to a desktop setting, the techniques need to be further investigated and adapted to distant large displays.

CONCLUSION

In this paper, we contributed several novel and practical ways for combining gaze and touch input from a mobile touchscreen for selection tasks on a distant display. According to the principle *gaze suggests* and *touch confirms*, we described five gaze-supported selection techniques ranging from a simple touch-enhanced *gaze-directed cursor* to novel *gaze-supported local zoom lenses* and our *MAGIC touch* and *MAGIC tab* techniques. While *MAGIC touch* allows for manually positioning the cursor via touch input, *MAGIC tab* allows for discretely going through a list of objects that are spatially close to the user's point-of-regard via a slide gesture. These techniques were evaluated in a user study providing important insights for further improvements. With the presented techniques we could overcome prevalent problems associated with gaze-based interaction, such as the *Midas touch* problem. Especially with our MAGIC techniques we could compensate eye tracking inaccuracies well. In this respect, the MAGIC techniques excel with their robustness against inaccurate gaze data, a high comfort as they are less straining for the eyes, and a high overall performance and perceived usability. In particular *MAGIC tab* shows a high potential for further investigations as it is suitable for quick and reliable selections of small, closely positioned and overlapping targets.

For future work, we will enhance the proposed gaze-supported techniques based on the collected user feedback and investigate possibilities to seamlessly combine them to take advantage of their particular strengths for different conditions. Furthermore, the revised techniques will be tested with large distant displays and in comparison with traditional input devices. Finally, the proposed selection techniques may also benefit target acquisition within virtual 3D environments, in which several objects may be positioned behind each other.

Therefore, as part of our future work we will investigate gaze-supported interaction in 3D environments.

ACKNOWLEDGMENTS

This research is supported by the German National Merit Foundation and the German Ministry of Education and Science (BMBF) project ViERforES-II (01IM10002B).

REFERENCES

1. Adams, N., Witkowski, M., and Spence, R. The inspection of very large images by eye-gaze control. In *Proc. of AVI'08* (2008), 111–118.
2. Ashmore, M., Duchowski, A. T., and Shoemaker, G. Efficient eye pointing with a fisheye lens. In *Proc. of Graphics Interface 2005*, GI '05 (2005), 203–210.
3. Bates, R., and Istance, H. Zooming interfaces!: enhancing the performance of eye controlled pointing devices. In *Proc. of Assets'02*, ACM (2002), 119–126.
4. Bieg, H.-J., Chuang, L. L., Fleming, R. W., Reiterer, H., and Bülthoff, H. H. Eye and pointer coordination in search and selection tasks. In *Proc. of ETRA'10*, ACM (2010), 89–92.
5. Castellina, E., and Corno, F. Multimodal gaze interaction in 3D virtual environments. In *COGAIN '08* (2008), 33–37.
6. Cho, S.-J., Choi, C., Sung, Y., Lee, K., Kim, Y.-B., and Murray-Smith, R. Dynamics of tilt-based browsing on mobile devices. In *Proc. of CHI'07*, ACM (2007), 1947–1952.
7. Drewes, H., and Schmidt, A. The MAGIC touch: Combining MAGIC-pointing with a touch-sensitive mouse. In *Proc. of INTERACT'09*, Springer-Verlag (2009), 415–428.
8. Fono, D., and Vertegaal, R. EyeWindows: evaluation of eye-controlled zooming windows for focus selection. In *Proc. of CHI'05* (2005), 151–160.
9. Hansen, D. W., Skovsgaard, H. H. T., Hansen, J. P., and Møllenbach, E. Noise tolerant selection by gaze-controlled pan and zoom in 3D. In *Proc. of ETRA'08*, ACM (2008), 205–212.
10. Hansen, J. P., Johansen, A. S., Hansen, D. W., Ito, K., and Mashino, S. Command without a click: Dwell time typing by mouse and gaze selections. In *Proc. of INTERACT'03*, IOS Press (2003), 121–128.
11. Jacob, R. J. K. What you look at is what you get: eye movement-based interaction techniques. In *Proc. of CHI'90*, ACM (1990), 11–18.
12. Kabbash, P., and Buxton, W. A. S. The prince technique: Fitts' law and selection using area cursors. In *Proc. of CHI'95*, ACM Press/Addison-Wesley Publishing Co. (1995), 273–279.
13. Kumar, M., Paepcke, A., and Winograd, T. EyePoint: practical pointing and selection using gaze and keyboard. In *Proc. of CHI'07*, ACM (2007), 421–430.
14. Lankford, C. Effective eye-gaze input into windows. In *Proc. of ETRA'00*, ACM (2000), 23–27.
15. Miniotas, D. Application of Fitts' law to eye gaze interaction. In *Proc. of CHI EA'00*, ACM (2000), 339–340.
16. Miniotas, D., Špakov, O., and MacKenzie, I. S. Eye gaze interaction with expanding targets. In *Proc. of CHI EA'04*, ACM (2004), 1255–1258.
17. Monden, A., Matsumoto, K., and Yamato, M. Evaluation of gaze-added target selection methods suitable for general GUIs. *Int. J. Comput. Appl. Technol. 24* (June 2005), 17–24.
18. Salvucci, D. D., and Anderson, J. R. Intelligent gaze-added interfaces. In *Proc. of CHI'00*, ACM (2000), 273–280.
19. San Agustin, J., Hansen, J. P., and Tall, M. Gaze-based interaction with public displays using off-the-shelf components. In *Proc. of Ubicomp'10*, ACM (2010), 377–378.
20. Skovsgaard, H., Mateo, J. C., Flach, J. M., and Hansen, J. P. Small-target selection with gaze alone. In *Proc. of ETRA'10*, ACM (2010), 145–148.
21. Smith, B. A., Ho, J., Ark, W., and Zhai, S. Hand eye coordination patterns in target selection. In *Proc. of ETRA'00*, ACM (2000), 117–122.
22. Stellmach, S., Stober, S., Nürnberger, A., and Dachselt, R. Designing gaze-supported multimodal interactions for the exploration of large image collections. In *Proc. of NGCA'11*, ACM (2011), 1–8.
23. Špakov, O. Comparison of gaze-to-objects mapping algorithms. In *Proc. of NGCA'11*, ACM (2011), 1–8.
24. Ware, C., and Mikaelian, H. H. An evaluation of an eye tracker as a device for computer input. In *Proc. of CHI'87*, ACM (1987), 183–188.
25. Yamato, M., Inoue, K., Monden, A., Torii, K., and Matsumoto, K.-i. Button selection for general GUIs using eye and hand together. In *Proc. of AVI'00*, ACM (2000), 270–273.
26. Yoo, B., Han, J.-J., Choi, C., Yi, K., Suh, S., Park, D., and Kim, C. 3D user interface combining gaze and hand gestures for large-scale display. In *Proc. of CHI EA'10*, ACM (2010), 3709–3714.
27. Zhai, S., Morimoto, C., and Ihde, S. Manual and gaze input cascaded (MAGIC) pointing. In *Proc. of CHI'99*, ACM (1999), 246–253.
28. Zhang, X., Ren, X., and Zha, H. Improving eye cursor's stability for eye pointing tasks. In *Proc. of CHI'08*, ACM (2008), 525–534.

Gaze-Augmented Think-Aloud as an Aid to Learning

Sarah A. Vitak
Joint Science Department
Scripps College
sarah.vitak@scrippscollege.edu

John E. Ingram
Math and Computer Science
Sewanee: Univ. of the South
ingraje0@sewanee.edu

Andrew T. Duchowski
School of Computing
Clemson University
duchowski@clemson.edu

Steven Ellis
Animal & Veterinary Sciences
Clemson University
ellis@clemson.edu

Anand K. Gramopadhye
Industrial Engineering
Clemson University
agramop@clemson.edu

ABSTRACT
The use of recorded eye movements, or *scanpaths*, has been demonstrated as an effective visualization for feed-forward visual search training, instruction, and stimulated retrospective think-aloud usability testing. In this paper we show that creation of a scripted or recorded video of an expert's think-aloud session augmented by an animation of their scanpaths can result in an effective aid for learners of visual search. Because the creation of such a video is relatively easy, the benefits-to-cost ratio may potentially be substantial, especially in settings where learned visual scanning strategies are indicators of expertise. We suggest that two such examples are examinations of Chest X-Rays and histological slides. Results are presented where straightforward construction of an instruction video provides measurable benefit to novice as well as experienced learners in the latter context.

Author Keywords
eye tracking; histology; visual search

ACM Classification Keywords
H.1 Models and Principles: User/Machine Systems; H.5 Information Interfaces and Presentation: User Interfaces; J.4 Computer Applications: Social and Behavioral Sciences

INTRODUCTION
Expertise manifests itself differently, depending on the given demands of the task. For example, expertise can involve expression of deep knowledge of a subject (e.g., scholarship), or physical prowess as demonstrated by consistency and precision of action (e.g., repeatable golf swing). In the particular execution of visual search, well defined strategies have been developed by domain experts. In certain approaches to pathology and other diagnostic disciplines that require image analysis, radiologists employ a partially endogenous, cognitive visual search strategy, related to top-down mechanisms that are based on prior expectations [15], which in turn are couched in training and experience. In the specific case of Chest X-Ray (CXR) reading, this strategy may be typified by the ABCDEFGHI method for CXR interpretation. The ABCDEFGHI mnemonic guides trainees and practitioners through a series of checks and assessments to inspect **A**irway, **B**ones, **C**ardiac silhouette, **D**iaphragms, **E**xternal soft tissues, **F**ields of the lungs, **G**astric bubble, **H**ila, and **I**nstrumentation. Figure 1 illustrates qualitatively the differences in expert and novice visual strategies: the expert executes the search quickly, tending to "check off" the ABCDEFGHI elements, not pausing excessively on any particular element (notice that in the abnormal CXR with left lung atelectasis, the expert does not devote an apparently greater proportion of fixations over the problematic left lung, clearly opaque in Figure 1(b)). Conversely, the novice tends to dwell longer on each of the elements, often revisiting previously examined regions of the film. If the expert's visual search strategy could be recorded, visualized, and taught to trainees, we hypothesize its adoption by novices is likely to be accelerated.

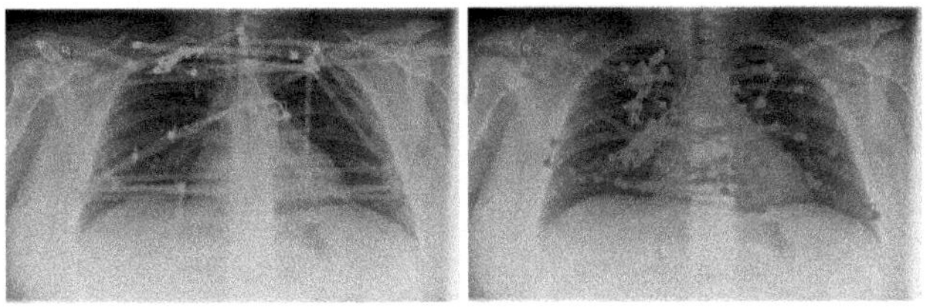

(a) expert (left) and novice (right) viewing normal CXR

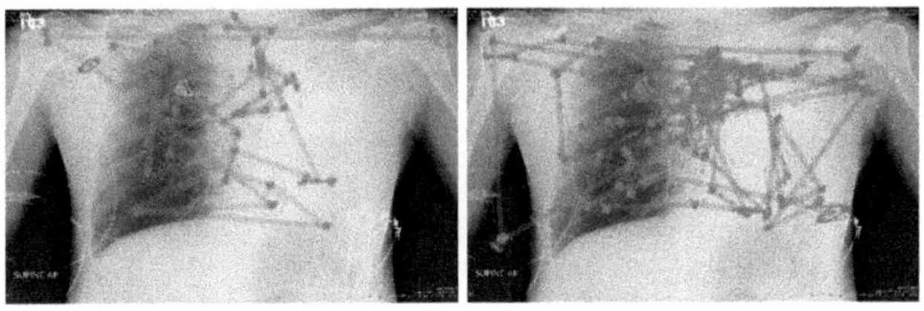

(b) expert (left) and novice (right) viewing abnormal CXR

Figure 1. Example of expert/novice scanpaths over CXR film: experts tend to execute the visual search task considerably faster than novices.

In this paper we test this hypothesis in a related visual search task, namely structured image analysis performed during the course of traditional histology instruction. Histology is the study of the microscopic anatomical structure of cells and tissue, and is usually performed by examining a thin slice or section of tissue under a light microscope or electron microscope. Histological stains are often used to enhance the ability to visualize or differentially identify microscopic structures. However, it is the ability of the histologist to differentiate between certain types of cells that is the most crucial aspect of the task. Thus a complementary understanding of structure and function is necessary for students to understand the core concepts in the biological sciences. Students who develop a comprehensive understanding of structure-function complementarity are better able to integrate concepts of biology across multiple scales of inquiry. Histology then, is a discipline perfectly suited to instruction in structure-function complementarity because it integrates physical and physiologic concepts from the chemical to the organismal scales.

Histology instruction still employs single-viewer microscopes and classical tissue staining methods that have not changed over many decades. There are tissue-specific classification systems (e.g., shape, arrangement, and specialization amongst epithelial tissues), but different systems are required for each tissue type (epithelial, connective, nervous, muscle) and peculiarities of arrangement or modification lead to confusion between some tissues and organs. Others have even reported that, in practice, the actual vernacular for histology differs from the structured classification systems espoused in the textbooks—in fact, Pani et al. [19] have described the development of histologic acumen amongst undergraduates and noted wide variation in the specific features used by the tested students for the identification of tissues or organs. Despite shared knowledge of a common syntax and vocabulary for histologic identification, the students used different visual cues for their identifications, with varying success.

Histology centers on the development of knowledge and skills required for the recognition of primary tissue types, identification of organs, and appreciation for structure-function complementarity. Following lecture discussion of specific tissues or organs, students inspect slides to develop visual recognition skills. Histologic proficiency is assessed through a combination of standard written tests and practical examinations where students are allowed a limited time to inspect an image or microscope field for subsequent identification. The development of effective visual search strategies is thus critical to student achievement.

BACKGROUND

Previous efforts have promoted a conceptual understanding of histology through abstraction and generalization of common biologic themes [3]. Unfortunately, there is still a great unmet need for organization in histology studies. Indeed, a survey of classic and contemporary histology texts yields little in the way of helpful advice other than admonitions to consider the plane of section, to mind the specific staining or visualization technique employed, and to be wary of artifacts caused by processing [5, 23, 25, 16]. Adherence to such guidelines requires trained interpretation and analysis of the micrograph. So, the advice is not always helpful to beginning histology students, who are then forced to develop methods for analysis independently.

Part of the challenge in developing a more effective approach to histology instruction is that little is known about exact visual scanpaths employed by students during the analysis of micrographs or microscope fields. However, understanding visual strategies for image or field analysis can be extremely informative.

Comparison of eye movements of experts and novices is surveyed by Ericsson et al. [4]. In this compendium, eye movement comparison methods are reviewed of soccer players, pilots, drivers, musicians, chess players, and laparoscopic surgeons. Among the many useful conclusions summarized in the volume, data are presented to illustrate that:

- expert soccer players use visual search to anticipate defenders' actions when playing against a video-taped opponent (expert search strategies are task dependent);
- expert pilots' gaze during simulated flight showed their landing performance less variable than apprentices' (experts' shorter dwell times were thought to reflect their skill level);
- apprentice drivers appear to concentrate their visual search in a smaller area, closer to the front of the vehicle (experienced drivers make better use of peripheral vision);
- minute ocular movements of musicians are modified considerably by training and that beginning text readers' eye movements differ from advanced readers (expert patterns of visual analysis develop with training, even across disparate visual stimuli);
- advanced chess players fixate more on the edges of squares than weaker players, exhibiting saccades of larger amplitude (more-skilled players use a larger area around fixation to detect changes);
- expert laparoscopic surgeons tend to fixate the target rather than the tip of the laparascope as novices do [11] (experts develop proficiency in the utilization of extra-foveal, i.e., peripheral, vision).

Additionally, O'Neill et al. [18] reported that glaucoma subspecialists develop a more systematic efficient and logical approach to examining optic disc images than trainees.

Previous studies on the analysis of visual scanpaths in histology are limited. Using a fixed magnification image and a head-mounted eye-tracker, Krupinski et al. [10] showed that expert observers spent less time scanning the whole image and identified regions of interest almost immediately. Medical students viewing the same images had a less-directed search pattern with more saccades, but failed to identify the same regions of interest and relied more heavily on foveal inspection than the peripheral visual recognition exhibited by trained pathologists. Predictable alterations in the pattern of saccades and increased reliance on peripheral vision may therefore serve as objective indicators of analytic proficiency, but little information presently exists to describe how much training is required for the development of such expert behaviors.

Elsewhere, eye tracking studies of scanpaths used by pathologists viewing virtual slides at a range of magnifications revealed that different expert individuals spent a large fraction of time viewing similar regions of interest [22]. Effectively, the study demonstrated that eye tracking can be used to reveal which features were most useful for diagnosis. Indeed, Krupinski et al. [10] specifically highlighted the possible development of a feed-forward training program similar to the program employed in this study.

Others [26] have reported high variation in eye-tracking data comparisons amongst a small group of pathologists, but utilized only a very limited image series (2 micrographs) and did not develop comparative metrics to analyze the differences reported. Instead, subjective assessments of differences in scanpaths were offered. The subjective assessments are difficult to extrapolate because of the limited image set used. Furthermore, the eye-tracking hardware employed in the study was relatively crude, consisting of a bulky head-mounted device, reflective surfaces, and other distracting elements that could have affected the outcome.

Sadasivan et al. [24] had previously shown that students can be trained in adoption of visual inspection strategies and the development of advanced analytical skills for aircraft inspection. While seemingly disparate, the analysis of aircraft images during inspector training closely mirrors histologic instruction in many ways. Aircraft inspectors and histologists must both orient themselves to the image by recognizing the field on the basis of regions of interest, detection of significant features (e.g., fuselage elements or epithelial tissues, respectively), and analyze component parts. In the aircraft inspection study, an eye tracker was used to record the pattern of visual inspection ("scanpath") used by expert inspectors reviewing images of aircraft parts. Novices viewing the same images were then guided with effective search/recognition strategies by the expert scanpath. In effect, the scanpath was used to train students *how to analyze* an image, not just *how to recognize* an image. The feed-forward instructional system was shown to improve training outcomes and reduce the time required for development of analytical proficiency.

While Sadasivan et al. used static (and stylized) scanpath depictions to guide attention, Nalanagula et al. [17] presented evidence for enhanced visual search training benefits from dynamic and hybrid gaze cues. Litchfield and Ball [12] have also shown that dynamic scanpaths can also promote attentional shifts that trigger insight problem solving.

In a series of experiments, Litchfield et al. [13] investigated whether radiographers benefit from knowing where others fixated when searching CXRs for pulmonary nodules. They showed that both novice and experienced radiographers' performance improved when shown the visual search behavior of either a novice radiographer or expert radiologist, while only novices' performance consistently improved when shown an expert's search behavior. In two experiments, participants were either "shown an eye movement recording of someone else examining the image" or "shown an eye movement recording indicating where an expert radiologists examined each image", with the latter instruction hypothesizing the *task-specificity* of eye movements as the primary factor effecting learning benefit. Although the second experiment confirmed the hypothesis of task-specificity, neither experiment explicitly identified or otherwise advocated a search task strategy to be learned by either expert or novice observers. Indeed, we believe that it is the task-specific search strategy that is essential for provision of a learning benefit, and that, for learning to occur, it must be presented to the observer in some fashion *a priori*, e.g., through mnemonic instruction such as with the ABCDEFGHI method, and/or through verbalization of the method. Eye movements are a means of visualizing the strategy, which, we believe, help identify search targets in the image thereby illustrating the process. We hypothesize that the combination of verbalized strategy along with expert eye movement depiction, akin to a graphically stimulated think-aloud protocol, will imbue a greater learning benefit than verbalization alone, however.

Guan et al. [6] examined the validity of Stimulated Retrospective Think-Aloud and found it to be a reliable and valid form of recording the participant's visual and verbal processes captured during task execution. This protocol, performed retrospectively, relies on re-examination of one's own scanpath in an effort to jog one's memory regarding visual elements inspected while performing the task. Although this protocol could be used to elicit retrospective commentary on the strategy employed by an expert, it is generally not used for this purpose, rather it is more popular for usability evaluation.

Combining an expert's verbal explanation with their eye movement recordings, termed Eye Movement Modeling Examples (EMME), is an effective method of highlighting aspects of dynamic stimulus (i.e., video) in an instructional setting (e.g., classification of fish locomotion patterns and diagnosis of neurological diseases in infants) [9, 7, 8]. Expertise task analysis precedes EMME composition so that salient regions of the video are highlighted by the superimposed expert's scanpath. We follow this approach in advocating task analysis prior to eye movement recording so that an expert's specific scanning strategy can be captured. In this particular instance, we do so for visual inspection of histological slides. We show that the superimposition of the expert's scanpath is effective in the simpler usage of still images used as stimuli. Moreover, our approach differs from EMME in that the objective is not only to highlight salient regions of the images, but to impart an expert's visual search *strategy* to the novice.

In this paper, we combine the ideas of feed-forward scanpath visualization, retrospective think-aloud, and EMME to a certain extent, and propose a Gaze-Augmented Think-Aloud protocol which we believe to be specifically suitable for use in the instructional (classroom) setting. The protocol calls for creation of a video depicting the recorded scanpath, augmented by an either scripted or recorded verbalization of the task as the scanpath was recorded. Scanpath visualizations are relatively easily obtained since most eye tracking software is generally capable of exporting such a video stream. Augmenting this video stream with an audio stream of the relevant verbalization is achieved with little complication by most video authoring tools (e.g., `iMovie`).

Beyond EMME, other approaches are somewhat less closely related but incorporate facets of visual search and involve ei-

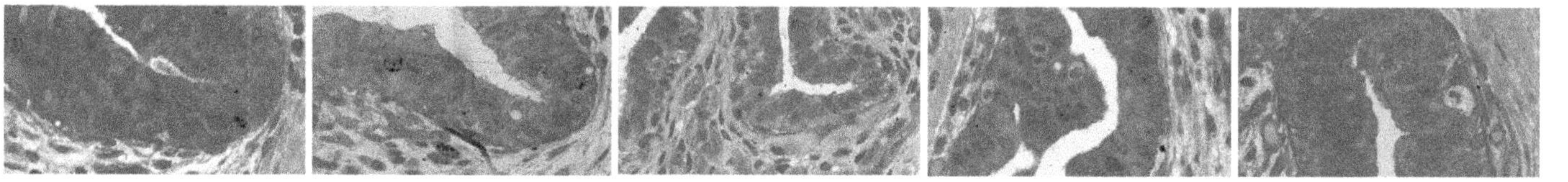

image 1:	*there's label on [counting] one cell, two cells, three cells*
image 2:	*this one has a very obvious label; there's some... label in connective tissue that doesn't count or isn't of interest for this study*
image 3:	*there's obvious epithelia but no discernible label*
image 4:	*labeling on the top on the right side; that's about it...there's a blood vessel on the left that you wouldn't count*
image 5:	*the BrdU is in the stroma not in the epithelia*

Figure 2. Training video (duration: 1:03 min): the five images used in the GATA video showing gaze locations (scanpath samples) on select frames along with excerpts from the transcribed audio stream synchronized with the scanpath visualization over the five images—it is important to note that the audio identifies both true and false positive target locations (marked cells that should and should not be counted).

ther highlighting salient regions of interest with a high-resolution foveated window [2], a variant of the moving window paradigm [14, 21], or mask out previously foveated regions to force the viewer to inspect previously unfixated regions [20].

In this paper we document a clear learning benefit of Gaze-Augmented Think-Aloud, as demonstrated by naïve and experienced learners in examining histological slides. We follow the EMME protocol's specification of a prerequisite task analysis, but diverge from EMME by requiring a specific visual search strategy for this particular domain.

METHODOLOGY

The key to learning visual search is to present learners with a *strategy* on which to rely on when scanning the visual stimulus, in the present case histological slides. To promote a visual strategy, we developed one that is analogous to what radiologists use when reading Chest X-Rays (CXRs), namely following the ABCDEFGHI mnemonic.

CXR reading depends roughly on two stages: evaluation of the CXR slide (noting exposure quality of film, orientation of the patient, e.g., whether the CXR is anteroposterior (AP) or posteroanterior (PA), etc.), and identification of the slide features following the ABCDEFGHI mnemonic (airway, bones, cardiac silhouette, diaphragms, external soft tissues, fields of the lungs, gastric bubble, hila, and instrumentation).

In the case of histological slides, a proposed search strategy is one that can be generalized across histology samples. We have distilled the advice and content offered to students in an Animal Histology course taught at our university down to a **STAMP** mnemonic to guide our initial efforts. Specifically, through recording of an expert's scanpath, students are advised to consider: **S**taining, **T**issue types, **A**rtifacts, **M**agnification, and **P**lane of section.

Training in the analysis of **S**taining techniques should include recognition of common histochemical indicators that can be used to calibrate expectations in the image (e.g., nuclei are generally basophilic, but erythrocyte cytoplasm is generally acidophilic). Instruction in recognition of **T**issue types should proceed by conventional methods (e.g., assessing cellularity, extracellular materials, lumenal spaces, and repeating structural patterns). Students should be reminded to be wary of **A**rtifacts that might confuse identification (e.g., spurious separation artifacts). Guidance on the estimation of **M**agnification should be offered through discussion of expected size ranges for common histologic reference elements (cell nuclei, erythrocytes, etc.). Finally, students should be taught to recognize the **P**lane of section as an aid in orienting their inspection patterns.

The **STAMP** approach closely and concisely approximates the advice offered in a wide range of introductory histology and pathology texts [5, 23, 25, 16], so it should serve as a useful basis for Gaze-Augmented Think-Aloud. However, because a great deal of visual image processing happens over a very short time scale when visual stimuli are encountered, even experts may not be consciously aware of more defined search patterns they use to analyze images. This is the main reason for recording eye movements (scanpaths) of an expert histologist as they perform the **STAMP** search strategy.

To assess the effectiveness of Gaze-Augmented Think-Aloud, scanpaths were recorded of the histology instructor as he viewed the stained histology images used in the study. The task that both instructor and learners were asked to perform required identification of immuno-gold marked epithelial cells in bovine mammary tissue. The instructor's (expert's) scanpath was recorded by commercial eye tracking software (Tobii Studio (v2.2.8)) and exported as a video clip. His accompanying verbalization was recorded by a digital recorder and synchronized to the scanpath video in a video editor (Apple's `iMovie`). The resultant Gaze-Augmented Think-Aloud (GATA) video was shown to one of two groups of participants in the study (see Figure 2). Although the video was short in duration (only 1:03 min), it identified both true and false target locations (marked cells that should and should not be counted) visually and aurally to participants in the experimental group; participants in the control group saw the training images but only heard the instructor's audio recording, and did not see the animated scanpath visualization.

Experimental Design

The experiment was designed as a 2 (presence or absence of scanpath visualization) $\times$ 2 (experienced or naïve participant) mixed factorial design with scanpath visualization serving as the between-subjects factor and eight stimuli images serving as the within-subjects factor. That is, only one of two groups of participants saw the scanpath visualization, but every participant saw eight stimuli images, shown in randomized order.

Two groups of participants were recruited. Both were given basic training in viewing histological slides, but only the experimental group was shown the gaze-augmented video clip. The control group saw the same training video along with the instructor's recorded verbalization, but with no scanpath visualization. Both groups were tasked with finding immuno-gold marked cells and their eye movements were recorded as they completed the task.

Stimulus

Eight stimuli images and five training images were provided by a histology expert (see Figure 3). All of the images were of immuno-gold (BrdU) stained cross-sections of bovine mammary tissue. Each image was categorized by its level of difficulty: "easy", "medium", or "hard", depending on the number of marked cells and how difficult they were to find. Images characterized as "negative", containing no marked cells, were also used. The eight images participants were shown were divided evenly across these four categories although level of difficulty was not considered in the analysis.

Participants

Participants, eventually 32 in number, with ages ranging from 19 to 57 (mean 24, median 22) took part in the study. The initial goal was to balance the number of participants within two population subgroups: students from an introductory-level anatomy class, knowledgeable about tissue images, and naïve participants with no prior knowledge of bovine anatomy. Fifteen participants were recruited from the introductory-level anatomy class—these participants could identify the types of cell layers in the images before the training segment of the study. To match this number, twelve participants were recruited from a neighboring computer science lab. These participants, for the most part, had no experience looking at histological slides and could, at the very most, identify a nucleus before training. An additional five participants—assorted other students and faculty—who were considered naïve in terms of the given task demands, were later recruited when, during the course of the experiment, data from two participants were removed because not enough gaze points were recorded during performance of the task (they probably shifted out of the video camera's field of view during testing; one participant was uncooperative and distracted, and, during the course of the experiment, was busy on his cell phone). For analysis, participants were categorized into two groups based on their prior experience of examining tissue samples.

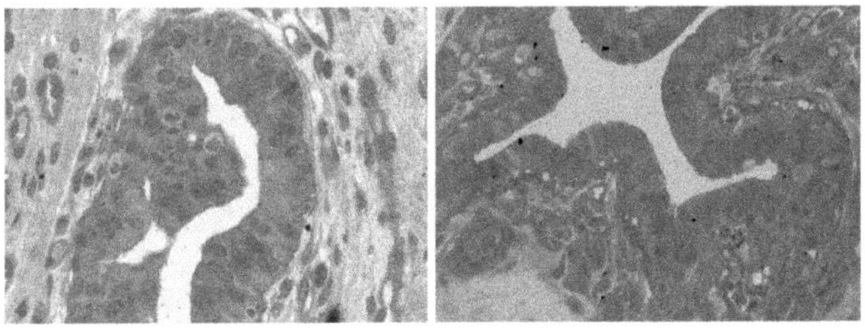

Figure 3. Examples of stimuli used for the study

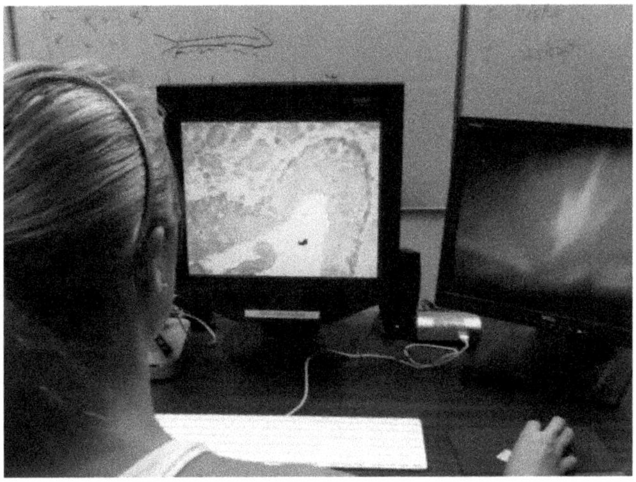

Figure 4. Example of study participant viewing stimulus.

Apparatus

Eye movements were captured using the Tobii 1750 eye tracker and Tobii's Studio software (see Figure 4). The Tobii 1750 eye tracker is binocular and samples at 50 Hz. Its 17-inch TFT-LCD monitor was set to 1280 × 1024 resolution. Participants sat naturally in front of the computer screen at a distance of about 50 cm. The Tobii Studio software was used to randomize and display stimulus images, collect eye movements while they were displayed, and to record mouse clicks as participants completed the assigned task.

Procedure

Participants were randomly assigned to either the control or experimental group. The training session for both groups was the same. Only the experimental group viewed the gaze-augmented video of an expert's eye movements with verbalization of what he was doing while completing the given task. Apart from the animated scanpath visualization, the video contained no information that was not presented in the training session. The expert's recorded verbalization was played back to both participant groups as they viewed the training slides.

Participants were welcomed and given a seat upon arrival. First, the experimenter asked the participant to review an informational letter concerning their participation. The participant was asked 4 demographic questions (age, occupation, previous experience with histology, and ability to identify any structures in an immuno-gold stained mammary tissue image). The experimenter then gave a short PowerPoint training session (see Figure 5).

The training highlighted the staining technique used to create the images, how to identify immuno-gold marked cells, how to identify the epithelial layer, and how to avoid artifacts

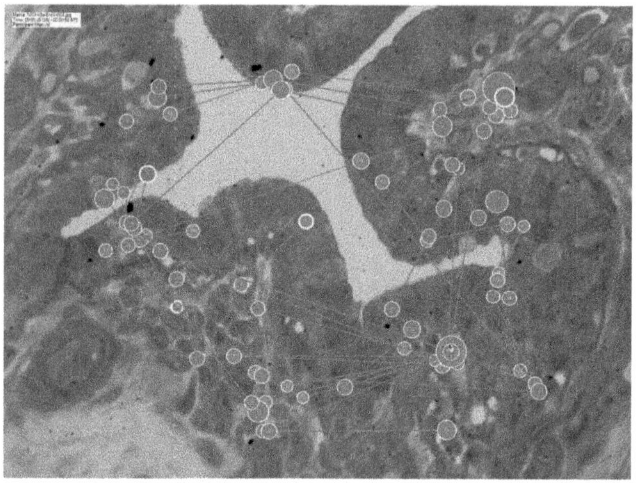

Figure 6. Examples of two captured scanpaths over the stimulus: the blue scanpath is by a participant who saw the GATA training video, the red is by a control participant who did not see the GATA video.

or mistakes in the images. After this the experimenter answered any questions the participant had about the information presented in the training. The experimenter then told the participant their task would be to "identify cells marked with immuno-gold in the epithelial layer" and answered any questions about the task. At this point, those in the experimental group were shown the GATA video of the expert's eye movements while those in the control group were shown the same video but without the animated scanpath (just the expert's audio track). Then, for both control and experimental groups, the Tobii 1750 was calibrated, participants were instructed to follow a moving red dot with their eyes. If the calibration was deemed unsuccessful by the experimenter (based on visualization of calibration error displayed by the eye tracker software), it was repeated. If the calibration was deemed successful, participants were then reminded of the task and instructed to make their selections using a left mouse click, and to use the space-bar to move on to the next image. The eight stimulus images were then displayed in a randomized order and with no time limit (self-paced). After making selections within each of the eight images the participant was thanked and dismissed.

Dependent Measures

Dependent measures consisted of performance metrics (speed and accuracy) as well as process (eye movement) measures:

1. Speed. Performance was measured as the time to task completion, tabulated per each of the eight images viewed by each participant and averaged.
2. Fixation count. Fixations are defined as a set of (raw) gaze points counted between two consecutive saccades (rapid eye movements used to reposition the fovea). This measure, tabulated by the number of fixations over each of the eight images viewed and averaged, generally corroborates the time to completion, assuming constant fixation durations, which indeed may not be constant, and often varies proportionately with cognitive load. See Figure 6 for examples of captured scanpaths, consisting of sequences of fixations, over a stimulus image.
3. Fixation duration. Longer fixation durations tend to suggest a higher level of cognitive load, e.g., often considered to be a consequence of increased information processing difficulty. This measure was tabulated as a mean of means: mean fixation duration per each of the eight images viewed, and then averaged.
4. Accuracy. Accuracy was measured by ratios of both true positives and false positives. A true positive (hit) was defined as a cell chosen by the participant that was, in fact, an immuno-gold marked cell in the epithelium. A false positive (miss) was defined as a cell selected by the participant that was not marked and/or not in the epithelium.

RESULTS

Although the between-group experimental design was initially balanced (15 participants per each of experimental and control cells), statistical analysis of speed, accuracy and eye movements was subject to removal of outliers beyond 3 standard deviations. Specifically, in analysis of each of time to completion, number of fixations made, and mean fixation duration, one outlier (from the A&VS group) was found to lie outside of 3 standard deviations and was removed. In terms of accuracy, one outlier was found and removed from the experimental group (those who saw the scanpath).

Time to completion

Analysis of performance via mean gaze time per image (essentially mean time to completion) was obtained by matching the experimental design's 2 (population group) $\times$ 2 (presence of the GATA instructional video) between-subjects factorial design, with image serving as a within-subjects fixed factor, group and video serving as the two between-subjects fixed factors, and time serving as the random factor [1]. Two-way

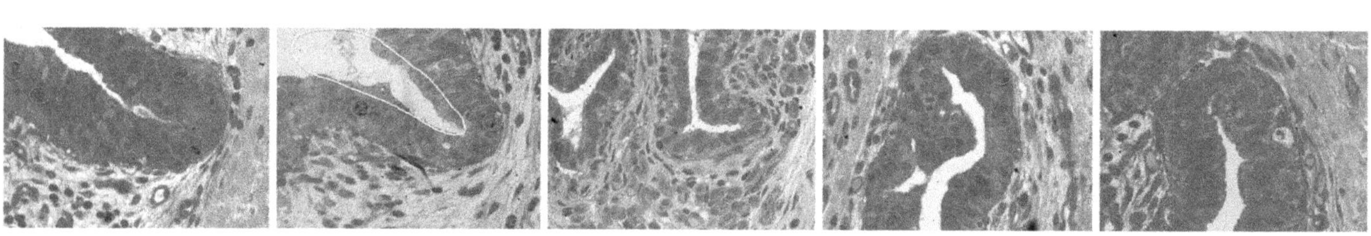

Figure 5. Training slides: the five PowerPoint slides used to train all participants. The first slide highlights the marked cells which participants were later tasked to identify. The second slide differentiates tissue types, e.g., lumen and the epithelial layer that contains marked cells. The third slides shows epithelia with no marked cells. The fourth slide again identifies marked cells. The fifth slide contains no obvious marked cells. Participants heard the same audio verbalization that was part of the GATA video (see Figure 2).

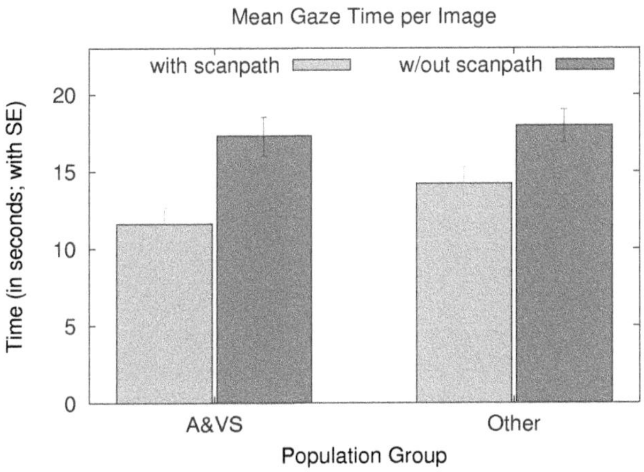

Figure 7. Results: mean gaze time per image.

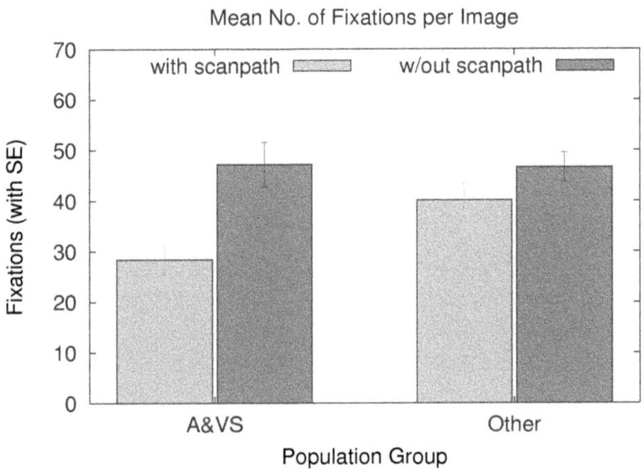

Figure 8. Results: mean number of fixations per image.

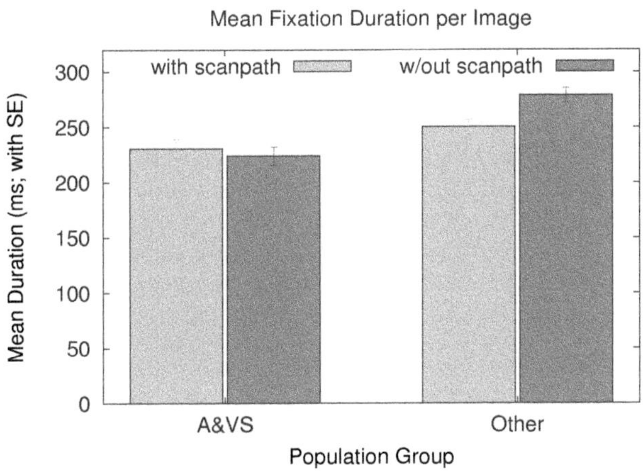

Figure 9. Results: mean gaze duration per image.

ANOVA of time to completion revealed a significant effect of video ($F(1,6) = 9.25$, $p < 0.05$) but not of population group ($F(1,6) = 0.01$, $p = 0.92$, n.s.).

Within-group pairwise comparisons using t-tests with pooled SD and Bonferroni correction show significant differences in time to completion by both naïve ($p < 0.05$) and experienced ($p < 0.01$) participant groups (see Figure 7). On average, experienced participants who viewed the scanpath performed faster ($M = 11.6$, $SD = 7.2$ seconds) than those who did not view the scanpath ($M = 17.3$, $SD = 9.1$ seconds); naïve participants who viewed the scanpath also performed faster ($M = 14.2$, $SD = 8.3$ seconds) than their cohorts who did not see the scanpath ($M = 18.0$, $SD = 8.2$ seconds).

Fixation count

Analysis of the mean number of fixations per image, considered in the same 2×2 experimental manner as time to completion, closely mirrors the time to completion results. Two-way ANOVA of the mean number of fixations revealed a significant effect of video ($F(1,6) = 8.93$, $p < 0.05$) but not of population group ($F(1,6) = 0.02$, $p = 0.90$, n.s.), as depicted in Figure 8.

Within-group pairwise comparisons using t-tests with pooled SD and Bonferroni correction show significant differences in number of fixations by the experienced ($p < 0.01$) viewers, but not by the naïve ($p = 0.14$) participants. On average, experienced participants who viewed the scanpath issued significantly fewer fixations ($M = 28.4$, $SD = 19.6$ fixations) than those who did not view the scanpath ($M = 47.2$, $SD = 31.4$ fixations); naïve participants issued about the same number of fixations whether they saw the scanpath or not ($M = 40.2$, $SD = 25.6$ fixations seeing the scanpath vs. $M = 46.7$, $SD = 22.2$ fixations not seeing the scanpath).

These results are not surprising as the number of fixations is generally related to viewing time spent, particularly during visual search, i.e., one completes visual search faster with fewer fixations, particularly if duration of fixations is constant (which it might not be). In the present case the number of fixations within groups suggests that scanpath visualization produces a stronger effect for the experienced group of viewers, but, in terms of numbers of fixations, offers little improvement benefit for naïve participants.

Fixation duration

Analysis of mean time to completion and mean number of fixations may suggest that fixation durations should not be expected to differ between groups. This is indeed so: analysis of the mean fixation duration, considered in the same 2×2 experimental manner as time to completion, shows no significant differences between participant groups. Specifically, two-way ANOVA of mean fixation durations shows no effects of either population group ($F(1,6) = 0.00$, $p = 0.56$, n.s.) nor of video ($F(1,6) = 0.00$, $p = 0.98$, n.s.), as depicted in Figure 9.

Within-group pairwise comparisons using t-tests with pooled SD and Bonferroni correction show significant differences in fixation duration by the naïve ($p < 0.01$) group but not the experienced ($p = 0.57$) participant group.

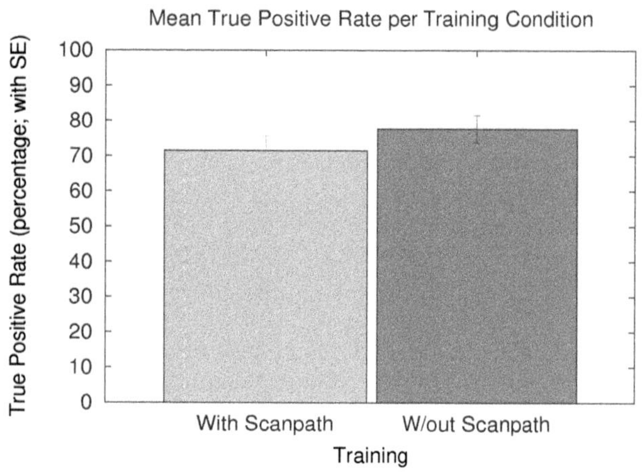

(a)

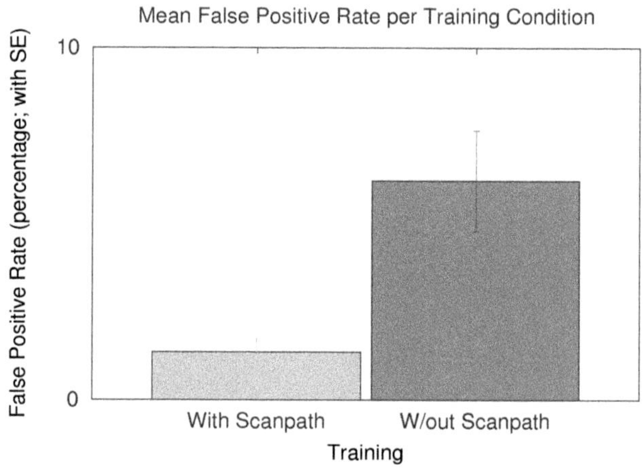

(b)

Figure 10. Results: accuracy in terms of true and false positive rates.

On average, experienced participants who viewed the scanpath issued fixations of about the same duration (M = 230.7, SD = 57.3 ms) as those who did not view the scanpath (M = 224.0, SD = 58.6 ms); naïve participants who saw the scanpath issued significantly shorter fixations (M = 250.2, SD = 51.8 ms) than those who did not (M = 278.9, SD = 50.8 ms).

These results suggest that provision of the training video reduced the fixation duration of naïve students, but not of the experienced Animal and Veterinary Science students.

Accuracy

Accuracy was measured in terms of true positive (hit) and false positive (miss) rates. A true positive was counted when a participant correctly marked an immuno-gold stained cell. A false positive was counted when a participant selected an unmarked cell. The true positive rate was computed as a ratio of true positive selections made by the participant over all possible correct selections (i.e., the number of marked cells) contained in all eight stimulus images. In all, there were 15 marked cells. The false positive rate was computed as a ratio of false positive selections made by the participant over all unmarked cells in all eight stimulus images. There were approximately 800 such cells.

In effect, the true and false positive rates report percentage of correct and erroneous responses, respectively. As shown in Figure 10, participants, on average, correctly identified marked cells at a rate of about 74.5%, with an average error rate of only about 3.8%.

Considering only the effect of the training video on both rates of correct and erroneous responses, i.e., ignoring the population groups, one-way ANOVA of true positive rates shows no significant effect of video on correct responses ($F(1,28) = 1.21$, $p = 0.28$, n.s.). However, the gaze-augmented video appears to significantly affect the error rate ($F(1,27) = 10.15$, $p < 0.01$). On average, participants who viewed it committed fewer errors (M = 1.3% error rate) than those who did not (M = 6.2% error rate).

DISCUSSION

Results suggest a fairly clear explanation for the effect of the scanpath video: the scanpath visually indicates examples of correct targets to search for. Participants who viewed the scanpath generally performed faster and made fewer errors. The effect was more strongly pronounced in the performance of participants who were already somewhat experienced or acquainted with the subject matter, corroborating to a certain extent previous results reported by Litchfield et al. [13].

Eye tracking data provides supporting evidence for the performance benefits: because the number of fixations generally coincides with time taken to complete visual search, participants who did not view the scanpath video took longer to complete the task because they had to issue a larger number of fixations. The difference in time to task completion might not have been evident had it simply been measured with a stopwatch (eye tracking data provides evidence of active visual search—participants were not simply daydreaming or staring at a fixed point).

Fixation duration, which is often associated with cognitive load, in this case suggests that it may also be an indication of expertise, insofar as it may be assumed that expertise relies on familiarity with the subject matter. In this instance, students already familiar with the subject matter, on average, took less time to inspect potential target cells than their counterparts who in general had not previously seen histological slides. Considering shorter fixation durations as indicators of *ambient* types of fixations [27], experienced viewers tend to scan familiar images faster. Longer fixation durations may suggest *focal* types of fixations which unfamiliar viewers need to make in an effort to better understand the stimulus.

Present results support the efficacy of eye movements as feed-forward training visualization previously reported [24, 13, 7, 18], however, the present construction of the Gaze Augmented Think Aloud video is simpler than the more elaborate (e.g., Sadasivan et al.'s [24]) visual codification of the scanpath. The cost-benefit ratio is thus increased by the video compilation's simplicity. Furthermore, our results indicate *why* the GATA protocol is effective: the scanpath visually indicates which targets to look for and which to avoid when augmented by a verbal description of the search strategy.

An obvious criticism of the interpretation of results may be that the observed effect is merely due to the provision of additional training in the form of the GATA video, e.g., the video contained extra material not taught to the control group. Indeed, only the experimental group of participants was presented with the scanpath video. However, apart from the animated scanpath visualization, no additional information was included beyond what was already provided in the training administered to both groups. Both groups heard the expert's recorded verbalization as they viewed the training video (PowerPoint slides). The only difference in training was the animated scanpath itself. The visualization imparts a scanning strategy that the control group did not see, therefore, the observed learning effect can be attributed solely to this visualization. Verbalization alone may only give a vague connection between what is being seen and what is heard. That is, without the benefit of the verbalizer's scanpath visualization, listeners may be "lost in space" when surveying the visual search field. Eye movement visualization provides the critical link between verbal instruction and visual stimulus.

CONCLUSION

Gaze-Augmented Think-Aloud is a relatively simple protocol based on the combination of recorded verbal description augmented with an animated depiction of the expert speaker's eye movements (the scanpath) recorded during the act of verbalization. Most modern eye trackers will readily produce a video animation of a recorded scanpath. Adding an audio track of the viewer's monologue is easily accomplished by modern video editing tools (e.g., `iMovie`, or, for the command-line savvy, `ffmpeg`). The learning benefit of viewing such an audio/video montage is drawn from simply seeing what an expert was doing visually when performing the given task. This form of visualization was empirically shown to significantly affect performance (increasing speed and accuracy by reducing error rate) in the context of histological visual examination. It is likely that this protocol will also carry similar benefit to other similar visual search tasks where a clear visual inspection strategy is employed, e.g., Chest X-Ray reading.

Acknowledgments

This work was supported in part by CNS grant #0850695 from the National Science Foundation (REU Site: Undergraduate Research in Human-Centered Computing).

We would also like to thank reviewers of this initial manuscript and their suggestions for improvement and, in particular, re-formulation of the statistical analysis, which we believe has significantly improved its clarity.

REFERENCES

1. J. Baron and Y. Li. Notes on the use of R for psychology experiments and questionnaires. Online Notes, 09 November 2007. URL: `http://www.psych.upenn.edu/~baron/rpsych/rpsych.html` (last accessed Jan. 2012).
2. M. Dorr, H. Jarodzka, and E. Barth. Space-variant spatio-temporal filtering of video for gaze visualization and perceptual learning. In *ETRA '10: Proceedings of the 2010 Symposium on Eye Tracking Research & Applications*, pages 307–314, New York, NY, 2010. ACM.
3. S. Ellis, M. Marsh, T. McNutt-Scott, S. Calcatera, and N. Balsone. "Design-an-alien" exercises in histologic instruction: A means to promote conceptualization and critical thinking. *Journal of Histotechnology*, 32:76–79, 2009.
4. K. A. Ericsson, N. Charness, P. J. Feltovich, and R. R. Hoffman, editors. *The Cambridge Handbook of Expertise and Expert Performance*. Cambridge University Press, New York, NY, 2006.
5. L. P. Gartner and J. L. Hiatt. *Color Textbook of Histology*. W. B. Saunders Co., Philadelphia, PA, 2nd edition, 2001.
6. Z. Guan, S. Lee, E. Cuddihy, and J. Ramey. The validity of the stimulated retrospective think-aloud method as measured by eye tracking. In *Proceedings of the SIGCHI Conference on Human Factors in computing systems*, CHI '06, pages 1253–1262, New York, NY, 2006. ACM.
7. H. Jarodzka, K. Scheiter, P. Gerjets, and T. van Gog. In the eyes of the beholder: How experts and novices interpret dynamic stimuli. *Learning and Instruction*, 20:146–154, 2010.
8. H. Jarodzka, K. Scheiter, P. Gerjets, T. van Gog, and M. Dorr. How to Convey Perceptual Skills by Displaying Experts' Gaze Data. In *Proceedings of the 31st Annual Conference of the Cognitive Science Society*, pages 2920–2925, Austin, TX, 2009. Cognitive Science Society.
9. H. M. Jarodzka. *In the Eye of an Expert: Conveying Perceptual Skills in Biological and Medical Domains via Eye Movement Modeling Examples*. PhD thesis, Eberhard Karls Universität Tübingen, Tübingen, Germany, April 2010. TR-91-049.
10. E. A. Krupinski, A. A. Tillack, L. Richter, J. T. Henderson, A. K. Bhattacharyya, K. M. Scott, A. R. Graham, M. R. Descour, J. R. Davis, and R. S. Weinsein. Eye-movement study and human performance using telepathology virtual slides. Implications for medical education and differences with experience. *Human Pathology* , 37:1543–1556, 2006.
11. B. Law, M. S. Atkins, A. E. Kirkpatrick, A. J. Lomax, and C. L. Mackenzie. Eye Gaze Patterns Differentiate Novice and Experts in a Virtual Laparoscopic Surgery Training Environment. In *Eye Tracking Research & Applications Symposium*, pages 41–47. ACM, 2004.
12. D. Litchfield and L. J. Ball. Using another's gaze as an explicit aid to insight problem solving. *The Quarterly*

Journal of Experimental Psychology, 64(4):649–656, 2011.

13. D. Litchfield, L. J. Ball, T. Donovan, D. J. Manning, and T. Crawford. Viewing Another Person's Eye Movements Improves Identification of Pulmonary Nodules in Chest X-Ray Inspection. *Journal of Experimental Psychology: Applied*, 16(3):251–262, 2010.

14. G. W. McConkie and K. Rayner. The Span of the Effective Stimulus During a Fixation in Reading. *Perception & Psychophysics*, 17:578–586, 1975.

15. C. Mello-Thoms, C. F. Nodine, and H. L. Kundel. What attracts the eye to the location of missed and reported breast cancers? In *ETRA '02: Proceedings of the 2002 Symposium on Eye Tracking Research & Applications*, pages 111–117, New York, NY, 2002. ACM.

16. A. L. Mescher. *Junqueira's Basic Histology Text & Atlas*. McGraw Hill, New York, NY, 12th edition, 2010.

17. D. Nalanagula, J. S. Greenstein, and A. K. Gramopadhye. Evaluation of the effect of feedforward training displays of search strategy on visual search performance. *International Journal of Industrial Ergonomics*, 36:289–300, 2006.

18. E. C. O'Neill, Y. X. G. Kong, P. P. Connell, D. N. Ong, S. A. Haymes, M. A. Coote, and J. G. Crowston. Gaze Behavior among Experts and Trainees during Optic Disc Examination: Dos How We Look Affect What We See? *Investigative Opththalmology & Visual Science*, 52(7):3976–3983, June 2011.

19. J. R. Pani, J. H. Chariker, N. M. Claudio, and R. D. Fell. Diagnostic visual information in the use of microscopes in histology. In *Proceedings of the 29th Annual Meeting of the Cognitive Science Society*, 2007.

20. P. Qvarfordt, J. T. Biehl, G. Golovchinsky, and T. Dunningan. Understanding the benefits of gaze enhanced visual search. In *ETRA '10: Proceedings of the 2010 Symposium on Eye Tracking Research & Applications*, pages 283–290, New York, NY, 2010. ACM.

21. E. M. Reingold, L. C. Loschky, G. W. McConkie, and D. M. Stampe. Gaze-Contingent Multi-Resolutional Displays: An Integrative Review. *Human Factors*, 45(2):307–328, 2003.

22. L. Roa-Pena, F. Gomez, and E. Romero. An experimental study of pathologist's navigation patterns in virtual microscopy. *Diagnostic Pathology* , 5(1):71–81, 2010.

23. M. H. Ross, E. J. Reith, L. J. Romrell, and L. V. Kibiuk. *Histology: A text and Atlas*. Williams and Wilkins, Baltimore, MD, 2nd edition, 1989.

24. S. Sadasivan, J. S. Greenstein, A. K. Gramopadhye, and A. T. Duchowski. Use of Eye Movements as Feedforward Training for a Synthetic Aircraft Inspection Task. In *Proceedings of ACM CHI 2005 Conference on Human Factors in Computing Systems*, pages 141–149, Portland, OR, 2005. ACM Press.

25. I. R. Telford and C. Bridgman. *Introduction to Functional Histology*. Harper Collins College Publishers, New York, NY, 2nd edition, 1995.

26. E. Tiersma, A. Peters, H. Mooij, and G. Fleuren. Visualising scanning patterns of pathologists in the grading of cervical intraepithelial neoplasia. *Journal of Clincial Pathology* , 56:677–680, 2003.

27. B. M. Velichkovsky, M. Joos, J. R. Helmert, and S. Pannasch. Two Visual Systems and their Eye Movements: Evidence from Static and Dynamic Scene Perception. In *CogSci 2005: Proceedings of the XXVII Conference of the Cognitive Science Society*, pages 2283–2288, 21-23 July 2005.

An Exploratory Study of Eye Typing Fundamentals: Dwell Time, Text Entry Rate, Errors, and Workload

Kari-Jouko Räihä and Saila Ovaska
School of Information Sciences, University of Tampere, Finland
{kari-jouko.raiha, saila.ovaska}@uta.fi

ABSTRACT
Although eye typing (typing on an on-screen keyboard via one's eyes as they are tracked by an eye tracker) has been studied for more than three decades now, we still know relatively little about it from the users' point of view. Standard metrics such as words per minute and keystrokes per character yield information only about the effectiveness of the technology and the interaction techniques developed for eye typing. We conducted an extensive study with almost five hours of eye typing per participant and report on extended qualitative and quantitative analysis of the relationship of dwell time, text entry rate, errors made, and workload experienced by the participants. The analysis method is comprehensive and stresses the need to consider different metrics in unison. The results highlight the importance of catering for individual differences and lead to suggestions for improvements in the interface.

Author Keywords
Eye typing; error analysis; adjustable dwell time; extended study; eye tracking; workload

ACM Classification Keywords
H.5.2. [Information interfaces and presentation]: User Interfaces - Evaluation/methodology;

General Terms
Experimentation, Measurement, Performance

INTRODUCTION
Eye typing refers to entering text for a computer with the eyes as the input device. Writing with the eyes is important for those user groups who find it difficult to use their hands in interaction with the computer. By using a computer equipped with an eye tracking device, people suffering from ALS, locked-in syndrome, or other motor disabilities can produce text by using the focus of gaze as a means of input [10, 12].

While there are several novel approaches [18, 19, 20, 23] for entering text with eye gaze, the traditional and still most common way of eye typing involves selecting characters from an on-screen keyboard. Earlier work has indicated that text entry speeds with eye typing on a virtual keyboard are rather low at first, starting at seven words per minute, but with practice and proper interface design the text entry speed rises considerably. Majaranta, Ahola, and Špakov [11] showed that if users are allowed to adjust the dwell time (the time needed to look at an on-screen key before it gets selected), text entry rates of more than 20 words per minute can be achieved within two and a half hours of practice over a 10-day period.

Our understanding of how eye typing works in detail is still limited. Obviously, the time needed to look at each letter accounts for some of the time needed, but where does the rest of the time go? How close to optimal performance is it possible to get with dwell-based eye typing? Does the time needed to enter a character depend on that character's frequency in the language? Does it depend on the distance from the previous key? A distinctive feature of eye typing is that it does not allow parallel processing as normal typing with the hands and 10 fingers does: there is no 'next finger' that can prepare for its task while the previous key is being pressed. Therefore, it is plausible that the distance between two consecutive keys has a role, except that the eyes are extremely fast and there is as yet no agreement on whether they obey, for example, Fitts' law for selection tasks on the desktop.

What about errors? Previous studies have reported overall error rates, but, again, this calls for more detailed analysis. Are some keys more error-prone than others? It is known that shortening the dwell time increases corrective actions – that is, characters being incorrectly entered and then being deleted via the Backspace key. But why does this happen? Are there inadvertent duplicate clicks of the same key because the eye has not left it in time? Are there inadvertent clicks of the next key because the eye did not land on it correctly after a long saccade and the adjacent key was selected instead? How much are the errors due to poor calibration of the eye tracker?

Finally, subjective impressions of how tiring it is to write by eye typing have not been explored in detail in previous studies. Metrics such as experienced eye fatigue before and after a test session are commonly applied (see, e.g., [11]), but also more detailed satisfaction questionnaires have been suggested – for instance, by Bates and Istance [2], who applied the NASA TLX rating scale [3] in their comparison of eye pointing technologies. We wanted to study it further: what factors cause feelings of extended workload in eye typing?

To shed light on these detail-level issues, we carried out a study of dwell-based eye typing over four weeks with 10 participants. To gain experience with a text entry technique, one needs to use it regularly and repeatedly over some time. In the study, we began with a learning phase similar to that described in [11, 18], with 10 sessions spread over 2–3 weeks. After the learning phase, the participants had some experience in eye typing, typically more than at the onset of any published eye typing studies [12]. This was followed by a controlled phase wherein the participants entered text under the same settings. The dwell times for the five sessions were set such that they extended from fast yet comfortable typing to very fast and error-prone typing, to illuminate the effects of reduced dwell time. In contrast with previous studies, our focus was on finding out how quickly and effortlessly people can type in several sessions in this advanced phase, after the initial learning phase. The final phase consisted of a typing session of one full hour, to reveal whether the duration of the task has a significant effect on performance.

We next present the method used for data collection and processing. Then, the results from each of the three phases are presented and discussed separately. We conclude by discussing the design implications of our findings.

METHOD

The study involved three consecutive eye typing phases, which took place at varying times of day in a laboratory with no windows.

Before launching the study, we ran a pilot study with two participants and similar procedures (i.e., almost five hours of typing per pilot, over several weeks) except that it was conducted in a normal office room with a window. So, for example, the amount of daylight in the room varied and was not controlled in the pilot. Since it was a likely cause for poor calibration (a problem observed in the pilot), this potentially confounding variable was controlled in the actual experiment that followed.

Participants

Altogether 10 participants (one female) took part in the study. The participants were 16 to 33 years old (mean: 25). They were recruited for the study as part of their summer internship at the university and received no compensation for their effort. Some of them had tried out an eye tracker, and one had taken part in a short-term eye tracking experiment before our study, but none could be considered to have extensive experience in eye typing.

Apparatus

The eye tracker used was a Tobii T60, integrated with a 17-inch TFT color monitor with 1280 × 1024 resolution.

The software used in the experiment was the same as that used in [11] but with a slightly modified layout of the function keys (see Figure 1). The model phrase to be written is shown in the top pane, and the characters entered by the participant appear below it in the entry area (in red). The letters of the alphabet are listed in the three-row QWERTY arrangement for Finnish keyboards (with 'ö', 'ä', and 'å' keys on the right). Common punctuation marks (',.!?') are on the third row.

The fourth and fifth row contain special characters. The fourth-row buttons, from left to right, are Shift, making the next letter chosen appear in uppercase; Space, for adding a space character; and Backspace, to delete a character ('←'). The bottom row has the tools for adjusting the typing speed (with buttons for '–' and '+' and a meter display between them) and the Ready key ('☺') for accepting the string entered and moving to the next one. All keys are displayed as round buttons.

When the user looks at a button to select it, visual feedback is displayed on the button. The animation of a closing circle indicates the elapsing dwell time (shown for the letter 'a' in Figure 1). When the circle is full, the key is shown 'pressed down' and a 'click' sound is heard to indicate that it was selected. Because of the space needed to make the feedback prominent, the letters on the keys look small in Figure 1, but there is no problem with legibility at their actual size (14 pt Arial bold).

To enter the same character twice, one can leave the gaze on the key after typing it for the first time, but the dwell time clock is started only after 150 ms has elapsed since entry of the first character. The reason is that this should aid in avoiding inadvertent double clicks caused by the eyes remaining on one key for too long.

The indicator for adjusting the typing speed works by relative increments and decrements of the dwell time. For a beginning typist, the increment is larger than when the setting is already far right for a fast typist. The actual dwell time is not shown in the interface, only in the experimental control settings.

Procedure

Our study consisted of three phases: the learning, advanced, and extended phase. The focus of this study was the advanced phase. The main role of the learning phase was to bring participants to a certain level, and the extended phase was included to get some feel of whether the short 15 minute sessions would differ from extended use. While the apparatus was the same in all phases, there were minor changes in procedure, as shown in Table 1.

In the learning phase, participants could change the dwell time by adjusting the typing speed whenever they wanted to. In the advanced phase, the dwell time was pre-set before the start of the session and the participant was instructed not to change the setting. Finally, in the extended phase the dwell time was set according to participant preferences.

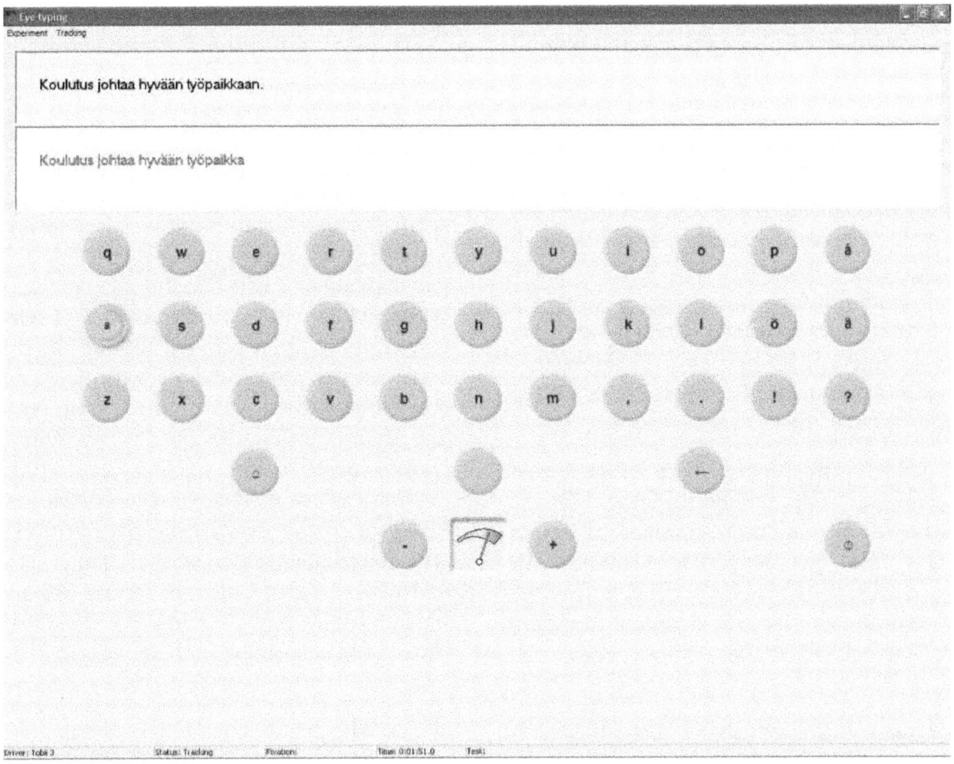

Figure 1. The QWERTY keyboard with Finnish layout used in the experiment.

The participants were seated such that their eyes were at arm's length (50–60 cm) from the on-screen keyboard. The eye tracker was calibrated for each session; in the extended phase, the tracker was recalibrated after every 15 minutes of use. Five-point calibration was used in all phases.

Phase	Session length (minutes)	Number of sessions	Calibrations	Dwell time	TLX
Learning	15	10	1 per session	adjustable	
Advanced	15	5	1 per session	pre-set	X
Extended	60	1	1 every 15 min	preference	

Table 1: Study phases in a nutshell.

The learning and advanced phases featured several sessions, each approximately 15 minutes long. If the participant was in the middle of a phrase when the 15 minutes ended, the software waited until the last phrase was entered in full. Comprehensive text-entry and eye-movement logs were saved after each session.

Subjective evaluations of the task workload were collected in the advanced phase with the NASA TLX workload scale [3]. A paper questionnaire[1] was created for rating of mental demand, physical demand, temporal demand, performance, effort, and frustration level. The participants filled it in after each session in the advanced phase. The rating scale definitions were provided to the participants to be consulted for clarification as needed. After the five sessions, participants weighted the factor dimensions.

Task

The goal was to enter text as quickly and accurately as possible. This is the standard instruction for participants in text entry studies [7, 9, 11, 18]. If the participant noticed immediately (within the same word) that there was an error in the characters entered, the error was to be corrected by deleting with the Backspace key and entering the correct letter(s) instead. However, if the error was further away in the string entered, the instructions were to move on without correcting it.

The model phrases used in the study come from a set of phrases used in studies for text-entry method comparisons in English [8] that were later translated into Finnish [7]. The Finnish phrase set contains 500 phrases, five of which were removed from the set for this experiment (e.g., because they contained characters that do not exist on our keyboard, such as ':'). The software selects phrases randomly and displays them in the top pane one after another. Pressing the 'Ready' key brings up the next phrase.

ANALYSIS AND DATA CLEANING

Metrics used

Text entry rate is measured in words per minute (WPM) [16, 21]. Here, 'word' means five characters; accordingly, the phrase 'Metrics used' forms 2.4 words. The value for

[1] Based on the questionnaire form available from http://humansystems.arc.nasa.gov/groups/TLX/.

the WPM metric is obtained by dividing the number of words entered by the number of minutes used for the text entry task. It is a normalized metric that accommodates text of varying length. WPM is the standard metric used for comparing the performance of different text entry methods.

Since we are also interested in the performance details, we use a metric that is in a sense an inverse of WPM. We call the metric *milliseconds per character* (MSPC). For each character entered, it is defined as the average time (in milliseconds) that it took to enter that character after the previous character was entered; Wobbrock [21] refers to a similar metric as intercharacter time. The smaller the MSPC value, the faster it was to enter the relevant character.

Speed is only one part of the picture. The other factor affecting the user experience is the number of errors. This is commonly measured with two metrics: number of errors remaining in the text that was entered and number of corrective actions (Backspace presses) needed in the process. Again, it is common to use not absolute numbers but figures that are normalized to take into account the length of the text.

For the errors that remain in the text, the normal metric is minimum string distance (MSD) [15, 22]: the minimum number of edit operations (insert character, delete character, and replace character) needed to transform the result string into the target string, divided by the length of the string.

For our study, a measurement that reflects the number of corrective actions is more interesting. Again, there is a standard metric that we will use: keystrokes per character (KSPC) [16, 21]. It is defined as the ratio of the number of key presses used to enter a phrase to the minimum number of key presses needed. With QWERTY-type techniques and with optimal performance, the KSPC value should be 1. This assumes that presses of the Shift key are not counted; we will follow this convention. The higher the KSPC value, the more erroneous characters were entered and had to be corrected.

Data cleaning

In our analysis of the text entry rate, we were interested in the limits achievable by experts. Although we collected typing data for almost five hours for each participant, that did not make the participants experts. To at least approximate expert behaviour as well as possible, we decided to analyze the character-level text entry rate only for characters entered correctly after another correctly entered character. Therefore, if a key was pressed in error and deleted through a press of the Backspace key, it was not included in the MSPC analysis, and neither was the next correct character. Furthermore, if the participant glanced at either the model line or the result line in between two key presses, the latter key press was again omitted from analysis (since the time for pressing it would have been affected by this artefact of the task, not only by the effort needed for pressing the key).

With this process, the remaining characters reflect error-free typing as reliably as possible. In word-level error analysis (i.e., with the MSD and KSPC metrics), all key presses were included as usual, unless otherwise indicated.

LEARNING PHASE

All participants started with a dwell time of 1000 ms. They were free to adjust the dwell time as they saw fit. Two participants (P2 and P5) did not change from the default of 1000 ms in the first session. Clearly they chose a conservative approach, decreasing the dwell time only after considerably more practice with the previous setting. Some participants tried to reach a high typing speed quickly: already in the first session, two participants (P3 and P4) had chosen dwell times of less than 400 ms. The average decrease in the first session was 320 ms. Figure 2 shows a box plot of the dwell time distribution after each session, with the median value shown as the divider within the box, and whiskers that indicate .25 and .75 quartiles extending to the minimum and maximum values. Accordingly, 50% of dwell time selections in the session fall within each box.

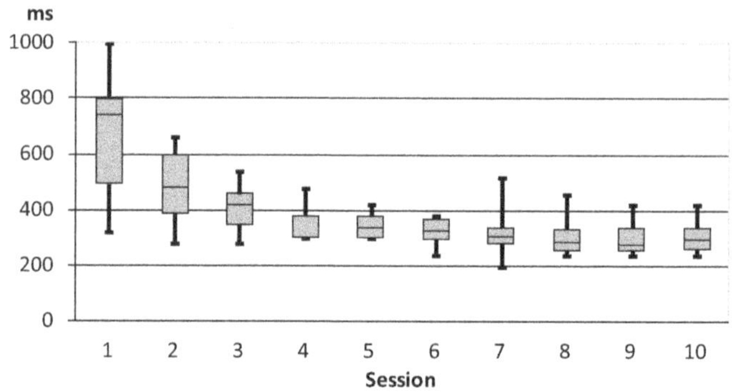

Figure 2. Dwell time (in ms) after each session.

Seven participants never increased the dwell time. The lowest end-of-session dwell time value (200 ms) was that of P4 in session 7, but he returned to 240 ms in session 8 and then stayed with it. Figure 2 does not indicate within-session changes of the setting, only the setting in use when the session ended. For one participant (P5), finding a good dwell time was hard: the data show changes from 380 to 520 ms and then lowering to 420 ms (with several phrases typed with each setting).

On average, the final dwell time in session 10 was around 300 ms; six participants worked with a shorter dwell time than 300 milliseconds and only one participant with more than 400 ms. In summary, the data set indicates that dwell times as short as 200 ms are reachable but not endured for longer periods, and that a workable setting for most participants is found already after four or five sessions.

Text entry efficiency increases in line with the rapid decrease in dwell times. It was typical for the WPM figure to grow until the fifth or sixth session but then level off. The highest WPM value reached was 22.18 (P8, session 10), and five participants, in total, reached 20 WPM; the average in the learning-phase sessions was 16 WPM. The

KSPC values show great variation, which becomes more apparent as one considers individual participants.

Figure 3 plots the WPM and KSPC values over the sessions for P7 and P5, who employed different strategies. P7 was more casual, soon opting for high WPM values, but at the expense of increased errors. His KSPC value in the 10th session was close to 1.2, meaning about one incorrect key press for every 10 characters (with another key press being needed for the Backspace key). P5, on the other hand, tried to carefully avoid incorrect key presses. His KSPC figure stayed low, but he never reached the text entry rate of P7.

It is worth noting that, overall, the participants were careful in their task. In 85% of the sessions, the average MSD was below 1, indicating that participants emphasized correcting errors while typing. Obviously, this affects KSPC numbers. In other words, participant conscientiousness [16] was high.

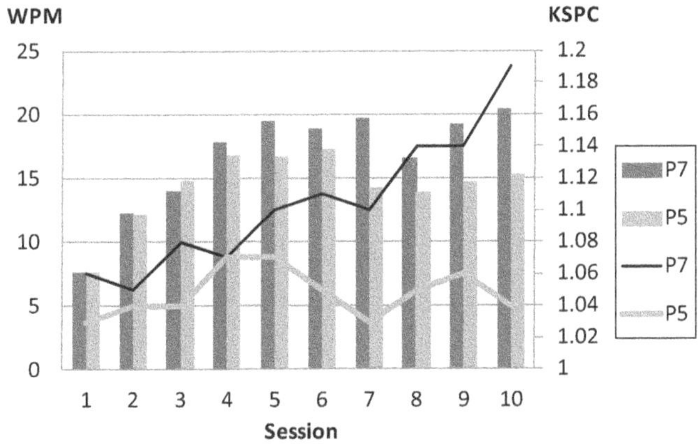

Figure 3. Learning phase: overall performance for P5 and P7 (bars for WPM, lines for KSPC).

Of particular interest to us was what affects the time for each key press, in addition to the dwell time threshold, and how good the actual performance was in comparison to the theoretical optimum allowed by the threshold. This is shown in Figure 4; as explained above, MSPC figures take into account only consecutive error-free key presses for characters. Figure 4 shows combined data from all participants.

In Figure 4, the light green (top) part of each bar represents the dwell time threshold in milliseconds. The darker, bottom part shows what we call 'slack', the time needed to enter a character in addition to dwell time. A small slack is an indication of fluent typing activity. The bar's total height shows the average MSPC figure for each condition. The values on the x-axis also show the decrements produced by pressing of the '–' key of the speed control interface.

We see that the slack decreases at first, then remains fairly stable at close to 300 ms. It does not significantly depend on the session (or, therefore, the dwell time). The jump at a dwell time of 220 ms (for both WPM values and slack) is caused by the fact that the data for the shorter dwell times come from only three participants. As noted, they all returned to higher dwell times by the end of a session.

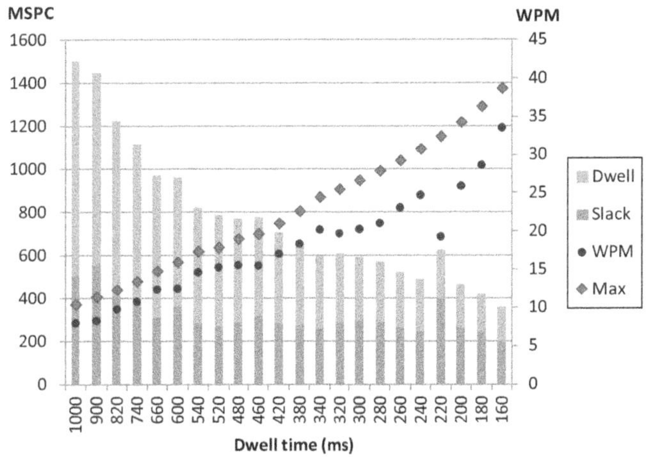

Figure 4. Learning phase: error-free performance (bars for MSPC, markers for WPM).

Figure 4 shows progress during the learning phase, and a similar but more in-depth analysis of performance will be presented for the data collected in the advanced phase.

The red diamond-shaped markers ('Max') in Figure 4 plot the optimal performance achievable, computed by adding to the dwell time 150 ms per character. For double characters, this is the actual minimum slack, and for others we use it to approximate the reaction and movement time needed for moving from one key to the next. Although in the beginning the error-free performance ('WPM') is close to the theoretical optimum, the difference grows as dwell time decreases.

ADVANCED PHASE

Overall performance measures

The five sessions in the advanced phase were on consecutive days, and each session lasted 15 minutes. The dwell time was pre-set for each session and the same for all participants. Figure 5 shows the dwell times used and the participants' minimum, average, and maximum performance.

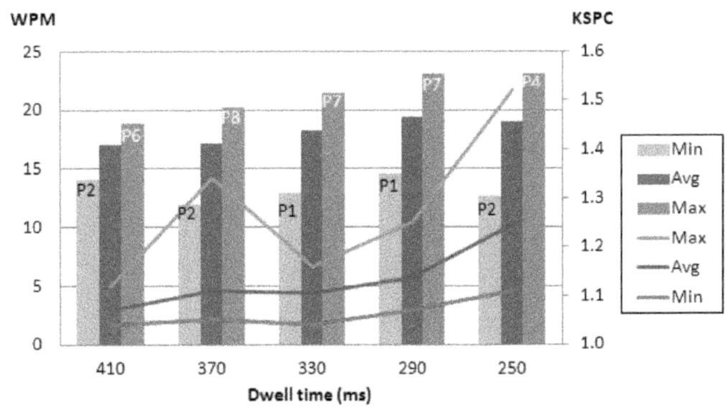

Figure 5. Advanced phase: overall performance (bars for WPM, lines for KSPC).

Comparing with the learning phase (partly depicted in Figure 3), we can see that the maximum entry rates achieved are in line with those at the end of the learning phase. The KSPC metrics show more modest numbers but start to grow as the dwell time approaches 250 ms, which only two participants had reached at the end of the learning phase. Interestingly, one-way ANOVA shows that in the learning phase the session had a significant effect on WPM ($F_{9,81} = 26.615$, $p < .0001$) but not on KSPC ($F_{9,81} = 1.573$, $p > .05$), whereas in the advanced phase the situation is largely reversed: here the session did have a highly significant effect on KSPC ($F_{4,36} = 13.978$, $p < .0001$) but much less so for WPM ($F_{4,36} = 4.310$, $p < .01$). This highlights the fact that when dwell times got inconveniently short, for many participants there was only slight improvement in WPM but a big increase in KSPC.

Figure 6 shows the performance when only error-free character sequences are taken into account, similarly to Figure 4 for the learning phase. The results are similar, and the trend is very consistent: the slack is almost constant, and decreased dwell time improves the WPM value, which, nevertheless, lags more and more behind the theoretical optimum, both in absolute and relative terms (with actual performance declining from 86,0% to 80,9%).

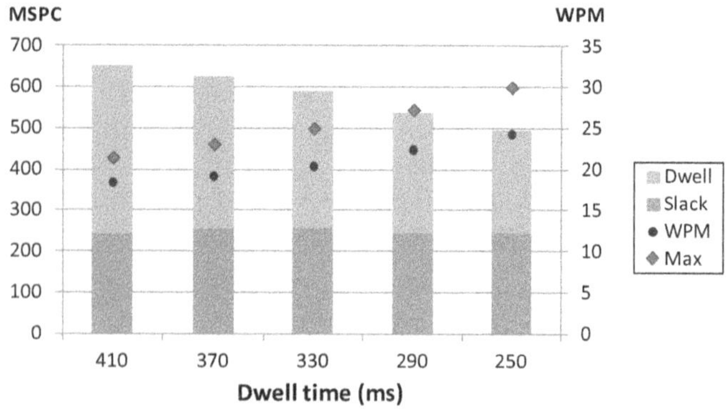

Figure 6. Advanced phase: error-free performance (bars for MSPC, markers for WPM).

Character-level analysis

Turning now to more detailed analysis of what causes the slack, we first inspect the effect of frequency of characters in the language. It is plausible that common characters take less time to enter, as people are used to pressing those keys a great deal. With ordinary typing, much of the keyboard layout is in motor memory; nevertheless, it can be expected that common letters are easy to find for the eyes as well.

Figure 7 shows the average slack for each letter. The letters are ordered according to their frequency in the Finnish language [13]. The dots denote the frequencies.

There are no big surprises in Figure 7. Of course, we did not expect the slack to be an exact functional inverse of frequency – instead, we expected that really rare letters might have a longer slack, and this is indeed the case: the frequency of 'b' in the Finnish language is 0.053% (one 'b' in every 1,900 characters), and from there on the search times get long. Characters 'c', 'å' and 'x' did not appear in the test phrases in this experiment.

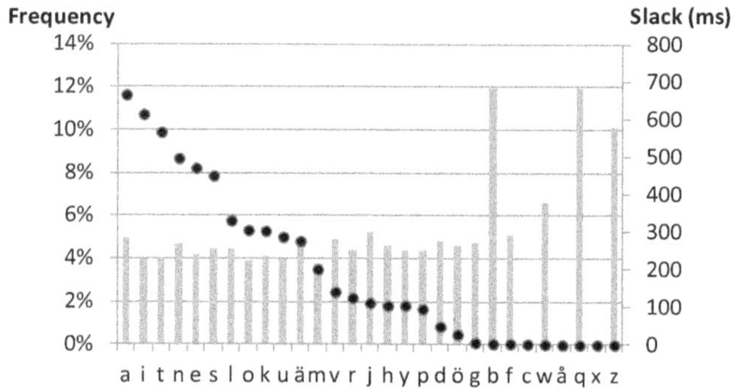

Figure 7. Slack vs. frequency of characters (bars for slack, markers for frequency).

Another possible explanatory factor for the slack is the distance of a letter from the previous letter. The average slack is plotted in Figure 8 for the letter pairs that appear in the data set. Four outliers, for which the slack was more than 500 ms, have been omitted for the sake of a clearer picture; these were for the letter pairs 'iz', 'lh', 'ös', and 'rb'.

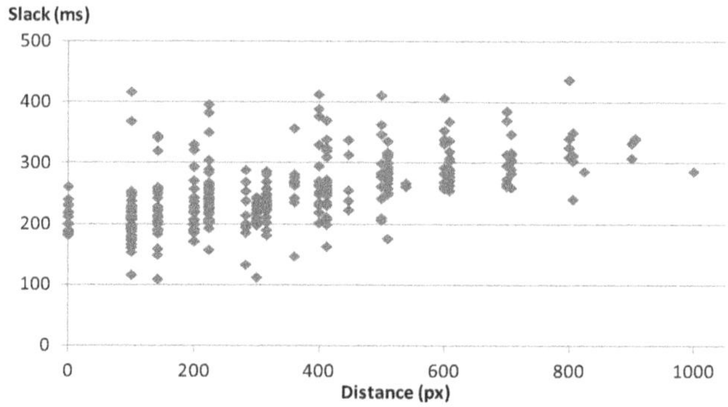

Figure 8. Slack vs. distance from previous character.

The dots at x-value 0 are for cases wherein the same character had to be typed twice. The slacks are not much higher than the minimum of 150 ms. This points to the fact (also supported by subjective experience) that the solution for such double letters worked well. Another approach used in some interfaces is to force the user to leave the letter and return to it, to avoid inadvertent double clicks. The data show that having to leave the key would have been an unnecessary burden: once the first letter was entered, the participant could be sure that the gaze point had been correctly recognised and could relax for the second letter.

The dots show a statistically significant trend: the greater the distance, the larger the slack value ($r = .574$, $t(325) = 12.637$, $p < .0001$). Variability also decreases with distance because of the decreasing number of letter pairs giving rise to each individual distance.

The outliers (omitted from Figure 8) have a logical explanation. For instance, the highest average slack (856 ms) was produced for the letter pair 'iz' (in the word 'pizzaa'). This word was entered several times, by various participants, with varying dwell times. The detailed eye-tracking log tells us that in one case (at 370 ms), P4, after typing 'i', started a visual search for 'z'. His gaze had swept, in turn, over 'j', 'v', 'c', 'x', and 'c' and 'x' again, before finally landing on 'z'. Clearly P4 had an idea of where the key was on the keyboard, but finding the exact location required reading the letters on the keys. Interestingly, in the background questionnaire, P4 indicated that he is a touch typist. As the very last step in the experiment, we asked participants to place the letters of the alphabet on a blank paper keyboard. P4 placed 'z' correctly but transposed 'c' and 'v'. Either the motor memory of touch typists does not fully carry over to eye typing, or people have a different idea of what it means to be a touch typist.

A detailed look at errors

In-depth analysis of the error logs reveals two issues. Some letters were difficult to enter; for instance, the letters 'a', 't', and 's' were often missed. The other issue is that the errors are clustered in some locations on the keyboard and not evenly spread across all letters. The two images in Figure 9 indicate the target letters and the letters that were selected in attempts to enter one of the target letters. The size of the bubble is relative to the number of misses (top) and incorrect selections (bottom). Wobbrock and Myers [22] show how to analyse the missed-hit interdependencies precisely; we adopt a simpler approach, since it suffices for highlighting the issues.

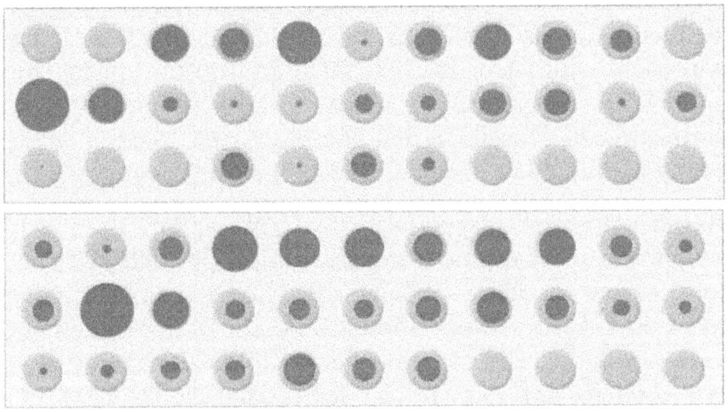

Figure 9. Total error count in the advanced phase. Top: misses of target letters. Bottom: erroneous selections.

Examining the clusters, we see that the misses tended to land to the right. For instance, the letters 'a' and 's', on the left end of the second row, were often missed while 's' and 'd' were often hit incorrectly. Both a closer inspection of the gaze log and subjective experiences confirm that here the reason was poor calibration. Participants had to struggle to enter 'a', though there certainly was no uncertainty as to which key needed to be pressed.

A second cluster, on the top row ('r', 't', and 'y' being hit instead of the intended 'e', 'r', and 't'), has another likely explanation. No calibration issues were experienced with these letters to the same extent. Instead, with short dwell times it often happened that the gaze had landed not on the correct key after a saccade but on its neighbouring key. Before the typist realized this, the software had entered the incorrect key. Complicating things further, many times the participant had already prepared a corrective saccade and proceeded to execute it – creating the need to address two key presses instead of just one. There is a high number of two consecutive presses of Backspace in the data.

Subjective impressions of workload

The NASA TLX rating scale takes into account that experiences of workload and the factors affecting it differ from one person to the next [3]. The individual values given *in situ* for each sub-scale are not accepted for analysis as such. Instead, participants consider the factors' magnitude in their workload in the task situation and the raw numbers are weighted accordingly. For instance, the temporal demands of the task might be greater cause for a participant's sense of the workload than the experimenters' performance expectations are. In total, there are 15 such pairwise factor comparisons. The factor loadings derived for the participants are shown in Figure 10. Only two of the sub-scale factors, physical demand and effort needed to produce the results, were rated high by all respondents.

A striking finding is that people experience the causes of workload quite differently. While P1 emphasized feelings of frustration as cause for experienced workload, for P4 and P7 the most important factor was the temporal demand set by the experimental conditions. The mental demands (need to focus on the task intensively without making errors) make the task especially challenging for P3, P5, P7, and P9.

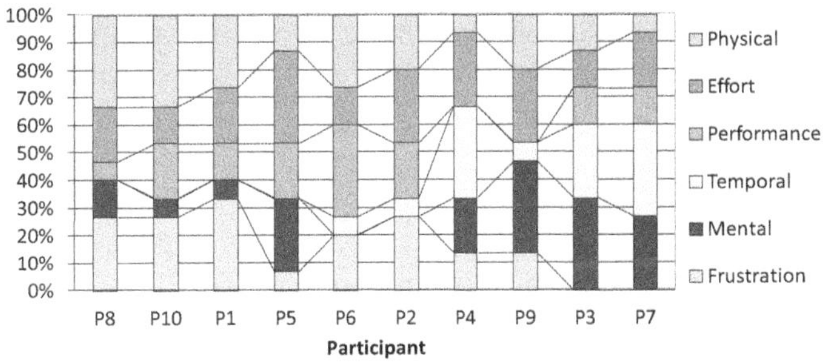

Figure 10. NASA TLX factor loadings for workload estimation.

The subjectively experienced workloads across the five sessions in the advanced phase are shown in Figure 11 as a box plot graph. The participants experienced quite different workloads, which is shown especially in the huge whiskers indicating the dispersion of values (from the .25 and .75 percentiles). The mean over all sessions is 40, which indicates a moderate workload experience.

The participants also ranked their level of eye fatigue before and after each of the five sessions, using a 10-point scale. Yet again the result was that there was great variation by individual. One participant (P5) reported the highest possible value (10) consistently after each test session but another participant (P9), equally consistently, no experiences of eye fatigue. On average, a 2.7-point increase

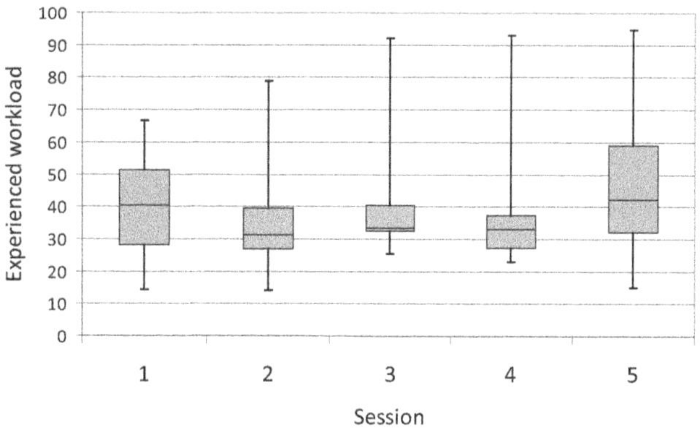

Figure 11. Subjectively experienced workload.

in eye fatigue was reported. Feelings of eye fatigue are caused partly by the need to focus on the task: there do not seem to be good moments for blinking or resting one's eyes when eye typing, especially in studies such as this.

EXTENDED PHASE

The extended phase consisted of a one-hour-long session of eye typing with a dwell time set to a level preferred by the participant. The participants did not take breaks other than as necessitated by recalibration and saving of data every 15 minutes. The experimental software was set such that it collected 15 minutes of data at a time, and then the data were stored by the experimenter and the session continued, with or without a new calibration.

Our motivation for the extended phase was twofold: to see whether there would be a performance difference from the beginning to the end of the session and whether the extended exposure to infrared light would cause significant eye irritation or fatigue.

Overall performance is plotted in Figure 12 in the now-familiar format. The graph is based on data from eight participants: P1 quit after 45 minutes and P5 after 15 minutes. Both complained about eye fatigue. Contrary to our expectations, performance remained fairly constant throughout the full hour for four participants, and two actually improved their performance. Maintaining a steady pace in eye typing seems possible for extended periods even with rates as high as 20–22 WPM. Still, some participants complained that the effort required felt greater in the extended phase than in a normal 15-minute session.

For KSPC, the trend in Figure 12 remains fairly even throughout the session. During a prolonged session, the participants got into a regular typing rhythm. Errors break the rhythm and slow the pace [10].

As for the exposure to infrared light, the T60 conforms to the standard on limits for exposure to IR light (as do all commercial eye trackers). Nevertheless, although safe, infrared light can cause dryness and irritation of the eyes over a long period of use. This was found to be true to some extent; participants were relieved when the extended

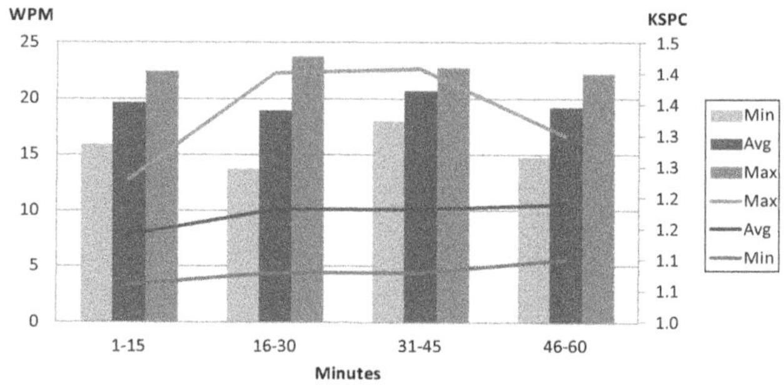

Figure 12. Extended phase: overall performance with dwell times set to 240 to 340 ms (bars for WPM, lines for KSPC).

sessions were over (with the intermediate calibration steps, they took about 75 minutes in total).

DISCUSSION AND DESIGN IMPLICATIONS

The text entry rates in our experiment reached 20–24 WPM. This is a good rate, similar to those reported in an earlier experiment [11]. However, the highest entry rates were achieved at the cost of a high number of corrections (KSPC). Therefore, most participants resorted to a somewhat higher dwell time setting than the one yielding the best WPM rate.

How could we reduce the number of incorrect key presses? We found that there were two main reasons for them: poor calibration and saccades landing on incorrect keys (and, consequently, corrective saccades that compounded the problem). Let us first consider the calibration issue. One approach suggested in the literature is to update the calibration dynamically. When a key is pressed, the software could assume that the user was looking at its centre and gradually improve the calibration accordingly.

Another possibility specific to the typing application is to keep track of the errors. If the application repeatedly detects, for instance, the letter 's' being cancelled and an 'a' entered instead of it (sometimes after several consecutive attempts, as we experienced), it could decide that the calibration is not good for that part of the screen and try to make life easier for the user (or to increase the quality of the data collected for the experimenter, as suggested in [5]). There are at least two options in the case of eye typing. One is to increase the dwell-time threshold for keys that are frequently pressed in error, so that they do not get pressed quite as easily. Thus, additional to user-adjustable overall dwell time, the application could make local modifications to reduce errors – somewhat similar to the suggestion of Špakov and Miniotas [17] except that the adjustments should be localized, not over the whole keyboard. The other option is to change the activation areas, as suggested by MacKenzie and Zhang [9]. The areas are already a bit larger than the visible rendering of the keys. In the example used above, the activation area for 'a' could be broadened and the area for 's' shrunk.

High-frequency eye trackers would allow additional techniques for coping with poor calibration, such as adjusting the cursor position and feedback based on a sliding average of raw data points [4].

The second source of errors was saccades that rested on the wrong key for too long. This is where predictive techniques could help to at least some degree. While predictive techniques in the traditional sense are difficult to implement with a fixed keyboard, an interesting idea was offered by MacKenzie and Zhang [9]. After a letter is entered, the most likely following letters could be highlighted (e.g., with a different border or highlight color for the key). This would still leave the user the possibility of entering any letters desired, but the more likely letters could draw attention and in most cases direct the gaze quickly to the correct target without intermediate clicks.

One issue not revealed by the character-level analysis is the effect of the screen design. We ruled out the use of optimized keyboards in lieu of the QWERTY keyboard, because they would have required a far longer learning phase. Moreover, the advantages might have been small, given the quickness of the eyes. But the QWERTY keyboard still leaves room for many design choices. In our layout, all keys were of equal size, which probably was not a good choice. At least the Space key could have been bigger, since it is the most common key in entry of text.

Probably a bigger time-saver for us than a large Space key would have been easier access to the Backspace key. The high error frequency with 'a' and 's', in particular, meant repeated trips across the keyboard from the left to the Backspace key, near the right edge. There is no reason there could not be several Backspace keys, perhaps one each below, above, to the left of, and to the right of the keyboard. This would force the actual text-entry keys into a smaller space, which would not necessarily be a bad thing, since (as often experienced) the calibration tended to be better toward the centre of the screen. Another possibility is to use offscreen targets (as suggested by Isokoski [6]) that could just be glanced at quickly for cancelling the previous character. This would not require any screen real estate.

The field of workload assessment is a broad one and much researched. In this study, the NASA TLX method provided a versatile (though not universally accepted) means to analyze the influential factors over a number of sessions. In many studies, these factors are not explored fully, and the relevant factors are hard to quantify in questionnaires. Although TLX has been recommended especially for predicting a particular individual's performance of a certain task [14], our current feeling is that understanding the factors that affect workload in a specific situation for the individual requires felt experience, not prediction.

The ratings collected with TLX point to large subjective differences in workload experience. Though eye fatigue (as part of physical demands) likely is one key issue in felt workload, the temporal demands of short dwell time in combination with the mentally taxing need for concentration is an important issue for some users. Furthermore, frustration caused by poor calibration adds to the experienced workload considerably.

Limitations of the study

The data collection was conducted over the course of four weeks. Though more time than is commonly used in experimental studies, it is still quite a short time for learning and becoming an expert user of eye typing.

The main intended user group for eye tracking software, people with motor disabilities, are not readily available for controlled experiments. Conducting such multi-phase studies with members of the intended user population would not be feasible, let alone motivating for the participants, for whom the main interest in eye tracking lies in empowerment in everyday life, not in learning about the limitations of eye tracking technology. Experimental studies of eye typing commonly use able-bodied participants [10], especially in those phases of research in which the software and hardware systems involved are in their early stages.

Finally, the standard instruction in text entry experiments ('type as quickly and accurately as possible') differs from what real-world users would need in everyday use.

CONCLUSION

In our three-phase experiment in eye typing, each participant typed with the eyes for four hours and 45 minutes, in total: more than in any other eye typing experiment we know of with a QWERTY keyboard. Aoki et al. [1] carried out another extensive eye typing study, but they used the Japanese alphabet and the hierarchical GazeTalk keyboard, which makes for a very different situation. The text entry rate we obtained was comparable to those found in a previous study, though somewhat slower [11]. The performance analysis underscores the role of individual differences and the importance of good calibration. It also stresses the need for an even longer study than the one done here, as the values of key metrics changed considerably between the different phases of the study.

We focused on the detailed analysis of expert performance. A new metric and new ways of visualising performance were suggested. These supplement other recent metrics, such as 'attended keys per character' [1], developed to allow fine-grained analysis of eye typing. In particular, our MSPC metric computed from data cleaned of errors allows estimation of expert performance with a reasonable learning time. This is important in a case in which real experts are hard to come by. The detailed analysis led to several suggestions for possible improvements to the interface.

Subjective experience and workload too were analysed systematically, which they typically have not been. The analysis showed that different participants find different aspects of the text entry process strenuous. Common to most participants was that the setting yielding the highest text entry rate in WPM was not considered the most convenient. A proper balance of speed and error-freeness is needed. Leaving the choice of the dwell-time threshold to the user is a key element in creating a satisfying experience.

ACKNOWLEDGMENTS

We are indebted to Heikki Kuivala for carrying out the data collection and for creating scripts for the analysis, and to the summer interns for participation in the experiment. We also thank Oleg Špakov for the experimental software, Poika Isokoski for the phrase set, I. Scott MacKenzie for the use of his Java tools in analyzing the results, and Harri Siirtola for help with the pictures. This work was supported by the Academy of Finland grants 1129335 and 1130044.

REFERENCES

1. Aoki, H., Hansen, J. P., and Itoh, K. Learning gaze typing: what are the obstacles and what progress to expect? *Univ. Access Inf. Soc.* 8, 4 (2009), 297-310.
2. Bates, R. and Istance, H. Zooming interfaces! Enhancing the performance of eye-controlled pointing devices. In *Proc. Assets 2002*, ACM Press (2002), 119-126.
3. Hart, S. G. and Staveland, L. E. Development of the NASA-TLX (Task Load Index): Results of empirical and theoretical research. In P. A. Hancock and N. Meshkati (eds.), *Human Mental Workload*. Elsevier (1988), 139-183.
4. Helmert, J. R., Pannasch, S., and Velichkovsky, B. M. Influences of dwell time and cursor control on the performance in gaze driven typing. *J. Eye Movement Research* 2, 4 (2008), 3:1-8.
5. Hornof, A. J. and Halverson, T. Cleaning up systematic error in eye-tracking data by using fixation locations. *Behavior Research Methods, Instruments, & Computers* 34, 4 (2002), 592-604.
6. Isokoski, P. Text input methods for eye trackers using off-screen targets. In *Proc. ETRA 2000*, ACM Press (2000), 15-21.
7. Isokoski, P. and Linden, T. Effect of foreign language on text transcription performance: Finns writing English. In *Proc. NordiCHI 2004*, ACM Press (2004), 109-112.
8. MacKenzie, I. S. and Soukoreff, R. W. Phrase sets for evaluating text entry techniques. In *CHI2003 Extended Abstracts*, ACM Press (2003), 754-755.
9. MacKenzie, I. S. and Zhang, X. Eye typing using word and letter prediction and a fixation algorithm. In *Proc. ETRA 2008*, ACM Press (2008), 55-58.
10. Majaranta, P. *Text Entry by Eye Gaze*. University of Tampere, Department of Computer Sciences, Dissertations in Interactive Technology, Number 11 (2009). Available at http://acta.uta.fi/pdf/978-951-44-7787-4.pdf
11. Majaranta, P., Ahola, U-K., and Špakov, O. Fast gaze typing with an adjustable dwell time. In *Proc. CHI 2009*, ACM Press (2009), 357-360.
12. Majaranta, P. and Räihä, K.-J. Text entry by gaze: Utilizing eye-tracking. In I. S. MacKenzie and K. Tanaka-Ishii (eds.), *Text Entry Systems: Mobility, Accessibility, Universality*. Morgan Kaufmann (2007), 175-187.
13. Pääkkönen, M. A:sta Ö:hön. Suomen yleiskielen kirjaintilastoja (From A to Ö. Letter frequencies in standard Finnish). *Kielikello* 1/1991, SKS (1991), p. 3.
14. Rubio, S., Díaz, E., Martín, J., and Puente, J. M. Evaluation of subjective mental workload: A comparison of SWAT, NASA-TLX, and Workload Profile methods. *Applied Psychology: An international review* 53:1 (2004), 61-68.
15. Soukoreff, R. W. and MacKenzie, I. S. Measuring errors in text entry tasks: An application of the Levenshtein string distance statistic. In *CHI2001 Extended Abstracts*, ACM Press (2001), 319-320.
16. Soukoreff, R. W. and MacKenzie, I. S. Metrics for text entry research: An evaluation of MSD and KSPC, and a new unified error metric. In *Proc. CHI 2003,* ACM Press (2003), 113-120.
17. Špakov, O. and Miniotas, D. On-line adjustment of dwell time for target selection by gaze. In *Proc. NordiCHI 2004*, ACM Press (2004), 203-206.
18. Tuisku, O., Majaranta, P., Isokoski, P., and Räihä, K.-J. Now Dasher! Dash away! Longitudinal study of fast text entry by eye gaze. In *Proc. ETRA 2008*, ACM Press (2008), 19-26.
19. Urbina, M. H., and Huckauf, A. Alternatives to single character entry and dwell time selection on eye typing. In *Proc. ETRA 2010*, ACM Press (2010), 315-322.
20. Ward, D. J., Blackwell, A. F., and MacKay, D. J. Dasher—a data entry interface using continuous gestures and language models. In *Proc. UIST 2000*, ACM Press (2000), 129-137.
21. Wobbrock, J. O. Measures of text entry performance. In I. S. MacKenzie and K. Tanaka-Ishii (eds.), *Text Entry Systems: Mobility, Accessibility, Universality*. Morgan Kaufmann (2007), 47-74.
22. Wobbrock, J. O. and Myers, B. A. Analyzing the input stream for character-level errors in unconstrained text entry evaluations. *ACM Trans. Comput.-Hum. Interact.* 13, 4, ACM Press (Dec. 2006), 458-489.
23. Wobbrock, J. O., Rubinstein, J., Sawyer, M. W., and Duchowski, A. T. Longitudinal evaluation of discrete consecutive gaze gestures for text entry. In *Proc. ETRA 2008*, ACM Press (2008), 11-18.

Increasing the Security of Gaze-Based Cued-Recall Graphical Passwords Using Saliency Masks

Andreas Bulling
University of Cambridge
Lancaster University
andreas.bulling@acm.org

Florian Alt
University of Stuttgart
florian.alt@vis.uni-stuttgart.de

Albrecht Schmidt
University of Stuttgart
albrecht.schmidt@acm.org

ABSTRACT
With computers being used ever more ubiquitously in situations where privacy is important, secure user authentication is a central requirement. Gaze-based graphical passwords are a particularly promising means for shoulder-surfing-resistant authentication, but selecting secure passwords remains challenging. In this paper, we present a novel gaze-based authentication scheme that makes use of cued-recall graphical passwords on a single image. In order to increase password security, our approach uses a computational model of visual attention to mask those areas of the image that are most likely to attract visual attention. We create a realistic threat model for attacks that may occur in public settings, such as filming the user's interaction while drawing money from an ATM. Based on a 12-participant user study, we show that our approach is significantly more secure than a standard image-based authentication and gaze-based 4-digit PIN entry.

Author Keywords
User authentication; Eye tracking; Gaze-based; Cued-recall graphical passwords; Saliency masks

ACM Classification Keywords
H.5.2 Information Interfaces and Presentation: User Interfaces—*Input devices and strategies*; K.6.5 Computing Milieux: Security and Protection—*Authentication*

General Terms
Experimentation, Human Factors, Security

INTRODUCTION
Graphical passwords have long been investigated as a means of user authentication (see [2, 22] for reviews). Cued-recall graphical passwords (also known as locimetric passwords) have considerable advantages over traditional approaches, such as text passwords, as they leverage the vast capacity and capabilities of the human visual memory system [1, 8]. In addition to improved memorability and thus usability [21], graphical passwords promise increased resistance to guessing attacks, due to the potentially larger theoretical password space. Despite these advantages, graphical passwords that rely on physical interaction with the authentication system are still susceptible to shoulder-surfing attacks [9]. Particularly in public spaces, e.g. in front of an ATM, direct observation techniques such as video cameras or fake keypads can easily be used to eavesdrop and steal passwords or PINs.

Figure 1: Sample images used in the study without (a) and with (b) saliency mask shown in red.

One solution to increase the security of graphical passwords is to use authentication schemes that do not require any physical contact with the system. Amongst the methods investigated in the past, the human gaze is particularly promising for implementing such schemes [14]. By its very nature, gazing does not require any physical contact and therefore, potentially works over greater distances. In addition, the human eye moves rapidly, which makes eavesdropping gaze-based passwords more difficult than touch-based input.

A key challenge in user authentication generally, and in graphical schemes in particular, is to define secure passwords. Previous research has shown that such schemes lead to hotspots, i.e. areas of the image that are more likely to be selected by users as password points. A password point is defined as a single fixation that is detected by the authentication system to be part of the chosen graphical password. These hotspots render such schemes more susceptible to dictionary attacks [24]. The only viable solution so far has been to select single password points across a sequence of several images [5].

In this present work, we present an alternative gaze-based authentication scheme that supports users in selecting secure gaze-based graphical passwords. To tackle the problem of hotspots, our scheme uses a computational model of visual attention – also known as saliency maps – to mask out those areas of the image most likely to attract visual attention (see Figure 1). We show that this approach significantly increases the security of gaze-based cued-recall graphical passwords.

The specific contributions of our research are 1) a shoulder-surfing resistant gaze-based authentication scheme that allows the user to select a sequence of arbitrary points in an image, 2) the introduction of computational models of visual attention to increase the security of gaze-based cued-recall graphical passwords, and 3) a security evaluation of three different gaze-based graphical passwords – PIN, picture without a saliency mask, and picture with a saliency mask – in a user study with 12 participants guessing passwords after watching close-up videos of the eye movements of other users.

RELATED WORK

Gaze-Based Authentication

Gaze has only recently started to be investigated as a means of user authentication. In one of the first works in this area, Kumar *et al.* presented an authentication system that mitigated the issues of shoulder-surfing by using gaze to enter a text-based password on an on-screen keyboard [18]. They found that gaze-based password entry required marginal additional time and that the error rates were similar to those of using a keyboard. Overall, the users in their study preferred gaze to traditional keyboard-based password entry.

One problem with text-based passwords is that they are more vulnerable to guessing attacks, due to the predictability of passwords, particularly for weak user-chosen ones. Several researchers have investigated gaze-based approaches that are less predictable and thus less vulnerable. For example, Maeder *et al.* demonstrated a graphical authentication scheme that requires users to look at pre-defined points in a single image [20]. Using a grid overlaid on the image, different sequences of these points were interpreted as different PINs. They evaluated different fixation thresholds and found that in all cases, users were able to successfully authenticate, using their own PIN sequence.

A key issue with gaze-based authentication schemes is the need for accurate point-of-regard gaze measurements. To address this issue, De Luca *et al.* proposed using sequences of relative eye movements, so-called eye gestures. They argued that gestures can be detected more robustly and are therefore better suited to real-world applications, such as public terminals or ATMs. De Luca *et al.* first demonstrated an authentication system in which each eye gesture corresponded to one digit of a standard pin [7]. In a subsequent work, they presented EyePassShapes – an authentication system that used a single eye gesture as the password [6]. The results of their usability studies indicated that EyePassShapes are more secure than common manual PIN entry and add less time to the login procedure than previous gaze-based authentication schemes. To assess the security of EyePassShapes, they performed a qualitative evaluation where a person familiar with their system tried to attack the password using video footage.

Security of Graphical Passwords

LeBlanc *et al.* identified eye tracking as a potential threat to the security of click-based graphical passwords [19]. They analysed participant gazes as they looked at images that had been used as the basis for passwords in an earlier study. They compared both datasets and analysed the likely success of guessing passwords. In their simulations, they found that the gaze data partly resembled the password click points. The authors argued that this might offer attackers an advantage over guessing click-based graphical passwords at random.

Others investigated means of making text-based and graphical passwords more secure. For example, Forget *et al.* developed a text-based password creation system that leveraged persuasive principles, in order to encourage users to select more secure passwords [10]. Their system randomly added characters to the passwords defined by the users. Afterwards, users were allowed to retrigger this process until they found a password they felt was easy to remember. The authors found that their approach significantly increased password security, but also that participants exhibited compensatory behaviour, by choosing weaker passwords in the first place.

Poorly chosen passwords in graphical password schemes like PassPoints [24] were found to lead to hotspots, i.e. parts of the image for which different users selected similar click-points as part of their passwords. These hotspots allowed attackers to mount more successful dictionary attacks [23]. Chiasson *et al.* addressed this issue by only using one click point on each of a sequence of different pictures; the next picture shown was determined by the location of the previous click point [5]. In subsequent research, they were able to successfully persuade users to select more secure passwords, by using a viewport positioned randomly on the picture that forced users to select a click point within its area [4].

Forget *et al.* conducted the only previous study on gaze-based graphical password entry via user-selected password points [9]. They described a shoulder-surfing-resistant gaze-based authentication scheme that relied on several points on a sequence of different images. They evaluated their scheme with respect to eye tracking accuracy, password entry time, as well as the number of successful logins by users with their own passwords. They also discussed some advantages, in particular the larger theoretical password space (TPS) and the cued-recall nature of their approach that helped users to more easily remember multiple passwords.

Summary

Previous research has investigated eye tracking for gaze-based authentication, as well as means of persuading users to select more secure graphical passwords. Only one study used a "guessing test" to qualitatively evaluate the security of gaze-based graphical passwords [6]. That study involved a single attacker and – like the study presented in [9] – required the user to press a key on a keyboard for several seconds to activate the password detection. In contrast, the current work presents a quantitative evaluation with a total of 240 password attacks from 12 users. In addition, we are the first to investigate computational models of visual attention in order to increase the security of gaze-based graphical passwords.

KEY IDEA

Visual attention is constantly attracted by different parts of the visual scene. Bottom-up computational models of visual

Figure 2: Sample images within the different image categories used in the studies: abstract image with low image complexity (a), abstract image with high image complexity (b), nature image (c), holiday image (d), and landscape image (e).

saliency aim at estimating the parts of a visual scene that are most likely to attract visual attention [15]. Given an input image or video, these models compute a so-called saliency map that topographically encodes for saliency at every location in the image. Visual saliency models were shown to predict human visual performance for a number of psychophysical tasks and have a large number of applications (see [11] for an extensive review). For example, in computer vision, saliency models were used for automated target detection in natural scenes, smart image compression, fast guidance of object recognition systems, or high-level scene analysis [16].

The key concept underlying this work is that by encouraging users to select password points that do not fall inside salient regions of the image, the security of gaze-based graphical passwords can be increased significantly. This is similar to the characteristics commonly required for text-based passwords, such as a minimum number of different alphanumeric or special characters.

Figure 1a shows one of the normal login images used in this work. Because the penguins' heads and feet are most likely to attract the user's visual attention – as predicted by the visual saliency model – these parts are masked out in Figure 1b. In a real-world authentication system, such masked images would be shown to the user in selecting the initial password. During operation, such as for authentication at a public terminal, the same image but without a mask would be used instead.

Method

To calculate saliency maps, we used a Graph-Based Visual Saliency (GBVS) model (see [13] for details on GBVS and [12] for the MATLAB toolbox we used). GBVS was shown to predict human fixations on natural images with superior performance to the original visual saliency algorithm presented in [16]. The saliency maps were calculated using the default parameters of the toolbox. The greyscale heatmaps returned by the GBVS algorithm were first normalised and a threshold applied at the 0.5 level so as to separate salient and non-salient areas. The salient areas were used as saliency masks that were overlaid in red onto the original images (see Figure 1b).

Hypotheses

In this work our aim was to compare gaze-based graphical passwords with and without saliency masks. As a baseline, we opted to use gaze-based PIN entry, which is a common approach for implementing gaze-based graphical passwords [18]. More specifically, we investigated the following hypotheses:

1. Gaze-based graphical passwords using several password points on an image are more secure, i.e. more difficult to attack, than gaze-based PIN entry.
2. Saliency masks increase the strength of gaze-based graphical passwords and thus the system's security.

APPARATUS

We designed and implemented a gaze-based authentication system consisting of a remote eye tracker and a custom login interface. The system allowed users to login using their gaze with two types of graphical passwords.

Hardware

For recording gaze data, we used a Tobii X120 remote eye tracker. The X120 has two integrated infrared cameras and was configured to track gaze at a sampling frequency of 60Hz. The login interface was shown to the participants on a 19 inch computer screen with a resolution of 1600x1200 pixels.

Login Interface

The login interface was implemented in Java and obtained gaze data from the eye tracker via TCP/IP. In addition, it recorded all events triggered by the user interacting with the system, such as the detection of password points or successful and failed login attempts. The interface included a standard 9-point calibration routine to adapt the tracking system to each user and a validation routine to assess the calibration quality. The testing routine involved the user looking at each of the calibration points in sequence until a fixation was detected by the system. Calibration quality was calculated for each participant as the mean Euclidean distance between all calibration points and the detected fixation points.

In the user study, depending on the type of graphical password, the interface showed two different screens:

- PIN: the login screen showed a grid of 10 tiles resembling a standard 10-digit keypad (see Figure 3). In order to perform a login attempt, the participant fixated at four of these tiles in sequence. Sequences of fixations to correct tiles in the correct order resulted in a successful login attempt; all other attempts were considered as failed.
- Image: the login screen showed a full-screen image. In contrast to PINs, the screen was not discretised by a grid, but arbitrary locations in the image could be selected.

We used a dwell-time-based method for selecting the password points of the graphical passwords, because this approach

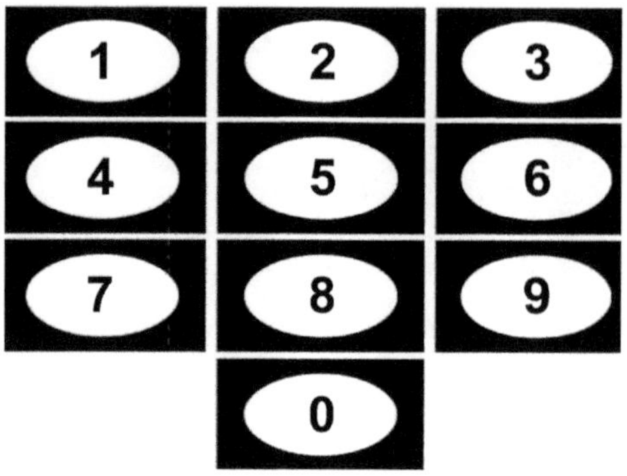

Figure 3: Standard 10-digit keypad used in the studies for gaze-based PIN entry.

is more natural and less error-prone than, for example, double blinks [17]. To select a password point, the participant had to fixate at a certain point in the image. The software continuously analysed the dispersion of the gaze points within a time window of 1.5 seconds. A fixation was detected by the system if at least 70% of the gaze points in this time window were inside a circular area with a radius of 1.7 degree of visual angle (about 75 pixels, the fixation detection threshold th_f).

EXPERIMENT

Study Design

The experiment consisted of a pre-study and a main study. In the pre-study, we asked one group of participants to define three different types of gaze-based graphical passwords (PIN, image with a saliency mask, image without a saliency mask). The goal of the main study was to assess the security of these passwords by asking a second group of participants to try to attack and guess these passwords by analysing close-up videos of the eyes recorded from the pre-study participants. The main study was designed as a randomised, controlled user study (repeated measures design).

For the main study, the binary output of all login attempts per image (successful: 1, unsuccessful: 0) was the dependent variable. The dependent variable was measured under three different conditions of the within-participants factor "graphical password": PIN-based, image-based without saliency mask, and image-based with saliency mask.

Image Selection

Selecting the images was an important step in the study preparation. Allowing participants to choose their own images would have made it difficult to control for similarity across images. In addition, pre-processing of the images would have been necessary to adjust for ratio and resolution. Finally, we expected side effects if people had chosen familiar images, for example containing family members or friends, for which certain areas in the image would have been more likely to be selected as password points.

Because they should also cover a realistic range of motifs and different visual complexities, we preselected all the images.

Figure 4: Experimental setup used in the pre-study. Participants selected image-based passwords, gazing at images with and without a saliency mask, as well as PINs on a standard 10-key keypad. Gazes were recorded using a remote eye tracker placed under, as well as a high-resolution video camera mounted above the computer screen.

We first downloaded a large number of images from the Internet with a resolution of 1600x1200 pixels and without any potentially offensive or sexual content. The images were then grouped into five different categories:

1. *Abstract images* showing *low-complexity* background images with several homogeneous areas (see Figure 2a).
2. *Abstract images* showing *high-complexity* scenes such as from computer games or star clouds (see Figure 2b).
3. *Nature images* showing mainly (multiple) animals in the wild, making it easy to select an individual or a feature of an individual, such as a leg (see Figure 2c).
4. *Holiday images* showing a beach or famous sites very similar to what we expected people to have among their own private holiday pictures (see Figure 2d).
5. *Landscape images* showing famous skylines or mountains (see Figure 2e).

We randomly chose four images per category and calculated a saliency mask version of each of these images, resulting in a total of 40 different images.

Pre-Study

The goal of the pre-study was to record a set of real gaze-based graphical passwords that would be attacked in the main study. For the pre-study, we recruited four participants (three male and one female), aged between 22 and 32 years (*mean* = 25, *sd* = 4.7), none of whom were familiar with the project. To have as wide a variety of faces as possible, we selected one participant wearing glasses, one with an Asian appearance, and one male as well as one female European.

The pre-study was performed in the lab using the setup shown in Figure 4. Participants were seated about 60 cm from the computer screen, facing its centre. The eye tracker was placed under the computer screen. Above the screen, we mounted a video camera with a resolution of 720x576 pixels to record close-up videos of the participants' eyes (see Figure 5).

Experimental Procedure

After arriving at the lab we first explained the task to the participants and asked them to sign a consent form. Then, participants were instructed how to use the login interface, in particular how to enter and verify their passwords. We calibrated the eye tracker, validated the calibration and started the login interface. The interface automatically guided each participant through a sequence of screens, each involving their entering and verifying one image or PIN-based graphical password.

Each sequence consisted of 10 different PINs with four digits and a subset of 20 out of the 40 images – 10 images with a saliency mask and 10 without – shown to the participants in randomised order. The PINs were randomly generated to avoid people choosing easy or PINs that they were actually using. Participants were asked to look sequentially at the digits read out by the experimenter (cf. Figure 3).

For each image we asked participants to choose one graphical passwords consisting of four password points, but did not give them any indication as to how to choose them. We made sure that none of the participants was shown both the saliency and the non-saliency mask version of the same image and that, over all pre-study participants, each image was shown equally often. For images with a saliency mask, we asked participants to choose passwords points outside the red areas but did not explain how these areas had been defined.

Main Study

The goal of the main study was to evaluate the security of the three types of gaze-based graphical passwords recorded in the pre-study. We recruited 12 participants (one female and eleven males), aged between 23 and 29 years ($mean = 25.9$, $sd = 1.7$) via University mailing lists and bulletins in the neighbourhood surrounding the University building. Three of the participants wore glasses, one used contact lenses, and five had already participated in an eye tracking study before.

A first test showed that attacking all 120 passwords recorded in the pre-study took too long and would have affected participants' motivation and ability to keep concentrated. Consequently, for the study to take at most one hour, we had to reduce the number of passwords. We deemed crucial to still use the same number of passwords from each pre-study participant in order to minimise potential effects from different password selection strategies. We therefore selected five passwords per pre-study participant. Counterbalancing these passwords for image category and study condition finally resulted in a set of seven PINs, as well as seven images with and six images without a saliency mask and the corresponding videos.

Each participant was asked to attack the passwords in this set in randomised order. We made sure that, overall, all passwords would be attacked the same amount of times. We did not reveal which passwords were originally defined with and without a saliency mask and ensured that the eyes could be well recognised in all videos. Participants were rewarded with 10 EUR for participating in the study. In addition, we offered them a 1 EUR bonus for each password they managed to guess successfully.

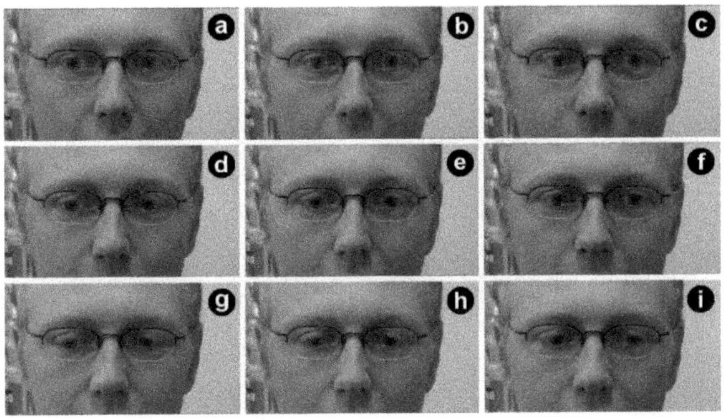

Figure 5: Sample images extracted from the video tutorial with the person looking at the top-left (a), top-centre (b), top-right (c), middle-left (d), middle-centre (e), middle-right (f), bottom-left (g), bottom-centre (h), and bottom-right (i) points of the calibration procedure.

Experimental Procedure

After the participants arrived at the lab, we introduced the study and asked them to sign a consent form. We asked them to complete the first part of the questionnaire on demographics and on their use of PINs and passwords. We guided them to the room where we had set up our authentication system.

All participants were first shown a video tutorial on how to guess gaze-based graphical passwords. In the first part of the tutorial, participants watched close-up videos of another person (who had not participated in the pre-study) looking at the nine points of the calibration procedure (see Figure 5). This was to give them a feeling of the maximum gaze range they could expect later on. In the second part of the tutorial, we showed them close-up videos of the person's gaze, while entering a PIN-based and an image-based password, and asked them to guess the password. In addition, we gave them some hints that we had discovered ourselves when trying to guess passwords using the same approach, e.g. to watch out for characteristic horizontal or vertical sequences of eye movements. All videos in the tutorial were mirrored horizontally, so that the gaze direction matched the on-screen gaze location.

After finishing the video tutorial, we ensured that participants were seated about 60 cm away from the computer screen and faced its centre. We calibrated the eye tracker, validated the calibration and started the login interface. The interface guided the participants through a sequence of login procedures, each involving their guessing one image or PIN-based password. For each password, the participants could watch the corresponding close-up video from the pre-study as often as they wished on a laptop placed next to the screen (see Figure 6). Participants could pause the video at any time so as to closely examine gaze direction. In addition, a printout of the image was provided for marking potential password points.

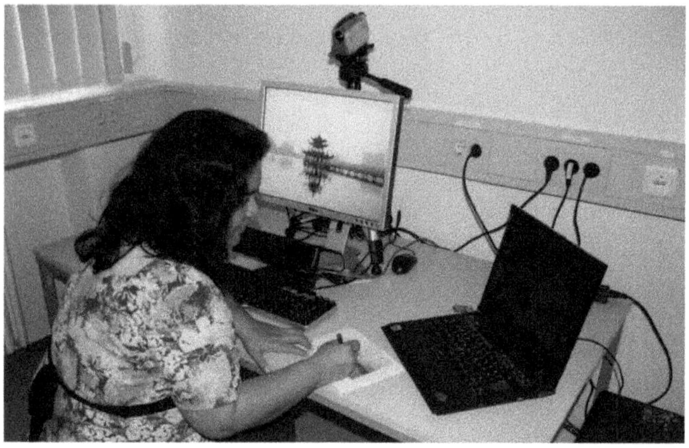

Figure 6: Experimental setup used in the main study. Participants tried to guess passwords by analysing close-up videos of other users' eye movements on the laptop. An additional printout of the image was provided to take notes and to mark potential password points.

Once participants thought they knew the password, they tried to log into the system using this password. For each image, participants were given a maximum of three login attempts before the interface automatically switched to the next image. If the password was guessed correctly, the system immediately switched to the next image. Participants were asked to guess as many passwords as possible while we recorded their gaze paths. We explicitly told them that guessing the passwords was more important than finishing the study quickly. However, when participants spent a lot of time watching the video, we applied a soft deadline of 2 minutes, after which the experimenter asked the participant to finish. Consequently, it was not possible to analyse post-hoc how quickly passwords could be guessed by the participants.

After the study, we asked participants to complete the second part of the questionnaire, with questions on the experiment and how they perceived the PIN-based and image-based graphical passwords with respect to robustness, security, and usability. In addition, we asked them how difficult it was to guess passwords, whether the tutorial had been useful, and whether they had noticed any differences in visual behaviour between the various people they had observed.

Data Analysis and Validation

In the main study, we collected quantitative and qualitative data. Quantitative data was recorded from participant interactions with the login interface and the questionnaires, using 5-point Likert scales. To verify that all login attempts were counted correctly in the post-hoc analysis, for each login attempt, we plotted the image with the password from the pre-study and the password guessed by the participants in the main study (see Figure 7 for an example). In total, we individually validated 541 images. Questionnaire responses were transcribed to a spreadsheet. Qualitative data was gathered from observations during the study, open questions in the questionnaire and from interviews following the study. This data was transcribed and important themes identified.

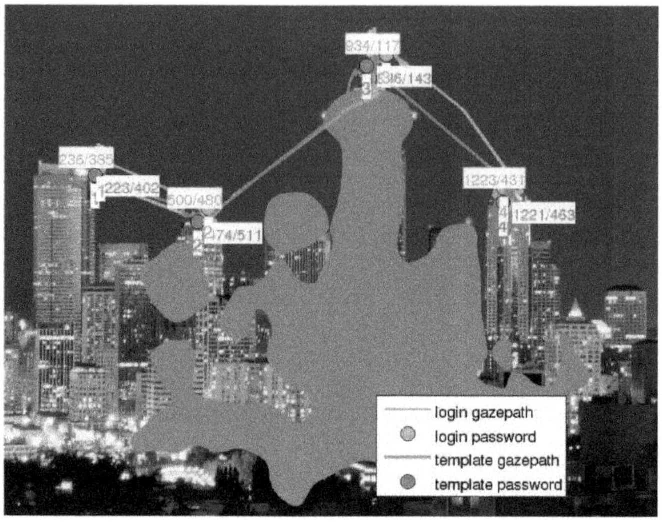

Figure 7: Image, password points as well as gaze paths of the password defined in the pre-study (template) and the login attempt (login) of the only successful login attempt on an image with a saliency mask.

RESULTS

Eye Tracking Accuracy

We first analysed the eye tracking accuracy (mean Euclidean distance between the calibration and detected fixation points) in the pre- and main study using the gaze data recorded during the validation routine after calibration. In the pre-study, the mean Euclidean distances ranged between 21 and 46 pixels ($mean$ = 33, sd = 10); in the main study the distances were between 22 and 52 pixels ($mean$ = 34, sd = 9). At a distance of 60 cm, these distances correspond to an accuracy of between 0.5 and 1.05 degree of visual angle – a range similar to the manufacturer-reported accuracy of the Tobii eye tracker.

Influence of Saliency Masks

Using the gaze data collected in the pre-study, we analysed whether the saliency masks actually influenced participant visual behaviour and thus the way they selected their password points. To this end, we compared the number of password points selected inside and outside the saliency regions for all images with and without a saliency mask. Figure 8 shows the results of this comparison for all pre-study images and participants. On average, for images without a saliency mask, 34.5% of the password points fell inside the saliency regions. For images with a saliency mask, this percentage dropped to 1.3%, a difference that was statistically significant ($p < .001$, one tailed Fisher's exact test).

Security of Graphical Passwords

We first calculated the theoretical password space, that is the total number of all possible distinct passwords in a system, for the different graphical password types. TPSs grow exponentially and are typically compared in log_2. The TPS for 4-digit PIN-based graphical passwords with a password length of four digits is $log_2(10^4) \approx 13.3$. An image size

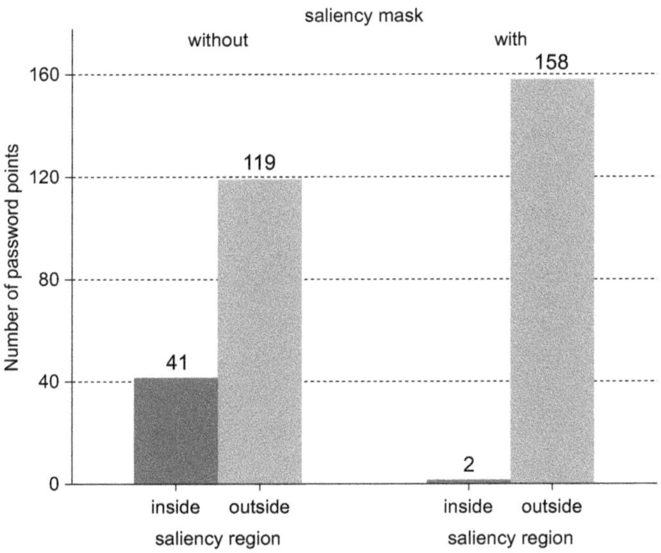

Figure 8: Number of password points inside and outside the saliency regions for images with and without a saliency mask. Values were calculated for all images shown to the four participants who took part in the pre-study.

Predictor	β	$SE\ \beta$	p	e^{β} (odds ratio)
intercept	-2.113	0.388	<0.001	N/A
saliency mask	-2.322	1.090	0.033	0.098
PIN	0.914	0.462	0.048	2.494

Table 1: Logistic regression analysis of 12 participants' performance in guessing three different types of graphical passwords. Both the "PIN" and image with a saliency mask ("saliency mask") conditions are significantly different to the "image without a saliency mask" reference condition.

of 1600x1200 pixels can contain 80 non-overlapping circles with a diameter of 150 pixels (fixation detection threshold th_f = 75 pixels). Thus, with the same number of password points per password, the TPS for image-based passwords is much larger, namely $log_2(80^4) \approx 25.3$.

We then evaluated the security of the different graphical passwords using the data recorded in the main study. Each successful login attempt was counted as a "1", whereas three failed login attempts on a single image were counted as a single "0". Overall, 19 out of 81 PINs were successfully guessed by the participants compared to 8 out of 72 images without a saliency mask and 1 out of 82 images with a saliency mask. We used a logistic regression to model the relationship between the password type and the relative probabilities of a successful login attempt. The regression was conducted using a generalized linear mixed effect model with "image without a saliency mask" as the reference condition. Participants was a random effect; the "PIN" vs. "image without a saliency mask", as well as "image with a saliency mask" vs. "image without a saliency mask" were fixed effects. As can be seen from Table 1, PINs are significantly less secure than

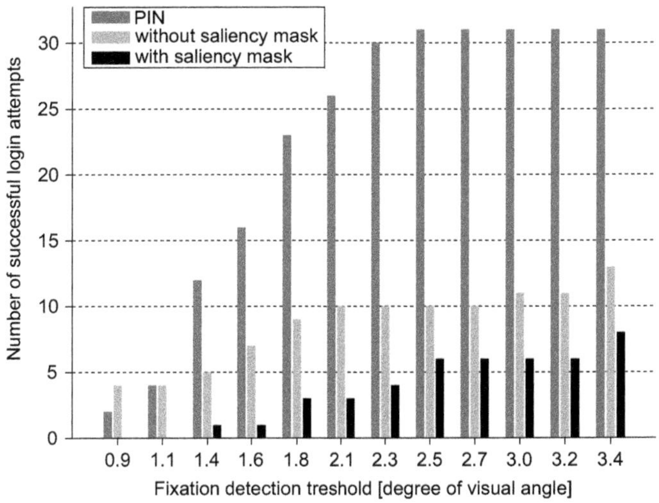

Figure 9: Number of successful login attempts for the different graphical password schemes for different values of the fixation detection threshold th_f.

image-based passwords without a saliency mask ($p = .048$) and saliency masks significantly increase password security ($p = .033$). A likelihood ratio test between the intercept-only (null) model and the logistic model was also significant (log-likelihood difference = 11.248, $\chi^2(2) = 22.497, p < .001$).

Influence of Fixation Detection Threshold

In the previous evaluation, the fixation detection threshold was fixed to th_f = 1.7 degree of visual angle. To analyse the influence of th_f on the number of successful login attempts, we simulated different thresholds by sweeping $th_f = 0.9 \ldots 3.4$ (in 12 steps). The lower bound of the sweep was motivated by the maximum eye tracking accuracy achieved after calibration. For login attempts in which one of these thresholds resulted in an earlier successful attempt than in the original study, all subsequent attempts on that image were excluded from the analysis. As can be seen from Figure 9, the fixation detection threshold exerts a considerable influence on the number of successful login attempts. Most importantly, the analysis shows that using saliency masks consistently, results in fewer successful login attempts and thus more secure passwords than without saliency masks or using PINs.

Questionnaires

From the questionnaires completed by the participants of the main study, we received valuable feedback on the perceived security and usability of the PIN-based and image-based graphical passwords, experiences with guessing them, preferred situations and devices, as well as general feedback on the study.

Security and Usability

We first analysed the perceived security and usability of the PIN-based and image-based passwords using a Friedman analysis of variance by ranks on the participant responses in both conditions (5-point Likert scale, 1: very low, 5: very high;

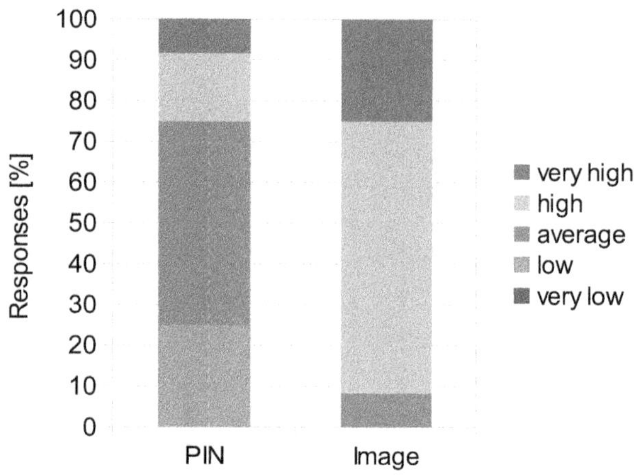

Figure 10: Distribution of responses to question "How do you rate the security of the different graphical passwords?".

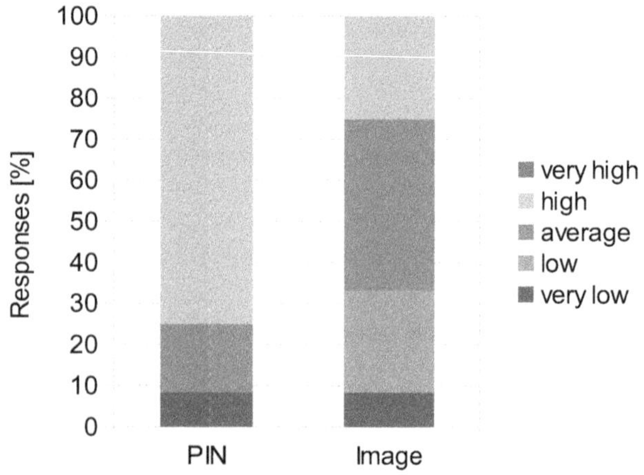

Figure 11: Distribution of responses to question "How do you rate the usability of the different graphical passwords?".

see Figures 10 and 11). Participants found image-based passwords to be significantly more secure than PIN-based passwords, $\chi^2(1) = 10.0, p < .05$. Yet, the password usability was rated significantly higher for PIN-based than for image-based passwords, $\chi^2(1) = 6.0, p < .05$.

Guessing Passwords

We then analysed the perceived ease of monitoring eye movements and guessing passwords from the videos for PIN-based and image-based passwords (1: very difficult, 5: very easy; see Figures 12 and 13). We again used a Friedman analysis of variance by ranks on participant responses in both conditions. Participants found it significantly easier to monitor eye movements for PIN-based passwords than for image-based passwords, $\chi^2(1) = 10.0, p < .05$. Consequently, participants found it significantly easier to guess PIN-based passwords ($\chi^2(1) = 8.0, p < .05$) and felt that they had to concentrate significantly more (1: had to concentrate intensively, 5: did not have to concentrate at all) when trying to guess image-based password, $\chi^2(1) = 4.5, p < .05$.

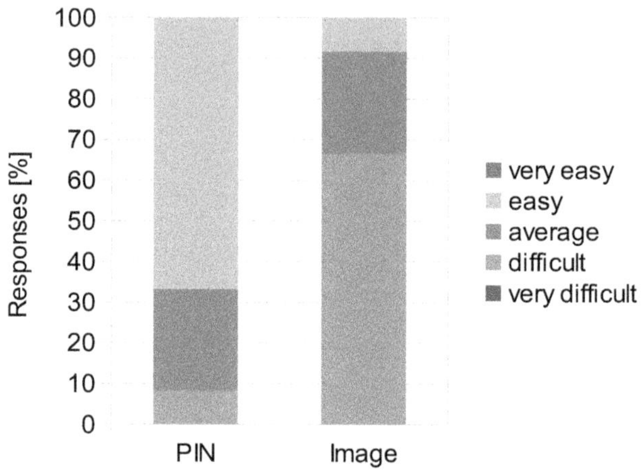

Figure 12: Distribution of responses to question "How do you rate the ease of monitoring eye movements in the videos?".

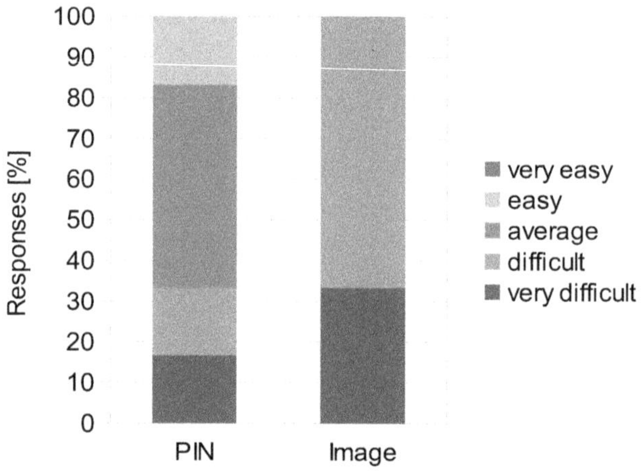

Figure 13: Distribution of responses to question "How do you rate the ease of guessing passwords from the videos?".

Although we did not elaborate on this, our results indicate that difficulties in guessing passwords may be related to the gender of pre-study participants. Participants consistently found the passwords of our female pre-study participant significantly easier to guess than those of the Asian male, $\chi^2(1) = 6.4, p < .05$, as well as the European male not wearing, $\chi^2(1) = 8.0, p < .05$, and wearing glasses, $\chi^2(1) = 5.4, p < .05$ (1: very difficult, 5: very easy).

Situations and Devices

We further analysed in which situations and with respect to which devices participants could imagine using the different graphical passwords. Although none of the following findings was statistically significant, they nonetheless raise some interesting questions for future work.

For situations (1: would definitely use, 5: would not use at all), we found that the image-based passwords were favoured in non-private situations, such as in a bank (*mean* = 3.58, *sd* = 0.79) or in public spaces (*mean* = 3.33, *sd* = 1.27). Image-based passwords were less favoured at home (*mean* = 3, *sd*

= 1.45) and at work (*mean* = 3.25, *sd* = 1.17). The favoured devices were ATMs (*mean* = 3.33, *sd* = 1.21) and access systems (*mean* = 3.64, *sd* = 1.17), while laptops (*mean* = 3, *sd* = 1.55), mobile phones (*mean* = 2.92, *sd* = 1.67), and desktop computers (*mean* = 3, *sd* = 1.55) were less popular.

By contrast, PIN-based passwords were most popular in private situations such as at home (*mean* = 3.42, *sd* = 1.57) and in the office (*mean* = 3.33, *sd* = 1.12), and less popular in public spaces (*mean* = 3, *sd* = 1.22) and a bank (*mean* = 3.08, *sd* = 1.1). PIN-based passwords were also preferred when used on laptops (*mean* = 3.42, *sd* = 1.13) and desktop computers (*mean* = 3.33, *sd* = 1.12) than on mobile phones (*mean* = 3.08, *sd* = 1.22) and ATMs (*mean* = 3.08, *sd* = 1.25).

User Study

Finally, participants reported that they found the user study moderately exhausting (*mean* = 3.08, *sd* = 1.16; 1: very exhausting, 5: not exhausting at all). The video tutorial was perceived as being helpful by all participants (*mean* = 4, *sd* = 1.18; 1: not helpful at all, 5: very helpful).

Qualitative Feedback

The qualitative feedback from the pre-study revealed that some participants developed strategies for selecting passwords. One participant constructed stories around the password points to make them more memorable. A second strategy reported by another participant was to select password points along vertical or horizontal lines, such as by choosing points at the intersection of foreground objects.

Participants from the main study found PINs easier to guess, due to the grid and thus the eye movements were more easily recognisable. P5 and P8 reported that having a reference point (e.g. by initially looking at the centre of the screen or using the glasses as a reference) or knowing the starting gaze position would make guessing easier. P2, P7, P8 found vertical eye movements more difficult to detect than horizontal ones. P2 reported looking for visual strategies, while P8 and P9 noticed that one pre-study participant had chosen password points in the direction of reading, i.e. from left to right.

DISCUSSION

The results of our study demonstrate that image-based graphical passwords are significantly more secure than PIN-based passwords, both in an actual attack and in terms of participant perception, hence verifying Hypothesis 1 (see Table 1 and Figures 10 and 13). Using computational models of visual attention to mask the most salient areas of the images does significantly increase security, compared to the standard image-based approach, hence verifying Hypothesis 2. In combination with the much larger theoretical password space, these results make saliency masks a promising means of increasing the security of gaze-based graphical passwords.

While image-based graphical passwords were perceived as significantly more secure than PIN-based passwords, the usability was rated lower by the participants in our study (see Figure 11). Participants preferred image-based passwords for public terminals, while PIN-based passwords were preferred for mobile devices such as laptops and mobile phones. These responses may have been caused by the fact that participants could not imagine mobile devices being equipped with robust eye trackers in the near future. While currently, application domains are indeed mostly limited to ATMs or similar stationary systems, the advent of mobile eye trackers will pave the way for gaze-based authentication on smaller and thus more mobile devices [3].

A proper analysis of password memorability requires a long-term study and was therefore beyond the scope of this work. However, when we asked two pre-study participants to log in with their image-based passwords two days later (whom we did not ask to remember their passwords in the first place) they correctly remembered 14 out of 40 passwords (five images with and nine without a saliency mask). 13 of these image-based passwords were remembered by the pre-study participant who had selected the password points in the direction of reading, i.e. from left to right. While using such strategies seems to improve password memorability this may come at the cost of reduced security. We plan to investigate this trade-off between memorability and security in more detail in future work and particularly how password memorability can be improved without compromising security. In terms of security, it will also be interesting to see how saliency masks compare to other approaches, such as selecting password points on a sequence of images [5].

Finally, the study also reveals some of the issues researchers may face in the real-world implementation of gaze-based graphical passwords. Participants in our pre-study reported having used visual strategies for selecting their passwords points in the images. Two main-study participants noticed and exploited this behaviour by specifically looking for characteristic eye movement sequences such as in a vertical or horizontal direction. This suggests that, in addition to the saliency masks presented here, measures need to be taken to prevent users from choosing closely related password points (similar to preventing PINs like "1111" or "1234"). Additional user studies will be required to investigate whether users should be allowed to choose their own graphical passwords (and potentially the images as well), or whether both should be provided by the authentication system during registration. In the latter case, it would be useful to identify what defines such "good" passwords and images.

CONCLUSION

In this paper we have proposed computational models of visual attention to increase the security of gaze-based cued-recall graphical passwords. We introduced saliency masks as a promising method for supporting the user in selecting more secure passwords and thus reducing the risk of hotspots in the authentication images. In a study with a realistic threat model, we showed that saliency masks significantly increase password security on a single image, compared to a standard image-based method and gaze-based 4-digit PIN entry. This result is promising, as saliency masks can easily be computed. It also raises the issue of the wider applicability of this approach, such as in the development of quantitative measures of the security of cued-recall graphical passwords.

ACKNOWLEDGEMENTS

This work was supported by the European Union 7th framework programme under grant agreements no. 215893 and 244011. We would like to thank Yordan Terziev, Andreas Kaiser, and Ken Pfeuffer for their help with implementing the authentication software, Brian Bloch for editing a draft of this paper, as well as Simon Byrne and Julian Mennenöh.

REFERENCES

1. Angeli, A. D., Coventry, L., Johnson, G., and Renaud, K. Is a picture really worth a thousand words? exploring the feasibility of graphical authentication systems. *International Journal of Human-Computer Studies 63*, 1-2 (2005), 128–152.
2. Biddle, R., Chiasson, S., and van Oorschot, P. C. Graphical passwords: Learning from the first twelve years. *ACM Computing Surveys* (2011). to appear.
3. Bulling, A., and Gellersen, H. Toward Mobile Eye-Based Human-Computer Interaction. *IEEE Pervasive Computing 9*, 4 (2010), 8–12.
4. Chiasson, S., Forget, A., Biddle, R., and van Oorschot, P. C. Influencing users towards better passwords: persuasive cued click-points. In *Proceedings of the 22nd British HCI Group Conference on People and Computers* (2008), 121–130.
5. Chiasson, S., van Oorschot, P. C., and Biddle, R. Graphical password authentication using cued click points. In *Proceedings of the 12th European Symposium on Research in Computer Security* (2007), 359–374.
6. De Luca, A., Denzel, M., and Hussmann, H. Look into my eyes!: can you guess my password? In *Proceedings of the 5th Symposium on Usable Privacy and Security* (2009), 1–12.
7. De Luca, A., Weiss, R., and Drewes, H. Evaluation of eye-gaze interaction methods for security enhanced pin-entry. In *Proceedings of the 19th Australasian Conference on Computer-Human Interaction* (2007), 199–202.
8. Everitt, K. M., Bragin, T., Fogarty, J., and Kohno, T. A comprehensive study of frequency, interference, and training of multiple graphical passwords. In *Proceedings of the 27th SIGCHI International Conference on Human Factors in Computing Systems* (2009), 889–898.
9. Forget, A., Chiasson, S., and Biddle, R. Shoulder-surfing resistance with eye-gaze entry in cued-recall graphical passwords. In *Proceedings of the 28th SIGCHI International Conference on Human Factors in Computing Systems* (2010), 1107–1110.
10. Forget, A., Chiasson, S., van Oorschot, P. C., and Biddle, R. Improving text passwords through persuasion. In *Proceedings of the 4th Symposium on Usable Privacy and Security* (2008), 1–12.
11. Frintrop, S., Rome, E., and Christensen, H. I. Computational visual attention systems and their cognitive foundations: A survey. *ACM Transactions on Applied Perception 7*, 1 (2010), 1–39.
12. Harel, J. Graph-Based Visual Saliency Toolbox for MATLAB, http://www.klab.caltech.edu/ harel/share/gbvs.php, 2006.
13. Harel, J., Koch, C., and Perona, P. Graph-based visual saliency. In *Proceedings of the 20th International Conference on Neural Information Processing Systems* (2006), 545–552.
14. Hoanca, B., and Mock, K. Secure graphical password system for high traffic public areas. In *Proceedings of the 2006 Symposium on Eye Tracking Research & Applications* (2006), 35–35.
15. Itti, L., and Koch, C. Computational modelling of visual attention. *Nature Reviews Neuroscience 2*, 3 (2001), 194–203.
16. Itti, L., Koch, C., and Niebur, E. A model of saliency-based visual attention for rapid scene analysis. *IEEE Transactions on Pattern Analysis and Machine Intelligence 20*, 11 (1998), 1254–1259.
17. Jacob, R. J. K. What you look at is what you get: eye movement-based interaction techniques. In *Proceedings of the 8th SIGCHI International Conference on Human Factors in Computing Systems* (1990), 11–18.
18. Kumar, M., Garfinkel, T., Boneh, D., and Winograd, T. Reducing shoulder-surfing by using gaze-based password entry. In *Proceedings of the 3rd Symposium on Usable Privacy and Security* (2007), 13–19.
19. LeBlanc, D., Forget, A., and Biddle, R. Guessing click-based graphical passwords by eye tracking. In *Proceedings of the 8th International Conference on Privacy Security and Trust* (2010), 197–204.
20. Maeder, A. J., Fookes, C. B., and Sridharan, S. Gaze based user authentication for personal computer applications. In *Proceedings of International Symposium on Intelligent Multimedia, Video and Speech Processing* (2004), 727–730.
21. Moncur, W., and Leplâtre, G. Pictures at the atm: exploring the usability of multiple graphical passwords. In *Proceedings of the 25th SIGCHI International Conference on Human Factors in Computing Systems* (2007), 887–894.
22. Suo, X., Zhu, Y., and Owen, G. S. Graphical passwords: A survey. In *Proceedings of the 21st Computer Security Applications Conference* (2005), 463–472.
23. Thorpe, J., and van Oorschot, P. C. Human-seeded attacks and exploiting hot-spots in graphical passwords. In *Proceedings of the 16th USENIX Security Symposium* (2007), 8:1–8:16.
24. Wiedenbeck, S., Waters, J., Birget, J.-C., Brodskiy, A., and Memon, N. Passpoints: design and longitudinal evaluation of a graphical password system. *International Journal of Human-Computer Studies 63*, 1-2 (2005), 102–127.

"You're Capped!" Understanding the Effects of Bandwidth Caps on Broadband Use in the Home

Marshini Chetty[1,2], Richard Banks[1], A.J. Bernheim Brush[1], Jonathan Donner[1] and Rebecca E. Grinter[2]

Microsoft Research[1]
{rbanks, jdonner, ajbrush}@microsoft.com

Georgia Institute of Technology[2]
{marshini, beki}@cc.gatech.edu

ABSTRACT

Bandwidth caps, a limit on the amount of data users can upload and download in a month, are common globally for both home and mobile Internet access. With caps, each bit of data consumed comes at a cost against a monthly quota or a running tab. Yet, relatively little work has considered the implications of this usage-based pricing model on the user experience. In this paper, we present results from a qualitative study of households living with bandwidth caps. Our findings suggest home users grapple with three uncertainties regarding their bandwidth usage: *invisible balances*, *mysterious processes,* and *multiple users*. We discuss how these uncertainties impact their usage and describe the potential for better tools to help monitor and manage data caps. We conclude that as a community we need to cater for users under Internet cost constraints.

Author Keywords

Bandwidth; metered use; data cap; Internet; pricing; usage-based pricing; usage-based billing; bandwidth cap

ACM Classification Keywords

H.5.m [Information interfaces and presentation (e.g., HCI)]: Miscellaneous;

INTRODUCTION

Faced with increased network congestion from both the rise in bandwidth intensive applications and the growing number of Internet users [19], many Internet Service Providers (ISPs) have imposed a data "cap" or monthly data limit on their subscribers [12]. These bandwidth caps vary from 1-250 GB and exist in nations such as Australia, Canada, Turkey, South Africa, the U.K., and the U.S. [10,24]. Data caps are not restricted to home broadband; they are also part of the pricing model used by cellular providers for mobile Internet users [25]. Since ISPs argue that caps help provide more consistent service to all their users (e.g., [4]), this pricing model is likely to persist. Yet, little work has directly considered the effects of bandwidth caps and costs on broadband users' Internet experiences.

We find this gap surprising because caps have implications for how we design and deploy networked technologies and content [18]. For example, how viable is a data intensive photo-sharing application in a home with a 150 GB data cap? As HCI and related fields increasingly design applications that rely on the Internet, we argue that it is time to re-examine the assumption that for end-users the only cost associated with network use is speed. Moreover, caps are another opportunity to explore how existing infrastructure shapes the ways in which people engage with the Internet, thus providing an opportunity to reflect on assumptions and imagine different future technologies [5].

In this paper, we describe how monthly bandwidth caps affect households' Internet use in South Africa—a country with roughly 480,000 broadband subscriptions for the population of 49 million [9]. We chose this country because prior to February 2010, all South African home broadband data subscriptions were capped so most users' experience of broadband was of a metered connection. Our goals were to learn (a) how bandwidth caps affect households' broadband use (b) how households manage a bandwidth cap during the month, and (c) what tools and information households desire to monitor and control their bandwidth usage.

To do this, we conducted a qualitative study of 12 households living with data caps. We found that households struggle with three uncertainties related to their bandwidth usage: *invisible balances, mysterious processes,* and *multiple users.* To overcome these uncertainties, households described wanting better ways to help them manage their bandwidth. Consequently, in a second study phase we gauged their reactions to designs for potential tools to address the uncertainties they raised. Our contributions include empirical evidence of how data caps shape Internet use and implications for the design of networked technologies and content.

BANDWIDTH CAPS AND RELATED WORK

Bandwidth caps are a form of usage-based pricing where Internet use is billed based on how much data is used rather than providing unlimited data access for a fixed cost. Usage-based pricing is not a new business model [11]. For some early dial-up home Internet plans, customers were charged for the connection and every additional hour of use above a certain time limit, on top of the cost of telephone calls [1]. In many countries such as the U.S., the shift from dial-up to broadband led to flat-rate pricing. By allowing users to pay a fixed rate for unlimited use, these plans enabled "always-on" Internet use [23]. Caps, however, pose a potential threat to this usage mode, one that remains under-examined in HCI and related fields.

Several studies have explored usage-based billing as a means of controlling network congestion. For example, Shenker et al. [4] investigated various usage-based pricing models and their effects on network traffic. Examples of pricing models include having a "smart market" where users are only charged for their traffic when the network is congested and priority-pricing where users indicate which packets should be prioritized over others [6]. These studies focused on how well each model managed network congestion and what technical challenges they presented. Most of these studies do not explicitly examine bandwidth caps as a form of usage-based billing. Moreover, the focus has largely been on optimizing pricing for the network infrastructure rather than understanding its effects on the user experience of the Internet.

Some exceptions exist. The Internet Demand Experiment (INDEX) in the late nineties exposed users to various usage-based pricing models including flat-rate pricing and paying per-byte used [18]. They found that people tended to use the Internet less when charged by the byte, as compared to when they paid a flat rate. Yet users embraced the idea of having rates change according to their own use and during times of high traffic congestion. Another report suggests that Internet users alter their behaviors in response to unlimited and limited Internet access [14]. These studies show that caps do cause people to modify their Internet usage, but they do not examine specific household Internet behaviors and practices in detail.

Since these studies, few have tackled the question of how cost as a constraint affects users' broadband experiences. Internet regulatory bodies have focused on how other Internet constraints shape Internet use, such as limited connectivity and slow speeds, or the absence of sufficient bandwidth to conduct online activities smoothly [7,16]. Additionally, some researchers have implemented visualizations for end-users to better manage Internet constraints such as speeds. For example, the *Kermit* system showed home users which devices were using up significant bandwidth and an estimate of the speed from the ISP to help users determine why the Internet was slow [3].

Constraints on speed and availability have also been a particularly salient part of the research discourse about Internet use in developing countries. For instance, Wyche et al. [26] studied how Kenyan Internet users, confronted with slow and sporadic connections at telecenters and cybercafés, orient to the web differently, with more deliberate, planned, and purposeful online interactions. Similarly, Chen et al. [2] found sporadic Internet connectivity and slow Internet speeds tend to frustrate users (e.g., during long page load times). In another study, Smyth et al. [20] discuss how users create innovative content distribution networks in situations of limited bandwidth and connectivity. They describe how mobile phone shops in India download media (e.g., video or voice clips) and resell it to others for entertainment use on their mobile phones.

In summary, we can draw two conclusions. First, previous work shows that cost affects how users use the Internet. Second, while empirical evidence exists for how certain users manage some types of constraints, the impact of bandwidth caps have not been explored in detail, nor widely discussed in the literature. For example, researchers do not typically consider how much data the applications we design consume or whether our field deployments take bandwidth away from other activities. Nor do studies explore bandwidth as a shared resource that must be allocated and negotiated as part of a family dynamic, with all the complexities of a household micro-economy. Moreover, although Internet usage may be likened to sharing energy resources or cell phone minutes, bandwidth is not a limited natural resource and multiple users and devices make tracking this commodity different than in these other domains. Our study was crafted to address these omissions. We focused specifically on how households experienced bandwidth caps, exploring the challenges they faced, discussing strategies they employed, and considering approaches that might make living with a cap easier.

FIELD STUDY SETTING AND METHODS

At the time of the research, Fall 2010, most South African ISPs offered "use-it-or-lose-it" data plans varying from 1-9 GB per month [15]. If a household did not use their allocation for the month, the unused data portion (which participants frequently referred to as "gigs") did not carry over to the following month. If a household ran out of gigs before the end of the month, they had to purchase additional gigs at higher cost to continue to access the Internet. These additional gigs were also "use-it-or-lose-it." At least one ISP did offer non-expiring "rollover" gigs at a slightly higher price, but only one of our participants mentioned having this type of plan.

To help users track bandwidth usage through the month, most providers such as Telkom[1] offered limited non-real-time tracking tools requiring users to login to their ISP's website. These tools could be configured to send a text message or email notification when the household was close to their cap. However, none of these tools offered a per device or per user breakdown of traffic usage. (Note, third-party tools for monitoring bandwidth usage such as NetLimiter[2] exist. However, these tools usually monitor usage per single machine and do not separate out internal home network traffic from bandwidth counts. Exceptions

[1] www.telkomsa.net

[2] http://en.wikipedia.org/wiki/NetLimiter

#	Household Composition	Annual Household Income (USD)	# PCs	Cap	Cost per month (USD)
H1	Mother [self employed], Son (Teen), Son (20s) Roommate (20s)	$35K+	4	U	$146
H2	Mother [Admin Assistant], Twin Daughters (Teens)	$35K+	3	3GB	$81
H3	Couple [sales, self employed], Daughter (Teen), Daughter (20s)	$35K+	3	5GB	$146
H4	Mother [Personal Assistant], Daughter (20s), Son (Teen)	<$35K	2	5GB	$22
H5	Couple [self-employed, finance], Son (20s), Son (Teen)	$35K+	4	3GB	$36
H6	Couple [Admin assistant, Manager], Daughters (2 Teens), Daughter (8)	$35K+	3	5GB	$36
H7	Couple [self-employed], Sons (10, 7), Daughter (2)	$35K+	5	6GB	$91
H8	Couple [Manager, finance], Daughter (12), Daughter (5), Nephew (24)	$35K+	3	3GB	$36
H9	Mother [self-employed], Daughter (Teen)	<$18K	3	3GB	-
H10	Couple [driver, teacher], Daughters (3 in 20s), Grandchildren (2 Toddlers)	<$18K	2	5GB	$146
H11	Couple [self-employed, translator], Daughter (Teen), Son (Teen), Son (8)	$35K+	3	U	$109
H12	Mother [retail], Son (Teen), Grandmother	<$18K	2	1GB	$29

Table 1. Participant Demographics (U is uncapped, Cost is self-reported and varies with phone line rental, data bundle, and ISP charges reflecting participant confusion over DSL vs. top ups vs. phone costs).

such as NetWorx[3] provide total bandwidth usage for a household but must be installed on every machine to be tracked and do not account for devices that do not support the software (e.g., an Xbox)).

Participants

Our goal was to recruit families reflecting different socioeconomic backgrounds. We recruited 12 households using word of mouth, email distribution lists, and through our network of contacts in the area. We compensated each family with dinner during the interviews and approximately 70 USD in gift certificates. Table 1 shows that our participants had a variety of broadband plans ranging from 1 GB per month to the more unusual (and new to South Africa) unlimited data plans. We interviewed families that tended to fall into higher income brackets and that owned two or more computers.

One household (H8) did not have Digital Subscriber Line (DSL), the main broadband technology in South Africa, and used two 3G (wireless) cards provided by a cellular service provider for Internet access, each with a data cap. Although our families had a range of speeds they paid for out of the offerings of 384 kbps, 512 kbps, or 4 Mbps, we focused discussions solely on their experiences of bandwidth caps.

Study Protocol

The study consisted of two parts. In part one, we visited the households and interviewed them about their broadband usage. We asked them about how they managed their Internet usage, whether they had ever exceeded their cap, and what had happened as a result. The two uncapped households commented on both their experiences living with and without a cap. Since we interviewed families as a group, their responses may have been affected by group dynamics. Each family also filled out a demographic questionnaire. We used these interviews to generate not just our empirical themes, but also to brainstorm concepts for ways to support cap management. We deliberately opted to create abstract low-fidelity designs to solicit feedback on the tool concepts [13].

In the second part of our study, we showed our designs to the families to get their opinions on the concepts. We presented the designs as a PowerPoint slide deck soliciting feedback on each concept. In addition, we provided each participant with printed copies of each design with space for them to add annotations and to sketch their own ideas. To complement the design feedback, we also created an exercise where participants estimated bandwidth costs of different online activities. Specifically we asked (1) how much 1 GB costs in Rands (the South African currency, ZAR) (2) how many times a YouTube video of a well-known song could be viewed with 1 GB of data, and (3) how large this particular song was in MB. Participants filled out their responses on paper and discussed them during a post-exercise interview.

We analyzed all the interviews, the feedback on the tool designs, cost exercise, and field notes, coding the data for relevant phenomena using established qualitative methods [22]. We then merged all the codes and resolved points of disagreement among our team. All of the codes were then arranged into higher-level categories presented here.

FINDINGS FROM INTERVIEW 1: LIVING WITH THE CAP

Participants had broadband for work, school, or their home business. The lower income families (H10 and H12 whose annual income was low relative to the number of occupants

[3] http://www.softperfect.com/products/networx/

[21]) had broadband for safety concerns (e.g., to avoid having to spend time at Internet cafes in unsafe neighborhoods), and as their "luxury" item to organize and do research online. All our families had reached or exceeded their caps, a process most referred to as "being (or getting) capped." For instance, H4 told us they were once capped three times in a month, H6 spoke of often being capped around 23rd or 25th of the month, and H5 had been capped twice in the month prior to the study, and every month before that.

Although our households paid for different speeds, none reported hitting their bandwidth quota any faster on higher speed plans. Instead, all the households always spoke of the cap as the overarching limiting factor on their browsing habits. Interestingly, the two households that had transitioned to uncapped plans spoke of how much slower these uncapped connections were compared to their capped plans. Yet, these uncapped households still preferred limitless consumption to having a fast capped connection.

In this section, we describe how families grappled with three uncertainties related to their bandwidth cap: *invisible balances, mysterious processes,* and *multiple users*. We also comment on the contrasting experiences of our two households on uncapped plans (H1 and H11).

Invisible Balances: Managing Use and Being Capped

Many of the issues our participants raised related to the inability to track their bandwidth balance or what was remaining of their cap at any time. In particular, our participants experienced bandwidth as a finite resource and highlighted the lack of warnings about when their data quota would be reached and the turmoil that resulted from being cut off from the Internet.

Lack of warnings and inadequate tools: Without a method to easily check their bandwidth balance, participants sometimes struggled to determine whether they had been capped. Often, the main sign of being capped was the inability to browse or access non-South African websites because certain providers offered a separate cap for local sites. For example, a participant in H9 told us: "*I can't access my Gmail account but I can go to the website for Telkom [ISP]. That's the only way I've managed to work it out.*"

Those without a separate cap for local sites complained that their "gigs" ran out suddenly, sometimes when they were in the middle of an online activity. To avoid this abrupt disconnection, several participants made an effort to use the existing ISP tools for managing their cap, such as configuring warning emails to alert them as they approached their limit. However, at least 5 households found those websites to be inadequate for their needs and "*not user-friendly*." For example, they complained that these sites required a login, forming a barrier to checking the usage at a glance. Even when warnings were issued, participants said that they came too late when there was insufficient bandwidth left (e.g., less than 5MB) to complete even basic tasks. Sometimes warning messages even arrived after the cap had already been reached when it was too late to prevent being cut off from the Internet.

Turmoil when cut off: Being capped or exceeding the invisible balance led to a variety of negative emotions. For instance, participants were exasperated when they wanted to do something online but then discovered that they were capped. In extreme cases, households felt "*incomplete*" without Internet access as the following participant in H4 said: "*It was awful realizing how dependent we were on technology. It was a big thing that we didn't have Internet. We were all psychotic.*"

This feeling arose in part to perceived expectations of responsiveness by friends, family, employers, and other institutions of those with home broadband access. H7 ran a home business and gave an example echoed by others: "*Suddenly I can't get [online] and I'm urgently getting an email, and there's a brief that has to go off now.*"

Forecasting and monitoring: Even before the end of the month, participants wanted to know if there was enough bandwidth for upcoming activities such as school projects. H6, a high school student, explained: "*It would be really useful for me, because then I know that I don't have to worry that I wouldn't have [the ability to go] on the Internet for a project or something, because I know I have the gigs.*"

Others wanted to know whether there were freeloaders on their wireless networks. For example, H11 noticed via their ISP usage tool that network activity had taken place at times when they were asleep. Additionally, their ISP told them that their network was insecure, making it possible for others to also use their cap, further depleting it.

Participants explained once they reached their caps they had three options: living with it until the next month, topping up their connection, or getting online via other channels.

Living with it: Those who lived with the cap (and limited Internet) told us they eagerly awaited next month's reset. Living with their cap was bearable for a few days, especially when there was a separate cap for local sites, allowing participants to still do online banking or check local email. However, sometimes constraints, such as economics, forced families to wait for the next month even if it was difficult. Even families who could afford more bandwidth described being tired of being forced to buy more gigs. A parent in H2 told us that she decided that living with being capped was a better option if they were close to the end of the month: "*Yes, initially it was a matter of we get capped, and then I would buy another gig. Until I realized, you know what, "No." So we got to the point of we kept [on going].*" Another mother in H4 said: "*Often I kind of stand firm and say, "We're not going to buy any more cap.*" Finally, the lack of information provided on bandwidth use was frustrating since parents could not use the opportunity to teach their children how to work within the budget.

Topping up: Families that wanted and could afford to, often chose to "top up" their balance or buy additional gigs, available in 1 GB increments. Topping up became part of a parenting strategy in the face of the invisible bandwidth balance; rules were set as to how many times this would occur. For example, the father in H3 said that he told his daughters to "*go a little bit slow*" with their usage and that he had a "*one top up on me for the month*" rule.

While topping up restored Internet access, participants complained that the process was exasperating. To top up, participants either had to call their ISP and wait in phone queues or they went online if that was an option. Some used creative solutions to make the process more convenient. For instance, one household (H10) had two ISP's with two plans and switched to the second plan when the first one was capped. Participants were also unhappy that top up gigs did not typically rollover into the following month.

Finding Internet access elsewhere: Families sometimes resorted to visiting friends and family members to access the Internet once capped. In H2, the mother told us her daughters often went to their aunt's house when it happened, but added that they usually ended up capping that connection too. Families also described using the Internet on their phones or using a 3G card on their computers, linked to their cell phone accounts or a pre-paid data bundle to avoid the cap. For example, the mother in H2 used her 3G card on her laptop to help the family stay within bandwidth limits: "*Before we used that final gig, I would use my phone as a modem. So I buy a data bundle.*"

Invisible balances frequently caused disruptions in connectivity, forcing users to either restore the network somehow, or live without it. Having timely visibility into the remaining balance was therefore desirable.

Mysterious Processes: Understanding and Optimizing

Our participants struggled with understanding what mysterious processes or applications and websites were using up bandwidth. In particular, families had difficulty identifying data-intensive Internet applications. For many, Internet terminology did not help. For example, H12 reported: "*With this MB and Kbps, I'm not clued up with it at all.*" Similarly confused, H5 correlated data used with time taken to download: "*Because I think what I understand is that the less time it takes, the less cap you can take.*"

Participants did not appear to understand that YouTube or downloading songs used up significantly more bandwidth relative to web browsing. Participants also did not comprehend how background or non-browser based activities consumed part of their monthly allotment. Specifically, they worried about these processes using up bandwidth but not being under their control, such as an application automatically sending usage data back to its manufacturer. To help with bandwidth budgeting, participants wanted to know prior to use whether a site was likely to consume a lot of their monthly data allowance. For example, a school child in H9 told us: "*I want to see—like when you are about to click [something], you can see how many gigabytes is in there.*"

Estimating bandwidth usage: Two households had downloaded third-party bandwidth monitoring tools such as Traffic Watcher[4], to help them budget their bandwidth. The remaining ten households did not use any tools other than the defaults provided by the ISPs. Our estimation exercise illustrated the lack of awareness of costs, both monetary and bandwidth wise. Twenty-two of 51 participants (43%) answered "I don't know" to the question of how much 1GB costs in Rands. Estimates of the number of videos they could watch for 1GB and how large a particular song was in MB also varied wildly.

In some ways, these responses were not surprising. ISPs imposed different charges for top-ups, line rental, modems, and data plans. Similarly, for estimating bandwidth costs, although a few respondents had an intuition that streaming media was more bandwidth intensive than browsing text and images, they were unlikely to know just "how much" a YouTube video would consume in MB, or how long they could surf the net for $10—the average cost of a 1 GB top-up. Data sizes are abstract concepts and in many cases difficult to find. However, forced by caps to create folk theories about how much data different activities consumed, our participants developed strategies to optimize use.

Avoiding updates: One surprising finding was that just under half of our households (H3, H4, H7, H8, and H11) chose not to do software updates because of the bandwidth required, despite the potential security risks. Even the few participants who reported applying updates were somewhat reluctant to use their precious cap for this purpose. A dad in H5 explained: "*Because it just uses up our gigs, so you know you can have three gigs of spin, one of the gigs [used up], downloading the latest version of everything, every month. And so I think I don't have to do it.*"

Setting Rules: In addition to software updates, families chose not to download anything they considered unnecessary unless they reached the end of the month and had a surplus of bandwidth. For example, many made a conscious effort not to download music. Others tried to curtail all downloads and prioritized files for work and school over personal or recreational downloads. Often, setting the rules involved negotiating what was allowed and what was not as well as what was prioritized, but there was no technical means to enforce these social rules.

Part of managing the cap was to set rules about home Internet usage in general. Some parents asked their children to stop using certain websites, avoid "*excessive gaming*" and to restrict media downloads and uploads. Other parents even banned certain sites such as Facebook and YouTube. Participants also self-monitored their online activities and purposefully reduced their usage of certain sites and software applications that they believed to be bandwidth intensive. One mom in H9 proudly told us of her child: "*I think [my daughter] is actually very sweet when she said she*

[4] www.codeproject.com/KB/IP/apptraffwatcher.aspx

won't have Facebook and all that because Facebook would suck it [bandwidth]. And I used to Skype full time with my friends in the UK [but] now [I] stopped doing that."

Often, because of the cap, participants became annoyed with family, friends, or colleagues who forwarded them emails with large attachments or images. These participants took care to be considerate when composing emails to their own contacts making sure not to send large files.

Using physical media and informal data sharing networks: Avoiding large email attachments led to increased use of physical media such as flash drives, DVDs, and CDs to send and receive files. H7 explained: "*But [my husband]'s dad for example has been taking photographs of our son. He did pictorials for us and I very much wanted him to upload them and get them to us, but practically he couldn't do that. So those have come through CDs a couple of times, he just popped them in post.*"

With capped usage curbing downloads, many households also spoke of informal data sharing networks. In these networks, friends, or family with uncapped or work connections would download videos, movies, and music to share with others using physical media such as CDs, DVDs, and flash drives. Our participants did not appear to have any qualms about whether this content was downloaded illegally or not. Rather the informal data-sharing network was seen as a type of favor on the part of the downloaders. One teenager in H9 told us she received music from one of her friends because: "*She's the one with the unlimited cap.*"

Maxing out the cap: After spending most of the month avoiding the cap, the last few days would be focused on using all the remaining bandwidth if the household tracked use with third party or limited ISP tools. Families spoke of downloading all the media they wanted (e.g., music), to ensure they used their entire cap. These binge downloads were a special treat and, to guarantee that the "use-it-or-lose-it" bandwidth did not go to waste, participants planned their wish lists. For example, H7's quote typified many we heard: "*If we've had a relatively good month and there's a lot of cap left over, then I'll start looking around at the end of the month for things that I might want to download which previously I would have not gone ahead and done.*"

The binge could even be competitive. H4 told us how a brother often did not remind his sister when the end of the month was approaching so that he could use any surplus bandwidth for his downloads. In other words, families swayed between avoiding and trying to reach their caps, depending on the time of month. Caps can and *do* shape usage patterns, creating routines that change over the month and with respect to the amount of bandwidth "left".

Multiple Users

Our families also had trouble understanding which household member was using up their bandwidth. Families of three or more especially complained that it was hard to identify heavy users. In many cases, a teenager was suspected of engaging in data intensive activities such as downloading media or playing games. However, the lack of accountability made accusations easy to deny; some children embraced this vague state and others with siblings felt unable to prove they were using only their fair share. While parents differed in the amount of information they desired about their children's Internet use, many expressed interest in seeing if the bandwidth was being used for educational or recreational purposes.

To explain the difficulties of tracking Internet usage, many participants compared it to managing their mobile phone use. Mobile phones, mostly used by a single person, were far easier to comprehend. People with pre-paid mobile plans spoke of checking how much phone credit in Rands (ZAR) or "airtime" they had left, in order to determine whether to call someone. Participants using the Internet on their phone also seemed to better understand the costs of bandwidth on these devices. For example, H10 said of her phone: "*A twelve rand would translate to about six megabytes I'm thinking. But it won't even last a full day, if you...I wasn't doing anything intensive. [If] I was just browsing text.*"

One reason participants felt they were able to more easily correlate their phone bandwidth usage with cost was because they tended to just browse or do a few online activities on these devices. Example activities included browsing Facebook, using MixIt (a chat messenger which is cheaper than SMS), or visiting reference sites. A teenage participant in H2, for example, compared the costs of different sites: "*When you Facebook from your phone, when you update, you just tap in then it says "connecting" and then it takes off your air time. And with Twittering, you tap your status and then it doesn't take off any air time even when you post it.*"

Overall, our participants appeared to be able to form better conceptual models of the costs of online activities on mobile devices used by a single user accessing a small number of applications. In contrast, multiple users on many devices sharing a broadband connection made it more difficult to correlate usage and costs.

Switching to Uncapped

In contrast to the capped households, the two households that recently switched to uncapped plans told us they stopped policing the Internet habits of their children and spoke of downloading more media because the threat of being capped was removed. More importantly, these households reported having fewer Internet related disputes about the cost of access. These differences highlight how capped plans change browsing behaviors.

FINDINGS FROM INTERVIEW 2: MANAGING THE CAP

Based on the themes from the first interview, we created tool design ideas to further explore issues around three uncertainties families were experiencing. Next, we describe the designs and participant reactions showing how difficult users find it to understand bandwidth costs and usage.

Invisible Balances: How much bandwidth is left?

To address invisible balances, we developed three designs including a line graph (e.g., Figure 1A), a bandwidth 'clock' and a simple number to answer the question of

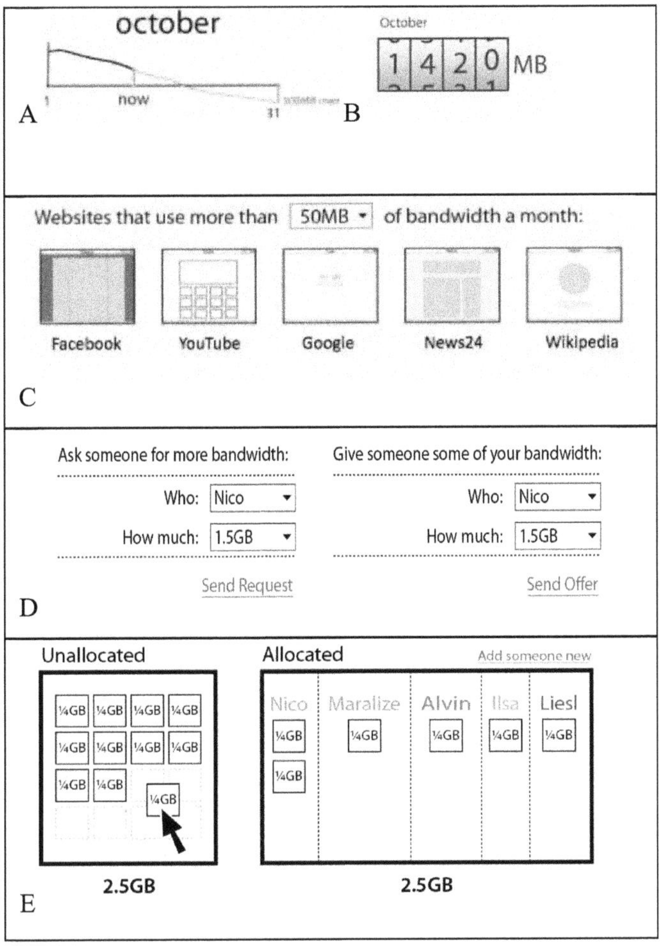

"How much bandwidth is left in a month?" We also created animations to elicit emotions around the fact that bandwidth is constantly running out such as a speedometer (e.g., Figure 1B). Participants varied in their affinity for the ways we visualized the bandwidth balance. Some told us that sometimes their use was erratic with lulls and spikes that our designs did not reflect. At least two participants also wondered if the calculations and predictions of when a home might run out of bandwidth were based on average use to date. One participant in H9 said of her daughter: "*It could be just one bad weekend that she spent all the time on Facebook, and then when you put the pie together, it looks like Facebook is the culprit. But it's not a daily culprit.*"

Our interactive animations were also met with varying opinions. The speedometer shown in Figure 1B garnered 22 positive comments, but participants raised concerns that the animations could be distracting depending on where they were shown. Participants for whom spending money on broadband was not an issue felt that the speedometer ticking down could be annoying creating a disturbing sense of urgency. For those who were more economically constrained, the meter ticking away was seen as a positive deterrence, with their goal being to restrict their usage and stay within their bandwidth budget without being capped.

Regardless of which representations participants preferred, they emphasized the need to know their balance in close to real time, when there was still time to change their usage pattern. Several also wished to know how much bandwidth was used in last 24 hours because access to recent data could make it easier to correlate usage with actions. Participants told us this would help them budget their time and prioritize work over recreational activities.

Mysterious Processes: What sites use most bandwidth?

For demystifying online processes and their bandwidth consumption, we created concepts to answer the question of "What sites are using up the most bandwidth?" (e.g., Figure 1C). In total, 19 participants made positive comments about this set of designs. Despite positive feedback, participants suggested that seeing monetary costs as opposed to bandwidth alone might help them curb their usage because it would likely be easier to understand. Moreover, many noted that in practice, costs would only become significant if aggregated over the month because web browsing may not use much bandwidth. One of our most interesting findings is that representing data usage requires careful presentation to show users that the time spent on a site does not necessarily equate to the amount of bandwidth used.

Multiple Users: Who is using the bandwidth?

To help users track multiple users, we created designs to answer the question of "Who is using the cap?" In particular, we focused on how bandwidth would be allocated to family members (e.g., Figure 1D), when this allocation would occur (e.g., Figure 1E), and around redistributing bandwidth during a month. Our designs for tracking use, allocating, and trading bandwidth, provoked the most spirited discussion. The tools we proposed extended beyond merely describing what the machine was doing; they described what its users were doing, and as such, created the opportunities for micro-economic behaviors and negotiations within the family.

Tracking Usage: Participants felt that having bandwidth usage information could become integral to their online habits. One participant from H4 summarizes this feeling: "*It's like always managing [or] the idea you have a battery on your laptop. You would have a battery for your Internet.*"

Yet, several participants were uneasy about the increased monitoring and collection of data about their Internet habits, a realm they previously considered private. One young adult in H4 for instance told us she was paranoid about being tracked and did not like the idea of her mother or brother knowing about her browsing habits or time spent on the web. Interestingly, at least two households did not feel that tool was out of bounds for tracking guests and student boarders or for shared households with roommates.

Our participants were also concerned that sharing bandwidth usage counts could lead to misperceptions about household users. A young adult in H1 gave the example: "*Let's say I'm doing research but you also go on YouTube just for a little bit. YouTube will use up to 50 megabits very, very quickly whereas your research might not even show up.*"

Clearly, making data caps more visible in the home can make household users accountable for their use of a shared resource and how they spend their time in a way that is not possible at present.

Bandwidth Allocation: Families differed in their responses to the idea of allocating gigs to household members. Some parents loved the concept of distributing the bandwidth like allowances, helping their children manage their time, or using it as a disciplinary tool. One parent in H6 told us she liked the idea of her kids being able to "earn more gigs." Allocation also appealed to participants who wanted their own Internet connection to work even if other householders were high bandwidth users. Similarly, those who had guests or boarders wanted to allocate a portion of bandwidth to them to avoid being capped by their use.

A few participants opposed allocation because they felt the feature went against the principles of sharing in the home. For example, the young female bill-payer for the Internet in H10 told us how her preference was that everyone should just use the Internet as they please. Her sisters disagreed and envisioned having an Internet café style home where everyone would be bargaining for bandwidth.

Families also wondered how the allocations would work in practice. Many saw the need for a login or password and felt this may be difficult to implement, given how different family members often get online on the same machines. Some were concerned that bandwidth would go to waste if someone did not use their allocation; others wondered who would be given rights to allocate the resource.

Others suggested assigning a cap for each site but this was usually met by protests from household members who did not want to share a cap for sites with their siblings (e.g., for Facebook (H10)). For some, trying to impose caps on children's website usage as opposed to restricting use by time seemed impractical. A father in H11 said: "*Ja [Yes], you not gonna be able to tell [my daughter] well you can only use 'x' percentage for Facebook. It's just not realistic.*"

Trading Bandwidth: Many of our families, particularly children, responded positively to the idea of being able to "*trade the cap*" with other family members or to "*sell bandwidth to each other,*" highlighting how this "*gives you something to bargain with*", as shown in Figure 1D. Several parents felt that allowing trading could mitigate fights if their children could give and take bandwidth from each other. For example, a mom in H6 felt that it would help her family use a shared laptop more fairly and that once she had finished the allocation, it was up to her kids to resolve their disputes. Participants did see downsides to trading including the potential for new forms of disputes: "[*my daughter] would inadvertently ask [my son], 'Can't I just use yours and I'll only use a quarter of a gig?'. And he'll come back and the whole lot would have been used.*" (H11)

"*Just a few megs [megabytes] man. I need my fix, I promise I'll pay you back next month.*" (H5)

Another family felt there would be nothing left to trade since the children would likely each use up their cap (H4). In these responses, it became clear that sharing bandwidth equitably was a major concern for tools to manage the cap.

In summary, exposing families to design ideas highlighted considerations for creating bandwidth management tools because families had to respond to concrete ideas as opposed to interview questions alone. Ultimately, making information about bandwidth balances, what applications, and people use up bandwidth was highly desired to help users form a better conceptual model of bandwidth and manage their caps more effectively. We are currently building a probe to investigate the technical challenges of bandwidth management tools and what the social implications of such tools might be on family relations.

DISCUSSION AND IMPLICATIONS FOR DESIGN

Our study findings show that families struggle with three uncertainties related to their bandwidth caps. Firstly, *invisible balances* make it hard to know when a cap will be reached and families must plan for inevitably losing connectivity. Secondly, *mysterious processes* mean that it is not easy to determine which applications are using up bandwidth. In the absence of this information, families have evolved strategies to avoid being capped. Thirdly, tracking *multiple users* sharing a data plan is difficult and exacerbates the process of dividing up the bandwidth. Overcoming these uncertainties is complicated by families' lacking a conceptual model of bandwidth as illustrated by their reactions to our designs. Thus, they desire improved ways to monitor and control their bandwidth caps.

To complement our findings, future research could explore how cost affects mobile broadband usage, particularly given that in resource constrained settings, Internet users are more likely to get online on their phones under this pricing model [17,23]. Other studies could examine whether users in countries with higher data caps react similarly to the users we studied. Despite the differing culture and context of use, we believe bandwidth intensive users with higher data caps may be subject to the same frustrations, even though cost may be less of a constraint. Next, we discuss the implications of our study for the HCI community.

The Case for Bandwidth Sensitive Design

At a minimum, our findings suggest capped users desire bandwidth management tools that show how much bandwidth is available and what users, devices, and applications are using up this resource both in near real-time and historically. This information could help users on usage-based pricing plans develop an improved mental model of bandwidth costs informed by real data and enable them to decide how their household wants to prioritize online activities. Presenting usage information that is easy to understand is challenging but offers new opportunities for creative user interfaces. For example, our participants struggled to comprehend that the time spent on a website does not correlate directly to the volume of data used.

Most importantly, we believe these tools need to move beyond simply visualizing information, instead allowing families to have more active control of the allocation of bandwidth to users, devices, and applications if they wish. For example, users could be given improved control over how "chatty" an application is, i.e., to configure how often it retrieves or sends data, or even calls its creator for updates. This model is akin to turning off data "push" notifications on a smart phone to avoid roaming charges. Users on capped or metered plans may also want to know upfront about bandwidth-lite content and how to consume only the most salient content without using too many 'gigs'.

Moreover, much like how developers account for access on a small screen or conditions of slow speeds, we believe there is value in creating content to save users bandwidth and associated monetary costs. For example, certain websites and services such as Netflix[5] (a streaming video service in the U.S.) already suggest a low-resolution version when a slow Internet connection is detected. Extending these design optimizations to users with data caps would be valuable. A trivial example might be to offer text only advertisements to reduce unnecessary bandwidth consumption. Other optimizations could be to delay downloading content immediately or to turn off browsers pre-fetching algorithms, all to minimize costs for those on the smallest of bandwidth plans.

Similarly, in the home, we could leverage the home network to share content. For example, in-home servers that download, store, and share content could make the roll-out of security patches, audio-visual content, and large software updates more efficient, e.g., by centralizing the distribution of one copy of a file to all machines requiring it. All of these features would enable families to make decisions about setting rules and priorities for content access, sharing access fairly, and budgeting monthly Internet costs.

While bandwidth sensitive design would make networking more usable for those with caps, it is important to consider why organizations would be motivated to provide such services. Although ISPs may actually profit from additional revenue when users buy more bandwidth, our suggestions could ultimately benefit them. Specifically, they will gain insight into whether their plan offerings match demand, whether the cap sizes they choose are within reason for average use, and whether users are being treated fairly across the board. In addition, they can more proficiently load balance their network resources and offer enhanced tools to decrease technical support costs.

On the consumer side, given the increasing network congestion from the rise of bandwidth intensive devices and applications we believe that practicing bandwidth sensitive design will provide a competitive advantage for operating systems, browsers, and application developers. As more and more users face the capped situation our participants struggled with, we expect given the choice people will seek out services that are respectful of bandwidth caps.

It is worth mentioning that bandwidth sensitive design also has social implications. As observed in participant reactions to our probes, households may or may not like having detailed usage charts made visible. For some, these charts may serve as a resource for discussions about managing Internet use. Others prefer the ambiguity around their consumption habits. Precisely how increased Internet monitoring and management affects household relationships is a topic for future research.

Moving Past Assumptions of "All You Can Eat" Plans

Aside from potential interventions, our study has highlighted how Internet pricing challenges the assumption that data is an unlimited resource and that what limits our activities is just the speed of the pipe. This has two sets of implications. Firstly and pragmatically, it may cause researchers to reconsider the types of interventions we make in the home. When we deploy probes and prototypes, we offer compensation to participants in part to offset both expenses and inconveniences of the system. Caps ask us to consider how our system interacts with their other data usage and how best to compensate for it. It may also encourage us to consider how our deployment uses the Internet and design in order to minimize that.

But the second and far more important take away is how caps press upon the pervasive assumption of "all-you-can eat" data consumption. Our families were mindful consumers of data, as they were about other consumables; decisions about today's use were considered in the light of what would happen tomorrow and for the rest of the month. Applications and people were in competition for the right to consume data from the network and data was perpetually scarce. Given this mindset, consider two examples of the implications of caps: smart homes and cloud computing. Visions of smart homes conjure up spaces filled with many interdependent networked technologies [8]. Yet, how would the occupants feel if their smart home and its devices cap their network? Would the home even function if capped, and how would we design it to be robust to this situation?

Caps and other forms of usage-based pricing also push on the idea of cloud computing. Pushing data into the cloud adds to competition for network access and with capped billing, storing data locally becomes a more attractive choice. Cloud computing also creates more complications for home users. For instance, households have to juggle data allocations increasingly, between people and devices such as Personal Video Recorders (PVRs) that call their manufacturer to update their television schedule. What alternatives can we envision instead?

In summary, the case of families living with broadband caps challenges assumptions of unlimited Internet and make clear the necessity of introspection in our community about limiting and prioritizing Internet activity, and the

[5] http://www.netflix.com

development of more bandwidth sensitive designs. Reflecting on caps offers an example of how the "messy" world of technology can inspire alternate futures for computing, and suggest that we attend to them if we are to have a truly global reach with our systems [5].

CONCLUSION

Bandwidth caps are likely to persist as ISPs and other Internet providers use tiers and limits to manage infrastructural constraints. In this paper, we explored the effects of data caps on home Internet usage in urban South Africa to show that users have three uncertainties with regards to their bandwidth usage: *invisible balances*, *mysterious processes,* and *multiple users*. Our results demonstrate the specific ways in which users orient to and manage their Internet access under cost constraints. Moreover, we suggest that the HCI community rethink assumptions about unlimited bandwidth in how we design our applications and devices to accommodate those who experience the Internet via usage-based pricing.

ACKNOWLEDGMENTS

We thank our participants. This work was supported by Microsoft Research and NSF IIS-090443.

REFERENCES

1. Andrew Odlyzko, "Internet Pricing and the History of Communications," *Computer Networks 36*, 5-6 (2001), 493-517.
2. Chen, J., Dhananjay, A., Amershi, S. and Subramanian, L. Comparing Web Interaction Models in Developing Regions *ACM DEV*, ACM, London, UK, 2010, Article 6.
3. Chetty, M., Haslem, D., Baird, A., Ofoha, U., Sumner, B. and Grinter, R.E. Why Is My Internet Slow?: Making Network Speeds Visible *CHI 2011*, ACM, Vancouver, Canada, 2011, 1889-1898.
4. Comcast. FAQs about Excessive Use, http://customer.comcast.com/Pages/FAQViewer.aspx?seoid=Frequently-Asked-Questions-about-Excessive-Use.
5. Dourish, P. and Bell, G., *Divining A Digital Future: Mess and Mythology in Ubiquitous Computing*. MIT Press, Cambridge, MA, 2011.
6. Falkner, M., Devetsikiotis, M. and Lambadaris, I., "An Overview of Pricing Concepts for Broadband IP Networks," *IEEE Communications Surveys Second Quarter* (2000), 2-13.
7. Federal Communications Commission, *Connecting America: The National Broadband Plan*, 2010.
8. Harper, R. (ed.), *Inside the Smart Home*. Springer-Verlag, London, 2003.
9. International Telecommunications Union. ITU Free Statistics, 2009.
10. Lasar, M. It Could Be Worse: Data Caps Around the World, Ars Technica,, 2011.
11. MacKie-Mason, J.K. and Varian, H.R., *Pricing the Internet*, in Public Access to the Internet, MIT Press Cambridge, MA, USA, 1995, 269-314.
12. MacKie-Mason, J.K. and Varian, H.R., "Some FAQs about Usage-Based Pricing," *Computer Networks and ISDN Systems 28*, 1-2 (1995), 257-265.
13. McCurdy, M., Connors, C., Pyrzak, G., Kanefsky, B. and Vera, A. Breaking the Fidelity Barrier: An Examination of our Current Characterization of Prototypes and an Example of a Mixed-Fidelity Success. *CHI 2006*, ACM, Montreal, Quebec, Canada, 2006, 1223-1242.
14. Middleton, C. and Chang, S., "The Adoption of Broadband Internet In Australia and Canada," in Dwivedi, Y.K., Papazafeiropoulou, A. and Choudrie, J. (eds.), *Handbook of Research on Global Diffusion of Broadband Data Transmission*, IGI Global, Harrisburg, PA, 2008, 818-840.
15. Naidoo, R., Kaplan, D. and Fransman, M. The South African Telecoms Innovation System and the Diffusion of Broadband *Globelics Africa 2005*, South Africa, 2005.
16. Ofcom. UK Broadband Speeds May 2010: The Performance of Fixed-Line Broadband Delivered to UK Residential Consumers, 2010.
17. Otsuka, Y., *Mobile Broadband: Pricing and Services*. OECD Publishing, 2009.
18. Public Knowledge. Letter to Federal Communications Commission, http://www.publicknowledge.org/letter-to-FCC-on-ATT-Data-Caps.
19. Shapiro, R., *The Internet's Capacity to Handle Fast-Rising Demand for Bandwidth*. US Internet Industry Association, 2007.
20. Smyth, T.N., Kumar, S., Medhi, I. and Toyama, K. Where There's A Will There's A Way: Mobile Media Sharing in Urban India *CHI 2010*, ACM, Atlanta, GA, USA, 2010, 753-762.
21. Statistics South Africa, *Income & Expenditure of Households 2005/2006*, 2008.
22. Strauss, A. and Corbin, J., *Basics of Qualitative Research Techniques and Procedures for Developing Grounded Theory*. Sage Publications, London, 1998.
23. The Berkman Center for Internet & Society, *Next Generation Connectivity: A Review of Broadband Internet Transitions and Policy From Around the World*. Harvard, 2010.
24. Wallsten, S. and Riso, J.L., *Residential and Business Broadband Prices Part 1: An Empirical Analysis of Metering and Other Price Determinants*. Technology Policy Institute,, 2010.
25. Wortham, J. As Networks Speed Up, Data Hits a Wall *NYTimes*, NYC, 2011.
26. Wyche, S.P., Smyth, T.N., Chetty, M., Aoki, P.M. and Grinter, R.E., "Deliberate Interactions: Characterizing Technology Use In Nairobi, Kenya," *CHI 2010*, ACM, Atlanta, GA, USA, 2010, 2593-2602.

Age Differences in Exploratory Learning from a Health Information Website

Jessie Chin and Wai-Tat Fu
University of Illinois at Urbana Champaign
405 N Mathews Avenue
Urbana, IL 61801
{chin5,wfu}@illinois.edu

ABSTRACT
An empirical study was conducted to investigate how older and younger users learned by performing exploratory search of health information using an interface that recommended relevant links based on browsing histories. While older and younger users gained both factual and structural knowledge about the health topics, significant age differences were observed. Our results showed that processing of recommended and regular Web links imposed distinct demands on cognitive abilities, which at least partially explained the observed age differences in the search process. The use of recommended links was positively associated with general knowledge, while the use of regular Web links was positively associated with processing capacity. Results also showed that the recommended links benefited both younger and older adults by broadening the exploration of information, which led to better learning. Implications on designs of health information interfaces that facilitate exploratory search and learning for different age groups were discussed.

ACM Classification Keywords
H.3.3 [Information Systems]: Information storage and retrieval-Search process; H.5.2 [Information Systems]:User interfaces- Theory and methods; J.4 [Computer Applications]: Social and behavioral sciences-psychology; J.3 [Computer Applications]: Life and medical science.

General Terms
Experimentation

Keywords
Aging; Exploratory Search; Knowledge Structure; Learning; Recommended Links

INTRODUCTION
According to recent Pew reports [1], in the United States, almost 80% of the Internet users have used the Internet to search for health information. At least 31% of the users claim that they have been significantly helped by following the medical advice or health information gathered from the Internet [7]. Indeed, online health information websites have become an important source from which people gather healthcare information from distributed Web pages to acquire relevant medical knowledge for self-care. Because older adults (age 60 or above) constitute a notable group of Internet users who regularly search for health information [1], research on the impact of age-related differences on search strategies and performance will highlight how information technologies should be designed to better fit the needs of this growing population of users.

People search for health information for various purposes. While there has been abundant research aiming at facilitating information retrieval, relatively little has been done to understand how information technologies can be designed to facilitate *both* searching and learning, such as when one is acquiring health knowledge about a broad topic (e.g., diabetes) to help them better understand and monitor his or her conditions, or to make treatment decisions [3]. The current study is focused on age differences in exploratory search and learning from a health information website that recommends links based on users' browsing histories. While previous research has primarily focused on how recommendation of links may widen the exposure of relevant information to users, our focus is on how older and younger adults may *use* the recommendations differently, how these differences may influence learning, and how the differences may lead to age-sensitive designs.

Age differences
Cognitive development has different trajectories across our life span. While processing capacity (broadly including processing speed, attentional span, and working memory) often declines with the aging process, crystallized knowledge (including general knowledge and domain-specific knowledge) tends to sustain [2]. The processing limitations influenced older adults' online information search routines in many levels, such as imposing extra difficulties in moving the mouse, tracking the cursors, anchoring the links, remembering browsing histories, etc. These difficulties may be reasons why older users are often believed to be less efficient in Web search, as studies showed that they tended to browse less information, spend more time to extract information, and give up search earlier than younger users [3,4,13,15].

Despite the limited processing capacity of older adults, crystallized knowledge tends to sustain and even grow as people age. While there are many ways that knowledge can be defined, for the current purpose we divide knowledge into *general knowledge*, which is the general verbal ability that we acquired from education or daily reading routines; and *domain-specific knowledge*, which is the topical knowledge that we accumulated from various sources in a specific domain, such as knowledge related to healthcare, finance, or others. Knowledge is important for people to effectively transform their information needs to query terms during search, as well as judge whether information (or links) is relevant.

Search processes

Research shows that the interplay of processing constraints and knowledge shapes users' information search processes and eventually impact performance [3,15]. For example, older adults may face a higher search cost, as measured by the longer time spent to click a link, than younger adults. The higher search cost may be one reason why older adults tend to look up less information and evaluate information more carefully than younger adults. Older adults may also rely more on their crystallized knowledge to evaluate the relevance of links than younger adults. Research has found that, compared to older adults, younger adults tend to adopt bottom-up interface-driven search strategies (following the information layout on the interface) to quickly visit many webpages until the target information is found. Older adults, on the other hand, tend to adopt top-down knowledge-driven search strategies by following their crystallized knowledge to evaluate the relevance of links. As a results, older adults are often found to click a smaller subset of, but more relevant, links as they perform exploratory search [3,4].

Recent research showed that, because of limited processing capacity, older adults could benefit more from a system that provided links across layers, in which the information could be accessed through multiple routes, than from a hierarchical system where information could be accessed only under certain predefined routes determined by the layers of directories dictated by the designer [13]. It is therefore possible that, if each page is linked to other relevant pages in ways that lower the search cost (such that the average number of clicks to go between any two pages is reduced), older adults may be able to access relevant information more efficiently to meet their needs.

Knowledge structures and learning

While a number of studies have showed age differences in information search [13,15], few have investigated its relation to learning, especially in terms of how users' knowledge structures (i.e., organization of knowledge in memory) are related to their search patterns, or how the organization of information on an interface may impact users' knowledge structures. This is particularly important for people who, for example, are chronically ill and need to repeatedly look for health information. Repeatedly searching for health information online may implicitly or explicitly lead to learning of health knowledge by, for example, learning of category and link structures among medical concepts (e.g., symptoms, disease) in a website, in addition to learning from contents of Webpages.

Users often have prior knowledge of health-related concepts, which may influence how they evaluate the relevance of links. For example, if a user knows that patients with obesity are prone to diabetes, the mental distance between the concepts of diabetes and obesity will be small, which may increase the likelihood that the user may actively look for information about diabetes when he or she is looking for information related to obesity. Without such knowledge, a user may learn that the two concepts are related if they are, for example, listed under the same category on a Web page. Therefore, in addition to contents, the link structures of a health website may also support users to learn the relationship among health concepts, which may also help them to guide their search.

Recommending links to users

There have been a growing number of methods to provide recommendation of information to users in different domains such as e-commerce, news, or online social networks. When users are navigating in a Web site, recommendation of links may allow users to explore more information that are believed to be relevant to the users. In general, recommendations can be determined by some forms of association between items. For example, in e-commerce, a company can estimate the associations between products by calculating how likely two products are purchased together, and when users purchase one of these two products, the other product can be recommended to the user. Other methods of association include the use of semantic relatedness of topics contained on two Web pages (such that pages that contain similar topics can be recommended), or similarities of social profiles (e.g., the overlap of social circles between two persons).

While there has been much success in developing new methods in these recommendation systems, the current focus is on how people with different cognitive profiles may *use* these recommendations differently. In particular, we are interested in how older and younger adults may use links recommended by a Web site differently, and to what extent these differences can be attributed to the differences in their cognitive profiles or background knowledge.

The current study

We implemented a link recommendation system to provide additional link structures based on users' browsing histories. We used a battery of cognitive tests to measure individual differences of older and younger adults, and we measured how these individual measures were associated with their search behavior (e.g., how they decided which links to click, how much time they spent on each page, how and when they decided to use the recommended links, etc), and how differences in search behavior could account for any learning effects after they performed exploratory search for different health topics using the Web site. Our goal is to unpack the complex interactions among individual differences between age groups, exploratory search behavior, and learning outcomes. Results will provide useful information for designs of intelligent health information systems that adapt to different demands of users with different profiles.

METHOD

Participants

Forty-seven participants were recruited. 27 college students (Mean=20.96, s.d.=2.07; 60% were female) and 20 older adults (Age of 60 and older, Mean=65.60, s.d.=7.30; 85% were female) were invited to this study. The gender imbalance was due to the random sampling of the study. (There were no main effect of gender or interaction of age and gender on cognitive measures or search behavior.) Data from one younger adult was lost due to a technical problem. All participants had completed high school education. Most (76%) younger adults were college students. Most (80%) older adults had more than high school degree.

Search interfaces

We created two versions of an interface mainly based on the materials from two well-known public medical information websites WebMD (http://www.webmd.com) and MedlinePlus.gov (http://medlineplus.gov). There were roughly 350 short essays about diseases and 100 short essays about how to maintain self-care including topics in nutrition, exercise, etc. In the *parts* interface, we categorized these symptoms based on body parts (e.g., head, chest, limbs); in the systems interface, we categorized symptoms based on the functional body systems (e.g., circulatory system, brain and nerve system, etc).

The two information organizations showed different associations between symptoms [4]. For example, in the systems interface, hearing problem and balance problem were clustered in the same category of "brain and nerve system". However, hearing problem and balance problem were organized in different categories in the parts interface, namely, "nose, mouth and ear" and "limb", respectively.

As Figure 1b and 1c showed, only the main page and symptom page were different in the two interfaces. The use

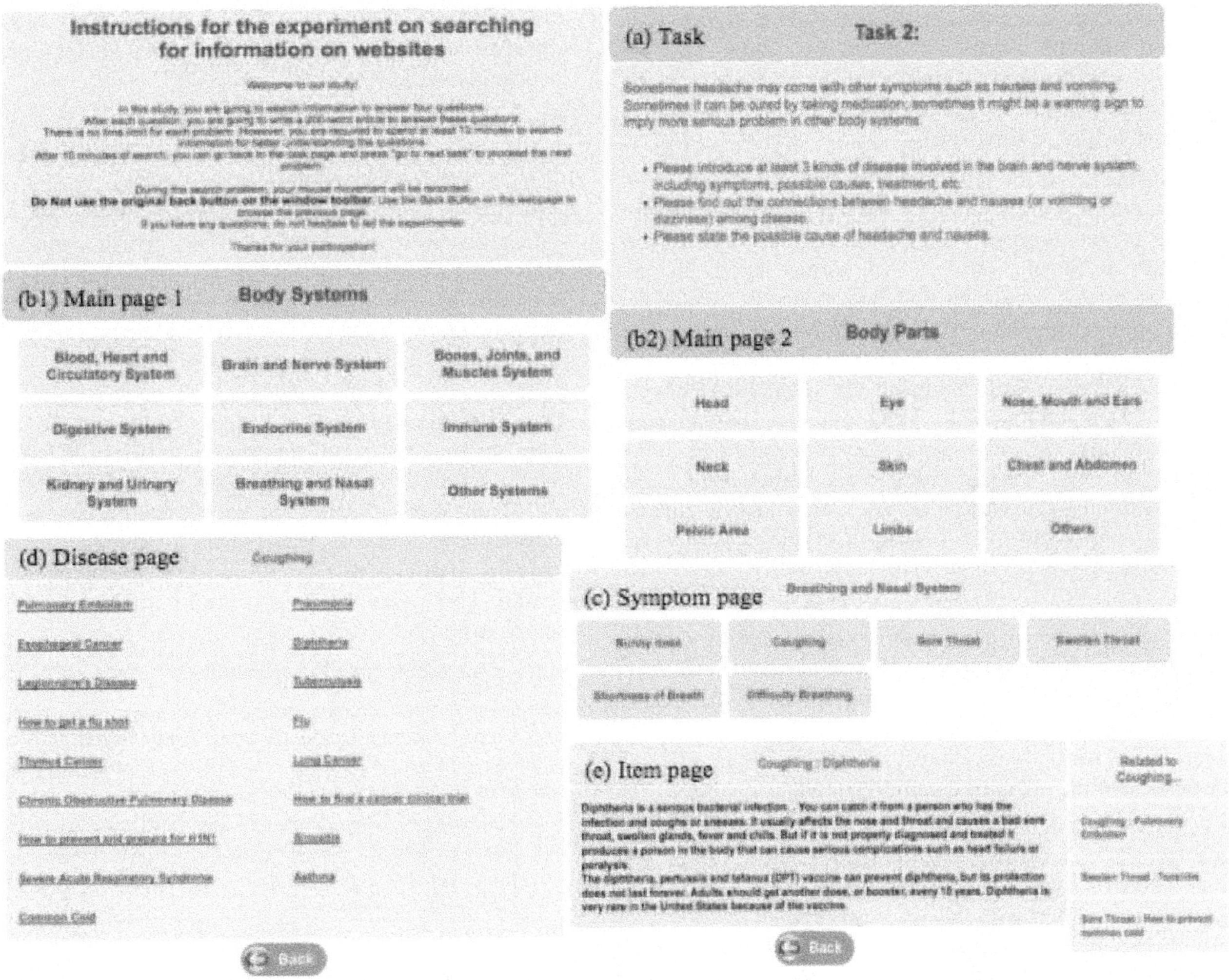

Figure 1. The flow of webpages in the website

of two interfaces was to test whether the change of structural knowledge was dependent on the information organization of the interface. The order of links presented on the website was randomized for each participant. There was no positional benefit for any of the links. Half of the participants from each age group performed the tasks in the parts interface, and the other half performed in the systems interface. For both interfaces, the contents were identical, only the categorization was different. Font size and font color also followed the guidelines for elderly-friendly design [6].

The recommended links

After participants clicked on the main category, they would be taken to the *symptoms* page, which listed symptoms that belonged to the chosen main category (part or system). For example, as shown in Figure 1c, participants could see "coughing" and "runny nose" after clicking on the main category "Breathing and Nasal System". When participants clicked on a symptom, they would be taken to the disease page, on which there was a list of diseases and related how-to tips that were associated with the chosen symptom (Figure 1d). Participants could then click on one of the diseases or how-to tips to see a brief description about this item, which would contain information about the disease definition, possible symptoms, prevalence rates, and the risk factors of this disease (Figure 1e). For how-to tips, the brief description would include a list of how-to procedures to establish self-care behavior.

The main feature to be tested was the recommended links, as shown on the right column of the item page (see Figure 1e). The presentation of recommended links on an item page was contingent on the symptom clicked by the participant prior to reaching that item page. For example, for the item page that described "Brain Cancer", the participant could reach this page after clicking on the symptom "Nausea", or clicking on the symptom "Balance Problem". Depending on the symptom that they clicked before reaching the item page, the recommended links could be different. In particular, the recommended links were symptoms and diseases that were related to the clicked symptom (see Figure 1e for an example). The exact calculations of the recommended links will be described below.

We were interested in how existing knowledge structures may interact with the information organization of the Web site as recommended links were used. Because the health information was categorized by symptoms in our website, we measured users' knowledge structures in terms of how they perceived the symptoms were related to each other.

To generate the recommended links, we first obtained the semantic relatedness matrix from the 53 X 53 symptoms using latent semantic analysis (LSA) [9]. Then each symptom was paired with the other two symptoms that had the highest semantic relatedness to it. The assumption was that the LSA scores would indicate how likely these symptoms co-occur in other contexts (thus were likely related to each other). Once people clicked on an item of a symptom, the program would display other three items under the selected symptom and the paired symptoms as the recommended links.

As an example, from LSA, we found that the symptom "headache" had the highest relevance to symptoms "dizziness" and "nausea". If a participants clicked on "headache", then the disease "Encephalitis", the interface would display "Headache: Stroke, Dizziness: Anemia, and Nausea: Brain cancer". In addition to the semantic relatedness among the symptoms presented in the recommended links, the symptoms could either be in the same or different categories as defined by the interface. Following the previous example, because "headache" and "dizziness" were under the same category "brain and nerve system" as defined by the interface, while "nausea" was under a different category "digestive system", we called the recommended link "dizziness" (after "headache" was clicked") an *interface recommended link*, while "nausea" a *non-interface recommended link*. By comparing how often older and younger participants clicked on the interface and non-interface recommended links, our goal was to test how different age groups may use these two types of links differently. About 60% of the recommended links were interface recommended links. The order of links presented was randomized.

Exploratory search tasks

Participants were given four health related open-ended search tasks in a random order. These tasks required participants to broadly explore a health topic in our website. The tasks were designed such that participants need to actively process information on the Web pages, and perform extensive integration and elaboration on the information. In contrast to simple fact retrieval tasks, the current tasks could not be solved by browsing a single web page or a single domain category (i.e., one body part or one body system). For each task, participants were required to spend at least ten minutes to search to better understand the topic. After each search task, participants answered open-ended questions about each search topic. To exclude the confounding factor of individual differences in memory capacity, participants were allowed to take notes during the search. There was no upper time limit for the exploratory search tasks.

Here is an example of the search task:

More than 80% of adults have low back pain at some time in their life. While back pain is usually acute (short-term), back pain can often be chronic. For those chronic back pain, they might be caused by other physical problems.

- *Find out the connections between back pain and other bone disease, such as osteoporosis, arthritis, osteoarthritis, etc.*
- *Find out the connections between back pain and health problems except bone disease.*
- *Provide some methods to relieve back pain.*

Cognitive measures

Three cognitive measures were given before the search

task. Processing speed was measured by Letter Comparison test [16]; working memory was measured by Letter Number Sequencing [18]; general knowledge (vocabulary) was measured by Advanced Vocabulary test [5].

Factual and structural health knowledge measures

Factual and structural health knowledge was measured by T/F questions and card sorting respectively. For factual health knowledge, we created 12 True/False questions about the search topics. All participants took this questionnaire before the search task. A false example item is," *The H1N1 swine flu virus spread in two ways. It is like the seasonal flu virus, can become airborne if you cough or sneeze without covering your nose and mouth. It can also spread by contacting or eating the contaminated pork".*

We also used card sorting to measure knowledge structures of the participants. Card sorting is a standard methodology to measure knowledge structures (e.g., [8,10,11,12]). In card sorting, participants were asked to use their own rules to put the paper cards into piles. Each card was written with a symptom. Participants were told that there was no correct answer for clustering and the purpose of the task was to understand how they think about the relationship among these symptoms. Twenty-three common symptoms were selected from the health information website, such as the balance problem and chest pain. Each participant did the card sorting twice, once before and after the search tasks..

Experimental design

A 2X2X2 mixed factor experimental design was conducted. There were two between-subject variables: Age (young/old) and Interface (parts/systems), and one within-subject variable (pretest/posttest). Half of the participants were assigned to perform the tasks in the parts interface and the other half in the systems interface. All participants completed four search tasks in their assigned interface.

Procedure

All participants completed the demographic questionnaire, performed the cognitive measures, and completed the health knowledge questionnaire. Then the card-sorting task was given before the search tasks. Participants would then be assigned to either the parts or systems interface. All participants first read the instruction page of the experiment (see Figure 1), and the first task problem would be presented (Figure 1a). Participants then clicked on "Begin" to start the task, which would take them to the main categories page. They could use the "Back" button anytime to go back to the previous page. After 10 minutes, participant could go back to the main page and click on "Done" button when they finished one task. After each task, participants answered a set of open-ended questions. After four search tasks, participants were given the card-sorting task again. The whole experiment took about 3 hours.

Figure 2. The theoretical approach of analysis

Table 1. A list of definitions of variables

Recommended links	The links listed on the item page with semantic relevance to the item
Interface Recommended links	The subcategory of the current recommended link (i.e. its symptom) was in the same category with the subcategory of previous item
Proportion of recommended links clicked	Number of recommended links clicked divided by the number of items clicked
Proportions of interface recommended links clicked	Number of interface recommended links clicked divided by the number of recommended links clicked
Mental Interface Match Index (MIMI)	Measures of harmony between the relational matrices of participants and the ideal sorting suggested by the interface
Semantic Index	Concordance scores between the relational matrices of participants and the ideal proximity matrix suggested by Latent Semantic Analysis

RESULTS

As guided by Figure 2, we first analyzed age differences in users' cognition, knowledge and search process. We then examined the associations between the search process and users' cognitive abilities and knowledge, before we analyzed effects of learning in factual and structural health knowledge (as measured by the open-ended questions and results from card sorting, respectively). Finally, we investigated the association between search process and learning outcome. A summary of the definitions of variables was in Table 1.

Cognitive abilities and internet experience

All participants used the Internet more than twice a week. However, younger adults used the Internet more often than older adults ($U=187.5$, $p<0.005$). Consistent with cognitive aging literature, younger adults performed better in the measures of processing capacity (speed and working memory) than older adults ($t(43)=4.79$ &3.06. p's<.01). Older adults, however, were better in the measures of general knowledge (vocabulary) than younger adults ($t(43)=-4.34$, $p<.01$).

Age differences in factual health knowledge

Older adults performed better in the health knowledge test in the questionnaire than younger adults ($t(43)=-2.09$, $p<.05$), showing that older adults had better understanding about the assigned medical topics than younger adults.

Age differences in structural health knowledge

We also used card sorting to examine the structural health knowledge of participants. Card sorting has been used to investigate the organization of knowledge in our memory and the amounts of learning in the psychology literature ([10, 11]). In our study, we used the free sorting procedure to measure the structural knowledge of medical symptoms. Participants put 23 symptom-cards into piles, and the number of piles was not limited. Based on the

Table 2. Age differences in the search process

Per search task	Young mean (s.d.)	Old mean (s.d.)	F(1,41)
Total clicks	37.18 (16.45)	28.13 (10.23)	4.85*
Total time (sec)	637.30 (132.77)	736.325 (185.55)	4.30*
Average time to decide a link click (sec)	7.93 (4.02)	12.01 (3.93)	12.97**
Number of items looked up	13.39 (5.09)	10.13 (3.83)	5.82*
Number of recommended links clicked	2.98 (1.99)	2.74 (2.13)	0.16
Proportion of recommended links	0.23 (0.13)	0.25 (0.15)	0.32
Proportion of interface recommended links	0.65 (0.04)	0.58 (0.1)	1.17
Average time to read an item (sec)	53.89 (42.84)	78.04 (51.05)	3.02^

**p<.01, *p<.05,^ p<.10

categorization of cards, we inferred the mental distance between each pair of symptoms in participants' knowledge. For example, if a participant put chest pain, difficulty breathing, and irregular heartbeats in the same pile, the symptoms of chest pain, difficulty breathing and irregular heartbeats might be closely connected or frequently co-occurred in his/her health knowledge structures, and thus the mental distance among them is small.

Semantic Index

We first transformed the clustering data into a 23X23 "relational matrix" with entries representing whether two items were put in the same category (1) or not (0). Based on the relational matrix, we calculated the *Semantic Index* to operationalize the measure of relational knowledge of the participants. The criterion knowledge structure used was the measure of semantic relatedness among symptoms generated from latent semantic analysis (LSA) [9]. LSA was shown to captured the general semantic relatedness of words well, and thus, we used it to further validate how well participants' judgment on how two terms were related was similar to the general semantic relatedness calculated by LSA.

We first created a proximity matrix consisted of the LSA scores obtained from each pair of symptoms used in the card sorting task. We then compared each participant's relational matrix to the LSA proximity matrix by calculating the inner products of the entries between the two matrices. The square root of the summation of these inner products was the *Semantic Index*. A higher semantic index would reflect that the judged relatedness among the symptoms was more similar to the semantic relatedness calculated by LSA.

We found that there was no age difference in the Semantic Index in the pretest (t(43)=-0.47, p=0.64) showing that older and younger adults do not differ in their relational health knowledge before the search. We will use the semantic index to compare the change of knowledge structures before and after the tasks.

Mental Interface Match Index

To quantitatively measure the extent to which the knowledge structures of health concepts matched those in the interface, we created another variable called the *Mental Interface Match Index (MIMI)* based on the measure of harmony ([17], cited in [11]). Similar to the semantic index, based on the card sorting data, we calculated the relational matrix, which was compared to the interface matrix, which represented the organization of information in the interface (the one that participants were assigned to). Similar to the relational matrix, the interface matrix was a 23X23 matrix with entries representing whether the pair of symptoms were presented in the same category in the interface (1) or not (0).

We created two interface matrices to represent the structures in the parts interface and the systems interface. The MIMI was calculated by the summation of the inner products between entries in the participant's sorting matrix and the interface matrix, then normalized by the sum of positive entries in the matrix from the interface. The MIMI index therefore indicated the extent to which the participants' knowledge structures of symptoms were similar to the information organization of symptoms in the interface. Therefore, participants with higher MIMI had the knowledge structures more similar to the information organization in the interface than those with lower MIMI. Older adults had higher MIMI in the pretest than younger adults showing that their internal knowledge structures were more similar to the interface before the search tasks (t(43)=-2.70, p<0.01). We will use the MIMI to measure the extent to which participants' knowledge structures became more similar to those in the interface before and after the tasks.

Age differences in the search process

Search process variables were summarized in Table 1 and Table 2, including the number of total links clicked in one task, the average time (measured in seconds) spent in one task, and the average time spent to decide on a link click. In addition to these global measures, we did further analysis on the item pages participants visited (Figure 1e). We first measured the number of items clicked in one task to measure the breadth of exploration. We then measured the number of recommended links clicked as well as the proportion of recommended links clicked (i.e., the number of recommended links clicked divided by the total number of items pages clicked) to examine the usage patterns of recommended links.

Older Users Conducted Less Exploration

A MANOVA was performed to investigate age differences in the search process (through variables in Table 2). We found that younger adults tended to click more links, leave a page more quickly, and decide to click more quickly than older adults. Older adults spent longer time to decide on a link and look up fewer items than younger adults, which replicated findings in previous studies [3, 4].

No Age Difference in Clicks of Recommended Links

The total number of item page visits (Figure 1e) included the case when people clicked an item on the disease page (Figure 1d) and when they clicked on one of the recommended links. Interestingly, younger adults visited more item pages than older adults. However, there was no age difference in both the number and proportion of clicks on recommended links, suggesting that older adults clicked the recommended links as frequently as younger adults (Table 2). Among all the item page visits, there were about a quarter of the item pages being accessed by the recommended links for both younger and older adults.

Individual differences and search process

Pearson Correlation was conducted to examine the relationship among the cognitive measures and search behavior. There was a significant association between the number of symptoms (subcategories) clicked and working memory (r=0.37, $p<0.05$). People with better working memory browsed more symptoms. This association confirmed that *people with higher capacity tended to look up more information*, which might be because they could mentally process more information and thus had lower cost in performing exploratory search (as they consumed less cognitive resources relative to their capacity).

Processing Demands, Knowledge, and Accesses to the Item Pages

Results showed distinct relations between cognitive abilities and the number of item page visits from either the disease page or the recommended links. *When participants visited the item pages from the disease page, there was a positive association between the number of item page visits and processing speed* (r=0.31, $p<0.05$). When participants visited the item pages through the recommended links, there was no association between the number of visits and the processing capacity measures. Rather, *there was a marginally significant association between item page visits and general knowledge* (i.e., verbal, r=0.29, $p=0.056$). The results were consistent with the notion that visiting the item page from the disease page required more processing capacity than through the recommended links, as participants who had higher processing capacity tended to visit the item page more from the disease page, but the same association was not found when participants visited the item pages through the recommended links. Rather, knowledge was related to how likely the recommended links were used, presumably because knowledge allowed participants to more correctly judge the relevance of the recommended links. Given that older participants tended to have lower processing capacity but better knowledge, it was possible that older adults benefited from the recommended links. We will come back to this idea later.

The Influence of Knowledge Structures on Clicks of the Interface Recommended Links

Table 3. Multiple regressions on the proportion of interface recommended links clicked with age and cognitive measures as predictors

Adjusted R square	Predictors	Standaradizd Beta Coefficients	t
0.195 (F=2.28, p=0.05)*	Age	-0.36	-1.69
	Speed	-0.29	-1.51
	Working memory	0.13	0.74
	General knowledge	0.35	1.96
	Medical knowledge	-0.37	-.2.25*
	Pretest MIMI	-0.13	-0.76
	Age X Pretest MIMI	0.44	2.68*

* $p<0.05$

As stated in the Introduction, we assumed that knowledge structures would influence how one would use the interface. To test this, we investigated who clicked the interface recommended links by a multiple regression model, which was conducted with the proportion of interface recommended links clicked as the dependent variable, and age, cognitive abilities, and structural knowledge before the task (pretest-MIMI) as the predictors. The model explained 19.5% of the variance (F=2.28, $p=0.05$) (See Table 3). There were two significant predictors: medical knowledge and the interaction term between age and pretest-MIMI while controlling for age, processing capacity (speed and working memory), and general knowledge (verbal ability). We found that people with less knowledge tended to click more interface recommended links. It was possible that participants with less knowledge might be more reliant on the suggested links, while those with better knowledge would tend to adopt a more top-down knowledge-driven strategy when searching for related information, which was consistent with previous findings (e.g., [3]).

The significant interaction between age and pretest-MIMI suggested that younger and older adults with different knowledge structures searched differently. We used Simple Slope Techniques [14] to visualize the interaction effect between age and pretest knowledge structures (i.e., pretest MIMI). The interaction term was decomposed into a simple regression of proportion of interface recommended links clicked onto pretest-MIMI for younger and older adults (Figure 3). Results showed that pretest-MIMI was positively associated with the proportion of interface recommended links clicked for older adults (B=1.81; B for the slope), but was negatively associated with proportion of interface recommended links clicked for younger adults (B=-1.41).

Results suggested that *older adults whose knowledge structures were less similar to the information organization in the interface tended to click fewer interface recommended links*. However, *younger adults whose knowledge structures were less similar to the information organization in the interface, were more likely to click on the interface recommended links*. There was no difference on the use of interface recommended links for people who have similar knowledge structures to the interface between two age groups. Therefore, younger adults were more exploratory, in the sense that they had a higher tendency to click on links when those links were clustered differently from their knowledge structures (perhaps to explore for information that they did not know). For older adults, on the other hand, they tended to be less exploratory, in the sense that they tended to click links that were consistent with their knowledge structures. Similar to previous findings (e.g., [3]), the search strategies of younger adults were more interface-driven (bottom-up), and the ones of older adults were more knowledge-driven (top-down).

Learning

Learning Factual Health Knowledge: Open-ended questions

Each participant answered 4 sets of open-ended questions. If participants answered comprehensively and accurately, they would get 1 point for each question in the task; if they answered partial questions, they would get 0.5 points for each question in the task. The answers were scored by two independent raters with good agreement (>90%). There was no age difference in the accuracy of answers (mean accuracy (SD) for younger and older adults: 0.88 (0.14) and 0.86 (0.11) respectively). Considering the accuracy scores for younger and older adults in the true/false health knowledge pretests, the mean accuracy for younger and older adults were 0.63 and 0.72 respectively. Although we did not use the same factual knowledge measures in the pretest and posttest (both have 12 questions), the growth in accuracy scores on the health knowledge measures suggested that participants had learned after performing exploratory search in the health information website.

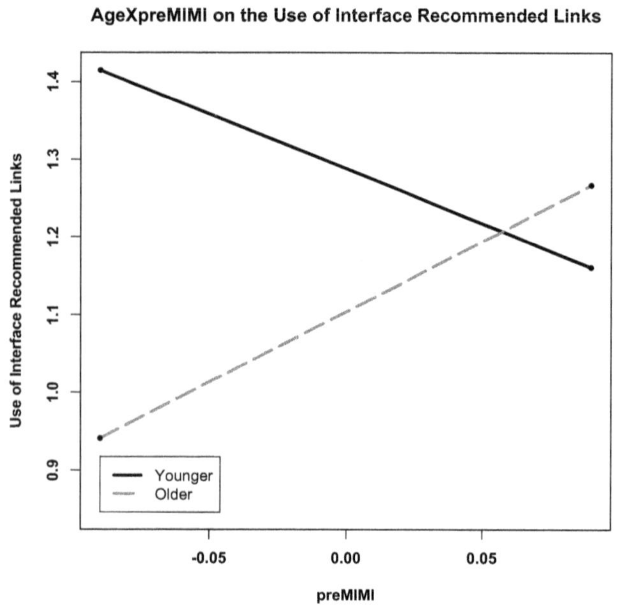

Figure 3. Relationship between proportions of interface recommended links clicked and pretest Mental Interface Match Index for younger and older adults

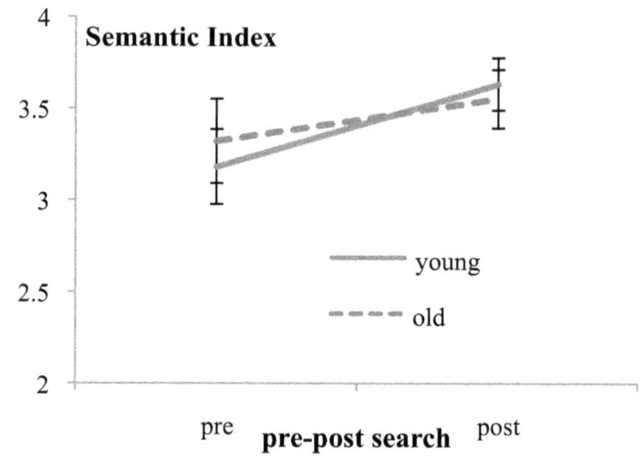

Figure 4. The semantic index for both younger and adults increased after the search tasks.

Learning Relational Knowledge: Semantic Index

Since participants did card sorting before and after the search tasks, we calculated the pretest and posttest semantic indices to investigate the learning effects in relational health knowledge. A 2X2 Repeated Measures ANOVA was performed on the pretest and posttest semantic indices, with age as the between-subject variable. The results showed a significant main effect in the difference between pretest and posttest semantic indices ($F(1,43)=8.13$, $p<0.01$) (See Figure 4). There was a main effect of age ($F(1,43)=.02$, $p=.90$), but the age X pre-posttest interaction was not significant ($F(1,43)=0.89$, $p=.35$). Older adults showed a generally higher semantic index than younger adults. However, for both younger and older adults, the semantic indices were higher in the posttest than the pretest. In other words, *both younger and older adults had more similar knowledge structures after the search tasks.* Results therefore showed learning effects in the relational health knowledge for both younger and older adults.

Learning the Information Structure from the Interface

A 2X2X2 Repeated Measures ANOVA was performed on the pretest and posttest of the MIMI with the between-subject variables of age and interface. There was no main effect or interaction effect associated with the interface. However, there was an interaction effect of age on the pretest and posttest MIMI ($F(1,41)=4.72$. $p<0.05$). As Figure 5 showed, the MIMI of younger adults increased after the search tasks, while there was no change for older adults. A post hoc test also confirmed that younger adults had higher MIMI after than before the search tasks ($t(1,24)=-2.46$, $p<0.05$); however, there was no difference in the pretest and posttest MIMI of older adults. Older adults started with a high MIMI and remained the same after the search tasks, while younger adults showed increase in the MIMI after the tasks, and reached the same level as older adults. Therefore, in addition to learning the semantic relatedness among health concepts during the exploratory search, *younger adults also acquired the information organization of the interface through the interaction with the interface.*

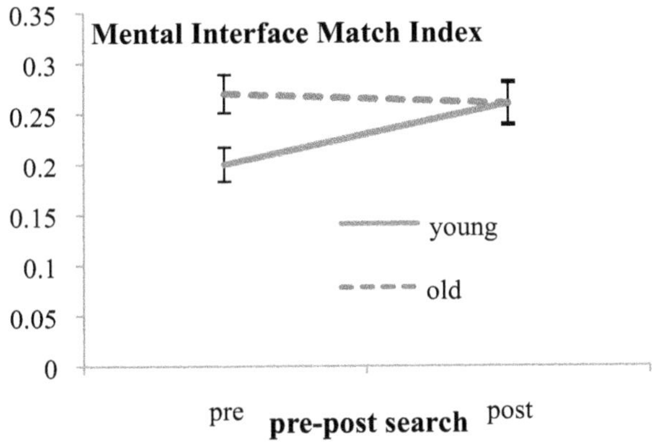

Figure 5. The interaction effect of age and pre-post test on the Mental Interface Match Index (MIMI)

Search process and learning outcome

Pearson correlations among accuracy scores of the open-ended questions and search behavior variables were calculated. Results showed that both younger and older adults who clicked on more relevant items (through both disease pages or recommended links) had higher accuracy scores for the open-ended questions ($r=.38$, $p<.01$). Relevant items referred to items that contained answers to the tasks. This at least partially validated the link between search and learning outcome – i.e., those who searched better (found more useful information) also learned better.

Although younger adults clicked more items than older adults, there was no age difference in the accuracy scores. *In other words, even though younger adults visited more item pages than older adults in total, only the relevant item pages helped them answer open-ended questions*. In other words, the more item pages that they browsed might not be all relevant. On the other hand, older adults browsed the same number of relevant item pages and achieved similar accuracy scores of the open-ended questions, even though the total number of visits of item pages was lower. This highlighted the reason why performance in open-ended search tasks was about the same for younger and older adults, which replicated the results from our previous study [3].

Learning the Interface's Information Structures through the Use of Interface Recommended Links

The final part of the results was the significant Age X Pre-Posttest intreaction on the MIMI. The effect suggested that, compared to older adults, the knoweldge structures of younger adults became more similar to the information organization of the interface after the search than older adults. To understand how this was related to the search process, we first calculated the deviance scores of MIMI (i.e., posttest MIMI minus pretest MIMI). Then we calculated the Pearson Correlation between the MIMI deviance scores and the search variables. We found that the *proportion of interface recommended links clicked* had the highest association with the MIMI deviance scores for younger adults ($r=0.53$, $p<0.05$). (Such association was not significant in the older group since there was no significant change in the MIMI scores before and after the search.) As we expected, *younger adults who clicked on the interface recommended links more were more likely to learn the information structures of the interface* because the interface recommended links and item pages were not only relevant, but also clustered in the same categories in the interface. As Figure 5 showed, for younger adults who used the interface recommended links more, their original knowledge structures were more different from the information organization of the interface. So the adoption of this search strategy led to more learning effects in MIMI scores for younger adults.

CONCLUSIONS and DISCUSSION

The current study examined age differences as older and younger participants learned by performing exploratory web search. We explained the age differences in terms of the relationship among users' background knowledge, search behavior, and learning outcomes. Consistent with previous research, we found age differences in cognitive abilities and health knowledge – younger adults had better processing capacity while older adults had better health knowledge (both factual and structural). We also found age differences in search behavior – younger adults were more exploratory, as they clicked more links, but visited and left a page more quickly, than older adults. Older adults did more focused search, as they clicked fewer (but more relevant) links and spent longer time deciding on a link.

Our results showed that search behavior was related to cognitive abilities. Specifically, we found that users who browsed more pages tended to have higher processing capacity. Perhaps because the use of the recommended links was associated with knowledge but not with processing capacity, older adults used and benefited from the recommended links as much as younger adults. It is also possible that, because younger adults tended to perform a broader exploratory search, they learned more from the information structures of the interface than older adults. Most interestingly, the amount of learning was associated with how often they clicked the interface recommended links (i.e., recommendations that were consistent with the interface's categorical structures of symptoms).

There were two main contributions of the current study. First, the study demonstrated the success of having recommended links as an intervention that aimed at supporting the use of *knowledge* for older users. As research has consistently shown, knowledge tends to be more resilient to the aging process, while processing capacity tends to decline with age (e.g., [2]). While testing the effects of different recommendation methods is not the focus of the current study, our results did demonstrate the benefit of recommendation methods that allow older adults to better utilize their often superior knowledge while minimizing processing demands and search costs (e.g., by reducing the number of clicks and the need to remember hierarchical link structures). Results have important implication for design of recommendation systems that better fit the needs and limits of older users.

The second major contribution of the study was the use of multiple measures to access exploratory learning. Our results showed that in exploratory search, not only did participants learned from the contents of Web pages, *they also could learn from the category and link structures in the Web site.* We found that while contents of Web pages could lead to learning of factual health knowledge, exploring for information by following links in a Web site could also lead to learning of relational knowledge about medical concepts, as the interface's categorical and link structures allowed users to infer the extent to which different concepts were related. This has important implication to design of health information systems, as when patients are exploring and learning about medical concepts from these systems, both factual and relational knowledge are important, as they are equally important for patients to make health-related inferences and decisions.

Human computer interaction research on designing senior-friendly technologies often focused on ways to offload processing demands to the interface, such as by providing browsing histories to aid older users' shorter span of working memory [6]. However, relatively little has been done to design intervention methods that facilitate the use of knowledge. Indeed, our results not only showed that the use of recommended links was associated with users' knowledge but not processing capacity, but also showed that these recommended links seemed to better fit the top-down knowledge-driven strategies adopted by older adults.

On the theory side, results from our study *highlighted the importance of understanding the reciprocal relation and coupling between search processes and knowledge structures*. This reciprocal relation is similar to the relation between reading comprehension and knowledge structures, as documented in the literature on text comprehension [11] – while knowledge structures may influence how a reader extracts topical structures of an essay, knowledge structures of the reader can also be influenced by the organization of texts. In our study, users learned and updated their knowledge structures through exploratory search in the Web site by interacting with its links structures, but it was also found that their knowledge structures influenced how they conducted the search.

Future research will investigate how to more intelligently cluster the information based on users' knowledge structures, such that the recommendation of health information can be adapted to the users' knowledge structures and their information needs to facilitate search and learning. Also, we will extend the topics to non-health contexts and low-domain-knowledge older samples to test if we can generalize our findings to whether interaction with the interface can induce direct and indirect learning.

Overall, the study guided interface design in two aspects, age-sensitive interfaces and learning through exploratory search. The study suggested that older users' search behavior might be promoted with more flexible information structures that adaptively estimated the ways users conceptualized the terms in their knowledge. User models that keep track of their interactions may therefore provide better recommendations of links to older adults. Given that repeated exposure to the interface would promote better learning, an interface that adapts to the user profiles over time will benefit knowledge acquisition for domains in which long-term gain in knowledge is useful, such as for chronic-ill patients.

REFERENCES

[1] American Life & Pew Internet Report, *Health Topics,* (2011).

[2] Beier, M. E. and Ackerman, P. L. Age, ability and the role of prior knowledge on the acquisition of new domain knowledge. *Psychology and Aging, 20,* (2005), 341-355.

[3] Chin, J. Fu, W-T. and Kannampallil, T. Adaptive information search: Age dependent interactions between cognitive profiles and strategies. In *Proc. CHI 2009*, ACM Press (2009), 1683-1692 .

[4] Chin, J. and Fu, W-T. Interactive effects of age and interface differences on search strategies and performance. In *Proc. CHI 2010*, ACM Press (2010), 403-412.

[5] Ekstrom, R. B., French, J. W., Harmon, H. H. and Dermen. *Manual for the Kit of Factor- Referenced Cognitive Tests.* Princeton, NJ: Educational Testing Service, 1976.

[6] Fisk, A.D., Rogers, W.A., Charness, N., Czaja, S.J., and Sharit, J. *Designing for Older Adults—Principles and Creative Human Factors Approaches.* CRC Press, Washington, DC, USA, 2004.

[7] Flynn, K.E., Smith, M.A., and Freese, J. When do older adults turn to the internet for health information? Findings from the Wisconsin longitudinal study. *Journal of General Internal Medicine, 21,* (2006), 1295-1301.

[8] Gliner, G., Goldman, S. R., and Hubert, L. A methodological study on the evaluation of learning from story narratives. *Multivariate Behavioral Research, 18,* (1988), 9-36.

[9] Landauer, T, Foltz P. W. and Laham, D. Introduction to latent semantic analysis. *Discourse Processes, 25,* (1998), 259-284.

[10] Mannes, S., and Kintsch,W. Knowledge organization and text organization. *Cognition and Instruction, 4,* (1987), 91-115.

[11] McNamara, D.S., Kintsch, E. Songer, N.B., and Kintsch, W. Are good texts always better? Interactions of text coherence, background knowledge, and levels of understanding in learning from text. *Cognition and Instruction, 14,* (1996), 1-43.

[12] Nelson, M. W., Libby, R., and Bonner, S. E. Knowledge structure and the estimation of conditional probabilities in audit planning. *The Accounting Review, 70,* (1995), 27-47.

[13] Pak, R. and Price, M. M. Designing the information search interface for younger and older adults. Human Factors, 50 (2008), 614-628.

[14] Preacher, K. J., Curran, P.J., and Bauer, D. J. Computational tools for probing interactions in multiple linear regression, multilevel modeling, and latent curve analysis. *Journal of Educational and Behavioral Statistics, 31* (2006), 437-448.

[15] Sharit, J., Hernandez, M., Czaja, S. and Pirolli, P. Investigating the Roles of Knowledge and Cognitive Abilities in Older Adult Information Seeking on the Web. *ACM Transactions on Computer-Human Interaction, 15,* (2008), 11-25.

[16] Salthouse, T. A. Mediation of adult age differences in cognition by reductions in working memory and speed of processing. *Psychological Science, 2,* (1991),179-183.

[17] Smolensky, P. Information processing in dynamical systems: Foundations of harmony theory. In D.E. Rumlhart & J.L.McClelland (Eds). *Parallel distributed processing* (vol1, pp194-281), Cambridge, MA: MIT Press, 1986.

[18] Wechsler, D. *Wechsler adult intelligence test manual* (3rd ed.), Psychological Corporation, San Antonio, TX, 1997.

Income, Race, and Class: Exploring Socioeconomic Differences in Family Technology Use

Sarita Yardi, Amy Bruckman
School of Interactive Computing
Georgia Institute of Technology
{yardi,asb}@cc.gatech.edu

ABSTRACT
Minorities are the fastest growing demographic in the U.S. and the poverty level in the U.S. is the highest it has been in 50 years. We interviewed middle to upper class, suburban, white American parents and low-income, urban, African-American parents to understand how each group incorporates technology into their lives. Participants had teens in their homes and devices like computers and cell phones played a powerful and preeminent role in family life. Our results show that socioeconomic differences both reflect and reinforce technology use at home. Specifically, low socioeconomic status families share devices more often and low socioeconomic status teens have more responsibility and independence in their technology use. We argue that that as low socioeconomic status families become the majority demographic, the CHI community needs to better understand how to design for these groups.

Author Keywords
Parents; teens; families; social computing; African American; race; income; class; socioeconomic status.

ACM Classification Keywords
H.5.m. Information interfaces and presentation (e.g., HCI): Miscellaneous.

INTRODUCTION
Demographers have long predicted that a dramatic shift would take place in the racial makeup of the population in the United States. This prediction came to fruition in early 2011. Data from the 2010 Census Bureau revealed that fewer than half of current three year-olds in the U.S. are Caucasian and more than half of them are races other than Caucasian [9]. As they grow up, this generation of non-Caucasian races will be over 50% minority. In other words, the rising new racial makeup is and will continue to be a *minority majority*.

At the same time, economic inequality is increasing in the U.S. The income gap between the richest and poorest Americans is the largest it has been since household income was first tracked in the 1960s [37]. In 2011, 15% of Americans and 22% of American children live below the poverty line [37]. In past decades, economically less advantaged individuals were arguably less relevant for HCI because computers were predominantly used only by the wealthy. Today, this has changed. Among families making under $30,000 per year, 59% have computers at home and 75% have mobile phones [29]. Taken together, these two trends mean that the typical HCI user is less and less likely to be white and middle class. These changes present an opportunity and challenge to the HCI community. To confront this emerging design space, HCI research will need to broaden its vision of the normative user.

We take a preliminary step towards this broad agenda through a qualitative study of how parents manage their teens' technology use. This provides a context through which to examine rules, priorities, and values that are deemed important by the family. Parent-teen relationships around technology use have been the focus of our research for a while and in this study, we wanted to use this familiar context to explore new territory around socioeconomic issues and technology use. We conducted interviews with 16 middle to upper class, white parents and 18 low-income, African American parents to explore how social structures bear on technology adoption. Prior research shows that low-income, African American populations tend to have different family structures and technology purchasing patterns; yet, little is known about how these differences impact technology use. The questions we ask are: does technology access and use differ across these two populations, and, to what extent are these differences pushed to the forefront by socioeconomic conditions?

As might be expected, we find that parents from both groups share many of the challenges in monitoring and managing their kids' use of technology. It is well-known that parents struggle with how much their teens use cell phones and the Internet, and with appropriateness of both teen behavior and the content they access [39] (see [23] for a detailed review of parenting concerns). However, we also find some novel, and perhaps surprising, relationships between socioeconomic status and sharing of devices, responsibility, and family structure. The results speak to themes that are too large to fully debate and theorize here. The goal of this paper is to contribute empirical data on the nature of the issues. This work brings two contributions to HCI. First, we show how technology uses relate to socioeconomic differences among two social groups. Second, we make a broader argument for moving the minority majority towards the center of the design process in future research.

RELATED WORK

To orient readers around this work, we first draw on research from Family Studies, Sociology, and large surveys to describe family structure and technology purchasing and adoption patterns. We then describe how our work builds on prior HCI studies of race and income as they relate to technology use.

Differences in technology use exist among different families and cultures. This section briefly highlights comparisons of technology ownership and use based on indicators of socioeconomic status, including race, income, and neighborhood. In this work, African American is defined as it is in the U.S. Census, as a person having origins in the black racial groups of Africa, and includes people who indicate their race as "Black or African American." This is a binary classification that doesn't take into account social and economic criteria that might affect the extent to which one identifies with this category. Similarly, White or Caucasian refers to people who identify as "White" on the U.S. Census and thus as having origins in Europe, the Middle East, or North Africa. Some participants identified as more than one race—White plus another race. No participants identified as mixed race of White and Black.

Like Ames et al. [1], we examine differences based on socioeconomic status (SES). SES relates to *class*, or *social class*, and is a function of many individual properties including income, education, employment, race, neighborhood, and lifestyle. Ames et al. argue that socioeconomic status and class are important but overlooked aspects in HCI research. Factors like race and income are at the heart of sociology and anthropology research but are often at the margins or even invisible in HCI.

Technology Purchasing and Adoption

Whites own desktop computers more than African Americans do and they go online using a computer more often. They also have Internet access and broadband Internet at higher rates than African Americans [15,30,31]. On the other hand, African Americans use mobile phones more often than Whites do, including for Internet use, to play games, and to use social networking sites [3,25,28,31,32] They also spend more time playing video games than Whites do, and spend more discretionary income on videogame hardware and software.

In terms of income, high-income families (>75k) own and use more technology than low-income families (<75k). Specifically, high-income families are more likely to use the Internet on any given day and to own multiple Internet-enabled devices. They also own more desktop and laptop computers as well as game consoles than low-income families [16]. Finally, patterns of use differ among urban, suburban, and rural Internet users. Urban users have three times as many friends on social networking sites as rural users [11] and they own smartphones at twice the rate of rural users [33]. Urban residents are more likely than suburban residents to use their mobile phones to play games, use social networking sites, or watch a video [34].

In general, African-Americans are the most active users of the mobile Internet and their use of it is growing the fastest [15]. Their heavy use of mobile devices offsets lower levels of access through traditional devices like desktop computers, laptops, and home-broadband connections [15]. African Americans spend more of their discretionary income on computers, cell phones, and other electronics than any other racial group. They remain somewhat less likely than whites to go online but the gap has decreased over the past 10 years [30,31].

Related Work in HCI

Recent work in HCI has increasingly focused on race and income in technology design and use. Research that has examined low-income demographics include Woelfer's studies of homelessness and technology use [38] and Dillahunt et al.'s studies of energy use in low-income communities [8]. Work that has examined race includes Grimes' series of studies which focused on eating patterns among African American populations [13] and DiSalvo et al.'s studies of young African American male game practices [7]. Nakanamura has examined the effects of race online and its consequences for offline behavior [22]. However, these studies of technology tend to focus on a particular demographic rather than a comparison of two demographics. Comparisons studies are difficult to conduct because technology deployments are often designed for a particular demographic and recruiting does not scale well if looking for two disparate types of participants. A notable exception is Ames et al.'s comparison study of screen time among working class and middle class families with young children [1]. They find that middle-class families restrict television and computer use whereas working-class families promote technology to their children.

We build on their work but focus on two new directions: 1) comparison of low-income, urban, African Americans and middle-upper class, suburban, white parents. They categorize middle and working class based on income alone whereas we also group by race and location. 2) study of families with pre-teens and teens (ages 10 and up). An overwhelming proportion of children get their first cell phones and online accounts during the middle school years [18]. Middle school is well-known as the time when children go through major developmental changes (e.g. biological transformations of puberty, educational transition out of elementary school, growing autonomy, and physical shifts with sexuality) [19,27]. Thus, we focus on this disruptive and transformative stage in families' lives. As others have done [35], our research problematizes a design process where the normative user is assumed to be white and middle class. The growing body of work on low-income and minority groups' use of technology reflects the research communities' interest in understanding users beyond white, middle class.

There is extensive work on family communication through technology in HCI, much of it focusing on systems to support family connectedness (see [36] for one example). In earlier work, we have described challenges parents face in managing their kids' use of social media, but we focused on middle and upper class parents [39]. Odum et al. (2010) report tensions around communication, coordination, negotiation, and identity in divorced families and consider ways of designing for these alternative families and their children [24]. Despite the range of prior work, there are gaps in this work that should be addressed. Little is known about the relationship between technology use and race and income and its implications in HCI. This is an important research direction with social, educational, and design implications in understanding the next generation of products and users.

METHODS

Participants were geographically split between north and south Atlanta. Atlanta has a rich history of diversity and struggle, and is representative of the diverse racial, ethnic, and economic backgrounds that we described in the introduction. Specifically, Atlanta has a high income equality rate and is 54% Black and 38.4% White according to 2010 U.S. Census data [40]. In this study, the middle and upper class, white parents live in North Atlanta and are referred to as high socioeconomic status (high SES). The low-income, African American parents in general live in South Atlanta and are referred to as low socioeconomic status (low SES). References to specific families are Family number + B or A to refer to high or low SES.

We partnered with a private school where most students are from middle or upper class families. At this school, students are tracked to go to college and parents keep their children involved in a number of after-school activities. We recruited parents through word of mouth, the school's parent board, and letters through the school. We interviewed 16 parents, two fathers and 14 mothers. The length of the interviews ranged from 40 minutes to 1.5 hours. Interviews were conducted at a time and location that was convenient for the participant such as the school, workplace, home, or a coffee shop. All participants were in a two-parent, heterosexual relationship with between 1-4 children. The recruiting pool we drew from was middle and upper class families. The average median income in the school we partnered with is just over twice that of the average median income in the U.S. This sample was biased towards parents who were economically able to buy new technologies.

	Low SES	High SES
Participants		
Mother	15	14
Father	3	2
Family Size		
1 child/family	3	0
2 children/family	8	2
3 children/family	5	7
4 children/family	1	4
Participants' Children		
(Total) Girls	20	22
(Total) Boys	18	19
Children's Ages		
<8	8	7
8-11	13	9
12-17	10	17
>18	7	8

Table 1: Participant demographics. Individual family structures have been aggregated to maintain privacy.

We also partnered with local community programs to recruit low-income, African American parents. Program I was a program for African American teen boys to learn computer programming skills. They had to be qualified as low-income as defined by the federal Free and Reduced Lunch Program. We interviewed 5 parents from Program I. These interviews took place in a mall food court, at Burger King, over the phone, and at a coffee shop.

Program II was a nationally recognized after-school program for youth with multiple sites in the city of our study. We visited two sites over multiple evenings and multiple weeks to interview 12 parents. We recruited by setting up a desk near the entrance and exit and invited parents to participate as they picked up their children.

All parents identified as African American in their interviews with us (five of the seven feeder schools into Program II are 100% Black [10]). Among the seven feeder schools into Program II, five have over 90% eligibility for

Free and Reduced Lunch (FRL). FRL is determined as a proportion of the Federal Poverty Guidelines (income has to be under 130% of FPG for eligibility for free lunch and 185% for reduced lunch). For example, for a 5-person family the FPG is $25,790; thus, families with an income less than $33,527 are eligible for free lunch and less than $47,712 are eligible for reduced lunch.

Interviews ranged in length of time from 15 minutes to one hour. Short interviews were in instances where parents were in transit while picking up their children and neither we nor they wanted to interrupt their day for too long without a prior scheduled appointment. We tried to recruit Program I parents for interviews but found it difficult to get them to return our phone calls or emails and thus resorted to the strategy at Program II. We did not pay any participants. We asked parents first about who was living in their home, then about what kinds of technology were there. As the interview progressed and parents became more comfortable, we asked about what kinds of rules they set at home around technology use, and what they found easy or difficult in enforcing such rules. All interviews were conducted in English and all participants were native English speakers. We refer to both parents and guardians as parents for simplicity, but note that the term "parent" may be more representative of some demographics than others.

We used a grounded theory approach to guide our data analysis [12]. We coded transcripts for high-level codes related to parenting, technology, and class. As we iterated over the interview transcripts and high level codes, we broke these codes down into more detail, such as strictness, values, rules, access, use, income, occupation, education, and family. We coded the interview transcripts again with the detailed codes and looked for high-level themes to emerge among interview transcripts. To do this, we highlighted themes throughout each transcript then aggregated them across transcripts and looked for the most common topics. The top themes were rules, monitoring, sharing, responsibility, economics, and status. We organized these into four major themes in the results section of the paper.

RESULTS

In general, the amount of use of technology and the appropriateness of content exchanged present challenges for parents. However, the exact form of those challenges differs in various ways.

Rules and Monitoring

Parents wanted their children to have cell phones to facilitate communication with parents and for safety and emergencies. High SES parents usually wanted their middle school kids to be able to coordinate after-school pick-ups and carpools real-time. Some low SES parents wanted their kids to be able to communicate when they took the bus to school or from after-school activities. Parents across demographics had similar approaches to rules about how their younger children (middle school and younger) could use social media.

Most of them looked to limit the amount of time their children spent on computers and mobile devices. Some parents limited television to a certain daily time limit or no TV at all during the week. A mother in Family 30A expanded the policy to include Facebook as her children grew older, though her children were upset that Facebook was not allowed. Her children shared a desktop between them (and she had her own desktop and laptop for herself). Though she had wanted to get them laptops for Christmas, she did not because she felt it was inviting more issues with Facebook. Her older son had Internet access on his cell phone so he could check Facebook anyway but she felt that cell phone use was different than a computer monitor, where people could chat for hours. The following quote from her was representative of many we heard about immediate families' use of cell phones:

> *It got to the point where they would email each other in the same house at the same time. They be emailing each other, he's upstairs, she's downstairs, the child's in another room.*

Parents recounted stories of other children's' parents calling them to tell them that their own child was engaged in inappropriate behavior. In one case, a parent had learned her child was writing that "nobody liked him" online and another girl told her mom who called the parent. In another case, a parent received a phone call from a father of an 8-year-old girl who said her 12 year-old son was playing games and chatting with the girl online late at night. In this case the girl had given the boy her home phone number and he called; the parents had callerID so they called the parent, who was previously unaware of his late night gaming and chatting.

Cutting off the Internet was a frequently used strategy for parents, though they accomplished this in different ways. Parents often did not have the right language for conveying the decisions they made. A parent in Family 11B told us she "cut off the Internet, for a long time." When asked how she did that, she said she "closed the laptop and took it downstairs." A parent in Family 14B, when asked the same question about how the computer turned off at 8:30pm, she could only say that "It just shuts off." High SES parents were more likely to tell us that they explicitly relied on other community members like parents and schools to help monitor and keep an eye on their children; however, this is likely in part because the school was private and tight-knit (as compared to the relatively disparate and under-funded public schools in the low SES neighborhoods).

Parents across demographics reported that it was hard for them to keep up with what their kids were up to. They assumed their kids knew more than they did about technology:

I have shut Facebook off completely because they were still going downstairs. If I go upstairs, where the kitchen and all that is, I can't see what they're doing. They were spending too much time on Facebook, so my computer friend showed me how to go in and block it. I just locked it within the last two weeks. They haven't said anything; I don't know if they've figured out how to get around it.

Parents were familiar with checking history as a tool for surveying their children's browsing activity. Many parents had tried blocking Internet use. A parent in Family 15A told us that she and her husband had blocks on their Internet browser. Her husband checked history and could tell that it was being erased. In low SES, a mother in Family 22 reported the same experience:

Researcher: How do you know where they've been?

Participant: I look over their shoulder. Sometimes I go back into their history but then they got real smart and they'll erase it as soon as I get up...

Researcher: How do you know?

Participant: When I check there's nothing there.

Researcher: How did you learn to check history?

Participant: From classes I've taken. From operating a computer myself.

Parents told us they had taken classes to learn about computers though where they accessed classes varied. The local Apple store was a source of information for some high SES mothers whereas local community centers were sources for some low SES parents.

Most parents knew that their kids were likely to be hiding search history in some way, especially as they got older. The low SES parents also knew that their kids were using private browsing (which means history is never logged and cannot be viewed later). In contrast, high SES parents we talked to did not mention private browsing and only a few mentioned deleting items from history. However, we observed that information tended to spread quickly and widely through parents at the high SES school and, thus, they often knew and were concerned about similar things. In both cases, parents acknowledged that their kids probably knew how to circumvent whatever rules they were setting up. Most parents were looking for effective ways to monitor their children's activities. Some wanted to monitor all the time, others just wanted the ability to monitor if they felt it was needed. Few families reported that their children were likely to tell them what they were doing.

There were some exceptions where families did communicate more openly among low SES families. One example indicates how family structure relates to attitudes towards technology. A low SES woman in her 50's was raising three of her nephews, the youngest of whom was a senior in high school. She became the legal guardian of the boys when they were 8-13 years old and the difference was discernable in the ways that she had raised them with respect to technology use. She gave them more freedom because they were not her own children. She also communicated with them more openly, and they with her.

I never had any kids of my own and I worked a lot. When I got them it was like one day I didn't have kids, the next day I had a bunch... I've heard some of my colleagues say they use Facebook to check what their kids are doing. My kids just tell me; sometimes it's too much information. Maybe it's because I'm their aunt and not their mom, I've always tried very hard to be not judgmental. If they bring it to me I try to be objective and show them why this is really not cool to be doing. So anything that they do, I basically already know.

Sharing Devices

Our findings suggest that low SES families are more likely to share devices like computers and cell phones than high SES families. Low SES parents reported that sharing posted challenges for them, such as the logistics of trying to share computer time. Parents were annoyed when children downloaded software and that slowed down the machine or when they changed settings. Some parents had rules about time of use, such as if children went over on their allotted time, the time would be taken from the next day's allotment. In most families, parents had their own computer(s) but children sometimes shared devices. In general, parents felt that sharing computers made it easier for them to monitor what their kids were doing on the computer.

Sharing of other technologies, like phones, also made it easier for parents to know what was going on. Most high SES children were given mobile phones around middle school time, at which point they no longer used the home phone line. For families who did still share phones, the sharing enabled parents to more easily "catch" their children. In Family 24A, the oldest son did not have a cell phone and a female friend called their home line at 4am. The son's parent intercepted the call before he could get to the phone. This transpired because he did not have a cell phone, but his female friend did, and thus imposed her own social protocols on his home landline. In Family 21A, a grandmother, who was the guardian of her grandchildren, caught her granddaughter's inappropriate sexual conversations after sharing a cell phone with the granddaughter. The granddaughter had borrowed the cell phone for a few days and the boys' texts kept coming. In these kinds of cases, shared devices left traces.

In contrast, high SES parents rarely shared personal desktops or laptops with their children, especially once the children reached middle school age and older. When parents decided their children needed a computer and a cell phone for homework and communication, respectively, high SES parents chose to purchase devices like laptops and cell phones for their children. We did not hear any parents say that they shared their devices with their children before purchasing children their own devices, though sometimes young children shared computers with one another. For high SES parents, middle school was when their children began to get their own devices and services (e.g. Facebook accounts). For these parents, transitioning into this new stage of parenting was a difficult and sometimes exhausting process [39].

How parents used technology also impacted their kids' uses. Family 17A consisted of a single mother of two young children who had gone back to school and did not have time to watch her daughter on the computer:

> *I'm really strict with her with the computer because she likes to explore places where she shouldn't. So she can only get on it if I'm going to be sitting there with her but that's really difficult because I use it for school.*

This single mother of two children was working a job and also going to school for a post-secondary degree. In her home, as was the case in many homes, the shared computer was for the parents' work first, and the children's play second. Parents felt that young children—roughly 5th grade and younger—didn't need computers for school work; computers were mostly for fun and play. Parents in both groups believed middle school was about when computers time should be allotted in the evening for homework.

The sharing of devices among high SES revealed important differences in participation. High SES parents were more likely to purchase their children individual laptops and cell phones around middle school while Low SES parents either prioritized sharing of existing household devices or passing down old ones to the kids, (though certainly some purchased devices for kids like high SES parents). Some Low SES families shared passwords for their email accounts, Facebook, and other online logins. One parent told us:

> *I have access, everybody has access to everybody's passwords. We have to have access to all passwords, FB, email, anything that is online.*

When asked how her children felt about it, she told us "They are okay with it." Another participant said she was friends with her children on Facebook. When asked if they were okay with it, she responded "Yeah, they don't have a choice." Many Low SES parents replied in similar tones, emphasizing their parental authority:

> *Participant: If they're using the computer in their room too much, we say something: "Why are you going to your room to use the computer? It's a laptop. Sit down here." You know, so, we don't allow too much private use. If we see a pattern of someone always wanting to go to their room, then we stop it.*
>
> *Researcher: And they're okay with that?*
>
> *Participant: They don't have a choice. I don't know if they're okay with it. It doesn't matter.*

Such responses like these were common and reveal the more authoritarian approach to parenting that has been described in earlier studies of African American parenting [23]. They can be more strict and demanding of their children, and reported this approach to us confidently. A grandmother of two teenagers told us she checked what the children were doing on the computer "whenever she felt like it." For her, privacy was a philosophical approach that undergirded day-to-day decisions in their home. When asked if they knew she was checking, she laughed and told us:

> *There's no such thing as privacy for them. They don't have privacy. We're just a very free-flowing kind of not uptight kind of family.*

Responsibility

Low SES parents consistently talked about responsibility as an important part of raising their children. Part of responsibility included getting a job as soon as teenagers were old enough, and transitioning towards independence as an adult, at age 18. In contrast, high SES parents rarely discussed jobs or economic independence (though that is undoubtedly a long-term goal they hold for their children [23]). These parents were more likely to talk about education and extracurricular activities—sports, music, and camps—than the low SES parents. An outcome of the emphasis on jobs and income among low SES participants was that low SES teens sometimes purchased their own devices, like games, and in those cases their parents and guardians granted them more agency over their uses. In Family 25A, an aunt who was guardian of three boys gave the youngest, a senior in high school, freedom with his laptop because he had purchased it himself. She didn't like the amount of time he spent on it but didn't feel it was her authority to tell him what to do it with it because he owned it. When we asked how he paid for it, she replied:

> *He bought it. He has money because when their dad died they received money every month until they were 18—a portion, a income, and I would give it to them every month because I thought it was only right. I find when kids don't have money to buy the little things, they tend to get into negative behaviors. I feel that at a certain age your parents are done. It gives you an opportunity to be on your own.*

Her philosophy had worked well for the older children she had raised but she was having trouble with the youngest one, who had just turned 18:

> *He spends an exorbitant amount of money on these games. He went out and bought with his graduation money, part of it, a flat screen TV. I'm talking a 42" flat screen TV and put it in his room. So you know*

'where's your money for your [college] room deposit'? Busted...

Her oldest boy had purchased handheld games and her middle boy purchased new cellphones, but for both she never felt it was an addiction. In contrast, she felt her youngest was addicted to the Xbox and at age 18, it was becoming his responsibility to take control of his future.

Getting a job and earning potential was important at an earlier age for low SES parents. A mother in Family 19A lamented that her teenage son spent his time playing games with a neighbor instead of getting a job or planning to go to school.

Lately, he's been going to another friend's house, guy that lives two doors down, they grew up together, and they play that game. He doesn't have a life either. He's about 21 years old, living in his mom's basement, and working at a McDonald's, not there's anything wrong with that, working at McDonald's is an opportunity. That guy has gained like 50 pounds, you can tell a young life going nowhere.

In Family 13B, the mother had gotten her oldest son a cell phone when he was in middle school but she took it away because he was using it too much. She got him one again for this 16th birthday. Her rule was that if she got any calls from school about him using it there or they confiscated it, he would not get it back. She did not want him using it during homework but knew he probably had it on vibrate and felt at age 16 he needed some leeway to use his own judgment.

Both high and low SES parents talked about taking away cell phones as punishment. Most parents felt that their child was their responsibility and there had to be consequences to actions. Taking away the cell phone was a supreme punishment for kids, and parents of all backgrounds appeared to be relieved to have at least one reliable leverage point over their kids.

Economics and Status

Many of the public schools attended by low SES children did not have working computers with Internet, and the local library was instead used as a computer and Internet resource center. The low SES local community also had parent centers available where parents could go to use the Internet. Parents' attitudes towards technology and educational opportunities varied. A Family 22A guardian lamented the fact that other parents thought it was more important to have cell phones than to have Internet service at home. For many families, there was status associated with having a "nice, shiny phone" that could take pictures and have Internet service rather than a home computer and Internet to do homework.

Status and stigma were associated with different devices and influenced purchasing decisions for families from all backgrounds. Low SES parents told us their children did not like prepaid cell phones because there was a stigma against them:

It's just considered an amateur phone. In the same way they might like Michael Jordan more than New Balance. It's a status symbol. –Family 9A

Phones like the TMobile and the Virgin Mobile both fit under this stigmatized category whereas the Blackberry and iPhone had higher status. Some low SES parents put their children on flat-fee plans like MetroPCS because they were worried about high cell phone bills. Low SES parents were concerned that their children would go over the monthly limit and they would be billed for their teenagers' heavy use. Low SES parents were also concerned about their children breaking devices, in part because they did not always have the financial resources to replace them. High SES parents were concerned about amount of use of cell phones as well, but their concerns were often related to the health and well-being of their children around excessive technology use.

The economic realities for low SES parents were that they had to make choices about what devices to buy and what services to pay for, especially during economic downturns. We spoke to a low SES participant who had worked at a neighborhood public library for over 20 years and who described the changes in patronage as the economy fluctuated:

Most of these people had the equipment before the economy went bad and the laptops, WalMart just about giving them way, people get their income tax, they go buy a laptop... It's incredible how many people do not know how to use the computer, how many people who were pushed out of the work force don't know how to do a resume. –Family 13A

At that particular library, patrons—up to 20 at a time—would come to the library before it opened and sit in the parking lot to use the wireless. Many low SES participants had laptops, or cell phones, or broadband, but not all three. Though they had some access to devices and Internet, they were hindered—especially lower income people—by the lack of a fully participatory engagement with technology. This was also the case for adults who were unemployed and could not look for jobs from home.

Results show that sharing of devices, financial responsibility, rules and monitoring, and changes in the economy relate to the ways that families use technology. The implications of these patterns are discussed in the next section.

DISCUSSION

Supporting Parent Literacy

The high SES families among our participants were two-parent families and often had at least one parent who was technologically literate. These families are better equipped to make informed decisions about how their children should be interacting with technology. In addition, low SES parents who are single parents or guardians may be constrained by first order priorities in their lives like inflexible work schedules, single parenting responsibilities, and ensuring food, shelter, and safety are satisfied first and foremost. Managing and monitoring social media use are secondary concerns.

Parents did not appear to have differences in terms of worldviews or moral panics about technology more generally. Some parents were pessimistic about the changes technology was bringing upon society and others were optimistic about the social and learning opportunities afforded. Most parents conveyed some amount of concern that their family was using social media too much. What we did observe was that parents who were often most concerned or confused were the least likely to be active users of social media themselves. For these parents, unfamiliarity bred uncertainty. It was hard for them to imagine what kinds of activities their children were engaging in on different sites, and thus, to imagine creative and effective approaches to teaching their kids how to use these sites.

However, while the issues are the same, how to address them within each group is different. Dual parent households often reported that one parent was the technical person and the other was less so (and this was often gendered). For single-parent families, the sole parent's ability to manage social media use was only as good as their knowledge of social media. For such parents, tools for quickly and easily keeping up with and staying on top of their children's behavior are needed. They need to be more lightweight and easy to use than existing monitoring software. They also should be less invasive of children's every move online, because neither parents nor children want such levels of surveillance.

Some families were more likely to share devices than other families, and the extent to which parents controlled devices varied by age and ownership. Older teens had more control over the devices and teens who bought their devices were afforded independence. In both cases, technological maturity is needed as teens gain ownership over their technology. As in other life transitions like driving, teens know how to use the tools, but their decision-making about what to do with them can be under-developed [19]. Teens are taught about social media in schools but more resources are needed for parents to know how to teach their teens age-appropriate decision-making skills around technology use.

Sharing and Ownership

High SES parents are likely to purchase devices for their children around middle school for communication or educational purposes. Low SES parents are also likely to buy devices for their middle school children, but have to make more choices about what products to get and what services to pay for on top of them. Among low SES families, teenagers are often encouraged to get jobs both for the income source and to prepare them for future employment. Teenagers with jobs and purchasing power can wield more independence from their parents in deciding what technology to use and how because they own their own devices. On the other hand, low SES parents of younger children also share devices more often which can make the monitoring process easier for the parent.

Our results and prior research [36] show that family members generally prefer not to share devices. Parents who do not want their young children to have full access and ownership will construct an environment in which the kids share a computer. However, for many low-income families, sharing a computer is not a choice. The device most parents and teens have is a mobile device. There are opportunities for developing mobile services that explore how low-income, minority groups can better connect to their immediate and extended families and local communities. There are opportunities to open communication channels within immediate and extended families that change some of the existing "get off my lawn" [5] paradigms of online family interaction. This builds on existing work towards connecting families and extended families but considers designing for different classes of users in the context of the kinds of devices they use regularly in their daily lives.

Status and Choices

Cell phones and video games are consistently purchased over desktops among low SES individuals. These devices offer entertainment, connectedness, and status at relatively affordable prices. However, lack of computers, Internet, and productivity software makes schoolwork and job searching difficult to do from home. Different social groups want devices that not only are pleasing for them to use, but that elicit status from their peer groups. Status has always been a lynchpin of adolescence but it is also a marker of class. Whereas families who are not economically constrained can *choose* to have certain styles of technology and not others, low-income families typically *have* to make choices.

An important factor that is also surfaced in our research is that class is dynamic. The use of the public library highlighted the wide swing that the economic downturn caused in library patronage and kinds of use. Some families had laptops but no home broadband, and others had broadband but only to connect to video games. The library was a central hub for computer access, wireless, and entertainment (movie rentals). Future work should also consider the dynamics of race and income and their (changing) economic realities.

Intersubjectivity and Implications for HCI

In this section we consider the implications of socioeconomic diversity for the HCI community. This research takes a microsociological approach to a macrosociological problem. It looks at things like parenting and technology—microsociological units—with the goal of understanding class and the participation gap—macrosociological issues. Though useful for our research, this approach has its drawbacks. There is a tendency to concentrate on the unfamiliar and frame it as the first order object of focus. This is the case in this work. Although two groups are compared as is done in comparative ethnography, this paper really examines an emerging majority minority group in relation to the status quo that has dominated HCI research.

Researchers have called for more reflexivity in HCI research [26]. Reflexivity refers to the ways in which the research approaches and outputs are impacted by the people doing the research [6]. As anthropologists have long known, it is impossible for researchers to write about other people without letting their own voice and preexisting biases into the writing [21]. Thus, we look to position our own presence in this research, recognizing the tension Bardzell describes between pursuing a socially conscious agenda and achieving scientific and moral objectives [4]. Even more importantly, we emphasize that it is not possible to determine in this research what is attributable to various features of class like race, income, education, or neighborhood from other aspects of participants' lives. None of these can be detached from the larger milieu in which participants live (see [20] for a discussion of intersectionality, or how socially constructed categories do not act independently of one another).

The results of our research are contextualized in an implicit set of values about what is right and desirable in terms of parenting and raising children. There are also values prescribed to technology adoption and its use in the home. These value judgments are inherent in any HCI study, but often fail to acknowledge the wide range of values that might exist across demographics. HCI research has a tendency to report observable characteristics like age and gender but ignore subtle cultural stereotypes like conversation style, self-presentation, or face-saving strategies. The class and culture researchers identify with is often different than that of the participants with whom they are interacting. As such, there is an inherent in-group and out-group formation, though power dynamics may vary fluidly depending on the number of researchers and participants and the nature of the research. Frequently, authors will identify with the race and education level of one group more than the other; yet, choices in conversation style, attire, and interview location can mitigate some of those differences.

Categories, social roles, and labels are dynamic. Researchers from a wide range of disciplines have wrestled with the use of race, in particular, as a scientific, socially constructed, and cultural categorization (and indeed, critical race theorists examine how researchers themselves participate in the social construction of race). Challenges include distinguishing between race as a risk factor or as a risk marker and finding a way to write about race that appropriately treats the we/they dichotomy [17]. Scholars also ask how to make sense of accounts in which race is silent or non-manifest [14]. In [2], Andersen warns against research inquiries that privilege the perspective of dominant group members. Andersen also warns against examining the experiences of minorities by holding them up to a set of norms that come from the dominant group or from any group different than their own. Moving forward, we encourage HCI researchers to consider both the observable and unobservable ideological structures within the research context. These impact the way technology is used and valued and broadens the scope and outcome of the research beyond the familiar normative user.

CONCLUSION

Race, income, and class affect access to devices, responsibility with those devices, and ability to monitor teens' use of them. Parents from all backgrounds share challenges in knowing what their children are doing online and how to best manage use, but low SES parents face particular challenges among single parents and teens with jobs and independence. On a micro level, this research indicates that training and resources are needed for parents to keep up with and keep ahead of the technology that their kids are using. On a macro level, this work exposes the limitations of HCI studies that marginalize or ignore completely the effects of socioeconomic status. HCI should attend to socioeconomic factors like race, income, and education of its users in it study design. Otherwise it risks conflating study results with socioeconomic factors, particularly around adoption and use which may be over or under reported depending on income, race, culture, and other factors. As low SES individuals and families become the majority demographic, the CHI community needs to acknowledge their differences and report on study results as a function of socioeconomic status.

ACKNOWLEDGMENTS

We thank all of the parents who participated in this research and the schools and community centers who supported our research. We thank Betsy DiSalvo for her intellectual contributions and help recruiting participants. We also thank Connor Graham and the anonymous reviewers who contributed extensive time and feedback to this work.

REFERENCES

1. Ames, M., Go, J., Kaye, J. "Jofish", and Spasojevic, M. Understanding Technology Choices and Values through Social Class. *CSCW '11*, (2011).
2. Anderson, M. Studying across difference: Race, class, and gender in qualitative research. In J. Stanfield and R. Dennis, eds., *Race and ethnicity in research methods.* SAGE, Newbury Park, CA, 1993, 39-52.
3. BET Networks. (2010). "African Americans Revealed: Black Family Study." http://bet.mediaroom.com/.

4. Bardzell, S., and Bardzell, J. Towards a Feminist HCI Methodology: Social Science, Feminism, and HCI. *CHI '11*, (2011).
5. Bruckman, A., Gurzick, D., Lampe, C., Stutzman, F., and Yardi, S. Get Off My E-Lawn: Mulching Youth and Technology. *CSCW '10*, (2010).
6. Davies, C.A. *Reflexive Ethnography: A Guide to Researching Selves and Others*. Routledge, London, 2002.
7. Dillahunt, T., Mankoff, J., Paulos, E., and Fussell, S.R. It's Not All About "Green": Energy Use in Low-Income Communities. *UbiComp'09*, (2009).
8. DiSalvo, B., Yardi, S., Guzdial, M., et al. African American men constructing computing identity. *CHI '11*, (2011).
9. Frey, W.H. *America's Diverse Future: Initial Glimpses at the U.S. Child Pop. from the 2010 Census*. 2011.
10. Georgia Department of Education. *Adequate Yearly Progress*. 2010.
11. Gilbert, E., Karahalios, K., and Sandvig, C. The network in the garden: an empirical analysis of social media in rural life. *CHI '08* (2008).
12. Glaser, B. and Strauss, A. *The Discovery of Grounded Theory: Strategies for Qualitative Research*. Aldine Publishing Company, NY, 1967.
13. Grimes, A., Bednar, M., Bolter, J.D., and Grinter, R.E. EatWell: Sharing Nutrition-Related Memories in a Low-Income Community. *CSCW '08* (2008).
14. Gunaratnam, Y. *Researching 'Race' and Ethnicity: Methods, Knowledge and Power*. SAGE, 2003.
15. Horrigan, J. Wireless Internet Use. *Pew Internet Research.* 2009.
16. Jansen, J. Use of the internet in higher-income households. *Pew Internet Research.* 2010.
17. Kaplan, J.B. and Bennett, T. Use of Race and Ethnicity in Biomedical Publication. *JAMA 289*, 20 (2003), 2709-2716.
18. Lenhart, A. Is the age at which kids get cell phones getting younger? *Pew Internet Research.* 2010.
19. Leon Mann, Ros Harmoni, C.P. Adolescent decision-making: the development of competence. *Journal of Adolescence 12*, 3 (1989), 265-278.
20. McCall, L. The Complexity of Intersectionality. *J. of Women in Cult. and Soc. 26*, (2007), 1771–1800.
21. Merton, R.K. *On social structure and science.* University of Chicago Press, 1996.
22. Nakamura, L. *Cybertypes: race, ethnicity, and identity on the Internet*. Routledge, 2002..
23. Nelson, M.K. *Parenting Out of Control: Anxious Parents in Uncertain Times*. NYU Press, 2010.
24. Odom, W., Zimmerman, J., and Forlizzi, J. Designing for dynamic family structures. *CHI '10* (2010).
25. Rideout, V.J., Foehr, U.G., and Roberts, D.F. Generation M2: Media in the Lives of 8- to 18-Year-Olds. *Kaiser Family Foundation.* 2010.
26. Rode, J.A. Reflexivity in Digital Anthropology. *CHI '11*, (2011).
27. Ryan, R.M. and Lynch, J.H. Emotional Autonomy versus Detachment: Revisiting the Vicissitudes of Adolescence and Young Adulthood. *Child Development 60*, 2 (1989), 340-356.
28. Selig Center. *African-American/Black Market Profile*. 2007.
29. Smith, A. Americans and their gadgets. *Pew Internet Research*. 2010.
30. Smith, A. Home Broadband 2010. *Pew Internet Research*. 2010.
31. Smith, A. Technology Trends Among People of Color. *Pew Internet Research*, .2010.
32. Smith, A. Mobile Access 2010. *Pew Internet Research*. 2010.
33. Smith, A. Platform differences in smartphone adoption. *Pew Internet Research*. 2011.
34. Smith, A. How Americans Use Their Cell Phones. *Pew Internet Research*. 2011.
35. Taylor, A.S. Out there. *CHI '11*, (2011).
36. Tee, K., Brush, A.J.B., and Inkpen, K.M. Exploring communication and sharing between extended families. *Int. J. Hum.-Comput. Stud. 67*, 2 (2009), 128-138.
37. U.S. Census Bureau. *Current Population Survey Annual Social and Economic Supplement*. .
38. Woelfer, J.P. and Hendry, D.G. Homeless young people's experiences with information systems: life and work in a community technology center. *CHI '10*, (2010).
39. Yardi, S. and Bruckman, A. Social and technical challenges in parenting teens' social media use. *CHI '11*, (2011).
40. U.S. Census Bureau. *2010 Population Report*. 2010. http://2010.census.gov/2010census/.

The eLabBench in the Wild – Supporting Exploration in a Molecular Biology Lab

Aurélien Tabard, Juan David Hincapié-Ramos, Jakob E. Bardram
The Pervasive Interaction Technology Laboratory – IT University of Copenhagen
{auta,jdhr,bardram}@itu.dk

ABSTRACT
In this paper we present a field trial of the eLabBench, a digital tabletop-based laboratory bench designed to support the exploratory practices of molecular biologists in the laboratory. The eLabBench supports the organization of personal information, capture of experimental work for later access, and the use of a variety of computational resources directly at the lab bench. We deployed the eLabBench in a biology laboratory for 16 weeks, and invited seven molecular biologists to run experiments on it. We report on how they used the bench and how it fitted within their larger experimental process. The main impact of the eLabBench lies in the changes it sparked off in preparing, running, and documenting lab experiments. By supporting computation at the bench and management of physical objects in the office, the eLabBench blurred the separation between office and laboratory work. Based on our observations, we discuss how interactive systems for laboratories such as the eLabBench can support a more exploratory or design-oriented way of 'doing' science.

Author Keywords
Design; field study; eLabBench; tabletop; digital bench; laboratory; experiment; research practices; biology; life-sciences.

ACM Classification Keywords
H.5.2 Information Interfaces and Presentation: User Interfaces – Evaluation/methodology; J.3 Computer Applications: Life and Medical Sciences – Biology and genetics

INTRODUCTION
The nature of synthetic biology work is changing in at least two significant ways. First, biology research increasingly relies on digital tools not only for everyday information management, but also for simulation and analysis of experimental conditions. Digital laboratory notebooks and laboratory information management systems are examples of the former, whereas bioinformatics and 3D visualization tools are examples of the latter. This digitalization creates opportunities for biologists, for instance by letting them virtually explore experimental parameters before running time-consuming laboratory experiments, or by offering much more powerful algorithms and datasets against which they can analyze collected data. Second, due to a better understanding of bio-

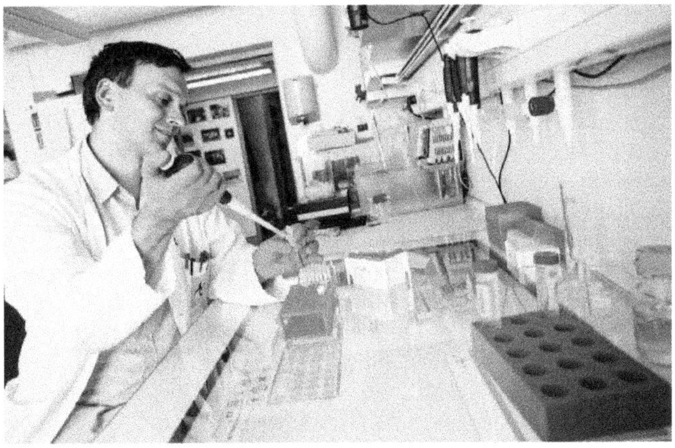

Figure 1. A biologist doing a lab experiment using the eLabBench.

mechanisms down to the nano-scale, a number of researchers are turning to *designing* synthetical biological matter. This shift from an analytical natural science to a design or engineering science changes the way many biologists work and surfaces research practices in which experimentation, exploration or trial and error play an important role.

Within HCI, we mainly addressed the first change by helping biologists handle digital resources in the lab or in the wild, for instance by augmenting laboratory notebooks with digital capabilities [12, 14, 20, 22] or supporting the experimental workflow with ubiquitous computing technology [1]. Such systems aimed at facilitating the transition to a more digital workflow. However, the changes in the way synthetic biologists 'do' science challenges the notion of a well defined workflow.

In this paper, we present a field study of the eLabBench and its supporting infrastructure, a set of technologies that aim at supporting exploration and computation in molecular biology laboratories. Figure 1 shows the eLabBench, an interactive tabletop system which supports browsing and annotation of digital resources, access to native applications and object tracking of test tube racks and other objects on its surface. The underlying infrastructure allows users to store, manage, move, share, and annotate digital resources both at the eLabBench and on their office computers. We presented the system and its technical implementation elsewhere [19]. The purpose of this paper is to report from a 16 week trial deployment of the system in a biology laboratory. The purpose of the deployment was to gauge the usefulness of the system 'in the wild', investigating how this type of technology can support analytical as well as synthetic experiments. Our study focused on a particular type of molecular biologists working on the design and construction of DNA nano structures. The deployment allowed us to better understand how to support these biologists' iterative workflow. The long term use of the eLabBench showed how computational resources are now a necessity at the bench and how capture mechanisms for physical samples are of great interests. As such, the eLabBench and its supporting infrastructure were able to support the molecular biologists in their work, without enforcing a strongly defined experimental process.

RELATED WORK

Many research projects exploring how to support experimental biology work have addressed the core problem of information management (capture, archival and access) of biologists. Here, the laboratory notebook captured much of the attention due to its status of de-facto standard for recording the execution of experiments, reflecting on the acquired data, and planning new experiments. For example, Mackay et al. presented a series of augmented paper notebook with search capabilities and bi-directional links between paper notes and digital data [12]. Hinting toward a deeper integration between field work and office (computer-based) activities, Yeh et al. designed ButterflyNet to support better gathering and analysis of field data through augmented paper notebooks [22]. Along the same line of research, Tabard et al. proposed PRISM [20] an online collaborative laboratory notebook that integrates data captured in Anoto-paper notebooks with data acquired from the biologist's PCs. Focusing on digital notebooks, Schraefel et al. created a tablet-based digital laboratory notebook aimed at streamlining and structuring information capture, in order to ease revisitation, re-use, security and archiving [14]. Even though the eLabBench aims at helping biologists manage, capture, archive, and move information used in biology experiments, it is not a lab notebook. Instead it integrates with a lab notebook and views it as but one resource in the ecology of resources used for biology experiments.

LabScape [1] is another related project that introduced a set of Ubicomp technologies in the laboratory environment, focusing on supporting the workflow of a protocol used for biology experimentation. By offering definition and execution of workflow-like experimental protocols, LabScape aimed at decreasing errors and improving efficiency in laboratory work. While LabScape focused on a more efficient execution of biology protocols, the eLabBench is designed to support an open-ended and less planned experimental approach. Moreover, we do not know how LabScape was accepted or used in the biology lab, since there is no report from any deployment study.

Recently, Echtler et al. have presented the BioTISCH [4], which illustrates how biology experiments can be run on an augmented multitouch laboratory bench. This work is in line with the research on the eLabBench and these two systems share goals and many features. The eLabBench is, however, more advanced in terms of features and comes with an underlying infrastructure that helps organize and distribute resources between several eLabBenches and the personal computers of the biologists. The BioTISCH has not – to our knowledge – been subject to any real-world trials.

Looking at the broader field of tabletops and interactive displays for eScience, Widgor et al. proposed a system for astrophysicists [21]. They designed a walk-up and share multi-surface for scientific meetings which goes beyond traditional meetings and encompasses different collaborative activities within astrophysicists' workflow. As a result, their work showed how introducing such new devices can lead to new scientific insights or help support existing hypotheses. Our work on the eLabBench is in line with this research but aimed at biologists. Finally, other experiments with tabletops within life-science explored how they could support *learning experiments* through the use of tangibles [18], and *learning abstract knowledge* through interaction and collaboration [16, 17].

Methodologically, we ground our work in the recent deployment studies of tabletops "in the wild". This naturalistic approach provides benefits at different levels. For example, at the design level, the MemTable [7] demonstrates that the perspective of long term usage forces designers to consider ergonomics constraints more carefully. From a research perspective, the outcomes of deployments in a tourist information center [13] or in homes [9] show how such a technological intervention can help uncover otherwise hidden social organizations.

EXPLORATION IN SYNTHETIC BIOLOGY RESEARCH

We designed and deployed the eLabBench in close collaboration with a group of molecular biologists working on DNA nano technology. Amongst other techniques, this group specializes in doing so-called DNA Origami, which is used to build 2D and 3D structures at a nanoscale [15]. The group consists one professor, four post-docs, three PhD students, and one lab technician.

We have been observing, interviewing, and working with this group of biologists in their lab over a period of two years. This collaboration has provided us with significant insights into the nature of biology work. The studies included task-centered observations of biology work; place-centered observations of work in the laboratory and in the office; and artifact-centered observations focusing on the use of digital and physical research resources [2]. Moreover, we took an observer-participant approach by experimenting with the biologists in the lab. In many places, our observations of biology work and technology use within laboratory work coincide with those previously documented in other HCI and Ubicomp research (e.g. [1, 20]). For example, biologists work in a messy lab environment with lab benches filled of racks, tubes, materials and documents; they are rather mobile moving in and out of labs, and they rely heavily on laboratory notebooks for situated capture of experimental details at the lab bench. Our observations have been incorporated in the design of the eLabBench system [19]. But in order to understand the deployment of the eLabBench system in this biology lab, is it worthwhile taking a closer look at the iterative and exploratory nature of biology work. Traditionally, biology research has been described and viewed as a deductive science, where biological phenomena can be inferred from general laws and experimentally verified (or falsified) following specific deductively designed experimental protocols. The biologists in this lab are, however, to a large degree thinking of their work as 'tinkering' and 'exploration'. As their research becomes increasingly geared toward 'making things', their workflow revolves around designing complex molecular shapes and optimizing their design in an iterative fashion[1].

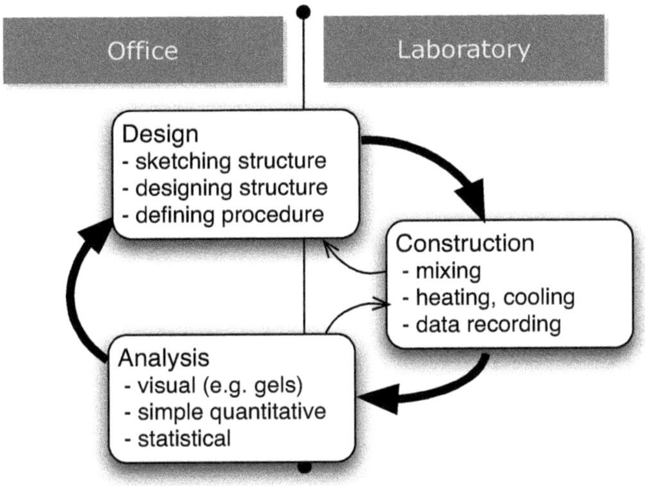

Figure 2. The exploratory workflow of synthetic biolgists.

Figure 2 illustrates this exploratory biology workflow consisting of three phases: (i) *designing* the nano-scale structures; (ii) experimental *construction* of the structures in the lab; and (iii) *analyzing* the produced structure using various tools in-and-out of the lab.

During the design phase, synthetic biologists focus on the structural design of new organic artifacts. This phase requires them to evaluate which building blocks (DNA or RNA primers) are to be used for the designed structure, how they fit into the whole structure, and their availability and cost. In this design phase, molecular biologists use novel types of computerized biology tools such as CAD Nano[2] and bioinformatics algorithms and visualization tools. These tools let them sketch the 2D and 3D structures and generate a list of compounds (oligos) to mix together and a protocol guiding the production of the nano structures. While designing organic structures in-silico, biologists try to take into account the details of the future laboratory work: e.g. whether the oligos needed are available or if they have to be ordered from external manufacturers.

[1]Constructivists ethnographers of science have described how scientists 'tinker' with their tools and objects of study [10, 11], and how scientists "produce order" through iterative selection, refinements and re-selection of processes and data. However, these statements have been subject to controversies and are not always recognized by scientists themselves. In our case – and perhaps because of the new type of research that this group is doing – they did actually think of their work as more exploratory and iterative.

[2]http://cadnano.org/

During the construction phase, biologists move to the lab and perform the hands-on activities of mixing, heating and cooling the basic organic materials which are the building blocks of their designs, transforming them into the designed structures. Biologists use the protocol made in the design phase, but often adaptations are needed and done during the experimentation in the lab. Adjustments to the protocol have to be done due to unexpected situations that arise while starting the laboratory work, e.g. when an experimenter realizes that the biological material she needs is missing, has to update her plan either by using a similar element with almost the same properties. Furthermore, incremental modifications to the protocol happen while doing the manual work at the bench, such as when the quality of a sample is questionable, unexpected results occur, or new questions arise leading the biologist to explore alternatives. Moreover, the protocol may be under-specified in places: some steps are simply too cumbersome to describe or too dependent on the sample that will be used. Simple adjustments are calculated and managed manually, whereas more complex adjustments require access to the computational tools used during the design phase. These kind of adjustments done on the computer motivates biologists to bring laptops into the lab, despite this being strictly prohibited for biohazard reasons. Finally, biologists seek to execute deliberate alternatives and explicitly explore as many alternatives as they can during the construction phase.

In the analysis phase, biologists analyze the experiment results in relation to the original design. Given that these organic structures are at a nano-scale, they are not directly visible and available for analysis and therefore biologists resort to tools that can capture the experimental results at different levels of fidelity (precision and confidence). Low fidelity measures, like a gel electrophoresis[3], give relative information about the size and weight of the constructed structure, from which biologists can infer whether the pieces assembled correctly or not. Low fidelity measures do not assure that everything went well, but provide relatively fast preliminary feedback on whether the biologist should return to the bench or go further in her analysis. Samples with noisy low fidelity measures often indicate procedural errors and force the biologist back to the lab to reflect on the experiment, whereas samples with clean low fidelity measures may trigger surprises that will lead back to other types of adjustments or push the biologist back to the design phase and explore new directions. High fidelity measures, like a 3D spectrometer image, require using specialized, expensive, and scarce equipment, and therefore biologists use them in few occasions: when previous low fidelity measures look consistent with what is expected, or when numerous low fidelity measures are consistently different from the expected values and the researchers have already ruled out the known possible mistakes. In the first case, biologists seek to confirm that they effectively obtained the structure they designed for and the level of accuracy. In the second case, biologists seek to uncover what really is happening with the mixed ingredients.

[3]http://en.wikipedia.org/wiki/Gel_electrophoresis

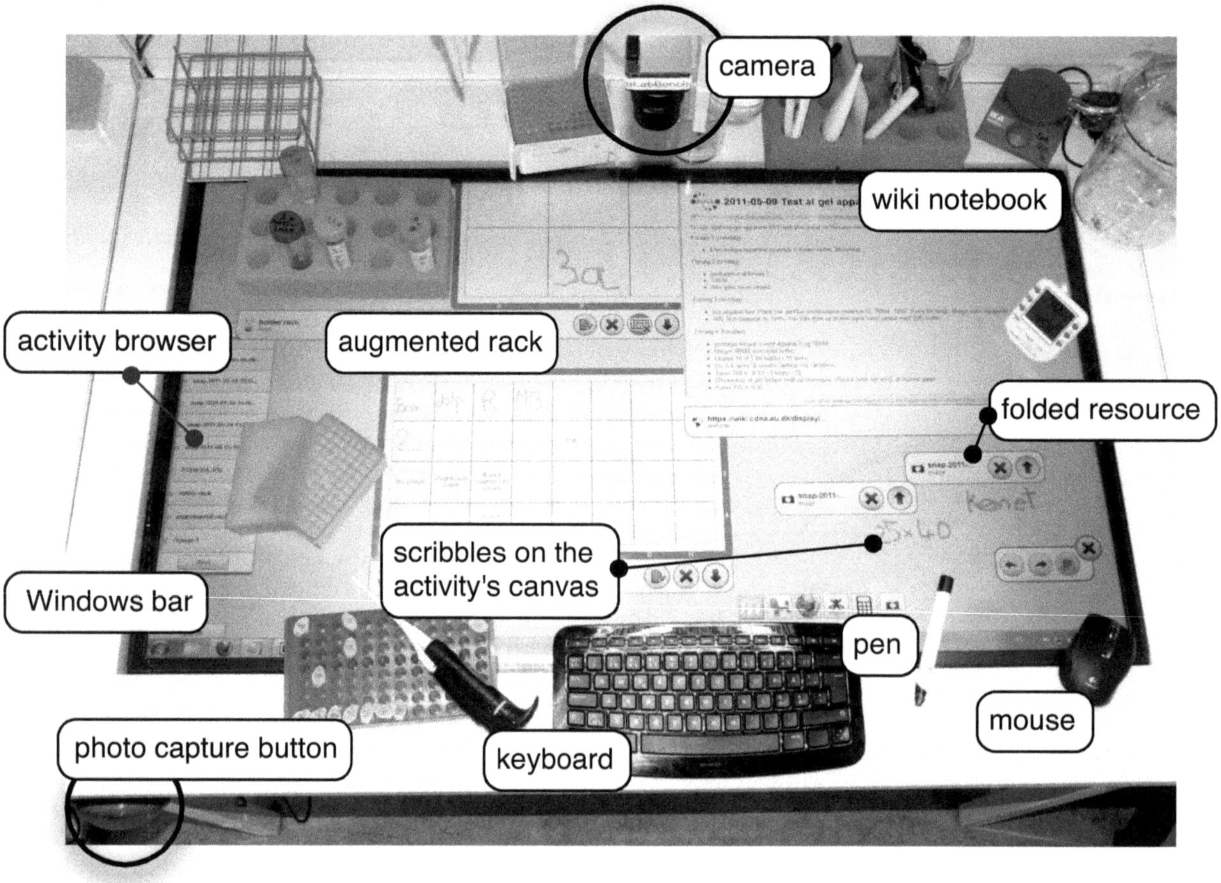

Figure 3. A top view of the eLabBench showing the interactive display, the activity browser, a resumed activity displaying a set of resources included two different types of augmented test-tube racks, and the top-mounted camera and its button.

ELABBENCH AND INFRASTRUCTURE

To support the exploratory type of work we observed, we designed the eLabBench and its supporting infrastructure [19]. The eLabBench is a tabletop-based laboratory bench supporting the phases of *design*, *construction*, and *analysis* of exploratory biology research. A distributed infrastructure enables users to move smoothly between their eLabBench and their office computers. Data and document management in this infrastructure is based on the notion of an 'activity' where the work of a biologist is organized in different activities. The eLabBench was designed through a user-centered process consisting of a series of collaborative workshops. This section summarizes the design considerations and system's features.

Design Considerations

We took into consideration two main elements in the design of the eLabBench, which we assessed and refined throughout the design process and the field deployment: 1) practical requirements of information access and management at the bench, and 2) considerations for supporting explorative biology at the bench.

The first set of considerations relates to information management and safety at a laboratory bench: the eLabBench should support access to relevant digital information at the bench or in the office, support capture of laboratory data in digital format, and provide seamless coverage throughout the experimental cycle (i.e. integration with activities happening out-of-the-lab). Moreover, the bench must accommodate the actual work conditions in a laboratory, such as safety regulations or the presence of many items laying on the bench. Finally, the bench should not be distractive and take into consideration that users' focus lay on the experimental products and tools rather than on the interaction with the tabletop.

The second set of considerations relates to supporting an open way of organizing the information necessary to the experiment, and hence, not pushing for a strict sequential or time-based organization often found in workflow-based or notebooks systems. Along this line the bench should support on-the-fly changes to the experimental cycle, easy forking of experiments and switching between them. Due to constant experimentation, the bench should provide mechanisms of *lightweight capture* for information that emerges while executing experiments, and mechanisms to execute computations directly at the bench rather than needing to move back to the office (e.g. concentration calculation or tube annotation). Finally, the bench should support the information needs that are pushing biologists to bring computers into the lab: this covers a set of office applications, browsers, PDF viewers, and bioinformatics tools for, e.g., consulting a molecule's 3D model.

System Design

Figure 1 shows the eLabBench in use in a molecular biology laboratory. Figure 3 shows a top view of the interactive tabletop surface with a set of digital resources and physical artifacts used by the molecular biologists while carrying out an experiment. On the left of the screen, the eLabBench lists a set of *activities*. Each activity contains links to data resources and services which are relevant for a specific experiment or other work tasks. An activity is 'resumed' by clicking its icon, and all its resources are then displayed on the tabletop. Users can switch between different activities by suspending one and resuming another. The eLabBench supports a wide variety of digital resources associated with an activity, including: images, text documents, a web-based digital notebook, and digital representations of test tube racks and other lab equipment. Moreover, when a resource is shown on the display, users can annotate it with hand-drawn scribbles and textual notes. Finally, the eLabBench integrates with native applications like the calculator, text editors, spreadsheets, and bioinformatics tools, in order to allow the biologist to work with their normal set of applications.

Users can interact with the eLabBench through different input mechanisms: a pen, a wireless mouse and keyboard, various forms of tangible interaction, and dedicated physical buttons. Most of the browsing of resources and annotations are carried out through pen interaction instead of direct touch. Pen interaction is necessary not only because of the contamination risks of touching the surface directly (the pen can be sterilized), but also as a way to decrease the false positives caused by all the objects usually standing on the bench. Pen-based interaction was well received by participants as it limited their worries of triggering actions by mistake (e.g. with their elbow resting on the bench while pipetting). Moreover, the eLabBench also has a wireless keyboard used for text entry, and a wireless mouse for those users who preferred this.

The eLabBench supports two types of tangible interaction; it tracks tagged-racks used to hold test-tubes and physical markers called 'machine tags' which represent the various machines used for biology experiments[4]. The tagged test-tube racks lets users annotate the content of specific tubes within a rack. When putting a rack on the bench, the eLabBench displays a grid-like interface and matches the spatial layout of the rack and the tubes it contains. The machine-tags are plastic squares which are associated with a wiki-page that describes the functioning of a particular machine in the lab. When putting the machine tag on the table, the wiki page is shown on the bench and the biologist can attach it as a permanent resource to the current activity. Finally, we placed a dedicated, physical, photo capture button on the front of the bench. When pushed, the eLabBench takes a picture from a top-mounted camera to capture the current state of the bench.

[4]Parallel to the two approaches herein described, we have investigated other mechanisms to integrated test tubes and tabletops through the notion of *mediated tabletop interaction* (MTI) [6]. For our MTI prototype we used RFID tagged-test tubes and a mediator to dynamically generate 2D codes for each tube, while the eLabBench uses static fiducial markers identifying the whole rack.

Figure 4. Dragging a picture in the activityDock in expanded mode

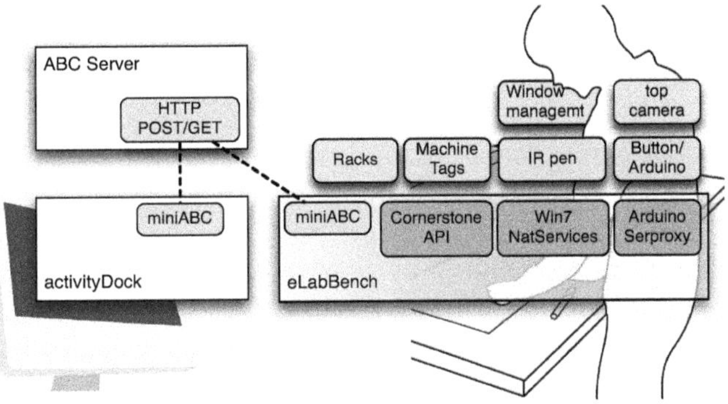

Figure 5. The activityDock, eLabBench and ABC server components.

Figure 5 illustrates the infrastructure behind the eLabBench system, consisting of two main components: (i) the activityDock, which is a desktop application running on personal computers; and (ii) the ABC server, which is a distributed data management infrastructure responsible for collecting digital data and distributing it between activityDocks and eLabBenches. Biologists can use the *activityDock*, shown in figure 4, to create and manage activities, and to add and remove resources to the activities on their computer. The activityDock supports any desktop documents and provides access to annotations made at the bench, for web pages, emails, images and pdf documents. The ABC server stores and manages access to the activities and their resources, and enables the roaming of activity data between multiple instances of the activityDock and of the eLabBench among different locations.

FIELD DEPLOYMENT

The main objective of our study was to observe how biologists used the bench. We were especially interested in the relationship between laboratory and office work. We also wanted to understand how the new possibilities offered at the interactive bench would influence participants' workflow, this included: the tangible integration of racks to the bench, the different capture and annotation mechanisms, and the use of native applications on the eLabBench.

Setting

We deployed the eLabBench in the laboratory of the group we have been collaborating with, a room equipped for eight scientists and one technician. We installed the eLabBench on week 1 by replacing a traditional bench as shown in figure 6. During the first three weeks, we presented the bench to many biologists within the department, gathered informal feedback, fixed stability and usability bugs, and fine-tuned the calibration for both object tracking and pen interaction. Between week four and nineteen, participants used the bench to run their biology experiments.

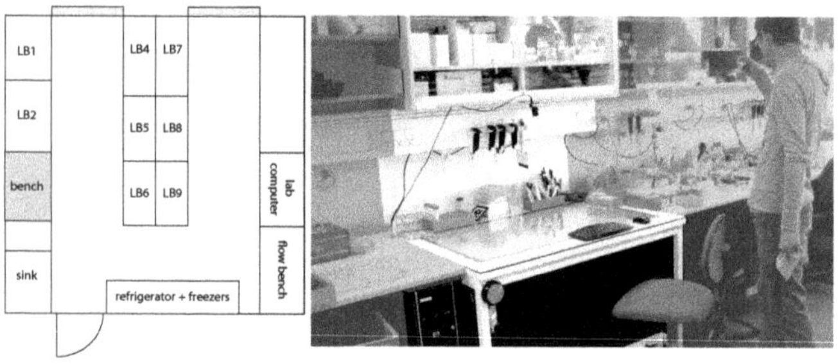

Figure 6. The laboratory plan to the left with the eLabBench in red, the eLabBench to the right.

Participants

We recruited seven users working primarily in the laboratory where the eLabBench was installed: three post-docs, two Ph.D students, and two bachelor students working on specific projects for shorter periods of time.

Method

We leveraged the lengthy nature of executing an experiment and had participants work on their own normal experiments instead of mock-ones prepared by us. In this way, we gathered data about a naturalistic use of the bench and minimized the disturbances to very busy students and post-docs. Although all seven participants ran experiments on the bench (most of them for about half a day to two days), one participant (P1) used the bench much more extensively than the others (19 days). The results we present next are grounded in a separate analysis of field data from all participants and the cases presented happened to more than one participant (except patterns 2 only to P5 and 3 to P1).

When participants logged in for the first time on the activityDock or the eLabBench, their account already contained a default activity with a web resource. We invited the participants to use this activity to explore the system. We excluded this activity and its resources from the results presented in the following section.

We developed and introduced new features as the deployment progressed; these features aimed at supporting activities that we did not anticipate in our original design. We report these changes in the results as they highlight lessons learnt from the deployment and relevant work practices that went un-noticed during our initial studies, sometimes because such behaviors where simply too complex or even impossible without the eLabBench.

Data analysis

We gathered data from three sources: 1) field notes including observations as well as pre- and post-interviews with the users before and after they ran their experiments on the eLabBench; 2) logs of in-app events[5]; and 3) state of the eLabBench every 10 seconds[6]. We ran through the interviews and field notes and looked at the automatically captured images (for context) to determine the usage patterns and the other qualitative results; we used the logs to retrieve specific events such as annotations on racks or on the notebook, and did simple statistical processing of events (e.g. log-in/out, resources changes, application switching) to measure the time spent on the bench or the applications used.

RESULTS

This section presents our observations on the usage of the eLabBench, usage patterns, and the eLabBench's impact on the experimental workflow, experiments' capture and interaction with tangibles.

Usage overview

After the 3 weeks of introduction and presentation, participants used the bench for 16 weeks. Figure 7 shows, for each week, the number of days the eLabBench was used, the number of times users logged-in, and the number of different users.

	Set-up and presentation			16 weeks of participants' eLabBench use															
Week #	1	2	3	4	5	6	7	8	9	10	11	12	13	14	15	16	17	18	19
Days Used	☒	☒	☒	1	2	0	2	1	1	0	0	1	2	4	1	1	1	2	1
Log-ins	☒	☒	☒	1	3	0	5	6	1	0	0	2	3	21	4	5	17	5	1
Participants this week	☒	☒	☒	1	2	0	2	2	1	0	0	1	1	1	1	1	1	3	1

Figure 7. Participants' activity over the course of the deployment.

During this period seven participants actively used the bench during 38 hours and 30 minutes. Table 1 details how much the different participants used the eLabBench.

User	Days	Hours	Activities	Resources	Racks
P1	19	17h10	5	15	2
P2	1	7h40	1	5	2
P3+P4	2	7h00	2	7	5
P5	2	1h50	1	4	3
P6	2	1h30	2	3	1
P7	1	2h20	1	2	1

Table 1. Overview of the bench use

Participant 1 (P1) was the main user of the bench using it on 19 different days. He worked on 5 different activities, 3 corresponding to real experiments; another was a test variation of an existing experiment; and the last one was used to explain

[5] login/out, create/display/hide/archive/delete activity or resource, pen annotation, typed annotation, bench image capture, tangibles coming in and out of the bench) and OS wide events (window switching)

[6] user logged-in, current activity, number of opened resources, number of archived resources, foreground application, screenshot, image from the top mounted camera

the eLabBench to the many people that visited the laboratory in order to see the eLabBench working. The fact that P1 started to use the bench first and was very involved in its deployment developed the impression of him owning the bench. In most laboratories benches are highly personal; scientists store the products or tools they use most often around *their* bench, stick reminders above it and even have written notes on the bench itself. As a result, the other participants would only use the eLabBench when P1 was explicitly not using it and we invited them to use it. The other participants used the bench for periods ranging from half a day to two days, and worked on one specific experimental procedure. These participants created one or two activities, each holding 2 or 3 resources including at least one protocol (or a short plan outline) and one rack resource.

Figure 8 shows the distribution of resources according to their type. The rack resources are the most numerous as all participants used and annotated them. The annotations went from comments on two or three key tubes, to extensive description of all the tubes in the rack. The web resources were the most used, either to provide quick access to the reference page of a material provider or to the collaborative notebook used by participants. In fact, the participants using the digital notebook relied heavily on it in order to document the experiment, whereas the ones not using it relied on Word documents or PDFs protocols to follow procedures (file or pdf resources in figure 8). Finally, participants captured snapshots from the top-mounted camera.

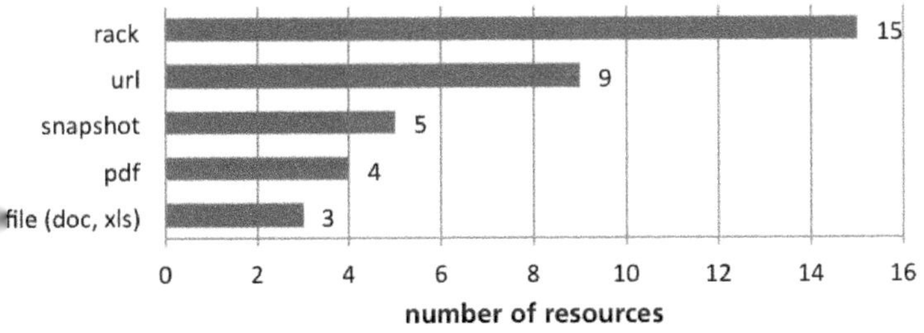

Figure 8. Distribution of resources

Usage Patterns

Based on the collected data and our interviews, we identified five usage patterns that matched the needs of our users:

Predefined experiment – This is mainly the case for junior people like bachelor students. P1, the most senior post-doc in the team, created an experiment originally for a summer school of high school students. Before the summer school, P1 invited P3 and P4 to run it in order to test both the completeness and intelligibility of the protocol and the complexity of the experiment. They executed the experiment following the instructions to the line. Moreover, the informal feedback collected during the first 3 weeks (demonstration weeks) from bachelor biology students found it very compelling to have access to some standard procedures such as a polymerase chain reaction (PCR) protocol, especially if it came with pre-annotated racks and resources.

Predefined experiment with changes on the way – We observed two instances of this situation e.g. when P5 prepared a laboratory procedure through the activity dock on his personal computer. Yet, when he came to the bench to run it, he decided to change so many parameters that it had little in common with the original plan. P5 did not use the digital notebook other participants relied upon for their protocols but MS Word files, therefore he edited the protocol Word document on the bench to fetch it later from the activityDock as he returned to his office.

Variation of an experiment done in the past – P1 used the bench to run a variation of a procedure he had done a few weeks before. He was at an early stage of his project and wanted to explore different alternatives for which he had to define similar bench activities. Based on this experience, we introduced the possibility to duplicate activities at the bench as a way to allow biologists to use past activities as templates for new ones.

Ad-hoc experiment, not prepared – P1 sat at the bench and created an activity from there and started to experiment, adding relevant resources as he went further, without any formal preliminary planning. He explained he had thought about it and wanted to quickly check whether it would work out. This particular lab procedure lasted half a day and involved the creation of a 'classical' substance to be used in many following experiments. For a different reason, P2 also just walked up to the eLabBench and started creating activities right there. P2 chose not to use the activityDock on his computer but rather defined his experiment on his digital notebook, which he then brought as a web resource to the eLabBench. For P2, the eLabBench served as a way to access the digital resources needed to run the experiment instead of a capture mechanism.

Collaborative experiment – P3 and P4 worked on an experiment together. They split their tasks at the bench, for instance one managed the physical rack while the other captured the information on the virtual one. This kind of coordination was helpful especially as they did not have the single user problem of switching between the handling of tubes and pipettes and the handling of the infrared pen or mouse.

Re-defining the experimental workflow

During the first half of the deployment (end of week eight), we gathered feedback from the three participants who had used the bench and from the many biologists working in other laboratories who came to see the eLabBench. This section describes the needs which arose during this period and how we accommodated them.

Blending laboratory and office work

A first occurrence of new practices the bench made possible is the ability to prepare the racks virtually in the office. Inline with current practices, we identified racks as completely belonging to the lab, where one would fill them with tubes and only then add digital notes. However, defining the content of key tubes can be a simple and efficient way to manage the biological compounds that biologists will need. P1 explained how it can help him prepare experiments, by *"lining up what I need, seeing what's available and order some things that I'm missing [from an external provider ...] also filling out something that does not exist yet"*.

Preparing a rack at the computer is more convenient, typing data more comfortable and it is possible to copy the information from biological providers directly into the rack interface. Without the eLabBench, rack preparation is less planned and involves a lot of back and forth between the laboratory and the office (find the tubes, find their data, contact the providers). We thus added the ability for creating and specifying racks in the office through the activityDock.

A second occurrence of new practices the bench made possible is the ability to describe experimental procedures directly while running them. Although we aimed at supporting open experiments, we initially envisioned that participants would prepare and organize information at their desk and use the bench as a browsing, annotation and capture device. Yet, we observed that on occasions participants would come to the bench with a very scarcely defined experimental plan or without plan at all and just a general idea of the experiment. On these occasions, participants (like P5 and P6) wanted to incorporate extra information into their activity while working at the bench; P1 faced a few situations where he wanted to directly work at the bench and set up the experiment from there.

Therefore, we added support for the creation of activities and addition of digital resources directly at the bench, rather than only from the activityDock. On the bench, users can drag and drop any type of document to the eLabBench canvas (from any applications) in order to add it to the current activity.

Computation in the laboratory

Besides allowing to organize information around activities, the eLabBench lets users run native Windows applications. Over an hour, participants switched on average 3 times between the eLabBench and another application which highlights the utility of other native/legacy applications on tabletops. Figure 9 shows that the most used applications alongside the bench were Web browsers, the Microsoft Calculator, a bio-informatics tool called CLC Workbench (CLC-WB), Word and Excel (mainly used by P5). Participants mainly used browsers for checking protocols, looking up products information and emails, the Calculator for computing the concentrations of tubes, the CLC-WB for data visualization, Word for following protocols, Excel and Notepad for data gathering. Finally, P7 set up TeamViewer[7] (a remote desktop application) to check the progress of his analyses running on a remote machine, while he worked at the bench.

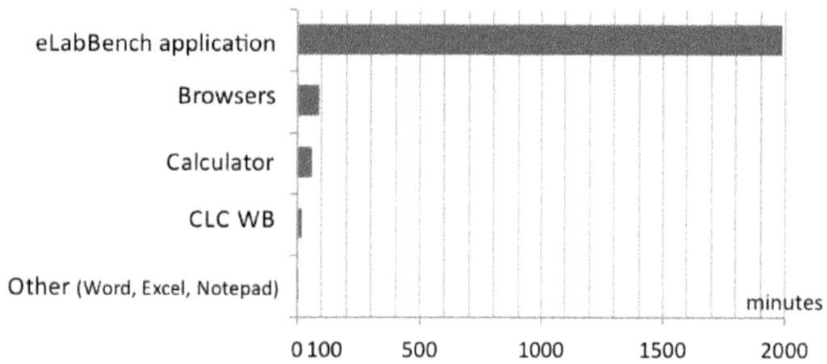

Figure 9. Usage of applications on the eLabBench.

[7]TeamViewer – `http://www.teamviewer.com/`

Changes in the plans

We observed that many participants (P1, P2 and P5) moved away from the experiments they originally planned: P5 modified his activity and his (Microsoft Word) protocol to reflect the last-minute changes in his plan, while P1 and P2 tried alternative of an original experiment. In both cases, participants lost the original organization within their activity as they shifted to the new one. To cope with these changes we introduced the ability to duplicate activities.

Refining capture

The eLabBench supports a variety of capture mechanisms: written and typed annotations, bench captures from its top mounted camera, and the ABC infrastructure as a whole for keeping relevant documents. These capture mechanisms did not conflict with the digital notebooks participants use to document their work. Rather, the two systems acted at different levels: the eLabBench was used to follow the progress of an experiment (i.e. which tube was last pipetted), organize the resources needed, among others; the digital notebook was used to keep important information for a later analysis of results (e.g. concentrations used). In other words, while the digital notebook acted as a formal record of the experiment, the eLabBench helped to keep track of the ongoing actions.

To better incorporate the digital notebook into the eLabBench, particularly for P1 and P6 as its most heavy users, we added the ability to drag into their notebook image captures of the bench, images of the racks and other files generated at the bench (e.g. spreadsheets of data). This feature lets biologists capture and annotate elements on the go and later, during some waiting time, properly reflect on what they did and describe it.

Interaction with tangibles (racks and machine tags)

All participants used the augmented racks while working at the bench, a fact that points out the lack of proper technical support to manage samples in the laboratory. Although tracking of tangibles elements was appreciated, nobody used the tangible shortcuts (machine tags) we offered. Even though biologists' reactions to the machine tags were positive, active participants felt that these physical markers took too much physical space on the bench (5x5 cm). As one participant pointed out: *"The whole idea with the bench is that you have less stuff on the table"*.

However, participants appreciated consulting the rack information on the bench without having to pull the rack from the fridge, but just looking at the racks' virtual instances, or checking the racks' content from their laptop via the activityDock. The ability of duplicate resources was highly appreciated for the racks as this allowed participants to create templates that could be reused across activities, without needing to re-input data. But this feature was restricted during the deployment since participants had to ask us to generate new 2D barcodes for racks as they could not create them by themselves.

Participants provided us with several ideas on a deeper integration of physical objects, particularly racks and tubes, into the bench: e.g. objects could act as reference points for activities and participants were eager to have the relevant activity show up when a specific rack or tube would be brought to the table.

DISCUSSION

We started this project with the idea of providing synthetic biologists with information management and computational resources in the laboratory. However, as we explored the setting and participants started using the eLabBench, we observed a much more open workflow than expected. This section discusses the challenges arising from such open workflows.

Supporting exploratory bench work

Our observations of participants' use of the eLabBench confirm previous social studies of scientific and engineering work. For instance, Bowker [3] discusses how instruments for capturing scientific work have an impact on the way of "doing science". Harmon and Nersessian [5] point out that even though laboratory work can be repetitive, efficiency may not be the most important advancement. They emphasize how technologies should act as "cognitive partners" which "embody the knowledge and hypotheses of the lab and promote and scaffold scientific exploration and creativity", and should be capable of evolving to accommodate the changing needs of scientists. Our deployment and the features we introduced along the way show both how the eLabBench had an impact in the way of "doing science" (e.g. defining racks at the office), but also how design decisions embody assumptions on the research practices of scientists.

This particular way of doing science and assumptions on research practices are embodied in the different phases of information capture supported by the eLabBench : A *tinkering* phase where scientists won't be held accountable for what they do. This is done through our activity based infrastructure which emphasizes actions and resources rather than workflow or temporal chronology, but also through the little efforts required to save information, whether by capturing a snapshot of the bench or just quickly annotating a digital rack. At this stage we aimed at making users feel free to explore and adjust, to *experiment* in the primary sense of the word. And a *reflective* phase where scientists could reason about what they did, what worked and did not (this normally happens within their notebook). These two phases can be intertwined but have different objectives, one is geared toward the present, the other toward the future. With the eLabBench we aimed at supporting these two stages and at facilitating the transition between them.

Moreover, the eLabBench does not only aim at supporting capture and access but also the increasing need for biologists to access computational resources at the bench. By providing native applications at the bench, users could shift some tasks they would have done in the office into the lab (e.g. checking details about a sample online, managing complex concentration calculations, or simply checking comments from a colleagues). Currently these practices imply that lab workers either overlook safety rules and bring in laptops or tablets into the lab, or constant move back and forth between the office and the lab.

Finally, the activity-based organization (which has been previously explored in other settings like offices or hospitals) offers smooth transitions between parallel experimental procedures. For instance, when one experiment requires the biologist to wait, she can shift to another experiment for preparation work or to improve the documentation.

Tangibles in laboratories

Introducing hybrid (physical+digital) objects in the laboratory provoked interesting behaviors. In the case of racks, it allowed participants to shift part of the work they do with tubes to their office. Machine tags on the other hand are a case where the digital instance fits better into the design than the tangible one. Looking back at Kirk et al.'s discussion on the design of hybrid interactive surfaces [8], the machine tags are a good illustration of a "a new and compelling user interface by [which] ultimately begins to wear thin in real use."

Tabletops in laboratories

The laboratories appear to be an interesting area to explore for the tabletop community as they offer a wide range of benefits compared to laptops or tablets: they can support existing applications and their flat surface affords objects laying on top, some of which can be tracked and augmented. Furthermore, their furniture-like form factor limits contamination problems (they stay in the lab) and facilitates cleaning.

Bringing tabletops into the synthetic biology lab allowed us to identify key points in the design of tabletop applications to be used in the workplace: (1) support for high resolutions so that different digital resources can be displayed alongside, (2) mechanisms for the UI to cope with the presence of inactive objects on the table, (3) support for native applications, and (4) pen-based interaction for quick, stable and natural input of information.

CONCLUSION

This paper presented the field deployment of the eLabBench, a digital tabletop-based laboratory bench for molecular biologists. Our interest in the eLabBench was triggered by the the fact that molecular biologists' are exploring many different alternatives for accessing digital data in the laboratory: from bringing their laptops in and out of the lab, to using tablets attached to mechanical arms on top of their benches. Even-though tabletop technology may still have to improve to be completely ready for everyday use in a laboratory, the eLabBench deployment allowed us to unpack the problems biologists are facing and how tabletops could support them.

As the research practices of some synthetic biologists shift toward engineering-like practices, their workflow become more iterative and exploratory. This shift is particularly acute with the molecular biologists we studied, who focus on the design of biological nano structures. The eLabBench lets them leverage computational resources at the bench and supports capture and access of digital resources and physical objects such as tubes. With this deployment, we hope to suggest a path where we, as researchers, are not only accommodating the changes our participants' are confronted with in their work practices, but where we actively take part in these changes.

Besides our presentations of the eLabBench in the first weeks of the deployment, the main user of the bench spent a significant amount of time also presenting the bench. Both university colleagues and visitors from other universities showed a special interest in this new technology. The biologists' interest was beyond simple curiosity toward a new gadget for the laboratory; their interest and questions highlighted how much they are in need for solutions that can help them with (1) to cope with management of digital data, and (2) to escape the many laboratory information management systems that enforce strict processes.

ACKNOWLEDGMENTS

Morten Esbensen and Thomas Berglund contributed to the implementation of the eLabBench. We thank Ebbe S. Andersen for his amazing support, Jesper, Rasmus, David, the Danish Nano Artists and all the molecular biologists who participated to the deployment and provided great feedback. This research was funded by the Danish Agency for Science, Technology, and Innovation under the project "PC Mini-Grids for Prediction of Viral RNA Structure and Evolution", #09-061856.

REFERENCES

1. Arnstein, L., Hung, C.-Y., Franza, R., Zhou, Q. H., Borriello, G., Consolvo, S., and Su, J. Labscape: A smart environment for the cell biology laboratory. *IEEE Pervasive Computing 1* (July 2002), 13–21.
2. Blomberg, J., Burrell, M., and Guest, G. The human-computer interaction handbook. L. Erlbaum Associates Inc., Hillsdale, NJ, USA, 2003, ch. An ethnographic approach to design, 964–986.
3. Bowker, G. C. *Memory Practices in the Sciences (Inside Technology)*. The MIT Press, 2006.
4. Echtler, F., Häussler, M., and Klinker, G. Biotisch: the interactive molecular biology lab bench. In *Proc. Ext. Abs. CHI 2010*, ACM Press (2010).
5. Harmon, E., and Nersessian, N. Cognitive partnerships on the bench top: designing to support scientific researchers. In *Proc. DIS 2008* (2008).
6. Hincapié-Ramos, J. D., Tabard, A., and Bardram, J. E. Mediated tabletop interaction in the biology lab: exploring the design space of the rabbit. In *Proc. Ubicomp 2011*, UbiComp '11, ACM Press (2011).
7. Hunter, S., Maes, P., Scott, S., and Kaufman, H. Memtable: An integrated system for capture and recall of shared histories in group workspaces. In *Proc. CHI 2011*, ACM Press (2011).
8. Kirk, D., Sellen, A., Taylor, S., Villar, N., and Izadi, S. Putting the physical into the digital: issues in designing hybrid interactive surfaces. In *Proc. 23rd British HCI Group Annual Conference on People and Computers: Celebrating People and Technology*, British Computer Society (Swinton, UK, UK, 2009).
9. Kirk, D. S., Izadi, S., Sellen, A., Taylor, S., Banks, R., and Hilliges, O. Opening up the family archive. In *Proc. CSCW 2010*, ACM Press (2010).
10. Knorr-Cetina, K. *The Manufacture of Knowledge: An Essay on the Constructivist and Contextual Nature of Science*. Pergamon Press, 1981.
11. Latour, B. *Science in Action: How to Follow Scientists and Engineers through Society*. Harvard University Press, 1988.
12. Mackay, W. E., Pothier, G., Letondal, C., Bøegh, K., and Sørensen, H. E. The missing link: augmenting biology laboratory notebooks. In *Proc. UIST 2002*, ACM Press (2002).
13. Marshall, P., Morris, R., Rogers, Y., Kreitmayer, S., and Davies, M. Rethinking 'multi-user': an in-the-wild study of how groups approach a walk-up-and-use tabletop interface. In *Proc. CHI 2011*, ACM Press (2011).
14. m.c. schraefel, Hughes, G., Mills, H., Smith, G., Payne, T., and Frey, J. Breaking the book: Translating the chemistry lab book into a pervasive computing lab environment. In *Proc. CHI 2004*, ACM Press (2004).
15. Rothemund, P. W. K. Folding DNA to create nanoscale shapes and patterns. *Nature 440*, 7082 (Mar. 2006), 297–302.
16. Shaer, O., Kol, G., Strait, M., Fan, C., Grevet, C., and Elfenbein, S. G-nome surfer: a tabletop interface for collaborative exploration of genomic data. In *Proc. CHI 2010*, ACM Press (2010).
17. Shaer, O., Strait, M., Valdes, C., Feng, T., Lintz, M., and Wang, H. Enhancing genomic learning through tabletop interaction. In *Proc. CHI 2011*, ACM Press (2011).
18. Song, K., Kim, G., Han, I., Lee, J., Park, J.-H., and Ha, S. Chemo: mixed object instruments and interactions for tangible chemistry experiments. In *Proc. Ext. Abs. CHI 2011*, ACM Press (2011).
19. Tabard, A., Hincapié-Ramos, J. D., Esbensen, M., and Bardram, J. E. The elabbench: an interactive tabletop system for the biology laboratory. In *Proc. ITS 2011*, ACM Press (2011).
20. Tabard, A., Mackay, W. E., and Eastmond, E. From individual to collaborative: the evolution of prism, a hybrid laboratory notebook. In *Proc. CSCW 2008*, ACM Press (2008).
21. Wigdor, D., Jiang, H., Forlines, C., Borkin, M., and Shen, C. WeSpace: the design development and deployment of a walk-up and share multi-surface visual collaboration system. In *Proc. CHI 2009*, ACM Press (2009).
22. Yeh, R., Liao, C., Klemmer, S., Guimbretière, F., Lee, B., Kakaradov, B., Stamberger, J., and Paepcke, A. Butterflynet: a mobile capture and access system for field biology research. In *Proc. CHI 2006*, ACM Press (2006).

How Students Find, Evaluate and Utilize Peer-Collected Annotated Multimedia Data in Science Inquiry with Zydeco

Alex Kuhn[1], Brenna McNally[2], Shannon Schmoll[2], Clara Cahill[2], Wan-Tzu Lo[2], Chris Quintana[2], Ibrahim Delen[2]

[1]Department of EECS
University of Michigan
2260 Hayward St.
Ann Arbor, MI 48109
kuhnalex@umich.edu

[2]School of Education
University of Michigan
610 East University
Ann Arbor, MI 48109
brenna.mcnally@gmail.com,{schmoll, claracah, loclaire, quintana, idel}@umich.edu

ABSTRACT
Scientific inquiry can be more authentic and meaningful to students when using personal and peer-collected data. The challenges of organizing and evaluating a potentially large amount of data can be overcome through the use of annotations (title, tags, and audio notes). We created Zydeco, a multi-component system that students use to collect annotated multimedia data from a museum (using a smartphone app), and then create a scientific explanation with their personal and peers' data (using a tablet app). We ran a classroom study with 54 students (ages 11-13) investigating how students searched for, evaluated, and used annotated data to construct a scientific explanation. We found that tags supported data interpretation, while title searching and panning through the unfiltered data set supported finding and using data.

Author Keywords
Learner-centered design; tagging; mobile computing; children and technology; science inquiry

ACM Classification Keywords
K.3.1 [Computers and Education]: Computer Uses in Education – Computer-assisted instruction

H.5.2 [Information Interfaces and Presentation]: User Interfaces - User-centered design

General Terms
Design

INTRODUCTION
Science inquiry, the act of posing questions and gathering and evaluating empirical evidence, is a critical component of science education in K-12 settings [1]. One important aspect of science inquiry involves collecting, managing, and analyzing different types of data to construct a scientific explanation that addresses the question that has been posed.

Traditionally, many K-12 science inquiry activities have been focused within the classroom. Explanation construction tools for science inquiry, such as SenseMaker and Belvedere, have been designed to support students in utilizing curated or web data in this context [18]. Field trips or similar experiences that take learners into informal environments are infrequent, and their complexity can make it difficult to engage in substantive scientific data collection. The new generation of mobile technologies, coupled with contemporary networking and cloud technologies, promise to provide new and enhanced opportunities for data collection by students and teachers in informal environments, such as museums, nature parks, etc. For example, students can collect and annotate multimedia data in the field and then return to the classroom to access their data as well as data collected by their peers, bringing the richness of these out-of-class experiences.

Using personal and peer-collected data can make inquiry tasks more authentic, motivating [15] and can enable students to view data they otherwise wouldn't have encountered in the field. The Participate project involved data collected by and shared amongst students (ages 13-15); using Google Earth and graphing software on a laptop in conjunction with data collection equipment, a GPS device, and a mobile phone [20], students were able to explore visualizations showing large amounts of numerical data. They found this student generated data was very engaging back in the classroom and provoked a lot of discussion. Fraser's SENSE project, which had students (ages 10-14) collect environmental data from the field and share this information back in the classroom with other students, found the process of viewing another classes' data helped students reflect and understand new perspectives on the data [9].

While using peer-collected data during science inquiry can be beneficial to students, and it may be advantageous to expand the ways that students can collect and review scientific data, using self-collected and peer-collected data can also pose distinct challenges to students who are not experienced with the science inquiry process. In addition to the constant challenge of reflecting upon and interpreting data for their explanations– where students must also deal with management issues as they organize and search through the large amounts of data – the entire process is made more difficult since the data is messier and potentially inaccurate due to being collected by peers, as opposed to utilizing a curated data source [3].

Mediating the search process with curated data sources or Internet data searches for young learners has been widely researched [8, 12]. Studies looking at how children search for information on the Internet have found them to have different strategies than adults, often having chaotic search habits that employ a variety of strategies, though they typically prefer and are more successful at browsing for data instead of using keyword searches [11]. Bilal ran three different trials with children (aged 12-13) searching on Yahooligans (a site designed for 7-12 year olds), looking at them doing a fact-based search, research-based search, and defining their own search task [4]. She found that students fared better with browsing strategies (misspelling and syntax issues hindered keyword searches), and also had a greater interest and task completion success when they defined their own search task versus being assigned a task. However, while students are best at browsing by categories, students would need to accurately assign large data sets into categories or otherwise organize the data during collection for this to be useful.

One method used to address the challenge of organizing and searching data has been the use of titles and tags as metadata, which is commonly used on social media websites such as Flickr and Del.icio.us [2]. There is a growing amount of research looking at the use of tags, the motivation behind why people use tags, and the impact of tags [2, 5, 10]. For example, Ames found that tags people applied to photos with Flickr and Zonetags helped people organize and describe their images, and tags help communicate the purpose of the image, both for personal recall later or to others viewing the image [2]. Without these identifiers, access to data can become tedious. OOKL (previously called Myartspace) is a handheld program that enabled users to record photos, audio or textual notes in a museum and access them later, though they were unable to link the text, audio, or photos to each other and had no metadata beyond the title [19]. While students enjoyed the activity, the lack of identifying metadata caused them to take a great deal of time reviewing data—more than was available for the activity. MobiTOP explored a very different approach: using hierarchical tagging to enable users to comment on photos by having a tag within a tag [17]. The tagging system received a mixed response from the college students who used it to collect data at geological sites while peers were in a lab suggesting tests. The complications of the tagging process and poor image quality made it difficult for students not involved with the collection process to understand the data.

But while research has focused on designing tagging systems and on the organizational and management aspects of tags, there has been little work on how learners search for, evaluate, and utilize peer-collected annotated data in an educational context. Tags have the potential to not only support data organization and retrieval, but also to support the evaluation and analytical tasks that students struggle with during the inquiry process. In this way, they could become an invaluable tool in connecting formal and informal learning contexts during inquiry, while supporting students in utilizing their peers' data.

THE ZYDECO PROJECT

We are exploring these possibilities within a project called Zydeco, which is examining the use of mobile computers (e.g., iOS devices) and cloud technologies to support students in engaging in science inquiry activities across formal classroom and informal field contexts, such as science museums, nature parks, etc. [6, 13, 14]. Zydeco consists of three components: (1) a website where students set up and access their investigation questions, hypotheses, and data, (2) a data collection/annotation component implemented as an iPhone/iPod app, and (3) an explanation construction component implemented as an iPad app where students view and use the data they and their peers have collected to construct a scientific explanation addressing the questions they are exploring.

We have implemented a version of the data collection component where students take photos or videos of interesting field artifacts and phenomena as appropriate, and then annotate those artifacts with (1) textual tags (previously created in the classroom with teachers or devised in the field), (2) textual titles (choosing from a pre-defined list or creating their own), or (3) audio notes. In previous work, we found that students were largely able to reflect upon the data they need to collect and tag accurate and potentially useful data with the Zydeco data collection app [13], and that recording audio notes encouraged some students to be more mindful while annotating their data [7]. We also found that the term "tags" was confusing to students and the term "labels" was more understandable.

We are now doing more work to explore the impact of these annotations (titles, tags, and audio notes), not only in terms of data management and organization, but also in terms of the reflective and analytical aspects of inquiry, where students need to assess their data in order to see whether it can be used for their scientific explanation, and how it might connect to the explanation. In this paper, we report on a study where we explored the following questions:

- What is the impact of annotations on how students search through and evaluate data?
- How do students find and choose the evidence they use in their explanation?

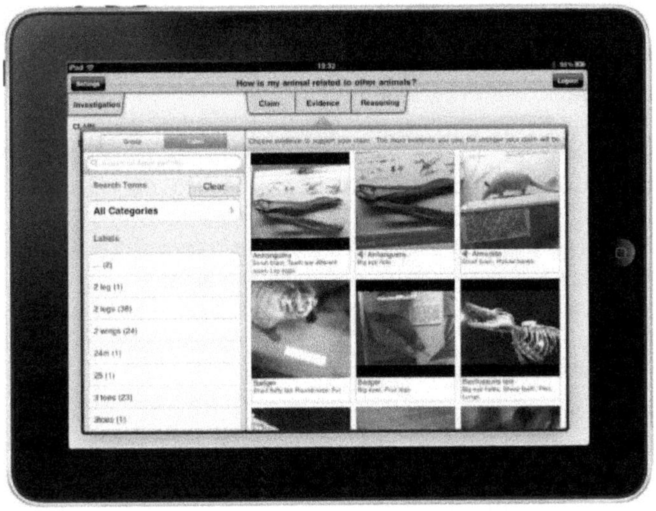

Figure 1. Browsing the entire data set.

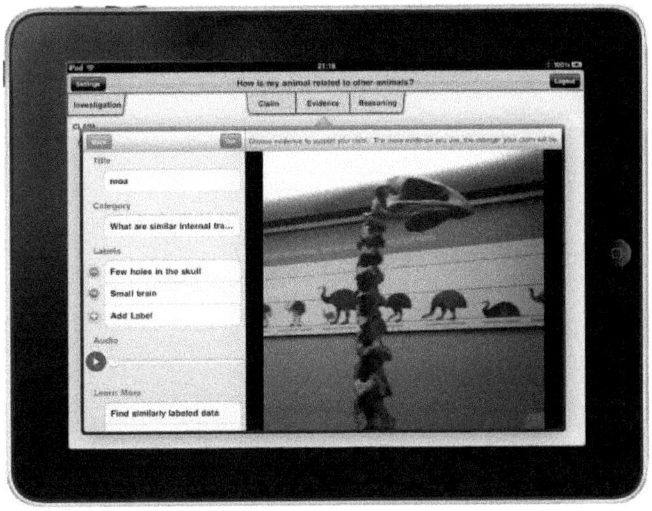

Figure 2. Detailed data view examining a Moa with an audio note attached.

How do Students Find and Choose the Evidence They Use in Their Explanation?

We ran a study in three public-school classrooms with middle school students who used Zydeco to collect data from a local natural history museum. Students spent 4 days (1 hour a day) using the explanation construction component to evaluate their data and use that data to create their explanations. We found that the annotations supported inquiry activities: tags supported data interpretation, titles supported data identification and searching. However, while audio notes showed the potential to convey additional meaning we found they were often not used appropriately.

USE SCENARIO

In the following scenario, we illustrate how a pair of students generated their explanation using the explanation construction component of Zydeco. While the focus is on how students manipulate and interpret data, we provide perspective for the activity by summarizing the preparation and inquiry leading up to explanation construction, as well as the activities after developing explanation, which includes peer critique and explanation presentation.

Classroom Preparation and Inquiry

Alice and her partner Bob are assigned an animal, the Sandhill Crane, and two investigations in their 6th grade science class: *Determine how three other animals are related to your animal*, and *Describe how these animals could survive in Michigan*. After spending several days doing pre-activities to learn about animal traits with their class, Alice and Bob research the internal and external traits of the Sandhill Crane. They create a list of these traits, which is combined with the lists from all of the other groups that were assigned the Sandhill Crane. This master list of traits is input into the Zydeco system as potential tags for students to use in the museum. After collecting a piece of data, they are provided the list of potential tags and can tap on a tag to apply it, or create their own tag. When adding a data title, the students can type in a title or select from a filterable list of the 165 exhibits at the museum that the students may visit, which provide potential title choices.

At the museum, Alice and Bob are each given an iPod Touch to use during for data collection at the museum [13] and they each collect 8 pieces of data. They tag each piece of data with 2-3 tags, and they each have two pieces of data that are additionally annotated with an audio note.

Explanation Synthesis

The teacher introduces the students to the claim—evidence—reasoning framework, which was developed to assist students in constructing explanations by breaking the task into manageable parts: making a claim, providing evidence to support the claim, and presenting reasoning that links the evidence to the claim. [16]. Then each group is given an iPad loaded with all their peers' data in the Zydeco explanation constructor system. After being introduced to the system and completing a short tutorial, Alice and Bob begin working on the first investigation, *Determine how three other animals are related to your animal*, which is always visible at the top of the screen. They are taken to the investigation guide, where they can see the steps they need to do to complete their investigation. Alice hits "Go Here" next to the prompt that tells them to review the data that was collected, and is taken to the Evidence page (Figure 1).

As Alice is scrolling down through thumbnails of the data collected by the class (Figure 1), Bob suggests that they look at the data they collected. By tapping "group" at the top of the screen, Alice and Bob are able to look at the 16 pieces of data that they cumulatively collected on their field trip. Just like in the class data, they are able to view the titles and tags they applied to each piece of data below each image thumbnail.

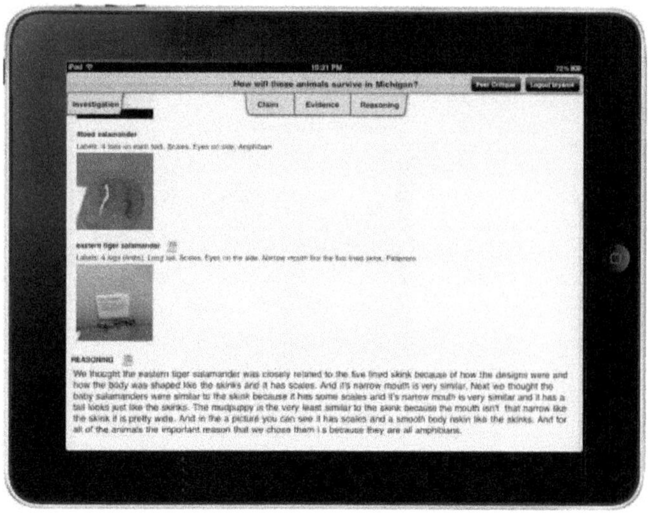

Figure 3. Partial view of an explanation created by a group in the trial.

Bob wants to take a better look at the data he collected on a Moa. He taps on the thumbnail to enlarge the image and can now listen to the audio note he took in the museum (Figure 2). Alice really likes the tag "small brain" that Bob had put on the Moa, and tells him that they should search for that tag in the class data. Scrolling through the tag cloud on the left of the screen (Figure 1), Alice finds and applies the tag "Small brain" as a search term. All the data annotated with that tag appear, including an image titled Deinonychus, which also has tags "backwards knees" and "feathers"—which matches the Sandhill Crane! Bob gets excited and does a title search for more Deinonychus data. There are two data with really good pictures of the animal, but one of them has a tag "fluffy" that Alice thinks is silly, so Bob selects the other picture. The tags on this picture are "backwards knees", "hollow bones", and "feathers"; Alice and Bob agree that this is a good piece of data because the tags match both the image and their animal and so they select "use". They create a group called "Deinonychus" and are taken back to their explanation page.

Alice and Bob continue searching for new evidence until they have three groups: Deinonychus, Moa and Pigeon. Alice taps on the Claim tab and, following the prompt, writes that, "The mostly closely related animal to the Sandhill Crane that we have is the Deinonychus, followed by the Moa and then the Pigeon". Bob agrees with her, and in the Reasoning text area writes that, "Because animals that have the most traits in common are more closely related, and the Deinonychus has six traits in common with the Sandhill Crane—such as backwards knees, eyes on side and feathers—that it is more closely related than the Moa or Pigeon because they have fewer in common. The Moa is next closest because it has five traits in common and the pigeon is last because it only has two." They now have finished their first draft of their explanation.

The evidence groups and reasoning from an explanation completed by a group in our trial can be seen in Figure 3.

Feedback and Presentations

Alice and Bob do peer critique with another group, using the system to provide feedback on specific components of the explanation their peers created. Once they received feedback on their explanation and made revisions for the relatedness investigation, they went on to the second investigation, which looked at how the animals they chose in the relatedness investigation would survive in Michigan. At the end of the week they presented both of their explanations to their peers.

FINDINGS

Our results come from a study with 54 students (ages 11-13) from three different classes at a diverse suburban school where 62% of the students get free or reduced lunch. Students had 6 hours of pre-activities to learn about animal traits (1 hour a day), 1 hour of data collection in a museum, and 5 hours (1 hour a day) of post-activities to create an explanation, four of which were spent using the tablet.

Of the 54 students, six pairs in each class (18 total pairs out of 27 across the three classes) were given approximately five-minute daily in-process interviews using a semi-structured interview protocol while they were using the tablet. This interview included daily questions and one-time questions asking about various aspects of the system. Fifteen of the pairs were randomly selected, while one pair from each class was chosen by the teacher for their ability to provide good feedback. Due to time constraints, only 18 pairs were selected for interviews and we were unable to get responses to every question from each pair.

Usage logs of the system, generated by all 27 pairs, were analyzed along with the field notes from four researchers who were present in the classroom. The data the students collected in the museum was analyzed and the students' explanations were graded following a rubric; the explanation grades are presented in this paper to provide context for the rest of the study.

Characteristics of the Data

In order to provide context for how the students were interpreting and using data, we first examined the quality and characteristics of the data set to assess the difficulties students would encounter finding and analyzing the data.

The three classes collected 676 pieces of data in total. The data included work from students in the class who were not part of this research study, which was excluded from further analysis. This left 474 pieces of data, 40 of which were audio notes that we requested of the students at the end of the field trip to tell us what they learned. Those 40 pieces of data were also excluded from analysis. Of the remaining 434 pieces of data, 327 were photos (75%), 9 were audio notes (2%), and 98 (23%) were a photo that had an audio note appended to it. There were a total of 1134 tags applied to the data (average of 2.6 tags per object) and out of these tags, 945 were tags generated during pre-activities (83%).

Tag Characteristics

Each of the tags was analyzed by a member of the research team and coded as to whether it was inaccurate or nonsensical in its representation of the data, accurate to the data, or if there was uncertainty regarding whether it was accurate or not. The breakdown of the tags was 1016 (90.1%) accurate, 84 (7.4%) inaccurate or nonsensical, and 27 (2.4%) uncertain (Cohen's Kappa=0.82).

The accurate tags were then analyzed as to whether they could potentially be useful to the investigation or not. For instance the tag "New to me", while accurate from the student's perspective, is not helpful in ranking animal relatedness or determining survivability. In fact, we found that all of the accurate tags were potentially useful to the investigation except for the one instance of "New to me" (100% IRR agreement). Overall the data was tagged well, the vast majority (90%) of the tags were both accurate and potentially useful to the investigation; though that left a portion of data (~10%) that students would be searching through that was incorrect or nonsensical.

Title Characteristics

Unlike tagging, students preferred to create their own titles, with only 152 (35%) data items being titled with the predefined exhibit names. Since some of the methods of searching through the data relied on accurate and correctly spelled titles, the titles were coded as to whether the title accurately described the animal and whether it was spelled correctly. All of the titles were first coded if it was giving the name of the animal (duck, t-rex, dino mastodon), a general family name for the animal (bird, dinosaur, dino), a general descriptor (predator, large), or gibberish (amm, ch) and had a Cohen's Kappa=0.93. The vast majority (80%) of the data was titled with the name of the animal, which we expected and encouraged given the activity and since it increased the ease of searching for the data. Of the remaining data, 5.3% were titled with a more generic classification of the animal (fish, canine), 9% were either named after a trait or short description of the animal, and 5.7% of the titles were gibberish (amn, ch).

Next all the titles (except those that were gibberish) were analyzed as to whether they were accurate (either naming the correct animal, family, or the description was accurate), not accurate, or unclear. Of these, 367 (89.7%) of the titles were accurate, 22 (5.4%) were unclear, and 20 (4.9%) of the titles were not accurate (Cohen's Kappa=0.86). Often the animal was incorrectly titled (for example, a possum was titled "owl"). In this case, extra effort and knowledge is needed on the students' part to identify and discard the data in these cases to avoid using incorrect evidence.

Lastly, we looked at the spelling of the titles. Most of the titles were correctly spelled, with 371 (90.7%) of the titles having the correct spelling, though the remaining objects were incorrectly spelled which would lower the chance that they would show up in the search results if looking for a specific animal (100% agreement between reviewers). The high percentage of accurate, correctly spelled titles that are the name of the animal will make the task of searching by title easier on the students as they don't have to try and guess the title of the data they desire, increasing the utility of searching on titles.

Audio Note Characteristics

The pieces of data that had an audio note were analyzed for accuracy and potential usefulness of the data. Each audio note was labeled as to whether what was said was accurate (no statements made that were inaccurate), partially accurate, or not accurate. Additionally, these notes were analyzed as to whether they were potentially helpful to the investigations or not helpful at all. For the audio notes, 81 (76.4%) were accurate, with 14 (13.2%) partially accurate and 11 (10.3%) inaccurate (Cohen's Kappa=0.79). From these notes, 69 (67%) were found to be potentially helpful in answering the investigation (Cohen's Kappa=0.89). Because the audio notes had lower accuracy and usefulness compared to titles and tags, it may be less helpful for students to review and listen to audio when evaluating data.

In summary, the data was overall quite accurate and in over 80% of the cases the data was annotated in the manner that the system was structured around supporting (accurate tags, titles with the name of the animal that are accurate and correctly spelled). However, in each of these categories there was still a fair amount of data that was not accurate or more difficult to search and find due to the nonstandard labeling or incorrect spelling. The audio notes were also less useful for interpretation of the data as they had the lowest accuracy (76.4%) and only 67% of the audio notes were potentially helpful in the investigation.

What Is the Impact of Annotations on How Students Search Through and Evaluate Data?

Students could use the data annotations as a mechanism to organize and filter the data, as well as analyze the data by looking at or listening to the annotations. Below we present the strategies students used to search and evaluate the data.

Annotations Impacting How Students Search

The different search strategies that were available to the students in this trial included: searching by the title of the data, searching by tags present in the data, looking at their own data, or looking at the entire data set. The groups employed a mix of strategies and spent radically different amounts of time viewing data (ranging from 16 to 113 minutes, median of 48 minutes). We analyzed the usage logs to determine the amount of time each group spent searching via each annotation type as well as without any filtering to see the effect annotations had on searching.

Using tags was the least common method of searching. While all but 2 groups tried tag searching, only 12 groups spent at least 5 minutes using this method. Only two groups spent over 25% of their time looking at data by tags (the heaviest user spending 38% of their time looking at data, a little over 22 minutes).

The next method that students used was browsing through their own data. Because of the small amount (average 16 pieces) of data collected by each group, all of the data could be viewed onscreen quickly and so annotations did not play a large role in search habits. Two groups spent the majority of their time browsing their own data, with a total of 14 groups spending 5 or more minutes browsing through their own data. All but one group spent time reviewing their own data, with 20 of the groups spending at least two minutes reviewing their data. The class average for time spent looking at their own data was 17% of their total time looking at data.

The next most common strategy that students used was title searching, with 17 of the groups spending 5 or more minutes searching by the title and a class average of 22% of their time looking at data being employed this way. Seven groups used title searching as their primary means of locating data (spending up to 42 minutes looking at data in this fashion). However, not all groups took this approach, one never using this feature and another five groups spent less than two minutes searching in this fashion.

With an average of 54% of their data browsing time being spent in this way, panning through tiled images of the entire data set without any filters applied was the most common method of reviewing data. Seventeen groups used this as their primary means of perusing data, and all groups spent at least 5 minutes using this tactic. Nineteen groups spent 20 or more minutes reviewing data via this method (two groups spending over an hour). This method did not use annotations for search purposes. Some students browsed through the entire data set to see what their peers' collected and found it enjoyable to see unrelated data, which could account for the high amount of time spent here.

While more students browsed through the entire data set without applying any annotations as search filters, a substantial portion used title searching to examine interesting data. Searching by tags was only popular with a small set of students, though the distribution of search strategies could be the result of the activity structure of finding similar animals: tag searches would be most useful to discover an animal related to their favorite animal, while title searches would locate an animal in mind.

Annotations Impacting How Students Evaluate Data

In order to see if any style of annotations helped students analyze data, we asked them, "How do you determine if the information you and your classmates collected is good?" Here, the tag annotations had a great effect. The majority, nine of the twelve groups responding to this question, indicated that they compared the tags to the associated images in order to evaluate their peers' data.

> *Student 1: It has good tags.*
> *Student 2: It has good tags and we kinda like look at the picture and see if it's like if its right.*
> *Student 1: If it goes with the animal.*
> *Student 2: Yep.*

After this, discussion between partners (4 groups) and using tags to find traits that were similar to their own animal (3 groups) were the most common approaches toward determining how good their classmates' data was.

> *Student 1: You should check the features of the animal the same traits that one animal has over the other...*
> *Student 2: You ah use the picture you click that you're gonna use it ah look for like the traits that the picture has ah if it has the same trait as your animal then that those are the right traits.*

To further look at the utility of tags (called labels to the students), and any effect they had on analyzing the data, we asked the students, "Did you find the labels describing individual animals helpful? Why?" All but one of the groups responding to this question reported the tags were helpful, primarily to see similarities in their animal (6 groups) or get more information than would be present in the image alone (5 groups). The group who didn't find the labels helpful felt this way, "*because, most of the stuff I would see by yourself so you don't really need labels.*"

> *Student: If there were no labels I would think what's the picture like what's the like what's all the things about it cuz I don't know anything about if there's no labels. Like turn that picture to the animal. Ok, then I didn't know what it was, there's no label on it so I don't know what it is still, and I don't know any facts about it or nothing.*

This implies that the tagged data greatly assisted students in evaluating their evidence, with some students believing they could not evaluate the data without tags being present.

However, audio notes were not mentioned in how students determined good data and we wanted to see if the students used this annotation. In looking at the usage logs, we discovered that while all but one group listened to audio notes, there was a high variance in audio playback. During the trial we had noted many students seemed to enjoy listening to audio notes other students collected, often wanting to identify who made the note. Additionally, there were two pieces of off topic audio data that several students found entertaining (one being a photo of a duck titled "Aflack" with an audio note that said Aflack, mimicking a TV commercial). Several students repeatedly played these audio notes; one group listened to the Aflack audio 85 times. This had caused a disruption to students nearby at

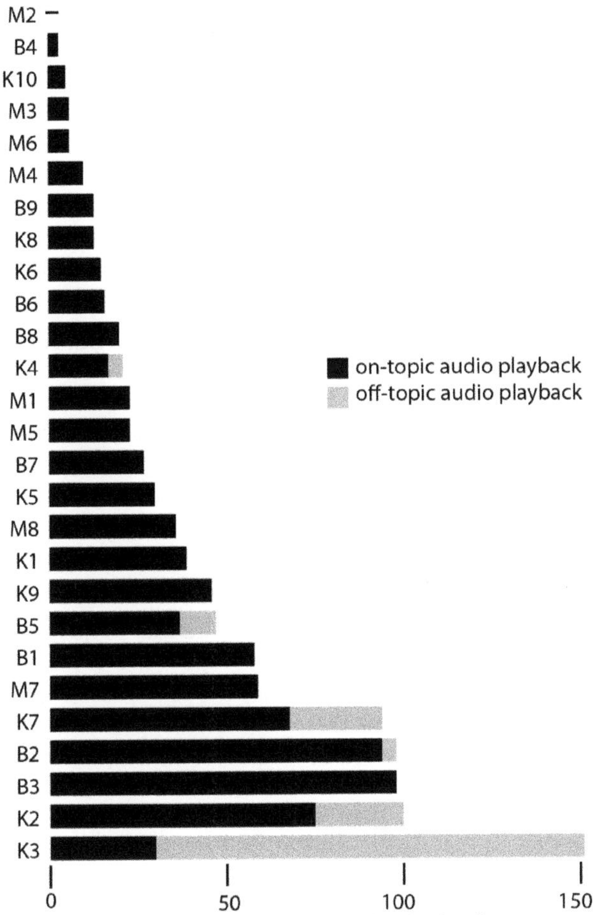

Figure 4. On and off-topic audio playbacks.

one point and the group was instructed to stop playing the audio by the teacher.

The breakdown of how many times each pair listened to audio notes can be viewed in Figure 4, which also separates out the two off-topic audio notes.

When students were asked, "Did you find audio playback on this page useful? Why?," several students found it useful, one student mentioned "because it explained details" and another group liked their own audio notes "because it kinda refreshed me why I kind of took it, the picture". However, one group mentioned not finding them useful because the audio notes say the same thing as the tags, showing a mixed impression of the utility of this annotation. Future work needs to be done to look at why particular groups of students avoided the audio notes and further exploring the effect that listening to audio notes has on evaluating and utilizing data.

How do Students Find and Choose the Evidence They Use in Their Explanation?

To understand how students found the data they applied to their explanation and how they ultimately chose this particular evidence, we examined how they first discovered each unique piece of evidence. In order to understand what

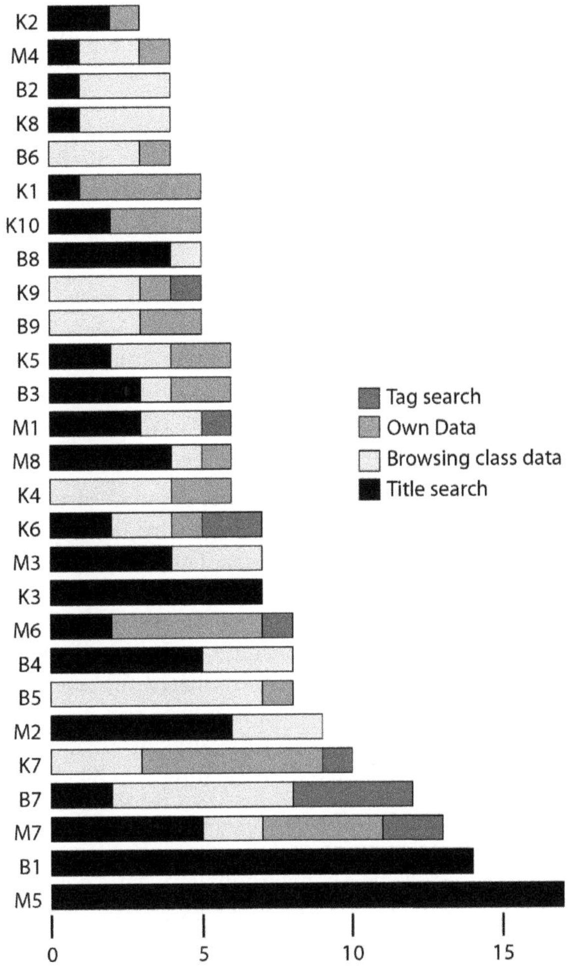

Figure 5. How students found data they used in their explanation.

they found important about the pieces of evidence included in their explanation, we asked them (1) how they might choose data they would want to use and, later, (2) how they chose the data that they did use in their investigation.

How Students Discovered Data

When we examined all the unique pieces of data students chose to use in their explanation, we categorized it by which search or browsing method they used to find the data (breakdown of the methods by group in Figure 5).

Only a few groups had spent any substantial amount of time looking at and evaluating their own data, and their usage also shows a lack of interest towards their own data, with only five groups using more than 50% of their own data while nine groups never used any of their personally collected data. This implies that most groups preferred evaluating and utilizing their peers' data, several mentioning that it was fun to look at what their peers collected. However, a few groups had heavy utilization of their personally collected data, showing it is valuable to support the filtering between personal and peers' data.

Finding data by searching titles was the most common means of adding data to the explanations, which groups did for a total of 88 times. Though students spent more time browsing the unfiltered full data set, the groups only utilized 57 pieces of data from this search method, showing the reduced effectiveness of trying to browse the unfiltered data set. As with time spent searching, tags were not used to discover much data they used, with only 12 pieces selected in this fashion.

When we looked at the characteristics of how students searched for data when they then chose to use a piece of data, several trends emerged. Whenever students found a piece of data to use with a tag applied, the tag was always a trait their favorite animal had, which is an ideal search behavior for discovering related animals.

For title searching, every search that resulted in a student adding data to their explanation began by looking up the animal name except for five cases. Three separate groups made queries on a more generic animal type (animal, fish, birds) and two different groups only typed in part of the animal name to retrieve the result (Q to find Quetzalcoatlus and gir for Giraffe). The system evaluated the search term looking to see if it matched the prefix of any word in the title, which in this case helped the student avoid spelling out Quetzalcoatlus (and avoid misspelling it in the process).

Student Perceptions on Choosing Data

While comparing pictures to tags was the main mode of judgment for students in determining what "good" data was, the criterion for, "How do you pick out which data you want to use?" was different. Though comparing pictures to their tags was still a notable strategy, the more prevalent strategy was comparing the tags to the traits of their chosen animal. Seven pairs explicitly named this as their strategy.

We expected that if students were being reflective about their work, then these methods of comparing the labels to the image, or to their chosen animal, would be their main strategies. Note that while image quality and asking an expert (such as a teacher or researcher) received mention as ways to determine good data and pick out what data to use, reviewing audio was never mentioned as a potential tool for evaluating the data. This may be due to the lower quality of the audio notes or the students' interpretation of the question, but it could indicate that audio notes are not seen as a useful means to interpret the data in this context.

An interesting phenomenon occurred when the students were asked, "How did you choose the specific pieces of data that you used in your explanation?" Several groups reported that picture quality became an important factor, even potentially surpassing the quality of the data.

> *Student: Well, its really one thing like this salamander picture it's actually a good picture... you can actually get better like you can get a bit more detail. Some other animals may be more closely related but still this gets back to the quality of the pictures*

This suggests that it would be helpful to have a method to swap the image that is associated with the annotations if a goal is to encourage using data with the best annotations.

In summary, students ended up finding the pieces of data they used for their explanations primarily from searching by titles, which was a more efficient use of time than browsing the unfiltered data set. The tags were primarily used to interpret the quality of the data, however a trend was noted that image quality was seemingly more important than quality of annotations for the data several groups included in their explanation.

Overview of Student Performance in Constructing Scientific Explanations

To provide context for the results presented in this paper about students' ability to find and use data, we evaluated their final explanations. Overall, students were able to find, evaluate, and utilize peer-collected, annotated, multimedia data to construct coherent scientific explanations for the two investigations they were assigned during this study.

Expectations

Previous research has shown students typically can articulate a claim and use some supporting evidence, but greatly struggle with providing reasoning that connects evidence to their claim [3]. We were working with students who have never engaged in such science inquiry investigations in school, only had a day introduction to the claims—evidence—reasoning framework, and were working in a difficult context with large amounts of peer collected data. Nonetheless, we wanted performance with the Zydeco system to be at least comparable to what is found in previous literature, particularly for the first investigation on animal relatedness due to it being an easier task for students to make a claim.

A rubric was created for each investigation modeled off McNeill's generalized claim—evidence—reasoning grading format [16]. We were defining success in this context as the majority of students completing the activity above a specific performance threshold. In investigation one the students were expected to create a complete claim, a piece of evidence for each ranked animal, and a reasoning that at least links the claim and evidence by repeating the evidence (Table 1). In the second investigation students were expected to have a claim answering the question, have at least one piece of appropriate evidence, and reasoning that at least links the claim and evidence by repeating the evidence. For each investigation, two reviewers independently graded 20% of the explanations and checked inter-rater reliability by percent agreements. Our inter-rater agreement was 100% for claim, above 94% for evidence, and above 83% for reasoning on each investigation.

Performance

In the first investigation, "*Determine how three other animals are related to your animal,*" the results exceeded our expectations with 18 (67%) of the pairs being

Claim	Evidence	Reasoning
0: Nothing/ not a claim	0: No evidence/ evidence not related to claim	0: Does not provide reasoning/ reasoning does not connect the evidence to the claim/ does not make sense
1: Partial claim/ ranks fewer than three animals	1: Some ranked animals without evidence	1: Provides reasoning that links the claim and the evidence by repeating the evidence
2: Complete claim- includes three ranked animals	2: One evidence for each ranked animal	2: Provides reasoning that explains why the evidence (traits) supports the claim
	3: Multiple evidence for some ranked animals	3: Provides reasoning that includes why the animals share traits through a scientific principle (i.e. shared ancestors)
	4: Multiple evidence for all animals	

Table 1. Grading rubric for the first investigation. Grey cells denote the minimum performance threshold for success.

successful on the first animal ranking investigation. The areas that held students back were failing to make a complete claim (5 groups), failing to use a piece of data for each animal (4 groups), and nonsensical reasoning (3 groups). Three of the groups that failed to make a complete claim had also failed to use evidence for each animal, showing they may not have understood the activity or how to use the system properly.

It was noted that 5 of the 9 groups that did not successfully complete investigation one were in the same class (groups with prefix K in the figures 4 and 5), which had numerous behavioral problems throughout the experiment. If the data from this class is discarded, 13 out of 17 (76%) of the groups hit the success bar.

For the second investigation, "*Describe how these animals could survive in Michigan*," 16 (59%) groups were successful at creating an explanation. Lack of time to complete the assignment was detrimental to their performance; if we judge completion by students asking for a peer critique, only 14 pairs were able to. However, all the groups' work was graded (partially complete or not), and 16 hit the baseline for at least one animal survival explanation (11 whom had a peer critique), and 11 (41%) groups were successful writing an explanation for two animals.

CONCLUSION

This work contributes to research on how to support finding and utilizing personal and peer-collected data for educational activities. It presents one of the first studies on how students, particularly those new to science inquiry, think about and utilize large quantities of annotated peer-collected image data, along with an effective interface design that enabled students to explore the data and create an explanation on a tablet.

Students were able to use different aspects of Zydeco to search through and evaluate their peers' multimedia data to create scientific explanations. This shows the potential for a variety of new rich activities for students, as they are able to engage in more authentic and personal inquiry activities through the use of systems built around their personal and peers' annotated photographic data. While they had the option to use their own data, almost every group primarily searched their peers' data set and used that data to make an explanation. The students' performance as they managed the over 650 pieces of data produced during this study implies that inquiry and collection activities can run concurrently across multiple groups (as was the case in this trial), or have activities that run over a longer duration and generate similarly large quantities of data.

Some lessons learned from this study were:

- Tags are a valuable tool in aiding students to evaluate peer-collected data
- Title searching and panning through the unfiltered data set are the preferred methods for finding data
- Evidence used in explanations are rarely the students own but primarily from their peers
- While audio notes were generally on topic, students saw mixed results in their utility for interpreting data

Previous research found that students were varied in their search strategies on the web [4] and they were better at browsing than keyword searching [4, 11]. This study suggests that while browsing is still the preferred method of exploring data, students were more efficient at finding data to use when they searched via the title. However, students had varying usage and preferences towards the different annotations for different tasks; for developers of data-rich systems, this can indicate there seems to be no all-encompassing annotation or search type and such systems would benefit from a range of annotations to assist students in finding, evaluating, and using data. Some students chose data based on the image quality instead of the annotation quality. For designers seeking to encourage appropriate annotation use, it would be useful to provide a mechanism to swap the image associated with annotations, to enable students to get the high quality image they desire matched with the appropriate annotations.

This work has some limitations in that it was only investigating one particular activity context (collecting data from a history museum investigating animal relatedness and survival), and future work will need to investigate how the use of annotations changes in varying contexts. Additionally, we will be adding in data probes to the system so students can gather numerical data and exploring how to support explanations using a combination of this data along with multimedia data. Future work will also include adding methods to incorporate information and articles from the Internet to further supplement the field data.

ACKNOWLEDGMENTS

We would like to thank Kira Berman and Amy Harris at the Exhibit Museum of Natural History for their support during our trials, the aid of team members on the Zydeco project, and the teachers and students who gave their time and advice to the project. This material is based on work supported by the National Science Foundation under Grant No. DRL-1020027. Any opinions and findings expressed in this material are those of the authors and do not necessarily reflect those of the National Science Foundation.

REFERENCES

1. American Association for the Advancement of Science *Benchmarks for Science Literacy*. Oxford University Press, New York, 2009.
2. Ames, M. and Naaman, M. Why we tag: motivations for annotation in mobile and online media. In *Proc. CHI 2007*, ACM (2007), 971-980.
3. Berland, L.K. and McNeill, K.L. Using a learning progression to inform scientific argumentation in talk and writing. *Learning Progression in Science*, 2009.
4. Bilal, D. Children's Use of the Yahooligans! Web Search Engine. III. Cognitive and Physical Behaviors on Fully Self- Generated Search Tasks. *Journal of the American Society for Information Science and Technology*, *53* (13), 1170-1183.
5. Bischoff, K., Firan, C.S., Nejdl, W. and Paiu, R. Can all tags be used for search? In *Proc. Information and Knowledge Management*, ACM (2008), 193-202.
6. Cahill, C., Kuhn, A., Schmoll, S., Lo, W.-T., McNally, B. and Quintana, C. Mobile learning in museums: how mobile supports for learning influence student behavior. In *Proc. Interaction Design and Children 2011*, ACM (2011), 21-28.
7. Cahill, C., Lo, W.-T., Kuhn, A., Quintana, C., McNally, B., Schmoll, S. and Krajcik, J., Student use of multimodal data and metadata tools during nomadic inquiry. In *Proc. Mobile and Contextual Learning 2011*.
8. Druin, A., Foss, E., Hutchinson, H., Golub, E. and Hatley, L. Children's roles using keyword search interfaces at home. In *Proc. CHI 2010*, ACM (2010), 413-422.
9. Fraser, D.S., Smith, H., Tallyn, E., Kirk, D., Benford, S., Rowland, D., Paxton, M., Price, S. and Fitzpatrick, G. The SENSE project: a context-inclusive approach to studying environmental science within and across schools. *In Proc. Computer Support for Collaborative Learning*, International Society of the Learning Sciences, 2005, 155-159.
10. Furnas, G., Fake, C., von Ahn, L., Schachter, J., Golder, S., Fox, K., Davis, M., Marlow, C. and Naaman, M. Why do tagging systems work? In *Proc. CHI 2006*, ACM (2006), 36-39.
11. Hutchinson, H.B., Bederson, B.B. and Druin, A. The evolution of the international children's digital library searching and browsing interface. In *Proc. Interaction Design and Children 2006*, ACM (2006), 105-112.
12. Jochmann-Mannak, H.E., Huibers, T.W.C. and Sanders, T.J.M. Children's information retrieval: beyond examining search strategies and interfaces. *The BCS-IRSG Symposium: Future Directions in Information Access*, British Computer Society, 2008, 64-72.
13. Kuhn, A., Cahill, C., Quintana, C. and Schmoll, S. Using tags to encourage reflection and annotation on data during nomadic inquiry. In *Proc. CHI 2011,* ACM (2011), 667-670.
14. Kuhn, A., McNally, B., Cahill, C., Quintana, C. and Soloway, E. Constructing scientific arguments with user collected data in nomadic inquiry. *Ext. Abstracts CHI 2011*, ACM (2011), 2167-2172.
15. Martin, S., Stanton Fraser, D., Fraser, M., Woodgate, D. and Crellin, D. The impact of hand held mobile technologies upon children's motivation and learning. In *Proc. Mobile and Contextual Learning 2010.*
16. McNeill, K.L. and Krajcik, J. *Supporting grade 5-8 students in constructing explanations in science: The claim, evidence and reasoning framework for talk and writing*. Pearson Allyn & Bacon, New York, NY, 2011.
17. Razikin, K., Goh, D.H.-L., Teng, Y.-L., Nguyen, Q.M., Kim, T.N.Q., Lim, E.-P., Chang, C.H., Chatterjea, K. and Sun, A. Sharing Mobile Multimedia Annotations to Support Inquiry-Based Learning Using MobiTOP. *Active Media Technology*, 2009, 171-182.
18. Scheuer, O., Loll, F., Pinkwart, N. and McLaren, B.M. Computer-supported argumentation: A review of the state of the art. *Computer-Supported Collaborative Learning*, *5* (1), 43-102.
19. Vavoula, G., Sharples, M., Rudman, P., Meek, J. and Lonsdale, P. Myartspace: Design and evaluation of support for learning with multimedia phones between classrooms and museums. *Computers & Education*, *53* (2), 286-299.
20. Woodgate, D., Stanton Fraser, D., Gower, A., Glancy, M., Gower, A.P., Chamberlain, A., Dillon, T. and Crellin, D. Using mobile and pervasive technologies to engage formal and informal learners in scientific debate. in Goh, T. ed. *Multiplatform E-Learning Systems and Technologies: Mobile Devices for Ubiquitous ICT-Based Education*, Information Science Reference, 2010, 196-214.

Phylo-Genie: Engaging Students in Collaborative 'Tree-Thinking' through Tabletop Techniques

Bertrand Schneider[1], **Megan Strait**[2], **Laurence Muller**[3], **Sarah Elfenbein**[4], **Orit Shaer**[5], **Chia Shen**[3]

Stanford University (Stanford, CA)[1], Tufts University (Medford, MA)[2], Harvard University (Cambridge, MA)[3], Yale University (New Haven, CT)[4], Wellesley College (Wellesley, MA)[5]

schneibe@stanford.edu, megan.strait@tufts.edu, lmuller@seas.harvard.edu, sarah.elfenbein@yale.edu, oshaer@wellesley.edu, chia_shen@harvard.edu

ABSTRACT
Phylogenetic trees are representations of evolutionary relationships amongst species. Interviews of instructors and students have revealed that novice biologists have difficulty understanding phylogenetics. Moreover, misinterpretations of phylogenetics are common among college-level students. In this paper we present Phylo-Genie, a tabletop interface for fostering collaborative learning of phylogenetics. We conducted an experimental study with 56 participants, comparing students' conceptual learning and engagement using Phylo-Genie as: 1) a multi-touch tabletop interface and 2) a pen and paper activity. Our findings show that the tabletop implementation fosters collaborative learning by engaging users in the activity. We also shed light on the way in which our design principles facilitated engagement and collaborative learning in a tabletop environment.

Author Keywords
Education; tabletop; collaborative learning; bioinformatics; multi-touch interaction; tangible user interface.

ACM Classification Keywords
H.5.2. Information interfaces and presentation: User Interfaces;

General Terms
Human Factors; Design.

INTRODUCTION
Phylogenetics, the science of constructing and evaluating hypotheses about historical patterns of descent, is at the very core of evolutionary theory. Thus, it has become pervasive inside and outside the field of biology [21]. Phylogenetic trees are the most direct representation of the principle of common ancestry, and as such, hold a prominent place in the public's understanding of evolution. It is common for biology professors to teach these representations in introductory classes. However, numerous studies indicate that evolutionary trees are difficult to comprehend for college-level students [32], and that many concepts are counter-intuitive and require a more in-depth understanding of evolution [15]. In addition, the field of phylogenetics depends on computational tools, such as Mesquite [30] and ClustalW [28], for creating and testing evolutionary trees. These tools are not appropriate for novice students since they do not support important aspects of college-level learning, such as collaborative learning or high-level reasoning. Instead, professors often turn to paper-based learning environments (textbooks or worksheets) for teaching phylogenetic principles. This approach does not provide sufficient support for novice students either because representations used in many textbooks have been shown to induce misconceptions [9] and because it lacks support for "active" learning.

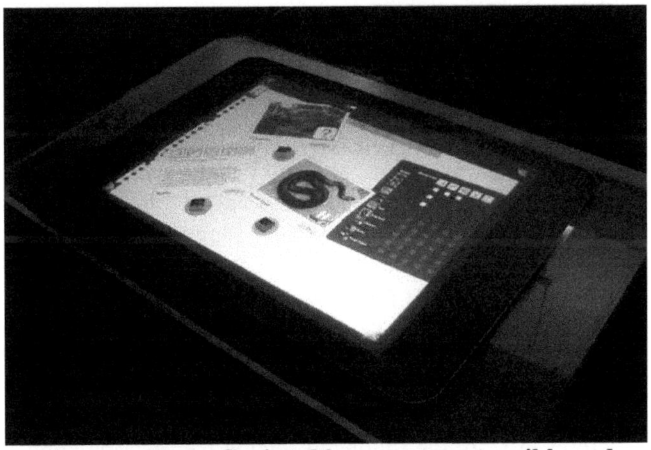

Figure 1. Phylo-Genie tabletop system: tangible and digital exploration of morphological characteristics of Australian snake specimen.

Recent investigations highlight common misconceptions held by students (e.g. [10]). These misconceptions illustrate fundamental barriers to understanding how evolution operates. Motivated by the need for computational support in college-level phylogenetics and by previous work demonstrating the potential of tabletop interfaces to facilitate learning [1, 3, 4, 7, 8, 13, 16, 17, 20, 23, 26, 37, 46], we developed Phylo-Genie (Figure 1). Phylo-Genie introduces tangible and multi-touch interactions on a horizontal surface. Its design is aimed at fostering collaborative learning and engagement in order to improve students' understanding of phylogenetics.

In this paper, we first discuss core concepts in phylogenetics and the misconceptions common to college-level students that have been reported in recent studies. We then review related work in the areas of tabletop and tangible user interfaces for science education, the evaluation of dyadic collaboration, and existing methods and tools for teaching phylogenetics. Next, we describe the Phylo-Genie learning environment and present findings from our comparative study that highlight the strengths and weaknesses of Phylo-Genie compared to traditional pen and paper interactions. Finally, we discuss the implications of our results for designing collaborative tabletop activities.

RELATED WORK

Phylogenetics, the study of evolutionary relatedness among species on earth, is based on morphological and genomic data. A phylogenetic tree shows that some species are more closely related than others because they share a more recent common ancestor. For example, in Figure 2, humans and chimps are more closely related than humans and gorillas. The ability to read and understand a phylogenetic tree is called tree-thinking [21]. More specifically, tree thinking refers to the ability to "(a) interpret and extract information about evolutionary history from phylogenetic trees and (b) use those diagrams to organize knowledge of biodiversity and make inferences to support one's decisions and actions" [34]. A significant number of studies ([5, 15, 21, 32]) suggest that tree-thinking is a crucial yet difficult skill to acquire, but it is necessary in order to fully grasp evolutionary principles.

Known Misconceptions

The framework of this paper is a constructivist view of the human mind whereby students hold an everyday understanding of a variety of topics and use their intuition to explain the world. This approach suggests that students use their prior knowledge to build new concepts [36]. The fact that students have pre-conceptions does not mean they are correct; in some cases, they may hold misconceptions that contradict experts' explanations of a phenomenon. Misconceptions are usually persistent and difficult to correct because they are deeply rooted in existing cognitive structures [15]. In the following section we describe known misconceptions in the field of phylogenetics.

Misconceptions are relatively well-documented in the field of teaching phylogenetics [10, 21, 32]. We review four major misconceptions held by college-level students [32]:

- *Incorrect Mapping of Relative Time:* Many are confused regarding the mapping of time to a phylogenetic tree. For instance, Meir et al. [31] found that some students, when given Figure 2, would draw an arrow from left (past) to right (present) based on the argument that humans descended from gibbons and gorillas. A correct mapping would define the root node of the tree as the oldest ancestor and the tips of the branches as living species.

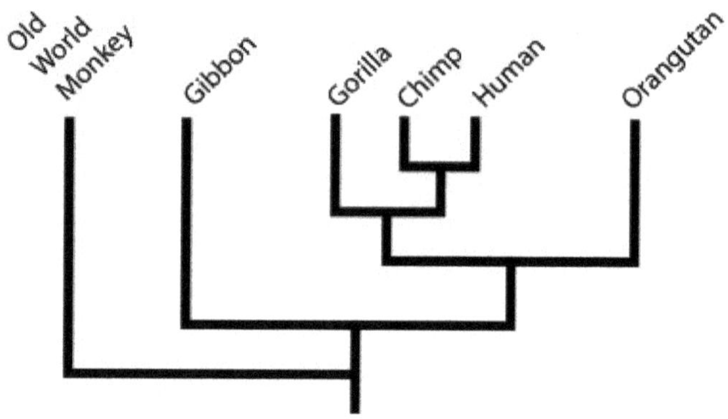

Figure 2. Example of a phylogenetic tree.

- *Proximity Indicates Relationship:* students often believe gorillas are more closely related to gibbons than to humans since they are spatially closer on the diagram. They fail to consider the most recent common ancestor (branching point) as an indicator of relatedness.
- *Node Counting:* a significant number of students also believe that counting internal nodes is the most efficient way to assess evolutionary closeness. Using this strategy would lead to the incorrect interpretation that orangutans are more closely related to gibbons (a distance of 2 nodes) than to humans (3 nodes). Again, a correct observation would consider the most recent ancestor as a sign of evolutionary closeness.
- *Straight Line Equals No Change:* a common misconception of Figure 2 is to interpret the first branching on the left (leading to old world monkeys) as a period where no change happened. This is erroneous since species continue to evolve along the lines of the tree, even though there is no branching.

In summary, misconceptions associated with phylogenetics are widespread and diverse. When designing Phylo-Genie we considered the misconceptions described above and sought solutions to avoid them through an interactive and engaging learning experience.

Existing Tools for Teaching Phylogenetics

The current approach for teaching phylogenetics relies heavily on textbooks and classroom instruction. Several studies outlined the weaknesses of this method: textbooks are often poorly designed (e.g. using a significant number of ambiguous or incorrectly constructed trees and a large number of cladograms in a ladder format [9]). Cladograms in a ladder format are known to be more difficult to understand and more likely to elicit misconceptions among students [33]. Additional studies have shown that college students [32] and even graduate students [41] hold strong preconceptions that reinforce alternative conceptions of macroevolution. As a consequence, new methods for teaching phylogenetics as well as carefully designed learning environments are necessary to ensure a better understanding of evolutionary principles. These methods should promote collaboration, active learning, and take into account students' prior knowledge, while using accurate representations of evolutionary trees.

Some prototypes embodying those ideas include the work of Halverson [22], who asked students to build their own phylogenetic trees by connecting pipe cleaners, and Matuk [48], who designed animated trees with multiple external representations to avoid erroneous interpretations. These studies differ from our work in that they have not been thoroughly evaluated, have produced mixed results [22], or do not propose a complete learning activity for teaching phylogenetic concepts [48]. Existing work has extensively studied how students perceive evolutionary trees [33,34], how small interventions can prevent specific misinterpretations [48] and documented students' misconceptions [10,21,32]. However to our knowledge no stand-alone activities that take advantage of recent technological advances have been thoroughly evaluated.

Proposition to correct existing misconceptions

In the design of Phylo-Genie, we adopted Smith, diSessa and Roschelle's [47] view on misconceptions. They propose to "move beyond simple models of knowledge and learning, where novice misconceptions are replaced by expert concepts". Indeed, while most instructional methods try to expose students to the truth hoping it will replace their previous knowledge with appropriate concepts, numerous studies have shown this approach ineffective and that misconceptions are deeply seated and resistant to change (e.g. [11]). As a consequence, replacement directly conflicts with the constructivist premise that learning is the process of adapting prior knowledge [47].

Smith, diSessa and Roschelle suggest a few ways to modify misconceptions in a constructivist fashion. First, they proposed that abstract representations should be removed. Instead, familiar situations where the students held a misconception should be utilized; indeed, novices are often able to exhibit expert-like behavior when describing highly complex systems with which they are familiar. They are more likely to revisit their understanding of concepts based on everyday objects and experience. Secondly, they emphasize the importance of using constructive discussions as a way to reformulate and re-conceptualize students' ideas. It is crucial to remove confrontation from the debate and validate students' pre-conceptions as an evolving structure that can be refined. We draw on Smith, diSessa and Roschelle's framework in the design of the Phylo-Genie learning environment. Misconceptions about phylogenetics need to be addressed in a familiar situation, where students have the opportunity to discuss their experiences in a collaborative and non-confrontational way.

Addressing Misconceptions With Collaborative Learning

In the past decade, research in education has focused much of its effort on social learning and small group cognition. The inspiration for this effort mainly comes from Piaget [36], who postulated that socio-cognitive conflicts cause major cognitive restructuration, and Vygotsky [49] who claimed that learning happens first on a social or cultural level and only then internalized. Those two theories coalesce under the umbrella of the socio-constructivist theory. This approach emphasizes the importance of collaborating and negotiating knowledge. As a consequence, socio-constructivist researchers have put their effort in analyzing group interactions and successful patterns of collaboration. From an empirical point of view, studies have shown mixed results of this approach [29,40]. As a consequence, we draw on Dillenbourg's view that collaboration works under some conditions, and it is the aim of research to determine the conditions under which collaborative learning is efficient [14]. Thus design guidelines are crucial for building suitable learning environments and activities. In the case of phylogenetic misconceptions, we propose that creating an engaging activity is a prerequisite for fostering positive collaboration.

Tabletops and Tangibles for Science Education

In this section we describe existing tabletops and tangible user interfaces (TUIs) for science education, present the theoretical foundations for our *system design,* and discuss techniques for fostering collaboration and engagement.

Several tangible and tabletop interfaces were designed to augment science education in areas where there is inherent physical structure or where abstract ideas can be clarified with physical representation. Ahmet et al. [1] explored children's learning of concepts in physics through mixed digital and physical interaction techniques. For molecular biology, Gillet et al. [19] created a TUI that employs augmented reality to enhance 3D molecular models. Shaer et al. [45] developed a TUI fostering inquiry-based learning of genomics (G-nome Surfer). Fjeld et al. [16] and Glaeser et al. [20] constructed TUIs for chemistry education. Schkolne, Ishii and Schroeder [41] developed a tangible immersive interface for the design of DNA molecules. Similarly, Involv [26] is a multi-touch tabletop interface for exploring biodiversity and the relationships among organisms. These systems have the potential to contribute to science education in areas related to phylogenetics. Some of those projects focus on the representation and manipulation of objects that have inherent physical structure, while others propose a purely digital output (G-nome Sufer, Involv).

Collaboration and Engagement

Most closely related to our work are two studies conducted by Shaer et al. [45] and Piper and Hollan [37]. Shaer et al. compared the affordances of multi-touch versus multiple and single mice on dyadic collaborative learning for undergraduate genomics. Piper and Hollan [37] studied pairs of undergraduate students, comparing the affordances of tabletop displays and traditional paper handouts. In both cases, they found that using a multi-touch surface increased the quality of collaborative processes. In a study comparing multi-touch and tangible interfaces, Schneider et al. [43]

found that the tangible interface fostered collaboration, playful learning and supported a larger exploration of the problem space. Our study draws largely upon this body of work in the context of enhancing learning of phylogenetics through interaction techniques that support collaborative processes. More specifically, we propose to blend multi-touch and tangible inputs to create a learning environment that engages users in collaborative problem-solving.

Other studies have focused on the linkages between engagement and learning [6, 8, 13, 39, 47]. Studies that focused on tangible interfaces found that physical objects fostered engagement and exploration among children [4] and apprentices in logistics [43]. Based on those studies, we propose that tangibles support users' engagement due to their aesthetic and affordances as physical objects.

PHYLO-GENIE

Phylo-Genie is a tabletop interface for supporting collaborative learning of phylogenetics. As a learning tool, Phylo-Genie targets the understanding of phylogenetic principles through engaging content and tabletop interaction techniques. Gregory [21] holds that lessons at the undergraduate level should de-emphasize the technical aspects of phylogeny reconstruction in favor of a focus on the concepts underlying 'tree-thinking'. For this reason, we designed the scenario of Phylo-Genie as a hands-on activity that focuses on exploratory and active learning.

Design Goals and Guidelines

To identify design elements for supporting engagement in learning of college-level phylogenetics, we collected data from a series of recurring individual 1.5-hour meetings with four instructors and two doctoral candidates in the field of evolutionary biology. These domain experts participated in brainstorming sessions and provided specific feedback on a series of prototypes. This iterative and participatory process allowed us to increase the fidelity and ecological relevance of our learning environment. Moreover, a review of related literature and teaching materials provided us with additional design requirements for the learning activity.

From the collected data we found that a learning environment focusing on phylogenetics needed to address the following questions: What is a phylogenetic tree? How do biologists build it (e.g. by combining morphological and genomic data)? How can it be interpreted (e.g. how closely related are two species)? It is also necessary to introduce a vocabulary for fostering discussion with a peer.

In addition to those requirements, we propose the following design principles to foster collaborative learning:

- Engagement: Providing an engaging learning experience supported by an interesting story, a visually appealing interface, and natural interactions techniques, so that students focus on discovering concepts.
- Territoriality: several studies [27, 44] suggest that territoriality is a crucial factor for supporting collaboration. A learning environment should provide ways to reinforce users' ownership of both physical objects and areas on top of the interactive surface.
- Opportunities for reflection: Clements [12] argues that the danger of concrete objects is to trap the students in an "action mode". Transitioning from physical action to abstract knowledge can be challenging for students. As a consequence our system needs to provide various "reflection stages" where users can step back and articulate their discoveries as formal concepts.
- Autonomy: traditional classroom exercises need a constant supervision from teachers. A more efficient system should provide automatic feedback and give users a strong sense of control and autonomy.

The next section describes how we addressed these requirements into the design of Phylo-Genie.

Scenario

The Phylo-Genie environment presents users with a scenario that motivates the learning activity. Participants 'travel' to Australia as researchers to assist in data collection and analysis. The trip is executed as a series of nine stages. During the trip, a user is bitten by a venomous snake. The users then have to choose between 4 equidistant hospitals; each hospital has only one type of anti-venom. They have time to reach only one hospital before the venom irreversibly affects the bitten user. Since the species of the snake is unknown, participants must learn tree-building techniques to assess the common ancestry of the Australian snakes. Closely related snakes share the same venom (and thus anti-venom). Successful tree construction and interpretation allows users to select a treatment. This scenario, anchored in a real life setting, provides participants with motivation for learning phylogenetics.

We developed a scenario that progresses in several stages to introduce and reinforce fundamental phylogenetic concepts in an engaging manner. First, participants receive and review several vocabulary notes and information in preparation for their trip to Australia. In Figure 3, users are introduced to the fundamental concepts and snake organisms by exploring and discussing 'sticky note' items. Phylo-Genie utilizes the metaphor of sticky notes to avoid overwhelming users with textual information: notes can easily be removed from the display with a swipe gesture, and retrieved by touching the corresponding area of the surface.

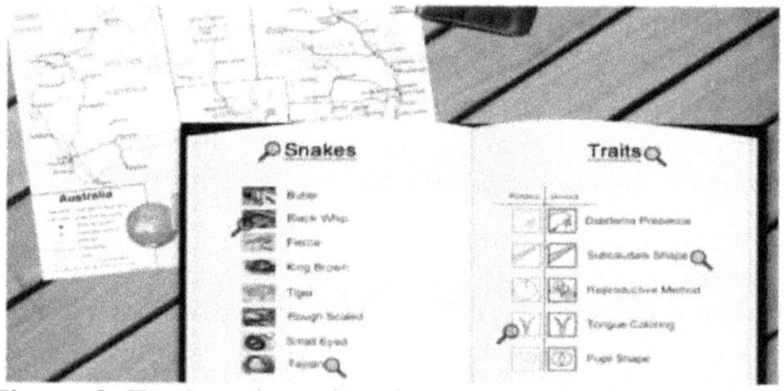

Figure 3. Exploration of basic concepts in phylogenetics, organized by virtual 'sticky notes'.

Organizing Heterogeneous Information

When constructing phylogenetic trees, scientists often involve more than a dozen variables. In this system, Phylo-Genie allows users to directly manipulate and explore the information relevant to each snake specimen of question. Snakes are embodied by small physical tokens and can be dropped on the table to access snakes' characteristics. Tokens are randomly distributed around the table at the beginning of the activity; this implicitly supports a sense of territoriality among participants, since they 'own' the tokens on their side of the surface. In addition, those tangibles facilitate sharing of data between partners because of their physical nature.

Figure 4 shows an image of simultaneous exploration of the information for three different snakes. Users fill in boolean values in a character table (right) to aggregate information for all snakes. Organizing the table allows users to create a matrix in a row echelon form; this, in turn, facilitates the tree building process. Snakes sharing a higher no. of characteristics are most closely related, while the species sharing only one or no feature with others represents the outgroup (Note that this is a simplified learning example.).

It should be noted that computational tools usually calculate these values for users; however, we propose that the physical completion of the task facilitates a connection between collecting real-world data and building a phylogenetic tree.

Constructing and Interpreting Scientific Representations

Phylo-Genie takes the users through two stages of construction, each employing one of two common methodologies: morphology-based and genomics-based. To build a tree, which shows the evolutionary relationships of 10 Australian snakes, participants place tangible tokens that represent species and character tokens that represent common traits.

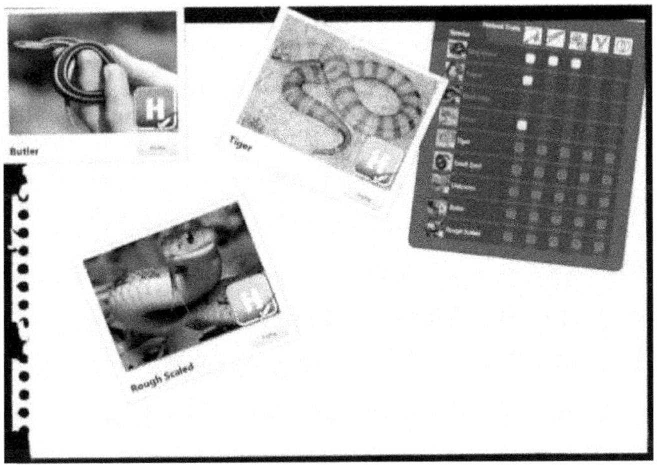

Figure 4. Collection and organization of morphological information of the Australian snake specimen.

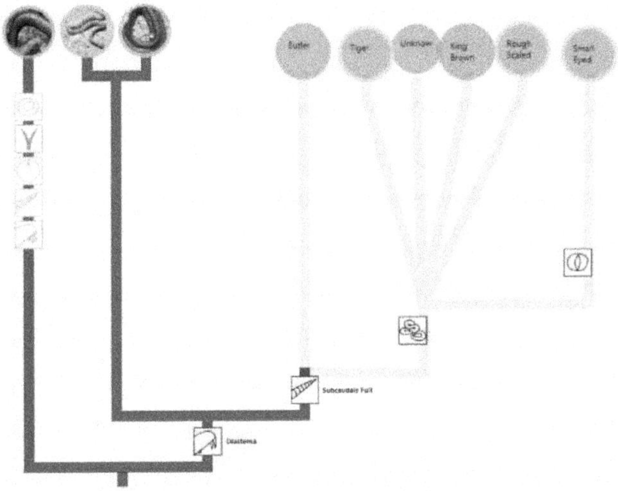

Figure 5. Construction of a phylogenetic tree based on the collected morphological information.

In the first step, the morphology-based method is used to build a basic phylogenetic tree. Since this tree does not provide enough information to resolve the evolutionary relationship amongst all snakes, users are motivated to learn genomic-based methods to choose the appropriate treatment for the bite.

Figure 5 shows a constructed tree based on morphological characteristics. The outgroup, the species most ancestral in the constructed tree, is shown (left) with all ancestral versions of the traits. In the Phylo-Genie scenario, traits refer to various characteristics of the snakes: being ovipara or vivipara (do they lay eggs or give live birth), having round or ellipse-shaped eyes, etc. Divergence is marked by the trait icons. The parts of the tree in dark gray are presented to the user prior to construction, and the items in light gray are those added by the participants.

Following each tree-building stage, participants reflect on the tree previously built to select an anti-venom for the bitten partner. This requires users to interpret the structure of the tree to derive and understand the historical relationships of the corresponding species. These steps are crucial for knowledge-building since they encourage users to reflect on their experience and formulate formal concepts. Reflection is encouraged by having users "step back" from their previous task (organizing information and building a tree): a new screen is presented, where users access the previously built tree in a non-editable format. This forces users to leave the "concrete mode" as defined by Clements [12], where manipulating objects is the focus of the activity and move to an "abstract mode" where they are required to think in abstract terms in order to correctly interpret the phylogenetic tree.

Interacting with Physical Tokens

In Phylo-Genie, students interact with physical tokens that represent various species of snakes. Users manipulate those tokens to accomplish two key actions: organizing heterogeneous information and building phylogenetic trees. In the first case, positioning a token on the surface will display the snake's characteristics and its outward appearance. Thus, the token becomes an embodiment of the snake and a self-contained object: information is easily retrievable by dropping a token on the table. Moreover, tokens are used to build the tree in the next step. By sliding a snake from a branch of the tree users can extend the given template and use the collected data to build their own phylogenetic tree. We designed those tokens as a way to foster collaboration: users implicitly "own" the tangibles situated on their portion of the table. Ownership, in turn, helps users to coordinate tabletop interactions [44].

Implementation

Phylo-Genie is written in C# using the Microsoft Surface SDK V1. The morphological and genomic information is adapted from Wallach [50] and material and exams from a course on Introductory Biology. Tangible objects are tagged with the Microsoft Surface fiducial tags.

EVALUATION

To evaluate Phylo-Genie's strengths and limitations in supporting collaborative learning of phylogenetics we conducted a between-subjects experiment with 56 undergraduate and graduate students. We compared the system implemented on a multi-touch tabletop to a traditional pen and paper implementation of the Phylo-Genie scenario. The rationale for this choice was to conduct an ecologically valid comparison of our system as pen and paper is the premier media used for teaching in college settings. In this study, we examined the similarities and differences of the two implementations in terms of quantitative performance and qualitative behavior.

Participants

56 undergraduate and graduate students (28 female, 28 male, average age = 21.28, SD = 3.70) volunteered to participate in the study, composing 28 dyads. None of the participants had received college-level instruction in evolutionary biology before the study. We also pre-screened students' knowledge in biology prior to the session with a basic 5-question quiz on phylogenetics; no participant correctly answered more than 2 questions.

Procedure

A between-subjects study design was used, in which 28 dyads were randomly assigned to one of the two experimental conditions. Sessions were held in two private laboratory spaces. Both spaces and conditions maintained the same spatial setup. Subjects received a 5-minute introduction on phylogenetics before the study task. Upon completion of the Phylo-Genie activity, participants individually filled out three post-task questionnaires: the NASA-TLX (a measure of the users' workload [24]), standard engagement questionnaire [35] and a test on phylogenetics (written by the same professor whose teaching materials were used to construct our learning activity). The session concluded with a short debriefing and the participants received $10 for their participation. Each session lasted approximately 60 minutes. All sessions were videotaped and observed by a researcher.

Paper Activity

The paper implementation of our learning scenario is identical to the tabletop implementation and contains similar stages and tasks. Instead of interactive screens users proceed through the pages of a booklet. Table 1 shows the differences between experimental conditions. The workspace was the same in both conditions. The display size in the paper condition was constrained to 8" x 11" pieces of paper; however, relative image and font sizes were consistent across conditions. Users accessed information by flipping pages of the booklet. In addition they built phylogenetic trees via traditional material (pen and paper).

	Paper	Tabletop
Workspace	42"	42"
Display size	8"	30"
Display orientation	Horizontal	Horizontal
Interaction style	Bimanual, multiple users	Multi-touch
Input	Direct	Direct
Tangible Interaction	No	Yes
Tutorials	Paper	Video

Table 1. Differences across experimental conditions.

Results

Learning Performance

We assigned a score on a scale of 0 to 100 to each subject's test based on the correctness of their answers (see Figure 6). We did not use a pre-test since none of our participants had received college-level instruction in phylogenetics. A between-subjects ANOVA of the learning performances from the two conditions showed that the subjects in the tabletop condition (mean = 90.3, SD = 11.3) obtained statistically significantly higher scores on the test than those in paper condition (Mean = 78.6 and SD = 15.8): $F(1,54) = 10.11$, $p = 0.002$.

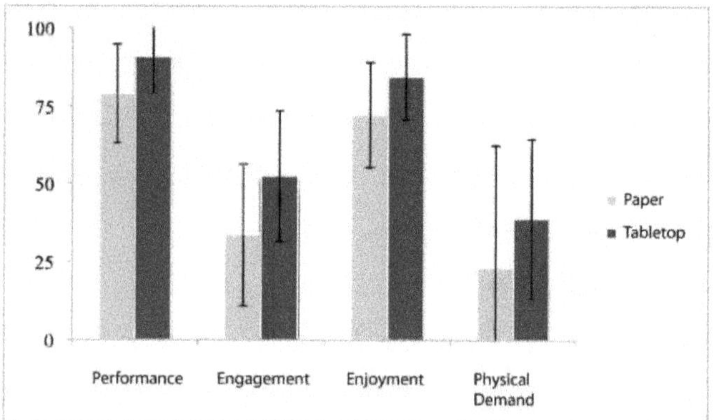

Figure 6. Average ratings of overall attitude measures and performance

Engagement

Using a five-step bipolar scale, participants gave a score from -2 to 2 on 56 questions adapted from O'Brien's measures of engagement [35]. This provides an estimate of users' engagement by aggregating answers on the following dimensions: focused attention, perceived usability, aesthetics, endurability, novelty and involvement. Ratings were normalized to a percentage out of 100 (Figure 6).

Overall, participants rated the task as being more engaging in the tabletop condition compared to the paper condition ($F(1,54) = 10.31$, $p = 0.002$). More specifically, participants gave higher ratings for the following factors: *Felt Involvement* - "how much fun users' were having during the interaction and how drawn in they were able to become" ($F(1,54) = 11.84$, $p = 0.001$), *Endurability* - "assessment of users' perception of success with a task, and their willingness to use an application in future or recommend it to others" ($F(1,54) = 5.14$, $p = 0.027$) and *Aesthetics* ($F(1,54) = 45.65$, $p < 0.001$). Finally, it should be noted that the difference in engagement was not influenced by a novelty effect ($F(1,54) = 2.08$, $p = 0.16$). Ensuring that subjects did not learn only because they were intrigued by the novelty of the interface is important.

Task Load

Task load was measured using a questionnaire adapted from Hart et al.'s NASA-TLX [24]. Using a twenty-step bipolar scale, participants gave ratings from 0 to 100 for each item of the questionnaire. A between subjects ANOVA of the task load's sub-dimensions indicate statistically significantly higher ratings of Engagement and Enjoyment on the tabletop condition ($F(1,54) = 10.31$, $p = 0.0022$ and $F(1,54) = 8.77$, $p = 0.0045$ respectively). Physical demand was also found to be significantly higher in the tabletop condition ($F(1,54) = 6.38$, $p = 0.015$). This is probably because questions of this dimension were formulated in terms of computer interface and not pen and paper activity (e.g. "How much physical activity was required (e.g. pointing, typing, pressing, turning, dragging, rotating)?"). It should be noted that questions from other dimensions were formulated in more general terms.

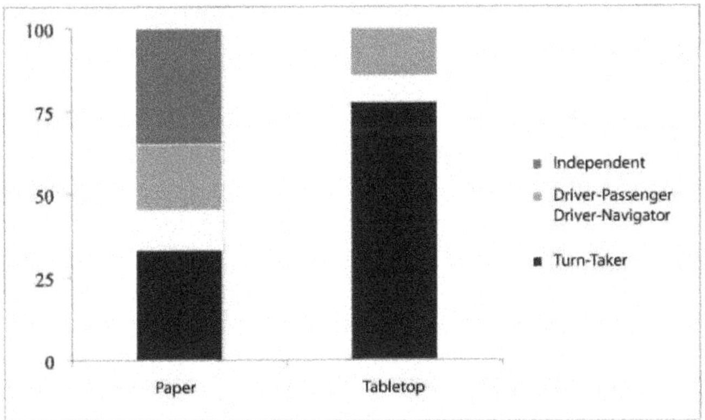

Figure 7. Average collaboration profile relative to total task stages.

Collaboration

Based on the collaboration profiles developed by Shaer et al. [45] we coded each dyad at each stage of the task, for nine total ratings per pair. A second judge double-coded 20% of the data; inter-reliability index using Krippendorff's alpha was 91%. An alpha higher than 80% is considered as a reliable agreement between judges [25]. Categories are defined as follows:

- Independent: users are absorbed in their own activity; there is a minimal verbal communication.
- Driver-Passenger: the driver is fully engaged; the passenger is not focused on the task.
- Driver-Navigator: both users are engaged. The navigator contributes with suggestions and observations.
- Turn-Taker: both users make and accept suggestions and observations.

The results of the average collaboration profile relative to the total number of task stages are shown in Figure 7.

Analysis of the profiles by total stages reveals the dyads in the paper condition were classified as Turn-Taker in only 33% of the stages in comparison to 78% for those assigned to the tabletop. Furthermore, an average 37% of the stages were classified as Independent in the paper condition in comparison to 0% of stages in the tabletop condition.

We further analyzed dyadic collaboration using the rating scheme developed by Meier et al. [31]. Each subject pair was assigned post-task a rating from -2 to 2 in nine process dimensions. Inter-reliability index using Krippendorff's alpha was 83% [25]. Figure 8 shows the results of the five aspects (aggregated from the nine process dimensions) of overall collaboration.

A between subject ANOVA of the overall measures revealed that the collaboration aspects of Dialogue management, Information Pooling, Technical Coordination, and Individual Task Orientation were all statistically significantly higher in the tabletop condition ($F(1,26) = 3.91$, $p = 0.0254$; $F(1,26) = 10.46$, $p = 0.0033$; $F(1,26) = 12.61$, $p = 0.0015$; $F(1,26) = 7.93$, $p = 0.0091$ respectively).

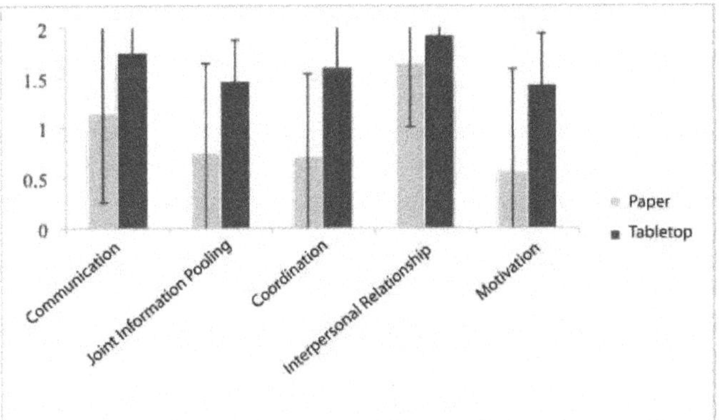

Figure 8. Average overall collaboration ratings by type.

It means that users in the tabletop condition had a smoother flow of communication (e.g. where turn-taking was facilitated by small questions like 'what do you think?'), they tried more intensively to collect and share pieces of information and better coordinated themselves. For instance, where participants in the paper activity tended to silently read the instructions, users in the tabletop condition actively shared information and spent more time discussing the best way to solve the problem at hand.

Mediatory Effect of Collaboration and Engagement on Learning

We conducted a mediation analysis [38] to isolate the factors associated with positive learning gains (see Figure 9). A mediation model assumes the existence of one or several variables (called "mediators") between the dependent (DV) and independent measure (IV). A meditational model assumes that the IV causes the mediator variable, which in turns causes the DV. Confidence intervals containing zero are interpreted as not significant; in other words, non-significant results mean that there are no causal relationships between the IV, the mediator and the DV. Our results show that a strong collaboration acts as a mediator between the two conditions and learning (CI:[0.074,5.95]), while engagement (CI:[-3.85,6.31]) and cognitive load (CI:[-0.66,5.54]) do not. If we consider collaboration as a dependent variable, our analysis shows that engagement acts as a positive mediator for an efficient collaboration (CI: [-0.75,-0.067]).

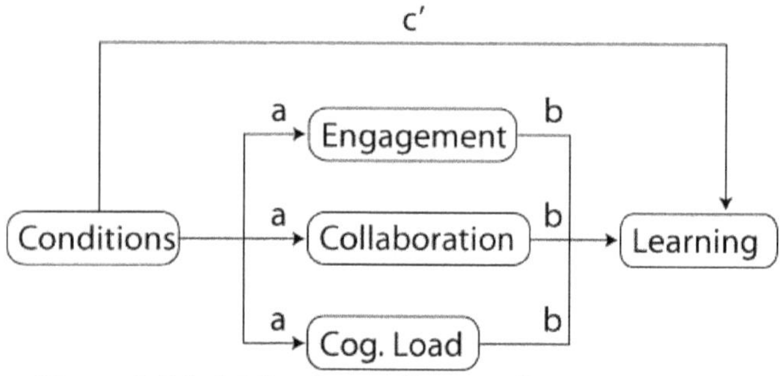

Figure 9. Model for the mediatory effects. Our results show that in our study only collaboration acts as a mediator for learning.

DISCUSSION

In this study we examined the similarities and differences of the two implementations in terms of quantitative performance and qualitative behavior. Our results suggest that our proposed design guidelines promoted a deeper understanding of phylogenetics.

More specifically, four guidelines shaped the design of our system: firstly, we focused on developing an activity that engaged and motivated students. Interactive technology helped reach this goal. We created rich and viscerally compelling contents that were not available in paper format (e.g. immersive videos, interactive contents, animated tutorials). The engagement questionnaire suggests that students felt more involved, viewed the learning experience more successful, and rated the task as being more aesthetic. Secondly, we supported collaboration through physical tokens and tabletop implementation embodying the main actors of this scenario. The goal was to reinforce users' ownership of both physical objects and areas on the interactive surface. We interpret the more balanced division of labor between users as an indirect evidence for this hypothesis: in the tabletop implementation, participants took more turns and spent more time collaborating (e.g. pooling information, coordinating activities) rather than working independently. The results are supported by other studies showing that territoriality plays an important role in tangible learning environments [27,44]. Thirdly, we dedicated a significant part of the learning activity for students to reflect on the content. Even though the paper activity also offered this opportunity, we argue that switching from a very active role (interacting with physical tokens on a multi-touch surface) to a more reflective stage (articulating discoveries as formal concepts) provided better opportunities for understanding and refining phylogenetic concepts. Fourthly, we tried to provide a sense of control and autonomy to our participants by building automatic feedback and scaffolding in our activity. Although we did not device any measures for this dimension, we believe that this principle played a major role in the learning process; in traditional classrooms, students often have a passive role and depend on the teachers for advancing in the domain taught. In Phylo-Genie, users control the pace of the activity and decide when to move to the next step without any social pressure. Future studies should develop metrics to measure this construct and investigate how it helped students' learning.

In summary, the four guidelines helped develop a strong learning activity. Additionally, we observed that the learning process took an indirect path. The mediation analyses revealed that collaboration was the strongest factor in supporting knowledge-building and that engagement acted as mediator for a productive collaboration. Thus, Phylo-Genie succeeded in supporting learning by increasing users' collaboration, which in turn was improved by a high engagement. It suggests that interactive environments can and should support learning in very diverse ways.

Limitations

There is one concern in using new technologies for education: a novelty effect may be responsible for the learning gain observed (e.g. students are more involved because they are intrigued by the interface). The main issue is that a novelty effect fades over time and brings the learning gain to the same level as with regular activities. Our results suggest that this is not the case for our system. More specifically, the "Novelty" dimension of the engagement questionnaire was not found to be significantly different across conditions. However, future studies should investigate this issue by using longitudinal measures.

This study has limitations: first, we did not take into account users' preconceptions; we assumed that the diversity of their pre-existing knowledge would be randomly distributed across both conditions. Future studies should better control for this dimension. Moreover, our evaluation of participants' knowledge only considered a few phylogenetic concepts and did not address the breadth and richness of evolutionary theory. In addition to assess students' knowledge more completely, future studies should investigate whether discovery learning activities on tabletops improves students' transfer of knowledge (e.g. in situations that seem different from our activity but share the deep structure of the base concept [18]).

CONCLUSIONS AND FUTURE WORK

While the domain of phylogenetics provides the frame for this work, this research makes four contributions to HCI in general and to tabletop interaction in particular: 1) we identify requirements and design principles for fostering collaborative learning through tabletop interaction; 2) we designed and implemented an interactive system, Phylo-Genie, which employs multi-touch and tangible interaction techniques to support the learning of college-level phylogeny; 3) we present findings from an experimental study that show that Phylo-Genie promotes engagement, collaboration, and learning to a greater extent than traditional learning tools (i.e. pen and paper); 4) we discuss implications for the design of tabletop user interfaces for promoting collaborative learning.

Future studies should explore the benefits of tabletops combining multi-touch and tangible interaction for longitudinal and less structured tasks and observe how students' thinking is impacted over longer periods of time.. Moreover, we plan to expand and explore Phylo-Genie's functionality to further support tree building and engagement in science learning through continued collaborations with domain scientists. We also intend to integrate Phylo-Genie into undergraduate biology courses for longitudinal measures of learning.

ACKNOWLEDGMENTS

Special thanks go to Professor Jonathan Losos (Organismic and Evolutionary Biology, Harvard University) whose teaching and exam materials were used as part of our learning activity. We thank our science advisors Hopi Hoekstra from the Department of Organismic and Evolutionary Biology at Harvard University, Andrea Sequiera and Emily Buchholtz from the Department of of Biological Sciences at Wellesley College. We also thank students Courtney Stepian from the Committee on Evolutionary Biology at University of Chicago, and Harriet Alexander from the WHOI program at Massachusetts Institute of Technology. This work was partially support by a grant from the Encyclopedia of Life Learning + Education group (http://education.eol.org/) and the Museum of Comparative Zoology at Harvard University. Finally, we thank the instructors and students that participated in our study.

REFERENCES

1. Ado, L. Ahmet, Z., Jonsson, M., Sumon, S.I., and Holmquist, L.E. Supporting embodied exploration of physical concepts in mixed digital and physical interactive settings. In *Proc. TEI '11.*

2. Anderson, M. L. Embodied cognition: A field guide. *Artificial Intelligence 149, 1* (2003), 91–130.

3. Antle, A.N., Bevans, A., Tanenbaum, J., Seaborn, K., and Wang, S. Futura: design for collaborative learning and game play on a multi-touch digital tabletop. In *Proc. TEI '11.*

4. Antle, A.N., Droumeva, M., and Ha, D. Hands on what?: comparing children's mouse-based and tangible-based interaction. In *Proc. IDC '09.*

5. Baum, D.A., Smith, S.D., and Donovan, S.S. The Tree-Thinking challenge. *Science 310, 5750* (2005), 979 –980.

6. Beeland, W.D. Student engagement, visual learning and technology: Can interactive whiteboards help. In *Annu Conf of the Assoc of IT for Teaching Edu '02.*

7. Bolchini, D., Finkelstein, A., Perrone, V., and Nagl, S. Better bioinformatics through usability analysis. *Bioinformatics 25*, 3 (2009), 406 –412.

8. Carini, R.M., Kuh, G.D., and Klein, S.P. Student engagement and student learning: Testing the linkages*. *Research in Higher Education 47, 1* (2006), 1–32.

9. Catley, K.M., and Novick, L.R. Seeing the wood for the trees: An analysis of evolutionary diagrams in biology textbooks. *BioScience 58, 10* (2008), 976.

10. Catley, K.M., and Novick, L.R. Digging deep: Exploring college students' knowledge of macroevolutionary time. *J of Research in Science Teaching 46, 3* (2009), 311–332.

11. Clement, J. The use of analogies and anchoring intuitions to remediate misconceptions in mechanics. (1987).

12. Clements, D.H. 'Concrete' Manipulatives, concrete ideas. *Contemporary Issues in Early Childhood 1, 1* (2000), 4560.

13. Corno, L., and Mandinach, E. The role of cognitive engagement in classroom learning and motivation. *Educational Psychologist 18, 2* (1983), 88–108.

14. Dillenbourg, P., Baker, M., Blaye, A., and O'Malley, C. The evolution of research on collaborative learning. In *E. Spada & P. Reiman (Eds) Learning in Humans and Machine: Towards an interdisciplinary learning science.* (1995), 189–211.

15. Evans, E.M., Spiegel, A.N., Gram, W., Frazier, B.N., Tare, M., Thompson, S., and Diamond, J. A conceptual guide to natural history museum visitors' understanding of evolution. *Journal of Research in Science Teaching 47, 3* (2010), 326–353.

16. Fjeld, M., Fredriksson, J., Ejdestig, M., Duca, F., Boetschi, K., Voegtli, B., and Juchli, P. Tangible user interface for chemistry education: comparative evaluation and re-design. In *Proc. CHI '07.*

17. Fleck, R., Rogers, Y., Yuill, N., Marshall, P., Carr, A., Rick, J., and Bonnett, V. Actions speak loudly with words: unpacking collaboration around the table. In *Proc. ITS '09.*

18. Gick, M.L., and Holyoak, K.J. Schema induction and analogical transfer. *Cognitive Psychology 15, 1* (1983), 1–38.

19.Gillet, A., Sanner, M., Stoffler, D., Goodsell, D., and Olson, A. Augmented reality with tangible Auto-Fabricated models for molecular biology applications. In *Proc. IEEE Visualization Conference '04.*

20.Glaeser, T., Franke, J., Wintergerst, G., and Jagodzinski, R. Chemieraum: tangible chemistry in exhibition space. In *Proc. TEI '09.*

21.Gregory, T. R. Understanding evolutionary trees. *Evolution: Education and Outreach 1, 2* (2008), 121–137.

22.Halverson, K. L. Improving Tree-Thinking one learnable skill at a time. *Evolution: Educ and Outreach 4, 1* (2011), 95–106.

23.Harris, A., Rick, J., Bonnett, V., Yuill, N., Fleck, R., Marshall, P., and Rogers, Y. Around the table: are multiple-touch surfaces better than single-touch for children's collaborative interactions? *Proc. CSCL '09.*

24.Hart, S., and Staveland, L. Development of NASA-TLX (Task load index): Results of empirical and theoretical research. *In Advances in Psychology, 52* (1988), 139–183.

25.Hayes, A.F. and Krippendorff, K. Answering the Call for a Standard Reliability Measure for Coding Data. *Communication Methods and Measures 1*, (2007), 77-89.

26.Horn, M. S., Tobiasz, M., and Shen, C. Visualizing biodiversity with voronoi treemaps. In Proc. *IEEE Symposium on Voronoi Diagrams in Science and Engineering '09,* 265–270.

27.Jermann, P., Zufferey, G., Schneider, B., Lucci, A., Lepine, S., and Dillenbourg, P. Physical space and division of labor around a tabletop tangible simulation. In *Proc. CSCL '09.*

28.Larkin MA, Blackshields G, Brown NP, Chenna R, McGettigan PA, McWilliam H, Valentin F, Wallace IM, Wilm A, Lopez R, Thompson JD, Gibson TJ, Higgins DG.(2007). Clustal W and Clustal X 2.0. *Bioinformatics, 23*, 2947-2948.

29.Lou, Y., Abrami, P. C., and d'Apollonia, S. Small group and individual learning with technology: A Meta-Analysis. *Review of Educational Research 71*, 3 (2001), 449–521.

30. Maddison, W.P., Maddison, D.R. Mesquite: A modular system for evolutionary analysis. *Evolution 62,* 5 (2005), 1103-1118.

31.Meier, A., Spada, H., and Rummel, N. A rating scheme for assessing the quality of computer-supported collaboration processes. *J of CSCL 2, 1* (2007), 63–86.

32.Meir, E., Perry, J., Herron, J. C., and Kingsolver, J. College students' misconceptions about evolutionary trees. *The American Biology Teacher 69*, 7 (2007), e71–e76.

33.Novick, L. R., and Catley, K. M. Understanding phylogenies in biology: The influence of a gestalt perceptual principle. *Journal of Experimental Psychology: Applied 13*, 4 (2007), 197–223.

34.Novick, L. R., Shade, C. K., and Catley, K. M. Linear versus branching depictions of evolutionary history: Implications for diagram design. *Topics in Cog. Sci. 3*, 3 (2011), 536–559.

35.O'Brien, H. L., Toms, E. G., Kelloway, E. K., and Kelley, E. Developing and evaluating a reliable measure of user engagement. *Proc. American Soc. for IS&T 45*, 1 (2008), 1–10.

36.Piaget, J. *The language and thought of the child.* Psychology Press, 1998.

37.Piper, A.M., and Hollan, J.D. Tabletop displays for small group study: affordances of paper and digital materials. In *Proc. CHI '09.*

38.Preacher, K. J., and Hayes, A. F. Asymptotic and resampling strategies for assessing and comparing indirect effects in multiple mediator models. *Behavior Research Methods 40*, 3 (2008), 879.

39.Roschelle, J., Tatar, D., Chaudbury, S. R., Dimitriadis, Y., Patton, C., and DiGiano, C. Ink, improvisation, and interactive engagement: Learning with tablets. *Computer 40, 9* (2007), 42–48.

40.Salomon, G., and Globerson, T. When teams do not function the way they ought to. *J of Educ Research 13*, 1 (1989), 89–99.

41.Sandvik, H. Tree thinking cannot be taken for granted: challenges for teaching phylogenetics. *Theory in Biosciences 127,* 1 (2008), 45–51.

42.Schkolne, S., Ishii, H., and Schroeder, P. Immersive design of DNA molecules with a tangible interface. In *Proc. IEEE Visualization Conference '04.*

43.Schneider, B., Jermann, P., Zufferey, G., and Dillenbourg, P. Benefits of a tangible interface for collaborative learning and interaction. *IEEE Trans.on Learning Technologies PP, 99,* 1–1.

44.Scott, S.D., Sheelagh, M., Carpendale, T., and Inkpen, K.M. Territoriality in collaborative tabletop workspaces. *Proc. CSCW '04.*

45.Shaer, O., Kol, G., Strait, M., Fan, C., Grevet, C., and Elfenbein, S. G-nome surfer: a tabletop interface for collaborative exploration of genomic data. In *Proc.* CHI '10.

46.Shaer, O., Strait, M., Valdes, C., Feng, T., Lintz, M., and Wang, H. Enhancing genomic learning through tabletop interaction. In *Proc. CHI '11.*

47.Smith, J., diSessa, A., and Roschelle, J. Misconceptions reconceived: A constructivist analysis of knowledge in transition. *J. of the Learning Sciences 3*, 2 (1994), 115–163.

48.Matuk, C.F. *Animated cladograms: Interpreting evolution from diagrams.* In: G. Stapleton, J. Howse, and J. Lee, (Eds.) Diagrams 2008 - Diagrammatic Representation and Inference - 5th International Conference 2008, 395-397.

49.Vygotskil, L. S. *Mind in society: the development of higher psychological processes.* Harvard University Press, 1978.

50.Wallach V. A cladistic analysis of the terrestrial Australian elapidae. In: Grigg G, Shine R,Ehmann H, eds. *Biology of the Australasian Frogs and Reptiles.* Sydney: Surrey Beatty and Sons, 223–253, 1985

The Impact of Communication Structure on New Product Development Outcomes

Marcelo Cataldo
Carnegie Mellon University
Pittsburgh, PA, USA
mcataldo@cs.cmu.edu

Kate Ehrlich
IBM Research
Cambridge, MA, USA
katee@us.ibm.com

ABSTRACT
New product development teams face important challenges to their performance due to the novelty of the work and the need to rapidly develop shared knowledge and goals. However, little is known about the relationship between the structural properties of communication and performance in these teams. This study examined the effect of communication structure, specifically hierarchical and small-world structures on the delivery performance and quality outcomes of a large-scale new product development project. Our longitudinal analyses revealed that structuring communication patterns in a hierarchical manner significantly improves delivery performance. However, hierarchical communication has a detrimental effect on quality while small-world communication structures improved the quality outcomes of development teams. We discuss the implications of these results for collaborative tools that support communication tradeoffs.

Author Keywords
Communication; New Product Development; Hierarchy; Small-World Networks; Social Network Analysis.

ACM Classification Keywords
H.5.3 [Group and Organization Interfaces]: Asynchronous Communication, Computer-supported Cooperative Work;

General Terms
Human Factors, Management, Measurement, Performance.

INTRODUCTION
Informal communication is a topic of long standing for project performance in product development teams [1, 6, 22]. As projects become geographically dispersed [9, 31, 32], communication as well as coordination and awareness can be impeded by the spatial and temporal barriers [17, 34], adversely impacting project productivity and quality outcomes [32, 35].

New product development (NPD) teams face additional challenges to their performance as a result of the novelty of the work, and new designs and processes [30]. Moreover, the need to ensure that the innovations are successful can result in different patterns of communication than for more routine or well-understood tasks [16, 40]. Research has established that team performance is associated with communication structure [27]. However, these studies have not addressed NPD issues and have been mostly cross-sectional., Further, ample evidence exists that interaction patterns evolve over the life cycle of a project (e.g. [1, 10, 16]).

The current study seeks to extend existing research on the effect of informal communication on performance, to new product development teams. We examined the effect of communication structure – specifically hierarchical and small-world structures – on: (a) planning and its execution and (b) the quality of the outcomes, in NPD projects. We depart from previous studies using surveys or retrospective reports, by relying on analysis of communication traces from to tasks performed in the project, collected as the work was being done in order to examine communication over time rather than at a particular snapshot.

Our work makes two valuable contributions to the new product development and CHI/CSCW literatures. Firstly, by examining the impact of communication structure on two distinct aspects of new product development performance, planning and quality, we begin to address the question of whether it is sufficient for a team to evolve a single communication structure or whether teams need to become more adept at trading off between communication styles. Secondly, we shed light on how the structure of informal communication evolves over the life cycle of new product development projects and how those patterns impact those projects, particularly geographically distributed ones.

The rest of the document is organized as follows. We first discuss the theoretical background leading to our hypotheses. Then, we describe the research setting and our empirical design followed by a discussion of the results. We conclude with a discussion of limitations of our study and the implications of our results for future research and tools.

INFORMAL COMMUNICATION AND OUTCOMES IN NEW PRODUCT DEVELOPMENT

In product development, project success or performance is often measured by outcomes such as product quality, time, cost and customer-oriented metrics [39]. When development projects focus on one outcome, e.g. high product quality, they face the need to make trade-offs in project length or functionality in order to deliver it on time [31, 39]. A key question for researchers and practitioners alike is whether it is in fact necessary for new product development (NPD) projects to trade one outcome for others, for instance, can projects achieve high levels of quality without impacting or minimally impacting product delivery plans? Research results are ambivalent in this regard. On the one hand, recent research showed that reducing defects and rework improves quality [24] suggesting that both quality and time could be optimized together. On the other hand, studies of geographically distributed software development projects has shown that team configurations that produce above average quality outcomes are different from those team configurations that exhibit high levels of productivity [13, 35].

One critical driver of new product development outcomes, is informal communication [6]. Most early research focused on the general aspects of communication within a project team such as adequate interaction among the key members or departments involved in the project and between the projects and external stakeholders [2, 6, 28, 38]. More recent work showed that the general patterns of interaction resemble the structure of the product being developed [37]. However, limited attention has been given to the relationship between the specific structural properties of the communication networks and different outcomes of NPD projects. Work in the areas of geographically distributed project teams and innovation suggests two particular communication structures that have been linked to project success: hierarchies and small-world networks [27, 40].

Hierarchical communication networks emphasize efficiency of information. In the context of communication networks, hierarchy considers the extent to which team communication flows outward from one person or a small group without flowing back [29]. Small-world networks are characterized by small densely interconnected groups of individuals which are themselves loosely interconnected through a small number of people. Unlike hierarchical networks, small-world networks emphasize the richness of the information exchange through the dense and redundant paths that link individuals. In this paper, we examine the impact of these two types of communications structures on two distinct outcomes of NPD projects: delivery performance and quality.

The Role of Communication in Delivery Performance

Delivery performance refers to planning development activities and executions of such plans in order to complete the tasks on time, and ultimately, deliver the final product on time. Poor delivery performance may have significant implications in a development organization such as failing to meet customer expectations, impact release of interdependent products and efficiently manage development resources. NPD teams face the challenge of structuring their communication across the various phases of the development process so that team members are well informed and engaged while the amount of communication required does not interferes with finishing the work in time.

Hierarchy

By centralizing communication responsibility to a few individuals, hierarchical structures can reduce the cost of establishing and maintaining communication particularly, in the context of geographically distributed teams [27]. Then, hierarchical communication may be especially well suited to the operational aspects of new product development by enabling efficient distribution of the relevant information to the team members who carry out the tasks.

> *H1a: NPD teams that have evolved a hierarchical communication structure will exhibit better delivery performance than those teams, which do not have that communication structure*

Small-World Communication

On the other hand, small-world communication structures are an important source of shared knowledge, collaborative efforts and innovation [40], factors of particular importance in new product development. However, considering the work involved in carrying out a set of development tasks, having communication clustered in several small, closely knit groups is likely to be detrimental to getting the work communicated, understood by the relevant people and, consequently, completed on time. Firstly, dense communication patterns can increase the amount of time spent on interactions, which can impact the time available for the work. Secondly, it moves communication away from project and technical leads who have responsibility for directing the work. Thirdly, it reduces the consistency of communication and messages to the whole team by reducing the role and voice of the project and technical leads.

> *H1b: NPD teams that have evolved a small-world communication structure will exhibit poorer delivery performance than teams, which do not have that communication structure*

The Role of Communication in Quality Outcomes

The quality of the outcomes is also a key factor in product development teams. Quality relates to the capabilities of the product development team to identify, integrate and bring to bear the right knowledge and information to make the right design or implementation decisions such that defects and mistakes are minimized [12, 19]. Despite the potential benefits of lean and efficient ways of conveying information there are important challenges associated with integrating, and leveraging such information in the context of novel development tasks [3]. Project members might struggle to make sense of new knowledge and effectively integrate it into the relevant context because of differences in perspectives, lack of common understandings and lack of familiarity working together [5]. Failure to adequately make sense of the knowledge and information can result, for instance, in unidentified dependencies, which lead to coordination breakdowns and ultimately, lower product quality [12, 26].

Hierarchy

Hierarchical communication centralizes communication to a few individuals, which reduces the amount of communication amongst people at the same level of the hierarchy. Lower levels of communication are associated with higher levels of coordination breakdowns [18] which ultimately results in poorer quality [26].

> *H2a: NPD teams that have evolved a hierarchical communication structure will exhibit poorer quality outcomes than teams, which do not have that communication structure.*

Small-World Communication

Small world communication structures may be especially well suited to development tasks, such as the need to coordinate the development of a crosscutting product feature, that are challenging and highly interdependent The richness of the communication makes it more likely for those people to share similar attitudes and norms and to trust each other and have strong relationships [7]. These commonalities may help reduce team problems due to miscommunication and conflict especially in distributed teams. They also make members more likely to give each other preferential access to important resources and knowledge, consider each other's information, integrated knowledge, and combine information effectively when making decisions [7, 40].

> *H2b: NPD teams that have evolved a small-world communication structure will exhibit better quality outcomes than teams, which do not have that communication structure*

RESEARCH SETTING

We examined the proposed hypotheses on data collected from the development of the first release of the Jazz software development environment on which the IBM[R] Rational[R] Team Concert[TM] (RTC) products are based[1]. Jazz is a development environment designed to make product development more collaborative through integration of information and tasks across the phases of the lifecycle [20]. RTC itself was developed using the Jazz environment; IBM made the data from project's software repositories for the first release available to us.

[1] IBM, the IBM logo, ibm.com, and Rational are trademarks or registered trademarks of International Business Machines Corporation in the United States, other countries, or both

Development activities started as early as May 2006. However, we focused our analysis on the 13 months prior to the release of the product's first version, which was the period of time between July 2007 and August of 2008 which corresponded to the main development period. A total of 161 developers, worked full time on the project during the period analyzed. There were 26 functional teams distributed in 21 different sites across U.S., Canada and Europe. Each team planned its own development work for the next iteration during the first week of the iteration and iterations began and ended at the same time for all teams. There were 14 iterations during the time covered by our data. See [19] for additional details.

Description of the Measures

In addition to the data from the software repositories, we also collected information about the project member's location from personnel records and conducted semi-structured interviews with 4 developers who were members of the project throughout the development, to validate our assumptions about the interpretation of the measures. The rest of the section is organized as follows. First, we describe our outcome measures. Second, we describe how we captured the interaction patterns as well as measures to assess the hierarchical and "small-worldness" nature of those communication networks.

Measuring Delivery Performance

In order to examine the role of the structure of communication patterns, we chose the pair <iteration, team> as the unit of analysis for our study. We measured *Delivery Performance* of an iteration as the number of tasks that were planned for the <iteration, team> pair but were rescheduled to the following iteration because they were not completed. This measure focuses on how well the team members that participated in the iteration were able to execute the planned set of activities as well as capturing aspects of the development process such as adequate planning and adequate handling of unexpected situations. Interviews confirmed that rescheduling was an adequate measure since it was an integral part of the development process. As one inteviewee said, "inevitably things didn't fit and then we moved them" referring to moving work items to the next iteration.

Measuring Quality

In order to assess the quality outcomes of an iteration, we examined the defects reported in each iteration with the following procedure. For a given iteration i_t, we first selected all the defects reported in the following iteration i_{t+1}. Our measure of *Quality* captured the number of defects that either impacted components changed during iteration i_t and took 1 or more days to get resolved or impacted components not changed in iteration i_t nor in iteration i_{t+1}. We validated this measure by analyzing a random sample of 527 defects corresponding to 10% of all the defects across all 14 iterations. We inspected the reports of those defects in order to understand if there were indicators that could assist us in the process of linking a defect to the iteration that introduced it. The analysis revealed that many defects consisted of work items that were created and resolved in a matter of hours. The comments in the reports suggested that there were issues found while working on other development tasks and the defects were blocking the other activities so they were resolved quickly but limited information existed to link the defect to prior changes in the source code except for the information about what files were changed.

Construction of the Communication Network

The RTC development environment has features that provides project members with contextualized interaction for work items. These interactions took the form of comments in a work item report and were stored in the tool's database, allowing us to identify the work items, the individuals that made the comment(s) as well as the content of the comment. A stated goal of the project was to make the development as transparent as possible to outsiders as well as internally, which led developers to use comments as the main channel of communication even with collocated colleagues. Moreover, good tracking reinforced developers' preference to use comments over other forms of interaction.

We constructed iteration-level communication networks as follows, We considered only those comments made in the work item reports that were within the time frame of the iteration. The first comment in the work item linked the person that made the comment with the owner of the task at the time the comment as made. If the owner and the commenter were the same person, the link was ignored. For the subsequent comments in the work item report, a link in the communication network between two project members was made if the comments were adjacent in the sequence of comments and they were associated with the task at hand. These comments also resulted in a link between the commenter and the owner of the work item at the time it was made. Additional details of the construction of the networks can be found in our previous work [19].

Measuring Hierarchical Communication Patterns

We computed the *Hierarchical Communication Pattern* measure based on the hierarchy metric proposed by Krackhardt [29]. Network hierarchy measures the direction of flow in the network. Krackhardt's approach counts the number of times there is a path from a node in the network to another but not a path back. In order for this measure to be computed, we consider the communication network as a dichotomous directed graph. We used the ORA tool [8] to compute the measure. There are other approaches to measure a central communication structure. A more traditional approach would have been to consider network centralization, which captures the extent to which one or a few individuals are highly connected to the rest of the individuals in the network. Although network centralization and network hierarchy share some similarities, as discussed by Hinds and McGrath [27], the two measures refer to two distinct constructs. Mainly, hierarchical network captures the flow of information. Furthermore, a network in which communication is centralized is not necessarily hierarchical because communication could be reciprocal between the central individuals and those in the periphery. On the other hand, hierarchical networks might not be centralized since information could be delivered through multiple nodes without reciprocal links.

Measuring Small-World Communication Patterns

Small world networks are those characterized by short average path lengths among any pair of nodes and high levels of a clustering coefficient [42]. Watts and Strogatz [42] proposed such a definition by comparing a class of networks to Erdos-Renyi random graphs. Then, establishing that a network is a "small world" requires a comparison between the focal network and random graphs. In order to measure the "small worldness" of our communication networks, we build on the approach proposed by Uzzi and Spiro [40] which is based on Watts and Strogatz's method [42] and utilizes two separate metrics: the clustering coefficient ratio (CC ratio) and path length ratio (APL ratio). Both ratios are determined by comparing the clustering coefficient and the average path length measures of our communication networks against the corresponding measures computed from random graphs with the same number of nodes and density. We computed 100 random graphs and then computed the average clustering coefficient and path length measures across those 100 graphs. Those averages were used in the comparison to the communication network metrics. The computation of the network metrics was done using the ORA tool. Once the clustering coefficient and average path length ratios were computed, the *Small World Communication Pattern* variable was calculated as *CC ratio* ÷ A*PL ratio* as proposed in Uzzi and Spiro [40].

Additional Control Factors

Past research work suggests a wide range of factors that may impact outcomes such as performance and quality in software development (e.g. [5, 12, 25]). We organized our control variables into five groups:

<u>*Controls for team-related factors*</u>: We computed several measures that capture attributes of the teams we studied. Since comments on work items associated with a pair (iteration *i*, team *t*) could also come from people outside the team we computed two measures: *Number of Project Members Involved* captures the total of team and non-team members that participated in the work associated with each pair (iteration, team) and *Number of Multi-Team Project Members* captures the subset of those individuals that were part of more than one formal team.

The project involved engineers in 21 different development locations, so geographical dispersion may play an important role in terms of communication and, consequently, in terms of delivery iteration performance and software quality. *GSD* is a dichotomous variable where 1 indicates that the project members involved in the work associated with a pair (iteration, team) were geographically distributed; otherwise it was set to 0.

We collected measures of experience based on the work by Boh and colleagues [5], which utilize the data in software repositories as the basis for assessing experience. We measured *Average Level of Technical Experience* as the average number of work items that the team member worked on prior to the focal iteration. Unfortunately, we did not have access to data to capture experience levels prior to the Jazz project. *Average Level of Shared-work Experience* measures the average number of times that team members worked together in work items prior to the beginning of the focal iteration. Finally, we measured *Average Level of Team Workload* as the average number of work items owned per team member during the iteration.

Controls for communication-related factors: Since our independent measures focus on patterns of communication, it is important to control for factors related to the propensity of the project member to communicate more or less with other project members or with particular project members. We also computed two measures that captured the project member's amount of interaction at the dyad level. *Amount of Intra-Team Communication* captured the number of dyads from the communication networks where both members belonged to the same team. On the other hand, *Amount of Inter-Team Communication* captured the number of dyads where at least one of the persons in the pair also belonged to a different team. However, a variance inflation factor revealed that the amount of intra-team communication measure was collinear with other control factors so we did not include it in our analysis.

Controls for task-related factors: Since iterations vary in the amount of work they generate and in the importance of the work, we measured the *Ratio of High Priority Work Items* that each team faced in each iteration as well as the *Average Size of Work Items* as the average number of files modified in the commits associated with the work items.

Controls for technical-related factors: Past work has shown that the technical dependencies that exist among the technical elements of a system under development are an important driver of dependencies among development tasks and consequently, of interaction among interdependent project members (e.g. [14, 37]. Building on past work [13] on the effect of technical dependencies on quality, we constructed an iteration-wide matrix containing the technical dependencies among system's components based on the commit information associated with the work items. Since the ownership of each architectural component was allocated to a single team, teams defined a relevant technical boundary. We combined such information with the dependency matrices to construct control measures that capture the nature of the project's technical dependencies. The *Internal Technical Coupling* measure refers to the density of the sub-matrix based on the set of relationships defined in the technical dependencies matrix that are contained within a team's area of responsibility. *External Technical Coupling* was operationalized as the number of components not under the responsibility of the focal team that had technical dependencies with those components changed by the focal team.

Controls for unobserved effects: Finally, we included a few additional controls for unobserved, team- and iteration-specific factors. These dummy variables effectively control for any factors, which we could not explicitly measure such as the cultural or organization aspects of the teams as well as temporal effects of the iterations. These were recorded as Dummy A through D for the teams and Dummy Iteration A through E for the iterations.

Finally, it is worth pointing out that we computed and evaluated other network measures such as density, which did not have any impact in our models. Therefore, we did not include them in the final results reported in the paper.

Description of the Model

Our two dependent variables, *Delivery Performance* and *Quality*, are count variables. Then, we used a multi-level Negative Binomial regression model. We examined our hypotheses by creating several negative binomial models, which included the different control variables as well as our independent measures as fixed effects. In addition, we added iteration, team and individuals as random effects. In order to assess the fit of each model, we report the log-likelihood of each model as well as the percentage of deviance explained by the model. The deviance of a model is defined as "-2 * log-likelihood of the model" and lower values are associated with a better fit of the model to the data. The percentage of the deviance explained is a ratio of the deviance of the null model (containing only the intercept) and the deviance of the final model. Although, regression coefficients are often reported as part of the results, we opted for reporting the incidence rate ratios (IRRs) associated with the fixed effect factors of the regression models because they simplify the interpretation of the results. IRRs indicate the rate at which the dependent variable would change for one unit change in one independent variable keeping the other factors constant.

RESULTS

Preliminary Analyses

In order to develop a robust dataset, we only included those teams who had at least 20 work items in an iteration and had work items planned in at least 4 iterations. We performed sensitivity analyses to examine the impact of such decision and we found that running our regression models including all the data resulted in overfitted estimates. Then, we considered that the decision to remove those data points was adequate. This resulted in data for 16 out of the 26 teams. The 14 iterations and 16 teams resulted in 197 pairs

<iteration, team>. Note that we did not have 224 pairs because each team did not necessarily have work items planned in all of the iterations.

We first computed descriptive statistics of the measures described in the previous section. All variables with the exception of our two independent measures and the GSD measure had skewed distributions so they were log-transformed. We also performed various collinearity diagnostics. We first ran a variance inflation factors (VIF) analysis and it showed that all the measures included in our models did not exhibit collinearity problems since they had VIFs below 5 as recommended guidelines suggest [23]. A pair-wise correlation analysis among those measures also showed levels of correlation that were not problematic.

The Impact on Delivery Performance

In this section we discuss the results pertaining to hypotheses 1a and 1b, which focused on the relationship between the hierarchical and "small-worldness" nature of communication patterns on *Delivery Performance*. Table 1 reports the results of the regression analyses. Models I and II show the incident rate ratios (IRRs) associated with the control factors. We separated the control factors in two different models because we wanted to assess the relative impact of the technical dependencies, a factor that has been shown to have major impact on coordination needs [11] and therefore, a major impact on software development productivity [11] and software failures [12]. The results reported by models I and II are consistent with past research (e.g. [5, 12, 25]). We also observe that several of the measures for unobserved factors associated with the teams and the iterations are statistically significant, suggesting there are idiosyncratic attributes of the teams as well as of the iterations that impact the performance outcomes of an iteration. Models III and IV test hypothesis 1A by introducing the *Hierarchical Communication Pattern* variable into the analysis. The IRR associated with our independent variable is statistically significant and between 0 and 1 suggesting that higher levels of hierarchy reduce the number of work items that are rescheduled In other words, increased hierarchical communication is associated with improved iteration performance providing support for H1a. Model IV emphasizes the robustness of that result since the effect remains significant after considering the role of the technical dependencies. It is also worth pointing out that the effect size of hierarchy (2.7% of deviance explained) is similar to the effect size of technical dependencies (3.1% of deviance explained).

Finally, models V and VI in Table 1 assessed hypothesis 1B that posited that small-world communication patterns would be associated with lower delivery performance in our specific case, associated with higher number of rescheduled work items. Our results show no clear support for the hypothesis. The IRR associated with the variable *Small-World Communication Patterns* are above 1 but the estimates are only marginally significant.

The Impact on Quality

We now turn our attention to hypotheses 2A and 2B, which posited that hierarchical communication patterns would be detrimental to quality outcomes while small-world communication patterns would be beneficial. Table 2 reports the results of our analyses. As before, Models I and II show the incident rate ratios (IRRs) associated with the control factors and, again, we separate the control factors in the two models to assess the specific impact of logical technical dependencies. The results are consistent with past research (e.g. [5, 12, 25]). Models III and IV examined hypothesis 2A by introducing into the models our independent variable, *Hierarchical Communication Patterns*. Our results provide strong support for hypothesis 2A suggesting that hierarchical communication patterns in computer-mediated communication are detrimental to the quality outcomes of iterations. An IRR above 1 indicates that increases in the hierarchical structure of the communication patterns are associated with increases in the number of defects, therefore, associated with poorer quality outcomes. In fact, when we compare models II and III, we see the negative effect of hierarchy is significantly larger than technical dependencies, which prior research suggested as a primary driver for software failures (e.g. [12, 13]). Finally, Models V and VI introduced the *Small-World Communication Pattern* variable into the analysis, which found support for H2b. Higher levels of "small-worldness" in the communication patterns reduces the estimated number of defects associated with the iteration since the IRR is below 1. It is worth pointing out that the effect size of the variable is not as high as our other independent variable (hierarchy) since it only explained 4.2% of the deviance.

DISCUSSION

This paper examined the effect of communication structure, specifically hierarchical and small-world structures on new product development delivery performance and quality. We measured delivery performance by the number of development tasks that needed to be rescheduled to a later iteration. There was a strong positive effect on performance for hierarchy providing evidence that structuring communication patterns in a hierarchical manner improves delivery performance (H1A). However, we found only a marginal negative impact for small-worlds communication structures on delivery performance, providing weak support for hypothesis 1B. We assessed quality by the number of defects that resulted from the work done during an iteration. We found that hierarchical communication structures have a significant detrimental effect on quality (H2A supported) while small-world communication structures improved the quality outcomes of an iteration providing support for hypothesis 2B. We especially draw attention to the significance of the findings after taking technical dependency structures into account. A number of research studies have established that dependencies can drive communication structure [14, 41]. The current study confirmed a positive effect of both intra- and inter-team dependencies on itera-

Table 1: The Impact of the Structure of Communication Patterns on the Number of Rescheduled Tasks

	Model I	Model II	Model III	Model IV	Model V	Model VI
Controls for unobserved effects						
Team Dummy A	1.291**	1.357**	1.085	1.364**	1.413**	1.327**
Team Dummy B	1.069	1.108	1.039	1.119	1.128	1.168
Team Dummy C	0.841+	0.921**	0.707**	0.920**	0.840*	0.928**
Team Dummy D	0.624**	0.934*	0.823*	0.911*	0.661**	0.752*
Iteration Dummy A	0.966	0.862	1.133	0.887	1.137	1.052
Iteration Dummy B	1.046	0.592	0.995	0.997	0.954	0.817
Iteration Dummy C	0.591**	0.514**	0.575**	0.515**	0.517**	0.462**
Iteration Dummy D	0.717+	0.388	0.872	0.400	0.702	0.465
Iteration Dummy E	0.139**	0.097**	0.101**	0.062**	0.116**	0.085**
Controls for Team-related factors						
Number of Project Members Involved	2.823**	5.801**	2.398**	5.710**	3.249**	4.263**
Number of Multi-team Project Members	0.568**	0.816*	0.740*	0.809*	0.590**	0.726*
GSD	2.631**	2.486**	2.238**	2.509**	2.280**	2.061**
Average Level of Technical Experience	0.937	1.013	0.992	1.041	0.983	1.011
Average Level of Shared-work Experience	0.857	0.675*	0.879*	0.601*	0.603*	0.618*
Average Level of Team Workload	1.643**	1.754**	1.792**	1.734**	1.382**	1.694**
Controls for Communication-related factors						
Amount of Inter-Team Communication	1.004**	1.022*	1.003**	1.012*	1.002**	1.003*
Controls for Task-related factors						
Ratio of High Priority Work Items	0.226**	0.701**	0.362**	0.639**	0.363**	0.331**
Average Size of Work Items	1.152	1.066	1.101	1.049	1.203	1.262
Controls for Technical-related factors						
Internal Technical Coupling		1.302		1.094		1.036
External Technical Coupling		2.331**		2.277**		1.869**
Independent Variables						
Hierarchical Communication Pattern			0.669*	0.843*		
Small World Communication Pattern					1.011+	1.016+
Log-Likelihood	-523.41	-502.08	-498.41	-480.71	-518.59	-500.63
Deviance Explained	24.8%	27.9%	28.4%	31.1%	25.5%	28.1%

(+ $p < 0.10$, * $p < 0.05$, ** $p < 0.01$)

tion performance and quality. More importantly, the impact of the communication structure remained strong, even after taking into consideration the effect of dependencies and other control factors. The longitudinal nature of our analysis suggests that the effects of the structure of communication patterns remain robust as the development effort evolves throughout the project.

These results confirm the importance of informal communication for software teams. They further promote the small but growing research on communication structures [27] by providing evidence of the role for hierarchy and small-world structures in the context of geographically dispersed teams interacting through computer-mediated means. The study also begins to address issues related to how teams can manage their communication by having enough communication without getting overloaded. As past research has noted, it is not the amount of communication that matters but how it relates to the task at hand [40]. In a hierarchical structure, there is less overall communication because the communication flows in a particular direction, which minimizes the communication between people at the same level of the hierarchy. This structure is suited to tasks associated with planning and executing against a plan. In contrast, there is a lot of localized communication within each small-world cluster although not necessarily much communication between clusters. This structure is better suited to tasks associated with individual development tasks that can benefit from the contextualization and trust that comes from high communication with a small group of people.

Our results highlight a potentially important trade-off between high delivery performance and high quality outcomes. An analysis of the evolutionary patterns of the communication networks suggested that certain teams were able to overcome the trade-off and achieve high performance and quality by combining hierarchical and small-world communication structures. More specifically, we examined the teams in the top 33 percentile in our outcome variables. These teams, also achieve high levels of both hierarchical and small-world communication. We observed this pattern

Table 2: The Impact of the Structure of Communication Patterns on the Number of Defects

	Model I	Model II	Model III	Model IV	Model V	Model VI
Controls for unobserved effects						
Team Dummy A	1.049	1.035	1.051	1.106	1.049	1.005
Team Dummy B	0.751**	0.802**	0.874**	0.923**	0.773**	0.831**
Team Dummy C	0.846**	0.739**	0.900*	0.875**	0.846	0.870**
Team Dummy D	0.983	0.798	0.975	0.828	0.936	0.835
Iteration Dummy A	0.423**	0.367**	0.417**	0.534**	0.431**	0.449**
Iteration Dummy B	0.921*	0.792*	0.972	0.895*	0.977	0.807*
Iteration Dummy C	1.239**	1.171**	1.401**	1.293**	1.281**	1.265**
Iteration Dummy D	0.445**	0.379**	0.364**	0.609**	0.487**	0.512**
Iteration Dummy E	0.136**	0.092**	0.067**	0.147**	0.102**	0.120**
Controls for Team-related factors						
Number of Project Members	1.374**	1.529**	2.701**	1.995**	1.351**	1.929**
Number of Multi-team Project Members	1.403**	1.091**	1.140	1.254**	1.463**	1.018*
GSD	1.336**	1.351**	1.039*	1.539**	1.282**	1.530**
Average Level of Technical Experience	0.998	0.868**	0.871**	0.881**	0.983+	0.942*
Average Level of Shared-work Experience	0.959	0.801**	0.799*	0.728**	0.894*	0.908*
Average Level of Team Workload	2.361**	1.958**	1.771**	1.554**	2.231**	1.901**
Controls for Communication-related factors						
Amount of Inter-Team Communication	1.001*	1.002	1.236*	1.001	1.001+	1.005
Controls for Task-related factors						
Ratio of High Priority Work Items	0.458**	0.377**	0.904+	0.243**	0.487**	0.230**
Average Size of Work Items	1.565**	1.953**	2.419**	1.983**	1.326**	2.248**
Controls for Technical-related factors						
Internal Technical Coupling		3.971**		2.441**		1.602**
External Technical Coupling		1.518**		1.502**		1.367**
Independent Variables						
Hierarchical Communication Pattern			2.230**	1.271**		
Small World Communication Pattern					0.884*	0.835*
Log-Likelihood	-735.95	-649.95	-521.13	-481.57	-691.09	-607.22
Deviance Explained	27.7%	36.1%	48.9%	52.7%	32.1%	40.3%

(+ $p < 0.10$, * $p < 0.05$, ** $p < 0.01$)

in at least 1 iteration for 13 teams, however, the pattern was more prevalent for 3 teams where they exhibited the pattern in more than 3 iterations. On the other hand, other teams developed only one particular pattern or they flip-flopped between the hierarchical and small-world patterns. These teams were never able to develop both high levels of delivery performance and quality within an iteration. Consequently, they faced a trade-off between performance and quality or both outcomes were not particularly high. Furthermore, in several instances those teams (9 out of the 26 teams) exhibited both low levels of delivery performance and quality in at least 1 iteration of the project.

Limitations

Our study has several limitations worth highlighting. First, we studied a single project, which might raise external validity concerns. Although we recognize such a risk, we think our research setting represents an unique opportunity to perform a longitudinal study of a new product development project and the communication patterns that emerge over time through computer-mediated-communication means. A second limitation of the study is the focus on the first release of the product. The project has continued to work together and produce other releases of the product. Then, we could expect maturation effects that might impact the patterns of communication and their evolution. Unfortunately, the data associated with subsequent releases are not currently available. Finally, several teams had collocated members and in our study we were not able to collect data to control for face-to-face interactions that might impact how the communication patterns in the work items reports evolve. However, our interviews confirmed that comments were the primary form of technical communication as befits a project that had transparency as a goal.

Implications for Tool Design

Although our research takes place in an NPD context, the relevance of this domain for the design of collaborative tools is well established in the CSCW literature (e.g. [18, 19, 34, 36]. The effect of distributed work on awareness and collaboration has been extensively studied in software engineering (e.g. [18, 36]) as well as other contexts (e.g. [34]). Our results provide two key contributions to the design of collaborative tools. First, current collaborative tools have been shown to be successful in small teams, however the current generation of designs is inadequate for large-scale and distributed projects [36]. For instance, existing technologies inform developers of a relatively large number of events of possible interest. However, in large-scale projects, such an approach will quickly exhaust attentional resources. The results of our study suggest an alternate approach in which collaborative tools target specific pairs or groups of people, to reduce the problem of information overload. Data on communication patterns – who talks to whom – can be used to focus presence, activity and other types of information relevant to a particular user as a way of reducing information load.

Second, and arguably more importantly, our work shows that two communication structures have different impacts on different product development outcomes, pointing to an important trade-off that collaborative tool designers need to understand in order to develop effective tools. The approach we used to construct the communication networks and our measures point to a potential technique that collaborative tools could leverage in order to better support the evolving nature of NPD projects

Implications for Additional Future Research

The results of our study have important implications for future research. First, our results point to a potential trade-off that development teams may face in terms of the structural properties of the communication patterns that emerge during an iteration and how those patterns impact two important outcomes in new product development: delivery performance and quality. Arguably, development teams could reap benefits in both performance and quality if they are able to modulate their communication in accordance with the type of work being done, as well as in alignment with the requirements imposed by technical dependencies [11]. However, a closer look at the teams in the dataset indicated that some of the teams were able to maintain above average delivery performance and quality. In those cases, we observe that the evolution of the hierarchy and small-worldness measures alternated between above average levels and average levels suggesting that those teams do seem to vary in their ability to change communication structures. Then, future research should examine these aspects and their implications on NPD outcomes.

Second, and in relation to the previous point, the trade-off challenge is augmented significantly in the context of geographically distributed product development. Ramassubu and colleagues [35] showed that the team configurations that are beneficial for productivity in geographically distributed development projects tend to be highly detrimental in terms of quality. Those results combined with those reported in the paper suggest that the trade-off between performance and quality could stem from the relationship of those outcomes with the structure of communication patterns as well as other important organizational factors such as the team configuration and the dispersion of expertise across the project's locations. Future research should examine the relative role of all those factors on NPD outcomes to gain insight into the specifics nature of the trade-off.

REFERENCES

1. Allen, T.J., *Managing the flow of technology*. MIT Press, 1977.
2. Ancona, D. and Caldwell, D. Bridging the boundary: External activity and performance in organizational teams. *Adm. Science Quarterly,* 37, 634-665, 1992.
3. Argote, L. *Organizational learning : creating, retaining, and transferring knowledge*. Kluwer Academic, 1999.
4. Bird, C. *et al.* Latent social structure in open source projects. In *Proc. of International Conference on Foundations of Software Engineering (FSE'08)*, Atlanta, GA, 2008.
5. Boh W.F. *et al.* Learning from Experience in Software Development: A Multilevel Analysis. *Management Science,* 53, 1315-1331, 2007.
6. Brown, S. and Eisenhardt, K. Product development: past research, present findings, and future directions. *Academy of Management Review,* 20, 343-378, 1995.
7. Burt, R. *Brokerage and closure: An introduction to social capital*: Oxford University Press, USA, 2005.
8. Carley, K.M. *et al.* Ora: Organization risk analyzer. Technical Report CMU-ISR-04-106, School of Computer Science, Carnegie Mellon Univerisity, 2004.
9. Carmel, E. *Global software teams: collaborating across borders and time zones*. Prentice Hall Upper Saddle River, NJ, 1999.
10. Cataldo, M. and Herbsleb, J.D. Communication networks in geographically distributed software development. In Proceedings of the 2008 ACM conference on Computer supported cooperative work, San Diego, CA, USA, 2008.
11. Cataldo, M. *et al.* Socio-technical congruence: a framework for assessing the impact of technical and work dependencies on software development productivity. In *Proc. of the 2nd international symposium on Empirical Soft. Eng. and Measurement (ESEM'08)*, Kaiserslautern, Germany, 2008.
12. Cataldo, M. *et al.*, Software Dependencies, Work Dependencies, and Their Impact on Failures. *IEEE Trans. Softw. Eng.,* 35, 864-878, 2009.
13. Cataldo, M. and Nambiar, S. The impact of geographic distribution and the nature of technical coupling on the quality of global software development projects. *Journal of Software Maintenance and Evolution: Research and Practice,* 2010.

14. Cataldo, M. *et al.* Identification of coordination requirements: implications for the Design of collaboration and awareness tools. In *Proc of the Int'l Conference on Computer Supported Cooperative Work (CSCW'06)*, Banff, Canada, 2006.

15. Crowston, K. and Howison, J. The social structure of free and open source software development. *First Monday,* 10, 2005.

16. Cummings, J.N. and Cross, R. Structural properties of work groups and their consequences for performance. *Social Networks,* 25, 197-210, 2003.

17. Cummings, J. N. *et al.* Crossing Spatial and Temporal Boundaries in Globally Distributed Projects: A Relational Model of Coordination Delay. *Information Systems Research,* 20, 420-439, 2009.

18. de Souza, C.R.B. and Redmiles, D.F. On The Roles of APIs in the Coordination of Collaborative Software Development. *Computer Supported Cooperative Work,* 18, 445-475, 2009.

19. Ehrlich, K. and Cataldo, M. All–for–One and One–for–All? A Multi–Level Analysis of Communication Patterns and Individual Performance in Geographically Distributed Software Development. In *Proc of the Int'l Conference on Computer Supported Cooperative Work (CSCW'12), Seattle, WA, 2012.*

20. Faraj, S. and Sproull, L. Coordinating Expertise in Software Development Teams. *Management Science,* 46, 1554-1568, 2000.

21. Frost, R. Jazz and the eclipse way of collaboration. *IEEE Software,* 114-117, 2007.

22. Gokpinar, B. *et al.* The Impact of Misalignment of Organizational Structure and Product Architecture on Quality in Complex Product Development. *Mgmt. Science,* 56, 468-484, 2010.

23. Hair, J.F., *et al. Multivariate data analysis, 5th Ed.* Upper Saddle River, NJ: Prentice Hall, 1998.

24. Harter, D.E. *et al.* Effects of Process Maturity on Quality, Cycle Time, and Effort in Software Product Development. *Manage. Sci.,* 46, 451-466, 2000.

25. Herbsleb, J.D. and Mockus, A. An Empirical Study of Speed and Communication in Globally Distributed Software Development. *IEEE Trans. Softw. Eng.,* 29, 481-494, 2003.

26. Herbsleb, J.D. *et al.* Collaboration in Software Engineering Projects: A Theory of Coordination. In *Proc. of the International Conference on Information Systems (ICIS '06)*, Milwaukee, Wisconsin, 2006.

27. Hinds, P. and McGrath, C. Structures that work: social structure, work structure and coordination ease in geographically distributed teams. In *Proc of the Int'l Conference on Computer Supported Cooperative Work (CSCW'06), Banff, Canada, 2006..*

28. Katz, R. and Tushman, M. Communication patterns, project performance, and task characteristics: An empirical evaluation and integration in an R&D setting. *Organizational Behavior and Human Performance,* 23, 139-162, 1979.

29. Krackhardt, D. Graph theoretical dimensions of informal organizations. In *Computational organization theory,* 89-111, 1994.

30. Loch, C. and Kavadias, S. *Handbook of new product development management.* BH Publishers, 2008

31. MacCormack, A. and Verganti, R. Managing the Sources of Uncertainty: Matching Process and Context in Software Development. *Journal of Product Innovation Management,* 20, 217-232, 2003.

32. McDonough III, E.F. *et al.* An investigation of the use of global, virtual, and colocated new product development teams *Journal of Product Innovation Management,* 18, 110-120, 2001.

33. Newman, M.E.J. Models of the small world. *Journal of Statistical Physics,* 101, 819-841, 2000.

34. Olson, G.M. and Olson, J.S. Distance Matters. *Human-Computer Interaction,* 15, 139 - 178, 2000.

35. Ramassubu, N. *et al.* Configuring Global Software Teams: A Multi-Company Analysis of Project Productivity, Quality, and Profits. In *Proc. of the Int'l Conference on Software Engineering (ICSE,11)*, Honolulu, Hawaii., 2011.

36. Sarma, A. et al. Empirical Evidence of the Benefits of Workspace Awareness in Software Configuration Mangement. In *Proc. of International Conference on Foundations of Software Engineering (FSE'08)*, Atlanta, GA, 2008.

37. Sosa, M.E. *et al.* The Misalignment of Product Architecture and Organizational Structure in Complex Product Development. *Mgmt. Sci.,*50,1674-1689, 2004.

38. Tushman, M. and Katz, R. External communication and project performance: An investigation into the role of gatekeepers. *Mgmt. Sci.,* 26, 1071-1085, 1980.

39. Ulrich, K.T. and Eppinger, S. *Product Design and Development.* New York, NY: McGraw-Hill, 2007.

40. Uzzi, B. and Spiro, J. Collaboration and creativity: The small world problem. *AJS,* 111, 447-504, 2005.

41. Wagstrom, P.A. *et al.* Communication, Team Performance and the Individual: Bridging Technical Dependencies. In *Proc. of Academy of Management Annual Meeting*, Montreal, Canada, 2010.

42. Watts, D.J. and Strogatz, S.H. Collective dynamics of small-world networks. *Nature,*393, 440-442, 1998.

43. Wolf, T. *et al.*, "Predicting build failures using social network analysis on developer communication". In *Proc. of Int'l Conference on Software Enginering (ICSE'09)*, Vancouver, Canada, 2009.

One of the Gang: Supporting In-Group Behavior for Embodied Mediated Communication

Irene Rae
University of Wisconsin–Madison
1210 W. Dayton St., Madison, WI
irene@cs.wisc.edu

Leila Takayama
Willow Garage, Inc.
68 Willow Rd., Menlo Park, CA
takayama@willowgarage.com

Bilge Mutlu
University of Wisconsin–Madison
1210 W. Dayton St., Madison, WI
bilge@cs.wisc.edu

ABSTRACT
As an emerging technology that enables geographically distributed work teams, mobile remote presence (MRP) systems present new opportunities for supporting effective team building and collaboration. MRP systems are physically embodied mobile videoconferencing systems that remote co-workers control. These systems allow remote users, *pilots*, to actively initiate conversations and to navigate the local environment. To investigate ways of encouraging team-like behavior among local and remote co-workers, we conducted a 2 (visual framing: decoration vs. no decoration) ×2 (verbal framing: interdependent vs. independent performance scoring) between-participants study ($n = 40$). We hypothesized that verbally framing the situation as interdependent and visually framing the MRP system to create a sense of self-extension would enhance group cohesion between the local and the pilot. We found that the interdependent framing was successful in producing more in-group oriented behaviors and, contrary to our predictions, visual framing of the MRP system weakened team cohesion.

Author Keywords
Embodied mediated communication; remote presence; in-group behavior

ACM Classification Keywords
H.5.3 Information Interfaces and Presentation: Group and Organization Interfaces – *computer-supported cooperative work*; H.4.3 Information Systems Applications: Communications Applications – *computer conferencing, teleconferencing, and videoconferencing*

General Terms
Design, Experimentation, Human Factors

INTRODUCTION
As geographically distributed collaboration becomes more commonplace, workplaces have been challenged to find ways of coordinating communication to ensure effective team outcomes. The productivity of group activity has been attributed to factors such as access to the communication behaviors of participants [40], knowledge of the environment and context of the situation [24], and a sense of membership within the organization [4]. Past approaches to facilitating geographically distributed teamwork have ranged from text-based communications to high-fidelity group videoconferencing. Research in computer-mediated communication has focused on carrying aspects of face-to-face communication over to remote collaboration using computing technology.

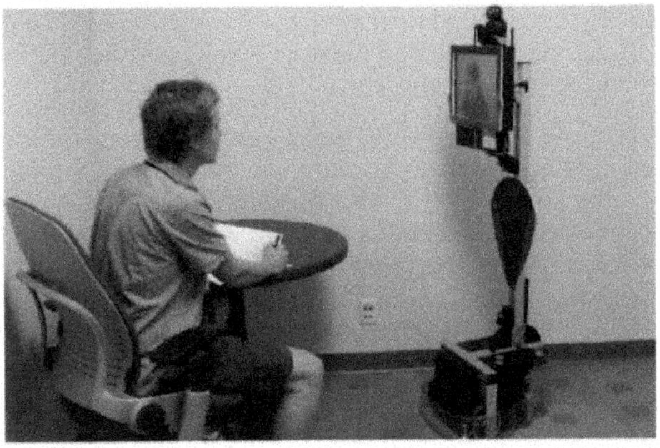

Figure 1. The Mobile Remote Telepresence (MRP) System used in our study shown with a participant.

One of the most recent demonstrations of this research are mobile remote presence (MRP) systems (see Figure 1). Although these types of mobile remote presence systems have been available for over 15 years (e.g., Personal Roving Presence [26]), they have only recently reached the consumer market. A number of these systems are now beginning to see use in a variety of business, medical, and educational settings [1, 10, 27, 30, 37]. Outside of work contexts, these systems have been used to enable sick children to attend school (e.g., PEBBLES [9]) and to participate in extracurricular activities after school (e.g., VGo [29]). Their potential applications for older adults [3, 33] and homecare [17] have also been explored. However, because these systems have been used most extensively in business settings (e.g., Bi-Reality [12], Texai [15], and VGo [34]), we have placed the current study within the context of geographically distributed work.

Mediated communication platforms are unique in two major ways. First, they provide a remote user, the *pilot*, the autonomy to drive and control the system, granting the ability to adjust his or her position to see the visual behaviors of the local users, the *locals*. This capability enables the pilot to explore the environment and points of interest, preventing feelings of disorientation or helplessness [24]. Second, in addition to the visual and aural information provided by the audio/video feed of the pilot, they provide the locals with a physical entity to interact with. This embodiment of the remote user provides supplemental cues of presence. For example, when the pilot changes the direction of the system to see the current speaker, locals become aware of the change in the pilot's orientation and the apparent shift in attention. While providing a physical representation of the remote user opens up new design opportunities for augmenting current modes of communication, it also has the potential to interpose a new barrier between users as those who are local to the system may perceive the MRP system as its own entity.

In this paper, we study how the physical presence of the MRP system affects the team dynamic between the local user and the remote user, as well as the impact this may have on collaborative work outcomes. In particular, we explore how the relationship between remote and local users might be manipulated to increase the local user's feelings of in-group membership with the pilot. In order to do this, we applied two different theoretical methods. In the first method, we use the physical embodiment of the system to improve the local user's perceptions of the pilot through the use of visual framing through self-extension [5, 11, 19, 31]. The second method focuses on the relationship between the local and the pilot as group members, verbally manipulating the framing of the pilot within the context of the team [35].

The next section outlines related work to provide background on how the creation and development of in-group identity in other media might inform our efforts toward achieving similar outcomes with MRP systems.

BACKGROUND

In organizations, the dynamics of group effectiveness are complex and influenced by a number of factors including access to communication behaviors of participants [40], awareness of the environment and the context of the situation [24], and sense of membership within the organization [4].

Computer-mediated communication (CMC) systems such as videoconferencing, support geographically distributed collaboration by enabling communicative behaviors through the implementation of movable [21] or multi-viewpoint directional displays [23]. Other systems improve knowledge of the environment and situational context through the use of immersive media spaces [16]. Each of these systems has treated the medium as a tool, using advances in technology to improve communication bandwidth, but they did not necessarily consider how the medium might be leveraged to promote a sense of membership between remote team members, an integral factor in deciding collaborative work outcomes.

Group cohesion is associated with promoting cooperation between group members, increased instances of people helping and training each other within the team, and improved productivity [4, 24]. In addition, groups with strong feelings of identity and membership tend to self-regulate, lessening the need for direct supervision and working more flexibly to resolve problems [4]. Conversely, the lack of group cohesion can sabotage organizational and team dynamics. People have been shown to be less cooperative and less trusting of those that they feel are out-group, and to deprive people that they do not identify with of positive consequences, acting against them [36].

Work on both human–human and human–computer interaction has shown *framing*—the presentation of information to encourage particular interpretations—to be effective in changing people's decisions [35] and their perceptions of others. For example, in studies where an opponent was *verbally framed* as a human as opposed to a computer [25], where a robot was presented as autonomous versus as being remote controlled [41], or where participants were told before the interaction that evaluation of their performance would either be interdependent with a team member or as an individual [22], the choice of framing had a significant effect on attitudes and behaviors toward the entity being framed.

In other examples, research in personality has shown that the use of *visual framing*, such as through the design and customization of objects, can increase group identity, improve judgments of the ease-of-use of an item, and promote *self-extension*—the feeling that a possession has meaning associated with a person's self-identity [5, 19]. These effects extend to objects or machines that have the ability to move autonomously or without the control of the person customizing them [11, 31].

In this paper, we will build on the concept that verbal and visual framing can be effective ways to manipulate perceptions by examining the effect framing has on the relationship between the locals and the pilot in the context of the MRP system. In our study, we employ a *verbal framing* variable and a *visual framing* variable to cultivate feelings of in-group identity and improve group cohesion with the goal of optimizing collaborative task outcomes.

In the next section, we present our research hypotheses and methodology, including both a pilot test and full laboratory experiment.

HYPOTHESES

We formulated our hypotheses based on previous work that focused on creating a sense of in-group identity between humans and computers [22]:

Hypothesis 1: Participants will perceive the pilot of the MRP system as more similar to themselves and as more trustworthy, exhibiting more signs of group identity through greater disclosure and more agreement with the pilot when the pilot is introduced with interdependent verbal framing as opposed to individual verbal framing.

Hypothesis 2: Participants will perceive the pilot of the MRP system as more similar to themselves and as more trustworthy, exhibiting more signs of group identity through greater disclosure and more agreement with the pilot when the system has been visually framed (decorated) by the participant than they will if the system is not visually framed.

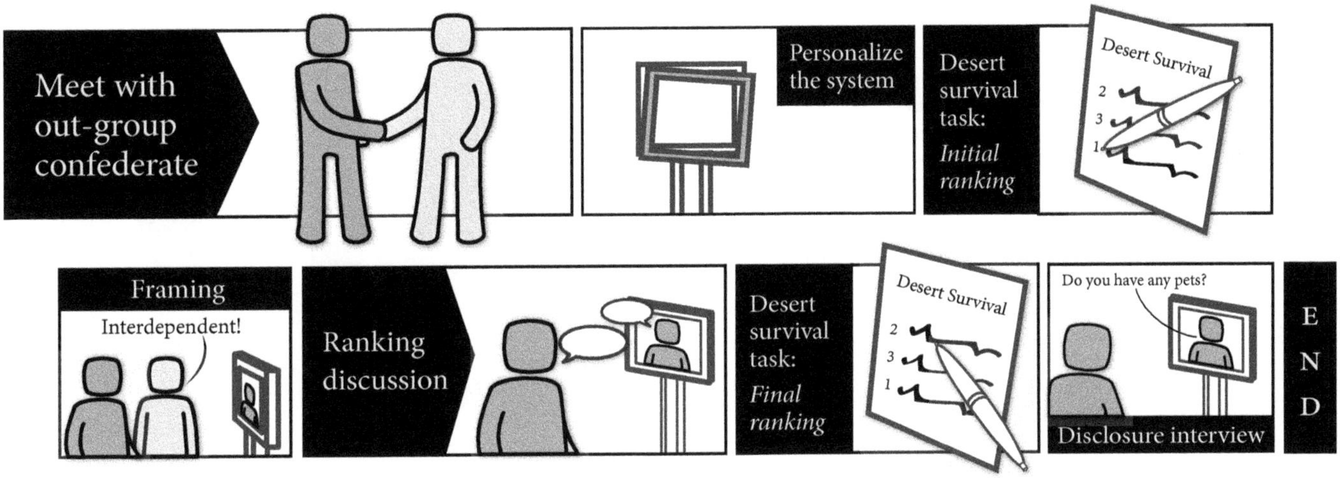

Figure 2. Storyboard of study procedure, depicting a participant's experience in the personalize and interdependent condition.

METHOD

We conducted a laboratory experiment to test these hypotheses and, due to the lack of previous work on MRP systems, we performed an extended pilot test to form a methodological basis for our experiment. This pilot test was based on related research in the fields of human–computer interaction, computer–mediated communication, and human–robot interaction. We used our observations from the pilot test as a guide for our final experimental design. Below we describe how the pilot test influenced each aspect of our study procedure.

Experiment Procedure

Participants were met at the lobby of Willow Garage by the experimenter and led to the room in which the study took place. There, the participant was introduced to an *out-group confederate*, who identified himself by name and stated that he was also participating in the study. This confederate's role was to provide an out-group member to compare against for an infrahumanization test in the experiment questionnaire. The experimenter explained to both the participant and the out-group confederate that there were two teams, a "blue team" and a "green team". The experimenter then told the participant that he/she was on the blue team, that the out-group confederate was on the green team, and that the teams would be separated. At that point, the experimenter led the out-group confederate out of the room. When the experimenter returned to the room, she had the participant complete a consent form.

After filling out the consent form, the experimenter instructed the participant on the Desert Survival Task (described in greater detail in our study measures) and asked the participant to perform an initial ranking of items in three minutes. Once completed, the experimenter introduced the participant to an *in-group confederate* who was logged in as the pilot of the MRP system. The participant and the in-group confederate then engaged in a ten minute discussion of their individual rankings of the Desert Survival Task items. After the participant and the pilot had concluded their discussion, the in-group confederate pilot exited the room and the experimenter asked the participant to do a second, three minute, final ranking of the task items. The participant then filled out a questionnaire, described in greater detail in our study measures. Following the questionnaire, the experimenter re-introduced the pilot (still logged into the MRP system) to the room and gave the participant a list of questions. The experimenter told both the pilot and the participant that they would be engaging in an untimed "getting to know you" (disclosure) task and that they had each received a list of questions, one odd numbered, one even numbered. They were instructed to alternate asking each other these questions after the experimenter left the room and to inform her when finished. After the disclosure task was complete, the pilot drove the MRP system out of the room and the participant was debriefed.

A full list of the disclosure task questions is available in Appendix I and a diagram of the full procedure is shown in Figure 2.

Modifications From Pilot Test. In pilot tests, two participants guessed that the pilot was a confederate. To counter this, we added a white backdrop to remove environmental cues. In addition, we found during the pilot test that some participants had taken an inordinately long time to rank the desert survival items and to discuss their rankings with the confederate; therefore, we found it necessary to add time limits to both the ranking and discussion portions of the Desert Survival Task.

Experiment Design

We used a MRP system with a touch screen mounted on a mobile platform, standing at approximately 1.58 meters or 5′ 2″ tall, as shown in Figure 1. If the participant was in the visual framing manipulation, immediately after completion of the consent form the experimenter gave the participant three items in the blue team's colors to use as decorations on the MRP system: a rectangular frame to be placed on the screen, a chest shaped body piece, and a magnetic name tag (see Figure 3). We positioned the MRP system in the hallway outside of the experiment room, asked the participant to write the *in-group confederate pilot's* name on the name tag and had him/her personalize the placement of the decorative pieces on the MRP system. After the participant finished placing the decorations, we asked him/her to return to the experiment room and continued by instructing him/her on the Desert Survival Task.

If the participant was in the interdependent framing condition, the experimenter explained that performance on the Desert Survival Task would be evaluated as a team. If the participant was in the independent framing condition, the experimenter explained that performance on the Desert Survival Task would be evaluated independently. During the study, participants interacted with two separate confederates, the *in-group confederate pilot* who was on their team and an *out-group confederate* who they were told was on the opposite team.

Modifications From Pilot Test. Because of the lack of related work in the field of embodied-mediated communication, we conducted a pilot test based on six different methods, each of which was informed by the manipulations used in previous studies on feelings of group identity or self-extension. Three of these methods sought to foster a sense of self-extension toward the embodied system through the use of visual framing or design elements and three attempted to build a stronger sense of group identity through the use of verbal framing. A total of 17 participants were pilot tested and three were eliminated, two due to a technical failure and one after guessing that the pilot was a confederate, leaving a total of two participants per condition ($n = 14$).

Visual framing: In Nass et al.'s study on creating a sense of team identity with a computer, people were found to act more collaboratively toward a computer visually framed with colored bands that matched the participant's group color [22]. We sought to create a similar manipulation by pre-decorating the MRP system in colors matching the participant's group, illustrated in Figure 3b. In this condition the procedure was the same as that of the full experiment and the MRP system was pre-decorated in blue.

Visual framing through self-extension: Blom et al. found that the personalization of mobile phones and web portals led to a feeling of self-extension among participants [5]. In this condition, we strengthened the visual framing manipulation by allowing people to choose where to place the colored markers, "personalizing" the system. Our goal was to create a sense of self-extension while limiting the level of customization to avoid possible confounds. In this condition, prior to being instructed on the Desert Survival Task, we gave participants the blue decorations and asked them to place them on the system, as shown in Figure 3a.

Mimicry: This condition was based on studies on mimicry [2] and the person-positivity bias [28] that concluded that similarity to an individual produces more trust and liking. In the case of the MRP system, creating human-like movement was an attempt to de-mechanize the appearance of the system, making it more similar to the participant. In this condition, the procedure was identical to that of the full experiment, but during both the desert survival and the disclosure tasks the pilot rotated the MRP system to the right and left by a small degree when stationary.

Choice: Demoulin et al. found that participants given a choice of what team they were on had a greater sense of team identity and favored their team members more than those who were assigned a team [8]. In order to reproduce this manipulation, we allowed the participant to choose his/her team color. In this condition, we asked participants which team they wanted to be on after informing them of the two team colors and assigned the out-group confederate to the opposite group.

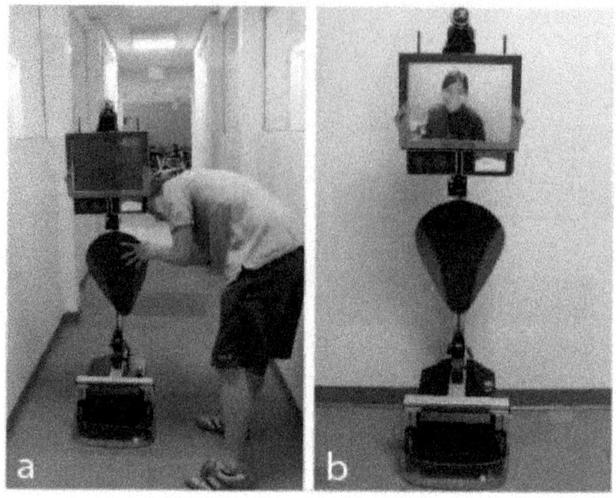

Figure 3. The MRP system (a) being decorated and (b) with decorations on.

Individuality: In his work on the person-positivity bias, Sears found that verbal framing of professors and politicians resulted in more positive or negative evaluations. When presented as individuals, professors and politicians received more positive evaluations than when presented as an aggregate. This result supported Sears's hypothesis that the more an entity resembles an individual person, the more positively people are inclined to judge it [28]. We similarly attempted to verbally frame the pilot as an individual by providing details on her interests. In this condition, when the pilot was introduced we told the participant "Your teammate will be [name], and she enjoys reading fiction novels, baking, and swimming. She said that she would one day like to bake the perfect cake."

Interdependency: Nass et al.'s study on creating a sense of team identity with a computer found that when participants were told that their performance would be dependent on how well they did as a team, their levels of cooperation and trust increased [22]. We replicated this by telling participants that they would be evaluated as a team. In this condition, when we instructed the participant on the Desert Survival Task the experimenter told the participant that their evaluation would be interdependent with that of the pilot.

Neutral: No manipulation of design or framing to serve as a control.

Using our observations of this pilot test, we determined that the visual framing through self-extension and the verbal framing manipulations were the most promising, as they nominally demonstrated the largest effects. The similarity of our pilot test results to Nass et al.'s experiment in building team identity between participants and computers [22] was also a factor in our choice of manipulations. The final experimental design

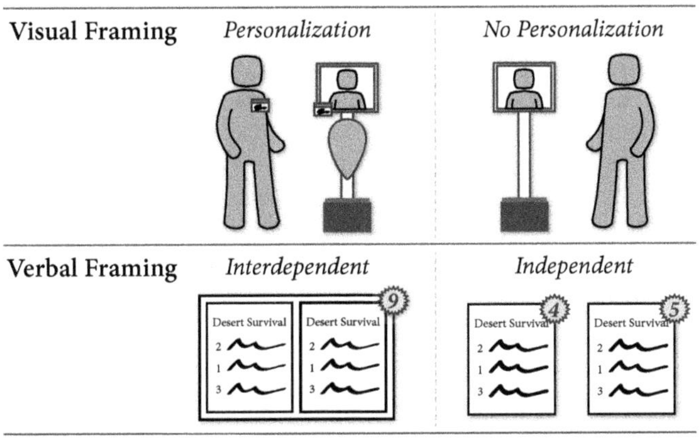

Figure 4. Diagram of study design conditions.

involved a 2 (visual framing: no personalization vs. personalization) ×2 (verbal framing: individual vs. interdependent) between-participants manipulation, as illustrated in Figure 4.

Participants

Twenty adult women (five in each condition) and twenty men (five in each condition), $n = 40$, whose ages ranged between 18 and 82 years, $M = 34.8$, $SD = 15.8$, volunteered to participate. They were recruited via a local university's online bulletin board, postings at two local newspapers, word of mouth from participants of previous studies, and posters placed around the neighborhood. Participants reported that on average they were somewhat familiar with robots, $M = 3.05$, $SD = 1.77$ (1 = not very familiar; 7 = very familiar), and were compensated $20 for each hour of their participation.

Measures

The measures we used for the study included video footage taken with a single camera of the personalization session, the Desert Survival Task, and the disclosure interview. We also collected attitudinal data using a three-part questionnaire and included a demographic information survey.

Desert Survival Task Rankings

The Desert Survival Task [14] is a collaborative decision-making task, modified from the original design to include items that would be relevant to a present-day survival situation. Participants were provided with a written scenario of a bus crash in the desert and were asked to do an initial ranking of nine items in order of importance for survival. The list of items included (1) a map of New Mexico, (2) the book "Edible Animals of the Desert", (3) duct tape, (4) first aid kit, (5) cosmetic mirror, (6) flashlight (four-battery size), (7) magnetic compass, (8) one 2-quart flask per person that is full of 180 proof vodka, and (9) one plastic raincoat per person.

We chose the Desert Survival Task primarily because it was used in Nass et al.'s study on creating a sense of team identity between a participant and a computer [22] and because it has been validated and tested for reliability. Related work has also used the Desert Survival Task as a measure of team alignment and agreement both because participants are inclined to believe that they should be good at the task and because a large amount of variance is regularly found in the ratings. After the initial ranking, the confederate and the participant discussed the differences in their orderings. For this discussion, we created a set of rankings for the confederate that would be consistently different across participants using an algorithm based on previous work [14], (see Appendix II). After the discussion, we asked participants to re-rank the nine items to create a final ranking.

Modifications From Pilot Test. In the pilot test, we used 12 items in the Desert Survival Task; however, we found that participants were spending a great deal of time ranking the items and there was confusion on what some of the items were, so we removed three from the task, resulting in a total of nine. In addition, we added a time limit of three minutes to perform rankings and of ten minutes for the discussion.

Questionnaires

Our questionnaire was split into three sections. In the first section, we used the assessment of perceived homophily developed and validated by McCroskey et al. to measure how similar the participant felt that the pilot was to himself or herself. This test consisted of nine adjective pairs (e.g., "similar to me vs. different from me" and "from a social class similar to mine vs. from a social class different from mine"), each in a seven-point semantic differential scale.

In the second section of the questionnaire, we used the interpersonal solidarity measure developed and validated by Wheeless [39] to measure how trustworthy the participant felt that the pilot was. This consisted of 23 statements (e.g., "This person has a great deal of influence over my behavior." and "We share a lot in common."), each paired with a seven-point ranking scale to indicate level of agreement ranging from 1 (strongly disagree) to 7 (strongly agree).

We based the third section of the questionnaire on measures used in studies of infrahumanization—the belief that members of one's group are more human than those outside of it [7, 8, 28, 36, 38]. This section consisted of two pages and was informed by the tests used in related infrahumanization work [7, 8, 36, 38]. Both pages included the following directions: "For the person listed on the left, draw lines connecting him/her with 8–10 words on the right that you think he/she may experience in a given day." Each page had sixteen words listed on the right side. These words were chosen from prior work which categorized and validated them as either primary (non-uniquely human) emotions (e.g., attraction, desire, excitement, pleasure, agitation, anger, fear, rage), or secondary (uniquely human) emotions (e.g., regret, disappointment, compassion, love, hope, admiration, bitterness, enthusiasm). The left side of the first page showed the name of the in-group confederate pilot and their team identification (*blue* team). The left side of the second page showed the name of the out-group confederate and their team identification (*green* team).

Modifications From Pilot Test. During our initial observations of these measures in the pilot test we found that the response to all three sections was promising, thus we kept all three sections. In our final questionnaire we added questions about the name of the in-group confederate and the team color as manipulation checks.

Disclosure Interview

The disclosure questions were developed and selected from related work that employed the disclosure task to test trust and group identity [6, 18, 32]. Similar to these previous studies, questions were asked on a gradually increasing scale of intimacy and the participant and in-group confederate pilot alternated asking questions. The confederate's responses to the questions were scripted (see Appendix I for the questions used in the study).

Modifications From Pilot Test. In our initial pilot test the disclosure task was a one-sided interview in which the pilot asked the participant questions and the participant responded. Feedback from the participants and our observations led to our changing the disclosure task to be two-sided, with the participant and pilot taking turns to ask questions.

Analyses

For the Desert Survival Task, we calculated Spearman's ρ—a rank-order correlation—to assess the similarity between the participant's final rankings and the confederate's rankings. This measure captured how much the participant changed his/her rankings to align more closely with those of the confederate. The distribution for our data from this measure showed a positive skew; therefore, we used Tukey's ladder of powers to take a $\log_{10}$ transformation of the dependent variable. Finally, we used an analysis of variance (ANOVA) to analyze the effects of personalization and framing (independent variables) on how much the participant aligned his or her final rankings to match the confederate's rankings (dependent variable).

The video data from the disclosure interview was transcribed and analyzed for the degree of self-disclosure, consistent with previous self-disclosure studies [6, 18, 32]. The breadth of disclosure was measured by the length of responses through word count and compared using an ANOVA.

We used an analysis of covariance (ANCOVA) to identify differences across conditions in each of the three sections of the questionnaire data.

RESULTS

The results of our data analyses showed that verbal framing of the situation as interdependent had a positive effect on performance ratings and group cohesion, which was consistent with the first hypothesis. However, we also found that visual framing of the MRP system unexpectedly had a negative effect, going in the opposite direction of our second hypothesis. All of the statistically significant results are shown in Figure 5.

Behavioral Measures

Decision making

In the collaborative decision making task, we found a trend of participants aligning to the confederate's scores less when the system was visually framed, but this effect was not significant at $p < .05$. Participants who did not have a visually framed MRP system tended to move their final decisions closer to the in-group confederate's, $M = \log(0.75)$, $SE = 0.12$, than participants in the visual framing through self-extension condition, $M = \log(0.65)$, $SE = 0.12$, $F(1, 36) = 2.83$, $p = .10$, $\eta_p^2 = .073$.

Disclosure

In the disclosure interview, participants who were told that performance would be interdependent with their teammate's performance disclosed more to the confederate, providing longer responses which were measured by word count ($M = 530$, $SD = 284$) than participants who were told that their performance would be judged independently ($M = 357$, $SD = 184$, $F(1, 35) = 4.85$, $p = .034$, $\eta_p^2 = .12$).

Attitudinal Measures

Perceived homophily

Our analysis of the first section of questionnaire data, which controlled for video-game experience[1] in all tests, showed several main effects that approached, but did not reach significance. Participants who did not participate in the visual framing condition seemed more likely to report that they and the pilot worked well together, $M = 6.05$, $SD = 1.15$, than those who adorned the robot with team colors in the visual framing through self-extension condition, $M = 5.30$, $SD = 1.42$, $F(1, 35) = 3.80$, $p = .059$, $\eta_p^2 = 0.098$. Participants who did not participate in the visual framing condition also seemed to show a tendency toward feeling that the pilot was more similar to them, $M = 5.05$, $SD = 1.23$, than participants in the visual framing through self-extension condition, $M = 4.35$, $SD = 1.46$, $F(1, 35) = 3.48$, $p = .070$, $\eta_p^2 = .091$.

Interpersonal solidarity

In the second section of the questionnaire, controlling for video game experience, we found that participants who did not participate in the visual framing condition were more interested in interacting with the pilot outside of the study, $M = 5.35$, $SD = 0.88$, than those who decorated the system in the visual framing through self-extension condition, $M = 4.65$, $SD = 1.14$, $F(1, 35) = 4.65$, $p = .038$, $\eta_p^2 = .12$. Participants to whom the system was not visually framed also made more of an effort to cooperate with the pilot, $M = 6.45$, $SD = 0.61$, than participants who personalized the system did, $M = 6.05$, $SD = 0.39$, $F(1, 35) = 5.68$, $p = .023$, $\eta_p^2 = .14$.

In contrast, participants who were told that evaluation of their performance was interdependent with that of the pilot's liked their teammate more, $M = 6.75$, $SD = 0.44$, than those who were told that their performance would be evaluated individually, $M = 6.20$, $SD = 0.70$, $F(1, 35) = 8.10$, $p = .007$, $\eta_p^2 = .19$.

Controlling for videogame experience, there was also an interaction effect between visual framing through self-extension and interdependence, $F(1, 34) = 4.40$, $p = .043$, $\eta_p^2 = .12$. For participants who did not decorate the MRP system in the visual framing condition, having interdependent scores made them feel more like they and the pilot did helpful things for each other, $M = 5.90$, $SD = 0.57$, than when their scores were verbally framed as being evaluated individually, $M = 4.60$, $SD = 1.08$, $F(1, 17) = 11.05$, $p = .004$, $\eta_p^2 = .39$. For participants who decorated the system in

[1] Video-game experience significantly correlates with people's perceptions of robots, as suggested by our previous research [20].

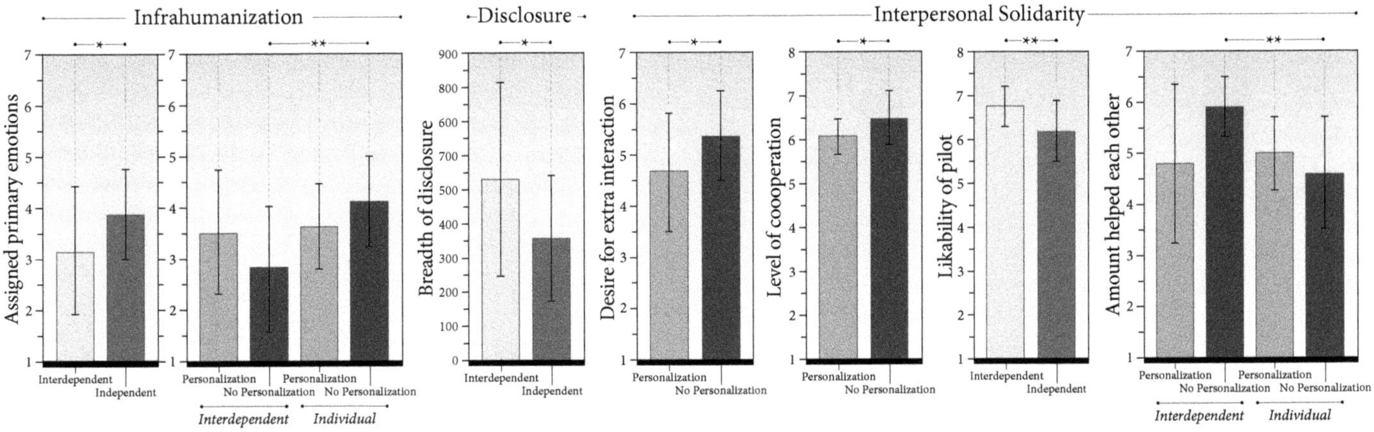

Figure 5. Results from the infrahumanization, disclosure, and interpersonal solidarity measures. (*) and (**) denotes $p < .05$ and $p < .01$, respectively.

the visual framing condition, having interdependent vs. individual scores did not significantly influence how much they felt that they and the pilot did helpful things for each other, $F(1, 16) = 0.16, p = .69, \eta_p^2 = .010$.

We also found several other marginal main effects, which approached, but did not reach significance at the $p < .05$ level. Participants with scores verbally framed as being judged interdependently with their teammate's scores appeared to cooperate more, $M = 6.40$, $SD = 0.50$, than those with individually framed scores, $M = 6.10$, $SD = 0.55$, $F(1, 35) = 3.63$, $p = .065$, $\eta_p^2 = .094$. Those who did not decorate the system in the visual framing through self-extension condition seemed to feel that they and the pilot understood each other more, $M = 5.75$, $SD = 0.97$, than those who did, $M = 5.05$, $SD = 1.36$, $F(1, 35) = 3.82$, $p = .059$, $\eta_p^2 = .098$. In addition, those who did not participate in the visual framing through self-extension condition seemed to feel that they had more in common with the pilot, $M = 4.90$, $SD = 0.91$, than those who did participate in the visual framing through self-extension, $M = 4.22$, $SD = 1.22$, $F(1, 33) = 3.79$, $p = .060$, $\eta_p^2 = .10$.

Infrahumanization

In the test for infrahumanization, controlling for video game experience across conditions, we found a main effect for verbal framing. Participants assigned more primary, non-uniquely human emotions to the pilot when told that performance was judged individually $M = 3.85$, $SD = 0.88$, than participants who were told that they would be judged interdependently, $M = 3.15$, $SD = 1.23$, $F(1, 35) = 4.32$, $p = .045$, $\eta_p^2 = .11$. This indicates that participants who believed that performance would be judged individually felt that the pilot was less human than those who believed that judgment of performance would be evaluated interdependently with their teammate's performance.

We also found an interaction effect between visual framing and verbal framing conditions. For participants not in the visual framing through self-extension condition, having individual scores caused them to assign more primary or non-uniquely human emotions to the pilot on average, $M = 4.10$, $SD = 0.88$, than having interdependent scores, $M = 2.80$, $SD = 1.23$, $F(1, 17) = 16.1$, $p = .001$, $\eta_p^2 = .49$. For participants for whom the system was visually framed through self-extension, having interdependent vs. individual scores did not significantly influence how many primary or non-uniquely human emotions they assigned to the pilot, $F(1, 17) = 0.07$, $p = .79$, $\eta_p^2 = .004$.

DISCUSSION

When the pilot's presence was verbally framed by instructing the participants that their performance would be interdependent with their teammate's, participants liked the pilot more and offered greater breadth of disclosure, showing more willingness to talk to the pilot. They also seemed to feel more cooperative and experienced weaker feelings of infrahumanization toward the pilot, meaning that they thought of the pilot as more human. These results support our first hypothesis.

Our results showed that participants who decorated the MRP system in the visual framing through self-extension condition were less inclined toward interacting with the pilot outside of the study and cooperated less with their teammate. They also tended to be less affected by the pilot's arguments in the Desert Survival Task and seemed to feel that they worked less well together, were less similar, understood each other less, and had less in common, than they did when the MRP system was not visually framed. This negative bias toward the pilot using the visually framed MRP system is inconsistent with our second hypothesis.

The results also showed that when participants did not personalize the MRP system in the visual framing condition and were told that their performance would be interdependent with the out-group confederate's, they felt greater group identity with the pilot and they believed that they had helped each other more as a team.

These results are consistent with some aspects of prior work (e.g., [22]); we found that interdependence between the task performances of the locals and the pilots increased in-group behaviors and attitudes. However, some of our results are also inconsistent with previous findings. Visually framing the MRP system by decorating it with the team's colors did not encourage the development of in-group behaviors and attitudes and decreased group cohesion and feelings of team identity.

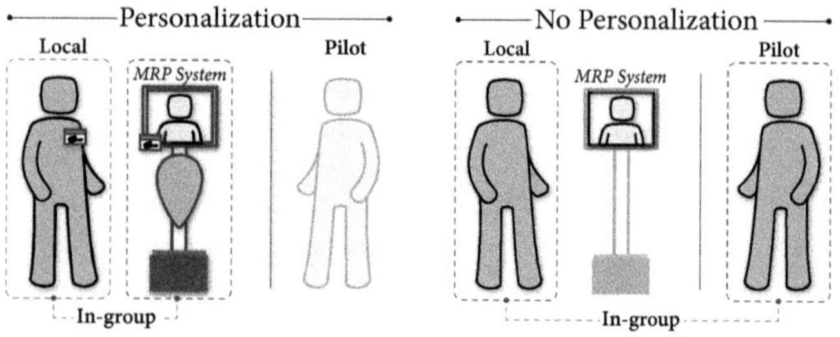

Figure 6. Our results suggest that personalization led participants to perceive the MRP system as an independent entity, diminishing collaborative outcomes between the local and the pilot.

This inconsistency with previous research on building group membership with machines [22] and creating a sense of self-extension through personalization [11] suggests a potential disparity between the local user's perception of the MRP system as a communication medium and the local's awareness of the system as its own entity.

The negative feelings that people expressed toward the pilot of the visually framed MRP system suggests that unlike communications facilitated by computer-mediated communications, embodied-mediated platforms such as MRP systems may be perceived as independent entities (see Figure 6). In previous work on personalization, people who put a face on an item in the process of customizing it experienced negative feelings of self-extension toward the the item; in contrast, those who did not put a face on the item attibuted a more positive bias toward it [13]. This negative reaction was attributed to the addition of the face, which was believed to have given the object a new identity as an individual in its own right. In the case of our study, the addition of the decoration step with the visual framing may have created a sense of self-extension or feelings of group identity between the local and the MRP system. The subsequent materialization of a face on the screen when the pilot logged on may have been perceived by the local as the intrusion of an out-group member on the in-group local-system team, thereby soliciting a hostile reaction. This creation of a relationship between the local and the MRP platform is a factor unique to embodied–mediated communication, requiring new research approaches.

In this study, we found that the physical presence of an embodied-mediated communication system creates a communication dynamic unlike that found in human–computer and computer–mediated communication. While the intricacies of this dynamic have yet to be fully explored, we have taken a first step toward understanding how both visual and verbal framing may impact the perceptions that local users have of the system, thus affecting their subsequent treatment of the pilot. Although we have not yet untangled the full consequences of highlighting or de-emphasizing the physical presence of the MRP system for the local, it is clear that this unique aspect of embodied–mediated communication has a number of implications for future design and research.

Design Implications

For designers of current and future MRP systems, there is a need to be aware that locals may perceive the MRP system as an independent entity and how this may impact their perceptions of pilots trying to use the system. In fact, although people often customize and personalize their domestic robots [31], this paradigm is not necessarily ideal for mobile mediums that are inhabited and controlled by remote users. A possible solution may be to design the system to be less obtrusive and to highlight the presence of the pilot while de-emphasizing the physicality of the system. Ways of accomplishing this may be to create systems that bear less of a resemblance to humans and are more generic in appearance. Other design heuristics for future MRP systems may include avoiding unique markers, actively discouraging decoration of the system by locals, or creating more mechanical physical interfaces; however, these approaches would require further study before implementation to ensure full understanding of their impact.

Organizational Implications

For businesses that use these systems, the importance of verbally framing the remote member as part of the team by reminding locals about the need to work together should not be underestimated. Managers of geographically distributed teams would benefit from communicating to the teams that their job performance will be judged in terms of team performance rather than being based solely on individual contributions.

Research Implications

For research in the field of embodied–mediated communication, our study has highlighted one of the critical key differences between other technological solutions and MRP systems. We have illustrated the importance of considering how the physical presence of MRP systems may significantly affect collaborative outcomes, ultimately leading to the success or failure of such systems in the future. We have also demonstrated that cultivating in-group identification can be a powerful tool for building successful teams across distances. Because of the unique dynamics between local users, remote users, and the MRP system itself, a great deal of further research is required to understand where the boundaries of the relationship between communicative actors lie. We outline a number of these new research questions in the following section.

FUTURE WORK

The nascency of work in the field of embodied–mediated communication and MRP systems offers potential for further research on the topic and deeper investigations into the interaction between the remote pilot, the local user, and the local system. The use of a more realistic task, longer exposure to the pilot, or repeated exposure to the pilot to simulate a real-world work environment may illuminate further differences or uncover changes in behavior toward the pilot or MRP system over time. Our findings may also affect the usage of MRP systems outside of business environments, such as in remote education or medical settings. Understanding the role of verbal framing may contribute to increased motivation and rapport in such settings, leading to better learning outcomes or increased follow-up by patients in treatment plans.

Further studies into how perceptions of the pilot or of the MRP system may be affected by the number of locals present during the interaction, the number of MRP systems in use, or the number of different pilots that share a system would provide a better understanding of the local user's view. From the pilot user's perspective, opportunities for future research include improving MRP system user interfaces, investigating how the perception of the locals by the pilot might change interaction dynamics, and exploring what the impact might be if the pilot personalizes the MRP system instead of the locals.

Future work must also strive to untangle how the physicality of the MRP system changes the local-system and local-pilot dynamic. For example, would visual framing without self-extension have facilitated more trust and cooperation on the local's side toward the pilot? Would visual framing of the system as more human-like or machine-like have created a different relationship between the local and the system, thus affecting the local's perception and attitude toward the pilot? From the pilot's perspective, the MRP system interface is similar to that of a videoconferencing system. How would the dynamic change if both parties were aware of the physical presence of the system? How do other physical characteristics of the MRP system such as height, speed, volume, width, and proportion change behavior toward the system and affect collaborative outcomes? These and many other questions remain to be resolved in future studies and have the potential to not only affect remote collaborators but also to provide mobility challenged individuals with a way to establish spontaneous communication while giving them control over the way that they are perceived.

LIMITATIONS

The relationship between the local user and the remote user and the relationship between the local user and the local MRP system has proven to be complex, imposing limitations on the depth at which these relationships could be examined in our study. We chose to use a confederate pilot to limit the amount of noise in our data that would have been caused by using two naïve participants. However, future work could explore truly dyadic interactions without the use of a confederate.

In the field, we observed that locals decorated the MRP systems with company-specific items (e.g., stickers, hats, expressions of inside jokes), but the current study used a fabricated identity of "the blue team." While limiting participants to pre-supplied decorations was necessary for the purposes of this study, allowing locals to decorate the MRP system with items that have more personal significance might generate a more externally valid understanding of the effects of visual framing through self-extension.

In light of our findings, we have learned that measuring the participant's sense of self-extension toward the MRP system *before* the pilot logged in would have allowed us to better detect whether or not the decoration of the system was the root cause of the negative bias that the locals expressed. In addition, the tasks used for detecting objective differences in team decision-making performance may not have been sensitive enough or of the correct design to successfully measure the manipulation effects.

Other possible limitations include imperfect capture of some of the disclosure tasks due to hardware errors (e.g., pauses in network connectivity), lack of rigorous qualitative analysis, and the difficulty in creating a convincing remote environment for the pilot to be situated in. Field observations suggest that some differences in behavior might occur if the local believes that the pilot is logged into the MRP system from a physically accessible location. A small number of participants voiced suspicions at some point in the interaction that the pilot may have been on-site and had to be reassured otherwise.

CONCLUSION

Research toward facilitating geographically distributed work teams is constantly evolving. One of the newest approaches to supporting distributed work is the mobile remote presence (MRP) system. As an emerging technology, these systems offer new opportunities for improving social and task outcomes in collaborative work. In this paper, we explored how the physical presence of the system affected group identity and collaborative outcomes using two different approaches: visual framing of the system using the placement of decorations on the system to create a sense of self-extension and verbal framing of the pilot with particular emphasis on the interdependence of evaluation. We found that verbal framing was successful in producing more in-group oriented behaviors such as willingness to work together and identification with the pilot and, contrary to our predictions, visual framing of the MRP system had a negative impact on levels of cooperation and feelings of team connectivity. By showcasing the effect that two different approaches have on group cohesion and collaborative task outcomes, we hope to inform designers of future MRP systems, to inspire others to explore research in this growing area of embodied-mediated communication, and to contribute to the direction of its future research.

ACKNOWLEDGMENTS

We would like to thank Bianca Soto for her help in conducting these studies. This research was supported by National Science Foundation award 1117652.

REFERENCES

1. Anybots, Inc. Qb. http://www.anybots.com, 2011.
2. Bailenson, J., Beall, A., Loomis, J., Blascovich, J., and Turk, M. Transformed social interaction: Decoupling representation from behavior and form in collaborative virtual environments. *Presence: Teleoperators & Virtual Environments 13*, 4 (2004), 428–441.
3. Beer, J. M., and Takayama, L. Mobile remote presence systems for older adults: Acceptance, benefits, and concerns. In *Proc HRI '11* (2011).
4. Blauner, R. *Alienation and freedom: The factory worker and his industry*. Chicago U. Press, 1964.
5. Blom, J., and Monk, A. Theory of personalization of appearance: why users personalize their pcs and mobile phones. *Human-Computer Interaction 18*, 3 (2003), 193–228.
6. Collins, N., and Miller, L. Self-disclosure and liking: A meta-analytic review. *Psychological Bulletin 116*, 3 (1994), 457.
7. Cortes, B., Demoulin, S., Rodriguez, R., Rodriguez, A., and Leyens, J. Infrahumanization or familiarity? attribution of uniquely human emotions to the self, the ingroup, and the outgroup. *Personality and Social Psychology Bulletin 31*, 2 (2005), 243.

8. Demoulin, S., Cortes, B., Viki, T., Rodriguez, A., Rodriguez, R., Paladino, M., and Leyens, J. The role of in-group identification in infra-humanization. *International Journal of Psychology 44*, 1 (2009), 4–11.
9. Fels, D. I., Waalen, J. K., Zhai, S., and Weiss, P. Telepresence under exceptional circumstances: Enriching the connection to school for sick children. In *Proc Interact '01* (2001), 617–624.
10. Giraff Technologies AB. Giraff. http://www.giraff.org/, 2010.
11. Groom, V., Takayama, L., Ochi, P., and Nass, C. I am my robot: The impact of robot-building and robot form on operators. In *Proc HRI '09* (2009), 31–36.
12. Jouppi, N. P., Iyer, S., Thomas, S., and Slayden, A. Bireality: Mutually-immersive telepresence. In *Proc ACM Multimedia '04* (2004), 860–867.
13. Kiesler, T., and Kiesler, S. My pet rock and me: An experimental exploration of the self extension concept. *Human-Computer Interaction Institute* (2004), 85.
14. Lafferty, J., Eady, P., and Elmers, J. The desert survival problem. *Experimental Learning Methods* (1974).
15. Lee, M., and Takayama, L. Now, I have a body: Uses and social norms for mobile remote presence in the workplace. In *Proc CHI '11* (2011), 33–42.
16. Luff, P., Yamashita, N., Kuzuoka, H., and Heath, C. Hands on Hitchcock: Embodied reference to a moving scene. In *Proc HCI '11*, ACM (2011), 43–52.
17. Michaud, F., Boissy, P., Labonte, D., Corriveau, H., Grant, A., Lauria, M., Cloutier, R., Route, M., Iannuzzi, D., and Royer, M. Telepresence robot for home care assistance. In *Proc AAAI Spring Symposia '07* (2007).
18. Moon, Y. Intimate exchanges: Using computers to elicit self-disclosure from consumers. *Journal of Consumer Research* (2000), 323–339.
19. Mugge, R., Schifferstein, H., and Schoormans, J. Personalizing product appearance: the effect on product attachment. In *Proc Design & Emotion* (2004).
20. Mutlu, B., Forlizzi, J., and Hodgins, J. A storytelling robot: Modeling and evaluation of human-like gaze behavior. In *Proc HUMANOIDS '06* (2006), 518–523.
21. Nakanishi, H., Kato, K., and Ishiguro, H. Zoom cameras and movable displays enhance social telepresence. In *Proc CHI '11*, ACM (2011), 63–72.
22. Nass, C., Fogg, B., and Moon, Y. Can computers be teammates? *International Journal of Human Computer Studies 45*, 6 (1996), 669–678.
23. Nguyen, D., and Canny, J. Multiview: Improving trust in group video conferencing through spatial faithfulness. In *Proc CHI '07*, ACM (2007), 1465–1474.
24. Olson, G., and Olson, J. Distance matters. *Human-computer interaction 15*, 2 (2000), 139–178.
25. Orcutt, J., and Anderson, R. Social interaction, dehumanization and the "computerized other". *Sociology & Social Research* (1977).
26. Paulos, E., and Canny, J. Delivering real world reality to the world wide web via telerobotics. In *Proc ICRA '96* (1996), 1694–1699.
27. RoboDynamics. Luna. http://robodynamics.com/, 2011.
28. Sears, D. The person-positivity bias. *Journal of Personality and Social Psychology 44*, 2 (1983), 233.
29. Smith, G. A boy and hit bot. *Sports Illustrated* (2011).
30. Suitable Technologies. Texai. https://www.suitabletech.com/, 2012.
31. Sung, J., Grinter, R., and Christensen, H. Pimp my roomba: Designing for personalization. In *Proc CHI '09*, ACM (2009), 193–196.
32. Taylor, D., and Altman, I. Intimacy-scaled stimuli for use in studies of interpersonal relations. *Psychological Reports* (1966).
33. Tsai, T.-C., Hsu, Y.-L., Ma, A.-I., King, T., and Wu, C.-H. Developing a telepresence robot for interpersonal communication with the elderly in a home environment. In *Telemedicine and e-Health*, vol. 13 (2007), 407–424.
34. Tsui, K. M., Desai, M., Yanco, H. A., and Uhlik, C. Exploring use cases for telepresence robots. In *Proc HRI '11* (2011), 11–18.
35. Tversky, A., and Kahneman, D. The framing of decisions and the psychology of choice. In *Science*, vol. 211 (1981), 453–458.
36. Vaes, J., Paladino, M., Castelli, L., Leyens, J., and Giovanazzi, A. On the behavioral consequences of infrahumanization: The implicit role of uniquely human emotions in intergroup relations. *Journal of Personality and Social Psychology 85*, 6 (2003), 1016.
37. VGo Communications, Inc. Vgo. http://www.vgocom.com/.
38. Viki, G., Winchester, L., Titshall, L., Chisango, T., Pina, A., and Russell, R. Beyond secondary emotions: The infrahumanization of outgroups using human-related and animal-related words. *Social Cognition 24*, 6 (2006), 753–775.
39. Wheeless, L. A follow-up study of the relationships among trust, disclosure, and interpersonal solidarity. *Human Communication Research 4*, 2 (1978), 143–157.
40. Whittaker, S. Theories and methods in mediated communication. *The handbook of discourse processes* (2003), 243–286.
41. Yamaoka, F., Kanda, T., Ishiguro, H., and Hagita, N. Interacting with a human or a humanoid robot? In *Proc IROS '07* (2007), 2685–2691.

APPENDIX I: DISCLOSURE INTERVIEW QUESTIONS

The questions used in the disclosure interview are listed below.

Participant Questions to Confederate:

1 How are you?
3 How old are you?
5 Do you have any siblings?
7 What's your favorite book and why?
9 What's your favorite type of food?
11 What's something that you want to accomplish before dying?
13 What's the craziest thing that you've ever done?
15 What's the worst thing that you've ever said to a friend?
17 What's a question that you wouldn't want to have to answer because it would be too embarrassing or personal?

Confederate Questions to Participant:

2 How are you?
4 Where are you from?
6 Do you have any pets?
8 What's your favorite movie and why?
10 What are your favorite things to do in your free time?
12 What are some of the things that make you angry?
14 What's your most negative childhood memory?
16 What is the meanest thing you've ever said to your parents?
18 What's a question that you wouldn't want to have to answer because it would be too embarrassing or personal?

APPENDIX II: DESERT SURVIVAL RANKING ALGORITHM

The confederate used the ranking algorithm below in the Desert Survival Task.

Participant Rank: 1, 2, 3, 4, 5, 6, 7, 8, 9
Confederate Rank: 5, 6, 1, 2, 3, 8, 4, 9, 7

Cross-Cutting Faultlines of Location and Shared Identity in the Intergroup Cooperation of Partially Distributed Groups

Amy Voida[1], Nathan D. Bos[2], Judith S. Olson[1], Gary M. Olson[1] & Lauren Dunning[1]
[1]Donald Bren School of Information and Computer Sciences
University of California, Irvine
{amyvoida, jsolson, gary.olson, ldunning}@uci.edu

[2]Johns Hopkins University Applied Physics Laboratory
nathan.bos@jhuapl.edu

ABSTRACT
This paper reports the results of a study comparing the relative influence of location and shared identity in partially distributed work. Using an experimental task called Shape Factory, groups of eight participants were configured such that in the baseline "strangers" condition only the location-based faultline was present while in the experimental "intergroup" condition, participants from two different shared identity groups engaged in distributed collaboration, creating an additional, cross-cutting faultline. The results showed that participants in the intergroup condition, with both location-based and shared identity faultlines, performed at a higher level than participants in the strangers condition, with only the location-based faultline. In the intergroup condition, the performance effects of location and shared identity were roughly equal and did not affect each other differentially in combination.

Author Keywords
Intergroup cooperation; faultline; partially distributed work; shared identity

ACM Classification Keywords
H.5.3. [Information Interfaces and Presentation]: Group and Organization Interfaces—Computer-Supported Cooperative Work

INTRODUCTION
Empirical studies of collaboration often find that subgroups form within workgroups, dividing workgroups into "us" and "them" [1, 5, 11, 15, 19]. Subgroups emerge along faultlines that have been attributed to a number of different factors including location, nationality, professional or organizational affiliation, shared group identity, power, information flow and diversity, subgroup size, resource distribution, values, race, gender, and age [1, 5, 6, 11, 15, 19, 21, 23, 25, 26, 32, 35].

Given the increasing prevalence of distributed teams, it is not surprising that location has been the most commonly cited subgroup faultline in the research literature on distributed teams. Distance and proximity have great influence over collaborative practices [22, 29].

Cramton offers one explanation for this tendency:

> *Shared location provides a natural basis for the development of strong subgroup identities because such clusters of people typically enjoy more interaction and more common information with each other than they do with remote partners* [11].

Armstrong and Cole call this location-based basis for subgroup identification the "metacontext of the locale" [1].

The presence of geographical faultlines within workgroups does not preclude the presence of additional faultlines, however. If other faultlines align with that of location (e.g., organizational faultlines in a team composed of members from two merging companies still working out of separate offices), subgroup tendencies could be even stronger [11]. But it is not clear what happens if other faultlines do not align with location (e.g., professional faultlines in a team composed of designers and developers who are both distributed across locations). Will these cross-cutting faultlines provide a "source of social integration for the dispersed team" [11] or will they serve to further fragment the composition of the workgroup?

The effects of two different factors—location and shared identity—have been examined separately in a series of laboratory studies of partially distributed teams. A study of the effect of *location* found that collocated participants interacted more with other collocated participants and formed a site-based in-group [5]. Similarly, participants working remotely from isolated settings interacted more with other isolated participants and formed their own in-group. Over the course of a series of studies related to subgroup faultlines, the isolated in-group, in some instances, was strong enough to perform as well as the collocated in-group, but more often the group of isolates performed less well [3, 4, 5].

In a follow-on study, the presence of *shared identity* in distributed teams was introduced to try to mitigate the subgroup faultline effects of location [2]. This study found that shared identity groups outperformed groups of strangers but that location still served as a significant faultline. Even within shared identity groups, collocated participants outperformed their isolated, remote counterparts; collocated participants took on more leadership roles within the group; and remote participants reported experiencing less affective group identity and less group efficacy.

While both location and shared identity have been found to significantly influence the work of partially distributed groups, we do not understand how these two factors interact. Nor do we understand the relative weight of their influence. What would happen if shared identity subgroups were split between collocated and remote locations? Would one faultline emerge as a more dominant influence? Would one factor help to mitigate the subgrouping influence of the other or further fragment the group?

In this paper, we present the results of an empirical study of partially distributed teams examining the mutual influence between and relative effects of two faultlines—location and shared identity.

RELATED WORK

The Influence of Location on Distributed Work

Location has a multidimensional influence on distributed work; differences in location result not just in geographic differences but time zone differences, organizational differences (e.g., different departments), and cultural differences (e.g., both national and office site cultures) [1, 29]. Each of these differences serves to influence distributed work, both for better and worse. Distributed teams, for example, are often formed in order to take advantage of diversity that is not present at a single site; as a result, the diversity within distributed teams is often greater than would be found in a collocated team, leading to an increased potential for the presence of additional or stronger faultlines [22].

Members of distributed teams lack the same kind of situational awareness about their colleagues' behavior that is available to collocated teams [11]. Team members have fewer cues with which to help them interpret their distributed colleagues' behavior; as a result, members of these teams tend to make harsher or more "uncharitable" attributions about their distributed colleagues [11, 15, 34].

Distributed teams also face a number of information-related challenges including communicating and maintaining contextual information across sites, managing the uneven distribution of information, cueing distributed colleagues about the importance of different kinds of information, overcoming differences in access to information and communication technology, interpreting silence during exchanges with colleagues at remote sites, and identifying sources of expertise and help from distributed colleagues [11, 16]. As a result of these challenges, some distributed teams have been found to fail to exchange necessary information with all relevant parties, misinterpret information (or focus on the wrong aspect of the information they have been given), and have less effective transactive memory [1, 11, 20, 28]. Indeed, researchers have identified instances in which members of distributed teams have expressed a reluctance to share information across sites [15]. Remote colleagues in distributed teams have reported feeling "cut off from key conversations" and even being ignored during tele- and video- conferences [1].

Location also influences the development of group identity within distributed teams. Individuals come to identify with a group by conforming to the norms of that group [37]. For remote collaborators, the process of observing and interacting with the group in order to discover those norms takes longer, and group identification is "diluted" through whatever medium is used to replace face-to-face collaboration [8]. Empirical studies of distributed work have, indeed, found that remote group members self-report significantly lower levels of affective group identity than their collocated colleagues [2] as well as problems forming groups and maintaining ties [1].

Finally, location has been found to cause the emergence of subgroups within distributed teams, with collocated colleagues forming one in-group and remote colleagues forming another [1, 5, 32]. The presence of location-based in-groups has been found to cause additional problems, as well, with location-based subgroups attending disproportionately to people and information within their in-group, leading to information bias and, ultimately, diminished performance [1, 4, 24]. More generally, biased dynamics between subgroups threatens group cohesion and can have significant negative consequences on the performance of the superordinate group [1, 18, 31].

The Influence of Shared Identity on Distributed Work

Shared (or group) identity is one aspect of an individual's social identity, "that *part* of the individuals' self-concept which derives from their knowledge of their membership of a social group (or groups) together with the value and emotional significance of that membership" [35]. Shared identity has three components: the cognitive component, characterized by social categorization; the affective component, characterized by interpersonal attraction; and the behavioral component, characterized by interdependence [14].

Shared identity has been posited to create a "psychological tie" among distributed team members, leading team members to have more faith in each other and be more likely to communicate about issues as they arise [17, 18]. Shared identity increases group cohesion, reduces conflict (particularly interpersonal and affective conflict), and increases motivation [13, 18, 21, 23, 27]. Additionally, shared identity has been found to correlate with increased employee compliance, increased job satisfaction, and decreased attrition [23].

Shared identity improves the performance of distributed workgroups, although empirical studies suggest that even within groups with strong shared identity, other faultlines can still influence work practices and perceptions of the work experience [2]. When location-based faultlines occurred within shared identity groups, for example, remote colleagues performed less well and reported less shared identity and trust than their collocated counterparts.

Research Questions

While there is ample literature exploring the influence of location and shared identity independently on distributed work, there is little research that explores the mutual influence between these two factors. This study, then, is exploratory in nature and motivated by two research questions: when shared identity and location are present as faultlines in distributed teams, (a) to what extent does each factor influence the productivity of teams and (b) in what ways do the two factors influence each other?

METHOD

Eighteen partially distributed groups of eight participants each played a serious game called Shape Factory, described in the next section, that has been designed to simulate distributed work. Each group was composed of four collocated players and four remote, isolated players (simulating telecommuters). Nine groups were composed entirely of strangers; half were collocated and half were remote. Nine groups were composed of members with shared identity from two different campus organizations; half of the individuals from each organization were collocated and half were remote. During each game, we logged messages exchanged in the game and recorded face-to-face interactions among collocated group members. Participants individually completed a post-game questionnaire. Researchers also took qualitative "field"notes about the collaboration strategies that they observed during each game.

Shape Factory

The experimental context for this research was a serious game, Shape Factory, designed to simulate the collaborative work of distributed teams [5]. We provide an overview of the game and then discuss the ways that it has been designed to simulate the dynamics of collaborative work.

Overview of Gameplay

In the Shape Factory game, groups of eight participants try to fill orders of strings of shapes, such as circle-circle-triangle. Players are assigned a specialty shape that they can build for $10. They can fill orders with their own specialty shape, they can opt to build any other shape in the game (their non-specialty shape) for $25, or they can buy shapes from other players who can make them more cheaply than they can.

Each participant manufactures shapes and sells them to other players, negotiating a price per shape anywhere between $10 and $30. Players who are able to fill orders earn game dollars commensurate with the length of the orders, from $35 for orders requiring two shapes to $220 for orders requiring eight shapes. Longer orders are more difficult to fill, requiring a greater amount of collaboration to acquire the necessary shapes.

Each group of participants played Shape Factory for ten rounds; each game lasted two and a half hours. During each round, players were given two new orders to fill and were allowed to build up to four shapes. Orders and shapes persisted for two game rounds before expiring.

All participants had access to a lightweight messaging system within the game. In the messaging system, participants could send requests for shapes, negotiate for the price of shapes, or send any other freeform messages that they desired. Collocated participants were also able to talk freely among themselves.

Simulated Real World Dynamics

Shape Factory is an established platform for conducting research on distributed work and provides a degree of ecological validity appropriate to an experimental context [2, 3, 4, 5, 10]. The game has been designed to simulate a number of key characteristics of workplace collaborations:

- As is typical in workplace collaborations, all group members had *individual expertise* that made them a valuable part of the collaboration. In Shape Factory, each participant's expertise is mirrored in their ability to make a shape inexpensively, either for their own orders or to sell to other players who need that shape.
- As is also typical in workplace collaborations, group members *work interdependently*, relying on the expertise of other group members in order to get their own work done. In Shape Factory, each group member was tasked with filling orders that included strings of shapes (e.g., square-circle-triangle), necessitating collaboration with other group members who could supply the needed shapes. Group members bought and sold shapes from each other in order to complete their own orders.
- Similar to the dynamic in workplace collaborations in which individuals have some degree of choice about with whom they collaborate, players of Shape Factory also have a degree of *choice among collaborators*. In each group, two participants have similar expertise, i.e., can build the same shape; players can choose the person from whom to buy that particular shape.
- As is typical in workplace collaborations, Shape Factory imposes *resource scarcity*. During each round of the game, each player is only able to build four shapes, enough to fill many, but not all, orders.
- Finally, participants were *incentivized in two ways* to most closely correspond with the incentive structure in typical work teams. Half of group members' compensation was based on a percentage of their individual performance in the game, while the other half was based on a percentage of their entire group's performance in the game.

Participants

We recruited participants from the undergraduate population at a large, public university. Each group of eight was composed of either all male or all female participants in order to avoid introducing gender as an additional faultline. Five groups in each condition were composed of male participants; four groups in each condition were composed of female participants. For the nine groups in the "strangers" condition, we recruited participants at new student job fairs and in large, introductory courses across campus. Participants in the strangers condition did not know any other participant in their session. For the nine groups in the "intergroup" condition (in which there were two different shared identity subgroups), we recruited participants who knew each other through participation in campus organizations that fostered shared identity among its members, either through shared housing and frequent group activities (e.g., fraternities and sororities) or through frequent collaborative activities that pitted members of their organization against others (e.g., club sports teams)[1].

Configuration of Participants

Half of the participants were collocated during the game, sitting around a conference room table. The other half of the participants played the game remotely, each in a separate room. In order to understand the relative influence of location on collaborative work, we ensured that one participant with the expertise to build each shape was present among collocated players and was also present among remote players, as shown in Figure 1.

Additionally, in the intergroup condition, half of the participants were members of one campus organization (A) and half of the participants were members of a second campus organization (B). In order to understand the relative influence of shared identity on collaborative work, we ensured that one member of each organization had expertise in building each shape (Figure 1). Members of each organization were divided equally between the collocated and remote conditions. Coarsely, then, a participant needing any particular shape had two options: to buy it from another player who shared his or her geographical characteristics (collocated or remote) or to buy it from another player with a common shared identity (from the same organization).

In the strangers condition, participants did not know each other beforehand and were randomly assigned to any one of the eight shape-location roles in the game.

[1] The groups we recruited for the shared identity condition had a number of co-occurring characteristics. In addition to shared identity, they also had individual relationships with each other (familiarity). Since they were both single-gender groups and belonged to organizations that usually self-select into houses based on personality and other interests, groups also had perceived similarity (homophily). In social psychology, these three constructs are distinct, albeit often co-occurring in the real world. Our research design mirrors real-world co-occurrence. The work of teasing apart the effects of these constructs would be an interesting challenge for future research.

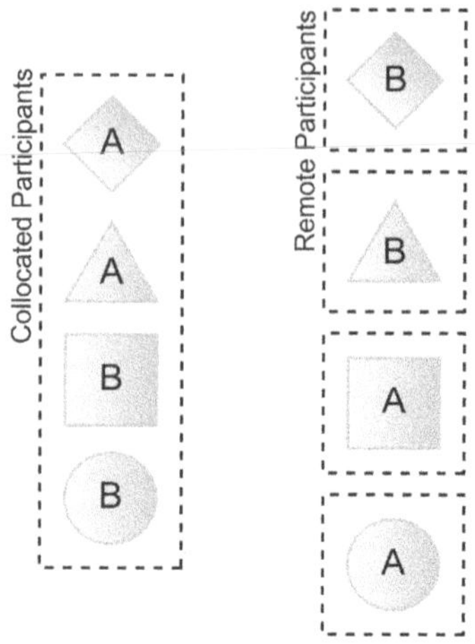

Figure 1. Configuration of participants in the intergroup condition. Dotted lines delineate rooms in which participants played the game, letters indicate shared identity subgroup membership, and shapes correspond to in-game expertise.

Procedure

Participants received instruction on how to play Shape Factory while in the same room. During instruction, two types of activities were interleaved[2]:

- Participants watched a series of videos explaining a particular aspect of the game (e.g., how to build shapes, how to buy shapes, or how to fill orders), and
- Participants logged into a "sandbox" version of the game and practiced that particular aspect of the game.

Afterwards, participants completed a quiz to ensure that they understood the rules of the game. The instructional phase of the study typically lasted about an hour. At this time, participants were also randomly assigned a shape expertise and location for gameplay within the constraints of shared identity and location as described above and shown in Figure 1. In the strangers condition, players were randomly assigned from among all eight possible shape-location permutations. In the intergroup condition, players from each campus organization were randomly assigned from among only the shape-location permutations allocated to their shared identity subgroup (e.g., For group A: collocated diamond, collocated triangle, remote square, and remote circle [Figure 1]).

Remote participants then moved to their individual rooms; collocated participants stayed together in the group room. Once situated, participants played ten rounds of Shape Factory, each lasting 15 minutes, for a total of 2 hours and 30 minutes of gameplay. Players took a short break between rounds five and six.

[2] The instructional phase of this study was different than the instructional phase of previous Shape Factory studies. The new instructional phase was designed to help participants understand the pragmatics of the game and its interface so that once the game had begun, they would be able to focus more on crafting and carrying out collaboration strategies.

Participants completed a post-game questionnaire, comprised of questions measuring the following constructs:

- *Shared Identity.* Participants rated four statements measuring affective group identity (e.g., "I enjoyed interacting with members of this group"). The group identity scale was developed by Henry et al. [14].
- *Group Efficacy.* Participants rated three statements measuring group efficacy, individuals' confidence in the group (e.g., "Our group worked well together"). The group efficacy scale was developed for a previous Shape Factory study [2] based on the concept described by Carroll et al. [9].
- *Reciprocity.* Participants rated seven statements measuring reciprocity, the extent to which individuals were motivated by a desire to dole out or receive "payback" (e.g., "I went out of my way to help players who had helped me"). The reciprocity scale was adapted for a previous Shape Factory study [2] based on a scale from Perugini et al. [30].
- *Individual versus Group Motivation.* Participants rated two statements about the extent to which they were motivated by individual incentives in the game (e.g., "My primary goal in the game was to maximize my own profit") and five questions about the extent to which they were motivated by group incentives in the game (e.g., "I sacrificed personal profits to help increase the overall group profit by helping other players fill longer orders"). The motivation scales were developed for a previous Shape Factory study by Bos et al. [2].
- *Trust.* For each other player in the game, participants rated their degree of trust in that individual along a five-point Likert scale (e.g., "Blue Square—I trust this player").
- *Leadership.* For each other player in the game, participants rated the leadership presence of that individual along a five-point Likert scale (e.g., Green Circle—"This player was one of the leaders of the group").

RESULTS

Comparison of Superordinate Group Performance Between Intergroup and Strangers Conditions

The superordinate groups[3] in the intergroup condition performed significantly higher, on average, than superordinate groups of strangers. In the intergroup condition, superordinate groups scored an average of 3520.00 points per game while in the strangers condition, superordinate groups scored an average of 3138.89 points per game (t[16]=3.21, p=0.005).

We performed a set of t-test comparisons on other measures to understand what led to higher superordinate group scores. Groups did not differ significantly on any of the following measures:

- The number of orders filled (for which participants would have been paid),
- The number of shapes sold in the process of trying to fill those orders,
- The price accrued for shapes sold, and
- The extent to which participants built their own specialty shapes at reduced cost (at $10 per shape) versus building non-specialty shapes (at $25 per shape).

What did vary was that superordinate groups in the intergroup condition filled significantly *longer* and therefore more lucrative orders. Filling longer orders required more coordination between multiple suppliers. Filling longer orders also required some trust and confidence in collaborators, because of the higher need for coordination and because the player stood to lose more money in unusable parts if the order couldn't be filled. Superordinate groups in the intergroup condition filled orders with an average length of 4.53 shapes while superordinate groups in the strangers condition filled orders with an average length of 4.09 shapes (t[16]=2.37, p=0.031). The average value of an order filled by a superordinate group in the intergroup condition was 106.46 while the average value of an order filled by a superordinate group in the strangers condition was 92.46 (t[16]=2.49, p=0.024). Participants in the intergroup condition engaged in more successful collaboration, then, because longer orders required more collaboration in order to be filled.

Comparison of Group Self-Report Measures Between Intergroup and Strangers Conditions

In order to examine whether participants in the strangers and intergroup conditions varied in their perceptions related to the collaboration, we compared self-report measures from post-game questionnaires. We used individual responses instead of group averages, which required consideration of possible effects at multiple levels. To test for effects at the superordinate group level we used the mixed model procedure in SPSS, constructing an 'empty' model for each scale with superordinate group first as a random effect, and then as both a fixed and random effect. In all cases, the superordinate group did not account for a significant amount of variance, indicating that it was not necessary to use a multilevel model including each variable as both fixed and random effects.

Instead, we used an ANOVA to compare responses to survey scales between participants in the strangers and intergroup conditions. Table 1 shows comparisons between conditions on questionnaire scales that had significant differences. Compared to participants in the strangers condition, participants in the intergroup condition reported

[3] In order to differentiate between the various groups and subgroups in our study, we refer to the full complement of eight participants in each study session as the superordinate group. Four-person subgroups based on location in both the strangers and intergroup conditions are referred to as the collocated and remote subgroups. Four-person subgroups in the intergroup condition based on organizational affiliation/shared identity are referred to as shared identity subgroups.

significantly higher affective group identity, group efficacy, and motivation to work for the group, with significantly lower demands for reciprocity and motivation for individual incentives. For each of these comparisons, df=(1,141). This pattern of results is similar to those found in Bos et al [2], where all members of the superordinate group were members of the same shared identity group.

Scale (Cronbach's alpha)	Intergroup Participants' Mean	Stranger Participants' Mean	F	p
Affective Group Identity (.64)	4.03	3.74	4.44	=.037
Group Efficacy (.70)	3.74	3.27	13.74	<.001
Reciprocity (.70)	2.96	3.19	5.20	0.024
Individual Motivation (.60)	3.22	3.79	14.07	<.001
Group Motivation (.80)	3.76	3.20	19.00	<.001

Table 1. Post-game questionnaire results

Comparison of Collocated and Remote Subgroup Performance within the Strangers and Intergroup Conditions

We next began to look for differences between collocated and remote team members. For these analyses, we examined the stranger and intergroup conditions separately. We first tested for superordinate group level effects using SPSS's mixed model procedure, as before, and found no significant effects of superordinate groups that would necessitate a multilevel model. We then compared scores using ANOVA. We found that within the strangers condition, collocated participants earned significantly higher scores than remote participants. Collocated participants averaged 424.17 points per game while remote participants averaged 360.56 points per game ($F[1,62]=4.85$, $p=0.031$). This finding replicates performance differences between collocated and remote participants found in some previous Shape Factory studies [2, 4].

In contrast, this performance difference did *not* manifest in the intergroup condition. The average difference in scores between collocated participants (440.83 points per game) and remote participants (439.17 points per game) was not significant. This result suggests that shared identity has an effect, reducing the impact of the location-based faultline on performance.

Relative Influence of and Interaction Between Location and Shared Identity on Collaboration Patterns

Next we examined trading patterns between participants in the intergroup condition to understand whether location or shared identity affected with whom players chose to collaborate. We constructed a matrix in which each vector represented a unique relationship between two players (e.g. Blue Square & Green Circle), excluding relationships between players with the same specialty shape (who rarely traded with each other). For each relationship, we aggregated the total number of shapes bought and sold (transactions occurring in both directions) as a measure of the amount of collaboration.

To examine what relationship characteristics predicted higher levels of trade, we created two Boolean variables, 'SameLocation' indicating whether the players were in the same location-based subgroup and 'SameIdentity' indicating whether they were both members of the same shared identity subgroup. As in the previous analysis, we first checked for superordinate group level effects using the mixed model procedure in SPSS; as before, there were no significant effects at this level that would necessitate a multilevel model. We analyzed the effects of these two variables with a two-way ANOVA in SPSS. We found that both being in the same location-based and shared identity subgroups were significant and fairly strong predictors of higher trade totals ($F[1,428]=90.45$, $p=<.001$ and $F[1,428]=122.105$, $p<.001$, respectively). The interaction between them was not significant. The adjusted R Squared for this model was a decent 0.268.

Having established these statistical relationships, we then inspected the trading patterns between players of different types. Turning to participants in the strangers condition, we found that, in line with previous Shape Factory studies, being in the same location-based subgroup led to a greater amount of trading between player pairs ($F[1, 430]= 450.7$, $p<.001$). The larger numbers of shapes in the upper left and lower right cells of Table 2 show the strong tendency for strangers to trade with other players in the same location-based subgroup.

		To Buyer	
		Collocated	**Remote**
From Seller	**Collocated**	973	267
	Remote	357	704

Table 2. Sum of shapes sold among collocated and remote players in the strangers condition

We then examined trading in the intergroup condition. In this condition, being in the same location-based subgroup was crossed with being part of a shared identity subgroup. Table 3 shows a much more equitable trading pattern between collocated and remote players in the intergroup condition. However, while the effects of location appeared to have been mitigated, they did not disappear. The effect of being in the same location-based subgroup was still a highly significant predictor of trading levels as reported above ($F[1,428]=90.45$, $p=<.001$). But being in the same shared identity subgroup was also highly significant ($F[1,428]=122.105$, $p<.001$). There was no significant interaction between these two factors.

		To Buyer	
		Collocated	Remote
From Seller	Collocated	692	497
	Remote	496	617

Table 3. Sum of shapes sold among collocated and remote players in the intergroup condition

Table 4 shows the average number of shapes exchanged by pairs with different permutations of subgroup affiliations. As expected, participants that shared both a location-based and shared identity subgroup traded the most (an average of 16.2 shapes exchanged) and those that shared neither subgroup affiliation traded the least (an average of 5.3 shapes exchanged).

	Same Shared Identity Subgroup	Different Shared Identity Subgroup
Same Location-Based Subgroup	16.2	10.0
Different Location-Based Subgroup	10.9	5.3

Table 4. Average number of shapes exchanged by pairs with varying subgroup affiliations

But comparing the effects of the two factors against each other, the effects were very similar. An average of 10.0 shapes were traded between pairs that shared location-based but not shared identity subgroup affiliations, and an average of 10.9 shapes were traded between pairs with the same shared identity but not location-based subgroup affiliation. That the two factors of interest, location and shared identity, were very similar in effect can be seen in their similar effects reported earlier and similar trading frequencies (10.0 vs 10.9) seen in Table 4. We explored the data using other methods (linear regression and multilevel regression) and found comparable effects; we also found no evidence of a significant interaction between the variables. Thus, within the intergroup condition, shared identity and location had roughly equal effects.

Superordinate Group Strategies

The Shape Factory game is designed such that if participants want to maximize their payoff, they must work together as a superordinate group. The most common superordinate group strategy involved players agreeing to buy and sell shapes for a standard amount (e.g., "sell everything for 10 next round so the group total goes up"). The second most common strategy (and the one most critical for optimizing superordinate group scores) involved players agreeing to sell shapes to others to fill the largest orders every round. For example, one participant sent the following message to other players:

> *why dont we just tell each other how big our orders are and take the highest four and fill those...i mean there are 8 of us so i figure half the orders per round or something u know, that way we"l be maximizing profits for each round...tell the girls your with :)*

Common variants of the largest-order strategy involved either asking everyone to fill only those orders worth more than 100 points or asking everyone only to fill only their largest order each round. Both of these variations are notable in that they demonstrate ways that players were attempting to balance the optimal strategy (of filling only the largest orders each round) with the overhead involved in having to continually maintain an awareness of who had what orders each round and which of those orders should be filled.

Of the nine superordinate groups in the intergroup condition, two did not discuss any superordinate group-level strategy with each other, two developed a superordinate group strategy among the four collocated subgroup members and shared it with their remote collaborators, and five had one or two people from the same shared identity subgroup work via the messaging system to advocate for a superordinate group strategy. In the latter case, if there were only one strategist, that strategist was always isolated and working remotely; if there were two strategists, at least one of the two worked remotely. Oddly, in all five of these latter cases, the shared identity subgroup to which the strategist(s) belonged performed less well than the shared identity subgroup without the strategist(s). Our data does not fully explain this phenomenon.

We know that groups generally did not run out of time during each round so we do not believe that the lower performance was due to coordination costs impinging on time constraints. We also know that, in most cases, the proposed superordinate group strategy was one of the variants of the optimal strategy that required less continual coordination so we do not believe that the lower scores were due to increased coordination overhead. We know, too, that the strategist was not always the lowest performing member of his or her shared identity subgroup, so we believe that the phenomenon is a subgroup-level effect and not the effect of the strategist(s) individually lowering the collective subgroup performance.

From the post-game questionnaire, we know that in four of the five groups, the strategists were rated more highly than non-strategists on the scale measuring leadership.

This phenomenon, if replicated, will require additional analysis in order to understand its underlying cause.

DISCUSSION

In this research, we studied the cross-cutting effects of location-based and shared identity faultlines on partially distributed work. We found that shared identity ameliorated some of the effects of the location-based faultline but both faultlines *still* had an effect on performance. Indeed, under the circumstances of this study, shared identity and location had roughly equal effects in shaping a team's performance. We did not identify any significant interactions between the two factors.

Shared identity affected performance by enabling greater collaboration as team members filled longer orders which had a higher payoff but required increased coordination. Increased coordination comes with costs [33], and adding multiple faultlines into the mix only accentuates this. Finally, we observed some puzzling trends in performance related to the coordination of superordinate group strategy in the intergroup condition, which suggest directions for future work.

Leadership and Subgroup Affiliations

The phenomenon we observed related to the lower performance of the superordinate group strategists' shared identity subgroup, although unexplained, does suggest the need to better understand leadership in teams that have been divided by subgroup faultlines. In a previous Shape Factory study in which all participants belonged to the same shared identity group, collocated participants typically collaborated to develop a superordinate group strategy and communicated that strategy to their remote counterparts [2]. In that study, the collocated subgroup formed a leadership team, making all strategic decisions and delegating many responsibilities to remote group members. The extent to which the collocated subgroup dominated superordinate group leadership raised concerns about the inequitability of leadership opportunities for remote colleagues in workgroups divided by a strong location-based faultline.

In the current study, the superordinate group strategists were more equitably distributed across location-based subgroup faultlines. Although the number of groups in this study is too small to generalize, half of the groups had strategists, rated by others as leaders, who were members of the remote subgroup. It may be the case, then, that the interaction between location and shared identity faultlines creates a working context in which remote colleagues are more likely to gain leadership experience than when a location-based faultline exists on its own.

However, it is troubling that the strategists' shared identity subgroups consistently underperformed relative to subgroups without strategists. Indeed, research has found that leadership can be challenging in the presence of shared identity faultlines, that "identical leadership behavior is interpreted differently depending on whether it is enacted by an ingroup or outgroup member" [12]. Further, it seems that the effectiveness of leaders depends on their ability to create shared identity among a workgroup:

> *The potential of leaders or managers to communicate and create a sense of shared identity is an important determinant of the likelihood that their attempts to energize, direct, and sustain particular work-related behaviors in their followers will be successful* [12].

If the prevailing shared identity within workgroups exists at the superordinate group level, then the leader may be more successful in his or her attempts to advocate for collaboration at the superordinate group level. If the prevailing shared identity within workgroups exists at the subgroup level, however, then the leader may have a more difficult time convincing colleagues to follow his or her lead.

In the present study, we do not have systematic evidence of the extent to which shared group identity existed at the superordinate- versus sub- group level. We can point to one instance in which participants became skeptical about the efficacy of a superordinate group strategy and decided, via backchannel messages to each other, that they would just focus on helping out the members of their shared identity subgroup:

> *...noone ever responds so idk what is going on anywhere! im just gunna try to fill orders*
>
> *wanna just help each other out? and still act like were trying to help the group? Lol*
>
> *Should we try to fill our own orders? within our group? the highest within our little area? or try to keep doing the mass group thing?*
>
> *lol im down, thats what kelly and i are doing anyways. our group profit isnt gunna take us anywehre, they used 20,000 as the group profit example...check ours out...FAIL*

Although our understanding of the causality and implications of this phenomenon is incomplete, it does suggest that more research is needed to understand leadership in workgroups with multiple faultlines. In the presence of cross-cutting location and shared identity faultlines, the shared identity faultline may be a double-edged sword. On one hand, it may help allow for more equitable leadership opportunities in distributed teams. On the other hand, if the shared identity faultline is strong enough that the subgroup identification dominates over the superordinate group identification, leaders may be faced with significant challenges in undertaking superordinate group-level collaborative work.

Design Challenges

While the emergence of subgroups can sometimes lead to in-group bias and negative effects on performance, researchers studying intergroup cooperation find that a balanced acknowledgement of the multiple superordinate and subgroup affiliations present in teams may, in fact, be the most productive way to overcome these negatively impactful biases:

> *An integrated perspective would involve the presence of a salient superordinate level of categorization that simultaneously preserves (allows for) subordinate differentiation (distinctive category identities) and individualization of members of both subgroups. Such a representation can be achieved by social structures*

that are not nested hierarchies but are characterized instead by cross-cutting roles and social categories [6].

It may prove useful, then, to explore the design space for systems that more explicitly acknowledge or support superordinate groups, subgroups, and the individual. That individuals maintain identities at multiple levels means that realistically, intergroup cooperation (at the superordinate group level) and in-group bias (at the subgroup level) are not mutually exclusive [36]. The challenge for design, then, may be in walking a very fine line between systems that simultaneously allow for a variety of categories of social identification to co-exist without fostering the negative effects that can sometimes result from in-group bias.

CONCLUSION

Researchers have become increasingly nuanced in their understanding of the ways that different configurations of the location faultline within distributed teams influences distributed work—that the effects on and challenges of distributed work are different in totally virtual teams than in partially distributed teams, for example (e.g., [13, 28]). Similarly, researchers have become increasingly nuanced in their understanding of the ways in which different configurations of the shared group identity faultline influence cooperative work—that individuals maintain layers of multiple shared group identifications as part of a complex social identity (e.g., [6, 7]).

Yet, while the field delves more deeply into understanding the nuances of individual faultlines and factors in distributed work, there is much less research that has focused on examining the interactions between multiple faultlines, particularly empirical laboratory studies that enable us to develop a more precise theoretical understanding of the relative weight and interaction of multiple factors.

Distributed teams are an undeniably complex phenomenon, and in the real world, multiple faultlines co-exist in a dizzying array of permutations and configurations. Corporations merge, for example, and distributed teams composed of new colleagues from different companies have to come together and function in the presence of different national, organizational or site cultures all while working from different locations or time zones and likely also taking into account a diversity of different disciplinary backgrounds and expertise. As merging companies are more fully integrated, each of these faultlines becomes a moving target, sometimes aligned with other faultlines and sometimes intersecting in different ways. Throughout, then, the need to understand the numerous (and evolving) permutations and configurations of faultlines becomes even more pressing.

In this research, we have begun to address this need and to more systematically study one of the many permutations and configurations of faultlines that co-exist in real-world distributed teams—the cross-cutting faultlines of location and shared identity. Much work still remains to be done to understand the effects of the many different permutations and configurations of faultlines present in real-world teams. The Shape Factory simulation has proven to be a productive context for exploring cross-cutting faultlines in collaborative work. However, the additional logistical complexity of recruiting and scheduling large groups of individuals with increasingly specific individual- and group- level characteristics makes this research trajectory a challenging enough enterprise to warrant the combined efforts of additional researchers who can bring a diversity of expertise to bear on this important and challenging problem.

REFERENCES

1. Armstrong, D.J. & Cole, P. (2002). Managing distances and differences in geographically distributed work groups. In P. Hinds & S. Kiesler (Eds.), *Distributed Work* (pp. 167–189). Cambridge, MA: MIT Press.
2. Bos, N.D., Buyuktur, A., Olson, J.S., Olson G.M. & Voida, A. (2010). Shared identity helps partially distributed teams, but distance still matters. In *Proc. Group 2010*. New York: ACM Press, 89–96.
3. Bos, N.D., Olson, J.S., Cheshin, A., Kim, Y.S. & Nan, N. (2005). Traveling blues: The effect of relocation on partially distributed teams. In *Proc. CHI 2005*. New York: ACM Press, 1917–1920.
4. Bos, N.D., Olson, J.S., Nan, N., Shami, N.S., Hoch, S., & Johnston, E. (2006). Collocation blindness in partially distributed groups: Is there a downside to being collocated? In *Proc. CHI 2006*. New York: ACM Press, 1313–1321.
5. Bos, N.D, Shami, N.S., Olson, J.S., Cheshin, A. & Nan, N. (2004) In-group/out-group effects in distributed teams: An experimental simulation. In *Proc. CSCW 2004*. New York: ACM Press, 429–436.
6. Brewer, M.B. (1996). When contact is not enough: Social identity and intergroup cooperation. *International Journal of Intercultural Relations*, 20(3–4), 291–303.
7. Brewer, M.B. & Gardner, W. (1996). Who is this "we"? Levels of collective identity and self representations. *Journal of Personality and Social Psychology,* 71(1), 83–93.
8. Burke, K., Aytes, K., Chidambaram, L. & Johnson, J.J. (1999). A study of partially distributed work groups: The impact of media, location, and time on perceptions and performance. *Small Group Research,* 30(4), 453–490.
9. Carroll, J., Rosson, M.B. & Zhou, J. (2005). Collective efficacy as a measure of community. In *Proc. CHI 2005*. New York: ACM Press, 1–10.
10. Cheshin, A., Rafaeli, A. & Bos, N. (2011). Anger and happiness in virtual teams: Emotional influences of text and behavior on others' affect in the absence of non-

verbal cues. *Organizational Behavior and Human Decision Processes,* 116(1), 2–16.

11. Cramton, C.D. (2002). Attribution in distributed work. In P. Hinds & S. Kiesler (Eds.), *Distributed Work* (pp. 191–212). Cambridge, MA: MIT Press.

12. Ellemers, N., de Gilder, D. & Haslam, S.A. (2004). Motivating individuals and groups at work: A social identity perspective on leadership and group performance. *Academy of Management Review,* 29(3), 459–478.

13. Fiol, C.M. & O'Connor, E.J. (2005). Identification in face-to-face, hybrid, and pure virtual teams: Untangling the contradictions. *Organization Science*, 16(1), 19–32.

14. Henry, K.B., Arrow, H. and Carini, B. (1999) A Tripartite model of group identity. *Small Group Research*, 30(5), 558–581.

15. Herbsleb, J.D. & Grinter, R.E. (1999). Splitting the organization and integrating the code: Conway's law revisited. In *Proc. ICSE 1999*. New York: ACM Press, 85–95.

16. Herbsleb, J.D., Mockus, A., Finholt, T.A. & Grinter, R.E. (2000). Distance, dependencies, and delay in a global collaboration. In *Proc. CSCW 2000*. New York: ACM Press, 319–328.

17. Hinds, P.J. & Bailey, D.E. (2003). Out of sight, out of synch: Understanding conflict in distributed teams. *Organization Science,* 14(6), 615–632.

18. Hinds, P.J. & Mortensen, M. (2005). Understanding conflict in geographically distributed teams: The moderating effects of shared identity, shared context, and spontaneous communication. *Organization Science,* 16(3), 290–307.

19. Huang, H. & Ocker, R. (2006). Preliminary insights into the in-group/out-group effect in partially distributed teams: An analysis of participant reflections. In *Proc. SIGMIS-CPR 2006*. New York: ACM Press, 264–272.

20. Jarvenpaa, S.L. & Keating, E. (2011). Hallowed grounds: The role of cultural values, practices, and institutions on TMS in an offshored complex engineering services project. *IEEE Transactions on Engineering Management*, 58(4), 786–798.

21. Jehn, K., Northcraft, G.B. & Neale, M.A. (1999). Why differences make a difference: A field study of diversity, conflict, and performance in workgroups. *Administrative Science Quarterly,* 44(4), 741–763.

22. Kiesler, S. & Cummings, J.N. (2002). What do we know about proximity and distance in work groups? A legacy of research. In P. Hinds & S. Kiesler (Eds.), *Distributed Work* (pp. 57–92). Cambridge, MA: MIT Press.

23. Kramer, R.M. (1991). Intergroup relations and organizational dilemmas: The role of categorization processes. In L.L. Cummings & B.M. Staw (Eds.). *Research in Organizational Behavior,* 13, 191–228. Greenwich, CT: JAI Press.

24. Kraut, R.E., Fussell, S.R., Brennan, S.E. & Siegel, J. (2002). Understanding effects of proximity on collaboration: Implications for technologies to support remote collaborative work. In P. Hinds & S. Kiesler (Eds.), *Distributed Work* (pp. 137–162). Cambridge, MA: MIT Press.

25. Lau, D.C. & Murninghan, J.K. (1998). Demographic diversity and faultlines: The compositional dynamics of organizational groups. *The Academy of Management Review*, 23(2), 325–340.

26. Li, J. & Hambrick, D. (2005). Factional groups: A new vantage on demographic faultlines, conflict, and disintegration in work teams. *Academy of Management Journal*, 48(5), 794–813.

27. Mortensen, M. & Hinds, P.J. (2001). Conflict and shared identity in geographically distributed teams. *International Journal of Conflict Management*, 12(3), 212–238.

28. O'Leary, M.B. & Mortensen, M. (2010). Go con(figure): Subgroups, imbalance, and isolates in geographically dispersed teams. *Organization Science*, 21(1), 115–131.

29. Olson, G.M., & Olson, J.S. (2000) Distance matters. *Human-Computer Interaction*, 15(2), 139–179.

30. Perugini, N., Gallucci, M., Presaghi, F., & Ercolani, A.P. (2002). The personal norm of reciprocity. *European Journal of Personality*, 17(4), 251–283.

31. Plotnick, L., Hiltz, S.R., Ocker, R., Ruthkowski, A.F. & Rossen, M.B. (2008). Leadership and trust in partially distributed software development teams. In *Proc. AMCIS 2008*.

32. Polzer, J.T., Crisp, B., Jarvenpaa, S.L. & Kim, J.W. (2006). Extending the faultline concept to geographically dispersed teams: How collocated subgroups can impair group functioning. *Academy of Management Journal,* 49(4), 679–692.

33. Steiner, I.D. (1972). *Group Process and Productivity*. New York: Academic Press.

34. Storck, J. & Sproull, L. (1995). Through a glass darkly: What do people learn in video-conferences? *Human Communication Research*, 22(2), 197–219.

35. Tajfel H. (1981). *Human groups and social categories: Studies in social psychology*. Cambridge, UK: Cambridge University Press.

36. Tajfel, H. (1982). The social psychology of intergroup relations. *Annual Review of Psychology,* 33, 1–39.

37. Turner, J.C. (1985). Social identification and psychological group formation. In H. Tajfel (Ed.), *The social dimension: European developments in social psychology* (Vol 2, pp. 518-538). New York: Cambridge University Press.

Time Travel Proxy: Using Lightweight Video Recordings to Create Asynchronous, Interactive Meetings

John C. Tang[*], Jennifer Marlow[*†], Aaron Hoff[*], Asta Roseway[*], Kori Inkpen[*]
Chen Zhao[*], and Xiang Cao[*]

[*]Microsoft Research
One Microsoft Way
Redmond WA 98008 USA
johntang|aaronho|astar|kori|chzha|xiangc
@microsoft.com

[†]Human Computer Interaction Institute
Carnegie Mellon University
5000 Forbes Ave
Pittsburgh, PA 15213 USA
jmarlow@cs.cmu.edu

ABSTRACT
Time Travel Proxy (TTP) enables participating in meetings that you cannot attend in real time, either because of time conflicts or global time zone differences. TTP uses lightweight video recordings to pre-record your contributions to a meeting, which are played on a tablet that serves as a proxy for you during the meeting. Reactions and responses in the meeting are also captured in video to give you feedback of what happened at the meeting. A working prototype of TTP was deployed and studied within four developer teams in their daily stand-up meetings. The study found that the affordances of video helped integrate the time traveler into the social context of the meeting, although the current prototype was better at enabling the time traveler to contribute to the meeting than it was in conveying the meeting experience back to the time traveler.

Author Keywords
Telepresence; asynchronous collaboration; video; meetings.

ACM Classification Keywords
H.4.3. [Information systems applications]: Communication applications---Computer conferencing, teleconferencing, and videoconferencing.

General Terms
Human Factors, Design.

KEEPING UP WITH MEETINGS
A growing concern in modern work life is keeping up with the number of requests to attend meetings. A survey of research on meetings [13] found that managers spent almost 70% of their time in meetings, which they expected to increase in the near future. This increasing demand for meeting time often makes it difficult to find times when all the participants can attend, resulting in challenges in resolving time conflicts among overbooked calendars. The increasing dispersion of work to other sites and time zones [3] adds to the temporal pressures. Working in global teams that span across time zone difference of eight hours or more adds to the challenge of scheduling meetings since there is no overlap in the typical workday [15].

Taken together, these trends in meeting pressure suggest an opportunity for "time-shifting" collaboration. Can we enable people to participate in meetings that they cannot attend in real time? Can we mitigate temporal distance by enabling asynchronous participation in meetings? While meetings have become a popular (perhaps even overused) mechanism for transferring information, they also provide a social context of creating a sense of belonging and working for the group [7]. Any tool to support meetings needs to support this social work as well as the communication functions of meetings.

We present the Time Travel Proxy (TTP) prototype which explores using lightweight video recordings to enable asynchronous meetings (see Figure 1). After reviewing related work, we describe the design of TTP and a field study of four developer teams using TTP in their daily stand-up meetings.

RELATED WORK
TTP builds on the work of Venolia et al. [17] in using a physical proxy to represent a geographically remote participant in hub-and-satellite teams. While their work

Figure 1. Time Travel Proxy prototype

showed the social and longitudinal benefits of physical proxies for spatially remote colleagues, we extend the proxy concept to include temporally remote colleagues.

In light of the maturing infrastructure for sharing video messages (e.g., YouTube), recent work has explored using lightweight, asynchronous video messaging to collaborate and communicate. VideoPal [5] enabled students between Greece and the U.S. to share "penpal-like" video messages to get to know each other in a conversational manner. We wanted to explore how recorded video messages could accomplish the work of business meetings.

There have been a few prior attempts at enabling time travel around meetings. Tucker et al. [16] developed Catchup, which allowed late-joiners to a meeting to get up to speed by reviewing condensed audio summaries of the meeting. Banerjee et al. [1] used mechanisms for annotating and indexing recorded meetings to enable quickly browsing and reviewing the meeting later. While this helped people who missed meetings quickly find the information they sought, it did not enable them to participate in the meeting.

The Time Independent Collaboration System [12] enabled students to complete a class project by exchanging asynchronous video messages. They used this prototype to study the effect of synchrony and high fidelity cues (e.g., video) on measures of social processes such as involvement, credibility, conversational effectiveness, etc. They found that synchrony, more than high fidelity, correlated with favorable social processes, emphasizing the challenge of creating an effective asynchronous conference experience. However, in their prototype, all participants viewed the video messages individually, as if they were never in the same place at the same time. In TTP, we designed for the case where most people met together with only one or two people who could not attend. We believe this "temporal hub-and-satellite" is a more common case where individuals may miss a meeting due to time conflict or global time zone differences.

Given the diverse activities that can occur in group meetings, ranging from decision-making to bargaining to discussing routine matters [11], we looked for an accessible meeting type to initially focus TTP's design. We thought that the relatively structured and short individual status reports presented at daily stand-up or scrum meetings used in the agile software development process [9] would be a good place to start exploring the concepts of TTP.

A case study of agile development in an industrial context [2] found that the prevalence of daily meetings led to a challenge of too many scrum meetings. A study of globally distributed scrum meetings [4] found that unsuccessful agile teams forced everyone to meet at very inconvenient times, leading to a resentment of scrum. Since these studies documented how these concerns arise in daily scrum meetings, we used those meetings as an initial focal point for the design concepts of TTP.

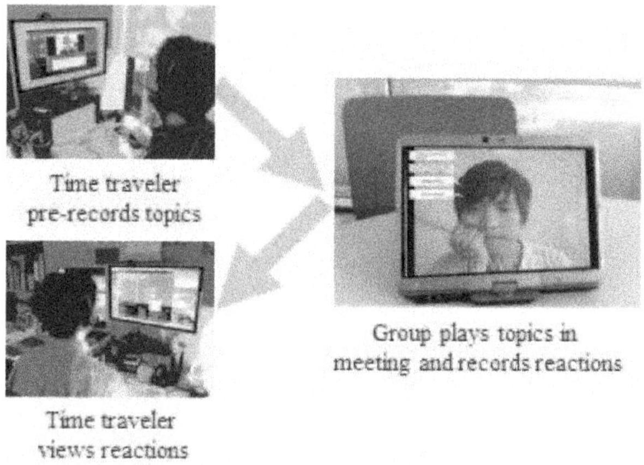

Figure 2. Using Time Travel Proxy

TIME TRAVEL PROXY PROTOTYPE

TTP is designed to enable a temporally distant person (*time traveler*) to participate in a meeting. Our design goals were to enable the time traveler to contribute to a meeting by pre-recording comments, to provide a physical proxy to represent the time traveler in a meeting that played those comments, and to capture the meeting's reactions and other comments to the time traveler and convey them back to the time traveler. This basic usage flow is depicted in Figure 2.

Asynchronously recorded video messages are used to enable a time traveler to contribute to a meeting. A time traveler selects an upcoming meeting scheduled in his online calendar and uses his computer to record video messages on topics that he would like to contribute to the meeting. These *topic* videos provide progress updates on his work or comments on issues that he anticipates will arise in the meeting. Pre-recording topics is easier if there is an agenda published in advance or a recurring structure to the meeting. Each topic has a subject line which describes the topic. Email notifications of his recordings are sent to all participants in the meeting, so they are aware of TTP topics to be presented at the meeting. In addition to the topic videos, the time traveler records about one minute of a video loop which serves as his *avatar* during the meeting.

During the meeting, a group member brings TTP running on a touch tablet, which serves as a physical proxy for the time traveler. After using the TTP software to select the recordings prepared for this meeting, the time traveler's avatar plays full screen on TTP, along with "thought bubbles" that contain the subject line of each recorded topic (Figure 3a). This avatar video loop provides an ongoing, dynamic representation of the time traveler's presence in the meeting to provide a proxy sense of actively participating in the meeting. TTP is set on the table such that the other meeting participants can see the TTP screen.

As a pre-recorded topic from the time traveler arises in the discussion, or whenever people in the meeting decide to play a topic, they can touch a thought bubble on TTP. The avatar changes to the full-screen replay of the recorded

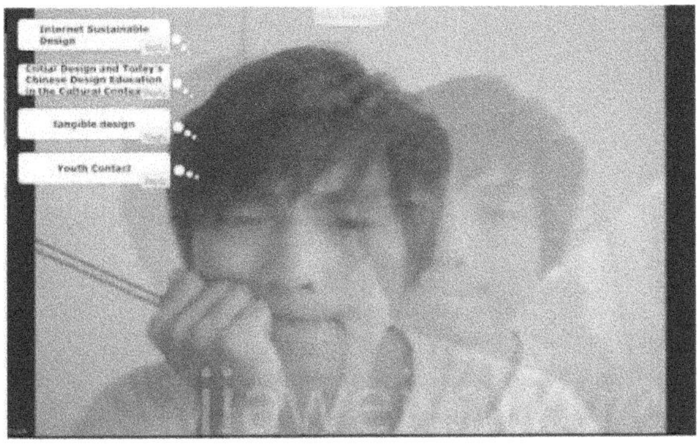

a. Time lapse of playing avatar video loop with topic "thought bubbles"

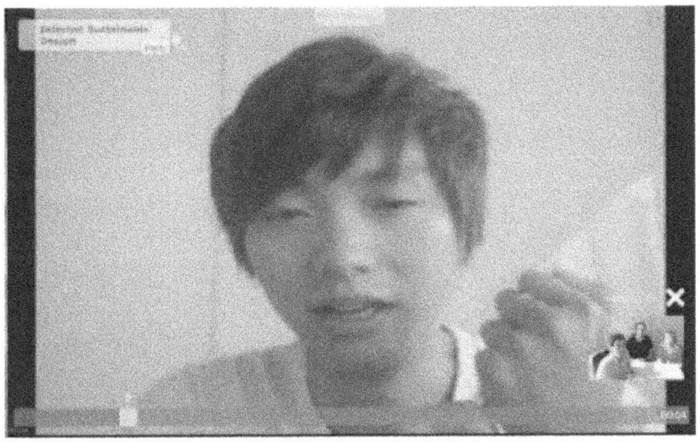

b. Playing topic while recording reaction video

Figure 3. Interacting with TTP

topic (Figure 3b). While the topic video is replaying, TTP also captures a *reaction* video of the meeting, to record the meeting participants' reactions to the time traveler's topic. The preview window in the bottom right corner of Figure 3b indicates that a reaction video is being recorded. By default, the reaction video extends for 60 seconds after replaying the topic to naturally capture the discussion presumed to immediately follow its replay. The reaction video recording can be ended before the 60 second timeout by touching an "X" close control. Our design rationale for the reaction videos was to capture a sense of the meeting members' verbal and non-verbal reactions, such as whether they understood the comment, agreed or disagreed, or any immediate responses to the pre-recorded topics.

Meeting members can also *reply* to a specific topic by touching a button embedded in its thought bubble. They can also record a *new message* to the time traveler, not related to any specific topic (Figure 4). In both cases, an interface for recording a video message (similar to that used by the time traveler to record topics) appears on TTP. The time traveler is notified via email when a reply or new message is recorded. Reactions, replies, and new messages provide ways for the meeting members to asynchronously interact with the time traveler through recorded videos.

When the time traveler has time, he can view the reaction, reply, and new message recordings directed toward him during the meeting. These recordings convey the group's reactions to his topics, responses, further questions, or other issues that arose in the meeting. He can then follow through on the collaboration using whatever means he chooses (email, groupware tool, or even another video message). He does not need to review the entire meeting, but can focus on just the interactions most directly relevant to him.

A working prototype of the TTP system was built using a standard three-tier architecture: a rich client, a web service, and a server back-end. The rich client (built using Microsoft Windows Presentation Framework) provided the interface for recording and playing back videos. Video operations were handled using Microsoft's Expression Encoder library. The video data were stored on a web server and metadata for the videos were stored in an SQL back-end. This architecture enabled videos to be recorded and played back by the meeting participants using clients that interfaced directly with the video web service. The TTP viewer client was designed specifically for touch-based tablets for portability and ease of operation in a meeting.

TTP FIELD STUDY

Using an iterative design approach to system development, we deployed an initial working prototype into actual use to get early experience and feedback on the concept. This approach enables studying how the technology interacts with the actual social context of the work activity being supported. To maximize the input we could get on TTP at this early stage, we focused on co-located agile development teams that have people who often miss meetings due to time conflicts. Studying co-located teams enabled members to experience both the time traveler and in-meeting experience of TTP. The daily frequency of the agile teams' stand-up meetings maximized the opportunity for using TTP for a member who could not attend.

Using an exploratory survey sent to randomly selected developers at a local U.S. site of our large global software company, we recruited four software development teams to participate in the TTP field study. Each team had between six and fifteen members involved in software or web

Figure 4. Recording a new message in TTP

feature development work. The teams followed an agile software development process, which included a daily stand-up meeting where everyone provided a status update on their completed tasks, discussed planned future work, and identified any issues that blocked their progress.

We deployed TTP in each team for about three weeks. Each team volunteered three or four members to serve as time travelers who participated in the meeting asynchronously three times each (one person scheduled per meeting). This repeated usage enabled gaining familiarity with using the system over time, allowing us to observe how usage evolved. Wherever possible, we identified volunteers who had naturally occurring time conflicts that caused them to miss meetings. We had 15 participants (13 male, 2 female) across four teams using TTP as a time traveler. Throughout the paper, time travelers will be referred to by number (P1-P15) and their teams by group number (G1-G4).

At the end of G2's field study, they wanted to try TTP with some contractors located in China working with their team. Previously, one U.S. team member served as a liaison with the team lead in China. G2 wanted to involve the Chinese colleagues more directly in their daily workflow and afford more interaction with the whole team. The 15-hour time zone difference between the U.S. West Coast and China made it very difficult to find a convenient time for everyone to meet during the workday. We extended the study with G2 to enable them to try using TTP to connect across global time zone differences to increase interaction with their Chinese colleagues. G2's Shanghai-based team lead used TTP to record and participate in the U.S. team's daily stand-up meeting twice a week for a total of five times.

Data collection

We collected a variety of quantitative and qualitative data about the teams' use of and reactions to TTP. For each group, we video-recorded two daily meetings prior to introducing the system to observe how they were normally conducted. We then continued to video record the meetings when using TTP one to two times per time traveler to capture the group's interaction with the system. These recordings captured the physical and behavioral interactions with the system and associated comments and conversations made by the group in reference to the proxy.

We also conducted two interviews each with all 15 time travelers: once prior to using the proxy system, to learn about current practices in their meetings and attitudes towards missing them, and a second interview after they had used TTP to asynchronously participate in two meetings. The second interview focused on their attitudes and reactions towards making recordings and viewing the reactions. Interviews were first open-coded for recurring themes, then analyzed by comparing specific instances of those themes across groups and participants. [14]

Additionally, all team members (time travelers and group members) were given a survey both prior to the team's use of TTP and at the conclusion of the study. The pre- and post- surveys both used Likert scale questions that measured attitudes towards the value, convenience, and importance of attending the daily stand-up meeting, and the post-survey also featured specific questions pertaining specifically to the experience with TTP.

For the extension to the team in China, we also sent before and after surveys to members in both the U.S. and China, and observed and video recorded four of their meetings using TTP. Finally, we interviewed the project leads in both geographical locations at the end of the team's usage to understand their perspectives on the experience.

Furthermore, we collected log data from TTP as a record of the participants' use of the system. This data helped us characterize the team's usage of TTP, such as the duration of topic and reaction videos and whether and when topic messages and reactions were viewed.

FIELD STUDY OBSERVATIONS

From the log data, we observed that the 15 time travelers made 51 sets of recordings for 48 unique meetings using TTP. Some time travelers elected to use TTP beyond the three times we had asked of them to participate in meetings when unexpected time conflicts arose. Three different teams also found a way to share TTP among two time travelers within the same meeting when an additional time conflict arose beyond the person scheduled to use TTP. They did this by using the tablet to play one time traveler's comments, then switching to the second time traveler. Table 1 summarizes the usage statistics of the number and duration of recordings made and viewed in TTP.

Time Traveler	Median avatar duration	29.5 secs
	Topics per meeting: mdn./avg.	1 / 1.9
	Median topic duration	38.5 secs
Meeting	Topics viewed	89%
	Median additional reaction duration	35.5 secs
	Median reply+new message duration	32.5 secs
Time Traveler Review	Reaction videos viewed	54%
	Replies+new messages viewed	57%

Table 1. Usage data from TTP log files

With a few exceptions, recordings made in TTP of any kind (topics, reactions, replies, and new messages) were short, with a median of less than 40 seconds. We use medians as a more representative way to describe the data due to some outlier long messages that skew the averages. Short messages worked well with people's expected attention span for TTP, and the teams quickly learned from observing TTP in use to keep the recordings clear and concise. One time traveler commented, *"Now when I do it I pre-think in my head 'OK I need to make these points, and try to be succinct about it, because people are going to listen to it, they don't want to hear me chatter'"* (P4).

Just over half (26) of the TTP recordings only had one topic, which is consistent with a status report meeting structure of going around the room and having each person give their status update. The other recording sessions had two (11) or three (also 11) topics, which corresponded to a meeting structure that separated input into different categories (e.g., what I did today, what I plan for tomorrow, what I am blocked on). The order of playing TTP comments in the meeting varied among the teams. A couple teams often played it first so as not to forget about it or to "get it out of the way". But others progressed in an alphabetic order or according to the category of topic, so TTP topics were played in an appropriate order.

For reaction videos recorded during the meeting, we looked at the length of the *additional* reaction beyond replaying the topic video (i.e., the total length of the reaction video minus the length of the topic video to which it was reacting). Besides the few cases where the topic video was stopped before completely playing it, the median additional reaction duration was 35.5 seconds (which is shorter than the default 60 second extension). There were only ten new messages recorded in meetings (and most of those were made by one team that did not notice the "Reply" mechanism for replying to a specific topic). Thus, we grouped reply and new message usage statistics together.

In scheduling participants' use of the TTP system, natural time conflicts were leveraged as much as possible to provide a realistic context for using TTP. Where there were no time conflicts, participants were scheduled at random to serve as time travelers. Out of the 51 recordings made, 16 of them reflected genuine time conflicts. Common reasons that participants cited for missing the meeting included working from home or other site (7), doctor/dentist appointments or illness (3), or a concurrently scheduled meeting (3). If there was no conflict, participants generally continued to work in their offices while the regularly scheduled meeting occurred. Thus, recordings were made under a mix of both realistic and artificial conditions.

Avatars

TTP's avatar loop was intended to give a dynamic presence for the time traveler in the meeting, encouraging a sense of participation and ensuring that they were not forgotten. In response to a survey question "I liked having a constant video representation of the person", team members rated an average of 4.8 (SD=.9) on a 7-point scale (7=strongly agree). This rating was supported by comments that it "*adds a bit more life*" (P8) and "*I'm actually somewhat pleased by the effect of it, it's a little bit of a hokey thing, but when the avatar is playing on the laptop in the meeting, it actually kinda looks like the person's there*" (P6)

We asked participants for a roughly 1-minute long avatar to give a long enough interval before looping back. This duration typically decreased over a time traveler's repeated use, as evidenced by the 29.5 second median avatar video duration. When asked about the avatar video recording experience, nearly half of the time travelers disliked having to record a new avatar for each meeting. A few considered it a "waste of time" (especially if the topic video was short) and others found it "forced" and awkward to sit in front of the camera for up to a minute. Some even "re-used" their avatar for subsequent meetings (even though that meant that their clothing changed between playing their avatar and topic videos in the meeting).

Four participants expressed some degree of being self-conscious about their appearance, whatever appeared in the background, or "tics" recorded as part of the avatar. Two participants mentioned that they noticed distracting or annoying behaviors in others' avatars in previous meetings that they avoided in their avatar recordings. Thus, time travelers expressed several concerns about the effort involved in recording the avatar loop.

Regarding viewing the avatars in the meetings, video recordings of the meeting showed that initial reactions to the avatar often exhibited some confusion as to whether the video loop was in fact a live video feed. Some participants greeted the time traveler's avatar as if they were under that impression, or explicitly asked "Is it live?" In three of the four groups, upon learning that it was a constantly playing loop, people mentioned that it was "creepy," "disturbing," or were uncertain of the purpose of the avatar video: "*So we just watch him fidget?*" These initial reactions quickly subsided as they gained familiarity with TTP, but the widespread initial reactions suggest that the avatar's rich sense of "presence" of the time traveler perhaps led to some tensions in expectations of interactivity.

The potentially distracting factor of the avatar was also noted, particularly in cases where actions in the recording occurred at random times in the meeting (e.g., head nodding or a "hmmm" grimace). A few people suggested that a still image would suffice (or that no avatar was needed). Nevertheless, there was evidence that the avatar succeeded in including and remembering the time traveler in the meeting. For example, participants frequently directly addressed the TTP as if the person was actually there: ("*[P3], do you have anything to say? We'll come back to you.*") And the avatar provided an opportunity to express some social playfulness with the team: "*I can clearly see how the creative minds of my team would from time to time do something incredibly silly on the screen just to see if we're paying attention. I'm not sure if that is intended, but it's certainly fun and enjoyable.*" (P4).

Topic videos

The topic videos enabled the time traveler to contribute information to the meeting. A total of 94 topic videos were recorded over the field study. Once they were familiar with the software and had addressed any technical issues with their computers and sound levels, time travelers generally reported that recording messages was fairly easy, often taking only a few minutes. No one reported any difficulty thinking of what to say in the messages, largely due to the well-known, standardized format and structure of the stand-up meetings: "*[it's] pretty practiced in terms of we do these every day, do these meetings so much that I know what I need to bring with me*" (P7). Thus, participants felt prepared and qualified to record their messages via TTP.

Nine participants re-recorded at least one of their messages, for various reasons, mostly because they reviewed their recording and decided they were either rambling, unclear, or otherwise not polished enough: "*Just wanted to say a quick message and realize I'm rambling on here and what I wanted to say was this…that wasn't clear, either not verbally clear or you could've said it in 2 sentences*" (P1). Others who did not re-record any messages deemed it unnecessary to worry about. One person mentioned that "*it wasn't a show,*" (P2) and another was unconcerned with appearances: "*If it looks funny, it looks funny*" (P14).

Although the content of the status updates were often intentionally "short and sweet", as one group member said, several time travelers interjected elements in their recordings to engage or otherwise add some level of interactivity with their recordings. Time travelers tried techniques such as: referring to individuals in the meeting by name and directing a comment specifically to them (either joking or serious), asking questions to a specific team member or the group as a whole, inviting discussion among the present group members ("*So, talk about that*"), or asking hypothetical questions and pausing to simulate a normal conversational flow ("*Guess what I did today? [pause] That's right, had a bunch of meetings*." (P8)).

Reaction videos

We expected that time travelers would be curious to see how the meeting reacted to their recordings, both while they viewed the topics and in the discussion immediately following. However, the log data show that only 54% of reaction videos made during the meetings were viewed by the time travelers. In the interviews, time travelers commented that unless they had intentionally embedded an attempt at interaction in the recording, they did not expect much reaction from the status updates that they were contributing. Furthermore, there were other feedback mechanisms shared among the team, such as emailed minutes, updating the bug-tracking spreadsheet in a shared repository, or even hallway conversations, that could confirm the team's receipt of the time traveler's contributions without having to watch the reaction videos.

Efforts to engage the audience in the topic video often yielded some sort of relevant response in the reaction video. For example, jokes were met with laughter and questions or invitations for discussion resulted in replies back to the time traveler in the reaction video (either with specific information or a request for later follow up). Time travelers commented that they were more likely to watch the reaction video when they had recorded something to elicit a response: "*If I do something goofy you want to see people's reactions to it*" (P6). Participants also reported receiving valuable information in the reaction videos that they would not have received in any other context: "*I guess historically I probably would not have gotten that bit of feedback from an email status I sent out*" (P6).

In most cases, participants generally felt that the message they were trying to convey in their recordings was understood by the group. However, in the case of G4, at least two participants found that their topic videos were misinterpreted, as evidenced by confusion and added discussion in the reaction videos and how they were documented in the team's official record. For both these members, watching the reaction videos provided "*some feedback that I should make my status update more clear*" (P14), which they consciously tried to do in the future.

Since these interesting reactions while viewing the topic videos in the meeting were relatively rare, time travelers expressed wanting some way to highlight any notable reactions that did occur so they could just watch those. Otherwise, they wanted to skip or scan toward the end of the topic video replay to hear when the group started to explicitly respond to the topic.

Reply and new message videos

Only 18 replies and 10 new messages were recorded for time travelers in the meetings. We expect that most of the meeting's feedback was captured in the reaction videos during the time (up to 60 seconds) automatically recorded after replaying the topic videos. Most of the new messages were recorded by one group that did not notice the reply mechanism for replying to a specific topic, so we grouped reply and new message usage data together. The median duration of these messages was short at 32.5 seconds.

It was disappointing to see that only 57% of the reply and new message videos created in the meeting were ever viewed by the time traveler afterwards. Given the explicit effort of creating replies and new messages (unlike the automatically captured reaction videos), and the email notification to the time traveler that they had been recorded, we would have expected that the time travelers would have viewed those recordings. It seems likely that since the groups were co-located, there were easier, more immediate ways of following up on the issues raised in the meeting, making it unnecessary to actually view the recorded videos.

Comparison to email

When we asked how teams typically dealt with absences at the stand-up meeting (without TTP), usually the absent member sent an email status update to the team as a whole or just to their manager. This led to exploring the question of whether participating via video through TTP was more effective than sending email. In the interviews, time travelers saw added benefit in using TTP over email, as one time traveler reflected:

"For the person who's playing it... maybe it's hard for them, but for the person doing it I think it's better than sending an email. It's a live perspective, because it feels to me more 'in' the meeting than with an email" (P12)

By contrast, email updates were often seen as ineffective because they were frequently either ignored by group members, or if they were only sent to the manager, they were not necessarily shared with the rest of the group. Furthermore, email may be subject to more mediation or interpretation by a spokesperson sharing the message to the group who "*may just highlight or paraphrase, may or may not get the whole context of what's going on*" (P19).

In commenting on listening to the time traveler's recordings in a meeting, many people mentioned the benefits of receiving the information in a richer medium. Often the richness came from cues including facial expressions and tone of voice. Two participants also noted that information was easier to process when delivered verbally as opposed to in written form. The usefulness of video was also more beneficial for more substantial messages than for status updates that were only one or two sentences long.

An additional benefit of TTP over email was related to the visible presence of the time traveler. TTP increased the visibility of absent team members, especially in the case of recurring absences. Prior to using TTP, one participant explained feeling annoyed when group members regularly missed the stand-up "*because I think they're valuable, and 80% of the team made the effort to be there... A lot of times it'll be like 'Oh where's that guy? He's missing. Did he tell anyone? No. I don't know what he did today'*" (P15). One such group member, who frequently missed daily stand-ups, mentioned the potential positive impact of TTP on teammates' perceptions of him: "*it's a more live thing that shows to the team that I am caring more*" (P12).

Two time travelers even cited the advantage of not having to worry about writing a formal, grammatically correct email: "*It's a lot easier to record, it's easier to talk to someone directly*" (P10). In summary, TTP was viewed as better than email due to the increased visibility of the sender and message, the fact that the message was not mediated and easy to process by listeners, and the relatively lightweight and low-effort process of recording video.

Extension with Chinese colleagues

While the team using TTP to connect with their Chinese colleagues used the system in the same way as the other groups, they also experienced some unique issues related to their geographic distribution. In the co-located teams, time travelers also had the experience of watching others' messages played back when they attended the meeting. Some mentioned that experiencing TTP from both sides informed the way they made recordings (e.g., avoiding distracting avatar behaviors). The Chinese time travelers, on the other hand, never experienced using TTP in a meeting, and this lack of feedback affected their behavior. For example, at first the Chinese time travelers recorded messages that were several minutes in duration, at a level that was too specific to be relevant to the entire U.S. team. As a result, the U.S. team liaison sent an email to the Chinese team lead suggesting ways to adapt their use of TTP to be more beneficial to the audience (e.g., breaking up recordings into smaller chunks, tips on avatar creation).

The international use of TTP also added some asymmetries in the communication. The Chinese team lead found TTP and video to be useful to share a large amount of information (particularly relating to software bug testing) in a way that was better than exchanging emails and pictures. However, he acknowledged that in terms of the U.S. team's response, "*they haven't done too many messages in the videos to share to us*" (P16). Rather, most follow up communication occurred via email. The U.S. team liaison felt that, from their perspective, it was not always clear how or if the Chinese team received any video responses that the U.S. team sent: "*If we give feedback or questions, don't have the real time 'I get that'...That's been a little uncertain in my mind, if everything kinda gets back*" (P8). This concern was compounded by the fact that the teams had different native languages, making comprehension more uncertain. Thus, TTP did not serve as a replacement for written communication, but rather a supplement: "*there are some things that don't quite get across so you have to follow up in email to make it clear*" (P8).

In terms of social presence, TTP enabled the two groups of people, who had never met in person, a richer means to communicate and interact via video. Aside from the detailed information being shared, TTP provided a higher-level, general awareness of the Chinese group that was viewed as beneficial from the U.S. side: "*There's an awareness of the teams... It's easy to forget about teammates that you don't see every day... This is the opportunity to get together with them that we wouldn't otherwise have, or make it feel that way I guess*" (P8). The advantages of video over written communication in this regard were echoed: "*TTP has been kinda a chance to bump up to a high level, share the important parts with the team who otherwise would not be interested in reading a 5 page document on what's going on*" (P8). The Chinese team lead also spoke to the reciprocal nature of awareness: both being able to "*share my face with the other team, that's cool...*" and to know what the other teammates were like allowed the two sites to get to know each other better.

REFLECTING ON THE FIELD STUDY

As an initial prototype in attempting "time travel" in meetings, we were encouraged that all the teams used TTP over the course of about three weeks each, and even found uses for TTP beyond what we had asked of them. Using TTP to include more than one person who could not attend the meeting and to include Chinese contractors who were time zone shifted from the team demonstrated needs that the teams recognized could be addressed by TTP. The field study also identified several issues to guide the iterative design of TTP and future work.

Role of video

A central feature of TTP is using video to represent the time traveler in the meeting and to communicate information into and back from the meeting. In deploying TTP into usage, we examined the role of video in its effectiveness, especially given the added effort needed to record and view video. While the design of TTP was intended to convey the more rich and nuanced interactions that video is good at supporting [6], limited opportunities for those kinds of complex interactions arose during daily stand-up meetings.

The TTP meetings we recorded did show some examples of rich reactions through TTP, especially in response to explicit attempts by time travelers to elicit interaction. Laughing at jokes, non-verbal expressions of agreement or confusion to what was being said, and responses to direct questions were all captured in the reaction videos. Video also enabled many of the playful interactions through TTP, largely through avatar recordings. Playful avatars included animating a stuffed animal across the screen, using an action figure as an avatar, and pretending not to be able to hear. These avatars used the richness of video to add some personality and social camaraderie to the meeting.

Perhaps the most practical use of video was to ensure attention to the time traveler's comments in the meeting. Interviewees mentioned that the time travelers felt like their recordings were heard in the meeting, unlike email messages that they could have sent about their progress. While email may have effectively communicated the content of their updates, they had no confidence that people would actually read them, whereas the video recordings projected their participation into the social context of the meeting where they did expect they would be viewed.

In summary, we see a few different ways that video provided a *social context* for the time traveler's contributions. The playful uses of video in TTP evoked more social connection across the asynchronous interactions. The social act of viewing a video as part of the meeting was more likely attended to than reading an email outside the context of a meeting.

Avatar video loops

One of the novel uses of video in TTP is the avatar video loop that gave the time traveler a dynamic, physical presence in the meeting. While the avatar contributed toward getting a high percentage of the time traveler's recorded topics played during the meeting, it also generated some negative reactions from both the meeting participants and the time traveler.

The common initial reaction of mistaking the avatar for a live video feed of the remote person evoked a "telepresence uncanny valley" reaction [10], where the avatar's lifelike representation of the time traveler misled viewers into trying to interact with it in real time. While understanding the purpose of the avatar was easily learned, it can be a confusing (if not embarrassing) first impression. This misperception probably contributed to several people's comments on the avatar as being "creepy" or "disturbing".

Furthermore, time travelers did not like having to re-record an avatar for each new meeting. We designed TTP to require a new avatar for each meeting to provide continuity from the avatar to replaying the topic videos. That is, the time traveler would be wearing the same clothes and recorded in the same lighting conditions for a smooth transition from playing the avatar loop to the topic videos. But many time travelers complained about the inefficiency of re-recording the avatar which, except for occasions when people used the avatars playfully, was a tedious effort.

One design implication of these reactions is to capture and represent the avatar in a different way. Rather than recording a minute-long video loop, the avatar could be created by individual frames abstracted out of the topic video recordings. Video analysis algorithms could be used to judiciously select individual frames from the topic videos and create a slow animation loop as an avatar. This approach would obviate having to explicitly record an avatar and would generate a dynamic, but animated, avatar that would not look like a live video conferencing feed but still maintain continuity with the topic video recordings.

Asymmetry of benefit

Looking across all of our data, our experiences indicate that we were more successful in integrating the time traveler's contributions into the meeting than we were in conveying the meeting back to the time traveler. The usage logs show that most topic videos (89%) were played in meetings, whereas much lower percentages of messages generated in the meeting (54% of reaction videos, 57% of replies and new messages) were reviewed by time travelers. While most of the survey responses did not show significant differences comparing before and after using TTP or between time travelers and meeting participants, one question that showed a significant difference according to a t-test was, "With TTP, our daily group meetings were helpful to me". On a 7-point scale with 7=strongly agree, time travelers rated the usefulness of the meeting when participating via TTP an average of 4.69 ($SD=.33$), while the average for other group members participating in the meeting was 5.64 ($SD=.30$) ($t=2.06$, $p=.05$).

Time travelers appreciated being able to share their information with the group, and receive directed comments in response to their items. However, despite being able to convey their information, time travelers almost unanimously agreed that they missed hearing their teammates' updates and wanted to be aware of what occurred in the rest of the meeting beyond what was recorded in the reaction videos. While acknowledging that sometimes they would find out relevant information one way or another if it was truly important, there was a general feeling of potentially losing something: "*I'm basically blind to what others are doing...I felt like I could be missing something or not, there is some uncertainty*" (P10).

Team members benefited from the TTP in that they were able to receive information from an absent member. One team manager even mentioned that TTP "obliged" members to record an update that they might normally forget to send to the group. However, many group members also commented that the inability to receive real-time replies to questions and responses was disappointing. According to G4's manager, "*If we hear their voice we feel they are more involved, but only for the 30 seconds [that they speak.] After that it's all one-way...We're talking TO them and there's no response, we don't feel that they're involved. We're sending messages to them and that's it.*"

Even though the time travelers received email notification of recordings made for them in the meeting, just over half of those recordings were viewed by the time traveler. This pattern underscores the point that email notifications do not engender the recipient's attention, in part because email by itself lacks the social context for focusing attention. Despite the effort invested in recording video messages from the meeting, there were not enough social cues to prompt the time travelers to view them.

Furthermore, while the time traveler could tell that the team had played their message by viewing reaction videos, the team had no such mechanism for determining if the time traveler had ever viewed the reaction videos (and, thus, may or may not have received their input and comments). The main reasons cited for not viewing the reactions included the fact that time travelers did not expect the group to provide feedback to their status, or the fact that there was little urgency to do so, as they expected colleagues would follow up with them later if important. G3's team manager described the effects of this break in the communication loop: "*The clarification questions we'd have to wait, and would not necessarily always get answered...[We] maybe didn't get a response to that, just get the next status. So the ball would get dropped.*".

Therefore, an imbalance in effort and benefit existed between the time travelers and group members. Time travelers were able to convey their messages but in return lacked information on what others had done. Group members received the recorded update but did not sense an illusion of further interaction, as any reactions from the group could not be responded to in real time (and were sometimes completely lost). Time travelers had to expend effort in pre-recording their topics, the meeting had to invest work in setting up and operating TTP in the meeting and time travelers had to invest additional work in reviewing the recordings from the meeting (although this often was not done). This imbalance between the relatively higher effort needed of the time travelers compared to the higher benefit received by the meeting leads to a classic CSCW obstacle to adoption [8].

We want to explore stronger, more socially visible feedback cues about whether recordings made are actually viewed as a way of creating more social context and sense of interaction through TTP. For example, while we could tell from analyzing the usage logs whether the recordings were actually played by the intended recipient, providing that viewing feedback within TTP itself might increase the social encouragement for playing back the videos. Future designs of TTP need to provide more interaction and feedback from the meeting to the time travelers.

Asymmetry of experience

Another dimension of asymmetry emerged in the group that included the Chinese contractors using TTP. Before adding time travelers that were geographically remote in China, all the time travelers were also able to experience how TTP was used in a meeting, which helped them tailor their recordings to be more effective (e.g., short videos, avatars that were not too distracting). However, the Chinese colleagues never had the opportunity to see TTP from the perspective of participating in a meeting, and relied on getting specific feedback on their recordings.

This asymmetry points to another issue that could benefit from richer feedback. Whereas meetings are mutual experiences where there is more shared sense of what is appropriate to say and do in a meeting, the asynchronous time travel in TTP creates a split between the experience for the time traveler and the meeting. Richer feedback between those experiences is needed to regain a sense of shared awareness. For example, if TTP provided implicit feedback to the Chinese contractors that their recordings were stopped before they were completely played, it might have given them a cue about needing to shorten their recordings.

Limitations of our field study

While we learned a lot from our field study, there are some limitations from how much we can generalize from the teams we studied. First of all, they were all developer groups within our software company that were comfortable with technology and using new software as early adopters. Furthermore, their daily stand-up status meeting had a pre-defined structure and short duration, which might be more conducive to TTP use than other types of meetings (e.g. those that involve discussions or brainstorming). Usage of TTP in different contexts may yield different findings that vary based on both the work and the group dynamics.

Another frequently-raised question was how TTP use would scale if several people could not personally attend the same meeting. Although the original design of TTP was intended to support just one remote user at a time, it could be possible that in larger teams, multiple tablets could be used to represent different people. Alternatively, if the avatar is modified to represent several people, then recordings from multiple time travelers could be played in a meeting. In fact, in at least three meetings during our study, two people sent in recordings. They "shared" the TTP tablet by switching it to represent each person in sequence during the meeting. While coordinating the playing of multiple comments could become an issue, groups were able to navigate shared use of TTP with little difficulty.

Additionally, the size of groups and the physical space in which their meetings occur could have an impact on the utility of TTP. The group that was least interactive with TTP (in terms of sending replies and curtailing reaction videos) was a larger team operating in a big space, so that TTP was both located farther away from the group and less able to capture the context of the audience.

We also observed that TTP relies on a certain amount of local overhead to bring in a touch tablet to a meeting, log on, and get the avatar running for the meeting. While the teams in our study seemed to master playing the time traveler's recordings at appropriate times in the meeting, some teams struggled more with the overhead effort of getting TTP started in the meeting. The least interactive group with TTP also had the most problems with starting TTP at the beginning of the meeting (perhaps related to setting it up in a big, public space rather than being able to keep TTP running in an office or more private space).

Future work

We plan to continue iterating on the design of TTP, incorporating the design implications that have arisen in our field study. We also want to deploy TTP in a broader range of contexts to exercise how it can work. Beyond the status update meetings where TTP showed some potential in including time travelers, we would like to see what benefits TTP could enable in other kinds of meetings or social chats.

While our field study focused primarily on missed meetings among a co-located team due to time conflicts, we got a preview of the potential and challenges of using TTP in supporting meetings among members in globally offset time zones. We would like to conduct further deployments in globally distributed teams to study their experiences.

While time travel still remains a physical impossibility, we believe that TTP shows potential for enabling "virtual" time travel to participate in work meetings. We hope that an iterative design process will continue to refine the proxy for time travel concept into one that can be practically used in meetings in the future… or perhaps even in the past.

ACKNOWLEDGEMENTS

We thank our anonymous study participant teams who gave of their time and effort to use TTP in their work. We thank interns Benjamin Koehne for his feedback on TTP use in China and Jiawei Gu, who helped generate the figures for the paper.

REFERENCES

1. Banerjee, S., Rosé, C., and Rudnicky, A. The necessity of a meeting recording and playback system, and the benefit of topic–level annotations to meeting browsing. *INTERACT 2005, 643–656.*
2. Begel, A., and Nagappan, N. Usage and perceptions of agile software development in an industrial context: An exploratory study. *Empirical Software Engineering and Measurement Conference 2007*, 255-264.
3. Carmel, E. *Global Software Teams: Collaborating Across Borders and Time Zones*. Prentice Hall, 1999.
4. Drummond, B. S., and Unson, J. Yahoo! Distributed Agile: Notes from the world over. *Agile 2008*, 315-321.
5. Du, H., Inkpen, K., Chorianopoulos, K.. Czerwinski, M., Johns, P., Hoff, A., Roseway, A., Morlidge S., Tang, J. and Gross, T. VideoPal: Exploring asynchronous video-messaging to enable cross-cultural friendships. *ECSCW 2011*, 273-292.
6. Finn, K., Sellen, A., and Wilbur, S. *Video-Mediated Communication*. Lawrence Erlbaum Associates, 1997.
7. Geyer, W., Richter, H., Fuchs, L., Frauenhofer, T., Daijavad, S., and Poltrock, S. A team collaboration space supporting capture and access of virtual meetings. *GROUP 2001*, 188–196.
8. Grudin, J. Why CSCW applications fail: problems in the design and evaluation of organizational interfaces. *CSCW 1988*, 85-93.
9. Larman, C. *Agile and Iterative Development: A Manager's Guide*. Addison-Wesley, 2004.
10. Mori, M. "Bukimi no tani The uncanny valley" (K. F. MacDorman & T. Minato, trans.) *Energy* 7, 4 (1970), 33–35.
11. Noll, A. Teleconferencing communications activities. *Communications Society* 14, 6, (1976), 8–14.
12. Nowak, K. L., Watt, J., and Walther, J. The influence of synchrony and sensory modality on the person perception process in computer-mediated groups. *Journal of Computer-Mediated Communication* 10, 3 (2005), Article 3.
13. Romano, N. and Nunamaker, J. Meeting analysis: Findings from research and practice. *Hawai'i International Conference on System Sciences 2001*, 1-13.
14. Strauss, A., and Corbin J. *Basics of Qualitative Research*. Sage Publications, 1998.
15. Tang , J., Zhao, C., Cao, X., and Inkpen, K. Your time zone or mine? A study of globally time zone-shifted collaboration. *CSCW 2011*, 235-244.
16. Tucker, S., Bergman, O., Ramamoorthy, A. and Whittaker, S. Catchup: A useful application of time-travel in meetings. *CSCW 2010*, 99–102.
17. Venolia, G., Tang, J., Cervantes, R., Bly, S., Robertson, G., Lee, B., and Inkpen, K. Embodied Social Proxy: Mediating interpersonal connection in hub-and-satellite teams. *CHI 2010*, 1049-1058.

Evaluation of Human Tangential Force Input Performance

Bhoram Lee, Hyunjeong Lee, Soochul Lim, Hyungkew Lee, Seungju Han, Joonah Park
Samsung Advanced Institute of Technology
San14, Nongseo-dong, Giheung-gu, Yongin-si, Gyeonggi-do, Korea
{ bhoram.lee, hyem.lee, soochul.lim, hyungkew.lee, sj75.han, joonah}@samsung.com

ABSTRACT
While interacting with mobile devices, users may press against touch screens and also exert tangential force to the display in a sliding manner. We seek to guide UI design based on the tangential force applied by a user to the surface of a hand-held device. A prototype of an interface using tangential force input was implemented utilizing a force sensitive layer and an elastic layer and used for the user experiment. We investigated user controllability to reach and maintain target force levels and considered the effects of hand pose and direction of force input. Our results imply no significant difference in performance when applying force holding the device in one hand and in two hands. We also observed that users have more physical and perceived loads when applying tangential force in the left-right direction compared to the up-down direction. Based on the experimental results, we discuss considerations for user interface applications of tangential-force-based interface.

Author Keywords
Force-based interface; mobile interaction; input devices

ACM Classification Keywords
H.5.2. [Information interfaces and presentation]: User Interface - *Interaction styles;*

General Terms
Design, Experimentation, Human Factors

INTRODUCTION
Sensor technologies and gesture interaction techniques provide a rich and intuitive user experience. Among such interfaces, touch-based and motion-based interfaces are widely used in mobile environments and well studied. The use of touch-based input has become especially prevalent in smart phone UIs. Motion user interfaces have also become popular since small motion sensors became affordable. However, interaction methods using a touch interface are limited by the small size of a touch screen with respect to the large and continuous virtual space being navigated. For example,

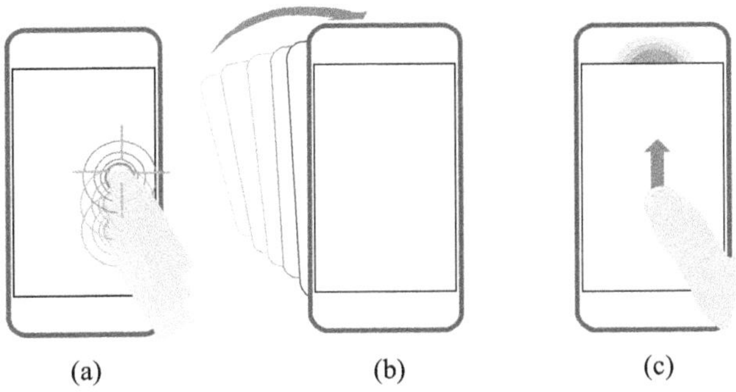

Figure 1. Input mechanism of gesture interfaces. (a) Touch input relies on 2-dimensional movement of the contact location; (b) Motion input is based on 3-dimensional spatial movement; and (c) Force input requires no movement but only application of force along the surface.

when we explore a long list, we have to repeat "flicking", that is moving down on the screen and up off the screen or vice versa. This quality of touch input makes it hard to control continuous parameters. Motion-based interactions are better suited for continuous control parameters; every human motion itself is inherently continuous. A motion controller for sports or action-based games at home is one of the best applications of it. Yet it tends to impose unnecessary physical burden on mobile users.

Besides touch and motion input, a "force" dimension can be added to mobile gesture interfacing so as to be free from spatial restrictions and the requirement of movement (Figure 1). Force input in normal and tangential directions on the surface of mobile devices can be applied and measured as shown in Figure 2. Compared with other gesture input means, users can statically input directional information of tangential force unless the finger slips. When combined with touch and motion gestures, force input can provide richer information including location, intensity, and direction.

This paper investigates the characteristics of continuous and directional user input of tangential forces on the contact surface. In the following section, previous works on force-based inputs will be reviewed. We then describe tangential force input and the implementation of the prototype for our study. After elaborating on our user experiment to examine user controllability of tangential force input and its results, we discuss further studies needed and guide the design of user interface applications adopting tangential force input.

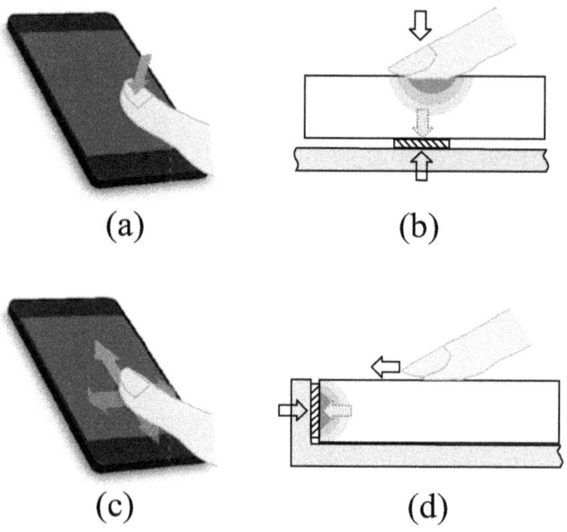

Figure 2. Force-based input: (a) Applying and (b) measurement of a normal force; and (c) Applying and (d) measurement of a tangential force. (Note: the thickness of the pad and the sensor is exaggerated in this figure.)

RELATED WORK

Force-based input initially has been studied primarily for stationary display and devices. Examples include utilizing strain gages around large displays and embedding them in rigid finger joysticks. For mobile devices, while many works have pioneered the study of pressure-based or normal-force-based input, the work on force input including tangential force for mobile interfaces is currently underexplored.

Among earlier studies on force input including tangential force, Herot and Minsky suggested multidimensional inputs such as position, velocity, and force on the surface for CRT monitors in 1978 and 1984 respectively. Herot et al. [7] employed eight strain gauges to derive the force vector and the torque, developed five input routines based on the outputs, and observed qualitative user ability while performing tasks. Minsky [10] also utilized four load cells to measure force and used gestures to control actions in interactive graphical environments. User investigation using isometric input devices can be also found. Selker et al. [20] investigated user motor control ability such as accuracy and precision of finger force, with a small joystick built in to a keyboard. In this work, it is reported that the accuracy of digit force control is limited in spite of long integration time, and that applying a force in 2D is observed no worse than the case of 1D. Transfer functions and performances of force input as rate control for isometric devices was studied in [19] and for elastic devices in [3]. For mobile interfaces, Heo et al. [5,6] demonstrated the feasibility of using 3-axis force in a touchscreen device equipped with multiple Force Sensitive Resistors (FSR). They defined five force gestures based on normal and tangential force as well as finger movement, implemented applications based on the gesture set, and reported user evaluation results on their experiences.

The majority of prior work on force input characteristics for mobile devices has focused on normal-force-based interfaces. Some previous works added force sensors to interface devices that we grasp or press for use. Ramos et al. [17] used pressure sensitive pen-type interfaces to study user control of force input and discussed the design space for pressure widgets. Shi et al. [21] attached to a mouse a FSR which the thumb makes contact on, and focused on evaluating discretization functions of pressure input. Clarkson et al. [4] placed force sensors on every key of a keypad to add extra dimensions of input. In this work, the authors first introduced an interaction technique, called PressureTap, adopting discrete pressure levels for "tapping". McCallum et al. [9] also suggested a similar hardware design and compared the user performance of pressure-based tapping and MultiTap.

Recently, there has been a move toward augmenting touch screens with pressure modality. In [23], two multi-touch enabled smart phones were physically overlapped and pressure sensors were attached to the surfaces. The study explored the effects of hand pose and multimodal feedback of pressure input. Miyaki et al. [11] also attached a FSR on the backside of a smart phone, covered it with an acryl case, and suggested the use of pressure input for zooming control. Rekimoto et al. [18] augmented a touch-pad with pressure sensors under the pad and tactile feedback actuators. In this study, both pressure values and the contact area on the touch pad were used to create positive and negative inputs. In [24], Wilson et al. used a commercial pressure-sensitive resistive touch screen in the pilot test and made a comparison of it with FSR-based input attached to a Perspex plate next to a mobile device in the main user evaluation. The research trends give a broad hint to the significance of studies on tangential force input, which this paper deals with. Because humans can apply only positive pressure on a surface, there is a lack of information with normal pressure. Thus, as Heo et al. explored the concept, adding tangential force to mobile devices also capable of sensing touch and normal force will enrich input modality.

This paper contributes to understanding of characteristics of tangential forces applied on the flat surface of a small device for utilizing richer information including direction and continuous intensity. It should be noted that the characteristics of force input may differ according to the site where sensors are attached and the way that sensors are pressed. Therefore, it is worthwhile to pay careful attention to the different hardware setups of previous works and then refer and apply their findings to our study.

TANGENTIAL FORCE INPUT

The tangential force in this context is actually *friction*, a friction force between the finger and the contact pad. When a user exerts force on the surface of the pad in a tangential direction, the contact force will tend to press against the side of the outer frame that supports the pad. Then we can measure the friction force magnitude transferred to a force sensitive layer as Figure 2.(d) shows. Although friction between the pad and the base was ignored for simplification, we should be careful of its existence as also pointed out in [6] for its prototype design. The friction resists the movement of the pad to recover its neutral position, which makes sensors produce non-zero output when a user releases force. It should be also noted that the friction force always accompanies the normal force, which is omitted for brevity in Figure 2.(d).

Tangential Force Input Device

The prototype of the interface device designed to measure the tangential force is shown in Figure 3. It is made of UV-curing resins and weighs 130 grams. The entire volume of the device is approximately 134 x 75 x 14 mm^3. The dimension of the contact pad is designed to be the same as a commercial smart phone. The base has approximately a 5mm thickness and thin holes for force sensors to be inserted between the base and the pad (Figure 3.(c)). Its bottom side is also designed to reduce the effect of friction (between the base and the pad) and for the contact pad to restore when it is released from slight movement. Specifically, there are 3×3 symmetrically distributed small bumps on the bottom to minimize the contact area. The bumps at the bottom are wrapped with a thin, 350 μm, rubber layer. Small thin rubber patches were also attached on sensor locations around the contact pad to fit in the base, providing restoring forces to the pad and applying the pre-bias pressure to sensors.

Commercially available force sensors with a sensing range of 0 to 4.4N (Tekscan FlexiForce® Model-A201) are chosen for our prototype. Physically healthy adults can apply force bigger than 4.4N, yet people may not like the frequent use of large force for interaction with mobile devices. Also, experiments in a study on finger properties in tangential directions were performed with a force range less than 5N [14,15], suggesting that the 4.4N range of finger force is reasonable for the user test of this study. Four sensors were attached in the middle of the inner sides of the base with a pre-biased pressure of about 0.1 V. The pre-biased pressure can eliminate a possible error caused by a strong nonlinear tendency of FSRs in the range of small values. Another force sensor was placed on the center bump of the bottom of the base to measure normal force. This was included to observe relative variations of normal force while users apply tangential force input. We made a drive circuit for force sensors to linearize sensor outputs and the output voltage ranged from 0 to 3.7 Volts. All sensors were wired to a drive circuit and sensor data was sampled by signal acquisition equipment at the rate of 100 Hz per channel on a desktop PC.

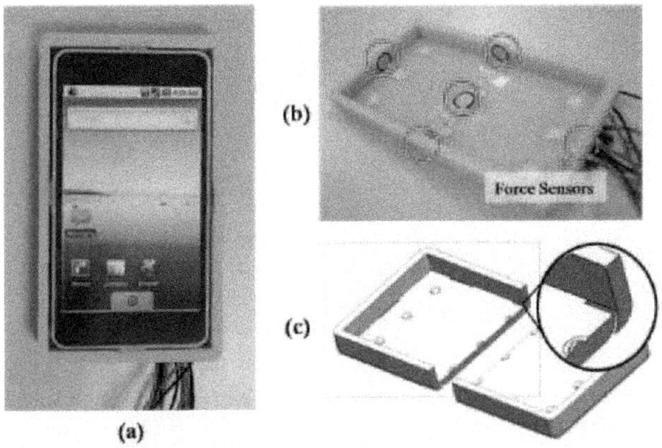

Figure 3. (a) Front view of the prototype. (b) Sensors attached on the base. (c) Cross-section view of the base.

FSRs have many advantages: they are cheap and able to be manufactured in thin and flexible shapes so that they can be easily embedded inside a mobile device. On the other hand, they are hard to handle in a quantitative analysis because the signal of FSRs tends to be noisy. This can be overcome to some extent by adding a low-pass in the software. In our implementation, a 2nd order Butterworth filter was used and the tradeoff was made between the delay and smoothness of the signal based on a preliminary test.

EXPERIMENT

The experiment was designed to evaluate user controllability of tangential force input. We intended to follow the experimental designs of relevant previous works on pressure input.

We investigated user controllability of force in four commonly distinguishable directions: up, down, left, and right. Each direction corresponds to the directional tendency of flexion, extension, abduction, and adduction for the case of anatomic movement [13]. Directionality of tangential force input was an important interest of our study. Since humans use different muscles from different joints for moving a finger in various directions, there may also be differences in physical or perceived loads to users. The task space differed depending on which direction input being tested (Figure 4). The orientation of the cursor was aligned with the direction of tangential force input. Participants held the device in their hands to input force while interacting visually with a LED monitor.

We tested two poses to see if different poses affect users' ability to reach and maintain the same force level. Users often hold mobile devices in both hands when they use more than one finger, for instance, when they *pinch* the screen. Users also use one hand when the other hand is busy. In this case, the thumb is used to touch and press the screen. In either pose, we only considered the thumb in the experiment since a pilot test indicated that it was difficult for a user to apply tangential force using the index finger. We did

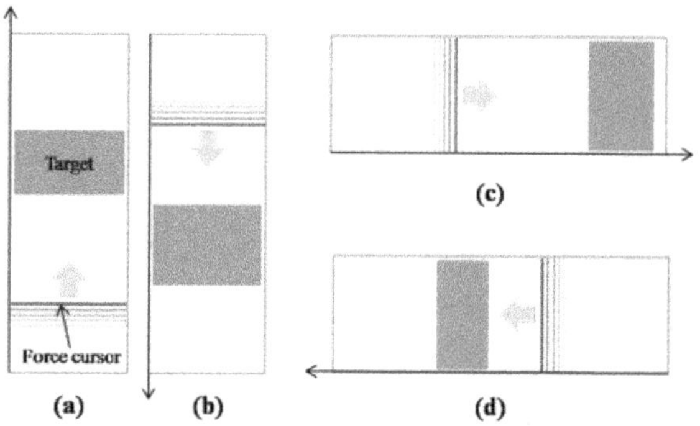

Figure 4. Orientation of task spaces according to the direction tested: (1) Upward; (b) Downward; (c) Rightward; and (d) Leftward.

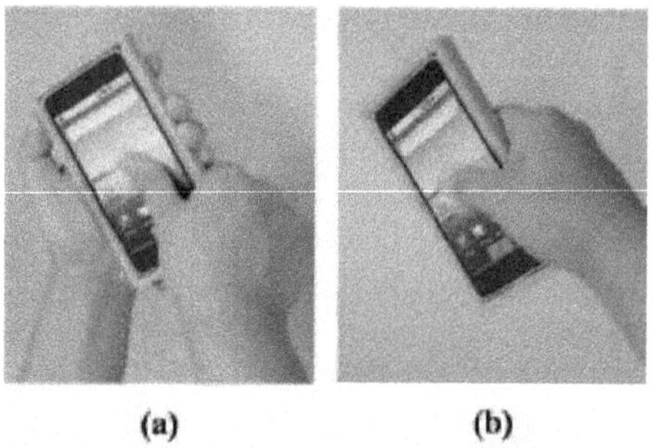

Figure 5. Pose variations. (a) Both-hands. (b) One-hand. (Note: modeled by a right-handed person.)

not consider the situation where the device is resting on a tabletop; because we expect that a generic device may slip without sufficient friction. In summary, two poses are tested (Figure 5): (1) holding and supporting the device in the non-dominant hand and using the thumb of the dominant hand for force input, and (2) holding the device in the dominant hand and using the thumb of the same hand.

Participants

17 Participants (13 males and 4 females) aged between 19 and 37 (32.1 years on average) were included in the experiment. One of them was left-handed and the rest were right-handed. They had no prior experience using pressure sensitive input devices.

Experimental Materials

It is reported that users have difficulties in controlling normal force when it is relatively small [17] and large [12]. To see if this tendency applies to tangential force input, we included four levels of force target, which is visually represented as four target distances. We also varied the target width in five steps at every predetermined target distance. The range of target widths was selected among the possible integer numbers of divisions of the target space from 4 to 8, based on a pilot test. Many GUIs in current mobile devices allow a continuous movement of 2D space so that an item of a menu can be displayed anywhere in the display. We rather fixed the target distance and observed the effects of distance and width variations (Figure 6).

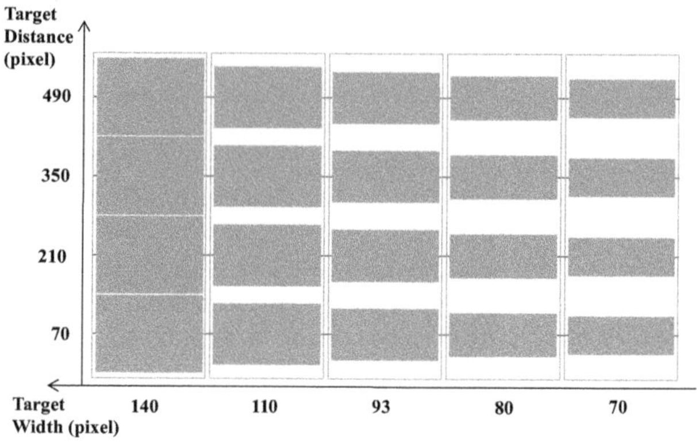

Figure 6. The target space.

- Target distance: 70, 210, 350, and 490 (pixel)
- Target width: 70, 80, 93, 110, and 140 (pixel)

Sensor voltage outputs were mapped to the cursor position linearly from 0 to 560 pixels space. Pre-biased force value was mapped to 0 and the maximum force (3.5V+biased voltage) to 560. Because of the gravitational effect in the vertical direction, we reset the bias offset for each sensor and participants were instructed not to change the tilt angle during the experiment.

Procedure

The experiment consisted of a single session of eight blocks. The first four blocks were performed in one pose and the rest in the other pose. Nine participants started the session using both hands and changed their pose after completing four blocks. The other participants started the session in the one-hand pose and changed to the both-hands pose for the remaining four blocks. They were instructed to apply force with the thumb of the dominant hand. Users had less than one minute of warm-up time before the task started. While warming up, they practiced freely moving the force cursor without appearance of the target and we observed if they had difficulty in reaching the maximum value of the force range. After practicing applying tangential force to the device, they were asked to complete tasks in the instructed direction for each block of the experiment. They had to control force so as to maintain the force level indicator within the target area for one second.

For the four blocks within the same pose, each block used a single direction but the block order was varied so every direction appeared evenly at each point in the order across the whole group of participants. Within a block, 20 trials were made with the target width decreased orderly. The target position of the same width was shuffled in a random way. There was no repetition of the entire session.

After the experiment finished, we asked users for their subjective feelings about the experience. All questions on the questionnaire were multiple choice and some questions were nested. Questions were designed to see if they had felt differences in difficulty between poses and directions and

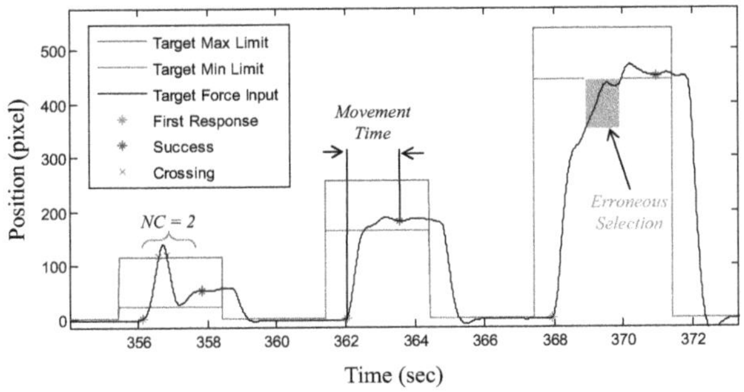

Figure 7. Definition of performance measurement indices: NC; MT; and ER.

when they started to feel fatigue. We also added a question to rank probable application candidates of the interface among a given list.

Performance Measures

To measure user performance of controlling tangential force input, three dependent variables are evaluated: Movement Time (MT), Error Rate (ER), and Number of Crossings (NC). They are visually illustrated in Figure 7 which is captured from experimental data. MT is defined as the time from the first user response after the target appears on the screen to the time when a successful selection (1-second dwell) was made. Note that negative values are seen in the figure as a result of low-pass-filtering. ER is defined as the percentage of erroneous selections with respect to the whole number of trials. This measure reflects how frequently inaccurate selections were made. An erroneous selection means that the 1-second dwell happened in another region, which is unseen to the user, having the corresponding target width. NC counts the number of times entering and exiting a target minus one. It is a measure of the user's ability to maintain a given force level for a period of time. Erroneous selections were not included when evaluating NC and MT. While both ER and NC are measures for accuracy of user control, MT measures speed of performing tasks.

RESULTS

We used trimmed data for Analysis of Variance on the dependent variables for testing conditions of pose and direction. In a 2 x 4 (pose x direction) repeated measures ANOVA, pose was not found to have a significant effect on any performance index ($F_{1,131}$=0.70, p>0.05 for MT; $F_{1,131}$=0.68, p>0.05 for NC; and $F_{1,131}$=0.01, p>0.05 for ER). Figure 8 shows the value of dependent variables according to pose variations.

Tangential force input direction was also not found to have a significant effect on the number of crossings ($F_{3,265}$=1.79, p>0.05) and error rates ($F_{3,265}$=0.93, p>0.05). It was found, however, to be significant for MT in a 4 x 4 (direction x target position) repeated measures ANOVA. Figure 9 shows each value of the dependent variables according to

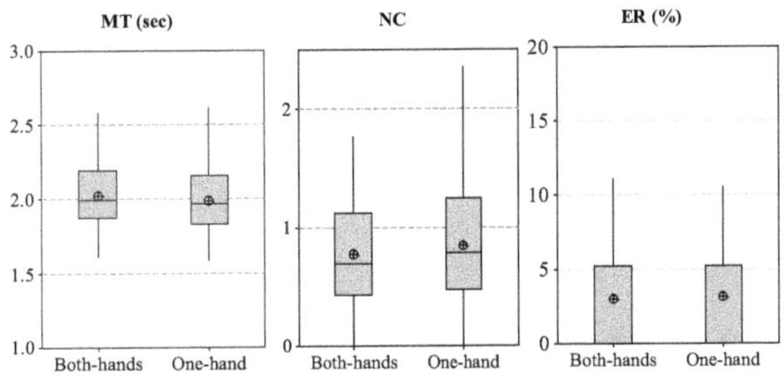

Figure 8. Effect of pose on MT, NC, and ER.

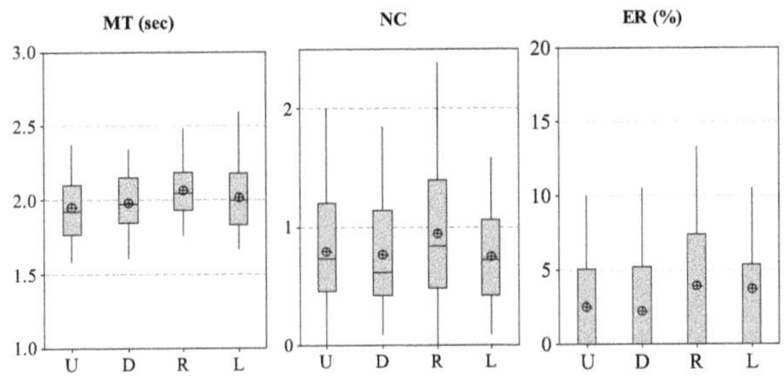

Figure 9. Effect of input direction on MT, NC, and ER.

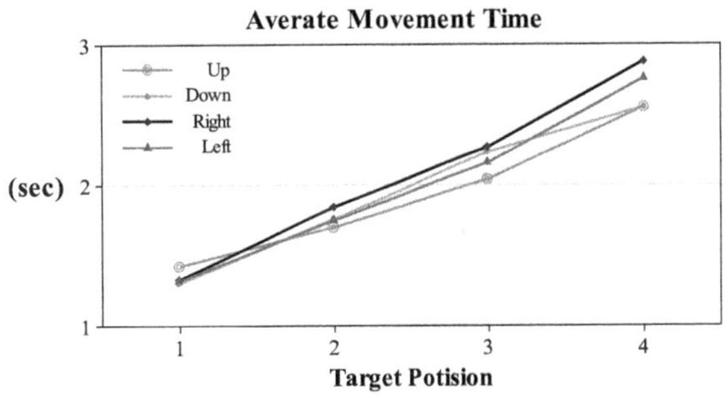

Figure 10. Average movement time of each input direction for all target positions.

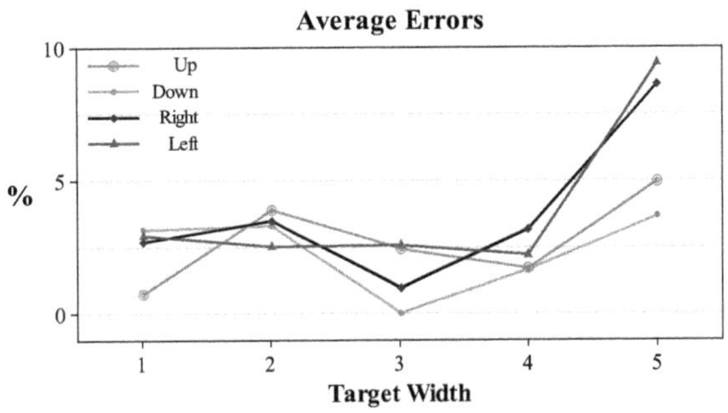

Figure 11. Average error rate of each input direction for all target widths.

directional variations. It showed that there existed a significant main effect of direction on MT ($F_{3,265}$=4.13, p<0.01) and a significant interaction between direction and the target position ($F_{3,265}$=2.38, p<0.05) (Figure 10). Directional variations did not have significant effects overall, but the results did show a tendency of lateral directions to deteriorate in ER more than the vertical direction at distant and narrow targeting in Figure 11.

The overall performance for all target positions and all target widths is plotted in Figure 12. The average of MT and NC are represented on the left axis and the average ER is represented on the right axis. A tendency of movement time and number of crossings to decrease in wider target is observed. They also clearly increase as the target distance increased. However, a distinct tendency is not visible in ER.

Even though we did not perform the experiment in a completely random order thereby preventing firm conclusion, it is noticeable that the measures in Figure 13 show better performance after 3 blocks from the start. Note that all variables increase, which means worse performances again, after 6 blocks.

To further analyze the experimental data, we examined if the target acquisition tasks using tangential force input reproduced Fitts' law. Fitts' law describes the relationship between the movement time to a target area and the quantitative properties of the target. It is modeled as,

$$MT = a + b \cdot ID.$$

ID represents the index of difficulty and is computed as,

$$ID = \log(1+D/W),$$

where D is the distance from the starting point to the target center and W is the target width. Fitts' Law is known to apply only to raw human motor response without any operation in software. We fit linear regressions of the average MT by ID and found a high correlation of the data with Fitts' Law for all input directions: r^2=0.90 for upward; r^2=0.94 for downward, r^2=0.93 for rightward; and r^2=0.93 for leftward (Figure 14).

Normal force was also measured while users performed the tasks. We assumed that applying tangential force generally requires more energy than applying pressure in the normal direction. Tangential force, which is friction between the finger and the contact surface, can be generated only if the normal force is bigger than zero. As expected from the relationship of friction (f=μN), normal force is shown to be linearly proportional to tangential force in Figure 15. However, the slopes of linear regression for normal force with respect to tangential force input are different for different directions. The slope of linear regression for the rightward direction was 1.5 times bigger than the slope of upward, 1.4 times for the leftward, and 1.06 times for the downward.

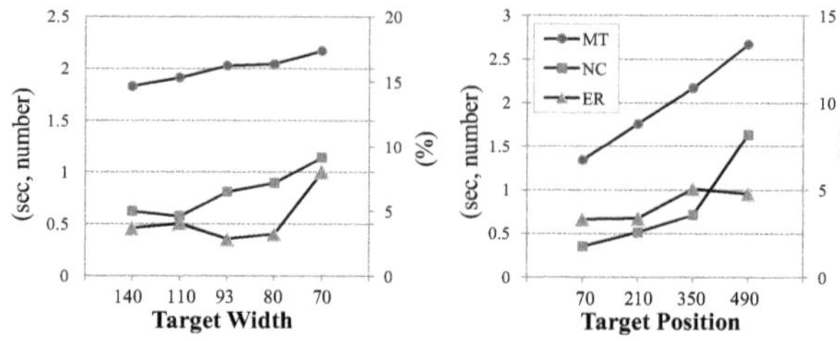

Figure 12. Average MT, average NC, and average ER for all target widths and all target positions.

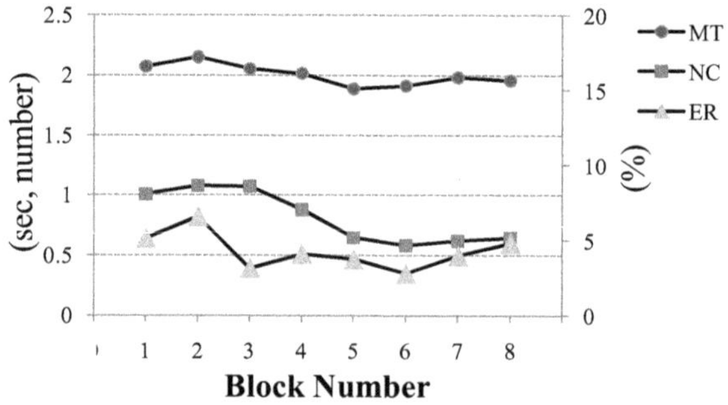

Figure 13. Performance variables *versus* block numbers. The block numbers are assigned according to the temporal order of the experiment.

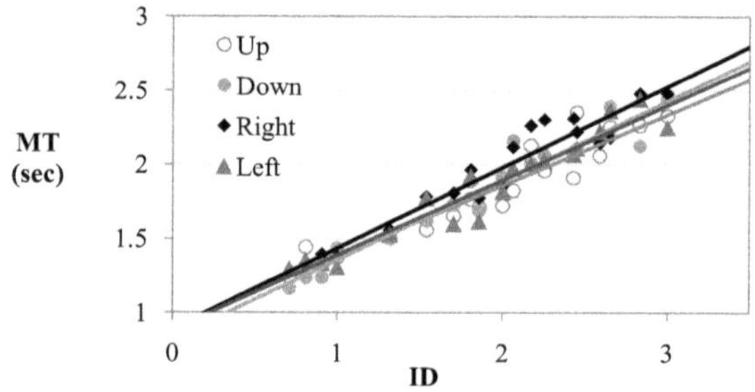

Figure 14. Linear regression of MT *versus* ID of all input directions.

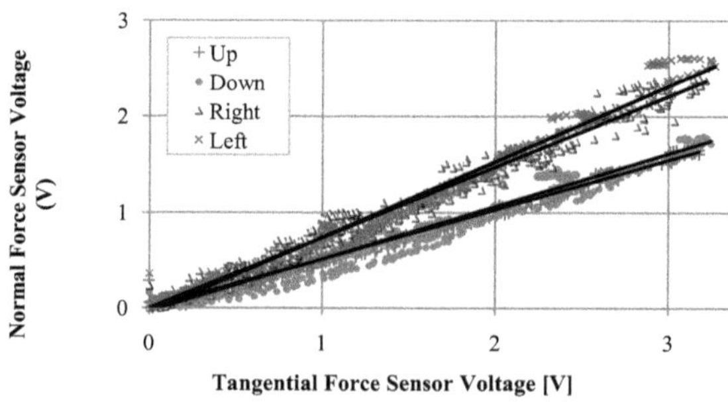

Figure 15. Normal force *versus* tangential force for all input directions (Plotted data are sampled from an individual data.)

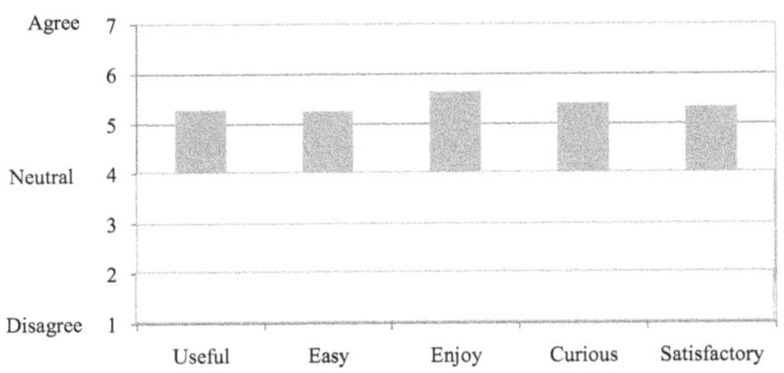

Figure 16. Responses to post-task Questionnaire on the Likert scale from 1("Disagree") to 7("Agree").

(The r-values for the regressions are r2=0.99 for upward; r2=0.96 for downward, r2=0.98 for rightward; and r2=0.98 for leftward.) Note that Figure 15 is the normal force versus tangential force measurement in voltages. The force sensor at the bottom was pressed on a bump which only made a partial contact with the sensor, which may lead the incorrect conversion of the voltage into the force unit. However, as the voltage output is to proportional to applied force, it is valid when we compare the tendency of up-down and left-right directions. Notice also that the plotted data are sampled from purely ascending intervals of force input log data of an individual. Because of the viscoelastic quality of rubber materials attached to the sides of the contact pad, a large hysteresis instead of a linear pattern was observed when it was quickly released.

Lastly, responses from the questionnaire indicate that people viewed tangential-force-based input positively (Figure 16). They rated between 5.3 and 5.6 on average for "enjoyable" (5.65), "curious" (5.41), "satisfactory" (5.33), "useful" (5.28), and "easy" (5.25) on the Likert scale from 1 to 7 scale.

DISCUSSION

In the experimental result, no significant effect of hand pose on performance indices was found and tangential force input direction was found to be significant for MT. Also, a tendency of movement time and number of crossings to decrease for distance and wider targets is observed. All directions of tangential force input had high correlations with Fitts' Law. However, applying tangential force in the rightward and the leftward directions required more normal force than the vertical directions.

The experimental study shows us an interesting result when it is compared to the post-task questionnaire we conducted individually. In the question about pose dependency, 14 people (82 %) answered "felt difference between the both-hands pose and the one-hand pose" and 4 (29 %) of them checked "one-hand" as the easier one. While 10 participants (59 %) answered that "It was easier to use two hands than one hand", the experimental result reveals that user performance was not significantly affected when a user uses one hand for inputting. From our observation, some individual participants with relatively smaller hands complained of the size of the device and tended to perform worse with one hand.

In another question, we asked if they felt any difference of directional conditions. Even though eight participants (47%) chose "not different", seven people who checked "different" chose the left (or the right if left-handed) as the hardest direction to input including three who answered both the right and the left. (We allowed multiple choices for the question.) In contrast, there were seven counts for "down" as the easiest direction for tangential input and five counts for the "up" choice. We can see an accordance of this result of the survey with the experimental data. In the user study, participants tended to perform worse when they apply tangential force in the leftward and rightward direction for forces above 3N. So they not only applied more force on the contact pad in the direction, but many of them also perceived that they did so.

In addition, we asked if they felt fatigue and when did they start to feel fatigue. Only three out of 17 participants (18%) answered "not felt fatigue" and seven of the rest answered (50% of all) "felt fatigue" after 4-6 blocks. These answers are consistent with Figure 13 which shows a slightly lifted curve of variables after the 6th block on the *x*-axis. Considering that the average time to complete a single block was about three minutes, this indicates that half of the participants started to feel fatigue after 12-18 minutes.

Compared to other studies on normal pressure input [4,21,24], erroneous selections seem to happen at a similar rate, approximately 5%, for tangential force input. However, relatively frequent wrong selections for the widest target in Figure 12 seem to have appeared owing to the 1-second dwell selection technique. For this target, approximately 1N tangential force was needed to move from a selection region to another. Since the user did not increase force fast enough to get out of a selection region it was recorded as a wrong selection. This indicates that a force rate of 1N per second may be too high for comfortable interaction.

Although we used a position control method to investigate user controllability of tangential force, it is more likely that the strength and direction of it is used for rate control. When we gave five common manipulation examples and asked respondents to rate the suitability of tangential force input for them in the questionnaire, eight of them (47%) ranked "map exploration" as the most probable application of tangential force input and "rapid scroll" was ranked to the very next position. On the other hand, 59% (10 people) replied that "moving a cursor" is least probable. Between the most and least probable application candidates were "map (image) zooming in and out" and "3-dimensional object manipulation". This result implies that users were able to understand intuitively that force input was better suited to rate control of parameters, even though we made no explanation about its usage. This result also agrees with the conclusion of the study on the finger force control for isometric joysticks that mapping force into velocity is more adequate than into position [20].

As described earlier, users experience less physical loads when applying tangential force with the thumb in the upward and downward direction. From this result, using tangential force in the vertical direction for controlling one-dimensional parameters would be the easiest way to implement without worrying about user performance degradation. One dimensional list searching and zooming-in-and-out is examples of such applications. UI design employing tangential force for 2-dimensional input should take careful consideration of our results about directionality of input. That is, user controllability in the direction of abduction and adduction may not be as good as other directions. To equally map tangential force input of all directions onto the virtual space, the force range of user interface needs to be adjusted for the worst performed direction. In the user study, directional difference became distinctly larger when the target force was bigger than 3N. Another approach to improve 2D input controllability could be using non-equal mapping functions for each direction.

Furthermore, tangential force input can be extended to the concept of sequential input and security input. It can be used like *double-click* for mice and any user defined gestures. Also the invisible property of applying force can be used as secured input gestures. While a touch-based or key-based passcode input method can be easily observed by others, a sequence of static force inputs may be more difficult to detect. In these usages, the variation of the force intensity will be regarded less important and recognizing the sequence of force directions may be a more important issue.

FUTURE WORK

Future works include hardware improvement, further usability test, and UI design for tangential force input. To improve hardware design, customized flexible PCBs or rubber-like materials that are force-resistive can be embedded within the mobile device. Current touch-sensitive devices can be easily utilized with tangential force input if the sensing layer is laid between the outermost glass and the casing of the device. If we integrate force sensors in smart phones, the effect of gravity can be eliminated using onboard accelerometers [8].

There are numerous areas of further user studies for better understanding of the characteristics of tangential force input applied to the surface. As done in prior works for force inputs for isometric joysticks or in normal direction, various transfer functions of force sensing voltages onto the virtual space can be examined [3,19,21,25], the target acquisition performance in a 2D space can be studied [1,20], and parameters of learning curves can be evaluated [2,20]. It will be also useful to study the effects of selection techniques [17] and multimodal feedback on tangential force interface [23].

User studies can also be designed to compare or combine the force input modality with other input techniques for the same UI implementation. Tangential-force-based interfaces may compete with touch and motion interfaces for better performance or better usability in navigation and zooming tasks.

CONCLUSION

In conclusion, this paper investigated user input based on tangential force applied on the surface of a mobile device. The main advantage of tangential force input is that it provides directional information and does not require movement. We presented considerations for hardware implementation of the input device; to compensate for friction between the base and the contact pad, we recommend inserting elastic parts to provide restoring force to the pad. User studies including objective data analysis and a subjective survey to understand tangential force input were conducted. The experimental results show that user controllability to reach and maintain tangential force does not significantly deteriorate when the device is held in one hand. We demonstrated that the target acquisition tasks using tangential force input follow Fitts' law. It is also revealed that users have more physical and perceived loads when applying tangential force in the lateral direction. Finally, we suggested and discussed design of user interface applications based on tangential force. Tangential force input is expected to enrich the user interface technology.

REFERENCES

1. Accot, J., Zhai, Z., Beyond Fitts' law: models for trajectory-based HCI tasks. In *Proc. CHI '97*. ACM (1997), 295–302.
2. Card, S., English, W., Burr, B., Evaluation of Mouse, Rate-Controlled Isometric Joystick, Step Keys, and Text Keys for Text Selection on a CRT. *Ergonomics* (1978). 21(8): 601-613.
3. Casiez, G. and Vogel, D. The effect of spring stiffness and control gain with an elastic rate control pointing device. *In Proc. CHI '08.* ACM (2008), 1709-1718.
4. Clarkson, E. C., Patel, S. N., Pierce, J. S., Abowd, G. D., Exploring continuous pressure input for mobile phones. *GVU Technical Report*. GIT-GVU-06-20, 2006.
5. Heo, S., Lee, G., Force gestures: augmented touch screen gestures using normal and tangential force. *Ext. Abstracts CHI '11*. ACM (2011), 1909-1914.
6. Heo, S., Lee, G., Force gestures: augmenting touch screen gestures using normal and tangential force. In *Proc. UIST '11*. ACM (2011), 621-626.
7. Herot, C., Weinzapfel, G., One-Point Touch Input of Vector Information from Computer Displays. In *Proc. SIGGRAPH '78*. ACM (1978), 210-216.

8. Luczak, W. Oleksiuk, M. Bodnicki, Sensing tilt with MEMS accelerometers. *IEEE Sensors Journal* (2006), 1669-1675.
9. McCallum D.C., Mak, E., Irani, P., Subramanian, S., PressureText: pressure input for mobile phone text entry. *Ext. Abstracts CHI '09*. ACM (2009), 4519-4524.
10. Minsky, M. R. Manipulating simulated objects with real-world gestures using a force and position sensitive screen. In *Proc. SIGGRAPH '84*. ACM (1984), 195-203.
11. Miyaki, T., Rekimoto, J., GraspZoom: zooming and scrolling control model for single-handed mobile interaction. In *Proc. MobileHCI '09*. ACM (2009), 81-84.
12. Mizobuchi, S., Terasaki, S., Keski-Jaskari, T., Nousiainen, J., Ryynanen, M., Silfverberg, M., Making an impression: force-controlled pen input for handheld devices. *Ext. Abstracts CHI '05*. ACM (2005), 1661-1664.
13. Moore, K.L., Dalley, A.F., Agur, A.M.R., *Clinically Oriented Anatomy*. 6th ed., Lippincott Williams & Wilkins (2010).
14. Nakazawa, N., Ikeura, R., Innoka, H., Characteristics of human fingertips in the shearing direction. *Biological Cybernetics* 82(3). Springer-Verlag (2000), 207-214.
15. Pataky, T.C., Latash, M.L., Zatsiorsky, V.M., Viscoelastic response of the finger pad to incremental tangential displacements. *Journal of Biomechanics*, 38 (2005). 1441-1449.
16. Quinn, P., Cockburn, A., Zoofing!: faster list selections with pressure-zoom-flick-scrolling. In Proc. OZCHI '09. ACM (2009), 185-192.
17. Ramos, G., Boulos, M., Balakrishnan, R., Pressure widgets. In *Proc. CHI '04*. ACM (2004), 487-494.
18. Rekimoto, J., Schwesig, C., PreSenseII: Bi-directional touch and pressure sensing interactions with tactile feedback. *Ext. Abstracts CHI '06*. ACM (2006), 1253-1258.
19. Rutledge, J.D., Selker, T., Force-to-motion functions for pointing, In *Proc. of Human-Computer Interaction - INTERACT'90*. Springer (1990), 701-705.
20. Selker, T., and Rutledge, J. Finger Force Precision for Computer Pointing. *IBM RC 17342* (1991), 2-7.
21. Shi, K., Irani, P., Gustafson, S., Subramanian, S., PressureFish: a method to improve control of discrete pressure-based input. In *Proc. CHI '08*. ACM (2008), 1295-1298.
22. Silfverberg, M., MacKenzie, I.S., Kauppinen, T. An Isometric Joystick as a Pointing Device for Handheld Information Terminals. In *Proc. Graphics Interface* 2001, 119-126.
23. Stewart, C., Rohs, M., Krats, S., Essl, G., Characteristics of pressure-based input for mobile devices. In *Proc. CHI '10*. ACM (2010), 801-810.
24. Wilson, G., Stewart, C., Brewster, S.A., Pressure-based menu selection for mobile devices. In *Proc. MobileHCI '10*. ACM (2010). 181-190.
25. Wilson, G., Brewster, S., Halvey, M., The effects of walking and control method on pressure-based interaction. *Ext. Abstracts CHI '11*. ACM (2011), 2275-2280

PocketNavigator: Studying Tactile Navigation Systems In-Situ

Martin Pielot, Benjamin Poppinga
OFFIS – Institute for Information Technology
Oldenburg, Germany
{pielot,poppinga}@offis.de

Wilko Heuten
OFFIS – Institute for Information Technology
Oldenburg, Germany
heuten@offis.de

Susanne Boll
University of Oldenburg
Oldenburg, Germany
boll@informatik.uni-oldenburg.de

ABSTRACT
In this paper, we report about a large-scale in-situ study of tactile feedback for pedestrian navigation systems. Recent advances in smartphone technology have enabled a number of interaction techniques for smartphone that use tactile feedback to deliver navigation information. The aim is to enable eyes-free usage and avoid distracting the user from the environment. Field studies where participants had to fulfill given navigation tasks, have found these techniques to be efficient and beneficial in terms of distraction. But it is not yet clear whether these findings will replicate in in-situ usage. We, therefore, developed a Google Maps-like navigation application that incorporates interaction techniques proposed in previous work. The application was published for free on the Android Market and so people were able to use it as a navigation system in their everyday life. The data collected through anonymous monitoring suggests that tactile feedback is successfully adopted in one third of all trips and has positive effects on the user's level of distraction.

Author Keywords
Handheld Devices and Mobile Computing; Tactile & Haptic UIs

ACM Classification Keywords
H.5.2 User Interfaces: Haptic I/O; I.3.6 Methodology and Techniques: Interaction techniques

General Terms
Human Factors; Design;

INTRODUCTION
In the automotive domain, navigation systems have proven to be successful and are widely accepted nowadays. Thanks to increasingly powerful and prevalent handheld devices, we now carry them with us all the time. Hence, the commodity of electronic navigation systems is now also available for pedestrians. More and more vendors consider pedestrian navigation as a growing market and promote pedestrian support as a key feature.

Figure 1. Examples for situation induced impairments (sunlight reflections and *head down* interaction) that can impede the use of common map-based navigation systems for pedestrians.

However, a significant body of research on interaction with handheld devices shows that visual and, to some extent, auditory user interfaces may not always be suitable for typical usage scenarios. Users may suffer from so-called situation induced impairments (see Figure 1), i.e. to loose awareness about the situation around them. For example, in a *PewInternet* study [9] one of six (17 %) cell-owning adults reported to have physically bumped into another person while being busy with their mobile phone. Using earplugs, frees the eyes but can lead to *iPod Zombie Trance*, which refers to the loss of situational awareness from listening to loud audio content. According to the Sydney Morning Herald, authorities in Australia are speculating that listening to loud audio content is one of the main contributing factors to the still increasing pedestrian fatalities.

As a solution for these challenges, several research groups have investigated using the sense of touch to convey the navigation information in a non-distractive manner. Examples are vibrating vests or belts [3, 14], vibration patterns [8, 18, 21], or using the mobile phone as a pointing device that vibrates when facing the direction to go [10, 19, 31]. These studies provide evidence that tactile feedback can significantly reduce the navigator's distraction. So far, these techniques have been studied in controlled field and lab studies. The navigation tasks were given by the researchers and limited in terms of usage time and geography. Hence, the external validity of the findings has yet to be shown, namely if tactile feedback for navigation systems will be helpful and beneficial in in-situ usage, i.e. situations where having to use a handheld navigation system arises from a real necessity rather than being a task given by a researcher.

In this paper, we report on the first large-scale in-situ study of tactile feedback for pedestrian navigation systems. We, therefore, developed a map-based pedestrian navigation application for Android phones. Based on tried and tested previous work, we included tactile feedback which guides the user along the route without the need to look at the display. The application was distributed for free via the Android Market and downloaded over 17,000 times. By monitoring how the application is used, we collected data from in-situ usage. In this paper, we report on findings of over 9,400 hours covering a period of eleven months.

RELATED WORK

Tscheligi and Sefelin [25] argue that considering the context of use appropriately is one of the main prerequisites for the success of pedestrian navigation systems. One of the main challenges is the distraction that emerges from the use of mobile devices on the move [13]. Pedestrians might lose their situation awareness, which may be dangerous when walking through lively, traffic-heavy areas [9].

A solution to this problem can be derived from Wicken's Multiple Resource Theory [30]. Each sensory channel has its own pool of attentional resources. When conveying two bits of information by different sensory channels it is more likely that both are perceived and processed. For example, when a user has to watch the traffic, it is easier to listen to navigation instructions than reading them from a small display. Since the sense of touch is hardly used to monitor the environment for dangerous traffic situations, it is best suited to communicate navigation information and avoiding dangerous distraction at the same time.

In 1997 Tan and Pentland [24] proposed a 3x3 array of tactile actuators worn on the back for conveying navigation information. E.g., a series of pulses moving from the left to the right of the display could be used to indicate "turn right" or "right-hand side". A more intuitive form of presenting directional information [23], by creating vibro-tactile stimuli on the torso that "point" in the direction to move, was proposed by van Erp et al. [28]. Such tactile display come in the form of belts [26, 29] or vests [22]. An early example by Tsukada and Yasumura [26] is the ActiveBelt, which is a waist belt equipped with eight vibro-tactile actuators. It allows creating tactile stimuli around the wearer's waist to "point" into a horizontal direction. By pointing into the direction the user has to go, such tactile displays can guide pedestrians along a route. This form of waypoint navigation has found to be effective and beneficial for the user's distraction [3, 14].

Tactile displays, such as tactile belts, might become common in the near future, but yet they might not always be available when the user is traveling. Therefore, researchers have investigated whether navigation support can also be provided with the most ubiquitous tactile display: the vibration alarm of mobile phones. There are two predominant solutions, which Frohlich et al. [5] refer to as the *magic wand* and *sixth sense*.

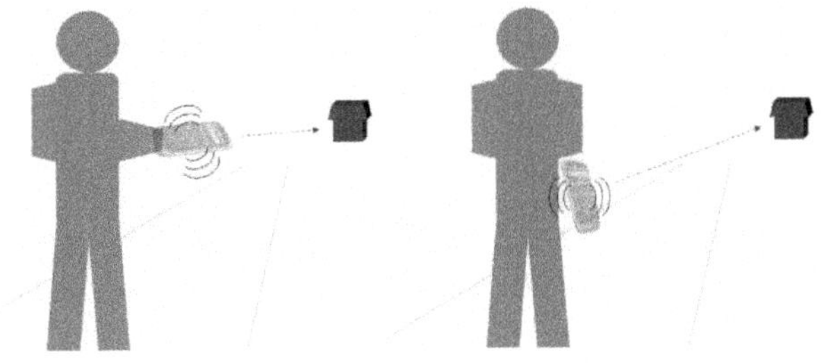

Figure 2. Left: Magic wand metaphor – the user *scans* for spatial information; the presence of an entity, such as a waypoint, in the pointing direction is indicated by vibration. Right: The sixth sense metaphor – the direction of a spatial entity, such as a waypoint, is encoded in vibration feedback itself, e.g. by using different pattern for different directions.

The *magic wand* metaphor (see Figure 2a) refers to pointing at a distant object with a handheld device to learn about its presence or access information about it. Technically, this has become possible since smartphones are increasingly more often equipped with digital compasses that allow obtaining a device's pointing direction. Recent implementations provide feedback when the user roughly points at a relevant spatial entity, such as the travel destination [10, 19, 31]. In the context of navigation support, users can stay aware of the general direction of their travel destination by actively scanning the environment for it. It has been shown that this technique is intuitive and allows users to effectively reach a given destination [10, 19, 31]. However, the intuitiveness is traded with the drawback that the techniques requires active pointing gestures, which might become cumbersome over time [19].

The *sixth sense* metaphor describes interaction techniques that use multimodal feedback to alert the user about changes in the environment, such as the location of a travel destination in relation to the traveler's location and orientation. (see Figure 2b). This has been applied by issuing turning instructions in vibration patterns [8] as well as cueing the direction of spatial entities in vibration patterns [10, 18, 17, 21] by the means of Tactons [1]. The advantage this approach is that users are not required to search for spatial entities via pointing gestures. However, it requires users to learn the meaning of the feedback, e.g. vibration patterns, first.

Further, it has shown that both approaches go well together [16, 10, 17]. These groups have successfully tested conveying the direction of a spatial entity relative to the devices pointing direction using vibration patterns. The combination of both approaches has the advantage that the design has the intuitiveness of the magic wand approach, but can also be used without doing pointing gestures.

In terms of situation awareness, previous field studies [3, 15, 14, 18, 17] have provided evidence that tactile feedback for navigation systems can significantly reduce the traveler's distraction. However, all of the above cited studies are field experiments where participants had to complete navigation tasks specified by the experimenters, which typically means reaching a given set of destinations. Thus, there are a number of imminent limitations. Using a navigation system was not a real need of the participants. All studies took place at one single location and with rather homogeneous user samples. These controlled setting ensure the internal validity of the results, but consequently they lack external validity. This means, that it is not clear, whether the intuitiveness and the benefits of tactile feedback in terms of distraction will translate to in-situ, real world usage [27]. The question remains, whether users will benefit from tactile feedback in all different kinds of situations, where navigation support is a real necessity of the user.

METHODOLOGY

The presented study aims at bringing the research on navigation systems from the lab into everyday life. The goal is to study how travelers use the tactile feedback and if there is a positive effect on the level of distraction. Furthermore, we aim at collecting data from as many usage scenarios as possible in order to provide evidence that the positive findings from previous studies translate to typical navigation situations.

So far, only few in-situ studies with tactile feedback have been conducted. Nagel et al. [12] report from a long-term study of a tactile belt showing North which four participants had to wear for sixth weeks. Hoggan and Brewster [6] conducted an in-situ study where nine participants were asked to use a handheld device with a multimodally enhanced keyboard for eight days. These studies were conducted with only a few participants because the implementation of long-term studies is resource intensive.

In order to tackle that problem, we applied the emerging approach of doing "research in the large" [2]. By using mobile application distribution channels, such as Apple's App Store or Google's Android Market, we bring our research apparatus "further into the wild" [11]. We, therefore, developed a navigation system for pedestrians with added tactile feedback. By providing this application for free via the Android Market, we hoped to encourage as many Android users as possible to use the application on their trips. To be able to collect evidence from a large amount of users with our given resources, and to avoid being obtrusive to our users, we used automated context sensing and logging to obtain our data.

Apparatus

As apparatus for the experiment we used the PocketNavigator [16], a map-based navigation system developed by our research group that is similar to Google Maps. The PocketNavigator, as shown in Figure 3, uses OpenStreetMap data which has highly detailed data on pedestrian paths in many countries. Further, the application provides all the essential navigation functionalities available as with Google Maps: an icon drawn onto the map indicates the user's position and orientation. The map can be set to automatically rotate and align itself with the environment, so the "up" direction on the screen corresponds to the device's orientation. Users can search for addresses or just select their destination via the map. The application uses two routing services, YOURS[1] and OpenRouteService[2] to calculate the shortest route to a given destination. The route is highlighted on the map.

Figure 3. Screenshot of the PocketNavigator. The user location and the route are shown on a map. The icon in the lower left provides a visual cue where to go.

Navigation Support

Besides calculating and showing a route on a map, most of today's navigation systems can also provide navigation instructions. In cars, navigation systems typically give turning instructions, such as "turn right in fifty meters". For pedestrians, this has a few disadvantages. Cars usually travel in confined lanes of a road. Pedestrians, however, can move freely and change direction at any time. Also, pedestrians move much slower, so the typical distances (turn right in 300, 100, 50 meters) are too big. For pedestrians, distances would have to be reduced to a few meters only. This, however, is difficult to achieve, since GPS is hardly accurate enough.

Previous work has suggested the concept of waypoint navigation as an alternative form of guiding pedestrians [4]. Routes are divided into sets of waypoints. Instead of a turning instruction, the system constantly conveys the direction of the waypoint that has to be reached next (e.g. 11 o'clock). Once this waypoint has been reached the system switches to the subsequent waypoint. In our application, the arrow in the lower left corner of the screen (see Figure 3) constantly points at the next waypoint. By walking into the indicated direction, users are guided along the route until reaching the destination.

Tactile Feedback

Since our goal is to study tactile feedback, we added a tactile user interface to indicate the direction of the next waypoint. In order to build on a proven technique we combined previously proposed instances of the Magic Wand and the Sixth Sense metaphor.

As instance of the Sixth Sense metaphor, we used the Tactile Compass design described in our previous work [18]. The basic idea is to map directions (ahead, left, right, behind, and

[1] `http://www.yournavigation.org/`

[2] `http://www.openrouteservice.org/`

the four intermediate directions) to individual vibration patterns. The patterns used in our prototype are illustrated in Figure 4. For example, when a user walks towards the next waypoint, two short vibration buzzes indicate "ahead". When the next waypoint is to the left hand side, a long buzz is followed by a short buzz. These directions are given in relation to the user's walking direction. The walking direction is obtained from the GPS signal. This has the advantage that the device can be left in the pocket and requires no potentially fatiguing gestures. The disadvantages are that the patterns have to be learned and that no walking direction can be determined when the user does not move.

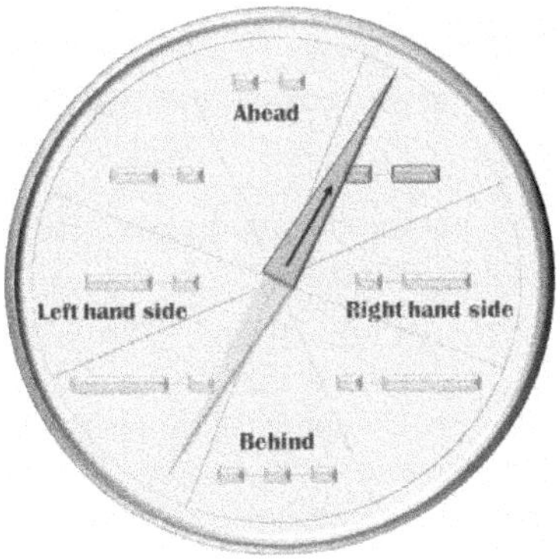

Figure 4. The vibration patterns that encode the four walking directions.

To compensate for these disadvantages, we added a Magic Wand design which closely follows the ones that were successfully tested in previous work [10, 19, 31]. When the device is held parallel to the ground it becomes a pointing device. This allows users to scan for the direction to go. For example, when the device points at the next waypoint, users receive the "ahead" signal, as in the Sixth Sense metaphor. Here, the application uses the magnetometer to obtain in which direction the device is pointing.

In both interaction designs, the vibration feedback is repeated every 3-4 seconds. In a previous experiment [17] we found that while some people appreciate the constant feedback, others were afraid to become annoyed over time. In order to not having to turn off the tactile feedback manually, we introduced two features that apply to the Sixth Sense mode. One feature is that the feedback mutes when the user stands still. Thus, when typically no information is needed the device remains silent. The other one is that we introduced a "silent corridor". As long as the user walks towards the next waypoint, the system remains silent. In the Magic Wand mode, we did not silence the vibration feedback since we believed that users would use this mode to actively sweep for directions and hence desire the information.

A further effect that played in our hands was that the vibration of typical devices is usually too weak to be perceived well in the pocket on the move. We found that users then just touch the pocket to feel the vibration with the fingers. This has the advantage that it allows users to receive tactile feedback on-demand by simply touching the device.

Waypoint Navigation Implementation

The pilot tests of our previous experiment [17] showed that a simple implementation of waypoint navigation which strictly requires reaching the waypoints in the given order will not work in the real world. Users may always skip waypoints, e.g. when the GPS signal is bad or when they find a shortcut. If the system does not react to such situations, users may be forced to go back to a missed waypoint. Our application, therefore, monitors the distance to several waypoints, and skips to a closer waypoint when applicable. If the user has left the route for too long, a new route is calculated.

The success of waypoint navigation also depends on how close the user needs to get to a waypoint until the system switches to the subsequent waypoint. Switching too late causes the user to reach a decision point without knowing where to turn. Switching to the next waypoint too early can result into direction information that may be hard to interpret, e.g. if the system points at a building. In a series of pilot studies, we optimized the switching algorithm to provide the new directional information in the most suitable moment. One of the tweaks we used was to switch to the next waypoint earlier, the faster the user walks and the less accurate the GPS signal becomes.

To help users to learn the vibration feedback, a tutorial was included that automatically popped up when starting the application. In a series of pictures it showed different routing situations and the according vibration patterns. Further, we added visualizations of the vibration patterns to the visual direction arrow (see Figure 4). Thus, users had sufficient hints to learn and understand the vibration patterns.

Design

Since our aim was to study the effect of tactile feedback on the level of distraction, the presence of the tactile feedback is considered as the independent variable. It has two levels: being turned on corresponds to the experimental condition, being turned off to the control condition. We first envisioned a between-group experiment design where the condition would be randomly assigned to the user. For half of the users the tactile feedback would have been always turned on, for the other half it would always been turned off. However, we discarded this approach, since we heavily advertised the application's vibration guidance feature. We were afraid to confuse or annoy users if they were not receiving the expected vibration feedback. Further, in our pilot studies we learned that turning off the tactile feedback is sometimes necessary, e.g. when just studying a route before actually leaving the house. Thus, we allowed the user to turn the tactile feedback on and off. Consequently, the experiment is not a true experiment, but a quasi-experiment.

Logging Strategy

To monitor the usage of the device, our goal was to recognize important events via the available sensors. Since important events, such as looking at the display, may be very short, our primary strategy was to continuously monitor the device's state. For practical reasons, the application takes snapshots of the current context once every second. These snapshots are stored on the device and transmitted to our server when a proper internet connection is available. To limit the use of bandwidth, we only stored and transmitted snapshots where a route was present.

One context snapshot consists of

- **Identifying information**, including the hash of the device ID, a time stamp, and the application version number
- **Status information**, including screen on, user centered, map rotated, route computed, watching tutorial, and tactile feedback enabled being true or false
- **Sensor information**, including location provider (GPS or WLAN), location accuracy, speed over ground, heading according to GPS, device orientation (pointing direction), light level, proximity, temperature
- **Route information**, including distance to destination, destination ID (hash), route length, destination reached
- **Usage information** = high level approximation of usage, including device in hand, device used for pointing, user follows route

Ethics
To avoid ethical issues we never stored any personal data, i.e. such data that would allow identifying or contacting the participant. To be able to match data to a certain phone, we calculated an MD-5 hash code from the phone's device ID and used this as an identifier. Hash codes have the advantage that they are not reversible but can be used as a unique identifier. Further, we never stored any GPS locations, nor the names or addresses of the travel destinations.

RESULTS
The PocketNavigator was uploaded to the Android Market in April 2010. It was advertised in blogs and social networks. The logging framework used for this study was added February 2011. The data we report reflects usage between this date and December 2011.

In the time between April 2010 and February 2011 the PocketNavigator has been subject to numerous pilot tests and a published field experiment [17]. Thus, during the study period the application had already been thoroughly tried and tested. Therefore, bugs or salient usability issues do not bias our findings.

Users
During the study period the application was started on 3,338 different devices. As shown in Figure 5 the locales reported by the devices lets us suggest that our sample mostly contains users from the so called *Western Countries*, i.e. North America and Europe. More than 58 % of the devices named English (en_US & en_UK) as system language.

Result Filtering
34,035,316 context snapshots were collected, each reflecting about 1 second of application usage. Thus, more than 9,400 hours of usage were recorded. Since context snapshots were only collected when the user had calculated a route we clustered the snapshots by route.

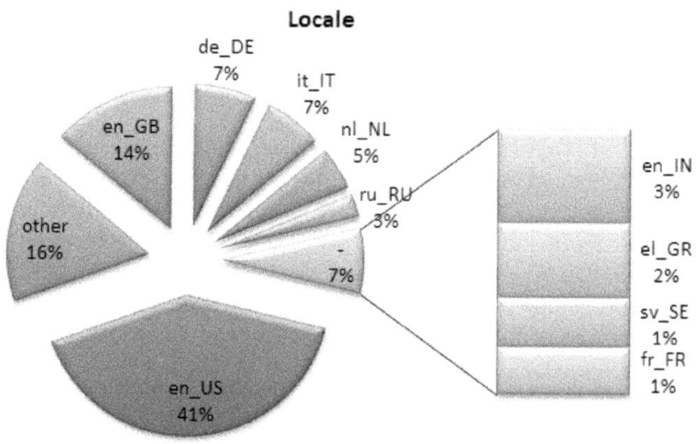

Figure 5. Users by locale.

8,187 different routes were found. The average characteristics of these routes suggest that the typical usage of the application was to browse and explore routes rather than using the application as navigation system. Users moved in only 13.0 % of all collected snapshots. Further, there is a huge contrast between the median (2082 m) and the mean (256,982 m) route lengths. Thus, most of the recorded routes do not reflect usage on the move by a pedestrian.

Since the aim of this work is analyzing usage on the move we applied a set of filters. The goal was to only keep those routes, which were part of a trip, i.e. the user was moving along it. We therefore kept only these routes that lasted longer than 30 seconds, were shorter than 40 km. Further, the user had to have moved at least 25 % of the time with a mean travel speed being below 8 km/h and a the maximum travel speed being below 20 km/h. By using these constraints we filtered out all routes that are not likely to be traveled by foot.

Trips Characteristics
301 routes by 112 distinct devices matched our filters, which we will call *trips* in the following. The mean/median number of trips per device is 2.5/1. Thus, most results reflect first-time usage. The maximum number of trips is 34 by a single device.

Measure	Mean (Std. Dev)
Travel time (min)	7.8 (21.2)
Travel distance (km)	1.32 (1.76)
Travel speed (km/h)	3.8 (1.3)
Destination reached (%)	15.6
User moving (%)	70.0 (22.3)
Following route (%)	87.2 (SD 18.2)

Table 1. Characteristics of trips traveled on foot.

Table 1 shows the average characteristics of a trip. The mean length of a trip was 1,111.7 m (SD 590.8 m). Most of the trips (75 %) represent distances below 1 km, which are easy to travel on foot in 6 to 12 minutes (assuming a walking speed of 5 km/h). In average, users walked 1.32 km in 7.8 min with an effective travel speed of 3.8 km/h. For the calculation of the effective travel speed we included only the context snapshots where the user was moving, so the result does not get biased when the user is standing.

For most of the time (89 %) users followed the calculated route. This means they stayed close to the shortest path between the previous and the next waypoint. Since the destination was reached on 15 % of all trips only, we updated logging framework by adding the distance to the destination as a parameter to the context snapshots. Judging from 130 trips containing this added parameter, the mean distance between the user and the travel destination was 874.7 m (SD 1,264.9 m) when the routing was discontinued.

Tactile Feedback Usage

29.9 % of the users used the tactile feedback, i.e. contributed to the experimental condition on at least one of their trips. It was turned on in about one forth of all context snapshots (mean 23.3 %). In terms of navigation performance, not statistically significant differences could be found between the conditions.

To understand how the tactile feedback was used we analyzed how often and how long users scanned for the next waypoint when the tactile feedback was turned on. A *scanning event*, i.e. the interaction technique described in [10, 19, 31], is assumed when the device is held roughly parallel to the ground. From our previous studies we can confirm that this is the typical posture when people scan for the next waypoints.

Measure	Mean	Median	SD
Count	12.4	6.0	16.1
Mean Duration	19.3	4.0	53.5
Ratio of Trip (%)	30.5	14.9	32.3

Table 2. Scanning events with tactile feedback turned on.

As shown in Table 2 scanning events occurred frequently but were rather short most of the time. The difference between the mean duration (19.3 s) and the median duration (4 s) of a scan shows that there were quite different usage strategies. One seems to involve frequent, but short scans, while the other means sustain scanning for the next waypoint.

Users used the scanning feature during one sixth to one third of the route (mean 30.5 %, median 14.9 %). Scanning occurred more often when the tactile feedback was turned on (mean 33.3 % for tactile feedback on versus 36.8 % for tactile feedback off), but the difference is not statistically significant ($p = .213$).

Level of Distraction - Amount of Touch Screen Interaction

To see in what way the user interacted with the device we analyzed the touch events generated by the touch screen. Whenever a touch event was recorded during a snapshot we counted an *interaction event* for the second that the snapshot represents.

Table 3 shows the detailed analysis of the interaction events. The median value shows that during many trips users touched the screen only once and briefly. This excludes the touch

Measure	Mean	Median	SD
Count	3.3	1.0	5.3
Mean Duration	4.8	1.0	23.7
Ratio of Trip (%)	6.3	2.9	9.0

Table 3. Interaction Events.

events needed to specify the route. Thus, users did not interact much with the device during their trips.

Yet, the tactile feedback had a significant effect on the amount of interaction ($p < .001$). With the tactile feedback turned on, users interacted with the device significantly less (Mean 2.0 %, Median 0.0 %) with the device than without the tactile feedback (Mean 4.8 %, Median 1.0 %)[3].

Level of Distraction - Looking at the Display

Related work argues that travelers are often distracted, since they spent a lot of time looking at maps and screens on the move [3, 15, 14]. Thus, we wanted to understand how often the users held the device in the hand so that they could see the screen. We call these *in hand* events. From our pilot tests we knew that users tend to hold the device nearly parallel to the ground with a slight tilt towards the face when looking at the display. Hence, whenever the screen was turned on and the device was held roughly as e.g. seen in Figure 1 we considered the device being held *in hand*.

Measure	Mean	Median	SD
Count	6.5	3.0	10.9
Mean Duration (s)	50.5	16.5	2416
Ratio of Trip (%)	53.5	50.5	34.6

Table 4. In Hand Events.

As shown in Table 4 users held the device *in hand* for more than half of the trip time in average. The tactile feedback had a significant effect on the time the device was held in hand ($p < .01$) The device was held significantly less in hand when the tactile feedback was turned on (Mean 60.1 %, Median 66.5 %) compared to when it was turned off (Mean 71.2 %, Median 92.0 %).

Level of Distraction - Display Turned Off

Further, we identified those events where distraction is highly unlikely, since the screen was turned off. Whether the screen is turned on or of can be determined from the lifecycle status of an Android application. Only when the status is *started* the screen is on.

Measure	Mean	Median	SD
Count	2.5	1.0	3.2
Mean Duration	136.4	27.0	653.8
Ratio of Trip (%)	55.4	57.5	35.1

Table 5. Screen Off Events.

Table 5 shows how often and how long participants turned off the screen. Usually this happened only a few times and lasted

[3] These numbers are lower than the overall average, since some users switched the tactile feedback on/off during their trips and thus contributed to both conditions

for about half a minute to 1.5 minutes. In total, the screen was kept off for nearly half of the trip time. The difference between mean and median duration and the high standard deviation of 351.3 s show that few users kept the screen turned off for several minutes, while the majority of the users turned it off for a short time (less than half a minute) only.

The tactile feedback had a significant effect on the time the screen was turned off ($p < .01$). With the tactile feedback the screen was turned off significantly longer (40.2 % of travel time) than without tactile feedback (28.6 % of travel time).

User Comments

From the initial release to the end of this study we received about 35 comments via the Android Market's rating facility. Six of them addressed the vibration guidance:

- *Good applet but consumes too much battery [Buena applet pero consume demasiada bater'a]*
- *Works fine on Legend. Nice if you don't want to stare at your mobile all the time to find the way. Needs a bit practice to interpret the vibration.*
- *Good idea. Bit laggy. Not sure how long my hero's battery will last with GPS on and my phone vibrating every second to indicate if on right track!?!*
- *Ahead pattern can't be muted on nexus one. Too annoying and so I didn't try it for navigation yet. Looks good though.*
- *The vibration seems a useful concept, but the program doesn't use a particularly good navigation system. No rerouting, and sends me back to points.*

We found three main take-aways: (1) the users' main concern is degrading the battery life by the vibration, (2) training is needed to make use of the tactile feedback, and (3) the idea is received well. We addressed the concern about the battery life by enabling the user to reduce the amount of vibration by turning on the silent corridor. The desire for more training was addressed by adding the tutorial demonstrating the vibration patterns. Both of these additions were in place when the data logging began.

Beyond that the user comments were not at all helpful with respect to our research questions. We believe that researchers should never rely on user comments alone when studying user interfaces via the Android Market or similar distribution channels.

DISCUSSION

We collected data from 8,187 routes and more than 9,400 hours of usage. Most of the time a route was calculated, the application was presumably not used as a navigation aid as the user did not move. Filtering our data according to the characteristics of a pedestrian traveler, we found 301 trips where pedestrians navigated along the calculated route. The tactile feedback was used in 29.9 % of the trips with no effect on the navigation performance. However, we found evidence that suggests statistically significant effects on the level of distraction: users interacted less with the touch screen, looked less often at the display, and turned off the screen more often.

Trips on Foot

The notable difference between the number of calculated routes and those that were actually navigated by the user indicates that the application was mainly used to explore environments with the help of the map. Browsing a map, therefore, seems to be the more frequent use case than navigation. This could be explained by previous findings suggesting that people appreciate the fact that maps provide them with an overview [7, 18, 20].

Further, the destination was only reached in one sixth of the trips. In average the distance was about 850 m away when the application was turned off. At the same time, users followed the route most of the time (90 %). One explanation might be that the application was mainly used to guide the users along parts of a route only.

Tactile Feedback Usage

The tactile feedback was used in roughly one third of the travel time and in one forth of all trips. Given the fact that the users had to learn the vibration patterns from the tutorial and the indications on the visual compass icon (see Figure 4) only, we consider this as a positive finding.

On the trips where tactile feedback was used, the Magic Wand technique, i. e. situations where users were sweeping the device for the direction of the next waypoint, was used more than one third of the travel time in average. About one third of the users scanned often but only for a few seconds, another third of the users scanned only a few times but for a longer time. However, these findings have to be handled with care. The application cannot decide whether the user actually intended to scan for the next waypoint, or maybe just checked the map and accidentally held the device parallel to the ground.

Distraction

All dependent measures related to the level of distraction show a positive effect of the tactile feedback and, therefore, confirm findings from previously reported field studies.

Previous results [7, 15, 20] indicate that navigators spent a significant portion of their attention on reading the map and navigation instructions. In [20], participants looked every 5.8 seconds on the map or the display of the navigation system. In [15], the participants looked at the map for about 25 % of the total trip in average — some participants for even half of the travel time. Our results suggest that users looked at the display for 53.5 % of the trip time, which shows that the results from previous work are not necessarily caused by the context of the user study. Given that the average trip was 7.8 minutes and during the averate trip user switched 6.5 times from a posture where s/he could look at the display to a posture where this was not possible, we infer that users checked the map at least every 72 seconds at the device. However, unlike Rukzio et al., we are not able to detect quick context switches between checking the display and checking the environment. Thus, there might have been many more context switches, which, however, did not cause the user to change the posture of the device. Yet, our results confirm that distraction is a challenge that also exists during in-situ usage and not only in field studies.

These findings from previous work [7, 15, 20, 17] also suggest that navigators consult their navigation system far more often than necessary. Instead of just checking the map or navigation instructions when approaching a decision point, users keep looking at the display throughout the trip. Hence, motivating travelers to turn off the display of the navigation system or to stow it away more often will make it less likely that users glance at it and, therefore, become distracted from the environment. Our results here show that the tactile feedback caused users to interact less with the touch screen, turn off the display more often, and hold the device less often in a way that users typically do in order to read the display's content. Thus, we conclude that adding the tactile feedback caused the users to be less distracted from the environment.

This confirms findings from previous field studies which have shown that replacing visual navigation cues by vibro-tactile navigation cues lower the travelers' level of distraction [3, 14, 17] or that conveying tactile navigation cues while navigating with a map can also reduce the level of distraction [15].

Limitations

With our study design of conducting a study on the Android market, we focus on the external validity of the findings. We gave up control over how our participants use the application and traded internal validity for external validity. Our results show that people use applications in other than the indented forms, such as exploring a route without going on the actual trip. This makes it harder to rule out confounding variables. However, our very strict set of filters ensures that we only analyzed situations, were travelers were navigating along the route on foot for a minimum of half a minute.

On the other hand, our findings reflect in-situ usage, and cover a wide range of users, usage environments and contexts. The controlled studies in previous work, in contrast, only reflect a limited set of usage situations and always required the user to fulfill a given navigation task. We believe that previous work and the presented study in combination cancel out each other's weaknesses. With this study we provide the missing evidence that allows reinforcing the external validity of these previous studies. Taken together, previous work and the study presented provide evidence that tactile feedback is usable and accepted by a good share of pedestrians, and has a positive effect on the level of distraction.

CONCLUSIONS

In this paper, we report on the first large-scale in-situ evaluation of tactile feedback for pedestrian navigation systems. We have enhanced a map-based navigation system with vibration patterns in order to deliver navigation cues in an eyes-free way. The system was published for free on the Android Market. The collected data provides evidence that tactile feedback was used in nearly one third of the usage time. When the tactile feedback was enabled, users interacted less with the touch screen, checked the display less, and turned off the screen more often.

These results are in line with findings from previous field studies. Furthermore, since we obtained these results from an application from the Android Market, this study is the first which provides results from in-situ usage and numerous different users and usage contexts. Using this novel study methodology, allows us the conclusion that users would accept tactile feedback in their handheld devices and are able to make sense of it with no help but a tutorial. These findings encourage incorporating tactile feedback into applications for handheld devices that are designed to be used on the move.

Future work will have to investigate how to assess and increase the internal validity of studies where the experimenter is not present. With the right kind of measurement tools and data collection strategies, we may be able to study novel interfaces in much broader contexts than we do today.

ACKNOWLEDGMENTS

The authors are grateful to the European Commission, which co-funds the IP HaptiMap (FP7-ICT-224675). We like to thank our colleagues for sharing their ideas with us.

REFERENCES

1. Brewster, S., and Brown, L. M. Tactons: structured tactile messages for non-visual information display. In *Proc. AUIC 2004*, Australian Computer Society, Inc. (2004), 15–23.

2. Cramer, H., Rost, M., Belloni, N., Bentley, F., and Chincholle, D. Research in the large. using app stores, markets, and other wide distribution channels in ubicomp research. In *Adjunct Proceedings of UbiComp 2010*, ACM (2010), 511–514.

3. Elliott, L. R., van Erp, J., Redden, E. S., and Duistermaat, M. Field-based validation of a tactile navigation device. *IEEE Transactions on Haptics 99* (2010).

4. Erp, J. B. F. V., Veen, H. A. H. C. V., Jansen, C., and Dobbins, T. Waypoint navigation with a vibrotactile waist belt. *ACM Trans. Appl. Percept. 2* (April 2005), 106–117.

5. Fröhlich, P., Oulasvirta, A., Baldauf, M., and Nurminen, A. On the move, wirelessly connected to the world. *Commun. ACM 54* (January 2011), 132–138.

6. Hoggan, E., and Brewster, S. A. Crosstrainer: testing the use of multimodal interfaces in situ. In *Proceedings of the 28th international conference on Human factors in computing systems*, ACM (2010), 333–342.

7. Ishikawa, T., Fujiwara, H., Imai, O., and Okabe, A. Wayfinding with a gps-based mobile navigation system: A comparison with maps and direct experience. *Journal of Environmental Psychology 28*, 1 (2008), 74–82.

8. Lin, M.-W., Cheng, Y.-M., Yu, W., and Sandnes, F. E. Investigation into the feasibility of using tactons to provide navigation cues in pedestrian situations. In *Proc. OZCHI '08*, ACM (2008), 299–302.

9. Madden, M., and Rainie, L. Adults and cell phone distractions. Tech. rep., Pew Research Center, 2010.

10. Magnusson, C., Rassmus-Gröhn, K., and Szymczak, D. The influence of angle size in navigation applications using pointing gestures. In *Proc. HAID '10*, Springer-Verlag (2010), 107–116.

11. McMillan, D., Morrison, A., Brown, O., Hall, M., and Chalmers, M. Further into the wild: Running worldwide trials of mobile systems. In *Proc. Pervasive '10* (2010).

12. Nagel, S. K., Carl, C., Kringe, T., Märtin, R., and König, P. Beyond sensory substitutionlearning the sixth sense. *Journal of Neural Engineering 2*, 4 (December 2005), R13+.

13. Oulasvirta, A., Tamminen, S., Roto, V., and Kuorelahti, J. Interaction in 4-second bursts: the fragmented nature of attentional resources in mobile hci. In *Proc. CHI '05*, ACM (2005), 919–928.

14. Pielot, M., and Boll, S. Tactile Wayfinder: comparison of tactile waypoint navigation with commercial pedestrian navigation systems. In *Proc. Pervasive '10* (2010).

15. Pielot, M., Henze, N., and Boll, S. Supporting map-based wayfinding with tactile cues. In *Proc. MobileHCI '09*, ACM (2009), 23:1–23:10.

16. Pielot, M., Poppinga, B., and Boll, S. Pocketnavigator: vibro-tactile waypoint navigation for everyday mobile devices. In *Proc. MobileHCI '10*, ACM (2010), 423–426.

17. Pielot, M., Poppinga, B., Heuten, W., and Boll, S. 6th senses for everyone!: the value of multimodal feedback in handheld navigation aids. In *Proc. ICMI '11*, ACM (2011), 65–72.

18. Pielot, M., Poppinga, B., Heuten, W., and Boll, S. A tactile compass for eyes-free pedestrian navigation. In *Proc. INTERACT '11*, Springer-Verlag (2011), 640–656.

19. Robinson, S., Jones, M., Eslambolchilar, P., Murray-Smith, R., and Lindborg, M. "i did it my way": moving away from the tyranny of turn-by-turn pedestrian navigation. In *Proc. MobileHCI '10*, ACM (2010), 341–344.

20. Rukzio, E., Müller, M., and Hardy, R. Design, implementation and evaluation of a novel public display for pedestrian navigation: the rotating compass. In *Proc. CHI '09s*, ACM (2009), 113–122.

21. Rümelin, S., Rukzio, E., and Hardy, R. Naviradar: a novel tactile information display for pedestrian navigation. In *Proc. UIST '11*, ACM (2011), 293–302.

22. Rupert, A. An instrumentation solution for reducing spatial disorientation mishaps. *Engineering in Medicine and Biology Magazine, IEEE 19*, 2 (Mar/Apr 2000), 71–80.

23. Srikulwong, M., and O'Neill, E. A comparison of two wearable tactile interfaces with a complementary display in two orientations. In *Proc. HAID '10*, Springer-Verlag (2010), 139–148.

24. Tan, H. Z., and Pentland, A. Tactual displays for wearable computing. In *Proc. ISWC '97* (1997).

25. Tscheligi, M., and Sefelin, R. Mobile navigation support for pedestrians: can it work and does it pay off? *Interactions 13* (2006), 31–33.

26. Tsukada, and Yasumura. Activebelt: Belt-type wearable tactile display for directional navigation. In *Proc. UbiComp '04* (2004).

27. van der Linden, J., Johnson, R., Bird, J., Rogers, Y., and Schoonderwaldt, E. Buzzing to play: lessons learned from an in the wild study of real-time vibrotactile feedback. In *Proc. CHI '11*, ACM (2011), 533–542.

28. van Erp, J. B. F. Tactile navigation display. In *Workshop on Haptic HCI*, Springer-Verlag (2001), 165–173.

29. van Erp, J. B. F. Presenting directions with a vibrotactile torso display. *Ergonomics 48* (2005), 302–313.

30. Wickens, C. D. Processing resources in attention. In *Processing resource in attention*. London: Academic, 1984.

31. Williamson, J., Robinson, S., Stewart, C., Murray-Smith, R., Jones, M., and Brewster, S. Social gravity: a virtual elastic tether for casual, privacy-preserving pedestrian rendezvous. In *Proc. CHI '10*, ACM (New York, NY, USA, 2010), 1485–1494.

Funneling and Saltation Effects for Tactile Interaction with Virtual Objects

Jaedong Lee, Youngsun Kim and Gerard J. Kim
Digital Experience Laboratory, Korea University
Anam-dong 5-ga, Seongbuk-gu, Seoul, Republic of Korea
{ jdlee@korea.ac.kr, zyoko85@korea.ac.kr, gjkim@korea.ac.kr }

ABSTRACT
Funneling and saltation are two major illusory feedback techniques for vibration-based tactile feedback. They are often put into practice e.g. to reduce the number of vibrators to be worn on the body and thereby build a less cumbersome feedback device. Recently, these techniques have been found to be applicable to eliciting "out of the body" experiences as well (e.g. through user-held external objects). This paper examines the possibility of applying this phenomenon to interacting with virtual objects. Two usability experiments were run to test the effects of funneling and saltation respectively for perceiving tactile sensation from a virtual object in an augmented reality setting. Experimental results have shown solid evidences for phantom sensations from virtual objects with funneling, but mixed results for saltation.

Author Keywords
Phantom sensation; Illusory feedback; Funneling; Saltation; Vibro-tactile feedback;

ACM Classification Keywords
H.5.2 [Information Interfaces And Presentation]: User Interfaces - Interaction styles;

General Terms
Human Factors; Experimentation.

INTRODUCTION
Vibro-tactile feedback is one inexpensive and effective way to enhance interaction experience. Tactile feedback is also often combined with other modalities to amplify its effect or produce phantom sensation. For instance, a mere vibration, synchronized with the sound and animated bouncing ball, can induce a phantom sensation of directional inertia [6]. Another illusory feedback techniques associated with vibro-tactility are funneling and saltation [5, 12]. Both techniques generate pseudo-tactile sensations by presenting two or more tactile stimuli directly to the parts of the body simultaneously (funneling) or with time delay (saltation). The locations of the pseudo-tactile sensation can be changed by modulating the intensities/duration (funneling) or inter-stimulus time interval (saltation). These two techniques have often been applied to reduce the number of tactile actuators on the body [15, 25]. Recently, Miyazaki has discovered that saltation could be extended to body-worn objects and to create phantom sensations from "out of the body" (see Figure 1) [21]. This means phantom tactile sensations can be felt as if coming from an external object, and it can be applied e.g. to designing of tactile feedback devices for hand-held mobile devices without direct contact (Figure 14).

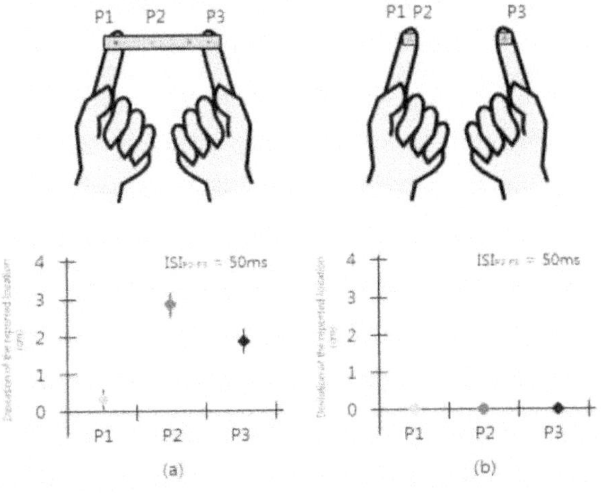

Figure 1. The concept of "out of the body" tactile experience (saltation) from a hand-held object (figure is a reproduced version from [21]). When vibrations are given to the fingertips with proper delay values, phantom tactile sensations are felt as if occurring in the middle of the hand-held ruler (a). No such sensations are felt without the physical medium (b).

In the same line of reasoning, we explore the possibility of the same out of the body experience using funneling or saltation, but when interacting with "virtual" objects without any physical medium (see Figure 2). Our motivation lies in realizing more flexible and inexpensive tactile/haptic feedback for interfaces for tangible interfaces. Conventional tangible interfaces employ physical props for the sense of tangibility and physicality, but being passive and fixed in shape, cannot effectively and realistically represent all different shapes or dynamic interactions.

Two usability experiments were carried out to test the effects of funneling and saltation respectively for perceiving tactile sensation from a virtual object in an augmented reality setting. If their existences are validated, these techniques can find good practical uses in designing hand-held or hand-worn props/interaction devices for virtual and augmented reality.

In the next section, we first review previous research literatures related to phantom tactile sensation and its application to practical interaction design. Then, we describe the two validation experiments and report the results. Finally, we conclude the paper with a discussion and directions for future research.

RELATED WORK

Phantom sensation refers to the phenomenon that user's perception does not match the stimulus' physical characteristics. Funneling and saltation are two major perceptual illusion techniques for vibro-tactile feedback. Funneling refers to stimulating the skin at two (or more) different locations simultaneously with different amplitudes and eliciting phantom sensations in the space between [5]. Figure 3 illustrates this very well.

Several researchers have applied this phenomenon to human interfaces, experimenting with different ways of modulating the vibration amplitudes for detailed controlling of the target phantom sensation locations [1, 4, 23]. Mizukami has used funneling to generate phantom sensations in 2D and applied it to tactile character recognition [22].

On the other hand, in saltation, the skin is stimulated at two locations (at P1 and P3) with proper time intervals (also known as inter-stimulus interval or ISI), and the phantom sensation is felt in between [12]. That is, with a phantom sensation would be felt at P2 in Figure 1(a) with timed stimulations at P1 and P3. Since the discovery of this peculiar phenomenon, several researchers have followed up, investigating in the effects of different values of ISI's and stimulation distances [24], combining saltation with visual feedback [11, 19], and applying saltation to non-continuous skin (e.g. from the right arm to the left) [10, 28]. The 1D saltation has been applied to actual user interfaces [16]. For instance, Hoggan et al. experimented with using three vibrators on a mobile device to emulate a tactile progress indicator [15]. Tan et al. applied saltation to implementing a tactile chair using a 3 x 3 tactile array for pattern recognition [27].

Recently, Miyazaki has discovered the saltation can be extended to body-worn (e.g. hand-held) objects and create "out of the body" tactile experience [21]. This form of saltation is appealing in its practical application because less direct contact would be needed between the device and user's body. For instance, in the case of the tactile chair, the user needed to maintain tight contact with one's entire part of the back to the tactile array, limiting its practical application [27]. This paper explores whether this phenomenon carries over to virtual objects as well.

EXPERIMENT I: FUNNELING FOR VIRTUAL OBJECT

Experimental Design and Set up

In this experiment, the user was given simultaneous tactile stimulations to one's two index fingers, one in the right and the other in the left. The two fingertips were tracked using small markers by a head mounted camera and an augmented reality video imagery was presented to the user as visual feedback in which a virtual ruler[1] was overlaid (to look as if being) on between the two fingers (see Figure 2).

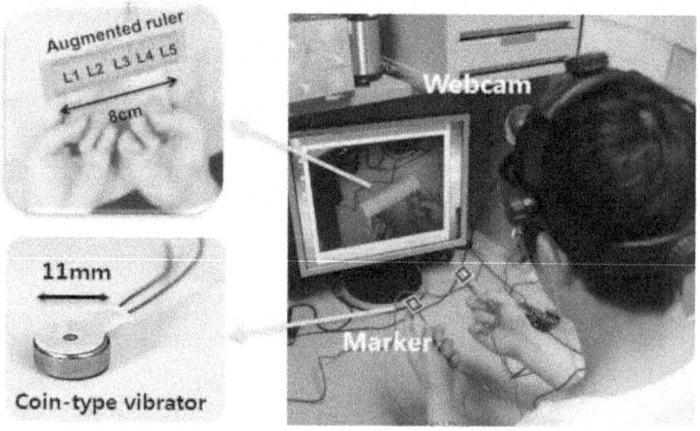

Figure 2. The experimental set up for Experiments I and II. Vibratory stimulations were given to the two index fingers and a user watched the monitor where an augmented virtual ruler was placed on the fingers.

The stimulations were given in different durations and relative amplitudes intended to create phantom tactile sensations at particular locations (see later subsections for details) and the user was asked where on the virtual ruler one felt the tactile feedback.

AR Toolkit [3] was used to recognize and track the small markers and generate the augmented video imagery. A webcam was worn on the head mounted fixture to produce a view close to one according to the actual line of sight. This set up was used to generate a natural feel of "holding" the object, by allowing small movements of the hands/fingers and still maintain natural augmented imagery. The holding distance for the virtual ruler (augmented imagery) was kept at 8cm by asking the user to maintain the finger positions stably. The ruler stayed augmented even if fingers became separated more than 8cm, but only to a limited degree (±2.5 cm). There was virtually no operational difficulty in this regard. The visual length of the virtual ruler was calibrated to match the physical units.

A common coin-type vibrator was used (placed on the respective fingertips) and controlled by an Arduino board

[1] A ruler (virtual object) and using the index finger as the place of stimulation were chosen to follow up on the work by Miyazaki [21].

[2] (and interfaced to and synchronized with the AR Toolkit based experiment software). The vibration motor used in our experiment has the same specification [17] as reported in [18], flat/circular and sized 11mm in diameter (see Figure 2). It is controlled by a voltage input using a pulse width modulation signal with an amplitude between 0 to 5V, which in turn produces vibrations with frequency between 0 and 250 Hz and associated amplitudes between 0 to 2G (measured in acceleration, or 0 to 18μm in position) respectively. According to [7, 18, 26], these values are well above the human's normal detection threshold (about 6 ~ 45db).

Detailed Procedure

Fourteen paid subjects (9 men and 5 women) participated in the experiment with the mean age of 24.5. After collecting one's basic background information, the subject was briefed about the purpose of the experiment and instructions for the experimental task. A short training was given for the subject to get familiarized to the experimental process. None of the participants were experienced in using AR systems nor aware of the phantom sensation phenomenon.

In addition to the head mounted fixture for the camera, the subjects wore ear muffs to prevent any bias from the sounds of the vibration. The ear muff was tested to make sure so that no sound could be heard during the experiment, and did not affect the outcome of the experiment. The small markers were attached to the respective fingers using a tape and the users were allowed to freely move or twist the fingers to some extent. During the short training session, subjects played with the markers (or virtual ruler) to get the natural feeling for interaction.

The levels of stimulations were given with the intention to create phantom and real sensations at 5 different places along the ruler (note that the stimulations at the two extreme ends of the ruler are real). The Linear variation of stimulus amplitudes methods of Alles [1] was used as shown in Figure 3. A preliminary pilot test also confired that the aforementioned linear method exhibited the best effect.

Each subject experienced a block of 40 positional feedbacks (with 10 seconds inter-stimulus rest interval) for three different stimulation durations (80, 140 and 200ms) resulting in a total of 120 trials in (all presentations balance ordered) [13,20]. The subjects were asked to indicate the place of phantom sensations in terms of the five prescribed positions. In addition, after all trials, they were asked to answer a short survey about their subject feelings (questions shown in Table 1).

The virtual ruler was created to appear as 10cm with the two fingers holding it at 1cm from the two ends (at 1cm and 9cm marks with the inter-stimulus distance = 8cm). The inter-finger distance of 8cm was set equal to the experimental condition used in [21].

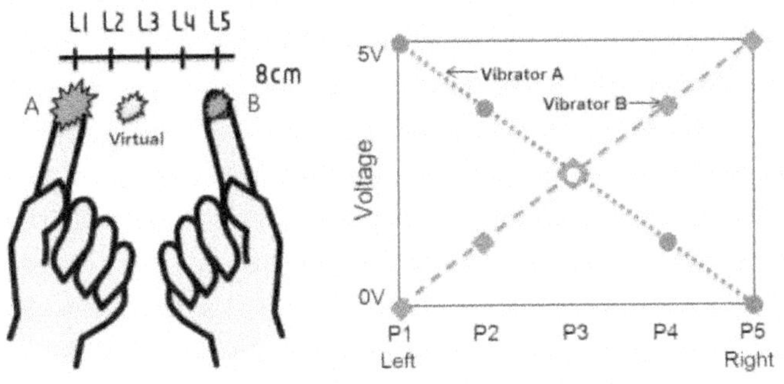

Figure 3. The amplitude rendering (as originally proposed by Alles [1]) for funneling to create phantom sensations at five different positions (L1 ~ L5).

Table 1. The four survey questions regarding the subjective feel for the phantom sensation answered in 7 Likert scale.

Q1	Rate how immersed you were in the AR testing environment (1: Not at all ~ 7: Very well)
Q2	Were you able to perceive phantom sensations? (1: Not at all ~ 7: Very much)
Q3	How certain are you about your answer to Q2? (1: Not confident at all ~ 7: Very confident)
Q4	How long did it take you to perceive the phantom sensation if any? (1: Instantly ~ 7: Few seconds)

Results

Figures 4, 5, and 6 show the user responses to the funneling stimulations at three different stimulation durations. All response groups in each duration group were differentiated with statistical significance (all p-values lower than < 0.001). This indicates solid and clear effects of phantom sensation from the virtual object elicited by funneling.

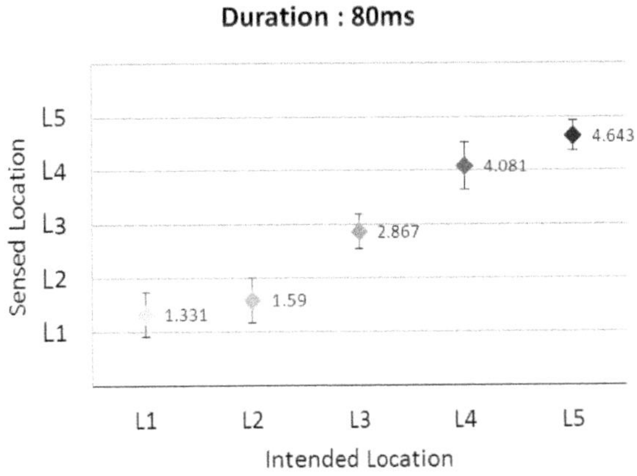

Figure 4. Effects of funneling with stimulation duration of 80ms. All location responses were distinguished with statistical significance (all relevant p-values were lower than 0.001).

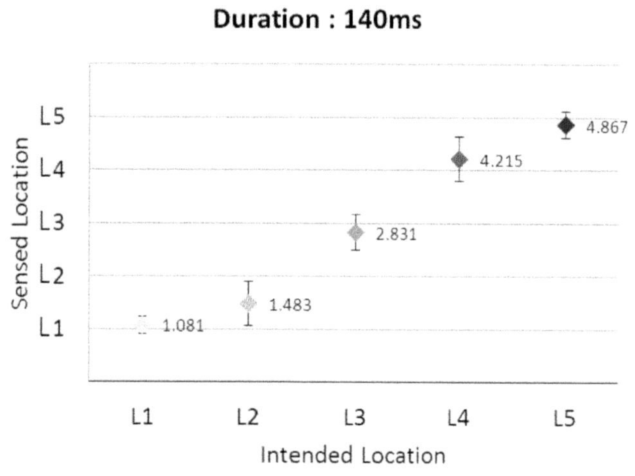

Figure 5. Effects of funneling with stimulation duration of 140ms. All location responses were distinguished with statistical significance (all relevant p-values were lower than 0.001).

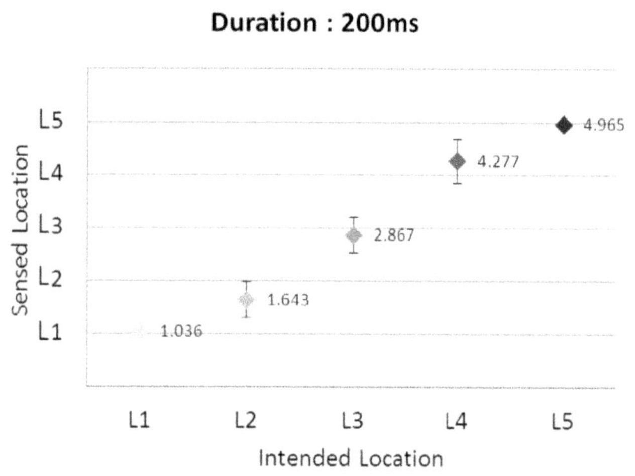

Figure 6. Effects of funneling with stimulation duration of 200ms. All location responses were distinguished with statistical significance (all relevant p-values were lower than 0.001).

Whether the Linear rendering model achieved the intended accuracy (e.g. average response for L3 should ideally be close to L3 = 4cm and so on) is difficult to assess. By naked observation of the average values and standard deviations and from the comparison graph across the different stimulation durations in Figure 7, it seems the performance was slightly better with longer stimulation durations (140ms or 200ms). Tendencies to confuse between L1 and L2, or L4 and L5 were observed with the duration of 80ms (i.e. higher variations). Performances with the longer durations (140ms or 200ms) had a statistically significant difference with those of when duration was 80ms at these locations (see Table 2).

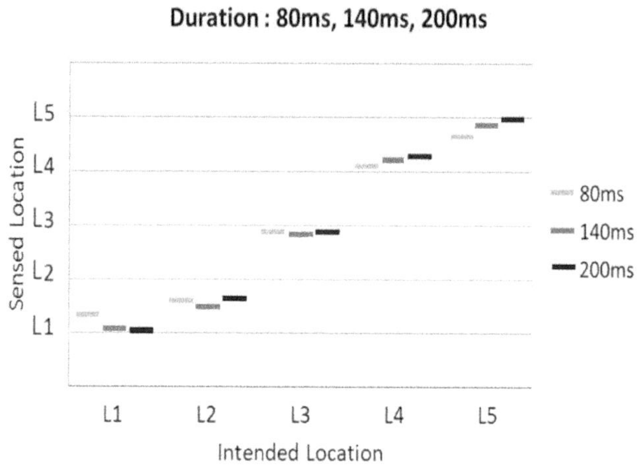

Figure 7. Comparison of the effects of funneling across different stimulation durations.

Table 2. The p-value statistics for effects of funneling across different stimulation durations.

	L1	L2	L3	L4	L5
80-140ms	**0.001**	0.140	0.577	0.062	**0.001**
140-200ms	0.187	**0.028**	0.616	0.374	**0.008**
80-200ms	**0.001**	0.466	1.000	**0.006**	**0.001**
80-140-200ms	**0.001**	0.081	0.828	**0.019**	**0.001**

The collective responses to the survey were all above average (> 4.0) for a reasonable credibility given to the experimental results (see Figure 8). Despite the use of a monitor, a non-immersive display, subjects still felt higher than average level of immersion and with such level of visual feedback, it is unclear whether the funneling effect can be uncoupled from the combined visual feedback. This aspect warrants further investigation [11,19].

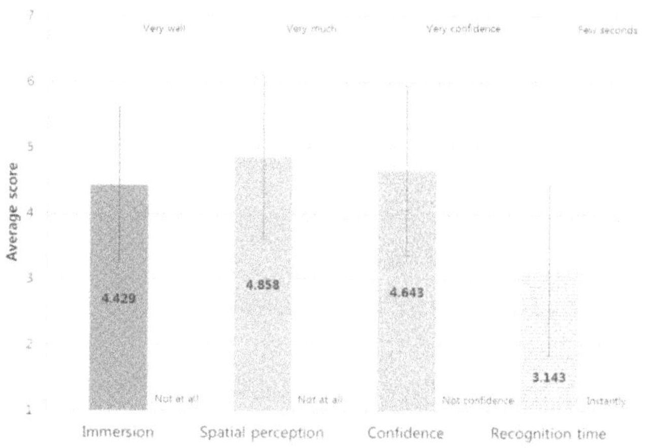

Figure 8. The collective responses to the general usability survey.

EXPERIMENT II: SALTATION FOR VIRTUAL OBJECT

Experimental Design and Set up

The experimental design and set up for the second experiment was mostly same as in Experiment I. The main difference was that "timed" tactile stimulations (saltation) were given instead of simultaneous funneling.

Detailed Procedure

Fourteen paid subjects (9 men and 5 women) participated in the experiment (different pool from the first experiment) with the mean age of 26.2. After collecting one's basic background information, the subject was briefed about the purpose of the experiment and instructions for the experimental task. A short training was given for the subject to become familiarized to the experimental process. None of the participants were experienced in using AR systems nor aware of the saltation phenomenon.

As was with Experiment I, subjects wore the head mounted camera and ear muffs, and were attached with the small markers on their fingers. The levels of stimulations were given with the intention to create phantom and real sensations at 5 different places along the virtual ruler. As shown in Figure 9, a total three timed stimulations were given, two (P1 then P2) at the left fingertip (L1) and then one (P3) at the right fingertip (L5). Note that half the trials were given in the direction from right to left and vice versa.

The intervals were varied each at three levels: P1-P2 (800, 400, 80ms) and P2-P3 (80, 50, 30ms). These intervals were chosen as recommended values based on the previous research results around which produced the best saltation effects (see Figure 1) [21]. Thus in total, a subject experienced a total of 144 trials (3 P1-P2 intervals x 3 P2-P3 intervals x 2 directions x 8 repetitions). Theoretically, these 9 combinations of intervals (see Table 4) would ideally produce phantom sensations at 9 different locations between the two fingers. The same vibration amplitude and frequency was used for all conditions (corresponding to 3.6V PWM input, approximate frequency 250Hz [7,18,26]).

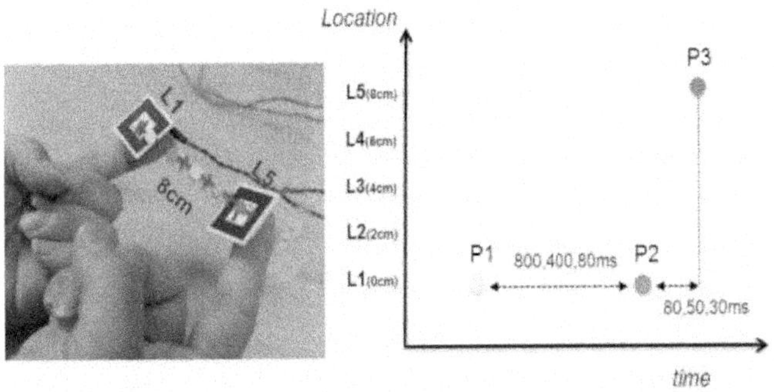

Figure 9. The rendering method for saltation stimulation. Three timed stimulations of P1, P2 (at location L1) and P3 (at location L5) were given with three varied intervals between P1 and P2 and between P2 and P3.

Note that in [21] (Figure 1), a phantom sensation was felt at about 3cm from the left finger with P1-P2 interval of 800ms and P2-P3 interval of 50 or 80ms (P1 and P2 at left finger first, then P3 at right finger). Thus, despite the theoretical assessment, it is much more likely that phantom sensations would be felt, if any, at a number of locations less than nine. Subsequently, the subjects were asked to indicate the place of phantom sensations in terms of the five equally spaced prescribed positions (as was in the Experiment I). Subjects were also asked to indicate the direction of the stimulation Subjects were given stimulations half times from left to right and vice versa. In addition, after all trials, they were asked to answer a short survey about their subject feelings (questions shown in Table 3).

Table 3. The four survey questions regarding the subjective feel for the phantom sensation answered in 7 Likert scale.

Q1	Rate how immersed you were in the AR testing environment (1: Not at all ~ 7: Very well)
Q2	Were you able to perceive phantom sensations? (1: Not at all ~ 7: Very much)
Q3	Rate the strength of the perceived feedback. (1: Very weak ~ 7: Very strong)
Q4	How certain are you about your answer to Q2? (1: Not confident at all ~ 7: Very confident)
Q5	How long did it take you to perceive the phantom sensation if any? (1: Instantly ~ 7: Few seconds)

RESULTS

Existence of Saltation Effect for Virtual Objects: Table 4 shows the effects of saltation felt with nine different combinations of P1-P2 and P2-P3 intervals. In all cases, the locations of sensation (L2) had statistically significant differences from the L1 or L3 where the actual stimulations were given. That is, phantom sensations were clearly felt.

Table 4: Effects of saltation. L2 (sensed location) were in all cases different from L1 or L3 with statistical significance indicating the existence of the saltation effect with the virtual object.

P1-P2 Interval	P2-P3 Interval	p-value L1-L2 (Stim. L→R)	p-value L3-L2 (Stim. R→L)
800ms	30ms	0.001	0.001
	50ms	0.001	0.001
	80ms	0.001	0.001
400ms	30ms	0.001	0.001
	50ms	0.001	0.001
	80ms	0.001	0.001
80ms	30ms	0.001	0.001
	50ms	0.001	0.001
	80ms	0.001	0.001

Locations of the Phantom Sensations: Having found that the saltation effect existed for virtual objects, we compared their locations with respect to the inter-stimulus intervals (ISI). Figure 10 (and Table 5) shows two locations of sensation (L2) felt with the nine different ISI's (statistically distinguished from L1 or L3, one around at 0.896cm (P1-P2 ISI = 80ms) and another at 1.268cm (P1-P2 ISI = 800ms) from the source of the stimulation).

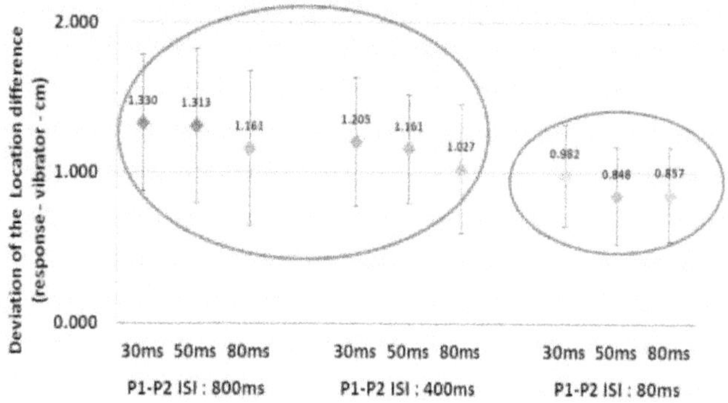

Figure 10. The two phantom sensation locations (distinguished with statistical significance): one at ~0.896cm from the P1 with P1-P2 ISI = 80ms, and another at ~ 1.268cm with P1-P2 ISI = 800ms. No statistically significant differences were found among the effects of three P2-P3 intervals.

Table 5: The statistics for effects of P1-P2 ISI to phantom sensation locations. Statistically significant differences were found between the 800ms/400ms and 80ms cases.

Effects of P1-P2 Interval	800-400ms	400-80ms	800-80ms
p-value	0.271	**0.001**	**0.001**

It is noteworthy to compare the results with that of [21] (i.e. "out of the body" effect for physical objects) which produced a phantom sensation at about 3cm from the left finger with P1-P2 interval of 800ms and P2-P3 interval of 50 or 80ms (See Figure 1). Figure 11 shows the case for when P1-P2 interval is 800ms and three values of P2-P3, 30, 50 and 80ms.

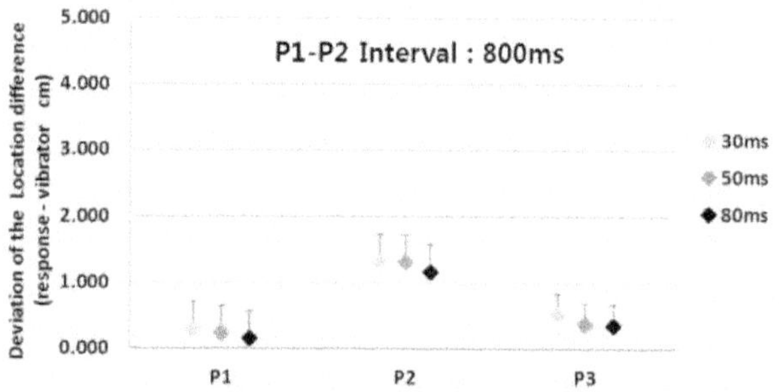

Figure 11. The phantom sensation locations (P2 ~ 1.3cm from the P1) for P1-P2 interval = 800ms. No statistically significant differences were found among the effects of three P2-P3 intervals.

While as already discovered, statistically significant differences are found between the locations P1, P2 and P3, there are no differences between when the P2-P3 intervals are varied. The average value of the P2 is around 1.3cm from the left (or right), contrast to about 3cm in the results of [21] where a physical medium was used for the out of the body experience. We can generally state that the saltation effect has diminished compared to when a physical medium is present. The trend is similar for when the P1-P2 intervals are 400ms and 80ms. This data shows that the P2-P3 interval data had no influence to the location of the phantom sensation. No statistical differences were found between when the stimulations were given from the left nor the right.

The same data is plotted from the reverse point of view, with the P2-P3 interval value fixed at three different values. For instance Figure 12 shows the locations of sensations with 50ms. Statistically significant differences were found among few sensation locations (e.g. those between when P1-P2 interval = 400ms and 80ms, marked bold in the table of Figure 12). The trend is similar for when the P2-P3 intervals are 80ms and 30ms. Thus, we conclude that the P2-P3 interval has some effect on the location of the phantom sensation elicited by the saltation.

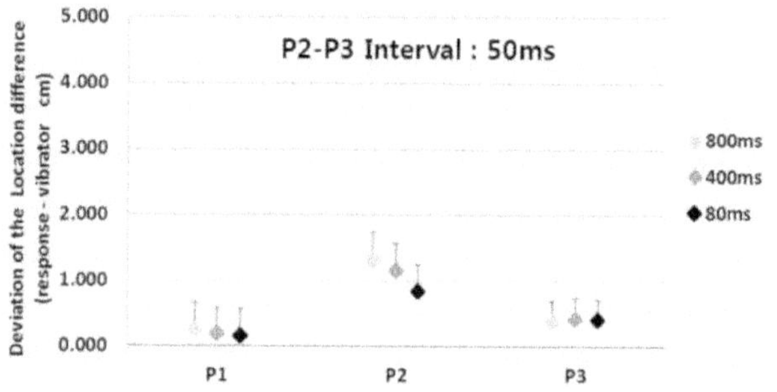

p-values

Effects of P2-P3 Interval	800-400ms	400-80ms	800-80ms
At P1	0.889	0.741	0.670
At P2	0.468	**0.011**	**0.003**
At P3	0.382	0.411	0.910

Figure 12. The phantom sensation locations (P2: 1~ 1.3cm from the P1) for P2-P3 interval = 50ms. Few values had statistically significant differences (whose p-values are marked bold).

The responses to the subjective survey did not reveal anything in particular (all answers were over the average values (4.0/7.0) but with relatively large variations). Based on this result, we separated the subjects into two groups: upper and lower half in terms of their collective responses to Q2~Q4 (e.g. how well they thought they felt the phantom sensations). The analysis showed an extreme polarization of the subject's ability as illustrated in Figure 13. With the subject data for the upper half percentile, the phantom sensation location moved up to about 2.2792cm (with P1-

P2 ISI = 800/400ms) and 1.4583cm (with P1-P2 ISI = 80ms), a result closer to the figures seen in work of Geldard and Miyazaki [12, 21].

Finally, we asked the subjects to describe the saltation induced tactile feedback. There were mainly three categories of answers: (1) soft bounce (7/14), (2) flow like (5/14), and hard/brittle bounce (2/14).

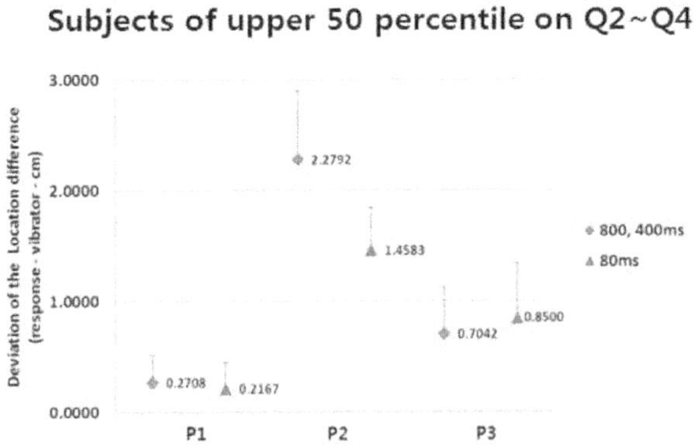

Figure 13. The saltation performance between the two subgroups of subjects: top 50% on responses to Q2~Q4. Diamond indicates P1-P2 ISI = 800 or 400ms, and triangle, 80ms. For those who subjectively rated themselves to feel the phantom sensation above the average, the performance figures were similar to the previous research done on physical objects or directly on the skin [12, 21].

DISCUSSION AND CONCLUSION

In this paper, we have newly verified for the first time that funneling and saltation, the two main perceptual tactile illusions exist also on virtual objects without any physical medium. Furthermore, based on the experimental data, it seems quite possible to modulate the locations of the phantom sensations with the funneling technique quite accurately. Out of body saltation, on the other hand, while shown to be existent even for virtual objects, only showed relatively low precision/resolution (only one or two phantom sensations created within 10 cm span). In addition, saltation exhibited more dependence on personal ability.

Such "out of the body" experience through funneling and saltation has a good application to future vibro-tactile interface for augmented and virtual reality with minimal number of actuators. Figure 14 show possible ways to interact with a physical, virtual and augmented objects. We hope to be able to simulate various indirect dynamic effects (e.g. holding a virtual bottle and feeling for the moving objects in it) using minimal number of vibrators and the effects of saltation and funneling.

In the future, we plan to further validate the phantom sensations for virtual objects through brain imaging [8, 9, 14] and develop practical interaction techniques based on it. Another avenue for future work is to investigate the multimodal effect, or the extent to which the visual feedback affects funneling or saltation. For instance, in Experiment II, we only rendered the virtual ruler, without visual indications of the intended location of sensations. The effects of funneling or saltation are expected to be further strengthened with such combined feedback.

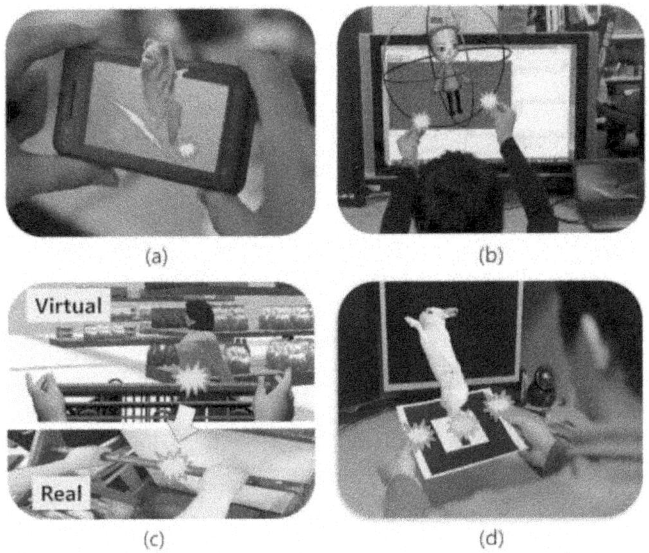

Figure 14. Applications of funneling or saltation to interacting with (a) physical, (b) virtual/direct, (c) virtual/indirect, and (d) augmented objects.

ACKNOWLEDGEMENTS

This research was supported in part by the NRF (ERC Program in Platform Technologies for Holo-Digilog Media) and the MKE/KIAT (Strategic Technology Lab. Program in Multimodal Entertainment Platform and the IT R&D Program in Digital Textile based Around Body Computing, (Project No. KI-10035619)).

REFERENCES

1. Alles, D.S. Information transmission by phantom sensations. *IEEE Transactions on Man-Machine Systems*, (1970), 11(1), 85–91.
2. Arduino. http://www.arduino.cc
3. ARToolKit. http://www.hitl.washington.edu/ARToolKit
4. Barghout, A., Kammerl, J., Jongeun, C., Steinbach, E., and Saddik, A. E. Spatial resolution of vibrotactile perception on the human forearm when exploiting funneling illusion, In *Proc. IEEE International Workshop on HAVE 2009.*
5. Bekesy, G.V. Funneling in the nervous system and its role in loudness and sensation intensity on the skin. *Journal of the Acoustical Society of America*, (1958), 30(5), 399–412.
6. Bouncing Ball on Nokia. http://bit.ly/x2-bouncingball
7. Burdea, G., and Coiffet, P. Virtual Reality Technology 2nd Ed, 2003.

8. Chen, L. M., Friedman, R. M., and Roe, A. W. Optical imaging of a tactile illusion in area 3b of the primary somatosensory cortex. *Science 302*, (2003), 881–885.
9. Chen, L. M., Turner, G. H., Friedman, R. M., Zhang, Na., Gore, J. C., Roe, A. W., and Avison, M. J. High-resolution maps of real and illusory tactile activation in primary somatosensory cortex in individual monkeys with functional magnetic resonance imaging and optical imaging. *Journal of Neuroscience*, (2007), 27, 9181-9191.
10. Eimer, M., Forster, B., and Vibell, J. Cutaneous saltation within and across arms: A new measure of the saltation illusion in somatosensation. *Percept Psychophys*, (2005), 67(3), 458-68.
11. Flach, R., and Haggard, P. The cutaneous rabbit revisited. *Journal of Experimental Psychology: Human Perception and Performance*, (2006), 717-732.
12. Geldard, F.A., and Sherrick, C.E. The Cutaneous Rabbit: A perceptual Illusion. *Science*, (1972), 178-179.
13. Geshelder, G. Psychophysics: The Fundamentals. Lawrence Erlbaum Associates, 1997.
14. Gross, L. Classic illusion sheds new light on the neural site of tactile perception. *PLoS Biology*, (2006).
15. Hoggan, E., Brewster, S., and Anwer, S. Mobile multi-actuator tactile displays. In *Proc. HAID 2007*, 22-33.
16. Israr, A., and Poupyrev, I. Control space of apparent haptic motion. *IEEE World Haptics Conference*, (2011), 457-462.
17. Jahwa Electronics, Korea. http://www.jawha.co.kr
18. Jung, J., and Choi, S. Perceived magnitude and power consumption of vibration feedback in mobile devices. In *proc, HCII 2007*, 354-363.
19. Kilgard, M. P., and Merzenich, M. Anticipated stimuli across skin. *Nature 373*, (1995), 663.
20. Kingdom, F., and Prins, N. Psychophysics: A Practical Introduction. *Elsevier-Academic Press*, (2010).
21. Miyazaki, M., Hirashima, M., and Nozaki D. The "Cutaneous Rabbit" hopping out of the body. *The Journal of Neuroscience*, (2010), 30(5), 1856-1860.
22. Mizukami, Y., and Sawada, H. Tactile information transmission by apparent movement phenomenon using shape-memory alloy device. *International Journal on Disability and Human Development*, (2006), 277–284.
23. Rahal, L., Cha, J., Kammerl, J., El Saddik, A., and Steinbach, E. Investigating the influence of temporal intensity changes on the apparent movement phenomenon. In *Proc. Int. Conf. Virtual Environments, Human-Computer Interfaces and Measurement Systems*, (2009), 310-313.
24. Raisamo, J., Raisamo, R., and Surakka, V. Evaluating the effect of temporal parameters for vibrotactile saltatory patterns. In *Proc. ICMI-MLMI 2009*, 317-326.
25. Richter, H., Hang, A., and Blaha, B. The PhantomStation: Towards funneling remote tactile feedback on interactive surfaces. In *Proc. AH 2011*.
26. Sherrick, C. E., A. Scale for rate of tactual vibration. *Journal of the Acoustical Society of America*, (1985).
27. Tan, H.Z., and Pentland, A. Tactual displays for wearable computing. In *Proc. IEEE ISWC 1997*, 84-89.
28. Warren, J. P., Santello, M., and Tillery, S. I. H. Electrotactile stimuli delivered across fingertips inducing the Cutaneous Rabbit Effect. *Exp Brain Res*, (2010), 206(4), 419-26.

Using Shear as a Supplemental Two-Dimensional Input Channel for Rich Touchscreen Interaction

Chris Harrison **Scott E. Hudson**

Human-Computer Interaction Institute and Heinz College Center for the Future of Work
Carnegie Mellon University, 5000 Forbes Avenue, Pittsburgh PA 15213
chris.harrison@cs.cmu.edu, scott.hudson@cs.cmu.edu

ABSTRACT

Touch input is constrained, typically only providing finger X/Y coordinates. To access and switch between different functions, valuable screen real estate must be allocated to buttons and menus, or users must perform special actions, such as touch-and-hold, double tap, or multi-finger chords. Even still, this only adds a few bits of additional information, leaving touch interaction unwieldy for many tasks. In this work, we suggest using a largely unutilized touch input dimension: *shear* (force tangential to a screen's surface). Similar to pressure, shear can be used in concert with conventional finger positional input. However, unlike pressure, shear provides a rich, analog 2D input space, which has many powerful uses. We put forward five classes of advanced interaction that considerably expands the envelope of interaction possible on touchscreens.

Author Keywords: Tangential force; handheld mobile devices; finger interaction; touchscreens; fat fingers.

ACM Classification Keywords: H.5.2 [Information interfaces and presentation]: User Interfaces – GUIs.

INTRODUCTION

Touch interaction is becoming pervasive, especially in the mobile domain, where there is limited room for static physical buttons. Conventional touch input is generally treated as binary – the user is touching or not touching. Further, touch points are typically reduced to a simple X and Y coordinate. This is not particularly high bandwidth – for comparison, a modern computer mouse provides X/Y position, a continuous 1D scroll wheel, and several buttons. Because of this, touch interaction can be unwieldy at times, requiring less-than-natural touch-and-hold [14] or multi-finger chording actions [12] to trigger secondary functions or switch modes.

In response, there has been tremendous work on sensing and processing additional dimensions of touch, for the purposes of enriching interaction on touchscreens, including pressure [15,18-23], finger orientation [27], finger posture [15], configuration of the hands [1], rolling motions of static fingers [24], and what part of the finger was used for input [6].

Handheld devices can also augment touch position with non-finger input dimensions (see [9] for overview), including tilt [28], acceleration [9], how the enclosure is being manipulated [25] and position relative to the user [13].

One dimension that has been underexplored is shear force. Shear stress (also called "tangential force" in the literature) arises from a force vector perpendicular to the surface normal of a touchscreen (i.e., parallel to the touchscreen surface). This is similar to normal stress – what is commonly called pressure – which arises from a force vector parallel to the surface normal.

Before we can discuss related work and shear applications, it is necessary to define four terms we use to describe finger movements. To describe traditional finger pointing and dragging, we use the term *move* or *drag* respectively (e.g., "the user *moves* their finger over an icon" or "*drags* an icon"). We call the application of force in the shear dimension a *push* (e.g., "the user *pushes* upward"; this is called a "pivot" in [7]). The finger does not slide during *pushes* due to static friction. Finally, a drag action performed with substantial pressure is called a *hard drag* (e.g., "a user *hard drags* an icon"). Shear forces are created due to sliding friction between the finger and screen. Of note, hard drags do not provide a secondary 2D input channel (i.e., you cannot drag in one direction and *push* in another), but rather provide an alternative drag mode.

The central contribution of this work is considering shear as a rich analog X/Y input channel. Importantly, this can operate in parallel with convention finger X/Y tracking, potentially affording touchscreens an additional 2D input channel. For example, a user can touch the screen (providing a 2D position) and *push* in any direction (providing a 2D shear vector). As we will discuss, this enables a variety of compelling interaction techniques and could be used to alleviate some of the input contention experienced in today's touchscreen devices.

RELATED WORK

Touchscreens able to capture finger shear forces date back at least as far as 1977 [8]. Exploration of the interaction space was limited, given that it predated popular use of graphical user interfaces. Minksy revisited touch+shear interaction in 1984 [16], suggesting uses for higher-fidelity digital painting and visual programming. Of note, they propose directional flicks, inferred from shear information, which could be used for sending items to different screens.

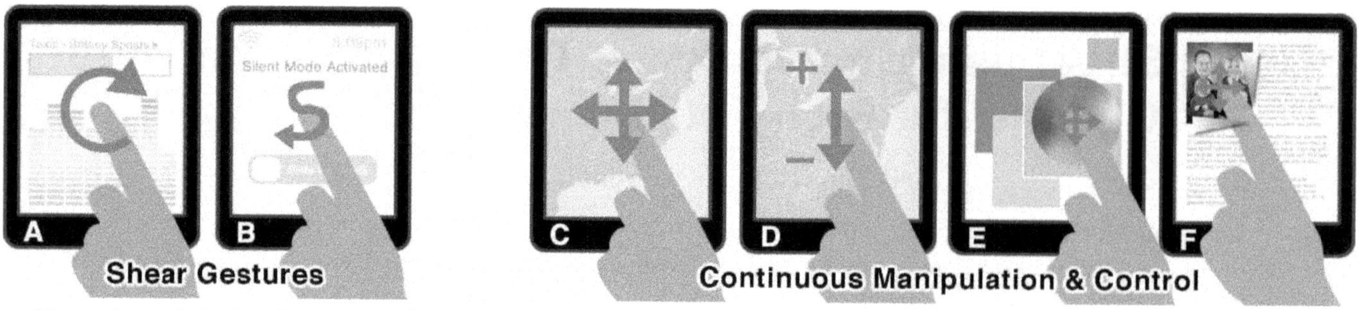

Figure 1. A: clockwise shear gesture increases volume. B: 'S' shear gesture sets phone to silent. C: In situ rate-controlled map panning, and D: zooming. E: In situ color selection using 2D shear. F: X/Y shear dimensions control brightness and saturation.

There have also been efforts to instrument the fingers with shear sensors [15], though this is particularly invasive. Most recently, Heo and Lee have taken the idea into the mobile domain, augmenting an iPod Touch [7]. The latter work describes a shear- and pressure-augmented web browser and eBook reader. These applications were primarily controlled by "force gestures" in the up/down/left/right directions (see e.g., Table 1 in [7]).

Pressure is much like shear, in that it offers a continuous input dimension that can operate in concert with conventional touch input [15,18-23]. The most significant difference is that pressure is one-dimensional. It should be noted that shear and pressure input are not entirely orthogonal. Although pressure can be provided without shear, shear force requires pressure, which alters the static and sliding friction of a finger on a touchscreen. For example, in order for users to produce a hard drag, they must press their fingers firmly to the screen. In combination with X/Y finger tracking, pressure sensors could determine a hard drag. However, for example, even with X/Y tracking, pressure cannot be used to determine the directionality of a push.

It seems likely that most interaction techniques built on top of pressure forces are immediately portable to shear input (and potentially enhanced further). For example, there has been considerable work on continuous scrolling [20,22] and zooming [18] using pressure. This is trivially implemented using shear [7,8,11], and can gain a directional component (e.g., scrolling up/down with up/down shear force).

Our prototype hardware is based on two self-centering, analog joysticks, which displace in response to shear forces roughly according to Hooke's law. Similar are isometric joysticks [26], which are essentially 2D shear force sensors. There is a substantial body of work assessing human motor performance in this input modality [2,3,5,7,11]. Results show humans are remarkably dexterous in shear-space, though performance is slightly worse than positional input, like a mouse. Further, shear input appears to be comfortable and intuitive [7,11]. This work does not contribute new empirical results, but rather pushes the envelope in interaction design.

UTILIZING 2D SHEAR INPUT

As described previously, shear has been primarily utilized for simple gestures, consisting of uni-directional *pushes* and *hard drags*. This is small subset of possible uses - we now describe five advanced interactions that fully realize shear as rich, secondary, 2D input dimension. To illustrate the unique capabilities of shear, we ground our discussion with many small examples. This simultaneously serves to highlight the utility of shear input. Please also see our Video Figure, which demonstrates a collection of applications utilizing complex force gestures, continuous and 2D control.

Shear Gestures

In much the same way as a touchscreen can support gestures, shear too can support a rich gesture set. These can be as simple as directional pushes [7], all the way up to full alphanumeric text entry [4]. A dedicated gesture input channel on touchscreens would be invaluable, and would allow functionality typically provided in buttons and menus to be removed from the screen, freeing valuable real estate.

One simple, but useful application we built was shear-augmented copy and paste – unwieldy on touchscreens at present. With shear input, a user highlights a section of text as usual, finishing with an up push, which copies the text to the clipboard. The user then moves their finger elsewhere, and with a down push, pastes in the text at that location.

A smartphone offers a more sophisticated gesture set. Writing a 'V' in shear-space triggers the voicemail. Clockwise and counterclockwise circling motions increase and decrease speaker volume, respectively (Figure 1A). An 'S' gesture puts the phone into silent mode (Figure 1B).

In-Situ Continuous Manipulation and Control

Two-dimensional shear input can be used in a rate-controlled manner. We implemented this for in situ, continuous scrolling of a web page. The more shear force that is applied, the faster the scroll rate. This would be useful on small screens, which often require repeated finger drags to navigate large content (e.g., maps; Figure 1C). Continuous zooming (in and out) can be handled with a single shear dimension, and with one finger (instead of +/- buttons or two finger pinches; Figure 1D).

There are many one- and two-dimensional manipulations beyond panning and zooming. For example, by moving ones finger onto a photograph, brightness and saturation can be adjusted with shear force (X and Y dimensions; Figure 1F). Note this operation is not global, but can be made to act solely on the element under the finger. This is a unique quality, in that both selection and manipulation can happen without fingers moving or lifting from the display.

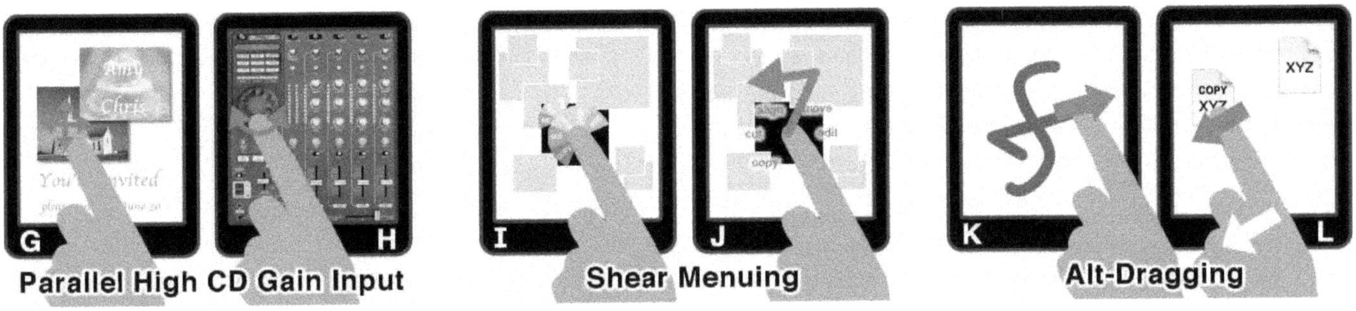

Figure 2. G: High precision positioning of graphical elements. H: Fine-grained tuning of knob. I: Shear-driven pie and J: marking menus. K: Freehand strokes with drags and line segments with hard drags. L: "Tearing off" a copy of a file with a hard drag.

Similarly, we built a demo application that allows users to change the color of a graphical element by placing their finger on it, and using shear forces to select a color from a popup color pallet, as depicted in Figure 1E.

Parallel High CD Gain Input

Touchscreen interaction generally operates with a 1:1 control-device (CD) gain. While providing a tight coupling between physical and digital manipulations, fine-grained operations are challenging. In mobile contexts, this problem is further compounded by small screens and "fat fingers".

Fine-grained manipulation is important in many digital tasks. For example, in graphic design, proper sizing, placement and alignment of objects and text is fundamental. In general, fine adjustments are common in tasks requiring continuous control, for example, when selecting colors or adjusting audio parameters.

Touchscreen inaccuracy could be mitigated by using shear as a parallel, high CD gain input means. For example, we built a demo application that lets users can place their finger on an object, and adjust its position by pushing it in the desired direction; a 1:10 CD gain is used (Figure 2G). Also consider a tuning knob that could be adjusted with great precision, without lifting the finger (Figure 2H).

Shear Menuing

Because shear operates in two dimensions, in situ navigation of pie or marking menus is possible [14,15,17] (Figure 2 I and J, respectively). For example, imagine a user wishing to align a figure to the top-left of a document. They could touch the figure and push up, which triggers a pie menu. Users could then push in the direction (e.g., 37°) of desired menu items; e.g., alignment→top-left→margins.

Alt-Dragging

In the same way a right mouse button provides an alt-click function, hard drags could serve as a natural alt-drag in touchscreen interaction, and in general, enable modal dragging [22,24]. For example, we created a freehand drawing application where finger drags produce strokes. Straight line segments are drawn with hard drags, without effecting freehand strokes (Figure 2K). Another example is organizing documents. In our proof-of-concept system, conventional dragging moves the item around the desktop; a hard drag, however, "tears off" a duplicate of the file (Figure 2L).

LIMITATIONS

Current shear-input-capable systems [7,8,11,16], including our own, have several limitations of note. Foremost, because a single rigid touchscreen is used, only a single shear reading can be captured at any instant. This precludes shear multitouch (i.e., where each finger has a separate shear vector), but does not preclude capturing a single shear force for multitouch gestures, which is still powerful (e.g., a two finger push). Multi-user input is similarly affected.

EXPLORATORY PLATFORM

To help us explore shear as an additional two-dimensional input dimension for touchscreens, we created a proof-of-concept handheld device, which we briefly describe for reference (Figure 3). The device consists of a Haier 7" LCD display, on top of which we mounted a 6.7" 3M capacitive touchscreen. Operating between the display and touchscreen are two, low-profile, self-centering, analog joysticks. These are affixed to the panels in the upper-right and lower-left corners with epoxy. When sufficient shear force is applied to the touchscreen, the joysticks displace in response to the force (roughly according to Hooke's Law), causing the touchscreen to translate relative to the display. Maximum translation in the X- and Y-axes is 2mm.

For rapid prototyping, our device is tethered to a conventional computer, which processes input and provides a graphical user interface. Single-finger touch input from the touchscreen is transmitted to the computer over USB using a 3M EXII controller. Values from our two joysticks are processed by an Arduino and also sent over USB. A series

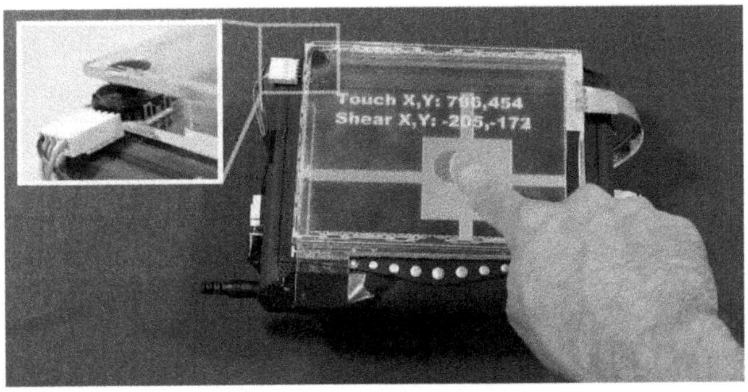

Figure 3. Our exploratory hardware captures 2D touch location and 2D shear force. The latter is captured by two joysticks operating between the display and touch panel (zoomed inset).

of custom Java programs handle touch and shear input data, and provide an interactive experience (see Video Figure).

Although our sensors are capable of digitizing 2mm of shear displacement with roughly 9-bits of resolution, functional precision is much lower due to lack of human motor precision at such small scales [20]. This is similar to results found in pressure input experiments, where humans are generally only capable of accurately providing six discrete levels of pressure [14,23]. Users can also push out to the maximum displacement (physical boundary) of our sensors. When used in this fashion, our system acts more like EdgeWrite [29]. However, as our (and most) joysticks have a radial maximum, there is a continuous circular periphery instead of sides and corners.

FUTURE WORK

There are many avenues of future work that would be interesting to pursue. For example, how effectively can shear, pressure and positional input be used in concert, and what advanced interactions can leverage all three? Our system is also capable of sensing static twisting forces of a finger (i.e., screen torque) – this is an unutilized input dimension at present and could have interesting applications. Finally, direct manipulation interfaces typically provide visual feedback about users' touch locations. How to design visual feedback for shear forces is an outstanding question.

CONCLUSION

We have shown that shear has many compelling uses when realized as a supplemental analog 2D input channel. Drawing on a range of inspirations, we have put forward five uses of shear input that significantly advances shear input beyond uni-directional force gestures.

ACKNOWLEDGMENTS

Funding for this work was provided in part by grants from the Center for the Future of Work, Heinz College, CMU, and also a Microsoft Ph.D. Fellowship. We also thank our reviewers for their many excellent comments.

REFERENCES

1. Cao, X., Wilson, A., Balakrishnan, R., Hinckley, K., and Hudson, S.E. ShapeTouch: Leveraging contact shape on interactive surfaces. In *Proc. TABLETOP '08*. 129-136.
2. Card, S., English, W., and Burr, B. Evaluation of Mouse, Rate-Controlled Isometric Joystick, Step Keys, and Text Keys for Text Selection on a CRT. *Ergonomics*, 1978. 21(8): 601-613.
3. Casiez, G. and Vogel, D. The effect of spring stiffness and control gain with an elastic rate control pointing device. In *Proc. CHI '08*. 1709-1718.
4. Chau, D., Wobbrock, J., Myers, B. and Rothrock, B. Integrating isometric joysticks into mobile phones for text entry. In *CHI '06 Ext. Abst.* 640-645.
5. Gibbs, C. Controller design: interactions of controlling limbs, time-lags and gain in positional and velocity systems. *Ergonomics*, 5 (1962), 385–402.
6. Harrison, C., Schwarz, J. and Hudson S. E. TapSense: Enhancing Finger Interaction on Touch Surfaces. In *Proc. UIST '11*. 627-636.
7. Heo, S. and Lee, G. Force gestures: augmented touch screen gestures using normal and tangential force. In Proc. UIST'11. 621-626.
8. Herot, C., Weinzapfel, G., One-Point Touch Input of Vector Information from Computer Displays. In Proc. SIGGRAPH '78. 12(3): p. 210-216.
9. Hinckley K. and Song, H. Sensor synaesthesia: touch in motion, and motion in touch. In *Proc. CHI '11*. 801-810.
10. Kurtenbach, G. and Buxton, W. The limits of expert performance using hierarchic marking menus. In *Proc. CHI '93*. 482-487.
11. Lee, B., Lee, H., Lim, S., Lee, H., Han, S. and Park, J. Evaluation of Human Tangential Force Input Performance. In *Proc. CHI '12*.
12. Lepinski, J.G., Grossman, T., and Fitzmaurice, G. The design and evaluation of multitouch marking menus. In *Proc. CHI '10*. 2233-2242.
13. Li, F., Dearman, D., and Truong, K. Virtual shelves: interactions with orientation aware devices. In *Proc. UIST '09*. 125-128.
14. Li, Y., Hinckley, K., Guan, Z., and Landay, J.A. Experimental analysis of mode switching techniques in pen-based user interfaces. In *Proc. CHI '05*. 461-470.
15. Mascaro, S. A. and Asada, H. H. Measurement of finger posture and three-axis fingertip touch force using fingernail sensors. In *IEEE Trans. on Robotics and Automation*, 2004.
16. Minsky, M. R. Manipulating simulated objects with real-world gestures using a force and position sensitive screen. In *Proc. SIGGRAPH '84*, pp. 195-203.
17. Mithal, A.K. and Douglas. S.A. Differences in movement microstructure of the mouse and the finger-controlled isometric joystick. In *Proc. CHI '96*. 300-307.
18. Miyaki, T. and Rekimoto, J. GraspZoom: zooming and scrolling control model for single-handed mobile interaction. In *Proc. MobileHCI '09*.
19. Omata, M., Kajino, M., and Imamiya, A. A multi-level pressure-sensing two-handed interface with finger-mounted pressure sensors. In *Proc. GI '09*. 199-202.
20. Quinn, P. and Cockburn. A. Zoofing!: faster list selections with pressure-zoom-flick-scrolling. In *Proc. OZCHI '09*. 185-192.
21. Ramos, G. and Balakrishnan, R. Pressure marks. In *Proc. CHI '07*. 1375-1384.
22. Ramos, G. and Balakrishnan, R. Zliding: fluid zooming and sliding for high precision parameter manipulation. In *Proc. UIST '05*. 143-152.
23. Ramos, G., Boulos, M., and Balakrishnan, R. Pressure widgets. In *Proc. CHI '04*. 487-494.
24. Roudaut, A., Lecolinet, E. and Guiard, Y. MicroRolls: expanding touch-screen input vocabulary by distinguishing rolls vs. slides of the thumb. In *Proc. CHI '09*. 927-936.
25. Schwesig, C., Poupyrev, I., and Mori, E. Gummi: a bendable computer. In *Proc. CHI '04*. 263-270.
26. Selker, T., and Rutledge, J. Finger Force Precision for Computer Pointing. IBM RC 17342, October 1991.
27. Wang, F. and Ren, X. Empirical evaluation for finger input properties in multi-touch interaction. In *Proc. CHI '09*. 1063-1072.
28. Wigdor, D. and Balakrishnan, R. TiltText: using tilt for text input to mobile phones. In *Proc. UIST '03*. 81-90.
29. Wobbrock, J., Myers, B. and Kembel, J. EdgeWrite: a stylus-based text entry method designed for high accuracy and stability of motion. In *Proc. UIST '03*. 61-70.

GyroTab: A Handheld Device that Provides Reactive Torque Feedback

Akash Badshah[1,2], Sidhant Gupta[1,3], Dan Morris[1], Shwetak N Patel[1,3], Desney Tan[1]
[1]Microsoft Research
Redmond, WA, USA
{dan, desney}@microsoft.com
[2]Massachusetts Institute of Technology,
Cambridge, MA, USA
akashbad@mit.edu
[3]University of Washington
UbiComp Lab, DUB Group
Seattle, WA, USA
{sidhant, shwetak}@uw.edu

ABSTRACT
Haptic devices that provide robust and realistic force feedback are generally grounded to counterweight the applied force, prohibiting their use in mobile devices. Many ungrounded force-feedback devices rely on the gyro effect to produce torques on the human body, but their active control systems render them extremely bulky for implementation in small mobile devices. We present GyroTab, a relatively flat handheld system that utilizes the gyro effect to provide torque feedback. GyroTab relies on the user to produce an input torque and provides feedback by opposing that torque, making its feedback *reactive* to the user's motion. We describe the implementation of GyroTab, discuss the kinds of feedback it generates, and explore some of the psychophysical results we obtained from a study with the device.

Author Keywords
Haptics; gyroscopic feedback

ACM Classification Keywords
H.5.2. [Information interfaces and presentation]: User Interfaces – Haptic I/O.

General Terms
Algorithms, Design, Human Factors.

INTRODUCTION
With the drive to enhance user experiences on general-purpose mobile devices, there is a growing trend to go beyond visual and auditory sensory channels, in particular to engage the sense of touch with haptic feedback. The most common type of haptic feedback is vibrotactile feedback, which uses vibrations or small surface changes to provide feedback. Although vibrotactile devices have been widely deployed in mobile phones and game controllers, they tend to be relatively weak and cannot actively convey forces. On the other hand, kinesthetic feedback, such as that generated by devices like the Phantom haptic device [4], actively replicates real-world forces and has been previously used to simulate large, rigid, and deformable objects. This feedback can be much stronger than that provided by vibrotactile feedback, but the vast majority of kinesthetic feedback devices rely on *grounding*: the physical attachment of the device to the ground or a large surface to act as a counterbalance for the forces it exerts.

Figure 1: GyroTab provides reactive torque feedback. Two masses (under the display) spinning in opposite directions are controlled to produce varying levels of feedback that oppose the user's movement.

In this work, we set out to create a kinesthetic force feedback device that we envision integrating into a practical mobile form factor. In order to create a flat system, we built a device that produces *reactive* feedback instead of actively generating torque. In this way the movement of the user acts as the input torque for the gyroscopes and no feedback is produced unless the user is moving. We call this device GyroTab (Figure 1). GyroTab consists of (1) a pair of flat, disk-shaped masses that are spun in opposite directions to create an adjustable angular momentum vector; (2) an inertial measurement unit (IMU) to detect device tilt and orientation; and (3) a small display that reflects the form factor of a mobile tablet or phone.

GyroTab produces torque on the user's hands that is dependent on the magnitude of the angular momentum when the user rotates the device. This feedback can be used to convey the feeling of weight or inertia. For example, in a gaming application where the user is tilting the device to drive a car, the feedback can simulate the mass and momentum of the car by resisting the user's attempts to make quick or impossible maneuvers. Similarly, the feedback could be used to convey the difference between a working car and one with a flat tire.

RELATED WORK

A number of haptic feedback devices, such as the Phantom [4] and HapticMaster, provide kinesthetic feedback like GyroTab. However, they require grounding to counterbalance the output force with an equal and opposite reaction force, thus limiting their applicability to mobile devices. There have also been efforts to produce body-grounded kinesthetic feedback devices like the HapticGear [2]; however, these require cumbersome fitting of the device on a user's body.

There has been some past work in ungrounded kinesthetic feedback in order to remove the need for a ground or counterbalance surface in strong force-feedback devices. TorqueBAR, for example, is a two-handed kinesthetic feedback system that uses a mass moving along a linear path to produce feedback effects like changes in center of mass [5]. Lead-Me creates a sensation of being pulled in a certain direction [1]. Both of these systems, unlike GyroTab, generate feedback in only one dimension.

Other types of ungrounded devices have taken advantage of similar properties of gyroscopes in order to produce feedback. Indeed this *gyroscopic feedback* is the same feedback used in large sea liners and spaceships to counteract the forces of the waves and induce precession as opposed to capsizing. Several devices take advantage of these gyroscopic effects, by either actively torqueing a spinning mass quickly [6] to create a push-pull sensation or rotating three disks at different speeds to produce angular momentum changes [8]. These devices, however, generate three-dimensional feedback, which makes them non-flat and hard to incorporate into mobile devices. The device presented in [3] also leverages the gyro effect by dynamically braking fast spinning masses to produce opposing torques, but produces relatively weak impulses on the arm. GyroTab, on the other hand, produces dynamic, strong feedback in a reactive manner, which reduces the mechanical requirements for the device.

In this paper, we describe the design and implementation of GyroTab, summarize the kinds of feedback we can generate with potential applications, discuss some initial psychophysical results we obtained from our user study, and conclude with a discussion on improvements.

THE GYROTAB

GyroTab leverages Newton's first law of physics, which states that objects in motion tend to stay in motion. In a rotational system, this law manifests itself as the *gyro effect*: spinning masses tend to continue spinning, in the same direction, along the same axis. Thus, any torque exerted on a spinning mass will result in the mass exerting a torque back, in a perpendicular direction from the input axis (see Figure 2). The magnitude of these torques is dependent on factors that influence the angular momentum of the device, namely mass, speed of rotation, and radius. Also of importance is the angular speed at which the masses are torqued, which depends on both the velocity and the length of the lever arm.

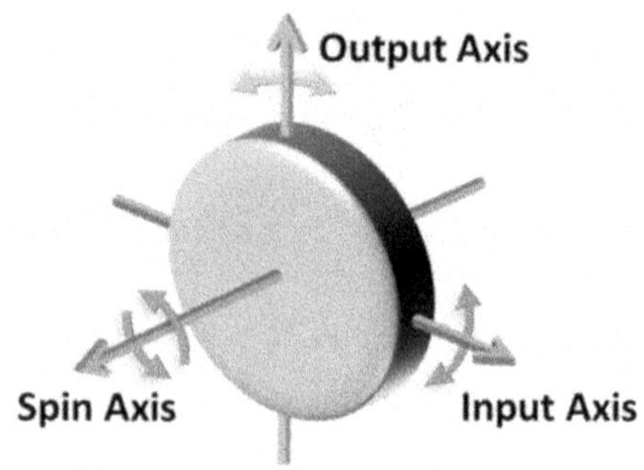

Figure 2: The *gyro effect* illustrated.

Prototype and Implementation Overview

GyroTab consists of a feedback system and a sensing system (Figure 3). The feedback system leverages the gyro effect by spinning two flat, disk-shaped masses along the same axis in opposite directions. When these masses rotate at the same speed, the net angular momentum vector is zero, and the device does not produce any feedback. When one mass is accelerated and/or the other is decelerated, the device produces feedback. In this case, the resultant angular momentum vector will produce an output torque whenever the user rotates the device along an axis other than the spin axis. GyroTab's rotating masses are aligned with the plane of the screen, allowing the prototype to be relatively flat.

Although the same effect could be achieved by accelerating and decelerating a single platter, spinning a mass from rest requires up to several seconds, introducing significant latency. By maintaining two masses in constant motion, GyroTab can vary the supplied feedback quickly by braking one motor and accelerating the other.

In our prototype, the spinning masses themselves are constructed from desktop computer hard drive components (Figure 3). Specifically, we removed the motor-and-platter assembly from several Western Digital WD2500 hard drives, added additional platters to increase mass (and thus increase feedback), and overclocked the motors from 7,200 to 11,000 RPM. The net result is an increase in total angular momentum of about two-fold relative to stock hard drives. In our prototype, the total mass of the platters in each hard drive assembly was 114.7g, and the radius was 4.75cm. Each assembly had a top speed of approximately 11,000 RPM for a maximum angular momentum of 0.0474J-s. Since low weight is of paramount importance to handheld devices, the weight of the system can be reduced without affecting the feedback by increasing the platter's speed.

We chose hard drives because their form factor was conducive to generating large angular momentums (large-radius platters and fast rotations). In addition, hard drive platters are machined and balanced precisely to prevent vibration at high speeds. Hard drives also use high-turn motors, which achieve speeds in excess of 10,000 RPM. We controlled the drive motors with Exceed-RC Proton-18A electronic speed

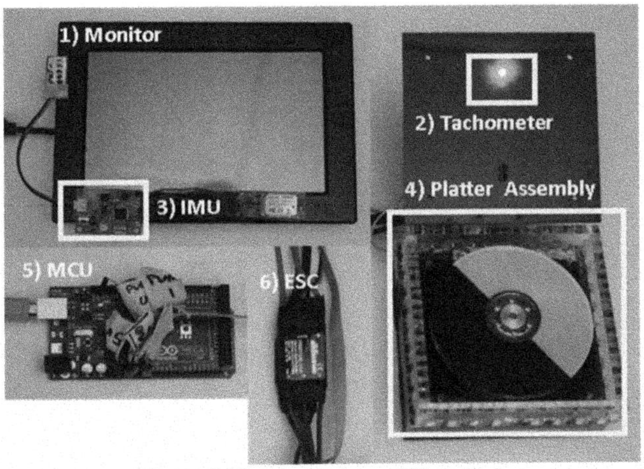

Figure 3: Internal view of GyroTab.

controllers (ESCs). These speed controllers allow us to dynamically vary the speeds of the masses and provide EMF-based braking.

The hard drive platters and drive motors are simply sandwiched together with a short standoff. Multiple platter units could be placed side-by-side to further reduce depth. The feedback system also includes a digital tachometer, which consists of an LED, a photoresistor, and a painted pattern on the hard drive platter to measure the rotational speed of the drives (see Figure 3). We used tachometers in order to provide precise feedback to the ESCs and thus allow consistent control of the motors. The feedback system was controlled using an Atmel ATmega2560 microcontroller connected to the PWM interfaces of the ESCs.

For tilt input, we used a SparkFun Razor 9-DOF inertial measurement unit, which includes an accelerometer, a gyroscope, and a magnetometer. Additionally, we attached a screen on top of the device to simulate the integration of GyroTab's feedback into a mobile form factor.

Although our current prototype is slightly large (currently 4cm thick), the device could conceivably be much smaller if we used custom components rather than hard drive parts. In our device, we reached the limits of speed and responsiveness with our motors. By including custom motors, speeds could easily be increased 3-5 fold without a loss of responsiveness; many commercial RC airplane motors have comparable specifications. By increasing the speed, the device could be made lighter and flatter. Using denser platters could also help reduce GyroTab's width, which would ease integration into a consumer tablet device.

ACHIEVABLE FEEDBACK

GyroTab is capable of achieving varying levels of feedback by varying the relative angular momentum of the spinning masses. In this section, we present the sensations that were presented to participants during our study, and we present anecdotal observations of additional sensations participants described when using GyroTab. This is not a comprehensive list, but provides a sense of how GyroTab may be incorporated into various applications.

Differences in weight

Output torques from the device are generally perceived as *resistance*, making a virtual object harder to move around. We found that increasing the angular momentum of the system could help to convey differences in the weight of a virtual object (for example, a vehicle in a game), with higher angular momentums corresponding to heavier weights. We envision applications in gaming or tilt-controlled user interfaces. This could also be built into handheld measurement equipment that requires restricting the rate at which users can tilt the device.

Path guidance

The torques from the device can also be used to create the feeling that the device is tugging the user's hands along a path. This perception is based on the fact that the output vector is perpendicular to the input vector defined by the user's own torque. We envision this sensation being useful in applications such as real-time remote navigation of a robot or robotic arm that is intended to follow a certain trajectory or avoid obstacles.

Simulated physical media

Varying GyroTab's feedback can simulate motion of a virtual object through different physical media. For example, more feedback (and thus more resistance to motion) corresponds to more viscous media. Similarly, the same mechanism can be used to simulate friction between a moving on-screen object and an on-screen surface. This could, for example, make a virtual ball easier or harder to control as the surface it rolls on changes. Beyond gaming, this could be extended to any tilt-controlled interface to allow the user to detect UI boundaries, for example.

Momentum

Finally, the device can be used to covey the momentum of a moving object. As described above, the feedback could be used to make it difficult to turn a car in a video game, just as the forward momentum of a physical car makes it physically resistant to quick turns. This is perhaps the most intuitive of these proposed effects, because the feedback itself originates from the momentum of physical masses.

STUDYING PERCEIVED FEEDBACK LEVELS

We conducted a small study to explore feedback levels users could perceive with GyroTab. Six participants (three female) aged 25 to 37 performed two tasks, in which we evaluated their ability to perceive *Absolute* and *Relative* levels of haptic feedback.

In the Absolute test, participants were asked to perform a simple gesture: tilting the device forward, back, left, and right, while they were presented with five levels of feedback (i.e., levels of net angular momentum). Participants performed the gesture as many times as necessary to allow them to analyze each level appropriately. They were first shown each of the five levels in order in a tutorial phase, and were then presented with 15 trials (three trials at each of the five levels) in a randomized order. They were asked to label the feedback level from 1 to 5 in each trial, and were required to place the device back on the table after each trial.

In the Relative test, participants were presented with sequences of two different feedback levels (not the same levels used for the Absolute test). During each presentation of a feedback level, participants performed the same gesture described above. After each pair, participants were asked to rate the second feedback level as higher than, lower than, or the same as the first. Participants were presented with six different deltas (the difference between the two levels): 50%, 40%, 30%, 20%, 10%, and 0% of the device's maximum. Participants performed 30 trials: five each of the six deltas. Participants put down the device before the feedback was changed and were fed white noise through headphones to ensure they did not exploit auditory queues.

For the Absolute test results, participants could very reliably (100%) differentiate between the two most extreme levels However, the average accuracy was not as high for precisely identifying a specific level (49%). This may have been because they were required to put the device down after each trial. However, most of the errors were only one-level errors. Thus, when remapping our feedback levels to a coarser resolution, the results are much better. With three absolute levels, the accuracy rises to 95%. Fewer errors occurred at the highest levels, which implies that a larger dynamic range with a bias toward the higher end may improve accuracy.

Results (Figure 4) suggest that participants were very effective in detecting high deltas (~90% accuracy at 50% and 40% deltas) and fairly effective in detecting low and no deltas (~75% accuracy at 30%, 20%, and 0% deltas), but ineffective in measuring very small deltas (~20% accuracy at 10% delta). This implies that users would be able to identify small changes in applications that have continuously changing torque, but also that applications might leverage relative delta changes, rather than encoding feedback using absolute amounts, when many levels are needed.

DISCUSSION AND FUTURE WORK

GyroTab is a device that produces reactive gyroscopic haptic feedback. The key contributions of this paper are: (1) the use of spinning masses to produce reactive gyroscopic feedback; (2) a discussion of the various kinds of feedback that can be generated with this approach; (3) initial results of the perceptibility of the feedback from a user study.

The study presented above provides early evidence that this approach produces several discernible feedback levels, but more work is needed to determine if the resolution accuracy could be improved with a higher dynamic range and different strategies for quantizing the feedback levels.

While conducting this quantitative exploration, we also received positive comments about the haptic feedback itself and the breadth of the perceptual space it suggests; in fact, most of the concepts described in the "Achievable Feedback" section were discovered by our participants. This

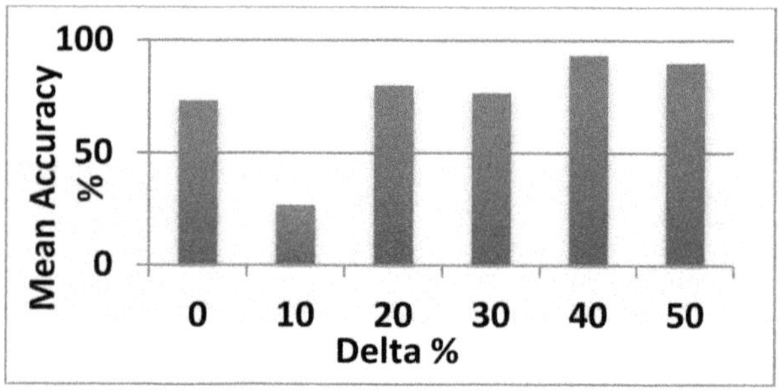

Figure 4: Results for the relative change experiment. Participants were able to discern small relative changes (20%).

space becomes even broader when we consider incorporating appropriate audio-visual cues to enhance the feedback.

The areas of improvement for this device lie primarily in making it truly mobile and increasing the speed at which the feedback can be created (i.e., the rate at which the angular momentum can be changed). In addition, the current device consumes just over 10W while spinning, so power reduction will be essential to integration into mobile devices. Strategically switching between completely off and idle mode could help alleviate some of the power concerns, but custom motors and smaller platters will likely be required.

REFERENCES

1. Amemiya, T., Ando, H., Maeda, T. Lead-me Interface for a Pulling Sensation from Hand-held Devices. *ACM Trans Appl Percept* 5, 3(15), 2008.
2. Amemiya, T., Yamashita, J., Hirota, K., and Hirose, M. Virtual leading blocks for the deaf-blind: A real-time way-finder by verbal-nonverbal hybrid interface and high-density RFID tag space. In Proc. of Virtual Reality Conference 165–172.
3. Ando, H., Obana, K., Sugimoto, Maeda, T. A Wearable Force Display Based on Brake Change in Angular Momentum. *Proc Artificial Reality and Telexistence 2002*, 16–21.Massie, T.H., Salisbury, J.K.
4. PHANToM Haptic Interface: A Device for Probing Virtual Objects. *Symposium on Haptic Interfaces for Virtual Environment and Teleoperator Systems*, 1994.
5. Swindells, C., Unden, A., Sang, T. TorqueBAR: An Ungrounded Haptic Feedback Device. *Proc ICMI 2003*, 52-59.
6. Tanaka, Y., Masataka, S., Yuka, K., Fukui, Y., Yamashita, J., and Nakamura, N. Mobile Torque Display and Haptic Characteristics of Human Palm. *Proc Artificial Reality and Telexistence 2001*, 115-120.
7. Winfree, K.N., Gewirtz, J., Mather, T., Fiene, J., Kuchenbecker, K.J. A High Fidelity Ungrounded Torque Feedback Device: The Torque 2.0. *Proc EuroHaptics 2009*, 261-266.
8. Yano, H., Yoshie, M., Iwata, H. Development of a Non-Grounded Haptic Interface Using the Gyro Effect. *Proc Symp on Haptic Interfaces for Virtual Environment and Teleoperator Systems 2003.*

Accurate Measurements of Pointing Performance from In Situ Observations

Krzysztof Z. Gajos, Katharina Reinecke and Charles Herrmann
Harvard School of Engineering and Applied Sciences
Cambridge, MA 02138, USA
{kgajos,reinecke,iherrmann}@seas.harvard.edu

ABSTRACT
We present a method for obtaining lab-quality measurements of pointing performance from unobtrusive observations of natural in situ interactions. Specifically, we have developed a set of user-independent classifiers for discriminating between deliberate, targeted mouse pointer movements and those movements that were affected by any extraneous factors. To develop and validate these classifiers, we developed logging software to unobtrusively record pointer trajectories as participants naturally interacted with their computers over the course of several weeks. Each participant also performed a set of pointing tasks in a formal study set-up. For each movement, we computed a set of measures capturing nuances of the trajectory and the speed, acceleration, and jerk profiles. Treating the observations from the formal study as positive examples of deliberate, targeted movements and the in situ observations as unlabeled data with an unknown mix of deliberate and distracted interactions, we used a recent advance in machine learning to develop the classifiers. Our results show that, on four distinct metrics, the data collected in-situ and filtered with our classifiers closely matches the results obtained from the formal experiment.

Author Keywords
Pointing; motor performance; machine learning; in situ studies

ACM Classification Keywords
H.5.2. Information Interfaces and Presentation: User Interfaces—*Evaluation/methodology*;

INTRODUCTION
We present a method for obtaining lab-quality measurements of pointing performance from unobtrusive observations of natural in situ interactions. In controlled laboratory studies, participants are instructed to focus entirely on the task at hand and proceed as quickly as possible while keeping error rates minimal. The measurements collected in such studies reflect primarily the motor abilities of the participants and the properties of the input device used. In contrast, in naturalistic settings people's pointing performance is also affected by a number of cognitive, perceptual, or environmental distractions such as deciding what task to perform next, looking for the right user interface element, or watching TV. Thus, data obtained from in situ observations of natural pointing interactions differs substantially from data collected in laboratory settings [2]. Yet, if lab-quality data could be collected in situ, it might enable measuring longitudinal fluctuations in a user's motor performance (e.g., due to medication, fatigue, or progression of a disease) [11], automatic detection of pointing problems and the need for assistive technology [10], automatic adaptation of user interfaces to the changes in the user's motor abilities [7], and more realistic assessments of novel input devices.

To enable such lab-quality measurements of pointing performance from in situ observations we have developed a set of user-independent classifiers for discriminating between deliberate, targeted mouse pointer movements and those movements that were affected by any extraneous factors. As illustrated in Figure 1, these classifiers can be used to effectively filter the naturalistic data such that the filtered in situ data is nearly indistinguishable from the data obtained from the same person through a formal experimental set-up.

To develop and validate our approach we developed logging software to unobtrusively record mouse pointer trajectories from 18 participants as they naturally interacted with their computers over the course of several weeks. Each participant also performed a set of pointing tasks using a formal study set-up. For each movement, we computed a set of measures capturing properties of the movement trajectory as well as the speed, acceleration, and jerk profiles. Treating the observations from the formal study as positive examples of deliberate, targeted movements and the in situ observations as unlabeled data with an unknown mix of deliberate and distracted interactions, we used a recent advance in machine learning [4] to develop user-independent classifiers capable of discriminating between trajectories of deliberate and distracted mouse pointer movements.

We evaluated our approach on four different tasks—estimating the mean of a measurement, conducting tests for statistically significant differences, estimating Fitts' throughput, and building Fitts' law models to generate movement

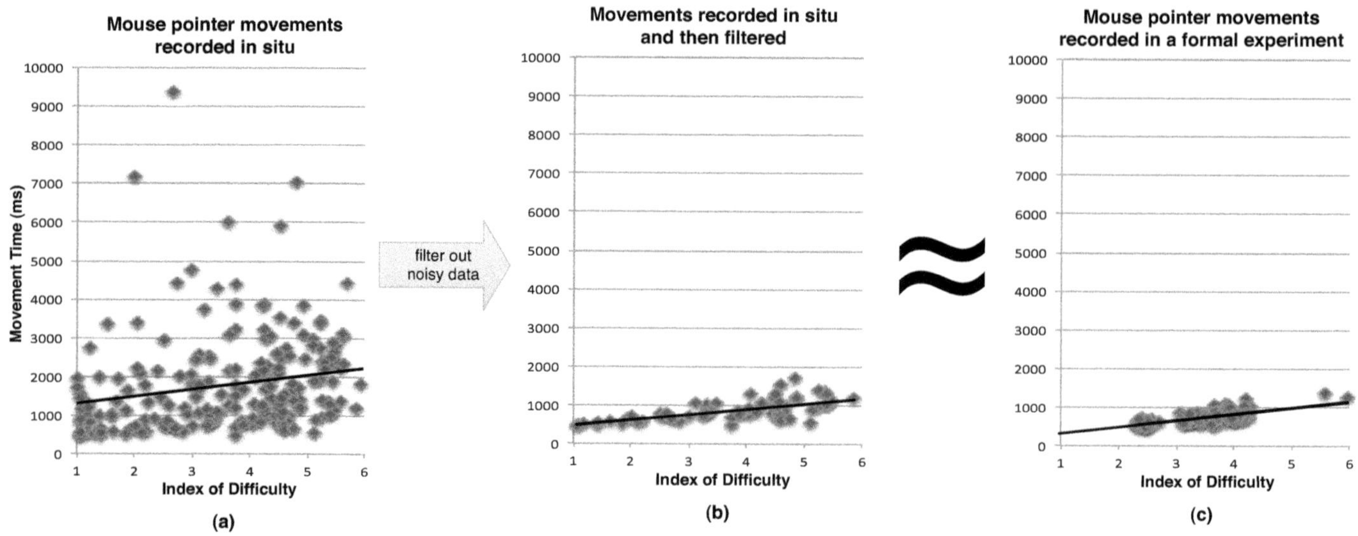

Figure 1. (a) Mouse pointer movements collected in situ from one participant by unobtrusively observing his interactions with the computer. (b) A subset of these movements classified by our system as deliberate targeted interactions; the distribution of these movements, as represented by the Fitts's law parameters computed from them, is nearly indistinguishable from (c) the movements collected from the same participant in a formal experiment. Trend lines are shown in black.

time predictions—and the results obtained from data collected in situ and filtered with our classifier closely matched the results obtained from a formal experiment.

The main contribution of this paper is the development and the evaluation of a machine learning–based method for discriminating between mouse pointer trajectories that came from deliberate, targeted movements and those that were produced when the person was distracted or not focused on the task. We also make available on our web site our data set of over 7800 mouse pointer trajectories, our source code, and the user-independent classifiers trained on these data.

PRIOR RESEARCH

Unobtrusive observations of user behavior have previously been used to characterize naturally occurring mouse pointer interactions [2]. The analysis of these data confirmed that naturally occurring pointing interactions have different properties from those observed in controlled laboratory studies. Meanwhile, Hurst and colleagues demonstrated that laboratory studies are insufficient for properly characterizing the motor performance of people with motor impairments because the motor abilities of these users tend to vary substantially over time due to medication, fatigue, and changes in the underlying medical condition [11]—longitudinal in situ measurements are needed instead. Hurst and colleagues also demonstrated that lab-quality pointing performance data could be used to automatically detect the certain kinds of motor impairments and to predict the benefit of particular assistive technologies [10] and, again, argued that their methods would be most useful if the data could be collected unobtrusively.

The SUPPLE system [6] uses models of an individual's motor performance to automatically generate user interfaces optimized for that user's unique motor abilities. Currently, lab-quality measurements are needed to build appropriate models of users' motor abilities. The data collection process used by SUPPLE can take up to an hour for people with moderate to severe impairments to complete. Such significant upfront effort will deter many users from adopting ability-based adaptations, especially if the effort has to be repeated each time a person's abilities fluctuate or their computing environment changes.

Unobtrusively collected behavioral measures—capturing temporal patterns in scrolling, mouse movements, clicks, text entry, and periods of apparent inactivity—have also been used to predict the reliability of contributions by workers on the Amazon Mechanical Turk crowdsourcing platform [19]. Our work could provide another mechanism for assessing participant effort (and therefore data quality) for tasks that involve pointing as part of the overall interaction.

The very recent work on the Input Observer [5] is aimed at developing a logging and analysis system for both keyboard- and mouse pointer–based interactions. It uses a conservative heuristic for identifying parts of movements that can be used to compute Fitts' model parameters characterizing a particular individual's motor performance. If combined with Input Observer, our work may enable more efficient use of the collected data.

GOALS AND APPROACH

Our high level goal, illustrated in Figure 1, is to obtain results from in situ observations that are of the same quality as the results obtained from controlled laboratory experiments.

Our approach is to relax requirements for how the data are collected and instead filter the observations by identifying deliberate, targeted mouse pointer movements and separating them from those that were affected by any extraneous factors such as cognitive effort related to a difficult choice, visual search for the correct target, lack of effort, or an environmental distraction.

Our approach hinges on the assumption — which our results confirm — that deliberate, targeted mouse pointer movements can be distinguished from "noisy" ones by a careful analysis of their trajectories as well as the speed, acceleration and jerk profiles.

To collect examples of deliberate, targeted mouse pointer trajectories, we asked each participant to perform a set of pointing tasks based on the ISO 9241-9 standard [12]. To obtain a broad and representative sample of mouse pointer trajectories affected by extraneous factors, we asked participants to install a Firefox browser plugin on their computers for a period of several weeks to record the trajectories of the mouse movements performed while participants were interacting naturally with their computers.

We evaluate the approach by examining its reliability on four representative tasks:

- estimating a mean of a directly measured variable for each participant (we use movement time divided by Fitts' Index of Difficulty);
- testing for statistically significant differences in the values of those means across participants;
- estimating the per-participant value of the Index of Performance;
- computing parameters of the Fitts' law model for each participant and using the model to make movement time predictions for a range of tasks.

We briefly review Fitts' law, and the related concepts of Index of Difficulty and Index of Performance in the Data Processing section.

Definitions

For ease of exposition, we will refer to the data collected from the formal pointing experiment test as *experimental* data or movements. *Natural* data or movements will denote the mouse pointer trajectories collected unobtrusively with the browser extension. Finally, our approach will classify the natural movements into *deliberate* and *distracted.*

DATA COLLECTION

Participants

18 participants (10 male, 8 female; aged 19 to 64) successfully completed all parts of the study. Participants were recruited nationally from the broad population through advertisements delivered via email or posted on various community portals. All participants were regular computer users. Almost all participants reported using a touchpad, a mouse, or a combination of the two as their primary input devices. Only one participant used a tablet. These data are summarized in Table 1.

No participants reported any major impairments or other factors that might affect their computer usage except for P48 who reported slightly reduced visual acuity (partially corrected with an anti-glare screen) and P44 whose mouse acted "sticky."

Participant	Pointing device used typically	Age	Gender
P02	touchpad	21	m
P03	mouse	52	f
P17	touchpad	30	m
P18	touchpad	32	f
P22	touchpad	20	f
P24	mouse/touchpad	24	m
P25	touchpad	30	m
P30	touchpad	19	f
P31	touchpad	22	m
P33	touchpad, sometimes mouse	27	f
P40	mouse	42	m
P41	mouse	29	m
P43	touchpad	20	f
P44	mouse	64	f
P48	mouse/touchpad	52	f
P49	mouse	52	m
P60	tablet	31	m
P63	mouse	32	m

Table 1. The Participants.

Participants received monetary compensation for taking part in the study.

Apparatus

We have built two data collection tools: a web-based formal experimental tool based on the ISO 9241-9 standard [12] (to collect the experimental data) and a Firefox browser extension to record trajectories of the mouse pointer movements that occurred naturally within the browser content window. The formal experimental tasks were presented as sets of targets arranged in a circular pattern. The next target to be clicked was highlighted in yellow. A number of task sets were presented to each user varying in target sizes (10, 15, 25, 40, and 60 pixels) and the distances between successive targets (three distances dependent on the size of each participant's screen). Up to 10 clicks were collected per condition and the conditions were presented in a random order.

The data recorded with both tools included all mouse movement events and clicks. The tools also recorded when the mouse left and re-entered the browser content window so that we could identify those movements for which the trajectory data was incomplete (our software had no access to mouse events triggered outside of the browser content window). For the explicit diagnostic tasks, we recorded whether a click was a hit or a miss. For data captured with the Firefox extension, we were able to identify only a subset of meaningful interactors (those that were marked with tags such as A, INPUT, SELECT, etc., and those with appropriate ARIAA [22] tags). When a click occurred on such a target, we recorded the target type, its dimensions and location. When a click occurred on any other part of the page, we also recorded it, but because we could not tell if the element clicked was a valid interactor, we could not reliably determine if the click was a miss or a deliberate interaction.

To maintain participants' privacy, our software did not collect the URLs or the content of the pages visited by the participants, nor did it capture any information entered by the users on the pages. All data collected on participants' computers were identified by a study code and were periodically automatically transmitted to our server over an encrypted and authenticated connection.

Procedure

Interested participants responded to our advertisements by visiting the study web site where they were presented with a brief overview of the study purpose and procedures, followed by an informed consent form. Participants who consented were asked to provide basic contact information and were given instructions on how to download and install the Firefox extension. They were then contacted by a researcher, who conducted a phone interview to collect basic demographic information and who confirmed the study procedures and helped resolve any technical issues.

The unobtrusive recording of a participant's mouse pointer movements began the moment a participant consented to participate in the study and installed the Firefox extension.

Participants were instructed to do the formal experiment at as quick a pace as possible and at a time when they would not be distracted. They were told that they could take a break from those tasks at any point they needed to. Our software automatically resumed where the participant had left off. Participants were encouraged to complete the diagnostic tasks as soon as possible, but were free to do so any time before the completion of the study.

After 4 weeks, participants were contacted again by a researcher with instructions on how to uninstall the Firefox extension.

DATA PROCESSING

Extracting Individual Mouse Movements

We parsed the collected sequences of mouse pointer events to extract individual *movements*. We defined a movement as a sequence of mouse move events starting immediately after a click that ended a previous movement or after a pause of at least 1 second. Valid movements ended with a click on a recognized interactive element. Because our software could not identify all interactors on every page, if a click occurred outside one of the recognized interactors, we could not reliably determine if such a click was a mistake or an intentional action — we did not include such movements in the analysis. We also discarded movements during which the mouse pointer left the browser content window, the user switched to a different tab, or a page load event was registered.

Because we could not always obtain the exact position of a clicked target, we calculated movement distance as the distance from the location of the first movement event to the location of the final click.

We used the following formulation of the Fitts' law to compute any Fitts' law–related measures:

$$\text{Movement Time} = a + b * \log_2\left(\frac{A}{W} + 1\right)$$

Where A is the movement *amplitude,* or distance, and W stands for the target size. Constants a and b are estimated from the data. The logarithm term is referred to as the *Index of Difficulty,* or ID and is measured in bits. The reciprocal of b is called the Index of Performance and is measured in bits per second, and is occasionally used as an informative diagnostic measure for comparing performance of devices or people [15, 21]. We used the smaller of the target width and height as the target size [17] (more sophisticated approaches are available [1, 8]; we chose the min model because it provides reasonable accuracy with minimal complexity).

Data Cleaning

We removed extreme outliers from the data collected during the formal experimental tasks. From each participant's data we removed those movements where the Movement Time divided by ID was two standard deviations or more away from that participant's mean. This resulted in removal of between 3 and 11 movements per participant (between 2% and 7% of each participant's data).

Filtering Trajectories

To enable robust computation of trajectory-related statistics, we first smoothed the pointer trajectories to remove any sampling-related artifacts. We started by resampling pointer position trajectories at regular time intervals (10 ms resulting in a 100 Hz sampling rate) and we subsequently filtered them with a 30 Hz low-pass NER filter [14]. To compute successive derivatives (speed, acceleration, and jerk), we used a differentiating filter [14]. Once the derivatives were computed, we passed position, speed, acceleration, and jerk time series again through a 7 Hz low-pass filter. This overall process has been used previously by a number of researchers (e.g., [21, 13, 18, 20]) to ensure that low-level sampling-related artifacts are removed, while significant phenomena are preserved.

Computing Movement Features

In addition to movement time, we recorded a number of other performance-related measures (or features) for each movement. These measures have been described, illustrated, and motivated more extensively by the researchers who originally proposed them, but we briefly summarize them below for completeness. In defining some of the measures, we will refer to the *task axis,* which is the straight line passing through the end points of the movement. The following measures refer directly to the movement trajectory:

Length to Distance Ratio [2] is the ratio of the length of movement's overall trajectory to the straight line distance between the movement's end points.

Number of Task Axis Crossings [16] captures how many times the pointer crossed the task axis.

Movement Direction Changes [16]—if the movement trajectory were rotated such that both end points were on the x-axis, this measure captures the number of times the y-component of the movement direction changed sign (i.e., it captures direction changes toward/away from the task axis).

Orthogonal Direction Changes [16]—as above, but for the x-component of the movement direction (i.e., it captures direction changes toward/away from the target).

Movement error [16] is computed as the average absolute distance of the mouse pointer from the task axis.

Movement variability [16] captures the standard deviation of the distance of the points on the trajectory from the task axis. Intuitively, it captures the level of "wiggliness" of the movement.

Speed, acceleration, and jerk profiles. Following [21], we also computed several measures of the speed, acceleration, and jerk profiles:

- the number of peaks
- the number of x-axis crossings
- time from the start of the movement to the first peak
- the relative time (with respect to the total movement duration) from the start of the movement to the first peak
- time from the start of the movement to the last peak
- the relative time to the last peak
- time from the start of the movement to the maximum peak
- the relative time to the maximum peak

Finally, we computed correlations between task properties (distance, target size, and the Index of Difficulty) and the values of each of the features. We found that 4 features (movement time, and the time of the last peak for each of speed, acceleration, and jerk) correlated substantially with the Index of Difficulty. Because our goal is to use these features to identify differences in participant performance that are independent of the task, we replaced each of these 4 features with a transformed version by dividing the original by the Index of Difficulty. Lastly, we added Movement Time divided by the movement distance, and Movement Time divided by a logarithm of the movement distance to the list of features.

Thus, for each movement we computed a total of 34 features.

Overview of the Data

In the end, we extracted a total of 7847 usable mouse pointer trajectories (2762 from the formal experimental tasks and 5085 from the browser extension). The browser extension was much easier to develop than recording tools that integrate directly with the operating systems, but it resulted in a relatively low data collection rate: A large fraction of the recorded movements were affected by the mouse pointer leaving the content window, slow page loads, or tab switches. Some sites also prevented recapturing of mouse click events. The extended data collection period ensured, however, that sufficient data were collected for the purposes of this study.

As a diagnostic check, we computed the Index of Performance for each participant's experimental movements. The results ranged from 4.1 bits/second for our oldest participant to 10.5 bits/second for the youngest, with the mean of 6.9 bits/second (a number that is consistent with the results from other studies, e.g., [21]).

CLASSIFYING MOUSE MOVEMENTS

Given the collected data, we aimed to develop a classifier capable of discriminating between mouse pointer trajectories corresponding to deliberate and distracted interactions. Note, however, that our data did not match the assumptions of typical classification approaches: while the experimental data could be assumed to contain mostly examples of deliberate movements, the natural data was an unlabeled mix of deliberate and distracted movements, and we could not even justify making assumptions about the relative proportions of the two types of movements. While typical classification approaches assume that all data are labeled and that all classes are represented in roughly equal proportions, our data set contained some positive labeled examples (the experimental data) and the remaining data had no labels at all (the natural data). Many other classification problems that arise in HCI would be most naturally treated as learning from positive and unlabeled examples (e.g., a user quickly inspects a large number of images and marks a small number as interesting — the remaining images will be more correctly treated as unlabeled rather than uninteresting). We therefore briefly summarize the state of the art in machine learning to support other researchers in adopting these techniques in their work.

The problem of learning from positive and unlabeled examples has been addressed by several machine learning researchers. Some early approaches involved using heuristics to identify an initial set of likely negative examples among the unlabeled data and then falling back on better understood semi-supervised learning techniques (e.g., [23]). Other approaches make assumptions about the relative proportions of the positive and negative examples in the unlabeled data (e.g. [3]). All of these approaches can be very sensitive to the accuracy of the initial guesses. A more recent approach [4] overcomes the limitations of the earlier work. This approach builds on the observation that if the labeled examples are drawn completely at random from the pool of all positive instances in the training data, then, informally:

$$p(\text{instance x is positive}) = \frac{p(\text{instance x would be labeled})}{\text{fraction of positive instances that are labeled}}$$

In other words, to learn from positive and unlabeled examples, we can first fall back on a more traditional classification problem where we assume that all unlabeled examples are in fact negative. Then $p(\text{instance x would be labeled})$ is a probability estimate that a mainstream classifier would return if trained on a data set where all unlabeled examples are temporarily given a negative label. This probability then needs to be adjusted by a constant specific to the data set: the fraction of positive instances that are labeled. This quantity cannot be observed directly, but the reader will find three methods for estimating it in Elkan and Noto's paper [4].

This overall method is well-motivated theoretically and is also easy to implement because it relies on existing classification methods for estimating the probabilities. The main requirement is that the underlying mainstream classification method produces well-calibrated probabilities. Many of the standard classification techniques used in the HCI community, such as decision trees, support vector machines, or naive Bayes, do not satisfy this requirement. Instead, logistic regression is an appropriate choice, and this is what we use in the work presented here.

EVALUATION PROCEDURE

Evaluation Measures

Intuitively, our goal is to measure how "alike" the data obtained from the formal experiment and the natural data filtered with our approach are. Formal measures of distribution similarity are unlikely to be illuminating, however. We therefore turn to four functional metrics that reflect common purposes for which such data might be used. Using the experimental data as the base line for all error computations, we compute per-participant error rates for the following primary measures:

Mean Movement Time divided by the Index of Difficulty (MT/ID). For each participant, we compute the difference in the estimates of the mean value of Movement Time divided by the Index of Difficulty (MT/ID) between the experimental data and the natural data classified as deliberate.

Tests for statistically significant differences. For each pair of participants, we test whether the difference in their mean values of MT/ID is significant. We use a t-test at $\alpha = .01$ and we log-transform the data before applying the test to correct for the non-normal distribution. We perform these tests separately for both data sets (the experimental data set and the data set being evaluated). To make the comparison between the two data sets meaningful, we randomly subsample the larger data set such that the two data sets have the same number of measurements for each participant. To make the results less susceptible to chance, we repeat each test 100 times redoing the resampling each time. We consider the outcome of the test as significant if more than half of the repetitions returned $p \leq .01$. We limited the testing to only those pairs where at least 50 data points were available for each participant.

Movement time predictions of Fitts' models. For each participant, we estimate the parameters of the Fitts' models separately from the experimental data and the natural data classified as deliberate. We compute the relative difference between the predictions of the two models with the model derived from the experimental data serving as the baseline of the comparison. We perform this comparison for a set of Index of Difficulty values ranging from 2 to 7 at intervals of 0.2. Because the models may cross (i.e., each model may produce higher estimates for a part of the range of the IDs considered), we calculate the mean *absolute* relative difference in the predictions.

Mean Index of Performance. For each user, we compute the relative difference between the estimates of the Index of Performance derived from the experimental data and the natural data classified as deliberate. This is the most sensitive of our measures because it is estimated with the least squares method, which is particularly sensitive to outliers for extreme values of ID.

In addition to the above error measures, we also compute three more informative statistics:

Standard deviation of the MT/ID. While the errors in the estimates of the mean value of MT/ID capture the systematic errors in the measurements, standard deviation captures the variance in the measurements and provides another indication of the data quality. We compute the mean per-user standard deviation.

Recall. Recall captures the fraction of the experimental movements that the classifier identifies as deliberate. Assuming that our participants completed the formal experimental tasks conscientiously and without distraction, it is desirable for this number to be close to 100%.

Fraction of natural movements classified as deliberate. This measure provides some insight into how generalizable the model used by the classifier is—a very small fraction of natural movements classified as deliberate may indicate that the classifier was overfitting to the data from the training set. This number is also informative for estimating how many more in situ observations would need to be collected than in a controlled experiment for similar quality of the results.

Cross-validation Procedure

We used a per-participant cross-validation procedure for evaluation: for any configuration tested, we trained the classifier on data obtained from all but one participant. We applied the resulting classifier to the data from the remaining participant to identify the deliberate movements and we computed the values of all of the evaluation measures on those filtered data. This procedure ensured that the results reflect the capability of this approach to make accurate classification decisions on data collected from previously unseen users.

Feature Selection Procedure

The choice of features impacts the ability of machine learning algorithms to generalize robustly. We have identified over 30 potential features (discussed in the Data Processing section), but which of them are actually useful for discriminating between deliberate and distracted movements?

We used a variant of the stepwise discriminant analysis as our feature selection algorithm. Starting with an initial (potentially empty) set of features to consider, our algorithm proceeded in the following steps: First, it removed one feature at a time from the current set of features. If removing any one feature resulted in an improvement, the best of such reduced feature sets was kept as the current best and the process was restarted with this set as the starting point. If removing features did not improve performance, the algorithm attempted to extend the model by adding one feature (trying each of the unused features in turn). If any of such expanded feature sets

	Unfiltered Natural Movements	*Approach 1* Filtered	*Approach 2* Normalized & Filtered	*Approach 3* Filtered, Target-Agnostic Features Only	*Approach 4* Normalized & Filtered, Target-Agnostic Features Only
Properties and assumptions					
Data requirements	n/a	movement trajectory + target size	movement trajectory + target size + a set of trajectories representative of the person's natural behavior	movement trajectory	movement trajectory + a set of trajectories representative of the person's natural behavior
Movement Time divided by Index of Difficulty					
Mean absolute error	172.10%	22.00%	19.05%	35.14%	25.12%
min	*70.78%*	*-33.20%*	*-20.41%*	*-3.24%*	*-4.43%*
max	*236.92%*	*51.42%*	*45.32%*	*77.97%*	*63.93%*
Mean per-participant standard deviation (value for experimental data: 62)	488.54	52.90	53.71	103.58	89.16
Statistical tests					
Fraction incorrect	49.67%	41.18%	16.67%		
chance of not detecting correctly a statistically significant difference if there is one	76.62%	51.33%	42.86%	6.82%	24.14%
chance that a statistically significant difference will be reported as significant but in opposite direction	*5.26%*	*0.00%*	*0.00%*	*0.00%*	*1.72%*
chance of detecting a statistically significant difference	22.37%	12.50%	10.34%	55.74%	59.57%
Movement time predictions of the Fitts' models					
Mean absolute error	149.38%	21.85%	19.42%	35.90%	21.48%
min	*67.18%*	*9.39%*	*0.79%*	*3.62%*	*2.67%*
max	*219.10%*	*54.96%*	*44.07%*	*75.21%*	*49.56%*
Index of Performance					
Mean absolute error	-27.27%	20.00%	16.82%	24.07%	29.08%
min	*-68.17%*	*-48.32%*	*-47.55%*	*-55.02%*	*-25.57%*
max	*78.05%*	*63.61%*	*38.01%*	*22.55%*	*81.04%*
Recall					
Mean recall on experimental data	n/a	89.03%	88.75%	84.98%	88.70%
min	*n/a*	*24.78%*	*64.60%*	*26.55%*	*69.12%*
max	*n/a*	*99.35%*	*99.45%*	*98.70%*	*98.35%*
Mean fraction of natural movements classified as deliberate	n/a	24.65%	23.12%	30.65%	24.77%
min	*n/a*	*3.90%*	*7.25%*	*11.11%*	*12.95%*
max	*n/a*	*58.70%*	*36.12%*	*55.80%*	*35.68%*

Table 2. Summary of the results. Errors are reported as percentages of the values derived from the experimental data.

resulted in an improvement, the process was restarted with the best of such expanded sets as the starting point. The process terminated when neither shrinking nor expanding the feature set resulted in an improvement. To reduce the chance that the final result would be a local minimum, the process was repeated with a number of different randomly chosen starting sets of features.

The numerical criterion used to evaluate the performance of classifiers trained on different subsets of the feature was the sum of the mean and worst-case values of the MT/ID error, error in the movement time prediction of the Fitts' models, and the error in the Index of Performance estimate.

RESULTS

In this section, we report on the performance of four variants of our approach, each making different assumptions about the type and quantity of the available data.

We begin by evaluating how informative the raw unfiltered natural data are for evaluating the quantities listed in the Evaluation Measures section. These and other results are summarized in Table 2. As expected, the natural data resulted in substantial overestimates of the mean value of MT/ID and much larger variance in the data. Next, nearly half of the pairwise statistical tests resulted in a conclusion different from what was obtained from experimental data: Not surprisingly, most of the errors were false negatives: nearly 77% of the statistically significant differences present in the experimental data were not detected in the natural data. Of larger concern are the false positives and the small fraction of tests that indicated the presence of a significant difference, but in the direction opposite to that observed in the experimental data. A larger number of natural observations may help correct the false negative errors, but the other two types of errors are likely due to the different distributions of "noise" in each participant's natural data and may not be correctable even if larger amounts of data were collected.

The natural data also resulted in Fitts' models that substantially differed in their predictions from the models calculated from the experimental data.

Index of Performance is the most indirect measure we collected from the data. The mean absolute difference between the estimates obtained from natural and experimental data is 27%. Closer inspection of the results shows a strong bias toward underestimates: for all but three participants the Index of Performance estimated from the natural data is lower than the ground truth.

Approach 1: Identifying Deliberate Movements

The first approach addresses the situation where movements have to be classified on-line, one-by-one. We assume that both the movement trajectory and the size of the target are available.

Approach 1 Filtered	*Approach 2* Normalized & Filtered	*Approach 3* Filtered, Target-Agnostic Features Only	*Approach 4* Normalized & Filtered, Target-Agnostic Features Only
1. Movement time divided by the Index of Difficulty	1. Movement time divided by the Index of Difficulty (normalized)	1. Movement time divided by movement distance	1. Movement time divided by movement distance (normalized)
2. Movement time divided by logarithm of movement distance	2. Movement time divided by logarithm of movement distance (normalized)	2. Movement error	2. Movement time divided by logarithm of movement distance (normalized)
3. Movement error	3. Movement error	3. Relative time to the first peak in speed	3. Movement error
4. Movement variability	4. Movement variability	4. Relative time to the first peak in acceleration	4. Movement variability
5. Relative time to the first peak in speed	5. Number of submovements	5. Relative time to the maximum peak in acceleration	5. Number of submovements (normalized)
6. Relative time to the maximum peak in speed	6. Number of submovements (normalized)	6. Relative time to the maximum peak in jerk	6. Relative time to the first peak in speed
7. Relative time to the first peak in acceleration	7. Relative time to the first peak in acceleration		7. Relative time to the first peak in acceleration
8. Relative time to the maximum peak in jerk			8. Relative time to the maximum peak in acceleration
			9. Relative time to the maximum peak in jerk

Table 3. Sets of features that resulted in best performance in the four approaches evaluated.

The result of the feature selection process was a classifier using 8 out of 34 available features (shown in Table 3). Two of the features relate to the speed of movement execution, two are related to the shape of the path, and four use information captured in the speed, acceleration, and jerk profiles.

On average, 25% of each participant's natural movements were classified as deliberate. The errors in estimating MT/ID and the Fitts' model predictions were reduced by factors of 8 and 7, respectively, to 22%. This improvement translated into more reliable results of statistical tests: the probability of declaring a statistically significant difference where none was present was reduced nearly by half and there were no cases where a statistically significant result was declared in the direction opposite to what was observed in the experimental data. The probability of missing a statistically significant result was reduced by a third, but still remained high.

The overall recall was 89%, meaning that on average 11% of each participant's experimental movements were classified as distracted. Because the data collection occurred in an unsupervised setting, this number may reflect the true quality of our experimental data. What is a source of concern is the fact that for one of the participants the recall was only 25%. This was the only such extreme outlier—the next lowest number was 69%. An inspection of the data revealed that the participant with the lowest recall was P44, who was the oldest person to take part in our study and who reported mechanical difficulties with her mouse. This participant was by far the slowest of the 18 as measured by the Movement Time divided by the Index of Difficulty. P44 was, unsurprisingly, also the outlier in terms of the fraction of natural movements classified as deliberate: only 4% of her movements were classified as such.

Approach 2: Mitigating the Impact of Individual Differences

The results presented above suggest that the approach, as presented so far, is sensitive to individual differences among participants: it identifies the best exemplars of deliberate movements across the population. Instead, in most situations the desired behavior would be to identify those movements that reflected a particular individual's best attempt at deliberate, targeted pointing movements.

To mitigate the effects of such individual differences, we propose a second approach where in addition to the movement trajectory and the size of the target, we also have available a set of trajectories representative of that user's typical natural computer behavior.

In this approach, we normalized each participants' data by subtracting (separately for each feature) the mean value of the feature over natural data and then dividing the resulting value by the standard deviation (also computed over the natural data). This normalization procedure eliminated participant-specific differences in magnitude while preserving the relative differences between natural and experimental data. We then created a new set of data that included both the original features and the per-participant normalized counterparts for a total of 68 features per movement.

We then re-run the feature selection procedure. The recall results for the resulting classifier indicate that the effects of differences in individual motor performance have been indeed attenuated: the recall is still the lowest for P44, but it is now at 65% — a value that may reflect the participant's problems with a "sticky" mouse more than the limitations of the algorithm. The fraction of P44's natural movements classified as deliberate is now at 27%.

Compared to the initial filtering method proposed, the normalization procedure improved both the averages and the outlier results for all the metrics. This provides further evidence that normalization improves the generalizability of the approach making it more robust to the individual differences in motor performance. The normalization procedure does, however, implicitly rely on there being a similar distribution of deliberate and distracted movements in each user's natural interactions with the computer.

Approaches 3 & 4: Filtering with Target-Agnostic Features

Because most operating systems make it easy to capture all pointer-related events, but reveal incomplete information about the presence, location, and size of interactors [2, 5, 9], in some cases researchers may not have access to the information about the locations and sizes of targets, but may still want to collect instances of lab-quality pointing movements. The earlier two approaches both made use of the information about the size of the target: Movement Time divided by

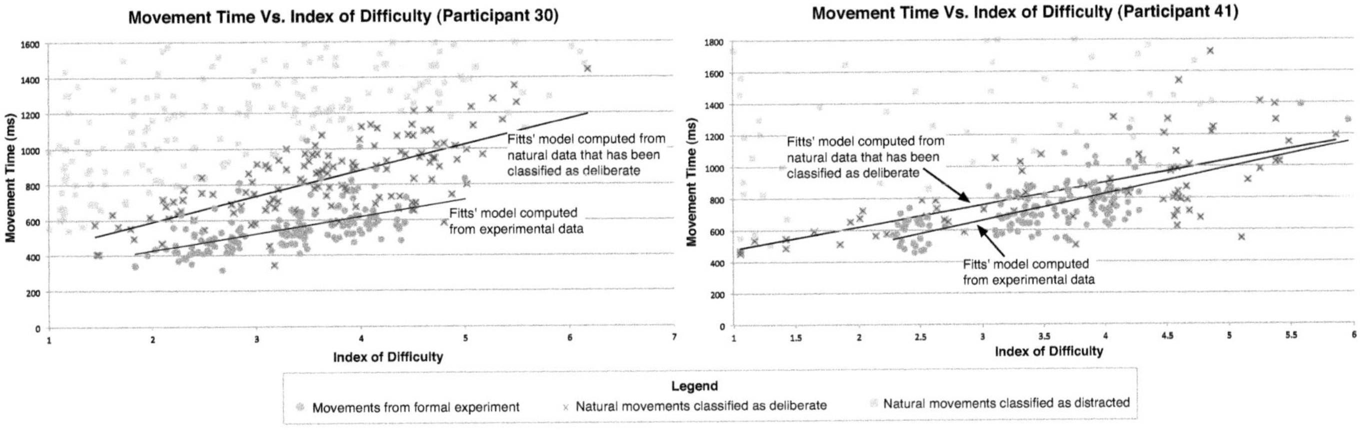

Figure 2. Understanding errors

the Index of Difficulty was a feature included in both models. Could we determine if a movement was deliberate in a target-agnostic manner?

To answer this question, we repeated our analysis using only target-agnostic features. We used the same evaluation criteria as in the previous analyses: although we recognize that target-agnostic classification will not be used for building Fitts' law models, these measures indirectly indicate whether deliberate, targeted movements are being identified correctly.

The result are two new approaches: Approach 3, which can perform classification based just on the movement trajectory information, and Approach 4, which (like Approach 2) requires a sample of trajectories representative of the user's natural interactions with the computer.

The features selected for the two resulting approaches are listed in Table 3 and the results are summarized in the last two columns of Table 2. Unsurprisingly, these approaches in general do not perform as well as the previous two. In particular, they result in a high rate of false positives in the tests for statistically significant differences. We have less confidence that these two approaches can be used to reliably filter individual interactions. However, we find that 86% of classification decisions of Approach 3, and 93% of Approach 4, agree with the predictions of Approach 2.

Understanding Sources of Error

Lastly, we take another close look at the results to understand the causes of the remaining errors — do they point to any specific limitations of our methods? To gain some insights, we review the data of Participant 30 for whom both Approach 1 an 2 resulted in consistently high errors in the estimates of MT/ID and Index of Performance — Participant 30 was not an extreme outlier like Participant 44 discussed earlier, but the error rates computed from her data were high and did not improve from Approach 1 to Approach 2. The left panel in Figure 2 contrasts the experimental data from this participant with her natural data classified as deliberate using Approach 2. What this figure makes apparent, is that Participant 30 rarely moved as quickly in a natural setting as she did during the experiment. A follow-up revealed that, when performing the formal experimental tasks, this participant "raced" a friend who had also signed up for our study. Thus, the apparent errors in our data can likely be explained by her extreme effort level during the formal experiment.

Our approach cannot compensate for such situations. In our data set, however, this was an unusual situation and the data from our other participants tended to look more like that of Participant 41 (illustrated the right panel of Figure 2), where the deliberate movements in the natural setting were similar to the movements observed in the formal experiment.

CONCLUSIONS AND FUTURE DIRECTIONS

We have developed and evaluated four user-independent classifiers (each making different assumptions about the type and quantity of data available) capable of discriminating between deliberate, targeted mouse pointer movements and those that were performed when the participant was in any way distracted.

Our results demonstrate that the classifiers we have developed can be used to filter pointing data collected in naturalistic settings such that the resulting data have properties very similar to the data typically collected in lab settings. This enables some of the measurements that are currently performed in laboratory settings to be conducted in situ, allowing for larger-scale and longer-term observations.

In accessibility-related settings, in situ pointing performance modeling can be used to adapt user interfaces to people's changing abilities [7, 6] and to understand how people's abilities change over time on different time scales (daily due to medication or fatigue and over longer periods of time due to progression of the disease or the effects of therapy) [11]. However, as the results for Approach 1 have demonstrated, our methodology will need further refinement before it can generalize to people with substantially atypical motor abilities.

The methods we have described here provide a blueprint that can be used to develop similar classifiers for other interactions (e.g., dragging, steering) and for different types of hardware (e.g., touch screens).

Lastly, the methods we have presented may be used to assess the quality of the data obtained from on-line experiments conducted with unsupervised remote participants: for experiments involving mechanical pointing tasks (i.e., tasks where participants are not simultaneously solving a complex cognitive task or need to engage in visual search), our classifier can be used used to identify and exclude from the analysis participants who appear to have been distracted during the experiment.

ONLINE APPENDIX

To enable others to use, validate and extend our results, we also make the following resources available from our web site at http://iis.seas.harvard.edu/resources:

- the user-independent classifiers already trained on more than 2000 deliberate movements and several thousands distracted movements collected in realistic conditions from 18 diverse participants;
- the data set containing 2762 experimental and 5085 natural movement trajectories;
- and the source code of the software used in this work.

Acknowledgments. Evan Greif led the implementation of the study apparatus. We thank Dimitrios Antos, Kanya (Pao) Siangliulue, Kenneth Arnold, Jennifer Mankoff, Tovi Grossman, and the anonymous CHI reviewers for helpful comments on earlier drafts of this manuscript. Katharina Reinecke was supported by the Swiss National Science Foundation under fellowship number PBZHP2-135922.

REFERENCES

1. Accot, J., and Zhai, S. Refining Fitts' law models for bivariate pointing. In *CHI '03: Proceedings of the SIGCHI conference on Human factors in computing systems*, ACM Press (New York, NY, USA, 2003), 193–200.
2. Chapuis, O., Blanch, R., and Beaudouin-Lafon, M. Fitts' law in the wild: A field study of aimed movements. Tech. Rep. 1480, LRI, Univ. Paris-Sud, France, December 2007. 11 pages.
3. Denis, F., Gilleron, R., and Letouzey, F. Learning from positive and unlabeled examples. *Theor. Comput. Sci. 348*, 1 (2005), 70–83.
4. Elkan, C., and Noto, K. Learning classifiers from only positive and unlabeled data. In *Proceeding of the 14th ACM SIGKDD international conference on Knowledge discovery and data mining*, KDD '08, ACM (New York, NY, USA, 2008), 213–220.
5. Evans, A., and Wobbrock, J. Taming wild behavior: The Input Observer for obtaining text entry and mouse pointing measures from everyday computer use. In *Proceedings of the ACM Conference on Human Factors in Computing Systems (CHI '12). Austin, Texas (May 5-10, 2012)*, ACM Press (2012). To appear.
6. Gajos, K. Z., Weld, D. S., and Wobbrock, J. O. Automatically generating personalized user interfaces with Supple. *Artificial Intelligence 174* (2010), 910–950.
7. Gajos, K. Z., Wobbrock, J. O., and Weld, D. S. Improving the performance of motor-impaired users with automatically-generated, ability-based interfaces. In *CHI '08: Proceeding of the twenty-sixth annual SIGCHI conference on Human factors in computing systems*, ACM (New York, NY, USA, 2008), 1257–1266.
8. Grossman, T., and Balakrishnan, R. A probabilistic approach to modeling two-dimensional pointing. *ACM Transactions on Computer-Human Interaction (TOCHI) 12*, 3 (2005), 435–459.
9. Hurst, A., Hudson, S. E., and Mankoff, J. Automatically identifying targets users interact with during real world tasks. In *Proceedings of the 15th international conference on Intelligent user interfaces*, IUI '10, ACM (New York, NY, USA, 2010), 11–20.
10. Hurst, A., Hudson, S. E., Mankoff, J., and Trewin, S. Automatically detecting pointing performance. In *IUI '08: Proceedings of the 13th international conference on Intelligent user interfaces*, ACM Press (Jan. 2008).
11. Hurst, A., Mankoff, J., and Hudson, S. E. Understanding pointing problems in real world computing environments. In *Assets '08: Proceedings of the 10th international ACM SIGACCESS conference on Computers and accessibility*, ACM (New York, NY, USA, 2008), 43–50.
12. International Organization for Standardization. 9241-9 Ergonomic requirements for office work with visual display terminals (VDTs)-Part 9: Requirements for non-keyboard input devices, 2000.
13. Jagacinski, R., Repperger, D., Moran, M., Ward, S., and Glass, B. Fitts' law and the microstructure of rapid discrete movements. *Journal of Experimental Psychology: Human Perception and Performance 6*, 2 (1980), 309–320.
14. Kaiser, J. F., and Reed, W. A. Data smoothing using low-pass digital filters. *Review of Scientific Instruments 48*, 11 (1977), 1447–1457.
15. MacKenzie, I. S. Fitts' law as a research and design tool in human-computer interaction. *Human-Computer Interaction 7*, 1 (1992), 91–139.
16. MacKenzie, I. S., Kauppinen, T., and Silfverberg, M. Accuracy measures for evaluating computer pointing devices. In *Proceedings of the SIGCHI conference on Human factors in computing systems*, CHI '01, ACM (New York, NY, USA, 2001), 9–16.
17. MacKenzie, S. I., and Buxton, W. Extending Fitts' law to two-dimensional tasks. In *CHI '92: Proceedings of the SIGCHI conference on Human factors in computing systems*, ACM Press (New York, NY, USA, 1992), 219–226.
18. Meyer, D. E., Abrams, R. A., Kornblum, S., Wright, C. E., and et al. Optimality in human motor performance: Ideal control of rapid aimed movements. *Psychological Review 95*, 3 (1988), 340–370.
19. Rzeszotarski, J. M., and Kittur, A. Instrumenting the crowd: Using implicit behavioral measures to predict task performance. In *Proceedings of the 24th annual ACM symposium on User interface software and technology*, UIST '11, ACM (New York, NY, USA, 2011).
20. Walker, N., Philbin, D. A., and Fisk, A. D. Age-related differences in movement control: adjusting submovement structure to optimize performance. *J Gerontol B Psychol Sci Soc Sci 52*, 1 (January 1997).
21. Wobbrock, J. O., and Gajos, K. Z. Goal crossing with mice and trackballs for people with motor impairments: Performance, submovements, and design directions. *ACM Trans. Access. Comput. 1*, 1 (May 2008), 1–37.
22. World Wide Web Consortium. Accessible Rich Internet Applications (WAI-ARIA) 1.0, 2011. Accessed on January 8, 2012.
23. Yu, H., Han, J., and Chang, K. C.-C. Pebl: positive example based learning for web page classification using svm. In *KDD '02: Proceedings of the eighth ACM SIGKDD international conference on Knowledge discovery and data mining*, ACM (New York, NY, USA, 2002), 239–248.

A General-Purpose Target-Aware Pointing Enhancement Using Pixel-Level Analysis of Graphical Interfaces

Morgan Dixon,[1] James Fogarty,[1] Jacob O. Wobbrock[2]
[1]Computer Science & Engineering, [2]The Information School
DUB Group, University of Washington
mdixon@cs.washington.edu, jfogarty@cs.washington.edu, wobbrock@uw.edu

ABSTRACT
We present a general-purpose implementation of a target-aware pointing technique, functional across an entire desktop and independent of application implementations. Specifically, we implement Grossman and Balakrishnan's *Bubble Cursor*, the fastest general pointing facilitation technique in the literature. Our implementation obtains the necessary knowledge of interface targets using a combination of *pixel-level analysis* and *social annotation*. We discuss the most novel aspects of our implementation, including methods for interactive creation and correction of pixel-level prototypes of interface elements and methods for interactive annotation of how the cursor should select identified elements. We also report on limitations of the Bubble Cursor unearthed by examining our implementation in the complexity of real-world interfaces. We therefore contribute important progress toward real-world deployment of an important family of techniques and shed light on the gap between understanding techniques in controlled settings versus behavior with real-world interfaces.

Author Keywords
Target-aware pointing; pixel-based reverse engineering; Bubble Cursor; Prefab; social annotation; real-world interfaces.

ACM Classification Keywords
H.5.2. [Information interfaces and presentation]: User Interfaces;

INTRODUCTION

The human-computer interaction literature includes many promising techniques for *target-aware pointing*, including deep studies of specific characteristics of those techniques in controlled laboratory settings. This important family of techniques can improve pointing for a variety of people on a range of devices in many applications. Target-aware techniques can significantly outperform other pointing facilitation techniques, and they ultimately have great potential to improve the efficiency of interaction.

Despite the promise of these techniques, few have been deployed or evaluated in real-world interfaces. The impact of target-aware pointing, and our understanding of its effectiveness, is currently limited by two challenges to *implementing* target-aware pointing in real-world interfaces.

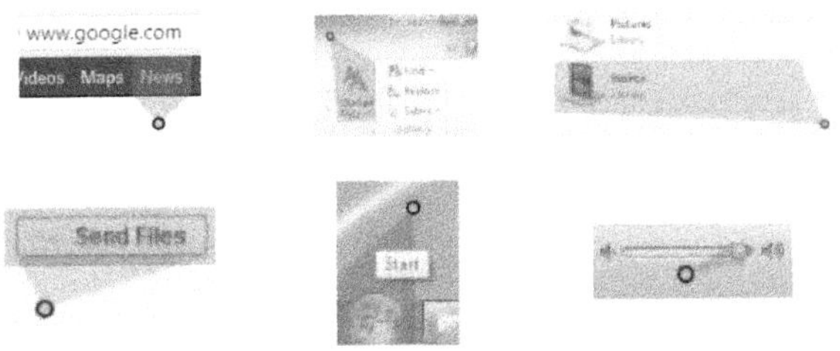

Figure 1: We present a practical implementation of a general-purpose target-aware pointing enhancement. Specifically we implement Grossman and Balakrishnan's Bubble Cursor across the Windows 7 desktop.

First, external pointing enhancements often cannot obtain reliable information about the size and location of interface elements [9,22]. Accessibility APIs attempt to provide some of the necessary information, but are inevitably incomplete due to developer failures to implement the API. For example, Hurst *et al.* found 25% of widgets are completely missing from the accessibility API [22]. The API also exposes widget *models*, not necessarily their on-screen view (e.g., the pixel coordinates of a slider's thumb are intentionally encapsulated). Techniques for dynamic code modification can also often be made to work in a single application or toolkit [13,14,32], but are generally too brittle for enhancement of the full desktop. Code injection techniques also sometimes fail (e.g., when a skinnable application uses pre-rendered images of widgets instead of meaningful graphics operations). Failures at these levels of applications can only be corrected by their developers, so many interface elements remain opaque.

Second, even a complete enumeration of interface elements is insufficient for determining how a targeting enhancement should behave. Studies of pointing facilitation techniques generally treat an interface as a field of abstract targets (e.g., gray circles), but the notion of a "target" is often not well defined in real-world interfaces. Targeting ambiguities are presented by calendars, paint canvases, text fields, and many other standard and custom widgets [41]. It is difficult or impossible for the developer of a general-purpose enhancement to foresee and address all such ambiguities.

We address these challenges in a general-purpose implementation of Grossman and Balakrishnan's *Bubble Cursor* [18], an area cursor that dynamically expands to

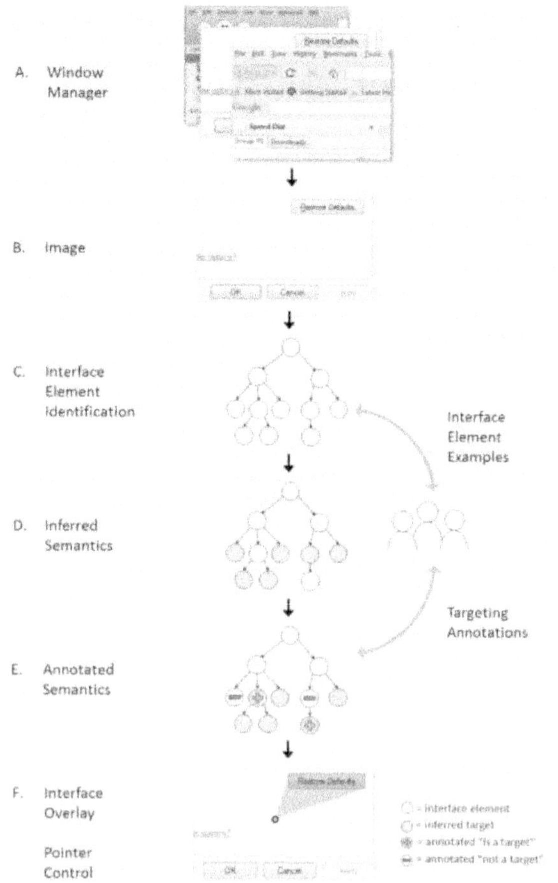

Figure 2: We implement a general-purpose Bubble Cursor in a novel architecture that combines pixel-based *identification* of interface elements with *interpretation* of their targeting. We emphasize a *human-driven* approach with interactive extension and correction of both implementation layers.

always capture the nearest target. Our implementation functions across the Windows 7 desktop, as illustrated in Figure 1. The methods we develop can be applied to any modern desktop, and they can be extended to support other target-aware techniques. Specifically, we architect our enhancement to separate *identification* of interface elements from *interpretation* of how to target those elements. We then implement identification using Prefab's pixel-based methods for reverse engineering interface structure [11,12]. We implement interpretation by annotating interfaces with desired targeting behavior. We also develop interfaces for correcting errors in both levels, and we argue that *social* mechanisms for identification and interpretation are essential to any broad target-aware deployment.

Figure 2 offers an overview of our system. We first query the window manager for images of targeted windows. We then *identify* elements using Prefab's pixel-based methods. This requires a library of Prefab prototypes, each created from one or more example images. Prefab creates a tree containing a node for each interface element (e.g., a leaf for a text label, a leaf for a slider thumb, or an inner node with children for a button and any interior icon or text). We then *interpret* the interface to determine potential targets, using annotations inferred from the interface structure and content together with annotations from prior interactive target correction. Finally, we walk the tree to determine what the Bubble Cursor should target and then overlay a translucent highlight over that target. Executing this process many times per second yields our general-purpose Bubble Cursor.

The specific contributions of our work include:

- An implementation of a general-purpose target-aware pointing enhancement. Specifically, we scale Prefab's [11] implementation of the Bubble Cursor using pixel-level analysis to target interface elements throughout Microsoft Windows 7.
- A novel architecture for general-purpose target-aware pointing enhancements. Informed by the insight that knowledge of interface element locations and dimensions is insufficient for a general-purpose target-aware pointing enhancement, we separate pixel-level *identification* of interface elements from higher-level *interpretation* of how to target those elements. Prior work has assumed identifying all elements is sufficient. We are the first to develop such a layering of semantics upon pixel-based methods.
- Two interfaces for users to correct the behavior of a general-purpose target-aware pointing enhancement. We examine the requirements and design space for such interfaces and develop two concrete designs that explore complementary approaches.
- A discussion of implications for the design and evaluation of target-aware pointing techniques in the complexity of real-world interfaces. Examining our implementation with real-world interfaces reveals both unexpected targeting behaviors not addressed in prior literature and new potential approaches to overcoming the limitations of current target-aware techniques.

RELATED WORK

We focus on Grossman and Balakrishnan's Bubble Cursor [18], but the Bubble Cursor is emblematic of a much larger body of target-aware techniques. This includes gravity wells [24], force fields [1], sticky icons [42], semantic pointing [5], area cursors [26], enhanced area cursors [15], bubble targets [10], object pointing [19], and drag-and-pop or drag-and-pick [3]. Such techniques offer great potential, but remain difficult to deploy in practice. The pixel-level analysis and social annotation methods we develop can help enable the broad deployment of these and future techniques.

The difficulty of deploying target-aware techniques motivates *target-agnostic* techniques, which aim to improve pointing without knowledge of targets. We are aware of only four such techniques: conventional pointer acceleration (cf., [6]), PointAssist [21], the Angle Mouse [41], and the Pointing Magnifier [25]. In addition, Hurst *et al.*'s [23] use of click history to approximate gravity wells can be considered a target-agnostic technique [23]. Despite the ingenuity of these techniques, they are inherently limited by their ability to consider only mouse kinematics and clicks. Our current work provides a foundation for the future deployment of target-aware techniques. This is especially promising because no target-agnostic technique has demonstrated performance superior to the best target-aware techniques.

Edwards *et al.* [13] and Olsen *et al.* [32] implement runtime modification of existing interfaces by replacing the toolkit drawing object and intercepting commands (e.g., draw_line, draw_string). Stuerzlinger *et al.* [37] present advanced customizations in their User Interface Facades, many based on interface introspection using the accessibility API. Eagan *et al.* [14] dynamically load code into program space with Scotty, developing runtime modifications based on greater access to the underlying interface model. Toolkit introspection and injection techniques can indeed enable runtime modifications that would otherwise be difficult or impossible, but with the consequence that enhancements are limited to interfaces that provide the required support.

Because all graphical interfaces ultimately consist of pixels, pixel-based methods are motivated by their independence from underlying application or toolkit requirements. Classic work by Zettlemoyer *et al.* [45,46] examined widget identification in IBOTS and VisMap for interface agents and programming by example [34,35]. St. Amant *et al.* [36] developed Segman for cognitive modeling applications. In an interactive context, Olsen *et al.*'s [33] ScreenCrayons links ink annotations to arbitrary screen elements. Tan *et al.*'s [39] WinCuts interactively subdivides windows via a copy-paste metaphor. Yeh *et al.*'s Sikuli [40] uses template matching and voting based on invariant local features to identify targets in interface scripting and testing applications. Dixon *et al.*'s [11,12] Prefab demonstrates real-time modification using input and output redirection together with pixel-based reverse engineering of interface content and structure. Our current work is informed and inspired by this prior research, contributing to pixel-based methods through deep implementation of our Bubble Cursor.

The strengths and limitations of application introspection versus pixel-based methods motivates synergies between the two approaches. Hurst *et al.* [22] studied and addressed the coverage of accessibility APIs, finding approximately 25% of widgets are completely missing from the API's view of many common interfaces. They developed a hybrid technique that improves target boundary detection using pixel-based methods together with interaction traces. Chang *et al.* [7] explored several synergies in PAX, including use of Sikuli to obtain paths to elements in the accessibility API, pixel-level analyses to locate screen text, and the use of Sikuli to find elements in portions of the screen where the accessibility API's representation is incomplete. Neither system developed methods capable of supporting the real-time demands of an interactive Bubble Cursor. More importantly, the current paper highlights that even complete *identification* of interface elements does not provide the *interpretation* required to enable target-aware pointing.

Dixon and Fogarty [11] present a rudimentary demonstration of target-aware pointing in their original Prefab research. Although they use pixel-based identification to target a handful of elements, they never examine the challenges of applying these techniques beyond the scope of simple, isolated interfaces. For example, they assume all necessary examples of interface elements have already been provided to Prefab, and they do not discuss the ambiguities of targeting in real-world interfaces. The current work is unique in its deep application of Prefab to a general-purpose Bubble Cursor. In addition to our direct contributions to this first deep implementation of general-purpose target-aware pointing, we also present the first tools for interactive correction and extension of Prefab's identification of interface elements. Our methods for interpretation of identified elements are also a clear advance over earlier Prefab research.

We draw inspiration from extensive interface customization research, including integration of sharing and other social mechanisms. Most of this research is limited to the web, where the DOM provides a model of interface elements. Classic examples are ChickenFoot [2] and CoScripter [29], and systems like Highlight [31] extend these ideas to task-centric re-authoring for mobile devices. Clip, Connect, Clone [17], d.mix [20], and Vegemite [28] demonstrate end-user mash-up methods. In the desktop context, Chapuis and Roussel's [9] UIMarks allow creation of macros invoked by targeting special marks within an interface. Tagaki *et al.* [38] develop social annotation methods for improving web content accessibility. Hurst *et al.*'s [23] use of click history also suggests a role for sharing that history.

A REAL-WORLD BUBBLE CURSOR

Among the variety of target-aware pointing techniques, we implement the Bubble Cursor for several reasons: (1) we believe it is the fastest general technique in the literature, (2) it can be implemented as an overlay, without modifying targeted elements, and (3) it is exemplary of the family of target-aware techniques, so the methods we develop should have broader relevance. Our discussion revisits this, emphasizing our work as a starting point for the real-world design and deployment of target-aware techniques.

Our methods are inherently *human-driven*, in that we focus on allowing people to improve targeting by interactively correcting erroneous behavior. We also expect any broad deployment will be *social*, with people sharing interactive corrections and receiving updates based on the corrections of others. Interfaces are procedurally generated, so their pixel-level appearance rarely changes. Familiar interfaces will therefore be thoroughly annotated and appear to "just work". But interactive correction will remain important, both to ensure individuals can correct private, niche, or unpopular interfaces and to allow communities to quickly annotate newly-released interfaces.

This section presents the primary technical components of our system: (1) *identification* of elements using Prefab's pixel-based methods, (2) *interpretation* of those elements via interactive and automatic annotation, and (3) *targeting* according to those annotations. We then briefly comment on details of our current Windows 7 implementation. This section focuses on responsibilities of each component and how they combine to enable a deployable Bubble Cursor. The next section then considers inevitable errors in such a system and introduces interfaces for interactively correcting those errors in terms of these underlying components.

Identifying Interface Elements

We identify interface elements using Prefab's pixel-based methods for reverse engineering interface structure [11,12]. Prefab's methods are a strong fit for several reasons, but the most important is they can be *corrected* and *extended* by providing additional examples of interface elements. This sharply contrasts accessibility APIs, where there is generally no recourse if an element is not correctly exposed. To enable our human-driven approach, we develop the first interactive tools for providing Prefab with examples at runtime.

More specifically, Prefab identifies interface elements via a library of *prototypes*. A prototype describes an arrangement of pixels, and each is learned from example images. Prefab uses two high-level strategies to identify interface elements: (1) exactly matching prototype pixels against an image, or (2) modeling prototype background and differencing pixels in an image to identify foreground interface elements. Prefab realizes these high-level strategies by varying how it generalizes from example images according to *models* of the *parts* of interface elements. Parts can be *features* (exact patches of pixels) or *regions* (methods for painting areas of variable size, such as gradients or repeating patterns). Figure 3 illustrates three prototypes selected to show a range of complexity in their underlying models.

The simplest are *exact-match* prototypes, which consist of a single feature exactly matching the pixels of an example. These do not generalize, but many interface elements also do not vary in appearance (e.g., checkboxes, icons, radio buttons). For example, the left prototype in Figure 3 identifies all unchecked Windows 7 Steel checkboxes.

A more complex *slider* prototype uses multiple parts to account for the variable length of the slider trough and the variable position of the thumb. Five parts characterize the appearance of the slider's thumb, the left and right ends of the trough, and a repeating trough pattern on either side of the thumb. The middle prototype in Figure 3 was generalized from the single illustrated example and identifies all occurrences of the standard Mac OS X slider. Prefab performs this generalization by searching for an assignment of pixels from the example to parts in the model minimizing the number of pixels in the resulting prototype. If multiple examples are provided, Prefab searches for the minimal prototype consistent with all examples. Additional discussion of this search is available elsewhere [11,12].

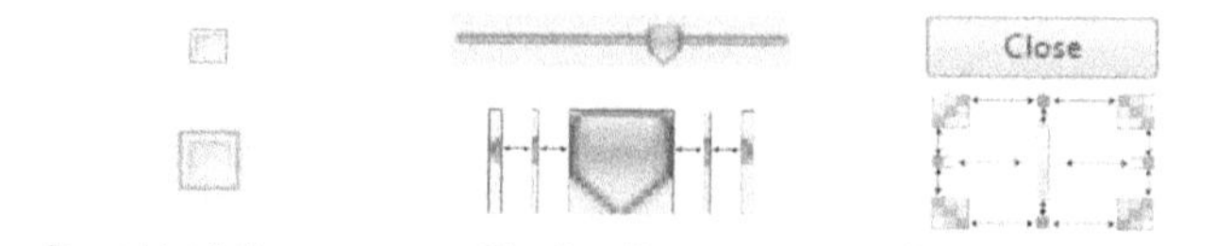

Exact-Match Prototype Windows 7 Checkbox — *Five-Part Prototype Mac OS X Slider* — *Nine-Part Prototype Windows 7 Steel Button*

Figure 3: Prefab uses examples of interface elements to generalize prototypes of the appearance of families of widgets.

A *nine-part* prototype adds the ability to model background and use runtime pixel differencing to identify unpredictable foreground elements. For example, the prototype at the right of Figure 3 identifies all Windows 7 steel buttons and any text or icons painted over their gradient background. It was generalized from the single illustrated example button. Nine-part prototypes are first identified by matching their four corners and four edges, similar to matching the five parts of a slider. Prefab then uses the interior *content region* to identify elements painted over the interior background. Additional discussion of content regions, including how Prefab generalizes a background from example images that include foreground elements, is available elsewhere [12].

Differencing the pixels between content regions and their backgrounds allows Prefab to identify elements that are not in its prototype library. For example, a nine-part prototype of a tab pane can allow identification of all elements within that pane (e.g., buttons, icons, text). If Prefab lacks prototypes for these elements, it can still identify them as connected sets of foreground pixels, represent them as children of the tab pane, and thus make them available for interpretation as potential targets.

Prefab generalizes the idea of containment within a content region by organizing the entire interface into a hierarchy. The root corresponds to the processed image, and identified elements are added as children to any element in which they are spatially contained. This *spatial hierarchy* is not strictly the same as an interface's logical hierarchy, but represents visible containment (e.g., buttons, group boxes, tab panes). The next subsection uses the hierarchy to robustly annotate identified interface elements with targeting information.

Interpreting Interface Elements

The above subsection described how Prefab identifies a hierarchy of elements, but any hierarchy is by itself insufficient for targeting. Even complete compliance with a typical accessibility API does not enable an effective Bubble Cursor. This is ultimately due to mismatches between available metadata and the needs of an external enhancement. Framework and application developers cannot foresee all potential external enhancements, so they cannot provide all relevant metadata. For example, current accessibility APIs are designed to provide access to the underlying data in each widget (i.e., the widget *model*). They therefore expose the value to which a slider is set, but not the screen location of the thumb (precluding targeting of that thumb). General targeting behavior is undefined for other elements (e.g., calendars, paint canvases, text fields), and will vary among techniques. We believe this mismatch between available metadata and the needs of enhancements is inherent, requiring a human-driven approach.

We therefore interactively *annotate* which elements of an interface hierarchy should be targeted by a Bubble Cursor. Any node can be marked as a *target*, can implicitly not be targeted due to other targets in the hierarchy, or can be explicitly marked *not a target*. We store annotations using an XPath-like path descriptor based on properties of an element, its location in the hierarchy, and properties of its ancestors. A library of annotations therefore consists of path descriptors with associated metadata. Annotations can be quickly retrieved for an element, and entire libraries can be stored, combined, and shared to enable social annotation.

A path descriptor needs to identify a *specific* element in a *specific* interface while being robust to changes in element size or position. The root of a hierarchy corresponds to the entire image processed by Prefab, so the root needs to include how an image was captured. We currently set root attributes for the application executable name and top-level window class. If this became insufficient, additional root attributes could be added for problematic applications (e.g., including the URL for images captured within web browsers). The remainder of the descriptor is based upon the unique identifier for each prototype along the path from the root to the annotated element. Elements identified via background differencing do not have a prototype, so we use a content attribute based on a hash of their pixels (which allows differentiation among sibling content elements). Finally, we use an index for otherwise identical descriptors.

Direct manual annotation likely can be sufficient in a broad deployment leveraging social mechanisms, but also can be expedited by even minimal inference. We currently employ two simple mechanisms. The first assumes every leaf is a target. This heuristic yields good behavior for many widgets (e.g., checkboxes, radio buttons). The second generalizes annotations of inner nodes to other nodes with identical subtrees. Scrollbars provide one example of this, as their thumbs vary in size and usually contain a knurling graphic. A nine-part model represents the thumb as a node with a single child (i.e., the knurling). Preferred behavior is to target the entire thumb, and annotation of one scrollbar can then generalize over other occurrences of that scrollbar. Arbitrarily sophisticated inference could identify likely targets, and our XPath-like descriptors suggest relevance of the deep literature on wrapper induction [27]. But any inference mechanism will sometimes fail, so we see these techniques as a powerful complement to human annotation.

Choosing a Target

We choose a target for the Bubble Cursor in a pre-order traversal of the hierarchy of the window nearest the pointer. We consider each *target* node to determine which is closest to the pointer, defining distance to be zero if the pointer is within a target. Recursion ends at target nodes, because the spatial containment represented by the hierarchy means any children will be further from the pointer. Recursion can therefore also end at non-target nodes that are further than the current best. Some arrangements require considering the possibility the nearest target is not in the nearest window, but other windows are typically ignored because their root is further from the pointer than the current best target.

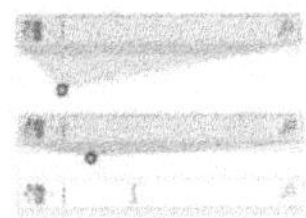

Our design for real-world interfaces also required subtle refinement of the Bubble Cursor. One important refinement is our degradation into the standard point cursor whenever within a target (illustrated here with a storyboard of the cursor approaching a textbox). On one hand, this is aesthetically simpler than crosshairs used to illustrate the center of the original Bubble Cursor with abstract targets [18]. But it is also important because it creates a *graceful degradation* in the face of unknown interface elements or ambiguous targets. If Prefab fails to interpret the pixels in a portion of an interface, or if the appropriate targeting behavior is genuinely ambiguous (e.g., as with a text field), then normal point cursor behavior is automatically restored in that region without requiring a hotkey or other modifier. Pointing can therefore be improved in many interactions without necessarily being penalized in others. We believe such *conservative* strategies are promising for the design of deployable external interface enhancements.

The cursor must also be capable of *dragging* targets while moving or sizing elements (e.g., scrollbars, sliders, windows). Dragging is implicitly supported by our conservative strategy, as moving into a target allows use of the point cursor to drag the target. We also enable dragging from outside a target. When the drag is initiated, the Bubble Cursor latches onto the target. Subsequent movement drags the target, and mouse release resumes standard targeting behavior. We currently do not use knowledge of potential drop targets during the drag, but could imagine strategies for target-aware drops.

Implementation Details

This section has focused on novel methods and strategies in our system, as these can be applied and extended in future research on target-aware pointing or external enhancement of existing interfaces. For completeness, we briefly discuss relevant details of our current Windows 7 implementation.

At the start of each cycle, we query the Windows 7 Desktop Window Manager for the bounding box, application executable path, class name, and z-order for each visible top-level window. We construct a hierarchy with the desktop at the root and top-level windows as children, and we then capture pixels for the window closest to the pointer. If two windows are at the same distance (typically due to overlap), we choose the front. As a performance optimization, we ignore entire windows that are marked as non-targetable (e.g., visible but non-interactive windows). We also infer target annotations during traversal, and only when there is no existing human annotation (i.e., our inferred annotations are lazily evaluated).

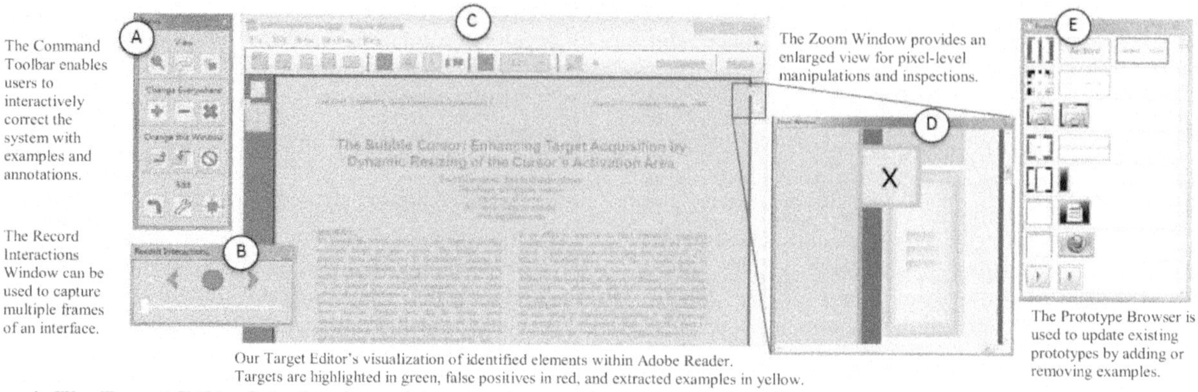

Figure 4: The Target Editor interface is used to extract examples, create and update prototypes, and manipulate annotations.

We render our Bubble Cursor as a translucent window, and update its z-order to render above the targeted window. We redirect input using a low-level hook to intercept mouse events and update the center of our Bubble Cursor instead of the system pointer. We use each mouse event to move the center of our Bubble Cursor, and we clip the system cursor to the center of our targeted element. If the target is partially occluded by another window, we clip to the center of a visible region (and adjust the size of our overlay).

Our associated video was captured on a typical laptop. Prefab is mostly single-threaded and unoptimized, but still processes an interface every 100 msec. Many optimizations described in [11,12] could improve performance, however our video shows the cursor is responsive and we have not found performance to be a concern.

INTERACTIVE TARGETING CORRECTION

We previously noted that many familiar interfaces will seem to "just work", but that interactive correction remains important to our approach. We identified six requirements for correcting target identification and interpretation:

- *Invoking Correction:* A person must be able to access an interface to correct erroneous targeting behavior.
- *Capturing an Interface:* Errors are caused by incorrect identification or interpretation of elements in images of an interface, so a person must be able to capture images that illustrate the failure condition.
- *Visualizing Identification and Interpretation:* A person must be able to understand what error occurred so that they can determine how it should be corrected.
- *Extracting Examples:* A person must be able to extract examples of the elements of an interface that should be identified by our pixel-based methods.
- *Creating Prototypes:* A person must be able to use extracted examples to create appropriate prototypes that can then be identified at runtime.
- *Authoring Annotations:* A person must be able to annotate desired targeting of an interface hierarchy.

These requirements imply a large design space. Because we focus on the first deep implementation of a general-purpose target-aware technique, we explore two initial points in the design space. The first is a full-featured design, called the *Target Editor*. The second is a lightweight interface for in-context annotation, called the *Annotation Menu*.

Correcting Behavior with the Target Editor

Figure 4 presents screenshots of the Target Editor. Its major components include the *window image*, colored *highlights* of identified elements, and the *command toolbar*.

Invoking Correction. The editor is always accessible via a system tray icon and a keyboard shortcut. When a person encounters erroneous targeting, they invoke the editor and then click a window on the desktop to "edit" that window.

Capturing an Interface. Selecting a window as part of invoking the editor triggers capture of an image of that window. The image is processed to identify and interpret interface elements, then displayed in the editor.

Some errors only occur during interaction with a *dynamic* interface, so a captured static image may be insufficient. For example, the blinking text cursor in a textbox can lead to erroneous targeting. When present, it is identified as a leaf and targeted. When absent, the textbox itself becomes a leaf and is targeted. The result is a Bubble Cursor that jumps between the blinking caret and the larger textbox. To determine why this occurs, a person may need to inspect multiple images captured at different times.

The editor addresses this need with a "Record Interactions" tool to capture videos of interaction. A record button starts and stops recording, a slider supports skimming captured video, and buttons advance individual frames. The blinking text cursor behavior is fixed by annotating the textbox as a target, thereby overriding the inferred targeting of the text cursor leaf.

Visualizing Identification and Interpretation. Translucent highlights visualize system identification and interpretation of interface elements. Green highlights are placed over elements that will be targeted (i.e., the first *target* node encountered on every path from the root, whether inferred or annotated). Red highlights are placed over elements explicitly annotated as *not a target*. Identification is thus encoded via the presence of a highlight, while interpretation is illustrated via color. Interactive selection is illustrated via a border, and elements can be manipulated individually or in batch using multiple selections with the toolbar.

Extracting Examples. Prefab often builds a good prototype from just a single example of an interface element. But it can also under-generalize, requiring additional positive examples to broaden its concept, or over-generalize, requiring negative examples to narrow its concept.

For example, this YouTube movie control causes Prefab to overgeneralize because its widgets are painted to share vertical edges. A single example creates a prototype that over-generalizes by identifying every group of k adjacent widgets (creating duplicate leaves and inner nodes that do not describe any true element). Providing any of these false detections as a negative example will correct the prototype, resulting in a prototype that detects the combination of the single-pixel edge and the adjacent interior pixel.

Examples can be specified by rubber-banding a yellow highlight. Each highlight can be moved, resized, or deleted. Because pixel-level selection can be tedious and error-prone, the editor provides "Zoom" and "Snap" tools.

"Zoom" opens an enlarged view of the image and highlights. The enlarged view receives input, so it supports pixel-level adjustment of highlights. As a shortcut, double-clicking in the image or on any highlight also opens the "Zoom" tool with its view centered at the double-click point.

"Snap" resizes highlights to tightly fit interface elements. Informed by a heuristic from the original Prefab work [11], it starts from the center of a highlight and uses gradient thresholds to search for possible bounding rectangles. Among the heuristically-identified rectangles, it chooses the one closest in size to the drawn highlight. This does not always snap exactly to interface elements, but is helpful for expediting extraction. When it fails, it usually snaps close to the desired size and can then be adjusted using "Zoom".

Two categories of examples can be automatically extracted: (1) positive examples of elements already identified by background differencing within a parent's content region, and (2) any negative examples. In both cases, Prefab has already identified the bounds of the element. There is no need to manipulate the highlight, so a person instead just adds the extracted element to a new or existing prototype.

Creating Prototypes. A new prototype is created using the "Add" tool. A dropdown menu allows model selection (e.g., the exact-match, five-part, and nine-part models discussed previously). For each selected highlight, the editor creates a new prototype from the highlighted positive example. Automated creation of the prototype from the example takes a few seconds, after which the user can immediately see the impact of the new prototype on identification and interpretation within the interface.

Existing prototypes are updated with additional negative examples using the "Mark Incorrect" tool. Note that the editor already knows which prototype should be updated: the prototype that falsely identified the example.

Updating existing prototypes with additional positive examples requires the selection of the prototype to receive the new example. The "Prototype Browser" visualizes the prototypes in the current library, together with the positive and negative example images used to create each prototype. A person selects an existing prototype, then uses "Add" to provide it with additional examples.

Bad examples or entire prototypes can be deleted via the "Prototype Browser". Bad prototypes can also be deleted directly in the editor by selecting a highlight and clicking the "Remove" tool. This removes the prototype that identified the highlight, and it is helpful for quickly deleting prototypes accidentally created from bad examples.

Authoring Annotations. Three tools are used together for annotation of the desired interpretation of targets.

The "Look Bigger" tool annotates the *parent* of a selected element as a *target*. The Bubble Cursor then targets that parent, thus no longer targeting the element. For example, this can be used to target a button instead of its text, a canvas instead of its content, or an entire window instead of any interior icons. The tool does not modify any annotations of the selected element or its children. Such annotations have no effect, as our Bubble Cursor targets downward from the root. Leaving them intact allows "undo" via "Look Smaller".

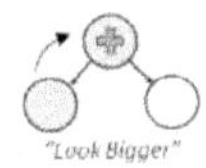

The "Look Smaller" tool annotates a selected element as *not a target*, which will cause the Bubble Cursor to consider its descendants as possible targets. Because we heuristically infer leaf elements to be targets, this is typically used to undo the "Look Bigger" tool. But it can also correct inferred targeting of inner elements and would likely see more use together with more extensive inference of targets.

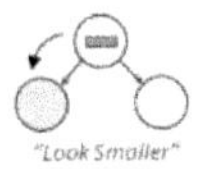

The "Not a Target" tool annotates a selected element and all descendants as *not a target*. This is used to ignore an entire subtree of non-targetable elements, such as labels or disabled buttons.

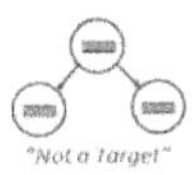

Lightweight Targeting with the Annotation Menu

The Annotation Menu examines a design that is less capable than the Target Editor, but can also be used without leaving the context of an interaction. Figure 5 storyboards the menu, which is embedded in the Bubble Cursor and *invoked* after a dwell of the pointer within a target.

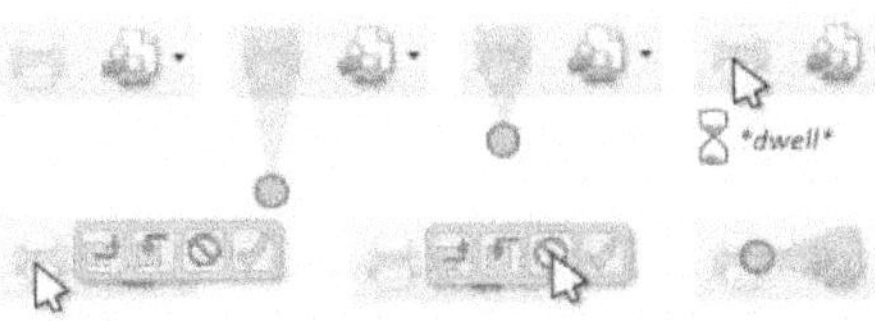

Figure 5: A storyboard of the Annotation Menu. It appears when the center of the Bubble Cursor dwells on a target.

Interface *capture* and *visualization* are implicit, as the Bubble Cursor itself conveys the current identification and interpretation. Editing is limited to *authoring annotations* using the same "Look Bigger," "Look Smaller," and "Not a Target" functionality from the editor. Each tool makes its edits to the annotations, closes the menu, and updates the Bubble Cursor to target the new nearest target.

The menu also provides a "Confirm" tool. When clicked, it applies a *confirmed* annotation to the selected interface element. The Annotation Menu then does not invoke itself upon dwell over *confirmed* elements.

Discussion of Interface Design

Figure 6 recaps our two designs in the context of our six requirements. They take different approaches to correction, but both are helpful and suggest additional possibilities. For example, we use simple visualizations of the identification and interpretation of elements, but other tree visualizations could be considered. Our *confirmed* annotation was developed for the Annotation Menu, but it would be a sensible addition to the Target Editor. Rapid batch confirmation of targeting would then prevent the Annotation Menu from appearing in interfaces that are already known to be correct. Greater collection of explicit confirmations would also provide additional data for use in training learning systems to automatically infer targets.

Our requirements and designs also suggest opportunities for fundamentally different approaches. Image *capture* might be automated through passive observation of interface use (e.g., as in Hurst *et al.*'s prior work [22]), with an interface *invoked* later to review targeting corrections inferred from the observed usage. Instead of focusing on the current interface, a design might focus on *creating prototypes*. Such a design could be organized around review, creation, and modification of prototypes and could retrieve images of specific interfaces from a large usage history to illustrate the targeting that results from the current prototype library. A crowdsourcing interface might focus on local *invocation* and *capture*, with other requirements addressed by remote workers. Because our designs require an understanding of pixel-based methods, other designs might explore a range of required *expertise*. Our initial focus has demonstrated effective interfaces, but a variety of additional approaches can be developed upon our underlying technology.

EXAMINING BEHAVIOR IN REAL-WORLD INTERFACES

The Bubble Cursor and other target-aware techniques are often designed, discussed, and evaluated using fields of abstract targets and distractors. Because our implementation provides a unique ability to deploy such techniques, we sought to examine what new insights we could gain from examining the Bubble Cursor in real-world interfaces. We identified and annotated elements in a variety of interfaces, including Microsoft Office applications, Mozilla Firefox, Adobe Reader, instant message clients, several web pages, and the file browser. We studied a total of 31 applications, creating a library of 754 prototypes and 714 annotations.

Requirement	Target Editor	Annotation Menu
Invoking	System Tray Keyboard Shortcut	Dwell
Capturing	Static Frame on Launch Record Interactions Tool	Implicit
Visualizing	Colored Highlights of Elements	Implicit
Extracting	Rubber-Band Zoom Snap Automatic via Prefab	N/A
Creating	Add / Remove / Mark Incorrect Model Selection Prototype Browser	N/A
Authoring	Look Bigger Look Smaller Not a Target	Look Bigger Look Smaller Not a Target Confirm

Figure 6: Our interfaces highlight two initial points in the design space of correctional interfaces for our system.

Our findings with real-world interfaces include insights into two important challenges: (1) the limitations of pointer proximity as a proxy for user intent within an interface, and (2) conflicts between target-aware behavior and the intentional design of interfaces for typical point cursors.

Pointer Proximity and User Intent

The Bubble Cursor and other target-aware techniques use pointer proximity as a proxy for user intent to manipulate interface elements. It is understood to be an imperfect proxy (hence the notion of distractors), but examining behavior in real-world interfaces gives new insight into limitations.

One example we found is that a person may expect similar elements to have similar targeting behavior. Rows of elements provide a good example, as the arrangement suggests each item is equally relevant. But placement of a menu bar next to a toolbar can create different effective targets for otherwise similar elements. The Voronoi overlay shows "Page Up" is more difficult to target than "Page Down", and "Help" behaves differently than the other menu items. The behavior is correct, but can be jarring.

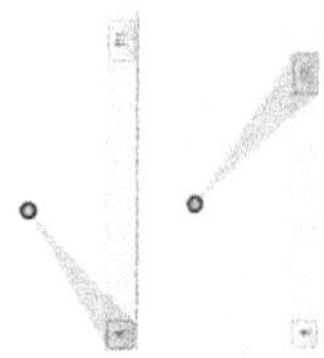

The dynamics of real-world interfaces also expose gaps between pointer location and user intent. Consider using a Bubble Cursor to click a scrollbar arrow. A person's intended focus is likely to remain upon the arrow after a click, but the movement of the scrollbar toward the cursor may now mean the thumb is the nearest target. Latching onto the thumb is the correct behavior for the Bubble Cursor, but it may be unexpected.

A third case emerges when interfaces act upon a notion of user intent that competes with the Bubble Cursor. For example, the Windows 7 taskbar contains a row of buttons for accessing windows of open applications. A hover over any opens a preview. Approaching the taskbar with the Bubble Cursor results in the cursor snapping to a button, invoking the preview, and then snapping to the preview. This is helpful if the desired window is captured, as clicking will activate the window. But if an adjacent taskbar button was desired in the first place, then the benefits of the Bubble Cursor are destroyed by snapping to the preview.

Conflicts Due to Intentional Design for a Point Cursor

Modern interfaces are carefully and intentionally designed for use with a typical point cursor. This section presents examples where the Bubble Cursor conflicts with that design, together with initial thoughts on how such conflicts could be resolved through extensions to our system.

Designers often use small elements for minor or infrequently-accessed functionality. The Bubble Cursor can greatly distort the importance of such minor elements. For example, the Windows 7 file browser includes several minor icons beneath its search box. These eclipse targeting of the search box itself when approaching from below, which is the typical direction of approach. Selection of the search box is therefore more difficult than intended. Extending the methods in this work, it is interesting to consider a *look past* annotation. This might indicate an element should be targeted only if the pointer is directly overhead. The Bubble Cursor could then look past these elements to allow easy targeting of the search box, but would still latch onto minor elements when the pointer was directly overhead. This seems preferable to a hotkey or some other method for disengaging the Bubble Cursor.

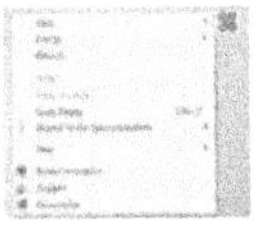

Another example is the design of typical context menus, which are dismissed by clicking in non-interactive space. Such a design is incompatible with a technique like the Bubble Cursor that always targets the nearest interactive element. This problem motivated creation of DynaSpot [8], which adjusts the maximum reach of a Bubble Cursor based on pointer speed. Examining this in the context of our system suggests additional strategies. For example, a *dismissable* annotation might overlay a close icon at the upper-right of an element. Upon selection, the system could use its identification and interpretation of the surrounding interface to click in non-interactive space.

A third example is the scrollbar. As pictured elsewhere, it is easy to imagine the utility of a Bubble Cursor attached to a scrollbar thumb. But the trough is also interactive, meaning the thumb can only be grabbed from a narrow horizontal channel. In our own use, we therefore annotate the trough as *not a target*. This allows easy capture of the thumb, but also prevents targeting the trough. It is interesting to realize that the same *look past* annotation discussed above would remove the need for this tradeoff (i.e., latching onto the thumb from outside, but targeting the trough from within). This also suggests a more general distinction between "major" versus "minor" targets, a theoretical perspective that can inform the design of future techniques. Such future techniques could be evaluated with a combination of laboratory studies and insights gained from examination in real interfaces using the methods we have developed here.

DISCUSSION AND CONCLUSION

Although we describe our approach to implementing a Bubble Cursor, we also provide a general strategy for implementing additional interface enhancements. Our separation of identification from interpretation, together with our approaches to each, can enable and inform a variety of future enhancements. For example, Prefab prototypes interactively created with our Bubble Cursor can be shared and re-used with any Prefab-based application. Similarly, our Bubble Cursor can benefit from Prefab prototypes created in other applications. At the interpretation level, target-aware enhancements may be able to directly share and re-use annotations (e.g., the notion of a *target* for Sticky Icons [42] may be the same as a *target* with our Bubble Cursor). Other techniques may have different interpretations of targets based on additional annotations, perhaps bootstrapped through inference based upon annotations collected with our Bubble Cursor or some other technique. Finally, our strategies also apply to non-pointing enhancements. For example, Findlater *et al.*'s [16] Ephemeral Adaptation could be implemented using analyses of interaction history together with explicit annotation of element groupings and other preferences.

This work is the most extensive application of Prefab's pixel-based methods to date. Our experiences validate Prefab's methods, but also suggest opportunities to advance pixel-based systems. For example, we found that Prefab would benefit from additional sophisticated models of the pixel-level appearance of complex elements (e.g., it could not deeply model complex text panes found in Microsoft Visual Studio 2010). We also sometimes found it tedious to create multiple prototypes for different appearances of the same interface element (e.g., multiple states of a button, checkbox, or radio button). Pixel-based methods could therefore benefit from additional modeling of the dynamics of interface elements. Our work has also not addressed the case where changes to a prototype might orphan existing annotations (i.e., might change the descriptor needed to retrieve existing annotations). We previously noted that wrapper induction techniques may help to infer descriptors that are robust to change [27], and we also believe we could explicitly migrate annotations between hierarchies obtained with different prototype libraries (e.g., by checking that they refer to the same spatial region in the captured image). Overall, we believe that deep applications like that pursued in this paper have a unique potential to inform future development of underlying pixel-based methods. Building out this application has also given us a better understanding of effective and sustainable abstractions for developing with Prefab, and we are currently exploring the best way to make this functionality available.

Looking forward, we believe the methods and findings of this work suggest future research opportunities in both interaction techniques and underlying systems. Our hope is to help more interaction research in escaping the laboratory, putting it into the hands of end-users who stand to benefit from the field's rich innovation.

ACKNOWLEDGMENTS

We thank Jon Froehlich and Shaun Kane for discussions related to this work. This work was supported in part by the NSF under awards IIS-1053868 and IIS-0811063, by Intel, and by the UW College of Engineering Osberg Fellowship.

REFERENCES

1. Ahlström, D., Hitz, M. and Leitner, G. An Evaluation of Sticky and Force Enhanced Targets in Multi Target Situations. *NordiCHI 2006*. 58-67.
2. Bolin, M., Webber, M., Rha, P., Wilson, T., and Miller, R.C. Automation and Customization of Rendered Web Pages. *UIST 2005*. 163-172.
3. Baudisch, P., Cutrell, E., Robbins, D., Czerwinski, M., Tandler, P., Bederson, B. and Zierlinger, A. Drag-and-Pop and Drag-and-Pick: Techniques for Accessing Remote Screen Content on Touch- and Pen-Operated Systems. *INTERACT 2003*. 57-64.
4. Baudisch, P., Cutrell, E., Hinckley, K. and Gruen, R. Mouse Ether: Accelerating the Acquisition of Targets Across Multi-Monitor Displays. *CHI 2004*. Extended Abstracts. 1379-1382.
5. Blanch, R., Guiard, Y. and Beaudouin-Lafon, M. Semantic Pointing: Improving Target Acquisition with Control-Display Ratio Adaptation. *CHI 2004*. 519-526.
6. Casiez, G., Vogel, D., Balakrishnan, R. and Cockburn, A. The Impact of Control-Display Gain on User Performance in Pointing Tasks. *Human-Computer Interaction 23 (3)*. 215-250.
7. Chang, T., Yeh, T., and Miller, M. Associating the Visual Representation of User Interfaces with their Internal Structures and Metadata. *UIST 2011*. 245-256.
8. Chapuis, O. Labrune, J., and and Pietriga, E. DynaSpot: Speed-Dependent Area Cursor. *CHI 2009*. 1391-1400.
9. Chapuis, O. and Roussel, N. UIMarks: Quick Graphical Interaction with Specific Targets. *UIST 2010*. 173-182.
10. Cockburn, A. and Firth, A. Improving the Acquisition of Small Targets. *HCI 2003*. 181-196.
11. Dixon, M. and Fogarty, J. Prefab: Implementing Advanced Behaviors Using Pixel-Based Reverse Engineering of Interface Structure. *CHI 2010*. 1525-1534.
12. Dixon, M., Leventhal, D., and Fogarty, J. Content and Hierarchy in Pixel-Based Methods for Reverse Engineering Interface Structure. *CHI 2011*. 969-978.
13. Edwards, W.K., Hudson, S.E., Marinacci, J., Rodenstein, R., Rodriguez, T. and Smith, I. Systematic Output Modification in a 2D User Interface Toolkit. *UIST 1997*. 151-158.
14. Eagan, J.R., Mackay, W.E., and Beaudouin-Lafon, M. Cracking the Cocoa Nut: User Interface Programming at Runtime. *UIST 2011*. 225-234.
15. Findlater, L., Jansen, A., Shinohara, K., Dixon, M., Kamb, P., Rakita, J., and Wobbrock, J.O. Enhanced Area Cursors: Reducing Fine Pointing Demands for People with Motor Impairments. *UIST 2010*. 153-162.
16. Findlater, L., Moffatt, K., McGrenere, J. and Dawson, J. Ephemeral Adaptation: The Use of Gradual Onset to Improve Menu Selection Performance. *CHI 2009*. 1655-1664.
17. Fujima, J., Lunzer, A., Hornbæk, K. and Tanaka, Y. Clip, Connect, Clone: Combining Applications Elements to Build Custom Interfaces for Information Access. *UIST 2004*. 175-184.
18. Grossman, T. and Balakrishnan, R. The Bubble Cursor: Enhancing Target Acquisition by Dynamic Resizing of the Cursor's Activation Area. *CHI 2005*. 281-290.
19. Guiard, Y., Blanch, R. and Beaudouin-Lafon, M. Object Pointing: A Complement to Bitmap Pointing in GUIs. *GI 2004*. 9-16.
20. Hartmann, B., Wu, L., Collins, K. and Klemmer, S.R. Programming by a Sample: Rapidly Creating Web Applications with d.Mix. *UIST 2007*. 241-250.
21. Hourcade, J.P., Perry, K.B. and Sharma, A. PointAssist: Helping Four Year Olds Point with Ease. *IDC 2008*. 202-209.
22. Hurst, A., Hudson, S.E. and Mankoff, J. Automatically Identifying Targets Users Interact with During Real World Tasks. *IUI 2010*. 11-20.
23. Hurst, A., Mankoff, J., Dey, A.K. and Hudson, S.E. Dirty Desktops: Using a Patina of Magnetic Mouse Dust to Make Common Interactor Targets Easier to Select. *UIST 2007*. 183-186.
24. Hwang, F., Keates, S., Langdon, P. and Clarkson, P.J. Multiple Haptic Targets for Motion-Impaired Computer Users. *CHI 2003*. 41-48.
25. Jansen, A., Findlater, L. and Wobbrock, J.O. From the Lab to the World: Lessons from Extending a Pointing Technique for Real-World Use. *CHI 2011*. Extended Abstracts. 1867-1872.
26. Kabbash, P. and Buxton, W. The "Prince" Technique: Fitts' Law and Selection Using Area Cursors. *CHI 1995*. 273-279.
27. Kushmerick, N., Weld, D.S, and Doorenbos, R. Wrapper Induction for Information Extraction. *IJCAI 1997*.
28. Lin, J., Wong, J., Nichols, J., Cypher, A. and Lau, T.A. End-User Programming of Mashups with Vegemite. *IUI 2009*. 97-106.
29. Little, G., Lau, T.A., Cypher, A., Lin, J., Haber, E.M. and Kandogan, E. Koala: Capture, Share, Automate, Personalize Business Processes on the Web. *CHI 2007*. 943-946.
30. McGuffin, M. and Balakrishnan, R. Acquisition of Expanding Targets. *CHI 2002*. 57-64.
31. Nichols, J. and Lau, T.A. Mobilizing by Demonstration: Using Traces to Re-Author Existing Web Sites. *IUI 2008*. 149-158.
32. Olsen, D.R., Hudson, S.E., Verratti, T., Heiner, J.M. and Phelps, M. Implementing Interface Attachments Based on Surface Representations. *CHI 1999*. 191-198.
33. Olsen, D.R., Taufer, T. and Fails, J.A. ScreenCrayons: Annotating Anything. *UIST 2004*. 165-174.
34. Potter, R. Triggers: Guiding Automaton with Pixel to Achieve Data Access. A. Cypher, eds. *MIT Press*.
35. St. Amant, R., Lieberman, H., Potter, R. and Zettlemoyer, L.S. Visual Generalization in Programming by Example. *Communications of the ACM 43(3)*. 107-114.
36. St. Amant, R., Riedl, M.O., Ritter, F.E. and Reifers, A. Image Processing in Cognitive Models with SegMan. *HCII 2005*.
37. Stuerzlinger, W., Chapuis, O., Phillips, D. and Roussel, N. User Interface Façades: Towards Fully Adaptable User Interfaces. *UIST 2006*. 309-318.
38. Takagi, H., Kawanaka, S., Kobayashi, M., Itoh, T., and Asakawa, C. Social Accessibility: Achieving Accessibility through Collaborative Metadata Authoring. *Assets 2008*. 193-200.
39. Tan, D.S., Meyers, B.R. and Czerwinski, M. Manipulating Arbitrary Window Regions for More Effective Use of Screen Space. *CHI 2004*. 1525-1528.
40. Yeh, T., Chang, T.-H. and Miller, R.C. Sikuli: Using GUI Screenshots for Search and Automation. *UIST 2009*. 183-192.
41. Wobbrock, J.O., Fogarty, J., Liu, S., Kimuro, S., and Harada, S. The Angle Mouse: Target-Agnostic Dynamic Gain Adjustment Based on Angular Deviation. *CHI 2009*. 1401-1410.
42. Worden, A., Walker, N., Bharat, K. and Hudson, S.E. Making Computers Easier for Older Adults to Use: Area cursors and Sticky Icons. *CHI 1997*. 266-271.
43. Zellweger, P.T., Bouvin, N.O., Jehøj, H., and Mackinlay, J.D. Fluid Annotations in an Open World. *Hypertext 2001*. 9-18.
44. Zhai, S., Morimoto, C. and Ihde, S. Manual and Gaze Input Cascaded (MAGIC) Pointing. *CHI 1999*. 246-253.
45. Zettlemoyer, L.S. and St. Amant, R. A Visual Medium for Programmatic Control of Interactive Applications. *CHI 1999*. 199-206.
46. Zettlemoyer, L.S., St. Amant, R. and Dulberg, M.S. IBOTS: Agent Control Through the User Interface. *IUI 1998*. 31-37.

Assisting Hand Skill Transfer of Tracheal Intubation Using Outer-Covering Haptic Display

Vibol Yem[1], Hideaki Kuzuoka[1], Naomi Yamashita[2], Hiroaki Yano[1], Ryota Shibusawa[1], Jun Yamashita[1]

[1] University of Tsukuba
Tsukuba, Ibaraki, Japan
{e0813116@edu.esys, kuzuoka@iit, yano@iit, r_shibusawa@edu, jun@iit}.tsukuba.ac.jp

[2] NTT Communication Science Laboratories
Kyoto, Japan.
naomiy@acm.org

ABSTRACT
Various systems for hand tool skill training have been developed in the domain of haptic displays. These systems typically present force to a learner's palm by directly actuating the tool. However, this approach is sometimes ineffective because learners have difficulty sensing the haptic feedback from the tool when they are holding it tightly. Thus, we propose a different approach (OCHD) that effectively guides the learner's hand by presenting force to the back of his/her hand as if an instructor is holding it. A preliminary experiment showed that OCHD effectively guides users with less actuator drive force than cases where the tool is directly actuated.

Author Keywords
Haptic display; tracheal intubation; hand skill training.

ACM Classification Keywords
H.5.2 [Information interfaces and presentation]: User Interfaces-Haptic I/O.

General Terms
Human Factors; Experimentation.

INTRODUCTION
Tracheal intubation is a medical procedure where a practitioner opens a patient's buccal capsule with an instrument called a laryngoscope (Fig. 1, left) and places a plastic tube into the trachea to secure an open airway for forced respiration (Fig. 1, right). This procedure "requires accurate manipulation of the laryngoscope blade [5]". If the laryngoscope is not properly manipulated, it not only results in incorrect intubation but it may also injure the patient's buccal cavity or break the patient's front tooth. Although recent development of mannequin simulators has enabled realistic training, they tend to focus on supporting a learner's assessment of the current status (e.g., [6]); they do not straightforwardly instruct them how to move their hands. As a result, the success rate of inexperienced paramedics remains low. It is thus important for system designers to find an efficient way to impart the hand skills for manipulating the laryngoscope.

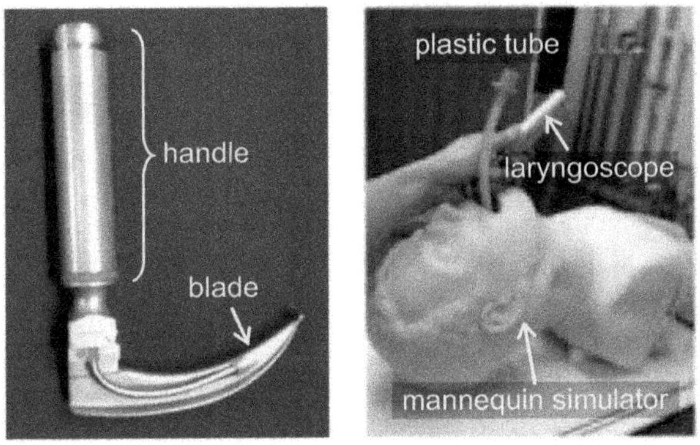

Figure 1. Laryngoscope (left) and tracheal intubation using a simulator (right).

Assisting skill transfers have been actively studied in the domain of haptic displays. Most previous studies have operated a tool so that learners can directly sense the guiding force from the tool itself [8]. However, this approach is not practical when applied to tools that require strength such as the laryngoscope. Since learners have to hold the laryngoscope tightly, it becomes harder to sense the haptic feedback from the tool itself.

Instead of presenting force to a learner's palm by actuating the laryngoscope, our idea is to present force to the back of his/her hand as if an instructor were holding it. The aim of this paper is to introduce a new haptic display called Outer-Covering Haptic Display (OCHD) that actualizes our idea and show its potential in a preliminary experiment.

In the remainder of this paper, we first explain the theoretical background of our approach and review related studies. Next, we introduce our new haptic display, and using it, we describe an experiment that assesses its potential. Finally, we conclude with a discussion about some remaining issues and future work.

BACKGROUND
A variety of systems are being developed to support hand skill transfer. The most common way to assist hand skill transfer using haptic displays is to operate a tool using

actuators so that learners can directly sense the guiding force from the tool itself. For example, Teo proposed a pen-like haptic display to assist the skill transfer of Chinese calligraphy [8]. This system records an expert's movements, and the recorded pen movements give novices proper feedback to stay on track, allowing them to effectively learn the correct hand movements for Chinese calligraphy.

However, this method may not be practical when applied to learning skills that require strength (i.e., when learners need to hold the tool tightly) because the guiding force inevitably increases, which typically increases the tool's size and cost. The key theory that supports this assumption is Weber's Law. Weber's Law states that the change in a stimulus that is "just noticeable" is a constant ratio of the original stimulus [9]. For example, one must shout to be heard in a noisy environment but a whisper works in a quiet room. This law can be applied to a variety of sensory modalities including strength. Consequently, we predict that the detection threshold of the guiding force increases as the learner holds the tool tighter.

Unfortunately, tracheal intubation requires practitioners to apply relatively strong force (about 40 N at the peak) and torque (about 4 Nm at the peak) to the laryngoscope [3], forcing the handle to be held tightly. According to Weber's Law, the actuators to manipulate the laryngoscope should have a much stronger drive force. As the required drive force of the actuators becomes stronger, the required motor performance becomes higher and the rigidity of the structure needs to be stronger, making the actuator heavier, more costly, and more dangerous to be used near humans.

To resolve this issue, we focus on previous works that apply stimulus to a person's outer skin to guide movement rather than moving the instrument itself. For example, Bark et al. proposed "a wearable haptic feedback device that imparts rotational skin stretch to provide feedback regarding movement of a virtual object [1]." Kuniyasu et al. also proposed a wearable haptic device that applies skin deformation to a person's forearm and found that it can give illusory external force to users [4].

Spurred by these previous studies, we developed the idea of applying guiding force to the back of a learner's hand. Since no other force is applied at its back, we expect that learners will be sensitive to relatively weak stimulus no matter how strong they hold the laryngoscope. However, note that the validity of our idea is unclear since palms are generally more sensitive than the back of the hand [2].

This study is important in two ways. First, it demonstrates the effectiveness of applying haptic sensations to the back of a person's hand when the tool manipulation requires strength. Second, it adds to our understanding of the use of a stimulus on the back of the hand. To the best of our knowledge, no studies have compared the detection threshold between the palm and the back of the hand when holding a tool with particular grasping powers.

OUTER-COVERING HAPTIC DISPLAY

OCHD applies haptic sensations to the back of a learner's hand. Fig. 2 shows OCHD's latest structure. Its main components are aluminum frames, silicon effectors, and silicon bands. It weighs about 80 g, which is much lighter than a typical laryngoscope that weighs about 500 g. The effectors attached to the frames are square, 1 cm on a side and 2-mm thick, and the distance between them is 1 cm. Since the effectors reduce the contact area, we expect them to effectively apply pressure to the learner's skin as well as enhancing the haptic sensation by deforming the skin [4].

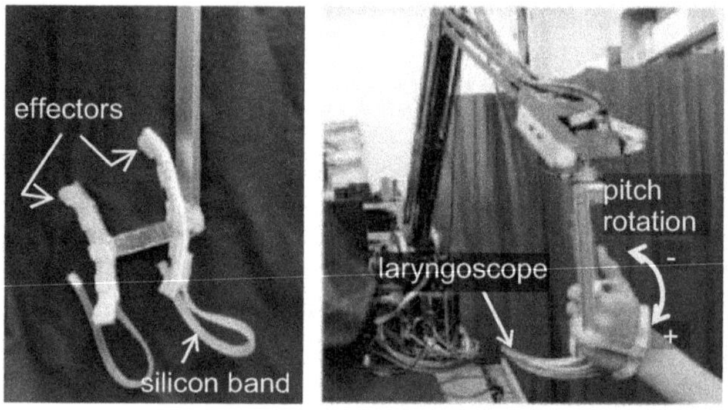

Figure 2. Left photo shows OCHD and right photo shows OCHD actuated by 6-DOF manipulator.

PRELIMINARY EVALUATION

We experimentally investigated the effect of OCHD for applying haptic sensations to subjects. We aimed to confirm that OCHD requires less drive force for the subjects to detect the haptic sensation around the pitch axis compared to the case where the laryngoscope was directly actuated. Our hypothesis argues that for the latter case, as the subject increases his grasp of the laryngoscope handle, a proportionally stronger drive force is required. In the former case, on the other hand, the required drive force will not change so much regardless of the grasping power. Note that since our study is still in its early stage, we only tested the effect of OCHD on pitch rotation. Also, we regarded the "drive force" equivalent to the motor torque that drove the apparatus because we only used one motor for this experiment.

Design

This experiment, which measured the minimum motor torque (detection threshold) for subjects to detect the haptic sensation around the pitch axis, was conducted using a 2x3x2 within-subjects design. The independent variables were *haptic display* {OCHD, laryngoscope}, *grasping power* {0 kgf, 1 kgf, 2 kgf}, and *rotation direction* {plus, minus}. For the *grasping power*, half of the subjects conducted the tasks in an incremental order (0 kgf → 1 kgf → 2 kgf) and the other half in a decremental order (2 kgf → 1 kgf → 0 kgf). For the *rotation direction*, the plus and minus directions of the pitch rotation were randomly presented several times to each subject. The orders of the *haptic display* and *grasping power* were counterbalanced across subjects.

Apparatus

Figure 3 shows the experiment's apparatuses. For the OCHD condition, the subjects wore it on their left hands and grasped the aluminum pipe. OCHD was driven by a motor. But the pipe was structurally disconnected from the motor, and thus the haptic sensation was only applied through the OCHD (Fig. 3 left). In the laryngoscope condition, since the subject grasped the same aluminum pipe structurally connected to the motor (Fig. 3 right), the haptic sensation was only given through the pipe.

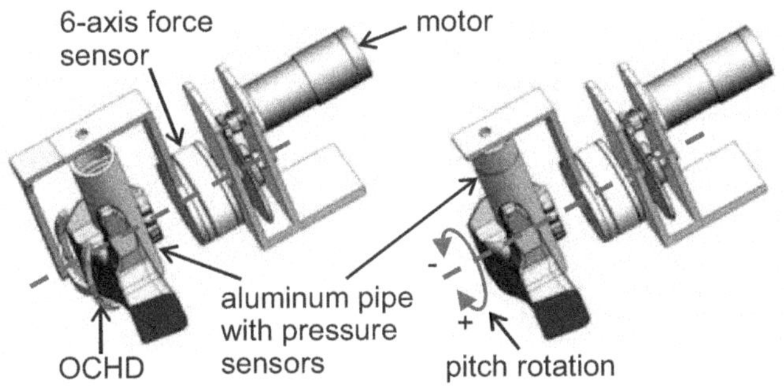

Figure 3. Apparatuses for OCHD condition (left) and laryngoscope condition (right).

The aluminum pipe was embedded with two pressure sensors inside (Fig. 4 left). The subject's grasping power was measured as the sum of two pressure sensor values. To eliminate the influence of silicon effectors between the conditions, we wrapped the pipe with a silicon sheet and attached the effectors in the same way as for OCHD (Fig. 4 right).

Subjects and Procedures

Eight males from 21-29 years participated in this experiment. None of the subjects had any experience in intubation. One subject was left-handed.

At the beginning of each task, they grasped the pipe with a designated grasping power. Then the detection threshold for the pitch rotation was measured using the simple up-and-down method [7]. The size of torque increment/decrement was 5 N-mm and there were six reversals.

Since keeping the grasp force constant is almost impossible*, we allowed +/- 0.035 kgf variation around the designated value and applied stimulation (pitch rotation) to the subjects when their grasping power was within this range.

* Our preliminary test with five subjects showed that, when they were told to hold the pipe with 2 kgf, their average grasp power and its standard deviation lied within $1.98 < \mu < 2.02$ and $0.027 < \sigma < 0.033$, respectively.

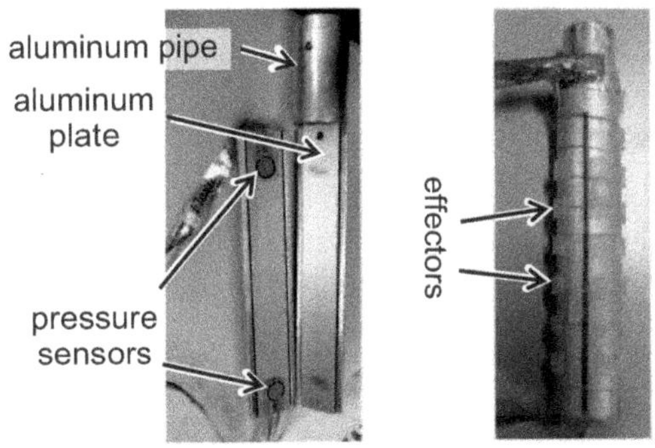

Figure 4. Internal structure (left) and outside view (right) of laryngoscope model pipe.

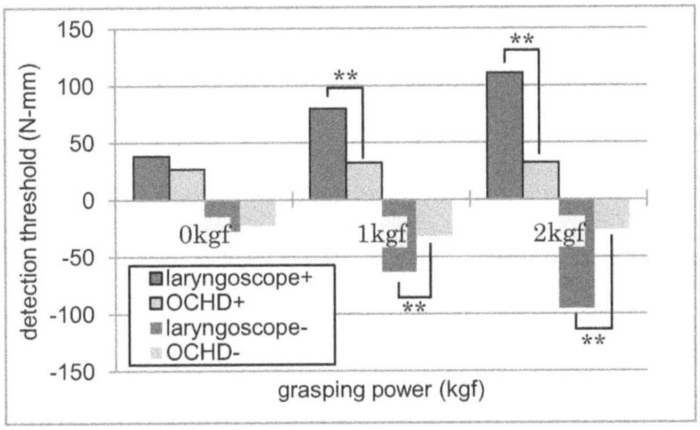

Figure 5. Average detection threshold for plus (indicated by +) and minus (indicated by -) directions: "" denotes significant difference at p<.01 level.**

For this experiment, the subjects were notified that they would be presented with the pitch rotation (it was specifically explained to the subjects). However, the subjects were not notified of how and when the stimulus would be presented (i.e. the number of trials, the timing, and the plus/minus directions). In this way, the detection threshold (i.e., minimum motor torque) was measured six times for both directions. For each direction, the average of six measured values was used as each subject's detection threshold.

RESULTS

Figure 5 shows the average detection threshold of two haptic display conditions for each grasping power. A 3-way repeated measures ANOVA indicated significant main effects for rotation direction ($F(1, 84)=5.7$, $p<.05$), haptic display ($F(1, 84)=116.51$, $p<.001$), grasping power ($F(2, 84)=34.23$, $p<.001$), and a significant interaction between *haptic display* and *grasping power* ($F(2, 84)=25.62$, $p<.001$). Also the simple main effect of *grasping power* at the laryngoscope condition was significant ($F(2, 84)=59.17$, $p<.001$) but not at OCHD condition ($F(2, 84)=.68$, $p=.51$). For grasping power of 1 kgf and 2kgf, Bonferroni post-hoc tests showed significant difference between the laryngoscope and OCHD conditions in both plus and minus directions (1 kgf plus: $F(1, 84)=26.56$, $p<.001$, 1 kgf minus: $F(1, 84)=11.88$, $p<.01$, 2 kgf plus: $F(1, 84)=73.19$, $p<.001$, 2 kgf minus: $F(1, 84)=56.55$, $p<.001$). A significant difference was not found for 0 kgf grasping power.

After the experiment, we asked the subjects how they felt when they were presented the guiding force. Most of them answered that they felt skin stretch for OCHD condition.

DISCUSSION

From this experiment, we have proven that the OCHD condition was superior to the laryngoscope condition in terms of the detection threshold. For the laryngoscope condition, the detection threshold significantly increased as the grasping power became stronger. In contrast, for the OCHD condition, the detection threshold remained almost the same regardless of the grasping power. Our results suggest that the OCHD is a promising device for learners to sense the guide force with less drive force.

Since the palm of the hand is more sensitive than its back, one might have predicted that for 0 kgf grasping power, the detection threshold would be lower in the laryngoscope case than the OCHD case. Surprisingly, however, we did not find any significant difference between the two cases. Since the number of effectors contacting the subject hands is fewer for the OCHD condition, we speculate that each OCHD effector yields more pressure and skin deformation to the hands than for the laryngoscope case, resulting in a similar detection threshold for the OCHD condition. This result also strengthens the effectiveness of our approach.

OCHD's advantage is not only in its low detection threshold. Since OCHD does not directly actuate the tools, a single OCHD could be applicable for various tools such as endoscopes and medical ultrasonic probes. One possible enhancement of the OCHD for versatile applications is to combine OCHD with wearable computers as in [4] where arm guidance using skin deformation is suggested to be implemented in wearable computers. Since OCHD does not occupy the palm, wearable OCHD may be used for guiding hand motion of various activities.

Further study is required to make such an application feasible and to expand the possibilities of OCHD. For example, we need to find an appropriate shape and control method for OCHD so that learners can sense 6-DOF of the guiding force. It is particularly important to design OCHD so that leaners can properly sense the combination of more than two axes.

CONCLUSION AND FUTURE WORK

As the first step toward developing a system to assist transferring hand skills for tracheal intubation, this paper proposed an Outer-Covering Haptic Display (OCHD) and proved that, although only for the pitch rotation, the display effectively reduces the detection threshold compared to the case where the laryngoscope was driven by a motor.

The next step of our study is to embed the OCHD as part of a hand skill transfer system for the tracheal intubation. We have two lines of OCHD usage under consideration: a master-slave control approach and an automatic guide approach. In the master-slave control approach, an expert applies a guiding force to a learner's hand with an OCHD (slave) by manually operating the master controller while a learner is conducting intubation with a laryngoscope. One of the advantages of the master-slave approach is that experts can guide the learners' hands without physically touching their actual hands. In the automatic guide approach, a computer automatically assesses the learner's hand motion and applies the guide force by operating the OCHD as needed. This approach is similar to the concept of wearable computer where computers monitor human movements and assist their activities. After implementing these systems, we will experimentally assess the effect of our system on actual tracheal intubation training.

ACKNOWLEDGMENTS

This work was supported by Grant-in-aid for Scientific Research (B) 20390148.

REFERENCES

1. Bark, K., Wheeler, J., Lee, G., and Savall, J., A Wearable Skin Stretch Device for Haptic Feedback, *World Haptics 2009*, IEEE Computer Society (2009), 464-469.
2. Brown, L., Morrissey, B., and Goodale, M., Vision in the Palm of your hand, *Neuropsychologia* 47 (2009), 1621-1626.
3. Hastings, R., Hon, E., Nghiem, C., and Wahrenbrock, E., Force, Torque, and Stress Relaxation with Direct Laryngoscopy, *Anesth Analg 1996;82* (1996) 456-461.
4. Kuniyasu, Y., Fukushima, S., Furukawa, M., and Kajimoto, H., Weight Illusion by Tangential Deformation of Forearm Skin, *Proc. AH 2011,* ACM Press (2011), 10: 1-10: 2.
5. Mayrose, J., Kesavadas, T., Chugh, K., Joshi, D., and Ellis, D., Utilization of virtual reality for endotracheal intubation training, *Resuscitation 59* (2003), 133-138.
6. Noh, Y., Segawa, M., Shimomura, A., Ishii. H., Solis, J., Hatake., K., and Takanishi, A., WKA-1R Robot assisted quantitative assessment of airway management, *Int J CARS 3* (2008), 543-550.
7. Over, R., A Comparison of Haptic and Visual Judgments of Some Illusions, *The American Journal of Psychology 79, 4* (1966), 590-595.
8. Teo C.L., Burdet E., and Lim H.P. A robotic teacher of Chinese handwriting. *Proc. HAPTICS 2002* (2002), 335-341.
9. Weber's Law of Just Noticeable Differences, USD Internet Sensation & Perception Laboratory, http: //people.usd.edu/~schieber/coglab/WebersLaw.html.

An Investigation of Fitts' Law in a Multiple-Display Environment

Dugald Ralph Hutchings
Computing Sciences Department, Elon University
Elon, North Carolina 27244 USA
dhutchings@elon.edu

ABSTRACT
We describe the design and analysis of a Fitts' law experiment, conducted in a multiple-display environment (MDE), in which the physical gap between displays and the proximity of targets to the gap systematically varied. Participants achieved decreasing throughput values (a combined measure of movement time and accuracy in a target acquisition task) under increasing gap sizes. Participants likewise performed relatively poorly in tasks involving monitor crossing over all gap conditions, especially so when motion either originates or terminates very close to the gap. Both results could be considered surprising since in either case, the amount of mouse movement needed to successfully execute the task does not change based on physical gap size or a target's proximity to the edge. Fitts' law may underestimate the difficulty of movement tasks in MDEs.

Author Keywords
Multiple-display environment; Fitts' law; throughput

ACM Classification Keywords
H.5.2 [Information interfaces and presentation]: User Interfaces - *Theory and Methods*

General Terms
Experimentation, Human Factors

INTRODUCTION
Fitts' law is a mathematical model that predicts a user's movement time (*MT*) to navigate from a known starting location to a known target. Although the forms of the specific Fitts' law equations vary for many reasons, the standard equation shown below for one-dimensional horizontal movement is known as the Shannon formulation [11]:

$$MT = a + b \log_2(D/W + 1),$$

such that W is the width of the target, D is the distance to the center of the target, and a & b are empirically determined constants relating to the pointing device used and relevant environmental characteristics such as mouse speed and acceleration. The term $\log_2(D/W + 1)$ is referred to as the index of difficulty (*ID*). Fitts' law is an intuitive model: smaller or distant targets are predicted to require more movement time than larger or nearby targets.

For many years HCI researchers have investigated the applicability of Fitts' law and it is considered by many researchers to be a fundamental HCI principle. A common element of almost all HCI-related past work on Fitts' Law is that experimenters used a single-display environment. Multi-display environments (MDEs) introduce a visual discontinuity ignored by navigation devices, *i.e.*, although there is a physical gap among the different displays, a mouse user need not move the mouse a distance commensurate with the gap in order to cross it. For example when two identical monitors rest on a flat desk, the physical monitor edges could be touching, separated by 1cm, or separated by 1m and the user would move the mouse the same distance to travel from the current position on the left-side monitor to click on a button on the right-side monitor.

Since the user controls the physical distance between displays, the UI designer must assume that the value of D in Fitts' law is to be measured by the amount of space traveled by the input device (equivalent to the number of actual pixels traversed). A question thus arises whether Fitts' law adequately predicts user movement times in an MDE, where the user-perceived distance is greater than the number of pixels. Before presenting an experiment design that addresses this question, we present and analyze key past work related to Fitts' law or navigation in MDEs.

RELATED WORK
In 2004 Soukoreff and MacKenzie provided seven recommendations for the design and analysis of Fitts' law experiments [11] based on a wide variety of past literature and on the ISO 9241-9 standard *Requirements for Non-keyboard Input Devices*. Our design follows the recommendations to the extent possible and key exceptions are noted in our description. Despite a standardized approach, there is still some disagreement about proper design. For example whereas Soukoreff & MacKenzie call for participants to experience a wide variety of D and W conditions so as to vary *ID*, Guiard argues that this introduces a confound and instead argues that D should be fixed and *ID* should be systematically varied [8]. Further, whereas Soukoreff & MacKenzie do not discuss display environment, Guiard indicates that his recommendations may not be feasible for

large displays. We have attempted to satisfy both sets of recommendations by varying *D* and *ID*, thereby deriving *W*.

MDEs are not just larger, but physically discontinuous. For monitor-crossing navigation tasks, part of *D* will be traveled on one display and the final part on another display, though the user will use a continuous mouse motion. In the extreme case, in which a target is located just over the gap, nearly all of the distance will be traveled on one monitor. Whereas in a single-display environment placing targets on actual screen edges can be beneficial [1], in MDEs it may be quite difficult to acquire such a target. Indeed, researchers such as Rodgers et al. have proposed slowing mouse acceleration or speed to ease the task [10]. To assess whether gap proximity affects performance, we have also varied the amount of distance allocated to each display within a particular setting of *D* and *ID*, but our experiment occurs in the absence of a manipulation of mouse speed or acceleration.

Other researchers have proposed ways to avoid crossing the gap altogether (which also decreases the actual value of *D* and should thus reduce *ID*). Techniques such as Multi-monitor Mouse [2] and Ninja Cursors [9], which provide the illusion of one or mouse cursors per monitor, and Drag-and-Pop [5], which temporarily re-locate likely targets near the current cursor position, all have the effect of reducing *D*. We are interested in measuring and analyzing performance when a user crosses a gap.

We finally note two studies closely related to our investigation. MDEs are not the only way for users to experience a mismatch between motor space (how far a mouse needs to move to reach a target) and visual space (the apparent distance to a target). Semantic pointing alters mouse speed & acceleration and target representation in the context of the task to reduce *ID* and a study of the technique reflects that motor space dimensions give the best indication of actual *ID* value [4]. We do not alter the mouse behavior or the target properties but instead alter physical display distance, finding that motor distance may in fact be inadequate for describing *ID*. Our configuration differs from that of Bi et al. where gap distance between monitors was not altered and all monitors were touching. Bi et al. indicated that in this grid configuration, tiny gaps between monitors had no effect on the predictive power of Fitts' law [3]. Bi et al. also were studying 2D movement and stated that their "study [was] not intended to be a general Fitts' law experiment."

EXPERIMENT DESIGN

The goal of this experiment is to explore whether user interface designers can reliably use Fitts' law to predict one-dimensional movement time and accuracy in a two-monitor MDE when physical proximity of the monitors is unknown.

System and Task Configuration

In a computing lab we created a two-monitor, single-mouse MDE on a desk. The mouse was a wireless Logitech M510 but used the standard Windows 7 operating system mouse configuration software and its default settings. The monitors were identical Dell U2311H models with a native resolution of 1920px × 1080px, interior dimensions of 51cm × 28.5cm, exterior dimensions of 55cm × 32.5cm, and an elevation of 15.5 cm from the desk's top. The left-side monitor never changed positions, but the experimenter would alter the position of the right-side monitor at predetermined points during the experiment in one of three ways:

- *GN*: (no gap) monitors are touching, side-by-side;
- *GF*: (full gap) the distance between the two monitors is exactly equal to the width of one of the monitors[1]; *or*
- *GH*: (half gap) the distance between the two monitors is half the distance of the GF condition.

In this within-subjects experiment, the 6 possible orderings of the *gap size conditions* were counterbalanced to minimize learning effects. In each gap condition, a participant would engage in 16 practice trials of a basic mouse move-and-click task similar to the configuration used in the original Fitts' law experiment [6]. In a single trial, experimental software displayed two areas on the screen: a light gray start area and a dark red target area. The software centered the mouse cursor in the start area. When the participant started moving the mouse, the software would begin timing and when the participant next clicked, timing stopped. If the participant did not click inside the target area, the computer system audibly beeped to indicate the error. Whether the participant was successful or erroneous, the software switched the positions of the target and start area (maintaining the distance) and a new trial began, facilitating a back-and-forth motion among targets.

Note that modern design recommendations call for a circular arrangement of targets and two-dimensional movement [11]. Our design is motivated by a desire to isolate movement direction based on the physical discontinuity in the display space, the very wide aspect ratio of the display environment (which limits the possible distances to be used in the circular arrangement), and the desire to avoid a target being placed so as to straddle the gap between the monitors (an unlikely occurrence in actual practice [7]).

In many Fitts' law experiments, participants experience a variety of values for *D* and *ID* organized into blocks and presented in a randomized order. We likewise used two *D* values (945px, 1785px) and three *ID* values (2, 4, 6), yielding six unique combinations. As previously stated, in MDEs the proximity of the target to the gap between displays may affect performance. We examined six conditions of *gap proximity* for each unique combination of *D* and *ID*. In four of six conditions, the start area and target area each appear on a separate monitor and the distance from the left edge of

[1] This is a considerable size and was selected as the *reasonable* theoretical boundary for monitor placement, not necessarily the *known* common practice of monitor placement.

the right-side area to the gap is 0%, 12.5%, 25%, or 50% of *D* (respectively designated *EZ*, *EE*, *EQ*, *EH*). For example, in condition *EQ* and regardless of mouse movement direction, about 25% of the distance travelled is on the right-side monitor and the remainder is on the left-side monitor. In the other two conditions, the task occurred entirely on the left-side or right-side monitor (*EL* and *ER* respectively). We examined all 36 combinations of *D*, *ID*, and gap proximity except for *ID*=2 and *D*=1785, where only the four conditions involving moving from one monitor to another can be examined (i.e., *EZ, EE, EQ, EH*) because the targets are too wide to fit on a single display.

Finally, our pilot tests did not reveal a common occurrence from the actual execution of the experiment: participants often shifted arm or chair position during the first or second trial of a new block, especially when the distance between targets dramatically changed. Due to the adverse effect on task performance, we omit the first two trials within each block in subsequent analysis. Summarizing, we recorded

2 values of distance *D* (1785px, 945px)
3 values of index of difficulty *ID* (6, 4, 2)
× 6 edge proximity conditions (*EZ, EE, EQ, EH, EL, ER*)
36 target configurations
− 2 target config. (*D*=1785, *ID*=2, only *EZ, EE, EQ, EH*)
34 target configurations
× 3 monitor gap conditions (*GN, GH, GF*)
104 total blocks of trials
× 14 timed trials per block
1428 total timed trials per participant.

Notes on Experimental Software

We instrumented a software application written in Visual Basic. The application covered the entire display space and used visual components that did not alter normal mouse behavior. In addition to timing participant actions as described in the previous subsection, the software recorded the *x* coordinate of the mouse cursor at the end of a trial.

Sequencing and Participant Interaction

An experimenter met each participant in the hallway outside the computing lab. The monitors' initial configuration was *GN*, with the participant seated in front of the left-side monitor and the experimenter seated to the left of the participant. The participant first provided informed consent using paper and pen and then responded to several demographic questions. The experimenter explained the purpose of the experiment and the task that the participant would execute. In particular, the experimenter informed the participant to be as fast and as accurate as possible, striving for an error rate of 4%. Experimental software notified the participant of the error rate every 7 blocks and encouraged the participant to speed up (if error rate was below 3.5%), slow down (if error rate was above 4.5%), or maintain speed. The experimenter also told the participant to rest for as long as desired in between trials or blocks in order to avoid fatigue.

The participant engaged in 6 practice blocks on the left-side monitor. The experimental software then indicated the gap condition for the experimenter to configure, the experimenter confirmed the configuration, and the software presented one practice block then 34 blocks of timed trials in a randomized order. This process repeated for the remaining two gap size conditions. Throughout the experiment, participants were free to adjust chair, arm, and head position.

EXPERIMENT RESULTS AND ANALYSIS

12 undergraduate students (9 female) at our institution participated in the experiment. Ages ranged from 19 to 21 with an average age of 19.9. All participants had at least some experience in using multiple-monitor computer systems, with 4 participants using such systems on at least a weekly basis. All participants used desktop or laptop computers for at least 4 hours per day. Further, all participants were right handed, used their right hand for everyday mouse or touchpad use, and had normal or corrected-to-normal vision. Total participation time was between 40 and 55 minutes.

Analysis Methods

We follow the Soukoreff and MacKenzie recommendations for analyzing our data [11], though due to space limitations[2] we only report error rates and calculated throughput values. For each participant *p*, each gap size condition *g*, and each block *b*, we calculated effective width We_{pbg} as 4.133σ, where σ is the standard deviation of the *x* coordinate of the end point among the trials in the block, and effective distance De_{pbg}, the mean number of pixels between the starting *x* coordinate and the final *x* coordinate. The effective *ID* is noted $IDe_{pbg} = \log_2(De_{pbg}/We_{pbg} + 1)$ and indicates the actual difficulty of the task completed. $TP_{pbg} = IDe_{pbg}/MT_{pbg}$, the throughput, provides a combined measure of speed and accuracy (where MT_{pbg} is the mean movement time).

Gap Size

To assess the effect of gap size, for each participant and each gap size condition, we averaged the throughput achieved on monitor-crossing tasks and performed an ANOVA on the resulting values, finding a significant difference ($F_{2,33}$=52.51, p<0.0001, η^2=0.76, see Table 1). The result suggests that the size of the physical gap between monitors significantly affects actual movement time and accuracy despite having no influence on the actual distance necessary for travel by the mouse to reach the target. In other words, it seems that visual distance, not motor distance, is a key factor for MDE navigation. Table 1 also indicates overall error rates in each of the gap size conditions; an ANOVA did not show significance ($F_{2,33}$=0.98, p=0.39).

Gap Proximity

Similar to the gap size analysis, we assessed the effect of gap proximity by calculating average participant throughput

[2] More analysis at http://facstaff.elon.edu/dhutchings/chi12

Cond.	GN	GH	GF
TP	5.22	4.59	4.09
s.d.(TP)	0.29	0.23	0.29
Err. (%)	4.5	3.8	4.2

Table 1. Gap Size Throughput and Error Rate

per proximity condition. An ANOVA likewise indicated a significant difference ($F_{5,66}$=29.56, p<0.0001, η^2=0.69). Table 2 illustrates the average throughputs and standard deviations for the various conditions and indicates two main findings: (1) tasks involving starting or stopping on the gap (condition *EZ*) are harder than any other; and (2) crossing a monitor in any fashion is relatively worse.

Table 2 also indicates overall error rate in each of the gap proximity conditions. An interesting trend is apparent (significant according to an ANOVA analysis ($F_{5,66}$=4.865, p=0.0008, η^2=0.27)). Error rates were highest when participants *did not* cross monitor boundaries (the highest throughput conditions), second highest for tasks involving starting or stopping at the gap (the lowest throughput condition), but lowest when the target was a short distance away from the gap (yet not the highest or lowest throughput condition). One possible explanation for this phenomenon is that the user's eyes locate the mouse cursor on the other monitor sometime just prior to 12.5% of the total distance travelled, resulting in a two-stage task in which the second stage has a relatively low *ID*. In instances when the gap is not crossed, the participant might be moving the mouse faster or farther than necessary, expecting the time needed to travel to be larger since most tasks involve gap crossing.

This observation about gap proximity poses a conundrum however in that our previous observation about the effect of monitor gap suggests that target distance be decreased or target width increased when the target is on a different monitor than the starting location. Placing a target right at the gap places it as close as possible but nevertheless appears to be the worst possible choice. Our results suggest that targets be placed some distance away from the gap but do not necessarily indicate the smallest reasonable distance.

SUMMARY AND FUTURE WORK

We have demonstrated that both the size of the gap between monitors and the proximity of a target to the gap impact actual target acquisition performance in a two-monitor MDE. In particular, increasing visual distance without increasing motor distance nevertheless increases predicted movement time, as does placing a target such that its edge abuts the gap. One line of future work thus involves generalizing the Fitts' law model to account for MDEs. Such a generalization may also benefit from other factors not explored in this work, such as two-dimensional movement tasks, MDEs with multiple gaps (possibly in multiple dimensions), heterogeneous displays (such as a laptop with second attached display), or degree of monitor tilt. Another line of future work involves using MDEs to re-evaluate novel input approaches first assessed only using a single display.

Cond.	EZ	EE	EQ	EH	EL	ER
TP	4.19	4.73	4.81	4.80	5.25	5.22
s.d.(TP)	0.25	0.19	0.20	0.25	0.32	0.24
Err. (%)	5.1	3.3	4.0	4.2	5.6	5.6

Table 2. Gap Proximity Throughput and Error Rate

REFERENCES

1. Appert, C., Chapuis, O. and Beaudouin-Lafon, M. Evaluation of pointing performance on screen edges. In *Proc. AVI 2008*, ACM Press (2008), 119-126.
2. Benko, H. and Feiner, S. Multi-monitor mouse. *Ext. Abstracts CHI 2005*, ACM Press (2005), 1208-1211.
3. Bi, X., Bae, S.-H. and Balakrishnan, R. Effects of interior bezels on tiled-monitor large displays of visual search, tunnel steering, and target selection. In *Proc. CHI 2010*, ACM Press (2010), 65-74.
4. Blanch, R., Guiard, Y. and Beaudouin-Lafon, M. Semantic pointing: Improving target acquisition with control-display ratio adaptation. In *Proc. CHI 2004*, ACM Press (2004), 519-526.
5. Collomb, M., Hascoet, M., Baudisch, P. and Lee, B. Improving Drag-and-Pop on wall-size displays. In *Proc. Graphics Interface 2005*, Canadian Human-Computer Communications Society (2005), 25-32.
6. Fitts, P. M. The information capacity of the human motor system in controlling the amplitude of movement. *J. Experimental Psych.* 47, 381-391 (reprinted in *J. Experimental Psych.: General 121*, 3 (1992), 262-269).
7. Grudin, J. Partitioning digital worlds: focal and peripheral awareness in multiple monitor use. In *Proc. CHI 2001*, ACM Press (2001), 458-465.
8. Guiard, Y. The problem of consistency in the design of Fitts' law experiments: Consider either target distance and width or movement form and scale. In *Proc. CHI 2009*, ACM Press (2009), 1809-1818.
9. Kobayashi, M. and Igarashi, T. Ninja cursors: Using multiple cursors to assist target acquisition on large screens. *Proc. CHI 2008*, ACM Press (2008), 949-958.
10. Rodgers, M., Mandryk, R. L. and Inkpen, K. Smart sticky widgets: pseudo-haptic enhancements for multi-monitor displays. In *Proc. Smart Graphics 2006*, Springer (2006), 194-205.
11. Soukoreff, R. W. and MacKenzie, I. S. Towards a standard for pointing device evaluation, perspectives on 27 years of Fitts' law research in HCI. *Int'l. J. Human-Computer Studies 61* (2004), 751-789.

Extending Fitts' Law to Account for the Effects of Movement Direction on 2D Pointing

Xinyong Zhang◇, Hongbin Zha†, Wenxin Feng◇
◇School of Information, Renmin University of China, Beijing, China
†Key Lab of Machine Perception, MOE, Peking University, Beijing, China
x.y.zhang@ruc.edu.cn, zha@cis.pku.edu.cn, fengwenxin@gmail.com

ABSTRACT
Fitts' law is the most widely applied model in the field of HCI. However, this model and its existing extensions are still limited for 2D pointing task especially when the effects of movement direction (θ) remain in the task. In this paper, we employ the concept of projection to account for the effects of target width (W) and height (H) on movement time so that we seamlessly integrate the four factors, i.e. θ, amplitude (A), W and H, into the new extension of Fitts' law, which can uncover not only the periodicity of the asymmetrical impacts of W and H with the variation of θ but also their interrelation. Carrying out two experiments, we verify that the vertical projection of W and the horizontal projection of H in the line of movement direction can be viewed as the determinants of movement time. Finally, we offer recommendations for 2D pointing experiments and discuss the implications for interface designs.

Author Keywords
Fitts' law; two-dimensional pointing; movement direction.

ACM Classification Keywords
H.5.2. [Information interfaces and presentation]: User interfaces - *evaluation, theory and methods*; H.1.2 [Models and principles]: User/machine systems - *human factors*

General Terms
Experimentation; Human Factors; Theory.

INTRODUCTION
In the field of human-computer interaction (HCI), predictive performance models often serve as theoretical tools to evaluate the user's capabilities of interacting with computers. On the one hand, performance models can offer substantial evidence to indicate whether or not a new technique or user interface is effective and efficient from a theoretical perspective, and, on the other hand, they can also provide inspiration for the designs of HCI. Up to now, a number of quantitative models have been proposed for different tasks, such as steering task [1], peephole pointing [8], menu selection [3] and navigation in scrolling and hierarchical lists [9].

Nevertheless, pointing and selecting visual targets to activate the corresponding commands is still the most dominant task in current graphic user interfaces. Therefore, it is very important to deeply understand the user's capabilities of pointing. Among the published models in the literature for this daily task, the most prevalent one is Fitts' law [10]. Regardless of its original expression, the widely-applied "standard" form of Fitts' law for movement time (MT) predictions is as follows [17, 21]:

$$MT = a + b\log_2(A/W + 1) \tag{1}$$

where a and b are two regression coefficients, and W and A denote target width and movement distance of the cursor, respectively. The logarithmic term is defined as the index of difficulty (ID) of pointing tasks. This equation expresses a linear relationship between ID and MT that the user takes when moving the cursor to acquire the desired target as quickly and accurately as possible.

With respect to the two-dimensional (2D) targets in conventional user interfaces, target position (including direction and distance) and size (including width and height) are all relevant to the time of target acquisition [13, 23, 6, 22]. However, Fitts' law and its existing extensions [16, 2, 4, 26] do not take account of these factors at the same time and also do not reveal the potential relationship among them. In this paper, therefore, we endeavor to provide a more appropriate extension of Fitts' law. We simply view the projections of target width and height (H) in the line of movement direction as the essentials to determine MT, and we find that the different impacts of W and H on MT will periodically vary with movement direction (θ). This periodicity can be expressed using a single weighted parameter in the new extension of Fitts' law, directly exposing the impact of movement direction on both of W and H.

RELATED WORK
The validity and reliability of Fitts' law for pointing task were confirmed in many different situations. Recently, for example, it was reported that Fitts' law effectively governed the performance under the conditions that the visual feedback was restricted [25] or that the motor movements included translational and rotational components [18].

In the field of HCI, Fitts' law is the defacto standard of user performance evaluation [21]. It can also serve as a theoretical foundation to deduce new models for different tasks, such as steering [1] and peephole pointing [8]. More importantly, Fitts' law itself can be extended for different situations, such as pointing with the need of manual obstacle avoidance [14] and pointing at targets accompanied with distractors [5]. Especially, there were a number of studies on extending Fitts' law for 2D pointing [16, 19, 2, 4] and on modeling it using different concepts [11, 26]. Next, we will give a review on those studies, which are highly related to our current work, as well as the investigations about the effects of movement direction on user performance.

Taking Account of Target Width and Height Together

MacKenzie and Buxton made the first effort to seek more accurate ID for 2D pointing tasks [16]. They tested each of the terms: $min(W, H)$, $W + H$, $W \times H$ and W' [1], in the place of W in Fitts' law, to capture the effect of H. They examined the accuracies of the redefined indexes of difficulty under different conditions of movement directions, including 0°, 45° and 90°. They found that both $min(W, H)$ and W' resulted in better data fitting than the others. W' appears to be theoretically appealing, but it could lead to unreasonable predictions of MT in some special cases as pointed out by themselves. In order to properly take account of the interaction effect between the two factors W and H, Accot and Zhai employed the methodology of weighted ℓ_r-norm to extend the standard Fitts ID [2] and got the general definition (denoted using ID_{az} in this paper) as follows:

$$ID_{az} = \log_2\left(\left[\omega\left(\frac{A}{W}\right)^r + \eta\left(\frac{A}{H}\right)^r\right]^{1/r} + 1\right) \quad (2)$$

where ω and η denote two positive weights, and as a real number of norm order, $r \geq 1$. This ID definition has five properties describing the effects of both W and H:

- *Scale Independency.* When the sizes of A, W and H are changed at the same rate, theoretically, the values of MT will be identical due to the unchanged ID_{az}.
- *Limit Tasks.* The 2D index of difficulty can converge to the one-dimensional (1D) form of Fitts ID when one of the variables W and H is increasingly close to infinity.
- *Dominance Effect.* When either W or H is gradually getting small, it will dominate the difficulties, and consequently weaken the impact of the other.
- *Duality of H and W.* The definition of ID_{az} includes both of W and H, indicating their similar contributions to MT in terms of functional relation.
- *Continuity.* The factors W and H do not stepwise or segmentally but continuously affect MT.

In order to remove unnecessary parameters, Accot and Zhai examined the accuracies of Equation 2 under twelve different parameterization conditions. They pointed out that when $r = 2$ and $\omega = 1$, the Euclidean form of ID_{az}, as the following Equation 3 expresses, was the most appropriate one.

$$ID_{az} = \log_2\left(\sqrt{(A/W)^2 + \eta(A/H)^2} + 1\right) \quad (3)$$

They reported that there was a strong linear correlation between ID_{az} and MT ($R^2 > 0.94$) when $1/7 \leq \eta \leq 1/3$. The values of η implied that W had greater impact than H on 2D pointing tasks. However, they did not evaluated the effectiveness of ID_{az} for the tasks performed in various movement directions but only in horizontal directions. Therefore, the implication was uncertain in different directions.

The ISO9241-9 standard recommends a multidirectional tapping task to neutralize the effects of different directions, but lots of studies (see the reference [4] for a brief review) took account of this factor when evaluating the user's capabilities of pointing. In this connection, Appert et al. treated the factor of movement direction as an explicit variable in their work [4]. According to the general form of ID_{az}, they simply set $\omega = \eta = r = 1$ due to the acceptable correlation coefficients ($R^2 > 0.89$) that Accot and Zhai's work presented under this settings [4]. At the same time, they introduced a special term related to movement direction to capture the dominant effect of the smaller of W and H. They proposed a new index definition as ID_ϕ expresses as follows:

$$ID_\phi = \log_2\left(\frac{A}{W} + \frac{A}{H} + 0.6cos(\phi)\frac{A}{min(W, H)} + 1\right) \quad (4)$$

where ϕ represents the absolute value of the angle between the approach line and the vertical axis. As their experimental results indicated, ID_ϕ appeared to be more accurate to express the difficulties of 2D pointing than ID_{az}.

As can be seen from the related work above, it is inevitable that the more the factors are taken into consideration, the performance model will be more complex. Therefore, there is another kind of efforts to address the issue of modeling 2D hand pointing. Grossman and Balakrishnan [11] proposed a generalized index of difficulty (ID_{Pr}) only based on the probabilities that targets are rapidly hit by users. They constructed a mapping relationship between the probabilities of hitting targets and the values of ID_{Pr}. Intuitively, the difficulty of pointing will decrease with the increase of the probability of hitting. According to the 2D spread of hits [20], it is possible to calculate the probabilities and then the values of ID_{Pr} of acquiring targets in different directions as well as targets with arbitrary shapes. The essence of this approach is to calculate the probabilities of hitting targets, without the need to explicitly interpret the impacts of different factors.

More recently, Yang and Xu employed a novel concept to interpret 2D pointing task [26]. They converted 2D pointing task from a complex state to a simple one, which could be described using fewer parameters without the loss of information. Concretely, for example, it is possible to describe a directional 2D pointing task without including a parameter of angle. Thus, in principle, the corresponding definition of ID could be devoid of the component related to movement direction. Regarding the different states of 2D pointing task, Yang and Xu derived several IDs. These indexes were defined as the logarithm of the inverse of the probability that the target was successfully hit. They picked out the one as expressed in Equation 5 (ID_{conf}) as the superior due to its accuracy and simplicity.

$$ID_{conf} = \log_2\left(\frac{1}{2}\sqrt{(A/W)^2 + (A/H)^2} + 1\right) \quad (5)$$

[1] The symbol W' represents the width along the line where the cursor approaches the target.

The methodology used by Yang and Xu does not need to introduce an arbitrary term into the definition of ID. Thus, the risk of overfitting raised by such an unexplainable term, like that in ID_{ϕ}, could be reduced.

Investigating the Effects of Movement Direction

Fitts' law does not take the factor of movement direction (θ) into account. In traditional 1D Fitts experiments, the tasks are reciprocally performed in horizontal directions, while ISO9241-9 recommends that pointing tasks should be performed in different directions. However, there is a common view that the difficulties of acquiring a given target from different directions are likely different. A number of studies [7, 16, 23, 22, 11, 4] have investigated the effects of movement direction on user performance or considered this factor in their experimental designs. For example, MacKenzie and Buxton took account of movement direction in their 2D pointing experiment and reported that target acquisition time in horizontal and vertical axes were almost the same, faster than that in diagonal axis [16]. Whisenand and Emurian systematically investigated the effects of movement directions in every 45° angle from 0° to 360°, with the consideration of target shape (circular vs. square) and task type (drag-drop vs. point-select) [23]. They reported that it was more efficient to point at horizontal targets than at vertical targets. Using circular targets and different control-display gains, Thompson et al. tested the validity of Fitts' law in eight different movement directions as used in Whisenand and Emurian's work. They also observed the best performance in horizontal pointing and the worse in vertical pointing in general [22]. Grossman and Balakrishnan further confirmed this point when they employed five movement directions from 0° to 90° at an interval of 22.5° in their work [11]. They found that when one of the two target dimensions (W and H) was parallel to movement direction, it was more critical than the other to determine MT, and that W and H would equally affect MT in the direction of 45°.

Theoretically, Grossman and Balakrishnan's model can accommodate the effect of movement direction (θ), but this factor is "invisible" without directly exposing how user performance can be affected by θ. At the same time, their model is difficult to be used to explicitly inform designers how user interfaces can be improved. If there is a hidden truth about θ in 2D pointing, how does it systematically affect MT? A general expectation is that this factor should be harmoniously integrated into the definition of ID unlike the form of Equation 4, which results in an unreasonable implication that only one of the two factors W and H could determine the effect of movement direction. Equation 4 also implies that ID_{ϕ} is not a continuous index, i.e. ID_{ϕ} does not have the property of continuity. Next, we will propose a new extension of Fitts' law to uncover the truth of 2D pointing, with the advantage that it can be conveniently applied.

A NEW EXTENSION OF FITTS' LAW

We can find a common theme in the prior literature [2, 26] that the two terms A/W and A/H are essential to the determination of ID for 2D hand pointing tasks. The effects of W and H could be accumulated to determine ID so as to ultimately determine MT. With respect to the work of Yang and Xu, we find that they calculated the probability of hitting target based on a uniform distribution of hits when deducing Equation 5. This pattern of hand pointing is inconsistent with the findings in other work [20, 11]. Furthermore, if the target only rotates ±90° at a given position (i.e. W and H are replaced by each other), the corresponding MT should almost be the same since the value of ID_{conf} is constant according to its definition. Unfortunately, as reported in the studies [2, 11], the performance differences were notable in this situations. That is to say, ID_{conf} is unable to interpret the usual cases of target transposition, which can cause significant differences of MT. Actually, ID_{conf} in form is the special case of Equation 2 when $\omega = \eta = 0.25$ and $r = 2$. Mathematically, the extension of Fitts' law made by Accot and Zhai for 2D pointing was sufficiently completed.

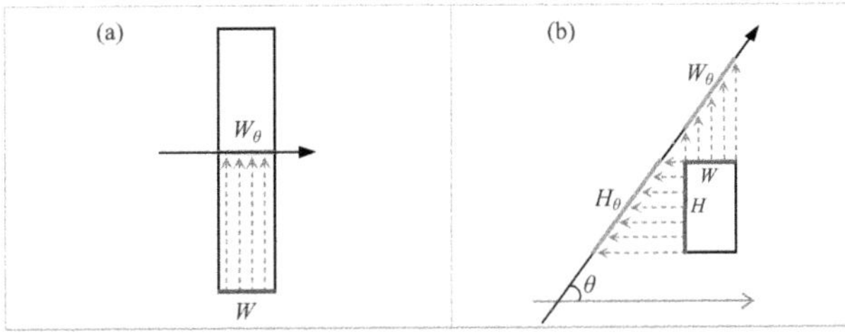

Figure 1. Projections of target width and/or height in the line of movement direction in (a) Fitts tasks and (b) general 2D pointing tasks.

Recall the traditional 1D Fitts task, which is reciprocally performed in horizontal directions. As Figure 1a depicts, we use W_θ to denote the vertical projection of target width W in movement direction. When $\theta = 0°$ or $180°$, $W = W_\theta$. Then, the traditional Fitts ID in Equation 1 can be replaced with the form $\log_2(A/W_\theta + 1)$. This means that the vertical projection W_θ can be viewed as the real determinant capturing the effect of target width. Extending this point of view to the situation of 2D pointing, we propose

Hypothesis 1: ***The vertical projection of W and the horizontal projection of H in movement direction are two essential target factors determining the difficulty of pointing.***

As shown in Figure 1b, the projections of target width and height, W_θ and H_θ, in general can be given by

$$W_\theta = W/\cos(\theta),\ H_\theta = H/\sin(\theta) \quad (6)$$

According to Accot and Zhai's work as well as that of Yang and Xu, the ℓ_2-norm extension of Fitts' law appears to be the pretty-much optimal form for 2D pointing. Then, substituting W_θ and H_θ for W and H, we can directly define:

$$ID_\theta = \log_2(\sqrt{(A/W_\theta)^2 + (A/H_\theta)^2} + 1) \quad (7)$$

Replacing W_θ as well as H_θ based on Equation 6, we have:

$$ID_\theta = \log_2\left(\sqrt{\cos^2(\theta)(\frac{A}{W})^2 + \sin^2(\theta)(\frac{A}{H})^2} + 1\right) \quad (8)$$

We can let $\omega = \cos^2(\theta)$ and $\eta = \sin^2(\theta)$ for 2D pointing task, leading to the constraint $\omega + \eta = 1$. Now, the two weighted parameters built an internal relation between the two terms A/W and A/H in the binomial. This is unlike the situation of Equation 2, where ω and η are independent from each other. In addition, the mutually constrained two parameters η and ω let ID_θ has a new property of backward compatibility (as explained later in this section). Equation 8 expresses the ideal situation of projection. However, this equation implies that MT would be relevant to only one of the target dimensions in horizontal or vertical movement directions. This point is not the case reported by different studies [2, 26]. A reasonable explanation is that there should be a constant component in the trigonometric functional relation between θ and ω or η. Thus, we further propose

Hypothesis 2: ***There should be simple linear transformation in the trigonometric functional relations to ensure that none of the target dimensions would be excluded to determine MT in any movement direction.***

That is to say, the trigonometric functions that express the weighted parameters ω and η should be generalized using linear transformations. Therefore, we have:

$$\omega = c_1 + c_0 \cos^2(\theta),\ \eta = c_2 + c_0 \sin^2(\theta) \qquad (9)$$

where c_0, c_1 and $c_2 \geq 0$. To maintain the backward compatibility, we still let $\omega + \eta = 1$. So, we can extend Fitts ID to express the effects of movement direction on 2D target acquisition as follows:

$$ID_\theta = \log_2 \left(\sqrt{\omega(\frac{A}{W})^2 + (1-\omega)(\frac{A}{H})^2} + 1 \right) \qquad (10)$$

where $\omega = c_1 + c_0 \cos^2(\theta)$ and $0 < \omega < 1$. In practice, the estimate of ω rather than c_0 or c_1 is the major concern. ω in form is a weighted parameter, but essentially it has inherent connection to movement direction, unlike the counterpart in Equation 2. The two components of ω imply that not only target dimensions themselves but also their projections are the determinants of ID_θ. We can look Equation 8 as a special case of Equation 10. Besides the aforementioned properties of ID_{az}, Equation 10 further emphasizes the following points:

- *Periodicity and Symmetry of movement direction's effects on both of H and W.* The factor θ does not affect one of W and H selectively, like Equation 4, but both of them simultaneously. More importantly, the trigonometric function expressing the relationship between ω and θ indicates how movement direction periodically affects H and W so as to determine the difficulties of 2D pointing.
- *Backward Compatibility.* Regardless of the concrete value of ω, Equation 10 will be exactly equivalent to the standard form of Fitts' law when $W = H$.
- *Proportionality of H and W.* The factors W and H proportionally contribute to ID via the quantities ω and (1-ω). The relative proportion of one factor still remains even when the other's contribution is close to zero. This is unlike Equation 3, which appears to imply that ID would be entirely dependent on the single factor W when H is close to infinity. Unlike Equation 5, different proportions also imply the inequality between W and H's effects.
- *Complementarity of H and W.* There is no more target property (e.g. aspect ratio, or area) than target width and height used to compose the whole determinant of ID. Increasing the weight of W's contribution will cause the equivalent decrease of H's weight, and vice versa.

Under the same conditions (A, W and H), the difficulties of pointing task in different directions are not same, since the freedoms of hand moving on a given plane, such as the horizontal desktop, range in different directions. Nevertheless, the freedoms of the hand as well as the movement difficulties should be equivalent in any pair of reciprocal movement directions. The point is supported by the periodicity of ω or η (i.e. π) as indicated in Equation 9.

Therefore, we maintain the meanings of ω unchanged when considering the following form of ID_θ to study whether or not there is another norm order that, mathematically, can result in better data fitting for 2D pointing.

$$ID_\theta = \log_2 \left(\left[\omega(\frac{A}{W})^r + (1-\omega)(\frac{A}{H})^r \right]^{1/r} + 1 \right) \qquad (11)$$

Equation 11 in form appears to be the result of subjecting Equation 2 to an additional constraint $\omega + \eta = 1$. But now, we have endowed ω with the ability to access the effects of movement direction. When the norm order r is close to infinity ∞, ID_θ can be expressed as follows:

$$ID_\theta = \log_2 \left(\max \left(\omega\frac{A}{W}, (1-\omega)\frac{A}{H} \right) + 1 \right) \qquad (12)$$

This form means that W and H are mutually exclusive to determine ID_θ, like the use of $min(W, H)$ in MacKenzie and Buxton's work [16]. The purpose of introducing Equations 11 and 12 is to explore how the accuracy of ID_θ depends on r and ω via curve fitting so as to indicate that ℓ_2-norm extension is the most appropriate choice for 2D pointing. Next, we present the results of two experiments to verify our hypotheses, especially the satisfying accuracy of Equation 10 under each of the twelve different θ conditions we tested.

EXPERIMENT 1: 2D POINTING TASK WITH DIFFERENT MOVEMENT DISTANCES

As an indirect pointing device, mouse separates motor space from visual space without the possibility of causing target to be obscured by hand in any movement direction. Thus, we carried out the experiment using a traditional mouse.

Apparatus and Participants

The experiment was performed on a HP Compaq DC7700 computer, which featured an Intel Core 2 Duo CPU at 2.0 GHz, 2.00 GB RAM, and a 17-inch LCD at 1280 × 960 resolution. A PS/2 mouse in its default settings was used as the pointing device.

Sixteen undergraduates (8 females and 8 males, with the average age of 20.3) participated in this experiment. All of them are right-handed.

Task and Experimental Design

For each trial, the participant needed to click a trial-start button and then moved the cursor to acquire a rectangular target as quickly and accurately as possible. The start button and the target were alternatively displayed. The effective diameter of the start button was 100 pixels, but it was visually rendered as a small 24-pixel-diameter circle. This form was helpful to concentrate the hits closer on the center of the button so as to prevent significant biases of actual movement

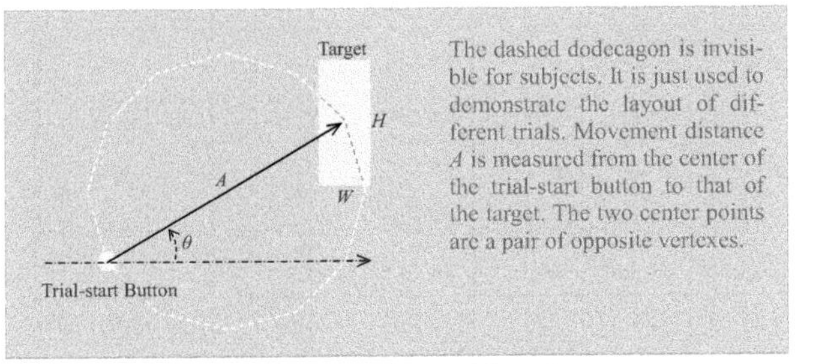

Figure 2. Experimental interface.

distance. As Figure 2 shows, the start button and the target were respectively placed at a pair of opposite vertexes of an invisible regular dodecagon, which was located at the center of the screen to control the layout. The duration from the start of trail by clicking the button to the moment the subject made a click for target selection was measured as MT. If the hit missed the target, an error trial was recorded. The trial settings would not be changed to the next combination of experimental factors until the success of the current one.

There were four experimental factors: movement distance A (250, 450, 650 pixels), target width W (30, 50, 80, 120 pixels), target height H (30, 50, 80, 120 pixels), and movement direction θ (i.e. approach angle, with 12 levels equally distributed from 0° to 360°, as determined by the centerlines of the vertex angles of the dodecagon, respectively). The core goal of the experiment was not to investigate the effects of the first three factors on user performance, like the studies [16, 2], but to test the validity of the new modification of Fitts' law. Therefore, the factors A, W and H were not fully crossed but manipulated to generate 25 combinations (as shown in Figure 4), with the requirement that the ID values calculated using Equation 5 were distributed throughout the corresponding range as evenly as possible because ID is the essential factor to determine MT [12]. A task block included 300 trials, resulting from the design of 25 combinations × 12 directions × 1 trial. These trials were presented in a predetermined random order. There were 6 blocks for each of the participants, who successfully completed the experiment within one session lasting about one hour.

Results

This experiment generated more than 29 thousand trials. The errors and outliers, which we at first excluded from our analyses, were about 3.69% of the whole data. This means that the subjects properly maintained an approximate 4% error rate required for Fitts' law studies [17]. As recommended by Soukoreff and MacKenzie [21], we used aggregated trial data for the analyses.

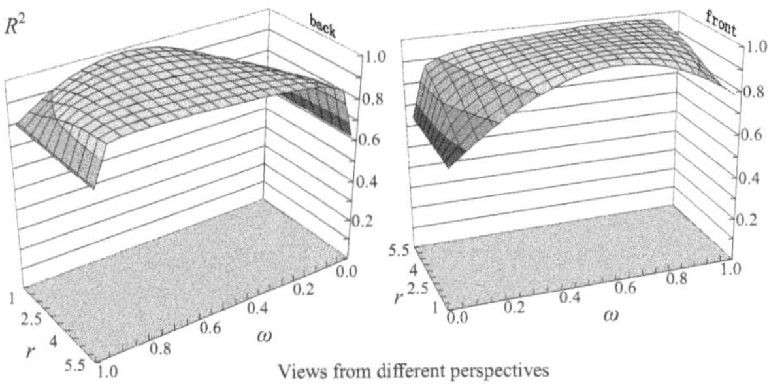

Figure 3. ID_θ **model's fitness plotted as a function of** ω **and** r.

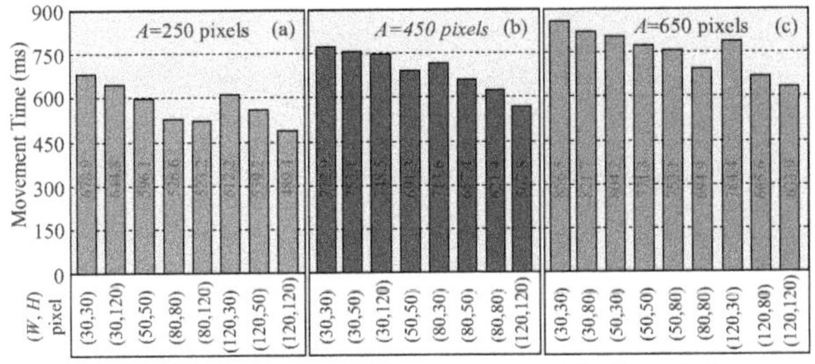

Figure 4. MT **by the combination of** W, H **and** A.

r	ω	a		b		ω		r		R^2
		Est.	*Std. Err.*	*Est.*	*Std. Err.*	*Est.*	*Std. Err.*	*Est.*	*Std. Err.*	
1	0.5	277.6	13.6	129.2	4.3	—	—	—	—	.977
	*	278.3	11.3	129.2	3.6	0.584	0.027	—	—	.984
2	0.5	276.4	11.7	127.4	3.6	—	—	—	—	.983
	*	277.2	8.2	127.5	2.5	0.616	0.023	—	—	**.992**
∞	0.5	359.1	18.3	128.8	7.1	—	—	—	—	.940
	*	343.7	13.0	132.3	4.9	0.563	0.013	—	—	.972
*	0.5	276.1	11.6	127.8	3.7	—	—	1.81	0.353	.983
	*	277.1	8.2	127.6	2.6	0.614	0.026	1.95	0.281	**.992**
Equation 3		250.6	9.1	123.9	2.4	0.62	0.061	*for* η	—	**.992**
Equation 5		311. 9	10.4	134.2	3.7	—	—	—	—	.983

Table 1. Results of model fitting. The asterisk denotes a free parameter.

Movement Time

Using repeated measures ANOVA, we found a significant learning effect among the task blocks ($F_{5,75} = 9.63, p < .001$) because of the significant differences between the first block and some of the others. Thus, we also excluded the data of the first block. Figure 4 depicts the averages of MT under the 25 different conditions of (A, W, and H). It indicates that for a given combination of $A \times W$ or $A \times H$, MT will decrease in general with the increase of H or W, and vice versa. This point directly reflects the duality of H and W. The results also reveal the dominance effect. In Figure 4a, for example, when $W = 30$ pixels, the difference of MT between the two H levels 30 and 120 pixels is obviously smaller than the difference when $W = 120$ pixels. In Figure 4c, we can also find a similar result when H increases from 30 to 80 pixels. Figure 4b illustrates a more direct evidence of the dominance effect that the difference between the two H levels (50 and 120 pixels) when $W = 30$ pixels is insignificant ($F_{1,15} = 0.363, p = .556$).

Model Fitting to Entire Data

When fitting the model of Equation 11 to the grand means of MT, we considered different parameterization schemes of ω and r. Similar to the method in Accot and Zhai's work [2], we also let the norm order $r \in \{1, 2, \infty, *\}$ to parameterize it, where the asterisk denotes being free for the best estimate. The weight ω was parameterized by setting it free or equal to 0.5, which denotes the equal impact of W and H. Therefore, there were 8 models resulting from the parameterization. Table 1 lists the schemes and summarizes the results of model fitting. As can be seen, the most suitable combination was that when $r = 2$, and ω was set as a free parameter (i.e. Equation 10), which resulted in a higher R^2 up to .99. We further plotted R^2 as a function of ω and r. As Figure 3 shows, the convex curved surface confirms the reliability of the estimates in Table 1. These results justified the derivation from our hypotheses to Equation 10. Comparing ID_θ with ID_{az} and ID_{conf}, we found that they all could accurately predict the grand means of MT. Next, we further present their performances under different θ conditions.

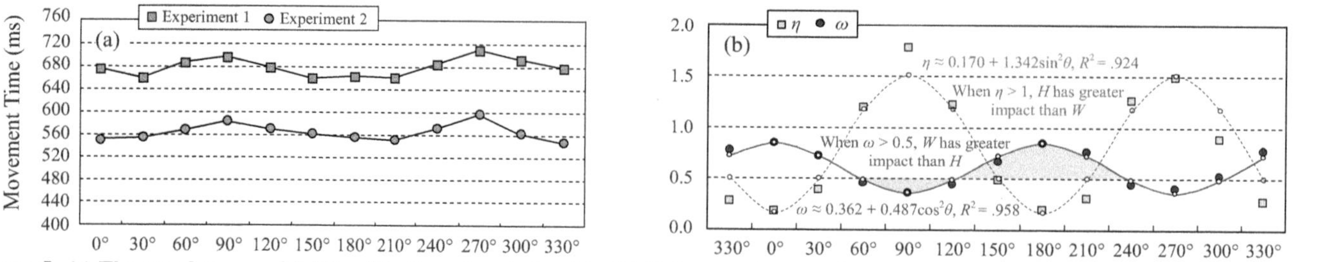

Figure 5. (a) The grand means of MT by θ in Experiments 1 and 2; (b) Estimates of ω as well as η by θ. It appears to be that there is a periodic function relationship between the parameter ω and the factor θ, matching the use of ω as the replacement of $c_1 + c_0 \cos^2\theta$ based on our hypotheses. Within a period (π), the area above the dashed line where $\omega = 0.5$ is obviously larger than that below (see the light green area and the gray one), indicating that target width W, overall, has greater contribution than target height H to hand pointing tasks' difficulties.

Effects of Movement Direction

The factor θ had a significant main effect on MT ($F_{11,165} = 11.79, p < .001$). Figure 5a shows the averages of MT at different θ levels. Post hoc pairwise comparisons indicated that there were 40 pairs of directions that generated significant differences of MT, but in general there was no significant difference between two opposite or axisymmetric directions. Table 2 summarizes the results of model fitting. As can be seen, there were some interesting results when the data were differentiated by movement direction. The R^2 values of the new modification and Equation 3 were very close to each other under every θ condition, and they were higher, in general, than those of Equation 5, especially under the horizontal conditions. In other words, the new modification and Equation 3 were able to effectively capture the effect of movement direction on MT via the introduced parameter ω or η, and they were better than Equation 5 when taking account of movement direction.

More importantly, it was implied that both ω and η were dependent on θ. As Table 2 indicates, the estimates of ω as well as η could be divided into two clusters. They consistently indicated that when θ leaned to the horizontal directions, W had greater weight affecting MT than H ($\omega > 0.5$, $\eta < 1.0$), otherwise the weight of H was greater ($\eta > 1.0$, $\omega < 0.5$). In general, the closer the movement direction to the horizontal axis is, the greater the weight of W for MT will be (compared to that of H and the weight of W under a different θ condition as well). The relationship between the estimates of ω and θ could be formulated using $\omega = 0.362 + 0.487\cos^2\theta$ ($R^2 = .958$), correctly matching the meanings of ω based on our hypotheses, while those of η could be expressed as $\eta = 0.170 + 1.342\sin^2\theta$ ($R^2 = .924$). Figure 5b plots the estimates and the calculated values of ω and η by θ. It seemed that the parameter ω was more accurate than η to reveal the symmetry and periodicity of the effect of movement direction on MT.

Figure 5b also indicates that the balanced directions where W and H theoretically have equal impacts ($\omega = 0.5$) are not the bisectors of the quadrants but biased to the vertical axis. Thus, within a period, e.g. from 60° to 240° (π), the area (i.e. the probability) of the θ conditions where $\omega > 0.5$ is obviously larger than the area where $\omega < 0.5$. That is to say, overall, target width W had greater contribution than H to MT as implied by the estimates of ω in Table 1 ($\omega > 0.6$).

We also plotted R^2 by ω under each of the θ conditions. As Figure 6 shows, it further reveals the following three points:

θ	Equation 12				Equation 3		Equation 5
	a	b	ω	R^2	η	R^2	R^2
330°	288.9	124.7	0.778	.981	0.284	.981	.925
0°	277.4	128.1	0.851	.975	0.174	.975	**.880**
30°	284.2	119.5	0.719	.969	0.386	.969	.933
60°	267.2	132.7	0.451	.963	1.195	.961	.963
90°	258.6	138.7	0.361	.936	1.772	.935	.925
120°	297.8	120.6	0.449	.972	1.224	.972	.970
150°	284.9	119.2	0.671	.963	0.487	.962	.941
180°	264.8	128.1	0.841	.971	0.189	.971	**.872**
210°	280.3	121.7	0.769	.983	0.299	.984	.931
240°	246	139	0.44	.965	1.267	.964	.963
270°	278.1	136.6	0.402	.957	1.491	.957	.952
300°	289.2	127.9	0.531	.956	0.888	.957	.953

Table 2. Summary of model fitting to the data under each of the θ conditions in Experiment 1.

- *R^2 has similar dependence on ω when θ is in axisymmetric or opposite directions.* As shown by the convex curves in each of the subfigures, ω apparently has similar impacts on the accuracies of ID_θ in each pair of axisymmetric or opposite directions due to the similar summits, with the curves themselves closely matched with each other. A reasonable explanation about this point is that the user performances in axisymmetric or opposite directions are similar to each other. Furthermore, the convexities of all the curves also confirm the reliabilities of the optimal estimates of ω under different θ conditions (see Table 2).
- *R^2 is more sensitive to W.* Comparing the curvatures near the summits, it is also clearly indicated that the accuracies are more sensitive to the variations of ω ($\omega > 0.5$) under the horizontal θ conditions than under the vertical conditions ($\omega < 0.5$). That is to say, W is prior to determine ID_θ for horizontal pointing tasks, but the corresponding priority of H is not stronger for vertical pointing tasks because the differences of R^2 are not obvious when ω is changed from the best estimate to 0.5 or beyond.
- *W is superior to H for the accuracies of ID_θ.* Comparing the differences between the R^2 values when $\omega = 0.5$ and the best estimate under different movement direction conditions, we can find that the improvements of the accuracies of ID_θ via increasing the weight of H under the vertical θ conditions are not as great as those via increasing the weight of W under the horizontal θ conditions.

Recently, Guiard argued that the linear relationship between MT and ID could be "contaminated" when using a crossed design of $A \times W$ [12]. In other words, the regression coefficients would be different under different movement distance (A) or target width (W) conditions. Accordingly, we calculated the regression coefficients for different A levels

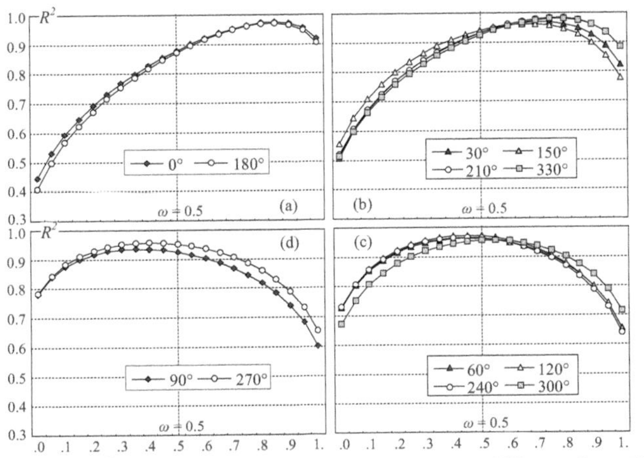

Figure 6. R^2 **plotted as a function of** ω **under every different** θ **condition in Experiment 1.**

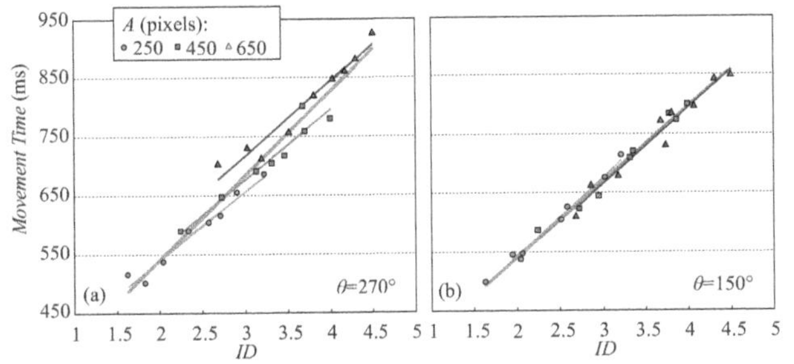

Figure 7. Regression lines at different A **levels when** $\theta = 270°, 150°$

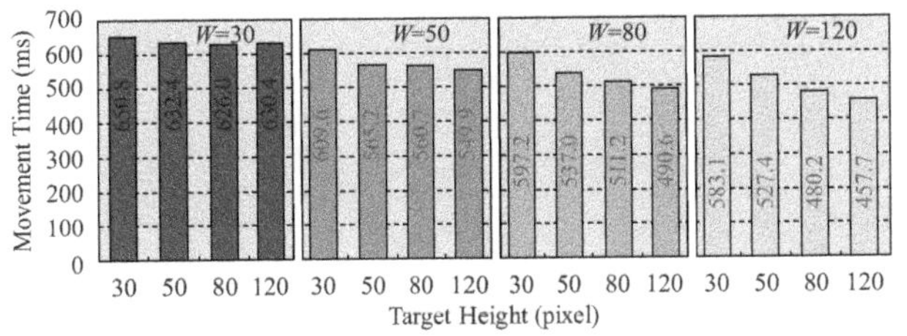

Figure 8. MT **by the combination of** W **and** H **when** $A = 550$ **pixels.**

θ	Equation 12				Equation 3		Equation 5
	a	b	ω	R^2	η	R^2	R^2
330°	169.2	109.3	0.771	.969	0.296	.969	.817
0°	208.9	100.5	0.877	.976	0.139	.976	.676
30°	198.9	103.2	0.791	.952	0.263	.953	.785
60°	226.9	97.70	0.484	.943	1.067	.942	.942
90°	176.1	117.2	0.386	.966	1.600	.967	.939
120°	187.2	109.9	0.536	.975	0.866	.975	.974
150°	163.7	115.5	0.786	.930	0.272	.930	.765
180°	138.1	122.0	0.857	.988	0.166	.988	.734
210°	168.3	111.0	0.785	.958	0.274	.958	.785
240°	176.2	113.6	0.419	.942	1.387	.941	.931
270°	158.9	125.7	0.396	.939	1.530	.940	.918
300°	174.7	111.3	0.489	.971	1.045	.971	.970
Total	182.3	110.0	0.644	.994	0.552	.994	.952

Table 3. Summary of model fitting to the data under each of the twelve θ **conditions and the entire data in Experiment 2.**

and further found that the contamination extents appeared to be relevant to the direction factor θ. As illustrated by the regression lines of the cases when $\theta = 270°$ and $150°$ in Figure 7, the contamination was noticeable in vertical directions, but, on the contrary, it was negligible in horizontal (or near-horizontal) directions.

Overall, this experiment suggests that the parameter ω can effectively capture the unequal effects of W and H in different movement directions, and that the parameter ω is a periodic function of θ. To substantiate these findings, we further carried out the following experiment.

EXPERIMENT 2: 2D POINTING TASK WITH A CONSTANT MOVEMENT DISTANCE

As Figure 7a indicates, the different slopes of the regression lines under different movement distance conditions also imply that using different A levels in 2D pointing experiments could probably bias the estimations of ω in some movement directions. In order to purify and highlight the effects of W and H, we employed a constant distance (550 pixels) in this experiment as Guiard recommended [12].

The apparatus was the same as in Experiment 1 but a 22-inch LCD at 1680×1050 resolution in place of the 17-inch LCD. The task as well as the procedure was also similar. The main difference was that the start button and the target, which was disabled at first, were both presented before the beginning of each trial. This was helpful for subjects to reduce the possible (maybe negligible) delay of target locating. Once clicked, the start button would disappear, with the target enabled immediately. Both of target width and height varied at four levels of 30, 50, 80 and 120 pixels. There were 7 task blocks, and each of them included 192 trials, resulting from a fully crossed design ($4\ W \times 4\ H \times 12\ \theta \times 1$ trial). Seventeen right-handed participants (8 females and 9 males, with the average age of 22) successfully finished this experiment. Only five of them took part in the first experiment.

Results

We recorded more than 23 thousand trials in this experiment, and when analyzing the results we left out the errors and outliers (3.49%) as well as the data of the first block due to the significant learning effect ($F_{6,96} = 19.99, p < .001$).

We found that the factor θ had a significant main effect on MT ($F_{11,176} = 10.25, p < .001$). Similar to the results of the first experiment, post hoc pairwise comparisons revealed that there was also no significant difference among almost all pairs of opposite directions but 150° and 330° ($p < .05$) as well as in all pairs of axisymmetric directions. This result clearly supported our explanation about the similarity of the relationships between R^2 and ω in opposite and axisymmetric directions. Consequently, the data under these θ conditions could be grouped together to construct a common model as shown in Figure 10. Furthermore, it was also indicated that the vertical directions generated significant differences compared with all the other non-vertical directions but 240° compared with 90° ($p = .108$). Figure 8 shows the means of MT by the combination of W and A, while the means by θ are also shown in Figure 5a. It indicates that the user performance would gradually deteriorate if θ varied from horizontal to vertical directions. This result is consistent with that presented in prior studies [23, 22, 11].

Table 3 summarizes the results of model fitting. We can see that ID_θ and ID_{az} almost had the same accuracies either for the entire data or the data grouped by θ, and that both of them were better than Equation 5, whose accuracies obviously deteriorated under the conditions that movement was in or near the horizontal directions. We rechecked the accuracy of Equation 5 under each of the three A con-

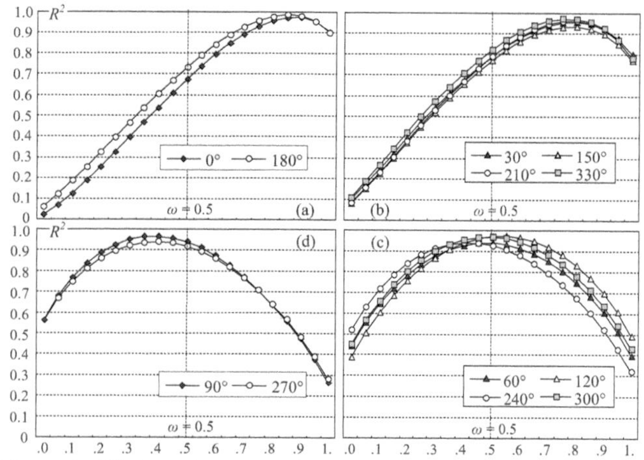

Figure 9. R^2 **plotted as a function of** ω **under every different** θ **condition in Experiment 2.**

ditions in Experiment 1 and found similar situations. These results substantially implied that W had greater impact on MT especially in the directions close to horizontal. The estimates of ω could be approximately expressed as $\omega = 0.372 + 0.518\cos^2\theta$ ($R^2 = .969$). Regarding the parameter η, the estimates could be approximately calculated using $\eta = 0.130 + 1.311\sin^2\theta$ ($R^2 = .913$). This means that η could capture the effects of movement direction on MT as accurate as ω, but its periodicity was not as strong as that of ω. We plotted R^2 as a function of ω as shown in Figure 9, which clearly demonstrates the superiority of W to determine MT, the stronger W-sensitivity of R^2 and the similarities that ω impacts R^2 in opposite or axisymmetric directions. As shown in Figure 9a&b, for example, if only use H ($\omega = 0$) to define ID_θ, there is almost no linear correlation, while it is still obvious if only use W ($\omega = 1$). Overall, this experiment strengthened our findings as we anticipated.

DISCUSSION

In this paper, we aim to uncover how movement direction affects user performance, although some other researchers [11, 26] prefer to accommodate this factor without directly interpreting it. With the following three points, the results of our study definitely justified our hypotheses.

First, the findings consistent with those in prior studies implied the reliability of the data. For example, our experiments indicated that 2D pointing could achieve the best performance in horizontal directions or their near directions and the performance would become increasingly degraded, as reported in the studies [22, 11], when θ was gradually transferred to vertical directions. Our experiments also indicated that the performance change pattern, especially in Experiment 2, regularly took place in the range from 0° to 360° like the result in Whisenand and Emurian's work [23]. Regarding the results of model fitting, the parameter η got similar estimates to those in the Accot and Zhai's work [2] when Equation 3 was used to model horizontal 2D pointing. The fitness of Equation 5 under the horizontal conditions in Experiment 1 was also as low as Yang and Xu themselves reported [26] and even lower in Experiment 2, which eliminated the effect of movement distance. These consistencies indirectly indicated that our experiments properly captured the performance features of 2D pointing.

Second, excluding the possible contamination of movement distance, Experiment 2 successfully reproduced and further strengthened the findings about the parameter ω. These findings included the good model fit to the data differentiated by movement direction and the entire data as well, the periodic variation of ω in the whole range of θ and the clear relationship between ω and the accuracy of ID_θ in each of the different movement directions. These repeated results substantially confirmed the validity of our hypotheses. Comparing the two approximate expressions of ω (i.e. $\omega = 0.362 + 0.487\cos^2\theta$ vs. $\omega = 0.372 + 0.518\cos^2\theta$) resulted from the empirical data of the two experiments, we further found that the parameters c_1 and c_0, calculated based on the estimates of ω, had little variations between the two experiments. It probably means that these two parameters are not dependent on subjects but on pointing devices. This property is desirable for the definition of ID as it can provide a new criterion for device comparisons.

Third, the weighted parameter η also exhibited an apparent periodicity with the variation of θ. In Equation 3, η is the only adjustable parameter so that it highlights the variations of the impact of target height as implied by the larger amplitude of the sine square wave in Figure 5b. The same change pattern of η and $1 - \omega$ (i.e. $c_2 + c_0\sin^2\theta$) directly confirms the potential connection between the impacts of target width and height as indicated in our hypotheses.

As can be seen in Tables 2 and 3, ID_θ and ID_{az} almost had the same power to model 2D pointing. The results clarified that ID_{az} did not only work for horizontal directions but also for every different direction. However, we need to point out that ID_{az} ***is incompatible with the standard Fitts*** ID. In Experiment 2, for example, when pointing at the rectangular target of 50 × 80 pixels along the movement direction $\theta = 0°$ and $270°$, the corresponding difficulties should be between the difficulties of pointing at two different square targets 80 × 80 and 50 × 50 pixels. As Figure 10a shows, however, the values of ID_{az} (3.62 and 3.90) are not in the Fitts ID range $(\log_2(\frac{550}{80}+1), \log_2(\frac{550}{50}+1))$ but larger than the upper bound. This means that the extension of Equation 3 leads to a distortion of IDs, making ID_{az} incomparable with Fitts ID and even with itself due to the different distortion caused by different η. On the contrary, it is easy to prove that for any rectangular target, its ID_θ value will always fall into a specific Fitts ID range, whose bounds are determined by the two dimensions of the rectangular target. In other words, we can find an equivalent square target for any rectangular target, whose ID_θ value is equal to the Fitts ID value of the square target, in a specific size range.

The incomparability of ID_{az} with itself under different η conditions can greatly bias or even reverse the results of user performance evaluation. As presented in Figure 10b, for example, the regression lines wrongly imply that the user performance in horizontal directions would get worse than that in vertical directions at the "same" level of ID_{az}. In addition, regardless of the effectiveness of data fitting using ID_{az}, this problem might bias and invalidate the dependent measure of throughput, which has been accepted by ISO9241-9 for the evaluation of pointing devices. We can find two different points of view about the definition of

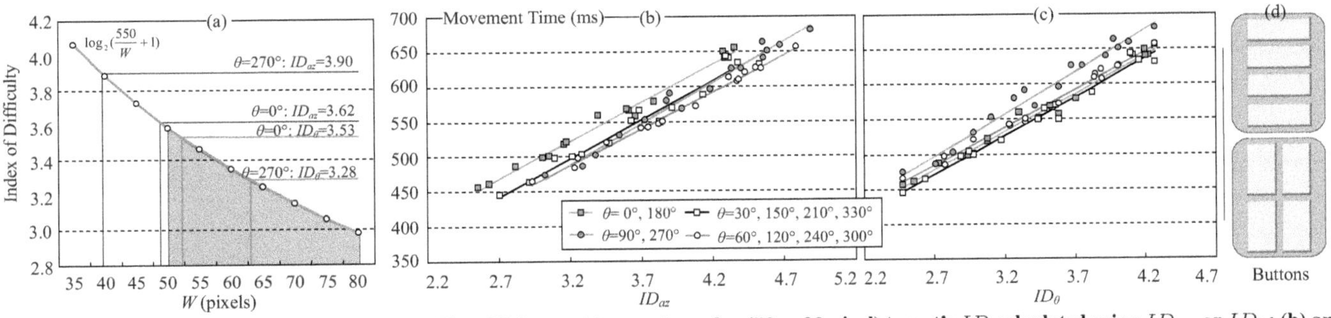

Figure 10. (a) Width of the square target whose Fitts ID is equal to a rectangular (50×80 pixel) target's ID calculated using ID_{az} or ID_θ; (b) and (c) Regression lines for the data in Experiment 2 based on ID_{az} and ID_θ, respectively; (d) Button groups arranged in the same limited area.

throughput [21, 27], but, anyhow, this measure is not independent from ID. Therefore, it is also necessary to maintain the consistency of different definitions of ID, like ID_θ, with the standard Fitts ID for the comparability of experimental evaluations [21]. Figure 10c clearly shows the benefit that the regression lines based on ID_θ can correctly represent the ranks of the user performance in different directions.

Design Recommendations for 2D Pointing Experiments

We have presented the reliability and advantages of ID_θ. Now, we make the following design recommendations for Fitts' law experiments that take account of 2D targets.

- *Use rectangular targets with various aspect ratios instead of circular targets.* ISO9241-9 recommends using circular or square targets so as to match the variables of the 1D Fitts' law. Our study indicates that it is no longer necessary to restrict the shape of targets. Accounting for the difficulties of pointing at general rectangular targets, ID_θ with an empirical constant ω to capture the different effects of W and H can offer more valuable information for interface designs and pointing device evaluations as Accot and Zhai previously mentioned [2].
- *Avoid the risk of contamination caused by the factor of movement direction.* The results of Experiment 1 confirmed that the use of different A levels could indeed result in the contamination of Fitts' law parameters [12]. Unfortunately, the use of different θ values could also cause contamination, as Figure 10c shows, even though the contamination caused by A were excluded. This means that multidirectional tapping tasks may be unsafe for model fitting. A simple way to prevent this potential risk is to use only a group of opposite or axisymmetric directions.
- *Use horizontal or vertical directions to highlight the asymmetrical impact of W and H on movement time.* Our findings about the asymmetry of W and H are consistent with those of the prior studies [2, 11]. Our work further reveal that the asymmetry, quantified using ω and 1-ω for W and H, respectively, is periodically varied with movement direction (i.e. $\omega = c_1 + c_0 \cos^2 \theta$). W achieves the maximum impact in horizontal directions, but so does H in vertical directions. When one of the target dimensions gets the maximum impact, the other gets the minimum.
- *Use diagonal directions to reveal the overall impacts of W and H.* If a target can be equally accessed from different directions (0° – 360°), the mathematical expectation of ω, which could be interpreted as the overall impact of W, will be equal to the value of ω in diagonal directions (e.g. 135°). The similarity between the estimate of ω for the entire data and the calculated value using the approximate expression (0.616 vs. 0.610 in Experiment 1; 0.644 vs. 0.631 in Experiment 2) supports this point.

Design Implications for User Interfaces

The findings of our study can benefit the development of user interfaces. First of all, it is more efficient to facilitate the acquisition of targets by elongating them in horizontal directions than in vertical directions unless the targets are usually acquired via vertical pointing. Comparing the impact of H in vertical directions and that of W in horizontal directions (e.g. 0.628 vs. 0.890 in Experiment 2), we can find that the user cannot make use of target height as fully as of width. Overall, W has greater impact ($\omega > 0.6$) than H. Secondly, the frequently used buttons should be placed in the left or right side of the workspace in user interfaces due to the better user performance in (or near) the horizontal directions. Thirdly, with respect to a group of icons or buttons that need to be arranged in a limited area (such as the case in Figure 10d), it is better to make them as wide as possible.

In addition, the results of our study indicate that when $\theta \approx 60°, 120°, 240°$ or $300°$, instead of 45° as Grossman and Balakrishnan reported [11], the two target factors W and H have equal impact on MT. This implies that increasing the widths of the targets placed at the corners of a window can still obtain greater benefits, especially when wide LCD monitors increasingly get popular today. The inconsistency between this implication and that in previous work [11] maybe resulted from the use of different pointing devices.

CONCLUSIONS AND FUTURE WORK

The experimental results we have presented above indicate that the projections of target width and height (W and H) on the line of movement can properly express their asymmetrical impacts on movement time; that the projection method can effectively uncover the inherent dependence of the impacts of W and H on movement direction and the internal relation between them. To summarize, the difficulty of pointing at 2D targets can be defined as:

$$ID_\theta = \log_2\left(\sqrt{\omega(A/W)^2 + (1-\omega)(A/H)^2} + 1\right)$$

where $0 < \omega < 1$, and it depends on movement direction θ, i.e. $\omega = c_1 + c_0 \cos^2 \theta$. In practice, it only needs several different angles to calibrate c_1 and c_0, and we believe that they will be consistent in different experiments when the same pointing device is used. Thus, the parameter ω can be used as a new measure for pointing device evaluation. The simplicity of ID_θ in form, the easy use and its compatibility with the standard Fitts ID can benefit the field of HCI as we have discussed. In the future, we plan to investigate the benefits of using effective width and height based on 2D joint probability distribution [19] or endpoint deviation [24], confirm the effectiveness of ID_θ for other pointing devices, evaluate target expansion in two dimensions and study the acquisition of rotated 2D targets.

ACKNOWLEDGMENTS

The authors thank the anonymous CHI reviewers for their detailed and valuable commentaries, especially the constructive recommendations to revise this paper. This work was supported by the National Natural Science Foundation of China (Grant No. 61070144).

REFERENCES

1. Accot, J. and Zhai, S. Beyond Fitts' law: Models for trajectory-based HCI tasks. In *Proc. CHI'97*, ACM Press (1997), 295–302.
2. Accot, J. and Zhai, S. Refining Fitts' law models for bivariate pointing. In *Proc. CHI 2003*, ACM Press (2003), 193–200.
3. Ahlström, D., Cockburn, A., Gutwin, C. and Irani, P. Why it's quick to be square: Modeling new and existing hierarchical menu designs. In *Proc. CHI 2010*, ACM Press (2010), 1371–1380.
4. Appert, C., Chapuis, O. and Beaudouin-Lafon, M. Evaluation of pointing performance on screen edges. In *Proc. AVI'08*, ACM Press (2008), 119–126.
5. Blanch, R. and Ortega, M. Benchmarking pointing techniques with distractors: Adding a density factor to Fitts' pointing Paradigm. In *Proc. CHI 2011*, ACM Press (2011), 1629–1638.
6. Bohan, M., Longstaff, M. G., Van Gemmert, A. W., Rand, M. K. and Stelmach, G. E. Differential effects of target height and width on 2D pointing movement duration and kinematics. *Motor Control*,Vol.7, No.3 (2003), 278–89.
7. Boritz, J., Booth, K. S. and Cowan, W. B. Fitts' law studies of directional mouse movement. In *Proc. Graphics Interface'91*, Canada (1991), 216–223.
8. Cao, X., Li, J.J. and Balakrishnan, R. Peephole pointing: Modeling acquisition of dynamically revealed targets. In *Proc. CHI 2008*, ACM Press (2008), 1699–1708.
9. Cockburn, A. and Gutwin, C. A predictive model of human performance with scrolling and hierarchical lists. *Human-Computer Interaction*, Vol.24, No.3 (2009), 273–314.
10. Fitts, P.M. The information capacity of the human motor system in controlling the amplitude of movement. *Journal of Experimental Psychology*, Vol.47 (1954), 381–391.
11. Grossman, T. and Balakrishnan, R. A probabilistic approach to modeling two-dimensional pointing. *ACM Transactions on Computer-Human Interaction*, Vol.12, No.3 (2005), 435–459.
12. Guiard, Y. The problem of consistency in the design of Fitts' law experiments: Consider either target distance and width or movement form and scale. In *Proc. CHI 2009*, ACM Press (2009), 1809–1818.
13. Hoffmann, E. R. and Sheikh, I. H. Effect of varying target height in a Fitts' movement task. *Ergonomics*, Vol. 37, No. 6 (1994), 1071–1088.
14. Jax, S.A. and Rosenbaum, D. A. Extending Fitts' law to manual obstacle avoidance. *Experimental Brain Research*, Vol. 180 (2007), 775–779.
15. MacKenzie, I. S. A note on the information-theoretic basis for Fitts' law. *Journal of Motor Behavior*, Vol.21 (1989), 323–330.
16. MacKenzie, I.S. and Buxton, W. Extending Fitts' law to two-dimensional tasks. In *Proc. CHI'92*, ACM Press (1992), 219–226.
17. MacKenzie, I.S. Fitts' law as a research and design tool in human-computer interaction. *Human-Computer Interaction*, Vol.7 (1992), 91–139.
18. Martin, F. S. Assessment of Fitts' Law for Quantifying Combined Rotational and Translational Movements. *Human Factors*, Vol. 52, No. 1 (2010), 63–77.
19. Murata, A. Extending effective target width in Fitts' law to a two-dimensional pointing task. *Int. J. Human-Computer Interaction*, Vol. 11, No. 2 (1999), 137–152.
20. Schmidt, R.A., Zalaznik, H.N., Hawkins, B., Frank, J.S. and Quinn, J.T. Motor output variability: A theory for the accuracy of rapid motor acts. *Psychology Review*, Vol.86 (1979), 415–451.
21. Soukoreff, R.W. and MacKenzie, I.S. Towards a standard for pointing device evaluation, perspectives on 27 years of Fitts' law research in HCI. *Int. J. Human-Computer Studies*, Vol.61 (2004), 751–789.
22. Thompson, S., Slocum, J. and Bohan, M. Gain and angle of approach effects on cursor-positioning time with a mouse in consideration of Fitts' law. In *Proc. the 48th annual meeting of HFES*, (2004), 823–827.
23. Whisenand, T.G. and Emurian, H.H. Analysis of cursor movements with a mouse. *Computers in Human Behavior*, Vol.15 (1999), 85–103.
24. Wobbrock, J.O., Shinohara, K. and Jansen, A. The effects of task dimensionality, endpoint deviation, throughput calculation, and experiment design on pointing measures and models. In *Proc. CHI 2011*, ACM Press (2011), 1639–1648.
25. Wu, J., Yang, J. and Honda, T. Fitts' law holds for pointing movements under conditions of restricted visual feedback. *Human Movement Science*, Vol. 29 (2010), 882–892.
26. Yang, H. and Xu, X. Bias towards regular configuration in 2D pointing. In *Proc. CHI 2010*, ACM Press (2010), 1391–1400.
27. Zhai, S. Characterizing computer input with Fitts' law parameters - the information and non-information aspects of pointing. *Int. J. Human-Computer Studies*, Vol. 61, No. 6 (2004), 791–809.

Perceptions of Facebook's Value as an Information Source

Cliff Lampe
University of Michigan
105 South State St. Ann Arbor, MI 48109
cacl@umich.edu

Jessica Vitak, Rebecca Gray, Nicole B. Ellison
Michigan State University
409 Comm Arts Bldg, East Lansing, MI 48824
[vitakjes, grayreb2, nellison]@msu.edu

ABSTRACT
Facebook has become an increasingly important tool for people engaging in a range of communication behaviors, including requesting help from their social network to address information needs. Through a study of 614 staff members at a large university, we show how social capital, network characteristics, and use of Facebook are related to how useful individuals find Facebook to be for informational purposes and their propensity to seek different types of information on the site. We find that bridging social capital and engagement with one's network through directed communication behaviors are important predictors of these dimensions of information seeking; furthermore, a number of demographic and usage behavior differences exist between those who choose to engage in information-seeking behaviors on Facebook and those who do not. Finally, when predicting information-seeking behaviors, we identify a significant interaction between users' perceptions of Facebook as appropriate for purposes beyond the purely social and their engagement with their network.

Author Keywords
Information-seeking, Facebook, social network sites, social capital

ACM Classification Keywords
H5.m. Information interfaces and presentation (e.g., HCI): Miscellaneous.

General Terms
Human Factors

INTRODUCTION
In this study, we seek to understand the extent to which Facebook users are likely to use the site for their information-seeking activities. With an expanding user base [20] and a wide variety of motivations driving site use [14], it is important to consider if and how users are employing the site's social and technical features to connect with their social networks when seeking information.

In everyday life, individuals encounter a wide range of information needs. These can include questions as wide-ranging as how to fix a printer, what to name a pet, or recommendations about a major purchase [6]. Models of information seeking around these daily uncertainties argue that people turn to those in their social network for information rather than going to formal sources [29]. As social network sites (SNSs) have been shown to connect individuals to people with whom they have a previously established offline connection [15], as well as to connections of different degrees of relational closeness [12], it is likely that people turn to SNSs as an efficient way to tap these connections for information-seeking purposes.

Facebook is increasingly used by a diverse group of people. Recent Pew data indicate that 65% of Internet using adults in the United States have a profile on at least one SNS [20]. The average age of SNS users has also increased in recent years: among American Internet users, 70% of 30-49 year-olds, 51% of 50-64 year-olds, and 33% of those 65 or older now have a profile on a SNS [20]. Facebook is the dominant SNS, with nearly all (92%) adult SNS users maintaining a profile on the site [9].

As diverse groups of users become Facebook members, they use the site in increasingly varied ways. Previous work has shown that Facebook users engage in multiple activities on the site and have different motivations for using the site [14, 23, 31]. Connecting with friends, seeking emotional support, playing games, and sharing pictures are just some of the ways people use Facebook [18]. In addition, research suggests that, increasingly, users are repurposing SNSs for purposes beyond the strictly social, including for networking and collaboration [17].

A few researchers have looked at how SNSs are used for information seeking, both in workplace settings [8, 30, 32] and, more generally, to fill common information needs [21]. The primary finding from these studies is that people turn to SNSs for information—as opposed to using formal channels like search engines or libraries—when the information need is best fulfilled by information from people who know and are known by the information seeker.

The present study extends this line of research by exploring the degree to which individuals find Facebook useful for information seeking, as well as the extent to which they engage in a range of information-seeking behaviors on the site. Existing research on the use of SNSs for "social search" functions differentiates information seeking from browsing, explores cultural differences in question-asking behaviors, and identifies different types of information seeking as well as factors influencing responses to information seeking [33, 36]. Another line of research has shown how Facebook use is related to perceptions of social capital [3, 11], a construct that captures how likely individuals feel they are able to convert network connections into things like favors or information. The contribution of this work is to extend scholarship on social search, provide additional evidence for the social capital implications of Facebook use, and synthesize these research streams to explicate how social capital affects social search.

LITERATURE REVIEW

Everyday Information Seeking

How people seek information—and the types of information they seek—is a complex interplay between characteristics of the information seeker, the properties of the information they are looking for, and the systems in which they seek information. For example, Dervin [4] developed a "sense-making" model of information seeking that argued people with information needs iteratively contextualize both the need and potential "bridges" (i.e., sources of information) for filling those needs. Likewise, Nardi and O'Day's [22] "information ecologies" perspective suggests people address information needs by incorporating multiple "species," including formalized systems like books, people, and practices. These perspectives incorporate information search not just as purposive seeking of information, but as a continual process where information that may be useful in the future is noted as people encounter it [35].

Theoretical work by Pirolli—specifically Information Foraging Theory [25] and the Social Information Foraging Model [24]—support these models of information seeking. The original Information Foraging Theory represents an economic approach to information search and argues that information seekers evaluate the benefit of their current access to information versus the cost of seeking additional information. With Information Foraging Theory, Pirolli argues that individuals' information-seeking performance can be improved by increasing network diversity, especially among those who would be willing to respond to an information request. In other words, social connections reduce many of the costs of information seeking.

Considering these perspectives on information seeking, it is clear that people with information needs go through an iterative search process that can include multiple sources, systems, and techniques. Thus, we suspect SNSs such as Facebook may play an important role in this "information ecology" by providing users with multiple outlets through which to request and access information from their Facebook networks.

Research on Facebook Use

Facebook contains a number of useful features related to information seeking. Users establish networks of "Friends"—often in the hundreds—and maintain those relationships through both passive consumption and active contribution of content to the system. Facebook contains multiple channels for information seeking, including dyadic and group messaging, as well as network-wide interaction via status updates. Facebook also enables users to passively view the information-sharing and -seeking activities of their network via the News Feed and can respond to network members' information requests, either by commenting directly on an update or through another channel.

Scholars in several fields have addressed how people use Facebook, as well as outcomes associated with use. Early work established that individuals used the site more to connect with pre-existing offline connections than to meet new people [15] and that specific types of profile information (e.g., those hard to fake, like contact information and organizational membership) predicted network size (number of Friends) [16]. More recent studies have established a typology of Facebook uses, including relationship maintenance, social surveillance, and social interaction [14, 23].

When considering potential outcomes derived from SNS use, several researchers have focused on the relationship between Facebook use and social capital [3, 4, 9]. Social capital can be understood as the cumulative resources—both actual and potential—that individuals have access to through their social network [2]. Social capital is exchanged through interactions with that network, both in the request for and provision of those resources. Researchers have identified specific uses of Facebook that positively predict two types of social capital: *bridging*, which includes the ability to access non-redundant information and diverse perspectives, typically through weaker ties; and *bonding*, which reflects the physical, social, and emotional support that close ties typically provide. For example, Burke and colleagues [4] found that increases in Facebook network size were positively correlated with increases in perceived social capital. Ellison and colleagues [11] found that the *type* of tie—operationalized as the number of "actual" friends users reported in their network—was more predictive of social capital than the *quantity* of ties (total number of Friends).

Researchers have also found specific Facebook usage behaviors to be predictive of social capital. While neither broadcasting updates nor passive consumption of information predicted bridging social capital, Burke et al. [3] found that directed communication—a measure that captures comments, likes, and tags individuals receive from others in their network—positively predicted it. This area of research has been extended by Ellison and colleagues [11], who argue that specific forms of directed communication, such as responding to a Friend's request for information or social support, serves as a signal of relational investment and highlights their presence in that person's social network. These relationship maintenance behaviors can be viewed as a form of social grooming [7] and may increase the likelihood that those network members will respond to resource requests in the future.

SNSs and Information Seeking

Social network sites are increasingly employed as "social search engines" because of the nuanced context in which question asking occurs. In a study of Microsoft employees, Morris and colleagues [21] analyzed how SNSs like Facebook and Twitter were employed for information-seeking purposes. They found that respondents often preferred asking questions on SNSs as opposed to Q&A sites or search engines for multiple reasons, including: the information need required responses that were tailored to the asker, the trust in the people answering the question was higher because they were known to the asker, the question could be framed in natural language, and the asker received secondary benefits like emotional support.

On most SNSs, users can ask their network questions through multiple channels, including private messages and more public broadcasts. Morris et al.'s [21] research on Facebook status updates provides insight into many different characteristics of the questions posed in Facebook members' status messages, such as the types of questions asked (e.g., rhetorical, factual knowledge), question topics (e.g., technology, current events), and motivations for asking questions this way (e.g., social connection, higher degree of trust). Recent research has begun to identify user characteristics—such as cultural differences [36]—that significantly predict question and answer behavior on SNSs as well as factors that influence characteristics of responses (such as quality and quantity) to information-seeking activities in these social online contexts [33].

Bridging Social Capital and Information Seeking

The performance of information-seeking behaviors within SNS contexts presents individuals with new methods of accessing and harnessing the resources embedded in their network of ties. Social information-seeking behaviors on Facebook, such as using the site to "check out" people one does not know well, have been linked to greater levels of bridging social capital in past research [7]. However, these activities typically involve more passive behaviors, such as browsing another user's profile to discover common interests, and do not include more active behaviors such as using Facebook to ask questions of another user.

Social capital research has also examined the role that network structure plays in bridging social capital. Burt [5] asserts that in order to reap the social capital benefits of a diverse social network, one must be able to recognize beneficial opportunities and communicate across multiple clusters, which requires particular analytic and communicative skills. Other social capital researchers have demonstrated that weak and "bridging" ties (those that span different clusters within a network) are the paths through which individuals are exposed to novel information [26, 27, 34]. Users with larger, more diverse networks should have greater access to non-redundant information than those with dense networks. Assuming users are aware of these benefits, users with larger networks may be more likely to use Facebook for information seeking and, subsequently, have more success accessing non-redundant information from their network.

ESTABLISHING CHARACTERISTICS OF FACEBOOK INFORMATION SEEKERS

The present study seeks to explicate the relationship between individuals' use of Facebook, their attitudes toward Facebook as a space for information seeking and sharing, and their propensity to turn to their Facebook network with questions.

Bridging social capital captures the benefits associated with a large network of loosely connected ties and reflects an individuals' ability to access resources embedded in their network [19]. Work by Granovetter [13] notes that weak ties in social networks are able to provide access to non-redundant information. Burt's [5] work has extended this thinking, arguing that specific types of ties—bridging ties—are especially important for information diffusion because they connect otherwise independent networks. Therefore, larger networks with more clusters should theoretically be more appropriate for meeting information needs.

H1: The greater users' perceptions of their Facebook bridging social capital, the greater their (a) perceptions of Facebook as useful for information purposes and (b) engagement in information-seeking behaviors.

Previous research has established a significant relationship between various measures of Facebook use and bridging social capital. For example, Burke et al. [3] found that users' total network size was positively correlated to their perceptions of bridging social capital. In more recent research, Ellison et al. [11] suggest that total network size may not be as important as the types of relationships those connections represent; in their study, the number of perceived "actual" friends Facebook users reported significantly predicted perceptions of bridging social capital, while total Facebook Friends did not. When considering the relationship between network composition and engagement in information seeking, it may be that users are more likely to trust their actual friends' opinions—which previous research has identified as a key reason for asking questions [21]. Therefore, it should be expected that individuals with more actual friends in their network would see the site as more useful for information purposes and engage in more information-seeking behaviors.

H2: As the number of actual friends on Facebook increases, so will users' (a) perceptions of Facebook as useful for information purposes and (b) engagement in information-seeking behaviors.

Another component of bridging social capital often discussed in the literature is the norm of generalized reciprocity, or giving to an individual or community without expectation of an immediate "payment"; rather, generalized reciprocity is driven by the belief that the favor will be repaid at some point in the future [26]. On Facebook, one way in which users may engage in generalized reciprocity is by responding to Friends' requests for information or other resources. Recent research [10] found a strong positive relationship between individuals' intent to respond to network members' requests for resources and their perceptions of bridging social capital. Therefore, it is also likely that individuals who engage in these kinds of behaviors are likely to view Facebook as useful for information purposes and engage in information-seeking behaviors themselves.

H3: As individuals' intent to respond to posts from their Facebook network increases, the greater their (a) perceptions of Facebook as useful for information purposes and (b) engagement in information-seeking behaviors.

METHOD

To analyze the relationship between Facebook users' perceptions of social capital and their engagement in information-seeking behaviors on the site, we emailed 2149 non-faculty staff at Michigan State University invitations to participate in an online survey regarding their use of online communication tools in February 2011; all participants were also invited to provide an email address to be entered into a raffle for one of fifteen $15 Amazon gift card. We received usable responses from 614 people; after removing a number of potential participants for technical reasons (email bounce-backs, out-of-office replies), the response rate was calculated to be 28.9%.

Participants

Participants tended to be female (66%), White (83.4%), and highly educated, with 75.4% holding at least a bachelor's degree and 33.2% having pursued additional training after college. The average participant was 45 years old (SD = 10.75 years) and, among those reporting income, the largest subset of the sample reporting personal annual income of $50,000-75,000 (33.7%), followed by $40,000-$49,999 (20.8%). Seventy-eight percent of participants reported having a Facebook account. When comparing demographic characteristics of users and non-users, only age emerged as significantly different, with Facebook users being significantly younger (M = 43.88, SD = 10.91) than non-users (M = 50.16, SD = 9.90), $t(592) = 5.78, p < .001$.

Survey Content

The survey contained scales for bridging social capital, information-seeking behaviors, measures of Facebook engagement and use, and demographics. Unless otherwise noted, scale items were measured on a five-point Likert-type scale (1 = Strongly Disagree, 5 = Strongly Agree).

Facebook-specific bridging social capital

This measure (10 items, alpha = .93, M = 3.33, SD = .76) was adapted from previous research [35] to reflect the ways in which people feel they can access novel information resources from their Facebook connections. Sample items include: "Interacting with people in my Facebook network makes me want to try new things" and "Talking with people in my Facebook network makes me curious about other places in the world."

Information Usefulness

In order to capture participants' sense of how useful Facebook is for information-seeking purposes, we include a single-item, scaled variable in some of the analyses. Information Usefulness (M = 3.54, SD = .89) was measured through the extent to which participants agreed with the item, "I feel I get useful information from Facebook."

Information-seeking behaviors

This measure (4 items, alpha = .85) is an original scale developed as part of this study to capture individuals' use of Facebook to seek information and support from their network. These four items were winnowed down from a larger list of 13 information-related behaviors using factor analysis to determine which items seemed to be capturing a similar aspect of information seeking. The original 13 items included in the instrument measured specific behaviors users can perform on the site (e.g., "I use Facebook to get business referrals"), perceptions of Facebook's use as an informational tool (e.g., "I use Facebook to get business referrals"), frequency of these behaviors (e.g., "How often do you use Facebook to ask questions of your Facebook friends?"), and users' reasons for requesting information from and providing information to their networks (e.g., "I ask questions on Facebook because my Facebook Friends provide me with better information than an Internet search").

Exploratory factor analysis of the 13 items regarding information behaviors on Facebook revealed a three-factor solution accounting for 68% of the variance. In this study, we focus on one of these factors: information-seeking behaviors. This scale originally included five items, but confirmatory factor analysis led to the removal of one item ("I use Facebook to ask for favors from my network"). The final, four-item scale (M = 2.30, SD = .82), was a good fit to the data, $X^2 = 4.46, p = .48$; RMSEA = .000; CFI = 1.00; GFI = .99. Full details of this scale, including item means and standard deviations, are provided in Table 1.

We believe our final four-item scale is a robust measure because the items address different aspects of information seeking. Asking health-related questions typically entails disclosure of potentially sensitivity personal information and is thus "higher risk" and more discriminating. The business and purchases items speak to financial investments

Item	Mean	SD
I use Facebook to get advice about something I want to buy.	2.32	.98
I use Facebook to get business referrals.	2.12	.93
I use Facebook to get answers to specific questions.	2.50	1.06
I use Facebook to ask questions about health issues.	1.98	.88
Scale Average	**2.30**	**.82**

Table 1. Items, means, and SDs for Information-Seeking Behaviors Scale

by the participant and explicit instances of social capital conversation that evidence trust in one's network. Finally, we included a measure that referenced "answers to specific questions," which probes instances of active information-seeking, as opposed to more opportunistic instances of information exposure via Facebook (e.g., happening to see something of interest in one's feed).

Signals of Relational Investment

This measure [10] (SRI; 5 items, alpha = .90, *M* = 3.55, *SD* = .83) captures the extent to which Facebook users attempt to engage in directed communication behaviors with their Friend network. Sample items include: "When I see someone asking for advice on Facebook, I try to respond" and "When a Facebook friend has a birthday, I try to post something on their wall."

Facebook Appropriateness

Facebook has always existed, first and foremost, as a social space, and the site centers around social connection and interaction. However, as the site—and its user base—has expanded, so have the possibilities for repurposing it for uses beyond simple social interaction. As information seeking can be considered a use of the site beyond the purely social, it is important to control for users' perceptions of the appropriateness of Facebook for non-social purposes.

To address this, the Facebook Appropriateness scale (alpha = .86, *M* = 2.82, *SD* = .78) was developed. Items asked participants the degree to which they agreed with the following statements: "Facebook is an appropriate place to ask (1) health-related questions; (2) for advice; (3) for emotional support; (4) for others' opinions; (5) for favors."

Facebook use variables

These measures capture the extent to which individuals engage with the site through three open-ended items. Time spent on Facebook (*M* = 33.9 minutes, median = 15, *SD* = 47.9) was measured through the item, "In the past week, on average, approximately how many minutes PER DAY have you spent actively using Facebook?" Total Facebook Friends ("Approximately how many TOTAL Facebook Friends do you have?") measures users' perceptions of their network size (*M* = 207, median = 120, *SD* = 288.16). Developed in earlier research [11], Actual Friends ("Approximately how many of your TOTAL Facebook friends do you consider actual friends?") attempts to capture more meaningful relationships within one's network (*M* = 76, median = 40, *SD* = 101.08). On average, participants in this sample considered 36.7% of their Facebook Friend network to be "actual" friends.

Controls

In addition to sex (women = 1), age, ethnicity (recoded as a dichotomous variable, 1 = White), and education, self-esteem [28] was included as a control because it has been linked to perceptions of social capital [9]. This seven-item scale (alpha = .86) had a mean score of 4.33 (*SD* = .56).

RESULTS

Facebook Information Usefulness

Table 2 shows the nested Ordinary Least Squares (OLS) regression model with perceived usefulness of information on Facebook as the dependent variable. Variables were added in blocks to show the individual contribution of each set of variables to the model. The final model explains 40% of the variance in users' perceptions of Facebook as useful for information seeking, which is robust.

The model shows that bridging social capital is positively related to perceptions of information usefulness on Facebook, supporting H1a. In other words, the more people feel they are exposed to a broader world-view through their Facebook networks, the more they feel the site is able to provide useful information.

We also hypothesized that the number of actual friends reported by respondents would positively predict perceived information usefulness (H2a). This hypothesis was initially supported (see Model 2); however, once bridging social capital was added as a predictor (Model 3), the actual friends variable dropped out as a significant predictor of information usefulness. It could be that actual friends, which has been shown to be related to bridging social capital in other research [11], is moderated by bridging social capital. Alternatively, it could be that respondents consider actual friends to be more similar to them and therefore less likely to provide access to novel information. Finally, H3a predicted SRI would be positively related to perceived information usefulness. The data support this hypothesis.

Time spent on Facebook was included as a control and emerged as significant in the model. In other words, users who spent more time on the site reported higher perceptions of Facebook as useful for information seeking. This could be because users who spend more time on the site are exposed to more content, including information exchanges. Because these data do not speak to causal direction, it could also be that these users see Facebook as being a good

	Model 1: Controls	Model 2: Time & Friend Variables	Model 3: Facebook-specific Bridging Social Capital	Model 4: SRI	Model 5: Appropriateness x SRI
Sex: Women	.095 (2.13)*	.077 (1.78)	.028 (.688)	.011 (.266)	.011 (.267)
Ethnicity: White	.008 (.189)	.025 (.597)	.024 (.618)	.033 (.843)	.033 (.843)
Age	-.079 (-1.73)	.007 (.160)	-.005 (-.126)	-.007 (-.163)	-.007 (-.158)
Education	-.009 (-.209)	.004 (.098)	.009 (.219)	.016 (.408)	-.016 (.409)
Self-Esteem	.087 (2.00)*	.064 (1.51)	.035 (.883)	.034 (.878)	.034 (.876)
FB Appropriateness	.436 (9.80)***	.374 (8.47)***	.222 (4.92)***	.180 (3.85)***	.187 (1.25)
FB Minutes Per Day		.180 (3.94)***	.148 (3.49)**	.123 (2.87)**	.124 (2.86)**
Total FB Friends		.079 (1.54)	.061 (1.28)	.054 (1.41)	.054 (1.14)
Actual Friends on FB		.114 (2.26)*	.067 (1.42)	.069 (1.47)	.069 (1.47)
Facebook-specific Bridging Social Capital			.373 (8.160)***	.309 (6.13)***	.308 (6.12)***
Signals of Relational Investment (SRI)				.154 (2.91)**	.160 (1.27)
Appropriateness*SRI					-.011 (-.048)
Constant	n/a (3.58)***	n/a (3.11)***	n/a (1.87)**	n/a (1.35)*	n/a (.884)**
	$F(409) = 21.06$***	$F(406) = 19.66$***	$F(405) = 27.22$***	$F(404) = 25.97$***	$F(403) = 23.75$***
Adjusted R^2	**.225**	**.288**	**.387**	**.398**	**.397**

*$p < .05$, **$p < .01$, ***$p < .001$

Table 2: Nested OLS regression with Facebook information usefulness as the dependent variable.

source of information, so they subsequently spend more time on the site.

Facebook Information-Seeking Behaviors

Table 3 shows the nested OLS regression model with "Information-Seeking Behaviors" as the dependent variable. Variables were added one step at a time to show how each contributes to explaining the variance in users' perceptions of their engagement in information-seeking behaviors on Facebook. The final model explains 39% of the variance in users' information seeking behaviors.

We proposed in H1b that there would be a positive relationship between perceptions of bridging social capital and perceived likelihood of seeking information on Facebook. The third block in the model describes the addition of bridging social capital. This variable is strongly related to the dependent variable, meaning that people who feel like they have more access to diverse people through the site are more likely to turn to their network when they have everyday information needs.

We also hypothesized that Facebook Information-Seeking Behaviors would be positively associated with the number of actual friends users reported in their Facebook network (H2b). The second block of variables measures perceptions of time spent on the site and size of network, including actual friends. These variables do not affect the dependent variable; thus, H2b is not supported.

H3b posited that users reporting greater engagement in SRI would report more engagement in information-seeking behaviors. In other work [10], SRI was positively related to bridging social capital, along with the number of "actual" friends users reported having in their Friend network. This hypothesis was supported, with greater engagement in SRI behaviors being associated with greater engagement in information-seeking behaviors (see Model 4).

In addition to the hypothesized relationships, age was negatively associated with perceived likelihood to seek information on Facebook in the final model. In all models, an increase in age was significantly associated with decreased likelihood to seek information through Facebook. Self-esteem, which has been a consistently strong predictor in models of Facebook use when social capital is the dependent variable [3, 9], was unrelated in these models.

Following analysis of the hypothesized relationships, we conducted additional analyses on some of the variables included in the models. First, we considered the appropriateness variable, which was significant ($p < .001$) across all four steps of each regression. As discussed above, users have a variety of motivations for using Facebook and, consequently, may experience significant variance in what content they perceive as appropriate to be shared through the site. The appropriateness variable was intended to control for variance across individual users—some of whom may see Facebook as a "strictly social" space while others may take advantage of the benefits of being able to communicate with a large network of connections and extract resources associated with that network. As seen in Step 5 of Table 3's model, we found a significant interaction effect between users' perceptions of appropriateness and their engagement in SRI behaviors on

	Model 1: Controls	Model 2: Time & Friend Variables	Model 3: Facebook-Specific Bridging Social Capital	Model 4: SRI	Model 5: Appropriateness x SRI
Sex: Women	.098 (2.21)*	.088 (2.03)*	.040 (.969)	.023 (.567)	.023 (.557)
Ethnicity: White	-.030 (-.702)	-.014 (-.329)	-.010 (-.259)	-.002 (-.058)	-.014 (-.350)
Age	-.188 (-4.17)***	-.109 (-2.33)*	-.124 (-2.82)**	-.126 (-2.90)**	-.135 (-3.12)**
Education	-.095 (-2.14)*	-.086 (-2.00)*	-.087 (-2.14)*	-.080 (-2.00)*	-.085 (-2.11)*
Self-Esteem	.005 (.122)	-.015 (-.348)	-.039 (-.986)	-.040 (-1.01)	-.038 (-.974)
FB Appropriateness	.414 (9.40)***	.368 (8.33)***	.233 (5.15)***	.194 (4.11)***	-.146 (-.965)
FB Minutes Per Day		.130 (2.85)**	.100 (2.33)*	.077 (1.77)	.067 (1.54)
Total FB Friends		.117 (2.28)*	.101 (2.10)*	.094 (1.97)*	.089 (1.88)
Actual Friends on Facebook		.068 (1.35)	.023 (.490)	.025 (.527)	.014 (.301)
Facebook-specific Bridging Social Capital			.344 (7.48)***	.286 (5.68)***	.288 (5.74)***
Signals of Relational Investment (SRI)				.142 (2.67)**	-.130 (-1.02)
Appropriateness*SRI					.545 (2.36)*
Constant	n/a (4.68)***	n/a (4.17)***	n/a (3.01)**	n/a (2.53)*	n/a (3.46)**
	$F(406)$ = 23.45***	$F(403)$ = 19.69***	$F(402)$ = 25.73***	$F(401)$ = 24.40***	$F(400)$ = 23.08***
Adjusted R^2	**.246**	**.290**	**.375**	**.384**	**.391**

*$p < .05$, **$p < .01$, ***$p < .001$

Table 3: Nested OLS regression with Facebook Information Seeking scale as the dependent variable.

the site. In other words, the degree to which users saw Facebook as an appropriate space to request emotional support, advice, and information moderated SRI's relationship with users' engagement in information-seeking behaviors. The positive beta suggests that, as engagement in SRI increases, those who think requesting these kinds of resources through Facebook is more appropriate are more likely to engage in information-seeking behaviors than those who see Facebook as less appropriate for these purposes. In order to visualize this relationship, we conducted a simple slopes analysis [1], presented in Figure 1. As the figure shows, increases in information-seeking behaviors rose at a greater rate for those with high appropriateness perceptions than for those with low appropriateness perceptions. This interaction was only found for the information-seeking behavior measure, not the variable measuring Facebook's usefulness as an information source (Table 2).

Difference between high and low info seekers

In order to further explore how characteristics of Facebook users affect their perceived likelihood of seeking information through the site, we divided the respondents into quartiles and examined those who were in the lowest quartile in responses to the Facebook Information-Seeking Behaviors scale ("low info seekers"), and those in the highest quartile ("high info seekers"), comparing user characteristics through independent samples t-tests. This method allows us to identify users who believe they engage (or do not engage) in information seeking on Facebook.

We found that several user characteristics, included as independent variables in the regression models, were significantly different between the low info seekers and the high info seekers. Table 4 summarizes the means and standard deviations of low info seekers (highlighted in gray) and high info seekers. T-scores explain the statistical strength of the distance between the groups. All t-scores presented are significant at p < .01.

Low info seekers were more likely to be older males. They had half the total and actual Facebook friends, spent half the amount of time on the site, had less perceived social capital, lower SRI, and were less likely to feel that seeking

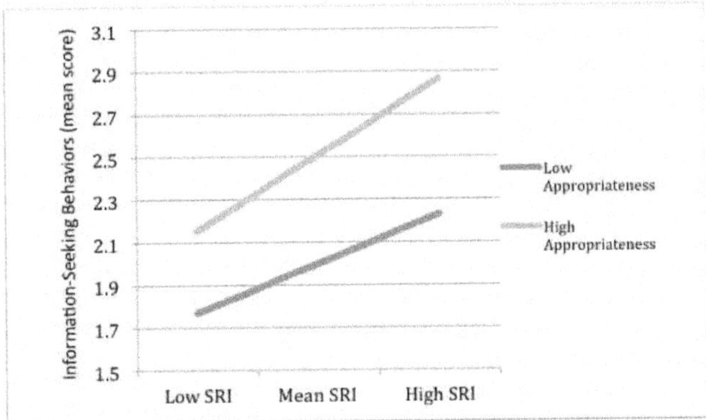

Figure 1: Simple slope analysis of relationship between Signals of Relationship Investment and appropriateness.

Variable	Mean	SD	t-score
Women	0.60	0.49	-2.55
	0.74	0.41	
Age	45.99	10.64	4.95
	40.22	10.14	
TOTAL Facebook Friends	147.05	73.10	-4.87
	311.75	133.19	
Actual Facebook Friends	49.42	73.10	-6.63
	123.17	133.19	
FB Minutes per day	21.48	38.39	-6.27
	54.78	59.51	
FB Bridging Social Capital	2.98	0.80	-9.74
	3.77	0.50	
SRI	3.15	0.90	-10.05
	4.02	0.51	
Appropriateness	2.60	0.78	-9.98
	3.38	0.54	

Table 4: T-test comparisons of user characteristics between low Facebook information seekers (shaded) and high Facebook information seekers.

resources on Facebook was appropriate. There were no differences between the groups in terms of ethnicity, education level, or self-esteem.

Other than gender and age, high reported use of Facebook for information seeking is associated with site engagement, including more Friends, more minutes per day, and higher reported SRI. Previous work has indicated that active use of Facebook was more associated with positive outcomes [4], which is consistent with these findings. In other words, it is not sufficient to be a member of Facebook to receive potential benefits, but rather requires the user to actively engage with the site across multiple dimensions.

DISCUSSION

The present study contributes to our understanding of how users perceive social network sites as venues in which to seek information. While previous work has established a typology of questions SNS users are likely to ask through the site [21], the analyses presented here help describe the characteristics of the type of person who is more likely to use Facebook to gather information, as well as the specific attitudinal and behavioral factors that contribute to engagement in Facebook information seeking.

Social capital researchers have often associated bridging social capital with access to diverse points of view and novel information from different clusters within a network [5, 13]. Participation on SNSs has been shown to be associated with social capital, with researchers arguing that sites like Facebook reduce the cost of accessing diverse clusters [3, 9, 11]. The study presented here extends this line of research by unpacking the concept of bridging social capital and exploring a specific way in which Facebook users might try to convert the social capital from their Friends into another form of capital: information. The types of people in information seekers' networks, and their engagement in reciprocal communication, may affect the types of information resources that can be converted from the social capital inherent in the relationships.

Our results indicate that Facebook users are not extremely likely to engage in information seeking with their Facebook network (M = 2.30, SD = .82). However, we did find that there are a number of shared user characteristics that are associated with people who have a higher propensity to seek information on the site. High information seekers are more likely to be female, younger, and have more total and actual Facebook Friends. They are also more likely to spend more time on Facebook and are more likely to engage in reciprocal communication (SRI) with members of their Facebook network. This could be related to the perspective that social capital is not just about network structure, but about a user's beliefs and behaviors in that network. Another factor that played an interesting yet unsurprising role on engagement in information-seeking behaviors was the perceived appropriateness of asking questions on Facebook. Those who do not see Facebook as a normative or appropriate venue to ask others for information were less likely to engage in information seeking and to perceive Facebook as a useful provider of information.

Additionally, the significant interaction of SRI and perceived appropriateness on information-seeking behaviors offers further insight into how both norms and usage patterns on Facebook may influence the likelihood to use Facebook for information seeking. Signals of relational investment indicate willingness to respond to resource requests from a Facebook Friend; however, the interaction of SRI and appropriateness renders SRI itself less predictive of actual information-seeking behaviors. For Facebook users who do not deem information seeking on Facebook appropriate, whether or not they engage these relationship maintenance behaviors with their network is of little consequence to their overall likelihood in seeking information through the site. However, for those who do find information seeking on Facebook appropriate, engaging in more SRI renders them much more likely to use Facebook to address their information needs. When users engage in SRI behaviors with other members of their network, they do so in order to provide support and, potentially, garner support for later needs of their own. It is possible that those who perceive information seeking on Facebook as more normative or appropriate are more willing to request favors back, as they believe it will not disrupt their reputation or the unspoken norms of the site. Future research should explore in more detail how perceived norms of Facebook use affect both member behavior and outcomes of use. For example, how do norms of privacy and disclosure affect reciprocal exchanges? More data regarding how norms are detected and sanctioned on sites like Facebook could further explain the benefits people receive from these sites.

Facebook users do think the site provides them with useful information (M = 3.54, SD = .885), slightly in contrast to their slightly lower reported propensity to seek information on the site. This difference may be due to the distinction between searching for a specific information need, which is what our information-seeking behaviors scale captures, versus encountering useful information incidentally.

In general, participants did not report that they were likely to use Facebook to seek information, as the mean for this scale (2.3) was well below the midpoint. Likewise, the mean response on the Appropriateness scale was below the midpoint (2.82). These findings suggest that even with the technical features available to manage and interact with a large network of connections, individual users may still struggle to view Facebook as meeting needs beyond the strictly social reasons for which they were likely to join—reconnecting with old friends and maintaining relationships with current friends.

Limitations

While the use of adult university employees provided access to a relatively diverse sample, they do not represent the general population of Facebook users. Survey responses are limited to people's perceptions of their behavior, rather than actual behavior. While the research community should continue to seek behavioral information, this study was largely concerned with users' attitudes about Facebook as an information source. In addition, while our constructs for "information" were derived from a large set of questions about possible information behaviors, we are only capturing a limited dimension of information needs, and other dimensions may show different effects.

Implications for Practice

One of the strongest relationships in our model was between bridging social capital and likelihood to use Facebook to seek information. While it is not clear how Facebook chooses which Friends to show in users' News Feeds, it is most likely related to aspects of their relationship unrelated to information seeking. It may be more productive to continue to adapt the News Feed based on what types of things people are posting, rather than the relationship between the members of the network. For example, a person who is posting messages and status updates that include questions could have their updates shown in the News Feeds of more diverse clusters in their Facebook network.

If users are receiving valuable incidental information by reading the posts of their Facebook Friends, this suggests designers should consider the content of a post and its responses when creating tools to filter information. For example, allowing users to promote a status update as "informative" could allow for a different type of filtering. Additionally, tools could be built that would allow users to bookmark informative Facebook exchanges they see, so they can return to them when a relevant information need becomes salient. Currently, Facebook exchanges are, to a large degree, ephemeral, and can disappear quickly for users with large networks.

CONCLUSION

We investigated how likely people are to use Facebook to fulfill their everyday information needs by conducting a survey of 614 staff members of a large university. We found that user characteristics predicted how likely they are to use Facebook to seek information. In particular, perceptions of their relationships with network members, as measured in scales for Facebook-specific bridging social capital and for behaviors that "groom" connections in a network, were significant predictors of how likely respondents were to turn to Facebook for their information-seeking activities.

ACKNOWLEDGMENTS

This work was supported in part by the National Science Foundation (HCC 0916019).

REFERENCES

1. Aiken, L.S. and West, S.G. *Multiple regression: Testing and interpreting interactions*. Sage Publications, Thousand Oaks, CA, 1991.
2. Bourdieu, P. Forms of Capital. in Richardson, J.G. ed. *Handbook of Theory and Research for the Sociology of Education*, Greenwood Press, New York, 1983.
3. Burke, M., Kraut, R. and Marlow, C. Social capital on facebook: differentiating uses and users *Proceedings of the 2011 annual conference on Human factors in computing systems*, ACM, Vancouver, BC, Canada, 2011, 571-580.
4. Burke, M., Marlow, C. and Lento, T. Social network activity and social well-being *Proceedings of the 28th international conference on Human factors in computing systems*, ACM, Atlanta, Georgia, USA, 2010.
5. Burt, R.S. *Network Neighbors: Competitive Advantage Local and Personal*. Oxford University Press, Oxford, UK, 2010.
6. Dervin, B. A Overview of Sense-Making Research: Concepts, Methods, and Results to Date *International Communications Association*, Dallas, TX, 1983.
7. Donath, J. and Boyd, D. Public Displays of Connection. *BT Technology Journal*, *22* (4). 71-82.
8. Dugan, C., Geyer, W., Muller, M., DiMicco, J., Brownholtz, B. and Millen, D.R., It's all 'about you': diversity in online profiles. in *ACM 2008 conference on Computer supported cooperative work*, (San Diego, CA, 2008), ACM Press, 703-706.
9. Ellison, N., Steinfield, C. and Lampe, C. The benefits of Facebook "friends:" Social capital and college students' use of online social network sites. *Journal of Computer Mediated Communication*, *12* (4). article 1.
10. Ellison, N., Vitak, J., Gray, R. and Lampe, C. Cultivating Social Resources on Facebook: Signals of

Relational Investment and their Role in Social Capital Processes. *iCS-OII, "A Decade in Internet Time" Symposium*, Oxford, UK, 2011.

11. Ellison, N.B., Steinfield, C. and Lampe, C. Connection Strategies: Social Capital Implications of Facebook-enabled Communication Practices. *New Media & Society*, *13*. 873-892.

12. Gilbert, E. and Karahalios, K. Predicting tie strength with social media *Proceedings of the 27th international conference on Human factors in computing systems*, ACM, Boston, MA, USA, 2009.

13. Granovetter, M.S. The Strength of Weak Ties. *Amerian Economic Review*, *78* (6). 1360-1480.

14. Joinson, A.N., Looking at, looking up or keeping up with people?: motives and use of facebook. in *Conference on Human Factors in Computing Systems (CHI)*, (Florence, Italy, 2008), ACM Press, 1027-1036.

15. Lampe, C., Ellison, N. and Steinfield, C., A Face(book) in the Crowd: Social Searching vs. Social Browsing. in *ACM Special Interest Group on Computer-Supported Cooperative Work*, (Banff, Canada, 2006), ACM Press.

16. Lampe, C., Ellison, N. and Steinfield, C., Profile Elements as Signals in an Online Social Network. in *ACM Conference on Human Factors in Computing Systems (CHI)*, (San Jose, CA, 2007), ACM Press.

17. Lampe, C. and Roth, R. Social Media in Public Sector Organizations: Strangers Among Us. Foth, M. ed. *Communities & Technologies 2011*, Brisbane, Australia, 2011.

18. Lenhart, A. Adults and Social Network Websites, Pew Internet & American Life Project, Washington, DC, 2009.

19. Lin, N. Building a network theory of social capital. . *Connections*, *22*. 28-51.

20. Madden, M. and Zickuhr, K. 65% of Online Adults Use Social Networking Sites, Pew Internet & American Life Project, Washington, DC, 2011.

21. Morris, M.R., Teevan, J. and Panovich, K. What do people ask their social networks, and why?: a survey study of status message q&a behavior *Proceedings of the 28th international conference on Human factors in computing systems*, ACM, Atlanta, Georgia, USA, 2010.

22. Nardi, B.A. and O'Day, V.L. *Information Ecologies: Using Technology with Heart.* MIT Press, Cambridge, MA, 1999.

23. Papacharissi, Z. and Mendelson, A. Toward a new(er) sociability: Uses, gratifications and social capital on Facebook. in Papathanassopoulos, S. ed. *Media perspectives for the 21st century*, Routledge, New Tork, 2011, 212-230.

24. Pirolli, P. An elementary social information foraging model *Proceedings of the 27th international conference on Human factors in computing systems*, ACM, Boston, MA, USA, 2009.

25. Pirolli, P. and Card, S. Information Foraging. *Psychological Review*, *106* (4). 643-675.

26. Putnam, R.D. *Bowling Alone*. Simon & Schuster, New York, 2000.

27. Resnick, P. Beyond Bowling Together: SocioTechnical Capital. in Carroll, J. ed. *HCI in the New Millenium*, Addison-Wesley, 2001.

28. Rosenberg, M. *Society and the Adolescent Self-image*. Wesleyan University Press, Middletown, CT, 1989.

29. Savolainen, R. Everyday life information seeking: Approaching information seeking in the context of "way of life". *Library & Information Science Research*, *17* (3). 259-294.

30. Skeels, M.M. and Grudin, J. When social networks cross boundaries: a case study of workplace use of facebook and linkedin *Proceedings of the ACM 2009 international conference on Supporting group work*, ACM, Sanibel Island, Florida, USA, 2009.

31. Smock, A.D., Ellison, N.B., Lampe, C. and Wohn, D.Y. Facebook as a toolkit: A uses and gratification approach to unbundling feature use. *Computers in Human Behavior*, *27* (6). 2322-2329.

32. Steinfield, C., DiMicco, J.M., Ellison, N.B. and Lampe, C. Bowling online: social networking and social capital within the organization *Proceedings of the fourth international conference on Communities and technologies*, ACM, University Park, PA, USA, 2009.

33. Teevan, J., Morris, M.R. and Panovich, K., Factors Affecting Response Quantity, Quality, and Speed for Questions Asked via Social Network Status Messages. in *ICWSM - International Conference on Weblogs and Social Media*, (Barcelona, Spain, 2011).

34. Williams, D. On and Off the 'Net: Scales for Social Capital in an Online Era *Journal of Computer Mediated Communication*, *11* (2).

35. Williamson, K. Discovered by Chance: The Role of Incidental Information Acquisition in an Ecological Model of Information Use. *Library & Information Science Research*, *20* (1). 23-40.

36. Yang, J., Morris, M.R., Teevan, J., Adamic, L. and Ackerman, M., Culture Matters: A Survey Study of Social Q&A Behavior. in *ICWSM - International Conference on Weblogs and Social Media*, (Barcelona, Spain, 2011).

WebCrystal: Understanding and Reusing Examples in Web Authoring

Kerry Shih-Ping Chang
Human-Computer Interaction Institute
Carnegie Mellon University
Pittsburgh, PA 15213
kerrychang@cs.cmu.edu

Brad A. Myers
Human-Computer Interaction Institute
Carnegie Mellon University
Pittsburgh, PA 15213
bam@cs.cmu.edu

ABSTRACT
Examples have been widely used in the area of web design to help web authors create web pages. However, without actually understanding how an example is constructed, people often have trouble extracting the elements they want and incorporating them into their own design. This paper introduces WebCrystal, a web development tool that helps users understand how a web page is built. WebCrystal contributes novel interaction techniques that let the user quickly access HTML and CSS information by selecting questions regarding how a selected element is designed. It provides answers using a textual description and a customized code snippet that can be copied-and-pasted to recreate the desired properties. WebCrystal also supports combining the styles and structures from multiple elements into the generated code snippet, and provides visualizations on the web page itself to explain layout relationships. Our user study shows that WebCrystal helped both novice and experienced developers complete more tasks successfully using significantly less time.

Author Keywords
Web Authoring; Examples.

ACM Classification Keywords
H.5.2 [Information interfaces and presentation]: User Interfaces - Interaction styles; D.2.6 [Software Engineering]: Programming Environments - Graphical Environments; Design Tools and Techniques - User interfaces.

General Terms
Design, Human Factors.

INTRODUCTION
Increasingly, Internet users with minimal technical training are creating their own web pages. This involves not only authoring the content, but also designing the appearance and behaviors of the web pages. Good design is important to improve the readability and usability of the pages, and also to reflect the unique personality of their creator. Using templates or a "wizard" interface to build a web site are common ways to create a well-designed web page without writing any actual code [7]. However, these techniques cannot fully satisfy every user's needs since people have different requirements and aesthetic preferences for their web pages [13].

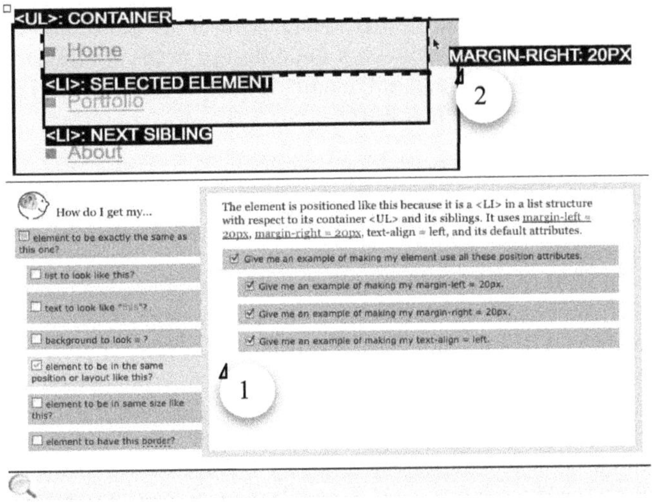

Figure 1: A WebCrystal user finds out how to lay out a list structure by inspecting an example web page, by (1) asking a position question of the selected list element in WebCrystal, and (2) inspecting the black area around the element on the web page.

Previous research has shown that one popular way for users to build a customized web page is through the use of examples, and that this results in pages with higher ratings [14]. It has also been reported that web designers in the real world often look at other people's websites, pick the pieces they like, and combine these pieces in their own designs [10]. In general, a popular way for developers to learn how to create code for any task is to look at examples [1]. One of the participants in our user study mentioned his own web design experience: "The best thing about web design is that all the code is open source... you can always go to the websites you like and see how they work." Potentially, every web page can serve as a design example for people who like some aspect of its design or want to learn how it achieved some effect. Assisting reuse of desired design elements from a web page could thus be very beneficial to many web designers.

Even after deciding on a design for a web page element, a person must know how to achieve that design. Thus, people must serve as both the *designers* for the style of a web page, as well as the *developers*, who write the code to implement the design. Reproducing a complex design from an example requires a person to have a decent knowledge about web development languages, even when using modern tools like Adobe Dreamweaver or Microsoft Expression Web. Furthermore, people often just want *part* of the design [10] and thus must identify which part of the code actually is responsible for the design aspect that is wanted. Consequently, to create a high-quality result, the ability to develop a web page to achieve the desired design can be as important as the ability to come up with a good design in the first place. Design examples are not useful if people cannot realize them in their own final work.

To help address this problem, we built *WebCrystal* (Figure 1), a tool that assists in the low-level programming tasks required to learn from and reuse examples as part of the web authoring process. "Examples" here can be anything built in HTML and CSS, the two most common languages used to create the static style of a web page. Currently, WebCrystal does not handle JavaScript, Flash, AJAX or other scripting languages. WebCrystal allows users to select any web element of a page that was created with HTML and CSS, and then choose from a set of "how" questions about how to recreate the different aspects of the selected element. The tool then answers the questions by (1) providing an automatically generated human-readable textual explanation using the element's HTML and CSS information, and (2) generating a customized code snippet for the users to recreate the design using the selected attributes.

WebCrystal makes the following contributions:

- A novel example-based web design tool for extracting and combining styling information from existing websites, and for helping designers understand how existing sites use HTML and CSS to create desired appearances. This includes how to achieve the positioning of elements.
- The novel use of automatically generated hierarchical questions and explanations about existing website styling information, in combination with element selection techniques to facilitate the extraction, combination, and understanding of existing website styling code. The explanations included generated code in a variety of user-selected formats (rather than code extracted from the source examples) that will reproduce the element.
- A between-subjects evaluation of the prototype system compared to standard tools for copying desired HTML and CSS from existing websites. This evaluation showed that WebCrystal users had significantly higher task completion rate and faster task completion time in reproducing web elements from a given web page, compared with people using Firebug [5], a state-of-the-art web development tool.

WebCrystal is inspired by previous systems Crystal [17] (which focused on desktop applications) and FireCrystal [19] (which focused on JavaScript). In WebCrystal, the goal is to make the construction of the HTML and CSS parts of web design "crystal clear" to the user, so that the user would be able to easily reuse them in their own pages. The tool was originally intended for novice and intermediate HTML and CSS developers, which we believe are the majority of the web authors today (and blog posts seem to indicate that even many "professional web designers" may not have particularly advanced coding skills—e.g., [8]). In fact, in our user study, we found that even advanced developers also benefited from and liked using WebCrystal.

RELATED WORK

WebCrystal was inspired by several previous systems that allow users to ask questions about a program's execution, as a way to provide more focused answers. Crystal [17] explains a word processor's behaviors by letting users ask about why elements look the way they do. Crystal not only provides a textual explanation, but also highlights the user operations that affect the element, so the user can more easily fix problems and control the operations. The Java Whyline [12] is a debugging tool that allows developers to ask "why" and "why not" questions about a Java program's output and leads developers backward to its causes. In WebCrystal, we adapted this idea of letting users ask questions in the different domain of web authoring.

WebCrystal allows its users to select the element they want from a rendered web page, and presents a code snippet that can recreate that element. Some prior systems have used a related approach in helping people make use of an example more efficiently by interacting with the output and displaying the corresponding source code. FireCrystal [19], for example, lets users record the interactive behavior of a web page and shows the JavaScript code that might be responsible for that behavior. Rehearse [2] is an extension for the Processing IDE that highlights each line of code in an example as it is executed to help programmers quickly identify which line of the code is relevant.

Many systems help with finding and presenting examples. Some systems allow users to specify layout information through sketches to retrieve desired designs [9], while others [14][15][20] support retrieving and browsing related designs from example galleries. WebCrystal helps *after* the examples have already been found, and assists users to incorporate desired examples into their own work. Some prior systems have focused on reusing examples without requiring users to look at or understand any code. CopyStyler [6] copies the style of text elements from one page to another. Adaptive Ideas [14] pre-annotates examples with metadata about properties and ranges of values, and then it can combine the user-selected attributes into a new page. Bricolage [13] maps some aspects of the style of one web page onto the content of another using an AI algorithm to rapidly generate a new web page. In contrast to these systems,

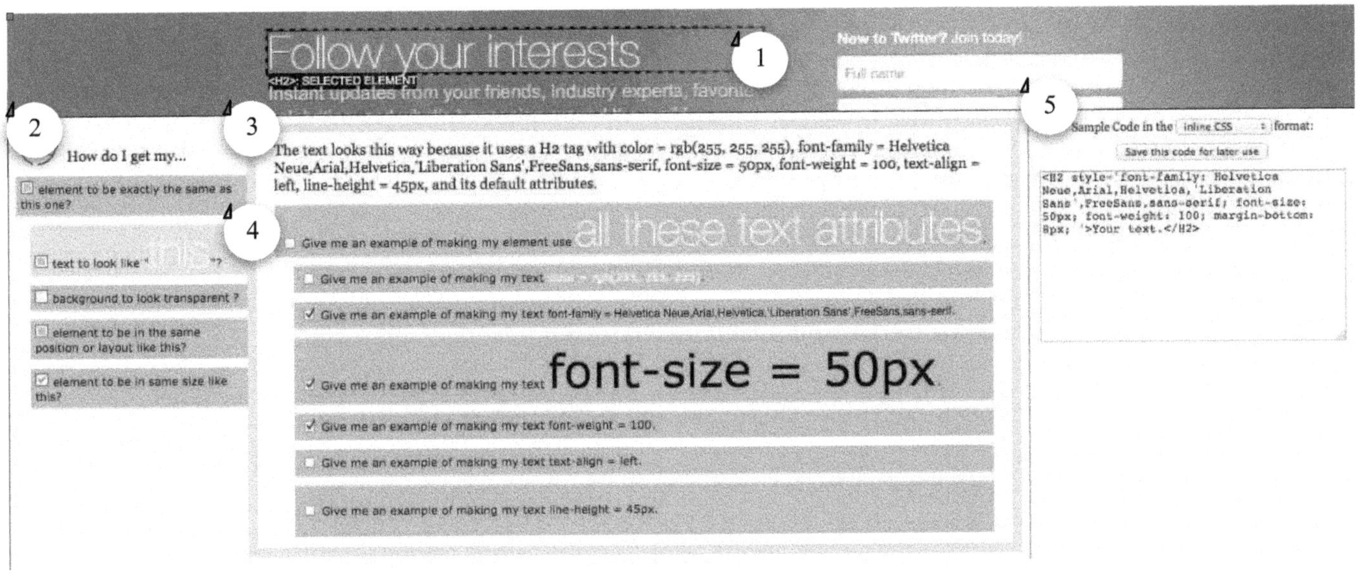

Figure 2: (1) is the web page under investigation, showing the purple highlight and the dotted box around the selected element. (2) is a list of questions the user can ask about recreating the selected element, with the selected question highlighted with a yellow background. (3) shows the textual response that answers the question selected in (2). Here, it explains the text properties. (4) is a sub-menu of commands that the user can pick to generate a code example using the selected properties. (5) shows the generated code.

WebCrystal gives users complete control of the results, since it does not use heuristic algorithms..It also exposes the underlying code to users, which might help them learn it.

THE WEBCRYSTAL USER INTERFACE

The main goal of WebCrystal is to enable the users to quickly reuse one or more aspects of an example in their own work. Ideally, WebCrystal would be integrated with a code editor, so the code extracted from the example could be directly inserted into the user's code. For now, in order to explore the appropriate user interface for discovering the appropriate code, WebCrystal instead runs as a plugin for the Firefox browser, and the user can copy-and-paste the code into a separate editor window. WebCrystal is a Firefox extension written in XUL [16] and JavaScript, using the jQuery [11] library. WebCrystal accesses the document object model (DOM) of the web page, and treats every DOM node in the web page as a web *element*. WebCrystal is activated by clicking on the magnifying glass icon button in the browser's status bar (Figure 1, bottom left). When activated, it tracks the current element under the mouse cursor as users move their mouse around the web page. The current element is highlighted using a semi-transparent box, with a small label showing the element's tag name (Figure 2 at 1). At the same time, a set of questions about how to recreate the various aspects of the underlying element are dynamically generated and displayed in the left of the WebCrystal window (Figure 2 at 2). The user can "freeze" a selection by left clicking on the desired element and then can start to inspect that element by browsing questions from the tool interface. A selection is "unfrozen" by left clicking anywhere on the web page.

Browsing the Elements Hierarchically

HTML is a hierarchical language. An element's position on the web page is related to its parents (containers) and siblings. For example, in Figure 1 the selected <li> is positioned relative to the position of its parent <ul>. Therefore, WebCrystal allows users to directly select any element using the mouse, but also allows users to move the selection around the hierarchical structure. Users can explore the hierarchy using the arrow keys to go up to the parents (containers) (e.g., from <li> to its <ul>), down to the children (<ul> to <li>), and left and right to the previous and next siblings (<li> to next <li>). In our user study, we found this feature also was useful for participants to select overlaid elements that have a similar size, by navigating up to parents and sideways to other siblings.

When WebCrystal is enabled, it disables the default function of mouse left button (navigating to hyperlinks) and arrow keys (scrolling the web page) so these events can be used to select and browse elements in WebCrystal. When the regular web page behavior is desired, WebCrystal can simply be disabled by clicking on its magnifying glass icon again to turn the tool off.

Asking Web Construction Questions

WebCrystal explains web construction by allowing users to select different "how" questions. All questions are in a similar form, such as "how do I get my … to be like this?" Previous studies in web design showed that when looking at an example, people only wanted *part* of the design and wanted to incorporate this specific part of the design in their own web page [10]. The key to successfully reusing an example is therefore to identify which lines of code are relevant to the user's needs, which is often difficult [2]. To address this requirement, WebCrystal generates questions on both how to recreate an element as a whole, and how to recreate each aspect of the element. The first question in the list is always "how do I get my element to be exactly the same as this one?", which shows users how to recreate everything about the element. Next is a set of sub-questions that allow users to ask about recreating more specific aspects of the element. WebCrystal reads the HTML and CSS attribute values of the selected element and uses them to generate sub-questions in 11 categories (see Table 1). For questions about text, background, and border, WebCrystal also dynamically renders the style of the element's text, background and border, and shows it in the question description (Figure 2 at 4). Besides showing the properties immediately, we found this particularly important when the selected element's style is caused by *other* elements. For example, when DOM elements overlay on each other, the look of an element can be caused by the element behind it. Another example is that a vertical line can be made by using a background image inside a table cell or by turning on the left border of the next cell. By showing the feedback in the questions themselves, the user can select the correct element to ask the questions about. See Figure 5 for more examples.

After selecting a question, the middle pane will update and show the answer (Figure 2 at 3). The first part of the answer is a computer-generated human-readable textual explanation of what tag and attributes the element uses to generate the aspect(s) selected in the left pane. WebCrystal compares each attribute with its default value, and only shows the attributes that have a value different from their defaults, and thus would need to be specified by the user.

Generated Code

Under the textual explanation is a set of checkboxes with which users can select specific aspects of the property they are interested in (Figure 2 at 4). WebCrystal automatically generates an item for each CSS attribute that is relevant. When the user selects one or more of these, the system generates an example code snippet that will cause an element to have the same values for those attributes as the example. These choices are phrased as requests of the form: "Give me an example of making my element *attribute* = *value*." As a shortcut, the first checkbox says "Give me an example of making my element have all the same attributes" to get a result the same as the example. Attributes are also rendered in their style when possible to help users quickly identify what they want and understand the effect of the attributes.

The generated code snippet is shown in the code window on the right of the WebCrystal's interface (Figure 2 at 5). WebCrystal can provide code snippets in either inline-CSS or separate-CSS formats, chosen by the drop down menu, to let users generate the most appropriate kind of code for their situation (Figure 3). For cases where inline CSS is not allowed (such as for hover dynamic behaviors explained below), then the inline CSS option is removed.

Property for "How do I get my … to look like this?"	This question is displayed when:
Text	Tag is not <img>
Background	Every time
Position and Layout	Every time
Size	Every time
Border or Outline	CSS attribute "border-style" or "outline-style" is not "none"
Input element	Tag is "input", "select, "textarea" or "button"
Link	Tag is <a>
List	Tag is <ul>, <ol>, <li>, <dd>, <dl>, or <dt>
Image	Tag is <img>
Table	Tag is <table>, <th>, <tr>, <td>, <thead>, <tbody>, or <tfoot>
Dynamic behavior	System detects there is a style change of the element before and after *mouseover* effect

Table 1: The 11 sub-question categories and their display conditions

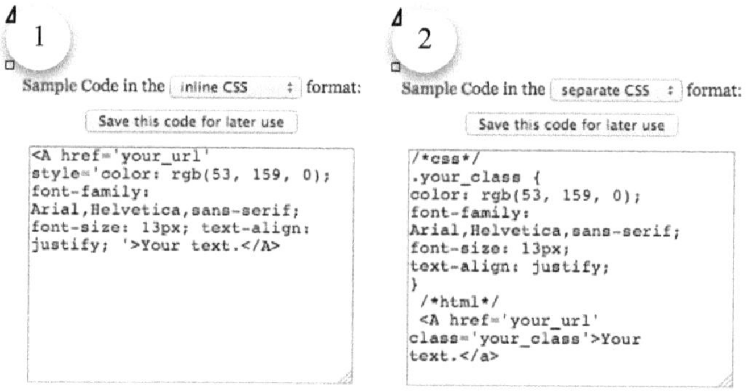

Figure 2: WebCrystal generates example code in both (1) inline CSS format and (2) separate CSS format.

The user can copy and paste the generated code into their editor to reproduce the effect. In addition, showing this code may help users learn the appropriate coding techniques. In a study of online code example usage [1], researchers found that using example code not only helped programmers finish their tasks more quickly, but also helped them learn new knowledge and clarify existing knowledge.

Explaining Position and Layout

WebCrystal provides additional questions and visualizations to explain the position and layout of elements by highlighting both the selected element's parent (container) and siblings on the web page (Figure 4 at 1), and allowing users to inspect the blank areas around the selected element that are generated by CSS layout attributes such as margin, padding, top, left, bottom, and right. Users can inspect a blank area by hovering the mouse on it, and WebCrystal will display a label with the CSS attribute that caused this blank space, along with its value (Figure 4 at 3). Alternatively, if the user hovers the mouse over the CSS attribute in the textual explanation on WebCrystal's interface, then the corresponding blank space will be highlighted (Figure 4 at 4).

Explaining Dynamic Behaviors

A key feature of web pages is that they are interactive, not just static drawings. CSS adds the ability to support hover behaviors that show different styles depending on the mouse location. Therefore, WebCrystal adds additional questions so the user can ask for an explanation and code for these behaviors.

For hover behaviors that change the style of an element, the user can demonstrate to WebCrystal the styles by first selecting the element and then moving the cursor on and off of the element, to cause the style change. During the interaction, WebCrystal detects that the element changes styles. In this case, WebCrystal will show a message in the textual area that tells the user that this is a dynamic element, and which style of the element is being used right now. The message also includes a toggle button with which the user can see the other style for this element; that is, alternating between showing a description of the hovered and not-hovered styles for a link. The questions also toggle so the user can find out the details of how each of the styles is achieved. WebCrystal also adds a question so the user can ask "how do I get my element to have this dynamic effect", and will then provide the HTML and CSS skeleton code for the appropriate hover effect as the answer (Figure 5 at 2).

Figure 3: When answering position questions, WebCrystal (1) highlights the container and the siblings of a selected element, and (3) allows user to inspect blank areas around the element on the web page or (4) inside the textual explanation using the mouse.

Storing and Combining Multiple Elements

Many web design examples consist more than one DOM element. For example, the 3-grid menu structure in Figure 6, or the text and image layout in Figure 4, both use multiple elements to achieve those designs. The positioning of these elements results from their CSS layout attributes and their nesting in the HTML hierarchy, such as being siblings or parent and children. WebCrystal enables users to investigate this kind of layout design of multiple elements, and

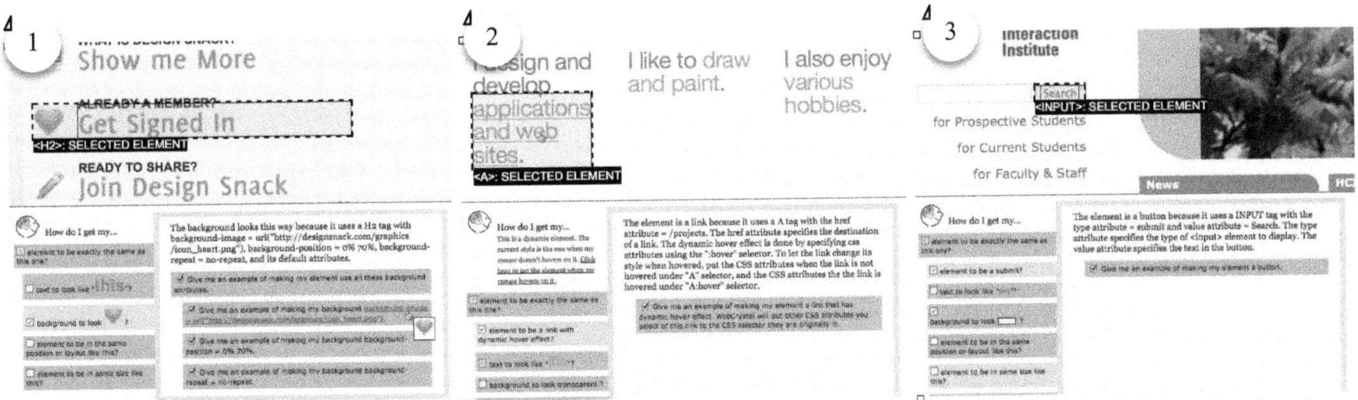


```
<H2 style='background-image:
url("http://designsnack.com/graphics
/icon_heart.png"); background-
position: 0% 70%; background-repeat:
no-repeat; '>Your text.</H2>
```

```
/*css*/
A.your_class {color: rgb(255, 102, 0);}
A.your_class:hover {text-decoration:
underline;}
/*html*/
<A class='your_class'
href='your_url'> Your text.</A>
```

```
<input type='submit' value='your
value' style='background-color:
rgb(240, 240, 240); '/ >
```

Figure 5: WebCrystal answers how to recreate (1) an image background, (2) an interactive link element, and (3) a search button, with the generated code snippets.

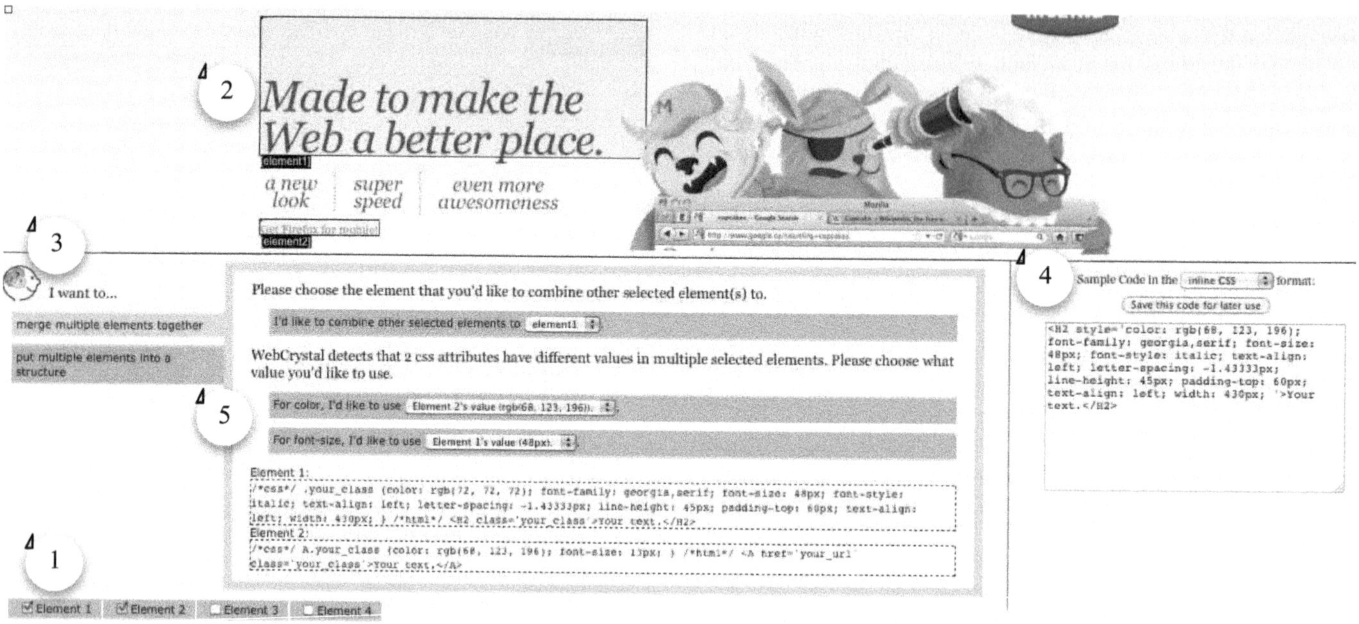

Figure 6: The interface for combining multiple elements. (1) the elements stored to be combined. (2) elements selected in (1) being highlighted in the web page in brown boxes. (3) the two commands of how to combine the elements. (4) the generated code for all selected elements merged together. (5) when an attribute is in multiple elements with conflicting values, the user can select which one to use.

even to select which specific aspects are desired from each element.

Another reason to investigate multiple web elements is to combine separate examples together. Inspired by Bricolage's approach of generating a new design by combining two web pages [13], WebCrystal supports creating a "style mashup" for users. For example, if the user likes the text style of one element, the background of another element and the size of a third element, WebCrystal can generate a code snippet for the user that creates a single element containing all of these desired design aspects.

The user interface for this feature is shown in Figures 2 and 6. First, the user selects the desired aspects of the first element in the usual way, which will cause the appropriate code for the first aspect to be displayed in the code pane. Then, the user selects the "save this code for later use" button (see Figure 2 at 5). The user then selects and shows the code for the other elements, and saves the code for each. The storing idea is inspired by the fact that designers in the real world often store the examples they like and retrieve them later in their design process [10].

Each saved code snippet is represented by a button with a system or user-defined name at the bottom of the WebCrystal window (see Figure 6 at 1). The user can select multiple snippets using the check boxes. The original element(s) from which the selected snippet(s) are copied from are highlighted on the web page in an orange semi-transparent box (Figure 6 at 2). Selecting multiple snippets takes users out from the question-asking interface to the "combining" interface, in which users give "I want to…" commands to the system to say how they want to combine the selected code (Figure 6 at 3). Clicking on "I want to merge multiple elements together" executes the "style mashup" feature, and WebCrystal generates code that has a single element with all the attributes in the selected code (Figure 6 at 4). If the saved snippets are elements of different types (e.g., one is a <span> and another is a <li>), then a menu is generated to allow the user to select which type is desired in the code. If the same attribute has different values in different selected snippets (for example, if one snippet used the color gray and another used blue), WebCrystal will generate a menu for users to select which value they want (Figure 6 at 5).

The other top-level command in Figure 6 at 3 is "I want to put multiple elements into a structure." This is used when multiple items at different levels are desired to be combined into a multi-level structure in the result. For example, if one snippet is a styled list <ul> and another snippet is a styled list element <li>, and the desired result is a <ul> with the <li> inside of it. WebCrystal uses the hierarchical relation of the elements, and generates new code that has the appropriate code in the same hierarchy. Currently, WebCrystal knows how to combine elements that are siblings or that are parent and children into the same structure. In the future, we will investigate support for creating sensible structures from elements with no well-defined relations to each other, such as a <dt> with a <ul> or a <div> with a <h1>.

USER STUDY

We evaluated the usefulness of WebCrystal in a small lab study. We polled a few web designers and web developers, and they reported that the most common ways that are used today to investigate code are the "View Source" menu item, along with tools such as Firebug [5] and the Chrome Developer Tool [4], which allow users to browse all of the HTML and CSS source code. Since WebCrystal is implemented as a Firefox plugin, we decided to compare it to Firebug in our user study.

Study Design

The study used a between-subject design. Participants were randomly assigned into two groups, the experimental group was given WebCrystal, and the control group was given Firebug [5]. In addition, both groups could use any of the standard FireFox features, such as View Source. Participants were also allowed to use any desired online resources to help with their tasks. In both conditions, the participants used the same special-purpose testing environment we created. This environment contains a text pane for entering the code, a "your output" pane that shows a preview of what a rendering of the code in the text pane will produce, and a "desired output" pane showing a preview of the correct answer (Figure 7). The participants' goal was to make the "your output" pane look and behave the same way as the "desired output" pane. Inside the text pane for each task, there was a small piece of code automatically inserted by the testing environment, for the participants to start from. Participants were told that they had to use this code as part of their answers. We did this to shrink the solution space and focus the task on just the reuse of the example code. We measured both the success rate and completion time on each task.

Participants

Both groups had 6 participants, all graduate students in our university. All participants had previous experience in writing HTML and CSS code. Participants rated their proficiency with both HTML and CSS language on a 4-point scale from "novice" to "superior". The average rating for HTML proficiency of all participants was 2.3 and for CSS was 2 out of 4. We also asked the participants to rate their level of experience with using Firebug or other web inspection tools on a 4-point scale of "none" to "expert". The average rating was 2.3. There were no significant differences in these measures between groups.

Tasks

All participants received the same 10 tasks in the same order. We designed the tasks to have 3 different levels of difficulty. The first 5 questions were the easiest, and were about reproducing the style of a single element. For example, one was to recreate a vertical separation line pointed to by the arrow in Figure 8 at 1. Next were 2 medium-difficulty questions, which were about reproducing the interactive behavior of an element. For example, one was to recreate a button that will change its style from green to red when hovered over by the mouse cursor like the one in Figure 8 at 2. The last 3 questions were the hardest, and were about reproducing the style of multiple elements. For example, recreating a same 3-grid structure like the one in Figure 8 at 3, but changing the color of the text to the blue color pointed by the arrow. The time limit for answering easy and medium tasks was 6 minutes and for hard tasks was 8 minutes. If users had not finished the task by the end of the time limit, they were marked as "uncompleted."

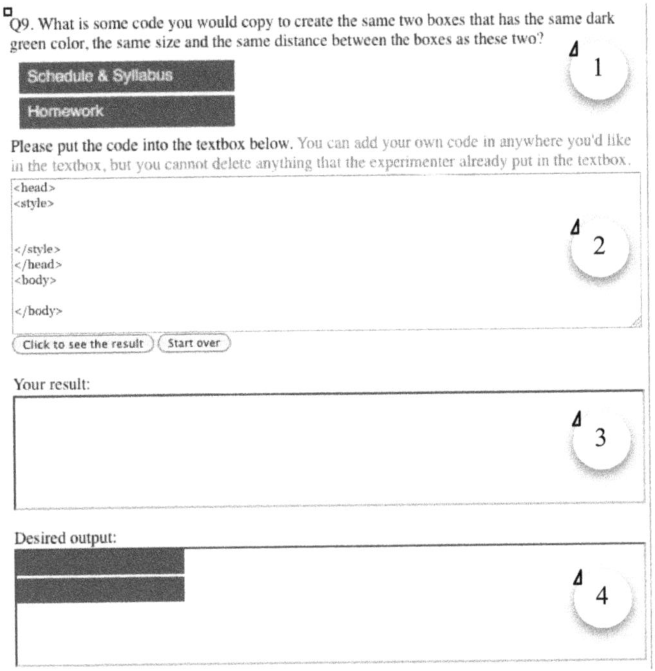

Figure 7: The testing environment contains (1) a question description, (2) a text pane for entering code. When clicking on the "Click to see the result" button, (3) will show a preview of (2). The correct output is shown at (4).

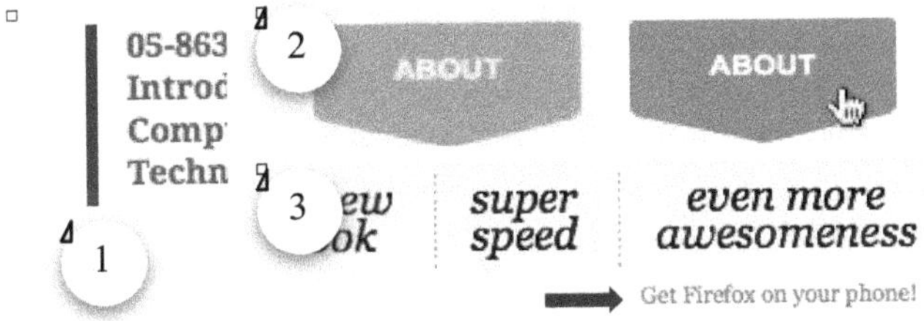

Figure 8: Tasks of 3 levels of difficulty.

Procedure

After giving consent to the study, the participants in both groups received a 15-minute tutorial on their tool (Firebug or WebCrystal) followed by a 5-minutes tutorial on the testing environment (Figure 7). The WebCrystal group was shown all the features described in the previous sections, and the Firebug group was shown all of its features that are relevant to HTML and CSS investigations, including view source, enabling and disabling CSS properties, and inspecting the CSS layout. We did not train participants in using other Firebug features , such as network monitoring or JavaScript debugging, since they were irrelevant to the tasks.

After the tutorials, participants started to do the first task. For each task, the experimenter would read the task description and then after reading the whole description would start timing. Participants were told to inform the experimenter when they thought they had the correct answer. The experimenter then stopped the clock, checked their work, and told them if they gave a correct answer. If the answer was wrong, participants could choose to work on it some more or give up. However, in our study, none of the participants chose to give up on any of the tasks. All participants worked until the time ran out or they succeeded. After attempting all the tasks, the participants answered a short interview to provide feedback. Participants were paid $15 after the study.

Results

We analyzed the data using a random-effect logit model to predict task completion rate, and a random-effect linear model to predict task completion time, with all the observation of one person as a group. The results are presented in Figures 9 and 10. Participants in the WebCrystal group completed an average of 9.67 (97%) of the tasks, whereas participants in the Firebug group completed an average of 7.83 (78%). The difference in task completion rate between two groups is significant (coef. = 2.49, p=.013).

We also analyzed the average time per task for all those participants who completed successfully. Participants using WebCrystal spent an average of 94.27 seconds (SD = 75.29) on tasks, whereas participants using Firebug spent 115.09 seconds (SD = 98.26). The difference is significant (coef. = -30.47, p = .036). As shown in Figure 10, the difference increases a bit as the tasks get more difficult. Taking the "hard" tasks alone, successful participants were 43% faster with WebCrystal (147.91 seconds vs 211.91 seconds).

The user study confirmed that our difficulty ratings were valid since across both groups, the main effect of task difficulty was significant on both task completion rate (coef. = -1.42, p < .001) and task completion time (coef. = 53.58, p < .001).

In the interviews, participants in the WebCrystal group expressed a great interest in using WebCrystal in real life:

"This is cool... are you gonna release it?"
"Can I have it?"
"Do you have this in Chrome?"
"This is definitely useful... I'll pay a little money for it."

Among the 6 WebCrystal users, 5 of them asked about the tool's availability, and 3 of them volunteered to help on testing and reporting bugs after its release. This is particularly encouraging since most of our participants have previous experience in using other web development tools.

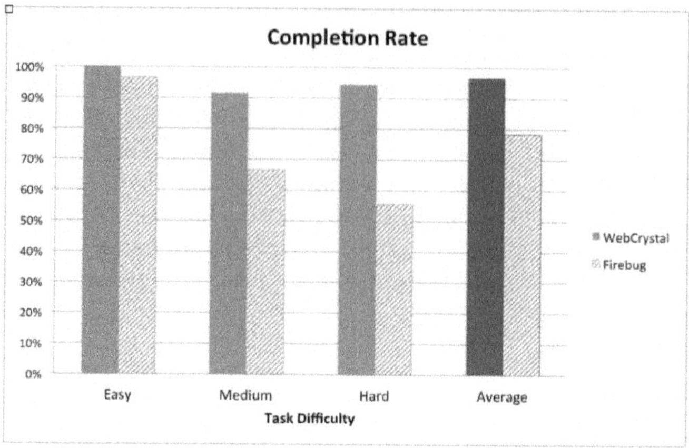

Figure 9: The completion rate of two groups in three levels of difficulty tasks and the overall average. Taller bars are better.

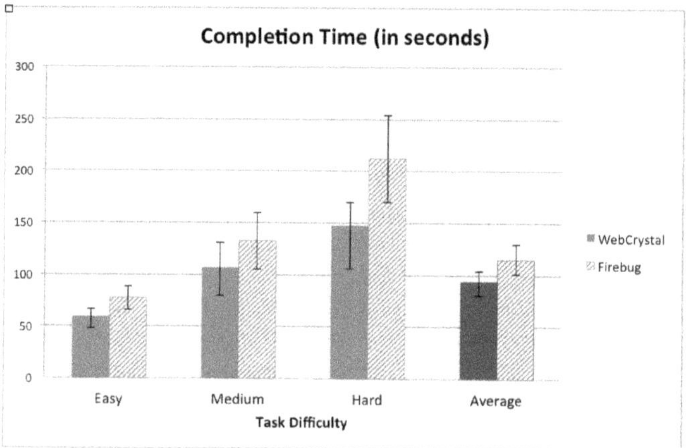

Figure 10: For the participants who completed the tasks, the average time they took in 3 levels of difficulty, and the overall average with standard errors. Shorter bars are better.

DISCUSSION

The key to successfully finishing the tasks in our user study is to quickly identify all of the required attributes and combine them to form usable code, while avoiding including inappropriate attributes. This is especially critical with the difficult tasks because they involve more attributes. We feel this study has external validity since reproducing a design aspect in real life almost always requires copying multiple related attributes. For example, to recreate text that has the same style as in Figure 2 at 1 requires users to specify 6 different text attributes. WebCrystal users took advantage of the way that attributes are already classified into different categories. They accessed the appropriate attributes by selecting different questions to ask the system to show them what they wanted. In contrast, the Firebug users were presented with all of the attributes by the system and needed to determine on their own which ones were related to the task.

When identifying an individual attribute, WebCrystal users viewed the rendered style of the attribute in each checkbox description to understand the effect of that attribute. Participants reported that this "graphical indicator" of an attribute and its effect were very helpful, because they actively provided the relevant information. This led the users to ask the right questions. On the other hand, Firebug users used the live editing feature in Firebug to turn the attributes on and off to view the changes in the web page. Although this feature also successfully explained the effect of an attribute to the user, it required the users to be the initiator of the inquiry process, and since it modifies the example page, it can interfere with appropriate rendering. In other words, with Firefox, all the attributes were passively waiting to be explored, and users had to first guess or know which attribute could be relevant and then decide if they wanted to use the live editing feature to check if it was truly the one they needed. We observed much trial-and-error clicking since users' first guesses were often not correct. We also found that for some of the tasks which Firebug participants failed to complete, there were attributes which participants never explored because they incorrectly assumed these attributes were irrelevant.

We observed that all WebCrystal users benefitted from the customized, ready-to-use code snippet generated by the system when doing both easy and hard tasks. Participants in the WebCrystal group liked using the checkboxes to select attributes to include in the code snippet, and thought it was very easy and efficient to use. Copying and pasting the generated code snippet prevented users from having any potential syntax errors and typos. In the Firebug group, some users chose to retype the attributes they thought were relevant rather than copying and pasting. This is because attributes are separated into different lines in Firebug, which would therefore require users to perform multiple selecting, copying and pasting operations. The result of this retyping was that more typos occurred, which users often did not notice at first. The typos often caused incorrect output, which made the users think that they had identified the wrong attribute. Then, instead of checking their code, users went searching in the example code again and got more and more confused, until they finally discovered that it was the typo that caused the wrong output. Conventional web editors such as Dreamweaver have the ability to check syntax errors for users, but still may not identify if there is a typo in an attribute name or value. These observations suggest that having a customized, ready-to-use code snippet extracted from the example file not only saves the users' time but also might result in higher-quality code.

When performing the tasks, we often observed very exploratory usage of sample code by the WebCrystal users. In WebCrystal, because selecting all attributes under a category was so easy (simply by checking one checkbox), when participants where not sure about the effect of individual attributes, some would just check everything that related to the task description, and see how the resulting code snippet worked using the preview pane in the answering environment. We observed fewer attempts like this in the Firebug group, because both identifying the relevant attributes and copying them were time-consuming.

Both WebCrystal and Firebug users considered the tool they used to be very helpful for their tasks. Some participants with advanced knowledge of HTML and CSS expressed that the textual explanations WebCrystal provided were less useful for them because they already knew most of the attribute names and effects. The main performance difference in completion time between expert users in the two groups seemed to be caused by the fast copy-and-paste ability in WebCrystal, which saved them from typing (and typos) and kept track of the attributes one by one. For novice and intermediate HTML and CSS users, WebCrystal's textual descriptions seemed to be more useful. Both expert and novice participants reported that they liked the question-asking style of the interface. They thought it was very intuitive to use and easy to learn. While novice and intermediate participants in the Firebug group struggled to identify the right attributes to use and even to form syntactically correct code, novice and intermediate participants in the WebCrystal group found the correct attributes by asking a higher-level question and directly copying the ready-to-use code as their answer.

LIMITATIONS

WebCrystal focuses on explaining HTML and CSS, and does not handle JavaScript, Flash, or other scripting languages for interactive behaviors. WebCrystal currently flattens any CSS inheritance in the example, and generates code that contains all the required attribute values together. Our motivation for this was to help users quickly reproduce a desired element by directly copying the example code into their own web page. The downside of this piece-by-piece styling approach is that it does not take advantage of the cascading nature of CSS, and might result in a difficult-to-maintain file as the number of copied elements become larger. Also, the style of an element is affected by its parents because some of the attributes can be inherited. Therefore, we cannot be sure whether the example code pasted from WebCrystal will work exactly the same in the target web page as in the example without knowing the hierarchical structure of where it is pasted. As a simple example, WebCrystal leaves out attributes which have their default value in the source file, and these attributes may have different default values in the target file. This could be addressed by integrating WebCrystal with a web editor to support the user's choice of whether to override or inherit any attributes that differ in the example and target files.

CONCLUSIONS AND FUTURE WORK

WebCrystal is a tool that helps users to understand how an example is constructed and to reproduce the example in their own web page. Its interaction techniques based on asking and answering questions proved effective, easy-to-learn and well-liked by both novice and experienced web developers. WebCrystal successfully allowed fast copying-and-pasting of desired attributes, and the storing and combining of attributes from multiple examples. The ability to specify the desired attributes and have the tool generate appropriate combined code for them proved to be an important advantage, compared to requiring users to combine the code by hand. WebCrystal is now available at http://www.cs.cmu.edu/~webcrystal/.

Future work could be in many directions. One is to integrate WebCrystal with web editing tools such as Dreamweaver or Eclipse to facilitate intelligent pasting of the example code in a way that would consider the hierarchy relations among elements, as described in the previous sections.

Another direction is to extend the system's ability to be able to explain the construction of interactive behaviors of a webpage. A previous system, FireCrystal [19], lets its users playback the interactions with web pages using a timeline and displays relevant code. From our user study, we observed that participants benefitted from selecting and augmenting desired code snippets through a hierarchical question-asking interface. Combining the interaction techniques in WebCrystal and FireCrystal, one could imagine a system that records interactions in a web page, divides complex interactions into smaller and easily understandable parts, and lets users access relevant code of each part by asking hierarchical questions.

Finally, we are also interested in observing web developers using WebCrystal for real-world tasks. What elements are most web developers interested in? What are the most common questions that web developers ask when recreating an element? How does WebCrystal affect on the design process? Understanding these questions would give us more insights on designing future tools that support reusing examples in web authoring.

ACKNOWLEDGMENTS

We would like to thank Ruogu Kang, Yanjin Long, Haiyi Zhu and Colleen Stuart for their help with the statistics for the paper, and Andrew Faulring for his help with the user study. This research was funded in part by the NSF under grant IIS-1116724. Any opinions, findings and conclusions or recommendations expressed in this material are those of the authors and do not necessarily reflect those of the NSF.

REFERENCES

1. Brandt, J., Guo, P. J., Lewenstein, J., Dontcheva, M., Klemmer, S. R. Two studies of opportunistic programming: interleaving web foraging, learning, and writing code. *Proc. CHI* (2009), ACM, pp. 1589-1598.
2. Brandt, J., Pattamatta, V., Choi, W., Hsieh, B., Klemmer, S. R. *Rehearse: Helping Programmers Adapt Examples by Visualizing Execution and Highlighting Related.* Tech. rep. CSTR 2010-05, Stanford, Oct. 2010.
3. Buxton, B. *Sketching User Experiences*. Morgan Kaufmann, 2007.
4. *Chrome Developer Tools*. http://code.google.com/chrome/devtools/
5. *Firebug*. http://getfirebug.com/
6. Fitzgerald, M. CopyStyler: Web design by example. Master Thesis, Dept. of EECS, MIT, May 2008.
7. Gibson, D., Punera, K., Tomkins, A. The volume and evolution of Web page templates. *Proc. WWW* (2005), ACM, pp. 830-839.
8. *Graphic Mania*. http://www.graphicmania.net/are-web-designers-required-to-know-how-to-code/
9. Hashimoto, Y., Igarashi, T. Retrieving web page layouts usingsketches to support example-based web design. 2nd Eurographics Workshop on Sketch-Based Interfaces and Modeling (2005).
10. Herring, S. R., Chang, C.-C., Krantzler, J., Bailey, B. P. Getting inspired!: understanding how and why examples are used in creative design practice. *Proc. CHI* (2009), ACM, pp. 87-96.
11. *jQuery*. http://jquery.com/
12. Ko, A. J., Myers, B. A. Finding Causes of Program Output with the Java Whyline. *Proc. CHI* (2009), ACM, pp. 1569-1578.
13. Kumar, R., Talton, J. O., Ahmad, A., Klemmer, S. R. Bricolage: Example-Based Retargeting for Web Design. *Proc. CHI (2011)*, ACM, pp. 2197-2206.
14. Lee, B., Srivastava, S., Kumar, R., Brafman, R., Klemmer, S. R. Designing with interactive example galleries. *Proc. CHI* (2010), ACM, pp. 2257-2266.
15. Marks, J. et al. Design galleries: a general approach to setting parameters for computer graphics and animation. *Proc. SIGGRAPH* (1997), ACM, pp. 389-400.
16. *MDC Doc Center*. https://developer.mozilla.org/en/xul
17. Myers, B. A., Weitzman, D. A., Ko, A. J., Chau, D. H. Answering why and why not questions in user interfaces. *Proc. CHI* (2006), ACM, pp. 397-406.
18. Nardi, B. *A small matter of programming*. MIT Press. 1993.
19. Oney, S., Myers, B. A. FireCrystal: Understanding Interactive Behaviors in Dynamic Web Pages. *IEEE Symp. On VL/HCC* (2009), pp. 105-108.
20. Ritchie, D., Kejriwal, A. A., Klemmer, S. R. d.tour: style-based exploration of design example galleries. *Proc. UIST* (2011), ACM, pp. 165-174.

Understanding Mobile Q&A Usage: An Exploratory Study

Uichin Lee, Hyanghong Kang, Eunhee Yi, Mun Y. Yi, Jussi Kantola
KAIST Knowledge Service Engineering Department
{uclee, hong.h.kang, eunhee.yi, munyi, jussi}@kaist.ac.kr

ABSTRACT
Recently questioning and answering (Q&A) communities that facilitate knowledge sharing among people have been introduced to the mobile environments such as Naver Mobile Q&A and ChaCha. These mobile Q&A services are very different from traditional Q&A sites in that questions/answers are short in length and are exchanged via mobile devices (e.g., SMS or mobile Internet). While traditional Q&A sites have been well investigated, so far little is known about the mobile Q&A usage. To understand mobile Q&A usage, we analyzed 2.4 million question/answer pairs spanning a 14 month period from Naver Mobile Q&A and performed a complementary survey study of 555 active mobile Q&A users. We find that mobile Q&A is deeply wired into users' everyday life activities—its usage is largely dependent on users' spatial, temporal, and social contexts; the key factors of mobile Q&A usage are accessibility/convenience of mobile Q&A, promptness of receiving answers, and users' satisficing behavior of information seeking (i.e., minimizing efforts and settling with good enough information). We also observe that users tend to seek more factual information attributed to everyday life activities than they do on traditional Q&A sites and that they exhibit unique interaction patterns such as repeating and refining questions as coping strategies in seeking information needs. Our main findings reported in the paper have significant implications on the design of mobile Q&A systems.

Author Keywords
Mobile Q&A System; Online Community; Ubiquitous Computing

ACM Classification Keywords
H.5.3 Information Interfaces and Presentation: Group and Organizational Interfaces

General Terms
Measurement; Human Factors; Design

INTRODUCTION
Question and answering (Q&A) sites such as Yahoo! Answers and Naver KiN facilitate knowledge sharing among users by leveraging the wisdom of crowds. Q&A sites complement existing Web search engines by supporting flexible query formulation and customized answer delivery. With the rising popularity of mobile phones, mobile versions of Q&A sites have recently been introduced to the market, including Naver Mobile Q&A, ChaCha, Jisiklog, and AQA. The popularity of mobile Q&A services has been increasing over the past several years. For example, by September 2011 ChaCha answered more than 1.7 billion questions, surpassing the number of answers made in Yahoo! Answers. In mobile Q&A, users post short questions using their cell phones to solicit answers from other users on the Web (e.g., via SMS). The main departure from conventional Q&A sites is that the length of questions and answers has a limit (e.g., 150 letters), and that a mobile phone has its own characteristics (i.e., small screen, portability, restrictive keyboard).

While conventional Q&A sites have received a lot of attention from the research community, and significant research has been conducted, so far little is known about the mobile Q&A usage. In this paper, we seek to improve our understanding of mobile Q&A usage with the following research questions:

- Why do people use mobile Q&A services? When compared to existing information sources that people often use, what are the key drivers of mobile Q&A usage?
- What kinds of questions are asked and (not) answered over mobile Q&A? Are there any factors that influence the likelihood of receiving answers? Are the types of asked questions different from those in other information channels?
- How do users interact with mobile Q&A to meet their information needs (e.g., coping strategies, asker-answerer social networks, etc.)?

We answer these research questions by studying Naver KiN, the largest Q&A service in Korea. Naver the most popular online search provider in Korea offers both conventional and mobile Q&A services, i.e., Naver KiN and Naver Mobile Q&A, respectively. Naver Mobile Q&A was launched in April 2010 and has become one of the largest mobile Q&A services in Korea. We analyze the crawled data set from Naver Mobile Q&A in the period of June 1, 2010 to July 31, 2011. We also perform a survey study with 555 active Q&A users to supplement a large scale data analysis. To the best of our knowledge, our work is the first large scale study on mobile Q&A services. The following are the main contributions of the paper.

- We find that mobile Q&A is deeply wired into users' everyday life activities, and its usage is largely dependent on spatial, temporal, and social contexts. When compared to traditional Q&A sites, mobile Q&A users tend to ask a much broader range of questions attributed to everyday life activities. The key factors of mobile Q&A usage are (1) accessibility and convenience of mobile Q&A, (2) promptness of receiving answers, and (3) users' satisficing behavior of information seeking (i.e., minimizing efforts and settling with good enough information).
- We classify questions based on types (e.g., fact, suggestion, opinion), topics, and personalness and investigate how those qualities are related to the chances of receiving answers. Our classification shows that in mobile Q&A, asking simple facts is more dominant than traditional Q&A—questions from everyday life activities are more likely to seek factual information. The types of questions significantly differ from one topic to another. Interestingly, personalness of questions does not improve the chances of receiving answers.
- We analyze macroscopic user interactions by analyzing the crawled data set. We find unique interaction patterns such as repeating and refining questions as coping strategies of seeking information needs. Asking/answering behavior is heavy-tailed, meaning that there are quite a few light/heavy askers/answerers. The length of an answer linearly scales with that of a question; i.e., a longer question tends to result in a longer answer.
- We discuss several design implications: (1) user interface design that lowers the cognitive burden of askers, (2) context sharing mechanism that permits answerers to know the previous interactions, (3) answerer's personalized user interface that potentially improves the answer speed and quality, and (4) privacy aware system design that protects the privacy of askers.

RELATED WORK

Conventional Q&A sites

Some of the large-scale Q&A sites analyzed in the research community include Yahoo! Answer, Naver KiN, Microsoft Live Q&A, Google Answer, and Mahalo. In the following, we review the related work that characterizes the Q&A sites.

Adamic et al. [4] showed that in Yahoo! Answers, interaction among users varies depending on the topic and is highly skewed, knowledge sharing patterns across different topic categories (i.e., experts in different domains help one another) exist, and best answers can be predicted based on reply/thread length. In their analysis of Naver KiN, Nam et al. [22] studied the user behavior of answerers and found that the level of participation is highly skewed, answerers' participation tends to be intermittent, and the expected level of their expertise is lower than that in specialized online forums.

Questions in Q&A sites are generally classified as soliciting facts, opinions, and suggestions [18]. Harper et al. [8] showed that the types of questions in Q&A sites can be broadly classified into two categories, namely informational questions (e.g., fact and advice) and conventional questions (e.g., opinions and self-expression). Rodrigues et al. [27] found that Q&A sites can also be used for socializing, such as by chatting and searching for entertainment (puzzles, riddles), and unlike Yahoo! Answer, a significant fraction of answers in Microsoft Live Q&A (16.4%) belong to such a category.

In Q&A sites, the response time tends to be fairly long. Hsieh and Counts [12] reported that in Microsoft Live Q&A, the average time to receive an answer was 2 hours and 53 minutes, and 20% of the questions never received an answer. Zhang et al. [36] showed that in a specialized Q&A site for Java program language, the average time to receive an answer was around 9 hours.

The motivation behind answering questions is largely dependent on a mixture of intrinsic factors (e.g., perceived ownership of knowledge, enjoyment and feelings of gratitude and respect) and extrinsic factors (e.g., monetary rewards, reputation systems) [25]. Online discussion forums such as Usenet groups do not offer any explicit incentive mechanisms and mostly rely on intrinsic factors. In contrast, Q&A sites typically employ incentive mechanisms to solicit users' participation. Nam et al. [22] showed that the motivation for answering in Naver KiN is due to both intrinsic and extrinsic factors; i.e., altruism is the leading factor, followed by business motives, learning, hobbies, and earning points (in its reputation system). When monetary rewards are involved, it is reported that fee-based sites elicit better answers than free sites (e.g., Google Answer vs. Yahoo! Answer), and that higher quality answers can be acquired by paying more money [9]. Hsieh et al. [13] analyzed Mahalo, a fee-based Q&A site and showed that askers wish to pay when requesting facts and will pay more when asking difficult questions.

Unlike that of existing work, our focus is to characterize the usage of mobile Q&A services. In particular, we study why people use a *mobile Q&A service* as opposed to other available information channels (including traditional Q&A sites and web search) and investigate such a service's social network graph, types of questions, and unique usage patterns.

Real-time Q&A systems

Real-time (or synchronous) Q&A systems typically support question answering in the following steps: (1) identify experts for a given question (e.g., by analyzing documents such as emails and Web pages [16]), and (2) solicit answers from the experts. Various strategies are used for soliciting answers: (1) broadcasting questions to all the users (no expert selection), e.g., mimir [12], (2) multicasting questions to the specific expert group for a given question, e.g., Aardvark [11] and IM-an-expert [26], and (3) topic-based publish-subscription (any users who subscribed to a certain topic group), e.g., ReachOut and Quora. For direct communication, real-time Q&A systems use emails (e.g., Aardvark, Quora) or dedicated instant messaging (e.g., mimir, IM-an-Expert, ReachOut). Mobile Q&A services deliver near real-time question answering as in real-time Q&A systems. However, this is achieved through *asynchronous* communications; i.e., as in conventional Q&A systems, answerers must visit mobile Q&A web sites.

	Interaction Method	Incentive	Mixed
Naver Mobile	SMS, Mobile App/Web	Reputation	No
ChaCha	SMS, Mobile App/Web, Web	ChaCha pays	-
Jisiklog	SMS, Mobile App	Asker pays	-
AQA	SMS, Mobile App	Asker pays	-
kgb answers	SMS, Mobile App	Asker pays	-
Ask People	Mobile App/Web, Web	Reputation	Yes
Daum Live	Mobile App/Web, Web	Reputation	No

Table 1. Classification of mobile Q&A services (ChaCha, Jisiklog, AQA, and kgb answers do not have conventional Q&A services)

Mobile Q&A Systems

Popular mobile Q&A services include ChaCha, kgb answers, Ask People in the US, AQA in the UK, and Jisiklog, Naver Mobile Q&A and Daum Live Q&A in Korea. Mobile Q&A services in the market can be classified based on the following dimensions: (1) whether question posting is limited to mobile devices (i.e., SMS/MMS and mobile App/Web), (2) whether there is a monetary incentive mechanism, and if any, who pays the fees, and (3) whether a mobile Q&A service is mixed with a conventional Q&A service (i.e., presented together). Table 1 summarizes the classification of various mobile Q&A services. Note that those services that only support mobile devices (ChaCha, AQA, kgb answers, Naver Mobile Q&A) have a length limit on questions/answers as SMS/MMS is mainly used (due to ease of billing), but a mixed service like Ask People does not have such a constraint. ChaCha originally accepted questions via SMS only, but this restriction was recently relaxed, and questions can now be posted via the Web. In this paper, we analyze the usage patterns of Naver Mobile Q&A, a representative mobile Q&A service as it supports only question posting via mobile devices. We believe that our work sheds light on understanding the overall usage patterns of mobile Q&A systems in general.

Mobile Web and Web Search Usage

The taxonomy of web tasks is generally classified as information seeking, casual browsing, communication (e.g., chatting), and transactions (e.g., bank services) [17]. In their recent study, Cui and Roto [6] reported that in mobile environments, tasks are rather limited to information seeking, communication, and transactions with an additional task of maintaining personal content as a part of personal space extension. User behavior studies about mobile Internet use show that such web tasks are largely dependent on users' contexts, e.g., personal context (e.g., goals) and environmental context (e.g., distractions, social interactions) [19, 6]. Kamvar and Baluja [15] performed quantitative analysis of mobile web search usage from the Google Mobile Search data set in 2004 (connected via mobile Internet). The overall topics are quite consistent with the desktop search statistics. Popular topics include adults (e.g., "free porn"), computer and communications (e.g., "free ringtones"), and entertainments (e.g.,"imdb"). The average number of words per query is 2.3, with an average letter length of 15.5. Users tend to perform a series of related queries by refining/repeating previous queries, including automatic spell correction. In their recent study of mobile search pattern evolution, Yi and Maghoul [35] reported that the query topics experienced significant change (consistent with desktop search) when comparing the data sets from year 2007 and 2010 (e.g., decrease of entertainment queries, increase of local and commerce queries). In this paper, we discuss mobile Q&A communities that are very different from traditional web search. Our work compliments the prior research on user behavior in mobile web search in that we use a large-scale mobile Q&A data set supplemented with a survey study of 555 active service users to characterize information seeking behavior with mobile Q&A.

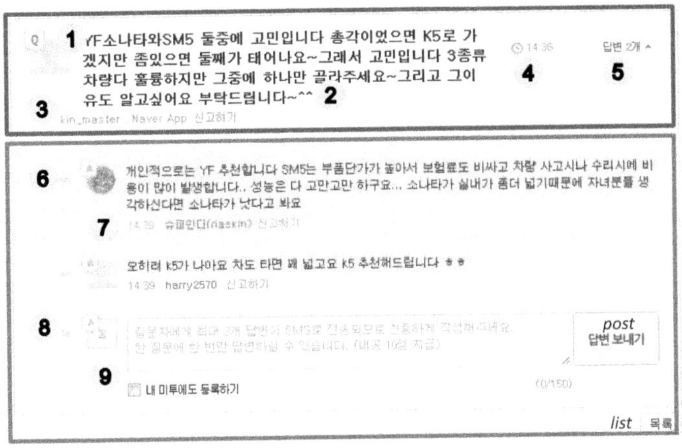

Figure 1. A question and its answers posted on the Naver Mobile Q&A Web site: (1) a user's profile image (if present), (2) question, (3) user ID, sent-from information (SMS, Mobile Web, Naver App), and abuse report, (4) posted time, (5) click to answer and the number of answers posted, (6) posted answers, (7) posted time, answerer ID, and abuse report (8) posting a new answer, (9) uploading the answer to the answerer's Me2day simultaneously (a Twitter-like service offered by Naver). If a user posts an image, its thumbnail will be shown next to the user's profile image.

INTERACTION IN NAVER MOBILE Q&A

In Naver Mobile Q&A, users can post questions only via mobile devices; a list of supported methods of communication includes SMS/MMS, Mobile Web, and Naver App. Since it basically uses SMS, there is a strict limit on the length of a question/answer, i.e., 150 letters. For a given question, users can also attach related images using MMS. Registered users of Naver can post their questions on the Web via such interaction methods. As shown in Figure 1, a requester's user ID is revealed along with the delivery method (e.g., SMS, Mobile Web, and Naver App). Naver currently restricts users to posting at most 30 questions a day.

The registered users can only post answers through the Naver Mobile Q&A Web site as in the traditional Q&A sites (see Figure 1). The front page of the Web site presents a list of the 20 most recent questions (in the form of the upper box in Figure 1 stacked). The old lists can be browsed by clicking the next button located at the bottom of the page. The questions are basically ranked on the basis of recency; whenever a new question arrives, the entire rank trickles down by one, and the 20th ranked question on the front page will be placed on the second page. Answerers can pause/resume real-time updates of questions using the pause/resume button located at the top of the page. Requesters can choose to receive answers via SMS (regardless of whether they posted questions via Mobile Web or Naver App). Due to the financial burden involved, Naver Mobile Q&A only delivers at most three answers via SMS. If more than three answers are made, the rest can be accessed via mobile Web and Naver App. Naver has a point-based reputation system for answerers. A user can earn 10 points for each answer. The following are the notable differences from the traditional Q&A: (1) a question expires after 24 hours, and expired questions cannot be answered; (2) users cannot edit the submitted questions/answers; (3) there is no option for selecting the best answer; and (4) there is no predefined question category.

METHODOLOGY

Our methodology is composed of two complementary parts: (1) automated crawling of publicly accessible questions and answers on Naver Mobile Q&A [3] and (2) email-based surveys. The crawl of millions of questions/answers allows us to gain comprehensive statistics about user behavior, whereas the email-based survey results from Mobile Q&A users help us to develop an in-depth understanding of the underlying factors that derive the observed usage behavior. As the reader will see later, such a combination has provided mutually supporting evidence on our findings.

Naver Mobile Q&A launched its service in April 2010. We crawled the Q&A data set from June 1, 2010 to July 31, 2011. The total number of questions and answers were 2,483,624 and 3,086,365, respectively. For a given question, we extracted a set of associated items for analysis, including user ID, posted time, and posted answers.

We supplemented the data set with the surveys of active Naver Mobile Q&A users. From the users who posted questions in July 2011, we randomly selected 9,000 Naver Mobile Q&A users on the basis of their usage level of high, moderate and low (3,000 each) and sent the survey questionnaire via the Naver email service in August 2011. The total number of participants was 223 (after removing duplicate/erroneous answers). To check whether there are nonresponse errors, we sent the first part of the survey questionnaire in November 2011 to those users who did not answer the earlier survey. The total number of participants in the second survey was 332 (after removing duplicate/erroneous answers). Our statistical analysis with chi-square goodness of fit tests reveals that in each usage level group, the two survey results are almost statistically identical.

The survey begins with demographic questions. The results of 555 participants show that 49.5% are males. The majority of participants (73.9%) are the teenagers, and 15% are in their 20s. 3.1%, 1.6%, and 0.4% are in their 30s, 40s, and 50s, respectively. When looking at their jobs, we have the following distribution: elementary school (5.6%), junior high school (33.5%), high school (33.3%), college (14.3%), and working (7.2%). 70.5% of participants use smartphones. As mobile Q&A is based on short messaging, we found that the age distribution is similar to that of SMS/IM usage—teenagers are the dominant user groups, and SMS/IM are preferred to emails and voice calls in these user groups [2]. Given that the Naver Mobile Q&A users were randomly selected, we believe that our survey participants are representative.

The rest of the survey was composed of two parts: (1) asking about the overall usage of Mobile Q&A, and (2) describing the detailed situations/reasons for the questions that participants actually asked in July 2011. In the first part, we asked users about the types of questions posted using Mobile Q&A, asking them to rate whether Mobile Q&A usage is different from that of Naver KiN. We also asked users to rate the perceived answer quality of Naver Mobile Q&A in general and to select alternative methods when the answers were less satisfactory. In addition, we asked a few questions to find out why Q&A services are preferred to other information sources. In the second part of the survey, to better understand why people use mobile Q&A, we showed the actual questions that the participants posted in July 2011 and asked them to describe the detailed situation/reason when they asked those questions. Due to privacy concerns, only 86 participants (38.6%) completed the second part of the survey.

WHY PEOPLE USE MOBILE Q&A

We illustrate the concept of everyday life information seeking and information practices which is closely related to the contexts of mobile Q&A usage; we then derive the key factors of mobile Q&A usage from the data set.

Everyday Life Information Seeking

Information seeking occurs in both work-related and non-work related contexts of everyday life. While work-related information seeking is self-explanatory, the concept of non-work related information seeking is rather elusive. To bridge this gap, a number of theoretical models have been proposed as summarized in the survey article [28]. One model of particular interest is information practice, which defines socially and culturally constituted (often *habitualized*) ways of identifying, seeking, using, and sharing information [20].

Everyday information practices are deeply embedded in spatio-temporal contexts of our everyday lives (e.g, watching TV news, reading newspapers and searching the Web) in order to deal with the *life projects* at large (i.e., information practices as caring activities of life projects or *mastery of life*) [29]. Some life projects are generic and routine in that they are common to most people (e.g., household care, entertainment), and other projects are specific in that they originate from an individual's life situation (e.g., hobbies, child rearing) [10]. Various activities associated with life projects are performed in our daily life places (e.g., home, café, clubs, and library) in which social interaction is likely to occur, and as a by-product, the needs for information seeking/sharing arise [23].

For everyday life information seeking, people rely on an information horizon that consists of a variety of information sources such as social networks, books, information retrieval tools, web pages, and Q&A services [29]. People typically judge the relevance of information sources available in the information environment, select a set of *preferred sources* to resolve the issue related to the everyday project, and consult the sources by following the preferred sequence, learned over time [14]. For information needs in mobile environments, readers can find more detailed information in recent diary studies [31, 5]. In the following, we analyze the role of a mobile Q&A service in a person's information horizon and present the key factors of mobile Q&A usage.

Factors of Mobile Q&A Usage

The types of information sources that are closely related to Q&A services are human resources over the social networks (e.g., family members/friends, members in Q&A site communities). First of all, mobile phones have greatly improved the accessibility of one's social network and have given users a great level of freedom in terms of mobility. Whenever information needs arise, a user's mobile phone provides a convenient way of accessing remote information sources at the user's finger tips. In this case, the availability of potential answers is of critical concern. Yet, mobile Q&A significantly improves the availability by tapping a large pool of users over the Internet as in traditional Q&A. Unlike traditional Q&A, mobile Q&A permits users to submit questions and receive answers via SMS which greatly lowers the cognitive burden (due to short in length with a small number of touches) when compared to accessing traditional sources (e.g., searching the Web using desktop computers and smartphones). Further, users can receive answers much faster (median delay of 2.1 minutes in Naver Mobile Q&A vs. mean delay of 2 hours 52 minutes in Microsoft Live Q&A [12]).

We carefully designed the survey questionnaire based on these observations. To examine why a traditional Q&A service is preferred to generic web search, we asked users to select all the reasons from the following options: (1) I am not good at web search (1.6%) (2) web search results were less satisfactory (27.6%), (3) it is more convenient (36.9%), (4) I can save time (46.5%), (5) I do not want to be distracted from the task at hand (25.2%), and (6) I can receive personalized answers (34.2%). If they had other reasons, we asked participants to write them, but we did not find any other significant reasons. As expected, users generally believe that Q&A sites allow them to conveniently interact with human answerers and to receive customized answers without spending much effort.

We then asked users why mobile Q&A is preferred to traditional mechanisms by presenting a set of reasons as before: (1) I can readily ask questions anytime anywhere (63.2%), (2) it is more convenient than accessing Q&A sites using PCs (35.6%), (3) it is more convenient than web searching with PCs and smartphones (32.3%), (4) it gives faster responses (43.1%), (5) it provides more satisfactory answers (7%), and (6) I do not want to be distracted from the task at hand (19.1%). If they had other reasons, we asked the participants to write them, but we did not find any other significant reasons. These results clearly show that the key factors are accessibility (portability), convenience, and promptness. In addition, regarding the answer quality of Mobile Q&A, as shown later most users believe that they are somewhat satisfied/dissatisfied. Yet, users' coping strategies are rather limited within mobile Q&A, and users tend to show satisficing behavior—accepting less satisfactory answers without spending further efforts. In the following, we further examine these factors by analyzing the data set.

Note that in our survey, we also asked participants to write why mobile Q&A is more useful than seeking information directly from other people (e.g., friends). Our manual classification reveals that the majority of participants (75%) believe that answerers in mobile Q&A are likely to have more expertise than their friends (availability of answerers) and can possibly deliver better answers. Promptness and convenience are mentioned by 20% and 16% of the participants respectively. Other minor reasons include seeking for more objective opinions from the crowd (5%), asking private questions that may be embarrassing if revealed to their friends (5%), and not disturbing one's friends (5%).

Accessibility and Convenience of Mobile Q&A

In our survey we asked users to describe the detailed contexts in which they posted the questions, by presenting at most five questions asked by the participants in the month of July 2011. We received detailed descriptions of 206 questions from 83 participants. Our manual investigation shows that information seeking is largely attributed to everyday life activities: (1) while watching TV and movies (12%), (2) while talking with someone (13%), (3) while studying (10%), (4) while planning something (18%), and (5) while performing other activities such as exercising and observing unusual conditions (42%). Several example questions and descriptions are the following:

Question: *"What's the name of an exercise device that looks like a jump rope, but you can hold your foot on it and pull it?"*
Description: *"When I was watching a diet program on TV, I saw that device and wanted to buy that device. But I didn't know the name."*

Question: *"What's the broadcast schedule of the all-star baseball game today?"*
Description: *"I knew that the game happened that day, but I didn't know the time and channel. Also, I didn't have enough time to go and check with my desktop PC."*

Since its usage is largely dependent on our everyday life activities, we expect that mobile Q&A usage will increase over the course of a day as people will perform more activities and experience more social interactions, which will greatly increase information seeking needs (e.g., morning vs. afternoon vs. evening). To confirm this, in Figure 2 we plot the percentage of hourly usage of mobile Q&A and juxtapose it with that of mobile web browsing and PC based *web browsing* measured by a large Internet portal service provider in Korea [1]. The figure shows that mobile Q&A usage continues to increase over time until it tapers off at 9PM. Interestingly, the usage pattern of mobile web browsing differs from that of mobile Q&A usage in that web browsing has a much higher usage level during the commuting hours in the morning (e.g., reading newspapers) and the usage drops after midnight. The role of PC and mobile devices appears to be complementary; more usage of mobile web during the commuting and evening hours, and dramatic drop of PC-based web browsing after 5PM. In Figure 3, we plot the daily usage pattern of mobile Q&A. The figure shows that the activity level on weekends is higher than that on weekdays, corrobo-

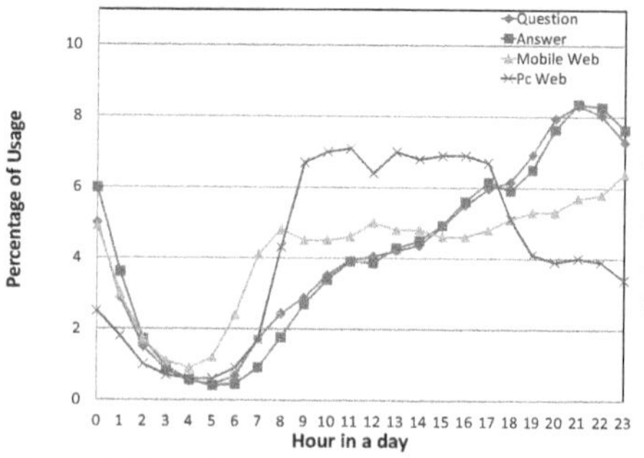

Figure 2. Hourly usage percentage: mobile web browsing, PC-based web browsing, and mobile Q&A

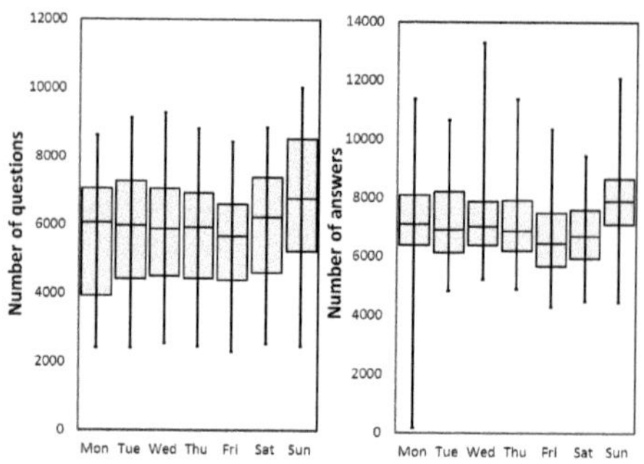

Figure 3. Daily usage pattern of mobile Q&A (left: questions, right: answers)

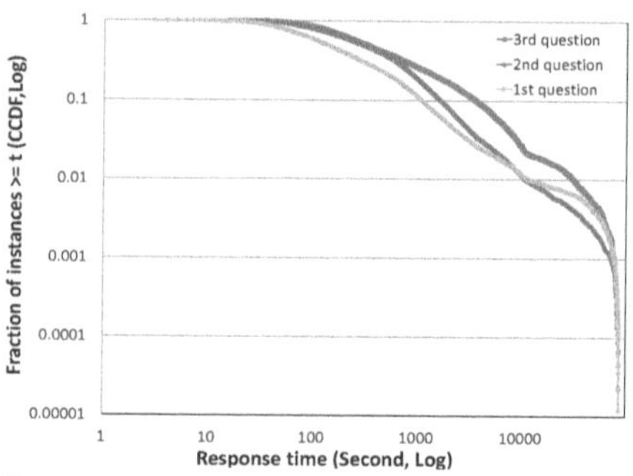

Figure 4. Response delay of Mobile Q&A (time to receive the first, second, third answer (log-log)

rating our observation that mobile Q&A usage is dependent on our everyday life activities.

Promptness of Receiving Answers

Unlike traditional Q&A, in which the response delay tends to be fairly long, we find that mobile Q&A delivers a much smaller response delay. In Figure 4 we plot the cumulative distribution of response delay of Naver Mobile Q&A under the following cases: time to receive (1) the first answer, (2) the second answer, and (3) the third answer. The shape of the graphs approximately follows a power law distribution with exponential cut-off. This exponential cut-off is due to the fact that Naver Mobile Q&A enforces a restriction according to which answers can be made only within 24 hours after posting. In the delay distribution graph of receiving the first answer, for instance, the average is 932.9 seconds (15.5 minutes), whereas the median is 127 seconds (2.1 minutes); the minimum is as small as 3 seconds, and the maximum is as large as 23.99 hours. The mean inter-arrival time between the first and second answer is 143.3 seconds, and that between the second and third answers is 911.6 seconds.

Users' Satisficing Behavior of Information Seeking

Simon defines satisficing as a decision-making process in which an individual forgoes the best solution in favor of one that is acceptable [30]. The concept of satisifcing has been applied to a number of disciplines in the social sciences. It was recently adopted in the information science field to explain how and when individuals stop looking for information—"the information is good enough to satisfy a need even though a full cost-benefit analysis was not performed" [24]. For instance, Warwick et al. [33] reported that university students strategically use satisficing behavior to minimize their efforts for time-saving.

As illustrated earlier, we received the detailed context information about questions posted by 83 users. In that part of our survey study, we also asked participants to rate urgency (in minutes), importance, and satisfaction (on a 5 level Likert scale) for each question. The expected urgency varies, ranging from less than 10 minutes (54%), to less than 1 hour (80%) to less than 1 day (90%). For importance, 46% answered important (4, 5), 33% answered somewhat important/unimportant (3), and 21% answered unimportant (1, 2). Our analysis shows that urgent questions are likely to be more important ($p < 0.001$, Gamma: .494). For satisfaction, 50% answered satisfactory (3, 4), 25% answered somewhat satisfactory/dissatisfactory, and 25% answered unsatisfactory (1, 2). In our survey, we also asked participants to select personal coping strategies for less satisfactory answers from the following options: (1) post the same question again (32.3%), (2) rephrase the question (36.8%), (3) wait for other answers (27.8%), (4) seek other information sources such as web search (41.7%), and (5) stop looking for information (39.8%). If there were other strategies, we asked to write them, but we did not find any other significant strategies. The results clearly show evidence of satisficing behavior in Mobile Q&A; i.e., participants want to minimize their efforts of searching (option 1, 2, 3) or even want to stop searching (39.8%). Given that not all the questions are considered important (only 46%), some of the questions would have never been asked if mobile Q&A were not available.

QUESTIONS IN MOBILE Q&A

We classify questions based on types, topics, and personalness and investigate how they are related to the chances of receiving answers. To this end, we randomly selected 1000 questions from the Naver Mobile Q&A data set. The questions were coded by two raters (600 each). We used 200 common questions and measured the inter-rater agreement with Cohen's Kappa statistic, which indicated substantial agreement: $\kappa = 0.711$. The following are the criteria used for classification. For question types, we used the classification proposed by Kim et al. [18], in which questions are classified into three types, namely information, suggestion, and opinion. Information is for finding specific facts (e.g., *"I am at the train station. Which bus should I take to go to Sadang?"*); suggestion is for seeking recommendation and advice (e.g., *"I need to go to Sadang from Seoul Station, which one is better: taxi or subway?"*); and opinion is for surveying other people's thoughts or tastes (e.g., *"I screwed up my finals. What should I do?"*). We extended this model with two additional types that are commonly used to describe the functions of dyadic interactions [7], i.e., request for resources or services (e.g., *"Please send me some interesting e-books"*), and expressive monologue (e.g., expression of joy, sorrow, anger). For question topics, we use the main topic categories in Naver KiN; i.e., living, computer & communications (C&C), education, entertainment, games, health, and sports. In terms of personalness, we judge that a question is personal if the question is narrated based on a personal account, (e.g., *"I need to get an X-ray of my foot. How much will it cost?"*). The coding results of 962 questions are presented in Table 2; the raters

	Type	Personal		Topic Category						
		Yes	No	Living	C&C	Edu	Entertain	Game	Health	Sports
Information	51.1%	26.6%	60.9%	41.1%	55.9%	72.3%	53.6%	34.4%	44.0%	94.3%
Suggestion	18.7%	25.9%	15.8%	21.1%	27.3%	9.5%	22.6%	26.2%	9.3%	3.8%
Opinion	23.4%	40.1%	16.7%	31.7%	14.3%	16.8%	14.3%	21.3%	45.3%	1.9%
Monologue	4.1%	3.6%	4.2%	4.5%	1.9%	.0%	2.4%	3.3%	1.3%	.0%
Request	2.7%	3.6%	2.3%	1.6%	.6%	1.5%	7.1%	14.8%	.0%	.0%
Count	962	274	688	375	161	137	84	61	75	53

Table 2. Breakdown of questions based on types, topics, and personalness

Answer	Type					Personal		Topic Category						
	Inf.	Sug.	Opi.	Mon.	Req.	Yes	No	Liv.	C&C	Edu.	Ent.	Game	Hea.	Spt.
No	41.1%	51.7%	35.1%	43.6%	65.4%	43.8%	41.9%	42.1%	49.7%	33.6%	53.6%	55.7%	30.7%	30.2%
Yes	58.9%	48.3%	64.9%	56.4%	34.6%	56.2%	58.1%	57.9%	50.3%	66.4%	46.4%	44.3%	69.3%	69.8%
Count	492	180	225	39	26	274	688	375	161	137	84	61	75	53

Table 3. Receiving answers vs. question type, personalness, and topic

failed to classify 38 questions because they are either unreadable (5) or incomplete (33).

Our results show that seeking information is the dominant usage (51.1%), followed by opinion (18.7%) and suggestion (23.4%). Given that questions in mobile Q&A are mostly attributed to everyday life activities (e.g., while watching TV or chatting with friends), it is more likely that users will seek for factual knowledge. This unique pattern significantly differs from that of traditional Q&A sites or status message based Q&A using social networking systems (SNS), where the role of suggestion is more significant. For instance, Kim et al. [18] showed that in Yahoo! Answer, the fractions of information, opinion, and suggestion questions are 35%, 23%, 39%, respectively (others: 3%); Morris et al. [21] showed that in SNS based Q&A, the fractions are 15.3%, 23.6%, 31.2%, respectively (others include rhetorical and invitation: 19.7%), and this pattern is quite consistent across different cultures [34].

The distribution of question types across various topics is significantly different. For instance, Information is more pronounced in Education (72.3%), and Sports (94.3%); suggestion is more pronounced in Games (26.2%), and Computer & Communications (27.3%); opinions are more important in Health (45.3%). Note that information questions in Sports (94.3%) are mostly to check current scores or the results. Finally, among the sample questions, we find that 26.3% are personal questions that are based on personal accounts. We find that the types of *personal* questions are very different from the general statistics; the dominant type is opinion (40.1%), followed by information (26.6%) and suggestion (25.9%).

We also investigated how this classification is correlated with the chances of receiving answers. When question types are considered, the answer rate of opinion questions is the highest (64.9%); the rate of answers for request questions is the lowest (34.6%). When the topic categories are considered, several topics, namely Health (69.3%), Sports (69.8%), and Education (66.4%) received higher answer rates than did the others. Interestingly, personalness does not have any statistically significant impact on the chances of receiving answers ($p = .585$). Personal questions typically have more detailed descriptions and are longer in length (personal average: 79.8 vs. overall average: 35.9), but, unfortunately, such efforts do not yield a better answering rate.

INTERACTION PATTERNS

We examine macroscopic user interaction patterns of mobile Q&A by analyzing the crawled data set. First, we present a unique pattern of user's interaction with answerers as coping strategies of meeting a user's information needs. Second, we analyze the inter-arrival patterns of questions/answers and the answer-to social network. Third, we show the relationship between the question length and the answer length to see whether short questions elicit short answers.

Interactive Behavior: Repeating, Refining Questions

For a given question, we can expect the following scenarios: (1) a user's question is not answered, (2) a user's question is answered, but it is less than satisfactory, and (3) a user's question is answered, and it is satisfactory. As shown earlier, our survey results indicate that people use various coping strategies to meet the information needs attributed to everyday life activities or tasks: posting the same question again, rephrasing or refining the previous question, waiting for other answers, seeking other information sources, or stopping information seeking. Among these strategies, we use our data set to perform a quantitative analysis of user behavior of repeating and refining questions.

We first take a look at the repeating behavior. In Naver Mobile Q&A, our results show that 34% of questions are never answered. To receive an answer, one strategy that a user can use is simply re-sending an unanswered question. This behavior can be modeled mathematically. Assuming that a question is answered with probability p, the number of trials (Y) to receive an answer simply follows a geometric distribution: $Pr(Y = k) = (1 - p)^k p$, and the expected number of trials is $1/p$. In the case of Naver Mobile Q&A, assuming that answering is an independent, identical process, we have $p = 0.66$, and thus, the expected number of trials is 1.5.

Besides repetition, we observe that users often refine a question into a new question that more accurately reflects the information needs attributed to life activities. In mobile Q&A,

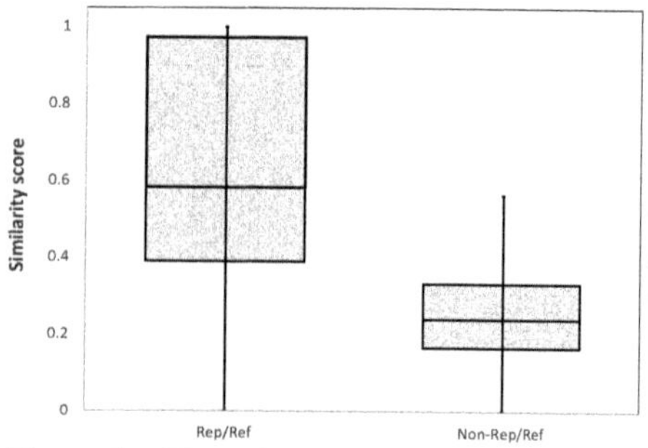

Figure 5. Manual classification results: similarity scores of repeating/refining and non-repeating/refining questions

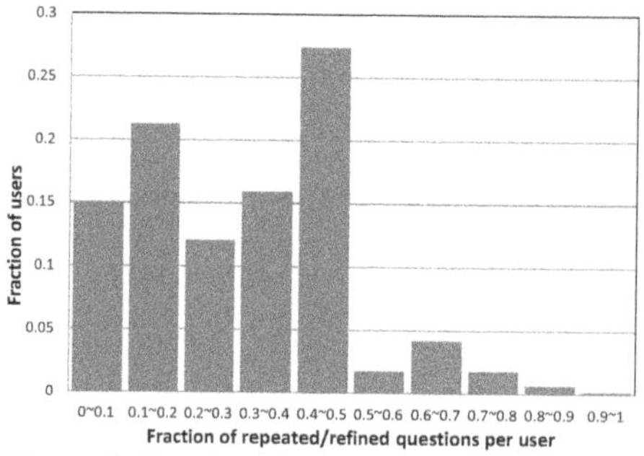

Figure 6. Fraction of users who have a specific fraction range of repeated/refined questions

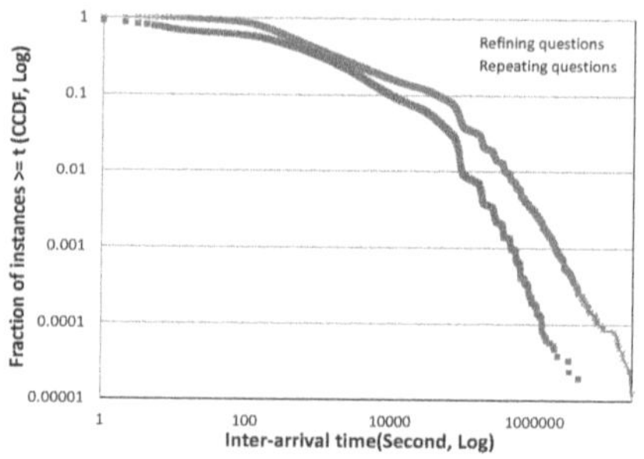

Figure 7. Inter-arrival time distribution of repeated (score=1) [bottom] and refined (0.6≤score<1) questions [top] (log-log)

we observe that users typically wish to interact with potential answerers to meet their information needs or complete their tasks at hand. The refining behavior could be as simple as rephrasing the question with more information or as complex as making some decision (e.g., choosing which smartphones to buy). Interestingly, this user behavior is somewhat similar to the query refinement behavior in information retrieval: when facing too many documents, a user narrows down the scope of search results by refining the previous query [32]. Due to its unique interactions, question refinement in mobile Q&A is very different from query refinement in traditional information retrieval. First of all, a series of answers is delivered in sequence to the users opportunistically, and yet a user cannot predict how many answers will be received. It usually takes a long time to receive an answer (on the order of minutes), and the time scale of the refining process is much greater than that in traditional information retrieval.

To illustrate an asker's interactive behavior, we present the following interaction example adapted from one of our participants. The question was originally sent while the asker was on the train bound to Seoul Station and was planning to travel to Sadang Station.

Question 1 (10:23AM): *"How do I get to Sadang Station from Seoul Station?"*
Answer 1 (10:25AM): *"Take a subway line number 4"*
Answer 2 (10:27AM): *"Just take a taxi"*
Question 2 (10:28AM) : *"How long does it take and how much does it cost to go to Sadang Station from Seoul Station by taxi?*
Answer 1 (10:30AM): *"About 31 minutes, and 9,400 Won"*

To quantify how often repeating or refining behavior occurs, we analyzed the data set as follows. For a given user, we examine a pair of consecutive questions in sequence and measure the cosine similarity. Each question is represented as a vector in which each element is a unique letter. Given two vectors $\vec{r_1}$ and $\vec{r_2}$, the *cosine of the angle* between $\vec{r_1}$ and $\vec{r_2}$ is given as: $sim(\vec{r_1}, \vec{r_2}) = \vec{r_1} \cdot \vec{r_2} / |\vec{r_1} \times \vec{r_2}|$. Here, a similarity score of 1 means a perfect match (i.e., repeated questions), and that of 0 means no match. Note that we used a rather simple cosine metric instated of semantic analysis due to the unique challenge; i.e., a large fraction of questions are worded without spaces, which is quite common when texting in Korean. Fortunately, our approach works well in practice as the total number of unique Korean letters is 11,172.

To choose a proper threshold value, we randomly chose three heavy users and manually classified 782 questions. Figure 5 clearly shows that the similarity score distributions are very different from one another. Given that the similarity scores of non-refinement questions are lower than 0.6, we use this value to automatically detect refined questions. While conservative, the automatic classification allows us to understand such behavior on a large scale. In Figure 6, we plot the fraction of repeated/refined questions per user. A large fraction of users utilize query refinement quite often (e.g., mode is 40-50% of all the questions). Interestingly, there are users whose questions are almost the same. These are the users who ask a few similar questions over the period of time; e.g., checking game scores such as *"today's baseball results?"* or repeatedly posting their concerns such as *"I have some problem with my girlfriend..."* Finally, we plot the inter-arrival time distribution of repeated (score=1) and refined (0.6≤score<1) questions in Figure 7. The figure shows that both repeated and refined distributions approximately follow a power-law distribution. The median inter-arrival time of repeated and refined questions (i.e., the time difference between two consecutive questions) is 250s (4.1 min) and 550s (9.2 min), respectively.

Questioning/Answering Process and Social Relationship

Given that a mobile Q&A service can be considered as a queueing system, we analyze the arrival process of questions and answers. We select five bins of hourly activities and plot the aggregated inter-arrival time distribution of questions and answers in Figure 8 and Figure 9. By inter-arrival time we mean the time difference between two consecutive questions or answers. These figures show that the arrival patterns of questions and answers approximately follow an exponential distribution (log-linear plot). The system can be simplified as an M/M/1 queueing model, and various math analyses can be performed, which we will defer as a part of future work.

To understand questioning/answering patterns, we analyze an answer-to social network in which a node represents a user, and a directed edge from user i to user j means that i gave an answer to j. Given this answer-to graph, we plot the indegree and outdegree distribution in Figure 10. Here, an indegree of a user means the number of answers that the user received, which is proportional to the number of questions asked, and an outdegree of a user means the number of answers that the user gave. Both distributions approximately follow the power law distribution. While quite a few users have a very low

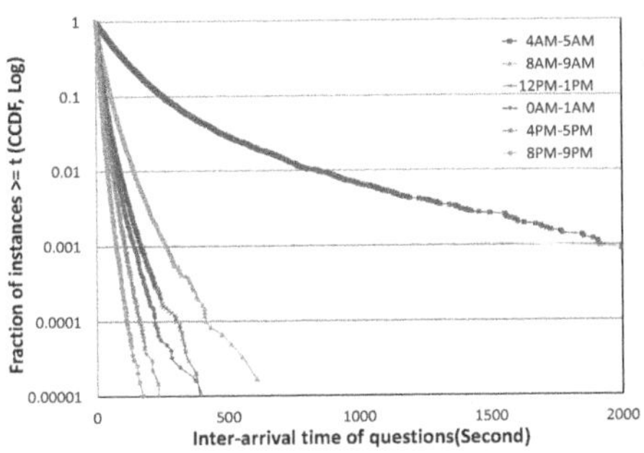

Figure 8. Inter-arrival time distribution of questions (log-linear)

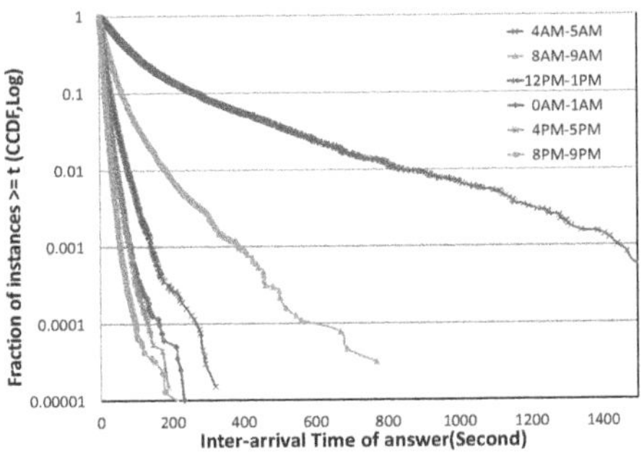

Figure 9. Inter-arrival time distribution of answers (log-linear)

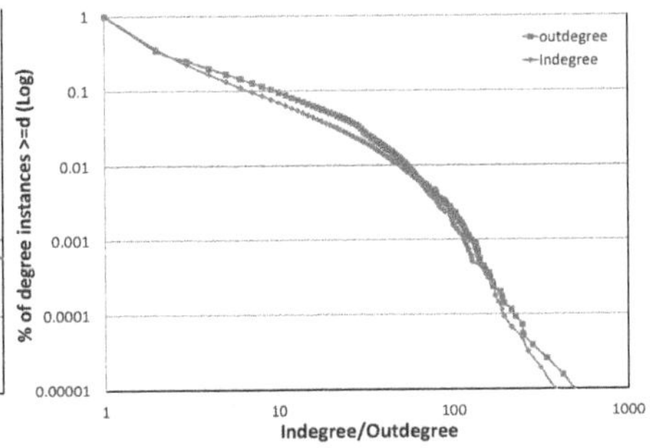

Figure 10. Indegree (bottom) and outdegree (top) distribution (log-log)

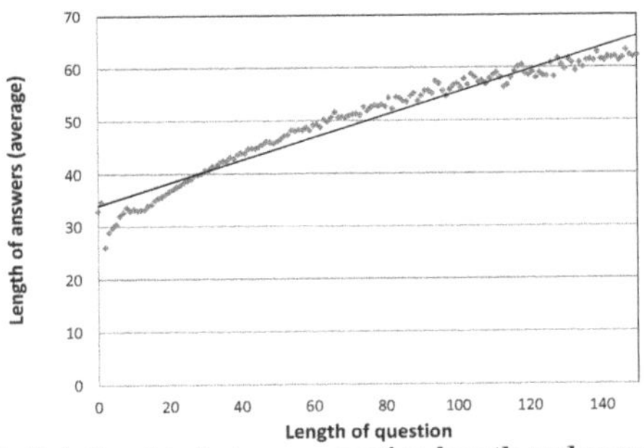

Figure 11. Relationship between question length and answer length

activity level, there are also a large fraction of users with relatively high activity levels. This behavior is also observed in the traditional Q&A site as well [4].

Question Length vs. Answer Length

Another interesting question is whether there is any relationship between the length of a question and that of an answer. As shown earlier, the average length of questions posted in Naver Mobile Q&A is 35.9 letters, which is much longer than that of mobile web search (e.g., Google Mobile Search: 15.5 letters). For a given question length, we calculate the average length of all the answers and plot the graph in Figure 11. The figure shows that the length of answers is strongly correlated with that of questions (Spearman's rho = 0.96, $p < 0.001$). The average answer length linearly increases. If a user texts a longer question, in general we expect that the user will receive a longer answer.

DESIGN IMPLICATIONS

In this section, we discuss several system design implications. First of all, we found that a significant fraction of users exhibit interactive behavior (i.e., repeating, refining questions) in mobile Q&A. One critical problem is that the asker knows the current context, but it is likely the case that the potential answerers do not have any information about the user's current context.[1] For instance, during the peak hours the inter-arrival time between questions is very short, and there are many answerers working together. The chance that an answerer can successfully select a follow-up question is fairly low. One simple way of solving this problem is to list the recently posted questions by a specific person in a reverse chronological order.

Another system design issue is to enhance the mobile user interface of mobile Q&A systems. For fast dyadic interaction with mobile devices, users should be able to browse and copy/paste previous questions—typing with mobile devices tends to be a slow and laborious task. This interaction is quite natural with the SMS interface, but the current systems lack such a feature. This partly explains why SMS is preferred to other methods among heavy mobile Q&A users. We analyzed the questions posted in the month of July 2011 (a total of 248,646 questions asked by 105,825 users). The fractions of SMS, Naver App, and Mobile Web were 7%, 55%, and 34% (the rest is the combination of those methods). If we restrict our scope to heavy users (say, those who send more than 20 queries in that month), we find that the distribution is significantly different; i.e., SMS (55%) is preferred to Naver App (25%) and Mobile Web (8%). Interestingly, 4% of heavy users utilize both SMS and Naver App/Web—SMS is much easy to interact with.

Enhancing answerer's user interface of mobile Q&A is necessary. In mobile Q&A, there are several trending topics, and some of the queries are repeatedly asked say over the course of a day (e.g., sports game results or some hot issues of a day). The system should help quickly answer those questions, which can improve the overall answering rate. For those questions, one can even design an answering system that automatically answers with a high level of accuracy. The system can treat users based on their communication methods; in particular, we can deliver additional search results along with answers to smartphone users. Another improvement is to personalize the question listing based on the answer's expertise. One simple way is to use topic categories to match answerer's expertise or interest.

Finally, our analysis reveals that a significant fraction of questions (26.3%) are based on personal accounts. Given that questions in mobile Q&A are mostly attributed to the asker's daily activities, those who are heavily using the service may suffer from potential privacy leakage. Our manual investigation shows that we were able to easily identify a fair amount of sensitive information about the askers (e.g., age, hometown, personal relationship, medical records). Existing mobile Q&A systems should at least anonymize user IDs to prevent the potential attacks. At the time of this paper write-up (September 2011), Naver changed its policy to reveal only

[1]Note that our investigation shows that only handful askers use answerers' IDs in the questions to solicit follow-up answers (e.g., "*asgsky12: I would really appreciate it if you recommend more songs!*").

first three letters of a user ID (e.g., *bmw*****) to prevent potential privacy attacks.

CONCLUSION

We studied Naver Mobile Q&A, a large-scale mobile Q&A service in Korea. To understand mobile Q&A usage, we analyzed 2.4 million question/answer pairs spanning a 14 month period from Naver Mobile Q&A and performed a complementary survey study of 555 active mobile Q&A users. We found that the usage of mobile Q&A significantly differs from that of conventional Q&A sites as it is deeply wired into users' everyday life activities. We characterized the key factors of mobile Q&A usage, namely accessibility/convenience, promptness, and satisficing behavior. Our query classification study revealed that in mobile Q&A asking simple facts is more dominant than it is traditional Q&A. Further, we analyzed the macroscopic user interactions and identified the interactive user behavior such as repeating and refining questions as coping strategies of seeking information needs, the questioning/answering process, and the relationship between query length and answer length. Finally, we discussed the system design implications such as user interface design, context sharing, and privacy-awareness. As with any qualitative or single-site work, the generalizability of this work is limited such that an additional work on similar mobile Q&A services such as ChaCha and AQA is necessary, which will be part of our future work.

REFERENCES

1. Comparison of Hourly Wireless Internet Usage. `http://mobizen.pe.kr/971`.
2. ExactTarget: Messaging Behaviors, Preferences, and Personas, 2008.
3. Naver Mobile Q&A. `http://kin.naver.com/mobileqna/listMobileQuestion.nhn`.
4. Adamic, L. A., Zhang, J., Bakshy, E., and Ackerman, M. S. Knowledge Sharing and Yahoo Answers: Everyone Knows Something. In *WWW* (2008).
5. Church, K., and Smyth, B. Understanding the Intent Behind Mobile Information Needs. In *IUI* (2009).
6. Cui, Y., and Roto, V. How People Use the Web on Mobile Devices. In *WWW* (2008).
7. Ervin-Tripp, S. An Analysis of the Interaction of Language, Topic, and Listener. *American Anthropologist* (1964).
8. Harper, F. M., Moy, D., and Konstan, J. A. Facts or Friends? Distinguishing Informational and Conversational Questions in Social Q&A Sites. In *CHI* (2009).
9. Harper, F. M., Raban, D., Rafaeli, S., and Konstan, J. A. Predictors of Answer Quality in Online Q&A Sites. In *CHI* (2008).
10. Hektor, A. What's the Use? Internet and Information Behavior in Everyday Life. *Linkoping University* (2001).
11. Horowitz, D., and Kamvar, S. D. Aardvark: The Anatomy of a Large-scale Social Search Engine. In *WWW* (2010).
12. Hsieh, G., and Counts, S. mimir: A Market-Based Real-Time Question and Answer Service. In *CHI* (2009).
13. Hsieh, G., Kraut, R. E., and Hudson, S. E. Why Pay?: Exploring How Financial Incentives are Used for Question & Answer. In *CHI* (2010).
14. Johnson, J. D. Fields and Pathways: Contrasting or Complementary Views of Information Seeking. *Information Processing and Management* (2006).
15. Kamvar, M., and Baluja, S. A Large Scale Study of Wireless Search Behavior: Google Mobile Search. In *CHI* (2006).
16. Kautz, H., Selman, B., and Shah, M. ReferralWeb: Combining Social Networks and Collaborative Filtering. *International Journal of Human-Computer Interaction* (1997).
17. Kellar, M., Watters, C., and Shepherd, M. A Goal-Based Classification of Web Information Tasks. In *ASIST* (2006).
18. Kim, S., Oh, J. S., and Oh, S. Best-Answer Selection Criteria in a Social Q&A Site from the User-Oriented Relevance Perspective. In *ASIST* (2007).
19. Lee, I., and Kim, J. Use Contexts for the Mobile Internet: A Longitudinal Study Monitoring Actual Use of Mobile Internet Services. *International Journal of Human-Computer Interaction* (2005).
20. McKenzie, P. J. A Model of Information Practices in Accounts of Everyday Life Information Seeking. *Jounal of Documents* (2003).
21. Morris, M. R., Teevan, J., and Panovich, K. What Do People Ask Their Social Networks, and Why? A Survey Study of Status Message Q&A Behavior . In *CHI* (2010).
22. Nam, K. K., Ackerman, M. S., and Adamic, L. A. Questions in, Knowledge iN?: A Study of Naver's Question Answering Community. In *CHI* (2009).
23. Pettigrew, K. E. Lay Information Provision in Community Settings: How Community Health Nurses Disseminate Human Services Information to the Elderly. *Library Quarterly* (2000).
24. Prabha, C., Connaway, L. S., Olszewski, L., and Jenkins, L. What is Enough? Satisficing Information Needs. *Journal of Documentation* (2007).
25. Raban, D., and Harper, F. M. Motivations for Answering Questions Online. In *New Media and Innovative Technologies* (2008).
26. Richardson, M., and White, R. W. Supporting Synchronous Social Q&A Throughout the Question Lifecycle. In *WWW* (2011).
27. Rodrigues, E. M., and Milic-Frayling, N. Socializing or Knowledge Sharing?: Characterizing Social Intent in Community Question Answering. In *CIKM* (2009).
28. Savolainen, R. Everyday Life Information Seeking. *Encyclopedia of Library and Information Science* (2005).
29. Savolainen, R. Everyday Information Practices: A Social Phenomenological Perspective. *The Carecrow Press* (2008).
30. Simon, H. A. Models of Thought. *New Haven* (1979).
31. Sohn, T., Li, K., Griswold, W., and Hollan, J. A Diary Study of Mobile Information Needs. In *CHI* (2008).
32. Veĺez, B., Wiess, R., Sheldon, M. A., and Gifford, D. K. Fast and Effective Query Refinement. In *SIGIR* (1997).
33. Warwick, C., Rimmer, J., Blandford, A., Gow, J., and Buchanan, G. Cognitive Economy and Satisticing in Information Seeking: A Longitudinal Study of Undergraduate Information Behavior. *Journal of the American Society for Information Science & Technology* (2009).
34. Yang, J., Morris, M. R., Teevan, J., Adamic, L. A., and Ackerman, M. S. Culture Matters: A Survey Study of Social Q&A Behavior. In *ICWSM* (2011).
35. Yi, J., and Maghoul, F. Mobile Search Pattern Evolution: The Trend and the Impact of Voice Queries. In *WWW* (2011).
36. Zhang, J., Ackerman, M. S., Adamic, L., and Nam, K. K. QuME: A Mechanism to Support Expertise Finding in Online Help-seeking Communities. In *UIST* (2007).

Author Index

www.ingramcontent.com/pod-product-compliance
Ingram Content Group UK Ltd.
Pitfield, Milton Keynes, MK11 3LW, UK
UKHW051455290926
15471UKWH00008B/1211